HISTORIANS OF THE AMERICAN FRONTIER

HISTORIANS OF THE AMERICAN FRONTIER

A Bio-Bibliographical Sourcebook

Edited by
JOHN R. WUNDER

GREENWOOD PRESS
New York • Westport, Connecticut • London

Library of Congress Cataloging-in-Publication Data

Historians of the American frontier : a bio-bibliographical sourcebook / edited by John R. Wunder.
p. cm.
Bibliography: p.
Includes index.
ISBN 0-313-24899-0 (lib. bdg. : alk. paper)
1. Historians—United States—Biography. 2. Frontier and pioneer life—United States—Bio-bibliography. 3. United States—Territorial expansion—Bio-bibliography. I. Wunder, John R.
E175.45.H57 1988
973'.072022—dc 19 88-5637
[B]

British Library Cataloguing in Publication Data is available.

Library of Congress Catalog Card Number: 88-5637
ISBN: 0-313-24899-0

First published in 1988

Greenwood Press, Inc.
88 Post Road West, Westport, Connecticut 06881

Printed in the United States of America

The paper used in this book complies with the Permanent Paper Standard issued by the National Information Standards Organization (Z39.48-1984).

10 9 8 7 6 5 4 3 2 1

Copyright Acknowledgments

The following have generously given permission to use extended quotations from the writings of historians treated in this work: Ohio Historical Society, selections from Randolph C. Downes, *Frontier Ohio, 1788-1803* (1935); University of Washington Libraries, the papers of Stewart H. Holbrook; Newberry Library, Chicago, D'Arcy McNickle Papers; Harriet C. Owsley, the papers of Frank Lawrence Owsley; Deanna Rundell, the papers of Walter Rundell, Jr.; George Arents Research Library for Special Collections at Syracuse University, the correspondence and manuscripts of Mari Sandoz; University of Nebraska–Lincoln Libraries, Mari Sandoz Papers.

for
VERNON CARSTENSEN

CONTENTS

PREFACE

Historians of the American frontier are a special group. They represent what is perhaps the most dynamic specialty in the history profession. Since the origins of the professionalization of history as an academic discipline, historians of the American frontier have contributed numerous theories and theses that have been taken so seriously they have altered how other historians and other disciplines view history.

This book is an attempt to provide a creative reference work devoted exclusively to American frontier historians. A bio-bibliography represents a unique opportunity for scholars in the field of American frontier history. Bibliographies and historiographical essays have been compiled and composed before, but this volume contains both extensive individual analyses and bibliographical information. Chapters on fifty-seven historians of frontier America are divided into four subsections: biography, themes, analysis, and bibliography.

The selection of the historians was predicated upon several factors. First, each historian had to have completed his or her work. In order to allow for as objective and complete an analysis as possible, the subjects chosen were deceased. Some of the historians only recently passed on, such as Robert G. Athearn (1983), Eve Ball (1984), and Lawrence Kinnaird (1985). Others died decades ago, such as Adolph Bandelier (1914), Hiram Chittenden (1917), and Hubert Howe Bancroft (1918). When I first contemplated this undertaking, Vernon Carstensen advised me to include this criterion for selection as a top priority, and he proved prophetic as always.

Second, historians were chosen because of contributions to the discipline. All of the historians made significant discoveries that have shaped further research, writing, and thought about the American frontier and American history in general. This is no mean achievement. This criterion, of course, is subjective, but the essays generally confirm this qualitative judgment.

Third, attention is paid to geographical and subject matter distribution. The frontier is broadly defined in terms of space, time, and process. Thus, it became important that historians of the colonial, trans-Appalachian, and trans-Mississippi frontiers be represented. Moreover, subfields exist within frontier studies. Agricultural history, the Borderlands, land policy, railroad history, Native American studies, and other subject areas are represented in the selections.

And fourth, historian is broadly defined so that those scholars who contributed to history even though they may have been more often identified with other disciplines are included. Consequently, ethnohistorians and anthropologists such as Edward Spicer, political scientists such as Benjamin Shambaugh, and agricultural economists such as Benjamin Hibbard are a part of this volume. Also, preprofessional historians have earned a place within this elite group.

This project took over four years to complete. I did not ever think it would take this long, but it has. Much credit goes to Greenwood Press and to the fifty-seven other authors whose patience has been a model for other presses and scholars. Most of the time needed to complete the volume has been spent on tracking down rare bibliographical entries, verifying bibliographical and biographical information, and coordinating fifty-seven authors toward a common goal.

Perhaps the most frustrating part of this endeavor, now that it is completed, is that more needs to be done. This is really volume I. There are still more very important frontier historians who need treatments similar to those included within this volume. These include Francis Parkman, Ernest Osgood, Clarence Alvord, Verner W. Crane, Clarence E. Carter, Le Roy Hafen and Ann Hafen, Reuben Gold Thwaites, Theodore Saloutos, and others who were assigned but whose essays were not completed. Others include John Bannon, Rodman Paul, and Ernest Wallace, examples of those frontier historians only recently deceased. These important contributors to the historiography of the American frontier have not been left out by design or accident. I regret that all have not been included.

Much of the credit for whatever is positive about this volume goes to many people. These include many persons from Clemson University, such as Marian Withington and her fellow librarians in interlibrary loan at the Clemson University Library; Fara Driver, Gina Crawford, Stephen Lowe, Christopher Poteat, Chandana Mozumdar, Laura Benjamin, Paul Peterson, Brian McKown, and Craig Friend, graduate students in the Department of History; and secretaries Sharon Barnes, Flora Walker, Trisha Herring, and Reba Brown. My former colleagues in the Department of History were most understanding of my dedication to this book, and I appreciate them immensely. Joseph Arbena and Alan Grubb were especially helpful with their confirmation of Spanish and French terms and with their advice concerning Clemson University's computer system to a beginner. Particular thanks should be bestowed upon Lawrence

Goodman of Scarsdale, New York, who helped me solve significant numbers of bibliographical puzzles during a summer of culture shock in South Carolina, and to his AP teacher, Eric Rothschild, who sent his talented, high school, Harvard-bound student for an intellectual outing. Special acknowledgment should be made to one of the contributors, William Graves, whose enthusiasm for the project was infectious and whose life was prematurely ended by a reckless driver on the mountainous roads of eastern Kentucky.

Special thanks go to my wife, Susan Anderson Wunder, and to my daughters, Amanda and Nell, who willingly let me retreat to my office or the library to check the seemingly endless details. Nell also helped organize and proof the manuscript. And I am particularly grateful for the education I received from my two mentors, Malcolm Rohrbough at the University of Iowa and Vernon Carstensen at the University of Washington. Through them I came to appreciate and cherish the writing of the history of the American frontier.

John R. Wunder
Lincoln, Nebraska

HISTORIANS
OF THE
AMERICAN FRONTIER

1

THOMAS PERKINS ABERNETHY

by William H. Graves

Biography

Thomas Perkins Abernethy was nationally recognized as the foremost authority of the frontier movement of the Old Southwest. Jack P. Greene said of Abernethy: "Few men have contributed more significantly to the study of the early South than Thomas Perkins Abernethy" *(Journal of Southern History* 31:326). Keith B. Berwick called Abernethy "the acknowledged dean of early southern historians" *(Virginia Magazine of History and Biography* 70:356). A student of Frederick Jackson Turner at Harvard University, Abernethy's historical training was nurtured in Turner's "frontier school" and shaped by the progressive interpretation of United States history, popular early in this century. Yet, Abernethy was destined to break with his mentor and to establish a national reputation in his own right.

Abernethy was born on August 25, 1890, in Lowndes County, Alabama. He received his B.A. from the College of Charleston in 1912, and earned his M.A. (1915) and his Ph.D. (1922) at Harvard, having served two years in the United States Army during World War I. After leaving Harvard, Abernethy taught at Vanderbilt University, the University of Chattanooga, and the University of Alabama before going to the University of Virginia in 1930. A native southerner, Abernethy devoted his life's work to the history of the formative period of that region. Author of five major books, numerous articles, lectures, and edited works, and dozens of book reviews, he taught for thirty-one years at the University of Virginia in Charlottesville before retiring as Richmond Alumni Professor of History in 1961. Abernethy was one of the founders of the Southern Historical Association, presided as its third president (1937-1938), and for many years served on the board of the *Journal of Southern History*. Abernethy was a masterful teacher and many of his graduate students were devoted to him. To honor their mentor, eleven of his former students published *The Old Dominion: Essays for Thomas Perkins Abernethy* in 1964. This *festschrift* stands on its own, its essays are provocative, and they ensure that Abernethy's influence will continue on succeeding generations of historians. Held in high esteem by his peers and loved by his former students, Abernethy died at home in Charlottesville on November 12, 1975. His death severed one of the last direct links to Frederick Jackson Turner and ended an era of Old Southwest frontier scholarship.

Themes

Thomas Perkins Abernethy evolved as a historian over some thirty-six years, from his first book, *The Formative Period in Alabama 1815-1828* (1925) to his last, *The South in the New Nation* (1961). His themes were Turnerian and beyond; his focus became succinctly regional.

In 1925 Abernethy published his first book, *The Formative Period in Alabama, 1815-1828,* which was a revised version of his dissertation. This monograph shows Turner's influence and is a traditional frontier study that relies upon primary documents to analyze the early development of Alabama. In it Abernethy argues that "the new conditions of the frontier" modified "old habits and old views," (p. 9) but that the product of this experience was not pure Turnerian democracy. Instead, Abernethy found that land speculators gained title to the most fertile lands, and the legislature of Alabama held the real reins of power, not the masses of the people. These two elements and not democracy, Abernethy stresses, were the product of the frontier experience. This was his first tentative proposal of a new frontier thesis. The book was favorably received; one reviewer called it "an unusually good study" and "the first chapter of a state history written as a state history should be written" *(Mississippi Valley Historical Review* 11:586-587).

From the present perspective, *The Formative Period in Alabama* has stood the test of time for its solid scholarship and the evolution of Alabama political institutions, but it has omissions that any modern study would have to include. The study is political and, for the most part, ignores social, ethnic, and cultural history. Women are absent from it, as are blacks, except as appendages to the white economy, and Indians, when treated, are stereotyped. Abernethy wrote that much more work needed to be completed on slavery because it was an integral part of Alabama's development, but he did not do the work and despite the existence of slavery as a major force in Alabama, Abernethy concludes that "Alabama was a state where democracy was the rule" (p. 169). About southern Indians, he writes, "they engaged in a crude method of agriculture" and that "their methods of culture were primitive" (p. 21). To Abernethy, the primary result of the Battle of Horseshoe Bend, which devastated the Creek Indians, was that "the Mississippi Territory was indebted to [Andrew] Jackson not only for safety but also for room in which to grow" (p. 24). This book shows the inconsistencies often found in a first study, and stereotypes of nonwhite peoples would appear again and again in Abernethy's later works.

After 1925 Abernethy continued to teach, research, and write. In the next five years he published several articles, each analyzing some phase of the early political and financial history of Tennessee. During this period he further developed and refined his views about Old Southwest democracy, views which would challenge his mentor Turner and challenge the traditional interpretation of Andrew Jackson and Jacksonian democracy.

In 1932 Abernethy published *From Frontier to Plantation in Tennessee: A Study in Frontier Democracy.* It was immediately hailed as a seminal study. One historian called it a "work of genuine originality," *(A History of American History,* p. 545), another, "a path-breaking book" *(History: The Development of Historical Studies in the United States,* p. 202). Abernethy dedicated the book to his mentor, but much of its thesis attacked Turner's frontier democracy; one reviewer said the book was "perhaps the most provocative interpretation" of Jacksonian democracy ever written by a critic of Turner *(Jacksonian Democracy and the Historians,* p. 41).

From Frontier to Plantation in Tennessee is a case study of the frontier experience of a single state. In it Abernethy analyzes not just the development of Tennessee's political institutions, but also "its development as a community" to "throw new light upon the growth of our democracy" (p. ix). He chose Tennessee because it had some of the earliest transmontane settlements, a varied economy, contributed a high percentage of the nation's early leaders, and was the first state to undergo the territorial process.

However, where Turner argued that democracy was the first product of the frontier experience, Abernethy counters that "the first offspring of the West was not democracy but arrogant opportunism" (p. 359). "Wealthy investors and speculators" ruled Tennessee, while the poor farmer "had to go to the back country or become dependent on the wealthy landlord" (p. 209). The lost state of Franklin was not "the cry of the West for Freedom," but "a game played between two rival groups of land speculators" (p. 89). Abernethy concedes that there was some advance towards democracy, but that "the advance was more apparent than real"(p. 136).

That sharp break with the mainstream of frontier and southern history, which Abernethy admitted was "a minority report, so to speak, against the 'frontier thesis' of my preceptor and friend," earned him a national reputation (p. v.). In the second half of the book, Abernethy broke more new ground by attacking Andrew Jackson, whom he characterized as "a westerner with a colorful personality and a transcendent military reputation" who "never really championed the cause of the people; he only invited them to champion his" (pp. 248-249). Arthur M. Schlesinger, Jr., Charles G. Sellars, Jr., and other prominent historians would attack this interpretation, but none could totally disprove it.

The 1930s was a decade of professional growth and accomplishment for Abernethy. He was appointed to the faculty at the University of Virginia and served as President of the Southern Historical Association in 1937-1938. His presidential address, delivered on November 19, 1937, in

Durham, North Carolina, was entitled, "Democracy and the Southern Frontier." It was published in the *Journal of Southern History* in February, 1938. Abernethy's major article, "Andrew Jackson," was published in the *Dictionary of American Biography* in 1932, the same year that *From Frontier to Plantation in Tennessee* appeared. Some have found it ironic that someone holding a minority view of Jackson would author such an important article.

In 1937 Abernethy published his third book, *Western Lands and the American Revolution*, in which he hoped "to bring together in a single narrative an account of the American West from the time when its exploration was begun by English colonists to the end of the Confederation period" (p. vii). Despite its ambitious title, the study is limited to the region south of the Ohio River, basically ignoring the land concerns of Pennsylvania, New York, and the other northern states. Again, this is a traditional institutional study, one that focuses on political concerns, ignoring social and cultural issues. The study is long and tedious and reviews of it were mixed. One reviewer writes that "nobody will ever read this book for sheer enjoyment," but no students of the period could ignore it either *(Political Science Quarterly* 53:469).

It is an important study, especially for Virginia and its role in frontier development, but it is not a complete study of western lands. As in *From Frontier to Plantation in Tennessee,* the role of the speculator is stressed, as is the emergence of nondemocratic elements. One of the book's strengths is its treatment of the intrigue caused by British and Spanish interests in the Southwest. The volume is a good sourcebook, but it should be used judiciously. Nevertheless, Theodore Pease wrote that it was "a fine piece of craftsmanship" *(Mississippi Valley Historical Review* 25:399).

In 1940 Abernethy delivered the Walter Lynwood Fleming Lectures in Southern History at Louisiana State University in Baton Rouge. These lectures were published later that same year as *Three Virginia Frontiers* and for the most part are distillations of his earlier findings and interpretations. Here Abernethy examines tidewater, piedmont, and transmontane Virginia because he felt these areas were representative of American frontier development. He believes that "the fascination of the frontier as applied to American history lies in the fact that it stresses a basic factor which has significantly influenced the development of our national habits and institutions" (p. 1). Abernethy admits that the frontier was not the only factor influencing American development, but that it was a significant one. His antidemocratic interpretation led one critic to conclude that Abernethy had "not thrown the Turner thesis into discard, but he had attempted to supplant it" *(Journal of Southern History* 7:550).

In 1954 Oxford University Press published Abernethy's *The Burr Conspiracy*, a narrative of the events of one of the most famous incidents in early United States history. James W. Silver characterizes the book as a "competent and scholarly volume" that is "an unadorned, complete narrative of events" in which Abernethy was "content to allow the facts to speak for themselves" *(American Historical Review* 60:127). Making good use of primary documents, including several volumes of previously unavailable Clarence E. Carter *Territorial Papers*, the book was the most "complete and objective work" on the conspiracy yet written *(Mississippi Valley Historical Review* 41:704).

The monograph is narrative and not interpretive. It effectively argues that Aaron Burr and General James Wilkinson were surely guilty of plotting treason against the United States, but Abernethy partly justifies their actions on the grounds that strong nationalism was lacking in the trans-Appalachian region, and Union disloyalty was not seen as a terrible act. Modern researchers might question his assumption about treason, but they would have difficulty disproving Burr and Wilkinson's complicity. The real importance of the book is its examination of the motives of President Thomas Jefferson and Chief Justice John Marshall, and the political-legal machinations at Burr's Richmond, Virginia, trial.

The Burr Conspiracy is a good example of Abernethy's strengths and weaknesses. His research and use of documents is very impressive, but, as with his other works, when he writes about people, his characterizations seem, by today's standards, very stereotyped. For Abernethy, the typical westerner of the Burr era "fought Indians, grew corn, and distilled whiskey"; they were "hardy backwoodsmen who had made a home for themselves on the Western waters" (pp. 3-4). What about frontierswomen, what were their roles, or blacks or Cajuns or Indians?

Abernethy's last book was published in 1961. *The South in the New Nation, 1789-1819,* represented the fourth volume of the *A History of the South* series, edited by Wendell H. Stephenson and E. Merton Coulter. Abernethy, the leading authority of the region and era, might have been the logical choice to write the first volume of the series that treated the South as a distinct, separate region. Nevertheless, in many ways this book falls short of expectations and is not as strong as his earlier monographs.

Much of *The South in the New Nation* is distilled from his earlier writings. Ten of the sixteen chapters chronicle Old Southwest expansion and one of the remaining six, on the Burr conspiracy, is lifted almost *in toto* from the 1954 manuscript. There is no chapter on slavery or its impact on the psychology or institutions of the South, and there are only seven references to slavery in the entire volume. For the most part the book ignores social, cultural, and ethnic history, and one cannot erase the feeling that the authorship of the volume was offered to Abernethy because of his past accomplishments and not because he could bring any new or vibrant interpretations to this major series.

In *The South in the New Nation* Abernethy argues that nationalism in the West was absent until the War of 1812 and when it was created, this spirit was resented by the Hamiltonian Federalists. To Abernethy, this, plus the fact that most citizens believed they had a right to leave the Union, proves that "sectionalism was not a product of the slavery issue, but that this issue was a product of sectionalism" (pp. ix-x). The real North-South difference, writes Abernethy, was not slavery, but the "puritanical attitude" of the North versus the "liberal Anglicanism" of the South (p. x). One is forced to ask, was Abernethy, as an ethnic white southerner, personally uncomfortable with the slavery issue? Did he not understand it, or did he, unlike almost all other historians, legitimately believe that slavery was not the crucial factor in early national southern development?

This book received more unfavorable reviews than all of his earlier books combined. Abernethy justified his de-emphasis of slavery on the grounds that "the problems connected with the conquest and settlement of the Southern and Western frontiers had made it impossible for him to trace the social and economical development of the region" and that Charles Sydnor's succeeding volume in the series, *The Development of Southern Sectionalism, 1819-1848*, adequately covered these aspects of southern development (p. xi). However, Chase C. Mooney was correct when he reviewed the book and wrote that these reasons do "not justify the omissions" *(Mississippi Valley Historical Review* 49:124).

Sydnor's volume, after all, covers a different time period than Abernethy's and while it does discuss slavery in some detail, slavery in the earlier period deserves major treatment. In the *Virginia Magazine of History and Biography,* Keith Berwick writes that it seemed as if Abernethy "had projected a volume three times as long, and then decided to publish the first sixteen chapters he completed" (70:356). The book is also a little more conservative than most of Abernethy's volumes. Here the southern planters are characterized as having "faults like most capitalists, they were engaged in exploitation, yet they were also builders. Without their leadership there would have been little progress" (p. 6). Even more than *Western Lands and American Revolution,* this book leaves the reader feeling that he or she has only learned part of the story. *The South in the New Nation* was Abernethy's last book. In the year of its publication he retired from teaching, though he continued to research and lecture.

Analysis

There can be no doubt that Thomas Perkins Abernethy significantly contributed to United States frontier history and broke new ground in Old Southwest frontier history. His writings were powerful and well-documented, but not accepted by all historians and following the publication of *From Frontier to Plantation in Tennessee*, his interpretations were vigorously challenged, especially his views of Andrew Jackson. In his preface to the second edition of *From Frontier to Plantation in Tennessee* (University of Alabama Press, 1967), Abernethy took the offensive against his critics. He writes that certain historians, such as Arthur M. Schlesinger, Jr., appeared "unfettered by any real understanding of the early history of Tennessee or of Jackson's part in it" and that the "politically oriented historians who are so strongly opposed to my interpretations . . . have yet to prove the inaccuracy of any statement" cited from sources in his books and articles (p. vi). These conflicting interpretations must be examined and evaluated.

To understand Abernethy, one must start with Turner. In 1893 Turner presented his famous thesis, "The Significance of the Frontier in American History." This radical interpretation argued that if one wanted to discover the origins of American democracy he or she should look to the frontier, not to Europe, as was generally held in that period. This proposal caused a revolution in United States historiography and the frontier thesis quickly become a mainstay of American historical writings.

Additionally, Turner was soon identified as a leading member of the Progressive School of American history, many of whose members came from the small town, middle class, rural West and South. Up to this point American history had been interpreted from the northeastern point of view, that is, that American institutions were formed in that area after a cloning of English ideas and exported to the rest of the country. Turner, Woodrow Wilson, Charles A. Beard, and Vernon L. Parrington, among others, interpreted American history from a southern and western point of view, challenging traditional scholarship. Together they advanced new points of view, some of which were not accepted, but all of which, taken together, forever altered the direction of American historiography.

It was into this environment that the young and impressionable Thomas Perkins Abernethy entered in 1912. Abernethy was born in Alabama, educated in southern public schools, and received his B.A. from a southern college; he was a fitting subject for Turner's ideas. At Harvard, Abernethy studied, learned, and matured under the tutelage of Turner. He accepted the frontier thesis and he devoted his life to learning as much as possible about the formative period of his native region. His dissertation examined the early history of Alabama, and later published as *The Formative Period in Alabama, 1815-1828,* it is a standard frontier study. There is little in it to indicate that Abernethy would later break with Turner and propose a different interpretation of the frontier movement, Andrew Jackson, and Jacksonian democracy.

Abernethy tentatively advanced his new findings in two articles that followed *The Formative Period in Alabama.* In "The Origins of the Whig Party in Tennessee," he argues that Jackson's "imperious and self-willed manner . . . became more and more irksome to his local supporters, and one by one several among them were alienated" (p. 505). In "Andrew Jackson and the Rise of Southwestern Democracy," Abernethy writes that Jackson was supported by rich speculators and aristocrats, not the masses of the people. An examination of Jackson's actions in Tennessee proved to Abernethy that "the truth of the matter is that Jackson had little to do with the development of the democracy of the West. The [democratic] movement made him President, but he contributed to it not one idea previously to his election in 1828" (p. 71). Abernethy accused Jackson of having no political philosophy, no political principals, and of being a Nashville aristocrat. He concluded that Jackson "thought he was sincere when he spoke to the people, yet he never really championed their cause. He merely encouraged them to champion his" (p. 76).

These charges do not seem to have created much controversy when they were first published, but Abernethy's next attack on Jacksonian democracy did. In *From Frontier to Plantation in Tennessee* Abernethy proposed a new interpretation of the origins of southwestern democracy and Jackson's role in that process. The study is a frontier history, but it sharply breaks with Turner. In it Abernethy argues that yes, the frontier experience in Tennessee did modify old institutions, but that "the rampant land speculation that prevailed on the frontier constitutes highly persuasive evidence that there were serpents in Professor Turner's egalitarian Eden" (p. v). Abernethy's analysis of early Tennessee institutional development proved that land speculators, rich investors, and their cronies soon came to dominate Tennessee politics. Only in a later stage of development did the masses of people in Tennessee gain some real voice in state political affairs. This interpretation was widely praised and soon accepted by many scholars. Abernethy's second thesis was not so easily accepted.

The second half of *From Frontier to Plantation in Tennessee* is largely an attack on Andrew Jackson, the Democrat. Scrupulously examining Jackson's career, attitudes, and ideas *prior* to his election as president in 1828, Abernethy presented an entirely different Old Hickory. Abernethy's Jackson was a military hero, land speculator, and Nashville elitist. He "was not a theorist. He was a man of action and an opportunist." He was "not a consistent politician, he was not even a real leader of democracy," but rather "the democracy of America called him to be its leader." He "never really championed the cause of the people; he only invited them to champion his." (pp. 248-249). The true Tennessee democrat, wrote Abernethy, was not Jackson, but Andrew Johnson, who Abernethy characterizes as "the only true and outstanding democrat produced by the Old South" and one who "never erred from his purpose of improving the conditions of the masses, politically, economically, and intellectually" (p. 357).

Abernethy concludes that Tennessee had had the typical American frontier experience, but instead of that experience producing Turner's democratic Eden, "the first offspring of the West was not democracy, but arrogant opportunism" (p. 357). The frontier experience gave Tennesseeans greater individual freedom, but "at the same time it took them out of contact with cultural influences and established the crass and superficial egalitarianism of the Jackson period" (p. 359). The result in Tennessee, he writes, was that the political voice of the people was negligible, state statutes were largely nondemocratic, and, in reality, "democracy was never applied to politics" (p. 363).

This interpretation did not cause as much of an uproar as did Turner's 1893 break with the mainstream, but it quickly brought Abernethy both support and criticism. One critic, Alfred Cave, said that Abernethy had written the most extreme interpretation of Jacksonian democracy yet to appear (*Jacksonian Democracy and the Historians*). Others saw the book as valuable and pathbreaking.

Many scholars were not so taken with Abernethy's thesis, but not until 1945 did the first comprehensive rebuttal to it appear in print. In 1945 Arthur M. Schlesinger, Jr., published his prizewinning study, *The Age of Jackson.* In it Schlesinger champions Jackson, the Democrat, and attacks Abernethy's interpretation directly. Schlesinger rejects Abernethy's thesis on largely methodological grounds. Abernethy was in error, Schlesinger argues, because he only analyzed Jackson's career in Tennessee, *not* his actions as president. Schlesinger believes that Jacksonian democracy must be evaluated on the basis of Jackson's actions *as* president and nothing else. His prepresidential career had some bearing, but his actions as chief executive were the real heart of Jacksonian democracy. Schlesinger continues: "The point about Professor Abernethy's thesis is that his conclusion is one to be established by evidence, not by deductive logic." Writes Schlesinger, "If Professor Abernethy were to use the same method on Lincoln, or Wilson, or Franklin Roosevelt--that is, to dogmatize on their presidencies on the basis of their pre-presidential records--his results would be self-evidently absurd" (p. 44). As further proof of Abernethy's anti-Jackson bias, Schlesinger points out that in Abernethy's article on Jackson in the *Dictionary of American Biography* only eight of twenty-six paragraphs dealt with Jackson's presidency.

The next scholar to attack Abernethy was Charles G. Sellers, Jr., in two articles published in the *Mississippi Valley Historical Review* (June, 1954, and March, 1958). Sellers writes that it was crucial to have a correct understanding of Jackson because Jackson "was intimately identified with the full flowering of American democracy" (44:615). He argues that Abernethy's interpretation was, in fact, not a new one, but a new form of the old Whig interpretation in which Jackson was a rich elitist. (Schlesinger also touches on this, but he uses the term, Republican-Whig.) The result of this, Sellers says, was that "students of the period have been misled by the interpretation . . . set forth in studies by Thomas Perkins Abernethy" (41:75).

Sellers refutes several of Abernethy's points about Jackson's early career and severely criticizes Abernethy for not proving that Jackson was involved in any land speculation after 1795. Sellers says that even if Jackson had been an opportunist and speculator in his Tennessee days, as President he was a true frontier champion of the people. Sellers concludes that since Jackson knew so many people in the right places and had so many favorable opportunities, if he was opportunistic, why should he "have made such meager use of his opportunities?" (41:78).

Abernethy, however, held firm to his views. Each of his later works in some way supported the thesis presented in *From Frontier to Plantation in Tennessee,* especially *Western Lands and the American Revolution* and *The South in the New Nation.* Abernethy's only direct answer to his critics is found in the preface to the second edition of *From Frontier to Plantation in Tennessee.* In it Abernethy dismisses the charges of his "liberal" critics, Schlesinger in particular, writing that "the politically oriented historians" are apparently "unfettered by any real understanding of the early history of Tennessee or of Jackson's part in it" (p. vi). The dispute proved a standoff. Both interpretations of Jackson are still held in high regard and neither can be totally disproven.

Thomas Perkins Abernethy clearly had an impact on American frontier history. His legacy is still debated. It remains in graduate schools where his views are learned and discussed, it remains in the teachings and writings of his former graduate students, and it remains in its rightful place on the shelves of college and university libraries.

Bibliography

Books

The Burr Conspiracy. New York: Oxford University Press, 1954.

The Formative Period in Alabama, 1815-1828. Montgomery: University of Alabama Press, 1925.

From Frontier to Plantation in Tennessee: A Study in Frontier Democracy. Chapel Hill, NC: University of North Carolina Press, 1932.

The South in the New Nation, 1789-1819. Baton Rouge: Louisiana State University Press, 1961.

Three Virginia Frontiers. Baton Rouge: Louisiana State University Press, 1940.

Western Lands and the American Revolution. New York: D. Appleton-Century Co., 1937.

Articles

"Aaron Burr in Mississippi." *Journal of Southern History* 15(February-November, 1949):9-21.

"Andrew Jackson."In *Dictionary of American Biography,* edited by Dumas Malone. New York: Charles Scribner's Sons, 1932. 5:526-534.

"Andrew Jackson and the Rise of Southwestern Democracy." *American Historical Review* 33(October, 1927):64-77.

"Democracy and the Southern Frontier." *Journal of Southern History* 4(February, 1938):3-13.

"The Early Development of Commerce and Banking in Tennessee." *Mississippi Valley Historical Review* 14(December, 1927):311-325.

"Journal of the First Kentucky Convention, Dec. 27, 1784-Jan. 5, 1785." Editor. *Journal of Southern History* 1(February-November, 1935):67-78.

"The Origins of the Whig Party in Tennessee." *Mississippi Valley Historical Review* 12(March, 1926):504-522.

"Social Relations and Political Control in the Old Southwest." *Mississippi Valley Historical Review* 16 (March, 1930):529-537.

"The Southern Frontier: An Interpretation."In *The Frontier in Perspective* edited by Walker D. Wyman and Clifton B. Kroeber. Madison: University of Wisconsin Press, 1957. Pp. 129-142.

Pamphlets

Historical Sketch of the University of Virginia. Richmond, VA: The Dietz Press, Inc., 1948.

More News From Virginia: A Further Account of Bacon's Rebellion. Editor. Charlottesville: University of Virginia Press, 1943.

A Summary View of the Rights of British America by Thomas Jefferson. Editor. New York: Scholar's Facsimiles and Reprints, 1943.

Selected Reviews

Abernethy wrote literally dozens of book reviews over five decades. His reviews may be found in the *Mississippi Valley Historical Review, Journal of Southern History, American Historical Review,* almost all of the state and regional journals of the South, and in other publications. Some of his more important reviews are included below.

The Atlantic Frontier: Colonial American Civilization by Louis B. Wright. *Journal of Southern History* 14(February, 1948):119-120.

Cavaliers and Pioneers: Abstracts of Virginia Land Patents and Grants, 1623-1800, volume I abstracted and indexed by Nell Marion Nugent. *Journal of Southern History* 1(February and November, 1935):82-83.

Early American Land Companies: Their Influence on Corporate Development by Shaw Livermore. *American Historical Review* 42(January, 1940):408-410.

Gentlemen Freeholders: Political Practices in Washington's Virginia by Charles S. Sydnor. *Mississippi Valley Historical Review* 39(March, 1953):752-753.

George Washington: Volume III Planter and Patriot and *Volume IV Leader of the Revolution* by Douglas Southall Freeman. *Virginia Magazine of History and Biography* 60(January, 1952):180-181.

A History of the College of Charleston, Founded 1770 by J. A. Easterby. *American Historical Review* 41(April, 1936):586-587.

James Madison, the Virginia Revolutionist by Irving Brant. *Journal of Southern History* 8(February and November, 1942):114-115.

Jefferson and Madison: The Great Collaboration by Adrienne Koch. *American Historical Review* 56(October, 1950):123-124.

John Sevier, Pioneer of the Old Southwest by Carl S. Driver. *American Historical Review* 39(October, 1933):138-139.

Lexington in Old Virginia by Henry Bailey. *Journal of Southern History* 2(August, 1936):409-410.

Patrick Henry: Patriot in the Making by Robert D. Meade. *Journal of Southern History* 23(November, 1957):529-530.

The Revolutionary Generation, 1763-1790 by Evarts Boutell Greene. *Journal of Southern History* 10(February, 1948):98-99.

The Slave States in the Presidential Election of 1860 by Ollinger Crenshaw. *Virginia Magazine of History and Biography* 55(April, 1947):181.

The South, New and Old by Francis Butler Simkins. *American Historical Review* 54(October, 1948):157-159.

Travels in the Old South: A Bibliography, 2 volumes, by Thomas Clark. *Mississippi Valley Historical Review* 43(December, 1956):479-481.

Valley of Democracy: The Frontier versus the Plantation in the Ohio Valley, 1775-1818 by John Barnhart. *Journal of Southern History* 20(May, 1954):257-259.

Studies of Thomas Perkins Abernethy

Berwick, Keith B. Review of *The South and the New Nation, 1789-1819* by Thomas Perkins Abernethy. *Virginia Magazine of History and Biography* 70(July, 1962):356.

Cave, Alfred A. *Jacksonian Democracy and the Historians*. Gainesville, FL: University of Florida Press, 1964.

Driver, Carl S. Review of *From Frontier to Plantation in Tennessee* by Thomas Perkins Abernethy. *Mississippi Valley Historical Review* 19(December, 1932):422-423.

Fleming, Walter L. Review of *The Formative Period in Alabama, 1815-1828* by Thomas Perkins Abernethy. *Mississippi Valley Historical Review* 11(March, 1925):586-587.

Greene, Evarts B. Review of *Western Lands and the American Revolution* by Thomas Perkins Abernethy. *American Historical Review* 43(July, 1938):896-898.

Greene, Jack P. Review of *The Old Dominion: Essays for Thomas Perkins Abernethy* edited by Darrett B. Rutman. *Journal of Southern History* 31(August, 1965):326-327.

Higham, John. *History: The Development of Historical Studies in the United States*. Englewood Cliffs, NJ: Prentice Hall, 1965.

Hofstader, Richard. *The Progressive Historians: Turner, Beard, Parrington*. New York: Alfred A. Knopf, 1968.

Hollon, W. Eugene. Review of *The Burr Conspiracy* by Thomas Perkins Abernethy. *Mississippi Valley Historical Review* 41(March, 1955):704-706.

Kraus, Michael. *A History of American History*. New York: Farrar and Rinehart, 1937.

Lynch, William O. Review of *Three Virginia Frontiers* by Thomas Perkins Abernethy. *Journal of Southern History* 7(November, 1941):550-551.

Mooney, Chase C. Review of *The South in the New Nation* by Thomas Perkins Abernethy. *Mississippi Valley Historical Review* 49(June, 1962):123-124.

"New Light on the Nature of Our Frontier Democracy." *New York Times Book Review* May 29, 1932, p. 3.

Nye, Russel B. Review of *The South in the New Nation* by Thomas Perkins Abernethy. *Journal of Southern History* 28(May, 1962):244-247.

Pease, Theodore C. Review of *Western Lands and the American Revolution* by Thomas Perkins Abernethy. *Mississippi Valley Historical Review* 25(December, 1938):399.

Rutman, Darrett B., ed. *The Old Dominion: Essays for Thomas Perkins Abernethy*. Charlottesville: University of Virginia Press, 1964.

Savelle, Max. Review of *Western Lands and the American Revolution* by Thomas Perkins Abernethy. *Political Science Quarterly* 53(September, 1938):469-470.

Schlesinger, Arthur M., Jr. *The Age of Jackson*. Boston: Little, Brown and Co., 1945.

Charles G. Sellers, Jr. "Andrew Jackson versus the Historians." *Mississippi Valley Historical Review* 44(March, 1958):615-634.

__________. "Banking and Politics in Jackson's Tennessee, 1817-1827." *Mississippi Valley Historical Review* 41(June, 1954):61-84.

Silver, James W. Review of *The Burr Conspiracy* by Thomas Perkins Abernethy. *American Historical Review* 60(October, 1954):127-129.

2

GEORGE L. ANDERSON

by Burton J. Williams

Biography

The bucolic town of Blue Rapids lies just south of the juncture of the Little Blue and Big Blue rivers in Marshall County, situated in northeast Kansas. Fifteen miles to the north near present-day Marysville, California-bound forty-niners forded or were ferried across the Big Blue by Frank J. Marshall as they headed northwest en route to Fort Kearney in present-day Nebraska. From that point they turned westward to travel along the Great Platte River Road in pursuit of their iridescent dreams of the California El Dorado. Frank Marshall's lasting legacy is assured by the county named for him. It was here in Blue Rapids that Anders Anderson settled in 1877. Leaving his native Denmark behind, he had joined those thousands of Scandinavians who migrated to America in the 1870s and 1880s. Blue Rapids had already attained the reputation of a milling town when Anders Anderson arrived there. Anders' brother, Peter, and sister, Carolina Anderson Christenson, had migrated from Denmark to America earlier, and Peter was engaged in the milling business at Blue Rapids when Anders joined him. Together they owned four mills along the Blue River; however, a flood in 1903 destroyed the one located in Blue Rapids.

Anders married shortly after settling in Blue Rapids, and to this union a son and daughter were born, Perry and Mary. Shortly thereafter Anders' first wife passed away and he remarried. His new bride was Mary E. Pitman, of Welsh ancestry, whose family had migrated from Alabama to Illinois, and then to Kansas. Three children were born to them, Lena, Bill, and George Anderson, who was the youngest of the children. George was born on February 27, 1905.

George Anderson's father died before George was three years of age, and his mother passed away the following spring. George, his brother Bill, and his sister Lena, were raised by his father's sister, Mary, and her husband, Soren Bertelson, who lived nearby. In addition, George's half-sister, Mary, also lived with Aunt Mary and Uncle Soren. Assuming the responsibility for rearing the Anderson children was particularly difficult for Aunt Mary as she was fifty-one years old at the time, but she insisted on keeping the children together. As a child George attended a country school near Barnes, Kansas. Later his aunt and uncle moved to a farm a few miles from Waterville, and George completed the elementary grades there and then graduated from Waterville High School.

Following graduation from high school, George attended the University of Kansas at Lawrence. Standing more than six feet tall, George was a handsome young man who possessed hands of near gargantuan size. A pencil held in his hand looked like a toothpick. The young man, with big hands and a heart to match, received his A.B. degree from K.U. in 1926. It was here, as an undergraduate, that George Anderson's interest in history was encouraged under the tutelage of Professors Frank H. Hodder and James C. Malin. And here also his love for a charming young coed was sparked. Her name was Caroline Miek. Upon graduation from college George taught school in Waterville for two years, 1926-1928, and in Waterville he married his college sweetheart, Caroline, on June 8, 1928. To them were born two children, Marianne Anderson Wilkerson and James LaVerne Anderson. Following in his father's footsteps, Jim Anderson also became a professor of history and now teaches at the University of Georgia.

In 1928 George became superintendent of the Washington County school system at Barnes, Kansas, for two years. In 1930 he decided to further his education, so he returned to the University of Kansas to do graduate study in history where he received his M.A. degree in 1931. George Anderson studied with Professor James C. Malin, who directed his master's thesis entitled "The Grant Administrations: John Sherman's Position in the Political System." This only whetted his appetite for still more education, and that fall he enrolled at the University of Illinois where he received his Ph.D. degree in history in 1933.

With the Ph.D. degree in hand Anderson took a teaching position at Colorado College in Colorado Springs, Colorado, where he remained until 1945. In that year he was invited to return to his alma mater at Lawrence, Kansas, to join the faculty of the history department. With a sense of mixed emotions, he took leave of the snow-capped Rocky Mountains of Colorado to return to his native state. The history department at K.U. was small in those days, consisting of but five faculty members. Four years later, in 1946, Anderson was selected to be chairman of the department which now numbered eight members. He was forty-five years of age at the time, and he was up to the challenge. Under his leadership the department increased in size from eight to forty faculty members. His growing administrative workload made heavy demands upon his time, but he continued what had already become a hallmark of his many fine characteristics -- his personal interest in students, not just while members of his classes, but for all the years that followed.

While teaching a short course dealing with the history of Southwest Kansas in Dodge City, Kansas, in 1970, he introduced himself to his students as follows: "I am Mr. Anderson - Jayhawker, man and boy, for nearly one half the history of the state. The better seven eights in the family (his wife Caroline) is from Ness County." In the process of making these introductory remarks to his class, he rather simply stated his own philosophy (*Essays on Kansas History in Memoriam*, p. 7):

> In a way I am a lineal descendant of the German historians who believed that simply to know what happened is task enough for any learner in the field of history--too much for some of us.
>
> At the conclusion of last year's course Mrs. Robinson asked each member (of the class) to fill out a questionnaire. Among the critical comments was a suggestion that I did not seem to know very much about the history of Southwest Kansas. That student was absolutely right. In proportion to what there is to know I know very little more than you people know--not as much as some. This makes us learners together--colleagues in the search for knowledge. Probably more because of age and experience I happen to be the leader in this process and unhappily, the judge of the outcome.
>
> Simply stated, history is knowledge of what has happened and the task of the historian is to reconcile as best he can the remembered series of events with the actual series of events.

Just a few days before his death George was hospitalized, but nevertheless, he was still thinking about his students. His wife, Caroline, in his hospital room, read aloud from theses and dissertations nearing completion under his supervision. He even chaired the final oral examination of one of his students from his hospital bed. And only a day before he died, Caroline was able to turn in the final grade for a master's thesis completed by one of his students. On May 5, 1971, George Anderson became a part of history which he so dearly loved.

Themes

George Anderson's primary historical concerns centered around frontier economic institutions. These institutions were regionally conceived, but they had broad human ramifications. He was especially intrigued by banking and railroading.

His Ph.D. dissertation reflected a new and growing interest in banks. It was titled "The National Banking System: A Sectional Institution," and was supervised by the eminent Civil War historian, James G. Randall. This title also reflected his interest in a sectional rather than a national approach to historical phenomena. At his first academic position in Colorado, he developed still another important research interest -- railroads. He turned his attention to the Colorado scene and completed one of his major publications on *General William J. Palmer: A Decade of Colorado Railroad Building, 1870-1880*, first published in 1936. It was reissued in 1963 under the title *Kansas West: An Epic of Western Railroad Building*.

After Anderson returned to the University of Kansas, his interest in banks and banking was rekindled and resulted in a book entitled *The Widening Stream: The Exchange National Bank of Atchison, 1858-1968*, published by Lockwood Press in 1968. His research in banking continued and resulted in still another book published by Coronado Press in 1972 entitled, *Essays on the History of Banking*. During these same years he took up still another major research project, the public lands. His research in this field of study led to the publication of another volume, *Essays on the Public Lands: Problems, Legislation, and Administration*, also published by Coronado Press in 1971. His meticulous research and writing raised a much broader question in his mind, to wit: What was the nature and purpose of history? Throughout his career he searched for a satisfactory answer to this question, and he called upon his students to join with him in pursuit of a satisfactory answer. His own efforts at supplying the answer resulted in his writing a number of essays that were published in book form under the title, *Variations on a Theme: History as Knowledge of the Past*. This, too, was published by Coronado Press in 1970. In these essays he vigorously challenged the popular subjective-relativism approach to history and any form of deterministic interpretation of history. History was not a subject that could be "used" to arrive at predetermined economic, political, or social ends. For history to remain pure and undefiled, it had to be essentially useless. This conviction on the part of George Anderson was no doubt influenced by his mentor, friend, and colleague, James C. Malin.

Malin had been pursuing answers to the questions of the nature and purpose of history long before Anderson took up the challenge. In 1954 Malin published a book, paid for out of his own pocket, entitled, *On the Nature of History: Essays About History and Dissidence*. In this book Malin states that "The historian should not apologize for the fact that history is useless. Not only is history useless, but the historian should take pride in its uselessness. Only in that way can he be free as a historian to pursue his study of history as intellectual enterprise in an objective sense -- his sole motivation being human curiosity, and his sole objective, to know" (p. 39).

George Anderson's interest in this broad topic of the nature and purpose of history led him to organize and direct three historical conferences that took place on the campus of the University of Kansas in 1955, 1956, and 1957. These conferences hosted invited scholars. Not surprisingly, the first of this series of conferences was entitled, "On the Nature and Writing of History." The second and third conferences dealt, respectively, with "The Progressive Period in Brief Perspective" and "Twentieth Century American Diplomatic History." The diplomatic history conference resulted in a volume of essays edited by George Anderson entitled, *Issues and Conflicts: Studies in Twentieth Century American Diplomacy*. It was published by the University of Kansas Press in 1959, and reissued by Greenwood Press in 1969. A fourth conference was held on the K.U. campus in 1969. Its purpose was to honor George for his nineteen years as departmental chairman. Ten leading scholars were invited to present papers which were subsequently published by the University of Kansas Press in 1971 under the title, *The Frontier Challenge: Responses to the Trans-Mississippi West.* Professor Anderson himself presented one of the papers entitled, "Banks, Mails, and Rails." It is a fascinating paper which demonstrates his refusal to accept unproven assumptions. It also reveals that George Anderson was an innovative historian.

Analysis

In reviewing the several thematic interests of George Anderson, it is ironic to note that the title of this reference book would make him uncomfortable. He was quick to declare "I am not a frontier historian!" What then was he, and why is he included in this book of prominent past frontier historians?

Here was a man who eschewed even the use of the term frontier. He could accept the plural of that term, frontiers, but even that made him grimace in discomfort. He much preferred to style himself as a regional historian with particular emphasis on state and local history. And Kansas, of course, was a major focal point of his historical interests. This is not to imply that Kansas was the limit of George Anderson's historical inquiries. The bibliography of his publications attest to a much wider field of historical interests. But the field of Kansas history was his first love. This dedication to state and local history was acquired from his mentor, friend, and colleague, the late, long-time professor of history at the University of Kansas, James C. Malin. Under the tutelage of Professor Malin, first as an undergraduate, then as research assistant while pursuing his master's degree, and finally as colleague, George Anderson began to see history much as Malin saw it. History was to be taught and written from the bottom up, not from the top down. As Malin wrote in 1957 for the *Wisconsin Magazine of History*:

> Local history has been in disrepute for a number of reasons, some of them valid as applied to prevailing practices. But the concept of local history as formulated here achieves a relevance which it is not usually accorded and one that should challenge the capacities of the ablest minds--history written, not from the top down, but from the bottom up--a recognition of the basic fact that all history of human activity must necessarily start from the individual at a particular time and place--locality (p. 227).

The term frontier, then, was much too broad, ill-defined, and vague to serve as an acceptable description of a field of history for Professor Anderson. But George Anderson taught frontier history, albeit by a different title. He regularly taught History 189 at the University of Kansas which was entitled, "History of the Trans-Mississippi West." The class, however, actually dealt with the trans-Missouri West, a title Anderson personally preferred. "Big George," as his students secretly but affectionately called him, taught the history of the American West as a region, a fixed place on the planet. He had little regard for the westward moving line of settlement approach to frontier history made so popular by Frederick Jackson Turner and his disciples. For Anderson this was little more than the beginnings of Anglo-American displacement of Indians which, according to Turner and his associates, came to an end in 1890 and with it came the end of the frontier and its alleged "safety-valve" opportunities. In short, the deterministic, closed-space doctrine of Turner's frontier thesis was a totally unacceptable approach to the history of the American West, at least to George Anderson.

Turner's thesis, with its sweeping generalizations, ignored the particulars, and without particulars, Anderson held no valid construction of history could take place. Anderson's commitment to historical detail was a pronounced characteristic of both his research methodology and his teaching. The syllabus he put together for his undergraduate course in the history of the trans-Mississippi West was twenty-one pages long--and this did not include the bibliography. In this course he stressed a particular geographical region; its geological considerations, land forms, drainage patterns, climatic considerations, and its flora and fauna. In short it was an ecological approach to the study of a region. Following this he stressed the relationships of the region's natural characteristics to the settlement and development of the region. This began with a discussion of the antiquity of Homo sapiens in America; where they came from, how long they had inhabited the continent, and the various stages of the cultural development of America's first true natives, its Indian population. He snorted at the "quickie" approach to frontier history which usually begins with the founding of Jamestown and concludes with the alleged passing or closing of the frontier in 1890.

George Anderson's primary objection to Turner's approach to frontier history was its closed-space, deterministic doctrines. Anderson detested the notion of determinism whether it be economic, political, social,or geographical. In brief he was tenaciously but politely independent. But what perturbed him to a point near exasperation were the disciples of Turner. These disciples suggested that with the passing or closing of the American frontier, it was the responsibility of the federal government to provide substitute opportunities for the American people who were no longer allegedly provided with the "free" lands of our nation's now vanished frontier. The direct applicaion of this sentiment produced the New Deal of the 1930s, with its emphasis on federally-sponsored programs of relief and recovery for the distressed citizenry of that depression decade. In George Anderson's eyes this was blatant political collectivism which struck at the very heart of our commonly held and cherished traditions of self-help, coupled with personal and corporate philanthropy. A deeply religious man himself, he, perhaps a bit too idealistically, preferred and practiced Christian charity. To him federal philanthropy could well mean the creation of a nation of federal dependents, and this in turn stymied individual initiative and with it a sense of personal responsibility not only for ourselves, but for our less fortunate needy citizenry. Anderson was deeply committed to the private or free enterprise system. But such a system was to be heavily laced with personal and corporate integrity, and this was to be coupled with a compassionate commitment to philanthropy.

George Anderson was also vigorously committed to the belief that history was a branch of the humanities--period! It was not social science. He elaborated on this conviction in considerable detail in an address he made to the Kansas History Teachers' Association in May, 1952. The brief title of that address alone made his position quite clear, it was "History vs. Social Science." In his opening remarks he calls for "a complete divorce, on grounds of intellectual incompatibility, of history from the social sciences; it is a plea directed to the historical profession to engage in a long overdue housecleaning so that the discipline for which it is responsible may be restored to a reasonable facsimile of its former self; and it is a plea that history be restored to a central place in the curricula of secondary schools, colleges, and universities" (p. 4).

Unfortunately, George Anderson's plea was but a voice crying in the wilderness. Professional and social science curricular pursuits in our nation's school system, at all levels, public or private, are firmly ensconced. History, as a discipline, has been bucked from the curricular saddle and lies sprawled in the dust in favor of a new rider (discipline), functional social science and professional pursuits. George Anderson believed "that the time has come when the assertion should be made deliberately and advisedly that functional social science programs are the concomitant if not the very foundation stone of totalitarian forms of government" (p. 8). Anderson saw this educational trend as always and only education *for* something, not education *in* something.

Professor Anderson buttressed his argument on behalf of history for history's sake by reference to an article written by V. A. McCrossen in 1941 entitled, "How Totalitarian Is Our Education" *(Association of American Colleges Bulletin* 25:827-845). In this article McCrossen asserts that Lenin and Trotsky, as well as many Russian educators, repeatedly stated that the way to make a good Communist out of a pupil is to have him deny God, love sex, and study the social sciences.

John Dewey, patron saint of professional educators, was particularly annoying to George Anderson. As Anderson saw it, history for its own sake was attacked with increasing vigor "by educators who were inspired by Dewey, and by sociologists who wanted to make history a more useful subject" ("History vs. Social Science," p. 9). According to at least one Dewey disciple, "The true starting point of history is always some present situation with its problems" (p. 11). This subjective-relativist approach to history reached its apex in our public schools with the nonsense notion that history could be taught in "reverse chronology."

It is obvious from the foregoing that George Anderson was deeply committed not only to the teaching and writing of history, but also to teaching and writing about history. This is made even more evident in his book entitled *Variations on a Theme: History as Knowledge of the Past* (1970). In this volume are chapters devoted to the discipline of history: "History in the Making," "The Nature and Learning of History," "Characteristics of Good Teaching in History," "History: Instant or Authentic," and "History: Global or Provincial." In these essays he expresses his disdain for "quickie" history which searched the past only for its usable parts which could then be applied to shape or justify a present position or proposed outcome. He also deplored the pathological emphasis given to violence in the American West. He exhorted his students to minimize their interest in "triggernometry," and encouraged them to study history in its entirety. In Anderson's view there was far too much emphasis given to a small minority of "bad guys," and not enough emphasis given to the vast majority of good folk, and he enjoyed using the word folk.

In analyzing George Anderson, the man and historian, appropriate attention must also be given to his strong religious faith. As a staunch member of the United Lutheran Church in America he played an active and important role. He served on that denomination's Board of Education for fourteen years. In addition, he served in several capacities of Lutheran student programs. He was also a lay minister and delivered countless sermons in Colorado and Kansas. Further, he wrote the history of several Lutheran churches, including Trinity Lutheran Church in Lawrence. And there is more--he served on a number of local and synod boards, and taught Sunday School in virtually every church he ever attended. In every sense of the word he was both a Christian gentleman and educator. He took his religion and history seriously, but neither church nor history was to be "used" to achieve devious ends.

As a historian, he lent his best efforts to the cause of history for history's sake at the local, state, and national levels. And above all he understood the vital place of local history within the larger framework of regional, national, and even world history. He provided leadership in organizations devoted to history at all levels.

At the national level he served from 1955 to 1957 as chairman of the Executive Committee of the Mississippi Valley Historical Association. He also served as a member of the editorial board of this association from 1957 to 1960. In 1956 he was elected president of the Agricultural History Society. At the state and local level he served as a member of the board of directors of the Kansas State Historical Society for many years, and was chosen to be the Society's president in 1961. That was the year of my arrival at the University of Kansas as a Ph.D. aspirant. As president of the state's historical society, he was preparing his presidential address for the annual meeting. The title of his address was "Atchison and the Central Branch Country, 1865-1874." This first year Ph.D. student was absolutely amazed when he was presented with a draft copy of the presidental address and asked to critique it. That was the measure of a real man.

In 1951 he was elected president of the Kansas History Teachers' Association, and in 1967 he was chosen as president of the Douglas County (Kansas) Historical Society. In addition, he served as both consultant and teacher of history at the Cultural and Heritage Arts Center in Dodge City, Kansas. He also served on the Research and Publication Committee of the American Association for State and Local History, and on the Advisory Council of the American History Research Center of the State Historical Society of Wisconsin.

Perhaps the ultimate measure of a professor's life is to be found in the accomplishments of his students, and perhaps the most accomplished of George Anderson's many students was the late John D. Unruh, Jr. Unruh wrote his doctoral dissertation under the supervision of Professor Anderson, and it resulted in the prize winning book, *The Plains Across: The Overland Emigrants and the Trans-Mississippi West, 1840-1860*. Before Unruh's untimely death at the age of thirty-nine, he penned in *Essays on Kansas History in Memoriam* (1977) the following tribute to his mentor-friend George Anderson:

> Our lives were enriched simply by knowing him. He was an example of what an administrator, historian, teacher and friend should be, a man of complete integrity who will always serve as a measure against which we can gauge our own success. I suspect that because we were privileged to know him we all came closer to understanding what history and life are all about (p. 18).

This was George Anderson, gentleman and teacher, probing scholar and true friend.

Bibliography

Books

Essays on the History of Banking. Lawrence, KS: Coronado Press, 1972.

Essays on the Public Lands: Problems, Legislation, and Administration. Lawrence, KS: Coronado Press, 1971.

Four Essays on Railroads in Kansas and Colorado. Lawrence, KS: Coronado Press, 1971.

General William J. Palmer: A Decade of Colorado Railroad Building, 1870-1880. Colorado Springs, CO: Dentan Publishing Company, 1936. Reprinted as *Kansas West: An Epic of Western Railroad Building*. San Marino, CA: Pacific Railroad Publications, Inc., 1963.

Issues and Conflicts: Studies in Twentieth Century American Diplomacy. Editor. Lawrence: University of Kansas Press, 1959. Reprint. Westport, CT: Greenwood Press, 1969.

A Petition Regarding the Conditions in the C.S.M. Prison at Columbia, SC Addressed to the Confederate Authorities by Col. John Fraser, Later Second Chancellor of the University of Kansas,. Editor. Lawrence: University of Kansas Libraries, 1962.

Trinity Lutheran Church, Lawrence, Kansas, 1867-1967. Lawrence, KS: Privately published, 1967.

Variations on a Theme: History as Knowledge of the Past. Lawrence, KS: Coronado Press, 1970.

The Widening Stream: The Exchange National Bank of Atchison, 1858-1968. Atchison, KS: Lockwood Press, 1968.

Articles

"The Administration of Federal Land Laws in Western Kansas, 1880-1890: A Factor in Adjustment to a New Environment." *Kansas Historical Quarterly* 20(November, 1952):233-251.

"Atchison, 1865-1886, Divided and Uncertain." *Kansas Historical Quarterly* 35(Spring, 1969):30-45.

"Atchison and the Central Branch Country, 1865-1874." *Kansas Historical Quarterly* 28(Spring, 1962):1-24.

"The Balm of History." *Christian Education* (now the *Christian Scholar*) 35(June 1951):146-150. Reprint. *Jayhawker* 63(1951):9ff.

"Banking and Monetary Problems." In *Colorado and Its People: A Narrative and Topical History of The Centennial State* edited by LeRoy R. Hafen. New York: Lewis Historical Publishing Co., 1948.

"Banks, Mails, and Rails, 1880-1915." In *The Frontier Challenge: Responses to the Trans-Mississippi West* edited by John G. Clark. Lawrence: University of Kansas Press, 1975. Pp. 275-307.

"Beginnings of Federal Land Machinery in Territorial Kansas." *Your Government* 9(1954):3-4.

"The Board of Equitable Adjudication, 1846-1930." *Agricultural History* 29(April, 1955):65-72.

"By Sea to the California Gold Fields, 1850-1851." *The Trail Guide* 13(1968):1-23.

"The Canon City or Arkansas Valley Claim Club, 1860-1862." *Colorado Magazine* 16(1939):201.

"A Century of Banking in Kansas." In *Kansas: The First Century* edited by John D. Bright. New York: Lewis Publishing Company, 1957. Chapter 39.

"Colorado." *Collier's Encyclopedia* 5(1952):485-494.

"Colorado." *Collier's Yearbook* (1946):132-133; (1947):143.

"The Diary of Thomas K. Mitchell." *Books and Libraries of the University of Kansas* 2(1961):2-3.

"Education for Democracy in Retrospect." *School and Society* 52(November 23, 1940):511-517.

"The El Paso Claim Club, 1859-1862." *Colorado Magazine* 13(1936):41-53.

"The Forty-fourth Annual Meeting of the Mississippi Valley Historical Association." *Mississippi Valley Historical Review* 38(September, 1951):251-278.

"Frank Heywood Hodder and the Kansas-Nebraska Act, 1854-1954." *Your Government* 9(1954):4.

"From Cattle to Wheat: The Impact of Agricultural Developments on Banking in Early Wichita." *Agricultural History* 33(January, 1959):3-15.

"General William J. Palmer, Anti-Imperialist, 1895-1905." *Colorado Magazine* 22(1945):7-23.

"General William Jackson Palmer: Man of Vision." *Colorado College Studies* (1960):1-23.

"History vs. Social Science." In *Studies in American History in Honor of James C. Malin.* Lawrence, KS: Coronado Press, 1973. Pp. 1-21.

"Kansas." *Collier's Yearbook* (1946):274; (1947):306; (1948):365; (1949):450-451; (1950):393-394; (1951):368; (1954):317-318.

"The Kansas Synod, 1868-1948."In *Minutes of the Eighteenth Annual Convention of the Evangelical Lutheran Synod of Kansas and Adjacent States.* Lawrence, KS: Outlook Publishing Co., 1948.

"Mechanical Aids in Historical Research." In *In Support of Clio: Essays in Memory of Herbert A. Kellar* edited by William B. Hesseltine and Donald R. McNeil. Madison: State Historical Society of Wisconsin, 1958. Pp. 77-105.

"A North-South Link: Missouri Pacific's Proposal: Union Pacific's Achievement, 1889-1910." *Kansas Historical Quarterly* 2(Summer, 1970):88-96.

"Some Phases of Currency and Banking in Territorial Kansas." In *Territorial Kansas: Studies Commemorating the Centennial.* Lawrence: University of Kansas Publication, Social Sciences Studies, 1954. Pp. 103-147.

"The South and Problems of Post-Civil War Finance." *Journal of Southern History* 9(May, 1943):181-195.

"The Territory of Kansas, 1854-1861." *Your Government* 9(1953):4.

"Western Attitudes Toward National Banks, 1873-1874." *Mississippi Valley Historical Review* 23(September, 1936):205-216.

Reviews

The Adams-Jefferson Letters: The Complete Correspondence between Thomas Jefferson and Abigail and John Adams edited by Lester J. Cappon. *The Historian* 23(May, 1960):433-435.

Agriculture and the Civil War by Paul Wallace Gates. *Journal of Political Economy* 74(December, 1966):643-644.

American Industry and the European Immigrant by Charlotte Erickson. A review essay published in a pamphlet by the National Bank Foundation, September, 1959.

The Cabinet and Congress by Stephen Hern. *Mid-Continent American Studies Journal* 3(1962):65.

California Ranches and Farms, 1846-1862 by Paul Wallace Gates. *American Historical Review* 74(October, 1968):291-292.

Can Representative Government Do the Job? by Thomas K. Finletter. *Pacific Historical Review* 14(September, 1945):361-362.

The Confederate Quartermaster in the Trans-Mississippi West by James L. Nichols. *Civil War History* 11(September, 1965):319-321.

The Decline of Agrarian Democracy by Grant McConnell. A review essay published in a pamphlet by the National Bank Foundation, September, 1959.

Essays on American Historiography: Papers Presented in Honor of Allan Nevins edited by Donald Sheehan and Harold C. Syrett. *Mid-Continent American Studies Journal* 3(1962):62.

Fabulous Empire: Colonel Zake Miller's Story by Fred Gipson. *Pacific Historical Review* 16(May, 1947):189-190.

Fifty Million Acres: Conflicts over Kansas Land Policy, 1854-1890 by Paul Wallace Gates. *Wisconsin Magazine of History* 34(Spring, 1956):220-221.

Foreign Relations of the United States: Diplomatic Papers, the Conference at Malta and Yalta 1945. World Affairs Quarterly 27(1957):388-391.

Frontier Doctor by Samuel J. Crumbine. *Pacific Historical Review* 18(May, 1949):258-259.

The Greenback Era: A Social and Political History of American Finances, 1865-1879 by Irwin Unger. *Agricultural History* 39(July, 1965):169-170.

Gulf to Rockies: The Heritage of the Fort Worth and Denver-Colorado and Southern Railways, 1861-1898 by Richard C. Overton. *Pacific Historical Review* 23(June, 1954):290-291.

Harry L. Russell and Agricultural Science in Wisconsin by Edward H. Beardsley. *American Historical Review* 75(October, 1970):1792.

History of Public Land Law Development by Paul W. Gates. *Western Historical Quarterly* 1(April, 1970):190-192.

Iron Road to Empire: The History of 100 Years of the Progress and Achievement of the Rock Island Lines by William Edward Hayes. *Mississippi Valley Historical Review* 42(December, 1955):344-345.

James Monroe: Public Claimant by Lucius Wilmerding, Jr. *Mid-Continent American Studies Journal* 3(1962):67.

Merchants and Planters by Richard Pares. *Journal of the Central Mississippi Valley American Studies Association* 1(1960):41.

The Molding of American Banking: Men and Ideas by Fritz Redlich. *Mississippi Valley Historical Review* 34(December, 1947):481-482.

Money and American Society, 1865-1880 by Walter T. Nugent. *Business History Review* 43(Spring, 1969):101-102.

Money at Interest: The Farm Mortgage on the Middle Border by Allan G. Bogue. *Mississippi Valley Historical Review* 43(June, 1956):143-144; also reprinted as a review essay published in a pamphlet by the National Bank Foundation, September, 1959.

Oil on Stream: A History of Interstate Oil Pipe Line Company by John Loos. *Nebraska History* 41(1960):157-159.

Oklahoma: Foot-loose and Fancy-free by Angie Debo. *Mississippi Valley Historical Review* 37(June, 1950):140-141.

Political Prairie Fire: The Nonpartisan League, 1915-1922 by Robert L. Morlan. *Indiana Magazine of History* 52(June, 1956):205-208.

Politics and Grass: The Administration of Grazing on the Public Domain by Phillip O. Foss. *History News* 26(1961):48.

Prairie Trails and Cow Towns: The Opening of the Old West by Floyd Benjamin Streeter. *Southern California Quarterly* (December, 1965):420-421.

The Public Lands: Studies in the History of the Public Domain edited by Vernon Carstensen. *Arizona and the West* 6(Summer, 1964):162-164.

Rebel of the Rockies: A History of the Denver and Rio Grande Western Railroad by Robert G. Athearn. *Mississippi Valley Historical Review* 50(June, 1963):133-134.

The Reluctant Farmer: The Rise of Agricultural Extension to 1914 by Roy V. Scott. *American West* 8(July, 1971):56-57.

Scholarship and Cataclysm: Teaching and Research on American History, 1939-1945 by Edgar Eugene Robinson. *The Historian* 10(Autumn, 1948):158-161.

Shelby M. Cullom: Prairie State Republicanism by James W. Neilson. *Mid-Continent American Studies Journal* 7(1966):72.

Steelways of New England by Alvin E. Harlow. *Mississippi Vallley Historical Review* 33(June, 1946):163-164.

Struggle for Equal Opportunity: Dirt Farmers and the American Country Life Association by Orrin L. Keener. *American Historical Review* 68(October, 1962):255.

Sunset Cox: Irrepressible Democrat by David Lindsey. *Mississippi Valley Historical Review* 47(June, 1960):144-145.

The Territories of the United States, 1861-1890: Studies in Colonial Administration by Earl S. Pomeroy. *American Historical Review* 52(July, 1947):751-752.

The Texas-Santa Fe Pioneer by Noel M. Loomis. *Mid-Continent American Studies Journal* 3(1962):69.

This Almost Chosen People by Russel B. Nye. *Indiana Magazine of History* 63(June, 1967):170-171.

The Tolerant Populists: Kansas Populism and Nativism by Walter T. Nugent. *Indiana Magazine of History* 49(September, 1963):395-396.

Western Yesterdays: Thomas Fitzpatrick, Railroadman by Forest Crossen. *Colorado Magazine* 45(1968):354-355.

The Wilderness Road by Robert L. Kincaid. *Mississippi Valley Historical Review* 34(March, 1948):679-680.

William Body Allison: A Study of Practical Politics by Leland L. Sage. *Wisconsin Magazine of History* 40(March, 1957):297.

Studies of George L. Anderson

Williams, Burton J., ed. *Essays on Kansas History in Memoriam.* Lawrence, KS: Coronado Press, 1977.

3

ROBERT G. ATHEARN

by Elliott West

Biography

It might seem that a historian born in a place called Kremlin would drift into Russian studies, but it was the land around this small Montana town, not its name, that influenced the life of Robert G. Athearn. Kremlin sits just west of Havre in the north central part of the state, near U.S. 2 and "Gentleman Jim" Hill's Great Northern Railroad. It is square in what once was Blackfoot hunting grounds, not far north and east of the course of Lewis and Clark, and close to the sites of Forts Assiniboine, Benton, and Union. During the generation before Athearn's birth on August 30, 1914, Scandinavian farmers had brought the farming frontier to this high plains region. It is country "layered in history from the day of the fur traders to modern missile bases," Athearn remembered (*Western Historical Quarterly* 2:125), an appropriate choice of words for a man who would write on western history from the earliest frontier until the present.

When he was still a small boy, Athearn's family moved to Havre, a market center that boasted department stores, banks, and a library, two movie theaters, speakeasies and a tea room--hardly a rude frontier outpost--but at seven Athearn was sent to live for a summer on his grandfather's ranch along the Missouri River. "Going there was like having the time machine slip a few cogs," he wrote more than sixty years later in *The Mythic West*. In and around the cottonwood log buildings he had a taste of the frontier West, helping break horses and playing in the isolated country along the Missouri breaks. He found the experience "suffocating" at the time, but it planted a seed of interest in the story of an older West and the passage of its people into the modern era.

After education in the Havre public schools, Athearn attended Northern Montana College for two years, then went on to the University of Minnesota. There he was drawn to Ernest Staples Osgood. A student of Frederic L. Paxson, Osgood was a dynamic teacher whose writing concentrated on the cattle industry and the frontier of the northern Great

Plains. His influence on Athearn, in his subjects of interest, approach and style, was profound: "He was the Pied Piper, and we followed him westward, unquestioningly and even devoutly" (*Western Historical Quarterly* 2:128).

Athearn received his B.A. at the University of Minnesota in 1936 and his M.A. in 1938. His doctoral work was interrupted by service as an officer in the Coast Guard from 1942 to 1945, but he returned to complete the degree in 1947, writing his dissertation on Thomas Francis Meagher, an Irish revolutionary who ended his life as territorial Secretary of Montana. In 1942 he married Claire Raney, whom he would come to regard as his best and most helpful editor. Two children, Dana and Frederic, would come from the marriage.

Upon graduation Athearn took a post at the University of Colorado at Boulder. There he remained throughout his career, leaving only for summer stints at the Universities of Maine and Montana, an appointment as a Fulbright lecturer in Wales in 1960, and a series of lectures in Italy, England, and the Netherlands in 1961. At Boulder he rose steadily through the ranks and emerged as a popular classroom lecturer. He also began to contribute to the deparment's graduate program, and in time his seminars attracted great numbers of students, many of whom chose to work with him toward their graduate degrees. By his retirement he had directed twenty-eight persons to completion of their doctorates, a number matched by few others in the field, and the University of Colorado had become known as an important center for the study of the West. As did their mentor, these students showed a great diversity of historical interests, writing on topics ranging from railroads and public policy, through dude ranches and mining, to saloons, baseball, and cats. In 1983, ten of his students published a collection of essays in his honor, *A Taste of the West*.

Athearn's first book, *Thomas Francis Meagher: An Irish Revolutionary in America*, an expansion of his dissertation, was published in 1949. Though he later would refer to Meagher as a "third-rate hanger-on," Athearn also acknowledged that this research led to more important subjects, William T. Sherman in particular. Meagher's experiences may also have piqued his interest in foreigners' views of the country beyond the Mississippi. In any case, *Westward the Briton*, a study of British travelers and their impressions, and a biography of Sherman appeared respectively in 1953 and 1956. He turned then to a synthesis of the history of his most familiar turf, the northern Plains and Rocky Mountains. The result, *High Country Empire*, was probably his most popular book; its easy style and masterful weaving of the various strands of western development demonstrate his most recognized talents.

Athearn's career then took a turn when officials of the Denver and Rio Grande Western asked him to write a history of that famous narrow gauge line. He agreed, and after *Rebel of the Rockies* appeared in 1962, he was approached by the president of the Union Pacific Foundation, who offered Athearn access to previously restricted files of the Union Pacific so he might produce a study of the first transcontinental on the centennial of its completion. This large undertaking led in 1971 to *Union Pacific*

Country, which traces both the building of the railroad and its impact on the land through which it passed. Together these two works convinced Athearn of the value of a broad approach to the relationship between corporate and western history.

Nonetheless he turned his attention back to military and regional history. It was "a great deal of fun to write" *Forts of the Upper Missouri*, he would say of this book set in the country of his boyhood (*Western Historical Quarterly* 2:130). Nine years later he published *The Coloradans*, a highly readable but interpretive history of the adopted home of his adult years. Then, spurred perhaps by the new interest in the black experience in the West, Athearn examined the exodus to the Kansas plains of recently freed southern slaves in 1879. Though he left another manuscript ready for publication, this foray into black history, *In Search of Canaan*, was the last book published during his lifetime. Adding to this prolific record were forty-eight articles written or edited for twenty different journals, most of them related to his book-length publications, and nearly 150 book reviews. He also edited a large collection of letters, co-authored texts on the history of the West and Colorado, and contributed to thirteen other books.

As his reputation as an author and scholar flourished, Athearn played a growing role in professional organizations. From its birth he was one of the guiding figures in the Western History Association (WHA), serving on its executive committee from 1962 until 1965, when he became its third president. Acknowledging both his service and his academic contributions, the WHA in 1982 established a biennial award in his name for the best book on the West in the twentieth century. He served also on the executive committee of the Mississippi Valley Historical Association, the advisory council of the Western Heritage Center, and the editorial boards of seven historical journals, including the *Western Historical Quarterly* and *Pacific Historical Review*. Athearn was also long associated with *Montana: The Magazine of Western History* as an informal adviser, vigorous and effective supporter, and book review editor from 1955 until 1978.

Along the way his remarkable list of publications and his many professional duties won Athearn wide recognition and numerous awards. In 1971 the American Association of State and Local History, after issuing awards of merit for three of his books, gave him a special award for his distinguished contribution to the history of the West. *High Country Empire* was a White House Library selection in 1965 as a book especially interpretive of American life, and in 1977 the Mountain-Plains Library Association issued to him its first Contribution Award. The University of Colorado recognized his accomplishments as author and teacher on several occasions, including the award of the University of Colorado Medal in 1982. Perhaps his greatest honor came in October, 1983, when the Western History Association named him as the first recipient of its award for a distinguished body of writing on western history. On November 13, 1983, he died of cancer at the age of sixty-nine.

Athearn's contributions went well beyond writing and formal professional service, however. Outgoing, accessible, a ready source of both opinion and praise, and an apparently bottomless reservoir of stories and jokes, he demonstrated that academic rigor, personal warmth, integrity, and a sense of humor could be lifelong, loving companions, With others such as Ray Allen Billington, he cultivated a tone of openness that became a tradition in gatherings of the Western History Association and other groups. His graceful writing style and his convivial personality helped maintain the wide public interest in western history. The awards committee of WHA best summed up his place among his peers:

> Many scholars are held in respect for their capacity to dig out material and publish, some are admired for their originality, fewer still win friends among their readers, but only a handful come in many ways to embody the field itself. Robert Athearn's zeal, large-mindedness, and generosity make him one of that rare handful (*Western Historical Quarterly* 15:134).

Themes

In fitting the work of Robert Athearn among that of other historians, it is important to begin by noting what he was not. In the work of Turner or Webb, a reader can find one or a few grand unifying ideas, but there is no single analytical framework tying together Athearn's many books and articles. He did not develop any highly original techniques as did, for instance, James C. Malin, to help us feel our way toward new insights in western history. Athearn often is called a social historian, but a reader will find in his work virtually none of the approaches taken by most scholars in that field today--quantification, the meticulous study of local history and the daily lives of ordinary folk, or an interdisciplinary weaving of economic, sociological, and psychological theory.

Instead of developing an "Athearn thesis" or refining an innovative methodology, he moved through a remarkable variety of subjects, from railroads and tourists to soldiers and black homesteaders, saying what he had to say in a smooth, almost conversational prose. This breadth of interests complicates somewhat the search for clear and consistent themes. Athearn, furthermore, rarely stood aside in the text to ruminate on the larger meaning of the subject at hand and belabor readers with the points he considered especially important. Nevertheless, anyone who reads his work will find certain threads running through the few thousand pages of his books and articles. Together these ideas offer a perspective on the West and its development that is peculiarly Athearn's.

Among these ideas, four themes stand out. One considers in a broad context the role of business and technology in the development of the West. The second, related to the first, emphasizes the part played by the national government in western growth and settlement. A third focuses upon issues of regionalism, the extent to which unique conditions have shaped the evolution of society and institutions in one part of the West in particular, the northern Plains and Rocky Mountains. Finally, pervading the first three themes is the question of myth and popular perceptions, the ways that beliefs and attitudes about the place, some correct and others wildly distorted, have themselves been powerful forces in the making of the modern West.

Analysis

A closer look at the themes in Athearn's work is certainly worthwhile, but in a sense such analysis misses an important point, for his reputation grew not only from what he wrote but also how he wrote it. From Robert Athearn's typewriter came some of the most readable and entertaining western history of his generation. The reader always can depend upon a vigorous yet smoothly flowing style, fresh turns of phrase, and vivid metaphors and images that bring the narrative to life. He cultivated a gift for choosing especially colorful and revealing quotations and examples. Through all this, finally, ran an engaging sense of humor so characteristic of Athearn, the man. The reader never knows when he might be ambushed in the middle of a paragraph by an unexpected--and often very funny--anecdote, such as the story of the Montana horse soldiers who eased their winter boredom by teaching Sioux warriors to play poker, only to discover the natives much preferred jacks ("chiefs") over kings and scorned queens ("squaws") altogether (*Forts of the Upper Missouri*, p. 45).

He also was one of the master synthesizers of his field. This talent was most evident in his texts on western and American history and in his broad regional and state studies, but it is there also in his treatment of more specific subjects. Thus the building of the Union Pacific Railroad is placed in the context of the changing land and society through which it passed, and in a few sentences or paragraphs that in turn is set within the larger story of national development. In this sense the reader always knows where he is, historically speaking; the bearings given in a few short passages are uncannily precise. The pieces fit so snugly and the story moves so easily that it is easy to miss the depth of understanding that supports it all.

In this sense Athearn should be placed squarely within the narrative historical tradition that has played such a prominent part in the writing on the frontier and the West. His approach invites the same criticism leveled at others who have chosen it--that narrative historians too seldom question the prevailing asssumptions of their subjects, for instance, and that their attention to the big picture obscures the varieties and complexities of life in the West.

Such complaints are to some degree justified in Athearn's case. But it should be emphasized that, though he sometimes is called a "traditionalist," the term is really far off the mark. He contributed to areas, such as black history, that had been largely ignored when he was writing, and he was among the first to heed the call for the study of the West in the twentieth century. And by placing the more traditional topics of business and military history always in the broader context of their surrounding societies, Athearn was arguing for what today is called a "holistic" approach to the past. At his best, then, Athearn entertained and amused his readers even as he urged them to think of the American West in new ways.

Among the themes he stressed in his writing, the importance of business and technology is perhaps the most obvious. He would never have denied the crucial role played in westward expansion by the ambitious, persevering frontiersman and his family, but he emphasized often that the pioneers had never acted alone. Always they were encouraged and aided by outside forces, and of these the eastern business establishment was among the most influential. Arm-in-arm with business, furthermore, was a technological revolution providing essential instruments of survival and connecting the newcomers with distant sources of support. While such outside support had been a factor throughout the history of the moving West, its significance increased during the late nineteenth century, years when an extraordinary economic expansion helped propel the wave of settlement into the demanding environment of the nation's final frontier.

Walter Prescott Webb and Fred Shannon, among others, already had written of the importance of technology and business in the settlement of the Great Plains, but Athearn's work still stands apart from theirs. Others, for example, typically emphasized the important role of new agricultural tools and devices in subduing the land, from steel plows and combines to windmills and barbed wire. Athearn focused instead upon the technological wonder of the age, the railroad. "The foundation of high plains civilization was made of steel . . . brought from industrial America in the form of rails," he writes in *High Country Empire* (p. 152), "Without rail service, the main army of frontiersmen--the farmers--could not have braved the arid, windswept plains." Reviewing a study of western railroads, Athearn portrayed the railroad as a tool consciously developed to help accomplish western settlement, a "great steel weapon" honed for the final assault on the last frontier (*Pacific Historical Review* 50:112).

Such ideas are found most obviously in his two volumes on railroad history, *Rebel of the Rockies* (1962) and *Union Pacific Country* (1971). The first in a way is uncharacteristic of Athearn, a sparklingly written but rather straightforward business history concentrating on the builders, promoters, and corporate wars of Colorado's famous narrow gauge line. The second, however, he intended not as the history of a company but as "one chapter in the larger story of how the American West was penetrated, settled, and developed with the aid of steam and iron" (p. 18). Throughout this book Athearn shows how the iron horse was the common element among the various developments that transformed the region, attracting farmers and cattlemen and miners, creating towns that in turn drew in capital and regional promoters, and providing military leaders the personnel, material, and mobility needed to control the native inhabitants. It is an artful weaving of social and economic history, one of the finest in western historiography.

Athearn's business history is set apart by another, subtler element--the role of image and myth. William Jackson Palmer, builder of the Denver and Rio Grande Railroad, for instance, initially was not inspired just by the lust for profits and fat dividends. To him, the railroad was merely the means to attract immigrants who would build along the Front Range of the Rockies idyllic communities free of social strife. Palmer was less a hard-nosed capitalist than another romantic drawn to the West as a land of personal and social regeneration. Similarly, leaders of corporations like the Union Pacific played upon and expanded the old idea of the West as a land of opportunity. They had good and practical reasons to do so, and their promotions and propagandizing helped mightily in the creation of the inflated visions of the Far West that thrilled the American public. In this way, too, business contributed to westward expansion, but Athearn, always a lover of irony, shows also how the myth might turn upon the businessmen. The glittering images that they themselves helped promote lured executives into questionable decisions, attracted competitors that bit into the company's market, and tempted settlers onto land that could not support them, thus paving the way to economic catastrophe and public rage against the railroad itself. The kingpins of the rail empires often seem as much victims as exploiters of the myth.

The Union Pacific was built only with massive economic assistance from the national government. This was only one of innumerable cases, Athearn wrote, in which Washington encouraged and supported the advance of the frontier, and though enterprises such as the Union Pacific often were hindered as well as helped by government policies, Athearn considered the influence of this outside aid over the years as generally beneficial. This second theme in Athearn's writing, the role of government in western history, in fact is often closely linked to the first, but its implications go far beyond the impact of business. The government in Washington, Athearn believed, always treated the settlers of the West like pampered children. Benefits were given the trans-Appalachian West in the form of support for roads and canals, but in the lands across the Missouri the support was both much greater and much more varied. To the cattlemen the free grass on the open range was "a kind of subsidy by default," while miners and lumbermen assumed the public domain would be available to them on extraordinarily generous terms (*Union Pacific Country*, p. 378). The Homestead and Pre-emption Acts, for all their shortcomings, still represented massive gifts of land that might have been held for sale at higher prices later. Indirectly Washington has propped up westerners and their economy from the nineteenth century until the present through subsidies to rail, road, and air transportation; research into baffling problems of agriculture; massive reclamation projects; sprawling military establishments; and the leasing of public land at cheap rates.

During the nineteenth century the role of one arm of the government--the military--was especially important. In his two books on this subject, *William Tecumseh Sherman and the Settlement of the West* (1956) and *Forts of the Upper Missouri* (1967), Athearn details the ways the army and its leaders encouraged the westering impulse. The soldiers protected prospective settlers, of course, and the campaigns against the Indians occupy much of this pair of volumes, but just as his railroad history is filled with a continuous interaction between business and the developing western society, so his military history unfolds within the larger process of the country's development. The story of military operations on the upper Missouri, for instance, is woven into that of the mining booms of Montana and the tentative development of the northern Plains.

His biography of Sherman provided Athearn with a much broader canvas to make his point, for the Civil War hero was in command first of the High Plains and then of the entire army during the crucial years between 1865 and 1883. In directing the army in the West, Sherman was moved by a Jacksonian belief in the rightness of expansion. He toured the West, commented upon it, and mixed with its restless people. He eagerly encouraged construction of the railroad--"the most important event of modern times," he thought--because he knew it would bring towns, farms, and businesses (*William Tecumseh Sherman and the Settlement of the West*, p. 344). In short, Sherman seemed to see no line between military activities and the transformation of the region by his countrymen. His directing policies were intricately--and, Sherman believed, benevolently--involved with western growth. Nonetheless, the settlers and journalists often turned upon him, criticizing the army's conduct and his own shortcomings. This, with his famous exploits during the Civil War, obscured Sherman's brilliant contributions to western settlement. Ironically, the man who saw himself as a great builder is mainly remembered as an angel of destruction and death, the destroyer of a southern state and the officer who supposedly thought that the only good Indians were dead.

This unjust impression of Sherman is part of a larger ironic point made frequently in Athearn's books. The national government has been rewarded for its encouragement and support of western growth by frequent and bitter condemnation by those being helped. The early complaints about the army's inadequacies were part of an ongoing refrain about Washington's supposed failures and mistreatment of the pioneers and their descendants. This puzzling reaction in turn is related to a more basic issue that has drawn the interest of other historians--colonialism, the question of whether the West has been unjustly exploited by powerful economic and political forces in the East. Athearn's emphasis upon the roles of business and government naturally led him to consider this issue. Although he never addressed systematically the question of class and the direction of western development by outside elites, he seemed to agree at several points with Walter Prescott Webb (*Divided We Stand: The Crisis in a Frontierless Democracy* [1937]) and Bernard DeVoto (*Harper's Magazine* 179:355-364) that from John Jacob Astor to Anaconda Copper, wealthy capitalists have profited enormously from the region's resources and the sweat of its people. Yet, like Gene Gressley more recently (*Twentieth Century West - A Potpourri* [1977]), he found the issue complex and full of ironic turns. For one thing, the helter-skelter scrambling for opportunities was never remotely within the day-to-day direction of even the most powerful outsiders. The railroad executives, utopian planners, and governmental agents like Sherman who appear in Athearn's books were frequently frustrated by the chaotic individualism of the trappers, prospectors, overconfident sodbusters, and hopeful cattle barons swarming into the land. Exploitation implies a degree of control, and that was just what these businessmen and administrators, for all their passion for order, did not have.

Athearn also makes an original contribution here by again putting the question within the context of the popular mystique of the West. The country beyond the Missouri traditionally has been perceived as a place of immeasurable abundance and limitless opportunity. It has attracted go-getters and promoters who have gone acourting, hat in hand, for outside investors with the wherewithal to realize the land's possibilities. If capitalists have exploited the West, he wrote, it has usually been at the eager invitation of westerners who, in the old horse-trading tradition, have seen themselves as equals at the bargaining block. Nowhere was this better demonstrated than in Athearn's adopted home; he entitled chapters in his history of the state, "The Selling of Colorado" and "The Recycling of 'Sell Colorado'."

The western mystique also has emphasized an independence of spirit and a spit-in-your-eye attitude toward authority, and with that had grown a hostility and suspicion toward the national government, particularly during good times when Washington seemed to be tugging back on the reins and restraining development. Yet for all their talk of independence, westerners have always depended upon and expected government support, and when the bad times came they called for more aid and protection against outside economic interests who, they said, had treated them so shabbily. Like "adolescents in the national family," Athearn writes late in his career, westerners like to roam, but they also put out their hand when allowances are given out (*The Mythic West*). So the mythic dimension of western history has often encouraged the colonial relationship and has enormously complicated attempts to deal with the issue realistically.

A third theme in Athearn's writing is that of regionalism. Much of his work centered on the country where he grew up and spent most of his adult life, the northern Plains and Rocky Mountains. As an admirer of Turner, Athearn told his story partly in terms of the advance into this country of the European-American frontier. But he made clear this land has certain unique characteristics, and these have continued to shape life and institutions long after the end of the frontier stage. Thus much of Athearn's work should be placed within the traditions of both Turner and the man most associated with western regional studies, Walter Prescott Webb. In 1958, in fact, at the height of the vitriolic attacks on Webb for his description of much of the West as a vast desert, the Texas historian and Athearn published articles back-to-back in *Montana: Magazine of Western History*. While Webb expanded on his earlier remarks, his younger colleague defended the "desert thesis" by putting it in historical perspective, documenting the repeated warnings of shrewd observers and surveying the frustrations of settlers who have wrestled with the region's deficiencies and climatic eccentricities until the present day (8:2-12, 13-29).

This regional approach he developed most clearly in the award-winning *High Country Empire* (1960), a history of the country drained by the Missouri River. Like Paul Horgan in his history of the southwestern Rio Grande country, Athearn finds through the Missouri a unity within this region's diverse geography. He found the uniqueness of the country in its resources, from bunch grass to uranium, and in its climate, from its crop-blighting aridity to the champagne air and powder snow so precious to tourists. And as always, perceptions of this country--the West of the mind--have played a prominent part. In *The Coloradans*, written sixteen years later, Athearn traces the history of one of the high country states in its centennial year, again stressing the interplay of resources, climate, and image. In both books he relies mainly on a broad range of secondary sources to weave together the various developments, such as the fur trade, exploration, overland migrations, gold and silver rushes, military conflicts, the coming of the railroad and industry, government aid and construction, and the rise of agriculture and the cattle kingdom, shaping this country. His treatment is smooth and concise, so much so that the reader can easily underestimate his mastery of the complex cause-and-effect relationships among these various changes.

In both these regionally-oriented works, Athearn, predictably, highlights the roles of business and government. The most persistent theme of *High Country Empire*, he writes, is the "exploitation and experimentation carried on by remote control from the more settled parts of America" (pp. vii-viii). But it is clear that all attempts to use the country conformed to what the land would allow. The conflict between expectations and reality contributed to the region's booms and busts, and with these shifting fortunes the original popular perceptions of the country flickered and changed, in turn influencing the flow of people and money and shaping the history of the high country. The continuing connection Athearn finds among the land, its resources, and its image, is rich with possibilities for future research.

In these books Athearn also developed one of the most important implications of regionalism. Since the regional approach is dictated by the unchanging characteristics of the place, the story does not stop with the end of the frontier era. Regional history necessarily takes us to the present, and Athearn devotes a good part of these two books to the history of the high country in the twentieth century. He includes perceptive overviews of the Depression and New Deal, modern tourism and promotion. At a time when many were calling for more research and writing on recent western history, Athearn was doing just that.

The fourth theme, that of the importance of myth and image, pervades much of Athearn's work, and two of his books deal with the subject directly. It is a commonplace that western history is really not one but two fields. There is the history of a place--that part of the country beyond the Mississippi River--and also the study of the moving frontier, a process that supposedly has helped shape our character and institutions. Since the publication in 1950 of Henry Nash Smith's *Virgin Land*, furthermore, historians have increasingly recognized that myth and popular perceptions should play a significant role in each of these approaches. Ray Allen Billington and others have looked at the ways the frontier experience and the geography of the Far West, with its sweeping vistas and looming mountains, have both become intricately entangled with outsiders' perceptions of this nation and Americans' own national consciousness, their sense of who they are.

Surely no historian of the West would deny these statements. It is just as clear that few have developed their implications in their work as consistently as Athearn did. His attention to myth went well beyond debunking, though he enjoyed setting straight some of the innumerable distortions of the western past. He seemed to argue, however, that it was more important to recognize how these very misconceptions have been a powerful shaping force, inspiring emigrants and investors, influencing the making of laws and policies, and sometimes leading to frustration, disillusionment, and mutual resentment between the West and the world outside. Over time the westerners themselves, especially recent transplants, have embraced popular images and acted them out. It is increasingly difficult to separate the mythic and the real West simply because the former has been believed so ardently and so long.

Anyone who reads his work closely will see an increasingly subtle and sophisticated appreciation of the western myth. Perhaps inspired in part by his dissertation on Thomas Francis Meagher, Athearn examined in *Westward the Briton* (1953) the impressions of British visitors to the region late in the last century. The most amusing of his books, it continually plays with the gap between the travelers' expectations and the West they found. Yet here the myth is the point of departure, not the main topic. As Athearn emphasizes in his opening chapter, the making of the mythic West was well underway when his tourists arrived; their observations are worth studying precisely because these outsiders were better able to cut through the haze and describe the land and people more accurately than the natives.

During the next quarter century Athearn concentrated upon the three themes already discussed, but as he did, he developed an increasingly complex and ironic idea of myth and its influence. He found in Sherman a man guided by a dream of national greatness fed by western growth, a vision he conjured up while a young man in California during the Mexican War and the gold rush. The many figures who walk through his other books, the railroad magnates and captains of industry as well as the sodbusters and overlanders, are after personal gain, to be sure, but they also are moved by the grand vision, and often enough they end up victims. Nowhere was this better shown than in the case of the "exodusters," whose story he told in *In Search of Canaan* (1978). These former slaves left the South for the Plains of Kansas in 1879-1880, fearing what was coming with the end of Reconstruction. Their migration was a variation on the lure of the frontier as a place of escape, freedom, and redemption, "an unreasoned, almost mindless exodus . . . toward some vague ideal, some western paradise, where all cares would vanish once the beckoning gates were reached" (p. 17). Instead most of these black pioneers found racism, sickness, suffering, and destitution.

Near the end of Athearn's career, the interplay between myth and reality, a consistent but subordinate theme thus far, came to the fore. In two articles, "The American West: An Enduring Mirage?" (*Colorado Quarterly* 26:3-16) and "The Ephemeral West" (*Colorado Quarterly* 28:5-14), he suggests how the end of the frontier had brought about something of a cultural crisis in this century. Americans continue to need a belief in opportunity and renewal, ideas long associated with the frontier and the West, yet there also has been a general recognition that with the settlement of the Plains and Southwest the long westering process was at an end. This has produced an unease, often vague but running deep, among those who have warned that the final victory of the pioneers spelled trouble--a loss of the individualism and moral toughness encouraged by the struggle with the new land. Paradoxically, however, others have insisted that opportunity, challenge, and limitless natural bounties still await to keep the country prosperous and to reaffirm the old virtues. These things are supposedly to be found in "the West," by which is meant not so much a part of the country as a place of grand possibilities, a testing ground for the national spirit.

Pinpointing this Shangri La precisely, however, has been a problem. Athearn insightfully draws an amusing parallel betweeen the sometimes frantic search for opportunity and escape "out there" and the difficulty many have had deciding just where, geographically, the West is. Floating like a mirage somewhere between Iowa and Reno, "a state of mind or an emotion" as much as a junction of coordinates on a map, the ephemeral West eludes the modern American, who nonetheless continues the search (*Colorado Quarterly* 26:3). Ironically, the general region of this quest, the country between the hundredth meridian and the Sierra Nevadas, actually is plagued by grave limitations. The real westerners, those who have learned the hard truths of the plains and mountains, might well serve as "new pioneers" to teach the rest of the country how to live with scarcity and dwindling resources. In the meantime, Americans still are fascinated by the vast arid stretches beyond the Missouri, drawn by "the ambient myth, the aura of history even when it isn't there, the excitement of a land that is foreboding, even dangerous, but always intriguing" (*Colorado Quarterly* 28:13).

At his death Athearn was nearing completion of his eleventh book, *The Mythic West* (1986). In it he brought together many of the various threads he had spun out during the previous thirty-five years. Gathering extensively from newspapers, periodicals, and other popular writing and drawing also from a lifetime of his own perceptive observations, he considered the image of the West in the twentieth century in its many manifestations. He examined fiction, films, and tourism as well as the ways the shifting perceptions of the region have influenced public policy through issues like conservation, land policy, and government aid to the western states. In many ways this highly personal work stands as a culmination, the logical destination of the thematic paths Athearn chose to take during his long and distinguished career.

Bibliography

Books

America Moves West. Co-authored with Robert E. Riegel. 5th edition. New York: Holt, Rinehart, and Winston, 1971.

The American Heritage New Illustrated History of the United States. With a foreword by John F. Kennedy and an introduction by Allan Nevins. 16 volumes. New York: Dell Publishing, 1963.

Centennial Colorado: Its Exciting Story. Co-authored with Carl W. Ubbelohde. Denver: E. L. Chambers, 1959.

The Coloradans. Albuquerque: University of New Mexico Press, 1976.

Forts of the Upper Missouri. Englewood Cliffs, NJ: Prentice-Hall, 1967. Paperback edition, Lincoln: University of Nebraska Press, 1972.

High Country Empire: The High Plains and Rockies. New York: McGraw-Hill, 1960. Paperback edition, Lincoln: University of Nebraska Press, 1965.

In Search of Canaan: Black Migration to Kansas, 1879-1880. Lawrence: Regents Press of Kansas, 1978.

The Mythic West in Twentieth-Century America. Lawrence: University Press of Kansas, 1986.

Rebel of the Rockies: The Denver and Rio Grande Western Railroad. New Haven, CT: Yale University Press, 1962.

Soldier in the West: The Civil War Letters of Alfred Lacey Hough. Editor. Philadelphia: University of Pennsylvania Press, 1957.

Thomas Francis Meagher: An Irish Revolutionary in America. Boulder: University of Colorado Press, 1949.

Union Pacific Country. Chicago: Rand McNally & Co., 1971. Paperback edition, Lincoln: University of Nebraska Press, 1975.

Westward the Briton. New York: Charles Scribner's Sons, 1953. Paperback edition, Lincoln: University of Nebraska Press, 1962.

William Tecumseh Sherman and the Settlement of the West. Norman: University of Oklahoma Press, 1956.

Articles

"Across the Plains in 1863: The Diary of Peter Winne." Editor. *Iowa Journal of History and Politics* 49(July, 1951):221-241.

"The American West: An Enduring Mirage?" *Colorado Quarterly* 26(Autumn, 1977):3-16.

"An Army Officer in the West: 1869-1890." *The Brand Book: Corral of the Denver Westerners* 6(1950):1-13.

"An Army Officer's Trip to Alaska in 1869." *Pacific Northwest Quarterly* 40(January, 1949):44-65.

"An Indiana Doctor Marches with Sherman: The Diary of James Comfort Patten." Editor. *Indiana Magazine of History* 49(December, 1953):405-423.

"Black Exodus: The Migration of 1879." *The Prairie Scout* 3(1975):86-98.

"A Brahmin in Buffaloland." *Western Historical Quarterly* 1(January, 1970):21-34.
"British Impressions of Early Rocky Mountain Towns." *Western Humanities Review* 6(Autumn, 1952):315-324.
"British Impressions of Western Railroad Service: 1869-1900." *Pacific Historical Review* 20(November, 1951):365-375.
"Chapter 4." In *The West of the American People* edited by Allan G. Bogue, Thomas D. Phillips, and James E. Wright. Itasca, IL: F.E. Peacock Publishers, 1970.
"Chapter 8." In *The Montana Past* edited by Michael P. Malone and Richard B. Roeder. Missoula: University of Montana Press, 1969.
"The Civil War and Montana Gold." *Montana: Magazine of Western History* 12(April, 1962):62-72.
"Civil War Days in Montana." *Pacific Historical Review* 29(February, 1960):19-33.
"Clippings on Early Colorado Education." *School and University* [of Colorado] *Review* 7(1977):3-6.
"Colorado and the Civil War." *Rocky Mountain News Centennial Issue*, April 19, 1959, pp. 14, 17.
"Colorado and the Indian War of 1868." *Colorado Magazine* 33(January, 1956):42-52.
"Contracting for the Union Pacific." *Utah Historical Quarterly* 37(Winter, 1969):16-40.
"The Cow Kingdom." In *The Great Plains Experience* edited by James E. Wright and Sarah Z. Rosenburg. Lincoln, NE: University of Mid-America, 1978. Pp. 173-185.
"A Dedication to the Memory of Colin Brummit Goodykoontz, 1885-1958." *Arizona and the West* 13(Autumn, 1971):217-221.
"The Denver and Rio Grande and the Panic of 1873." *Colorado Magazine* 35(April, 1958):121-138.
"The Denver and Rio Grande Railway: Colorado's 'Baby Road'." *Colorado Magazine* 35(January, 1958):35-51.
"The Diary of John Wilson Phillips." Editor. *Virginia Magazine of History and Biography* 62(January, 1954):95-124.
"Early Territorial Montana: A Study in Colonial Administration." *Montana: Magazine of Western History* 1(July, 1951):15-23.
"The Education of Kit Carson's Son." *New Mexico Historical Review* 31(April, 1956):133-139.
"The Ephemeral West." *Colorado Quarterly* 28(Autumn, 1979):5-14.
"The Fifty-Niners." *American West* 13(September/October, 1976):22-25, 60-61.
"The '59ers and After." Co-authored with Carl Ubbelohde. *Colorado Wonderland* 8(1959):18-26.
"The Firewagon Road." *Montana: Magazine of Western History* 20(April, 1970):2-19.
"The Fort Buford 'Massacre'." *Mississippi Valley Historical Review* 41(March, 1955):675-685.

"From Illinois to Montana in 1866: The Diary of Perry A. Burgess." Editor. *Pacific Northwest Quarterly* 41(January, 1950):43-66.
"Frontier Critics of the Western Army." *Montana: Magazine of Western History* 5(Spring, 1955):16-29.
"General Sherman and the Montana Frontier." *Montana: Magazine of Western History* 3(January, 1953):55-65.
"General Sherman and the Western Railroads." *Pacific Historical Review* 24(February, 1955):39-49.
"George Gould and the Rio Grande System." *University of Colorado Studies* 2(1961):1-20.
"The Great Plains in Historical Perspective." *Montana: Magazine of Western History* 8(January, 1958):13-29.
"The Independence of the Denver and Rio Grande." *Utah Historical Quarterly* 26(January, 1958):3-21.
"Life in the Pike's Peak Region: Letters of Matthew H. Dale." Editor. *Colorado Magazine* 32(April, 1955):81-104.
"Little England Beyond the Missouri." *Colorado Quarterly* 1(Winter, 1954):328-337.
"Major Hough's March into Southern Ute Country." Editor. *Colorado Magazine* 25(May, 1948):97-110.
"The Montana Volunteers of 1867." *Pacific Historical Review* 19(May, 1950):127-137.
"Opening the Gates of Zion: Utah and the Coming of the Utah Pacific Railroad." *Utah Historical Quarterly* 36(Fall, 1968):291-314.
"The Oregon Short Line." *Idaho Yesterdays* 13(1969-1970):2-18.Reprint. In *The Idaho Heritage* edited by Richard W. Etulain and Bert W. Marley. Pocatello: Idaho State University Press, 1974.
"Origins of the Royal Gorge Railroad War." *Colorado Magazine* 36(January, 1959):37-58.
"Part 3." In *The Gilded Age: America, 1865-1900* edited by Richard A. Bartlett. Reading, MA: Addison-Wesley Publishing Co., 1969.
"The Promised Land: A Black View." *The Record* [Washington State University] 34(1973):5-22.
"Railroad Renaissance in the Rockies." *Utah Historical Quarterly* 25(January, 1957):1-26.
"Railroad to a Far Off Country: The Utah Northern." *Montana: Magazine of Western History* 18(October, 1968):2-23.
"The Sod Busters." In *The Great Plains Experience* edited by James E. Wright and Sarah Z. Rosenburg. Lincoln, NE: University of Mid-America, 1978.Pp. 244-253.
"Utah and the Coming of the Denver and Rio Grande Railroad." *Utah Historical Quarterly* 27(April, 1959):129-142.
"A View from the High Country." *Western Historical Quarterly* 2(April, 1971):125-132.
"War Paint Against Brass: The Army and the Plains Indians." *Montana: Magazine of Western History* 6(July, 1956):11-23.
"West of Appomattox: Civil War Beyond the Great River." *Montana: Magazine of Western History* 12(April, 1962):2-11.

"A Winter Campaign Against the Sioux." Editor. *Mississippi Valley Historical Review* 35(September, 1948):272-285.

Introductions, Forewords, and Contributions to Other Books

Commentary on "A Comparison of Military Frontiers." In *The Military on the Frontier* edited by James P. Tate. Proceedings of the Seventh Military History Symposium, USAF Academy, 1976. Washington, DC: 1978.

Consultant to *The Townsmen* by Keith Wheeler. Time-Life Series. New York: Time-Life Books, 1975.

Contributor to *Indian-White Reliations: A Persistent Paradox* by Jane F. Smith and Robert M. Kvaskicka. Washington, DC: Howard University Press, 1976.

__________ to *The Red Man's West* edited by Michael S. Kennedy. New York: Hastings House, 1965.

"Foreword." In *Fairmount and Historic Colorado* by David Fridtjof Halaas. Denver: Fairmount Cemetery Association, 1976.

__________. In *Silver Saga: The Story of Caribou, Colorado* by Duane A. Smith. Boulder, CO: Pruett Publishing Co., 1974.

__________. In *The West: An American Experience* by David Phillips and Robert A. Weinstein. Chicago: Henry Regnery and Co., 1973.

"Introduction." In *City of the Saints* (also *The Look of the West*) by Richard Burton. Lincoln: University of Nebraska Press, 1963.

Verbal Publications

"Voices of History." Tape cassette, "The Age of Exploration," C-2. Wilmington, DE: Michael Glazier, Inc., 1979.

__________. Tape cassette, "The Age of Settlement," C-3. Wilmington, DE: Michael Glazier, Inc., 1979.

Selected Reviews

America's Frontier Culture: Three Essays by Ray Allen Billington. *Journal of American History* 65(December, 1978):765-766.

America's New Frontier: The Mountain West by Morris E. Garnsey. *Pacific Historical Review* 19(November, 1950):426-427.

Bill Sublette: Mountain Man by John E. Sunder. *American Historical Review* 65(October, 1959):189.

The Bonanza Kings: The Social Origins and Business Behavior of Western Mining Entrepreneurs, 1870-1900 by Richard H. Peterson. *Pacific Historical Review* 48(May, 1979):301-302.

British Immigrants in Industrial America, 1790-1950 by Rowland T. Berthoff. *Mississippi Valley Historical Review* 41(September, 1954):348-349.

British Investments and the American Mining Frontier, 1860-1901 by Clark C. Spence. *American Historical Review* 64(July, 1959):972-973.

The Civil War in the Western Territories: Arizona, Colorado, New Mexico, and Utah by Ray C. Colton. *American Historical Review* 65(April, 1960):630-631.

The Custer Myth: A Source Book of Custeriana compiled by W. A. Graham. *Mississippi Valley Historical Review* 40(March, 1954):745-746.

Custer's Luck by Edgar I. Stewart. *Mississippi Valley Historical Review* 42(September, 1955):338-339.

Edward Kern and American Expansion by Robert V. Hine. *American Historical Review* 68(October, 1962):246.

Exploring the Northern Plains, 1804-1876 edited by Lloyd McFarling. *Mississippi Valley Historical Review* 42(June, 1955):121-122.

Fighting Indian Warriors: True Tales of the Wild Frontiers by E. A. Brininstool. *Pacific Historical Review* 23(February, 1954):64-65.

The First Hundred Years: An Informal History of Denver and the Rocky Mountain News by Robert L. Perkin. *Pacific Historical Review* 28(November, 1959):396-397.

Frontier America: The Story of the Westward Movement by Thomas D. Clark. *Pacific Historical Review* 29(May, 1960):179-180.

The Frontier Challenge: Response to the Trans-Mississippi West edited by John G. Clark. *Journal of American History* 58(December, 1971):765-767.

Gentlemen Emigrants: From the British Public Schools to the Canadian Frontier by Patrick A. Dunae. *Western Historical Quarterly* 14(January, 1983):101-102.

Grassland Historical Studies: Natural Resources Utilization in a Background of Science and Technology by James C. Malin. *Pacific Historical Review* 19(November, 1950):427-429.

The Great Platte River Road: The Covered Wagon Mainline Via Fort Kearny to Fort Laramie by Merrill J. Mattes. *Journal of American History* 57(September, 1970):439-440.

Grenville M. Dodge: Soldier, Politician, Railroad Pioneer by Stanley P. Hirshson. *Pacific Historical Review* 36(August, 1967):228-229.

A History of Steamboating on the Upper Missouri River by William E. Lass. *Mississippi Valley Historical Review* 50(September, 1963):321-322.

History of the Westward Movement by Frederick Merk. *American Historical Review* 84(June, 1979):835-836.

Ho! For the Gold Fields: Northern Overland Wagon Trains of the 1860s edited by Helen McCann White. *American Historical Review* 72(April, 1967):1099-1100.

The Indian Journals, 1859-1862 by Lewis Henry Morgan edited by Leslie A. White. *American Historical Review* 65(July, 1960):995.

Iron Road to the West: American Railroads in the 1850s by John F. Stover. *Pacific Historical Review* 50(February, 1981):112-113.

John Spring's Arizona edited by A. M. Gustafson. *Journal of American History* 53(December, 1966):604-605.

The Last Days of the Sioux Nation by Robert M. Utley. *American Historical Review* 69(January, 1964):553.

The Last War Trail: The Utes and the Settlement of Colorado by Robert Emmitt. *Pacific Historical Review* 24(May, 1955):186-187.

Leland Stanford: Man of Many Careers by Norman E. Tutorow. *American Historical Review* 77(December, 1972):1512.

The Long Death: The Last Days of the Plains Indians by Ralph K. Andrist. *Journal of American History* 52(September, 1965):379-380.

The Lost Pathfinder: Zebulon Montgomery Pike by W. Eugene Hollon. *Pacific Historical Review* 18(November, 1949):517-518.

The Matador Land and Cattle Company by William M. Pearce. *American Historical Review* 69(July, 1964):1168-1169.

The Military Conquest of the Southern Plains by William H. Leckie. *Mississippi Valley Historical Review* 50(March, 1964):705.

The Mountain Men and the Fur Trade of the Far West: Biographical Sketches, vol. 1, edited by LeRoy R. Hafen. *American Historical Review* 71(January, 1966):683-684.

The Nevada Adventure by James W. Hulse. *American Historical Review* 71(January, 1966):685-686.

On the Arkansas Route to California in 1849: The Journal of Robert B. Green of Lewisburg, Pennsylvania edited by J. Orin Oliphant. *American Historical Review* 62(October, 1956):255-256.

On the Oregon Trail: Robert Stuart's Journey of Discovery edited by Kenneth A. Spaulding. *American Historical Review* 59(April, 1954):745-746.

Pacifying the Plains: General Alfred Terry and the Decline of the Sioux, 1866-1890 by John W. Bailey. *Western Historical Quarterly* 11(July, 1980):344-345.

The Plainsmen of the Yellowstone: A History of the Yellowstone Basin by Mark H. Brown. *Pacific Historical Review* 31(February, 1962):74-76.

Prairie and Mountain Sketches by Matthew C. Field. *American Historical Review* 63(October, 1957):243.

The Reader's Encyclopedia of the American West edited by Howard R. Lamar. *Western Historical Quarterly* 9(October, 1978):510-511.

Relations with the Indians of the Plains, 1857-1861: A Documentary Account of the Military Campaigns and Negotiations of Indian Agents edited by LeRoy R. Hafen and Ann W. Hafen. *American Historical Review* 65(January, 1960):431-432.

The Rockies by David Lavender. *Journal of American History* 55(December, 1968):662.

The Rocky Mountain Journals of William Marshall Anderson: The West in 1834 edited by Dale L. Morgan and Eleanor Towles Harris. *American Historical Review* 73(June, 1968):1640-1641.

The Transportation Frontier: Trans-Mississippi West, 1865-1890 by Oscar O. Winther. *Pacific Historical Review* 34(February, 1965):94-95.

Travelers on the Western Frontier edited by John Francis McDermott. *American Historical Review* 76(December, 1971):1600-1601.

Tough Trip Through Paradise, 1878-1879 by Andrew Garcia edited by Bennett H. Stein. *American Historical Review* 73(April, 1968):1247.

The Unregimented General: A Biography of Nelson A. Miles by Virginia W. Johnson. *American Historical Review* 68(January, 1963):552.

War Drums and Wagon Wheels: The Story of Russell, Majors and Waddell by Raymond W. Settle and Mary Land Settle. *American Historical Review* 72(October, 1966):307-308.

The Water and the Power: Development of the Five Great Rivers of the West by Albert N. Williams. *Pacific Historical Review* 21(May, 1952):177-178.

Where the Old West Stayed Young by John Rolfe Burroughs. *Pacific Historical Review* 32(May, 1963):199-200.

Whoop-Up Country: The Canadian American West, 1865-1885 by Paul F. Sharp. *Pacific Historical Review* 25(May, 1956):192-194.

William Tecumseh Sherman: Gold Rush Banker by Dwight L. Clarke. *Western Historical Quarterly* 9(October, 1978):510-511.

Studies of Robert G. Athearn

DeVoto, Bernard. "The West: A Plundered Province." *Harper's Magazine* 179(August, 1934):355-364.

Eagan, William T. Review of *The Coloradans* by Robert G. Athearn. *Western Historical Quarterly* 8(October, 1977):459-460.

Lapp, Rudolph M. Review of *In Search of Canaan: Black Migration to Kansas, 1879-1880* by Robert G. Athearn. *Western Historical Quarterly* 10(October, 1979):495-496.

Limerick, Patricia Nelson. Review of *The Mythic West in Twentieth-Century America* by Robert G. Athearn. *Western Historical Quarterly* 18(July, 1987):343-344.

Lowitt, Richard. Review of *The Mythic West in Twentieth-Century America* by Robert G. Athearn. *Montana: Magazine of Western History* 37(Summer, 1987):77-78.

Ridge, Martin, Norris Hundley, and Clark C. Spence. "Western History Association Prize Recipient, 1983: Robert G. Athearn." *Western Historical Quarterly* 15(April, 1984):133-137.

Smith, Duane A., ed. *A Taste of the West: Essays in Honor of Robert G. Athearn.* Boulder, CO: Pruett Publishing Co., 1983.

Smith, Henry Nash. *Virgin Land: The American West as Symbol and Myth.* Cambridge, MA: Harvard University Press, 1950.

Webb, Walter Prescott. *Divided We Stand: The Crisis of a Frontierless Democracy.* New York: Farrar and Rinehart, 1937.

___________. "The West and the Desert." *Montana: Magazine of Western History* 8(January, 1958):2-12.

White, Gerald T. Review of *Union Pacific Country* by Robert G. Athearn. *Western Historical Quarterly* 3(January, 1972):85-86.

4

EVE BALL

by Kimberly Moore Buchanan

Biography

Katherine Evelyn Daly Ball was born March 14, 1890, in Clarksville, Tennessee. Her family moved to Kansas when Eve was very young. Her mother, Gazelle Gibbs Daly, was a strong influence in her daughter's life. Daly was the first woman licensed to practice medicine in Kansas, and she instilled in Eve an appreciation of education and a persevering sense of independence and initiative.

Eve's mother may have been the first to turn Eve's attention toward the Southwest and Native Americans. Eve Ball eventually became an educator and a writer. She chose the historic town of Ruidoso, New Mexico, to make her home, as the Southwest and the Apache Indians became her consuming avocation. Her extensive oral history research with numerous southwestern pioneers and Apache Indians make her a significant and unique frontier historian. She continued her writing and research until her death on December 24, 1984.

Ball received her Bachelor of Science Degree in Education from Kansas State Teachers' College in Pittsburg, Kansas, in 1918. She completed her Master's Degree in Education at Kansas State University in 1934. Artesia College awarded her an Honorary Doctorate in the Humanities in 1972. She taught on the elementary, secondary, and college levels. She served as the president of the New Mexico Folklore Society, and she was a member of Western Writers of America.

Eve Ball began her writing career around the age of sixty and published more than one hundred articles and six books. Her books include *Ruidoso, The Last Frontier* (1963), *Bob Crosby, World Champion Cowboy* (1966), *Ma'am Jones of the Pecos* (1969), *In the Days of Victorio, Recollections of a Warm Springs Apache* (1970), *My Girlhood Among Outlaws* (1972), and *Indeh, An Apache Odyssey* (1980).

The Western Writers of America awarded Ball the Golden Spur Award in 1975 for best nonfiction short story and the Saddleman's Award for *Indeh, An Apache Odyssey* in 1981. Ball was also awarded the New Mexico Press Women's ZIA Award. In April, 1982, she was inducted into the Cowgirl Hall of Fame and Western Heritage Center in Hereford, Texas. Perhaps her most prestigious honor came when United States Senators Pete Domenici and Jeff Bingaman from New Mexico introduced a U.S. Senate resolution commending Eve Ball and her value as a historian of the Southwest. The resolution was adopted on October 7, 1983, approximately one year before her death.

Themes

First and foremost, Eve Ball was a historian of the Southwest. Her works revolve around individuals who settled the area which is now New Mexico. Four basic themes are evident in her writing. They include the value of oral history in historical methodology, the study of "unsung heroes and heroines," the importance of women on the frontier, and the demythification of the Apache Indians.

Eve Ball was a historian ahead of her time. She recognized the tremendous value and validity of oral history long before it was universally recognized as a legitimate historical resource. In an article from *New Mexico Magazine*, Lynda A. Sanchez, a close friend and research assistant to Ball, writes of Ball's untimely belief in oral history:

> "If nothing else is said about me," Eve told me recently, "I want people to know of my long struggle to get my books published! Oral history was laughed at then. Ph.D.'s never accepted the intrinsic value of oral history until the last few years. Now that it has come of age, most of the old ones who experienced the history are gone" (p. 33).

All of Ball's works are primarily oral history. Each of her books incorporates the main character's actual words and reminiscences or those of his or her family and friends. *Indeh, An Apache Odyssey* is especially unique in that it is a compilation of interviews given to Ball by some sixty-seven Apache living on the Mescalero Indian Reservation. She gained their trust as had no other person, and they confided in her their experiences, anecdotes, and tribal culture. Ball's extensive use of oral history makes her work as a frontier historian especially valuable and unique.

The people that Eve Ball writes about are the genuine, independent, unpretentious people--merchants, innkeepers, cowboys, teachers, wives, mothers, warriors, and children. She enjoyed listening to their tales and recording their adventures. She did not necessarily gravitate toward the most sensational and famous historical figures; instead she chose those who actually *lived* southwestern history, but were generally unrecognized as being historically significant. The studies of Bob Crosby, James Kaywaykla, the Jones family, Lily Klasner, Asa Daklugie, and countless others reflect Ball's love and interest in the ordinary, and yet extraordinary, individuals who shaped the Southwest.

Ball's books are undeniably social history. She focuses on individuals and their relationships with society. She especially liked to study women's roles on the frontier. Many southwest historians neglect to recognize women as central and vital figures in frontier history, but Ball pays special attention to females. *Ma'am Jones of the Pecos* and *My Girlhood Among Outlaws* examine two remarkable southwestern women. *Bob Crosby, World Champion Cowboy* is written from the reminiscences of Crosby's widow, Thelma Crosby, and much of the story surrounds her activities and emotions. Ball's work with Apache women is unprecedented. She examines them in a way that defies the preconceived myths that characterized them as secondary characters in the history of their people. She presents them as vital participants in the Apache struggle for survival and independence.

Perhaps the most significant theme in Ball's writing is the demythification of the Apache. Her work demands a revision of previously written Apache history. Much of this was written by and from a predominantly non-Apache viewpoint. Her love for the Apache people is clearly evident in her work, but she is also an objective and professional historian. Most significantly, she is a writer of "the truth." She is careful to call attention to differing accounts and discrepancies. Above all, she presents the Apache story as no other historian has ever done.

Analysis

United States Resolution 230 (1983) recognizes the value of Eve Ball's historical writings:

> Resolved, That it is the sense of the Senate that the people of the United States owe Eve Ball a tremendous debt of gratitude for writings which enrich our knowledge of the Indian, the West, and those courageous persons who settled that vast land and for the invaluable legacy such writings will be for future generations.

Eve Ball's use of realism to describe the lives of the settlers of the Southwest is most commendable. Her works are painstakingly exhaustive. She spent forty years researching the settlers of New Mexico and the Apache. She became their friend, earned their respect, and recorded their stories for posterity. Her writings reflect her first-hand knowledge and genuine interest in her subjects. Her in-depth oral history research gives the readers of her works a rare glimpse of the individuals who made southwestern history.

The extensive uses of oral history in all of Ball's works place her writing in a unique historical class. Few, if any, frontier historians utilize oral history as extensively and successfully as has Eve Ball. This quality makes Ball's writings an especially significant contribution to the history of the frontier. Many settlers, and especially the Apache, never kept written journals or diaries and seldom, if ever, wrote letters. As a result, much frontier history was irrevocably lost when they died. Ball's timely interest in many southwestern pioneers and her preservation of their reminiscences present a facet of the frontier that otherwise would have gone unrecorded and unrecognized.

Many of the people Eve Ball writes about could be classified as "unsung heroes and heroines." They are all remarkable individuals in their own right, but largely unrecognized in southwestern history. Perhaps the most famous, and one of the most colorful, of Ball's subjects is Bob Crosby, a world champion cowboy from New Mexico. *Bob Crosby, World Champion Cowboy* is not an enlightening scholarly treatise, but it is replete with colorful anecdotes and important moments in rodeo and western history.

James Kaywaykla, a Warm Springs Apache, tells his story in *In the Days of Victorio, Recollections of a Warm Springs Apache.* Kaywaykla was with Victorio's band in the 1880s. He was a young boy when the band fled from the San Carlos Reservation in Arizona, and when Victorio was killed at Tres Castillos in 1881. Kawaykla's story encompasses every aspect of Indian life. He tells of living on the run--fearing for his life with every step, captivity on the reservation and in Florida, school in Pennsylvania, and a new reservation life in Oklahoma and New Mexico. This first-hand account of Indian life is a one-of-a-kind historical achievement.

Women are a favorite subject in Eve Ball's writings. *Ma'am Jones of the Pecos* is the story of Barbara "Ma'am" Jones and her family. They were the first Anglo family to settle permanently in the Pecos River Valley. Ball describes Ma'am Jones as "epitomizing the diverse and demanding roles played by the pioneer woman on the New Mexican frontier" (p. i). Ma'am Jones's story is told through the recollections of five of her nine sons. Ball interviewed them with the intention that "the true history of Lincoln County should be told" (pp. xi-xii). She saw the Jones family as an excellent medium for this task. Each son shared his own version of his youth while Ball took notes. Upon occasion she even rode horseback along the ranch while interviewing one of the sons. The resulting synthesis of these interviews presents a picture of a strong woman who held her family together during an especially turbulent period in New Mexico history. Ball observes that Barbara or Ma'am was "mother, homemaker, nurse, storekeeper, and teacher. She could handle a cookfire, a needle, a bandage, a rifle, or a square dance with equal competence" (p. i). She was the backbone of the family and was respected by everyone in the territory. Ball aptly recognizes Ma'am Jones as a true pioneer woman--powerful, resourceful, and resilient.

My Girlhood Among Outlaws is an unusual primary historical source. It is the story of Lily Casey Klasner, a remarkable nineteenth-century western woman. She was, among other things, a teacher, telegrapher, rancher, and writer. Her family traveled from Texas to New Mexico in 1867 and when her father was murdered in 1875, Lily became the leader of the family. Klasner's obituary from the *Roswell Record* reflects just what an extraordinary woman she was:

> She was truly a woman of the West living here when there were only a few people and no law and order, where most of the travelers were outlaws and Indians. She was able to hold her own with any of them (p. 6).

Lily's story is taken from her personal writings. She had planned to write the saga herself, but she was unable to complete it. Ball was fortunate enough to locate Klasner's original notes and complete the work. Perhaps the most valuable contribution in this work is the diary and papers of James Chisum, who was known as the New Mexico Cattle King. Klasner was a close friend of Chisum's and obtained his writings from his niece, Sallie Chisum Robert. This book contradicts many other western accounts of the period, and presents a very human and interesting side of the remarkable Lily Casey Klasner.

The Apache are a people who have been explored by many writers, and although there is an abundance of material dealing with them, many voids and misconceptions still exist. Eve Ball's work fills many of these voids and clears up numerous misconceptions. One such area is the role of Apache women. Usually Indian women are regarded and portrayed as dull and passive, but Ball presents evidence that defies this "drudging squaw" stereotype. She reveals that many Apache wives accompanied their husbands on raiding and warring parties and, on the whole, exercised a tremendous amount of freedom and power. Ball pays special attention to one exceptional Warm Springs Apache woman known as Lozen, "The Woman Warrier." She was an unmarried sister of the noted Warm Springs chief Victorio. After Victorio's death, she joined Geronimo's band. Her prowess as a warrior and her extraordinary supernatural ability to locate the enemy earned for her a legendary status among her people. The revelation of Lozen and the respected status of Apache women as a whole are directly attributable to Ball's oral history research.

Eve Ball is most famous for her work with the Apache. Her books are used as texts in classes throughout the United States and in England. Ball began interviewing the Mescalero and Chiricahua Apache living on the Mescalero Apache Reservation near her Ruidoso home in the 1930s and 1940s. Fortunately Ball's research recorded the memories of many Apache who had lived off the reservation before the famous surrender of Geronimo in 1886. These interviews are priceless as all those who had lived this traditional nomadic lifestyle are now dead. *Indeh, An Apache Odyssey* is a compilation of these interviews. Ball states, "this is not an attempt to write a definitive history - many people and events aren't known by informants - lost forever - nobody was sufficiently interested in securing it while there were living participants and witnesses to relate their experiences" (p. xix). The immense value of *Indeh, An Apache Odyssey* is the demythification of the Apache. Many have recognized this contribution. A review in *Publisher's Weekly* states, "Not only do we get a fresh view - the Indian side - of historical events, we come to understand and respect the Apache as a people" (217:205).

Eve Ball's admiration for the Apache and other southwestern pioneers is apparent in her work, but she is always a professional historian. She notes conflicting accounts, and she points out that her informants are not infallible. She presents intricate and secretive Apache religious and cultural beliefs, their everyday lifestyle, their motivations and fears, their joys and strong familial relationships, the immense and tragic pressures they faced, and their innermost feelings. She describes them as caring human beings and refutes the popular stereotype that labeled them as less. She places pioneer women in respected and resourceful roles. She examines her subjects through their own stories and words, and she brings her characters to life. In *Indeh*, Ball sees her obligation to her subjects and their memories as, "to present it as I have received it. I am neither the judge nor the jury. Though I do have opinions,I leave to the readers the freedom to make their own decisions"(p. xix). Therein lies the strength of Eve Ball as a frontier historian.

Bibliography

Books

Bob Crosby, World Champion Cowboy. Clarendon, TX: Clarendon Press, 1966.

In the Days of Victorio, Recollections of a Warm Springs Apache. Tucson: University of Arizona Press, 1970.

Indeh, An Apache Odyssey. Provo, UT: Brigham Young University Press, 1980.

Ma'am Jones of the Pecos. Tucson: University of Arizona Press, 1969.

My Girlhood Among Outlaws. Tucson: University of Arizona Press, 1972.

Ruidoso, The Last Frontier. San Antonio, TX: Naylor Press, 1963.

Articles

"1867 Apache Raid." *Old West* 28(Summer, 1971):32-34.

"The Apache Scouts: A Chiricahua Appraisal." *Arizona and the West* 7(Winter, 1965):315-328.

"Andale Gringo." *Frontier Times* 104(November, 1976):24-26.

"Angela Gonzales' Change of Heart." *True West* 85(February, 1968):28-30.

"Apaches Run Cattle." *True West* 63(June, 1964):32-33.

"A Badman's Long Exile." *True West* 150(December, 1978):22-24.

"Bar W and Block Ranches." *Frontier Times* 113(May, 1978):16-17.

"Big Mouth, Apache Scout." *Frontier Times* 2(Spring, 1958):14-16.

"Big Old Red Ants of Cow Country." *Old West* 12(Summer, 1967):29-31.

"Billy Swingle's Dishes." *Frontier Times* 123(January, 1980):36-37.

"Blizzard on Hog Eye Mesa." *True West* 134(April, 1976):41-43.

"Bob Olinger As I Knew Him." *True West* 98(April, 1970):10-12.

"The Boyds of Carretas." *Old West* 45(Fall, 1975):18-19.

"Boyhood of a Choctaw." *True West* 129(June, 1975):22-24.

"Bronco Apache." *Frontier Times* 105(January, 1977):26-29.

"The Buried Money." *True West* 123(June, 1974):12-13 and 130(August, 1975):60-63.
"The Capture of Jesse James." *True West* 74(April, 1966):42-45.
"Carl Collins Could Take It From Scratch." *True West* 127(February, 1975):34-36.
"The Case of the Smuggled Bear." *True West* 125(October, 1974):28-30.
"Charlie Siringo and 'Eat Em Up Jake'." *True West* 93(June, 1969):36-38.
"The Chennault Plane Crash." *True West* 124(August, 1974):26-28.
"A Choctaw's Friend." *True West* 145(February, 1978):51-54.
"Cibicu, An Apache Interpretation." In *Troopers West: Military and Indian Affairs on the American Fronter* edited by Ray Brandes. San Diego: Frontier Heritage Press, 1970. Pp. 121-133.
"Clell Lee--Greatest Living Hunter." *Frontier Times* 36(July, 1965):16-19.
"The Connell Murder Case." *Frontier Times* 86(November, 1973):22-24.
"A Cowboy Goes Prospectin'." *True West* 28(August, 1958):58-60.
'The Crazy One." *True West* 144(December, 1977):8-10.
"The Desert Will Do Its Part." *True West* 29(October, 1958):64-66.
"Dissertation on the Cow Chip." *True West* 73(February, 1966):26-27.
"Don Florencio of Lincoln County." *True West* 28(August, 1958):74-76.
"Double Hanging at Lincoln." *Frontier Times* 79(September, 1972):10-12.
"Early Days at Blazer's Mill." *Frontier Times* 120(July, 1979):28-30.
"Early Days at Mobeetie." *Frontier Times* 126(July, 1980):36-37.
"Early Days in Lincoln." *True West* 29(October, 1958):20-23.
"Edge of Settlement." *Old West* 52(Summer, 1977):45-47.
"Election Shootout in Magdalena." *True West* 159(June, 1980):44-45.
"The Fight for Ojo Caliente." *Frontier Times* 18(Spring, 1962):22-24.
"Fight for the Bosque Redondo." *True West* 106(August, 1971):36-39.
"George Mayes, Cherokee." *Frontier Times* 130(March, 1981):15-17.
"Gold in the Bottom of the Well." *Frontier Times* 87(January, 1974):21-23.
"Greatest Medicine Man." *True West* 38(April, 1960):30-32.
"The Hall Murders." *True West* 115(February, 1973):30, 62-63.
"Headwaters of the Gila." *True West* 148(August, 1978):18-20.
"Hell on the Largo." *Frontier Times* 75(January, 1972):6-8.
"Henry Record was My Hombre." *Frontier Times* 100(March, 1976):16-19.
"A House by the Side of the Road." *True West* 29(October, 1958):38, 49-50.
"I Survived the Massacre of Tres Castillos" by James Kaywaykla. Editor. *True West* 8(March-April, 1955):22, 38.
"Interpreter for the Apaches." *True West* 108(December, 1971):26-28.
Juh's Stronghold in Mexico." *Journal of Arizona History* 15(Spring, 1974):74-84.
"Kedinchin." *True West* 64(August, 1964):28-29.
"Kidnapped by Bandits." *True West* 28(August, 1958):26-28.
"Lady Flo." *Frontier Times* 22(March, 1963):35-36.
"The Last Open Range in New Mexico." *Frontier Times* 94(March, 1975):6, 42-44.

"Law of Survival." *Frontier Times* 125(May, 1980):29-31.
"Lawman of the Pecos." *True West* 81(June, 1967):20-22.
"Legendary Apache Women." *Frontier Times* 128(November, 1980):8, 42-43.
"Lon Megargle--Maverick Painter." *Frontier Times* 55(September, 1968):38-40.
"The Long Walk Escapees." *True West* 29(October, 1958):20-22.
"The Lowest Form of Murder." *True West* 158(April, 1980):12-14.
"McGonagill Pays Off." *Old West* 33(Fall, 1977):27-28.
"Massai-Broncho Apache." *True West* 34(August, 1959):7-9.
"Matter of Survival." *True West* 146(April, 1978):26-28.
"Mexico Bound." *True West* 154(August, 1979):13-15.
"Murder on Credit." *Frontier Times* 112(March, 1978):35, 61-62.
"Nana's People" by James Kaywaykla. Editor. *True West* 10(July-August, 1955):20-21, 66-67.
"The Nester and the Law." *Frontier Times* 101(May, 1976):34-35.
"New Mexico's Tully Family." *Old West* 66(Winter, 1980):18, 43-44.
"Old Time Singing School." *True West* 149(October, 1978):49-51.
"One Hundred Thirty-Seven Years Old." *True West* 130(August, 1975):21-23.
"Peyote Priest." *Frontier Times* 44(November, 1966):28-30.
"The Posse that Killed." *True West* 29(October, 1958):12, 33-34.
"The Price Was Right." *Old West* 40(Summer, 1974):17-19.
"Punching Chihuahuas for the Nations." *Frontier Times* 89(May, 1974):22-23.
"A Ramblin' Cowboy." *True West* 160(August, 1980):13, 43-44.
"The Real Pat Garrett." *Frontier Times* 28(March, 1964):31, 51-52.
"Revival at Seven Rivers." *Frontier Times* 17(Winter, 1961):25-27.
"Richard Merchant--Cowboy's Cowboy." *True West* 77(October, 1966):18-20.
"The Rise and Fall of a Cattle Baron." *Frontier Times* 127(September, 1980):20, 46-47.
"Rodeo in Magdalena." *Frontier Times* 102(July, 1976):28-30.
"Sacred Color of the Sun." *True West* 162(December, 1980):46-47.
"Salty John Cox and Bronco Bill." *True West* 141(June, 1977):24, 51-52.
"Search for a Family." *True West* 31(February, 1959):52-54.
"Starvin' Out in Quemado." *True West* 109(February, 1972):32-34.
"Stop-Over at Caudill's Ranch." *Old West* 35(Spring, 1973):30-32.
"Tom Bragg of New Mexico." *True West* 153(June, 1979):14, 41-42.
"Treasure of Alamo Canyon." *True West* 120(December, 1973):34-35.
"The Varmint." *Frontier Times* 51(January, 1968):24, 50-51.
"Viva Villa." *Frontier Times* 16(Fall, 1961):20, 47-48.
"What Became of Jesse Evans." *True West* 151(February, 1979):14, 38-39.
"Witchcraft." *Frontier Times* 34(March, 1965):26-28.
"You Can't Raise Cows with a Whiskey Bottle." *True West* 54(December, 1962):28, 49-50.

Book Review

The People Called Apache by Thomas E. Mails. *Arizona and the West* 17(Summer, 1975):181.

Studies of Eve Ball

Akwesasne Notes. Review of *In the Days of Victorio* by Eve Ball. (Early Summer, 1974):54.

American Book Collector. Review of *In the Days of Victorio* by Eve Ball.21(May, 1971):6.

The Amerindian. Review of *In the Days of Victorio* by Eve Ball. (November-December, 1971):123.

Anderson, Kenneth Edwin. Review of *My Girlhood Among Outlaws* by Eve Ball. *Journal of the West* 13(April, 1974):112.

The Book Exchange. Review of *In the Days of Victorio* by Eve Ball. (December, 1970):167.

Books and Bookmen. Review of *In the Days of Victorio* by Eve Ball. 18(July, 1973):140.

Books of the Southwest. Review of *In the Days of Victorio* by Eve Ball. (October, 1970):131.

Davisson, Lori. Review of *Indeh: An Apache Odyssey* by Eve Ball. *Journal of Arizona History* 22(Spring, 1981):154-155.

Denver Westerners Roundup. Review of *In the Days of Victorio* by Eve Ball. (May-June, 1971):61.

Disantis, John. Review of *Indeh* by Eve Ball. *Best Sellers* 40(October, 1980):257.

Donlon, Walter J. Review of *Indeh: An Apache Odyssey* by Eve Ball. *Southwestern Historical Quarterly* 85(April, 1982):468-470.

Edmunds, R. David. Review of *Indeh: An Apache Odyssey* by Eve Ball. *Utah Historical Quarterly* 49(Winter, 1981):98-99.

Griffen, William B. Review of *Indeh: An Apache Odyssey* by Eve Ball. *American Indian Quarterly* 7(1983):86-88.

Hamburger, Susan. Review of *Indeh* by Eve Ball. *Library Journal* 105(July 1980):1511.

Hitchcock, Catherine. Review of *Ma'am Jones of the Pecos* by Eve Ball. *Arizona and the West* 14(Spring, 1972):93-94.

Hutchinson, W. H. "Theseus in Leather Leggins." Review of *Bob Crosby, World Champion Cowboy* by Eve Ball. *American West Review* 1(Spring, 1967):13, 23.

Munkres, Robert L. Review of *Indeh: An Apache Odyssey* by Eve Ball. *Journal of the West* 20(July, 1981):92-93.

Oglesby, Richard E. Review of *In the Days of Victorio* by Eve Ball. *Arizona and the West* 14(Spring, 1972):93-94.

Publisher's Weekly. Review of *Indeh* by Eve Ball. 217:205.

Sanchez, Lynda A. "Eve Ball." *New Mexico Magazine* (April, 1981):33.

Southwestern Lore. Review of *In the Days of Victorio* by Eve Ball. (December, 1970):77.

Stevenson, Joan W. Review of *In the Days of Victorio* by Eve Ball. *Library Journal* 96(February, 1971):468.

Thrapp, Dan L. Review of *In the Days of Victorio* by Eve Ball. *Journal of Arizona History* 12(Spring, 1971):90-91.
Turcheneske, John A. Review of *Indeh: An Apache Odyssey* by Eve Bell. *New Mexico Historical Review* 57(July, 1982):297.
The Westerners Brand Book. Review of *In the Days of Victorio* by Eve Ball. (September, 1970):37.
Worcester, Donald E. Review of *Indeh: An Apache Odyssey* by Eve Bell. *Arizona and the West* 23(Summer, 1981):177-178.

5

HUBERT HOWE BANCROFT

by Jo Tice Bloom

Biography

Hubert Howe Bancroft was a bookman. From age sixteen when he went to work for his brother-in-law in upstate New York until his death at age eighty-five, he was involved with books. He gained renown for his histories of western North America and for his collection of books, pamphlets, documents, and newspapers which were used to produce those histories.

Born in 1832 in Granville, Ohio, Bancroft grew up in a large family. In 1848 he moved to Buffalo, New York, where he clerked for his brother-in-law, George Derby. After working in Derby's bookstore for almost a year, he became a peddler in Ohio, selling books from his wagon. A successful summer was followed by a return to Buffalo. But the 1849 gold rush in California brought changes to his family as it did to many families in the eastern United States. In 1850 his father went west to search for gold, followed by a son, giving the family more thoughts about El Dorado.

George Derby decided that there was money to be made from the gold rush without searching for the precious metal, so he sent young Bancroft and $5000 worth of books and stationery to California in February, 1852. Bancroft persuaded another clerk, George L. Kenny, to join him on the trip via the Isthmus of Panama. They established their first store in Sacramento. But business did not go well. Derby died. Sacramento suffered from massive flooding and a devastating fire. Moving to San Francisco, Bancroft sold his stock and looked for another job. After working in the city for several months, he moved to Crescent City where he set up a bookstore and kept accounts for a general store. Within two years he had assets of at least $6000. He continued this business in Crescent City until 1855 when he returned to New York.

By the fall of 1856 he had arranged for a stock of $10,000 worth of books and stationery on long-term credit. His sister, Mrs. Derby, invested an additional $5000 and Bancroft left again for California. On December 1, 1856, he opened H. H. Bancroft & Co. in San Francisco with his old partner, George L. Kenny.

From this time on he remained in business in San Francisco. During the 1850s he had several partners, but in 1859 his brother, Albert, joined him in business, and they stayed together for many years, using business names of H. H. Bancroft & Company, A. L. Bancroft Company, and the Bancroft Company. The business expanded from selling books and stationery into the publishing of blank books, textbooks, trade books, and law books, and the printing of stationery, cards, and labels.

In 1870 the company moved into a new building. The brothers planned to house the various functions of the company and to allow room for expansion. At that time the company was the largest book and stationery house west of Chicago, and it included printing, engraving, lithography, and bookbinding departments. The law department had published more than one hundred volumes and dominated legal publishing on the West Coast. Not only did the education department publish readers and spellers, it also provided a placement service for teachers. The lithography department, in addition to producing letterhead stationery, printed millions of labels for canneries and food processors. The Bancroft Company was a prosperous, expanding business serving a vital function in the development of the West Coast. Bancroft himself continued as an active member of the firm until the 1890s.

Themes

In many ways Hubert Howe Bancroft was one of the first historians of the trans-Mississippi West. He predated historical training, and he predated historical theoretical analysis. Bancroft was a collector and an organizer. He was a fact man.

Bancroft's historical work began in 1859 with the publication of a Pacific handbook. During the process of preparation, it seemed reasonable to collect all the books on California and the Pacific Coast in the company onto one shelf to aid the editor of the handbook. The result was a shelf of fifty to seventy-five books. Bancroft was surprised and interested. Slowly his interest in collecting was piqued as he purchased more items for the shelf in San Francisco. He recognized that many ephemeral items might disappear unless collected, and he began purchasing pamphlets, documents, and maps.

A trip to New York and another to London in the early 1860s convinced him that secondhand bookstores had a wealth of material for his collection. As he contemplated the work yet to be done, his conception of what to collect also began to expand, and he saw the necessity for collecting material covering areas beyond the boundaries of California -- rather he decided to collect books, documents, maps, and ephemera applicable to the whole geographic area from Panama to Alaska and from the Pacific Ocean east to the Rocky Mountains and Texas. Thus, he planned his trip to Europe in 1866 as a major collecting expedition. He scoured bookstores in England, Scotland, France, Spain, Italy, Switzerland, and Germany, buying voluminously. Thousands of volumes and documents were shipped to San Francisco. In ensuing years he purchased large portions of major collections on Mexico which were on the auction block, as well as hundreds of items from smaller auctions and catalogs. By 1880 he estimated that he owned 60,000 volumes on western North America.

As his interest and activity in writing history quickened, he also began collecting items in which few people were interested. He saw, for instance, that newspapers contained vital first-hand documentation of local history, and he began to purchase newspapers in quantities. Eventually he collected the equivalent of five thousand volumes. As the pioneers began to disappear, he started taking "dictations" or interviews with pioneers and prominent people all over the West. This was the Bancroft approach to oral history, preserving first-hand accounts of many people. In addition, he received manuscript collections from many people all over the West who wanted to help in writing and collecting, or who felt that their material would be safe in Bancroft's collections. Prominent among those donating papers was General Mariano Guadalupe Vallejo, a leading personality in California history from the 1830s to the 1890s. Bancroft also sent copyists to various archives in California to copy or abstract the provincial, mission, church, and land office records. He used the notes in preparation of his histories. These copies and abstracts were added to his collection, providing important additional primary resource material. Thus, the Bancroft collection pioneered in the preservation of primary materials and provided an outstanding resource for future research.

The collection outgrew the company building, and in 1881 a new fireproof building was constructed to house the library and to provide working space for researchers and writers at work on the histories. By 1886 Bancroft considered selling the collection, but there were no purchasers and the plan died. He renewed the idea in 1892 when the histories were completed, and he was considering retirement from an active business and historical life. A bill was introduced into the California state legislature for the state to purchase the collection at his estimated cost of purchase--$250,000--but the bill failed to pass. In 1898 he revived the project to sell it to the state, and this time the university librarian appraised the collection at $130,000. Again the state was not interested, but a new president at the University of California, Benjamin Ide Wheeler, was interested. He pursued the project, bringing Reuben Gold Thwaites, director of the State Historical Society of Wisconsin, to California in 1905 to appraise the collection. Thwaites valued it at $300,000 and identified more rare books than Bancroft had claimed. Thwaites recommended the university make the "bargain" purchase, which was completed. One of the terms of sale was that the University would maintain the collection separate from the general university library holdings. Thus, the University of California established the Bancroft Library, one of the finest collections of materials, primary and secondary, on the history of western North America.

As he was collecting material on western North America, Bancroft began to think about writing history. With his growing collection, he had the source material. In 1871 he first developed the idea of an encyclopedia on the Pacific states with many contributors and collaborators, but it was soon apparent that he would have to do the work of writing as well as editing the work. He discarded the idea.

Instead he determined to write a comprehensive history of the Pacific states. Obviously he could not hope to read everything in his library as it was too massive. So he decided in the fall of 1871 to hire readers, copyists, abstractors, and writers to do much of the research and drafting of the manuscripts. The process began with sorting and classifying the material and then making a subject index for the material on the Pacific states. Then assistants would outline or abstract the material, gather data, and write drafts. Bancroft himself did the final editing and polishing of the work prior to publication. At times he employed as many as fifty people, sometimes as few as twelve. No one person, other than himself, was employed in the entire project, which took more than twenty years. His most significant assistants were Henry L. Oak, William Nemos, Thomas Savage, Frances Fuller Victor, and Enrique Cerruti. Oak, Savage, and Fuller made significant contributions, and in later years both Oak and Fuller claimed authorship of several volumes. Oak worked for Bancroft longer than any of the others, about eighteen years.

Analysis

When Hubert Howe Bancroft began his histories in the 1870s, there were few historians with doctorates in the country. Most historians at the time were self-taught and Bancroft joined the group, feeling that common sense, willingness to work, and knowledge of the sources were most important. He began his writing by working on the conquest of Mexico, but he was soon dissatisfied with the product and tore up the manuscript. He then turned to a history of Central America and the Isthmus of Panama. As he worked on the early European conquest, he realized that the history of the Indians needed to be written first. There was no field of anthropology in the 1870s, nor any trained anthropologists. So he became one as he worked in the sources. By 1874 *Native Races* was ready for publication. As the five volumes were coming off the press, he took copies and headed east to obtain good reviews for his first history. Most of the reviews were positive on both the East and West Coasts, and Bancroft was recognized as a competent writer and publisher of history.

During the 1880s more volumes came off the presses of the Bancroft Company--histories of Central America, Mexico, California, the northern Mexican states, Texas, the Pacific Northwest, Utah, and the Rocky Mountain states. Many were multivolume editions, the *History of California* going to seven volumes between 1884 and 1890. Also included in the thirty-nine volumes of Bancroft's regional *Works*, in addition to these histories and *Native Races*, were *Popular History of the Mexican*

People, Popular Tribunals, California Pastoral, California inter pocula, Essays and Miscellany, and his own description of his work, *Literary Industries*.

After the completion of his regional histories, he published the seven-volume *Chronicles of the Builders of the Commonwealth: Historical Character Study* in the 1890s. This was a subscription biography series which included most of the important men who had developed the Pacific states. Essays on various aspects of the economy and culture were interspersed throughout the volumes, and they are fine historical essays. In the following years Bancroft wrote short essays on the World's Fair in Chicago, on the Pacific Basin, and on San Francisco. He also produced the ten-volume *The Book of Wealth* (1896-1908). But his most valuable contributions to the field of history are the thirty-nine volumes of his *Works*.

Bancroft's histories, voluminous, exhaustive, almost encyclopedic, grace the shelves of many libraries, both public and private. The *Works* are a place to begin research and often provide the only documentation on people and events during the early periods of European settlement. From the beginning there has been controversy over the quality of the research and writing, as well as over the methods employed to produce the volumes and sell them. When the first volumes appeared, the reviews were generally good and reviewers continued to provide favorable reviews over the years, but as time passed many critics surfaced and have continued.

Negative criticism has come from many sources. The developing field of anthropology contributed critics of *Native Races*. The new anthropologists pointed out that Bancroft's methods and conclusions did not agree with theirs; therefore he was wrong. But in a field where everything was new, especially methodology and theory, it is hard to fault Bancroft for following his own common sense. Bancroft did not call himself an anthropologist and certainly expected that further research and study of the aboriginal population would provide new knowledge and interpretation. He was one of the first to provide much basic material for others to use as well as a useful outline of Native American culture prior to European domination.

As a result of his recognition of the continuous history of northern Mexico and the southwestern United States, he wrote the *History of Texas and the North Mexican States*, and thus began the study of the Spanish Borderlands. Not until Herbert E. Bolton began similar studies at the University of California was Bancroft's approach truly appreciated.

His eleven-volume compendium of the history of California was the most important of his histories. The seven-volume *History of California* covered the state's history from 1769 to the 1880s with the emphasis upon the earlier periods. Appended to Volume I is an alphabetical listing of all non-Indian inhabitants of California from 1769 to 1800, giving date of arrival and indicating an occupation. A similar list of those arriving before 1830 was included in Volume II. Added to the "Pioneer Register and Index," a dictionary of California biography from 1542 to 1848, these lists form a particularly significant part of the history. Here historians have a unique roster of early settlers, a record not easily available for most frontier states or territories.

Bancroft, in preparing the *History of California* and its accompanying volumes, used a tremendously wide variety of sources for his day. Newspapers were scrupulously studied and extensive use was made of interviews with pioneers and prominent persons. Much material was drawn from archives created during the Spanish and Mexican period. By using so much first-hand material, Bancroft and his assistants were able to present a history that was relatively honest in its portrayal of California's beginnings. In fact, his work was greeted with such positive feelings that the California Society of Pioneers elected him an honorary member. However, when some members read his descriptions of John Sutter, John C. Fremont, Robert Stockton, and the Bear Flag Revolt, in particular, they felt that he was destroying their sacred heroes. And in the 1880s the Society attacked Bancroft vociferously and vehemently, eventually withdrawing his honorary membership. Over the years since, most historians of California have found that Bancroft's portrayal of the men and events of the 1848 to 1850 period was closer to the truth than that of the Society.

The other volumes in his series on California did not draw as much negative criticism. *California Pastoral* is the description of folkways and life in California from 1869 to 1888, and preserves the flavor of the period. In *California inter pocula*, Bancroft treats the gold rush period similarly, providing a wealth of information on the times, the men, and their lives. His history of the San Francisco Vigilance Committee, *Popular Tribunals*, was laudatory and drew only minor criticism. This was probably because he knew and talked with many men involved in those days of extralegal justice, and consulted the newspapers before writing the two-volume history. In addition, the minutes of the committee and other vigilante records were in his library.

Bancroft was criticized for his methods of production, some critics saying that it was not a proper way to write history. One suspects that part of such criticism is sour grapes, for good history was produced, and the critics were envious of his ability to organize, edit, and publish so much material in such a short time. He had ample money at his disposal which made it much easier to mobilize an army of workers for the purpose. In the late nineteenth century professional training for historians was just beginning, and even that training was not really equivalent to the rigorous research training of historians in the late twentieth century. Bancroft did a good job of production for his times and should be recognized for that.

Because the *Works* were sold by subscriptions throughout the West, Bancroft has been faulted for his marketing procedures. Again, it was a successful ploy to send salesmen throughout the West selling subscriptions to the entire series. It meant a guaranteed market for each press run. Costs could be held down because the inventory was not great and there was little need for advertising after the *Works* had been published. Bancroft devised a good method of selling his product, and the people of the Pacific states benefited from it.

Over the years since Bancroft completed his publications, his work has grown in stature. In 1960, Earl Pomeroy in *Arizona and the West* (2:111) observed:

> It is seldom that a writer so innocent of literary and philosophical distinction influences later generations, but countless state historians have quarried from Bancroft, perpetuating his proportions, his errors, and sometimes even his style. The very qualities that made his history unreadable when published have made it indispensable ever since. . . . Copying from Bancroft is not plagiarism; it is doing research from published notes and calendared sources. To ignore him is folly; to attempt alone to do again the research of his staff of assistants is impossible . . . . Bancroft may have influenced the shape of our Pacific Coast historiography not only by publishing the raw material of it but by establishing the greatest of the libraries of Far Western history. He had made the Bancroft Library so strong, so nearly adequate in pioneer Pacific Coast history, that no university librarians could bring their holdings on the post-pioneer years to equal strength.

Hubert Howe Bancroft was a bookman, and he left the world a legacy of books.

Bibliography

Books

Achievements of Civilization: The Book of Wealth: In Relation to Material and Intellectual Progress and Achievement; Being An Inquiry into the Nature and Distribution of the World's Resources and Riches, and a History of the Origin and Influence of Property, Its Possession, Accumulation, and Disposition in All Ages and among All Nations, as a Factor in Human Accomplishment, an Agency of Human Refinement, and in the Evolution of Civilization from the Earliest to the Present Era. 10 volumes. New York: The Bancroft Co., 1896-1908.

Annals of Early Central America. New York: The Bancroft Co., n.d.

The Book of the Fair: An Historical and Descriptive Presentation of the World's Science, Art and Industry, as Viewed through the Columbian Exposition at Chicago in 1893. 5 volumes. San Francisco and Chicago: The Bancroft Co., 1893.

California inter pocula. San Francisco: The History Co., 1888.

California Pastoral. San Francisco: The History Co., 1888.

Chronicles of the Builders of the Commonwealth: Historical Character Study. 7 volumes. San Francisco: The History Co., 1890-1891.

Essays and Miscellany. San Francisco: The History Co., 1890.

A Golden Wedding. New York: A. L. Bancroft and Co., 1872.

History of Alaska. San Francisco: A. L. Bancroft and Co., 1886.

History of Arizona and New Mexico. San Francisco: The History Co., 1889.

History of British Columbia. San Francisco: The History Co., 1887.
History of California. 7 volumes. San Francisco: The History Co., 1884-1890.
History of Central America. 3 volumes. San Francisco: A. L. Bancroft and Co., 1882-1887.
History of Mexico. 6 volumes. Volumes 1-5, San Francisco: A. L. Bancroft and Co., 1883; Volume 6, San Francisco: The History Co., 1888.
History of Nevada, Colorado, and Wyoming. San Francisco: The History Co., 1889.
History of Oregon. 2 volumes. San Francisco: The History Co., 1886, 1888.
History of Texas and the North Mexican States. 2 volumes. San Francisco: The History Co., 1884, 1889.
History of the Northwest Coast. 2 volumes. San Francisco: A. L. Bancroft and Co., 1890.
History of Utah, 1540-1886. San Francisco: The History Co., 1889.
History of Washington, Idaho, and Montana. San Francisco: The History Co., 1890.
In These Later Days. Chicago: Blakely-Oswald, 1917; supplement, Chicago: Blakely-Oswald, 1918.
The Life of Porfirio Diaz. 2 volumes. San Francisco: A. L. Bancroft and Co., 1885.
Literary Industries. San Francisco: The History Co., 1890.
Native Races. 5 volumes. New York: D. Appleton, 1874-1875.
The New Pacific. New York: The Bancroft Co., 1899; revised, 1912.
Popular History of the Mexican People. San Francisco: The History Co., 1887.
Popular Tribunals. 2 volumes. San Francisco: The History Co., 1887.
Resources and Development of Mexico. San Francisco: The Bancroft Co., 1892.
Retrospection. New York: The Bancroft Co., 1912.
Society--Past and Present: Education in the Western United States, Central America, and Mexico; Science, Art, and Literature in Mexico; The Church in the Western United States, Central America, and Mexico. San Francisco: n.p., 1892.
Vida de Porfirio Diaz: Resena historica y social del pasado y presente de Mexico. San Francisco: The History Co., 1887.

Pamphlets
Analysis and Valuation of the Bancroft Library. San Francisco: The Bancroft Co., 1891.
The Early American Chroniclers. San Francisco: A. L. Bancroft Co., 1885.
Evolution of a Library. San Francisco: n.p., 1901.
A Few Words Concerning the Historical Publications of Hubert Howe Bancroft. San Francisco: The History Co., 1882.

The Historical Works of Hubert Howe Bancroft in Their Relation to the Progress and Destiny of the Pacific States. San Francisco: The History Co., n.d., also in Spanish.

Modern Fallacies. New York: The Bancroft Co., 1915.

Resurgam. New York: The Bancroft Co., 1907.

Reviews of Hubert H. Bancroft's History of the Pacific States from the British Quarterly Review and the London Times. San Francisco: The History Co., 1886.

Some Cities and San Francisco. New York: The Bancroft Co., 1907.

Why a World Centre of Industry at San Francisco Bay. New York: The Bancroft Co., 1916.

Article

"California's Biography." In *Contemporary Biography of California's Representative Men* edited by Alonzo Phelps. San Francisco: A. L. Bancroft and Co., 1881.1:7-26.

Studies of Hubert Howe Bancroft

Caughey, John W. *Hubert Howe Bancroft: Historian of the West.* Berkeley: University of California Press, 1946.

Clark, Harry. *A Venture in History: The Production, Publication, and Sale of the Works of Hubert Howe Bancroft.* Berkeley: University of California Press, 1973.

Cutter, Donald C. "A Dedication to the Memory of Hubert Howe Bancroft, 1832-1918." *Arizona and the West* 2(Summer, 1960):105-106.

Lewis, Oscar. "The Launching of Bancroft's 'Native Races.'" *Colophon* n.s. 1(1936):322-332.

McCarthy, John R. "Wholesale Historian: Hubert Howe Bancroft." *American Heritage* 1(Spring, 1950):17-19.

Morris, William A. "The Origin and Authorship of the Bancroft Pacific States Publications: A History of a History." *Oregon Historical Quarterly* 4(1903):344-345.

Oak, Henry L. *"Literary Industries" in a New Light: A Statement on the Authorship of Bancroft's Native Races and History of the Pacific States, with comments on These Works and the System by Which They were Written.* San Francisco: n.p., 1893.

Pomeroy, Earl S. "Hubert Howe Bancroft." In *Reader's Encyclopedia of the American West* edited by Howard R. Lamar. New York: Thomas Y. Crowell Co., 1977. Pp. 68-69.

____________. "Old Lamps for New: The Cultural Lag in Pacific Coast Historiography." *Arizona and the West* 2(Summer, 1960):107-126.

6

ADOLPH BANDELIER

by Mark W. T. Harvey

Biography

On August 6, 1889, Adoph Bandelier celebrated a birthday in Santa Fe, New Mexico, with family and friends. Having received "a number of useful presents" including a travel bag, a pair of suspenders, and a cigar case, he thought "that I cannot but be very, very grateful to all and to God." Yet there was an element of dissatisfaction accompanying his contentment. That evening, after all the guests had gone, he wrote in his diary in a more contemplative frame of mind: "I am now 49 years old and:-- What have I done? Nothing" (*Southwestern Journals* 4:78). Coming from a man who had spent years of travel and research in Mexico and the southwestern United States, had established an impressive bibliography of publications, and ranked among the chief scholars of the American Indian and Spanish Southwest, the remark seems a bit surprising.

However, contrasting emotions and ideas were most indicative of Bandelier's personality. He took great satisfaction in his work at times, but he worked tirelessly at research and writing, always in pursuit of more facts which could help solve the puzzle, always ready to synthesize them into the broader picture he had in his mind. In the realm of the historian's craft, Bandelier believed pursuit of "the sources" must lead to the impartial truth, yet he spent much of his scholarly life in the shadow of the esteemed anthropologist Lewis Henry Morgan, whose theories about humankind included the notion that all cultures were identifiable by certain stages of development and that history might be written according to a rigid formula. Bandelier always tried to be aware of the richness of history, to approach his story with knowledge from a variety of fields, and to allow each to contribute to an integrated whole. Yet he often became overwhelmed with details, and sometimes he found it difficult to establish the broader patterns in history. He had a selfish and self-centered streak about him, while he also had much compassion for those around him and for native peoples whom he observed. He was truly a man of contrasts. And though he ranks today as a pioneering scholar of the Far Southwest, only recently has his reputation been brought into clear view.

Bandelier spent his lifework studying the Spanish frontier and pre-Columbian and contemporary Indians of the Southwest, Mexico, and South America. Given his background, he might well have followed a different path. Adolph Francis Alphonse Bandelier began his life in Bern, Switzerland, on August 6, 1840. His father was a lawyer, a "pompous gentleman" who decided his family should move to the United States when Adolph was still young. The Bandeliers settled in Highland, Illinois, built a large brick home with a wine cellar, surrounded themselves with expansive orchards, and became well-respected citizens. His father achieved notable success as a banker in Highland. He was active in community and church. The elder Bandelier ensured that his family lived well on their estate, with servants in the house.

The young Bandelier developed a strong will and sharp intellectual interests under his father's influence, and he twice returned to the University of Bern to study geology and the law. However, Bandelier's time abroad was short, and it appears that most of his formal schooling came through private tutors and from his parents, who possessed a broad range of interests including natural history and the study of foreign languages, particularly French and Spanish. When Adolph returned from Switzerland, he took a position in his father's banking business. His future, however, did not lie in private enterprise in a small midwestern town. Given his upbringing, it was not difficult for Bandelier to see the attractiveness of a scholarly career. Nearby was the Mercantile Library of St. Louis, where he found an exciting collection of documents on Spanish America. After marrying Josephine Huegy, daughter of one of his father's banking associates, Bandelier settled into life in Highland where his interests would lead him to the study of history.

Themes

Bandelier, it should be said at once, understood "history" very broadly, which helps explain why he has always been difficult to classify. Many have considered him primarily an anthropologist and archeologist, and a pioneer in the field of ethnology. He clearly had an interest in each of these, but he also considered himself a historian and chronicler of contemporary events. His writings, which include four published volumes of journals, show his variety of interests. Bandelier spent several years in archives in Mexico, and published articles on the social organization, government, land system, and mode of warfare among the Mexican people before the Spanish Conquest. Later, he followed the routes of Spanish friars into the borderlands, and explained their motives for settlement and their relations with Indians.

His overriding interest centered on the Pueblo Indians of the Southwest, and he was fascinated with many periods of their long history. His work took him out into hundreds of ancient dwellings where he took copious notes, drew countless sketches, and recorded with meticulous care every artifact and the structure of every ruin. He spent time among the living Pueblo, too, which allowed him to explore his keen interest in the religious life of the Indians. He learned an immense amount from them about the nature of their dances, language, and pottery styles, and he made a point of collecting Pueblo stories of their ancestors. He took a delight in many aspects of the history of the Southwest, and his rich storehouse of publications and journals do not allow him to be placed easily into any definable pigeonhole.

Bandelier made use of many sources--personal interviews, documents, artifacts--to learn everything he could. He was equally comfortable investigating ruins centuries old with a sketch pad and ruler as in working his way through faded, dusty documents in libraries. Any source was grist for his mill. One scholar has noted how Bandelier possessed "a tremendous appetite for data--field data, archival data, any kind of data. He had very little ability to look beyond the surfaces of things (*Southwestern Journals* 4:46)."

That is true to a large degree, but Bandelier did not lose sight of larger issues, and the total weight of his work made a substantial contribution to scholars' knowledge of the Southwest. Though he filled his books, articles, and journals with incredible detail, he seemed intent on reaching broader conclusions. Besides, being a kind of intellectual pack rat was not necessarily the wrong approach during the time that Bandelier engaged in his studies, particularly in light of the common image of Indians. Through most of the nineteenth century, views of the American Indian followed those of the classic historians of the Americas, Hubert H. Bancroft, William Prescott, and Francis Parkman. These historians painted fanciful portraits of some Indian civilizations, particularly those of Mexico and South America, and glorified their way of life. At the other extreme, they pictured some Indians as brutal savages, who lived the lives of animals. Given this intellectual climate, Bandelier's method of amassing information served scholars well.

Analysis

The first major figure who challenged the classic mythical views of the American frontier was the learned and authoritative Lewis Henry Morgan, whose *Ancient Society* established a new paradigm for interpreting history. Morgan argued that all forms of government fell into two categories, *societas*, based upon personal relations alone, and *civitas*, which developed in cultures founded upon territory and property rights. Morgan asserted that societas or simple forms of government were dominant among America's Indians. In fact, he contended that no Native American peoples had advanced beyond this stage; institutions such as feudalism, aristocracy, or monarchy never existed in the New World's native cultures.

Morgan based his conclusions to a large degree upon extensive research of the Iroquois Confederacy, from which he decided other Native Americans followed the same pattern of society and government. He was convinced that all Indian peoples had simple democracies, even the once mighty Aztecs. The notion that the Aztecs were monarchical had come from Spanish observers during the Conquest, but Morgan thought their observations were greatly distorted. As a corrective, he portrayed the Aztecs as peasants living in a communal system. Montezuma, the great Aztec chief, did not live in a palace, but in a modest dwelling with many others, while the city of Tenochtitlán had been a "humble Pueblo." Similar forms of government and society existed across the Americas. Morgan did not believe that all Indians were totally alike, but in his mind, no Indian community attained the institutional complexity of the dominant nations of western civilization (*Aztec Image*).

Morgan's view was obviously too simplistic, but it discredited the common romantic image of noble savages, and his conclusions also molded the mind of Adolph Bandelier. During a research trip to the University of Rochester, Bandelier obtained an introduction to Morgan. The two men took an immediate liking to one another, and soon established a correspondence and professional relationship which had a profound influence on the young scholar from Illinois. Morgan took Bandelier under his wing, and Bandelier's life work was in many ways a product of Morgan's views. In Mexico, where Bandelier began his travels and research, there was an abundance of scholarship waiting to be done, and he engaged in his work with Morgan's ideas foremost in mind.

At first, Bandelier disagreed with his intellectual father. He was struck, for example, at how Morgan's ideas could not be applied to the Aztecs. Combing the Spanish documents, Bandelier developed a different view, concluding that Aztec society had not been communal or "democratic" but decidedly monarchical, with a full conception of a body politic. He thought feudalism had been an integral part of early Mexico, and he concluded Aztec organization was more complex than a simple societas. Bandelier disagreed with Morgan, thinking that early Spanish accounts of Mexico's Indians had much merit.

Yet the relationship that began with the apprentice Bandelier challenging the master Morgan gradually changed. As time went on, Bandelier increasingly echoed Morgan's ideas, even as he did laborious research which Morgan could not claim to have done (*Pioneers in Anthropology*, pp. 15-16). After Morgan died in 1881, Bandelier continued to test the validity of the author's ideas against archival sources and cultural observations, all the while finding himself more inclined to accept them. Precisely why he came to adopt Morgan's views remains unclear. Certainly Bandelier found it easier to be accepted by other scholars the less he disagreed with Morgan. Whatever the explanation, he came to believe that Morgan's sweeping interpretations had a good deal of merit, and that with some exceptions, many of Morgan's thoughts about democracy and simplicity in Indian life could usefully be applied to the Indians of the Southwest.

Bandelier wrote articles and books on a variety of subjects, though his special interest centered on the Pueblo Indians of the United States. He spent the decade of the 1880s studying them, and he made his living writing articles for the *Nation* and as an employee of the Archeological Institute of America. Later, he joined the Hemenway Expedition to the Southwest as its chief historian. Unfortunately, none of his employers paid him well or offered him a secure living. So Bandelier came to resemble Mozart: while he complained constantly about his financial woes, he did not allow material considerations to prevent him from undertaking the work he loved, or from producing a staggering amount of written material. After nearly ten years among the Pueblo, Bandelier published his most important work: the two volume *Final Report of Investigations Among the Indians of the Southwestern United States.* In 1890, he also published his most famous work, a novel of early Pueblo culture titled *The Delightmakers.*

The *Final Report*, not well known, contains Bandelier's central ideas. The volumes show the results of years spent living among and talking with the Indians of northern Mexico, New Mexico, and Arizona. Bandelier begins with an overview of the region's geography and topography. He draws a portrait of the land with broad strokes, showing in crisp prose its climatic extremes, sparse vegetation, and the harsh effects of soil erosion and flash flooding on the fragile lands. He points out that Indians in this region relied on a variety of plants and animals and developed a keen sense of their availability in order to survive.

Bandelier recognizes that Indian religion reflects this intimate association with the environment, that the whole apparatus of rites, dances, and ceremonies functioned as a way to establish harmony with nature. On the other hand, Bandelier's conversion to Catholicism in 1881 shaped his perceptions, too. Imbued with the notion of a single God and a hierarchical church, his remarks about Southwest Indian rites and ceremonies are not surprising. He thought of them as "fetishism of the grossest kind," in which the Indians bowed before gods of a different kind each season of the year. Rites which paid homage to spirits of animals seemed abhorrent to him, for they placed many beasts "on a footing of equality with mankind" (*Final Report* 1:41).

Bandelier believed such rites made the Indian a slave. Deification of nature and the worship of many gods created moral chaos, he thought, for there seemed to him no code of conduct toward one's fellow human beings. Religion called upon the Indian only to bow before the gods of the elements, and from Bandelier's point of view, "these voices stifle the silent throbs of conscience; they are no guide to the heart, no support for the mind" (p. 41).

One detects the influence of Morgan. In Bandelier's mind, a central problem with Pueblo rites was their "democratic" conception of gods and of religious organization. Social organization and religious creed, that is, went hand in hand. Caciques, for example, had strong religious influence, yet lacked authoritarian power. Caciques who abused their power could be judged by war captains, then punished, and shamans then appointed new caciques. The cacique was not a hereditary position, and for Bandelier, this kind of tenuous authority in a religious leader was peculiar and inexplicable (pp. 284-285).

Most Pueblo developed their religious societies precisely because they wished to disperse such authority; theocracies were unwanted. Bandelier could not see the rationale behind this organization. In his words are Morgan's influence, the mind of a European, and the faith of a Catholic: "The separation of the family into two halves by exogamous marriage excluded all thought of heredity and dynasty. The organization of the esoteric clusters themselves, their number, and the numbers of those who constituted them, maintained the democratic principle in their midst, and rendered it impossible for one or a few to obtain more than a temporary and transient power" (p. 284). Pueblo religion and society were far removed from institutions founded upon private property, and Bandelier was unable to grasp why. He only knew that the religious rites and close-knit pueblo apartment structures suggested communal living and a democratic politic, a way of life which he believed unified all native peoples of the Southwest.

Still, it is not accurate to think of Bandelier as a clone of Lewis Henry Morgan, just as it is unfair to characterize his work as a search for evidence to substantiate a particular "theory." Bandelier was intellectually indebted to Morgan, but he is more often remembered as "an expeditionist" and prodigious researcher, more excited about uncovering a long lost fact about a Pueblo corn dance than about advancing any bold interpretation of the Southwest. Bandelier was essentially a modest individual, who took advantage of what he saw as a marvelous opportunity to record valuable information about hundreds of years of Southwest Indian life. He was a latter-day George Catlin, determined to learn as much as possible about the myths and lifeways of a culture centuries old. Even after years of research, he advanced tentative oonclusions about many aspects of the Indian past and present. His views about Pueblo "democracy" certainly had their origin in Morgan; but if they carried along a measure of European ethnocentrism, it must be said that Bandelier was a historian in the best sense of the word, never convinced that all the answers had been found, never fully satisfied with his own understanding. Perhaps this is why he felt less than pleased with his work on his forty-ninth birthday.

This much is clear. Bandelier's intense labors among the living and ancient Pueblo left to the following generations a sounder, more realistic body of material from which to work. His method of research--a combination of archival and archeological technique--and his passion for thoroughness became the norm among students of the Indian Southwest, Jesse Walter Fewkes, Clark Wissler, Frederick Hodge, and others. Bandelier's approach toward studying native peoples made him an important transitional figure in scholarly circles. By insisting the historian must blend careful research with sound writing, he helped sweep away remnants of the romantic tradition of Prescott and Bancroft. Charles Lummis once said of Bandelier that "he has driven the last nail in the coffin of the Romantic School of American History, whose head was the noble, brilliant but unfortunate Prescott. . . . We need him now to sit down and write . . . before his learning shall die with him, the digest of his unparalleled research. Now, that it not be lost" (*Arizona and the West* 2:22).

Furthermore, Bandelier's indebtedness to Morgan does not detract from the fact that he helped to lift the study of Indians up from the condescendingly theoretical approach of Morgan. Although he never attacked Morgan's ideas outright, his own work established one fact as indisputable: there could be no substitute for research. The irony of the close relationship between the two scholars is that Bandelier's own work gradually discredited Morgan's method of advancing grand theses on the basis of limited research. Thereafter, historians and anthropologists were obliged to do "field work." Bandelier helped focus students of the Southwest on the sources, less on theory. He accomplished this not by his own analytical brilliance, but through methodical, plodding, and sometimes grueling work.

Thanks to his many articles in the *Nation*, Bandelier also comes to us as a historian of Indian-white conflict in his own time. In order to bring in some money, he wrote a number of short articles, which tried to shed light on the tragic aspects of the far western frontier, and enlighten the journal's "cultivated" readers from the East. Bandelier often found himself defending the Indian, and he had no hesitation pointing out injustices inflicted upon them from the past. In 1886, he suggested that depredations upon Navajo lands and seizure of Navajo irrigation ditches and water was a sure way to provoke another war on the southwestern frontier. He defended Indian rights to land and water, partly because he knew well the probable consequences of provocation: thousands of Navajo and Apache might fight if only a few were disturbed.

On the whole question of Indian removal, Bandelier thought it most unwise to rush. He knew that southwestern Native Americans would strongly resist attempts to remove them, and this would generate additional military conflict. He knew, too, that any agreement between councils of Indians and officials from Washington might be difficult to put into effect, for gaining strict adherence from an entire nation was a tricky business. Each leader had many contending constituents, and could not claim to speak for an entire nation. Bandelier also realized that pressure to remove Indians usually came from settlers in pursuit of land and minerals, more than it did from their own fears (*Nation* 43:209).

All of this is to say that Bandelier did not belong to that group of Protestant reformers concerned with Indians. Their formula was easy: eliminate all communal property, carve Indian lands into individual plots, instill in the Indian mind the sanctity of private holdings, and build schools and teach Indians good American and Protestant values. Fundamentally, he agreed with them, that "the Indian, as Indian, must disappear" (*Final Report* 1:316). Indian language and some traditions might be kept so long as the young learned English and accepted mores of Anglo-American society. It was the speed of the Protestant reform program that Bandelier thought unrealistic. He sensed that such an idealistic approach carried with it a naive understanding of Indian peoples, and he thought it hypocritical.

Bandelier believed that neither Indians' manner of speech nor physical traits distinguished them from any other people. To make the Indian into a good American did not mean their skin color must be changed. They were different in a spiritual sense, and Bandelier knew this fact had been overlooked by Protestant reformers. They did not perceive that Indians'

> social organization and . . . creed . . . are so intimately interwoven as to have become inseparable. These are out of place in the march of civilization, and they must perish. But they are also rooted so deeply in the mental and moral nature of the Indian, so closely connected with his material existence, that no violent extirpation can be attempted without endangering also the purely human part of his being. To the latter, he is entitled, and above all from our national standpoint, by the formal declaration "that all men are created equal" (*Final Report* 1:316).

Bandelier was never satisfied with his own grasp of Pueblo culture and religion, but he believed that the reformers woefully lacked an understanding of Indian life. He showed a good deal of sympathy and perceptivity regarding Indian-white conflicts in his own nineteenth century. He undoubtedly had a more sophisticated understanding of the dynamics of that conflict than did most in his day.

Given Bandelier's determination to look beyond the conventional interpretations of contemporary and past events, it is easy to see why he also developed himself as a student of the Spanish in the Southwest. The Black Legend, which depicted the Spanish and their descendants as a cruel and conniving people, had a stronghold in the nineteenth-century American mind, so that anyone who undertook a serious study of Spanish history had to be courageous. Other histories of Spain and her New World empire existed, but Bandelier was one of the first to examine expeditions into the Borderlands, and how they established Spain's sovereignty in the present-day Southwest.

He took great pride in his studies of Cabeza de Vaca, Fray Marcos de Niza, Coronado, and Fray Juan de Padilla, though the modern reader can become frustrated with his narrative detail, and perhaps lose sight of Bandelier's purpose in approaching these figures. Each of them was a leader of exploratory parties in the Southwest during the sixteenth century. Bandelier determined to follow their routes closely, find out which Indian peoples they met, what geographic features they discovered, and how each helped spur additional explorations into the Borderlands. He wanted to set the facts of Spanish exploration straight, in order to bring to light the underlying motives behind it. Bandelier's scholarship in this area combined his passion for unearthing facts with an equally sharp interest about what the Spanish thought they were doing in their explorations. Prominent among the works devoted to this subject are a book entitled *The*

Gilded Man (1893), pertinent chapters in his *Final Report* for the Archeological Institute of America, and several articles in the *Nation.*

Of course, it has almost become a cliché to note that the Spanish mind was filled with dreams of gold and other riches, and that the expeditions sent to the Borderlands in the sixteenth century were expected to find long lost wealth. Bandelier was not the first historian to write about this subject, but he helped to clear away some of the cobwebs of misunderstanding. For example, he exerts a good deal of effort defending Fray Marcos de Niza, who claimed to have discovered one of the Seven Cities of Cibola in 1539, the walls of the city embroidered with rich stones. Bandelier concludes that de Niza had actually stumbled onto Zuni pueblo in western New Mexico which did not equal the size of Mexico City as de Niza had thought, nor were its walls made of pure gold as some of the stories emanating from de Niza's party suggested. Nevertheless, Bandelier thought de Niza had not lost all of his senses wandering through the deadly hot climate. There was indeed a tradition at Zuni to place turquoise in the doors. Nor would it have been difficult for someone standing at a distance from Zuni pueblo to see it as a large settlement, given the tightly compacted pueblos swarming with people (*The Gilded Man*, pp. 136-162).

The merits of de Niza's claim aside, Bandelier recognized the power of myth and fantasy in the history of the Borderlands. He knew that quite apart from the controversy surrounding de Niza's claim of finding one of the famed Seven Cities, the claim itself excited Spanish leaders in Mexico City. Thus, de Niza's return led to Coronado's expedition and soon there was an equally compelling story and powerful myth in the Southwest: that of Quivira. Coronado was given to believe that Quivira was a land to the north with inhabitants who possessed fantastic amounts of gold and silver. Yet he did not find such wealth in the north, only wandering Plains Indians in Kansas. So the myth of Quivira changed and beheld an opposite image. For many years after Coronado, Quivira became "merely one section of the immense steppes of the North--devoid of mineral resources, thinly inhabited, cold, and principally roamed over by enormous herds of strangely shapen wild cattle" (*Nation* 49:348). Still, the myth of Quivira as a land of gold refused to go away. After the myth was all but forgotten for generations, it was revived in the eighteenth century with the Escalante expedition into the Southwest. Now, Quivira took on the same image as de Niza's Seven Cities of Cibola: a lost land and people once rich beyond compare (p. 365).

Bandelier was fascinated with these myths, and he went to great lengths to explain their origin and significance. Because of his unsurpassed knowledge of the land and peoples of the Southwest in his present and the past, he could explain the development of these stories with accuracy, showing for example, which Pueblo ruins had been seen by the Spanish as the lost cities of gold. He tried to ascertain the truth behind the legends, where Spanish explorers actually went and what they said, and he tried to recreate the process by which myths had been made. Bandelier realized, most importantly, how stories of wealth took on a reality of their own, and gave rise to Spanish settlements and missions. The legacy of chasing myths of gold was the addition of substantial knowledge about the Borderlands and its native peoples.

Adolph Bandelier's portrayal of Spain and her empire was not wholly dispassionate, nor did he cover all aspects of the Borderlands frontier which historians today regard as vital to grasp the region's history. Another generation of scholars would be left to analyze Spanish influence on Indian religion and culture, successes and failures of Spanish settlements, and Spain's relations with other nations in North America. Bandelier had an obvious bias, too, viewing the Church and missionaries in an overly favorable light. His treatment of that subject really did not go beyond an assessment of individual clerics, whom he noted for their special courage and faith. Bandelier had relatively little to say about the mission system itself, which surely had a more significant influence on the region than did the wanderings of Fray Marcos de Niza or Juan de Padilla.

Yet if he left much unsaid, he also contributed a substantial body of knowledge to the history of the Far Southwest. A bibliography of his books, articles, and reviews would fill a volume, and these writings provide a treasure of information to present scholars, just as they established a foundation for historians, ethnologists, archeologists, and anthropologists of the past. It is perhaps trite to credit any student of the past with leaving an important body of scholarship for the future, but that is certainly true of Adolph Bandelier. He laid the groundwork for serious research of the Southwest Borderlands a generation before Herbert Eugene Bolton, and he built a framework for students of the Indian past.

Bibliography

Books

Contributions to the History of the Southwestern Portion of the United States. Cambridge, MA: Papers of the Archeological Institute of America, 1890. American Series V.

The Delightmakers. New York: Dodd, Mead & Co., 1890. Reprint. New York: Harcourt Brace Jovanovich, 1971.

Final Report of Investigations Among the Indians of the Southwestern United States, Carried on Mainly in the Years From 1880 to 1885. Parts I and II. Cambridge, MA: Papers of the Archeological Institute of America, 1890-1892. American Series III and IV.

The Gilded Man (El Dorado) and Other Pictures of the Spanish Occupancy of America. New York: D. Appleton & Co., 1893. Reprint. Chicago: Rio Grande Press, 1962.

Historical Documents Relating to New Mexico, Nueva Vizcaya, and Approaches Thereto, to 1773. Collected with Fanny R. Bandelier. Edited by Charles Wilson Hackett. 3 volumes. Washington, DC: Carnegie Institution of Washington, 1923-1927.

Indians of the Rio Grande Valley. Co-authored with Edgar L. Hewitt. Albuquerque: University of New Mexico School of American Research, 1937. Reprint. New York: Cooper Square Publishers, Inc., 1973.

Selected Articles

"Aboriginal Myths and Traditions Concerning the Island of Titicaca, Bolivia." *American Anthropologist* n.s. 6(April-June, 1904):197-239.

"The Aboriginal Ruins at Stillustani, Peru." *American Anthropologist* n.s. 7(January-March, 1905):49-68.

"Aboriginal Trephining in Bolivia." *American Anthropologist* n.s. 6(June-September, 1904):440-446.

"Alvar Nu ez Cabeza de Vaca, the First Overland Traveler of European Descent, and his Journey from Florida to the Pacific Coast--1528-1536." *Magazine of Western History* 5(July, 1886):327-336.

"The Apache Outbreak." *Nation* 41(July 2, 1885):8-9.

"Archeological Chronology." *Nation* 43(August 12, 1885):132-133.

"Archeological Work in Arizona and New Mexico During 1888-1889." In *Tenth Annual Report of the Archeological Institute of America.* Cambridge, MA: Archeological Institute of America, 1889. 3:106-108.

"The Basin of Lake Titicaca." *Bulletin, American Geographical Society* 37(1905):449-460.

"The Betrayer of LaSalle." *Nation* 47(August 30, 1888):166-167.

"Boundary Readjustments in South America." *Nation* 79(August 25, 1904):155-156.

"The Cross of Carabuco in Bolivia." *American Anthropologist* n.s. 6(October-December, 1904):599-628.

"Documentary History of the Rio Grande Pueblos of New Mexico." In *Papers of the School of American Research.* Lancaster, PA: Archeological Institute of America, 1910. 13:1-28.

"Existing Cave Dwellers." *Nation* 53(November 26, 1891):408-409.

"Fray Juan de Padilla, the First Catholic Missionary and Martyr in Eastern Kansas, 1542." *American Catholic Quarterly Review* 15(July, 1890):551-565.

"Historical Introduction to Studies Among the Sedentary Indians of New Mexico." In *Papers of the Archeological Institute of America.* Boston: Archeological Institute of America, 1881. 1:1-33.

"An Important Discovery for Mexican Antiquities." *Nation* 29(November 20, 1879):347-348.

"The Indians and Aboriginal Ruins near Chachapoyas in Northern Peru." In *Historical Records and Studies of the United States Catholic Historical Society.* New York: United States Catholic Historical Society, 1907. 5:Part 1.

"The Industrial Condition of Mexico." *Nation* 50(May 29, 1890):427-429.

"Irrigation in the Southwest." *Nation* 45(December 15, 1887):474.

"Kin and Clan." *New Mexico Historical Review* 8(July, 1933):165-175.

"The 'Montezuma' of the Pueblo Indians." *American Anthropologist* 5(October, 1892):319-326.

"Must We Have Another Indian War?" *Nation* 42(May 13, 1886):397-398.

"The National Museum of Mexico and the Sacrificial Stone." *American Antiquarian and Oriental Journal* 2(July-September, 1879):15-29.

"New Mexican Spanish Antiquities." *Nation* 48(March 28, 1889):265-266.

"Notes on the Bibliography of Yucatan and Central America." In *Proceedings of the American Antiquarian Society.* Worcester, MA: American Antiquarian Society, 1880-1881. 1:82-118.

"On the Art of War and Mode of Warfare of the Ancient Mexicans." In *Tenth Annual Report of the Peabody Museum of American Archeology and Ethnology.* Cambridge, MA: Peabody Museum, 1877. Pp. 95-161.

"On the Distribution and Tenure of Land, and the Customs With Respect to Inheritance, Among the Ancient Mexicans." In *Eleventh Annual Report of the Peabody Museum of American Archeology and Ethnology.* Cambridge, MA: Peabody Museum, 1878. Pp. 385-448.

"On the Relative Antiquity of Ancient Peruvian Burials." In *Bulletin, American Musuem of Natural History.* New York: American Museum of Natural History, 1904. 20:217-226.

"On the Social Organization and Mode of Government of the Ancient Mexicans." In *Twelfth Annual Report of the Peabody Museum of American Archeology and Ethnology.* Cambridge, MA: Peabody Museum, 1879. Pp. 557-699.

"An Outline of the Documentary History of the Zuni Tribe." *Journal of American Ethnology and Archeology* 3(1892):1-115.

"Po-s , a Tale of San Ildefonso Pueblo." *New Mexico Historical Review* 1(July, 1926):335-349.

"The Progressive Indian: What Advanced Civilization and the Winchester Have Done for the Red Man." St. Louis [MO] *Globe-Democrat,* December 26, 1885.

"Quivira-I." *Nation* 49(October 31, 1889):348-349.

"Quivira-II." *Nation* 49(November 7, 1889):365-366.

"Removal of the Apaches From Arizona." *Nation* 43(September 9, 1886):208-209.

"Report by A. F. Bandelier on his Investigations in New Mexico During the Years 1883-1884." In *Fifth Annual Report of the Executive Committee, Archeological Institute of America.* Cambridge, MA: Harvard University Press, 1884. Pp. 55-98.

"Report by A. F. Bandelier on his Investigations in New Mexico in the Spring and Summer of 1882." In *Bulletin of the Archeological Institute of America.* Boston: Archeological Institute of America, 1883. Pp. 13-33.

"Report of an Archeological Tour in Mexico in 1881." In *Papers of the Archeological Institute of America.* Boston: Harvard University Press, 1884. 2:1-326.

"The Ruins of Casas Grandes, I." *Nation* 51(August 28, 1890):166-168.

"The Ruins of Casas Grandes, II." *Nation* 51(September 4, 1890):185-187.

"The Ruins at Tiahuanaco." In *Proceedings, American Antiquarian Society.* Worcester, MA: American Antiquarian Society, 1911. Pp. 218-265.

"Sources of Spanish American History." *Nation* 28(April 17, 1879):265.

"The Southwestern Land Court." *Nation* 52(May 28, 1891):437.

"Southwestern Pine Timber." *Nation* 43(July 1, 1886):8.

"Traditions of Precolumbian Landings on the Western Coast of South America." *American Anthropologist* n.s. 7(April-June, 1905):250-270.

"Traditions of Precolumbian Earthquakes and Volcanic Eruptions in Western South America." *American Anthropologist* n.s. 8(January-March, 1906):47-81.

"The Truth About Inca Civilization." *Harper's Magazine* 110(March, 1905):632-640.

"A Visit to the Aboriginal Ruins in the Valley of the Rio Pecos." In *Papers of the Archeological Institute of America.* Boston: Archeological Institute of America, 1881. 1:34-133.

"Why New Mexico Does Not Flourish." *Nation* 42(January 28, 1886):70-71.

Selected Reviews

Aboriginal America edited by Justin Winsor. *Nation* 49(August 15, 1889):134-135.

An Apache Campaign in the Sierra Madre by John G. Bourke. *Nation* 42(March 11, 1886):222.

Ancient Nahuatl Pottery by David G. Brinton. *Nation* 46(February 2, 1888):102-103.

Ancient Society by Lewis H. Morgan. *Nation* 25(August 9, 1877):92-93.

The Arapahoe Sun Dance by George A. Dorsey. *Nation* 78(June 23, 1904):497.

Around the Caribbean and Across Panama by Francis C. Nicholas. *Nation* 77(November 19, 1903):411.

California and Its Missions by Bryan J. Clinch. *Nation* 80(May 18, 1905):404.

Die Culturlander des Alten Amerika by Ad. Bastian. *Nation* 28(May 22, 1879):357-358.

Indian Basketry: Studies in a Textile Art Without Machinery by Otis T. Mason. *Nation* 80(March 16, 1905):219.

The Indians of the Painted Desert Region by George W. James. *Nation* 78(February 25, 1904):156-157.

The Journey of Coronado by George P. Winship. *Nation* 78(June 2, 1904):439-440.

The Land of Little Rain by Mary Austin. *Nation* 78(May 19, 1904):391-392.

The League of the Ho-De-No-Sau-Nee or Iroquois by Lewis H. Morgan. *Nation* 79(November 3, 1904):362-363.

Life, Letters, and Travels of Father Pierre Jean DeSmet, S.J., 1801-1873 by Hiram Martin Chittenden. *Nation* 80(April 6, 1905):274-275.

The Mystic Mid-Region: The Deserts of the Southwest by Arthur J. Burdick. *Nation* 78(May 19, 1904):391.

Narratives of the Career of Hernando de Soto edited by Edward G. Bourne. *Nation* 80(March 9, 1905):197.

The Palenque Tablet in the U.S. National Museum by Charles Rau. *Nation* 30(June 3, 1880):423-425.

Pioneer Spaniards in America by William H. Johnson. *Nation* 77(December 10, 1903):473.

The Primitive Family in Its Origin and Development by C. N. Starcke. *Nation* 48(June 13, 1889):493-494.

Primitive Manners and Customs by James A. Farrer. *Nation* 30(January 8, 1880):33-34.

Researches into the Early History of Mankind by E. B. Tylor. *Nation* 28(March 6, 1879):170.

Spanish Institutions of the Southwest by Frank W. Blackmar. *Nation* 54(February 4, 1892):94.

The Story of New Mexico by Horatio O. Ladd. *Nation* 54(March, 24, 1892):237.

Studies in Ancient History by John F. McLennan. *Nation* 43(December 9, 1886):483.

William Hickling Prescott by Rolle Ogden. *Nation* 78(May 5, 1904):357.

Studies of Adolph Bandelier

Bandelier, Adolph F., Papers. Vatican Library, Rome, Italy. Manscripts include "Historie de la Colonisation et des Missions de Sonora, Chihuahua, Nouveau-Mexique, et Arizona jusqu'a l'an e," 4 vols., 1887-1888.

Brandes, Ray. "Archeological Awareness of the Southwest, As Illustrated in Literature to 1890." *Arizona and the West* 2(Spring, 1960):7-22.

Colley, Charles C. Review of *Adolph Bandelier's The Discovery of New Mexico by the Franciscan Monk, Friar Marcos de Niza in 1539* by Adolph F. Bandelier and translated and edited by Madeleine Turrell Rodack. *Western Historical Quarterly* 13(January, 1982):64-65.

Cushing, Frank Hamilton. "The Villard-Bandelier South American Expedition." *American Anthropologist* 5(July, 1892):273-276.

Fontana, Bernard L. "A Dedication to the Memory of Adolph F. A. Bandelier, 1840-1914." *Arizona and the West* 2(Spring, 1960):1-5.

Goad, Edgar F. "A Study of the Life of Adolph Francis Alphonse Bandelier, With An Appraisal of His Contributions to American Anthropology and Related Sciences." Ph.D. diss., University of Southern California, 1939.

Hodge, Frederick W. "Biographical Sketch and Bibliography of Adolph Francis Alphonse Bandelier." *New Mexico Historical Review* 7(October, 1932):353-370.

Keen, Benjamin. *The Aztec Image in Western Thought.* New Brunswick, NJ: Rutgers University Press, 1971.

Lange, Charles H., Carroll L. Riley, and Elizabeth M. Lange, eds. *The Southwestern Journals of Adolph F. Bandelier.* 4 volumes. Albuquerque: University of New Mexico Press, 1966-1984.

Noll, Arthur Howard. Review of *The Delightmakers* by Adolph Bandelier. *The Dial* 12(August, 1891):104-107.

Review of *Final Report of Investigations Among the Indians of the Southwestern United States, Carried On Mainly in the Years From 1880 to 1885, Part II* by Adolph Bandelier. *Nation* 56(January 19, 1893):54-55.

Review of *The Gilded Man and Other Pictures of the Spanish Occupancy of America* by Adolph Bandelier. *Nation* 57(December 28, 1893):489-490.

Rodack, Madeleine Turrel, trans. and ed. *The Discovery of New Mexico By the Franciscan Monk, Friar Marcos de Niza in 1539.* Tucson: University of Arizona Press, 1981.

White, Leslie A. *Pioneers in American Anthropology: The Bandelier-Morgan Letters, 1873-1883.* Albuquerque: University of New Mexico Press, 1940.

7

JOHN BARNHART

by Deborah J. Hoskins

Biography

His friends remembered John Barnhart as a devoted teacher and a generous colleague. This scholar of the Old Northwest dedicated himself to rigorous standards in his own scholarship and trained his students to that same rigor. Yet Donald Carmony once distinguished his friend "for his sympathy and tenderness toward frailties of others" (*Indiana Magazine of History* 61:251). As his books, articles, and reviews demonstrate, John Barnhart insisted on solid research and demanded analysis and interpretation beyond simple narrative. Nevertheless, he "always exercised patience and restraint in his evaluation of others" (p. 252).

The son of John Dale Barnhart and Effie Frances Clothier, John Donald Barnhart was born September 22, 1895, in Decatur, Illinois, and grew up in that state. He earned his A.B. in 1916 from Illinois Wesleyan College and both his B.D. from Garrett Biblical Institution and his A.M. from Northwestern in 1919. He entered the doctoral program at the University of Minnesota and served as a teaching assistant for the next two years. In 1921, Barnhart taught for a summer at Moorhead State Teachers College, and took over as chair of the history department at Nebraska Wesleyan College, a post he held until 1923.

John Barnhart longed to write his doctoral thesis under the historian whose work had made what would prove to be a lifelong impression on him--Frederick Jackson Turner. With that hope in mind, Barnhart wrote to Turner at Harvard late in 1922, indicating his desire to complete his doctorate at Harvard and proposing Nebraska Populism as his thesis subject. Turner offered some instruction to the young scholar:

> I regard *intra*-state sections, by counties (or precincts where possible) as an important aspect of state politics. These political sections should be studied *along side of* soil topography, rainfall, distribution of crops, ranch areas, peoples, &c. An

> analysis of distribution of wealth, mortgages, interest rates & the like economic data and density of populations would help (Barnhart Papers).

In this paragraph lay the germs for an analysis that Barnhart was only beginning to construct. Turner's emphasis on "sections," an identification that modern researchers might more easily define in economic, sociological, or cultural terms, challenged students like Barnhart to investigate a vast array of factors that influenced the character of a particular social order. Barnhart would spend his life researching two of these factors in the light of sectionalism and attempting to fit them into the mold of current historical analysis.

But this may well have been the extent of Barnhart's contact with the senior scholar. Turner retired in 1924, and John Barnhart remained in Nebraska until Harvard granted him a teaching assistantship for the academic year of 1924-1925. Life as a graduate student meant self-support for Barnhart since he had married Zella Marie Petty early in 1917 and already had three children, John Dale, Frank Allen, and Frances Mary. When Indiana University offered a one-year replacement position at a salary of $3100 for 1925-1926, the Barnharts accepted happily. The need to teach kept Barnhart remote from his advisers, especially Turner, and slowed his progress.

Turner had suggested a number of new sources to the younger man, but at the time Barnhart lacked, as Turner may have as well, a vision of what those sources might yield. Furthermore, perhaps because he felt intellectually closer to Turner, Barnhart had considerable difficulty deciding under which of the remaining faculty to write his thesis. Eventually he decided to work under Arthur M. Schlesinger, Sr., and he received considerable advice from Frederick Merk as well. But his correspondence indicates that he did not develop a particularly close relationship with either Schlesinger or Merk.

Schlesinger also hinted at a new path that Barnhart might explore. In a letter to his student then in the throes of a major effort to complete his thesis, Schlesinger suggested that Barnhart "go through the farm papers with the social point of view in mind. . . . Someone is going to revolutionize the story of Populism sometime by doing just this" (Barnhart Papers). Apparently Barnhart's thesis was not the revolutionary interpretation of the Populist movement toward which Schlesinger had pushed him, because only two minor publications, including an article co-authored with John D. Hicks, came from it (*American Political Science Review* 14:527-540; *North Carolina Historical Review* 6:254-280). Barnhart earned his Ph.D. in 1930.

The Indiana position proved uniquely satisfying for the Barnharts because it included the use of university president James A. Woodburn's home. The family made friends quickly in Bloomington, and Barnhart felt comfortable among the faculty in the history department. Perhaps even more importantly for his research, the job kept Barnhart generally in the Midwest, the area of his primary interest.

But Indiana could not offer another position after the replacement job expired, and the Barnharts accepted an offer from West Virginia University. Here tragedy struck the family. Their eldest son John died from a sudden illness in the winter of 1929. To compound their difficulties, the nation's mounting economic instability hit the ivory towers of academe, and the university began to threaten cutbacks in 1932, drawing up a list of professors whose contracts would be renewed only in the event that funding was available. John Barnhart's name was on that list. Despite the tireless efforts of his best supporter, John D. Hicks, publishers felt that the cost of printing Barnhart's massive thesis would be too high under the economic conditions they faced. By 1933, West Virginia was forced to release Barnhart, whose frantic efforts to secure another position failed. The young scholar greeted the new term without a job.

The impossibility of procuring a new position did not prevent Barnhart from pursuing new research. He launched a new project exploring the effect of industrial development on politics and folkways in the southern Appalachian states. Finding his access to the necessary source materials restricted by his financial situation, he turned to local themes, biding his time during the interval between jobs. During this period, Barnhart submitted yet apparently failed to publish articles on "Political Sectionalism in Maryland since 1865" and "Geographic Sectionalism of National Politics in Maryland, 1865-1928," edited the letters of Captain J. A. Payne of Ohio, and delved into the records of John Fairfax, George Washington's overseer.

He also presented his work to colleagues in the American Historical Association in 1933. Dumas Malone solicited his contributions on Jere Hungerford Wheelwright, the "West Virginia Coal King," and Thomas Willey, West Virginia senator, for the *Dictionary of American Biography*. The picture that emerges from Barnhart's correspondence during this period indicates that his early career was most difficult. No doubt his ability to stay active and visible in the profession and to draw upon the support of the older and more established scholars who knew him enabled Barnhart to reassert himself in the job market. Nevertheless, this hiatus in his career necessarily produced some publications that lay outside the logical flow of his main interest.

Finally the job drought ended, although the next several years took the Barnharts to several more institutions. A temporary position for the summer of 1934 at Colorado State Teachers College brought Barnhart back into the academic environment, but the fall term took the family to West Liberty State Teachers College in West Virginia where Barnhart served as head of the social sciences department for two years. Louisiana State University offered a position as associate professor in 1936, the College of William and Mary offered a summer post in 1939, and in 1941 the Barnhart family finally returned to Indiana University, an environment they had found congenial and to which they had longed to return.

Indiana again proved hospitable. Barnhart was promoted to full professor in 1946, and two years later began a five-year term as chair of the history department. He also edited the *Indiana Magazine of History* from his arrival in 1941 until 1955. He chaired the Indiana War Historical Committee during World War II, served as president of the Indiana Teachers' Association for the academic year 1947-1948, and chaired the Indiana Territorial Sesquicentennial Committee in 1950. The executive committee of the Indiana Historical Society benefited from his services from 1949 until his death in 1967, and he presided over the Society from 1957 until 1959. Barnhart was active in the local chapter of the Rotary Club as well.

Indiana was not the sole beneficiary of Barnhart's professional service. He also labored at both the regional and the national levels in addition to his massive devotion to state work. He held memberships in both the Southern Historical Association and the Mississippi Valley Historical Association, served on the board of editors for the *Journal of Southern History* from 1936 to 1940, the executive board of the Mississippi Valley Historical Association from 1942 to 1946, and the board of editors for the *Mississippi Valley Historical Review* from 1954 to 1956. Throughout the 1950s and 1960s, he lent his services to the nation as a member of the Advisory Committee on History to the Secretary of the Navy.

In 1965, John Barnhart retired, and the University promoted him to Emeritus. In his brief retirement time Barnhart demonstrated great forbearance during his battle with Parkinson's disease, but on Christmas Day, 1967, he lost the war. He is buried in the city of his birth, Decatur, Illinois.

Themes

Even a cursory examination of the list of books that Barnhart reviewed over his career indicates the astounding breadth of his interests. In part, this range reflected his position as editor of the *Indiana Magazine of History*, a journal of relatively small resources at the time. But it also reflected the particular perspective with which he viewed the historical question that most fascinated him: the creation of a national political culture. Barnhart's interests might be categorized into three primary subjects: cultural conflict, economic development, and sectionalism. These, in turn, defined the parameters of the question Barnhart sought to answer.

Cultural conflict, to John Barnhart, included political, social, and even military struggles. The American Revolution constituted a struggle between political philosophies that resulted from the differences in cultural development between the Old World and the New. In *Henry Hamilton and George Rogers Clark in the American Revolution in the West*, Barnhart studies the war primarily as it was pursued in the West, and he views the leaders on both sides as products of the two political cultures that had come into conflict. In *The Impact of the Civil War on Indiana*, he characterizes the Civil War as the culminating conflict between an aristocratic plantation society and a democratic national society that had emerged out of the crucible of westward frontier settlement. This conflict took such a central position in Barnhart's interpretation of American history that he might well have considered the Civil War inevitable. Other forms of cultural conflict, such as religious and class conflict, commanded Barnhart's attention, especially those that played out in the West. The result, Barnhart believed, of domestic wars and other struggles between competing political cultures had been to strengthen American institutions of government, and while he did not integrate this conclusion into a complete synthesis of his work, it clearly fit.

Barnhart viewed differences in economic development as perhaps the most important cause of cultural conflict. The economies that developed in each section of the nation determined in large measure the character of that section's political culture (*Mississippi Valley Historical Review* 17:581-594; *North Carolina Historical Review* 17:237-248). The South, characterized by its plantation economy with a servile labor force and dependence on a staple crop, came into conflict with the northeastern economy based on a free labor force and a more diverse foundation in manufacturing, banking, commerce, and agriculture (*Journal of Southern History* 7:19-36). In Barnhart's view, these two sections vied with one another for control over the developing West, and each endeavored to impose its economic priorities on new territories (*Valley of Democracy*, p. 226).

Barnhart adopted Turner's concept of sectionalism to help him draw the boundaries of particular political cultures. The North and the South seemed, if not homogeneous, at least dominated by particular socioeconomic structures, but the West, actually the Old Northwest, juggled immigrating influences from both sections. The West not only had to meet the physical challenges of fashioning a viable economy in a new remote area, but also to satisfy the demands of its new residents whose cultural baggage included whole sets of economic expectations. The new territories eventually arrived at their decisions from an assessment of their internal needs, rather than of the desires of the two competing sections east of the Appalachians. To westerners, construction of transportation networks and revision of land policies outweighed the priorities of either northeastern or southern politicians. Barnhart considered the Old Northwest the section most vital to the story he sought to explain.

Barnhart defended without question Turner's theory of the process by which American pioneers pragmatically adapted various institutions to their primitive conditions. Rather than criticizing Turner, Barnhart believed historians needed to expand and explain Turner's argument. "The Turner interpretation with its emphasis on American and frontier influences needs to be tested by the history of a definite place and time" (p. 224), and Barnhart undertook to do just that. He accepted that the pioneers' interaction with their raw environment required the adaptation of virtually every social, cultural, and political institution. Settling the West was a cooperative venture in institution building for the nation. Tentatively, Barnhart was pursuing an analysis of that elusive quality, the "American character."

Analysis

The most important key to understanding John Barnhart's perspective on American frontier history comes from remembering that all historians are, in one way or another, products of their times. Barnhart's life spanned decades that many Americans perceived as a confusing challenge to the American spirit both at home and abroad. Those challenges resonated through the events of Barnhart's own life. Moreover, Turner's influence on Barnhart's world view should not be underestimated. The older historian had struggled to help his nation define its place in the world, and the nation's lack of confidence had not disappeared as Barnhart entered the profession. Barnhart's analysis of American history, therefore, did not constitute a departure from the historiography of his contemporaries. Instead he responded to the national cohesion that accompanied the hardships of World War II and the optimism and expectation that grew as the war neared its end. With the buoyant mood brought on by the Allied victory, Barnhart sought to provide, not a new basis for Americans to understand themselves, but a solid historical foundation upon which to consolidate the nation's rising spirit. He envisioned that foundation to be the peculiar result of the way Americans had institutionalized a democratic system.

The historical problem that captivated Barnhart was nothing less momentous than explaining the rise of American democracy. He believed that the American system differed from European democracies primarily in its rejection of theoretical solutions to problems in favor of broadly based problem solving by those governed. To Barnhart, the settlement of the American West had actively created a "composite nationality, the particular type of democracy which has become an article of faith with the American people" (pp. vii-viii). American democracy did not spring full-blown from the sentiments of the Declaration of Independence. Rather, men had struggled with one another to establish a particular new article of faith.

Barnhart sought evidence for his interpretation in constitutional change at the state level, since here democratization seemed most likely to be visible. In a series of articles, each devoted to a different state and dealing with the process of creating a constitutional government for that state, Barnhart examined the minutiae of state constitution making throughout the trans-Appalachian West of the early national period. By comparing various elements of state constitutions with their predecessors in older states both North and South, he thought he detected a definite trend toward "democracy." He discovered concerted but unsuccessful efforts to reform the governments of older southern states, to "secure freedom from older governments" (p. 219), by frontiersmen in the western reaches of the original South. New states formed before the cession of western lands to the federal government adopted constitutions that restricted suffrage and officeholding, inequitably represented the West in state legislatures, restricted religious freedom, and adopted policies that limited the ability to purchase land to large, wealthy planters. Few provisions to protect settlers against Indian attack or to construct necessary transportation networks further demonstrated the power of southeastern control to southwesterners.

Ultimately Barnhart developed his magnum opus, *Valley of Democracy: The Frontier Versus the Plantation in the Ohio Valley, 1775-1818*, by synthesizing these state studies and integrating another series of articles that explored changes in national policies. Once the federal government had taken over administration of the western territories, land policy stabilized and grew progressively less attuned to the desires of large landholders and speculators. Indian policy promised to clear that threat and permit more rapid and stable expansion. The Ordinance of 1787 firmly abolished the colonial status of westerners and replaced it with a gradual means toward political equality with older states.

Under these national guidelines, the next states to organize produced constitutions far more egalitarian than their western predecessors, including

> white manhood suffrage, the removal of property qualifications for office holding, the apportionment of representation in the state legislatures according to numbers, and the disestablishment of the Anglican church (p. 217).

Part of the West's significance lay in the impact it had on national policy to overcome the "struggle" of the planter class "to perpetuate the colonial aristocracy" (p. 217). The presence of an expanding frontier altered the character of the national culture away from its mercantilistic parent country with the intent of simple exploitation. Instead, federal policy granted the West a degree of self-determination in achieving parity with older states. To Barnhart, the process seemed to embody the promise of America: equality of opportunity.

Barnhart's explanation for this triumph of western egalitarianism lay in the migratory process that had "sifted the people" (p. 218). The result was that, while "population movements created sectional settlements . . . they tended to counteract each other, and the established customs of any one section were not able to dominate the entire territory" (p. 136). Moreover, the stability imposed by a strengthened federal government eliminated "that uncertainty from which springs radical agitation" (p. 137). But most importantly, Barnhart determines that the emergent national state building scheme "offered hope for the future" (p. 137). Perhaps more by reflecting his times than by conscious effort, Barnhart identified a primary contribution of the western experience to the American character: optimism.

With the benefit of hindsight, today's scholars might find much to criticize in Barnhart's work. Some would surely take issue with his conclusion that the East did not perceive the West as a colonial possession. Others would disagree with the declaration that frontiersmen were "generally poor." Many historians would doubt the assumption that the frontier was intrinsically more democratic than older regions, and most would frown at the conclusion that American society was all that homogeneous.

Barnhart's own contemporaries split their opinions based on their regard for Turner's thesis, and *Valley of Democracy* was most chastized for its uncritical embrace of Turner. One argues that "the three states north of the Ohio were [not] necessarily more democratic than the two south of the river" and notes that such reforms as "expanded suffrage and less strict office-holding requirements appeared in many eastern states even before new western states formed" (*Mississippi Valley Historical Review* 41:506-507).

Nevertheless Barnhart's work has stood scrutiny. Some historians would agree with Barnhart that because the frontier was economically fluid it may well have been more egalitarian than eastern cities. Others would agree that the spirit of optimism and hope for the future constituted the most important contribution of the frontier to the nation. Still newer scholarship would find that the culture of the planter class was less egalitarian in its philosophy than upper classes elsewhere in the nation, and that southerners in general celebrated hierarchy to a greater degree than the rest of the nation. And no one who lives in the region of the Old Northwest can deny the presence of a southern cultural influence. Barnhart had drawn a different image of the influence of the western territories. He did not explore its impact on the individual, as Turner had. Rather, he explored its impact on national policy. Therein lies both the fundamental weakness and the enduring strength of his work.

Barnhart's work endures because of its emphasis on cultural conflict. He pioneered a route through the maze of factors that seemed to influence changes in political culture and explored the establishment of institutionalized means to deal with conflict. Out of the equalizing experience of survival in the West came a democratic spirit. That spirit still exists, wrapped in the belief that those who are governed should actively demonstrate their consent by participating in the process at least insomuch as casting a vote. Even the disaffected nonvoting majority in the United States today still perceives the right to vote as the most fundamental privilege of a democratic system.

But Barnhart's formative years were spent in an era of insecurity with the notion of democracy. The succession of wars and economic crises through which he lived seemed to require ideological unity, yet Barnhart knew from his own historical research that at least two conflicting visions had once existed. His analysis endeavored to trace the creation of consensus out of conflict, but Barnhart's vision did not extend far enough to throw off the metaphors of war that are still used to define the democratic process. Barnhart thus discovered winners and losers in the past. He, like many of today's researchers, believed that majority rule, the inevitable result of any struggle for dominance in a democracy, was the legitimate foundation of consensus.

The problem was, and remains, that the concept of a "good loser" is not and never has been a very viable cultural value upon which to stake the consent of the governed. Barnhart certainly did not prove that the planter culture was eliminated as a result of its defeat. The Civil War is obvious proof that it was not. But this is in fact the crux of Barnhart's enduring legacy, because in the United States, various bureaucracies function as ideological homogenizers, an arena in which conflicting ideas and values are hammered into compatibility with each other as well as with the dominant political culture. Barnhart explained how and why at least one set of those bureaucratic institutions was established.

But Barnhart did not demonstrate that the "article of faith" that emerged from the bureaucracy of the national government was actually *forged*, rather than dictated. He did not demonstrate the active consent of either of his cultural types. Because he focused on government, rather than on people, he ultimately could not identify some of the most critical factors involved in describing either political culture, the frontier or the planter. By accepting Turner too uncritically, he did not examine the intricacies of regional class culture or class structures, but instead defined his most powerful groups too simplistically. Southern aristocrats were "men who were or who aspired to become large landholders, masters of slaves, and founders of established families. Their ideals did not include democracy or faith in the common people" (*Valley of Democracy*, pp. 233-234). Barnhart provided no evidence for this image, and his description of the "democratic" frontiersmen was even less specific, aside from their poverty. Not only was the political culture that emerged as the final product in Barnhart's analysis homogeneous, but, given his vision, it could not have been otherwise. Barnhart celebrated the institutionization of the democratic process, assuming that victory, the successful domination of one political culture, could, through a bureaucracy, create agreement and consensus.

But defeat does not create consensus, although it can create attitudes ranging from disaffection to resignation to bitterness to revolt. Defeat is not an assimilative process, and voting is neither a source nor an exercise of power. Voting presupposes winners and losers. Access to the system is the only legitimate way to exercise consent in a bureaucratized democracy, but heterogeneous ethnic and racial cultures with their distinctive values still persist, refusing to admit defeat. Much of the recent work in American social history demonstrates all of this.

But here lies the key to understanding our national history of domestic political scandals, power brokering by economic elites, foreign policy administered by private enterprise, all accompanied by an ever-dwindling rate of voter participation and frequent recurrences of violence and mass dissent. What remains of the democratic spirit continues to give notice that the bureaucracy cannot ignore the consent of the governed and cannot dictate it either. Barnhart's tendency to define American ideals--democracy, egalitarianism, equality of opportunity--in institutional terms reflects his own times, but ours as well. The time has come for a new historical vision.

In the final analysis, Barnhart left three enduring legacies. First, he pointed the direction for later historians to explore the effects of migration and settlement patterns on western institutions, from religious institutions to education to commerce, and certainly politics. The next stage in his analysis might have been, as he suggested, to explore the impact of the planter and the frontier influences in the political and economic arena that the passing of frontier conditions left in its wake (pp. ix, 232). Heirs to Barnhart's focus on cultural difference needed only to reverse his perspective, from top down to bottom up. A careful observer might have been able to predict the recent work on homogeneous European settlements and separate black communities in the West as well as studies that emphasize interaction between cultures, the unique cultural structures among women, and the cultural conflicts between different classes.

Secondly, Barnhart focused the attention of today's historian on issues of nationalism. The Old Northwest played a crucial role in the development of a national spirit, according to John Barnhart, because it influenced national policy in the direction of constitutional democracy. Today's researchers might ask different questions about nationalism. The spirit of optimism, ideal of equal opportunity, and pervasive hope for the future that Barnhart identified as frontier traits may actually contribute to economic policies that require constant economic growth at the expense of quality, equality, and social services. The same national ideals that underpin the pressure for ever higher profits suffer from the pressures of that growth spiral.

Finally, Barnhart opened a door to discussion of the historical origins of issues that are just now being addressed. Barnhart focused on political culture. Whether the focus is social or regional, diplomatic or political, most historians seek a new model to synthesize the disparate findings of their various fields. A few envision an even broader synthesis that will give meaning to the course of American history across disciplines. For John Barnhart, that meaning lay in the progress of democratic institutions that served to unite the nation in a set of common beliefs. Today's historians face a much different set of challenges. The heterogeneity of our society has been proven without a shadow of a doubt. One cultural group's vision is not necessarily the same as that of another, nor can our institutionalized methods for mediating those conflicts solve our most intractable problem--inequality. The challenge now for historians is not to reject the work of a John Barnhart but to return to the search for the origins of our various political cultures and to trace the course of their interactions with one another.

Bibliography

Books

Henry Hamilton and George Rogers Clark in the American Revolution in the West, with the Unpublished Journal of Lieutenant Governor Henry Hamilton. Editor. Crawfordsville, IN: R. E. Banta, 1951.

Indiana: From Frontier to Industrial Commonwealth. Co-authored with Donald F. Carmony. 2 volumes. New York: Lewis Historical Publications, 1954.

Indiana: The Hoosier State. Co-authored with Donald F. Carmony, Opal M. Nichols, and Jack E. Weicker. Indianapolis: Indiana Historical Society, 1959. Revised, 1963.

Indiana to 1816: The Colonial Period. Co-authored with Dorothy L. Riker. The History of Indiana Series, vol. 1. Indianapolis: Indiana Historical Bureau and Indiana Historical Society, 1971.

Valley of Democracy: The Frontier Versus the Plantation in the Ohio Valley, 1775-1818. Social Science Series, No. 11. Bloomington, IN: Indiana University Press, 1953. Reprint. Bison Books, Lincoln, NE: University of Nebraska Press, 1970.

Pamphlets

The Impact of the Civil War on Indiana. Indianapolis: Civil War Centennial Commission, 1962.

Indiana's Century Old Constitution. Co-authored with Donald F. Carmony. Indianapolis: State Constitutional Centennial Commission, 1951.

Articles

"The Democratization of Indiana Territory." *Indiana Magazine of History* 43(March, 1947):1-22.

"The Democratization of the Northwest Ordinance." In *Journals of the General Assembly of Indiana Territory, 1805-1815*. Vol. 32. Indiana Historical Collections. Indianapolis: Indiana Historical Society, 1950. Pp. 1-17.

"The Farmers' Alliance." Co-authored with John D. Hicks. *North Carolina Historical Review* 6(July, 1929):254-290.

"Frontiersmen and Planters in the Formation of Kentucky." *Journal of Southern History* 7(February, 1941):19-36.

"A Hoosier Invades the Confederacy: Letters and Diaries of Leroy S. Mayfield." Editor. *Indiana Magazine of History* 39(June, 1943):144-191.

"The Impact of the Civil War on Indiana." *Indiana Magazine of History* 57(September, 1961):185-224.

"The Indiana War History Commission." *Indiana Magazine of History* 40(September, 1944):227-242.

"The Letters of Decius." Editor. *Indiana Magazine of History* 43(September, 1947):263-296.

"Letters of William H. Harrison to Thomas Worthington, 1799-1813." Editor. *Indiana Magazine of History* 47(March, 1951):53-84.

"Lieutenant Governor Henry Hamilton's Apologia." Editor. *Indiana Magazine of History* 52(December, 1956):383-396.

"The Migration of Kentuckians Across the Ohio River." *Filson Club History Quarterly* 25(January, 1951):24-32.

"A New Diary of Lieutenant-Governor Henry Hamilton." *Missouri Historical Society Bulletin* 12(October, 1955):10-24.

"A New Evaluation of Henry Hamilton and George Rogers Clark." *Mississippi Valley Historical Review* 37(March, 1951):643-652.

"A New Letter About the Massacre at Fort Dearborn." Editor. *Indiana Magazine of History* 41(June, 1945):187-199.

"Rainfall and the Populist Party in Nebraska." *American Political Science Review* 19(August, 1925):527-540.
"Recent Industrial Growth and Politics in the Southern Appalachian Region." *Mississippi Valley Historical Review* 17(March, 1931):581-594.
"Reconstruction on the Lower Mississippi: Letters of Captain James A. Payne from Baton Rouge." Editor. *Mississippi Valley Historical Review* 21(December, 1934):387-396.
"Report of the Committee on American History." *Indiana Magazine of History* 40(March, 1944):67-72.
"Some New Aids for Historians." *Indiana Magazine of History* 41(March, 1945):88-92.
"Sources of Indiana's First Constitution." *Indiana Magazine of History* 39(March, 1943):55-94.
"Sources of the Southern Migration into the Old Northwest." *Mississippi Valley Historical Review* 22(June, 1936):49-62.
"Southern Contributions to the Social Order of the Old Northwest." *North Carolina Historical Review* 17(July, 1940):237-248.
"The Southern Element in the Leadership of the Old Northwest." *Journal of Southern History* 1(May, 1935):186-197.
"The Southern Influence in the Formation of Illinois." *Journal of the Illinois State Historical Society* 32(September, 1939):358-378.
"The Southern Influence in the Formation of Indiana." *Indiana Magazine of History* 33(September, 1937):261-276.
"The Southern Influence in the Formation of Ohio." *Journal of Southern History* 3(February, 1937):28-42.
"The Tennessee Constitution of 1796: A Product of the Old West." *Journal of Southern History* 9(November, 1943):532-549.
"A Virginia Steamboat Captain on the Sacramento." Editor. *Pacific Historical Review* 9(December, 1940):445-459.

Reviews
Abraham Lincoln and the Widow Bixby by F. Lauriston Bullard. *Indiana Magazine of History* 44(June, 1948):200-201.
Arthur St. Clair, Rugged Ruler of the Old Northwest, An Epic on the American Frontier by Frazer Ells Wilson. *Indiana Magazine of History* 41(March, 1945):83-84.
Background to Glory, The Life of George Rogers Clark by John Bakeless. *Indiana Magazine of History* 53(December, 1957):438-440.
Behind the Lines in the Southern Confederacy by Charles W. Ramsdell. *Indiana Magazine of History* 40(June, 1944):183-185.
A Bibliography of Indiana Imprints, 1804-1853 by Cecil K. Byrd and Howard H. Peckham. *Indiana Magazine of History* 52(December, 1956):399-400.
Boom Copper: The Story of the First U.S. Mining Boom by Angus Murdoch. *Indiana Magazine of History* 40(December, 1944):398-399.

The Buffalo Trace by George R. Wilson and Gayle Thornbrough. *Indiana Magazine of History* 44(June, 1948):204-205.

Bullets by the Billion by Wesley H. Stout. *Indiana Magazine of History* 42(June, 1946):199-200.

The Catholic Church on the Kentucky Frontier (1785-1812) by Mary Ramona Mattingly. *Journal of Southern History* 3(May, 1937):217-218.

The Civil War Era, 1850-1873 by Eugene H. Roseboom. *Indiana Magazine of History* 40(December, 1944):393-394.

Climate of Indiana by Stephen Sargent Visher. *Indiana Magazine of History* 41(September, 1945):305-306.

Colonel Dick Thompson, the Persistent Whig by Charles Roll. *Indiana Magazine of History* 44(June, 1948):202-204.

Congregational Work of Minnesota, 1832-1920 edited by Warren Upham. *Mississippi Valley Historical Review* 8(December, 1921):288-289.

David Dale Owen, Pioneer Geologist of the Middle West by Walter Brookfield Hendrickson. *Indiana Magazine of History* 40(June, 1944):179-180.

The Diary of a Public Man: An Intimate View of the National Administration, December 28, 1860 to March 15, 1961, and a Page of Political Correspondence, Stanton to Buchanan edited with notes by F. Lauriston Bullard. *Indiana Magazine of History* 41(September, 1945):304.

The Dixie Frontier: A Social History of the Southern Frontier from the First Transmontane Beginnings to the Civil War by Everett Dick. *Indiana Magazine of History* 45(June, 1949):196-198.

Economic and Social Problems and Conditions of the Southern Appalachians by the U.S. Bureau of Agricultural Economics, Bureau of Home Economics, and Forestry Service. *Mississippi Valley Historical Review* 22(December, 1935):457-458.

Edward Eggleston by William P. Randel. *Indiana Magazine of History* 43(March, 1947):90-92.

Executive Proceedings of the State of Indiana, 1816-1836 edited by Dorothy Riker. *Indiana Magazine of History* 44(June, 1948):204.

The Exploration of Western America, 1800-1850 edited by E. W. Gilbert. *Indiana Magazine of History* 30(June, 1934):202-203.

Fabulous Hoosier, A Story of American Achievement by Jane Fisher. *Indiana Magazine of History* 44(March, 1948):116.

The Farmer's Last Frontier: Agriculture, 1860-1897 by Fred A. Shannon. *Indiana Magazine of History* 41(December, 1945):403-405.

The Fiery Epoch, 1830-1877 by Charles Willis Thompson. *Mississippi Valley Historical Review* 19(September, 1932):285-286.

The Foundations of Ohio by Beverley W. Bond, Jr. *Indiana Magazine of History* 37(September, 1941):279-282.

The Free Produce Movement, A Quaker Protest Against Slavery by Ruth Ketring Nuermberger. *Indiana Magazine of History* 42(September, 1946):286-287.

French Catholic Missionaries in the Present United States States (1604-1791) by Mary Doris Mulvey. *Journal of Southern History* 3(May, 1937):217-218.

The Frontier in Perspective edited by Walker D. Wyman and Clifton B. Kroeber. *Mississippi Valley Historical Review* 45(June, 1958):115-116.

The Frontier State, 1803-1825 by William T. Utter. *Indiana Magazine of History* 38(June, 1942):214-215.

The Harmonists, A Personal History by John S. Duss. *Indiana Magazine of History* 41(March, 1945):82-83.

The Hidden Civil War: The Story of the Copperheads by Wood Gray. *Mississippi Valley Historical Review* 29(December, 1942):437-438.

An Historian's World, Selections from the Correspondence of John Franklin Jameson edited by Elizabeth Donnan and Leo Stock. *Indiana Magazine of History* 53(September, 1957):320-322.

Historiography and Urbanization: Essays in American History in Honor of W. Stull Holt edited by Eric F. Goldman. *Journal of Southern History* 8(May, 1942):259-260.

A History of American History by Michael Kraus. *Journal of Southern History* 4(August, 1938):384-385.

A History of Minnesota by William Watts Folwell. *Indiana Magazine of History* 27(March, 1931):58-61.

A History of Oberlin College, From Its Foundation Through the Civil War by Robert Samuel Fletcher. *Indiana Magazine of History* 41(June, 1945):204-205.

A History of the Indiana State Teachers College by William D. Lynch. *Indiana Magazine of History* 43(September, 1947):298-301.

History of the Little Church on the Circle: Christ Church, Indianapolis, 1837-1955 by Eli Lilly. *Indiana Magazine of History* 54(March, 1958):74-75.

A History of West Virginia by Charles Henry Ambler. *Journal of Southern History* 1(February, 1935):79-81.

The Holmans of Veraestau by Israel George Blake. *Indiana Magazine of History* 39(June, 1943):196-198.

Hoosier City: The Story of Indianapolis by Jeanette Covert Nolan. *Indiana Magazine of History* 40(March, 1944):74-75.

Hoosier Training Ground: A History of Army and Navy Training Centers, Camps, Forts, Depots, and Other Military Installations Within the State Boundaries During World War II compiled by Dorothy Riker. *Indiana Magazine of History* 50(March, 1954):75-76.

Indiana: An Interpretation by John Barlow Martin. *Indiana Magazine of History* 44(September, 1948):308-309.

Indiana Scientists: A Biographical Directory and an Analysis by Stephen Sargent Visher. *Indiana Magazine of History* 49(March, 1953):96.

Industrial State, 1870-1893 by Ernest Ludlow Bogart and Charles Manfred Thompson. *Mississippi Valley Historical Review* 8(June-September, 1921):210-211.

The Intimate Letters of John Cleve Symmes and His Family, Including Those of His Daughter, Mrs. William Henry Harrison, Wife of the Ninth President of the United States edited by Beverley W. Bond, Jr. *Mississippi Valley Historical Review* 44(June, 1957):131-132.

J. Sterling Morton by James C. Olson. *Indiana Magazine of History* 39(June, 1943):201-203.

Kaskaskia Under the French Regime by Natalia M. Belting. *Indiana Magazine of History* 44(December, 1948):431-432.

King Cotton is Sick by Claudius T. Murchison. *Mississippi Valley Historical Review* 18(September, 1931):295-296.

Land of Promise: The Story of the Northwest Territory by Walter Havighurst. *Indiana Magazine of History* 43(December, 1947):406-407.

The Last Trek of the Indians by Grant Foreman. *Indiana Magazine of History* 42(June, 1946):201-202.

Lincoln Bibliography, 1839-1939 compiled by Jay Monaghan. *Indiana Magazine of History* 41(September, 1945):303.

The Lincoln Reader by Paul M. Angle. *Indiana Magazine of History* 43(June, 1947):187-189.

The Making of an American Community: A Case Study of Democracy in a Frontier Community by Merle Curti et al. *Indiana Magazine of History* 56(March, 1960):83-85.

The National Road by Philip D. Jordon. *Indiana Magazine of History* 44(September, 1948):311-312.

Ohio Comes of Age, 1873-1900 by Philip D. Jordon. *Indiana Magazine of History* 40(June, 1944):182-183.

The Ohio Company: Its Inner History by Alfred P. James. *Mississippi Valley Historical Review* 46(December, 1959):499-500.

The Ohio Company Papers, 1753-1817: Being Primarily Papers of the "Suffering Traders" of Pennsylvania edited by Kenneth P. Bailey. *Mississippi Valley Historical Review* 34(December, 1947):477-478.

Ohio in the Twentieth Century, 1900-1938 compiled by Harlow Lindley. *Indiana Magazine of History* 40(September, 1944):310-311.

Old Indiana and the New World: Address at the Opening of the Library of Congress Exhibition Commemorating the Territory of Indiana, November 30, 1950 by Elmer Davis. *Indiana Magazine of History* 47(December, 1951):391.

The Old Northwest as the Keystone of the Arch of American Federal Union: A Study in Commerce and Politics by Albert L. Kohlmeier. *Indiana Magazine of History* 34(December, 1938):468-470.

__________. *Journal of Southern History* 5(February, 1939):112-113.

The Old South: The Founding of American Civilization by Thomas Jefferson Wertenbaker. *Indiana Magazine of History* 39(September, 1943):304-306.

The Older Middle West, 1840-1880 by Henry C. Hubbart. *Journal of Southern History* 3(February, 1937):108-110.

Our Landed Heritage: The Public Domain, 1776-1936 by Roy M. Robbins. *Indiana Magazine of History* 38(September, 1942):307-310.

The Passing of the Frontier, 1825-1850 by Francis P. Weisenburger. *Indiana Magazine of History* 38(March, 1942):86-91.

Pioneer Life in Kentucky, 1785-1800 by Daniel Drake, M.D. edited by Emmet Field Horine. *Mississippi Valley Historical Review* 35(December, 1948):500-501.

Pioneer Sketches of the Upper Whitewater Valley, Quaker Stronghold of the West by Bernhard Knollenberg. *Indiana Magazine of History* 42(March, 1946):89-90.

The Plain People of the Confederacy by Bell Irvin Wiley. *Indiana Magazine of History* 40(June, 1944):183-185.

Pontiac and the Indian Uprising by Howard H. Peckham. *Indiana Magazine of History* 43(December, 1947):403-404.

Religion on the American Frontier: The Presbyterians, 1783-1840, A Collection of Source Materials compiled by William Warren Sweet. Vol. 2. *Journal of Southern History* 3(November, 1937):504-506.

Revolution in America: Confidential Letters and Journals, 1776-1784, of Adjutant General Major Baurmeister of the Hessian Forces translated and annotated by Bernhard A. Uhlendorf. *Journal of Southern History* 23(August, 1957):381-382.

The Road to Reunion, 1865-1900 by Paul H. Buck. *Journal of Southern History* 3(August, 1937):377-379.

Scientists Starred, 1903-1943, in "American Men of Science": A Study of Collegiate and Doctoral Training, Birthplace, Distribution, Backgrounds, and Developmental Influences by Stephen Sargent Visher. *Indiana Magazine of History* 44(September, 1948):318-319.

A Shelf of Lincoln Books: A Critical Selective Bibliography of Lincolniana by Paul M. Angle. *Indiana Magazine of History* 42(December, 1946):413-414.

The Southern Colonies in the Seventeenth Century, 1607-1689 by Wesley Craven. *Indiana Magazine of History* 45(December, 1949):427-429.

The Story of Illinois by Theodore Calvin Pease. *Indiana Magazine of History* 46(September, 1950):330-331.

The Territorial Papers of the United States: The Territory of Illinois, 1814-1818 compiled and edited by Clarence E. Carter. Vol. 17. *Mississippi Valley Historical Review* 38(June, 1951):106-107.

The Territorial Papers of the United States: The Territory of Michigan, 1829-1837 compiled and edited by Clarence E. Carter. Vol. 12. *Indiana Magazine of History* 43(March, 1947):92.

Theory and Practice in Historical Study: A Report of the Committee on Historiography. *Indiana Magazine of History* 42(December, 1946):414-416.

Thomas Worthington: Father of Ohio Statehood by Alfred Byron Sears. *Indiana Magazine of History* 55(March, 1959):73-74.

Threescore Years and Ten: A Narrative of the First Seventy Years of Eli Lilly and Company, 1876-1946 by Roscoe Collins Clark. *Indiana Magazine of History* 42(June, 1946):199-200.

The Trans-Mississippi West: A Guide to Its Periodical Literature by Oscar O. Winther. *Indiana Magazine of History* 38(December, 1942):427-429.

A Transylvania Trilogy: The Story of the Writing of Harry Toulmin's 1792 "History of Kentucky," Combined with a Brief Sketch of His Life and a New Bibliography by Willard Rouse Jillson. *Mississippi Valley Historical Review* 20(June, 1933):156-157.

The United States, 1830-1850: The Nation and Its Sections by Frederick Jackson Turner. *Journal of Southern History* 1(November, 1935):525-527.

The Vincennes Donation Lands by Leonard Lux. *Indiana Magazine of History* 45(September, 1949):295-296.

War, Peace, and Resistance by Guy Franklin Hershberger. *Indiana Magazine of History* 41(December, 1945):405-406.

West Virginia: The Mountain State by Charles Henry Ambler. *Journal of Southern History* 6(November, 1940):559-560.

The Western Reserve: The Story of New Connecticut in Ohio by Harlan Hatcher. *Mississippi Valley Historical Review* 36(March, 1950):695-696.

William Blount by William Masterson. *Indiana Magazine of History* 52(March, 1956):95-96.

William Henry Harrison, His Life and Times by James A. Green. *Indiana Magazine of History* 39(March, 1943):99-100.

With Sherman to the Sea: The Civil War Letters, Diaries & Reminiscences of Theodore F. Upson edited by Oscar O. Winther. *Indiana Magazine of History* 39(June, 1943):195-196.

Studies of John D. Barnhart

Barnhart, John D., Papers. Lilly Library, Indiana University, Bloomington, IN.

[Carmony, Donald]. "Tribute to John D. Barnhart." *Indiana Magazine of History* 61(September, 1965):251.

Clark, Thomas D. Review of *Valley of Democracy: The Frontier Versus the Plantation in the Ohio Valley, 1775-1818* by John D. Barnhart. *American Historical Review* 60(January, 1955):383-385.

Glazer, Sidney. Review of *Indiana to 1816: The Colonial Period* by John D. Barnhart and Dorothy L. Riker. *Journal of American History* 58(March, 1972):1007-1008.

Green, Fletcher M. Review of *Valley of Democracy: The Frontier Versus the Plantation in the Ohio Valley, 1775-1818* by John D. Barnhart. *Mississippi Valley Historical Review* 41(December, 1954):506-507.

Volwiler, A. T. Review of *Henry Hamilton and George Rogers Clark in the American Revolution, with the Unpublished Journal of Lieutenant Governor Henry Hamilton* edited by John D. Barnhart. *American Historical Review* 58(January, 1953):391-393.

8

RAY ALLEN BILLINGTON

by Richard E. Oglesby

Biography

There was little in his background to suggest that Ray Allen Billington would one day become the principal interpreter of the history of the American frontier, the Turner thesis, and the father of frontier studies, Frederick Jackson Turner. Born in Bay City, Michigan, on September 28, 1903, the only child of Cecil and Nina Allen Billington, Ray progressed through the local school system at a normal pace. Possessed of a natural talent, and encouraged, perhaps, by the fact that his father worked for one of the Detroit dailies, he early demonstrated a flair for writing. The exciting experience of having several of his offerings published in the high school newpaper determined him to become a journalist, and, after graduation, he headed for the University of Michigan in pursuit of that goal. There he learned that journalism had within it an element of danger when, while he was working for the *Michigan Daily,* Billington produced a separate publication which not only scandalized the university community but also got him expelled.

Losing his enthusiasm for journalism, Billington transferred to the University of Wisconsin, and there, in the classes of Carl Russell Fish and Frederic Logan Paxson, discovered the fascination of historical study. He completed his undergraduate work in 1926 and returned to Ann Arbor the following year to earn an M.A. in history. The graduate program at Harvard took him in, and, after a successful first year, Ray Billington married Mabel R. Crotty on September 6, 1928, thus establishing the partnership which would provide the support and stability upon which his career was founded and prospered.

At Harvard, Billington participated in the seminar in frontier history, offered on that occasion jointly by Frederick Merk, Turner's successor, and James B. Hedges, but found his inspiration in the seminar of Arthur M. Schlesinger, Sr., then engaged in producing a generation of historians destined to reinvigorate the study of the United States. In particular,

Billington was attracted to the emerging areas of intellectual history, and focused his dissertation research on a study of American nativism in the nineteenth century. In 1931, before he had completed his work at Harvard, Billington accepted a position in the history department at Clark University, and his collegiate career was launched. Two years later, Harvard awarded him the Ph.D., and, in 1937, he joined the faculty of Smith College. His first book, *The Protestant Crusade, 1800-1860: A Study of the Origins of American Nativism* was published by Macmillan a year later, and, at that point, he was approached by Professor Hedges to become a co-author of a proposed text in frontier history.

Challenged by the prospect of writing a text in a subject about which he knew very little, Billington plunged into a regimen of reading that carried him far and wide into the field. In the midst of reading and writing, Northwestern University lured the Billingtons back to the Midwest in 1944, and there they were at home for the rest of Ray's college career. As the frontier project progressed, Hedges gradually withdrew, and when *Westward Expansion: A History of the American Frontier* was published in 1949, it was, with the exception of three chapters, Billington's book. *Westward Expansion* not only gave coherence to a floundering field, but set Billington's course firmly on the star of the West. Though he taught a heavy load at Northwestern, new major publications quickly followed: *The Far Western Frontier, 1830-1860* (1954); *The Westward Movement in the United States* (1959); *Frontier and Section* (1961); and the like. But when he left Northwestern to become senior research associate at the Henry E. Huntington Library in San Marino, California, in 1963, his prodigious production increased in both volume and insight. *America's Frontier Heritage* (1966), the key volume in the Histories of the American Frontier series, which he created and edited; *The Genesis of the Frontier Thesis* (1971); the prize-winning *Frederick Jackson Turner: Historian, Scholar, Teacher* (1973); and, ultimately, *Land of Savagery, Land of Promise* (1981), all interpreted the meaning of the frontier experience to the development of the nation.

As his standing in the profession grew, so too did the honors and awards bestowed upon him by his appreciative colleagues. These ranged from a Guggenheim Fellowship, to a Harmsworth Professorship at Oxford, to the presidencies of the American Studies Association (1959), the Organization of American Historians (1962), and the Western History Association (1962), the latter of which he was founding president. The long list of publications and the visible honors placed him in great demand as a speaker, and Billington rarely turned down an opportunity to spread the gospel of history, becoming, in the process, one of the greatest ambassadors to the general public the historical profession has ever had. But the greatest measure of how far Ray Billington had taken frontier history came in 1975, when the American Historical Association asked him to deliver the plenary address to the first ever meeting of the International Congress of Historical Sciences on American soil; the subject, "Cowboys, Indians, and the Land of Promise: The World Image of the American Frontier."

Ray Billington was planning still further frontier studies when death took him in his sleep on March 9, 1981.

Themes

Ray Billington did not come to frontier history as a trained specialist in the field, and, although he was certainly aware of the acrimonious dispute between the disciples of Frederick Jackson Turner and the critics of the frontier thesis, he had taken no part in the argument. Billington was, first and foremost, an intellectual and social historian, and there his perspective remained. Yet the publication of *Westward Expansion* thrust him to the first rank of frontier historians, and it was almost incumbent upon him to get involved in the debate. Moreover, the extensive reading he had done in preparation for *Westward Expansion*, evidenced in the massive bibliographic essay at the end of the volume, convinced him that while Turner may have been guilty of a number of sins, his basic notion that the frontier had a great and ongoing influence on the development of the nation and the character of its people was valid.

His basic approach became readily apparent. One was to place Frederick Jackson Turner in his proper place in American historiography. To do that meant that Billington had to deal with Turner's overstatements, difficult, if not impossible to rebut (the existence of an area of free land, its continuous recession, and the advance of American settlement westward explain American development), and, more importantly, confront two Turnerian concepts in particular--that the frontier altered the basic character of frontier peoples and that those acquired traits then helped shape the general American character. Both of those ideas, that environment altered character, and that acquired characteristics could be inherited, had been proven to be scientific nonsense, and somehow Billington had to show that Turner was not guilty of scientific quackery if he was to have legitimacy as a historian. But having done that, Billington then had to demonstrate how the frontier did indeed influence the character of its human participants, and how that influence had continued, albeit with diminished force, down to the present.

There is one other theme, more important to Billington, and to posterity, that permeates his writing. As a result of a lifetime of research, he came to believe that the frontier shaped the character and institutions of the American people. Access to generous resources helped pioneers gain confidence in democracy and equality, favor physical mobility and adaptability, and distrust intellectualism and other nonfrontier peoples. The idea, of course, bred its opposite--that people of other nations need to know what the unique experience of frontiering did for America and the people who came to its shores so that they might better understand us.

Ray Billington addressed all of these themes with greater or lesser success, and always felt, particularly as a result of reviewers' comments, that he had somehow failed to convince both his colleagues and the general public of the validity and vital importance of his interpretations. He may well have succeeded better than he believed.

Analysis

As he researched and wrote *Westward Expansion* (1949), a process that consumed his energies for more than nine years, Ray Billington not only launched himself on a career in western and frontier history, he also discovered the various themes and problems in the subject that would emerge eventually in his writings. Since *Westward Expansion* was, by definition, based on the lecture outlines developed by Frederick Jackson Turner for his famous course on the History of the West at Harvard, Billington was obligated to introduce his subject along Turnerian lines. In so doing, there was no possibility of avoiding the rather acrimonious debate then raging between Turner's disciples and critics over the validity of the frontier thesis. Eschewing the histrionics so typical of the controversy, Billington, in the honest and straightforward manner that would characterize most of his interpretations, ignored the charges and counter charges, and, while coming down on the side of Turner and his defenders, inevitable, perhaps, under the circumstances, pointed out that "the most carping critic will agree that the unusual environment, and the continuous rebirth of society in the western wilderness, endowed the American people and their institutions with characteristics not shared by the rest of the world" (*Westward Expansion*, p. 3). That theme became part of all his subsequent writing.

Better than that, after presenting the geographical definition of the frontier used by Turner in his famous essay, Billington went on to state, simply and succinctly, his own interpretation of Turner's meaning: "The frontier can be pictured more accurately as a series of contiguous westward-migrating zones, each representing a different stage in the development of society from simple to complex forms" (1st ed., p. 3). That statement remained intact in the second edition (1960), but by the time the third edition (1967) came off the press, Billington had researched and written *America's Frontier Heritage* (1966) and his thinking had changed. Eschewing the Turnerian concept of succeeding zones, he embraced a better, more accurate and useful definition, one which remained through editions four (1974) and five (1982): "The frontier can be pictured meaningfully as a vast westward-moving zone, contiguous to the settled portions of the continent, and peopled by a variety of individuals bent on applying individual skills to the exploitations of unusually abundant resources" (3rd ed., p. 3). Thus his research indicated the importance of the interaction between people of the frontier and the resources of their environment, and fixed the individual as the most important ingredient in the westward movement itself and the theory surrounding it.

The importance of the individual was stressed in the concluding chapter of *Westward Expansion*, "The Frontier Heritage," as well, but with a twist that indicated that not only had Turner's critics had an impact on his thinking, but that times had changed, and Billington was aware of it. Thus the lessons of frontier history had immediate relevancy, a concept which colors all of his writing: history meant nothing unless it informed the present and prepared the future. "The hardy self-reliant men and women who through three centuries conquered the continent have played their role in the drama of American development; as they pass from the scene a new generation, freed from the prejudices of an outworn past where the needs of individuals transcended the needs of society, will blaze the trails into the newer world of cooperative democracy that is America's future" (1st ed., p. 756). That remained his ultimate statement on the meaning of the frontier experience until the publication of the fifth edition, the last in which he would participate.

There Billington felt that after a lifetime of study which had confirmed his initial impression, the lesson of the frontier legacy needed to be driven home more emphatically:

> The hardy self-reliant men and women who through three centuries conquered the continent have played their role in the drama of American development; the new generation must escape the prejudices of an outworn past and build on the lasting values of the frontier experience. It is now clear that social democracy, economic opportunity, and political freedom are not contingent on national expansion, nor must the ecological structure be permanently damaged to maintain a satisfactory standard of living for the American people. There are more rational long-term solutions to the problems faced by this generation and those to come. There must be a recognition that the strong desires of individuals do not transcend the requirements of society. The pioneers of the future will need more than primitive tools and ambitions to blaze the trail into the newer world of cooperative democracy that is America's future; they must retain their sense of optimism, their profound faith in themselves, their willingness to innovate, and their abiding trust in democracy, for on the new frontier men and women shall go forward together or they shall not go forward at all (5th ed., pp. 697-698).

So the times had indeed changed, and with them the meaning of the frontier experience. In adding this peroration to the most important text in the field, Billington hoped to continue to impress upon another generation of students the need to understand the history of the American frontier and to draw the conclusions necessary for their own society. It was this successful attempt to break the bounds of the Turner thesis that caused the initial reviewers of *Westward Expansion* to praise the volume, and to state, in the words of Martin Ridge, "He had pulled Turner's bow; he had written Turner's book" (*Western Historical Quarterly* 12:248).

It was a source of ironic amusement to Ray Billington that the second half of *Westward Expansion*, the trans-Mississippi West, received the most praise from reviewers. He had originally agreed to do the cis-Mississippi section, and had spent much of his time putting that together. When James Blaine Hedges had had to pull back from the project, Billington did all but three chapters of the remaining eighteen, more superficially, he thought, than the rest. Not only were the reviewers impressed, but the editor of the New American Nation Series invited him to do a volume in that series, *The Far Western Frontier, 1830-1860* (1954). In keeping with the nature of the series, Billington worked strictly from printed sources. Reviewer Earl Pomeroy noted that fact, but credits Billington with summing "up the state of knowledge in the field, and no one had done it better, or more clearly or readably" (*Journal of American History* 43:676.). But it was narrative rather than analysis, a detailed expression of the same kind of voluminous reading that had gone into *Westward Expansion*, and a book which continues to stimulate students to probe more deeply into various aspects of the western experience.

America's Frontier Heritage (1966) is a book of another sort. Billington had been asked to become consulting editor to Rinehart and Company, and one of his duties was to develop a multivolume history of westward expansion. He recruited many of the leading scholars in the field to participate, but wrote the lead volume himself. His research began about the time the Turner papers were opened at the Huntington Library, and, for the first time, Ray Billington immersed himself in primary sources. Not only that, but aware that the old arguments about the validity of Turner's thesis or the impact of the West upon the American character and institutions no longer attracted much attention, he knew that if he was to restore Turner to his appropriate place in the pantheon of great American historians, and demonstrate the validity of the field of western history, he would have to apply some of the newer methodologies and findings, not only of the historical profession but others as well. Thus he read widely in anthropology, sociology, economics, social psychology, and demography, among others, and examined the utility of theories of spatial mobility, social organization, and the like.

In short, it was a research *tour de force* of Turnerian proportions. Only, unlike Turner, Billington produced the book. In it he dropped the conventional organization of the westward movement in favor of dividing those who migrated west into two categories, the "users," and the "subduers," a much more comprehensible and useful approach, and dealt in depth with those aspects of the western legacy he felt most affected modern life. He clearly composed and validated the idea that while learned attributes cannot be transmitted genetically, as Turner had suggested, they can be taught, and they were taught. Thus characteristics learned on the frontier were passed down to the present generation, and not always to this generation's benefit.

Billington not only accomplished his purpose in restoring the Turner thesis and western history to a repectable position, but, in the words of Robert Dykstra, "managed to shift the debate to new ground, to a much more useful realm of analysis than we have yet possessed. This book is, in short, the book Turner himself should have written" (*New Mexico Historical Review* 43:67). Other historians were equally lavish in praise of *America's Frontier Heritage*: "More than any other historian, Billington has brilliantly evaluated the frontier heritage in all its complexity" (*American West Review* 1:23); Billington "relates the frontier experience to American character traits more persuasively than Turner without ever claiming that our character was the result of the frontier experience" *American Historical Review* 72:1477); and many more. Not all historians, however, were convinced. To Robert Berkhofer, perhaps the best spokesman of the new, social science oriented members of the profession, Billington's analysis was simply the same old Turnerian wine in a new bottle (*Agricultural History* 41:313-315).

Though the reaction to *America's Frontier Heritage* was generally excellent, Ray Billington was disappointed. He had hoped to reach out, indeed to "convert," two groups he believed needed to understand the influence of the frontier on the American character and on present thoughts, attitudes, and outlooks: the general public and social science historians. He felt he had failed. *America's Frontier Heritage* received scant notice in those publications which tend to inform general readers, the *New York Times Book Review*, the *Saturday Review* and the rest, and without such notice Billington assumed that the general public would simply remain unaware of its existence. More disappointing was the reaction of historians like Berkhofer, for Billington felt he had clearly demonstrated, using all the modern tools, "the scientific validity of the modern significance of the pioneer era of our history" (*Western Historical Quarterly* 1:17).

But while he may have been discouraged by what he perceived as the indifference of some of his colleagues and the general public, Billington did not cease to try to educate or carry on the major themes that still needed explication, particularly his analysis of Frederick Jackson Turner and the Turner thesis. In working through the Turner papers, it became evident to Billington that Turner was far from the monocausationist he had been accused of being. Indeed, he was considerably ahead of the profession in his examination of the themes, works, and tools of economists, sociologists, geographers, and others. Further, Turner always spoke from the best scientific viewpoint of his own generation, and while his words might sound like arrant nonsense to moderns, since scientific knowledge had increased dramatically since Turner's day, it was perfectly valid at the time. This Billington had done in *America's Frontier Heritage* from a study of the frontier and the reactions of foreign and eastern visitors to it, and he reaffirmed and expanded upon this theme in three books: *"Dear Lady": The Letters of Frederick Jackson Turner and Alice Forbes Perkins Hooper, 1910-1932* (1970); *The Genesis of the Frontier Thesis: A Study in Historical Creativity* (1971); and *Frederick Jackson Turner: Historian, Scholar, Teacher* (1973).

In *"Dear Lady"*, and, particularly, *Genesis*, Billington follows Turner's intellectual odyssey, which, in the words of one reviewer, carried Turner "through and ahead of the historiographical fashions of the time" (*American Historical Review* 78:175). But more than simply following Turner's pathways, Billington brought to bear modern psychological theories of creativity to shed light on Turner's evolution of thought. All of this was beautifully brought together in the Bancroft Prize winning *Frederick Jackson Turner*, a biography of monumental proportions, described by one reviewer as "a major event in the history of higher education and of American historiography" (*American Historical Review*

78:1542). Abundantly detailed, the biography went far beyond the man to depict his times, the academic worlds in which he flourished, both in the Midwest and on the East Coast, and offered a sympathetic view of Turner's attempt to comprehend the entire American experience. It was the latter, a frustrating if not impossible task, which made Turner a pioneer in so many areas of history, diplomatic, social, and economic, as well as frontier.

Though this long awaited book seemed to some to be the capstone of Billington's outstanding career, he was not yet through with his attempt to reach the general public and educate it to the legacy of the frontier past and its profound influence on the present. In *America's Frontier Heritage* he did it through the eyes of visitors to the frontier. In *Land of Savagery, Land of Promise* (1981), his "most significant and original work" (*Western Historical Quarterly* 13:64), he approached the subject from the viewpoint of European writers who had fictionalized the American frontier for generations, translating their perceptions of the American experience to the European population. That most of these authors had never been to America, let alone experienced its westering activities, apparently mattered little to their audiences. They created America for the rest of the world, and did it to their own image. As a consequence, two contrasting pictures of America grew up, that of a land of promise, with freedom, equality, and opportunity abounding, a concept abetted by the constant presence of legitimate "America letters," and a land of savagery, where, particularly on the frontier, lawlessness, racism, and violence held sway. By the innovative use of European popular literature, made available by the dedicated work of a devoted corps of European investigators and translators, Billington was able to depict the shifting image of the frontier over time, how it attracted and repelled, and why, and pointed up the lesson that in the modern world the image of America as a land of savagery predominated, not only because of that view of our frontier past, but also because the image of the land of savagery had been amplified by certain international activities in the present.

Land of Savagery, Land of Promise was a stunning achievement, but here too, Billington, now driven by the need to alert Americans to the mainsprings of their actions and attitudes which emanated from the frontier past, felt he had gone unheeded. He was only partially correct, for reviews in the *National Review* and the *New York Review of Books* appeared after his death. But he had done a superlative job, not only in *Land of Savagery, Land of Promise*, but in all of his works, of restoring the notion of frontier history and the history of the West as not only legitimate, but critical areas of study, and had raised the level, not only of frontier history, but all American history by emulating Frederick Jackson Turner in his broad outlook, utilizing materials, theories, ideas, and findings from disciplines other than history. He had analyzed some fundamental facets of the American character, noting those that had evolved from the frontier experience, and demonstrated clearly both their persistence and their direct impact upon the present. His written contribution to history is immense.

Ray Billington had a too modest estimate of the impact of his ideas and interpretations. In his career he had taught literally thousands of students, and, through his own graduate students, thousands more, a generation he liked to call his "intellectual grandchildren." Other thousands of people, businessmen, members of historical societies, Westerners, and others, heard him express those ideas in an unending series of speaking engagements throughout his career. Whereas Turner shot off an intellectual rocket which awed almost everyone immediately, and was almost as completely rejected at one point, Billington planted the seeds of historical truth on all sorts of ground, nurtured and stimulated them over the years, and thus ensured that the frontier cannot be neglected as a source of fundamental knowledge regarding the foundations of America. His may well be the greater legacy.

Bibliography

Books

Allan Nevins on History. Editor. New York: Charles Scribner's Sons, 1975.

The Apaches of the Rio Grande: A Story of Indian Life by Wilhelm Frey. Editor. Glendale, CA: Arthur H. Clark Company, 1978.

The American Frontier. Washington, DC: Service Center for Teachers, American Historical Association, 1958.

The American Frontier Thesis: Attack and Defense. Washington, DC: American Historical Association, 1971.

American History after 1865. Ames, IA: Littlefield, Adams & Co., 1950.

American History before 1877. Ames, IA: Littlefield, Adams & Co., 1951.

America's Frontier Culture: Three Essays by Ray A. Billington. College Station: Texas A&M University Press, 1977.

America's Frontier Heritage. New York: Holt, Rinehart & Winston, 1966.

America's Frontier Story: A Documentary History of Westward Expansion. Editor with Martin Ridge. New York: Holt, Rinehart & Winston, 1969.

Anti Movements in America. Consulting editor, 41 volumes. New York: Arno Press, 1977.

The Armenians in Massachusetts. Editor. Boston: Federal Writers Project, 1937.

"Dear Lady": The Letters of Frederick Jackson Turner and Alice Forbes Perkins Hooper, 1910-1932. Editor with the collaboration of Walter Muir Whitehill. San Marino, CA: Huntington Library, 1970.

Education and Student Life in the United States. Editor. Evanston, IL: Northwestern University Press, 1958.

Excursion Through America by Nicholas Mohr. Editor. Chicago: R.R. Donnelly & Sons, 1973.

The Far Western Frontier. Editor, 47 volumes of selected Western Classics. New York: Arno Press, 1973.

The Far Western Frontier, 1830-1860. New York: Harpers, 1954.

Frederick Jackson Turner: Historian, Scholar, Teacher. New York: Oxford University Press, 1973.

The Frontier Thesis: Valid Interpretation of American History? Editor. New York: Holt, Rinehart & Winston, 1967.

Frontier and Section: Selected Essays of Frederick Jackson Turner. Editor. Englewood Cliffs, NJ: Prentice-Hall, 1961.

The Genesis of the Frontier Thesis: A Study in Historical Creativity. San Marino, CA: Huntington Library, 1971.

Histories of the American Frontier. Editor, 10 volumes. New York: Holt, Rinehart & Winston, 1964-1970 and Albuquerque: University of New Mexico Press, 1978-1979.

The Journal of Charlotte L. Forten. Editor. New York: Dryden Press, 1953.

Land of Savagery, Land of Promise: The European View of the American Frontier. New York: W.W. Norton, 1981.

The Making of American Democracy: Readings and Documents. Editor with Bert J. Loewenberg and Samuel H. Brockunier. New York: Rinehart & Co., 1950.

People of the Plains and Mountains: Essays in the History of the West Dedicated to Everett Dick. Editor. Westport, CT: Greenwood Press, 1973.

The Protestant Crusade, 1800-1860: A Study of the Origins of American Nativism. New York: Macmillan, 1938.

The Reinterpretation of Early American History: Essays in Honor of John Edwin Pomfret. Editor. San Marino, CA: Huntington Library, 1966.

The United States: American Democracy in World Perspective. Co-author with Bert J. Loewenberg and Samuel Brokunier. New York: Rinehart & Co., 1947.

Western Americana: A Collection of 1012 Books and Documents of the 18th, 19th, and Early 20th Centuries. Editor. Ann Arbor, Xerox University Microfilms, Microfiche Edition, 1975.

Westward Expansion: A History of the American Frontier. New York: Macmillan, 1949.

The Westward Movement in the United States. Princeton, NJ: D. Van Nostrand, 1959.

Westward to the Pacific: An Overview of America's Westward Expansion. St. Louis: Jefferson National Expansion Historical Association, 1979.

Articles

"American Catholicism and the Church-State Issue." *Christendom* 5(Summer, 1940):335-366.

"The American Frontier." In *Beyond the Frontier* edited by Paul Bohannon and Fred Plog. Garden City, NJ: Doubleday, 1968. Pp. 3-24.

"The American Frontier Thesis." *Huntington Library Quarterly* 23(May, 1960):201-216.

"American History." In *The Case for Basic Education: A Program of Aims for Public Schools* edited by James D. Koerner. Boston: Little-Brown, 1959. Pp. 27-48.

"Americans on the Move." In *We Americans.* Washington, DC: National Geographic Society, 1975. Pp. 133-160.

"Americans Spread Out." In *Visiting Our Past: America's Historylands.* Washington, DC: National Geographic Society, 1977. Pp. 191-208.

"The Anti-Catholic Position." In *American Nativism, 1830-1860* edited by Ira N. Leonard and Robert D. Parmet. New York: D. Van Nostrand, 1971. Pp. 159-161.

"Anti-Catholic Propaganda and the Home Missionary Movement, 1800-1860." *Mississippi Valley Historical Review* 22(December, 1935):361-384.

"An Anti-Catholic Riot: The Burning of the Ursuline Convent in Charlestown, Massachusetts, August 11-12, 1934." In *American Violence* edited by Richard M. Brown. Englewood Cliffs, NJ: Prentice-Hall, 1970. Pp. 38-42.

"Books that Won the West: The Guidebooks of the Forty-Niners and Fifty-Niners." *American West* 4(August, 1967):25-32, 72-75.

"The Burning of the Charlestown Convent." *New England Quarterly* 10(March, 1937):4-24.

"Carl S. Dentzel: A Profile." In *Carl S. Dentzel: A Perpetual Spirit of the American Southwest, 1913-1980.* Los Angeles: private printing, 1980. Pp. 1-3.

"Carl Schaefer Dentzel (March 20, 1913-August 21, 1980)." *The Masterkey* 54(October-November, 1980):125-129.

"Charlotte F. Grimke." In *Notable American Women* edited by Edward James. Cambridge, MA: Belknap Press, 1971. 2:95-97.

"Charlotte Forten Experiences Integration." In *The Human Side of American History* edited by Richard C. Brown. Boston: Ginn & Co., 1962. Pp. 125-127.

"Charlotte Forten Grimke." In *Black Women in Nineteenth Century American Life* edited by Bert J. Loewenberg and Ruth Bogin. University Park: Pennsylvania State University Press, 1976. Pp. 283-291.

"Charlotte L. Forten." In *Cavalcade: Negro American Writing From 1760 to the Present* edited by Arthur P. Davis and Sounders Redding. Boston: Houghton-Mifflin, 1971. Pp. 108-119.

"Charlotte L. Forten: 'The Difficulty of Being a Christian Negro.'" In *The Negro in American History: III, Slaves and Masters.* Chicago: Encyclopedia Britannica, 1968. Pp. 3-6.

"Collector and Scholar: Frederick Jackson Turner on How to Build a Usable Library." *Hoja Volante* 122(August, 1975):6-7.

"The Coming of the Europeans." In *Story of the Great American West.* Pleasantville, NY: Reader's Digest, 1977. Pp. 6-14.

"Cowboys, Indians, and the Land of Promise: The World Image of the American Frontier." In *Proceedings of the XIV International Congress of the Historical Sciences.* New York: 1976. Pp. 79-99. Reprinted, *Representative American Speeches, 1975-1976* edited by Waldo W. Braden. New York: H. W. Wilson, 1976. Pp. 176-192.

"Cry from the Heart of a Black Girl." In *Diary of America* edited by J. and D. Berger. New York: Simon & Schuster, 1957. Pp. 402-407.

"Cultural Contributions versus Cultural Assimilation." In *The Cultural Approach to History* edited by Caroline F. Ware. New York: Columbia University Press, 1940. Pp. 78-82.

"Culture in the Changing West." In *The Flavor of the Past* edited by Leland D. Baldwin. New York: D. Van Nostrand, 1968. Pp. 354-368.

"David Humphreys Miller: Westerner Extraordinary." San Diego Westerners *Brand Book* 6(1979):175-178.

"A Dedication to the Memory of James Blaine Hedges, 1894-1965." *Arizona and the West* 10(Summer, 1968):105-110.

"Driving the Last Spike: The Northern Pacific Railroad." Chicago Westerners *Brand Book* 30(March, 1973):1-3, 7-8.

"English and American Education." In *American Education: The Thirty-Second Discussion and Debate Manual* edited by Bower Aly. Columbia, MO: University of Missouri Press, 1958. Pp. 187-190.

"Environment or Inheritance: Frontier Democracy." In *The American Political Experience: What is the Key*? edited by Edward Handler. Lexington, MA: D.C. Heath, 1968. Pp. 59-71.

"An Ethnic War: Native Americans versus Irish Immigrants in the Philadelphia Riot, May 3-8, 1844." In *American Violence* edited by Richard M. Brown. Englewood Cliffs, NJ: Prentice-Hall, 1970. Pp. 38-42.

"The Fort Stanwix Treaty of 1768." *New York History* 25(April, 1944):182-194.

"Franklin D. Scott: Teacher, Scholar, and Ambassador of International Goodwill." *Swedish Pioneer Historical Quarterly* 25(July, 1974):169-182.

"Frederick Jackson Turner." In *An American Primer* edited by Daniel J. Boorstin. Chicago: University of Chicago Press, 1966. 2:522-550.

"Frederick Jackson Turner: The Image and the Man." *Western Historical Quarterly* 3(April, 1972):137-152.

"Frederick Jackson Turner: Non-Western Historian." *Transactions of the Wisconsin Academy of Sciences, Arts and Letters* 59(1971):7-21.

"Frederick Jackson Turner and the Closing of the Frontier." In *Essays in Western History in Honor of Professor T.A. Larson* edited by Roger Daniels. Laramie: University of Wyoming Publications, 1971. 37:45-56.

"Frederick Jackson Turner and the Interpretation of American History." *California Social Science Review* 3(February, 1964):7-16.

"Frederick Jackson Turner and Logan's 'National Summer School,' 1924." *Utah Historical Quarterly* 34(Summer, 1969):307-336.

"Frederick Jackson Turner and Walter Prescott Webb: Frontier Historians." In *Essays on the American West* edited by Harold

Hollingsworth and Sandra Myres. Austin: University of Texas Press, 1969. Pp. 89-114.

"Frederick Jackson Turner Comes to Harvard." *Proceedings of the Massachusetts Historical Society* 74(1962):51-83.

"Frederick Jackson Turner in Southern California." Los Angeles Westerners *Brand Book* 15(1978):216-229.

"The Frederick Jackson Turner Papers in the Huntington Library." Co-authored with Wilbur Jacobs. *Arizona and the West* 2(Spring, 1960):73-77.

"Frederick Jackson Turner Visits New England." *New England Quarterly* 41(September, 1968):409-436.

"A Free Negro in the Slave Era," In *Black Heritage in Social Welfare* edited by Edyth L. Ross. Metuchen, NJ: Scarecrow Press, 1978. Pp. 70-73.

"From Association to Organization: The OAH in the Bad Old Days." *Journal of American History* 65(June, 1978):75-84.

"The Frontier and I." *Western Historical Quarterly* 1(January, 1970):5-20.

"The Frontier and the American Character." In *The Sweep of American History* edited by Robert R. Jones and Gustav Seligmann, Jr. New York: John Wiley, 1969. Pp. 61-73. Reprint. *Historical Viewpoints: Notable Articles from American Heritage* edited by John A. Garraty. New York: Harper & Row, 1979, 3rd Edition. Pp. 64-75.

"The Frontier and the Teaching of American History." In *The Westward Movement and the Historical Involvement of the Americas in the Pacific Basin.* San Jose, CA: San Jose State College, 1966. Pp. 29-41.

"Frontier Democracy." In *The American Political Experience* edited by Edward Handler. Lexington, MA: D.C. Heath, 1969. Pp. 59-71.

"The Frontier Disappears." In *American Story* edited by Earl S. Miers. New York: Channel Press, 1956. Pp. 253-258. Reprint. *The Building of the Nation* edited by Gordon E. Bigelow. Seibido, Japan: n.p., 1967. Pp. 55-63.

"The Frontier in American Thought and Character." In *The New World Looks at its History* edited by Archibald R. Lewis and Thomas F. McGann. Austin: University of Texas Press, 1963. Pp. 77-94.

"The Frontier in Illinois History." *Journal of the Illinois State Historical Society* 43(Spring, 1950):28-45. Reprint. *American History: Recent Interpretations* edited by Abraham S. Eisenstadt. New York: Crowell, 1962. 1:337-349; *An Illinois Reader* edited by Clyde H. Walton. Dekalb: Northern Illinois University Press, 1970. Pp. 89-102.

"Frontiers." In *The Comparative Approach to American History* edited by C. Vann Woodward. New York: Basic Books, 1968. Pp. 75-90.

"Full Speed Ahead and Damn the Tomorrows: Our Frontier Heritage of Waste." *American Heritage* 29(December, 1977):4-12.

"The Garden of the World: Fact and Fiction." In *The Heritage of the Middle West* edited by John J. Murray. Norman: University of Oklahoma Press, 1958. Pp. 27-53.

"The Genesis of the Research Institution." *Huntington Library Quarterly* 32(August, 1969):351-372. Reprint. *The Founding of the Huntington Library and Art Gallery*. San Marino, CA: Huntington Library, 1969. Chapter IV.

"Government and the Arts: The WPA Experience." *American Quarterly* 13(Winter, 1961):466-479.

"The Graduate Student's Haven." In *A Seidle for Jake Wirth* edited by Walter M. Whitehill. Boston: n.p., 1964.

"A Greeting and a Challenge." *American West* 1(October, 1964):6-7.

"Guides to American History Manuscript Collections in Libraries of the United States." *Mississippi Valley Historical Review* 38(December, 1951):467-496.

"A Historian Views the Everett Graff Collection." *Newberry Library Bulletin* 5(December, 1960):214-226.

"Historians and the Northwest Ordinance." *Journal of the Illinois State Historical Society* 40(December, 1947):397-413.

"History is a Dangerous Subject." *Saturday Review* 49(January 15, 1966):59-61, 80-81. Reprint. *Principles of Sociology: A Reader in Theory and Research* edited by Raymond W. Mack and Kimball Young. New York: American Book Co., 1968. Pp. 2-8; *Teaching History in Canada* edited by Geoffrey Milburn. Toronto: n.p., 1972. Pp. 76-79; *Ahead of Us the Past: History and the Historian* edited by Eunice Jones and Warren L. Hickman. New York: n.p., 1975. Pp. 26-28.

"History is a Dangerous Subject: Bias in History Textbooks." *The Education Digest* 31(April, 1966):37-40.

"How the Frontier Shaped the American Character." *American Heritage* 9(April, 1958):4-9, 86-89. Reprint. *The American Past: Conflicting Interpretations and Great Issues* edited by Sidney Fine and Gerald S. Brown. New York: Macmillan, 1961. 2:117-128; *Readings in Intellectual History: The American Tradition* edited by C. K. McFarland. New York: Holt, Rinehart & Winston, 1971.

"How the Frontier Shaped the American Character: Turner's Frontier Hypothesis." In *The Craft of American History* edited by A. S. Eisenstadt. New York: Harper & Row, 1966. 1:135-149.

"Image of the Southwest." *Westways* 70(January, 1978):43.

"The Indian Barrier." In *The Great Plains Experience: Readings in the History of a Region* edited by James E. Wright and Sarah Z. Rosenberg. Lincoln, NE: University of Mid-America, 1978. Pp. 142-157.

"An Informal Chronicle of the Western History Association." *American West* 14(September-October, 1977):30-31, 66.

"An Informal Chronicle of the Westerners." *American West* 15(September-October, 1978):32-33, 58-59.

"James Forten: Forgotten Abolitionist." *The Negro History Society Bulletin* 13(November, 1949):31-36, 45. Reprint. *Blacks in the Abolition Movement* edited by John H. Bracey. Belmont, CA: Wadsworth, 1971. Pp. 4-6.

"James Thorpe: The First Decade." *Huntington Library Calendar* (September-October, 1976):142.

"John Hawgood: A Memorial Tribute." *Journal of American Studies* 6(April, 1972):53-54.

"The Know-Nothing Uproar." *American Heritage* 10(February, 1959):58-61, 94.

"A Letter to the Editor that Got Unexpected Results." *Together* 3(April, 1959):46-48.

"Local History is Alive and Well." *Pomona Valley Historian* 12(Fall, 1976):139-150.

"Manuscripts and the Biographer."` *Manuscripts* 16(Summer, 1964):30-35.

"Maria Monk." In *Notable American Women* edited by Edward James. Cambridge, MA: Belknap Press, 1971. 2:560-561.

"Maria Monk and Her Influence." *Catholic Historical Review* 22(October, 1936):283-296.

"Memorial Tribute to Edward Everett Dale." *Hoja Volante* 109(August, 1972): 4-5.

"Memorial Tribute to Oscar Osburn Winther." *Indiana Magazine of History* 67(March, 1971):57-61.

"The Middle Ages and Comparative Frontiers: A Corrective Footnote." *Comparative Fronter Studies: An Interdisciplinary Newsletter* 2(Spring, 1976):1-2.

"Middle Western Isolationism." In *Understanding the American Past: American History and its Interpretation* edited by Edward N. Saveth. Boston: Little-Brown, 1954. Pp. 451-471.

"The Miners' Frontier Moves Eastward." In *Images of America* edited by Alastair Cooke. New York: Knopf, 1978. Pp. 243-268.

"The Mission as an Agent of Civilization." In *The Rebirth of a Library: Addresses Given at the Formal Dedication of the Bibliotheca Montereyensis-Angulorum Dioceseos* edited by Francis J. Weber. San Fernando, CA: Mission San Fernando, 1970. Pp. 5-10.

"The Mormons Move Westward." *American Heritage* 7(October, 1956): 20-25, 116-117.

"Nativism and Prejudice." In *The Social Setting of Intolerance* edited by Seymour J. Mandelbaum. Chicago: Scott-Foresman, 1964. Pp. 282-299.

"Nelson Manfred Blake: Pioneering Historian." In *Remember the Ladies: New Perspectives on Women in American History. Essays in Honor of Nelson Manfred Blake* edited by Carol V. R. George. Syracuse, NY: Syracuse University Press, 1975. Pp. xiii-xvi.

"The New Western Social Order and the Synthesis of Western Scholarship." In *The American West: An Appraisal* edited by Robert G. Ferris. Santa Fe: Museum of New Mexico Press, 1962. Pp. 3-12.

"Now and Then: The Uses of Local History." *American Heritage* 32(December, 1980):84-85.

"Old Bill Williams." In *The Unforgettable Americans* edited by John A. Garraty. Great Neck, NY: Channel Press, 1960. Pp. 149-154.

"Oregon Epic: A Letter That Jarred America." *Pacific Historian* 12(Summer, 1968):30-37.

"The Origin of the Land Speculator as a Frontier Type." *Agricultural History* 19(October, 1945):204-212.

"The Origins of Harvard's Mormon Collection." *Arizona and the West* 10(Autumn, 1968):221-224.

"The Origins of Middle Western Isolationism." *Political Science Quarterly* 60(March, 1945):44-64. Reprint. *Historical Vistas: Readings in United States History* edited by Robert Wiebe and Grady McWhinney. Boston: Allyn & Bacon, 1964. Pp. 282-299; *Pivotal Interpretations of American History* edited by Carl B. Degler. New York: Harper & Row, 1966. 2:246-263.

"Oscar O. Winther." In Oral History Association, *Fifth and Sixth Annual Colloquium Proceedings*. New York: n.p., 1972.

"The Overland Ordeal." *Westways* 59(May,1967):12-15, 58.

"The Plains Country." In *Lands and People.* New York: The Grolier Society, 1947.

"The Plains and Deserts Through European Eyes." *Western Historical Quarterly* 10(October, 1979):467-486.

"Politics and Patriotism." In *Forging a Nation* edited by Monroe Billington and Duane M. Leach. Berkeley: University of California Press, 1968. Pp. 199-210.

"Protecting the Frontier: Forts and Frontiers in Illinois." *Illinois History* 12(April, 1959):163-165.

"The Return of the Amateur Historian." In *The Big Smoke* compiled by Stuart B. Bradley. Chicago: Pflum Press, 1980. Pp. 2-7.

"The Roots of Anti-Catholic Prejudice." In *Religion and Politics* edited by Peter H. Odegard. New Brunswick, NJ: Oceana Publishers, 1960. Pp. 26-35.

"San Diego's Role in Western Transportation." San Diego Westerners *Brand Book* 5(1978):11-14.

"The Santa Fe Conference and the Writing of Western History." In *Probing the American West: Papers from the Santa Fe Conference* edited by K. Ross Toole, John Alexander Carroll, Robert M. Utley, and A. R. Mortensen. Santa Fe: Museum of New Mexico Press, 1962. Pp. 1-16.

"Selling the West." In *The Power of Print in American History*. New York: St. Regis Paper Co., 1976. Pp. 74-88.

"A Social Experiment: The Port Royal Journal of Charlotte L. Forten, 1862-1863." *Journal of Negro History* 35(July, 1950):233-264.

"Some Aspects of Turner's Thought." *Agricultural History* 32(October, 1958):250.

"Sources of American Resistance to International Involvement." In *The Shaping of Twentieth Century America* edited by Richard M. Abrams and Lawrence Levine. Boston: Little, Brown Co., 1965. Pp. 176-192.

"A Speaker's Use of Examples: The Wild West is Alive and Well." In *Speech: A Text with Adapted Readings* edited by Robert C. Jeffrey and Owen Peterson. New York: Harper and Row, 1980. Pp. 176-192.

"Stanley Pargellis: Newberry Librarian, 1942-1962." In *Essays in History and Literature Presented by the Fellows of the Newberry Library to Stanley Pargellis* edited by Heinz Bluhm. Chicago: The Newberry Library, 1965. Pp. 3-18.

"Tempest in Clio's Teapot: The American Historical Association Rebellion of 1915." *American Historical Review* 78(April, 1973):348-369.

"Tentative Bibliography of Anti-Catholic Propaganda in the United States (1800-1860)." *Catholic Historical Review* 18(January, 1933):492-513.

"The Trial of Anthony Burns." In *The Black American*, revised edition, edited by Leslie Fishel and Benjamin Quarles. Glenview, IL: Scott-Foresman, 1970. Pp. 199-202.

"Turner and the Frontier Hypothesis." Chicago Westerners *Brand Book* 14(November, 1957):71-75.

"The Uses of Local History." *American Heritage* 32(December, 1980):84-85.

"The West of Frederick Jackson Turner." *Nebraska History* 41(December, 1960):261-279.

"Westward Expansion and the Frontier Thesis." In *Interpreting American History* edited by John A. Garraty. New York: Macmillan, 1970. Pp. 251-275.

"Why Some Historians Rarely Write History: A Case Study of Frederick Jackson Turner." *Mississippi Valley Historical Review* 50(June, 1953):3-27.

"The Wild West in Norway." *Western Historical Quarterly* 7(July, 1976):272-278.

"The Wild, Wild West Through European Eyes." *American History Illustrated* 14(August, 1979):16-23.

"Young Fred Turner." *Wisconsin Magazine of History* 46(Autumn, 1962):38-54.

Forewords and Introductions

"Foreword." In *Abe Lincoln Laughing: Humorous Anecdotes from Original Sources by and about Abraham Lincoln* edited by P. M. Zall. Berkeley: University of California Press, 1982. Pp. ix-xi.

__________. In *Blacks in the West* by W. Sherman Savage. Westport, CT: Greenwood Press, 1976. Pp. ix-xiii.

__________. In *The California Gold Rush Diary of Byron N. McKinstry, 1850-1852* edited by Bruce L. McKinstry. Glendale, CA: Arthur H. Clark, 1975. Pp. 11-16.

__________. In *The Conference on Education and Student Life in the United States*. Evanston, IL: Northwestern University Press, 1957. Pp. i-ii.

__________. In *The Conquest of the American West* by Major John Selby. London: Allen & Unwin, 1975. Pp. 7-10.

__________. In *Exploration in the West: Catlin, Bodmer, Miller*. Omaha: Joselyn Art Museum, 1963. P. 4.

__________. In *Forth to the Wilderness: The First American Frontier* by Dale Van Every. New York: Morrow, 1961. Pp. v-ix.

__________. In *The Frontier in American History* by Frederick Jackson Turner. New York: Holt, Rinehart & Winston, 1962. Pp. vii-xviii.

__________. In *The Immigrant Upraised* by Andrew Rolle. Norman: University of Oklahoma Press, 1968. Pp. vii-x.

__________. In *The Making of an American: An Adaptation of Memorable Tales by Charles Sealsfield* by Ulrich S. Carrington. Dallas: Southern Methodist University Press, 1974. Pp. ix-xii.

__________. In *The Middle West in American History* by Dan Elbert Clark. New York: Crowell, 1966. Pp. iii-v.

__________. In *Negro Slave Songs in the United States* by Miles M. Fisher. Ithaca, NY: Citadel Press, 1953. Pp. vii-x.

__________. In *Jews on the Frontier* by Rabbi I. Harold Sharfman. Chicago: H. Regnery, 1977. Pp. ix-xii.

__________. In *Schoolboy, Cowboy, Mexican Spy* by Jay Monaghan. Berkeley: University of California Press, 1977. Pp. ix-xii.

__________. In *A Select Bibliography to the California Missions* by Francis J. Weber. Los Angeles: Dawson's Book Shop, 1972. Pp. 1-2.

__________. *Trails West.* Washington, DC: National Geographic Society, 1979. P. 5.

__________. In *Wheels West, 1590-1900* by Richard Dunlop. Chicago: Rand McNally, 1977. Pp. 7-9.

"Foreword: California and the Bicentennial, Its History and Historical Collections." In *Who's Who in California, Golden State Bicentennial Edition.* Los Angeles: Who's Who Publishing Co., 1976. Pp. vii-ix.

"Foreword: How This Book Was Written." In *Rise of the New West* by Frederick Jackson Turner. New York: Collier Books, 1962. Pp. 7-20.

"Foreword: One Moment Please." *Massachusetts: A Guide to Its Places and People.* Boston: Federal Writers Project, 1937. Pp. ix-xi.

"Foreword to 1973 Edition." In *Brigham Young the Colonizer* by Milton R. Hunter. Salt Lake City: Peregrine-Smith, 1973. Pp. vii-viii.

"Introduction." In *The American and Canadian West: A Bibliography* edited by Dwight L. Smith. Santa Barbara, CA: ABC Clio Press, 1979. Pp. ix-x.

__________. In *The Great Salt Lake* by Dale L. Morgan. Albuquerque: University of New Mexico Press, 1973. Pp. vii-xxviii.

__________. In *No Tears for the General: The Life of Alfred Sully, 1821-1879* by Langdon Sully. Palo Alto, CA: American West Publishing Co., 1974. Pp. 9-12.

__________. In *Soldier and Brave: Military and Indian Affairs in the Trans-Mississippi West* by the National Park Service. New York: Harper & Row, 1963. Pp. xii-xvi.

__________. In *The Walter Prescott Webb Memorial Lectures: Essays on Walter Prescott Webb* edited by Kenneth P. Philip and Elliot West. Austin: University of Texas Press, 1976. Pp. xvii-xii.

"Introduction: *The Awful Disclosures* in Historical Perspective." In *The Awful Disclosures of the Hotel Dieu Nunnery* by Maria Monk. Hamden, CT: Archon Books, 1962. Pp. ii-xxviii.

Selected Reviews

American Catholic Opinion in the Slavery Controversy by Madeline Hooke Rice. *American Historical Review* 50(January, 1945):404-405.

The American Churches: An Interpretation by William Warren Sweet. *American Historical Review* 54(January, 1949):438.

American Opinion of Roman Catholicism in the Eighteenth Century by Mary Augustina Ray. *American Historical Review* 43(October, 1937):211-212.

Autobiography of Peter Cartwright edited by Charles L. Wallis. *American Historical Review* 62(January, 1957):477-478.

Barton Warren Stone: Early American Advocate of Christian Unity by William Garrett West. *American Historical Review* 60(April, 1955):685-686.

Bibliography and the Historian: The Conference at Belmont of the Joint Committee on Bibliographical Services to History, May, 1967 edited by Dagmar Horna Perman. *Journal of American History* 55(September, 1968):373-374.

The Character and Influence of the Indian Trade in Wisconsin: A Study of the Trading Post As An Institution by Frederick Jackson Turner and edited by David Harry Miller and William W. Savage. *Journal of American History* 64(March, 1978):1096-1097.

Comparative Frontiers: A Proposal For Studying the American West by Jerome Q. Steffen. *American Historical Review* 85(December, 1980):1252.

Empire on the Pacific: A Study In American Continental Expansion by Norman A. Graebner. *American Historical Review* 61(April, 1956):661-662.

Eugene C. Barker: Historian by William C. Pool. *Journal of American History* 58(March, 1972):1043-1044.

The Exploration of the Colorado River in 1869 and *The Exploration of the Colorado River and the High Plateaus of Utah in 1871-72. American Historical Review* 56(January, 1951):360-361.

The Foundations of Nativism in American Textbooks, 1783-1860 by Marie Leonore Fell. *American Historical Review* 47(July, 1942):686.

The Frontier: Comparative Studies edited by David H. Miller and Jerome Q. Steffen. *Pacific Northwest Quarterly* 69(July, 1978):135-136.

The Frontier Re-Examined edited by John Francis McDermott. *American Historical Review* 73(February, 1968):906-907.

A Guide to Archives and Manuscripts in the United States edited by Philip M. Hamer. *American Historical Review* 66(July, 1961):1049-1051.

The Half-Blood: A Cultural Symbol in Nineteenth-Century American Fiction by William J. Scheick. *Register of the Kentucky Historical Society* 79(Winter, 1981):88-89.

Herbert Eugene Bolton: The Historian and the Man, 1870-1953 by John Francis Bannon. *Arizona and the West* 21(Summer, 1979):187-188.

History and American Society: Essays of David M. Potter edited by Don E. Fehrenbacher. *Journal of American History* 60(December, 1973):762-763.

History as High Adventure by Walter Prescott Webb. *Journal of American History* 57(December, 1970):680-681.

History of Bigotry in the United States by Gustavus Myers. *American Historical Review* 49(April, 1944):482-483.

A History of Chicago: The Rise of a Modern City, 1871-1893, vol. 3, by Bessie Louise Pierce. *American Historical Review* 63(October, 1957):146-148.

James Alphonsus McMaster: A Study in American Thought by Mary Augustine Kwitches. *American Historical Review* 56(October, 1950):222-223.

Major Trends in American Church History by Francis X. Curran. *American Historical Review* 52(October, 1946):190-191.

The Man Who Made News: James Gordon Bennett by Oliver Carlson. *American Historical Review* 48(April, 1943):606-607.

My Life With History: An Autobiography by John D. Hicks. *Journal of American History* 56(June, 1969):165-166.

Nativism in Connecticut, 1829-1860 by Carroll John Noonan. *American Historical Review* 44(July, 1939):999-1000.

The Old Northwest: Pioneer Period, 1815-1840, 2 vols., by R. Carlyle Buley. *American Historical Review* 56(July, 1951):907-909.

Political Nativism in Tennessee to 1860 by Mary De Lourdes Gohmann. *American Historical Review* 44(July, 1939):999-1000.

The Rancher: A Book for a Generation by Stan Steiner. *American West* 17(November-December, 1980):57.

The Readers' Encyclopedia of the American West edited by Howard R. Lamar. *Western Historical Quarterly* 9(October, 1978):509-510.

Regeneration Through Violence: The Mythology of the American Frontier, 1600-1860 by Richard Slotkin. *American Historical Review* 78(October, 1973):1116-1117.

The Rhetoric of History by Savoie Lottinoille. *Western Historical Quarterly* 8(January, 1977):68-69.

Stanley Vestal: Champion of the Old West by Ray Tassin. *Southern California Quarterly* 56(Fall, 1974):321-322.

The Story of Illinois by Theodore Calvin Pease. *American Historical Review* 55(April, 1950):705.

Walter Prescott Webb: His Life and Impact by Necah Stewart Furman. *New Mexico Historical Review* 51(October, 1976):338-340.

We Who Built America: The Saga of the Immigrants by Carl Wittke. *American Historical Review* 46(October, 1940):154-155.

What is the Good of History? The Selected Letters of Carl L. Becker edited with an introduction by Michael Kammen. *New York History* 55(January, 1974):115-116.

Studies of Ray Allen Billington

Abramowitz, Jack. Review of *The Journal of Charlotte L. Forten* by Ray Allen Billington. *American Historical Review* 59(April, 1954):726.

Akers, Charles W. Review of *The Reinterpretation of Early American History: Essays in Honor of John Edwin Pomfret* edited by Ray Allen Billington. *Journal of American History* 54(June, 1967):88-89.

Athearn, Robert G. Review of *Land of Savagery, Land of Promise: The European Image of the American Frontier* by Ray Allen Billington. *Montana: Magazine of Western History* 32(Spring, 1982):81-82.

Atherton, Lewis. Review of *Frederick Jackson Turner: Historian, Scholar, Teacher* by Ray Allen Billington. *Western Historical Quarterly* 4(July, 1973):327-328.

Barth, Gunther. Review of *America's Frontier Heritage* by Ray Allen Billington. *Pacific Northwest Quarterly* 58(July, 1967)155-156.

Berkhofer, Robert F., Jr. Review of *America's Frontier Heritage* by Ray Allen Billington. *Agricultural History* 41(July, 1967):313-315.

__________. Review of *The Frontier Thesis: A Valid Interpretation of American History?* edited by Ray Allen Billington. *Agricultural History* 41(July, 1967):313-315.

Billington, Ray Allen, Papers. Huntington Library, San Marino, CA.

Bloom, John Porter. Review of *America's Frontier Heritage* by Ray Allen Billington. *Journal of Southern History* 33(May, 1967):244-245.

Bogue, Allan G. "*Frederick Jackson Turner: Historian, Scholar, Teacher*; An Essay Review." *Pacific Northwest Quarterly* 64(October, 1973):175-177.

Brewer, Thomas B. Review of *America's Frontier Story* by Ray Allen Billington. *Southwestern Historical Quarterly* 73(April, 1970):560-561.

Carey, John. Review of *The Reinterpretation of Early American History: Essays in Honor of John Edwin Pomfret* edited by Ray Allen Billington. *American Historical Review* 72(July, 1967):1478-1479.

Caughey, John W. Review of *The Genesis of the Frontier Thesis: A Study in Historical Creativity* by Ray Allen Billington. *Montana: Magazine of Western History* 23(Winter, 1973):63.

__________. Review of *Frederick Jackson Turner: Historian, Scholar, Teacher* by Ray Allen Billington. *Pacific Historical Review* 42(August, 1973):419-421.

Content, Robin. "The Emergence of the American Professor." *History of Education Quarterly* 14(July, 1974):430-434.

Craven, Avery. Review of *Westward Expansion: A History of the American Frontier* by Ray Allen Billington. *Journal of Southern History* 16(February, 1950):77.

Cravens, Hamilton. Review of *The Genesis of the Frontier Thesis: A Study in Historical Creativity* by Ray Allen Billington. *Pacific Northwest Quarterly* 64(July, 1973):119.

Cunliffe, Marcus. Review of *The Far Western Frontier, 1830-1860* by Ray Allen Billington. *Manchester Guardian* (February 1, 1957):6.

Curti, Merle. Review of *"Dear Lady": The Letters of Frederick Jackson Turner and Alice Forbes Perkins Hooper, 1910-1932* edited by Ray Allen Billington. *Journal of American History* 58(September, 1971):488-490.

Dee, Ivan R. Review of *Frederick Jackson Turner: Historian, Scholar, Teacher* by Ray Allen Billington. *New York Times Book Review* (March 11, 1973):31-32.

Diggins, John R. Review of *America's Frontier Heritage* by Ray Allen Billington. *American West Review* 1(1967):15-23.

Dilliard, Irving. Review of *Westward Expansion: A History of the American Frontier* by Ray Allen Billington. *Illinois State Historical Society Journal* 42(December, 1949):472-473.

Dippie, Brian W. Review of *America's Frontier Culture: Three Essays* by Ray Allen Billington. *American Historical Review* 83(December, 1978):1091-1092.

Dykstra, Robert. Review of *America's Frontier Heritage* by Ray Allen Billington. *New Mexico Historical Review* 43(January, 1968):66-67.

Earle, Carville. Review of *Frederick Jackson Turner: Historian, Scholar, Teacher* by Ray Allen Billington. *William and Mary Quarterly* 31(January, 1974):146-149.

Ellsworth, S. George. Review of *Allan Nevins on History* edited by Ray Allen Billington. *Western Historical Quarterly* 7(October, 1976):425-426.

Fletcher, Robert Samuel. Review of *The Far Western Frontier, 1830-1860* by Ray Allen Billington. *Agricultural History* 41(July, 1967):66-67.

Frantz, Joe B. Review of *People of the Plains and Mountains: Essays in the History of the West Dedicated to Everett Dick* edited by Ray Allen Billington. *Journal of American History* 61(June, 1974):207-208.

__________. Review of *Frederick Jackson Turner: Historian, Scholar, Teacher* by Ray Allen Billington. *Montana: Magazine of Western History* 23(Autumn, 1973):63.

Fritz, Henry. Review of *America's Frontier Heritage* by Ray Allen Billington. *Arizona and the West* 9(Summer, 1967):169-170.

Gibson, Arrell M. "America's Frontier Heritage: A Review Essay." *Civil War History* 14(July, 1968):250-258.

Goodykoontz, Colin B. Review of *Westward Expansion: A History of the American Frontier* by Ray Allen Billington. *Pacific Northwest Quarterly* 41(January, 1950):69-70.

Goetzmann, William H. "Billington's Gift." Review of *Land of Savagery, Land of Promise: The European Image of the American Frontier* by Ray Allen Billington. *Reviews in American History* 10(April, 1982):149-157.

Grant, H. Roger. Review of *America's Frontier Culture: Three Essays* by Ray Allen Billington. *Western Historical Quarterly* 10(January, 1979):72.

Gressley, Gene M. Review of *"Dear Lady": The Letters of Frederick Jackson Turner and Alice Forbes Perkins Hooper* edited by Ray

Allen Billington. *American Historical Review* 78(February, 1973):173-175.

__________. Review of *The Genesis of the Frontier Thesis: A Study in Historical Creativity* by Ray Allen Billington. *American Historical Review* 78(February, 1973):173-175.

Hansen, Klaus J. Review of *Land of Savagery, Land of Promise: The European Image of the American Frontier* by Ray Allen Billington. *Journal of American History* 69(June, 1982):120-121.

Hicks, John D. Review of *Westward Expansion: A History of the American Frontier* by Ray Allen Billington. *Saturday Review of Literature* 32(July 30, 1949):27.

Hockett, Homer C. Review of *Westward Expansion: A History of the American Frontier* by Ray Allen Billington. *Journal of American History* 36(December, 1949):551-552.

Hollon, W. Eugene. Review of *Land of Savagery, Land of Promise: The European Image of the American Frontier* by Ray Allen Billington. *Western Historical Quarterly* 13(January, 1982):63-64.

Jackson. W. Turrentine. Review of *America's Frontier Heritage* by Ray Allen Billington. *Pacific Historical Review* 36(August, 1967):349-350.

Johansen, Dorothy O. Review of *The Far Western Frontier, 1830-1860* by Ray Allen Billington. *Pacific Historical Review* 26(May, 1957):180-182.

Karl, Barry D. "Frederick Jackson Turner: The Moral Dilemma of Professionalization." *Reviews in American History* 3(January, 1975):1-7.

King, Nicholas. Review of *Land of Savagery, Land of Promise: The European Image of the American Frontier* by Ray Allen Billington. *National Review* 33(April 3, 1981):368-369.

Kirby, David. "Jim Der Trapper and Other Heroes of the Old West." Review of *Land of Savagery, Land of Promise: The European Image of the American Frontier* by Ray Allen Billington. *Virginia Quarterly Review* 58(April, 1982):333-339.

Lamar, Howard R. Review of *America's Frontier Heritage* by Ray Allen Billington. *American Historical Review* 72(July, 1967):1476-1477.

McPherson, Harry. Review of *Frederick Jackson Turner: Historian, Scholar, Teacher* by Ray Allen Billington. *New Republic* 168(April 7, 1973):26-28.

Morrow, Ralph E. Review of *Frederick Jackson Turner: Historian, Scholar, Teacher* by Ray Allen Billington. *Journal of Southern History* 39(August, 1973):426-428.

Nevins, Allan. Review of *Westward Expansion: A History of the American Frontier* by Ray Allen Billington. *New York Times Book Review* (August 21, 1949):17.

Paul, Rodman W. Review of *People of the Plains and Mountains: Essays in the History of the West Dedicated to Everett Dick* edited by Ray Allen Billington. *American Historical Review* 79(April, 1974):565-566.

Peterson, Richard H. Review of *Frederick Jackson Turner: Historian, Scholar, Teacher* by Ray Allen Billington. *Agricultural History* 48(June, 1974):456-457.

__________. Review of *The Genesis of the Frontier Thesis: A Study in Historical Creativity* by Ray Allen Billington. *Agricultural History* 46(October, 1972):556-557.

Pomeroy, Earl. Review of *Frederick Jackson Turner: Historian, Scholar, Teacher* by Ray Allen Billington. *American Historical Review* 78(December, 1973):1541-1542.

__________. Review of *The Far Western Frontier, 1830-1860* by Ray Allen Billington. *Journal of American History* 43(March, 1957):676-677.

__________. Review of *The Genesis of the Frontier Thesis: A Study in Historical Creativity* by Ray Allen Billington. *Pacific Historical Review* 41(August, 1972):374-375.

Rawley, James A. Review of *Allan Nevins on History* edited by Ray Allen Billington. *Journal of American History* 63(March, 1977):1080-1082.

Ridge, Martin. "Frederick Jackson Turner, Ray Allen Billington, and American Frontier History." *Western Historical Quarterly* 19(January, 1988):5-20.

__________. "Ray Allen Billington, 1903-1981." *Western Historical Quarterly* 12(July, 1981):245-250.

__________. "Ray Allen Billington, Western History and American Exceptionalism." *Pacific Historical Review* 56(November, 1987):495-511.

Riegel, Robert E. Review of *America's Frontier Heritage* by Ray Allen Billington. *Montana: Magazine of Western History* 17(January, 1967):72.

__________. Review of *The Far Western Frontier, 1830-1860* by Ray Allen Billington. *Montana: Magazine of Western History* 7(April, 1957):47, 50.

Rundell, Walter, Jr. Review of *Frederick Jackson Turner: Historian, Scholar, Teacher* by Ray Allen Billington. *Journal of American History* 60(December, 1973):832-833.

__________. Review of *The Genesis of the Frontier Thesis: A Study in Historical Creativity* by Ray Allen Billington. *Journal of American History* 59(September, 1972):435-436.

__________. Review of *Westward Expansion: A History of the American Frontier*, 5th edition by Ray Allen Billington and Martin Ridge. *Western Historical Quarterly* 13(October, 1982):429-430.

Schafer, Boyd C. Review of *Frederick Jackson Turner: Historian, Scholar, Teacher* by Ray Allen Billington. *Arizona and the West* 15(Autumn, 1973):275-277.

Smith, Henry Nash. Review of *Land of Savagery, Land of Promise: The European Image of the American Frontier* by Ray Allen Billington. *American Historical Review* 86(October, 1981):933-934.

Spence, Clark C. Review of *America's Frontier Heritage* by Ray Allen Billington. *Journal of American History* 54(June, 1967):92-93.

__________. Review of *Essays on the American West* edited by Ray Allen Billington. *Southwestern Historical Quarterly* 74(October, 1970):275-276.

__________. Review of *The Genesis of the Frontier Thesis: A Study in Historical Creativity* by Ray Allen Billington. *Arizona and the West* 15(Summer, 1973):175-176.

Stephenson, George M. Review of *The Protestant Crusade, 1800-1860: A Study of the Origins of American Nativism* by Ray Allen Billington. *American Historical Review* 44(July, 1939):930-931.

Strout, Cushing. Review of *Frederick Jackson Turner: Historian, Scholar, Teacher* by Ray Allen Billington. *History and Theory* 13(July, 1974):315-325.

Watanabe, Masaharu. Review of *The Genesis of the Frontier Thesis: A Study in Historical Creativity* by Ray Allen Billington. *Western Historical Quarterly* 3(October, 1972):421-422.

Winther, Oscar Osburn. Review of *The Far Western Frontier, 1830-1860* by Ray Allen Billington. *American Historical Review* 62(April, 1957):638-640.

Woodward, C. Vann. Review of *Land of Savagery, Land of Promise: The European Image of the American Frontier* by Ray Allen Billington. *New York Review of Books* (June 11, 1981):33-35.

Wyllys, Rufus Kay. Review of *Westward Expansion: A History of the American Frontier* by Ray Allen Billington. *Pacific Historical Review* 18(November, 1949):511-512.

9

WILLIAM CAMPBELL BINKLEY

by Michael Q. Hooks

Biography

Texas is fortunate to be the focus of outstanding historians. Among those who have directed their scholarly attention to the Lone Star State was William Campbell Binkley, a nonTexan who spent almost his entire career in Tennessee and Louisiana.

Binkley, a physician's son, was born on April 30, 1889, in Newbern, Tennessee. At the age of fourteen, the Binkley family moved west to California, where William attended public school. After high school graduation, he enrolled briefly in the University of California. Although his studies at the Berkeley campus were interrupted for several years, during which time he married Vera B. McGlothin, he eventually earned all three of his academic degrees there, receiving the B.A. in 1917, the M.A. in 1918, and finally the Ph.D. in 1920 (*Arizona and the West* 23:313-314).

Binkley entered college intending to become a public school teacher. However, through the influence of historian Herbert Eugene Bolton, he changed his sights to becoming a historian, and a historian he became. Upon completing his doctorate, the Tennessee native embarked on a long and distinguished career teaching and writing history, and editing the efforts of others in his discipline. Over the next fifty years his jobs took him to Texas, Colorado, Tennessee, and finally Louisiana. In Texas he was an instructor of political science at the University of Texas from 1920 to 1921. After a year in Austin, the young scholar moved to Colorado College, where from 1921 to 1930 he was a member of the Department of History and for five years its chairman. Next, he returned home to Tennessee to join the faculty at Vanderbilt University. There he was professor of history, chairman of the department, and director of the Social Sciences Division. While at Vanderbilt, this busy teacher and administrator was also an editor, first of the *Tennessee Historical Quarterly* and then of the *Journal of Southern History*. Finally, he moved south to Tulane University, remaining on the faculty from 1953 to 1963, when he retired.

Once again, he edited a journal, this time the *Mississippi Valley Historical Review (Journal of Southern History* 36:645).

Although he retired in 1963, Binkley did not stop working. He conducted research at the University of Texas and taught at the University of Houston and Tulane. He died in New Orleans on August 19, 1970, at the age of eighty-one.

During his career Binkley was recognized for his contributions to historical scholarship. His peers not only elected him president of the Southern Historical Association, but also of the Mississippi Valley Historical Association. He was also selected a member of The Philosophical Society of Texas and a Fellow of the Texas State Historical Association. In 1964 Tulane awarded him the Honorary Doctor of Laws. The Mississippi Valley Historical Association (MVHA) established the Binkley-Stephenson Prize for the best scholarly article published each year, an award now given by the Organization of American Historians, the successor to the MVHA (*Philosophical Society of Texas Proceedings* 34:47).

Themes

Binkley wrote two books and edited two more. He also wrote eight major articles and numerous book reviews. From these writings three major themes are evident: the interrelationship of national events and regional developments, cultural differences as a cause for conflict, and the historian's responsibility in the search for truth. Although the third theme is not limited to frontier studies, the search for the truth was important to Binkley as he researched and wrote about the first two themes.

Analysis

The interrelationship of national events and regional developments can be traced to two areas of Binkley scholarship: revolution and the expansionist movement. For William C. Binkley, the focus was on Texas, specifically the Revolution of 1836 and the western boundary issue of 1836-1850.

In studying the Texas Revolution Binkley points out that the events in Texas were part of larger events. He argues that the revolution was important to relations between the United States and Mexico, with the end result being war. But it also had larger implications. Binkley views the Texas Revolution as a continuation of the fight for independence from a ruling nation, in this case Mexico, just as American colonists had fought for freedom from England (*The Texas Revolution,* p. 131).

The boundary controversy between Texas and New Mexico was tied to the national expansionist desires prevalent in the mid-nineteenth century. In Binkley's first book, *The Expansionist Movement in Texas 1836-1850,* published in 1925, he concludes that the "expansionist desires of the United States had a direct influence upon the territorial ambitions of the Texans during their existence as an independent republic--the Texans working at times to accommodate, at other times, to thwart those desires" (pp. v-vi). After Texas achieved statehood, the boundary question continued to be so important that Mexico, which opposed Texas' annexation to the Union, went to war against the United States. The boundary issue was resolved with the Compromise of 1850, which established the present boundary of Texas and awarded Texas $10 million for the claimed territory in New Mexico it lost.

The expansionist movement, however, was not simply the desire of Texans to move into New Mexico. Rather, it was part of a larger picture involving Texas, Mexico, and the United States. Texas received funds to pay its national debt, while Mexico lost one-third of its northern domain. But for the United States, expansionism had two results. First, it opened the way to acquire California, thereby ending the European presence on the West Coast. Second, according to Binkley, "the refusal of Texas to surrender her claims without compensation, together with the problem of organizing the newly acquired territory, accentuated the sectional strife which was to culminate in a civil war" (p. 222). Lastly, it was a part of the American frontier process at work as Anglo-Americans looked westward to carry out their dreams (p. 131).

The westward movement involved people from both the North and the South, according to Binkley, and any study of western development would be incomplete without examining the influence of southerners. "Although it has been more than half a century since Frederick Jackson Turner made us conscious of the importance of the West in American development," Binkley notes, "one still looks in vain for a systematic study of the part which the South may have played in determining the character of that West" *(Journal of Southern History* 17:6). Rather than study the American West, or any region for that matter, as if development came without outside influences, historians should study all the resources available to determine what factors were evident. They would find in "the search for the whole truth" that southerners made contributions to the economic, social, and cultural development of the region. He concludes that the interests of southerners certainly went beyond the question of slavery, for the "participation [of the South] in the development of the West continued undiminished long after slavery was gone" (p. 10).

The second major theme in Binkley's works is that the Texas Revolution was a clash of cultures rather than a conspiracy of interests, meaning slaveholders wanting to extend their system or land speculators desiring to control a new government. He sees the revolution as "the result of the difference between the racial and political inheritances of the two groups of people who came into contact with each other on Mexican soil" *(The Texas Revolution,* p. 129). On the one hand, the Anglo-American Texans brought with them the belief in a democratic system of government and the impatience to see it operational. On the other, the Mexicans, although professing to have such a system, were not prepared for it. A compromise agreeable to both sides could not be reached because the "prevailing atmosphere of racial distrust" hindered any efforts.

Underlying these two themes is the belief that the historian's responsibility is the search for truth. This responsibility is evident in all of Binkley's works, as he searched exhaustively and extensively all available sources and then based his conclusions on an objective analysis of the facts he uncovered. "History," writes Allan Nevins in *The Gateway to History* (1938), "is any integrated narrative or description of past events or facts written in a spirit of critical inquiry for the whole truth" (p. 22). The search for truth, for the whole truth as Nevins calls it, was the heart and soul of historical scholarship, Binkley believed. The historians must make an exhaustive and thorough search for the facts, which in turn provides the evidence on which the past is studied. But to study the evidence was not enough. The historian must examine it and understand it in an objective manner. In examining the facts, the true historian must not allow his own beliefs to distort or influence what he sees or what he writes. For when the historian explains the fact, or the record, he is writing history (*Journal of Southern History* 37:359-360).

All historians obviously did not share Binkley's strict view of his colleagues' responsibility, and he took note of this. In his 1946 presidential address to the Mississippi Valley Historical Association, Binkley reviewed changes in historical scholarship brought on by the two world wars, particularly the Second World War. One change certainly conflicted with his concept of history. Binkley lamented the insistence of the public to give more attention to current, or contemporary, history. This brought a confusion of current events with history. Although he recognized this trend as a pragmatic approach to scholarship demanded by the times, he did not like the trend because there was more interest in putting forth a point of view than with producing scholarly works. In the printed version Binkley accuses "important segments of the historical profession--which should have seen the difference . . . of blindly following the trend, shifting the center of their attention from the past to the present" *(Mississippi Valley Historical Review* 33:14). In his mind, historians were becoming too concerned about interpreting contemporary problems.

Binkley was not a prolific writer. Although he made important contributions to the study of Texas history, his primary influence came in his editorship of two major historical journals. Through his critical eye and attention to detail, he brought the best out of authors who attempted to publish their articles. He insisted that scholars be conscientious historians in searching for the truth and objective in presenting their conclusions.

Bibliography

Books

The Expansionist Movement in Texas, 1836-1850. Berkeley: University of California Press, 1925.

New Spain and the Anglo-American West: Historical Contributions Presented to Herbert Eugene Bolton. Vol. II. Edited with Cardinal Goodwin and J. Fred Rippy. Lancaster, PA: Lancaster Press, Inc., 1932.

Official Correspondence of the Texan Revolution, 1835-1836. Editor. 2 volumes. New York: D. Appleton-Century Company, 1936.

The Texas Revolution. Baton Rouge: Louisiana State University Press, 1952.

Articles

"The Activities of the Texan Revolutionary Army after San Jacinto." *Journal of Southern History* 6(August, 1940):331-346.

"Charles William Ramsdell." *Mississippi Valley Historical Review* 29(September, 1942):314-315.

"The Contribution of Walter Lynwood Fleming to Southern Scholarship." *Journal of Southern History* 5(May, 1939):143-154.

"The Last Stage of Texan Military Operations Against Mexico, 1843." *Southwestern Historical Quarterly* 22(January, 1919):260-271.

"Louis Pelzer, Scholar, Teacher, Editor." *Mississippi Valley Historical Review* 33(September, 1946):201-202.

"New Mexico and the Texan Santa Fe Expedition." *Southwestern Historical Quarterly* 27(October, 1923):85-107.

"The Question of Texan Jurisdiction in New Mexico Under the United States, 1848-1850." *Southwestern Historical Quarterly* 24(July, 1920):1-38.

"Reports from a Texan Agent in New Mexico, 1849." In *New Spain and the Anglo-American West: Historical Contributions Presented to Herbert Eugene Bolton* edited by William C. Binkley, Cardinal Goodwin, and J. Fred Rippy. Volume II. Lancaster, PA: Lancaster Press, Inc., 1932.

"The South and the West." *Journal of Southern History* 17(February, 1951):5-22.

"Two World Wars and American Historical Scholarship." *Mississippi Valley Historical Review* 33(June, 1946):3-26.

Reviews

America's Naval Challenge by Frederick Moore. *American Historical Review* 34(July, 1929):894-895.

America's Tragedy by James Truslow Adams. *Journal of Southern History* 1(March, 1935):226-228.

The Animating Pursuits of Speculation: Land Traffic in the Annexation of Texas by Elgin Williams. *Mississippi Valley Historical Review* 36(December, 1949):517-519.

As Our Neighbors See Us: Readings in the Relations of the United States and Latin America, 1820-1940 edited by T. H. Reynolds. *Mississippi Valley Historical Review* 27(March, 1941):669-670.

Bibliography of Texas, 1795-1845 by Thomas W. Streeter. *Journal of Southern History* 23(February, 1957):105-107.

Bolton and the Spanish Borderlands edited by John Francis Bannon. *Journal of Southern History* 51(December, 1964):485-487.

Check List of Texas Imprints, 1846-1860 edited by Ernest W. Winkler. *Journal of Southern History* 16(February, 1950):122-123.

Colonel Jack Hays: Texas Frontier Leader and California Builder by James Kimmins Greer. *Journal of Southern History* 18(November, 1952):554-556.

Diplomacy and the Borderlands: The Adams-Onis Treaty of 1819 by Philip C. Brooks. *Mississippi Valley Historical Review* 27(December, 1940):465-466.

Felix Grundy, Champion of Democracy by Joseph Howard Parks. *Journal of Southern History* 6(August, 1940):409-411.

Francisco de Ibarra and Nueva Vizcaya by J. Lloyd Mecham. *Southwestern Historical Quarterly* 31(October, 1927):188-190.

George W. Littlefield: Texan by J. Evetts Haley. *Mississippi Valley Historical Review* 30(March, 1944):605-606.

Historical Societies in the United States and Canada: A Handbook compiled and edited by Christopher Crittenden and Doris Godard. *Journal of Southern History* 10(November, 1944):495-498.

Journals of the Fourth Congress of the Republic of Texas, 1839-1840 to which are added the Relief Laws edited by Harriett Smither. 3 volumes. *American Historical Review* 37(October, 1931):133-134.

Mexico and Texas: 1821-1835 by Eugene C. Barker. *Mississippi Valley Historical Review* 16(June, 1929):114-117.

Mirabeau Buonaparte Lamar, Troubadour and Crusader by Herbert Pickens Gambrell. *American Historical Review* 41(October, 1935):198.

Municipality of Brazoria, 1832-1837 prepared by the Historical Records Survey, Works Progress Administration. *Southwestern Historical Quarterly* 41(July, 1937):113-115.

New Mexico History and Cities by Lansing B. Bloom and Thomas C. Donnelly. *Southwestern Historical Quarterly* 37(January, 1934):228-231.

The Papers of Mirabeau Bonaparte Lamar edited by Adams Gulick, Jr. Volume I. *Southwestern Historical Quarterly* 25(July, 1921):76-78.

Readings in Texas History for High Schools and Colleges edited by Eugene C. Barker. *Mississippi Valley Historical Review* 16(December, 1929):424-425.

Rehearsal for Conflict: The War with Mexico, 1846-1848 by Alfred Hoyt Bill. *Mississippi Valley Historical Review* 34(March, 1948):687-688.

Robert E. Lee in Texas by Carl Coke Rister. *Mississippi Valley Historical Review* 33(September, 1946):330-331.

The Romantic Story of Texas by Peter Molyneaux. *Journal of Southern History* 3(August, 1937):370-372.

Sectionalism and Internal Improvements in Tennessee: 1796-1845 by Stanley J. Folmsbee. *Mississippi Valley Historical Review* 27(June, 1940):106-107.

Southern History in the Making: Pioneer Historians of the South by Wendell Holmes Stephenson. *Journal of Southern History* 31(February, 1965):91-94.

Texan Statecraft, 1836-1845 by Joseph William Schmitz. *Mississippi Valley Historical Review* 28(June, 1941):101-102.

The Texas Rangers: A Century of Frontier Defense by Walter Prescott Webb. *Journal of Southern History* 2(August, 1936):419-421.

Texas Republic Postal System: A Brief Story Relating to the Post Office and Postal Markings of the Republic of Texas by Harry M. Konwiser. *Mississippi Valley Historical Review* 21(September, 1934):283-284.

The Western Military Frontier, 1815-1846: A Dissertation in History by Henry Putney Beers. *Mississippi Valley Historical Review* 23(June, 1936):102-103.

Writing Southern History: Essays in Historiography in Honor of Fletcher M. Green edited by Arthur S. Link and Rembert W. Patrick. *Journal of Southern History* 32(August, 1966):368-370.

The Writings of Sam Houston, 1813-1863 edited by Amelia W. Williams and Eugene C. Barker. Volume I. *Journal of Southern History* 5(May, 1939):259-261; Volume II. *Journal of Southern History* 6(May, 1940):268-270; Volume III. *Journal of Southern History* 7(February, 1941):111-112; Volume IV. *Journal of Southern History* 7(August, 1941):408-409; Volumes V-VI. *Journal of Southern History* 8(May, 1942):270-271; Volumes VII-VIII. *Journal of Southern History* 9(November, 1943):572-574.

Studies of William C. Binkley

Ashford, Gerald. Review of *The Texas Revolution* by William C. Binkley. San Antonio *Express*, September 14, 1952.

Barker, Eugene C. Review of *The Expansionist Movement in Texas, 1836-1850* by William C. Binkley. *American Historical Review* 31(January, 1926):366-367.

_________. Review of *Official Correspondence of the Texan Revolution, 1835-1836* edited by William C. Binkley. *Southwestern Historical Quarterly* 40(April, 1937):336-338.

Billington, Ray Allen. Review of *The Texas Revolution* by William C. Binkley. *Mississippi Valley Historical Review* 39(December, 1952):557.

Binkley, William C., Papers. University Libraries, Vanderbilt University, Nashville, Tennessee.

Carroll, H. Bailey. Review of *The Texas Revolution* by William C. Binkley. *American Historical Review* 58(July, 1953):1014.

Christian, A. K. Review of *The Expansionist Movement in Texas, 1836-1850* by William C. Binkley. *Southwestern Historical Quarterly* 29(October, 1925):159-160.

Frantz, Joe B. Review of *The Texas Revolution* by William C. Binkley. Dallas *Morning News*, January 11, 1953.

_________. Review of *The Texas Revolution* by William C. Binkley. *Southwestern Historical Quarterly* 56(January, 1953):472-473.

H., W. R. "William Campbell Binkley, 1889-1970." *Philosophical Society of Texas Proceedings* 34(1971):47.

Henry, Robert S. Review of *The Texas Revolution* by William C. Binkley. *Journal of Southern History* 19(February, 1953):87-89.

"Historical News and Notices: Deaths." *Journal of Southern History* 36(June, 1971):645.

Nance, J. Milton. "A Dedication to the Memory of William Campbell Binkley, 1889-1970." *Arizona and the West* 23(Winter, 1981):313-314.

"Obituaries." *Journal of Southern History* 58(June, 1971):260.

Owsley, Frank L. Review of *The Texas Revolution* by William C. Binkley. *Tennessee Historical Quarterly* 12(June, 1953):185-186.

Richardson, Rupert N. Review of *Official Correspondence of the Texan Revolution, 1835-1836* edited by William C. Binkley. *Journal of Southern History* 3(May, 1937):220-222.

Swint, Henry L. "William Campbell Binkley, 1889-1970: Historian, Editor, Teacher." *Journal of Southern History* 37(August, 1971):353-366.

10

HERBERT EUGENE BOLTON

by David J. Langum

Biography

The rural Midwest has produced more than its share of celebrated historians. Such names as Hubert Howe Bancroft (Granville, Ohio), Carl L. Becker (Blackhawk County, Iowa), and James Willard Hurst (Rockford, Illinois) alone confirm this. It is, therefore, a matter of note, but not great surprise, that the hilly woodlands of south central Wisconsin gave birth to not one but two of the greatest of American historians. Frederick Jackson Turner was born in 1861 in the small town of Portage. Herbert Eugene Bolton came into the world July 30, 1870, on an eighty-acre farm along a wooded ridge between Tomah and Wilton, less than ten years after Turner and only one hundred miles to the northwest.

The regularity of life on the farms and in the small midwestern towns close to the land produced habits and attitudes of stability, clarity of vision, and industry. At least this was once true. When these traits combined with the mental acuity and inquisitiveness needed to raise an outlook beyond the farmland provincial, the resulting accomplishments were spectacular. These rural scholars often traveled far beyond the geographic borders of the Midwest, to the great universities of the East or to California.

Bolton was a product of both new and old American lineages. His father, Edwin, was a native of Leeds, England, and had immigrated as a youth with Bolton's grandfather. His mother, Rosaline, traced her ancestry to the Mayflower. She was the daughter of a Methodist minister and had received a formal education. Edwin's schooling had ended when he was about fifteen, although he continued a rugged, serious self-education throughout his life. Herbert was one of eight children who survived to maturity.

Education was stressed in Bolton's childhood, along with the usual duties of rural youth--planting, harvesting, and all the other farm chores. Until Herbert began at Tomah High School, his learning was under his father's tutelage. It was more than an adequate preparation as he became the class valedictorian. By graduation both Herbert and Frederick, an extremely close older brother, had decided to become teachers. At what level and in what field was still to be determined.

Funds were a serious problem, however. Herbert's father died at the beginning of his high school years. Following Herbert's graduation from Tomah High School in 1889, he and Frederick began a pattern of alternating education with work. One would work as a high school teacher or principal to help finance the other's university studies for a year or two, and also gather additional funds for his own education. Then they would reverse positions. In this manner the two brothers achieved their university degrees, but this necessary process explains Herbert Bolton's somewhat delayed entry into the world of scholarship.

Bolton enrolled in the State Normal School at Milwaukee and graduated in June, 1891, with a teacher's certificate. Then there was an interlude of work as principal of the Fairchild, Wisconsin, High School. He entered the University of Wisconsin in the fall of 1893, taking courses from such leading historians as Charles Homer Haskins and Frederick Jackson Turner.

1895 was a momentous year. Bolton's bachelor's degree came to hand in June, just weeks before his twenty-fifth birthday. Later that summer he married Gertrude Janes of Tunnel City, Wisconsin, a sweetheart for a number of years and an acquaintance since high school. Also, in 1895, he determined on history as a field and the highest level, requiring a doctorate, as his objective.

But first there was another period of financial recoupment, and in the academic year 1895-1896 Bolton served as principal of the Kaukauna, Wisconsin, High School. He also began to work in absentia on a master's program through the University of Wisconsin, and was in residence during 1896-1897. The first of Bolton's seven children arrived on January 26, 1897. Money, tight before that, was now a prime consideration. Bolton had been working with Turner and had wished to complete the doctorate under his direction. However, the University of Pennsylvania offered a better financial inducement, a fellowship with the munificent sum of $600. It was for this reason that Bolton earned his doctorate from Pennsylvania under John Bach McMaster in May, 1899. Bolton was just short of twenty-nine years of age.

Herbert Bolton's first postdoctoral teaching began where he had earlier begun his own postsecondary education, State Normal School at Milwaukee. He worked there for two years, teaching economics, civics, and European history. A major break came with an offer from the University of Texas to replace an ailing history professor with the additional prospect of a permanent position.

Bolton's years at Texas, fall 1901 to spring 1909, were crucial. They saw the development of his interest in the Spanish settlement and exploration of Texas, his early research in the archives of Mexico, and the publication of his first major articles and his first book. One article, "Some Materials for Southwestern History in the Archivo General de Mexico," published in the *Quarterly* of the Texas State Historical Association (1902), caught the eye of an experienced scholar, J. Franklin Jameson. Jameson was then preparing a series of books under the auspices of the Carnegie Institution, designed to survey those contents of foreign archives bearing on the history of the United States. He commissioned Bolton to write the renowned *Guide to Materials for the History of the United States in the Principal Archives of Mexico* (1913). The publication of this book established Bolton as the nationally recognized master of the history of the southwestern region of the United States during the time of the Spanish domination.

Then young Stanford University called Bolton in 1908 and he began there in the fall of 1909, now with the rank of full professor and a mission to take charge of the field of the Spanish history of the Southwest. In the summer of 1910, two tempting offers were placed before Bolton: the headship of the Department of History at Texas and a professorship at the University of California. He accepted the Berkeley professorship, influenced primarily by the excellence of California's Bancroft Library, the leading American collection in his field, and also by his wife's strong dislike of the Texas climate.

Bolton began at the University of California in the fall of 1911 and remained there until his first "retirement" in spring, 1940. Most of his major publications date from this period. The graduation of the first of numerous doctoral progeny was at California, in 1912, although he had turned out some masters at Texas and Stanford. Bolton rose to head of department at California, and it was here that he became a widely acclaimed teacher and developed his famous pan-American course, History of the Americas.

After his retirement in 1940 Bolton collaborated with the National Park Service to commemorate the historical aspects of their domains. However, the wartime shortage of teachers at California prompted his recall to teaching duty, and Bolton again taught at Berkeley, from January, 1942, until his second and final retirement in March, 1944. Neither retirement meant much slackening of Bolton's creative pace. He retained his university office throughout and continued his scholarly publications. His final book, the Escalante work, *Pageant in the Wilderness*, was published in 1950, the year he turned eighty. By that time, however, he was slowing down from a lifetime of hectic scholarly activity. In June, 1952, while working at his desk at the University of California, Bolton suffered a stroke. After a temporary recovery of short duration, a series of subsequent strokes proved fatal. Herbert Eugene Bolton died on January 30, 1953.

Two further personal traits must be recorded. Those are his dedicated devotion to scholarship, largely to the exclusion of other interests, including family, and his incredible capacity for work. Sundays were given over to wife and children, and included many outings throughout the Bay Area in the family Hupmobile. Sometimes Bolton spent Saturdays on family affairs as well. Around the house he was utterly undomesticated and with no mechanical abilities whatsoever.

His wife, Gertrude, burdened with seven children to raise (six girls, one boy) without much help from her spouse, may be entitled to academic sainthood for tolerating Bolton's absorption in his work. Bolton typically worked a full day at the University, and was then picked up by his wife for dinner around 6:00. He thereafter drove himself back to his office around 8:00, quite regularly working until 11:00 or midnight. At times he was trapped overnight by newly employed janitors who did not realize that one of their duties was to chase Bolton out before locking the building at midnight. Whether this engrossed immersion in scholarship by a father of seven is good or bad, it is a fact that Bolton's many accomplishments are due in large measure to a tolerance and selfless support from his wife.

Themes

The three hallmarks of Bolton's writings are their exciting, adventuresome qualities, especially in the narrative, introductory volumes, their direct reliance on archival manuscripts, and finally, their feeling and tone of authoritativeness. The first of these distinguishing features, the reader's excitement, depends on vivid writing, and Bolton developed this quality early in his career. His 1921 *Spanish Borderlands* volume had been heavily edited by his publisher to achieve a lighter and more readable style. Bolton learned a lesson and wrote his later books, especially *Outpost of Empire* (1931) and the biographies of Kino (1936) and Coronado (1949), with a light unpedantic touch. The second cachet, reliance on archival research, derives from Bolton's extensive work in the Mexican archives where he personally uncovered so many documents from the Spanish colonial period.

The third hallmark is the authoritative tone to Bolton's writings. This quality comes to the reader gradually, and by means of the footnotes. The notes to the translations of the diaries of exploration, the narrative introductions, and the biographies are not tangential, arcane observations. The great majority of them are notes specifically identifying the location of the action being described--where de Anza ran into a terrible storm, where Kino baptized particular Indians, where Coronado skirmished with a certain tribe. Often the location is given in terms of the modern county, the distance and direction from today's village, road, or other landmark.

This detailed specificity accumulatively assures the reader that Bolton as editor or author is in absolute command of the manuscript and the geography. This is particularly true of his later writing and editing, on the de Anza, Kino, Coronado, and Escalante accounts. The explanation for this is quite simple. Bolton personally retraced the expeditions of these missionaries and explorers on the ground, by automobile where possible, by burro where necessary. He identified the landmarks mentioned in the diaries and knew them directly, not as mere words read in a library, and he shares this with his readers through numerous references.

Analysis

The term "Spanish Borderlands" is today a historical commonplace. It refers broadly to those positions of the United States which were once under Spanish domination, but with a special connotation of such portions of the American Southwest. It is not a narrow or rigid term, and its historical meaning comfortably embraces the later Mexican control of the same region. When the unity of historical study requires it, the Spanish Borderlands are readily extended beyond the international border into northern Mexico.

Herbert E. Bolton virtually defined the Spanish Borderlands as a distinct field for historical study. The term itself is derived from the title of one of his books, *The Spanish Borderlands: A Chronicle of Old Florida and the Southwest* (1921). But the creation of this distinctive field was far more than a mere definition. Bolton made the field by dint of hard efforts and archival discoveries, themselves comparable to the exertions and findings of the early Spanish explorers about whom he wrote so many accounts.

Bolton labored extensively in the Mexican archives and unearthed many manuscripts of early Spanish exploration which had previously been unknown, lost, or thought nonexistent. He encouraged his students to do likewise. Bolton himself made numerous transcripts and photostats of manuscript collections, both in Mexican and Spanish archives, and urged students to emulate his example. These copies were then added to the riches of the Bancroft Library at the University of California, over which Bolton presided as director in addition to his professorial duties. One of Bolton's primary accomplishments as a historian was to acquaint the profession with these overlooked treasures.

Throughout his career Bolton mined these archival lodes. They served as the source material for the bulk of Bolton's publications: the translation and editing of diaries of exploration kept by notable Spanish missionaries and explorers such as Juan Bautista de Anza, Francisco Vásquez de Coronado, Fray Juan Crespi, Fray Eusebio Francisco Kino, and many others. From the same materials he wrote biographies, such as those of Kino and Coronado, and published extensive historical introductions, such as in Fray Francisco Palóu's *Historical Memoirs of New California* (1926).

Often the narrative introductions preceding multivolume works, such as the Palóu set or the five-volume collection of diaries titled *Anza's California Expeditions* (1930), were so extensive and intrinsically interesting that Bolton published them as separate volumes. One of Bolton's most popular and enduring books is his *Outpost of Empire: The Story of the Founding of San Francisco* (1931). This narrative account of the de Anza expeditions first appeared as the introductory volume of the five-volume set.

Bolton was as successful in his teaching as in his scholarship. His undergraduate course, History of the Americas, regularly drew over a thousand students. His graduate students, although obviously fewer in numbers, prized him even more. In his seminars Bolton was warm and encouraging, always enthusiastic. His consuming interest in history was infectious, and Bolton guided 104 students to their doctorates, and perhaps twice that many to master's degrees.

Bolton's graduates spread throughout the nation and thought so much of him that they presented him with two separate *festschrifts*. The first was published in 1932, and the second came in 1945. A second *festschrift* is highly unusual, if not unique, but was almost compelled because of the length of Bolton's career and the large number of students he had guided. Bolton had turned sixty-two in the year of his first *festschrift* in 1932. Between then and 1945 forty-nine more of his students achieved doctorates, of whom twenty-six contributed essays in the second *festschrift*.

As a historian Bolton has been criticized from two different and somewhat contradictory perspectives. The first charge is that Bolton concerned himself with narrow, almost antiquarian, projects. He translated and edited documents, primarily diaries of Spanish soldiers and missionaries, and neglected analytical effort. In short, so the criticism goes, Bolton provided little conceptual meaning to the documents he unearthed from the archives; there was no synthesis.

Ironically, the second critical perspective concedes that Bolton did synthesize rather grandly, but charges that his analysis was wrong. This involves a critique of the so-called Bolton thesis, which Bolton himself never claimed, concerning commonality in the history of the Americas. This theory is said by critics to hold that the various national histories of the American nations, north, south, and central, are but parts of a unified history. An example would be to view the American revolt from England and the Latin American revolutions from Spain as being all segments of a larger picture of the separation of the American continents from Europe.

The two criticisms appear to be mutually exclusive, yet one writer, John Higham, in *History, The Development of Historical Studies in the United States* (1965), attempted to join them together:

> He [Bolton] attracted many students into research on Spanish soldiers and missionaries in the borderlands, where Spanish settlement impinged on that of other empires. Those studies gave Bolton the idea that all of the Americas have a unitary history shaped by common experience. Every year he preached this pan-Americanism to a thousand students in his course on the History of the Americas, and his numerous disciples took up the refrain. Bolton lacked the analytical ability to make his concept fruitful; he gave a specious appearance of significance to a program of fragmentary research (quoted in *Herbert Eugene Bolton: The Historian and the Man*, p. 188).

Of these two critiques, lack of analytical writing as one and unity of pan-American history as the second, the former is more justified than the latter. Bolton *did* spend most of his scholarly energies in translating and editing, and it is true that these efforts were, in the main, confined to Spanish soldiers and missionaries, and in their roles as explorers. Even his very sympathetic biographer and former student, John Francis Bannon, seems sensitive to this issue. In his excellent study, *Herbert Eugene Bolton: The Historian and the Man* (1978), Bannon claims that Bolton often planned to write analytical essays, "to sit back and isolate a theme running through his pioneering factual researchings and highlight the institution. But as time passed, he found so many basic Southwestern stories untold and in need of telling that he never quite had time for that job" (p. 108).

In truth, however, Bolton neither ignored nor deprecated analysis or synthesis. He himself penned two very fine interpretive essays, "The Mission as a Frontier Institution in the Spanish-American Colonies," (1917) and "Defensive Spanish Expansion and the Significance of the Borderlands" (1930). He subsequently published these and two other essays as *Wider Horizons of American History* (1939). Still, it is a matter of regret that Bolton left behind so little work describing the larger significance and contours of the separate field of historical study he almost single-handedly opened up and defined. With this reservation, Bannon's biographical conclusion is sound:

> He felt that it was the job of some historians, pioneers particularly, to furnish the facts by dint of consistent and careful probings into the archives. He devoted himself to this aspect of his craft. He was not unaware of the value and need for interpretive history. . . . (H)e showed his skill in this kind of history writing. . . . But primarily he went on to the end looking for more and new facts to enlighten his favorite pasts. He did not feel that being able to tell an historically sound and fulsome story was in anywise demeaning (p. 256).

The second criticism, challenging the so-called Bolton theory, attacks a straw man, since Bolton never had any "common history of the Americas" theory. The idea for Bolton having had such a thesis is derived from two disconnected sources. One was Bolton's personal participation in many pan-American historical conferences and Latin American historical causes in the late 1930s and early 1940s. Another was his 1932 presidential address before the American Historical Association meeting in Toronto. The first can be answered quickly: Bolton's personal interest in pan-American scholarship was motivated more by his belief in the contemporary Good Neighbor Policy toward Latin America than by his scholarly views of any commonality of past history.

In the Toronto speech Bolton came close to expressing the historical unity of the Americas the critics have attacked. At one point, according to Lewis Hanke, Bolton declared, in the context of a discussion of colonialism and independence:

> Our national historians, especially in the United States, are prone to write of these broad phases of American history as though they were applicable to one country alone. It is my purpose, by a few bold strokes, to suggest that *they are but phases common to most portions of the entire Western Hemisphere;* that each local story will have clearer meaning when studied in the light of the others; and that much of what has been written of each national history is but a thread out of a larger strand (*Do the Americans Have a Common History?*, p. 69; emphasis added).

In context, however, Bolton meant little more than that historians should not wear national blinders. Some topics can and should be studied on a hemispheric scale rather than from within sovereign borders. He mentioned as possibilities such disparate topics as "the history of shipbuilding and commerce, mining, Christian missions, Indian policies, slavery and emancipation, constitutional development, arbitration, the effects of the Indian on European cultures, the rise of the common man, art, architecture, literature, or science" (pp. 99-100). But the main point was merely to stimulate national historians to write in a context broader than that defined by national boundaries. Indeed, at the end of his speech Bolton expressed a "wish to repeat with emphasis that I do not propose such a synthesis as a substitute for, but as a setting in which to place, any one of our national histories" (p. 99).

In particular, Bolton was critical of many American historians' attitudes that American history began at Jamestown in 1607, and consisted essentially of the spread of Anglo-American culture across the continent. Such an approach ignored the efforts and accomplishments of the other nationalities, including Bolton's Spanish explorers, missionaries, and colonists, who arrived earlier and in many respects achieved greater triumphs than the English. Thus, he charged that "in my own country the study of thirteen English colonies and the United States in isolation has obscured many of the larger factors in their development, and helped to raise up a nation of chauvinists" (p. 68).

Bolton was correct in his accusation. The charge still rings true in that American historical studies at the secondary and collegiate levels excessively emphasize the English colonies and almost ignore the French in the Midwest and along the Mississippi and the Spanish in Florida and the Southwest. It is a splendid example of historical presentism to treat the early English colonies as more "important" than the early Spanish colonies simply because the English colonies thereafter in some sense "prevailed."

Be all this as it may, a call for hemispheric context is not a theory of historical unity. Critics of the Bolton theory have attacked a thesis he never uttered and never claimed.

These criticisms amount to very little alongside Bolton's accomplishments. Of course, many American historians had used foreign archives before Bolton. However, he was the first to point out the wealth of materials located in Mexico, and their utility for studying the Spanish activities that took place on lands now within the United States. Few American historians have had so great an influence on graduate students, attracting so many and creating a school with so distinctive a stamp. In this achievement Bolton ranks second only to Turner. Probably no historian has so deeply authenticated his scholarship by field work than Bolton. The reliability of his locations and landmarks through personal tracings of his subjects' trails is manifest in his writing.

Most distinctive of Bolton's accomplishments is his creation of the Spanish Borderlands as a separate historical field. Invention, it has been said, is the finding of a need and the filling of it. Certainly Bolton found the need in his discovery of a significant lacuna in American history, the period of Spanish and Mexican domination. The work of filling that need, of writing all the narrative and analytical histories, political, social, and legal, of that period, is an ongoing task. But Bolton did more than simply describe the job to be done. In his archival unearthings, training of students, and numerous documentary translations and editings, Herbert Eugene Bolton dominated, and to this date continues to dominate posthumously, the very undertaking of the task he defined.

Bibliography

Of the books listed in this bibliography, only the original issues, not reprint editions, are included. Nonetheless, there is some overlap as Bolton frequently published the introductory volume of a set of documentary translation as an independent book as well as the first volume of a set. Since these would both be original editions, both are indicated here.

Books

Anza's California Expeditions. 5 volumes. Berkeley: University of California Press, 1930.

Arredondo's Historical Proof of Spain's Title to Georgia :A Contribution to the History of One of the Spanish Borderlands. Berkeley: University of California Press, 1925.

Athanase de Mézières and the Louisiana-Texas Frontier, 1768-1780. 2 volumes. Cleveland: Clark, 1914.

California's Story. Co-authored with Ephraim D. Adams. Boston: Allyn and Bacon, 1922.

The Colonization of North America, 1492-1783. Co-authored with Thomas M. Marshall. New York: Macmillan, 1920.

Coronado, Knight of Pueblos and Plains. New York: Whittlesey House, 1949.

Coronado on the Turquoise Trail, Knight of Pueblos and Plains. Albuquerque: University of New Mexico Press, 1949.

Cross, Sword and Gold Pan. Los Angeles: Primavera Press, 1936.

The Debatable Land: A Sketch of the Anglo-Spanish Contest for the Georgia Country. Co-authored with Mary Ross. Berkeley: University of California Press, 1925.

Font's Complete Diary: A Chronicle of the Founding of San Francisco. Berkeley: University of California Press, 1931.

Fray Juan Crespi, Missionary Explorer on the Pacific Coast, 1769-1774. Berkeley: University of California Press, 1927.

Guide to Materials for the History of the United States in the Principal Archives of Mexico. Washington, DC: Carnegie Institution of Washington, 1913.

Historical Memoirs of New California, by Fray Francisco Palóu. Editor. 4 volumes. Berkeley: University of California Press, 1926.

History of the Americas: A Syllabus with Maps. Boston: Ginn and Co., 1928.

Kino's Historical Memoir of Pimería Alta: A Contemporary Account of the Beginnings of California, Sonora, and Arizona, by Father Eusebio Francisco Kino, S. J., Pioneer Missionary Explorer, Cartographer, and Ranchman, 1683-1711. 2 volumes. Cleveland: Clark, 1919.

Outpost of Empire: The Story of the Founding of San Francisco. New York: Knopf, 1931.

A Pacific Coast Pioneer. Berkeley: University of California Press, 1927.

The Pacific Ocean in History. Co-edited with Henry M. Stephens. New York: Macmillan, 1917.

The Padre on Horseback: A Sketch of Eusebio Francisco Kino, S.J., Apostle to the Pimas. San Francisco: Sonora Press, 1932.

Pageant in the Wilderness: The Story of the Escalante Expedition to the Interior Basin, Including the Diary and Itinerary of Father Escalante. Salt Lake City: Utah State Historical Society, 1950.

Palóu and His Writings. Berkeley: University of California Press, 1926.

Rim of Christendom: A Biography of Eusebio Francisco Kino, Pacific Coast Pioneer. New York: Macmillan, 1936.

The Spanish Borderlands: A Chronicle of Old Florida and the Southwest. New Haven: Yale University Press, 1921.

Spanish Exploration in the Southwest, 1542-1706. New York: Charles Scribner's Sons, 1916.

Texas in the Middle Eighteenth Century: Studies in Spanish Colonial History and Administration. Berkeley: University of California Press, 1915.

Wider Horizons of American History. New York: Appleton-Century, 1939.

With the Makers of Texas: A Source Reader in Texas History. Co-edited with Eugene C. Barker. New York: American Book Company, 1904.

Articles

"The Admission of California." *University of California Chronicle* 15(October, 1913):554-566.

"Affairs in the Philipinas Islands, by Fray Domingo de Salazar," [1583]. Translator. In *The Philippine Islands, 1493-1803* edited by Emma Helen Blair and James Alexander Robertson. 55 volumes. Cleveland: Arthur H. Clark, 1903-1909. 5:210-255.

"Anza Crosses the Sand Dunes." *Touring Topics* 23(May, 1931):7.

"Archives and Trails." *California Monthly* 37(October, 1936):19, 40-42.

"The Beginnings of Mission Nuestra Señora del Refugio." *Southwestern Historical Quarterly* 19(April, 1916):400-404.

"The Black Robes of New Spain." *Catholic Historical Review* 21(October, 1935):257-282.

"The Capitulation at Cahuenga." *Touring Topics* 23(November, 1931):7.

"Coming of the Cattle." *Touring Topics* 23(March, 1931):7.

"Coronado Discovers Zuñi." *Touring Topics* 23(January, 1931):8.

"Cultural Cooperation with Latin America." National Education Association *Journal* 29(January, 1940):1-4. Reprint. *Hispanic-American Historical Review* 20(February, 1940):3-11; *International Quarterly* 4(Autumn, 1940):21-24, 59; *Southwest Review* 25(January, 1940):115-125.

"'De los Mapas.'" Texas State Historical Association, *Quarterly* 6(July, 1902):69-70.

"Defensive Spanish Expansion and the Significance of the Borderlands." In *The Trans-Mississippi West* edited by James F. Willard and Colin B. Goodykoontz. Boulder: University of Colorado, 1930. Pp. 1-42.

"Description of the Philipinas Islands," [1618]. Translator. In *The Philippine Islands, 1493-1803* edited by Emma Helen Blair and James Alexander Robertson. 55 volumes. Cleveland: Arthur H. Clark, 1903-1909. 18:93-106.

Dictionary of American Biography. Articles on Juan Rodríguez Cabrillo, García López de Cárdenas, Francisco Vázquez Coronado, Juan Crespi, Eusebio Francisco Kino, Athanase de Mézières y Clugny, and Francisco Palóu. 20 volumes. New York: Scribner's, 1928-1936.

Dictionary of American History. Articles on "Alta California," "California, Russians in," "California, Spanish Exploration of," "California Missions," "California under Mexico," and "California under Spain." 6 volumes. New York: Scribner's, 1940.

"The Early Explorations of Father Garcés on the Pacific Slope." In *The Pacific Ocean in History* edited by Henry Morse Stephens and Herbert Eugene Bolton. New York: Macmillan, 1917. Pp. 317-330.

"The Epic of Greater America." *American Historical Review* 38(April, 1933):448-474.

"Escalante Way--An Opportunity for the National Park Service." In *American Planning and Civic Annual* edited by Harlean James. Washington, DC: American Planning and Civic Association, 1939. Pp. 266-273.

"Events in the Filipinas Islands, from the month of June, 1617, until the Present Date in 1618." Translator. In *The Philippine Islands, 1493-1803* edited by Emma Helen Blair and James Alexander Robertson.55 volumes. Cleveland: Arthur H. Clark, 1903-1909. 18:65-92.

"Expedition to San Francisco Bay in 1770: Diary of Pedro Fages." Editor and Translator. *Academy of Pacific Coast History Publications* 2(July, 1911):141-159.

"Father Escobar's Relation of the Oñate Expedition to California." Editor and Translator. *Catholic Historical Review* 5(April, 1919):19-41.

"Father Kino's Lost History, Its Discovery and Its Value." *Bibliographical Society of America Papers* 6(1911):9-34.

"The Founding of Mission Rosario: A Chapter in the History of the Gulf Coast." *Texas State Historical Association Quarterly* 10(October, 1906):113-139.

"The Founding of San Diegò Mission." *Touring Topics* 23(April, 1931):7.

"The Founding of the Missions on the San Gabriel River, 1745-1749." *Southwestern Historical Quarterly* 17(April, 1914):323-378.

"Francis Drake's Plate of Brass." In *Drake's Plate of Brass: Evidence of His Visit to California in 1579*. San Francisco: California Historical Society, 1937. Pp. 1-16.

"Fremont Crosses the Sierra." *Touring Topics* 23(October, 1931):7.

"French Intrusions into New Mexico, 1749-1752." In *The Pacific Ocean in History* edited by Henry Morse Stephens and Herbert Eugene Bolton. New York: Macmillan, 1917. Pp. 389-407.

"General James Wilkinson as Advisor to Emperor Iturbide." Editor. *Hispanic American Historical Review* 1(May, 1918):163-180.

"Gold Discovered at Sutter's Mill." *Touring Topics* 23(December, 1931):9.

Handbook of American Indians North of Mexico edited by Frederick Webb Hodge. Over 100 articles on the Indian tribes of Texas and Louisiana. Washington, DC: Government Printing Office, 1907-1910.

"In the South San Joaquin Ahead of Garcés." *California Historical Society Quarterly* 10(September, 1931): 211-219.

"The Iturbide Revolution in the Californias." Editor. *Hispanic American Historical Review* 2(May, 1919): 188-242.

"Jedediah Smith Reaches San Gabriel." *Touring Topics* 23(June, 1931):7.

"The Jesuits in America: An Opportunity for Historians." *Mid-America* 18(October, 1936):223-233.

"José Francisco Ortega." *Grizzly Bear* 38(January, 1926):1.

"Juan Crespi, a California Xenophon." *Touring Topics* 19(July, 1927):23, 48.

"The Jumano Indians in Texas, 1650-1771." *Texas State Historical Association Quarterly* 15(July, 1911):66-84.

"Letter from Francisco de Otaço, S.J., to Father Alonso de Escovar" [1620]. Translator. In *The Philippine Islands, 1493-1803* edited by Emma Helen Blair and James Alexander Robertson. 55 volumes. Cleveland: Arthur H. Clark, 1903-1909. 19:35-39.

"The Location of La Salle's Colony on the Gulf of Mexico." *Mississippi Valley Historical Review* 2(September, 1915):165-182. Reprint. *Southwestern Historical Quarterly* 27(January, 1924):171-189.

"Massanet or Manzanet." *Texas State Historical Association Quarterly* 10(July, 1906):101.

"Material for Southwestern History in the Central Archives of Mexico." *American Historical Review* 13(April, 1908):510-527.

"Mexico, Diplomatic Relations with [the United States, 1821-1914]." In *Cyclopedia of American Government* edited by Andrew Cunningham McLaughlin and Albert Bushnell Hart. New York: Appleton, 1914. 2:422-425.

"The Mission as a Frontier Institution in the Spanish-American Colonies." *American Historical Review* 23(October, 1917):42-61.

"The Mormons in the Opening of the West." *Utah Genealogical and Historical Magazine* 16(January, 1926):40-72.

"The Native Tribes about the East Texas Missions." *Texas State Historical Association Quarterly* 11(April, 1908):249-276.

"New Light on Manuel Lisa and the Spanish Fur Trade." *Southwestern Historical Quarterly* 17(July, 1913):61-66.

"Notes on Clark's 'The Beginnings of Texas.'" Texas State Historical Association, *Quarterly* 12(October, 1908):148-158.

"The Obligation of Nevada toward the Writing of Her Own History." *Nevada Historical Society Third Biennial Report . . ., 1911-1912* (1913):62-79.

"The Old Stone Fort at Nacogdoches." *Texas State Historical Association Quarterly* 9(April, 1906):283-285.

"Oñate in New Mexico." *Touring Topics* 23(February, 1931):8.

"Pack Train and Carreta." *California Monthly* 33(November, 1934):4, 6.

"Papers of Zebulon M. Pike, 1806-1807." Editor. *American Historical Review* 13(July, 1908):798-827.

"Records of the Mission of Nuestra Señora del Refugio." *Texas State Historical Association Quarterly* 14(October, 1910):164-166.

"Relation of Events in the Philipinas Islands and Neighboring Provinces and Kingdoms, from July, 1619, to July, 1620." Translator. In *The Philippine Islands, 1493-1803* edited by Emma Helen Blair and James Alexander Robertson. 55 volumes. Cleveland: Arthur H. Clark, 1903-1909. 19:42-70.

"Relation of the Events in the Filipinas Islands and in the Neighboring Provinces and Realms, from July, 1618, to the Present Date in 1619." Translator. In *The Philippine Islands, 1493-1803* edited by Emma Helen Blair and James Alexander Robertson. 55 volumes. Cleveland: Arthur H. Clark, 1903-1909. 18:204-234.

"Some Materials for Southwestern History in the Archivo General de México." *Texas State Historical Association Quarterly* 6(October, 1902):103-112; 7(January, 1904):196-213.

"The Spanish Abandonment and Re-occupation of East Texas, 1773-1779." *Texas State Historical Association Quarterly* 9(October, 1905):67-137.

"Spanish Activities on the Lower Trinity River, 1746-1771." *Southwestern Historical Quarterly* 16(April, 1913):339-377.

"The Spanish Occupation of Texas, 1519-1690." *Southwestern Historical Quarterly* 16(July, 1912):1-26.

"Spanish Resistance to the Carolina Traders in Western Georgia, 1680-1704." *Georgia Historical Quarterly* 9(June, 1925):115-130.

"Tienda de Cuervo's Ynspección of Laredo, 1757." *Texas State Historical Association Quarterly* 6(January, 1903):187-203.

"Trade between Nueva España and the Far East." [1617]. Translator. In *The Philippine Islands, 1493-1803* edited by Emma Helen Blair and James Alexander Robertson. 55 volumes. Cleveland: Arthur H. Clark, 1903-1909. 18:57-64.

"Trapper Days in Taos." *Touring Topics* 23(July, 1931):7.

"Two Letters to Felipe II," [Gerónimo de Guzmán and Jhoan de Vascones, 1585]. Translator. In *The Philippine Islands, 1493-1803* edited by Emma Helen Blairand James Alexander Robertson. 55 volumes. Cleveland: Arthur H. Clark, 1903-1909. 6:76-80.

"The Writing of California History." *Grizzly Bear* 19(May, 1916):4.

Selected Reviews

A Concise History of New Mexico by B. L. Bradford. *American Historical Review* 21(January, 1916):375.

Die Spanier in Nordaamerika von 1513-1824 by Von Ernst Daenell. *American Historical Review* 17(January, 1912):380-381.

Documentos Históricos Mexicanos: Obra Commemorativa del Primer Centenario de la Independencia de México. La publica el Muséo Nacional de Argueologia, Historia y Etmologia, bajola Dirección by Genaro García. *American Historical Review* 17(April, 1912):640-643.

Don Juan de Palafox y Mendoza, Obispo de Puebla y Osma, Visitador y Virrey de la Nueva España by Genaro García. *American Historical Review* 24(October, 1919):126-128.

Don Juan de Palafox y Mendoza, Su Virranato en la Nueva España, Sus Contiendas con los PP Jesuitas, Sus Partidarious en Puebla, Sus Apariciones, Sus Escritos Esrogidos [Documentos Imeditos o'muy Raros para la Historia de México] edited by Genaro García and Carlos Pereyna. *American Historical Review* 12(January, 1907):425-426.

The Explorers of North America by John Bartlett. *American Historical Review* 40(April, 1935):517.

Historia de Nuevo Leon con Noticias Sobre Coahuila, Téjas y Nuevo México. Por el Capitan Alonzo de Leon, un Auto Anonimo, y el General Fernando Sánchez De Zamora [Documentos Ineditos o'muy Raros para la Historia de México] edited by Genaro García. *American Historical Review* 15(April, 1910):640-642.

The Journey of the Flame: Being An Account of One Year in the Life of Señor Don Juan Obrigón by Antonio de Fierro Blanc, translated by

Walter de Steiguer. *Mississippi Valley Historical Review* 20(March, 1934):581-583.

Juan María de Salvatierra of the Company of Jesus; Missionary in the Province of New Spain, and Apostolic Conqueror of the Californias by Miguel Venegas, translated and edited by Marguerite Eyer Wilbur. *American Historical Review* 35(October, 1929):171-172.

Las Ordines Religiosas de España y la Colonización de América en la Segunda Parte del Siglo XVIII Estadísticas y Documentos Publicados by P. Otto Maas. *American Historical Review* 26(January, 1921):366.

The Leading Facts of New Mexican History, vol. 1, by Ralph Emerson Twitchell. *American Historical Review* 17(April, 1912):636-638.

Missions and Pueblos of the Old Southwest, Their Myths, Legends, Fiestas, and Ceremonies, with some Accounts of the Indian Tribes and Their Dances; and of the Penitentes by Earle R. Forrest. *American Historical Review* 35(April, 1930):681-682.

Spanish Alta California by Alberta Johnson Denis. *Mississippi Valley Historical Review* 14(December, 1927):397-399.

Viajes de Misioneros Franciscanos a la Conquista del Nuevo México by P. Otto Maas. *American Historical Review* 22(January, 1917):447.

Studies of Herbert Eugene Bolton

Bannon, John Francis. "Herbert Eugene Bolton: His *Guide* in the Making." *Southwestern Historical Quarterly* 73(July, 1969):35-55.

_________. *Herbert Eugene Bolton: The Historian and the Man, 1870-1953*. Tucson: University of Arizona Press, 1978.

_________. "Herbert Eugene Bolton--Western Historian." *Western Historical Quarterly* 2(July, 1971):261-282.

_________., ed. *Bolton and the Spanish Borderlands*. Norman: University of Oklahoma Press, 1964.

Binkley, William C., Cardinal Goodwin, and J. Fred Rippy, eds. *New Spain and the Anglo-American West: Historical Contributions Presented to Herbert Eugene Bolton*. Vol. 2. Los Angeles: n.p., 1932.

Bolton, Frederick E. "The Early Life of Herbert E. Bolton: From Random Memories of an Admiring Brother." *Arizona and the West* 4(1962):65-73.

Carew, Harold D. "Bolton of Bancroft." *Touring Topics* 20(November, 1928):28-30, 40.

Caughey, John Walton. "Dedication to Herbert Eugene Bolton." *Arizona and the West* 1(Summer, 1959):102-104.

_________. "Herbert Eugene Bolton." *Pacific Historical Review* 9(April, 1953):108-112.

_________. "Herbert Eugene Bolton." In *Turner, Bolton,and Webb - Three Historians of the American Frontier* by Wilbur R. Jacobs, John W. Caughey, and Joe B. Frantz. Seattle: University of Washington Press, 1965. Pp. 41-74.

Cleland, Robert G. Review of *Coronado on the Turquoise Trail, Knights of Pueblos and Plains* by Herbert E. Bolton. *American Historical Review* 55(October, 1950):948.

Cox, Isaac Joslin. Review of *Athanase de Mézières and the Louisiana-Texas Frontier, 1768-1870* by Herbert E. Bolton. *American Historical Review* 20(February, 1915):168.

_________. Review of *Guide to Materials for the History of the United States in the Principal Archives of Mexico* by Herbert E. Bolton. *American Historical Review* 19(June, 1914):638.

Crane, Verner W. Review of *Arrendondo's Historical Proof of Spain's Title to Georgia: A Contribution to the History of One of the Spanish Borderlands* by Herbert E. Bolton. *American Historical Review* 26(June, 1921):540.

_________. Review of *The Debatable Land: A Sketch of the Anglo-Spanish Contest for the Georgia Country* by Herbert E. Bolton. *American Historical Review* 31(February, 1926):176.

"Deceased: Herbert Eugene Bolton." *American Historical Review* 58(April, 1953):791-792.

Dunn, William Edward. "Portrait of a Teacher: Herbert Eugene Bolton." *The Alcalde* 42(November, 1953):54-56.

Emery, Edwin. "Bolton of California." *California Monthly* 47(September, 1941):12-13, 39-43.

Escudero, Carlos R. "Historian in Action--An Historical Adventure Story." *California Monthly* 47(September, 1941):14-16, 43-44.

Friend, Llerena B. "Herbert Eugene Bolton and the Texas State Library." *Texas Libraries* 35(Summer, 1973):48-64.

Gilbert, Hope Elizabeth. "He Followed the Trails of the Desert Padres." *Desert Magazine* 13(July, 1950):27-31.

Griffith, William J. "Herbert Eugene Bolton." *Mississippi Valley Historical Review* 46(January, 1953):185-186.

Hackett, Charles W., George P. Hammond, and J. Lloyd Mecham, eds. *New Spain and the Anglo-American West: Historical Contributions Presented to Herbert Eugene Bolton.* Vol. 1. Los Angeles: n.p., 1932.

Hammond, George Peter. "In Memoriam: Herbert Eugene Bolton." *The Americas* 9(April, 1953):391-398.

Hanke, Lewis, ed. *Do the Americas Have a Common History? A Critique of the Bolton Theory*. New York: Knopf, 1964.

Healey, Miriam. "Great Historical Sketches: Herbert Eugene Bolton." *The Pacific Historian* 13(Summer, 1969):76-78.

Hodge, Frederick W. Review of *Kino's Historical Memoir of Pimeria Alta: A Contemporary Account of the Beginnings of California, Sonora, and Arizona, by Father Eusebio Francisco Kino, S. J., Pioneer Missionary, Explorer, Cartographer, and Ranchman, 1683-1711* by Herbert E. Bolton. *American Historical Review* 26(April, 1921):340.

Hunt, Rockwell, D. "Herbert Eugene Bolton: An Appreciation." *Bancroftiana* Issue No. 8(May, 1953):1-2.

Jacobsen, Jerome V. "Herbert E. Bolton." *Mid-America* 24(April, 1953):75-80.

Kinnaird, Lawrence. "Bolton of California." California Historical Society *Quarterly* 32(June, 1953):97-103.

_________. "Our Distinguished Faculty: Professor Herbert E. Bolton." *California Monthly* 61(February, 1951):16, 30-31.

Lockwood, Frank C. "Adventurous Scholarship." *Catholic World* 188(November, 1932):185-194.

Magnaghi, Russell M. "Herbert E. Bolton and Sources for American Indian Studies." *Western Historical Quarterly* 6(January, 1975):33-46.

Ogden, Adele, and Engel Sluiter, eds. *Greater America: Essays in Honor of Herbert Eugene Bolton.* Berkeley: University of California Press, 1945.

Parish, John C. Review of *Anza's California Expeditions. American Historical Review* 36(October, 1931):839.

Powell, Lawrence Clark. "California Classics Reread: *Anza's California Expeditions.*" *Westways* 61(October, 1969):24-27, 43.

Rippy, J. Fred. "Herbert Eugene Bolton: A Recollection." *Southwest Review* 39(Spring, 1954):166-171.

_________. Review of *Outpost of Empire: The Story of the Founding of San Francisco* by Herbert E. Bolton. *Pacific Historical Review* 1(November, 1932):494.

Robertson, James Alexander. Review of *The Spanish Borderlands: A Chronicle of Old Florida and the Southwest* by Herbert E. Bolton. *American Historical Review* 27(June, 1922):580.

Ross, Mary. "Writings and Cartography of Herbert Eugene Bolton." In *New Spain and the Anglo-American West: Historical Contributions Presented to Herbert Eugene Bolton* edited by William C. Binkley, Cardinal Goodwin, and J. Fred Rippy. Volume 2. Los Angeles: n.p., 1932.

Shepherd, William R. Review of *The Pacific Ocean in History* edited by Herbert E. Bolton and Henry M. Stephens. *American Historical Review* 22(October, 1917):846.

Thomas, Alfred Barnaby. Review of *The Padre on Horseback: A Sketch of Eusebio Francisco Kino, S.J., Apostle to the Pimas* by Herbert E. Bolton. *Pacific Historical Review* 2(November, 1933):454.

Treutlein, Theodore E. "Necrologias: Herbert Eugene Bolton (1870-1953)." *Revista de História de América* 37-38(January-December, 1954):299-302.

11

BEVERLEY W. BOND, JR.

by Andrew R. L. Cayton

Biography

The great contribution of Beverley W. Bond, Jr., was the collection of information about the history of the Ohio frontier in the eighteenth and early nineteenth centuries. His meticulous and authoritative works, particularly *The Civilization of the Old Northwest* (1934), remain indispensable starting places for students of the settlement of the region north of the Ohio River.

Beverley Bond's early life contained little to suggest that he would become a historian of the Midwest. The son of a minister, he was born in Blacksburg, Virginia, on July 31, 1878. After attending Randolph Macon College, from which he received a B.A. in 1900 and an M.A. in 1901, Bond's interest in history took him to Johns Hopkins University in Baltimore, Maryland. Johns Hopkins had been a pioneer in developing intensive training for professional historians since its founding in 1876; among its famous graduates were Charles McLean Andrews, John Franklin Jameson, Woodrow Wilson, and Frederick Jackson Turner. Particularly emphasized at Johns Hopkins were a profound respect for the sanctity of primary sources and a scientific approach to historical scholarship. The ideal writer told the unadorned truth as one saw it, without embroidering or moralizing. The lessons Bond learned at Hopkins were never forgotten. As late as 1939, he would praise a historian for resisting the temptation "to draw extensive generalizations. Rather he has presented the facts, with much intelligent running comment, and has left future historians to make elaborate interpretations" *(Mississippi Valley Historical Review* 25:567).

When he received his Ph.D. in history in 1905, Bond faced the difficult task of finding an academic job. He managed to obtain temporary appointments in the history department at the University of Mississippi (1905-1906) and in the English department at Southwestern Presbyterian University (1906-1907). Finally, he landed a job in the history department at Purdue University. Bond stayed in West Lafayette for thirteen years, rising in rank from instructor to associate professor.

The most important change in Bond's career came in 1920 when he left Purdue for the University of Cincinnati. In the Queen City, the middle-aged scholar found his niche, both personally and professionally. He married his wife, Louisa S. Worthington, there in 1933 and became an active member of the Cincinnati Country Club and supporter of cultural institutions such as the Cincinnati Symphony Orchestra. At the university, Bond prospered. Appointed a full professor in 1926, he became department chairman two years later, a position he held until his retirement in 1948.

Involvement in both national and local historical societies took up much of Beverley Bond's time during his tenure at Cincinnati. In the 1920s he became an active member of the recently created Mississippi Valley Historical Society (now the Organization of American Historians). He served on the group's executive committee from 1924 to 1927 and from 1932 to 1938 and was a member of the board of editors of the *Mississippi Valley Historical Review* (now the *Journal of American History*) from 1926 to 1929 and from 1937 to 1938. The high point of his association with the Mississippi Valley Historical Society was his term as the organization's president in 1931.

Locally, Bond had always been interested in the affairs of the Historical and Philosophical Society of Ohio (now the Cincinnati Historical Society), a somewhat moribund group with an extensive collection of papers relating to the history of Cincinnati and the Miami Valley. In 1939, Bond began to devote much of his attention to reviving and improving this organization. Abandoning his interests in national associations, he became curator of the Historical and Philosophical Society in 1939. Three years later, he was elected the group's president and served until 1945, when he declined to run for reelection. During these years, membership increased, progress was made toward finding a home for the group's collections (which were housed in the library of the University of Cincinnati), consolidation and better cataloging of the collections themselves were initiated, and the *Bulletin* (now *The Queen City Heritage*) was established in 1943. After his retirement from the university in 1948, Bond held positions as curator emeritus and professor emeritus until his death on February 1, 1961. His wife, Louisa, preceded him in death by only three months.

Basically, Bond's long scholarly career can be divided into two major periods. The first, running from his years at Johns Hopkins until his arrival at Cincinnati, involved the publication of thorough but uninspired studies of rather traditional political topics like *State Government in Maryland, 1777-1781* (1905) and *The Monroe Mission to France, 1794-1796* (1907). The great achievement of Bond's early career was the publication of *The Quit-Rent System in the American Colonies*, with an introduction by Charles McLean Andrews, by Yale University Press in 1919. This exhaustive study of a somewhat arcane but important topic reflected the character of Bond's mature work. It is impressive in its wealth of information and its thoroughness but limited in analysis and imagination. Influenced heavily by Andrews, Bond's colony-by-colony examination showed that the quit-rent was a feudal charge on land instituted by the Crown in America both to raise revenue and to assert its authority in its colonies. Not surprisingly, the Americans resented the quit-rent. With the American Revolution, their "latent antagonism" became "open hostility." The quit-rent, Bond concludes, was "altogether out of keeping with the increasing spirit of individual freedom" (pp. 459-460). Like most of Bond's works, *The Quit-Rent System in the American Colonies* was a solid, reliable piece of scholarship, but it was not especially insightful.

The second major period of Bond's career began with his arrival in Cincinnati in 1920 and continued until his death in 1961. During these forty years, he devoted much of his time to preserving and promoting the early history of the Ohio frontier, especially that of the Miami Valley. By the mid-1920s, Bond was publishing edited materials in the *Mississippi Valley Historical Review* and in the *Publications* of the Historical and Philosophical Society. The most significant of his edited works were *The Correspondence of John Cleves Symmes, Founder of the Miami Purchase* (1926) and *The Intimate Letters of John Cleves Symmes and His Family* (1956). Symmes, a New Jersey judge who purchased hundreds of thousands of acres in the Miami Valley from Congress in the late 1780s, was the dominant figure in the early history of the region. As in all of his works, Bond performed his editorial duties with skill and accuracy. And in the cases of the two Symmes volumes, he provides useful information in brief introductions that today are standard reference works on Symmes and his purchase.

Meanwhile, after extensive research in Europe as well as the United States, Bond published two major works of original scholarship. *The Civilization of the Old Northwest* (1934) is an encyclopedic examination of many aspects of life in the region from the 1780s through the War of 1812. While it lacks the erudition and craft of R. Carlyle Buley's *The Old Northwest: Pioneer Period, 1815-1840*, *The Civilization of the Old Northwest* has become the standard work on its subject. Another book, *The Foundations of Ohio*, published in 1941, was the first volume in a six-volume history of the state of Ohio commissioned and published by the Ohio State Archaeological and Historical Society. Bond provides a reliable narrative of the Ohio settlements in the territorial period as well as an extensive study of British, French, and Anglo-American conflicts in the region before and during the American Revolution. These two books, along with the extensive materials he edited for publication, made Beverley W. Bond, Jr., a leading authority on the Ohio frontier. Few people have known the history of that region more thoroughly and none has done more to advance the study of it.

Themes

The principal themes of Bond's writings on the Old Northwest are dispassionate and qualified statements of points writers had been making with more zeal and fewer facts for decades. Bond contends that the Old Northwest was vitally important in American history for a number of reasons--all of which echoed throughout his publications. First, the Northwest Territory was where the colonial policy of the United States had first been tested; second, the early civilization of the Ohio Valley was the product of a cultural synthesis of peoples and practices from all parts of the Atlantic seaboard states; and third, the so-called "democratic" society of the Old Northwest was the product of a dynamic interaction between eastern ideals and western practices. Bond states these themes most fully in *The Civilization of the Old Northwest* and in an article he wrote in 1931 for a *festschrift* for Charles McLean Andrews entitled "Some Political Ideals of the Colonial Period as They were Realized in the Old Northwest" (pp. 299-325).

Bond claimed that the central question of *The Civilization of the Old Northwest* had to do with the nature of the colonial policy of the United States. Would it be developed along "the time-honored mercantilist principles of the British colonial government" or would it "support the liberal ideals of the [American] Revolution in a more democratic land system?" The Old Northwest was of critical importance in American history, Bond believes, because it had been "the one available laboratory in which an American colonial policy could be worked out" (pp. 5, 7).

He praises the "farsighted and democratic" guarantees of the Northwest Ordinance of 1787 as "steps in the right direction." True, the ordinance was conservative because it denied the "masses a voice in the government." But frontier conditions soon demonstrated the flaws in the territorial government. By the time Ohio became the first state created from the Northwest Territory in 1803, Bond argues that "American policy . . . recognizing actual conditions . . . [had] modified 'itself' to meet popular demands." In the end, then, the experiences of people living on the Ohio frontier had, in Bond's view, contributed significantly to the formation of a colonial policy that made land and political power readily available to the majority of American citizens (*The Foundations of Ohio*, pp. 475-476).

Another major theme in Bond's work was the diversity of early settlers of the Ohio frontier. He describes the settlements at Marietta in 1788 and in the Western Reserve in the early 1880s as the homes of New Englanders who brought an emphasis on religion, public education, and gentility to the frontier. Bond also notes the importance of people from Virginia, Kentucky, and Pennsylvania in settling the Ohio Country. Drawing on his own birthright and the work of Robert Chaddock in *Ohio Before 1850* (1908), he highlights the southerner's supposed insistence on democratic individualism (at least for white men). Finally, he points out that the Miami Valley--the region including and north of Cincinnati--had been developed by people from New Jersey and other states in between New England and the South.

Bond believes that the interaction of people from these diverse regions had produced--after an initial period of tension--a cultural melting pot. Refusing to champion any region or group, Bond argues that emigrants from all over America had founded in the Old Northwest "a civilization that combined in a notable degree the ideals and the points of view of the various elements of population from which these immigrants had sprung." Frontier society was a new and synthetic society. Ultimately, the mingling of peoples of such different types had produced "a cosmopolitanism and a tolerant and democratic spirit that has always characterized the Old Northwest" (*The Civilization of the Old Northwest*, pp. 16, 508).

Finally, Bond argues that the Old Northwest was the place where what he called the "liberal" principles of the American Revolution had most fully been put into practice. While he believes that the "thoroughgoing democracy" of the Old Northwest was partly the product of a militant western frontier spirit, Bond contends that it was also the fulfillment of "the liberal political ideas that had been only partially realized in the Revolutionary constitutions of the other states." Liberal democracy did not originate on the frontier, but it flourished there as nowhere else. According to Bond, "liberal" ideas included antislavery, religious freedom, a weak judiciary and executive, a strong Bill of Rights, public education, and popular sovereignty. All of these he found in the Ohio Constitution. Indeed, it contained almost "all the important political ideals of Revolutionary liberalism as they had been developed in the colonial period" (*Essays in Colonial History Presented to Charles McLean Andrews by his Students*, p. 306). What had been theory in many eastern states had become reality in Ohio in the early 1800s.

Here Bond, putting his vague terms and generalities aside for the moment, is saying something worth pursuing. In a way, he is attempting an historiographical synthesis of his own. Drawing on two decades of experience as a historian of colonial and revolutionary America while working in a field dominated by the frontier thesis of Frederick Jackson Turner, Bond is implicitly trying to combine the two, to find a connection between what he calls the "liberal" ideas that had appeared in the cities and on the plantations of the East and the so-called democractic spirit of the frontier. Characteristically, Bond is steering a middle course. But unfortunately, his ideas remain undeveloped.

Still, Bond successfully makes the point that more than local pride made the study of the frontier of the Old Northwest imperative. He drew attention to it as a true crossroads of Americans and American ideas. It was an important place because it had been settled by so many different kinds of Americans in the aftermath of the defining event of American history, the Revolution. The notions that the Old Northwest was a laboratory of cultural conflict and colonial government and its civilization the fulfillment of the Revolution remain ideas very much worth exploring.

Analysis

Contemporary reviewers' most frequent criticism of Beverley Bond's works was that they were lacking in interpretation. James B. Hedges, a professor of American Civilization at Brown University, for example, praises *The Civilization of the Old Northwest* as a "work of exposition and description," but laments that "it presents no thesis and offers no new or startling conclusions." Hedges wishes that Bond had found "a pattern by which to weave the multitude of separate threads into a completed fabric" (*New England Quarterly* 7:598). Randolph C. Downes, the author of *Frontier Ohio, 1788-1803* and later a professor of history at the University of Toledo, agreed with Hedges. Downes calls *The Civilization of the Old Northwest* "a storehouse of information representing a tremendous amount of work in the widest range of sources. It is encyclopedic in scope." But he thinks Bond had failed to make convincing arguments (*American Historical Review* 40:148). A reviewer in the *English Historical Review* was not as gentle as Hedges or Downes. He characterizes Bond's major work as "neither a detailed chronological narrative, nor a closely reasoned analytical study, but a digest of information . . . . The result is a useful collection of notes" (50:371). Unfortunately, these criticisms were largely on the mark. Bond's books present an almost numbing variety of facts; his research was thorough and impeccable. But the reader is often left to make of the facts whatever one wishes.

To be fair, Bond's work seems more significant when viewed in the context of the historiography of the Ohio frontier. As Carl Wittke, the editor of the six-volume *History of the State of Ohio*, noted in 1941, Ohio had been "strangely backward in the preserving of her historical materials and in the writing of her history." More crucial was the fact that, as Wittke put it, writers too often exalt "local pride at the sacrifice of impartial, scholarly judgment and method" (*The Foundations of Ohio*, p. v). Surely the history of every state suffers, to one degree or another, from an excess of boosterism. But Ohio had a particularly severe case, precisely because of a reason Bond noted in his histories--the diversity in origins of the state's original settlers.

It is not much of an exaggeration to say that the history of the Ohio frontier in the nineteenth century was a battleground between partisans of New England settlers in the Muskingum Valley and the Western Reserve and the champions of southerners who occupied much of the rest of the state, especially the Scioto Valley. Early historians, including Jacob Burnet, Caleb Atwater, and Samuel Prescott Hildreth, extolled the New Englanders as carriers of culture, religion, and social order to the frontier while ignoring or disparaging the contributions of settlers from other regions. In the late nineteenth and early twentieth centuries, several writers, especially David Massie, W. H. Hunter, and Robert Chaddock, worked to rehabilitate the southern and frontier influence. In particular, they pointed to the political contributions of the latter, arguing that southern-born settlers had upheld individual rights and the democratic process in the face of puritanical pressure from New Englanders. All of these writers tended to see the struggle for statehood for Ohio, which climaxed with Ohio's admission to the union in 1803, as a contest between these two kinds of people. It was, depending upon one's perspective, either a fight between order and anarchy or a contest between tyranny and democracy.

Beverley Bond brought some order to this historiographical and genealogical controversy with the skills and judgment of a professional historian. Expertly trained at Johns Hopkins and well versed in the art of research, Bond labored throughout his career at Cincinnati in the causes of accuracy and scholarly objectivity. He was meticulous in his research and balanced in his writing. In a word, his professionalism gave his work an authority that lifted it--and the history of the Ohio frontier--well above the quality of much of what had preceded it. In his two major books on the Ohio frontier, Bond combined the arguments of the two local schools of interpretation. He did not argue that New Englanders were more important than southerners or vice versa. Instead, he chose the middle course of describing the Ohio Valley as a cultural melting pot, thereby defusing local boosterism by attempting to see the civilization of the Old Northwest as a mosaic, as the sum of many diverse parts.

So, the reviewers were not entirely correct in claiming Bond's books were lacking in interpretation. He did state themes. But having looked at the historiographical context of Bond's studies, it remains to be said that his skills at making an argument lagged far behind his talents for research. Bond was not a bad writer. But he seems to have been incapable of developing his ideas. His method was to state generalizations at the beginning of a work and to summarize them at the end. In between were massive amounts of information. But the relationship between the facts and the generalizations was rarely made clear.

The failure to develop ideas makes them seem extremely vague and superficial. Bond tends to use phrases like the "liberal" ideas of the Revolution and crucial terms like "democracy" and "civilization" without fully explaining what he meant by them. Thus he left himself open to easy criticism. Randolph Downes got to the heart of the matter in his review of *The Civilization of the Old Northwest* when he notes that Bond lacked "an organic conception of what constitutes a civilization. One cannot understand the coming of law to the Northwest by summarizing in chronological order the output by meetings of the lawmaking bodies" (*American Historical Review* 40:149).

Time and time again, Bond made a very general statement and then tried to prove it by accumulating all the available facts on the subject. A good example is his discussion of the ordinances of the 1780s. He characterizes them in the introduction to the book; he summarizes how they were modified in the end. But he never shows his readers how this process of tranformation occurred. Another example is his repeated contention that diverse emigrants "mingled together in the Old Northwest to form a new civilization that combined the customs and the points of view of their original homes." There is a lot of merit to this idea, but Bond does not do anything with it; he simply tries to support it with long descriptions of settlements and lists of achievements. And, even with his efforts to bring balance to his subject, stereotypes abound. New Englanders were "austere

Puritans." Southerners had an "easy-going urbanity" and "political acumen," while settlers from the middle states were tolerant and practical (*Mississippi Valley Historical Review* 19:4). One wonders, in addition, whether the nineteenth century Midwest was as cosmopolitan and tolerant as Bond believed. Again, Bond does not demonstrate any of those generalizations; he merely asserts them.

Given these basic problems of organization, it is not surprising that Bond's work seems to have been little informed by the writings of other historians. It is little short of amazing how small a shadow Frederick Jackson Turner casts on these studies of the frontier of the Old Northwest written in the 1920s and 1930s. Clearly, Turner's influence is implicit in Bond's notion of sectional synthesis in the Northwest Territory and in statements such as "the liberal constitution of Ohio represented the definite triumph of Western democracy over Eastern conservatism" (*The Civilization of the Old Northwest*, p. 527). Bond, of course, had spent several pages earlier in the book asserting that the civilization of the Old Northwest was a fulfillment of the liberal ideas of a revolution that had its seeds in the colonies of the Atlantic Coast. But, that inconsistency aside, Bond was employing Turnerian phrases as a kind of deus ex machina when he wanted to tell his readers the significance of what they had read.

The superficial, incomplete nature of Bond's arguments and the encyclopedic nature of his works make him an easy target for criticism and a difficult historian to analyze. To some extent, it should be remembered, Bond's failure to develop sophisticated ideas was a product of the historiographical backwardness of Ohio. He had few monographs on which to build. He had to dig for sources that, in a few cases, he then made widely available by editing and publishing them. As Bond himself complained in 1930, "Anyone who has done real work in Ohio history knows the crying need" for "more publication." Historians had to "travel from place to place and then you move because some more material crops up somewhere else" (*Ohio Archaeological and Historical Society Publications* 39:454). *The Civilization of the Old Northwest* was, in every sense of the word, a pioneering study.

It is important to remember that Bond saw himself as a member of a first generation of professional historians. He believed himself to be part of a community working toward a common goal--historical truth. "I think what we need," he told a group of Ohio historians in 1930, "is to get together--not one man to work a thesis in one line and somebody in something else, but we need more cooperation" (pp. 453-454). So, he gathered facts, produced reliable, sound history, and published edited material while leaving "elaborate generalizations," as he puts it in a review of a book, to "future historians" (*Mississippi Valley Historical Review* 25:567).

Still, the inescapable conclusion is that Beverley Bond was a conscientious, competent, but unimaginative and limited historian. His forte never was the development of ideas. His earlier work on the quit-rent system, for example, shows the same depth of research and the same superficiality of interpretation. On occasion, he had the ability to see possibilities in uniting the story of frontier Ohio with political and social developments in the original states, of tying together the Revolution and the frontier. But he never found the ability to carry his ideas beyond the realm of generalizations. In the end, Beverley Bond, Jr., was a historian whose career was a triumph of research over argument.

Bibliography

Books

The Civilization of the Old Northwest: A Study of Political, Social and Economic Development, 1788-1812. New York: Macmillan, 1934.

The Correspondence of John Cleves Symmes, Founder of the Miami Purchase. Editor. New York: Macmillan for the Historical and Philosophical Society of Ohio, 1926.

The Courses of the Ohio River Taken by Lt. T. Hutchins, Anno 1776, and Two Accompanying Maps. Editor. Cincinnati: Historical and Philosophical Society of Ohio, 1942.

The Foundations of Ohio. Columbus: Ohio State Archaeological and Historical Society, 1941.

The Intimate Letters of John Cleves Symmes and His Family, Including Those of His Daughter, Mrs. William Henry Harrison, Wife of the Ninth President of the United States. Editor. Cincinnati: Historical and Philosophical Society of Ohio, 1956.

[James Smith] *Some Considerations of the French Settling Colonies on the Mississippi.* Editor. Cincinnati: Historical and Philosophical Society of Ohio, 1928.

The Monroe Mission to France, 1794-1796. Baltimore: Johns Hopkins University Press, 1907.

The Quit-Rent System in the American Colonies. New Haven: Yale University Press, 1919.

The Relation of Civil Service Reform to the Appointment of Teachers in the Public Schools. Boston: Women's Auxiliary of the Massachusetts Civil Service Reform Association, 1904.

State Government in Maryland, 1777-1781. Baltimore: Johns Hopkins University Press, 1905.

Articles

"The Aim of the General Course in American History and Its Place in the College Curriculum." *Historical Outlook* 14(March, 1923):93-98.

"American Civilization Comes to the Old Northwest." *Mississippi Valley Historical Review* 19(June, 1932):3-29.

"An American Experiment in Colonial Government." *Mississippi Valley Historical Review* 15(September, 1928):221-235.

"Andrews, Sherlock James." In *The Dictionary of American Biography* edited by Allen Johnson. 20 volumes. New York: Charles Scribner's Sons, 1928-1936. 1:297.

"Burnet, Jacob." In *The Dictionary of American Biography* edited by Allen Johnson. 20 volumes. New York: Charles Scribner's Sons, 1928-1936. 3:294.

"The Captivity of Charles Stuart, 1755-1757." Editor. *Mississippi Valley Historical Review* 13(June, 1926):58-81.

"The Colonial Agent as a Popular Representative." *Political Science Quarterly* 35(September, 1920):372-392.

"A Colonial Sidelight." Editor. *Sewanee Review* 19(January, 1911):87-107.

"A Colonial Sidelight, Second Paper." Editor. *Sewanee Review* 20(April, 1912):213-234.

"A Course for the Better Understanding of Latin-America." *Historical Outlook* 10(October, 1919):374-375.

"Dr. Daniel Drake's Memoir of the Miami Country, 1779-1794." Editor. *The Quarterly Publication of the Historical and Philosophical Society of Ohio* 18(April-September, 1923):39-117.

"Memoirs of Benjamin Van Cleve." Editor. *The Quarterly Publication of the Historical and Philosophical Society of Ohio* 17(January-June, 1922):3-71.

"Monroe's Efforts to Secure Free Navigation of the Mississippi River during his Mission to France, 1794-1796." *Mississippi Historical Society Publications* 9(1906):255-262.

"Notes on Proposed Settlements in the West, 1755-1757." Editor. *Publications of the Historical and Philosophical Society of Ohio* 2(1925):37-58.

"The Old Northwest to Eastern Eyes." *Ohio Archaeological and Historical Society Publications* 38(June, 1929):542-555.

"Our Society." *Bulletin of the Historical and Philosophical Society of Ohio* 1(March, 1943):1-2.

"Putnam, Rufus." In *The Dictionary of American Biography* edited by Dumas Malone. 20 volumes. New York: Charles Scribner's Sons, 1928-1936. 15:284-285.

"The Quit-Rent System in the American Colonies." *American Historical Review* 17(April, 1912):496-515.

"Some Political Ideals of the Colonial Period as They Were Realized in the Old Northwest." In *Essays in Colonial History Presented to Charles McLean Andrews by his Students.* New Haven: Yale University Press, 1931. Pp. 299-325.

"Symmes, John Cleves." In *The Dictionary of American Biography* edited by Dumas Malone. 20 volumes. New York: Charles Scribner's Sons, 1928-1936. 18:258-259.

"Two Westward Journeys of John Filson, 1785." Editor. *Mississippi Valley Historical Review* 9(March, 1923):320-330.

"A Vital Problem of the Rural High School." *History Teacher's Magazine* 7(November, 1916):309-312.

"William Henry Harrison and the Old Northwest, 1799-1811." *Bulletin of the Historical and Philosophical Society of Ohio* 7(January, 1949):10-17.

"William Henry Harrison in the War of 1812." *Mississippi Valley Historical Review* 13(March, 1927):499-516.

Reviews

The American Colonies, 1492-1750 by Marcus Wilson Jernegan. *Mississippi Valley Historical Review* 16(September, 1929):263-265.

The American Colonies in the Eighteenth Century, Vols. I and II by Herbert L. Osgood. *Mississippi Valley Historical Review* 11(September, 1924):274-277.

The American Colonies in the Eighteenth Century, Vols. III and IV by Herbert L. Osgood. *Mississippi Valley Historical Review* 12(December, 1925):423-426.

Evolution of Executive Departments of the Continental Congress, 1774-1789 by Jennings B. Sanders. *Mississippi Valley Historical Review* 37(September, 1935):284-285.

Fifty Years of Party Warfare by William O. Lynch. *American Historical Review* 37(October, 1931):135-136.

The Genesis of Western Culture: The Upper Ohio Valley, 1800-1825 by James M. Miller. *Mississippi Valley Historical Review* 25(March, 1939):566-567.

History of Economic Legislation in Iowa by Ivan L. Pollock. *Mississippi Valley Historical Review* 5(March, 1919):494-496.

History of Indiana by Logan Esarey. *Mississippi Valley Historical Review* 6(June, 1919):131-133.

The Indiana Company, 1763-1798 by George E. Lewis. *American Historical Review* 48(January, 1943):348-349.

John Hanson and the Inseparable Union by Jacob A. Nelson. *Mississippi Valley Historical Review* 26(September, 1939):252-253.

John Hanson of Mulberry Grove by J. Bruce Kremer. *Mississippi Valley Historical Review* 26(September, 1939):252-253.

The John Tipton Papers, Volumes I-III edited by Nellie Armstrong Robinson and Dorothy Riker. *Mississippi Valley Historical Review* 39(December, 1943):421-422.

The Kentucky Land Grants by Willard Rouse Jellison. *American Historical Review* 31(April, 1926):586.

Land Title Origins by Alfred N. Chandler. *American Historical Review* 52(October, 1946):148-149.

Letters of Members of the Continental Congress, Vol. III: January 1 to December 31, 1778 edited by Edmund C. Burnett. *Mississippi Valley Historical Review* 13(March, 1927):568-570.

Letters of Members of the Continental Congress, Vol. IV: January 1 to December 31, 1779 edited by Edmund C. Burnett. *Mississippi Valley Historical Review* 15(March, 1929):538-540.

Letters of Members of the Continental Congress, Vol. V: January 1, 1880 to February 28, 1781 edited by Edmund C. Burnett. *Mississippi Valley Historical Review* 19(September, 1932):272-273.

Letters to Members of the Continental Congress, Vol. VI: March 1, 1781 to December 31, 1782 edited by Edmund C. Burnett. *Mississippi Valley Historical Review* 20(September, 1933):275-276.

Letters to Members of the Continental Congress, Vol. VII :January 1, 1783 to December 31, 1784 edited by Edmund C. Burnett. *Mississippi Valley Historical Review* 22(June, 1935):90-91.

Letters to Members of the Continental Congress, Vol. VIII: January 1, 1784 to December 31, 1784 edited by Edmund C. Burnett. *Mississippi Valley Historical Review* 23(March, 1937):562-563.

The Life and Times of Colonel Richard M. Johnson of Kentucky by Leland Winfield Meyer. *American Historical Review* 38(January, 1933):381.

Method in History for Teachers and Students by William H. Mace. *Mississippi Valley Historical Review* 2(September, 1915):300-302.

The New Purchase by Robert Carlton. *Mississippi Valley Historical Review* 4(June, 1917):127-129.

Old Somerset on the Eastern Shore of Maryland by Clayton Torrence. *Mississippi Valley Historical Review* 23(June, 1936):87-88.

The Papers of Henry Bouquet, Vol. II edited by S. K. Stevens, Donald H. Kent, and Autumn L. Leonard. *American Historical Review* 57(July, 1952):1048-1049.

A Pioneer College: The Story of Marietta by Arthur C. Beach. *Mississippi Valley Historical Review* 2(March, 1936):573-574.

The Planting of Civilization in Western Pennsylvania by Solon L. Buck and Elizabeth Hawthorn Buck. *American Historical Review* 44(July, 1940):894-896.

Pope's Digest, 1815, Vol. I edited by Francis S. Philbrick. *Mississippi Valley Historical Review* 26(December, 1939):258-259.

Pope's Digest, 1815, Vol. II edited by Francis S. Philbrick. *Mississippi Valley Historical Review* 27(December, 1940):469.

Proceedings and Debates of the British Parliaments Respecting North America, Vol. II: 1689-1702 edited by Leo Francis Stock. *Mississippi Valley Historical Review* 14(December, 1927):392-393.

Proceedings and Debates of the British Parliaments Respecting North America, Vol. III: 1702-1727 edited by Leo Francis Stock. *Mississippi Valley Historical Review* 17(March, 1931):607-608.

Washington the Lover by Laura Aline Hobby. *Mississippi Valley Historical Review* 20(September, 1933):300.

Studies of Beverley W. Bond, Jr.

Ambler, Charles H. Review of *The Courses of the Ohio River* edited by Beverley W. Bond, Jr. *American Historical Review* 48(April, 1943):670.

Barnhart, John D. Review of *The Foundations of Ohio* by Beverley W. Bond, Jr. *Indiana Magazine of History* 37(September, 1941):279-282.

__________. Review of *The Intimate Letters of John Cleves Symmes and His Family* edited by Beverley W. Bond, Jr. *Mississippi Valley Historical Review* 44(June, 1957):131-132.

Bellott, H. H. Review of *The Civilization of the Old Northwest* by Beverley W. Bond, Jr. *English Historical Review* 50(April, 1935):371.

Benton, Elbert J. Review of *The Foundations of Ohio* by Beverley W. Bond, Jr. *Mississippi Valley Historical Review* 28(December, 1941):443-445.

"Beverley W. Bond, Jr." *Mississippi Valley Historical Review* 48(September, 1961):359-360.

Brown, George W. Review of *The Civilization of the Old Northwest* by Beverley W. Bond, Jr. *Canadian Historical Review* 16(March, 1935):84-85.

Carter, C. E. Review of *The Correspondence of John Cleves Symmes* edited by Beverley W. Bond, Jr. *American Historical Review* 31(July, 1926):806-807.

Downes, Randolph C. Review of *The Civilization of the Old Northwest* by Beverley W. Bond, Jr. *American Historical Review* 40(October, 1934):148-149.

Green, Fletcher M. Review of *The Civilization of the Old Northwest* by Beverley W. Bond, Jr. *Political Science Quarterly* 50(September, 1935):454-456.

Hedges, James B. Review of *The Civilization of the Old Northwest* by Beverley W. Bond, Jr. *New England Quarterly* 7(September, 1934):597-598.

"In Memoriam: Beverley Waugh Bond, Jr." *Bulletin of the Historical and Philosophical Society of Ohio* 19(April, 1961):159-160.

Kimball, Everett. Review of *The Quit-Rent System in the American Colonies* by Beverley W. Bond, Jr. *American Political Science Review* 13(November, 1919):692-693.

LaFollette, Robert. Review of *The Civilization of the Old Northwest* by Beverley W. Bond, Jr. *Indiana Magazine of History* 30(March, 1934):104-106.

Monaghan, Jay. Review of *The Foundations of Ohio* by Beverley W. Bond, Jr. *American Historical Review* 48(October, 1942):129-131.

Pease, Theodore C. Review of *The Civilization of the Old Northwest* by Beverley W. Bond, Jr. *Mississippi Valley Historical Review* 21(June, 1934):90-91.

"Proceedings of the Ohio History Conference, February 7, 1930." *Ohio Archaeological and Historical Society Publications* 39(1930):453-454.

Root, W. T. Review of *The Quit-Rent System in the American Colonies* by Beverley W. Bond, Jr. *American Historical Review* 26(July, 1921):802-804.

Smith, William E. Review of *The Intimate Letters of John Cleves Symmes and His Family* edited by Beverley W. Bond, Jr. *American Historical Review* 62(July, 1957):1009.

Utter, William T. Review of *The Intimate Letters of John Cleves Symmes and His Family* edited by Beverley W. Bond, Jr. *Bulletin of the Historical and Philosophical Society of Ohio* 15(April, 1957):162-164.

Weaks, Mabel C. Review of *The Correspondence of John Cleves Symmes* edited by Beverley W. Bond, Jr. *Mississippi Valley Historical Review* 13(September, 1926):270-272.

Weatherford, John D. Review of *The Intimate Letters of John Cleves Symmes and His Family* edited by Beverley W. Bond, Jr. *Ohio Historical Quarterly* 66(October, 1957):422-423.

12

R. CARLYLE BULEY

by Carl Ubbelohde

Biography

R. Carlyle Buley was born on July 8, 1893, at Georgetown in Floyd County, Indiana, the son of Dr. David Marion Buley and his wife, Nora Kiethley Buley. From this southern Indiana town, across the Ohio River from Louisville, Kentucky, his family moved to Vincennes. He graduated from the high school there in 1910. He chose to major in history (with minors in government and economics) at Indiana University from which he received his A.B. degree in 1914. He taught high school in Delphi, Indiana, the next year and then returned to Bloomington as a research fellow in Midwest Historical Studies. He completed a thesis on "Indiana in the Mexican War" and was awarded his A.M. degree in 1916. After teaching high school in Muncie for two years, he entered the United States Army. He was discharged at the rank of sergeant from the 329th F.S. Battalion in 1919. He moved to Springfield, Illinois, where he taught high school until 1923. He was married in 1919 to Esther Giles; she died in 1921. He married Evelyn Barnett in 1926.

In 1923 Buley began graduate work at the University of Wisconsin studying especially with Frederic Paxson. Buley completed his dissertation on the "Political Balance in the Old Northwest, 1820-1860" and was awarded his Ph.D. in 1925. He returned to Indiana University where he would spend the rest of his professional career. An instructor in history from 1925 to 1929, he was then advanced to an assistant professorship. He became an associate professor in 1937 and a professor in 1945. He retired in 1964.

Buley was a very popular teacher, always available for conversation and consultation with students and colleagues. His courses--survey and post-Civil War United States history--did not give evidence of his principal research interests, which were the pre-1840 Old Northwest and business history. His national reputation dates from 1951 when he was awarded the Pulitzer Prize in history for *The Old Northwest: Pioneer Period, 1815-1840.*

He also was honored with the Elizur Wright Award by the American Association of Teachers of Insurance for *The American Life Convention* (1953), and an honorary D. Litt. from Coe College in 1958.

Buley died on April 25, 1968.

Themes

Buley's work in business history, especially his studies of life insurance and the Eli Lilly Company, fall outside the scope of this essay. His writings about the frontier are best exemplified in his two-volume *The Old Northwest: Pioneer Period 1815-1840* and a book he co-authored, *The Midwest Pioneer: His Ills, Cures and Doctors*. There are essays that provide additional evidence of his interests and focus.

Buley attempted to be, in many ways, a "compleat historian." He was not content to limit his interest in the historic past by narrow definitions. Everything that happened in the lives of the people was of concern, and since others had been especially attentive to political and economic development, Buley's own work appeared to open new avenues into social and cultural history. Thus, a first theme of significance may be identified as recognition of the complexities of human lives and human history and the accompanying attempts to write about the past in the most inclusive manner possible. This, in fact, turned sometimes to unusual descriptive passages, such as attempts to describe the smells and odors of a time and place, or to represent in print the common pronunciations of frontier people.

A second theme that Buley stressed was the individual man or woman and the capacity of each person to overcome the hardships and the perils of a frontier existence. It was the ordinary person, the common folk, that most elicited his attention. He was inclined to be a bit skeptical of the way heroism is traditionally viewed by biographers and historians; he concludes an essay with these words about the pioneers: "In estimating these people and their work, the contempt of superiority is no less to be guarded against than the idealization which ascribes superabundance of vision, courage, industry, and virtue to them. After all, they were just folks, doing their day's work, and caring little for the verdict of history"(*Mississippi Valley Historical Review* 23:510).

Another theme of Buley that he himself once identified as characteristic of the frontier is the concept of the way a "sense of individual responsibility and the spirit of cooperation . . . went hand in hand on the frontier" (*Mississippi Valley Historical Review* 27:295). This is a rather conventional equation for a man like Buley, who grew up in the era of progressivism but was sufficiently conservative to scourge the "progressives" and to condemn and lament the New Deal. Buley defines progressives "as piebald a conglomerate of balmy idealists, hero worshipers, out-faction city bosses, office seekers, pro-tariff anti-trusters, anti-tariff pro-trusters, egotists, puzzlewits, 'apostates,' revivalists, 'honeyfuglers,' and 'reformers' as ever staged a pitch on the American scene" (*Mississippi Valley Historical Review* 33:328). Yet Buley was realistic and patriotic enough to understand some of community's claims on individual freedom.

In fact, others have identified a persistent effort to integrate two "superficially incongruous" themes--materialism (or realistic) and idealism (or romantic) approaches in a story of progress. The increasing scale and wealth of the society, as he saw it, came together with continuing efforts to achieve an ideal of peace and freedom.

A final but less pronounced concern was Buley's idea of a recurring process of planting society into frontier areas--the replication of activities and enterprises as the stream of westering persons moved from Ohio through Illinois and Indiana, Michigan and Wisconsin.

Analysis

Buley's objective in the *The Old Northwest* (1950) was to relate the lives of people of the past in their entirety--in a "wholeness," to use Gene E. McCormick's word--in which all facets were treated with equal significance. "However small the detail or large the event, it had context, and thus history could not be grasped through test drilling the evidence nor the recorded through the 'psychic impulses' of the author. 'I just want to give them the facts,' he would often say, 'and let them draw their own conclusions'" (*Indiana History Bulletin* 45:67).

His technique was to depict "comprehensively all phases of human activity . . . political and economic backgrounds, religion, literature, utopian experiments, education and health, agriculture, developments in transportation, habits of courtship, songs, and the slang expressions of the time" (*Current Biography 1951*, p. 74). From this came such "uncommon fullness, competence, wealth of source material and authentic flavor--that it may be considered unique" (quoted *New York Times* in *Current Biography 1951*, p. 74).

Where Buley's work fit within the literature of his era is easier to state than where or how he came to his research and writing strategies. As Harry P. Stevens pointed out in 1958, Buley's work filled most of the (then) gaps between two earlier studies, Beverley W. Bond's *Civilization of the Old Northwest, 1788-1812* and Henry C. Hubbart's *The Older Middle West, 1840-1880*. But Buley's book was a fuller, more detailed, and differently-textured history.

As for the origins of the idea for *The Old Northwest*, it is unclear at what point Buley began to accumulate the enormous quantity of information that forms its basis. It must have been quite early--perhaps a quarter-century before the book was finished. One possibility is that, as a graduate student at Wisconsin, he absorbed some of Joseph Schafer's thinking about the projected, but never completed, *Wisconsin Domesday Book* project--a complicated and inclusive enterprise centered in the State Historical Society of Wisconsin in the 1920s. Then, again, he might have been encouraged to take up the unfinished work of his teacher and colleague, Logan Esarey, who had wanted to write the history of the Old Northwest from earliest times to the Civil War, but had never finished nor published the first volume, intended to carry the history to 1815.

Everywhere, of course, Frederick Jackson Turner's work provides threads of possibilities. Turner lectured in Bloomington a few years before Buley entered Indiana University and Turner's analysis of the frontier influences probably formed a component in the history instruction Buley received. When Buley chose to pursue doctoral studies he elected Wisconsin as his school and Frederic Paxson, Turner's successor there, as his mentor. In 1947-1948, as he neared completion of the long-term project, Buley once again was in Madison as a visiting professor. Merle Curti, holder of the Turner professorship, soon began his pioneering quantitative testing of Turner's concepts that resulted in the publication of *The Making of an American Community*. Almost all of this is circumstantial, not direct, linkage, but like all others of his generation, if Buley intended to be a historian of the frontier, there could be no escape from the potent Turner concepts.

Critics have been divided in their evaluation of Buley's effort. Fulmer Mood believed that Buley accomplished his purposes "superlatively well"; that he had "harmoniously and tellingly interwoven" economic, social, and political strands, the facts patterned together in such a way as to mirror "the taking place," so to speak of the processes. In fact, Mood considers Buley's accomplishment superior to Frederick Jackson Turner's, his method more mature than Turner's (*Indiana Magazine of History* 48:7-8, 13, 19). Earl S. Pomeroy was less certain, calling attention to the difficulties of "episode and chronology overshadow[ing] conclusion . . . much appears as accumulation rather than illumination, and without weakening the book might have been shuffled, assigned to footnote and appendix, or simply deleted" (*Mississippi Valley Historical Review* 38:113).

It is no one's fault, certainly not Buley's, that the social historian of today finds his work a rather cluttered miscellany that asks few questions of current interest, constructed with old-fashioned and limited methods. The persons of the past who interest contemporary historians--women, minorities, the inarticulate and disadvantaged--did not particularly concern Buley. His common folk were mostly male and white, free and probably propertied. Nor were reforms and reformers among his favorite topics. Numbers and counting--precomputer-era quantification--was not a technique he entertained. (It is the impressionistic commentary, often lacking the shadow of statistical evidence, that frustrates and annoys.) And the possibilities of comparative analysis as a way to examine the Old Northwest--a region from which five contiguous states were created within a half-century, alike and yet different--is nowhere evident in Buley's publications.

Buley was a man of strong personal convictions. It is not surprising that from time to time some of his attitudes found expression in his historical writing. Although this was more likely to occur in reviews he wrote of others' publications, there are scattered places in the pages of *The Old Northwest* where the author's assumptions color the otherwise neutral record of the past. One area where this is likely to occur is when he approaches gender differentiation on the frontier. The same assumptions undoubtedly guided others' thoughts but Buley chose to describe life in all its aspects and this led him to construct (now) archaic descriptions such as: "The pioneer's world was essentially a man's world, and life possessed that robustness of flavor, that element of gusto and spontaneity which characterized the activities of people engaged in the harsher pursuits and in more direct contact with nature" (*The Old Northwest* 1:315-316). Not only was Buley's frontier masculine; it was a macho masculinity: "There were few weak or effeminate men in the West. Physical and military courage were taken for granted" (*The Old Northwest* 1:31).

Sometimes the assertations blend pseudo-science with nastiness to produce footnote commentary like: "The 'good-sized' families still exist among the remnant of some of the pioneer stock of feeble-minded strain in some of the counties of southern Indiana and Illinois. Social workers and attendance officers can supply some appalling information of families of a dozen or more children, with the usual conditions of disease, idiocy, illegitimacy, juvenile delinquency, incest, and all the rest. The maintenance charges on the public treasury are likewise sizeable, but the true pioneer spirit of individualism and *laissez-faire* still prevails" (*The Old Northwest* 1:310).

There also is in Buley's writings topics which he approached as a generous person, indicating merit and demerit therein in immediate proximity to each other. The historian who saw the frontier as a masculine sphere and believed twentieth-century feeble-minded families with many children a connection with the past, surprises the reader with a sympathetic, liberal attentiveness to both Indian and settler as their worlds collided. His narrative account of Black Hawk's War reflects fully the perceptions of a scholar who understood the perils of reliance on sources reflecting a limited point of view. Buley, of course, predated what now we would expect--use of the anthropologists' methods to help us see interior cultural perceptions. For his time and place, however, he thought and wrote from an informed and reasonable position. Something of this is observable in his short account of settlers' attitudes:

> though the expression "the only good Indian is a dead Indian" never truly represented the attitude of a majority of the pioneers over any length of time, nevertheless, between 1825 and 1830 the people of the region became convinced that the Indian should go--the farther the better. It was no longer, after 1832 at least, fear of the Indian; nor was it merely a desire for his lands. It was the belief in the final inability of the Indian to make the grade of the higher white civilization (or so the white man regarded it) and to live in adjustment within or alongside it. Though the "Indian hater," not an uncommon type in the earlier period of border wars, was becoming rare in the Middle West, he had left a heritage of a double standard of behavior in the minds of many--two consciences as it were, one for the white man and another for the red man.

One of the most attractive attributes of Buley's uncommon comprehensiveness is what he has recorded about the past from experiential--as well as documentary--evidence. When he began to study history as an undergraduate, he was as close in time to the quarter-century (1815-1840) of *The Old Northwest* as one is, today, to his era. In many ways he was closer. He had lived in small town, semirural, agrarian communities. He understood the cycles of the farming seasons. He had some sense of the order of values that pioneers might apply to land acquisition, childbearing, church services, and village taverns--and all the other institutions, commodities, and processes that made up the routines of life in the newly settled West. He has enriched our understanding, and more so with each year as ever fewer professional historians come to their labors with experience in agricultural or small town routines. Buley's evocative descriptions of plowing, planting and harvesting, butchering, soap making and distilling, of children's games and holidays, involve urbanized, dependent modern-day readers in a rural and more independent past. The affectionate care Buley devoted to these descriptions mark what may well be his most valuable and valued achievements as a historian.

Buley was a very careful craftsman who both recognized and appreciated precision in historical writing. He wrote reviews of historical novels as well as professional history; he stressed the importance of accuracy in historical information even, if necessary, at the expense of good writing. But he preferred publications that combined both. As he put it: "Historians can dig; writers can write; now and then one can do both" (*Indiana Magazine of History* 37:400-401). Often there was a nice lightness of touch, a snippet of humor, to illustrate the point, such as this sentence from a 1939 review: "In a period in which the world seems bent on going to hell on wheels, the general reader should find relief in idling with the folks who had only varmints, Indians, the devil, Yankee dudes, and serious horse problems to worry about" (*Mississippi Valley Historical Review* 26:262).

What might he have said about the present in relation to the past he learned to know so well?

Bibliography

Books

The American Life Convention, 1906-1952: A Study in the History of Life Insurance. 2 volumes. New York: Appleton-Century-Crofts, Inc., 1953.

The Equitable Life Assurance Society of the United States, 1859-1959. New York: Appleton-Century-Crofts, Inc., 1959.

The Equitable Life Assurance Society of the United States, 1859-1964. 2 volumes. New York: Appleton-Century-Crofts, 1967.

The Indiana Home by Logan Esarey. Editor. Crawfordsville, IN: R. E. Banta, 1943.

The Midwest Pioneer: His Ills, Cures and Doctors. Co-authored with Madge E. Pickard. Crawfordsville, IN: R. E. Banta, 1945.

The Old Northwest: Pioneer Period, 1815-1840. 2 volumes. Indianapolis: Indiana Historical Society, 1950.

The Romantic Appeal of the New West, 1815-1840. Detroit: Wayne State University Press, 1961.

Articles

"The Campaign of 1888 in Indiana." *Indiana Magazine of History* 10(June, 1914):30-53 [162-185].

"Glimpses of Pioneer Mid-West Social and Cultural History." *Mississippi Valley Historical Review* 23(March, 1937):481-510.

"Indiana in the Mexican War." *Indiana Magazine of History* 15(September, December, 1919):260-326; 16(March, 1920):46-68.

"Lilly: Heritage in Health--The Story Behind the Wonder Drugs." *American Heritage* 2(Autumn, 1950):28-31, 72.

"Logan Esarey, Hoosier." *Indiana Magazine of History* 38(December, 1942):337-381.

"The Middle West--Its Heritage and Its Role." *Wabash Bulletin* 41(December, 1943):11-14, 19-22.

"Origin of the Republican Party." Indianapolis, IN *Sunday Star*, June 26, 1914.

"Pioneer Health and Medical Practices in the Old Northwest Prior to 1840." *Mississippi Valley Historical Review* 20(March, 1934):497-520.

"The Pioneer Mid-West in the Depressions." *Proceedings of the Seventeenth Annual History Conference* (*Indiana History Bulletin*) 13(February, 1936):77-91.

"The Political Balance in the Old Northwest." *Studies of American History* (*Indiana University Studies*) 12(June, September, December, 1925):405-455.

"Water (?) Witching Can Be Fun." *Indiana Magazine of History* 56(March, 1960):65-77.

Reviews

Agricultural Dissent in the Middle West, 1900-1939 by Theodore Saloutos and John D. Hicks. *Mississippi Valley Historical Review* 38(December, 1951):530-532.

America is West--An Anthology of Midwestern Life and Literature edited by John T. Flanagan. *Indiana Magazine of History* 42(March, 1946): 90-92.

The American Heritage Book of the Pioneer Spirit by Richard M. Ketchum. *Indiana Magazine of History* 56(March, 1960):85-86.

Angel in the Forest: A Fairy Tale of Two Utopias by Marguerite Young. *Mississippi Valley Historical Review* 32(September, 1945):269-271.

Architecture of the Old Northwest Territory by Rexford Newcomb. *Indiana Magazine of History* 47(September, 1951):299-301.

Boom Copper: The Story of the First U.S. Mining Boom by Angus Murdock. *Indiana Magazine of History* 40(December, 1944):398-399.

The Critical Period, 1763-1765 edited by Clarence Alvord and Clarence E. Carter. *Indiana Magazine of History* 11(December, 1915):380.
David Ross--Modern Pioneer by Fred C. Kelly. *Indiana Magazine of History* 42(March, 1946):88-89.
Frontier Doctor by Urling C. Coe. *Mississippi Valley Historical Review* 27(September, 1940):294-295.
Half That Glory by Stanley E. Gray. *Indiana Magazine of History* 37(December, 1941):400-401.
James Hall, Literary Pioneer of the Ohio Valley by John T. Flanagan. *Indiana Magazine of History* 39(September, 1943):302-304.
Lake Erie by Harlan Hatcher. *Indiana Magazine of History* 42(June, 1946):200-201.
Lake Michigan by Milo Quaife. *Indiana Magazine of History* 40(December, 1944):396-398.
Lake Superior by Grace .L. Nute. *Indiana Magazine of History* 40(September, 1944):396-398.
Land of Promise, The Story of the Northwest Territory by Walter Havighurst. *Mississippi Valley Historical Review* 33(March, 1947):649-651.
Mid-Country edited by Lowry C. Wimberly. *Indiana Magazine of History* 42(March, 1946):90-92.
Midwest at Noon by Graham Hutton. *Indiana Magazine of History* 43(June, 1947):184-187.
Mentor Graham: The Man Who Taught Lincoln by Duncan Kunigunde and D. F. Nickols. *Mississippi Valley Historical Review* 31(March, 1945):605-606.
Pioneers of Morgan County: Memoirs of Noah J. Major edited by Logan Esarey. *Indiana Magazine of History* 11(December, 1915):382-383.
The Rampaging Frontier: Manners and Humors of Pioneer Days in the South and the Middle West by Thomas D. Clark. *Mississippi Valley Historical Review* 26(September, 1939):261-262.
Theodore Roosevelt and the Progressive Movement by George E. Mowry. *Mississippi Valley Historical Review* 33(September, 1946):328-329.
This Land is Ours by Louis Zara. *Indiana Magazine of History* 37(March, 1941):72-73.
Via Western Express and Stagecoach by Oscar O. Winther. *Indiana Magazine of History* 42(June, 1946):203.

Studies of R. Carlyle Buley

Billington, Ray Allen. Review of *The Old Northwest* by R. Carlyle Buley. *American Historical Review* 56(April, 1951):907-909.
Carmony, Donald F. "Tribute." *Indiana Magazine of History* 60(December, 1964):353-354.
Davis, Paul M. Review of *Midwest Pioneer: His Ills, Cures, and Doctors* by R. Carlyle Buley. *Mississippi Valley Historical Review* 32(December, 1945):442-443.

Hedges, J. Edward. Review of *The American Life Convention, 1906-1952: A Study in the History of Life Insurance* by R. Carlyle Buley. *Indiana Magazine of History* 52(December, 1956):407-410.

Kek, Evan R. Review of *The Equitable Life Assurance Society of the United States* by R. Carlyle Buley. *Indiana Magazine of History* 56(March, 1960):93-94.

McCormick, Gene E. "R. Carlyle Buley." *Indiana History Bulletin* 45(May, 1968):67.

Montagu, M. F. Ashley. Review of *The Midwest Pioneer: His Ills, Cures and Doctors* by R. Carlyle Buley. *New York Times Review of Books* (March 18, 1945):4.

Mood, Fulmer. "The Theory of the History of an American Section and the Practice of R. Carlyle Buley." *Indiana Magazine of History* 48(March, 1952):1-22.

Myers, Burton D. Review of *The Midwest Pioneer: His Ills, Cures, and Doctors* by R. Carlyle Buley. *Indiana Magazine of History* 41(June, 1945):200-201.

Norwood, William Frederick. Review of *Midwest Pioneer: His Ills, Cures, and Doctors* by R. Carlyle Buley. *American Historical Review* 51(January, 1946):329-330.

Notice of Pulitzer Award and account of tribute dinner in Buley's honor. *Indiana Magazine of History* 47(June, 1951):216.

"Obituaries." *Journal of American History* 55(September, 1968):459-460.

Pomeroy, Earl S. Review of *The Old Northwest* by R. Carlyle Buley. *Mississippi Valley Historical Review* 38(June, 1951):112-114.

"Private Preface (Purely Purloined)" to *The Old Northwest.* Typescript, Indiana University Press, Bloomington, IN.

"R. Carlyle Buley." In *Current Biography 1951.* 15 volumes. New York: H. W. Wilson Co., 1952. 12:74.

Solt, Leon, Donald Carmony, and Chase Mooney, "Memorial Tribute." *Indiana Magazine of History* 64(December, 1968):323-326.

Stalson, J. Owen. Review of *The American Life Convention 1906-1952: A Study in the History of Life Insurance* by R. Carlyle Buley. *Saturday Review of Books* 37(September 4, 1954):18, 31.

Unsigned review notice. *The Old Northwest* by R. Carlyle Buley. *Indiana Magazine of History* 59(December, 1963):403.

__________. *The Old Northwest* by R. Carlyle Buley. *Saturday Review of Books* 34(May 5, 1951):40.

__________. *The Romantic Appeal of the New West, 1815-1840* by R. Carlyle Buley. *Indiana Magazine of History* 57(September, 1961):274.

Watson, Ralph. Review of *The Indiana Home* edited by R. Carlyle Buley. *Indiana Magazine of History* 39(September, 1943):301-302.

Wellborn, Fred W. Review of *The American Life Convention, 1906-1952: A Study in the History of Life Insurance* by R. Carlyle Buley. *American Historical Review* 61(April, 1956):735-736.

White, Gerald T. Review of *The Equitable Life Assurance Society of the United States, 1859-1964* by R. Carlyle Buley. *Journal of American History* 55(December, 1968:)651-652.

__________. Review of *The Equitable Life Assurance Society of the United States* by R. Carlyle Buley. *Mississippi Valley Historical Review* 46(March, 1960):739-740.

Williamson, Harold F. Review of *The American Life Convention, 1906-1952: A Study in the History of Life Insurance* by R. Carlyle Buley. *Mississippi Valley Historical Review* 41(September, 1954):355-356.

13

CARLOS EDUARDO CASTAÑEDA

by Francisco E. Balderrama

Biography

Carlos Eduardo Castañeda was born the seventh child of Timoteo and Elisa Andrea Castañeda on November 11, 1896, in Camargo, Tamaulipas, Mexico. By virtue of its location in northern Mexico, Carmargo was a very appropriate birthplace for a life devoted to studying the history of the Mexican North and American Southwest. Even though he was born on the Mexican side of the border, Castañeda's parents had spent considerable time in Texas, for his father, Timoteo, had received an education in San Antonio and the city of the Alamo was also the site of the wedding of his parents. Carlos began his life in Texas at the young age of ten when he crossed the international border with his family to live in Brownsville.

Castañeda's Mexican birth and Texas residence were dominant forces shaping the direction of his historical scholarship. Don Carlos later described himself when beginning the work on his monumental multivolume study, *Our Catholic Heritage in Texas*, as "a graduate of the University of Texas and though a Mexican by birth, I feel that I am a Texan in spirit" (*Pacific Historical Review* 42:320).

Equally significant to Castañeda's development as a historian was his positive childhood schooling experience. This was accomplished even though young Castañeda was ordered to repeat two grade levels when he was initially enrolled in the Brownsville School District because of his limited command of English. Nevertheless, education was prized in the Castañeda family, especially by the father, who had worked as an instructor in Mexico before their arrival in the United States. His parents, therefore, registered Carlos for summer classes to master English, and he soon rejoined students of his own age and grade level. This parental concern, advice, and support for education inspired Carlos to become an energetic and enthusiastic student. It was apparent throughout his schooling in South Texas but it was especially noticeable during his high school years when he was involved in various academic as well as extracurricular activities. The crowning academic achievement of Castañeda's years in Brownsville was his graduation as valedictorian of the Brownsville High School class of 1916. This honor would be prized as an important accomplishment for any student, but this award was even more exceptional for Castañeda. He was not only the first student of his class, but he was also the only Mexican-American graduate of that year in this border town with a large Mexican population.

The University of Texas recognized Castañeda's extraordinary accomplishments by awarding him a scholarship upon his being admitted to the university. Still, he had to delay his educational plans for a year because of financial difficulties--property taxes were overdue on the family home. Castañeda earned the needed tax money by teaching at a Texas country school. This financial obstacle was the first of many monetary barriers blocking Castañeda throughout his career as a historian. Don Carlos himself underscored this dilemma when he was honored by the Academy of American Franciscan History: "To the young men and young women of today who desire a comfortable living, I do not recommend history as a career. There is much work, much self-satisfaction, some recognition, some honor, but no money" (*The Americas* 8:483).

Even though Castañeda realized that there were few financial rewards in the historical profession, he preferred this career to an earlier choice of the more lucrative field of engineering. This decision was made after serving as a research assistant for Texas historian Eugene C. Barker, who introduced Castañeda to the exciting work of historical research by assigning him the difficult task of translating rare documents about Spanish and Mexican Texas. Father John Elliot Ross, chaplain for the local Newman Roman Catholic Club, was aware of Castañeda's work as a research assistant and suggested that the young scholar pursue this type of work as a career. Ross also thought Castañeda could make use of his native knowledge of Spanish for translating and interpreting the historical experience of Latin America for American society. Even though Ross and Barker encouraged Castañeda to study history as his professional calling, military service during World War I and then family responsibilities interrupted his professional preparation. Nevertheless, Castañeda confronted these challenges, in his own words, as a "Spanish Toronado" of energy and enthusiasm, when earning the following degrees in history: B.A. (1921), M.A. (1923), and Ph.D. (1930). These achievements were formidable accomplishments, especially if one realizes that Castañeda studied and later taught during a time when there were no other Americans of Mexican descent professionally trained and employed as historians in the United States.

Carlos Castañeda's talent and dedication as a scholar were apparent early in his career, for while studying for the doctorate he was appointed the director of the Latin American Collection at the University of Texas. Don Carlos therefore played a critical role in laying the foundations of what was to become the leading Latin American collection in the United States. It was largely through his efforts that the University of Texas acquired thousands of important manuscripts and documents for the American Southwest, Mexico, and Latin America. Such important administrative responsibilities at the library never stopped Don Carlos's research and writing, for he produced some twelve monographs and book-length translations as well as numerous articles, pamphlets, reviews, and book notes.

Professor Castañeda also devoted considerable time and energy to instructional responsibilities, for he taught not only at his home institution of the University of Texas, but he was also a guest lecturer at the University of New Mexico, Catholic University of America, and the National University of Mexico. Acknowledgment of his work as a historian was widespread, with tributes forthcoming from various professional associations and learned academies in this country and throughout the world. Even though Carlos Castañeda was first and foremost a historian, he was associated with various community organizations concerned with the needs and problems of the Mexican population in Texas and in the American Southwest. His dedication as well as leadership in assisting the Mexican community was also apparent in his service as director of the Texas Fair Employment Commission during World War II. This role as an able representative for the local Mexican community was recognized with numerous commendations and honors.

Themes

The reason why Don Carlos was the worthy recipient of such countless honors was apparent in his first book, *The Mexican Side of the Texas Revolution.* This work presented for the first time in English the testimony of such major Mexican participants as generals Antonio López de Santa Anna and José María Tornel. Moreover, his translation of these documents was skillfully done with particular care for portraying the thought of the authors in a readable and understandable manner. This first book publication was the beginning of a significant series of historical translations establishing Castañeda as a leading translator of the Spanish-Mexican periods for the American Southwest.

Castañeda again made use of his translation talent when writing his doctoral dissertation. This project began when the National Library of Mexico asked Don Carlos and other scholars to classify newly discovered archival documents. While sorting through these materials, Castañeda uncovered a "lost" history of Texas written by Father Juan Agustín Morfi. The discovery of this manuscript was truly an important find, for some scholars had questioned the existence of Morfi's history. Castañeda therefore decided to translate and edit *Juan Agustín Morfi: History of Texas, 1673-1679*, with an extensive introduction and lengthy notes, as his dissertation.

To select the translation of a history of Texas by a Franciscan missionary as a dissertation topic was also indicative of Don Carlos's dedication to uncovering and interpreting the historical presence of Catholicism in the American Southwest and particularly in Texas. Castañeda ranked this interest as an important responsibility, for he was a practicing Roman Catholic and active in his church. The Catholic church recognized these efforts by bestowing on him honors from such organizations as the Order of the Holy Sepulchre of Jerusalem, the Order of Isabel the Catholic, and the Academy of American Franciscan History. Another Catholic association, the Knights of Columbus men's organization, funded the publication of Don Carlos's monumental seven-volume series, *Our Catholic Heritage in Texas*.

Concern with frontier Catholicism and the editing of little-known or neglected primary documents were not the only substantive themes characterizing Castañeda's work. Of even greater significance were his focus upon the Bolton School emphasis on missions and his reinterpretation of the Texas Revolution from the perspective of Mexican Texans.

Analysis

Carlos Eduardo Castañeda's scholarship contributed greatly to understanding the history of Spanish and Mexican rule in the American Southwest, especially in the state of Texas. Castañeda wrote during the time when the Bolton Borderlands School was an innovative and exciting framework for investigating the history of the United States-Mexico border region, and his writings should be analyzed and assessed as part of this historical school. In studying the American frontier, Herbert Eugene Bolton emphasized the Spanish presence in the American Southwest and also developed a hemispheric approach to the history of the United States. Bolton trained a generation of scholars to pursue these themes, and even though Castañeda never studied under Bolton he liked to describe himself as an "'adopted' boy" of Bolton's. Don Carlos's membership in the Borderlands School was particularly evident in his focus upon Bolton's frontier institution of the mission as a primary theme in his writings, especially for Texas. Castañeda portrayed the missions as noble institutions and the missionaries as heroic individuals. Even though one suspects that Castañeda's religious background as a Roman Catholic influenced his viewpoint, this interpretation is the explanation favored by most Bolton scholars at the time. Borderlands historians rarely challenged or questioned the objectives or actions of the missionaries seeking to Christianize and to "civilize" the Indians of the American Southwest and Mexican North.

Even though Castañeda was a major contributor to the Bolton School, Don Carlos also employed his professional skill for accurate investigation and sound analysis to introduce a new interpretation for American historians. Don Carlos's Mexican birth, Texas schooling, and love of the Lone Star State led him to reexamine the history of Texas and the borderlands from 1810 to 1836. A new interpretation was first presented in the translated testimony of the major Mexican participants in the Texas Revolution. In *The Mexican Side of the Texas Revolution* (1928), Castañeda selected documents showing how the Mexican republic was defeated not simply by military force but also by internal dissent. American scholars, and especially Texas historians, had previously overlooked this view of the 1836 conflict. This finding was later expanded and refined in his multivolume chronicle of Texas history. He describes the era of 1810 to 1836 as a "fight for freedom." Castañeda defines this fight in his volume VI of *Our Catholic Heritage in Texas, Transition Period: The Fight for Freedom, 1810-1836* (1950), as having various rounds of action, first against Spain, and then against Mexico. The battle for freedom is deemed essential "not because either the Spanish or the Mexican people were tyrannical, but because their respective governments had fallen into the hands of tyrants" (p. i). Castañeda therefore challenged the prevalent historical interpretations and contemporary views stereotyping Mexicans and Latin Americans as inherently incapable of democratic government. By focusing upon this nineteenth-century issue, Castañeda exposes the roots of twentieth-century misunderstandings and tensions between Anglos and Mexicans in the Lone Star State. Moreover, Don Carlos demystifies the heroic images of the Texas Revolution and places this event within a proper historical perspective.

In presenting his various interpretations, Castañeda always wrote a clear and precise narrative reflecting careful analysis as well as a detailed understanding of the pertinent sources. An additional hallmark of his scholarship was his talent as a skilled translator in presenting the meaning of key passages in a readable manner. Even though Don Carlos's publications are numerous, the best reflection of his scholarship is his extensive and rigorous seven-volume *Our Catholic Heritage in Texas, 1519-1936.* The title is somewhat misleading, for this is no simple ecclesiastical history. Rather, new primary sources were uncovered and employed to provide a systematic and detailed accounting of Texas history from the days of discovery to the early twentieth century, with the church remaining the major focus of attention. Moreover, this work provided new historical information on significant events, figures, and developments. In presenting this vivid picture of early Texas history, *The Catholic Heritage* did not consider only local events and circumstances, as many state and regional histories frequently do. Rather, Castañeda gave full attention to international forces, especially European power struggles, in describing and analyzing the evolution of Texas. Carlos Eduardo Castañeda was a master of extensive research, exact translation, careful analysis, and precise writing.

Bibliography

Books

Early Texas Album: Fifty Illustrations with Notes. Co-authored with Frederick C. Cabot. Austin: Privately printed, 1929.

Excerpts from the Memories for the History of Texas . . . of Fray Juan Agustín Morfi. Co-edited and translated with Frederick E. Cabot. San Antonio: Naylor Publishing Co., 1932.

La Guerra de Reforma Según el Archivo del General Manuel Doblado, 1857-1860. San Antonio: Casa Editorial Lozano, 1930.

Guide to the Latin American Manuscripts in the University of Texas Library. Co-edited with Jack Autrey Dabbs. Cambridge, MA: Harvard University Press, 1930.

Historia de Todos los Colegios de México desde la Conquista hasta 1780 by Félix Osores y Sotomayo. Editor. Mexico City: Talleres Gráficos de la Nación, 1929.

A History of Latin America for Schools. Co-authored with Samuel Guy Inman. New York: Macmillan, 1944.

Juan Agustín Morfi: History of Texas, 1673--1679, With an Introduction and Biographical Sketch of Morfi. Translator and editor. 2 volumes. Albuquerque: The Quivira Society, 1935.

The Lands of Middle America. Co-authored with E. C. Delany. New York: Macmillan, 1948.

The Mexican Side of the Texas Revolution. Dallas: P. L. Turner Company, 1928.

Our Catholic Heritage in Texas, 1519-1936. Austin: Von Boeckmann-Jones Company. 7 Volumes. Reprint. New York: Arno Press, 1976. Vol. I, *The Finding of Texas, 1519-1693* (1936); Vol. II, *The Winning of Texas, 1693-1731* (1936); Vol. III, *The Missions at Work, 1731-1761* (1938); Vol. IV, *The Passing of the Missions, 1762-1782* (1939); Vol. V, *The End of the Spanish Regime, 1780-1810* (1942); Vol. VI, *Transition Period: The Fight for Freedom, 1810-1836* (1950); Vol. VII, *The Church in Texas since Independence, 1836-1950* (1958).

A Report on the Spanish Archives in San Antonio, Texas. San Antonio: Yanaguana Society, 1937.

Three Manuscript Maps of Texas by Stephen F. Austin. Co-authored with Early Martin, Jr. Austin: Privately printed, 1930.

Selected Articles and Pamphlets

"Algunas Tendencias en la Poesía Mexicana Contemporanea." *La Prensa* (San Antonio, TX), November 9, 1931.

"Almonte's Statistical Report on Texas, 1834." *Southwestern Historical Quarterly* 24(January, 1925):177-222.

"Archival Needs: Latin America." *Inter-American Bibliographical Review* 2(Spring, 1942):10-13.

"The Beginning of Printing in America." *Catholic Library World* 10(May, 1939):243-252, 259-260. Reprint. *Catholic Digest* 3(July, 1939):36-40; *Hispanic American Historical Review* 20(November, 1940):671-685.

"The Beginnings of University Life in America." *Preliminary Studies of the Texas Catholic Historical Society* 3(July, 1938):5-26.

"The Bounds of Church and State in Education." Commencement Address, Saint Mary's College, Xavier, KS. *The Southern Messenger* 17(August, 1950):6.

"The Broadening Concept of History Teaching in Texas." In *Inter-American Conference on Intellectual Interchange*. Austin: University of Texas, 1943. Pp. 97-108.

"Carta de la Emperatriz Carlotta." *Revista de Estudios Hispánicos* 2(January-March, 1929):27-28.

"A Chapter in Frontier History." *Southwest Review* 28(Autumn, 1942):31-52.
"La Colección Latinoamericana de la Universidad de Texas." *Umbral* 1(March, 1944):3-9.
"The Coming of the Augustinians to the New World." *Records of the American Catholic Historical Society of Philadelphia* 60(December, 1949):189-196. Reprint. "Souvenir Program of the Dedication Ceremonies of the Villanova College Library," April, 22, 1949.
"Communication to the Congress." In *La Universidad y la revolución.* Mendoza, Argentina: Ministerio de Educación de la Nación, Universidad National de Cuyo, 1949. P. 130.
"Communications between Santa Fe and San Antonio in the Eighteenth Century." *Texas Geographic Magazine* 5(Spring, 1941):17-38.
"The Corregidor in Spanish Colonial Administration." *Hispanic American Historical Review* 9(November, 1929):446-470.
"Cuarto Entenario de la Imprenta en México." *Investigaciones Históricas* 1(January, 1939):319-322.
"Customs and Habits of the Texas Indians." *Mid-America* 14(July, 1931):47-56.
"El Dilema de México." *Revista Mensual, Universidad de México* 1(November, 1930):47-51.
"Earliest Catholic Activities in Texas." *Catholic Historical Review* 17(October, 1931):278-295.
"The Educational Revolution in Mexico." *Educational Review* 68(October, 1924):123-125.
"The Fiesta of Mexican Independence." Printed and distributed by the Committee for the Celebration of Mexican Independence Day, San Antonio, Texas (September, 1948).
"The First American Play." *Preliminary Studies of the Texas Catholic Historical Society* 3(January, 1936):5-39.
"First European Settlement on the Rio Grande." *Texas Geographic Magazine* 9(Autumn, 1945):28-31.
"The First Printing Press in Mexico." *Publisher's Weekly* 137(January, 1940):50-53.
"Foreword." In *La Salle's Occupation of Texas* by Walter J. O'Donnell. *Preliminary Studies of the Texas Catholic Historical Society* 3(April, 1936) :i.
"Fray Juan de Zumárraga and Indian Policy in New Spain." *The Americas* 5(January, 1949):296-310.
"Fray Junípero Serra, Pioneer and Saint." *The Serran* (May, 1950):1-4.
"The Genius of the Race." Printed by the Columbus Day Committee, San Antonio, Texas (October, 1948).
"History: Caribbean Area, The National Period." In *Handbook of Latin American Studies: 1939* edited by Lewis Hanke and Miron Burgin. Cambridge: Oxford University Press, 1940. Pp. 263-272.
"The Human Side of a Great Collection." *Books Abroad* 14(Spring, 1940):116-121.

"Inter-American Cultural Relations." *Catholic Library World* 19(October, 1947):26-30.

"The Irristible Challenge of the Pueblos." In *Jesuit Beginnings in New Mexico, 1867-1882* edited by M. Lilliana Owens. El Paso, TX: Revista Catolica Press, 1950. Pp. 11-14.

"Is Mexico Turning Bolshevik?" *Catholic World* 123(June, 1926):366-372.

"José María Sánchez: A Trip to Texas in 1828." *Southwestern Historical Quarterly* 29(April, 1926):249-288.

"The Latin American in Texas." Address delivered at the Annual Convention of the G.I. Forum, McAllen, Texas. McAllen, TX *Valley Evening Monitor*, August 20, 1950, p. 2.

"Latin America's First Great Educator." *Current History* 22(May, 1925):223-225.

"Life in the Old Mission of San Jose." In *San Jose, Queen of the Missions*. San Antonio, TX: Private printing, 1937.

"The Manuel E. Gondra Collection of Manuscripts." Co-authored with J. Autrey Dabbs. In *Handbook of Latin American Studies: 1940* edited by Miron Burgin. Cambridge: Oxford University Press, 1941. Pp. 505-517.

"Los Manuscritos Perdidos de Gutiérrez de Luna." *Revista Mexicana de Estudios Históricos* 2(September-October, 1928):170-176.

"Mexican Faith and Hope." *The Sign* 21(January, 1942):337-338.

"The Missionary Years in Texas History." In *Diocese of Galveston Centennial, 1847-1947*. Galveston, TX: Private printing, 1947.

"Modern Language Instruction in American Colleges, 1779-1800." Pamphlet for the College of William & Mary. Washington, DC: National Capital Press, 1925.

"The Oldest University in America." *Hispania* 13(May, 1930):247-249.

"Our Latin American Neighbors." *Catholic Historical Review* 26(January, 1940):421-433.

"Pioneers in Sackcloth." *Catholic Historical Review* 25(October, 1939):309-326.

"Pioneers of Christian Culture." Mexico City: Editorial Jus., 1950. Pp. 1-30.

"Pioneers of Christian Culture in Texas: An Address." Waco, TX: Private printing, 1949.

"Pioneers of the Church in Texas." *Diamond Jubilee of the Archdiocese of San Antonio, Texas*. San Antonio, TX: Private printing, 1950.

"Pioneers of Mathematics, Astronomy, and Astrology in America." *Texas Mathematics Teacher Bulletin* 15(May, 1931):5-8. Reprinted, *Eleusis of Chi Omega* 34(February, 1932):34-38.

"El Primer Optimista del Nuevo Mundo: Columbus." Columbus Day Celebration Pamphlet. San Antonio, TX: Pan American Club, 1945.

El Proceso del General Scott por sus Relaciones con el General Santa Ana." Pamphlet. Mexico City: Private printing, 1949.

"Recent Mexican Bibliographies." *Southwestern Historical Quarterly* 35(January, 1932):252-254.

"Relations of General Scott with Santa Anna." *Hispanic American Historical Review* 24(November, 1949):455-473.

"El Rev. P. Don José Antonio Pichardo." In *Pichardo, Vida y Martiro del Protomártir Mexicano San Felipe de Jesús de las Casas* edited by Francisco Orozco y Jiménez. Guadalajara, México: Private printing, 1934. Pp. v-xiv.

"The Rhythm of History." *Man* 1(February, 1949):27-28.

"Santa Anna as Seen by His Secretary." *Dallas Morning News*, May 12, 1928.

"The Second Rate Citizen and Democracy." In *Are We Good Neighbors?* edited by Alonso Perales. San Antonio, TX: Artes Gráficas, 1948. Pp. 17-20.

"Silent Years in Texas History." *Southwestern Historical Quarterly* 38(October, 1934):122-134. Reprint. *Preliminary Studies of the Texas Catholic Historical Society* 2(April, 1935):5-15.

"The Six Flags of Texas." *Preliminary Studies of the Texas Catholic Historical Society* 2(April, 1932):5-15.

"Social Osmosis, The Process of Incorporation." In *Report of the Conference on the Mexican American in Chicago.* Chicago: The Community Relations Service, 1950. Pp. 32-46.

"The Sons of Saint Francis in Texas." *The Americas* 1(January, 1945):289-302.

"Sor Juana Inés de la Cruz, Primera Feminista de América." *Revista mensual de la Universidad de México* 5(March-April, 1933):365-379.

"Sources for Spanish American Church History." *Catholic Library World* 10(December, 1938):99-102.

"Statement of Dr. Carlos E. Castañeda, Regional Director, Fair Employment Practice Committee, Region 10, San Antonio, Texas, before the Senate Committee on Education and Labor, March 13, 1945." In *Fair Employment Practices Act Hearings.* Washington, D.C.: Government Printing Office, 1945. Reprint. *Are We Good Neighbors?* edited by Alonso Perales. San Antonio, TX: Artes Gráficas, 1948. Pp. 92-104.

"Statement of Dr. Carlos E. Castañeda, Special Assistant on Latin-American Problems to the Chairman of the President's Committee on Fair Employment Practice, before a Senate sub-committee on Education and Labor, September 8, 1944." In *Fair Employment Practices Act Hearings.* Washington, DC: Government Printing Office, 1944. Pp. 205-212.

"Statement on Discrimination against Mexican-Americans in Employment, before the President's Committee on Civil Rights." In *Are We Good Neighbors?* edited by Alonso S. Perales. San Antonio, TX: Artes Gráficas, 1948. Pp. 58-63.

"Statistical Report on Texas by Juan H. Almonte." Translator. *Southwestern Historical Quarterly* 28(January, 1925):177-222.

"The Teaching of History in the Secondary Schools of Mexico." *The Historical Outlook* 24(May, 1933):246-252.

"Why I Chose History." *The Americas* 8(January, 1952):475-483.

Selected Reviews

Academic Culture in the Spanish Colonies by John Tate Lanning. *Catholic Historical Review* 27(October, 1941):370-371.

After Coronado, Spanish Exploration Northeast of Mexico, 1697-1727: Documents from the Archives of Spain, Mexico, and New Mexico edited by Alfred Barnaby Thomas. *Southwestern Historical Quarterly* 4(July, 1937):111-113.

Anales del Mueso Nacionalde Arqueología, Historia y Etnographía, Tomo II, Quinta Epoca. *Southwestern Historical Quarterly* 45(July, 1941):105-106.

At the End of the Santa Fe Trail by Blandina Segale. *Southwestern Historical Quarterly* 53(April, 1950):499-500.

Bibliografía de Coahuila, Historia y Geografía by Vito Alessio Robles. *Southwestern Historical Quarterly* 33(July, 1929):86-87.

Books of the Brave, Being an Account of Books and Men in the Spanish Conquest and Settlement of the Sixteenth Century by Irving A. Leonard. *Catholic Historical Review* 36(October, 1950):327-329.

Catálogo de la Colección de Manuscritos Relativos a la Historia de América, Formado por Joaquín García Icazbalceta by Federico Gómez de Orozco. *Southwestern Historical Quarterly* 31(January, 1928):293-294.

Colombian Government Publications compiled by James B. Childs. *Catholic Library World* 13(February, 1942):152.

Coronado on the Turquoise Trail: Knight of the Pueblos and Plains by Herbert E. Bolton. *Journal of Southern History* 16(November, 1950):519-520.

El Correo en las Provincias Internas by Fernando B. Sandoval. *Hispanic American Historical Review* 30(May, 1950):234-235.

Cosas Pocas Conocidas Acerca de Este Hombre y de su Heráldica by Carlos Pérez Maldonado. *Hispanic American Historical Review* 24(November, 1944):676.

Cronistas e Historiadores de la Conquista de México: El siglo de Hernán Cortés by Ramón Iglesia. *Hispanic American Historical Review* 23(February, 1943):84-85.

Crusaders of the Rio Grande: The Story of Don Diego de Vargas and the Reconquest and Refounding of New Mexico by J. Manuel Espinosa. *Southwestern Historical Quarterly* 46(January, 1943):285-287.

Culture Conflicts in Texas, 1821-1836 by Samuel Herman Lowrie. *Hispanic American Historical Review* 13(November, 1933):482-484.

Diego de Vargas and the Reconquest of New Mexico by Jessie Bromilow Bailey. *Southwestern Historical Quarterly* 45(July, 1941):105-106.

The Discovery of New Spain in 1518 by Juan de Grijalva edited by Henry R. Wagner. *Hispanic American Historical Review* 23(May, 1943):306-307.

Disquisiones Bibliográficas: Autores, Libros, Bibliotecas, Artes Gráficas by Juan B. Iguíniz. *Hispanic American Historical Review* 24(May, 1944):331-332.

Documentos Históricos de Nuevo Leon Anotados y Comentados, 1596-1811 by Carlos Pérez Maldonado. *Hispanic American Historical Review* 28(May, 1948):276-278.

Educational Foundations of the Jesuits in Sixteenth Century New Spain by Jerome V. Jacobsen. *Hispanic American Historical Review* 19(November, 1939):521-523.

Franciscan Awatovi: The Excavation and Conjectural Reconstruction of the 17th Century Spanish Mission Establishment at a Hopi Indian Town in Northeastern Arizona by Ross Gordon Montgomery, *et al. The Americas* 7(July, 1950):108-109.

Franciscan History of North America: Report of the Eighteenth Annual Meeting. Pacific Historical Review 6(June, 1937):197-199.

Fray Juan de Zumarraga, O. F. M. by Frederick C. Cabet. *The Americas* 5(January, 1949):355-356.

Fray Margil de Jesús by Eduardo Enrique Ríos. *Hispanic American Historical Review* 23(February, 1943):109-110.

Handbook of Latin American Studies: 1936 edited by Lewis Hanke. *Southwestern Historical Quarterly* 41(April, 1938):361-362.

Handbook of Latin American Studies: 1942 edited by Miron Burgin. *Hispanic American Historical Review* 27(February, 1946):71-72.

A Historical, Political, and Natural Description of California by Pedro Fages, Soldier of Spain translated and edited by Herbert Ingram Priestly. *Southwestern Historical Quarterly* 41(July, 1937):116-117.

The History of Lower California by Sara E. Lake and A. A. Gray. *Southwestern Historical Quarterly* 43(January, 1939):284-285.

History of Mexican Literature by Carlos González Peña. *The Americas* 1(October, 1944):246-247.

A History of Mexico by Henry B. Parkes. *Catholic Historical Review* 27(April, 1941):106-108.

The Horses of the Conquest by R. B. Cunninghame Graham. *American Historical Review* 55(April, 1950):712-713.

Indian Labor in the Spanish Colonies by Ruth Kerns Barber. *Southwestern Historical Quarterly* 37(July, 1933):64-65.

Indice de Documentos de Nueva España Existentes en el Archivo de Indias de Sevilla by Francisco del Paso y Toroncoso. *Southwestern Historical Quarterly* 33(July, 1929):87-88.

Latin America and the Enlightenment by Arthur Whitaker. *Catholic Historical Review* 28(October, 1942):402-403.

The Lost Pathfinder: Zebulon Montgomery Pike by W. Eugene Hollon. *The Americas* 7(July, 1950):122-123.

Men of Mexico by James A. Magnier. *Hispanic American Historical Review* 24(May, 1944):317-319.

Mexican Government Publications: A Guide to the More Important Publications of the National Government of Mexico, 1821-1936 compiled by Anita Melville Ker. *Catholic Library World* 13(February, 1942):152. Reprint. *Southwestern Historical Quarterly* 46(July, 1942):102-103.

La Primera Imprenta en las Provincias Internas de Oriente: Texas, Tamaulipas, Nuevo León y Coahuila by Vito Alessio Robles. *Hispanic American Historical Review* 20(February, 1940):126-127.
Proceso Histórico de la Metrópoli Guanajuantense by Fulgencio Vargas. *Hispanic American Historical Review* 23(August, 1942):517-518.
Real Cédulas de la Real y Pontifica Universidad de México le 1551 a 1816 by John Tate Lanning. *Hispanic American Historical Review* 27(November, 1947):667-669.
Religious Aspects of the Conquest of Mexico by Charles S. Braden. *Catholic Historical Review* 17(July, 1931):224-229.
Revolt of the Pueblo Indians of New Mexico and Otermin's Attempted Reconquest, 1680-1682 by Charles W. Hackett. *Southwestern Historical Quarterly* 46(April, 1938):361-362.
San Antonio and Its Beginnings, 1691-1731 by Frederick C. Cabot. *Southwestern Historical Quarterly* 35(October, 1931):250-252.
Siglo y Medio de Cultura Nuevoleonense by Héctor González. *Hispanic American Historical Review* 37(August, 1947):557-558.
The Story of the Mexican War by Robert Selph Henry. *Pacific Historical Review* 19(August, 1950):289-291.
Texas: An Informal Biography by Owen P. White. *The Americas* 2(April, 1946):531-532.
Viaje a la Nueva España by Juan Francisco Gemelli Carreri. *Southwestern Historical Quarterly* 31(January, 1928):392-393.
Viaje a Texas en 1828-1829 José María Sánchez. *Hispanic American Historical Review* 23(February, 1943):111-112.
With the Makers of San Antonio: Geneologies of the Early Latin, Anglo-Mexican, and German Families by Frederick G. Cabot. *Southwestern Historical Review* 41(October, 1937):190-191.

Studies of Carlos Eduardo Castañeda

Almaráz, Félix D., Jr. "Carlos Eduardo Castañeda, Mexican American Historian: The Formative Years, 1896-1927." *Pacific Historical Review* 42(August, 1973):319-334.
__________. "The Making of a Boltonian: Carlos E. Castañeda of Texas--The Early Years." *Red River Valley Historical Review* 1(Winter, 1974):329-350.
Barcarisse, Charles A. "A Dedication to Carlos Eduardo Castañeda, 1896-1958." *Arizona and the West* 3(Spring, 1961):1-6.
"Obituary." *New York Times*, April 6, 1958.
"Obituary Notice." *Hispanic American Historical Review* 38(August, 1958):385.

14

HIRAM MARTIN CHITTENDEN

by Gordon B. Dodds

Biography

Hiram Martin Chittenden was born on a farm in Cattaraugas County, New York, on October 25, 1858. Growing up on a farm, educated in country schools and the Ten Broeck Free Academy in neighboring Franklinville, young Hiram sought wider scope for his undoubted intellectual talents than that provided by his rural neighborhood. After some rounds of teaching school, in 1878 he received both a scholarship to the new Cornell University and an appointment to the United States Military Academy. He decided to take advantage of the liberal arts offerings at Cornell for one year before moving on to the more circumscribed intellectual regimen at West Point. Chittenden's higher education gave him some advantages that would be useful in his later career as a professional historian. At Cornell he worked with William C. Russel, who had been taught the modern methods of scientific history in Germany; at West Point he gained a reading knowledge of both the French and Spanish languages. In 1884 Chittenden graduated (third in a class of thirty-seven) from the Military Academy and received an assignment in the Corps of Engineers.

His first station was at Willett's Point in the harbor of New York City. There he resided with his bride, Nettie Parker, his childhood sweetheart, carrying out routine military duties but with sufficient time to acquire a law degree on the side. In 1887 he first saw the trans-Mississippi West on duty with the Department of the Platte in Omaha, Nebraska. His next post was in St. Louis with the Missouri River Commission beginning in 1889. Then, from 1891 to 1893, he began the first of two tours of duty building roads in Yellowstone National Park. One result of the assignment was the publication of a book in 1895 entitled *The Yellowstone National Park: Historical and Descriptive.* The work was a combination of history and guidebook that equipped the tourist to enjoy a stay in the park. Although described by Chittenden later as a "somewhat amateurish and freakish" effort, *The Yellowstone National Park* was based upon written sources and oral interviews as well as its author's personal observations and experiences.

Chittenden wrote his first history while doing routine duty at Louisville, Kentucky, and investigating canal routes in Ohio from 1893 to 1896. He then returned to the Missouri River Commission, but was soon detached to prepare a survey of reservoir sites in Colorado and Wyoming. His report, published in 1897, led to the Newlands Act in 1902, the first direct venture of the federal government in irrigation and reclamation. Chittenden served (within the United States) on active duty during the war with Spain, then returned to St. Louis and the Missouri River Commission. He did some routine work at this station and--in the summer construction seasons of 1899-1906--completed the construction of roads in Yellowstone Park. During these years--in the winter seasons, on weekends, and in the evenings--Chittenden worked on three historical works which were published between 1902 and 1905: *The American Fur Trade of the Far West,* 3 volumes; *History of Early Steamboat Navigation on the Missouri River,* 2 volumes; and *Life, Letters and Travels of Father Pierre-Jean De Smet, S. J., 1801-1873,* 4 volumes.

From 1906 to 1910 Chittenden was Seattle district engineer until retired for disability. During his last assignment Chittenden took time to publish a critique of the forestry conservationists' theory that reforestation would control stream flow on hillsides and mountains. His article brought him national publicity (much of it unfavorable). From 1911 to 1915 Chittenden served as the first president of the newly created Seattle Port Commission. Throughout his retirement years Chittenden wrote articles on a variety of public issues and in 1911 published a book entitled *War or Peace: A Present Duty and a Future Hope.* This last was not a book of history but a set of proposals to prevent war, a genre popular at the time. Chittenden died in Seattle on October 9, 1917.

Themes

Hiram Martin Chittenden was a transitional figure in American historical writing. He was affected by the older romantic school of narrative writers whose ranks included William H. Prescott and John Lathrop Motley and whose practitioners of frontier history numbered Washington Irving, Francis Parkman, and Theodore Roosevelt. But he also partook at times of the spirit and methods of the newer "scientific" historians, trained in the German method of respect for the accuracy of factual materials based upon original sources. His writings on historical subjects bridged the gap between these two significant methods of interpreting the past.

Chittenden's first historical work was an article about the history of Fort Benton that appeared in the *Magazine of American History* in 1890. It described the rise and fall of the city as a river port, the demise of which was due to the coming of the transcontinental railroad. A large portion of the article was a composite account, drawn from actual logs of steamboats, of a "typical" journey on the Missouri River. *The Yellowstone*

National Park, published in 1895, forced Chittenden to delve into source materials and led to his acquaintanceship with two professional historians, Elliott Coues and Frances Fuller Victor. The book, although in part a contemporary guidebook, included memorable passages on geology, geography, the Indians, and the mountain men.

What first turned Chittenden into a distinguished historian was discouragement with the value of his river and harbor assignments on the Missouri River. As he remembered his frustration many years later: "Now began the experience which has been a source of astonishment to me ever since. I didn't care enough about the Missouri River to waste any unnecessary energy thereon, for I felt as certain then as I do now that it would all be labor lost. I, therefore, had no compunction in directing as much of my time as I could to work which I believed would be of a great deal more use to my countrymen" (Chittenden Papers). The first product of this determination was *The American Fur Trade of the Far West,* a three-volume work finished in 1902. This was truly a pioneering endeavor, for Chittenden had no monograph on the fur trade for a guide. Washington Irving had written about a portion of the western trade, but his *Astoria* and *Captain Bonneville* were more modest than Chittenden's effort.

Chittenden decided on large proportions. The five major sections of his work are a combination of narrative and topical approaches. The first part of the book, only seventy pages, deals with the organization and financing of the fur trade. Following this introduction, Chittenden presented the most important section of the work--almost half the book--entitled "Historical." It traces the origins of the fur trade in North America and develops in detail the histories of the major companies that operated in the trans-Mississippi West. Part III of *The Fur Trade* discusses "Contemporary Events Connected with the Fur Trade" and part IV contains "Notable Incidents and Characters in the History of the Fur Trade." The final part of the text, "The Country and Its Inhabitants," includes a scientific description of the mountains, plains, watercourses, flora, fauna, and Indian life of the Plains and Rockies. Following the text is a series of eight appendixes that encompasses sources such as newspaper accounts of "The Flathead Deputation" of 1832 and miscellaneous materials including the author's lists of trading posts in the West.

Chittenden's second work, *History of Early Steamboat Navigation on the Missouri River,* was published in 1903. Its genesis was his friendship with a retired river pilot, Joseph La Barge, whom Chittenden met in St. Louis while on duty with the Missouri River Commission. La Barge interested him in the history of commerce on the great river and Chittenden decided to use the skeleton of La Barge's personal experiences to reconstruct a history of steamboat navigation. The organization of *Steamboat Navigation* reflects the tension between the biographical and institutional aspects of the topic. The subtitle, *Life and Adventures of Joseph La Barge,* was the most accurate description of the text of the book. Chittenden presented LaBarge's life in chronological order interspersed with topical analysis of various themes, such as the types of river craft employed in the fur trade, the art of steamboat navigation, the use of the steamboat in the fur trade, a description of the Indians of the Missiouri Valley, and the role of the United States Army on the Missouri. Chittenden analyzed in depth the effect of events of the 1840s upon the river: The Mormon migration upriver to Council Bluffs from 1845 to 1847; the transportation of troops during the Mexican War; the gold seekers who used the Missouri Route; and the government exploring parties of the West.

Chittenden's final major historical work was *Life, Letters and Travels of Father Pierre-Jean De Smet, S.J., 1801-1873*. Chittenden had as a collaborator in this work Alfred T. Richardson, whom he had met in Yellowstone National Park. Chittenden chose Richardson because he regarded him as a better linguist than himself. *The Life and Letters* appeared in 1905 in a four-volume edition. Chittenden and Richardson divided the book into two parts. The first was a 144-page biography of De Smet written by Chittenden. The second part was a translation of about thirty percent of De Smet's letters. The letters section is divided into nine portions. Parts I through VI cover the missionary's career and provide an itinerary of his major activities. Parts VII and VIII contain letters descriptive of the life of the Indians among whom De Smet lived on his long Indian missions in the West. Part IX contains miscellaneous letters on a variety of topics that could be compressed neatly into any framework. This book was the least popular of Chittenden's works, and the least professional. The biography did not attempt to place De Smet either in the larger context of Catholic missionary efforts or, except superficially, in the context of American Indian policy and Indian-white relations. Although he did not entirely ignore the latter topic, Chittenden's treatment was not exhaustive. So far as the correspondence section goes, the editors missed the holdings of De Smet letters in several repositories; they transposed or deleted paragraphs in the letters without indicating the alterations to the reader; and they made several poor translations, especially on matters of theology and religious practice.

Analysis

So far as his own published works were concerned, Chittenden never gave any thought whatsoever to a formal philosophy of history. It was not easy for an intellect like his, turned always to practical tasks, to publish any profundities on the nature of the discipline of history. What he was attempting, therefore, emerges from the nature of his work rather than from his explicit declarations. In a methodological sense, Chittenden was most certainly a scientific historian. He relied insofar as possible upon source materials. He credited his information in footnotes. He weighed authorities objectively. Beyond these methods, Chittenden was scientific in a larger sense.

Chittenden was frequently affected by Darwinian evolutionary thought when he made large explanations of historical events and developments. Chittenden found especially useful the offshoot of Darwinism that proclaimed the capacity of certain races or nations to assert themselves at particular periods. Like many scholars of his time in the United States,

Great Britain, and Europe, he was suspicious of "non Anglo-Saxon" peoples. He himself was alarmed over the great wave of immigration to the United States from southern and central Europe. He was a full-fledged Anglo-Saxon imperialist, arguing that nations must grow and expand. He cheered Britain's victory in the Boer War and the United States's acquisition of the Philippines and the Panama Canal Zone. When he contemplated the cession of Louisiana to the United States, Chittenden described the sentiments of the inhabitants in racial terms: "The new order of things was by no means generally acceptable to the foreign element of the population, either Spanish or French. They saw in it the death knell of their peculiar customs and laws, and they knew that the enterprising spirit of the Anglo-Saxon race would crowd them out of the avenues of industry and commerce even on the very soil where they had lived and toiled from infancy"(*The American Fur Trade of the Far West* I:79). This evolutionary view of race is also evident in Chittenden's rebuke to humanitarians who wished Indians and whites to share the land as equals. Although Chittenden mourned the passing of the Indians, he believed that the humanitarians were operating upon a false assumption: "It ignores the operation of that evolutionary process by which a weaker race disappears before a superior in spite of all that laws or military force can do to prevent"(I:11).

Although his historical methods were scientific, Chittenden was interested mainly in the romantic aspects of history. He admired the heroic figures, the movers and shakers and adventurers, who epitomized the industry and aggressiveness of the nineteenth century, although he recoiled from those who broke moral boundaries to gain their ends. In spite of the fact that only one of his historical works is even superficially a biography, all indicate Chittenden's admiration for the romantic individualist. Chittenden praises Astor's strength and wisdom, his courage, and his business sagacity. "John Jacob Astor," he declares, "although an alien by birth, is one of America's best examples of self-made men--men of humble beginnings, who, by sheer native ability, have risen to the foremost rank in their respective callings" (I:163). He praises the business morality and the accomplishments in the field and counting house of Joseph La Barge and Ramsay Crooks. He sprinkles throughout *The Fur Trade* anecdotes and brief biographical sketches of the primitive hero: Jim Bridger, Hugh Glass, and John Colter.

Romantic institutions and scenes also drew Chittenden's attention and admiration. He writes of the steamboat: "It has seldom happened in history that the introduction of labor-saving devices has not robbed society to some extent of what was poetic and sentimental, and replaced it by something more prosaic and matter of fact. The Missouri river steamboat was an exception, for with all the romance that attached to the old keelboat, its own history was more romantic still" (I:35). He evoked the Oregon Trail in the same vein: "There are few more impressive sights than portions of this old highway today. It still lies there upon the prairie, deserted by the traveler, an everlasting memorial of the human tide which once filled it to overflowing. Nature herself has helped to perpetuate this memorial, for the prairie winds, year by year, carve the furrow more deeply, and the wild sunflower blossoms along its course, as if in silent memory of those who sank beneath its burdens"(I:462).

In the frontier era Chittenden discovered a period in which the individual had large scope to govern her or his own destiny, a power which Chittenden saw possible in his own career. Although he saw in the frontier period many imperfections, Chittenden never acknowledged that the individual of character and ability was helpless to set his own course. In the end, then, in spite of his Darwinian gestures, Chittenden's determinism was rather mild, really not very fatalistic at all, a convenient way of interpreting some unsavory episodes like the expulsion of the Indian, but of little value for explaining most of the individuals, events, and developments that he characterized.

Chittenden's historiographical ambiguity clearly illustrates his transitional place in American historical writing. In many ways he was a follower of the first great frontier model, the dramatic, narrative, heroic approach of Washington Irving, Francis Parkman, and Theodore Roosevelt. Chittenden's romanticism, his faith in the superior virtues of the Anglo-Saxon race and his concern with the exploits of individuals, all resemble closely this original genre of frontier historical writing.

But Chittenden was not simply one who concentrated upon, as Frederick Jackson Turner derisively dubbed it, "border warfare and the chase." Although Chittenden never seemed to be influenced by Turner's more sophisticated ideas about social evolution in different physiographic regions, he, like Turner, did take a broad approach to his study. He consciously attempted to place the narrative against the background of the environmental setting. He showed more sympathy for the customs and fate of the Indians than did Parkman or Roosevelt (or Turner, for that matter). He did attempt to analyze business records. While neither a Turnerian nor a practitioner of what would soon be called the "new history," Chittenden did try to include data from several sciences and social sciences, but he did not view historical study, as did Turner and the "new historians," as being particularly applicable to the solution of current problems.

Chittenden's spirit was that of the trained, contemporary historian, seeking scientific objectivity. Although his preference was for the narrative of great deeds, his conscience and perhaps his lifetime of experience with the interests that bore upon any officer of the Corps of Engineers, helped him to recognize that history was not simply the exploits of colorful men. In coming to this recognition that romantic history was not the sum of historical pursuits, Chittenden took his place as one who helped shape the writing of the history of the West in ways that it would follow in the future, when Turner's multiple-hypothesis, multiple-discipline guidelines would stimulate a multitude of writings about the westward movement, which, while not abandoning entirely dramatic narrative and individual deeds of greatness, would increasingly hold up as significant the activities of men in the "ordinary" pursuits that the narrative, romantic historians had considered mundane.

Whatever later historians might think of his place in historiography, Chittenden himself never claimed to be a theoretician and he certainly had no school of followers as did Turner. Yet one great scholar of the fur trade, Dale L. Morgan, wrote of Chittenden's influence:

> Very few, I suspect, would place Hiram Martin Chittendenin the same class with Turner and [Walter P.] Webb. . . . Yet anyone disposed to inquire into the historiography of the past sixty years will find that Chittenden's *The American Fur Trade of the Far West* has influenced nearly everything written about the history of the west in the first half of the nineteenth century--that it has, indeed, been more largely influential than the only general work Turner himself ever published. . . . The idea may affront the professional historians, but it can be seriously maintained that neither Turner nor Webb has had an impact on the writing of western history comparable to Chittenden's (*American West* 3:28-29).

In any case, Chittenden was a historian more akin to Parkman, Hubert Howe Bancroft, and Webb, who attempted a large subject on a grand scale without bothering ever to define profoundly the purposes of history or its cosmic implications. If Chittenden ever did reflect on the objective of the historian or the meaning of history, he did not commit these thoughts to paper, perhaps because he thought they were too obvious to discuss. Or perhaps his general optimism about man's rational powers and the upward course of history was never shadowed by doubt about the value of the past or the purposes of its students. What remains of Chittenden's historical reflections is not abstract speculation but three solid histories of the West, one a masterpiece, achievements sufficient to place him among the giants of frontier historiography.

Bibliography

Books

The American Fur Trade of the Far West: A History of Pioneer Trading Posts and Early Fur Companies of the Missouri Valley and Rocky Mountains and of the Overland Commerce with Santa Fe. 3 volumes. New York: F. P. Harper, 1902.

History of Early Steamboat Navigation on the Missouri River: Life and Adventures of Joseph La Barge. 2 volumes. New York: F. P. Harper, 1903.

Life, Letters and Travels of Father Pierre-Jean De Smet, S.J., 1801-1873. Co-authored with Alfred T. Richardson. 4 volumes. New York: F. P. Harper, 1905.

War or Peace: A Present Duty and a Future Hope. Chicago: A. C. McClurg Co., 1911.

The Yellowstone National Park: Historical and Descriptive. Cincinnati: The R. Clarke Co., 1895.

Article
"The Ancient Town of Fort Benton in Montana." *Magazine of American History* 24(1890):409-425.

Studies of Hiram Martin Chittenden
Chittenden, Hiram, Papers. Washington State Historical Society. Tacoma, WA.
Dodds, Gordon B. *Hiram Martin Chittenden: His Public Career.* Lexington: University Press of Kentucky, 1973.
Le Roy, Bruce, ed. *H. M. Chittenden: A Western Epic.* Tacoma: State Historical Society of Washington, 1961.
Morgan, Dale L. "The Fur Trade and Its Historians." *American West* 3(Spring, 1966):28-35, 92-93.

15

ROBERT GLASS CLELAND

by Gordon Morris Bakken

Biography

Born in Shelbyville, Kentucky, in 1885, Robert Glass Cleland became a lifelong Californian in 1889. A graduate of Occidental College in 1907, Cleland joined the distinguished Occidental faculty in 1911 after graduate education at Princeton, where he received his Ph.D. in 1912. While a member of the Occidental faculty, he also served as vice president and dean of the faculty. Retiring in 1943, Professor Cleland joined the staff of the Huntington Library and, like so many others, continued a distinguished career as a scholar. When he died in 1957, he left behind over a dozen volumes that brought to life the history of California and aspects of the American West.

Cleland credited Robert M. McElroy and Herbert Bolton for influencing his dissertation and a later article entitled "The Early Sentiment for the Annexation of California." Despite this academic shepherding, it is clear from Cleland's writing that his early days roaming the hills around Azusa and later travels throughout California aroused his love of landscape and words.

Themes

Robert Cleland was known as a personable individual and his interest in people came through clearly in his writing. History was people in action. In his *A History of Phelps Dodge, 1834-1950* (1952), Cleland saw as the shapers of the frontier "men of initiative and imagination . . . [with] strong convictions and upright character . . . [who] held fast to simple virtues and traditions of the days when America was young." In Cleland's *California Pageant* (1946), his history focuses upon "their lives and ambitions, their accomplishments and failures, the spectacular adventures and heroic sacrifices." These were the people who transformed a wilderness into an empire, the state of California.

Cleland also had the gift to make his history spring to life for the reader, and he makes the point time after time. History was intended to bring the whole landscape to life, to render the exploration of the humblest village an adventure of thrilling possibilities, to give voice to the masses and to enrich the past with memories. Andrew F. Rolle credited Cleland with being a "popularizer of Western history" through a "vigorous and colorful style, and by the broad humanity reflected in his writings" (*Arizona and the West* 3:307). History to Cleland was written to be read by the general public as well as the scholars.

Analysis

Cleland accomplished his popularization of the history of the West with stirring prose. The governance of the rough and tumble mining camps of gold rush California took on heroic proportions in Cleland's hands:

> Here, along the American, the Feather, the Yuba, the Stanislaus, and a hundred kindred streams, a new chapter was written in American history. Life was lived for a few brief years without the restraints of civilization. Democracy, as literal as the world has ever known, flourished on every hand. Romance came down and walked openly among men, leaving behind a record of heroic accomplishment that can never be blotted from American tradition (*A History of California*, p. 263).

While the mind of a reader could be easily seized by the exploits of the forty-niners, it was harder to grind meaning out of a grist mill, but Cleland uses his facile pen to scratch significance out of the old mill of Mission San Gabriel:

> Its good, stout walls have sheltered men of many creeds and kinds . . . heard the melancholy verse of a soldier of fortune . . . seen comedy and tragedy, birth and death, festive and mourning . . . endured earthquake and storm, sun and rain, vandalism and neglect. Today, in a world of confusion, uncertainty and fear, they stand as a symbol of things not temporal but eternal--a pledge and promise of the ancient but half-forgotten truth that if a man builds in integrity and faith his handiwork will somehow survive the ruin of the years (*El Molina Viejo*, p. 57).

Stone walls could see and hear just as well as "romance" could walk among our forefathers.

Cleland was the master of personifying objects and using them as observers of people making history. He applied this technique extensively in his textbooks and less frequently in his scholarly monographs. Another technique worthy of note was his tendency to tease the reader into reading outside of the textbook. After opening the discussion of some event, he would find that he did not have enough space to continue. So he would tell the reader that "to go into details of all such revolts would require much more space," or "to go into detailed discussion . . . is impossible here" (*A History of California*, pp. 154, 415, 418). The reader knew that there was more to an already interesting story and would need to go to the library to continue the quest for knowledge.

Substantively, Cleland observed that California history was significant because of its national and international impact. Further, the most important part of that history was its transformation from a Mexican province into an American state. In Cleland's eyes California was initially "sparsely inhabited by an unambitious, pastoral people who were seemingly . . . indifferent to all material progress." The gold rush changed that and the forty-niners enabled the "dramatic transformation" and "the material progress of California" (*March of Industry*, p. 1). To Cleland, the Anglo population and their values, particularly the work ethic, brought the prosperity that California came to enjoy.

Cleland's California history textbooks, *A History of California* (1922), *From Wilderness to Empire* (1944), and *California in Our Time* (1947), set the standard for subject matter consideration for future text writers. Cleland wrote of the politics of the day, but he concerned himself with social and economic history as well. He saw the significance of agriculture and industrialization in the larger social and economic framework. Oil, water, electric power, and financial institutions were all part of his California story. Social arrangements, whether on the rancho or in Hollywood, were fit subjects for the historians of the state. The greatest weakness of the text histories was his treatment of minorities and women.

To Cleland, minorities were more often problems in California society, and women were not a major part of history. This approach to state and western history for the period 1915 to 1957 is not particularly surprising. Cleland may have thought the 1940s or 1950s were filled with "confusion, uncertainty, and fear," but, not having the benefit of the 1960s, Cleland did not have the drive to look beyond the captains of industry or to the underside of the history of the West to find its significance. As a result Cleland concludes that labor unrest in the copper industry was caused by Mexicans and the Industrial Workers of the World (IWW), rather than looking to the root of the unrest among Mexicans and IWW members. The 1940s and 1950s did have heroes who loomed larger than life, and it was not difficult to find their cultural forebears in the sweep of the western experience.

One of Cleland's most dramatic literary feats is his narrative history of the fur trapper, *This Reckless Breed of Men: The Trappers and Fur Traders of the Southwest* (1950). His extensive research in primary sources and command of the secondary literature join forces to follow the likes of Jedediah Strong Smith, James O. Pattie, and Joe Walker across the trackless waste to "the other side." The exploration of the trans-Mississippi West and the exploits of the explorers and fur men were the stuff of high adventure and great literature. Cleland ably gave his public the flare the subject deserved. Dale Morgan's *Jedediah Smith and the Opening of the West* (1953) would give the readers of *This Reckless Breed of Men* the scholarly notation and analysis that Cleland's work lacked. William H. Goetzmann would give the western explorer his greatest scholarly due in 1966 in *Exploration and Empire.*

Cleland as a western writer was a master of the language, and as a historian of our heritage he was a promoter as well as a contributing scholar. His *Cattle on a Thousand Hills* (1941) is a well-researched monograph describing the southern California cattle industry. Based on extensive use of manuscript material at the Huntington Library, the book analyzes the rise and fall of a key industry in early California history. Further, the book puts the regional industry in a broader context and assesses its contribution to the state's economic advancement. At the time of his death, Cleland was working on another book with Frank B. Putnam. Although Cleland did not live to see the book in print, in 1965 the Huntington Library staff brought out *Isaias W. Hellman and the Farmers and Merchants Bank.* It is an institutional and economic history of a banking institution that spanned the period of wilderness and brought in the empire of southern California enterprise. It is a fitting tribute to a scholar who moved in two dimensions: the popular literature of textbooks and narrative history and the historical monograph. California was like its financial institutions that Cleland observed in 1929. They and the state grew "like the mustard seed from insignificant beginnings to a position of strength and stability" (*March of Industry*, p. 9).

Bibliography

Books

Apron Full of Gold: The Letters of Mary Jane Megquier from San Francisco, 1849-1856. Editor. San Marino, CA: Huntington Library, 1949.

California in Our Time, 1900-1940. New York: Alfred A. Knopf, 1947.

California Pageant. New York: Alfred A. Knopf, 1946.

Cattle on a Thousand Hills. San Marino, CA: Huntington Library, 1941.

The Early Sentiment for the Annexation of California. Austin: Texas State Historical Association, 1915.

From Wilderness to Empire: A History of California, 1542-1900. New York: Alfred A. Knopf, 1944.

A History of California: The American Period. New York: Macmillan Company, 1922.

The History of Occidental College, 1887-1937. Los Angeles: Ward Ritchie Press, 1937.

A History of Phelps Dodge, 1834-1950. New York: Alfred A. Knopf, 1952.

The Irvine Ranch of Orange County, 1810-1950. San Marino, CA: Huntington Library, 1952.

Isaias W. Hellman and the Farmers and Merchants Bank. Co-authored with Frank B. Putnam. San Marino, CA: Huntington Library, 1965.

March of Industry. Co-authored with Osgood Hardy. Los Angeles: Powell Publishing Company, 1929.

The Mexican Yearbook. Los Angeles: Mexican Yearbook Publishing Company, 1934.

El Molina Viejo. Los Angeles: Ward Ritchie Press, 1950.

A Mormon Chronicle. Co-authored with Juanita Brooks. 2 Volumes. San Marino, CA: Huntington Library, 1955.

One Hundred Years of the Monroe Doctrine. Los Angeles: Times-Mirror Press, 1923.

Pathfinders. Los Angeles: Powell Publishing Company, 1929.

The Place Called Sespe: The History of a California Ranch. Los Angeles: Privately printed, 1940. Reprint. San Marino, CA: Huntington Library, 1957.

This Reckless Breed of Men: The Trappers and Fur Traders of the Southwest. New York: Alfred A. Knopf, 1950.

Articles

"California: The Spanish-Mexican Period." *Antiques* 64(November, 1953):368-395.

"Drought, Lawlessness, and Smallpox: Letters from Cave Couts to Abel Stearns, 1852-1863." Editor. *Southern California Quarterly* 36(March, 1953):3-10.

"The Early Sentiment for the Annexation of California." *Southwestern Historical Quarterly* 18(July, 1914):1-40; (October, 1914):121-161; (January, 1915):231-260.

"An Exile on the Colorado." Los Angeles Westerners *Brand Book* 6(1956):17-29, 153.

"The First Expedition of Jedediah S. Smith to California." *Historical Society of Southern California Annual Publications* 9(1914):200-203.

"Foreword." In "The San Francisco Committee of Vigilance of 1856: An Estimate of a Private Citizen" by Minor King. *Southern California Quarterly* 31(December, 1949):291-298.

__________. In *Sketches of Scenery and Notes of Personal Adventure in California and Mexico* by William McIlvaine. San Francisco: Book Club of California, 1951.

"From Louisiana to Mariposa." Editor. *Pacific Historical Review* 18(February, 1949):24-32.

"Introduction." In *California, From the Conquest in 1846 to the Second Vigilance in San Francisco: A Study of American Character* by Josiah Royce. New York: Alfred A. Knopf, 1948.

__________. In *Constitution of the State of California, 1849*. San Marino, CA: Friends of the Huntington Library, 1949.

__________. In *Eldorado, or Adventures in the Path of Empire* by Bayard Taylor. New York: Alfred A. Knopf, 1949.

__________. In *From the Kennebec to California: Reminiscences of a California Pioneer* by Henry Hiram Ellis, selected and arranged by Lucy Ellis Riddell, edited by Laurence R. Cook. Los Angeles: W. F. Lewis, 1959.

__________. In *Historic Spots in California: Counties on the Coast Range* by Mildred Brooke Hoover. Stanford, CA: Stanford University Press, 1937.

__________. In *Historic Spots in California: The Southern Counties* by H. E. and E. G. Rensch. Stanford, CA: Stanford University Press, 1932.

__________. In *Historic Spots in California: Valley and Sierra Counties* by H. E. and E. G. Rensch and Mildred Brooke Hoover. Stanford, CA: Stanford University Press, 1933.

"John Bidwell's Arrival in California." *Historical Society of Southern California Annual Publications* 10(1915-1916):110-113.

"Larkin's Description of California." Editor. *Historical Society of Southern California Annual Publications* 10(1918):70-75.

"Los Angeles: The Transition Decades, 1850-1870, an Exhibition at the Huntington Library." Los Angeles: Ward Ritchie Press, 1937.

"On the Sale of Liquor to the Indians: Proclamation of Governor [Richard B.] Mason, dated November 29, 1847." Editor. In *Attention Pioneers! . . . Facsimile Reproductions of Twelve Rare California Broadsides or Posters, with Explanatory Comment by Various Authorities.* San Francisco: Book Club of California, 1952.

"Transportation in California Before the Railroads, with Especial Reference to Los Angeles." *Historical Society of Southern California Annual Publications* 11(1918):60-67.

"The Writings of Phillip Ashton Rollins." *Princeton University Library Chronicles* 9(June, 1948):205-210.

Reviews

California Letters of Lucius Fairchild edited by Joseph Schafer. *Mississippi Valley Historical Review* 19(December, 1932):426-427.

Cape Horn to the Pacific: The Rise and Decline of an Ocean Highway by Raymond A. Rydell. *Pacific Historical Review* 21(August, 1952):296-297.

Coronado, Knight of the Pueblos and Plains by Herbert E. Bolton. *American Historical Review* 55(July, 1950):948-950.

Death Valley and Its Country by George Palmer Putnam. *Mississippi Valley Historical Review* 34(December, 1947):500-501.

Earth Horizon, Autobiography by Mary Austin. *Mississippi Valley Historical Review* 20(March, 1934):591-592.

The Establishment of State Government in California, 1846-1850 by Cardinal Goodwin. *Southwestern Historical Quarterly* 18(January, 1915):330-332.

Founding of Spanish California: The Northwestward Expansion of New Spain, 1687-1783 by Charles Edward Chapman. *Mississippi Valley Historical Review* 3(March, 1917):564-566.

History of California from 1542 by A. A. Gray. *Mississippi Valley Historical Review* 23(September, 1936):301-302.

History of the San Francisco Committee of Vigilance of 1851 by Mary Floy Williams. *Mississippi Valley Historical Review* 9(September, 1922):170-172.

Hubert Howe Bancroft, Historian of the West by John Walton Caughey. *Pacific Historical Review* 16(February, 1947):91-93.

Jedediah Smith and His Maps of the American West by Dale L. Morgan and Clark I. Wheat. *Pacific Historical Review* 24(May, 1955):179-181.

Leland Stanford, War Governor of California, Railroad Builder, and Founder of Stanford University by George T. Clark. *Pacific Historical Review* 1(November, 1932):498-499.

The Pacific Ocean in History edited by H. Morse Stephens and Herbert E. Bolton. *Mississippi Valley Historical Review* 4(March, 1918):534-536.

Studies of Robert Glass Cleland

Banfield, Edward C. Review of *A Mormon Chronicle: The Diaries of John D. Lee, 1848-1876* edited by Robert G. Cleland and Juanita Brooks. *Mississippi Valley Historical Review* 43(June, 1956):122-124.

Bieber, Ralph P. Review of *Pathfinders* by Robert G. Cleland. *Mississippi Valley Historical Review* 20(June, 1933):124-126.

Caughey, John W. Review of *California In Our Time, 1900-1940* by Robert G. Cleland. *Mississippi Valley Historical Review* 34(March, 1948):662-663.

__________. Review of *The Cattle on a Thousand Hills: Southern California, 1850-1880* by Robert G. Cleland. *Mississippi Valley Historical Review* 38(December, 1951):510-511.

__________. Review of *From Wilderness to Empire: A History of California, 1542-1900* by Robert G. Cleland. *Mississippi Valley Historical Review* 31(September, 1944):281-282.

Cleland, Robert Glass, Papers. Huntington Library, San Marino, CA.

__________. Occidental College Library, Occidental College, Los Angeles, CA.

Cooke, W. Henry. Review of *The History of Occidental College: 1887-1937* by Robert G. Cleland. *Pacific Historical Review* 6(May, 1937):387-388.

Hammond, George P. Review of *Apron Full of Gold: The Letters of Mary Jane Meqguier from San Francisco, 1849-1856* edited by Robert G. Cleland. *Mississippi Valley Historical Review* 36(December, 1949):520-521.

Richman, Irving B. Review of *A History of California: The American Period* by Robert G. Cleland. *Mississippi Valley Historical Review* 10(June, 1923):83-85.

Rister, Carl Coke. Review of *This Reckless Breed of Men: The Trappers and Fur Traders of the Southwest* by Robert G. Cleland. *Journal of Southern History* 16(August, 1950):356-357.

Rolle, Andrew F. "A Dedication to the Memory of Robert Glass Cleland, 1885-1958." *Arizona and the West* 3(Autumn, 1961):307-310.

Schafer, Joseph. Review of *A History of California: The American Period* by Robert G. Cleland. *American Historical Review* 28(January, 1923):334-336.

Vestal, Stanley. Review of *This Reckless Breed of Men: The Trappers and Fur Traders of the Southwest* by Robert G. Cleland. *American Historical Review* 55(July, 1950):919-920.

Wright, Louis B. Review of *This Reckless Breed of Men: The Trappers and Fur Traders of the Southwest* by Robert G. Cleland. *Mississippi Valley Historical Review* 37(September, 1950):329-330.

16

ROBERT S. COTTERILL

by Steven C. Schulte

Biography

His birthplace on the old Kentucky frontier influenced Robert Spencer Cotterill's decision to become a historian. Fleming County rests in the heart of some of the most colorful and dramatic scenes in early Kentucky history. Blue Licks Battlefield, the site of one of the last military confrontations of the Revolutionary War, is only a short distance from Cotterill's birthplace.

While Cotterill's Kentucky pioneer past guided much of his historical activity, unlike many early writers of state and local history, Cotterill transcended the antiquarian themes so common to them. He also focused his energy on larger historical subjects of regional, national, and international interest. His broad vision and the respect he attained in the scholarly community is reflected in the honors and positions he achieved during a career spanning over forty years.

After taking his A.B. at Kentucky Wesleyan College in 1904, Cotterill moved to Charlottesville, Virginia, where he completed an M.A. degree at the University of Virginia in 1907. His course of study emphasized economics, philosophy, Greek, and Latin. After a brief teaching stint in Louisiana, Cotterill returned to his alma mater in 1910 to teach Latin and chair the department of history. In 1915 he moved to Western Maryland College, where he also served as department chair. While at Western Maryland, Cotterill received his history doctorate from the University of Wisconsin, where he studied with Frederic L. Paxson (Cotterill Papers, Vertical File).

Paxson had succeeded Frederick Jackson Turner at Wisconsin in 1910 after the latter had left for Harvard University. Paxson made a strong impression on Cotterill's approach to history. Frederic Paxson has been called a master of historical synthesis. Not associated with a pioneering interpretation or a significant thesis, Paxson contented himself with writing the broad monograph. Cotterill absorbed much from Paxson, including his love for historical synthesis. As with Paxson, Cotterill's many articles concerned subjects with which he felt free to be more speculative.

The publication of *History of Pioneer Kentucky* (1917) marked Cotterill's progress from small college teacher to a young historian with a growing national reputation. To his good fortune, Cotterill became involved with the Mississippi Valley Historical Association in its infancy. Paxson probably encouraged his charge's participation and early articles in the *Mississippi Valley Historical Review*. By 1928, Cotterill held the position of associate editor of the *Review*. The Mississippi Valley Historical Association served as a lifelong scholarly outlet for Cotterill (Cotterill Papers, Cotterill to Arthur Williams, August 4, 1928).

In 1920, Cotterill joined the faculty of the University of Louisville. Though he took his doctorate in American history, his Louisville appointment was in European history. After three years he was named professor of American history and department head. Cotterill served at Louisville with a group of talented historical scholars, including Louis R. Gottschalk and Norman C. Ware. While at Louisville, Cotterill's career grew in other significant ways. In 1926, the University of Louisville and the Filson Club, a local historical society, established a quarterly journal with Cotterill as its managing editor. The *Filson Club History Quarterly* published articles dealing primarily with the history of Kentucky and the Ohio River Valley. Cotterill also began to specialize in the research and teaching of the history of the South and southern frontier history. He offered graduate seminars which resulted in more than a half dozen M.A. theses (*Filson Club History Quarterly* 34:166-167).

Cotterill became embroiled in a controversy with the University of Louisville administration which contributed to his resignation in August, 1928, and his relocation to the Florida State College for Women (today's Florida State University). The trouble started when recently named University of Louisville President George Colvin attempted to reorganize the College of Liberal Arts. Many faculty members, including Cotterill and Gottschalk, launched a protest because they sensed that Colvin's actions threatened accepted tenure procedures. They also feared a lowering of academic standards. The American Association of University Professors investigated the matter, and its report discredited Colvin's administration. The controversy ended with Colvin's death in 1928, but not before many faculty members had become alienated from the administration and several more had resigned or been forced to leave the university. The exact relationship between Cotterill's role in the controversy and his resignation in August, 1928, can only be surmised. Clearly, the negative feelings generated by the event made Cotterill glad to accept a professor's position at the Florida State College for Women at Tallahassee (Cotterill Letters, Deborah Skaggs to the author, June 28, 1985).

Tallahassee represented the final stop in Cotterill's academic career. His reputation continued to grow as he became an established scholar with an enviable publication record. He produced three major books within eighteen years: *The Old South* (1936), *A Short History of the Americas* (1939), and *The Southern Indians* (1954). He continued a steady outpouring of articles, book reviews, and scholarly papers. Active in the formation of the Southern History Association in 1934, he served as its president in 1948. Cotterill also taught summer sessions at such schools as the University of Kentucky, University of Pennsylvania, University of Virginia, and George Washington University. He often used summer appointments as an opportunity to do local research (Cotterill Letters, Deborah Skaggs to the author).

Cotterill's sole teaching responsibility at Florida State University was in United States history. Specifically, he taught the United States survey classes and a two-semester course on the American frontier. He also offered classes on the Old and New South. In addition, Cotterill participated in the university's small graduate program, directing several master's theses on subjects close to his personal research interests--the Indian traders Panton, Leslie, and Company; Creek leader Alexander McGillivray; and the black industrial workers in the New South (Cotterill Papers, Susan Hamberger to the author, September 11, 1985).

Students and colleagues found Robert Cotterill to be a pleasant and genteel man, with a delightful, dry sense of humor. Formal, and always properly dressed, Cotterill reportedly never removed his suit coat even during the steamy Florida summer. Soft-spoken, he could hold his classes spellbound with stories of the old frontier. He always encouraged superior students at Tallahassee. Cotterill and his wife never had any children, but, according to one former student, they seemed to "adopt" some of his best pupils wherever he taught. The Cotterills were widely known for entertaining his classes and students (Cotterill Papers, Daisy Flory interview, July 11, 1979; Earl Beck to the author, September 18, 1985).

Cotterill's active publication record becomes all the more impressive when it is considered that he regularly taught fifteen hours per week. He showed great dexterity in avoiding academic committee assignments and administrative duties--probably out of a sense of self-preservation and a commitment to his research. A quiet man, a good listener, given to the wry remark in both personal conversation and in his writings, Cotterill's personality made a strong impression on several generations of students and colleagues.

Retiring in 1951, Cotterill's final two years at Florida State University were spent as Research Professor of History. Cotterill used this time to finish the manuscript which became *The Southern Indians*. He also worked on manuscripts on Panton, Leslie, and Company as well as a documentary history of Kentucky. In his retirement years, Cotterill remained active by occasionally reviewing a book and by researching his home area, Fleming County, Kentucky. He died in 1967 without seeing his final projects through to completion.

Themes

Several major ideas emerge from any consideration of Cotterill's writings. Consciously or not, Cotterill's scholarship succeeded in recasting many time-worn ideas and myths. Examples of his revisionism include Cotterill's balanced approach to Indian leadership in the Southeast, especially his discussion of Shawnee leader Tecumseh. Cotterill also treated the history of his home state with great scholarly care, thereby avoiding some of the boosterism and chauvinism common to many state histories. His *History of Pioneer Kentucky* is a model of economy in writing and balance between narrative and interpretation.

A deep concern with the Indian nations of the American southern frontier also animates much of his writing. Cotterill originally earned his reputation as a frontier historian through his writings which illuminate the early history of his home region, the South. He always retained a deep interest in his home state's history. Cotterill also wrote extensively on the Anglo-American westward movement. In particular, he studied the transportation frontier and communications networks which made early settlement possible.

Cotterill's four books, several dozen articles, and countless book reviews provide ample documentation to consider his scholarly interests. Several of his first major articles--on the development of railroads in the Old Southwest--appeared in the *Mississippi Valley Historical Review*'s early volumes. In addition to his role in the early years of the Mississippi Valley Historical Association, he was a pioneer member of the Filson Club and the Southern History Association. He served on the editorial board of the *Mississippi Valley Historical Review, Journal of Southern History*, and *Filson Club History Quarterly*. He wrote numerous articles and book reviews for each journal. Thus, Cotterill's career paralleled the birth, rise, and maturation of several of the most important historical associations in the region and nation.

Cotterill's broadest yet best developed theme is a concern for the history of the frontier South. Though from a Civil War "border state," Cotterill considered himself a loyal son of the South (Cotterill Papers, Daisy Parker Flory to the Author, October 8, 1985). Cotterill's writing on the frontier South is characterized by careful scholarship, much of it derived from research collections in state archival institutions from all across the South. He also used materials from the National Archives and important collections of frontier Americana such as the State Historical Society of Wisconsin's Draper Collection.

A scholarly approach to such emotional subjects as early pioneering in the South enabled Cotterill to move beyond the almost deified status the white pioneer had attained in previous historical studies. Cotterill respected the white frontiersman, but a fine sense of historical justice coupled with an extraordinary interest in the American Indian made Cotterill one of his era's most knowledgeable historians of the Native American. His perspective toward the American Indian evolved over time, becoming increasingly sophisticated and informed. At a time when few professionally trained historical scholars were concerned with American Indians, Cotterill adopted a sensitive, pluralistic view reminiscent of Boasian cultural anthropology. While his perspective remained in continuous evolution, one aspect of Cotterill's scholarship never changed: his basic sympathy for the Indian as a victim of both historical circumstances and unfair dealings (*A Final Promise*, pp. 135-141).

Cotterill, like his mentor, Paxson, retained a love for the scholarly synthesis. Today, when scholars are often encouraged to take a micro-historical perspective, Cotterill's broad works of synthesis on *The Old South* or *The Southern Indians* appear almost naive if compared with modern research methodology. His writings, however, retain a vitality and usefulness because they represented tentative attempts at synthesis, while serving as a barometer for what research yet needed to be done.

Analysis

Cotterill's writings earned him both the respect of his contemporaries and the continued accolades of modern scholars. The respected southern frontier scholar Thomas D. Clark notes that Cotterill had an "insight into both southern and frontier history which was provocative." Clark considers Cotterill's *The Southern Indians* the "crowning achievement" of his career (Cotterill Papers, Clark to the author, July 16, 1985). Bennett H. Wall, longtime secretary-treasurer of the Southern History Association, believes that Cotterill's *History of Pioneer Kentucky* and *The Old South* continue to be important studies. Cotterill's scholarly contributions are more significant when it is considered that few great research libraries and collections existed in the South during Cotterill's heyday. "I marvel at the high quality of both volumes," Wall has remarked. "[T]he conclusions he drew seemed to me to have held up very well indeed" (Cotterill Papers, Wall to the author, July 29, 1985).

Cotterill's most outstanding achievements in the study of the American frontier occurred in two areas. He contributed a series of valuable articles and monographs on the history of the southeastern frontier. Also, perhaps as significant as his scholarly production, was Cotterill's work for the advancement of the historical profession. A highly effective teacher, Cotterill inspired several generations of students. Through his activity as a founder and booster of historical associations, Cotterill also served as an early promoter of professional historical scholarship in the South. His efforts helped scholarly inquiry on the American southern frontier attain a respected status within the historical profession.

Cotterill, along with contemporaries William E. Dodd, Walter L. Fleming, Ulrich B. Phillips, and others represented the first generation of southern historians who worked with a great respect for the canons of critical scholarship. As a broad group they made southern history--as well as each other's special subdisciplines--a mainstream part of American historiography (*The South Lives*, p. 118).

In addition to his active publication record and successful teaching career, Cotterill's personality, sociability, and concern with professionalism contributed to his excellent reputation. An integral part of most meetings of the Southern History Association, he regularly read papers, attended business meetings, and commented during scholarly sessions. Cotterill's commanding, yet soft-spoken presence made him a favorite of every group he chose to join. He had the rare ability to make the appropriate remark in a wry manner, or to relate an amusing yet revealing anecdote. Colleagues enjoyed his presence and students found him spellbinding.

Any consideration of Cotterill's writings must begin with his *History of Pioneer Kentucky* (1917). His first significant publication, it did little to foreshadow the broad historical vision its author would later demonstrate. Nevertheless, it is a model for early state and local history. At a time when many books on state and local topics often were exercises in filial piety, Cotterill's study stands in marked contrast. Though in places biased toward his home state, Cotterill makes a sincere attempt to demythologize aspects of Kentucky's past. In the process, Cotterill produces a concise and eminently readable study of early Kentucky.

Pioneer Kentucky reflects both Cotterill's upbringing and his maturation as a history scholar during the Progressive Era. Published two years before he received his doctorate, the book links Cotterill intellectually with Progressive historical scholarship. Progressive Era historians such as Frederick Jackson Turner, Charles A. Beard, and others had been conditioned by a keen awareness of the disappearance of frontier conditions. They had witnessed the disruptions caused by the depression of the 1890s, and had thought deeply about the role of industrialism in American life. "They were disposed," according to Richard Hofstadter, "to think more directly about the economic issues of society, and to look again at the past to see if economic forces had not been somewhat neglected" (*The Progressive Historians*, p. 42). In addition, Progressive Era scholars pioneered the use of interdisciplinary perspectives in historical analysis, incorporating insights from fields such as geography, economics, and sociology. As James Harvey Robinson, the "prophet" of the "old" new history asserted, historians must "surrender all individualistic aspirations" and cooperate with other disciplines (p. 72). Only by following this directive, according to Robinson, could history offer useful insights into contemporary problems.

Cotterill's topical choices and methodology in *Pioneer Kentucky* closely reflect his Progressive Era training. A mecca for Progressive thought, the University of Wisconsin shaped Cotterill's perspective toward historical analysis. Always comfortable with cross-disciplinary approaches, Cotterill used the tools and viewpoints of the different social sciences to enhance his research. His University of Wisconsin dissertation committee members, Frederic Paxson and noted economic historian Richard Ely, made sure their charge was well versed in the latest social scientific insights.

Pioneer Kentucky contains numerous pages devoted to discussing the state's archaeology, flora, and fauna. Unlike many state histories of this era, Cotterill's study is not a roll call of pioneer heroes. Instead, it narrates Kentucky's early story to statehood from a unique and often controversial position. Cotterill insists that the development of Kentucky should not be viewed as a mere offshoot of the Virginia story, as other writers had concluded. In the manner of Frederick Jackson Turner, Cotterill argues that the environment of Kentucky helped produce a unique character. The migration of people west into Kentucky was "for the most part a direct result of their economic environment" (p. 21). The original white settlement of Kentucky represented much more than a Virginian enterprise; settlers moved from Virginia, but from Pennsylvania and North Carolina as well. With sardonic wit, Cotterill concludes that had only Virginians attempted the settlement of Kentucky, it would be "at this moment, a kingdom of the Red Indian and a pasture for the wild buffaloes" (p. 25).

Much of *Pioneer Kentucky* is anti-Virginian in tone. This perspective undoubtedly reflected Cotterill's graduate school experience at the University of Virginia and his feelings that the South needed to declare its intellectual independence from the Old Dominion State. Using the analogy of Britain and America during the Revolutionary era, Cotterill argues that Virginia's western policies fueled the movement which culminated in Kentucky statehood. After all, during the American Revolution, western settlers cared little for such abstract principles as "taxation without representation." "They were Kentuckians first and Virginians afterward," Cotterill observes. "They were intensely interested in rendering their own home safe from the Indians, but were profoundly unwilling to fight England" based upon abstract rationales (pp. 175-176). *Pioneer Kentucky* captures the energy, scope, and original turn of mind that characterized most of Cotterill's later writings.

Cotterill's study of early Kentucky explores other subject areas which became his scholarly staples. Most significantly, an interest in American Indian history and the southern frontier is apparent. Cotterill's Ph.D. dissertation, "Improvement of Transportation in the Mississippi Valley, 1845-1850," also deals with topics which would become subjects for further examination. For example, he explores the agitation for a Pacific railroad and the heated sectional rivalry to obtain it. Cotterill observes that the status of the West played a vital role in every issue facing American national life during these years.

The southeastern frontier occupied a central place in Cotterill's writings from 1920 to 1936. A series of articles on southern frontier topics culminated in the publication of *The Old South* in 1936. Cotterill always views the development of the Old South through the eyes of a frontier historian. In Turnerian style, he depicts southern history as a series of distinct, successive stages. After an obligatory discussion of southern geography, Cotterill analyzes the Indian frontier, the Anglo-Saxon economic penetration of the Old South, and the expansion of white political institutions.

Many of Cotterill's statements sound archaic and strangely conservative to modern ears. He accepts the arguments of U. B. Phillips wholeheartedly. In *The Old South* (1936) Cotterill argues slavery was justifed as "the only possible solution" to the South's need for a labor supply (p. 80). One of Cotterill's goals in writing *The Old South* was to provide a textbook for a subject that had been neglected by publishers. He also viewed it as a showcase for summarizing the exciting scholarly work of his generation of southern historians. From his perspective in the early twentieth-century South, slavery appeared as a benevolent institution. "That the slave of the South was reasonably contented may well be believed," Cotterill argues (p. 269). Furthermore, Cotterill's views on slavery and the southern racial dilemma matched the perspective of most of his peers, including Phillips.

Other conclusions in *The Old South* sound equally discordant. Cotterill downplays the contributions of various ethnic groups in southern settlement, noting that the Scotch-Irish, Germans, and others "were quickly assimilated by the Englishmen" (p. 264). Cotterill, a devoted Democrat, allows his personal politics to influence his assessment of the party of Lincoln. The Republicans resembled a "heterogeneous mass of oppositionists" animated only by the "hope of plunder" (p. 245).

The Old South contains an abundance of information about the frontier South. Land speculators "marshalled and ordered" the march to the West. In southern history, the land speculator was the entrepreneur of the westward movement: "He fixed the time, chose the destination, and determined the routes" (p. 141).

Lauded by some reviewers as an important pathbreaking synthesis, *the Old South* was criticized by others as "naive." Another reviewer notes that Cotterill had de-emphasized the role of slavery in southern development. Cotterill, another reviewer observes, said as much about Indian affairs as about the "peculiar institution." Interestingly, Cotterill, in a review of Clement Eaton's *Freedom of Thought Struggle in the Old South* scorns that work on opposite grounds. Eaton, according to Cotterill, devotes "five-sixths of the lump . . . to the alleged hidebound mentality of Southerners on the slavery question" (pp. 299-300). Another reviewer of *The Old South* questions Cotterill's emphasis on Indians and the westward movement at the expense of such vital topics as southern constitutional theories, party alignment, and the proslavery argument. Still, despite its somewhat dated views, *The Old South* remains a worthwhile introduction to its subject, especially for readers interested in the southern frontier.

Cotterill ventured into other areas of frontier southern history. He wrote extensively about the railroad convention movement of the 1840s. Cotterill's research into the national land system of the South revealed the extent to which cotton culture had taken hold as far west as Mississippi before the War of 1812. He pioneered the study of the New South, offering courses on the subject while exploring possible avenues for its interpretation. His presidential address to the Southern Historical Association in 1948, "The Old South to the New," stressed the continuities of southern history. The New South, he argued, had more in common with the antebellum era than had previously been supposed. "It was not a Phoenix rising from the ashes of the Old; not a revival; not even a reincarnation: it was merely a continuation of the Old South" (*Journal of Southern History* 15:8). Cotterill stressed elements of southern continuity, ranging from economic development to racial prejudice, in his address.

His broadest work, *A Short History of the Americas* (1939), attempts to interpret more than 500 years of inter-American history in a single, short text. Tackling such a project was consistent with Cotterill's love of the grand historical synthesis. *A Short History* stresses the "forces and influences" common to the Western Hemisphere at the expense of local details. While it emphasizes North America, Cotterill devotes perhaps a disproportionate amount of space to topics dear to him: the frontier, economic development, and territorial expansion. His dominant frontier interest, however, from his earliest publication to his final book review, remained the study of the American Indian.

Cotterill's passion for frontier history is reflected in his early infatuation with the local Indian history near his boyhood home. This interest came to dominate his research following the publication of *The Old South* in 1936. Cotterill was one of the first academically trained historians to specialize in Indian history. His doctoral program at the University of Wisconsin had emphasized American frontier studies and European history. At this time, few scholars received training in American Indian history. Native Americans remained the academic domain of the cultural anthropologist or the interest of the professional writer and frontier "buff."

Cotterill's early writings on Native American subjects reflected the Progressive Era's ambiguity toward Indians. Negative Progressive Era attitudes toward all nonwhites helped justify a harsh evaluation of Indians, both contemporary and historical. Nevertheless, Cotterill demonstrated an early fascination with American Indians. His *History of Pioneer Kentucky* contains almost two full chapters on that state's Indian population. Indians dominate most of the decisive scenes from the remainder of the book as well.

Besides indicating an early interest in Indians, Cotterill takes a distinctly advanced view of Native American culture. At a time when much of American society regarded Indians as vanishing nonentities, Cotterill expresses a sympathetic view of the Indian past. Through the years, Cotterill's attitude toward Native Americans became more advanced and sophisticated as he absorbed the viewpoints of cultural anthropology and numerous ethnological studies.

In 1917, however, his attitude toward Indians remained ambiguous. In *Pioneer Kentucky*, after calling the Shawnee a "fierce and unforgiving tribe," a page later he refers to the same group as "not a savage or nomadic people" (p. 17). His early writings are littered with phrases such as "the Chickasaws lived in savage independence." His admiration for the white Kentucky frontiersman is evident. This explains such phrases as "the savages who infested the forests near Boonesborough" (p. 30). Like other followers of Frederick Jackson Turner, Cotterill had an early tendency to view the Indians as part of the landscape--as mere consolidating agents for the white settlement process.

As Cotterill's career lengthened, the study of American Indians increasingly became the focus of his research. As he remarks in the 1954 preface to his study, *The Southern Indians*, "This book has been written in self-defense. The writer on beginning his teaching of Southern history found that he needed a knowledge of Southern Indians and failed to find it in the books then in print" (p. ix). Beginning in the 1920s, Cotterill began to collect source material in almost every southern state to illuminate his Native American lectures for southern history courses. *The*

Southern Indians and several important articles are the result of his prolonged search for Indian source material.

In addition to the more general *Southern Indians*, Cotterill explored a diverse range of Native American topics in his articles. He examines Indian and white leadership, trade relationships, the impact of white westward expansion, and Indian diplomacy. Early in his career, Cotterill recognized the importance of the Indian trade as a forerunner of English expansion. His study of Panton, Leslie, and Company among southern Indians elaborates upon this theme. As a book reviewer, Cotterill attacks any book on early Indian policy which did not discuss trade relationships.

As Cotterill became more deeply involved with his study of American Indians, he became a critic of federal policy toward the first Americans. He views Jacksonian Indian Removal as a tragedy, a "lurid episode, full of hypocrisy and broken faith on one side, and of suffering and misery on the other" (*The Old South*, p. 172). Cotterill admires fair dealings between Indians and whites, but all too often a sincere Indian agent's activities were undermined by unscrupulous traders or other policymaking personnel. In 1933, Cotterill published an important article which opened his assault on federal Indian policy. He refers to the post-War of 1812 era as "prolific in Indian treaties and consequently in land cessions secured by force, fraud, and chicanery." Policymakers often articulated high sounding, altruistic motives, but "in its very nature, Indian management meant Indian spoliation" (*Mississippi Valley Historical Review* 20:350).

Cotterill continues his criticisms of federal Indian policy in *The Southern Indians*. Cotterill labels the years 1803 to 1811 as the era of "Debts, Bribes, and Cessions." United States treaty commissioners made extensive use of bribery and intimidation to effect their ends. Cotterill had perceptive insights into how federal Indian policy often exacerbated tribal factionalism. In *The Southern Indians*, in contrast to his earlier *Pioneer Kentucky*, Cotterill is not always in sympathy with white settlers in their disputes with Indians. He tends, however, to blame the United States government for most frontier Indian problems. In particular, Cotterill casts Andew Jackson and other rapacious whites as villians. He seems to take a great delight in documenting Jackson's perfidy, bribery, and use of corrupt negotiating practices in a series of treaties with the southern Indian nations after 1812. With glee, Cotterill tells the story of Jackson, the military man against the Creek Red Sticks in 1813: "No amount of [pro-Jackson] rhetoric can disguise the fact that Jackson, although leading an overwhelming force, a well-armed and equipped army against a foe reduced to dependence on bows and arrows, was twice beaten back by his fanatical adversaries" (*The Southern Indians*, p. 186). Very late in his career, Cotterill began questioning the moral underpinnings of Jacksonian Indian policy.

Critics received *The Southern Indians* with general approbation. William T. Hagan, in his American Historical Association pamphlet *The Indian in American History* (1971), calls it "a good" survey of the preremoval period in the South. Hagan especially admires Cotterill's analysis of the complicated diplomatic dealings between Indian nations and the English, Spanish, and Americans. Contemporary assessments noted the book's pioneering role, as well as Cotterill's sensitivity to the persistence of Native American institutions--in an era of profound cultural stress. One critic cites Cotterill's revisionist view of Tecumseh, the Shawnee leader. In *The Southern Indians*, Cotterill anticipates the recent findings of R. David Edmunds, who de-emphasizes Tecumseh's role at the expense of the broad movement started by his brother, the Prophet, Tenskwatawa. Cotterill avoids idealizing Tecumseh, a trap which Edmunds argues most writers have failed to avoid. Cotterill understood the spiritual significance of the Tecumseh/Tenskwatawa Indian movement far better than most previous historians.

Cotterill is a significant, though unrecognized early scholar of the Native American. His research on the Indian nations of the South before removal remains a standard contribution to American history. His use of ethnological studies and attempts at understanding the Indian viewpoint demonstrates Cotterill's early, pioneering position in American Indian historiography. Cotterill believed that scholars must first understand the deep-seated effects of tribal factionalism before the true results of any specific Indian policy could be assessed. A persistent critic of the history of American Indian policy, he differed from other early pro-Indian writers because his criticism was balanced, scholarly in tone, and well documented.

From the modern perspective, Cotterill looms as an important early frontier scholar. Beginning with rather provincial concerns, he matured intellectually, absorbing modern historical and anthropological viewpoints. His crowning achievement, *The Southern Indians*, is relatively free of negative stereotyping of Indians and the paternalism that characterized most histories of American Indians until the 1960s. His role as a pioneer scholar in the South has not been adequately recognized. Cotterill's career parallels the rise and development of several of the most important American historical associations. Robert Spencer Cotterill combined an early interest in his home state with wider historical concerns to become one of his generation's most respected frontier historians.

Bibliography

Books

History of Pioneer Kentucky. Cincinnati: Johnson and Hardin, 1917.

The Old South: The Geographic, Economic, Social, Political, and Cultural Expansion, Institutions, and Nationalism of the Ante-Bellum South. Glendale, CA: Arthur H. Clark, 1936.

A Short History of the Americas. New York: Prentice-Hall, 1939. Second edition, 1945.

The Southern Indians: The Story of the Civilized Tribes Before Removal. Norman: University of Oklahoma Press, 1954.

Articles

"Beginnings of Railroads in the Southwest." *Mississippi Valley Historical Review* 8(March, 1922):318-326.

"A Chapter on Panton, Leslie, and Company." *Journal of Southern History* 10(August, 1944):275-292.

Dictionary of American Biography. 20 volumes. New York: Charles Scribner's Sons, 1928-1936. Articles on Francis Robert Beattie, Clement Biddle, Joseph Clay Styles Blackburn, Jeremiah Tilford Boyle, Alexander Scott Bullitt, James Clark, Leslie Combs, Joseph Alexander Cooper, John Covode, Reuben Thomas Durrett, Walter Evans, John Filson, James Garrard, William Goebel, William Cassius Goodloe, Norvin Green, James Guthrie, John Francis Hamtranck, James Harlan, George Hay, Leonard Henderson, Richard Henderson, Robert Perkins Letcher, Joseph Horace Lewis, William Littell, Benjamin Logan, Augustus Emmett Maxwell, Benjamin Mills, John Milton, Thomas Patrick Moore, Samuel Pasco, Edward Aylesworth Perry, George Pettus Raney, David Shelby Walker, Harvey Magee Watterson, Charles Anderson Wickliffe, Augustus Everett Willson, Alva Woods, and David Levy Yulee.

"Early Agitation for a Pacific Railroad." *Mississippi Valley Historical Review* 5(March, 1919):396-414.

"Federal Indian Management in the South, 1789-1825." *Mississippi Valley Historical Review* 20(December, 1933):333-352.

"The Louisville and Nashville Railroad, 1861-1865." *American Historical Review* 29(July, 1924):700-715.

"Memphis Railroad Convention." *Tennessee History* 4(June, 1918):83-94.

"The National Land System in the South, 1803-1812." *Mississippi Valley Historical Review* 16(March, 1930):495-506.

"The National Railroad Convention in St. Louis, 1849." *Missouri Historical Review* 12(July, 1918):203-215.

"The Old South to New." *Journal of Southern History* 15(February, 1949):3-8.

"The Professor Has An Idea." *Harper's Monthly Magazine* 131(June, 1930):118-120.

"The South Carolina Land Cession." *Mississippi Valley Historical Review* 12(December, 1925):376-384.

"Southern Railroads, 1850-1860." *Mississippi Valley Historical Review* 10(March, 1923):396-405.

"Southern Railroads and Western Trade, 1840-1850." *Mississippi Valley Historical Review* 3(March, 1917):427-441.

"The Telegraph in the South, 1845-1850." *South Atlantic Quarterly* 16(April, 1917):149-154.

"Transylvania." *Kentucky Progress Magazine*, October, 1935, pp. 395-400.

Selected Reviews

Abraham Lincoln and Walt Whitman by William E. Barton. *Mississippi Valley Historical Review* 15(September, 1928):282.

American Railroads by John F. Stover. *American Historical Review* 68(April, 1963):828-829.

Annals of Southwest Virginia: 1769-1800 by Lewis Preston Summers. *Mississippi Valley Historical Review* 17(June, 1930):150-152.

A Bibliography of Kentucky History by J. Winston Coleman, Jr. *Mississippi Valley Historical Review* 37(June, 1950):128-130.

The Big Sandy Valley: A Regional History Prior to the Year 1850 by Willard Rouse Jillson. *American Historical Review* 30(January, 1925):405.

The Borderland in the Civil War by Edward Conrad Smith. *Mississippi Valley Historical Review* 14(March, 1928):551-553.

Buffalo Days by Homer W. Wheeler. *Mississippi Valley Historical Review* 13(June, 1926):109-110.

Confederate Mississippi: The People and Policies of a Cotton State in Wartime by John K. Bettersworth. *Pennsylvania Magazine of History and Biography* 67(October, 1943):423-424.

A Description of Kentucky in North America: To Which Are Prefixed Miscellaneous Observations Respecting the United States. Journal of Southern History 12(August, 1946):436-437.

The Development of Methodism in the Old Southwest, 1783-1824 by Walter Brownlow Posey. *Mississippi Valley Historical Review* 20(March, 1934):603.

Down the Santa Fe Trail and Into Mexico: The Diary of Susan Shelby Magoffin, 1846-1847 edited by Stella M. Drumm. *Mississippi Valley Historical Review* 14(June, 1927):100-101.

Economic Aspects of Southern Sectionalism, 1840-1861 by Robert Royal Russel. *American Historical Review* 30(January, 1925):402.

Florida during the Territorial Days by Sidney Walter Martin. *Journal of Southern History* 11(May, 1945):267-268.

Freedom of Thought Struggle in the Old South by Clement Eaton. *Mississippi Valley Historical Review* 27(September, 1940):299-300.

Garcia's Chronological History of the Continent of Florida translated with an introduction by Anthony Kerrigan. *Mississippi Valley Historical Review* 38(March, 1952):695-696.

Henry De Tonty: Fur Trader of the Mississippi by Edmund Robert Murphy. *Pennsylvania Magazine of History and Biography* 66(July, 1942):356-357

A History of the South by Francis Butler Simkins. *Mississippi Valley Historical Review* 40(March, 1954):763-764.

Indian Agents of the Old Frontier by Flora Warren Seymour. *Journal of Southern History* 8(May, 1942):265-266.

The Indians of the Southwest: A Century of Development Under the United States by Edward Everett Dale. *Journal of Southern History* 16(February, 1950):108-110.

Journey into the Wilderness: An Army Surgeon's Account of Life in Camp and Field during the Creek and Seminole Wars, 1836-1838 edited by Jacob Rhett Motte. *Journal of Southern History* 20(February, 1954):121-123.

Liberal Kentucky, 1780-1828 by Niels Henry Sonne. *Journal of Southern History* 5(August, 1939):393-394.

McGillivray of the Creeks by John Walton Caughey. *Journal of Southern History* 5(February, 1939):106-107.

Memories of Long Ago by O. L. Hein. *Mississippi Valley Historical Review* 13(June, 1926):109-110.

North Carolina: The Old North State and the New by Archibald Henderson. *Journal of Southern History* 8(February, 1942):108-110.

On the Ohio by H. Bennett Abdy. *Mississippi Valley Historical Review* 7(March, 1920):395-396.

Red Carolinians by Chapman J. Milling. *Journal of Southern History* 7(February, 1941):110-111.

Red Men Calling on the Great White Father by Katherine C. Turner. *Journal of Southern History* 17(May, 1951):255-256.

The Road to Disappearance by Angie Debo. *Journal of Southern History* 8(August, 1942):431-432.

Sectionalism and Internal Improvements in Tennessee, 1796-1845 by Stanley John Folmsbee. *Journal of Southern History* 6(February, 1940):115-116.

Sixty Years of Indian Affairs: Political, Economic, and Diplomatic by George Dewey Harmon. *Journal of Southern History* 7(November, 1941):561-562.

The Southern Frontier by Verner W. Crane. *Mississippi Valley Historical Review* 16(June, 1929):102-104.

Stage Coach Days in the Bluegrass by J. Winston Coleman, Jr. *Journal of Southern History* 1(November, 1934):522-523.

They Came Here First: The Epic of the American Indian by D'Arcy McNickle. *Mississippi Valley Historical Review* 36(March, 1950):681-682.

The Transylvania Colony by William Stewart Lester. *Journal of Southern History* 2(February, 1936):109-110.

Uncle Sam's Stepchildren: The Reformation of United States Indian Policy, 1865-1887 by Loring Benson Priest. *Journal of Southern History* 8(August, 1942):431-432.

The Virginia Frontier, 1754-1763 by Louis K. Koontz. *Mississippi Valley Historical Review* 13(June, 1926):90-92.

The Westward Crossings: Balboa, Mackenzie, Lewis and Clark by Jeanette Mirsky. *Mississippi Valley Historical Review* 33(March, 1947):646-647.

Studies of Robert S. Cotterill

Caughey, John W. Review of *The Southern Indians* by Robert S. Cotterill. *Journal of Southern History* 20(August, 1954):406-407.

Channing, Steven A. *Kentucky: A Bicentennial History*. New York: W. W. Norton, 1977.

Cole, Arthur C. Review of *The Old South* by Robert S. Cotterill. *Journal of Southern History* 3(August, 1937):355-356.

Cotterill, Robert Spencer, Letters. Personal recollections and biographical information by Thomas D. Clark (July 16, 1985), Deborah Skaggs (June 28, 1985), Susan Hamberger (September 11, 1985), Earl Beck

(September 18, 1985), Bennett H. Wall (July 29, 1985), and Daisy Parker Flory (October 8, 1985). In private possession of Steven C. Schulte, College of the Ozarks, Clarksville, AR.

__________, Papers. Strozier Library, Florida State University, Tallahassee, FL.

Dale, Edward Everett. Review of *The Southern Indians* by Robert S. Cotterill. *Mississippi Valley Historical Review* 41(September, 1954):329-331.

Dumond, Dwight L. Review of *The Old South* by Robert S. Cotterill. *Mississippi Valley Historical Review* 23(December, 1936):412-413.

Edmunds, R. David. *The Shawnee Prophet.* Lincoln: University of Nebraska Press, 1983.

__________. *Tecumseh and the Quest for Indian Leadership.* Boston: Little, Brown and Co., 1984.

Hagan, William T. *The Indian in American History.* Washington, DC: American Historical Association, 1971.

Harrison, Lowell H. "The Filson Club History Quarterly." *Filson Club History Quarterly* 34(April, 1960):166-167.

Hofstadter, Richard. *The Progressive Historians: Turner, Beard, and Parrington.* New York: Vintage Books, 1968.

Hoxie, Frederick E. *A Final Promise: The Campaign to Assimilate the Indians, 1880-1920.* Lincoln: University of Nebraska Press, 1984.

Kincaid, Robert L. Review of *The Southern Indians* by Robert S. Cotterill. *Tennessee Historical Quarterly* 13(June, 1954):179-180.

Kinnaird, Lawrence. Review of *The Southern Indians* by Robert S. Cotterill. *American Historical Review* 61(October, 1955):145-146.

Library of Congress. *A Guide to the Study of the United States of America.* Washington, DC: Library of Congress, 1960. Analysis of *The Old South* by Robert S. Cotterill. P. 492.

Paredes, J. Anthony. "Robert Spencer Cotterill." In *Dictionary of Southern History* edited by David C. Roller and Robert W. Twyman. Baton Rouge: Louisiana State University Press, 1979. P. 300.

Stephenson, Wendell Holmes. *The South Lives as History: Southern Historians and Their Legacy.* Baton Rouge: Louisiana State University Press, 1955.

17

ISAAC JOSLIN COX

by Daniel H. Usner, Jr.

Biography

To those familiar with the work of Isaac Joslin Cox, it seems very auspicious that he began his long career as a historian on a bicycle journey from San Antonio, Texas, to Mexico City in 1898. That research trip on what was then America's most popular vehicle presaged some of Cox's major contributions to historical scholarship. He was a vigorous researcher who equalled Herbert Eugene Bolton in his enthusiasm for Spanish records. Traveling across the Mexican countryside during the Spanish-American War amplified for him the importance of better understanding the Hispanic presence in North America. And the object of his trip with Walter F. McCaleb--to follow leads on Aaron Burr's intrigue in the Mississippi Valley--persisted as a lifelong endeavor for Cox.

Born in West Creek, New Jersey, in 1873, Isaac Joslin Cox graduated from Kimball Union Academy in 1892 and from Dartmouth College in 1896. This well-schooled young man from the Northeast then spent his next six years in San Antonio, Texas, teaching at the recently established San Antonio Academy. Founder and principal William Belcher Seely, who himself had left New Jersey for the Southwest to improve his health, admired Cox's devotion and skill so much that he planned for him to become his successor. But in the summer of 1898, Isaac undertook that fateful bicycle trip to Mexico City with Walter McCaleb. McCaleb had graduated from San Antonio Academy in 1892, attended the University of Texas, and embarked upon graduate studies at the University of Chicago. With a traveling fellowship from Chicago, he planned to continue research on the Burr Conspiracy, which he had begun while exploring the long neglected Bexar Archives back in 1892. Cox was no less interested in the frontier machinations of that controversial native of New Jersey, so he accompanied McCaleb. "We covered about 1500 miles searching through what archives there were," McCaleb recalled years later, "always intent on the Conspiracy. This was done to some hazard due to the fact that the United States was at war with Spain." In other summers between teaching at the academy, Cox studied with George P. Garrison at the University of Texas, Edward G. Bourne at the University of Chicago, and Frederick Jackson Turner at the University of Wisconsin (*The Aaron Burr Conspiracy*, pp. vi-vii).

Anxious to proceed with his own graduate career, Cox received a Harrison Fellowship at the University of Pennsylvania in 1902. With a Ph.D. from Pennsylvania, Herbert E. Bolton had recently joined the University of Texas department of history and perhaps influenced the promising academy teacher's choice. Isaac Cox wrote from Philadelphia to an instructor in the Texas history department, Eugene C. Barker, "I like the work pretty well, especially with Cheyney. Professor McMaster is very pleasant in personal conferences . . . but his seminar is not equal to Cheyney's" (*Eugene C. Barker*, pp. 40-41). Barker left Austin to begin his studies at Pennsylvania in 1906, two years after Cox received his Ph.D. In Bolton, Cox, and Barker, the University of Pennsylvania Department of History--in the vanguard of graduate training under Edward Potts Cheyney and John Bach McMaster--produced three of the early twentieth century's most eminent scholars of Texas history.

Isaac Cox taught at the University of Cincinnati from 1904 to 1919, during which time he industriously produced his major works on North American frontiers and established his reputation for professional service. He edited *The Journeys of Rene Robert Cavelier Sieur de la Salle* (1905) in two volumes and published his doctoral thesis on Jeffersonian expeditions as *The Early Exploration of Louisiana* (1906). Cox's vast geographical and chronological knowledge was further exhibited in several articles on early United States relations with Spanish Florida and Texas and in his editorship of a series of documents portraying commerce and politics in the Ohio River Valley. In 1918 he published *The West Florida Controversy, 1798-1813: A Study in American Diplomacy*, which originated in his Albert Shaw Lectures on Diplomatic History at Johns Hopkins University in 1911-1912 and became his most familiar book among American historians.

Over this same period Cox participated in professional organizations with an energy that did not diminish in later years. Expressing regrets over not joining his friend at the American Historical Association meeting in Charleston, Herbert Bolton told Cox early in 1914 that "The whole profession makes a great mistake by too much 'associating,' thinking that somebody will remember them, having seen them. This is one of the reasons why American scholars do not produce more work" (*Quarterly of the Texas State Historical Association* 2:94). Cox did not take Bolton's admonition to heart, nor did he allow meetings to inhibit his work. In addition to reading papers frequently at conferences, he served both the American Historical Association and the Mississippi Valley Historical Association in various capacities. He was president of the MVHA in 1914-1915 and the chairman of its executive committee from 1916 to 1920. At the 1916 AHA meeting in Cincinnati, for which he worked as secretary of the Local Committee of Arrangements, Cox was one of thirty individuals who participated in the meeting that founded the *Hispanic American Historical Review*. He also served on its first board of editors. Altogether over his career, further reflecting his professional activism, Cox wrote some one hundred book reviews for the *American Historical Review*, the *Mississippi Valley Historical Review*, the *Hispanic American Historical Review*, and the *Journal of Southern History*.

By the time of his appointment to Northwestern University in 1919, Isaac J. Cox was a leading spokesman for the importance of Hispanic American history. Along with a partial outline of his History of Hispanic America course printed in the August, 1919, issue of the *Hispanic American Historical Review*, Cox expressed the hope that colleges in the United States would "train teachers and men of affairs who will interpret our history from a wider point of view--one that includes Hispanic factors among those of European origin affecting our development--and who will treat our inter-American relationships with more definite and sympathetic knowledge of fundamental economic and racial conditions" (p. 399). This student of early nineteenth-century North American frontiers was himself turning his attention to twentieth-century Latin America. During the 1920s he wrote *Nicaragua and the United States, 1909-1927* with the same thorough detail and dispassionate analysis that had gone into *The West Florida Controversy*. By the following decade Professor Cox was considered a leading authority on Chile, and in 1941 his translation of Luis Galdames's *A History of Chile* was published in the Inter-American Historical Series.

In shifting the focus of his research to modern Latin America, Cox did not abandon his interest in earlier Spanish-United States borders in North America. As indicated in his many reviews of scholarship in both areas, he actually found them to be reciprocally informative fields for historical understanding. Cox's continuing interest in what he once called "that uncertain frontier that marked the meeting of Anglo-American and Hispanic American civilizations" (*American Historical Review* 39:338-339) was manifested in the additional essays that he wrote on Aaron Burr and in the work of many of his graduate students. Among those students who wrote dissertations under Cox on areas of Anglo-Hispanic relations were Kathryn T. Abbey, "Florida as an Issue during the American Revolution" (1926); Harris G. Warren, "New Spain and the Filibusters, 1812-1821" (1927); Harvey T. Prentiss, "The Mission of Andrew Ellicott: Some Events Incident to the Demarcation of the Spanish-American Boundary of 1795, 1796-1800" (1929); Eric J. Bradner, "Jose Alvarez de Toledo and the Spanish American Revolution" (1931); Elizabeth Warren, "The Contribution of Oliver Pollock to the Revolution in the West" (1932); and Percy W. Christian, "General James Wilkinson and Kentucky Separation" (1935). Another student of Cox, John Preston Moore, devoted his early career to colonial Peru, but eventually he contributed significant works on Spanish Louisiana during his tenure at Louisiana State University.

Cox's retirement from Northwestern in 1941, after being department chairman since 1927, did not reduce his enthusiasm for teaching, researching, and participating in conferences. He taught as visiting professor at the University of Chile, Tulane University, and Louisiana State University before moving to his beloved San Antonio, where he continued to instruct at Trinity University. Cox regularly attended Texas State Historical Association meetings in Austin and served as an advisory editor for the *Hispanic American Historical Review* from 1946 to 1955. Meanwhile he was researching New York politician and land speculator Charles Williamson, another shady figure in the Aaron Burr imbroglio. At the 1950 meeting of the Mississippi Valley Historical Association in Oklahoma City, Cox presented some of his findings on a panel that included papers by Alfred B. Thomas and Lawrence Kinnaird. Amidst a younger and more self-conscious generation of "borderlands" historians, the inspirational trailblazer of North American Hispanic frontiers was greeted with what the conference secretary described as "a spontaneous and heartwarming round of applause" (*Mississippi Valley Historical Review* 37:272). Before completing his work on Williamson, Isaac Cox died on October 31, 1956.

Themes

Cox approached North American frontiers principally as a historian of diplomacy, yet underlying all of his work was a belief that the people living on international borders played a more significant role in United States territorial expansion than did their national leaders. In one of his early essays on the Louisiana-Texas frontier, Cox explicitly distinguished between two groups influencing the evolution of all frontiers: "the men who at the forefront bear the brunt of the national struggle for expansion or self-defense; and the rear guard, composed of legislators, executives, or diplomats who strive to make sure of the national prestige won by the former, and who often unjustly obtain credit for the other's work" (*Proceedings of the Mississippi Valley Historical Association, 1909-1910* 3:198). Ironically though, Cox was at his best when focusing on the international setting of territorial pretensions and acquisitions. A flourish of details about political intrigues and negotiations was usually accompanied by a less documented counterpoint about the determination of settlers and traders to push westward.

Cox's unique exploration of important themes was fully introduced in *The Early Exploration of Louisiana* (1906). The few years during which Lewis and Clark, Hunter, Pike, and Freeman explored parts of the Louisiana Purchase territory were exceptional in the early republic, the author reports, because the federal government did not encourage exploration for another two decades. Cox closely examines the motives and actions that went into these United States expeditions, as well as those constituting the Spanish response to them. He explains the seesaw reactions among Texas and Florida officials as reflections of Spain's "divided and decaying power" in the western hemisphere during this period, a recurring theme throughout Cox's scholarship. But his assessment of United States policy is no more flattering. Cox emphasizes the modest scientific and political results of President Thomas Jefferson's reconnaissance projects and observes that subsequent U.S. policy "was almost as nerveless as that of the vice-regal court of New Spain" (p. 34). But then comes the contrapuntal theme, when he states that "fortunately, our government had in its unofficial service a class of citizens that New Spain lacked after the age of the *Conquistadores.*" The years following 1806 belonged to them, according to Cox, and "it was the fur trader and pioneer settler, rather than casual explorer, who really opened up our great West and made the Louisiana Purchase an important element in our national strength" (pp. 73-74).

The discrepancy between blundering diplomats and sure-footed frontiersmen was more elaborately underscored in *The West Florida Controversy, 1798-1813* (1918). Although themes are largely submerged in 668 pages of deeply detailed text, Cox attempted in this book to relate the two theaters of action that independently transferred territory situated west of the Perdido River from the Spanish Empire to the United States. While James Monroe and other United States ambassadors pursued a tenuous claim to this area, based upon ambiguous language in the Louisiana Purchase treaty, a mixed group of Anglo-American planters and U.S. Army deserters seized Spanish garrisons along the Mississippi River and declared their independence from Spain. But while U.S. territorial officials in Orleans and Mississippi clearly encouraged this action, the federal government annexed West Florida only under its stubborn pretense of rightful title. After taking his readers through a long, complicated journey back-and-forth between European capitals and gulf coastal towns, Cox concludes by attributing the outcome to "the natural phases of a popular movement into the wilderness:"

> The pioneers who took part in it had pressed into an area that physiographically belonged to the United States and they undertook to make this relation a political one also. They occupied the territory by peaceful means, dispossessing few that had any legitimate claim for redress. They outstripped the diplomat and forced his hand, and in the final settlement their deeds, though obscured under a cloud of words, formed the determining factor (p. 668).

The familiar themes of geographical inevitability and pioneer indomitability pervade Cox's studies; in this regard he was very much a common frontier historian of his generation. But on another level of analysis, Cox rose above the simplistic and self-serving glorification of Anglo-American territorial aggression. Altogether his work on North American borders between Spain and the United States keenly interprets the formative development of the foreign policy of Pan-Americanism, enhancing our understanding of how territorial expansion to the Gulf of Mexico and into the Southwest related to other forms of intervention in Hispanic America. A desire to expand commerce combined with a fear of French or British circumspection, amidst colonial rebellions against Spain, strongly influenced early American designs on more territory. These conditions created a political climate rife with duplicity both inside and outside the government, and not even Thomas Jefferson escapes Cox's incriminating treatment of frontier diplomacy. The broader implications of his work on the early nineteenth century were clearly understood by Cox, who in 1915 told his audience at the AHA presidential address in New Orleans that investigation into the Anglo-American advance across Hispanic regions "will not prove flattering to ourselves, but it may give us a much-needed corrective view of 'manifest destiny,' and serve to explain the sentiment which certain Spanish-American peoples cherish toward their great northern neighbor" (*Proceedings of the Mississippi Valley Historical Association, 1909-1910* 8:178).

In addition to these recurring themes, Isaac Cox always applies an analytical scheme to frontiers. Although never pushing the idea very far, he argues that frontiers pass through three distinctive stages of development. Today it might be called a model of geopolitical change. Cox calls the first phase a period of *definition*, when various national claims to territory are gradually defined through conquest, settlement, and diplomacy. The period of *delimitation* occurs when the spheres of influence are made more definite by fixed boundaries. This phase of development usually relies most intensively upon international diplomacy. Then comes the period of *demolition*, when unstoppable influences destroy diplomatic constructs. This evolution, of course, occurred at different rates and over different periods of time for various frontiers. Cox outlined the geopolitical history of the lower Mississippi Valley, for example, as follows. Definition happened over the century before 1763, when France governed the region across rough borders with Spanish and British colonies. Delimitation lasted from 1763 to 1798, during which time treaties first defined the boundary between Spanish and British provinces and then delineated the border between the United States and Spanish Louisiana and Florida. With the organization of the Mississippi Territory in 1798 and the Louisiana Purchase in 1803, these borders began to break down or be demolished--as Cox illustrates most closely in *The West Florida Controversy*.

Analysis

Isaac Cox's greatest contribution to frontier historiography was the example he left of extensive and thorough research. Beginning with his early work in Texas and Mexico, he realized the importance of manuscript collections left by the Spanish provinces of North America. His intimate knowledge of archives in both Europe and the United States made his scholarship on frontier diplomacy more balanced and comprehensive than many previous and subsequent studies. For *The West Florida Controversy* he researched in the Archivo General at Seville, the Archivo Histórico Nacional at Madrid, the Archives des Affaires Étrangères at Paris, the British Public Record Office at London, the National Archives and Library of Congress at Washington, D.C., and the Mississippi State Archives at Jackson. In his numerous reviews of books about the Old Southwest, Cox was quick to notice which collections in Spain or Mexico had been neglected by the authors.

Unfortunately Cox's writing style was less than exemplary, even stifling the vitality of his important arguments. Like many first-generation professional historians, he seems to have intentionally avoided lively prose for the sake of scientific legitimacy. In a review published in the *Mississippi Valley Historical Review* in 1916, Cox emphasized that the book under discussion was a "study," his definition of which best serves to describe his own work: "Consequently one may expect a straightforward narration of facts, without special distinction of style, and nothing more" (3:401-402). Reviewers of *The West Florida Controversy* all agreed that ponderous details encumbered the book, Clarence E. Carter wishing that it "had been compressed to about one-third its present length" (*Mississippi Valley Historical Review* 5:489). After noting that Cox was "better fitted in temperament and training to unravel the complicated story than any other scholar in the United States," Thomas Maitland Marshall observed, "In style the book is heavy, for Professor Cox is always willing to sacrifice style for accuracy. Seldom does he allow his pen to flow freely. Those who admire the severe, the academic, the painstaking, the continual striving for exactness, will find enjoyment in this book" (*Hispanic American Historical Review* 1:327-329).

The subjects chosen by Cox posed special problems that also contributed to the "heaviness" of his work. *The Early Exploration of Louisiana* and *The West Florida Controversy* move their readers across multiple spheres of action, from European capitals to American hinterland outposts to cabinet meetings in Washington. To Cox's credit, few historians have dared follow decisions and other influences across so much distance. Had he focused on any one stage, though, Cox might have been able to make his characters more vivid and his messages more lucid. But he was interested in the borderland in its truest sense, pursuing those interests and intrigues that brought Anglo-America face-to-face with Hispanic America. Peggy L. Liss's *Atlantic Empires: The Network of Trade and Revolution, 1713-1825* is a recent effort in this rare endeavor, further illustrating both the importance and the difficulty in untangling what was indeed a complex web of politics and commerce. In his own lifetime Cox appreciated the skill of Arthur P. Whitaker, whose *The Spanish-American Frontier: 1783-1795* (1927) and *The Mississippi Question, 1795-1803* (1934) superceded in style and partly in content the work of the older scholar. And since then Thomas P. Abernethy, J. Leitch Wright, Jr., and Frank Lawrence Owsley have greatly improved our understanding of international diplomacy and intrigue in the gulf coastal region of North America.

The value of Cox's work today also suffers from his dependence upon racial character to explain frontier affairs, in this regard reflecting American historiography over the course of his career. Although he was an early advocate for the importance of the Spanish colonial experience in North America and became increasingly committed to improving United States-Latin American relations, Isaac Cox never completely abandoned stereotypes that long pervaded American history. In his early work there was a tendency to juxtapose the feebleness of Spanish American colonists with the energy of Anglo-American pioneers, and throughout his essays and reviews one finds references to American Indians as "savages" and "barbarians." More important than the labels, Cox's examination of borderlands diplomacy totally neglected the active role of Indians and, one should add, of Afro-Americans in shaping commercial and political issues in frontier regions.

A glance at the list of articles published will reveal that Isaac Cox's most enduring interest in Anglo-Hispanic frontiers rested in the ambitions of Aaron Burr and James Wilkinson toward the American Southwest. Given the number of essays that he wrote about these two men, one must wonder why Cox never wrote a biography of either controversial figure. Perhaps the profusion of such biographies, several of them reviewed by Cox in major journals, discouraged him from a similiar project. Perhaps his own work on the Charles Williamson papers in the Newberry Library was an attempt to contribute to the Burr-Wilkinson literature by shedding light on a more obscure agent of early filibustering. This speculation aside, there is no doubt that the clandestine operations and plans of Aaron Burr in particular fascinated Isaac Cox and influenced the focus of his studies. Before the Mississippi Valley Historical Association in 1910, he stated in a very revealing way that on the Louisiana-Texas frontier "the questions of jurisdiction, of Indian alliance, of border explorations, of escaping slaves, and of inter-settlement trade, were all cast into the shade by the rumor of Burr's daring project to invade the Spanish domains of Mexico" (*Proceedings of the Mississippi Valley Historical Association, 1909-1910* 3:208).

Cox spent much of his career trying to salvage the complicated behavior of Burr from detractors, in the Henry Adams tradition, and from defenders who followed Walter McCaleb. In another essay he declares about this "fascinating, but baffling" figure that "In ancestry and in personal endowment he represents the best traditions of early national life; in character and in performance some of the worst" (*Transactions of the Illinois Historical Society, 1928*, p. 73). While Cox stalked the secretive doings of alleged spies and opportunists, those other, supposedly overshadowed, questions about Indians, trade, and slavery still awaited attention. Fortunately Abraham Nasatir, Mattie A. Hatcher, and other students of the Spanish borderlands did attend to some of the broader processes of exploration, diplomacy, settlement, and commerce west of the lower Mississippi River. And the current work of Dan L. Flores on early nineteenth-century southwestern exploration and trade in *Jefferson and Southwestern Exploration* (1984) is adding even more insight to the work begun by Isaac J. Cox.

In 1904 Frederick Jackson Turner wrote in the *Atlantic Monthly* that "the diplomatic intrigues for the possession of the Mississippi, the Ohio, and the Great Lakes were of higher significance in world history than many of the European incidents which have received more attention" (93:676-691). Isaac Joslin Cox was already closely attending to those intrigues of the early nineteenth century, and his early scholarship did more than anyone else's to prove their significance. With the eyes of a detective, he combed manuscripts written in Spanish, French, and English to trace the not-always candid actions of statesmen and frontiersmen. Although not as forceful and intelligible as modern scholars might like, Isaac Cox's studies on diplomacy across the Anglo-Hispanic frontier will continue to serve as informative and inspiring groundwork for historians of the lower Mississippi Valley.

Bibliography

Books

The Early Exploration of Louisiana. Cincinnati: University of Cincinnati Press, 1906.

A History of Chile by Luis Galdames. Translator. Chapel Hill: University of North Carolina Press, 1941.

The Journeys of René Robert Cavelier Sieur de la Salle. Editor. Two volumes. New York: A.S. Barnes & Co., 1905.

Nicaragua and the United States, 1909-1927. Boston: World Peace Foundation, 1927.

The West Florida Controversy, 1798-1813: A Study in American Diplomacy. Baltimore: Johns Hopkins University Press, 1918.

William Belcher Seeley: Founder and First Principal of San Antonio Academy. San Antonio: The Naylor Company, 1948.

Articles

"The American Intervention in West Florida." *American Historical Review* 17(January, 1912):290-311.

"The Border Missions of General George Matthews." *Mississippi Valley Historical Review* 12(December, 1925):309-333.

"The Burr Conspiracy in Indiana." *Indiana Magazine of History* 25(December, 1929):257-280.

"Chile." In *Argentina, Brazil, and Chile Since Independence* edited by A. Curtis Wilgus. Washington, DC: George Washington University Press, 1935. Pp. 279-414.

"Courses in Hispanic American History." *Hispanic American Historical Review* 2(August, 1919):399-403, 419-430.

"Documents Relating to Zachariah Cox." *Quarterly Publication of the Historical and Philosophical Society of Ohio* 8(April/June and July/September, 1913):29-114.

"The Early Settlers of San Fernando." *Quarterly of the Texas State Historical Association* 5(October, 1901):142-160.

"Educational Efforts in San Fernando de Bexar." *Quarterly of the Texas State Historical Association* 6(July, 1902):27-63.

"The Exploration of the Louisiana Frontier, 1803-1806." In *Annual Report of the American Historical Association for the Year 1904*. Washington, DC: Government Printing Office, 1905. Pp. 149-174.

"Father Edmond John Peter Schmitt." *Quarterly of the Texas State Historical Association* 5(January, 1902):206-211.

"Florida, Frontier Outpost of New Spain." In *Hispanic American Essays: A Memorial to James Alexander Robertson* edited by A. Curtis

Wilgus. Chapel Hill: University of North Carolina Press, 1942. Pp. 150-166.

"The Founding of the First Texas Municipality." *Quarterly of the Texas State Historical Association* 2(January, 1899):217-226.

"General Wilkinson and His Later Intrigues with the Spaniards." *American Historical Review* 19(July, 1914):794-812.

"Hispanic American Phases of the 'Burr Conspiracy.'" *Hispanic American Historical Review* 12(May, 1932):145-175.

"The Indian as a Diplomatic Factor in the History of the Old Northwest." *Ohio State Archeological and Historical Quarterly* 18(October, 1909):542-565.

"The Louisiana-Texas Frontier." *Southwestern Historical Quarterly* 10(July, 1906):1-75; 17(July, 1913):1-42; 17(October, 1913):140-187.

"The Louisiana-Texas Frontier during the Burr Conspiracy." *Mississippi Valley Historical Review* 10(December, 1923):274-284.

"Monroe and the Early Mexican Revolutionary Agents." In *Annual Report of the American Historical Association for the Year 1911.* Washington, DC: Government Printing Office, 1913. 1:197-215.

"The New Invasion of the Goths and Vandals." *Proceedings of the Mississippi Valley Historical Association for the Year 1914-1915* 8(1916):176-200.

"Opening the Santa Fe Trail." *Missouri Historical Review* 25(October, 1930):30-66.

"The Pan-American Policy of Jefferson and Wilkinson." *Mississippi Valley Historical Review* 1(September, 1914):212-239.

"Reprint of *View of the President's Conduct Concerning the Conspiracy of 1806* by J. H. Daveiss (1807)." Co-edited with Helen A. Swineford. *Quarterly Publication of the Historical and Philosophical Society of Ohio* 12(April and July, 1917):49-154.

"Selections from the Torrence Papers." *Quarterly Publication of the Historical and Philosophical Society of Ohio* 1(July, 1906):61-96; 2(January and July, 1907):1-36, 93-120; 3(January, 1908):65-102; 4(July, 1909):91-138; 6(April and July, 1911):1-88; 13(July, 1918):79-130.

"The Significance of the Louisiana-Texas Frontier." *Proceedings of the Mississippi Valley Historical Association for the Year 1909-1910* 3(1911):198-213.

"The Southwest Boundary of Texas." *Quarterly of the Texas State Historical Association* 6(October, 1902):81-102.

"Thomas Sloo, Jr., A Typical Politician of Early Illinois." *Transactions of the Illinois State Historical Society for the Year 1911.* Springfield: Illinois State Historical Library, 1913. Pp. 26-42.

"Trailways to the Momentous Transfer." *Louisiana Historical Quarterly* 27(April, 1944):329-342.

"Western Reaction to the Burr Conspiracy." In *Transactions of the Illinois State Historical Society for the Year 1928.* Springfield: Illinois State Historical Library, 1928. Pp. 73-87.

"Wilkinson's First Break with the Spaniards." In *Eighth Annual Report of the Ohio Valley Historical Association.* Charleston, WV: Ohio Valley Historical Association, 1915. Pp. 46-56.

"'Yankee Imperialism' and Spanish American Solidarity: A Columbian Interpretation." *Hispanic American Historical Review* 4(May, 1921):256-265.

Selected Reviews

Aaron Burr, a Biography by Nathan Schachner. *Journal of Southern History* 4(February, 1938):103-105.

_________. *Mississippi Valley Historical Review* 24(March, 1938):541-543.

Aaron Burr: The Proud Pretender by Holmes Alexander. *Journal of Southern History* 3(November, 1937):508-510.

_________. *Mississippi Valley Historical Review* 24(December, 1937):388-390.

The Admirable Trumpeter: A Biography of General James Wilkinson by Thomas Robson and M. R. Werner. *American Historical Review* 47(July, 1942):883-885.

At the End of the Santa Fe Trail by Blandina Segale. *Mississippi Valley Historical Review* 36(December, 1949):541-542.

Athanase de Mézières and the Louisiana-Texas Frontier, 1768-1780 by Herbert Eugene Bolton. *American Historical Review* 20(October, 1914):168-170.

The Austin Papers edited by Eugene C. Barker. *American Historical Review* 30(July, 1925):839-840.

The Beginnings of Spanish Settlement in the El Paso District by Anne E. Hughes. *Mississippi Valley Historical Review* 1(December, 1914):474-475.

Breaking the Wilderness by Frederick S. Dellenbaugh. *American Historical Review* 11(October, 1905):169-170.

Cavalier in the Wilderness: The Story of the Explorer and Trader, Louis Juchereau de St. Denis by Ross Phares. *American Historical Review* 58(January, 1953):388.

Charles Williamson, Genesee Promoter--Friend of Anglo American Rapprochement by Helen I. Cowan. *American Historical Review* 48(April, 1943):581-582.

Chicago and the Old Northwest, 1673-1835 by Milo Milton Quaife. *Mississippi Valley Historical Review* 1(September, 1914):305-307.

Colonial Records of Spanish Florida: Letters and Reports of Governors, Deliberations of the Council of the Indies, Royal Decrees, and Other Documents. Volume II, 1577-1580 translated and edited by Jeanette Thurber Connor. *Mississippi Valley Historical Review* 18(March, 1932):551-552.

The Coming of the White Man, 1492-1848 by Herbert Ingram Priestly. *American Historical Review* 35(January, 1930):374-376.

Descriptive Catalogue of the Documents Relating to the United States in the Papeles Procedentes de Cuba deposited in the Archivo General de

Indias at Seville by Roscoe R. Hill. *American Historical Review* 22(July, 1917):875-877.

Development of the United States From Colonies to a World Power by Max Farrand. *Mississippi Valley Historical Review* 6(December, 1919):404-406.

Diary of a Journey through the Carolinas, Georgia, and Florida from July 1, 1765, to April 10, 1766 by John Bartram and annotated by Francis Harper. *Hispanic American Historical Review* 23(November, 1943):740-741.

Diplomacy and the Borderlands: The Adams-Onis Treaty of 1819 by Phillip Coolidge Brooks. *American Historical Review* 46(April, 1941):676-677.

Documents Relating to the Commercial Policy of Spain in the Floridas with Incidental References to Louisiana translated and edited by Arthur P. Whitaker. *Mississippi Valley Historical Review* 20(June, 1933):113-114.

Early Diplomatic Relations between the United States and Mexico by William R. Manning. *Mississippi Valley Historical Review* 3(December, 1916):401-402.

The Finished Scoundrel: General James Wilkinson, Sometime Commander-in-Chief of the Army of the United States, Who Made Intrigue a Trade and Treason a Profession by Royal Ornan Shreve. *Mississippi Valley Historical Review* 20(March, 1934):573-574.

Florida, Land of Change by Kathryn Trimmer Abbey. *Journal of Southern History* 8(February, 1942):106-108.

Guide to the Materials for the History of the United States in the Principal Archives of Mexico by Herbert E. Bolton. *American Historical Review* 19(April, 1914):638-640.

Historical Documents Relating to New Mexico, Nueva Vizcaya, and Approaches Thereto, to 1773 collected by Adolph F. A. Bandelier and Fanny R. Bandelier and edited by Charles Wilson Hackett. Vol. I. *Mississippi Valley Historical Review* 11(December, 1924):426-429.

Jose de Galvez, Visitor-General of New Spain (1765-1771) by Herbert Ingram Priestly. *Mississippi Valley Historical Review* 4(September, 1917):232-234.

Journals of Captain Meriwether Lewis and Sergeant John Ordway Kept on the Expedition of Western Exploration edited by Milo M. Quaife. *Mississippi Valley Historical Review* 4(September, 1917):268-270.

Kino's Historical Memoir of Primeria Alta edited by Herbert Eugene Bolton. *Mississippi Valley Historical Review* 6(December, 1919):428-429.

The Lost Pathfinder: Zebulon Montgomery Pike by W. Eugene Hollon. *Mississippi Valley Historical Review* 36(March, 1950):706-707.

Manifest Destiny: A Study of Nationalist Expansion in American History by Albert K. Weinberg. *Mississippi Valley Historical Review* 23(December, 1936):421-422.

The Mississippi Question, 1795-1803: A Study in Trade, Politics, and Diplomacy by Arthur Preston Whitaker. *Mississippi Valley Historical Review* 21(December, 1934):400-401.

The Monroe Doctrine, 1826-1867 by Dexter Perkins. *Mississippi Valley Historical Review* 20(March, 1934):576-577.

The Monroe Doctrine, 1867-1907 by Dexter Perkins. *Mississippi Valley Historical Review* 25(September, 1938):285-286.

New Spain and the Anglo-American West: Historical Contributions Presented to Herbert Eugene Bolton. 2 volumes. *American Historical Review* 39(January, 1934):338-339.

_________. *Mississippi Valley Historical Review* 20(September, 1933):298.

Official Letter Books of W. C. C. Claiborne, 1801-1816 edited by Dunbar Rowland. *American Historical Review* 23(January, 1918):404-407.

The Ohio Country between the Years 1783 and 1815, including Military Operations that Twice Saved to the United States the Country West of the Allegheny Mountains after the Revolutionary War by Charles Elihu Slocum. *American Historical Review* 16(October, 1910):173-174.

Our Rising Empire, 1763-1803 by Arthur Burr Darling. *Hispanic American Historical Review* 22(February, 1942):110-111.

Pichardo's Treatise on the Limits of Louisiana and Texas translated and edited by Charles Wilson Hackett. Vol. IV. *Mississippi Valley Historical Review* 35(June, 1948):121-123.

Pinckney's Treaty. A Study of America's Advantage from Europe's Distress, 1783-1800 by Samuel Flagg Bemis. *American Historical Review* 32(April, 1927):616-618.

_________. *Hispanic American Historical Review* 7(August, 1927):336-339.

Spanish and French Rivalry in the Gulf Region of the United States, 1678-1702: The Beginnings of Texas and Pensacola by William Edward Dunn. *Hispanic American Historical Review* 2(August, 1919):458-459.

The Story of the West Florida Rebellion by Stanley Clisby Arthur. *Journal of Southern History* 2(November, 1936):532.

Tarnished Warrior: Major-General James Wilkinson by James Ripley Jacobs. *Journal of Southern History* 4(November, 1938):521-523.

The Writings of Sam Houston, 1813-1863 edited by Amelia W. Williams and Eugene C. Barker. *American Historical Review* 45(January, 1940):414-415; 46(October, 1940):165-166; 47(January, 1942):359-362; 48(April, 1943):586-587; 49(January, 1944):306-308.

Studies of Isaac Joslin Cox

Carter, Clarence E. Review of *The West Florida Controversy, 1798-1813: A Study in American Diplomacy* by Isaac Joslin Cox. *Mississippi Valley Historical Review* 5(March, 1919):488-490.

Hamilton, Peter J. Review of *The West Florida Controversy, 1798-1813: A Study in American Diplomacy* by Isaac Joslin Cox. *American Historical Review* 24(October, 1918):105-107.

Hasbrouck, Alfred. Review of *Nicaragua and the United States, 1909-1927* by Isaac Joslin Cox. *Hispanic American Historical Review* 9(February, 1929):99-103.

Marshall, Thomas Maitland. Review of *The West Florida Controversy, 1798-1813: A Study in American Diplomacy* by Isaac Joslin Cox. *Hispanic American Historical Review* 1(August, 1918):327-329.

McCaleb, Walter Flavius. *The Aaron Burr Conspiracy and a New Light on Aaron Burr.* New York: Argosy-Antiquarian Ltd., 1966.

"Notes and Fragments." *Quarterly of the Texas State Historical Association* 2(July, 1898):84.

"Obituary." *American Historical Review* 62(April, 1957):799.

________. *Hispanic American Historical Review* 37(February, 1957):138-139.

________. *Mississippi Valley Historical Review* 43(March, 1957):714-715.

________. *Southwestern Historical Quarterly* 61(July, 1957):167.

Pool, William C. *Eugene C. Barker: Historian.* Austin: Texas State Historical Association, 1966.

Schmitz, Joseph W. Review of *William Belcher Seeley: Founder and First Principal of San Antonio Academy* by Isaac Joslin Cox. *Southwestern Historical Quarterly* 54(January, 1951):369.

Warren, Harris Gaylord. "Isaac Joslin Cox, 1873-1956." *Hispanic American Historical Review* 37(February, 1957):138-142.

Williams, Mary Wilhelmine. Review of *A History of Chile* by Luis Galdames, translated and edited by Isaac Joslin Cox. *American Historical Review* 47(January, 1942):398-399.

18

EDWARD EVERETT DALE

by David J. Murrah

Biography

"I haven't taught history so much as I've lived it," Edward Everett Dale once told a reporter, and in so doing, summarized his major contribution to American historiography (Dale Papers, *Norman Transcript,* May 31, 1972). His life bridged two centuries, and as a boy he experienced the vanishing American frontier. As a student of history he carried those experiences into Frederick Jackson Turner's classrooms at Harvard. As a teacher and writer he communicated those experiences throughout a long and distinguished career at his beloved University of Oklahoma, and at the age of eighty-seven he produced one of his best works, based on his boyhood years.

Born February 8, 1879, in a log cabin between Roanoke and Keller in north Tarrant County, Texas, Ed Dale spent his first thirteen years on his father's farm, which was nestled in the edge of the eastern Cross Timbers country of north Texas (*Chronicles of Oklahoma* 45:290). His mother died when he was five, but before her death she taught her youngest son to read, which he did avidly. Left to the general care of his older brother George, five years his senior, young Ed enjoyed a relatively comfortable and happy farm life with his father and brother. In 1892, the Dales followed older members of the family who had located on 160-acre homesteads in what was then Greer County, Texas, later to become a part of Oklahoma Territory (*Great Plains Journal* 18:80). The move changed the course of Ed Dale's life, removing him from the drudgery of agrarian labor into the midst of a romantic cattle frontier on the rolling plains (*Frontier Historian,* p. 10).

The new Dale place lay near the border of the Kiowa-Comanche Indian Reservation and along the route of a popular cattle trail. A keen observer even as a boy, Dale learned quickly the skills of a cowboy by working cattle for his father, for neighbors, and for Texas drovers moving cattle into northwestern Oklahoma to the Cherokee Outlet. The seasonal ranch work also gave young Dale more leisure time, and as a result he attended a nearby four-week summer camp school, promoted by a Greer County teacher and prohibitionist. Dale credited the experience for improving his reading, memory, and oratorical skills (*Great Plains Journal* 18:82).

At age nineteen, Dale began his long teaching career in a rural Oklahoma school and at the same time entered the cattle business with his brother, George. In his unpublished autobiography, Dale notes that, at the time, teaching "appealed to me for, although I had no thought at this time of making teaching my life work, it seemed that it might be interesting to teach three or four terms and use my savings to buy calves" (*Frontier Historian,* p. 15). After attending a four-week certification program in 1898, he began teaching near Navajoe in a rural school, and helped his brother with the cattle as time allowed. But low prices and a hard winter in 1900 forced the partners out of business and Ed Dale into a serious academic career.

From 1901 to 1913, Dale taught in several rural schools and used his summers to do college work. In 1909, he received an associate degree from the Oklahoma Territorial Normal School at Edmond and, two years later, a B.A. in history from the University of Oklahoma. After graduation, Dale taught for two summers at the Normal School, an experience which whetted his appetite for college teaching. Determined to pursue a graduate education, he applied for a teacher's scholarship at Harvard University and was accepted into its history program (pp. 16-17).

Dale spent the 1913-1914 school year in Cambridge, where he encountered Frederick Jackson Turner, whom Dale says "opened a new Heaven and a new earth in the field of American History" (p. 17). Finishing a master's degree, Dale returned in 1914 to accept a teaching position at the University of Oklahoma and began an association that was to last for nearly sixty years. He returned to Harvard periodically, where he completed the Ph.D. in 1922, at the age of forty-three. Incidentally, while at Harvard in 1919, Dale received national attention by carrying his own six-gun while serving as a volunteer policeman during the infamous Boston police strike (p. 346).

Dale's Harvard degree also gained him stature at home, and he quickly rose through the ranks of the University of Oklahoma, becoming chairman of the history department in 1924, a post he held for eighteen years. He also established the Frank Phillips Research Collection in the 1920s, which later became the nucleus for the university's famous Western History Collections. Dale also served as a visiting professor at several other universities, including Texas, William and Mary, Nebraska, Missouri, Ohio State, Duke, and Wyoming. Although he formally retired in 1952, he taught as a Fulbright Lecturer at the University of Melbourne, Australia (1953-1954), and as a visiting professor at the University of Houston (1954-1955, 1958-1959). Dale died May 28, 1972, at the age of ninety-three.

Themes

Dale's accomplishment of moving from the cattle range to a Fulbright lectureship came as a result of his writing a great corpus of historical literature--nearly 100 books, articles, and edited works. Except for an occasional foray into national history, most of Dale's work centered on Oklahoma, primarily on the cattle country in the western Oklahoma of his boyhood. Certainly his scope was broader than his corner of the territory, but the prairie plains of Greer County in reality were the heart of Dale's cow country and, therefore, the heart of his best work.

Most of Dale's writing reflects a strong romantic approach to history. His first major published work, *Tales of the Tepee* (1920), was a book of Indian folk tales written as a children's reader. In its introduction, Dale reveals his personal fascination for those who had been his neighbors in southwestern Oklahoma, the Kiowa, Comanche, and Wichita. Dale's view of Indians is romantic: "Here I became acquainted with many Indians of these tribes; rode with them, hunted with them, visited them in their lodges, and joined in their sports and games" (p. iii).

Another early work was even more romantic. From childhood, Dale loved rhyming verse, and in 1929 he published a book of his own poetry, entitled *The Prairie Schooner and Other Poems.* His introduction serves as an example of the romantic images Dale visualizes:

> First the Indian, gaudy in paint and feathers as he rides his spotted pony o'er the boundless plains. . . . And then the cowboy with this boots and spurs, his wide-brimmed hat and trusty forty-five. . . . Then the homesteader in the prairie schooner, his toil worn wife beside him on the seat, his ragged offspring peeping out beneath its cover (p. 11).

Two of Dale's books came directly as the result of his work as curator of the Phillips Collection at the Universtity of Oklahoma. In 1930, he published *Frontier Trails: The Autobiography of Frank M. Canton,* based on a manuscript Dale discovered in Canton's papers which had been given to the new Frank Phillips Collection. Certainly a romantic character, Canton was a frontier peace officer who, among other things, participated in the Johnson County War, chased outlaws, and served as a cattle inspector, deputy U.S. marshal, and adjutant general of Oklahoma.

In 1939, with Gaston Litton, Dale produced *Cherokee Cavaliers.* This constituted the publication of a body of letters of the Ridge-Watie-Boudinot family, the minority leaders of the Cherokee nation, centered on the activities of Stand Watie. Collectively, the letters consist of an informal history of the Cherokee nation from 1832 to 1872 and reveal the private lives and thoughts of a people. Dale, who discovered the letters in 1919 in an old farmhouse, was instrumental in getting the letters transcribed through a Works Progress Administration project.

One of Dale's largest and more laborious books was his biography (with James D. Morrison), *Pioneer Judge: The Life of Robert Lee Williams*. Williams was a strange and tough individual who became Oklahoma's third governor. Apologetic and, of course, romantic in nature, the work is far less objective than Dale's other writing.

Analysis

Dale wrote five books which can be considered outstanding and which reflect what Dale's biographer, Arrell Gibson, termed Dale's "formal dissemination of his frontier experience" (*Great Plains Journal* 18:83). Four of the five, *The Range Cattle Industry* (1930), *Cow Country* (1942), *Frontier Ways* (1959), and *Cross Timbers* (1966), are drawn primarily from his rich personal experiences and memories gained on the Texas and Oklahoma frontiers. His fifth major work, *Indians of the Southwest* (1949), was by far Dale's most challenging work, and is probably the most scholarly of all of his books.

Dale's *Range Cattle Industry* was a pioneer effort in that it is one of the earliest scholarly studies of the midwestern cattle business and remains a classic to this day. He was one of the first to distinguish the ranching history of different geographical sections of the industry. Dale credits the range cattle industry with being "one of the most significant events in the economic history of the United States during the latter half of the nineteenth century" (p. 72). He notes that the industry provided an outlet for the energies of Civil War veterans, it furnished a field of investment for eastern and foreign capital, and it caused "in large measure" the development of the meat packing industry, which in turn provided a cheap food supply for growing American cities and for export.

Dale also terms the industry's rapid expansion as a "minor South Sea bubble." During the 1880s, thanks to the voluminous investment of foreign capital, the industry mushroomed and, for a few years, some cattlemen made good profits, but "it was not long until there came the bursting of the bubble, a collapse of prices, and a general decline in the whole movement, which brought to the ranchmen dire distress and, in many cases, complete financial ruin" (p. 91).

Generally, *Range Cattle Industry* was well received by the academic community. However, Louis Pelzer notes that Dale's work recorded "results and effects rather than processes. One misses adequate accounts of cattle associations, of the routine of ranching, of great cattle companies, and of the early financing of ranches" (*American Historical Review* 36:658). Another reviewer chides Dale for paring away "so ruthlessly the interesting details that he could have given. . . . He keeps to himself altogether too much of his rare knowledge of cowboy lore. . . . The rarest humorist in the Mississippi Valley Historical Association has written a book without a laugh in it" (*Mississippi Valley Historical Review* 17:647).

Dale must have taken the latter critic's comments to heart. His later works were lighter, yet packed with his rich personal experiences on the range. His next major work, *Cow Country,* perhaps his best, was also his most romantic, and certainly was more personal than his previous writing.

Influenced heavily by his major professor at Harvard, Frederick Jackson Turner, Dale sees the formation of the Great Plains cattle industry as a "natural and logical development in the economic history of the United States." The plains were ripe for develpment because the "farmers had hesitated, daunted by the broad stretches of plains which lay beyond and which obviously could not be dealt with in the same fashion as could the more humid, wooded, or partially wooded regions farther east" (p. 14).

For a book in which each chapter originally was produced as an independent article or essay over a twenty-five-year period, *Cow Country* has remarkable subject consistency. Yet some chapters reflect extensive research while others are based almost entirely on Dale's personal experiences. His chapter on cowboy humor is an excellent work which reveals not only the lighter side of cow work, but also a glimpse of the everyday lifestyle of the plains cowboy.

Academic reviewers praised *Cow Country* but the New York press was not as kind. The *Herald Tribune* noted that Dale had nothing new to offer, that others had covered the topics more ably, and, with an air of disdain, noted that folk in the West "still raise cattle, and people still, apparently, like to read about it" (October 11, 1942). The *Times* was less critical, citing that "Dale's particular contribution is in his own particular field--the significance of the great days of the cow country. For this, his book deserves a place on the top shelf" (August 2, 1942).

Dale's last few years as a professor at the University of Oklahoma were by far his most productive. In 1948, he co-authored two college textbooks, one state and one national. The following year he wrote a high school state history and a study of federal Indian policy, entitled *The Indians of the Southwest: A Century of Development under the United States.* The latter book is by far his most scholarly. Not only did Dale prove his ability to work with detailed research materials, but he also convinced reviewers that he could write very well. Joseph C. Green notes in the *American Historical Review* that Dale "succeeded in giving the specialist a scholarly work of exposition and reference, and he writes so well that he has almost accomplished the feat of making administrative history interesting to the general reader" (55:948).

Dale's late retirement years produced two other quality books. For his *Frontier Ways: Sketches of Life in the Old West,* published in 1959, Dale followed the successful format of *Cow Country,* drawing upon a wealth of articles he had produced since the 1940s. More personal than *Cow Country, Frontier Ways* included memories of Dale's boyhood life in a log cabin in Texas and in sod houses in western Oklahoma. Although he flatly states that he had no intention of entering the then-raging debate over the Turner thesis, his production of *Frontier Ways* was clearly an effort to substantiate the philosphy of his mentor. He notes, for the sake of the Turner critics, that "for two and a half centuries large numbers of American people did remove west to settle and develop unoccupied lands on the frontier, . . . that their new environment differed radically from that which they had known in the past . . . [and] that it was especially true for those who left the wooded areas to establish new homes on the western prairies" (pp. xi-xii).

Dale's last book, published in 1966 when he was eighty-seven, was *The Cross Timbers: Memories of a North Texas Boyhood.* Probably his most readable, the book recalls his first thirteen years of life and the many details of his farm home and furnishings, food, labors, neighbors, relatives, superstitions, and religion. An appropriate way to complete his life's work, *Frontier Ways* filled the last gap of Dale's colorful memoirs, as he was able to record the remainder in the pages of *Cow Country.*

At least five southwestern frontier historians, Walter Prescott Webb, Carl Coke Rister, Rupert Richardson, William Curry Holden, and Everett Edward Dale, spent their formative years within a 120-mile radius on the semiarid rolling plains of west Texas and Oklahoma. All became disciples of Turner's thesis in varying degrees; Dale and Webb especially emphasized the environmental impact of the frontier upon society. Dale, more than any of the others, truly experienced Turner's frontier long before he ever met the historian, and it was Turner, his professor, who taught him to recognize the thesis at work: "I had lived so close to all these things that they were conditions to be accepted as a matter of course," writes Dale. "Proof of virtually every theory which Turner advanced I had witnessed in practice, though at the time it had been meaningless" (*Mississippi Valley Historical Review* 30:339).

Dale firmly believed in Turner's frontier concept because he had experienced it. Having moved from the woods of north central Texas to the plains of Oklahoma, Dale witnessed first-hand the dramatic change in lifestyle that accompanied the venture. "Such violent changes of lifeways could hardly fail to affect the [frontier] man's mental processes; his manner of thought, ideas and ideals. These effects become more pronounced as the years went by" (*Frontier Ways,* pp. xii-xiii).

Arrell Gibson notes that Dale was "a social historian, more interested in people than presidents," one whose greatest contribution to historiography was his ability "to share what he had already experienced. Dale must be regarded less than a hard nosed professional historian and more of a romantic interpreter of the frontier milieu" (*Great Plains Journal* 18:84). It was Turner who had opened for Dale a "new Heaven and new earth." Perhaps it was this process of Dale's being taught by Turner to recognize the significance of his frontier boyhood experiences that made Dale the "romantic interpreter" of the American West.

Bibliography

This bibliography was adapted in part from Jimmie Hicks, "Edward Everett Dale: A Biography and Bibliography, *Chronicles of Oklahoma* 45(Autumn, 1967):290-306.

Books

Cherokee Cavaliers. Co-edited with Gaston Litton. Norman: University of Oklahoma Press, 1939.

Cow Country. Norman: University of Oklahoma Press, 1942.

The Cross Timbers: Memories of a North Texas Boyhood. Austin: University of Texas Press, 1966.

Frontier Trails: The Autobiography of Frank M. Canton. Editor. Boston: Houghton Mifflin Company, 1930.

Frontier Ways: A Ladder Edition at the 3,000 Word Level. Adapted by Edward A. Symans. New York: Popular Library, 1963.

Frontier Ways: Sketches of Life in the Old West. Austin: University of Texas Press, 1959.

Grant Foreman: A Brief Biography. Norman: University of Oklahoma Press, 1933.

History of Oklahoma. Co-authored with Morris L. Wardell. New York: Prentice-Hall, Inc., 1948.

A History of Oklahoma. Co-authored with James Shannon Buchanan. Chicago: Row, Peterson and Company, 1924.

History of the United States. Co-authored with Dwight L. Dumond and Edgar B. Wesley. Boston: D. C. Heath and Company, 1948.

The Indians of the Southwest: A Century of Development under the United States. Norman: University of Oklahoma Press, 1949.

The Journal of James Akin, Jr. Editor. Norman: University of Oklahoma Bulletin, 1919.

Lafayette Letters. Editor. Oklahoma City: Harlow Publishing Company, 1925.

Oklahoma--A Pageant. Bartlesville, OK: Bartlesville Pageant Association, 1923.

Oklahoma: The Story of a State. Evanston, IL: Row, Peterson and Company, 1949.

Outline and References for Oklahoma History. Co-authored with Morris L. Wardell. Norman, OK: Peerless Printing Company, 1924.

Pioneer Judge: The Life of Robert Lee Williams. Co-authored with James D. Morrison. Cedar Rapids, IA: The Torch Press, 1958.

The Prairie Schooner and Other Poems. Guthrie, OK: The Co-Operative Publishing Company, 1929.

The Problem of Indian Administration. Co-authored with Lewis Meriam et al. Baltimore: Johns Hopkins Press, 1928.

The Range Cattle Industry: Ranching on the Great Plains from 1865 to 1925. Norman: University of Oklahoma Press, 1930; new edition, 1960.

Readings in Oklahoma History. Co-edited with Jesse Lee Rader. Evanston, IL: Row, Peterson and Company, 1930.

A Rider of the Cherokee Strip By Evan G. Barnard. Editor. Boston: Houghton Mifflin Co., 1936.

Tales of the Teepee. Boston: D. C. Heath and Co., 1920.

Territorial Acquisitions of the United States. Blair, OK: Privately Printed, 1912.

Pamphlets

Critiques of Research in the Social Sciences: III. An Appraisal of Walter Prescott Webb's "The Great Plains: A Study in Institutions and En-

vironment." Series edited by Fred A. Shannon. New York: Social Science Research Council, 1940.

An Exhibition of Paintings and Bronzes by Frederick Remington and Charles M. Russell. Tulsa, OK: Thomas Gilcrease Foundation, 1950.

The Government of Oklahoma. A supplement to *Elementary Community Civics* by R. O. Hughes. Boston: Allyn and Bacon, 1928.

Articles

"Additional Letters of General Stand Watie." Editor. *Chronicles of Oklahoma* 1(October, 1921):131-149.

"America's Mary and Martha." *The Southwestern* 6(February and March, 1922):193-201, 229-232.

"An American Looks at Australia." *Walkabout Magazine* (Melbourne, Australia) 20(May, 1954):10-15.

"Arkansas: The Myth and the State." *Arkansas Historical Quarterly* 12(Spring, 1953):8-29.

"Arkansas and the Cherokee Indians." *Arkansas Historical Quarterly* 8(Summer, 1949):95-114.

"Blue Blood on the Vast Western Plains." *American Hereford Journal* 27(December 15, 1936):5-7, 70-71.

"The Cherokee Strip Live Stock Association." In *Proceedings of the Fifth Annual Convention of the Southwestern Political and Social Science Association.* Austin, TX: Southwestern Political and Social Science Association, 1924. Pp. 97-115. Reprint. *Chronicles of Oklahoma* 5(March, 1927):58-78; *The Cattleman* 12(June, 1925):21-28; and *Cow Country.*

"The Cherokees in the Confederacy." *Journal of Southern History* 13(May, 1947):159-185.

"The Cheyenne-Arapaho Country." *Chronicles of Oklahoma* 20(December, 1942):360-371.

"The Cow Country in Transition." *Mississippi Valley Historical Review* 24(June, 1937):3-20. Reprint. *The Cattleman* 24(March, 1938):35-44; Louis B. Wright and H. T. Swedenberg, Jr., eds., *The American Tradition* (New York: F. S. Crofts and Co., 1941), pp. 146-159; and *Cow Country.*

"Cow Custom." *American Hereford Journal* 52(July 1, 1961):156, 160, 162, 772-773. Reprint. Pamphlet by Don Ornduff, Kansas City, MO, 1961.

"Cow Horses of the Great Plains." *Hoofs and Horns* 30(February, 1961):10-11, 29, 38.

"Cowboy Cookery." *American Hereford Journal* 36(January 1, 1946):37-42, 46, 49, 52, 54, and 58. Reprint. *Frontier Ways.*

"Culture on the American Frontier." *Nebraska History* 26(April-June, 1945):75-90. Reprint. *Frontier Ways.*

"David Ross Boyd: Pioneer Educator." *Chronicles of Oklahoma* 42(Summer, 1964):2-35.

"A Dedication to the Memory of Grant Foreman, 1869-1953." *Arizona and the West* 6(Winter, 1964):271-274.

"Editorial on John Young Bryce, New Secretary of the Oklahoma Historical Society and Editor of the *Chronicles of Oklahoma*." *Chronicles of Oklahoma* 4(March, 1926):14-15.

"End of Heroic Age Came When Oklahoma Ranches Gave Way to Homesteads." *The Cattleman* 26(February, 1940):63-69. Reprint. Oklahoma City *Daily Oklahoman*, April 23, 1939.

"The End of the Indian Problem." In *Annual Report of the American Historical Association for the Year 1942*. Washington: Government Printing Office, 1944. 3:305-317.

"The Food of the Frontier." *Journal of the Illinois State Historical Society* 40(March, 1947):38-61. Reprint. *Frontier Ways*.

"Foreword." In *Always the Prairie: A Book of Verse* by Laressa Cox McBurney. Guthrie, OK: Co-Operative Publishing Company, 1949.

"From Log Cabin to Sod House." *Journal of the Illinois State Historical Society* 38(December, 1945):383-413. Reprint. *Frontier Ways*.

"The Frontier Literary Society." *Nebraska History* 31(September, 1950):167-182. Reprint. *Frontier Ways*.

"History of the Ranch Cattle Industry in Oklahoma." In *Annual Report of the American Historical Association for the Year 1920*. Washington: Government Printing Office, 1925. Pp. 307-322. Reprint. *The Cattleman* 12(December, 1925):15-25; and *Readings in Oklahoma History*.

"The Humor of the Cowboy." *The Cattleman* 22(January, 1936):11-12, 14, 16, 17. Reprint. *Cow Country*; and T. M. Pearce and A. P. Thomason, eds., *Southwesterners Write* (Albuquerque: University of New Mexico Press, 1946), pp. 82-92.

"The Indians of Oklahoma." *Outdoor Oklahoma* 1(April, 1939):8.

"Introduction." In *Experiences of a Special Indian Agent* by E. E. White. Reprint. Norman: University of Oklahoma Press, 1965.

__________. In *Fifty Years on the Owl Hoot Trail* by Harry E. Chrisman. Chicago: Sage Books, 1969.

__________. In *My Life on the Range* by John Clay. Reprint. New York: Antiquarian Press, Ltd., 1961.

"John Rollin Ridge." *Chronicles of Oklahoma* 4(December, 1926):312-321.

"Letter Concerning Doans' Crossing." Editor. *Southwestern Historical Quarterly* 56(July, 1952):137-138.

"Letters of the Two Boudinots." Editor. *Chronicles of Oklahoma* 6(September, 1928):328-347.

"Medical Practices on the Frontier." *Indiana Magazine of History* 43(December, 1947):307-328. Reprint. *Frontier Ways*.

"Memories of Frederick Jackson Turner." *Mississippi Valley Historical Review* 30(December, 1943):339-358.

"Oklahoma's Last Run." *Prairie Lore* 1(January, 1965):74-83.

"Old Navajoe." *Chronicles of Oklahoma* 24(Summer, 1946):128-145. Reprint. *Frontier Times* 24(February, 1947):307-320; and *Frontier Ways*.
"The Passing of the Range Cattle Industry in Oklahoma." *The Cattleman* 11(November, 1924):9-17. Reprint. *Readings in Oklahoma History*.
"Pioneer Speech." In *The John H. Hauberg Historical Essays* edited by O. F. Ander. Rock Island, IL: Augustana Book Concern, 1954. Pp. 29-40.
"Ranching in the Cherokee Strip." *American Hereford Journal* 29(March 1, 1939):5-6, 48B, 48C, 48F, 48G.
"Ranching on the Cheyenne-Arapaho Reservation, 1880-1885." *Chronicles of Oklahoma* 6(March, 1928):35-59. Reprint. *The Cattleman* 15(December, 1928):22-27, 30-32; and *Cow Country*.
"The Ranchman's Last Frontier." *Mississippi Valley Historical Review* 10(June, 1923):34-46. Reprint. *The Cattleman* 11(March, 1925):75-83.
"The Romance of the Range." *West Texas Historical Association Year Book* 5(June, 1929):3-23. Reprint. *The Cattleman* 16(November, 1929):33-40; and *Frontier Ways*.
"Romance Rode With Development." *The Cattleman* 12(March, 1926):15-21.
"A Sketch of the History of the University of Oklahoma." *The Southern Magazine* 3(August-September, 1936):18-20.
"The Social Homesteader." *Nebraska History* 25(July-September, 1944):155-171. Reprint. *Frontier Ways*.
"Some Letters of General Stand Watie." Editor. *Chronicles of Oklahoma* 1(January, 1921):30-59.
"The Speech of the Frontier." *Quarterly Journal of Speech* 27(October, 1941):353-363.
"The Speech of the Pioneers." *Arkansas Historical Quarterly* 6(Summer, 1947):117-131.
"The Spirit of Oklahoma." In *Oklahoma: A Guide to the Sooner State*. American Guide Series. Norman: University of Oklahoma Press, 1941. Pp. 3-6.
"The Spirit of Sooner Land." *Chronicles of Oklahoma* 1(June, 1923):167-178. Reprint. *Readings in Oklahoma History*.
"The Spirit of the West." *The Sooner Magazine* 4(May, 1932):269-270, 280, and 282.
"Teaching on the Prairie Plains, 1890-1900." *Mississippi Valley Historical Review* 33(September, 1946):293-307. Reprint. *Frontier Ways*.
"Those Kansas Jayhawkers." *Agricultural History* 2(October, 1928):167-184. Reprint. *The Cattleman* 16(June, 1929):28-37; *Cow Country*; and *Frontier Times* 29(July, 1952):284-294.
"A Trip to the Railroad." *Prairie Lore* 2(April, 1966):146-154.
"Turner--The Man and Teacher." *University of Kansas City Review* 18(Autumn, 1951):18-28.
"Two Mississippi Valley Frontiers." *Chronicles of Oklahoma* 26(Winter, 1948-1949):366-384.

"When Southerners Were Moving West." In *Mustang Gray*. Southern Life and Literature Series, Book 1. St. Louis: Webster Publishing Company, 1941. Pp. 37-47.

"Wood and Water: Twin Problems of the Prairie Plains." *Nebraska History* 29(June, 1948):87-104. Reprint. *Frontier Ways*.

"Work and Play of the Range Riders." *American Hereford Journal* 29(January 1, 1939):14-16, 70-71.

Selected Reviews

The American Tradition by John D. Hicks. *Mississippi Valley Historical Review* 48(September, 1956):342-343.

The Catholic Indian Missions and Grant's Peace Policy, 1870-1884 by Peter J. Rahill. *Southwestern Historical Quarterly* 58(July, 1954):186-188.

The Colorado Range Cattle Industry by Ora Brooks Peake. *Chronicles of Oklahoma* 12(March, 1939):97-98.

The Early Writings of Frederick Jackson Turner: With a List of All His Works compiled by Everett E. Edwards. *Southwestern Historical Quarterly* 43(October, 1939):265-266.

Indian Removal: The Emigration of Five Civilized Tribes of Indians by Grant Foreman. *Mississippi Valley Historical Review* 20(December, 1933):424-425.

J. Sterling Morton: Pioneer, Statesman, Founder of Arbor Day by James C. Olson. *Southwestern Historical Quarterly* 47(July, 1943):78-80.

The Last Trek of the Indians by Grant Foreman. *Mississippi Valley Historical Review* 33(September, 1946):343-344.

Names on the Land: A Historical Account of Place-Naming in the United States by George R. Stewart. *Mississippi Valley Historical Review* 32(September, 1945):274-275.

Narrative of the Coronado Expedition edited by George P. Hammond and Agapito Rey. *Chronicles of Oklahoma* 19(December, 1941):401-408.

Red Men Calling on the Great White Father by Katherine C. Turner. *Mississippi Valley Historical Review* 38(June, 1951):108-109.

Relations with the Indians of the Plains, 1857-1861: A Documentary Account of the Military Campaigns, and Negotiations of Indian Agents--with Reports and Journals of P. G. Lowe, R. M. Peck, J. E. B. Stuart, S. D. Sturgis, and Other Official Papers edited by LeRoy R. Hafen and Ann W. Hafen. *Chronicles of Oklahoma* 37(Winter, 1959-1960):513-515.

The Southern Indians: The Story of the Civilized Tribes Before Removal by Robert S. Cotterill. *Mississippi Valley Historical Review* 41(September, 1954):329-331.

A Traveler in Indian Territory: The Journal of Ethan Allen Hitchcock, Late Major-General in the United States Army edited by Grant Foreman. *Mississippi Valley Historical Review* 18(June, 1931):81-82.

The Typical Texas: Biography of an American Myth by Joseph Leach. *Southwestern Historical Quarterly* 57(July, 1953):144-145.

Studies of Edward Everett Dale
Borland, Hal. Review of *Cow Country* by Edward Everett Dale. *New York Times Book Review,* August 2, 1942, p. 4.
Clark, Thomas D. "The Cross Timbers: Memories of a North Texas Boyhood." *Journal of American History* 54(June, 1967):172-173.
_________. "Frontier Ways: Sketches of Life in the Old West." *American Historical Review* 66(July, 1961):1143.
"Cowboy Professor Describes Romance of Cattle Drivers." *Columbia Missourian,* October 20, 1932.
Dale, Edward Everett, Papers. Manuscript Collection (176 linear feet), Map Collection, Library, and Photograph Collections, University of Oklahoma. Norman, Oklahoma.
Dick, Everett. Review of *Cow Country* by Edward Everett Dale. *Mississippi Valley Historical Review* 29(September, 1942):269-270.
"Dr. Edward Everett Dale (1879-1972) As His Oklahoma Knew Him." *The War Chief of the Indian Territory Posse of the Oklahoma Westerners* 7(December, 1973):1-21.
"Former Cow Boy is Now University Professor." *Daily Oklahoman* (Oklahoma City), August 8, 1915.
Frost, David. "Dean of Oklahoma Historians Still Retains Interest in County." *Kiowa County Star Review,* April 27, 1967, pp. 1,4.
Gibson, Arrell M. "Edward Everett Dale." *Great Plains Journal* 18(1979):79-84.
_________, ed. *Frontier Historian: The Life and Work of Edward Everett Dale.* Norman: University of Oklahoma Press, 1975.
Gibson, Charles. Review of *The Indians of the Southwest: A Century of Development Under the United States* by Edward Everett Dale. *Mississippi Valley Historical Review* 36(March, 1950):715.
Green, Joseph C. Review of *The Indians of the Southwest: A Century of Development under the United States* by Edward Everett Dale. *American Historical Review* 55(July, 1950):947-948.
Hicks, Jimmie. "Edward Everett Dale: A Biography and A Bibliography." *Chronicles of Oklahoma* 45(Autumn, 1967):290-306.
Hicks, John D. Review of *The Range Cattle Industry* by Edward Everett Dale. *Mississippi Valley Historical Review* 17(March, 1931):645-647.
Loughlin, John. "New Frontier Down Under." *Daily Oklahoman* (Oklahoma City), August 30, 1953, p. 16.
Pelzer, Louis. Review of *The Range Cattle Industry* by Edward Everett Dale. *American Historical Review* 36(April, 1931):658.
[Unsigned] Review of *The Range Cattle Industry* by Edward Everett Dale. *New York Times,* October 12, 1930.
Walker, S. Review of *Cow Country* by Edward Everett Dale. *New York Herald Tribune,* October 11, 1942, p. 14.
White, Mike. "Dr. Dale Stays Active Even in His Retirement." *The Oklahoma Daily* (Norman), July 9, 1965, pp. 1-2.

19

BERNARD DEVOTO

by William L. Lang

Biography

Some ten miles from the crest of the Bitterroot Mountains in central Idaho alongside the roaring Lochsa River stands a darkly beautiful congregation of cedars. Steep canyon walls plunge practically to the river's edge, barely leaving room for a modern roadway and an alluvial bar where centuries-old large-girthed cedars dominate the view. In this place there is a sense of the American wilderness, a feeling, if one allows imagination space enough, of the wilderness that Lewis and Clark must have experienced when they struggled through this challenging landscape in 1805-1806. Walking in the cathedraled wood one senses something of the personal and dramatic.

A U.S. Forest Service sign at this wayside along U.S. Highway 12 informs motorists that Bernard DeVoto camped in this grove several times while he was tracing the Lewis and Clark trail, and that his ashes are scattered here. A beautiful, almost haunting campsite, the grove was one of DeVoto's favorite places along Lewis and Clark's route. He also might have chosen this spot because it evokes and characterizes some of the major themes of his intellectual life: the beauty and power of the western landscape, the dramatic intensity of western history's great moments, and the importance of western resource conservation. During three decades of professional life, DeVoto wrote books, articles, and essays about these subjects. He wrote passionately as a partisan westerner about the West, believing that the region and its history had changed America.

Born in Ogden, Utah, in 1897, DeVoto grew up in the arid Great Basin when it still could be called a frontier. He briefly attended the University of Utah in 1914 before going east to Harvard University. With time out for military service, he graduated Phi Beta Kappa from Harvard in 1920. Two years of teaching junior high school in Ogden followed; then DeVoto entered academic ranks as an English instructor at Northwestern University, where he taught until 1927.

DeVoto's future did not lay in university teaching; he wanted more than anything else to be a writer of fiction. After publishing one novel, *The Crooked Mile,* and a couple of journal articles, DeVoto returned to Cambridge and its intellectual community to try his luck as a freelance writer. He taught occasionally at Harvard during the next few years, but made his living by his pen, writing stories and articles under his own name and pseudonyms for *American Mercury, Saturday Evening Post, Atlantic, Collier's, Woman's Day,* and other publications. He published his first important work, *Mark Twain's America,* in 1932, and three years later he wrote his first "Easy Chair" column for *Harper's* magazine, beginning a monthly responsibility he met with elan and delight for more than twenty years.

As a critic, essayist, teacher of writers at the famous Breadloaf conferences in Vermont, and historian, Bernard DeVoto had enormous stature in the American world of letters. Although DeVoto considered himself primarily a novelist--he wrote five novels under his own name and four under a pseudonym--his success came as a critic and historian.

The publication of *Mark Twain's America* almost instantly made DeVoto a force in the study of American literature. With unerring and caustic frontier aim, DeVoto zeroed in on Van Wyck Brooks's *The Ordeal of Mark Twain* (1920), which had applied a Freudian interpretation to Twain's life and writings. DeVoto objected in sharp-tongued language. He chastised Brooks and the eastern clan of critics for ignoring Twain's frontier realism and for forgetting that Twain was a westerner and a humorist. DeVoto's blast against a literary critic's ignorance of history, especially western history, reverberated throughout American academic circles. The book became the most prominent critical work on Twain and landed DeVoto the job of curatorship of the Twain Papers, a position he held from 1938 to 1946.

In the wake of *Mark Twain's America,* DeVoto began to direct his scholarly attention to western history. In 1940 came *Mark Twain in Eruption,* an edition of Twain's papers, and in 1942 he compiled three of his critical essays on Twain in *Mark Twain at Work.* Throughout his studies of Twain, DeVoto became more and more fascinated with the history of the American West. He also took advantage of his friendships with historians Frederick Merk, Arthur Schlesinger, Sr., Garrett Mattingly, and Perry Miller to focus his historical ken. The result was *The Year of Decision: 1846* (1943), an impressively written and exciting historical vignette, which shoved DeVoto from the relative battleground of literary criticism into the often nit-picking arena of historical scholarship. Uncomfortable with the historian's label, DeVoto defended his literary approach to history by claiming he was really a novelist, while he combatively challenged historians to make judgments and quit hiding behind facades of adulterated objectivity.

DeVoto's literary production was staggering. While writing the "Easy Chair" columns, he edited books, wrote essays, novels and stories, book reviews, and vitriolic defenses of conservation, politics, and civil liberties. He also found time to write three more histories: *Across the Wide*

Missouri (1947), which many rank as the best portrait of the American far western fur trade and won the Pulitzer Prize in history; *The Course of Empire* (1952), a tour de force on the exploration of North America; and a one-volume abridgment of *The Journals of Lewis and Clark* (1953), which won the National Book Award.

DeVoto's reputation as a historian rests on his four books of history and on the hundreds of reviews and essays he wrote in defense of his historical viewpoint. In his histories, as in his essays, DeVoto was ever the combatant and the competitor. But it was his demand for accuracy, judgment, and verve in written history, not his curmudgeonly personal style, that became his trademark in historical writing. In 1955, he was at the height of his career, with the study of history and the defense of western natural resources dominating his literary and intellectual interests. DeVoto's death in that year deprived American historiography of one of its most creative and stimulating writers.

Themes

DeVoto wrote in a peculiarly western voice. Shrill at times in his defense of things western, he did not miss an opportunity to state and underscore his primary theme: the West was a distinctive region whose history must be understood if one is to make sense of the American past. Turnerian in viewpoint and phraseology, DeVoto defended a misunderstood West. "We are undoubtably a race, we Westerners," he writes in passionate partisanship, meaning that there had always been something exclusively distinctive about people who lived in the West (*Harper's Magazine* 155:713). In his famous essay, "The West: A Plundered Province" (*Harper's Magazine* 179:355), DeVoto tells readers: "The Westerner remains a bewildering creature to the rest of the nation." In DeVoto's mind, this bewilderment about the West and a people he labeled a "race," evolves from easterners' ignorance of western history and the region's landscape.

Taking a page from Walter Prescott Webb, who he greatly admired, DeVoto emphasized another theme that also proved the West's distinctiveness. The region's expansiveness and aridity, he explains, had much to do with the course of western history. A correlative emphasis in his writings underscored the decisive importance of geography in historical development. Referring to westerners, he claims, "We are far more than any other part of the country, in touch with the earth and subject to it" (*Harper's Magazine* 155:717). For DeVoto, the westerner and the westering individual was more virtuous than his eastern cousin.

If DeVoto saw the West through Turner's and Webb's glasses, he also cast a critical eye toward what westerners had done. Demythologizing the West became another prominent theme in DeVoto's historical writings. He argues persuasively against the Zane Grey and Hollywood versions of western history and character. He debunks the idea that the West was explored, settled, and developed by individuals. In *Across the Wide Missouri,* for example, DeVoto points out that the fur trade was not an individual enterprise, that it had operated as part of an organized, international business. And in *The Course of Empire,* DeVoto tells readers that nations, business ventures, and organized expeditions, not Daniel Boone-types, opened the continent to European settlement.

There is irony in DeVoto's methodology, however, because he invariably focuses his books on individuals, using the biographies of representative figures to carry the story lines. In *Across the Wide Missouri,* he spotlights Sir William Drummond Stewart; in *The Year of Decision,* he singles out mountain man James Clyman as the symbol for an era. For DeVoto these men were representatives of that power of accomplishment that he so admired in the history of the westward movement, a historical development that DeVoto considered inevitable.

The inevitability of the exploration and settlement of North America and the inherent drama of this story dominated DeVoto's historical writings. It stands out as the second most important theme in his work. The development of what he calls the "continental mind" fascinated DeVoto. Thomas Jefferson had that kind of vision, DeVoto argues in *The Course of Empire,* and James K. Polk acted on it in *The Year of Decision.* The story of the migration of people and civilization westward is central to DeVoto's histories. His books create and ride a crest of excitement about expansionism. In patriotic and theatrical language, he injects immediacy and excitement into his panoramic recitation of America's acquisition of the western territories. Never once did he question its inevitability.

Analysis

Bernard DeVoto wrote narrative history. His perspective runs to the pageant of American history, without the romantic fluff that so often distorted popular history while avoiding the tediousness of analytical history. Perhaps because he came to the study of history from two distinct but legitimate directions, he found a path that kept him safe from falling into banal and wrongheaded discourse or flamboyant and groundless hyperbole about America's greatness. One influence was his youth in Utah, where he learned about the limitations of an arid environment and a theocratic approach to political and community life. Another influence was his study of Mark Twain's cultural milieu, which taught him that any discussion not based on facts, especially the facts of history, should be questioned. He also learned, as he explains to Catherine Drinker Bowen, "Ours [America's] is a story mad with the impossible, it is by chaos out of a dream, it began as dream and it has continued as dream down to the last headline you read in a newspaper" (*The Letters of Bernard DeVoto,* p. 286).

DeVoto saw American history as romantic, powerful, and new to the world. With a consistency that spanned three decades of professional writing, he pursued questions he had about the westward migration of Europeans and Americans. "I see history as primarily a process of individuals," he wrote Henry Steele Commager in 1946. But DeVoto's individuals always acted in concert with an army of migrating Americans. His great strength as a historian was his ability to paint a large picture that portrayed the movement of a people. He introduces Oregon Trail pilgrims in *The Year of Decision* in unforgettable prose:

> These people were greenhorns: what the West came to call tenderfeet. Most of them were schooled in the culture that had served American pioneering up to now. The unfitness for the West of that experience shows at the beginning of the journey. The mountain men had mastered the craft of living off the country, finding grass, managing the stock, making camp, reading buffalo sign and Indian sign. All such matters were hidden from the emigrants (p.148).

As deftly as a playwright, DeVoto sets the historical stage for his readers and then moves his characters from scene to scene, emphasizing the humorous, the tragic, and the remarkable. Because he began as a novelist and always considered himself a novelist, DeVoto focuses on character development and plots. His characterizations are masterful. In a paragraph, DeVoto could form, dress, and set in motion one of his players, as he did with Oregon missionary Jason Lee in *Across the Wide Missouri:*

> Jason Lee is a hard man to make out and his great importance in American history is seamed with ambiguity. That is not because he had any of the malaises that rioted in the souls of so many missionaries to the Indians. He had experienced the earthquake of evangelical conversion but he appears, as Samuel Parker and Marcus Whitman also appear, never to have belonged to the twice-born. Manifest Destiny had selected a thorough extravert as the advance point of its religious expansionism. No conviction that he was a miserable sinner depressed Jason Lee for a moment (pp. 179-180).

DeVoto's technique is cinematic, as elusive and frustrating as it is illuminating. He skillfully weaves his characters and scenes into a compelling and seamless historical damask, but in accomplishing it he is prone to overstatements and unsupported generalizations. In communicating the excitement of historical developments, he often cut off the interpretive and analytical line that historians must follow if they are to make sense out of the past. Rather than marshal facts and organize them into systematic arguments, DeVoto selects facts and announces conclusions. Writing about Jefferson's desire to create a continental nation, for example, DeVoto boldly states the truth of the proposition, but he provides no analytical argument in its defense:

> It is true that he [Jefferson] did not expect to obtain all of Louisiana. . . . But to suppose that he did not fully expect the extension of American settlement across Louisiana, or to suppose that he did not expect extension of settlement to produce

> extension of sovereignty as well, is to ignore the most massive facts about the nation his administration governed (*Journal of Lewis and Clark*, p. xxiv).

Readers can hardly argue with such confident prose, and that is part of DeVoto's magic. He could bring historical events into sharp focus by selecting one representative or key individual and playing out his or her role in a salient event. Using the Wilmot Proviso as the political linchpin of his dissection of the year 1846, for example, DeVoto fearlessly treads where historians would shudder. "At some time," he writes in *The Year of Decision,* "between August and December, 1846, the Civil War had begun" (p. 489). DeVoto often simplified history to distortion. By creating a context for his history, DeVoto often ignored or destroyed a context for causal relationships in history. Rather than analyze the politics behind David Wilmot's famous resolution, DeVoto writes: "The motives of David Wilmot and his supporters do not matter. The thing he did must have been done by someone at some time--but he did it here and now" (p. 292).

What others might have called a cavalier approach to historical argumentation DeVoto labels as honest and forthright exposition. He criticizes historians for their conservatism: they hesitated too much at the gate; they retreated from making judgments. As he writes in a *Harper's Magazine* essay in 1939, "professional historians have increasingly come to prefer research to the synthesis and utilization of research and, what is more serious, they have increasingly avoided passing judgment. The reverence for fact that is the necessary condition of research has too often become a screen for timidity" (180:111).

Despite his criticisms of historians for hugging the facts too closely and not venturing forth as commentators, DeVoto had immense respect for the facts. "I am, if you must have words," he self analyzes, "a pluralist, a relativist, an empiricist. I am at home with the concrete inquiries of historians and scientists, and uneasy among the abstractions of critics and metaphysicians" (*Minority Report,* pp. 164-165). He railed more at authors who skimped on facts than he did at historians who failed to judge.

DeVoto was a Turnerian. He accepted Turner's outline of the frontier settlement process. When the trappers left the country, DeVoto tells his readers in *Across the Wide Missouri,* the overlanders crossed their path on their way west. "The equinoctial," Devoto writes, "had intersected the ecliptic. Thus the old West and the new West passed each other" (p. 383). DeVoto also agrees with Turner that the western experience helped free the nation from a debilitating stasis and that westerners had a certain virtue because of their struggles to carry civilization westward. Where he differed with Turner was in his emphasis on organized rather than individual action in the winning of the West.

DeVoto was also influenced by the writings of Walter Prescott Webb. Although DeVoto did not need Webb to tell him that aridity was the key to understanding western environment, Webb's emphasis on geographical factors in the settlement of the West buttressed DeVoto's geopolitical view of western history. Not quite a geographical determinist--he never allowed himself to be captive of any rigid interpretive viewpoint--DeVoto put geography first in his list of historical factors. "I believe, and I think I can establish," he wrote Frederick Merk, "that geographical factors adding up to a very powerful force indeed had their part in determining the size, shape, and government of the United States. I believe that Lincoln was speaking the exact, literal truth, literal as all hell, when he said, on the basis of the geographical data he summarized, that the land itself demanded Union" (*Letters of Bernard DeVoto*. p. 317).

In this way, in *The Course of Empire,* DeVoto describes the geopolitical core of French North America in 1682:

> Thus Louisiana was half of the hinge on which possession and mastery would turn. It was also a bastion necessary to the defense of New France, which sea power could throttle by blockading the mouth of the St. Lawrence. The St. Lawrence and the Mississippi were the compass of the New World (p. 133).

Applying the same geopolitical sense to the acquisition of the American Southwest, DeVoto describes our war with Mexico in geographical terms:

> The war that made them [Mexican provinces] American soil has the ugliness of any war, and no powerful nation looks admirable while imposing its will on a weaker one. But the injustice to Mexico was slight and the provinces fell not so much to conquest as to the geographical system of North America. If there is a guilt it must be assigned to geography, and the conquest was determined when the first American canoe crossed the Mississippi to the Louisiana Purchase. Or when the first British and French adventurers paddled westward of the Charles and the St. Lawrence (*Harper's Magazine* 182:558).

DeVoto insists that there were those places on the map of western America, such as St. Louis, South Pass, the salt desert, and the falls of the Columbia, that channeled the speed and direction of western historical development.

Aside from his adherence to Turner's or Webb's interpretations of western history, DeVoto contributed to American historiography in an important way. He challenged historians to take in the sweep of history and be brave in their assessments. And he brought to western history a narrative flair that compares with Parkman and a sense of the dramatic that rivals the best in historical novels. DeVoto expressed his viewpoint forthrightly. As he tells his readers in the preface to *Across the Wide Missouri,* "I shall have succeeded if the reader gets from the book a sense of time hurrying on while between the Missouri and the Pacific a thousand or so men of no moment whatever are living an exciting and singularly uncertain life, hurrying one era of our history to a close, and thereby making possible another one" (p. xiv). He succeeds and gives us some of the most dramatic and effective prose in western historiography. DeVoto's histories carry us high on the tide of a continental expansion he pictures as inevitable.

Bibliography

Books

Across the Wide Missouri. Boston: Houghton Mifflin Co., 1947.

The Course of Empire. Boston: Houghton Mifflin Co., 1952.

The Journals of Lewis and Clark. Editor. Boston: Houghton Mifflin Co., 1953.

The Literary Fallacy. Boston: Little, Brown, and Co., 1944.

Mark Twain at Work. Cambridge: Harvard University Press, 1942.

Mark Twain in Eruption. Editor. New York: Harper and Brothers, 1940.

Mark Twain's America. Boston: Little, Brown, and Co., 1932.

Minority Report. Boston: Little, Brown, and Co., 1940.

The Portable Mark Twain. Editor. New York: The Viking Press, 1946.

The Year of Decision: 1846. Boston: Little, Brown, and Co., 1943.

Selected Articles

"The Anxious West." *Harper's Magazine* 193(December, 1946):481-491.

"Brave Days in Washoe." *American Mercury* 17(June, 1929):228-237.

"Footnote on the West" *Harper's Magazine* 155(November, 1927):713-722.

"Manifest Destiny." *Harper's Magazine* 182(April, 1941):557-560.

"The Real Frontier: A Preface to Mark Twain." *Harper's Magazine* 176(June, 1931):60-71.

"The West: A Plundered Province." *Harper's Magazine* 179(August, 1934):355-364.

"The West Against Itself." *Harper's Magazine* 194(January, 1947):1-13.

"What's the Matter with History?" *Harper's Magazine* 180(June, 1935):109-112.

Selected Reviews

Before Lewis and Clark: Documents Illustrating the History of the Missouri, 1785-1804 edited by Abraham P. Nasatir. *American Historical Review* 58(July, 1953):933-934.

The Journals and Indian Paintings of George Winter, 1837-1839 edited by Howard H. Peckham. *Mississippi Valley Historical Review* 36(June, 1949):136-138.

Picture Maker of the Old West: William H. Jackson by Clarence S. Jackson. *American Historical Review* 53(April, 1948):649-650.

The Wild Horses of the West by Walker D. Wyman. *American Historical Review* 51(October, 1945):174-175.

Studies of Bernard DeVoto

Bower, C. D., E. R. Mirrielles, Arthur M. Schlesinger, Jr., Wallace Stegner, and J. P. Barclay. *Four Portaits and One Subject: Bernard DeVoto.* Boston: Houghton Mifflin Co., 1963.

Carter, Harvey Lewis. Review of *The Journals of Lewis and Clark* edited by Bernard DeVoto. *Mississippi Valley Historical Review* 40(March, 1954):732-733.

Goodykoontz, Colin B. Review of *The Year of Decision: 1846* by Bernard DeVoto. *Mississippi Valley Historical Review* 30(September, 1943):263-264.

Nute, Grace Lee. Review of *The Course of Empire* by Bernard DeVoto. *American Historical Review* 58(July, 1953):935-936.

Paxson, Frederic. Review of *The Year of Decision: 1846* by Bernard DeVoto. *American Historical Review* 49(October, 1943):120-121.

Sawey, Orlan. *Bernard DeVoto.* New York: Twayne Publishers, Inc., 1969.

Shoemaker, Floyd C. Review of *Mark Twain in Eruption: Hitherto Unpublished Pages About Men and Events* edited by Bernard DeVoto. *Mississippi Valley Historical Review* 28(June, 1941):117-118.

Stegner, Wallace. *The Uneasy Chair: A Biography of Bernard DeVoto.* New York: Doubleday and Co., 1974.

__________. Editor. *The Letters of Bernard DeVoto.* New York: Doubleday and Co., 1975.

Winther, Oscar O. Review of *The Course of Empire* by Bernard DeVoto. *Mississippi Valley Historical Review.* 40(December, 1953):519-520.

20

RANDOLPH C. DOWNES

by James H. O'Donnell III

Biography

Randolph C. Downes was a New Englander by birth, born in South Norwalk, Connecticut, on July 26, 1901. For his undergraduate education he remained in New England, enrolling at Dartmouth College, from which he graduated in 1923. The attraction of Wisconsin's history faculty drew him westward to become a student at Madison, where he completed his M.A. in 1924. In the following year he married and took up his first teaching position as instructor in history and economics at Marietta College. Two years in the hinterlands, however, were sufficient motivation to push him back to graduate school, this time at Ohio State University, where he completed his Ph.D. in 1929.

The major portion of Downes's teaching career was spent in Ohio and Pennsylvania. After finishing his doctorate, he was appointed an assistant professor at the University of Pittsburgh, where he remained until 1936. While Downes taught and at the same time revised his dissertation for publication, he was also a fellow of the Social Science Research Council (1931-1932) and a research associate at the Historical Society of Western Pennsylvania. As a result of these labors he was promoted to associate professor in 1932. Nevertheless, he left Pittsburgh in 1936 for a decade of work as both public historian and teacher. During the next ten years Randolph Downes worked for the Works Progress Administration Writers Project in Ohio, consulted with the American Association on Indian Affairs, and lectured at Centenary Junior College, Hartwick College, and Smith College. In 1946 he accepted a position at the University of Toledo, where he would spend the next twenty-five years researching and writing Ohio history.

Wherever he taught or worked, Randolph Downes was an assiduous scholar. Chapters from books often appeared first as articles in scholarly journals at the local, state, and national levels. After he became editor of the *Northwest Ohio Historical Quarterly* in 1946, most of his work was published in that periodical.

Themes

Downes's primary research interest themes were frontier Ohio and the Old Northwest, a devotion reflected in his books, articles, and academic connections. His publications fall into four roughly chronological periods: (1) dissertation and scholarly monographs, 1930-1940; (2) sponsored research activity, 1940-1946; (3) editorial publications, 1946-1971; and, overlapping the third, (4) research in defense of Warren G. Harding, 1955-1968, which this essay will not explore.

Narrative was Randolph Downes's basic style, an event by event account based on research in documents. He was not given to long insightful analysis, but his opinions were extremely strong. There was, moreover, a moralistic, didactic tone in his works which left no room for doubt about who was right. Ironically, that edge was the sharpest in both his first and his last major publications: *Frontier Ohio, 1788-1803* and *Rise of Warren G. Harding*. In each case Downes's frontier heroes, whether the product of the first Ohio frontier or the small town Ohio frontier, were valiant stewards to be defended.

Analysis

Randolph C. Downes's two major frontier history publications, *Frontier Ohio, 1788-1803* and *Council Fires on the Upper Ohio,* placed him firmly in the tradition of Frederick Jackson Turner. Turner had established the frontier school of American history in his seminal essay at the Chicago meeting of the American Historical Association in 1893. In Turner's view, the frontier, defined as both place and process, had been the single most important influence in shaping the people and the institutions of the United States during the country's first three centuries.

Frontier Ohio, 1788-1803, written by Downes almost a half-century after Frederick Jackson Turner's initial statement, adhered closely to the frontier hypothesis. Paragraph two of the preface reflects the Turnerian influence:

> The central theme throughout is the frontier. All of the early institutions of Ohio were the product of frontier conditions. Its religious life was dominated by schism and the spread of the evangelical denominations. Its commercial life developed a dependence on the downstream trade that weakened its relation to the East. In their relation to the soil the people universally insisted on free or cheap lands because of the rigorous frontier conditions to which they were subjected. In their political life they built up a democracy that revealed every weakness of the Ordinance of 1787 as an instrument of frontier government (p. xiii).

From the title of the first chapter onward, it is evident that Randolph Downes accepts the notion that Ohio was part of the progress of white civilization as its people engaged in the "conquest" of the Indians who inhabited the Ohio country between 1788 and 1795. Although he did mention the existence of an "Indian standpoint" in chapter 1, he assumes that the Native American perspective was really of no consequence. Indian resistance was merely a temporary delay in the inevitability of white victory. Unfortunately, his prowhite attitude undermines any attempt at telling a balanced story (he has in the preface acknowledged the assistance of a colleague in helping him understand the Indian point of view). "Obsequious" whites are contrasted with "rash" Indians as the two parties discuss treaties. The villains of the piece, furthermore, are the British because they sided with the Indians.

As if it were insufficient for the young historian to be influenced by one established scholar, Downes reflects the ideas of Charles and Mary Beard in his second chapter:

> As the discovery, settlement, and expansion of America, to use Charles A. and Mary R. Beard's phrase, form "merely one phase of the long and restless movement of mankind on the surface of the earth," so the beginnings of Ohio are but an incident in the great westward course of the American people (p. 55).

This passage fits quite comfortably with Downes's Turnerianism.

With the Beards acknowledged, Randolph Downes clung tightly to Turner. American settlers, who were regarded by the Indians as invaders, are praised as "intrepid frontiersmen. . . approaching the Ohio River" (p. 55). This was a natural occurrence, explains Downes, agreeing with Turner that population growth always took place along the frontier zone:

> Pennsylvania and Kentucky frontier communities furnished many settlers for the first Ohio settlement. Each of the early Ohio frontier settlements, although under the immediate direction of easterners, depended to a large degree on western frontiersmen to provide the industry and experience necessary in founding new communities in the rugged environment of the wilderness and the Indian country. There were plenty of settlers, dissatisfied with their holdings not far from the Ohio country, ready, at the earliest opportunity, to pack up their meagre possessions and seek for [sic] better luck farther west (pp. 59-60).

Indeed, he argues, even the cities were the result of frontier population movements. "Cincinnati, even more than Columbia, illustrates, in its settlement, the debt Ohio owes to the old frontier and the insistence of the latter on free lands" (p. 62). One can envision the face of Frederick Jackson Turner smiling down on Professor Downes's faithful recitation of the frontier litany as applied to early city growth. Cincinnati in its beginnings was influenced by the Kentuckian

> William McMillan, who was immediately chosen magistrate of the squatter government set up by the pioneers. It is not without significance that the superior advantages that were to make Cincinnati the emporium of the Old Northwest were perceived by Kentucky pioneers while Symms still sought for the site of the "City" (p. 63).

And as one would expect from any study in the Turnerian mold:

> The pioneer pressure of free or cheap lands . . . [was] of the utmost significance. It was one of the few weapons the frontiersman had in economic and political life, and it was a powerful one. With a universality that made them a political force with which to be reckoned, these frontiersmen sought every opportunity to get cheap lands (pp. 63-64).

However few the weapons of the frontiersman, they were effective, for in the contest for territory and control, frontier tactics triumphed. Against the Indian possessors, for example, the frontiersman triumphed because the Indian could be "out-Indianed" and blocked from successful retaliation by the effective use of frontier "stations." Indeed, observes Randolph Downes, "if the Ohio Company [not a frontier organization] had had such efficient guards against Indian attack, historians of the Muskingum Valley would not have to chronicle such a horrible massacre as the one that occurred at Big Bottom in December, 1791" (p. 69).

Frederick Jackson Turner's frontier as process model, likewise, is copied by Downes in his description of the earliest "squatter" settlers:

> Most of this class of "first settlers" were squatters, characters common to all frontiers from early times, individuals whose right to a claim was the mere fact of being the first to locate. The granting of patents to squatters, based on "tomahawk" or settlement rights, had long been part of Pennsylvania and Virginia law. The settler had but to be the first to make his clearing, or to plant his crop of corn, or to construct his cabin, in order to establish a right that frontier justice recognized as valid. Much of even so-called legal settlement partook of these squatter characteristics (p. 73).

Further, concludes the author:

> Squatter settlement required squatter government, and so there appeared another of those innumerable local associations, on the model of Marietta, Columbia, and Cincinnati, where respectable and "substantial men" for several years acted as

magistrates and sheriffs, keeping order in a region technically closed to settlement (p. 77).

Both frontier individualism and cooperation are reflected in Downes's description of organization by persons preparing to enter newly opened lands. All who intended to be adventurers in the new lands were to meet "at John Lyons tavern on Mill Creek, to enter into articles of regulation, elect a foreman and inform each other who will furnish wagons, oxen or horses, so that by unity, assistance may be given to the whole . . . [then the party would march overland] in a body with their wagons, pack-horses, cattle, sheep and hogs" (p. 84).

Turner's metaphor suggesting how layers of civilization were stripped away as part of the frontier deculturation process is embodied in Professor Downes's account of frontier churches:

> Frontier religious expression was, of course, crude, and the reason for this is the pathological condition created in the individual by the crudeness of his life. Indian fighting, the overshadowing importance of the struggle for a living, the lack of any refinements in material, intellectual and social conditions, and the empty loneliness of life, all helped to build an environment that left its unfortunate victim incapable of appreciating the joys of a calm, dignified and cultured reaction to the mysteries of life and death (p. 58).

Dramatically he contrasts the description of a simple Quaker meeting in 1792 with the uproar of a frontier revival ten years later. Of the latter he asks:

> Where is that eloquent silence of days gone by? What tragic testimony to the ravages of frontier isolation! Mrs. Ludlow was alone at Ludlow Station for long periods while her husband was out on surveying trips, on one of which, in 1804, he was killed. In her loneliness she undoubtably heard many frontier preachers, and not only absorbed their frontier theology, but adopted their terminology. *Vae victis!* (p. 89).

Given the impact which the Second Great Awakening was having along the frontier and the seaboard from Kentucky to New York, one does wonder about the validity of applying the Turnerian paradigm.

Downes observes further about religion that the frontier shaped the independence of those who called themselves "New Lights":

> The doctine of this New Light faith is a perfect example of frontier influence. In a word, it was the equality of all human beings before God. . . . Their form of church government, like their creed, was a perfect product of the frontier. Thus they abolished their own Presbytery. . . . They abolished all elders.

> . . . In short, they sought to establish a perfect democracy (pp. 93-94).

Democracy, emphasizes Downes, was the end product of frontier oriented religion. He observes: "If this be an impossible Utopia, the important thing is, not that it is the mere figment of a preacher's imagination, but that it was a *real product of frontier conditions*" (p. 94).

In turning from the spiritual to the temporal side of life, Downes concludes that the economy of the frontier was dominated in the early years by at least one major factor created by frontier conditions and two decidedly positive (albeit temporary) ones. In the first instance, commerce between the West and the settled areas resulted in an unfavorable balance of trade, thus draining off the precious specie which was always in short supply. There were, however, brief respites from this condition through two economic activities: supplying troops sent to conquer the Indians, and trading with the new settlers driven to conquer the lands. Once the armies withdrew and the new immigrants ran out of cash, however, the bugbear of tight money returned.

The frontier economy functioned nevertheless, as entrepreneurs and land speculators accepted country produce, especially wheat, corn, pork, and beef, in payment for land and services. The opportunists erected mills and warehouses in which grains could be stored for later shipment and sale. So, explains Randolph Downes, the mill and its warehouses became the "key institutions of the Northwest." Recognition of how important mills became was reflected in the "Federal Land Law of 1800 which granted preemption to all those who had begun to erect grist mills or sawmills on public lands prior to the passage of the act." Downes proposes this action as "the first step in the official surrender of the Federal Government to the squatter" (p. 120).

In the process of government capitulation to the inevitabilities of frontier pressures, argues Downes, the frontier process was advancing through its stages of development. "The old frontier gave way to new ones, the bankers; the merchants; the shippers; and the ship-builders, ... Life in Ohio was 'settling down' around new routines and the less glamorous occupations, i.e., to 'business as usual'" (p. 121).

Part of the uniqueness of the frontier, as Downes sees it, came from the unusual people of the frontier. "No group of people," he observes, "especially frontier people, is ever entirely satisfied. There is always striving. There are always tyrants to overthrow, windmills to assail, and worlds to conquer. And frontier environment in Ohio presented tyrants, windmills and worlds aplenty for its children to struggle with" (p. 127).

Not everyone, of course, was suited for the frontier environment. Such was Randolph Downes's assessment of Northwest Territory Secretary Winthrop Sargent: "No American frontier ever has had to submit to the rule of a more autocratic civil government than did frontier Ohio in the years from 1790 to 1795. [Sargent] was utterly unfit for the office [of acting governor]" (p. 127). In Turnerian fashion Downes explains that frontier Ohio asserted its political sovereignty too early to have its democratic tendencies constrained by a New England Puritan. Indeed, it was often the simple "natural quarrelsomeness of the frontiersmen" which Sargent confronted. The territorial secretary repeatedly sought conflict between frontier democratic traditions and his own preference of paternalistic authority. Further, writes Downes, the entire frontier period in Ohio was a microcosm of the struggle between frontier democracy expressed by the people and eastern authority reflected in the Northwest Ordinance of 1787. That Ohio triumphed in the end as a state is largely credited to the "frontiermen's resourcefulness--'plain good sense'" (p. 157).

The story of frontier Ohio Downes tells has a happy ending, because:

> From the first frontier days beyond the Ohio River, there had existed this strongest of frontier desires for self-government. It has been evident in every period of the Territorial era--in every phase of frontier life. Self-government was sought in all political affairs, in township, county and territory. And now every element of this frontier democracy, either accomplished or hoped for, received explicit sanction in the first Constitution of Ohio--which represents, therefore, the first political fruit of its frontier experience (p. 247).

Among the frontier inspired features of the new state constitution were suffrage for taxpaying white males over twenty-one, provisions for the impeachment of civil officers, limited terms of office, and stated maximum salaries for office holders. Finally, believes Downes, with Ohio's adoption in 1804 of an act

> placing the main burden of government of each county in the hands of a board of popularly elected commissioners, and of an act extending the civil jurisdiction of single justice of the peace to thirty-five dollars, the ultimate goal of complete frontier government may be said to have been attained (p. 251).

Parallel to this conclusion about the laws of early Ohio was his assessment from a 1931 review of *The Laws of Indiana Territory, 1801-1809*: "The laws themselves reveal the radical tendencies so characteristic of frontier life" (*Mississippi Valley Historical Review* 18:78-79).

Randolph C. Downes's second major work, *Council Fires on the Upper Ohio,* was published in 1940 by the University of Pittsburgh Press as part of a series dealing with western Pennsylvania history. For a historian to write a book about Indians in 1940 was rather unique. But for that writer to attempt the Indian point of view (or so he professes in the preface) was nothing short of astonishing. Downes explains: "The author has assumed the attitude that the Indian civilization was neither better nor worse than that of the white man, but that it was a distinctive civilization and that the Indians believed it worth defending" (p. x).

In order to accomplish his stated purpose, Downes resorts to an imaginative introduction in which the reader witnesses an unidentified council, attended by both whites and Indians. Unfortunately, the author's non-Indian perspectives are too powerful to suppress. His stated intentions are soon obscured. The hypothetical Indian speaker relates a dream to his hearers, a vision in which the essentials of Indian-white conflict were outlined, including the assertion that the Indians thought that the whites were gods when they arrived. That somewhat ethnocentric slip is not totally damaging to the author's purpose, but then Downes has the Indian feel shame because he was telling resplendently uniformed soldiers about a dream. What Downes was relating was his view of what he assumed the Indian thought, not a description of realistic Native American responses. To the Native American of eastern North America, few things were more important than a vision; there was indeed nothing embarrassing about relating it to any council, even one including warriors representing a European army.

Randolph Downes did not help his case any by referring to the Native Americans as "naive savages." In that two word description he already contradicts his assertion from the preface that "Indian civilization was neither better nor worse than that of the white man" (p. x).

On the credit side of Professor Downes's ledger, however, is his understanding of how the Indian viewed the whites with distrust by 1774. Indeed, Native American fear of invasion by the settlers was a point which no one who reads the sources could possibly miss. The white frontier as a place, for example, was seen by Native Americans as "a place of drunkenness, debauchery, and disease. . . . The triumph of the white man on the frontier came to be synonymous to the Indian with the triumph of chicanery and of false values" (p. 10). Intruding beyond the frontier, moreover, came the long hunters who wantonly slew the game on which Native American life in part depended.

Whenever Downes strays from a straightforward narrative drawn from documents, he steps onto shaky ground. Such was the case when he has a Delaware leader say: "We are Allegheny Indians" (p. 75). Although the narrative written by a frontier inhabitant might have included such an expression, it is doubtful that any Delaware ever called himself an "Allegheny Indian."

Generally it was Professor Downes's style to mine documents for a phrase summarizing the story and then move sequentially to another topic and its corresponding sources. So long as he adheres to that approach his narrative presents few real problems. Even in such straightforward passages, however, the author's ethnocentrism creeps in with such statements as that describing Indian speeches as including "promises to be good" (p. 108). "To be good" is so egregiously paternalistic that one cannot see how the author escaped recognizing it. Credit should be given to Downes, however, for letting the record of white attacks against Indians in 1777 speak for itself. In this instance at least it was the whites whose attacks were "brutal" and the "innocent" Indians those who suffered.

In his chapter on "Indian War," Randolph Downes analyzes the relationship between the pressure felt by white settlers on the frontier and their ability to support the war effort of the Continental Congress. At this point in the book, one is especially mindful of the author's first book, as he attributes numerous responses to the conditions of frontier life. The independent minded frontier militia, for example, would not volunteer for Continental service since they might be needed at home; these same persons were outraged, furthermore, by the attempts of the military establishment to impress supplies. However necessary that step may have been, it was onerous in the extreme to the folk of the frontier. Their independence of thought turned to offensive action, however, when they decided to punish the Ohio Indians on their own. This disastrous undertaking in 1782 culminated in the death by torture of Colonel William Crawford, who had been elected commander of the expedition by the militia from the Pennsylvania frontier counties of Westmoreland and Washington.

Downes's assessment of the Ordinance of 1783 is as forthright as had been his description of anti-Indian violence in 1777. "For imperial aggressiveness and outright effrontery this document takes a front rank in the annals of American expansion" (p. 284). Yet just when the reader has silently congratulated the author for his forthrightness, Downes does an about face. Much attention, for example, had been given by Downes to the Iroquois activity during and after the revolution throughout *Council Fires*. Yet in the final analysis Randolph Downes concludes that the Iroquois were "completely lacking in diplomacy" (p. 291).

Randolph C. Downes's Indian book, as it might be termed, remains a unique publication for its times. While the author never overcame his basic ethnocentric assumptions, he did at least allow the documents to reflect the existence of Indian peoples. Anyone studying the revolutionary or postrevolutionary frontier of the old Northwest is unwise to ignore Downes's patient narratives based on the sources.

Bibliography

Books

Ashland's Eternity Acres. Ashland, OH: N.P., 1942.

Canal Days, 1812-1850. Lucas County Historical Series, vol. II. Toledo: Historical Society of Northwestern Ohio, 1949.

The Cincinnati Guide. Cincinnati: American Guide Series, 1943.

The Conquest, Beginnings to 1812. Lucas County Historical Series, vol. I. Toledo: Historical Society of Northwestern Ohio, 1948.

Council Fires on the Upper Ohio: A Narrative of Indian Affairs in the Upper Ohio Valley until 1795. Pittsburgh: University of Pittsburgh Press, 1940.

Frontier Ohio, 1788-1803. Columbus: Ohio Historical Society, 1935.

Guidebook of Historic Sites in Western Pennsylvania. Pittsburgh: University of Pittsburgh Press, 1938.

Industrial Beginnings, 1875-1900. Lucas County Historical Series, vol. IV. Toledo: Historical Society of Northwestern Ohio, 1954.

Lake Port, 1850-1875. Lucas County Historical Series, vol. III. Toledo: Historical Society of Northwestern Ohio, 1951.
Lake Shore Ohio. 3 volumes. New York: Lewis Historical Publishing Company, 1953.
The Maumee Valley, U.S.A. Co-authored with Catherine G. Simonds. Toledo: Historical Society of Northwestern Ohio, 1955.
Navajo Report, 1946. New York: Association on American Indian Affairs, 1946.
Rise of Warren G. Harding, 1865-1920. Columbus: Ohio State University Press, 1970.

Articles
"An American Art Student Abroad: Selections from the Letters of Karl Kappes, 1883-1885." Editor. *Northwest Ohio Quarterly* 23(Winter, 1951):26-45.
"Cherokee-American Relations in the Upper Tennessee Valley, 1776-1781." *East Tennessee Historical Society Publications* 8(1936):35-53.
"Civil War Diary of Fernando E. Pomeroy."Editor. *Northwest Ohio Quarterly* 19(Summer, 1947):129-156.
"Creek-American Relations, 1782-1790." *Georgia Historical Quarterly* 21(June, 1937):142-184.
"A Crusade for Indian Reform, 1922-1934." *Mississippi Valley Historical Review* 32(December, 1945):331-354.
"Death of Warren G. Harding." Co-authored with Kenneth R. Walker. *Northwest Ohio Quarterly* 35(Winter, 1962):7-17.
"Dunmore's War: An Interpretation." *Mississippi Valley Historical Review* 21(September, 1934):311-330.
"Evolution of Ohio County Boundaries." *Ohio State Archaeological and Historical Quarterly* 36(July, 1927):340-477.
"Foundations of Toledo Public School System." *Northwest Ohio Quarterly* 29(Spring, 1957):9-26.
"George Morgan: Indian Agent Extraordinary, 1776-1779." *Pennsylvania History* 1(Winter, 1934):202-216.
"The Harding Muckfest: Warren G. Harding--Chief Victim of the Muck-for-Muck's-Sake Writers and Readers." *Northwest Ohio Quarterly* 39(Winter, 1967):5-37.
"How Andrew Jackson Settled the Ohio-Michigan Dispute of 1835." *Northwest Ohio Quarterly* 23(Winter, 1951):23-31.
"Indian War on the Upper Ohio, 1779-1782." *Western Pennsylvania Historical Society Magazine* 17(June, 1934):93-115.
"Jesup W. Scott Family and the Idea of a Municipal University." *Northwest Ohio Quarterly* 21 (Autumn, 1949):149-168.
"Jones and Whitlock and the Promotion of Urban Democracy." *Northwest Ohio Quarterly* 28(Winter, 1956):26-37.
"Judicial Review Under the Ohio Constitution of 1802." *Northwest Ohio Quarterly* 25(Autumn, 1953):140-170.

"Letters to George Creel by Brand Whitlock." Editor. *Northwest Ohio Quarterly* 28(Autumn, 1956):170-180.

"Nathan Brown: A Conference With Abraham Lincoln." Co-authored with N. Worth Brown. *Northwest Ohio Quarterly* 22(Spring, 1950):48-63.

"Negro Rights and White Backlash in the Campaign of 1920." *Ohio History* 75(Spring, 1966):85-107, 184-185.

"A Newspaper's Childhood: The *Marion Star* from Hume to Harding." *Northwest Ohio Quarterly* 36(Autumn, 1964):134-145.

"Ohio Population Trends, 1920-1940." *Ohio State Archaeological and Historical Quarterly* 51(July, 1942):219-232.

"Ohio's First Constitution." *Northwest Ohio Quarterly* 25(Winter, 1953):12-21.

"Ohio's Local History Law." *Northwest Ohio Quarterly* 25(Winter, 1953):69-70.

"Ohio's Second Constitution." *Northwest Ohio Quarterly* 25(Winter, 1953):71-78.

"Ohio's Squatter Governor, William Hogland of Hoglandstown." *Ohio State Archaeological and Historical Quarterly* 43(October, 1934):273-282.

"Opportunities for Immigration in Western Pennsylvania in 1831 by John A. Roebling." Editor. *Western Pennsylvania Historical Society Magazine* 18(June, 1935):73-108.

"The Ottawa Indians and the Erie and Kalamazoo Railroad." Editor. *Northwest Ohio Quarterly* 24(Summer, 1952):136-138.

"President Making--Harding." Editor. *Northwest Ohio Quarterly* 31(Autumn, 1959):170-178.

"Problems of Trade in Early Western Pennsylvania." *Western Pennsylvania Historical Society Magazine* 13(October, 1930):261-271.

"The Rapid Transit and Electric Power Problems in Toledo in the 1890's." *Northwest Ohio Quarterly* 26(Autumn, 1954)171-190.

"Some Correspondence Between Warren G. Harding & William Allen White during the Presidential Campaign of 1920." Editor. *Northwest Ohio Quarterly* 37(Summer, 1965):121-132.

"Squeezing the Water Out of the Toledo Railway and Light Company, 1907-1913." *Northwest Ohio Quarterly* 30(Winter, 1958):26-48.

"The Statehood Contest in Ohio." *Mississippi Valley Historical Review* 18(June, 1931):155-171.

"The Story of Camp Perry." *Northwest Ohio Quarterly* 22(Autumn, 1951):185-190.

"Thomas Jefferson and the Removal of Governor St. Clair in 1802." *Ohio State Archaeological and Historical Quarterly* 36(January, 1927):62-77.

"Toledo and the Ohio Centennial of 1902." *Northwest Ohio Quarterly* 25(Autumn, 1953):189-200.

"Toledo Political-Religious Municipal Election of 1913 and the Death of the Independent Party." *Northwest Ohio Quarterly* 30(Autumn, 1958):137-163.

"Toledo's History: A Bird's Eye View." *Northwest Ohio Quarterly* 34(Spring, 1964):71-81.

"Trade in Frontier Ohio." *Mississippi Valley Historical Review* 16(March, 1930):467-494.

"The Treatment of Indians in the Coshocton Campaign of 1781." *Western Pennsylvania Historical Society Magazine* 17(December, 1934):287-290.

"The Vulgar Newspaper World of Cross-Roads Ohio, 1865-1884." *Northwest Ohio Quarterly* 37(Spring, 1965):61-73.

"Wamba Week: The End of an Era in Toledo Civic Promotionalism." *Northwest Ohio Quarterly* 27(Autumn, 1955):160-172.

"Wanted: A Scholarly Appraisal of Warren G. Harding." *Ohioana* 2(Spring, 1959):18-20.

"Watered Securities and the Independent Revolution in Toledo Politics, 1901-1907." *Northwest Ohio Quarterly* 28(Spring, 1956):88-105; 28(Summer, 1956):143-156.

"William Henry Machen, Pioneer Local Colorist of Northwestern Ohio." Co-authored with Edwin A. Machen. *Northwest Ohio Quarterly* 20(Spring, 1948):58-81.

"Zophar Case: Migration from Cleveland to Vandalia, 1829-1830." *Northwest Ohio Quarterly* 24(Summer, 1952)83-91.

Selected Reviews

The Civilization of the Old Northwest: A Study of Political, Social, and Economic Development, 1788-1812 by Beverley W. Bond, Jr. *American Historical Review* 40(October, 1934):148-149.

Culture in Crisis: A Study of the Hopi Indians by Laura Thompson. *Mississippi Valley Historical Review* 38(December, 1951):549-550.

The Effect of Smallpox on the Destiny of the American Indians by E. Wagner Stearn and Allen E. Stearn. *Mississippi Valley Historical Review* 32(March, 1946):627-628.

Feather in a Dark Sky by Ray Wilcox. *Mississippi Valley Historical Review* 29(June,1942):126-127.

George Croghan's Journal of His Trip to Detroit in 1767, With His Correspondence Relating Thereto: Now Published For the First Time from the Papers of General Thomas Gage in the William L. Clements Library edited by Howard H. Peckham. *Mississippi Valley Historical Review* 26(September, 1939):251-252.

Hear Me, My Chiefs! by Herbert R. Sass. *Mississippi Valley Historical Review* 28(June, 1941):135-136.

Indian Art of the Americas by Leroy H. Appleton. *Mississippi Valley Historical Review* 38(June, 1951):97-98.

The Indian of the Americas by John Collier. *Mississippi Valley Historical Review* 35(September, 1948):287-288.

King of the Delawares: Teedyuscang, 1700-1763 by Anthony F. C. Wallace. *American Historical Review* 56(January, 1951):413-414.

Laws of Indiana Territory, 1801-1809 edited by Francis S. Philbrick. *Mississippi Valley Historical Review* 18(June, 1931):78-79.

Mutiny in January: The Story of a Crisis in the Continental Army, Now for the First Time Fully Told from Many Hitherto Unknown or Neglected Sources Both British and American by Carl Van Doren. *American Historical Review* 49(October, 1943):113-114.

Pioneer Life in Western Pennsylvania by J. E. Wright and Doris S. Corbett. *Mississippi Valley Historical Review* 27(December, 1940):460-461.

The Pioneer Merchant in Mid-America by Lewis E. Atherton. *American Historical Review* 45(January, 1940):490.

Squawtown: My Boyhood among the Last Miami Indians by Will M. Hundley. *Mississippi Valley Historical Review* 26(September, 1939):271-272.

Tecumseh and His Times: The Story of a Great Indian by John M. Oskison. *Mississippi Valley Historical Review* 26(June, 1939):82-83.

This Land Is Ours by Louis Zara. *Mississippi Valley Historical Review* 27(December, 1940):502.

Uncle Sam's Stepchildren by Loring B. Priest. *Ohio State Archaeological and Historical Quarterly* 51(April, 1942):145-147.

The Wars of the Iroquois: A Study in Intertribal Relations by George T. Hunt. *Mississippi Valley Historical Review* 27(September, 1940):287-288.

Wilderness Chronicles of Northwestern Pennsylvania edited by Sylvester K. Stevens and Donald H. Kent. *Mississippi Valley Historical Review* 28(March, 1942):635-636.

The Winnebago-Horicon Basin: A Type Study in Western History by Joseph Schafer. *American Historical Review* 43(July, 1938):904-905.

Studies of Randolph C. Downes

Blodgett, Geoffrey. Review of *Rise of Warren G. Harding* by Randolph C. Downes. *American Historical Review* 76(December, 1971):1608-1609.

"Downes, Randolph C." *Directory of American Scholars*. New York: R. R. Bowker, 1968. 1:80.

Huckett, Homer C. Review of *Frontier Ohio, 1788-1803* by Randolph C. Downes. *American Historical Review* 41(July, 1936):819-820.

Kellogg, Louise Phelps. Review of *Council Fires on the Upper Ohio: A Narrative of Indian Affairs in the Upper Ohio Valley until 1795* by Randolph C. Downes. *American Historical Review* 47(April, 1942):618-619.

Murdock, Eugene C. Review of *Rise of Warren G. Harding* by Randolph C. Downes. *Journal of Southern History* 37(November, 1971):664-665.

"Randolph C. Downes." *Northwest Ohio Quarterly* 46(Summer, 1964):120-121.

21

GRANT FOREMAN

by Michael D. Green

Biography

Ulysses Grant Foreman was a historian of Oklahoma. He was not the first, but he was the most prolific. No serious student of Oklahoma history today would end any studies of Oklahoma without consulting Foreman.

Foreman was born June 3, 1869, in the American Bottom country of western Illinois. The son of a small town physician, Foreman grew up in White Hall, Greene County, Illinois, where he attended and then taught in the public schools. With no undergraduate training, he entered the University of Michigan's law school in 1889 and two years later won the Bachelor of Laws degree. For the next eight years Foreman practiced law in Chicago, ending up in the offices of United States Senator William E. Mason. Delicate health, however, forced him to seek a warmer climate, and in 1899 he abandoned Chicago to join the staff of the Dawes Commission at its headquarters in Muskogee, Indian Territory.

The Commission to the Five Civilized Tribes, the proper name of the Dawes Commission, was created by Congress in 1893 to negotiate allotment agreements with the governments of each of the Five Tribes. Chaired in its first years by Henry L. Dawes, retired senator from Massachusetts and author of the 1887 General Allotment Act, the commission underwent several modifications during the 1890s as Congress expanded its authority to force the unwilling tribes to agree to allotment. By the time Foreman joined the group, the Curtis Act, passed by Congress in 1898, had empowered the commission to compile censuses of the tribes, select and appraise land, and proceed with allotment regardless of the desires of the Indians. Foreman's duties with the commission began as an appraiser and classifier of land; later he worked with the commission's legal staff as an arbitrator of conflicting claims.

As it applied to Indian Territory, Congress's allotment legislation stipulated that once each enrolled citizen received a tract, it was held subject to restrictions forbidding the sale of the land. This was done to protect Indians from the swindles of crafty whites. Following allotment, any undivided land remaining in the hands of the nations could be sold to others. Foreman witnessed the sale of the surplus lands belonging to Creek freedmen (the descendents of black slaves owned by Creeks and counted in the Dawes Commission census roles as full Creek citizens) and observed the sale of allotments by Creek mixed bloods whose restrictions had been lifted. These sales set off an "orgy of speculation" in which "grafters dispossessed guileless freedmen and mixed bloods of their holdings" which, according to a biographer, made a "deep impression" on Foreman. Disgusted by what he saw, Foreman joined the reformist Indian Rights Association and participated in its campaign against the hasty removal of restrictions on the lands of Indian allottees (*Chronicles of Oklahoma* 31:227).

In 1903, Foreman left the Dawes Commission to enter the law offices of John R. Thomas, a former federal district judge assigned to Indian Territory. Their association lasted until Thomas's death in 1914 and was probably instrumental in forging Foreman's personal and professional partnership with Thomas's daughter, Carolyn. They married in 1905. It is difficult to separate the historical contributions made by Carolyn Foreman from Grant Foreman. In addition to working with her husband in his research, in which he published over 100 books and articles, Carolyn Foreman wrote nearly 100 books and articles under her own name. *Oklahoma Imprints: A History of Printing in Oklahoma before Statehood, 1835-1907* (1936) was probably her most important book; *Indians Abroad* (1943) is probably her best known. Carolyn and Grant remained together until he died in 1953 at the age of eighty-four.

Themes

Presumably, Foreman's experiences with the Dawes Commission, his general exposure to life and conditions in and around Muskogee in the early years of the twentieth century, his outrage at the unprincipled, if not illegal, treatment of allotted Indians, and his deep interest in history all came together to work a change in his priorities. Judge Thomas's death in 1914 gave Foreman an excuse to cut back his practice, and highly profitable investments in agricultural and oil lands provided a good income. By the early 1920s, it was possible for Foreman to retire and devote the remainder of his life to scholarship. Thus was born, in his middle age, Grant Foreman, the historian.

In his pursuit of the history of his adopted state, Foreman explored two fundamental topics in his writings. One was his captivation with the Three Forks region of eastern Oklahoma where the Verdigris, Grand, and Arkansas Rivers meet. Eighteen books appeared between 1926 and 1947 with Foreman's name on them. Four are edited works--three travel accounts and one transcript of a Cherokee court case--and fourteen are monographs. With one exeception they all deal with Oklahoma history and most focus on eastern Oklahoma, particularly the Three Forks region. "As a trading center and theatre of military and more peaceful operations in the winning of this country, [the area of the Three Forks] was second to none west of the Mississippi." The seat of Fort Gibson, U.S. military headquarters in eastern Indian Territory and the center of U.S. political authority in its relations with the eastern Indian tribes exiled to the West, the Three Forks was the hub from which "the conquest of a large part of the Southwest was achieved" (*Pioneer Days in the Early Southwest,* p. 17). A second topic involved Foreman in the history of Native Americans of the Indian Territory. Foreman concentrated on the Osages and the Five Civilized Tribes. While showing sympathy and respect for Oklahoma's Indians, Foreman subscribed to the concepts of cultural evolution. Moreover, in both of his topical concerns, the themes of development, progress, and assimilation emerge as positive forces in Foreman's mind.

Analysis

Foreman first makes the argument for the significance of the Three Forks country in his *Pioneer Days in the Early Southwest* (1926). His first book, *Pioneer Days,* is an anecdotal history of the exploration of the region, trade with the Indians (mostly the Osages), the early history of Fort Gibson, and of wars involving the Osages, the Fort Gibson soldiers, and the Plains Indians of western Oklahoma and Texas. Concentrating on the 1820s and 1830s, Foreman used this book to set the stage for his major work--the four books published between 1930 and 1934 that combine to detail the history of Indian Territory before the Civil War. This body of scholarship is among the earliest systematic efforts to describe and explain the Indian history of Indian Territory and together they demonstrate a remarkable accomplishment.

Yale University Press published *Indians and Pioneers: The Story of the American Southwest before 1830* in 1930. Focusing on present Arkansas and Oklahoma, *Indians and Pioneers* is largely Osage history. Beginning with their early contacts with the Spanish and the French, covering the American missionary and military occupation, and ending with the early nineteenth century immigration of the eastern tribes into the Arkansas and Red River valleys, Foreman recounts a story of repeated incursions and stiff Osage resistance. Osage warriors "terrorized" the countryside, "massacred" white hunters and traders, "tolerated" missionaries, "stole" from the army, and "regarded with bitter animosity" the Delaware, Cherokee, Shawnee, and Kickapoo refugees who encroached on their hunting grounds.

Foreman dramatizes the richness and complexity of the pre-1830 history of the region, but he saw it largely in terms of what was to follow. It was a "period of preparation" before a "dramatic experiment with a race of people, unsurpassed in interest and pathos in our history." "A wild and lawless expanse of beautiful country," Congress made the home of the Osages Indian Territory and settled there a people of "fixed and domestic habits" who would "dot the landscape with farms and settlements, . . . establish new homes, governments, and schools, and [whose] habits and achievements [would] win for them the name of The Five Civilized Tribes" (*Indians and Pioneers,* p. 274). Never one to hide his enthusiasm for the replacement of "savagry" by "civilization," Foreman's lyricism uncovers the irony that in early Oklahoma this beneficient transformation occurred when one group of Indians supplanted another.

Indian Removal, first published by the University of Oklahoma Press in 1932, is the second volume of Foreman's history of Indian Territory. Here he depicts the expulsion of the Choctaws, Creeks, Chickasaws, Cherokees, and Seminoles from their southeastern homes. Released as the second volume in the press's widely acclaimed "Civilization of the American Indian Series," *Indian Removal* is beyond all doubt Foreman's most important book. It is the first to describe, systematically and in horrifying detail, the human cost of the removal policy of President Andrew Jackson. And it remains today, after a half century of scholarship, the standard source on the "Trail of Tears."

Foreman divided the book into five parts, one for each of the Five Tribes. Each part begins with the negotiation of the "removal" treaty, covers the efforts of the government to organize and prepare for the trek, and then describes the trip west. His themes are the hardship and suffering of the Indians, the confusion, waste, fraud, and unpreparedness of the government, and the humanity, generosity, and sympathy of many individual white officials.

Foreman shows that the native people of the Southeast were settled agriculturalists, not the "wandering nomads" of popular misconception. They had institutions of government, some patterned after that of the United States. Many were Christian, some were educated, and schools trained the youth in "civilized" pursuits. These were not people who held their lands lightly, and unlike the more "adaptable" white race, they did not continually move about looking for greener grass and better opportunities over the next hill.

Building on this foundation of stability, Foreman characterizes the treaties each tribe concluded with the United States to trade their lands for acreage in the West as the work of fraud, bribery, and deception. Crooked federal agents and crooked or naive tribal leaders agreed to the exchange over the expressed but suppressed opposition of the majority in every tribe. While the specifics of each arrangement differed, the pattern was so clear that twice in his three page preface Foreman warns his readers that his purpose is neither "to excite sympathy for the Indians" nor "to indict the people of the South for [their] mistreatment" of them.

The heart of the book is Foreman's "day-by-day recital of events." Told separately for each tribe, these "recitals" take the form of long, multipage quotes copied from the journals and reports of the military and civilian agents and physicians who accompanied the groups of exiles west. They tell a story of pained, hungry, cold, and sick people stumbling in long lines through mud and snow, or of people packed into rented river boats. They tell of the dead, mainly children and the aged, hastily buried along the way. And they tell of the heroic efforts of others, whites as well as Indians, to ease the suffering, to find food or blankets, to provide medical care. These "recitals" are moving accounts that Foreman let stand untouched.

Despite his announced intention to avoid an "interpretation of these events or of the actions and motives of the people connected with them," Foreman made no effort to hide his outrage at the needless and painful suffering inflicted on the southeastern Indians by the removal policy and its architects. Nevertheless, he found "a wistful hope" in their exile--the hope:

> that in this remote country they would find surcease from the cruelty, sordidness, and rapacity of the frontier white man. . . . With this hope after their arrival they resolutely attacked the problems of pioneering in the strange country that confronted them. The rehabilitation of these five Indian nations, their readjustment to their new surroundings, the recovery of their national spirit and enterprise, the building of their farms and homes, their governments and schools upon the raw frontier, bringing into being a higher civilization of Indians, this was an achievement unique in our history that compares favorably with the best tradition of white frontier civilization (p. 386).

This is classic Foreman. Nothing better captures the ironic contradiction in his thinking. His heart bleeds for the suffering of Indian people but his respect is for the "higher civilization" of the emigres and his highest praise is to measure them favorably against the achievements of the "white frontier"--the very force that expelled them from their homes.

The next two books in Foreman's history of Indian Territory deal with the postremoval history of the Five Tribes. The first to appear, *Advancing the Frontier* (1933), discusses the relations during the 1830s and 1840s between the exiles and the resident Prairie tribes into whose midst removal had dropped them. The argument here is that in the absence of effective military protection the leaders of the exiled nations had to work out policies of accommodation with the resident tribes or else be locked in bloody conflict with them. In a series of large intertribal conferences, in which the Creeks and Cherokees took the lead, delegates from both groups aired their grievances and struggled to find satisfactory ways to share the region and its limited resources. At the same time, the army erected a chain of small forts. Isolated and weak, they could neither protect the farmers nor scare the hunters. Whatever effective resolution occurred during these years was at the initiative of the Indians.

Foreman sees this confrontation between "civilized" eastern Indians and "wild" Plains hunters as the classic frontier conflict. If it was somewhat less violent than Indian-white collisions under similar circumstances usually were, it was because the people on both sides were Indians and therefore presumably understood each other. But the fundamental clash of "civilization" against "savagery" was present and as always "civilization" won. "The immigrant Indians came to exercise a profound influence on the denizens of the prairies that hastened the civilization of the western country and prepared it for the occupancy of the white man" (p. iii).

The Five Civilized Tribes (1934), the fourth volume in Foreman's history of Indian Territory, is organized like *Indian Removal* with a distinct part for each tribe. In these minihistories, Foreman describes the problems each faced in its new land and the efforts and policies each developed to regain prosperity and social stability and to reestablish its necessary public institutions.

Foreman's chief interest remains riveted on the degree to which these Indians were different from the Plains hunters. "Civilized" before their removal, the Five Tribes continued their "progress" in Indian Territory. Their rate of "progress" generally amazes Foreman, who repeatedly points to their "remarkable" development. "Achieved at a cost it has been the lot of few people to experience," Foreman writes, "their progress year after year and their achievements in the field of culture and government have no parallel in the history of our Indians" (*The Five Civilized Tribes,* p. 421).

Foreman mentions, at least in passing, most aspects of the histories of the Five Tribes. He notes their agricultural efforts and recites with approval the yield figures reported by their agents. He identifies the major native traders and businessmen and cites the profitability of their enterprises. He describes housing and settlement patterns and looks at the growing networks of roads. But Foreman is primarily interested in their institutions--particularly their schools and governments.

Education, Foreman asserts, was the first priority of each tribe once the primary needs for housing and food had been met. Except for the Seminole, each of the tribes had hosted schools in the East. After removal, even the Seminole joined in the universal cry for education. With the devoted aid of a large and growing corps of Protestant missionaries, the tribes embarked on educational policies designed to train their young men and women in the arts of "civilization." "Enlightened" tribal leaders encouraged, prodded, and propagandized for schools, but the credit for their existence and success, Foreman believes, lies with the missionaries.

Institutions of government equally interested Foreman. Visible evidence of the "civilization" of the Five Tribes, the constitutional governments of most of the tribes (the Creek did not write a constitution until 1859 but they did enact a body of written law), the laws, and the court and police systems represented order and justice in a region only recently rescued from chaos. Each of the tribal histories contains descriptions of these institutions, lists of laws, and anecdotes depicting the rule of law. And everywhere Foreman reiterates his respect for the ways these efforts dramatized the "civilization" of the exiles. For example, Foreman edited *Indian Justice: A Cherokee Murder Trial at Tahlequah in 1840 as Reported by John Howard Payne* (1934) to show "an Indian people . . . well on the road from a primitive life to a high state of civilization" (pp. ix-x).

Taken together, these four books constitute an elaborate, detailed, and carefully documented history of Indian Territory. Foreman meant them to be read and considered together, and one suspects that he viewed them as his most significant work. They are certainly his best known books. Generations of younger historians have found in them their introduction to western Indian history.

The balance of Foreman's monographs can be considered in two categories: short pieces of primarily local and antiquarian interest, and books that moved beyond the Three Forks country. *Down the Texas Road: Historic Places along Highway 69 through Oklahoma* (1936), *Fort Gibson: A Brief History* (1936), *Lore and Lure of Eastern Oklahoma* (1947), and *Muskogee: The Biography of an Oklahoma Town* (1943) fall into the first category. Foreman knew intimately the Three Forks country and in these brief publications (except for *Muskogee* they run from forty-five to eighty pages) he shares with local people the stories and legends of the area. Because they identify and locate trails, fords, villages, farms, trading posts, stores, churches, and such, these little gems are gold mines of obscure information for scholars doing research on eastern Indian Territory.

Even when Foreman's interest strayed beyond the confines of the Three Forks country, his books retained the links to the region. For example, Sequoyah was an Old Settler Cherokee who migrated to eastern Indian Territory in 1818. He had begun work on the development of a Cherokee syllabary in the East but perfected it in the West. As any scholar knows who has attempted the difficult task of Native American biography, the paucity of sources results in works that are sometimes strangely distorted. Foreman's *Sequoyah* (1938) is no exception. It concentrates almost exclusively on the syllabary, clearly Sequoyah's most significant accomplishment. The many accounts and legends describing how he decided to attempt the enormous challenge of reducing the Cherokee language to writing, how he overcame the skeptical resistance of his fellow Cherokee, how he perfected the system, and how he demonstrated its value comprise the bulk of Foreman's slim volume. Massively impressed by the enormity of Sequoyah's achievement, Foreman presents to the public of Oklahoma and elsewhere its first glimpse of "the only man in history to conceive and perfect in its entirety an alphabet or syllabary" (p. 3.). That this person was an Oklahoma Indian no doubt surprised many.

Foreman was extremely interested in the exploration of Indian Territory and the Southwest and published several books on the subject. *Marcy and the Gold Seekers: The Journal of Captain R. B. Marcy, with an Account of the Gold Rush Over the Southern Route* (1939) is a printing of Marcy's 1849 report to the War Department interspersed with large sections of commentary and explanatory material written by Foreman. In addition, Foreman edited three exploration and travel accounts: *Adventure on Red River: Report on the Exploration of the Headwaters of the Red River by Captain Randolph B. Marcy and Captain G. B. McClellan* (1937); *A Pathfinder in the Southwest: The Itinerary of Lieutenant A. W. Whipple during His Explorations for a Railway Route from Fort Smith to Los Angeles in the Years 1853 and 1854* (1941); and *A Traveler in Indian Territory: The Journal of Ethan Allen Hitchcock, Late Major-General in the United States Army* (1930). Hitchcock's journal concentrates on Indian

Territory and is a particularly valuable source for the history of the Five Tribes in the 1840s.

Foreman's last two major books were published in the 1940s. *The Last Trek of the Indians* (1946) is in many ways a companion to his earlier *Indian Removal.* Tribal dispossession and relocation remain the subjects but in this case the Indians who underwent this experience came from north of the Ohio River. "Fragments of once powerful and colorful nations," among them Potawatomis, Miamis, Shawnees, Sauks, and others from the Old Northwest, "were induced to enter into treaties by which they gave up their homes and agreed to remove . . . farther west" (pp. 8-9). Resettled in Missouri and Kansas, most of these groups were then shunted into Indian Territory after the Civil War. *Last Trek* recounts their experiences in short sections tribe after tribe, along with extended discussions of federal Indian policy and the western economic and political interests that influenced that policy.

A History of Oklahoma (1942) falls into a class by itself. Much of the material on eastern Indian Territory had, of course, been the subjects of earlier books, but in design, organization, structure, and coverage, this was by far his most ambitious book. And from the perspective of the 1980s and current standards of historiography, it is Foreman's most professional.

As the title suggests, this is a comprehensive history. The first third covers the Antebellum period and is the most repetitious of Foreman's earlier works. Here Foreman summarizes removal, the postremoval recovery of the Five Tribes, their relations with the Plains tribes, and the emergence of Indian Territory as a staging area for the war with Mexico and particularly for the postwar exploration of the Southwest. Next comes two chapters on the Civil War in Indian Territory, a period of conflict and devastation that is still not well appreciated. The balance of *A History of Oklahoma* covers the Reconstruction era of growing competition between Indians and whites for possession of the lands and resources of Indian Territory. Foreman's coverage of this nasty and often violent period ends with Oklahoma's statehood in 1907 and the legislative history of the new state for the next fifteen years. This is followed by two catchall chapters that sketch in the non-political events between statehood and the 1920s.

Grant and Carolyn Foreman had the money and desire to devote the last decades of their lives to history. Working as a team, they spent years in the major libraries and archives of the United States and Europe, copying letters, newspapers, diaries, and journals, buying documents and books to amass an enormous private library, and employing scores of secretaries to transcribe additional materials. They mined the Indian Office and War Department collections before the establishment of the National Archives and copied or acquired thousands of federal reports and documents, but he was one of the very few historians before World War II to use them so deeply and rely on them so heavily.

Foreman's dependence on federal records, supplemented with mission records, newspapers, travel accounts, and other sources, explains both the strengths and the weaknesses of his work. He covered virtually all the written sources, mastered them, and pieced together narratives rich in detail. He quoted extensively from the documents, he carefully identified his sources, and his bibliographical essays are models for guiding researchers to the richest collections. Though untrained as a historian, his legal education and practical experience schooled him in research. No professional historian could have done better.

Nevertheless, Foreman was not a good historian. Many of his faults were common to his period and were shared by others. (This does not excuse Foreman, it simply suggests that many historians have not been very good.) Foreman was, for example, fully convinced that cultures evolve from lower to higher states, the process of which he repeatedly describes as "progress toward civilization." This unquestioned assumption pervades his history of Indian Territory, it explains the histories of the Five Tribes, their relations with the hunting tribes of the Plains, and their relations with white people and the federal government. The struggle between "civilization" and "primitive Indians" was as inevitable as the triumph of "civilization" over the Indians.

Indians had only one hope for survival, to become "civilized." Their attempts to do so were "crude" and "simple" and their progress was necessarily slow, but Foreman's respect for the accomplishments of the Five Tribes suggests that he was honest in his belief that equality was possible. While Foreman's books reek with ethnocentric bias, one finds little, if any, racism.

The ethnocentric assumptions underlying Foreman's research and writing blinded him to the first and most difficult task of a good historian--to evaluate his sources critically. This Foreman rarely did. Indeed, he often quoted long passages from the documents, letting them stand as representing his views without comment. This technique succeeds fairly well in *Indian Removal* because his purpose was to describe the march of the refugee Indians west. It does not work to explain intertribal relations, relations between tribes and the federal government, or internal tribal history. Thus the contemporary explanations of government agents, missionaries, travelers, traders, indeed anyone who left a record, became Foreman's own. Everything is taken at face value, nothing is evaluated.

In Foreman's day, some Native American historians critically analyzed their sources and presented interpretations of events free from such glaring and inhibiting ethnocentric bias. Annie Abel and Angie Debo, both contemporaries of Foreman, worked on the history of the Indians of Indian Territory. Foreman's Indian history does not meet the careful, critical historical scholarship that marks their books.

Foreman's only book to approach a standard of analytical, interpretive history is his *History of Oklahoma.* Apparently unable to see or accept the depth and complexity of Indian history, he foundered in the sea of disconnected minutia contained in the mass of government documents he studied. The Reconstruction era contest for Indian Territory, on the other hand, presented him with a conflict he could understand. Fueled by motives of ambition, greed, and the desire for opportunity, the "sooners," "boomers," developers, grafters, lawyers, and government officials who increasingly came to control events in Indian Territory were people Foreman recognized. He had, indeed, been one of them. He groans at their excesses, but he never doubts the propriety or inevitability of the outcome, and his almost boyish enthusiasm for the exciting times he witnessed and participated in tends to transcend his everpresent ethnocentrism. His language becomes more vivid and his descriptions more interpretive. Though marred by a preoccupation with political detail, his wonder at the creation of Oklahoma is infectious.

Ultimately, however, *A History of Oklahoma*, along with Foreman's other books, disappoints the modern reader. Perhaps the special disability of the untrained historian is an unwillingness to argue a position from the sources. Perhaps he did not understand that the job of a historian is to analyze and interpret. Maybė his refusal grew out of a misplaced humility. At any rate, Foreman's books are all middles with no beginnings or endings. He was a historian because he wrote books and articles on historical subjects, and he published in such profusion that the very mass of his work commands attention.

Bibliography

Books

Advancing the Frontier, 1830-1860. Norman: University of Oklahoma Press, 1933.

Adventure on Red River: Report on the Exploration of the Headwaters of the Red River by Captain Randolph B. Marcy and Captain G. B. McClellan. Editor. Norman: University of Oklahoma Press, 1937.

The Adventures of James Collier, First Collector of the Port of San Francisco. Chicago: Black Cat Press, 1937.

Beginning of Protestant Christian Work in Indian Territory. Muskogee: Star Printing, 1933.

Down the Texas Road: Historic Places along Highway 69 through Oklahoma. Norman: University of Oklahoma Press, 1936.

The Five Civilized Tribes. Norman: University of Oklahoma Press, 1934.

Fort Gibson: A Brief History. Norman: University of Oklahoma Press, 1936.

A History of Oklahoma. Norman: University of Oklahoma Press, 1942.

Indian Justice: A Cherokee Murder Trial at Tahlequah in 1840, as Reported by John Howard Payne. Editor. Oklahoma City :Harlow Publishing Co., 1934.

Indian Removal: The Emigration of the Five Civilized Tribes of Indians. Norman: University of Oklahoma Press, 1932.

Indians and Pioneers: The Story of the American Southwest before 1830. New Haven: Yale University Press, 1930.

The Last Trek of the Indians. Chicago: University of Chicago Press, 1946.

Lore and Lure of Eastern Oklahoma. Muskogee: Muskogee Chamber of Commerce, 1947.

Marcy and the Gold Seekers: The Journal of Captain R. B. Marcy, with an Account of the Gold Rush over the Southern Route. Norman: University of Oklahoma Press, 1939.

Muskogee: The Biography of an Oklahoma Town. Norman: University of Oklahoma Press, 1943.

A Pathfinder in the Southwest: The Itinerary of Lieutenant A. W. Whipple during His Explorations for a Railway Route from Fort Smith to Los Angeles in the Years 1853 and 1854. Editor. Norman: University of Oklahoma Press, 1941.

Pioneer Days in the Early Southwest. Cleveland: The Arthur H. Clark Co., 1926.

Sequoyah. Norman: University of Oklahoma Press, 1938.

A Traveler in Indian Territory: The Journal of Ethan Allen Hitchcock, Late Major-General in the United States Army. Editor. Cedar Rapids, IA: Torch Press, 1930.

Articles

"Antoine Leroux, New Mexico Guide." *New Mexico Historical Review* 16(October 1941):367-378.

"The Bank Deposit Insurance Law of Oklahoma." *The Independent* 65(August 20, 1908):418-419.

"Bird-Feeding Towers of Ahmedabad." *Bird Lore* 25(September, 1923):302-303.

"The California Overland Mail Route through Oklahoma." *Chronicles of Oklahoma* 9(September, 1931):300-317.

"Captain John Stuart's Sketch of the Indians." *Chronicles of Oklahoma* 11(March, 1933):667-672.

"Captain Nathan Boone's Survey, Creek-Cherokee Boundary Line." *Chronicles of Oklahoma* 4(December, 1926):356-365.

"The Centennial of Fort Gibson." *Chronicles of Oklahoma* 2(June, 1924):119-128.

"A Century of Prohibition." *Chronicles of Oklahoma* 12(June, 1934):133-141.

"Clarence W. Turner." *Chronicles of Oklahoma* 10(March, 1932):18-20.

"Clifton R. Breckenridge." *Chronicles of Oklahoma* 12(March, 1934):118-119.

"The Constitutional Convention of Oklahoma." *Colliers Weekly* 38(January 12, 1902):20.

"Dwight Mission." Editor. *Chronicles of Oklahoma* 12(March, 1934):42-51.

"Early History of Spavinaw." *Chronicles of Oklahoma* 9(March, 1931):166-170.

"Early Post Offices of Oklahoma." Editor. *Chronicles of Oklahoma* 6(March, 1928):4-25, 6(June, 1928):155-162, 6(December, 1928):428-444, 7(March, 1929):7-33.

"Early Trails through Oklahoma." *Chronicles of Oklahoma* 3(June, 1925):99-119.

"Education among the Five Civilized Tribes in Early Days." *Indians at Work* 4(June 15, 1937):29-35.
"Edward Merrick." *Chronicles of Oklahoma* 13(March, 1935):127-128.
"English Emigrants in Iowa." *Iowa Journal of History and Politics* 44(October, 1946):385-420.
"English Settlers in Illinois." *Journal of the Illinois State Historical Society* 34(September, 1941):303-333.
"Fort Davis." *Chronicles of Oklahoma* 17(June, 1939):147-150.
"Frank C. Hubbard." *Chronicles of Oklahoma* 8(December, 1930):454-456.
"Frederick Simplich." *Chronicles of Oklahoma* 28(Autumn, 1950):365-366.
"Historical Background of the Kiowa-Comanche Reservation." *Chronicles of Oklahoma* 19(June, 1941):129-140.
"Historical Marker at Three Forks." *Chronicles of Oklahoma* 11(March, 1933):635-636.
"Historical Phases of the Grand River Valley." *Chronicles of Oklahoma* 25(Summer, 1947):141-152, 172.
"The Home of the Red Man in Statehood." *Overland Monthly* 54(October, 1909):368-374.
"The Honorable Alice M. Robertson." *Chronicles of Oklahoma* 10(March, 1932):13-17.
"Horace Speed." *Chronicles of Oklahoma* 25(Spring, 1947):5-6.
"Illinois and Her Indians." *Papers in Illinois History and Transactions for the Year 1939* (1940):66-111.
"In Search of the Comanches (The Journal of J. C. Eldredge)." Editor. *Panhandle-Plains Historical Review* 7(1934):7-41.
"The Indian and the Law." *Journal of the Oklahoma Bar Association* 17(1946):82-91.
"Inspection Tour." *Katy Employees Magazine* (December, 1946):4-5.
"J. George Wright: 1860-1941." *Chronicles of Oklahoma* 20(June, 1942):120-123.
"Jesse Bantley Milam." *Chronicles of Oklahoma* 27(Autumn, 1949):236-237.
"John Bartlett Meserve." *Chronicles of Oklahoma* 21(June, 1943):121-122.
"John Howard Payne and the Cherokee Indians." *American Historical Review* 37(July, 1932):723-730.
"John Leaf Springston." *Chronicles of Oklahoma* 27(Autumn, 1949):333-334.
"John Randolph Frazier." *Chronicles of Oklahoma* 13(September, 1935):367.
"John Taylor Griffin." *Chronicles of Oklahoma* 27(Spring, 1949):120-122.
"A Journal Kept by Douglas Cooper of an Expedition by a Company of Chickasaw in Quest of Comanche Indians." Editor. *Chronicles of Oklahoma* 5(December, 1927):381-390.
"The Journal of Elijah Hicks." Editor. *Chronicles of Oklahoma* 13(March, 1935):68-99.
"The Journal of Hugh Evans, Covering the First and Second Campaign of the United States Dragoon Regiment in 1834 and 1835: Campaign of 1834." Edited by Fred S. Perrine with additional notes by

Grant Foreman. *Chronicles of Oklahoma* 3(September, 1925):175-219.

"The Journal of the Proceedings of Our First Treaty With the Wild Indians, 1835." Editor. *Chronicles of Oklahoma* 14(December, 1936):394-418.

"Journey of a Party of Cherokee Emigrants." Editor. *Mississippi Valley Historical Review* 18(September, 1931):232-245.

"The Lady From Oklahoma: The Story of the Honorable Alice M. Robertson, the Representative of Women in the United States Congress." *The Independent* 105(March 26, 1921):311-326.

"The Last of the Five Civilized Tribes." *Overland Monthly* 49(March, 1907):196-198.

"The Law's Delays." *Michigan Law Review* 13(December, 1914):100-112.

"Legislative Curiosa." *Journal of the Oklahoma Bar Association* 18(1947):1912-1917.

"The Life of Montfort Stokes in the Indian Territory." *North Carolina Historical Review* 16(October, 1939):373-403.

"Lo, the Rich Indian." *Sunset Magazine* 22(June, 1909):647-650.

"Missionaries of the Latter Day Saints Church in Indian Territory." Editor. *Chronicles of Oklahoma* 13(June, 1935):196-213.

"The Murder of Elias Boudinot." Editor. *Chronicles of Oklahoma* 12(March, 1934)19-24.

"Nathanial Pryor." *Chronicles of Oklahoma* 7(June, 1929):152-163.

"The New State of Oklahoma." *The World Today* 11(August, 1906):796-802.

"Notes (G.F.)." *Chronicles of Oklahoma* 12(June, 1934):214-221.

"Notes and Documents: Pioneer Recollections." *Chronicles of Oklahoma* 18(December, 1940):371-396.

"Notes from the Indian Advocate." *Chronicles of Oklahoma* 14(March, 1936):67-83.

"Notes of a Missionary Among the Cherokees (Journal of Charles Cutler Torrey)." Editor. *Chronicles of Oklahoma* 16(June, 1938):171-189.

"Notes of August Chouteau on Boundaries of Various Indian Nations." Editor. *Missouri Historical Society, Glimpses of the Past* 7(October-December, 1940):119-140.

"Oklahoma." *State Government--The Magazine of State Affairs* 19(May, 1946):127-132.

"Oklahoma and the Indian Territory." *The Outlook* 82(March 10, 1906):550-552.

"Oklahoma's First Court." *Chronicles of Oklahoma* 13(December, 1935):457-469.

"Our Indian Ambassadors to Europe." *Missouri Historical Society Collections* 5(February, 1928):109-128.

"Plight of the Full Bloods." *Overland Monthly* 63(March, 1914):240-243.

"Protecting the Indian." *The Independent* 74(January 2, 1913):39-42.

"Red River and the Spanish Boundary in the United States Supreme Court." *Chronicles of Oklahoma* 2(September, 1924):298-310.

"Reminiscences of Mr. R. P. Vann, East of Webbers Falls, Oklahoma, September 28, 1932. As Told to Grant Foreman." *Chronicles of Oklahoma* 11(June, 1933):838-844.

"Report of Material Secured and Deposited with the Archives of the Oklahoma Historical Society." *Chronicles of Oklahoma* 14(March, 1936):3-8.

"Report of Placing a Marker in the National Cemetery of Fort Gibson for Col. John Nicks, Veteran of the War of 1812." *Chronicles of Oklahoma* 10(December, 1932):553-555.

"Report of the Cherokee Deputation into Florida." Editor. *Chronicles of Oklahoma* 9(December, 1931):423-438.

"River Navigation in the Early Southwest." *Mississippi Valley Historical Review* 15(June, 1928):34-55.

"Salt Works in Early Oklahoma." *Chronicles of Oklahoma* 10(December, 1932):474-500.

"Settlement of English Potters in Wisconsin." *Wisconsin Magazine of History* 21(June, 1938):375-396.

"Some New Light On Houston's Life Among the Cherokee Indians." *Chronicles of Oklahoma* 9(June, 1931):139-152.

"Sources of Oklahoma History." *Chronicles of Oklahoma* 5(March, 1927):42-57.

"Statehood for Oklahoma." *The Independent* 63(August 8, 1907):331-335.

"The Story of Sequoyah's Last Days." Editor. *Chronicles of Oklahoma* 12(March, 1934):25-41.

"Survey of a Wagon Road From Fort Smith to the Colorado River." Editor. *Chronicles of Oklahoma* 11(March, 1934):74-96.

"A Survey of Tribal Records in the Archives of the United States Government in Oklahoma." *Chronicles of Oklahoma* 11(March, 1933):625-634.

"The Texas Comanche Treaty of 1846." *Southwestern Historical Quarterly* 51(April, 1948):313-332.

"The Three Forks (of the Arkansas)." *Chronicles of Oklahoma* 2(March, 1924):37-47.

"Thrilling Story of First Indian Ambassadors in Europe." *The American Indian* 5(December, 1930-January, 1931):2-3, 16.

"The Trial of Stand Watie." *Chronicles of Oklahoma* 12(September, 1934):304-339.

"The Trusts and the People Get Together." *The Independent* 88(December 11, 1916):454.

"The U.S. Court and the Indian: Where the Red Man Gets a Square Deal." *Overland Monthly* 61(June, 1913):573-579.

"The University of Oklahoma." *Southwest Review* 27(Summer, 1942):411-424.

"An Unpublished Report by Captain B. E. E. Bonneville." Editor. *Chronicles of Oklahoma* 10(September, 1932):326-330.

Reviews

And Still the Waters Run by Angie Debo. *American Historical Review* 46(July, 1941):936-937.

__________. *Mississippi Valley Historical Review* 27(March, 1941):636-637.

Arkansas, A Guide to the State by Writers Program of the WPA. *Chronicles of Oklahoma* 19(December, 1941):408-409.

Around Tahlequah Council Fires by T. L. Ballenger. *Chronicles of Oklahoma* 13(September, 1935):357-358.

Beacon on the Plains by Mary Paul Fitzgerald. *Chronicles of Oklahoma* 18(December, 1940):395.

Chief Joseph: The Biography by Chester A. Fee. *Mississippi Valley Historical Review* 24(September, 1937):253.

Dawn of Tennessee Valley and Tennessee History by Samuel Cole Williams. *Chronicles of Oklahoma* 15(December, 1937):484-486.

Diary and Letters of Josiah Gregg edited by Maurice Fulton. *Chronicles of Oklahoma* 19(December, 1941):410.

The Early Far West, A Narrative Outline, 1640-1850 by W. J. Ghent. *Chronicles of Oklahoma* 10(December, 1932):434.

The Earth Speaks by Princess Atalie. *Chronicles of Oklahoma* 18(December, 1940):307.

Federal Indian Relations, 1774-1788 by Walter H. Mohr. *American Historical Review* 39(April, 1934):585-586.

Geronimo's Story of His Life by S. M. Barrett. *Mississippi Valley Historical Review* 25(December, 1938):419-420.

Henry de Tonty, Fur Trader of the Mississippi by Edmund Robert Murphy. *Arkansas Historical Quarterly* 1(Spring, 1942):83-85.

The Historic Trail of the American Indians by Thomas P. Christensen. *Mississippi Valley Historical Review* 21(September, 1934):271-272.

Indian-fighting Army by Fairfax Downey. *American Historical Review* 47(April, 1942):693-694.

The Life and Times of Colonel Richard M. Johnson of Kentucky by Leland Winfield Meyers. *Chronicles of Oklahoma* 10(December, 1932):435.

New Sources of Indian History, 1850-1891: The Ghost Dance, The Prairie Sioux -- A Miscellany by Stanley Vestal. *Mississippi Valley Historical Review* 21(December, 1934):420-421.

Oklahoma, A Guide to the Sooner State by Writers Project of the WPA. *Chronicles of Oklahoma* 20(March, 1942):72-73.

Old Frontiers: The Story of the Cherokee Indians from Earliest Times to the Date of Their Removal to the West, 1838 by John F. Brown. *Mississippi Valley Historical Review* 25(December, 1938):416-417.

Pueblo Indian Religion by Elsie C. Parsons. *Mississippi Valley Historical Review* 26(March, 1940):586-587.

The Pulse of the Pueblo: Personal Glimpses of Indian Life by Julia M. Seton. *Mississippi Valley Historical Review* 27(June, 1940):146-147.

Southern Trails to California in 1849 edited by Ralph P. Bieber. *Chronicles of Oklahoma* 15(December, 1937):483-484.

Springplace, Moravian Mission, and the Ward Family of the Cherokee Nation by Muriel H. Wright. *Chronicles of Oklahoma* 18(December, 1940):396.

Straight Texas by J. Frank Dobie and Mody C. Boatright. *Mississippi Valley Historical Review* 24(December, 1937):411.

Tixier's Travels on the Osage Prairies edited by John F. McDermott. *Mississippi Valley Historical Review* 27(December, 1940):470-471.

Zachary Taylor, Soldier of the Republic by Holman Hamilton. *Chronicles of Oklahoma* 19(June, 1941):192-194.

Studies of Grant Foreman

Abel-Henderson, Annie Heloise. Review of *The Five Civilized Tribes* by Grant Foreman. *Mississippi Valley Historical Review* 22(June, 1935):96-97.

_________. Review of *The Last Trek of the Indians* by Grant Foreman. *American Historical Review* 52(January, 1947):336-337.

_________. Review of *A Traveler in Indian Territory: The Journal of Ethan Allen Hitchcock, Late Major-General in the United States Army* edited by Grant Foreman. *American Historical Review* 37(October, 1931):138-139.

Bieber, Ralph P. Review of *Pioneer Days In The Early Southwest* by Grant Foreman. *Mississippi Valley Historical Review* 14(June, 1927):98-100.

Briggs, Harold E. Review of *A History of Oklahoma* by Grant Foreman. *Mississippi Valley Historical Review* 29(June, 1942):111-112.

Clark, J. Stanley. "Carolyn Thomas Foreman." *Chronicles of Oklahoma* 45(Winter, 1967-1968):368-375.

_________. "Grant Foreman." *Chronicles of Oklahoma* 31(Autumn, 1953):226-242.

Cosgrove, Elizabeth Williams. "The Grant Foreman Papers: Indian and Pioneer History." *Chronicles of Oklahoma* 37(Winter, 1959-1960):507-510.

Dale, Edward E. "A Dedication to the Memory of Grant Foreman, 1869-1953." *Arizona and the West* 6(Winter, 1964):271-274.

_________. *Grant Foreman: A Brief Biography*. Norman: University of Oklahoma Press, 1933.

_________. Review of *Indian Removal: The Emigration of the Five Civilized Tribes of Indians* by Grant Foreman. *Mississippi Valley Historical Review* 20(December, 1933):424-425.

_________. Review of *The Last Trek of the Indians* by Grant Foreman. *Mississippi Valley Historical Review* 33(September, 1946):343-344.

_________. Review of *A Traveler in Indian Territory: The Journal of Ethan Allen Hitchcock, Late Major-General In the United States Army* edited by Grant Foreman. *Mississippi Valley Historical Review* 18(June, 1931):81-82.

Debo, Angie. "A Dedication to the Memory of Carolyn Thomas Foreman, 1872-1967." *Arizona and the West* 16(Autumn, 1974):214-218.

Ellison, William H. Review of *A Pathfinder in The Southwest: The Itinerary of Lieutenant A. W. Whipple During His Explorations for a Railway Route 1853-1854* edited by Grant Foreman. *American Historical Review* 47(April, 1942):632-633.

Fisher, Lillian Estelle. Review of *Indian Justice: A Cherokee Murder Trial at Tahlequah in 1840, as Reported by John Howard Payne* edited by Grant Foreman. *Mississippi Valley Historical Review* 21(September, 1934):273-274.

Foreman, Grant, Papers. Oklahoma Historical Society. Oklahoma City, OK.

__________. Thomas Gilcrease Institute of American History and Art. Tulsa, OK.

Goodwin, Cardinal. Review of *Marcy and the Gold Seekers: The Journal of Captain R. B. Marcy, with an Account of the Gold Rush Over the Southern Route* by Grant Foreman. *Mississippi Valley Historical Review* 26(September, 1939):263-264.

Green, Joseph C. Review of *Indian Removal: The Emigration of the Five Civilized Tribes of Indians* by Grant Foreman. *American Historical Review* 39(January, 1930):349-350.

__________. Review of *Indians and Pioneers: The Story of the American Southwest before 1830* by Grant Foreman. *American Historical Review* 36(July, 1931):838-839.

Kelly, Lawrence C. "Indian Records in the Oklahoma Historical Society Archives." *Chronicles of Oklahoma* 54(Summer, 1976):227-244.

Lewis, Anna. Review of *Sequoyah* by Grant Foreman. *Mississippi Valley Historical Review* 25(September, 1938):277-278.

Malin, James C. Review of *Advancing the Frontier 1830-1860* by Grant Foreman. *Mississippi Valley Historical Review* 20(March, 1934):580.

Riegel, Robert E. Review of *A Pathfinder in the Southwest: The Itinerary of Lieutenant A. W. Whipple during His Explorations for a Railway Route from Fort Smith to Los Angeles in the Years 1853 and 1854* edited by Grant Foreman. *Mississippi Valley Historical Review* 28(September, 1941):302-303.

Sheldon, Addison E. Review of *Pioneer Days in the Early Southwest* by Grant Foreman. *American Historical Review* 32(October, 1926):146-148.

Smith, G. Hubert. Review of *Adventure on Red River: Report on the Exploration of the Headwaters of the Red River by Captain Randolph B. Marcy and Captain G. B. McClellan* edited by Grant Foreman. *Mississippi Valley Historical Review* 25(June, 1938):106-107.

Whitaker, Arthur P. Review of *Indians and Pioneers: The Story of the American Southwest Before 1830* by Grant Foreman. *Mississippi Valley Historical Review* 17(March, 1931):618-619.

Wiesendanger, Martin W. *Grant and Carolyn Foreman: A Bibliography.* Tulsa: University of Oklahoma, 1948.

Wyllys, Rufus Kay. Review of *Advancing the Frontier, 1830-1860* by Grant Foreman. *American Historical Review* 39(July, 1934):789-790.

22

GEORGE BIRD GRINNELL

by Thomas R. Wessel

Biography

The American West of the post-Civil War era attracted a host of explorers, hunters, scientists, entrepreneurs, naturalists, anthropologists, friends of the Indians, and eastern aristocrats seeking the "manly life." To a remarkable degree George Bird Grinnell was all of these. Grinnell enjoyed the privileged life and education of the eastern elite in the late nineteenth century. He was the complete American Victorian, at ease in a corporate board room in New York or a hunting camp in the Rockies. He lived by a code of conduct he associated with the sportsman. The code demanded that his peers be treated with respect and his lessers with kindness and understanding. Within that context Grinnell easily counted among his friends Theodore Roosevelt, the rough hewed western writer J. Willard Schultz, Indian fighters Charlie Reynolds and Frank North, and numerous Indian leaders among the Blackfeet, Cheyenne, and Pawnee.

Intellectual curiosity, rectitude, a vigorous physical life, and public service were for Grinnell the requisites of a sportsman. His friend Roosevelt sought elected office to fulfill that obligation. Grinnell served by becoming a joiner and often founder of numerous scientific and naturalist societies. He organized the first local bird preservation society and named it after John James Audubon; he helped found the New York Zoological Society and proposed the site of the society's animal collection in the Bronx. He was a trustee of the Hispanic Society of America, a fellow of the American Association for the Advancement of Science, and a member of the American Ornithologists Union, the Council on National Parks, the American Geographic Society, the American Society of Mammalogists, the New York Academy of Science, the National Parks Association, the Archeological Institute of America, the Genealogical and Biographical Society, the Mayflower Descendents, the Society of Colonial Wars, and cofounder with Theodore Roosevelt of the Boone and Crockett

Club. To all of these organizations he lent his name, his time, and his financial support.

Grinnell was born in 1849 in Brooklyn, New York. While still an infant, his family moved to Manhattan to the former estate of John James Audubon. His father, a successful businessman with connections to the Vanderbilts and other financial movers of the time, saw that his son gained a rigorous and complete education, first at a military school in upstate New York, then as a tutorial student of the widow of John James Audubon, and finally at Yale University. Probably his time with Mrs. Audubon stimulated his initial interest in nature, and later his association with Othniel Marsh, the paleontologist at the Yale Peabody Museum, solidified his intellectual curiosity.

Following his graduation from Yale in 1870, Grinnell accompanied Marsh on one of the first scientific expeditions to the central Great Plains and Rocky Mountain region. The fossil expedition took him through the Platte River Valley, to the Sand Hills of western Nebraska, and on to the Green River country of Utah, areas then largely unmapped and little explored.

On return to the East, Grinnell began a conventional life as an apprentice businessman in his father's office, although he continued to visit the Great Plains nearly every summer. In the meantime he wrote a series of articles describing his western trip of 1870 for the new journal *Forest and Stream* under the pseudonym Ornis (Greek for "bird"). The articles appealed to the journal's editors and prompted them to offer Grinnell the position of natural history editor in 1876. Two years earlier Grinnell had returned to Yale to work as an assistant to Marsh and pursue a graduate degree in osteology.

The return to Yale provided Grinnell the opportunity for another expedition in the West. That year at his own expense he accompanied the expedition of George Armstrong Custer to the Black Hills as the command's official naturalist. His work there recommended him to Captain William Ludlow, who was charged with mapping Yellowstone Park. The next summer, in 1875, Grinnell went to Yellowstone for the first time. His contributions on animal and bird life to Ludlow's report became standard works on the region. Later, in 1899, he acted as the naturalist with the Harriman expedition to Alaska.

Following completion of his Ph.D. degree in 1880, Grinnell purchased controlling interest in *Forest and Stream* and became the magazine's editor-in-chief. For the next thirty years Grinnell divided his time between trips to the West and New York, where he wrote of his travels, published Indian stories he had recorded, and turned the magazine into a crusading journal promoting the protection of the nation's parks and wild life. Grinnell remained editor of *Forest and Stream* until 1911 and a member of the magazine's board of trustees until 1925. In 1902, at the age of fifty-three, Grinnell married Elizabeth Curtis Williams. Elizabeth accompanied Grinnell on his many trips west and acted as his official photographer. Her pictures informed most of his later works.

In 1921 Yale University awarded Grinnell an honorary Litt.D. degree, and in 1925 he received the Theodore Roosevelt Medal from President Calvin Coolidge. A series of illnesses in the 1930s effectively ended Grinnell's active life. He died at the age of eighty-nine in 1938 at his home in New York City. Grinnell left an unmatched publishing record among American writers on the West. Of the thirty-four books published under his name, twelve remain in print as of 1985.

Themes

George Bird Grinnell was not a trained historian, but his work influenced many historians. Rather he was an acute observer and faithful recorder of the western experience in the late nineteenth century. His training as an osteologist sharpened his eye, but did not incline him to draw explicit conclusions. He generally limited his writing to those things he had personally experienced or had directly heard from participants. His nonfiction work stands unadorned and without editorial frills. His writing has endured principally because it has the ring of authenticity, reflecting the people he knew and the unembellished accounts of his travels.

Grinnell wrote or edited over thirty books, over 300 articles, and over 200 unsigned editorials. His work ranged from highly technical descriptions of prehistoric fossils to juvenile adventure stories. In his long career he edited or wrote ten books on hunting, twelve books of Indian stories and life, seven books of fiction and three books on early western exploration. Many of his books first appeared as serials in *Forest and Stream.*

Although diverse in character Grinnell wrote of only one topic, the natural environment and those who inhabited that environment. In his own lifetime the western environment changed dramatically. He witnessed the passing of the buffalo and antelope, the confinement of the horse-mounted warrior Indian nations to reservations, and an end to the life of the free-traders and guides.

From the time of his first trip into the wilderness in 1870 he carried on a love affair with the untrampled land and free spirited people of the unsettled West. Yet, it was not an uncritical love affair; he was no romantic. Like many in love, however, he felt compelled to share his experience with others, and in that way preserve the land and people for whom he felt such affection.

His many books on hunting were intended to instill a sense of sportsmanship in hunters as well as increase their skills. His last hunting book, *Hunting and Conservation* (1925), particularly emphasized the hunter's responsibility. "We have on the one hand descriptions of hunting--of the killing of animals," he wrote, "and on the other the advocacy of measures by which these animals may be preserved from being killed. There is no conflict between these two views. Animals are for man's use, and one of these uses is recreation, of which hunting is a wholesome form. So long as it does not interfere with the maintenance of a permanent breeding stock of any species this recreation is legitimate and praiseworthy" (p. xi). Grinnell devoted much of his effort to promoting the protection of game animals, particularly in the national parks. He conducted a long crusade in the pages of *Forest and Stream* for federal legislation providing for the integrity of Yellowstone Park and worked to expand the park to include the Grand Tetons. He successfully lobbied to create Glacier Park.

Throughout his writing one theme consistently emerges. The West meant freedom--freedom from the constraints of civilized life. In Grinnell's West the elemental confrontation between good and evil was clear. Those who meld with the environment, living within it and respecting its bounty, were people of character, while those who exploited the land and slaughtered the game were the true barbarians. In the West survival put a premium on physical endurance, the ability to cope, and personal character. He found and admired those traits in both the early explorers and the Indians of the Great Plains and Rocky Mountains. Throughout his life he was torn by a patrician's sense of responsibility and a longing for the free, adventurous, and unrestrained life he witnessed among the explorers, hunters, and Indians. The contrast of civilization defined by restraint and the life of the free westerner exists in all of Grinnell's work, but finds its clearest expression in his writing on the Pawnee, Blackfeet, and Cheyenne.

Analysis

In his first published article in *Forest and Stream* in 1873, Grinnell expresses the sense of freedom and excitement that big game hunting held for him. "We rushed to the spot and there lay the cow [elk] in her death agony. That was for me the supreme moment. As I stood over her, all the trouble and annoyance of the trip; all the worries and cares of everyday life were forgotten, and I was absorbed in the proud contemplation of the graceful creature lying before me" (1:116). The freedom of the hunt and the reliance on his own skill and daring never left him. That same summer on the Nebraska plains, he joined the Pawnee on a buffalo hunt and witnessed the same skill and abandon among the Indian hunters. Here were men of character and ability as much a part of the environment as the buffalo they hunted. The Indian life contrasted sharply with his own background yet there on the open plains they were one. "Hunting big game in the wilderness," he wrote, "is above all things, a sport for a vigorous and masterful people. The rifle-bearing hunter . . . must be sound of body and firm of mind, and must possess energy, resolution, manliness, self-reliance, and capacity for hardy self-help. In short, the big game hunter must possess qualities without which no race can do its life-work well" (*Forest and Stream* 33:222-223).

Grinnell could not abandon his eastern life but he admired those who had, like Charley Reynolds and Frank and Luther North. If business and personal obligations drew him back to the city, he could nevertheless relive that sense of freedom in writing about the West and working to preserve as much of the old life as possible.

By the mid-1880s the buffalo days on the Plains had come to an end, and Grinnell witnessed on the Blackfoot Reservation the desperate condition of Indians forced into dependence on government rations. He hunted with the Blackfeet in 1885 in the midst of a tragic starving time for that nation and played a significant role in gaining government relief for the Blackfeet. While he recognized that the old days could not be recovered, he was moved to see that those who had lived on the Great Plains were helped toward a new life with dignity.

Government policy toward the Indians became fixed in the Dawes Act in 1887. Grinnell originally opposed allotment of Indian lands, but ultimately agreed that farming and stock raising were the only future available for his old hunting companions. Much of his editorial writing and several of his books were intended to inform the public of Indian reservation conditions while forcing the government to take a more compassionate attitude toward their charges. In his *The Story of the Indian* (1895), he writes that "we are apt to forget that these people are human like ourselves; that they are fathers and mothers, husbands and wives, brothers and sisters; men and women with emotions and passions like our own, even though these feelings are not well regulated and direct in the calm, smoothly flowing channels of civilized life" (p. ix). Nevertheless, for Grinnell, "the most impressive characteristic of the Indian is his humanity. For in his simplicity, his vanity, his sensitiveness to ridicule, his desire for revenge and his fear of the supernatural, he is a child and acts like one" (p. x). In a series of books each titled *The Indians of Today* (1900, 1911) he compiled statistical information and reported on conditions on the reservations in the hope that public awareness might ease the transition from the old life. "As Indians are only grown-up children," he wrote, "they must be taught, as children are taught, all the knowledge which is unconsciously absorbed by the white man from his early associations and his reading" (1900 ed., p. 4). His reference to children was not meant to be pejorative, but reflective of the free unrestrained life he so much admired.

Shortly after the passage of the Dawes Act, J. Willard Schultz observed in *Forest and Stream*, "The recent act of Congress providing for the taking of land in Severalty by the Indians, is sure to break up all tribal relations. In a short time the ancient traditions and customs will have been forgotten. Before it is too late, then, let those of us who can save from oblivion such accounts of religious, social life and language of the different tribes as we may be able to obtain" (29:2). Grinnell agreed.

In 1889 he published through *Forest and Stream* his first collection of Indian stories, *Pawnee Hero Stories and Folk-Tales*. His first effort was eventually followed by four more collections, *Blackfoot Lodge Tales: The Story of a Prairie People* (1892), *The Punishment of the Stingy and Other Indian Stories* (1901), *Blackfeet Indian Stories* (1913), and *By Cheyenne Campfires* (1926). In each of these collections Grinnell follows a familiar pattern. He acts as reporter, not interpreter, of the Indian's cosmic view. His own thoughts appear only at the end of his first two books in a short description of the current condition of his storytellers. Here Grinnell contrasts the old free life with the constraints of civilization. He notes in

Pawnee Hero Stories and Folk-Tales that the Pawnee had endured difficult times after the buffalo days and had diminished in number. He is optimistic about their future, "but the character of the people has changed," he observes. "In the old barbaric days they were light-hearted, merry, makers of jokes, keenly alive to the humorous side of life. Now they are serious, grave, little disposed to laugh. Then they were like children without a care. Now they are like men, on whom the anxieties of life weigh heavily. Civilization, bringing with it some measure of material prosperity, has also brought to these people care, responsibility, repression. No doubt it is best, and it is inevitable, but it is sad, too" (pp. 407-408). In *Blackfoot Lodge Tales*, Grinnell makes much the same observation. Speaking of the Blackfeet of 1892, he observes, "It is the meeting of the past and the present, of savagery and civilization. The issue cannot be doubtful. Old methods must pass away. The Blackfeet will become civilized, but at a terrible cost. To me there is an interest, profound and pathetic, in watching the progrèss of the struggle" (p. 180).

Grinnell was anxious that others find in the Indians the same traits of dignity and character that he had encountered. That was particularly true of the Cheyenne. Unlike the Pawnee, who could claim white sympathy as former allies, the Cheyenne had warred with white settlers and had been one of the major obstacles to white penetration of the Great Plains. Perhaps for that reason Grinnell wrote of the Cheyenne only when memories of the past conflict had dimmed. With his *The Fighting Cheyennes* (1915) he meant to set the record straight. "Since the Indians could not write," he notes, "the history of their wars has been set down by their enemies. . . .[A]nd, since the wars are now distant in time, the Indians' own description of these battles may be read without much prejudice" (p. x).

It was important to Grinnell that the other side of the story be told, not just to maintain a sense of historical accuracy, but because the Cheyenne were deserving of no less. "The old time Cheyennes," he wrote, "possessed in high degree the savage virtues of honesty, trustworthiness, and bravery in the men, and of courage, devotion, and chastity in the women. Of the older people who took part in the fighting with the white troops some are still living and today are the only source of original information concerning the former ways of the wild Cheyennes, the old free life of the Western plains" (p. xi). Once again Grinnell acts the faithful reporter of a time and place that had disappeared.

Grinnell discovered that men of character existed among the civilized and uncivilized alike. Even if it were not possible to preserve the old free life for the Indians and for himself, it was possible to preserve some semblance of it. To that end he organized the Audubon Society and, with his friend Theodore Roosevelt, the Boone and Crockett Club. Civilized men of character had such responsibilities. Big game hunting was "manly" only when conducted for the trophy much like Indians who hunted only what they could eat. On the hunt the civilized sportsman and the uncivilized Indian shared a common bond. He wrote eloquently of the relationship in "Disappearance of Western Big Game" (1895), "The Native American

Hunter" (1897), "When Antelope were Plenty" (1911), and "What We May Learn from the Indian" (1916), and other articles in *Forest and Stream.*

Grinnell never wrote an autobiography, although he started the task. Yet, his fictional accounts of a young eastern boy's adventures in the West come near to being autobiographical. In *Jack in the Rockies* (1904), Grinnell's fictional hero, Jack Danvers spent the previous summer with the Piegans in Montana and was preparing to return. "Jack had gone East, to spend the winter in New York. He had had a year of hard work at school, for his experience of the previous winter had taught him that it paid well to work in school, and to make the most of his opportunities there. This made his parents more willing to have him go away to this healthful life, and he found that if he did his best he enjoyed all the better the wild, free life of the prairie and the mountains, which he now hoped would be his during a part at least of every year" (p. 10). Later young Jack, looking at the tall buildings of New York City and the bustling crowds of people, notes in awe that "only a few days journey distant, there was a land where there was no limit to the view, where each human being seemed absolutely free, and where it was possible to travel for days and days without seeing a single person" (p. 11). Young Jack is Grinnell. For much of his life the wilderness was only a few days journey distant, and for the all of his life it was as near as his pen.

Bibliography

Books

American Big Game Hunting. Co-edited with Theodore Roosevelt. New York: Forest and Stream Publishing Co., 1893.

American Big Game in Its Haunts. Editor. New York: Forest and Stream Publishing Co., 1904.

American Duck Shooting. New York: Forest and Stream Publishing Co., 1901.

American Game-Bird Shooting. Editor. New York: Forest and Stream Publishing Co., 1911.

Audubon Park: The History of the Site of the Hispanic Society of America and Neighboring Institutions. New York: Hispanic Society of America, 1927.

Bent's Old Fort and Its Builders. Topeka: Kansas State Historical Society, 1923.

Beyond the Old Frontier: Adventures of Indian-Fighters, Hunters, and Fur-Traders. New York: Charles Scribner's Sons, 1913.

Blackfeet Indian Stories. New York: Charles Scribner's Sons, 1913.

Blackfoot Lodge Tales: The Story of a Prairie People. New York: Charles Scribner's Sons, 1892.

By Cheyenne Campfires. New Haven, CT: Yale University Press, 1926.

The Cheyenne Indians, Their History and Way of Life. 2 volumes. New Haven, CT: Yale University Press, 1923.

The Fighting Cheyennes. New York: Charles Scribner's Sons, 1915.

Hunting and Conservation. Co-edited with Charles Sheldon. New York: Forest and Stream Publishing Co., 1925.

Hunting at High Altitudes. Editor. New York: Harpers, 1913.

Hunting in Many Lands. Co-edited with Theodore Roosevelt. New York: Forest and Stream Publishing Co., 1899.

The Indians of Today. Chicago: Hubert S. Stone, 1900.

__________. New York: Duffield, 1911. Revised editions, 1915 and 1921.

Jack among the Indians, or a Boy's Summer on the Buffalo Plains. New York: Frederick A. Stoke Co., 1900.

Jack in the Rockies, or a Boy's Adventures with a Pack Train. New York: Frederick A. Stoke Co., 1904.

Jack the Young Canoeman. New York: Frederick A. Stoke Co., 1906.

Jack the Young Cowboy. New York: Frederick A. Stoke Co., 1913.

Jack the Young Explorer. New York: Frederick A. Stoke Co., 1908.

Jack the Young Ranchman, or a Boy's Adventure in the Rockies. New York: Frederick A. Stoke Co., 1899.

Jack the Young Trapper. New York: Frederick A. Stoke Co., 1907.

Musk-Ox, Bison, Sheep and Goat. Co-edited with Owen Wister and Casper Whitney. New York: Macmillan and Co., 1904.

Pawnee Hero Stories and Folk-Tales. New York: Forest and Stream Publishing Co., 1889.

The Punishment of the Stingy and Other Indian Stories. New York: Harper and Brothers, 1901.

The Story of the Indian. New York: D. Appleton, 1895.

Trail and Camp-Fire. Co-edited with Theodore Roosevelt. New York: Forest and Stream Publishing Co., 1897.

Trails of the Pathfinders. New York: Charles Scribner's Sons, 1911.

Two Great Scouts and Their Pawnee Battalion. Cleveland: Arthur H. Clark Co., 1928.

When Buffalo Ran. New Haven, CT: Yale University Press, 1920.

The Wolf Hunters, A Story of the Buffalo Plains. Editor (arranged from the manuscript account of Robert M. Peck). New York: Charles Scribner's Sons, 1924.

Articles

"Account of the Northern Cheyenne Concerning the Messiah Superstition." *Journal of American Folk-Lore* 4(January, 1891):61-69.

"Albinos." Ornis (Pseudonym). *Forest and Stream* 2(February 19,1874):22.

"Alpine Climbing in America." *Harper's Weekly* 41(October 2, 1897):979-980.

"American Wildfowl and How to Take Them" (from *Forest and Stream*): "The Duck Family" 55(September 8, 1900):186-187; "Swans" 55(September 15, 1900):206; "Geese and Brant" 55(September 22, 1900):225; "The White-Fronted Goose" 55(September 29, 1900):246; "Canada Goose" 55(October 13, 1900):286; "Barnacle Goose" 55(October 20, 1900):308; "Tree Duck" 55(October 27, 1900):327; "The True Ducks" 55(November 3, 1900):346; "Black Duck and Dusky Duck" 55(November 10, 1900):366-367; "Gadwall"

55(November 17, 1900):385; "American Wedgeon-Bald-Pate" 55(November 24, 1900):404-405; "Green-Winged Teal" 55(December 1, 1900):425; "Cinnamon Teal" 55(December 8, 1900):446-447; "Pintail" 55(December 15, 1900):466-467; "Diving Ducks" 55(December 22, 1900):492; "Canvasback Duck" 55(December 29, 1900):506-507; "Redhead Duck" 56(January 5, 1901):5; "Broadbill" 56(January 12, 1901):25; "Ring-Neck Duck, Tufted Duck" 56(January 19, 1901):46; "Bufflehead Duck" 56(January 26, 1901):67; "Harlequin Duck" 56(February 2, 1901):87; "Spectacled Eider" 56(February 9, 1901):108-109; "American Scoter" 56(February 16, 1901):129; "The American Velvet Scoter" 56(March 2, 1901):164; "Buddy Duck" 56(March 9, 1901):185; and "Fish Ducks" 56(March 16, 1901):207-208.

"Antelope Hunting Thirty-Years Ago and Today." *Outing* 43(November, 1903):196-204.

"As to the Wolverine." *Journal of Mammalogy* 1(August, 1920):182-184.

"Ashbel's Goat." Yo (Pseudonym). *Forest and Stream* 59(December 27, 1902):510-511.

"A Band of Bears." Yo (Pseudonym). *Forest and Stream* 67(September 1, 1906):334-335.

"A Blackfoot Cheyenne." *Forest and Stream* 72(May 15, 1909):774.

"A Blackfoot Sun and Moon Myth." *Journal of American Folk-Lore* 6(January-March, 1893):44-47.

"A Bloodless Coup." *Forest and Stream* 70(March 28, 1908):488-489.

"Blue Geese on Long Island." *Auk* 35(April, 1918):222.

"Bluejay Visits the Ghosts." *Harper's Weekly* 101(November, 1900):540-545.

"A Boy in Indian Camp, L. H. Garrard's Experiences--The Plains in 1846--Life Among the Cheyenne Indians." *Forest and Stream* 75(December 3, 1910):888-892.

"Brazilian Tree-Duck in New Jersey." *Auk* 30(January, 1913):110.

"A Brood of Partridges." *Forest and Stream* 76(June 10, 1911):896.

"Buffalo Hunt with the Pawnee." Ornis (Pseudonym). *Forest and Stream* 1(December 25, 1873):305-306.

"Buffalo Memorials" (from*Forest and Stream*): "The Bones" Stream 68(February 16, 1907):253-255; "The Buffalo Chip" 68(March 2, 1907):329-330; and "The Trail and Wallow" 68(March 9, 1907):368-369.

"A Buffalo Sweatlodge." *American Anthropologist* New Series 21(October-December, 1919):361-375.

"Building the Northern Pacific." *Forest and Stream* 18(February 9, 1882):37-39.

"The Butterfly and the Spider among the Blackfeet." *American Anthropologist* 1(January, 1899):194-196.

"Bye-ways of the Northwest." Yo (Pseudonym). (from *Forest and Stream*): 16(July 14, 1881):469; 17(August 4, 1881):4-5; 17(September 22, 1881):144-145; 17(September 29, 1881):163-164; 17(October 13, 1881):204-205; 17(October 20, 1881):224-225;

17(November 3, 1881):265-266; 17(November 24, 1881):324-325; 17(December 15, 1881):384-385; 17(December 29, 1881):424-425; 17(January 19, 1882):484-485; and 17(February 9, 1882):524-525.

"A Chapter of History and Natural History in Old New York." *Natural History* 20(January-February, 1920):23-27.

"Charley Reynolds." *Forest and Stream* 47(December 26, 1896):503-504.

"Chase of the White Goat." Co-authored with John Fannin. *Forest and Stream* 35(August 21, 1890):88.

"The Cheerful Buffalo Hunters of Fifty Years Ago." *Forest and Stream* 74(June 18, 1910):968-970.

"The Cheyenne Medicine Lodge." *American Anthropologist* New Series 16(April-June, 1914):245-256.

"Cheyenne Obstacle Myth." *Journal of American Folk-Lore* 16(April, 1903):108-115.

"Cheyenne Stream Names." *American Anthropologist* New Series 8(January-March, 1906):15-22.

"Cheyenne Woman Customs." *American Anthropologist* New Series 4(January-March, 1902):13-16.

"Chief Mountain Lakes: Disagreement as to Location." *Science* 20(August 12, 1892):85.

"Childbirth among the Blackfeet." *American Anthropologist* 9(August, 1896):286-287.

"Climbing Blackfoot." *Forest and Stream* 51(October 8, 1898):282-283.

"Climbing for White Goats." *Scribner's Magazine* 15(May, 1894):643-648.

"Concerning Black Bears." *Forest and Stream* 74(March 12, 1910):415-416.

"The Corsair of the Woodlands." *Forest and Stream* 87(December, 1917):592-593.

"Coup and Scalp Among the Plains Indians." *American Anthropologist* New Series 12(April-June, 1910):297.

"A Crow Victory." *Forest and Stream* 73(July 31, 1909):171.

"Crown of the Continent." *Century* 62(September, 1901):660-672.

"A Day with Sage Grouse." *Forest and Stream* 1(November 6, 1873):196.

"Death of General Anderson." *Forest and Stream* 84(April, 1915):234-235.

"Deformed Buffalo." *Forest and Stream* 71(September 12, 1908):412.

"Development of a Pawnee Myth." *Journal of American Folk-Lore* 5(April, 1892):127-134.

"Disappearance of Western Big Game." *Harper's Weekly* 39(March 16, 1895):261.

"Dog-Wolf Partnership." *Forest and Stream* 69(November 16, 1907):772.

"The Dun Horse, A Pawnee Folk-tale." *Forest and Stream* 33(November 28, 1889):362.

"Eagle Prey." *Journal of Mammalogy* 10(February, 1929):83.

"Early Blackfoot History." *American Anthropologist* 5(April, 1892):153-164.

"Early Cheyenne Villages." *American Anthropologist* New Series 20(October-December, 1918):359-380.

"Elk Hunting in Nebraska." Ornis (Pseudonym). *Forest and Stream* 1(October 2, 1873):116.

"Falling Star." *Journal of American Folk-Lore* 34(July-September, 1921):308-315.

"Feathers and Tariff." *Forest and Stream* 81(July 12, 1913):43-44.

"Fighting Brutes." Yo (Pseudonym). *Forest and Stream* 57(July 27, 1901):65.

"The Fleetness of Crow Chief." *Forest and Stream* 71(December 26, 1908):1010-1011.

"Foxes in Captivity." *Journal of Mammalogy* 4(August, 1923):184.

"A Fur Trader of the North." *Forest and Stream* 71(December 12, 1908):928-930.

"A Generous Leader." *Forest and Stream* 71(October 3, 1908):529-530.

"Girl Who Was the Ring." *Harper's Magazine* 102(February, 1901):425-430.

"Glimpses at Canvasbacks." *Forest and Stream* 54(January 20, 1900):45-46.

"Gossip about the Pronghorn." *Forest and Stream* 67(July 14, 1906):50-52.

"The Great Fight with the Kiowas and Comanches." *Forest and Stream* 64(March 18, 1905):211-212.

"The Great Mysteries of the Cheyenne." *American Anthropologist* New Series 12(October-December, 1910):542.

"The Green River Country." Ornis (Pseudonym). *Forest and Stream* 1(November 13, 1873):212.

"Habits of the Buffalo Bird." *Forest and Stream* 55(November 3, 1900):344.

"Habits of the White Goat." Co-authored with John Fannin. *Forest and Stream* 35(July 31, 1890):27-28; 35(August 7, 1890):47; and 35(August 14, 1890):67.

"The Harriman Alaskan Expedition" (from *Forest and Stream*): "Itinerary" 54(February 24, 1900):142-143; "A Small Talk About Glaciers" 54(March 3, 1900):165-166; "Big Game Hunters" 54(March 10, 1900):183-184; "Prince William Sound" 54(March 17, 1900):205-206; "Some Fur Bearers" 54(March 24, 1900):222-223; "Indians" 54(March 31, 1900):243-245; "In Uyak Bay" 54(April 7, 1900):262-263; "Salmon Destruction" 54(April 21, 1900):302-303; "Some Life on Sea and Shore" 54(April 28, 1900):323-324; "To Bogoslof and Pribilofs" 54(May 5, 1900):343-344; "The Fur Seals of the Pribilof Islands" 54(May 12, 1900):363-364; "Destruction of the Fur Seals" 54(May 19, 1900):382-383; "Eskimos" 54(June 2, 1900):422-423; "Life on Shipboard" 54(June 16, 1900):463-464; and "Homeward Bound" 54(June 23, 1900):482-483.

"Hawking on the Plains." *Forest and Stream* 75(September 10, 1910):456.

"The Horse and the Indian." *Forest and Stream* 68(June 22, 1907):971-972.

"The Indian Buffalo Piskun." *Forest and Stream* 39(September 29, 1892):268-269.

"Indian Camp-fire Tales." *Forest and Stream* 71(September 19, 1908):450-451; 71(October 10, 1908):570; and 71(November 14, 1908):771.

"Indian Stream Names." *American Anthropologist* New Series 15(April-June, 1913):327-331.

"Indians and the Outing System." *Outlook* 75(September, 1903):167-173.

"Indians on the Reservation." *Atlantic Monthly* 83(February, 1899):255-267.

"Keeping the Wolves Down." *Forest and Stream* 86(December, 1916):1242.

"A Land of Plenty." *Forest and Stream* 74(May 14, 1910):773.

"Land of the Antarctic." *Forest and Stream* 76(June 17, 1911):930-933.

"Last of the Buffalo." *Scribner's Magazine* 12(September, 1892):267-286.

"A Letter to Audubon." *Journal of Mammalogy* 5(November, 1924):223-230.

"Little Friend Coyote." *Harper's Magazine* 102(January, 1901):288-293.

"The Lodges of the Blackfeet." *American Anthropologist* New Series 3(October-December, 1901):650-668.

__________. *Forest and Stream* 61(November 14, 1903):374; 61(November 21, 1903):395-396; and 61(November 28, 1903):415-416.

"Lynx and Wildcat." Yo (Pseudonym). *Forest and Stream* 69(July 6, 1907):13.

"Marriage among the Pawnee." *American Anthropologist* 4(July, 1891):275-281.

"Medicine Grizzly Bear: Indian Folk-Tale." *Harper's Magazine* 102(April, 1901):736-744.

"The Missouri River Wild Turkey." *Forest and Stream* 77(December 2, 1911):811.

"Mountain Sheep." *Journal of Mammalogy* 9(February, 1928):1-9.

"The Native American Hunter." *Forest and Stream* 49(October 9, 1897):284; 49(October 16, 1897):304; 49(October 23, 1897):322; 49(October 30, 1897):342; 49(November 13, 1897):382; 49(December 4, 1897):442; and 49(December 11, 1897):462.

"The Natives of the Alaska Coast Region." In *Harriman Alaska Expedition.* New York: Doubleday, Page, and Co., 1901. 1:137-164, 171-178.

"Natural Enemies of Bird Life." *Forest and Stream* 87(January, 1917):25.

"News of the Fur Seals." *Forest and Stream* 80(January 11, 1913):43.

"North American Indians of Today." *Review of Reviews* 19(March, 1899):357.

"Northern Rocky Mountain Glaciers." *Science* New Series 8(November 18, 1898):711-712.

"Notes on Cheyenne Songs." *American Anthropologist* New Series 5(April-June):312-322.

"Notice of a New Genus of Annelids from the Lower Silurian." *American Journal of Science and Arts* 14(September, 1877):1-2.

"An Old Story of Astoria." *Forest and Stream* 72(January 23, 1909):129-130.
"The Old West." Yo (Pseudonym). *Forest and Stream* 56(April 27, 1901):322.
"An Old-Time Bone Hunt." *Natural History* 23(July-August, 1923):329-336.
"Old-Time Range of Virginia Deer, Moose, and Elk." *Natural History* 25(March-April, 1925):136-142.
"On a New Crinoid from the Cretaceous Formation of the West." *American Journal of Science* 3rd Series 12(July, 1876):81.
"On a New Tertiary Lake Basin." Co-authored with Edward S. Dana. *American Journal of Science* 3rd Series 11(January, 1876):126-128.
"Othniel Charles Marsh." In *Leading American Men of Science* edited by David S. Jordan. New York: Henry Holt and Co., 1910. Pp. 283-312.
"Over Old-Time Trails." Yo (Pseudonym). *Forest and Stream* 67(December 22, 1906):978-979; 67(December 29, 1906):1019-1020; and 68(January 5, 1907):11-12.
"Pawnee Mythology." *Journal of American Folk-Lore* 6(April, 1893):113-130.
"Pawnee Star Myth." *Journal of American Folk-Lore* 7(July, 1894):197-200.
"A Peculiar People, The Red River Halfbreeds--A Vanished Race--The Cheerful Buffalo Hunters of Fifty Years Ago." *Forest and Stream* 74(June 18, 1910):968-970.
"Portraits of Indian Types." *Scribner's Magazine* 27(March, 1905):259-273.
"Present Distribution of Big Game in America." *Outing* 37(December, 1900):250-259.
"Primitive American Hunting." *Forest and Stream* 64(June 17, 1905):475.
"Primitive Bows and Arrows: Their Character and Uses in North America and the Wounds Caused by Them." *Forest and Stream* 69(November 23, 1907):808-810 and 69(November 30, 1907):848-851.
"Pronghorn Antelope." *Journal of Mammalogy* 10(May, 1929):135-141.
"Punishment of the Stingy." *Harper's Magazine* 101(August, 1900):323-328.
"Range of the Mountain Goat." *Forest and Stream* 50(May 7, 1898):366.
"Recollections of Audubon Park." *Auk* 37(July, 1920):372-380.
"The Return of a War Party." *Forest and Stream* 48(January 30, 1897):82-83.
"The Rock Climbers." Yo (Pseudonym). (Some articles in this series were written by another author.) (from *Forest and Stream*): 29(December 29, 1887):442-443; 29(January 12, 1888):482-483; 29(January 19, 1888):502-503; 30(January 26, 1888):2; 30(February 9, 1888):42-43; 30(February 16, 1888):62-63; 30(February 23, 1888):82; 30(March 1, 1888):102; 30(March 15, 1888):142-143; 30(March 22, 1888):162;

30(March 29, 1888):182-183; 30(April 5, 1888):202; 30(April 19, 1888):242; 30(April 26, 1888):266-267; and 30(May 3, 1888):286.

"Roosevelt in Africa." *Review of Reviews* 42(October, 1910):457-461.

"Ruddy Shelldrake on the Atlantic Coast." *Auk* 36(October, 1919):561-562.

"Ruffed Grouse." *Bird Lore* 15(January, 1913):63-66.

"Shed Horns of the American Antelope." *Journal of Mammalogy* 2(May, 1921):116-117.

"Slide Rock from Many Mountains." Yo (Pseudonym). (Some articles in this series were written by another author.) (from *Forest and Stream*): 34(January 23, 1890):2; 34(March 6, 1890):122; 34(April 10, 1890):226; 34(May 22, 1890):346; 35(September 4, 1890):126; and 35(October 2, 1890):206.

"Social Organization of the Cheyennes." In *Proceedings of the International Congress of Americanists, 1902.* Easton, PA: Eschenbach Printing Co., 1905. 13:135-146.

"Snipe Shooting." *Century* 4(October, 1883):921-925.

"Some Audubon Letters." *Auk* 33(April, 1916):119-130.

"Some Autumn Birds of the St. Mary's Lake Region." *Forest and Stream* 30(May 24, 1888):348-349 and 30(May 31, 1888):368-369.

"Some Cheyenne Plant Medicines." *American Anthropologist* New Series 7(January-March, 1905):37-43.

"Some Cheyenne Tales." *Journal of American Folk-Lore* 20(April-June, 1907):169-194 and 21(July-September, 1908):269-320.

"Some Habits of the Wolverine." *Journal of Mammalogy* 7(February, 1926):30-34.

"Some Indian Natural History Comments." *Forest and Stream* 52(May 6, 1899):345.

"A Stampede." *Forest and Stream* 91(June, 1921):248-249.

"Starving Deer of the Kaibob Forest." *Outlook* 136(January 30, 1924):186-187.

"A Summer Hunt with the Pawnee." *Forest and Stream* 33(October 10, 1889):222-223.

"Swallows." *Forest and Stream* 75(December 31, 1910):1052.

"Tenure of Land among the Indians." *American Anthropologist* New Series 9(January-March, 1907):1.

"Theodore Roosevelt as a Sportsman." *Country Calendar* 1(November, 1905):623-626, 666.

"Trails of the Pathfinders" (from *Forest and Stream*): 62(February 27, 1904):162-163;"Alexander Henry" 62(March 5, 1904):182-185 and 62(March 12, 1904):206-207; "Jonathan Carver" 62(March 26, 1904):246-248; "Alexander MacKenzie" 62(April 9, 1904):290-291, 62(April 23, 1904):330-331, and 62(May 7, 1904):370-373; "Lewis and Clark" 62(May 21, 1904):414-415, 62(June 4, 1904):457-458, 62(June 18, 1904):499-500, 63(July 2, 1904):5-6, and 63(July 23, 1904):67-68; "Zebulon H. Pike" 63(August 6, 1904):106-109, 63(August 13, 1904):132-133, and 63(August 20, 1904):150-151; "Alexander Henry (The Younger)" 63(September 3, 1904):190-194,

63(September 10, 1904):215-217, and 63(October 1, 1904):277-278; "Ross Cox" 63(November 19, 1904):424-425 and 63(November 26, 1904):444-445; "The Commerce of the Prairies" 63(December 3, 1904):465-466 and 63(December 10, 1904):488-489; "The Rambler in North America" 63(December 24, 1904):529 and 63(December 31, 1904):546-547; "Townshend Across the Rockies" 64(January 7, 1905):6-7 and 64(January 14, 1905):28; "Samuel Parker" 64(January 28, 1905):66-67; "Thomas J. Farnham" 64(February 18, 1905):131 and 64(February 25, 1905):150-151; "Fremont" 64(April 22, 1905):311-312, 64(April 29, 1905):332; 64(June 3, 1905):432-433, 65(July 15, 1905):43, and 65(July22, 1905):63-64; "George Frederick Ruxton, Mexico and the Rocky Mountains" 65(October 7, 1905):288-289 and 65(October 21, 1905):327-328.

"Trappers of Oregon Territory." *Forest and Stream* 65(August 26, 1905):166-167 and 65(September 2, 1905):186.

"The Tree-Climbing Wolverine." *Journal of Mammalogy* 2(February, 1921):36-37.

"A Trip to North Park." Yo (Pseudonym). (from *Forest and Stream*): 13(September 4, 1879):611-612; 13(September 11, 1879(:631; 13(September 18, 1879):651; 13(September 25, 1879):670-671; 13(October 2, 1879):691; 13(October 9, 1879):711-712; 13(October 16, 1879):730-731; 13(October 23, 1879):751-752; and 13(October 30, 1879):771-772.

"Two Pawnian Tribal Names." *American Anthropologist* 4(April,1893):197-199.

"The 'Unprovoked' Attack by a Bear." *Journal of Mammalogy* 4(February, 1923):52-53.

"Unusual Antelope Horns." *Forest and Stream* 75(August 13, 1910):251-252.

"Was I Lost or Not?" Yo (Pseudonym). *Forest and Stream* 72(November 13, 1909):768-769.

"Western Big Game Preserves." *Harper's Weekly* 39(February 23, 1895):190.

"Western Range of the Wild Turkey." *Forest and Stream* 73(August 14, 1909):251.

"What About the Yellowstone Elk?" *Forest and Stream* 88(June, 1918):336-337.

"What We May Learn from the Indian." *Forest and Stream* 86(March, 1916):845-846.

"When Antelope Were Plenty." *Forest and Stream* 77(October 14, 1911):582-583.

"When Beaver Skins Were Money" (from *Forest and Stream*): "Bent's Fort, Pioneer Settlement of Colorado--Stirring Scenes in the Southwest" 74(January 1, 1910):8-11; "Charles Bent, Captain of Santa Fe Trains and Governor of New Mexico--His Tragic Death--The Fight at Arroyo Hondo" 74(January 8, 1910):48-50; "Amusements of the Traders--Kit Carson's Fights with Indians--The Passing of the Old Fort" 74(January 15, 1910):88-91; and "Life at Bent's Fort--Bull

Teams on the Road--Trading with the Indians--One-Eyed Juan--Frolics at the Fort" 74(January 22, 1910):128-131.

"When the Ducks Flew." *Forest and Stream* 54(February 3, 1900):84.

"White Buffalo." *Forest and Stream* 57(December 21, 1901:484.

"Who Were the Padouca?" *American Anthropologist* New Series 22(July-September, 1920):248-260.

"Wild Horses and Indians." *Forest and Stream* 71(August 8, 1908):209-210; 71(August 15, 1908):248-249; and 71(August 22, 1908):290-291.

"Wild Indians." *Atlantic Monthly* 82(January, 1899):20-29.

"Wild Life Protection." *Forest and Stream* 87(February, 1917):73-74.

"The Wild Turkey." *Forest and Stream* 73(November 27, 1909):852-854 and 73(December 4, 1909):891-892.

"Willets in Migration." *Auk* 33(April, 1916):198-199.

"Winter War Stories" (from *Forest and Stream*):"The Prophecy of Bear Man" 74(February 26, 1910):330-332; and "A Trader's Story" 74(March 5, 1910):368-371.

"With Goats and Sheep in British Columbia." Ornis (Pseudonym). *Forest and Stream* 72(April 10, 1909):574-575; 72(April 17, 1909):613-614; 72(April 24, 1909):653-654; and 72(May 1, 1909):695-696.

"Woman's Work." *Forest and Stream* 66(March 3, 1906):340-342.

"Young Dog's Dance." *Journal of American Folk-Lore* 4(October, 1891):307-313.

Studies of George Bird Grinnell

Connelley, William E. Review of *Two Great Scouts and the Pawnee Battalion* by George Bird Grinnell. *Mississippi Valley Historical Review* 16(December, 1929):426-428.

Dunn, J. P. Review of *When Buffalo Ran* by George Bird Grinnell. *Mississippi Valley Historical Review* 7(March, 1921):409.

Hedges, James B. Review of *Two Great Scouts and Their Pawnee Battalion* by George Bird Grinnell. *American Historical Review* 34(July, 1929):890-891.

King, James T. "George Bird Grinnell." In *The Reader's Encyclopedia of the American West* edited by Howard R. Lamar. New York: Thomas Y. Crowell Co., 1977. P. 468.

Linton, Ralph. Review of *The Fighting Cheyennes* by George Bird Grinnell. *Mississippi Valley Historical Review* 3(December, 1916):417-418.

Mooney, James. Review of *The Fighting Cheyennes* by George Bird Grinnell. *American Historical Review* 21(April, 1916):612-614.

23

BENJAMIN HORACE HIBBARD

by Thomas Huffman

Biography

When six-year-old Benjamin Horace Hibbard heard that the Grange leader O. H. Kelly was due to speak in an organizational rally near the Hibbard family farmstead in central Iowa, he pleaded with his father for leave from chores to attend. Young Ben never went. The elder Hibbard believed such things were best for adults, and there were very few with time to spend on such social activities. Yet, despite these early parental restrictions, Hibbard pursued his interest in the social and political side of agriculture as a schoolboy and as a young farmer.

Hibbard was born on January 9, 1870, in Bremer County, Iowa. Seven years later his family moved to O'Brien County. Here Benjamin and his three sisters grew up in a still-rugged frontier community, struggled to break the sod, and worked among the German immigrants who had settled near them. Here also he came to understand the varying characteristics of rural America that so influenced his later writings: cultural differences, cooperation, alienation, and the realities of agricultural supply and demand.

Due to the increasingly poor health of his father, Hibbard took on the responsibilities of operating the one-quarter section farm at an early age. However, the young farmer was also an incipient scholar, and he blended cultivation of the soil with cultivation of the mind by teaching country school in his free time, often reading through the dictionary during lunch to increase his burgeoning vocabulary. At the age of twenty-five, and with only thirty-five weeks of formal education behind him, Ben seized a chance to attend Iowa State University at Ames. He graduated with honors in 1898 and enrolled in graduate school in September, 1899, at the University of Wisconsin. There he fell under the spell of Frederick Jackson Turner, Richard Ely, and the growing progressive ferment of the state's political scene.

By the time Hibbard finished his Ph.D. in 1902, with a dissertation on the "History of Agriculture in Dane County," his professional life course had been set. For the next fifty-three years, despite recurring health problems, Hibbard followed a dual career in agricultural economics and history. Failing to land a position at Massachusetts Institute of Technology, partially because his mentor Turner warned the school that Hibbard was "insufficiently experienced in a city environment to be at home in Boston," Benjamin accepted an offer at Iowa State. At Ames he chaired the Department of Economics, developing generalized courses in agricultural economics. More formative study followed at the University of Halle in Germany and in 1911 as a special agent for the Agricultural Division of the U.S. Bureau of Census, where he perfected much of his statistical thinking. In 1913, another Iowa farmboy, college roommate, Turner votary, and lifelong colleague, Henry C. Taylor, lured Hibbard to the University of Wisconsin. While spending the rest of his career at Wisconsin, Hibbard helped consolidate the newly formed Department of Agricultural Economics, serving as chair from 1919 to 1932, and finally retiring as Professor Emeritus in 1940. Hibbard continued summer session teaching and research until death at eighty-five on August 11, 1955, in Madison, Wisconsin.

Much like Turner, Hibbard influenced a number of graduate students who found jobs teaching, researching, and in government. His lectures were sprinkled with wit and down-home aphorisms embedded in content that demonstrated prodigious learning in all the classics. Indeed, Hibbard once claimed in later life that he had read every book of importance in the English language. In his professional career he became involved in many organizations, including the American Economic Association and the American Farm Economic Association. And, like so many activist American intellectuals, his love of ideas led him directly into politics and policy-oriented research. Friendships with the LaFollette brothers, John Commons, Henry A. Wallace (one of his Iowa State students), and Gifford Pinchot revealed his sympathy for the progressive tradition. Ties to the U.S. Chamber of Commerce, the Republican Party, the National Association of Manufacturers, and his consistent attacks on the Non-Partisan League demonstrated his more conservative tendencies.

Themes

By 1921, as a seasoned agricultural economist and historian, Hibbard admitted that his early life with farming would permit only a sympathetic view of farmer problems. The seeds of Hibbard's rural past developed to maturity over the years in the soil of an intellectual life dedicated to understanding and promoting agrarian America. Moreover, his preoccupation with the agricultural side of American history and economics stemmed not only from the practical experience obtained in growing up on a nineteenth-century Iowa farm but also from a passionate commitment to ideas gleaned from Frederick Jackson Turner and Richard Ely while Hibbard was a graduate student at the University of Wisconsin in Madison. With these ideas in mind he produced five books and many articles and reviews on agricultural economics, policy, and history. For the historian of the American frontier, then, the multifarious work of Benjamin Hibbard is primarily important for its consistent reliance on Turnerian theory, a quality found especially in important studies of public land policy, and farmer movements.

Hibbard's scholarly writings and lectures covered agricultural policy, marketing, rural taxation and credit, farmer movements, and land policy. His popular writings and lectures disclosed concern for the social aspects of rural life, child labor, conservation, poetry, horticulture, livestock raising, Christianity, and the ethics of democracy. As a consequence of these broad-ranging interests, he, like many mainstream academics, was often accused simultaneously of being a "communist" and a "tool of business." But Hibbard consistently avowed that he had "always been known as a radical," and stopped voting Republican after Theodore Roosevelt moved to the Bull Moose Party.

Hibbard made his greatest impact as a pioneer in agricultural economics and as a popularizer of rural American life. But his historical conceptions depended more upon two major themes which he then intertwined with traditional western and agricultural history topics. The first, something he called the "value" or "concept" of land, led to *A History of Public Land Policies* (1924), an ambitious attempt to summarize the disposal and use of the public domain. This focus on the environmental impact of the land on American society and culture pervaded all of Hibbard's interaction with Clio. The second, a romantic but often critical perception of the socioeconomic role of the American farmer, led to one of the first critical works on farmer organizations and helped set the framework within which subsequent historians worked.

Analysis

Hibbard began his innovative career as land historian when introduced to the economic theories of Richard Ely and Frederick Jackson Turner. Although Ely remained Hibbard's main advisor and lifelong colleague, Turner, to Hibbard, was the consummate historian and the primary influence in his writing on public lands and farmer movements. He took every course Turner offered to graduate students and considered Turner the most inspirational teacher he had ever met. Hibbard believed that "how people lived, how they became landowners, and what sort of general thinking they did respecting politics and government" was the key historical concept Turner gave to economists (Hibbard Papers, December 11, 1946). At Wisconsin, the interrelation of the history and economics departments impelled many graduate students to take interdisciplinary study in both areas. Turner believed that economists should use history in their research, and in doing so, many of the graduate students, like Hibbard, made Wisconsin a leader in the use of historical and geographic approaches in the study of agricultural economic problems in the early part of the century. With this training, Hibbard became an agricultural historian and agricultural economist concurrently.

After two years of seminar study with Turner, Hibbard started and completed his dissertation in one year. "The History of Agriculture in Dane County" (1902) became a pioneer work as a case study in local agricultural history. In the thesis, Hibbard outlined many of the thematic motifs which he would later use in his public land studies: a critique of the role of speculators, the process of land entries under federal laws, an analysis of soil and crop types, and the selection and use of land by settlers. He based all this on a discussion of the "simple pioneer's life," which confronted environmental or agricultural changes caused first by economic factors and later by social influences and politics in late nineteenth-century Wisconsin. Together with a 1904 essay, "Indian Agriculture in Southern Wisconsin," Hibbard provided cogent descriptive studies of economic forces in action in a dynamic frontier community. Moreover, in this work he fashioned a Turnerian pattern of historical interpretation that influenced the new field of agricultural economics as well as public land history.

Richard Ely advised Hibbard to begin his career by cultivating the goodwill of the historical profession and by educating historians of the importance of economic research. Hibbard was able to demonstrate such goodwill and continue his interest in agricultural research when he was offered the opportunity to write the history of "Federal and State land policies as influential in economic development" by the Carnegie Institution in 1906. Thus began work on *A History of Public Land Policies*, the first complete, critical synthesis of public land policies; a book that Paul Gates said "marked the beginning of modern writing on public land history," and which solidified Hibbard's position as the most influential early land scholar (*Agricultural History* 55:103).

Despite some difficulties with funding the project, Hibbard sent the first draft to Turner in 1916. In the first draft of *Public Land Policies*, he drew from preliminary study done by historians, like Payson Treat in *The National Land System* (1910), and undertook to sketch the provisions of land laws to show how they worked when settlers actually used them in acquiring the public lands of the federal government and nonpublic land states from colonial times to date. By final publication in 1924, Hibbard had further processed these themes and a "stupendous mass" of information into a comprehensive depiction of American land history.

As an institutional agricultural economist writing on public land policy, Hibbard signified a new interest among scholars in the relation between land law and agriculture. He wanted to know western sentiment and how land laws actually worked and how Congress reflected them. Hibbard's economic interpretation then was essentially new, that is, that "the constant pressure of the economic law might disturb the arrangement made by political law" in influencing the direction of land policy (p. 550). He proved this to be historically accurate in discussions on the physiographic character of land, the problem of markets, the impulses of western emigration, the effect of policy and land sales, the effect of the national debt on land policy, and the conflict among regions. By focusing on "the economic impact of American public land policy in terms of national growth rates and income distribution" and its impact on settlers he was able to pose hitherto unasked questions on the historical development of the use of the American environment (*Journal of Land and Public Utility Economics* 1:238-241).

As a result of Hibbard's inclusive research, *Public Land Policies* is a compendium of statistics and abstractions of the various land laws, discussing the use of the public domain as a source of revenue, as a basis for national development, and as conservation policy. This made it more like a reference work than a logically argued monograph. Yet, in his treatment of the entire period after the passage of the Homestead Law, he was moving into new territory. And the new material contained in the chapters on speculation, homesteading, land classification, and, especially, the final chapter, "The Public Land Policies Reviewed and Criticized," greatly influenced other land historians. In this last chapter, Hibbard offered a novel analysis of the precise problems of the federal role in the public domain, and urged policies later implemented in the Taylor Grazing Act as well as the retention of public control over the remaining domain a decade before they came to pass.

The intellectual source and the driving force for the scope and content of *Public Land Policies* first came from the education in social and agricultural matters Hibbard received while a young farmer and graduate student. Later, when writing the book as a LaFollette progressive, Hibbard emphasized equity questions in the study of land history, particularly focusing on whether land policy favored the rich at the expense of the poor. The concern over speculation and land taxation rates, the impact of large land holders and corporate transgressors, the failure of a laissez-faire federal land policy, and his sympathy for the plight of the small farmer placed Hibbard in the first generation of professional land historians reflecting an agrarian viewpoint. The ongoing debate in intellectual circles over the single tax writings of Henry George reinforced this progressive interpretation of land policy. Unable to accept fully the anticapitalist ideas of George, however, Hibbard maintained, "I am not a single taxer because I believe in private property in land. For the state to confiscate these values looks to me like the most unethical proposal being made in modern times" (Hibbard Papers, January 23, 1924). He disparaged later land historians like Roy Robbins who tended to blame the collapse of federal land policy solely on the evil influence of business monopoly. He spent much of his career mulling over the ramifications of the single tax and progressive ideas, playing them off against the traditional beliefs in property ownership that he thought were deeply ingrained in the character of the American people.

Many of the Turnerian interpretations in *Public Land Policies* have been questioned by modern historians; especially those on the suitability of land laws, the impact of democracy and free land, the Homestead Law, speculation, slavery, and political parties. His use of sources and statistics was often incomplete, something contemporary reviewers also criticized. But the social science methodology, perhaps even more than the critical focus on the problems of the land laws, left a strong legacy. Turner himself recognized that Hibbard had reexamined "the sources for the subject as a whole bringing out many new aspects thereby . . . and furnishing analytical treatment such as an economist like yourself can supply" (Hibbard Papers, February 1, 1925).

Hibbard provided the first statistical analysis of the actual operation of the land disposal system by employing new quantitative evidence culled from county deed registers and federal land office records. And with thirty-six tables and eleven charts and maps he underscored the necessity of buttressing land history with numerical data. Hibbard was aware of the inadequacies of the book and, fearful of the competition increasingly posed by young land historians, spent the remainder of his life importuning for funds to be used in revision.

Modern land historians have had to recognize the original quality of *Public Land Policies* despite the oft-cited theoretical weakness of the book. In *Marketing Agricultural Products* (1921) Hibbard made some historical references to the industrial revolution and the settlement of land. But the slowness with which *Public Land Policies* proceeded through its first printing meant that the book was superseded in time by a number of other works on public lands. Such authors as Raynor Wellington, George Stephenson, and John Ise had already finished land policy treatises started after and published before Hibbard, who, apparently, failed to consult these works for the writing of his book. However, in scope and content they foreshadowed the later importance of *Public Land Policies*.

Not only did Hibbard influence his peers but his insightful research laid the foundation for the entire modern school of land history promulgated by Paul Gates. From Gates's work, starting in the 1930s, to the present, a long line of scholars, including such disparate historians as Merle Curti, Roy Robbins, Vernon Carstensen, Louise Peffer, Everett Dick, Margaret and Allan Bogue, and Robert Swierenga have continued to expand the boundaries of Hibbardian land history. Although initially inspired by Hibbard's signpost book, and also working from the ideas of Turner, Walter Prescott Webb, and James Malin, recent land historians have revised the original methodological direction and interpretation in *Public Land Policies*. Since the 1950s the new economic historians have produced "value-free" land studies using statistical theory and methods less tied to the emotional and polemical fervor of Hibbard's era. *Public Land Policies* helped start a scholarly debate that lasts to this day.

One interesting consequence of Hibbard's study of land policy was that it made him an ardent conservationist. Having rejected the nineteenth-century laissez-faire federal land policy as about as helpful "as were the incantations used in the manufacture of Damascus blades," he set himself squarely in the group of early twentieth-century intellectuals who not only advocated the wise use of nature but who also saw land as embodying aesthetic and symbolic value. Drawing both from Gifford Pinchot's practical and John Muir's "cosmic" conservation attitudes, Hibbard argued for agricultural profit while at the same time pointing out that land "in a very real sense becomes the basis of life;" that "every one or two percent of land which can be used to good purpose in making life more enjoyable is a step in the direction of a more stable basis of values of other lands" (Hibbard Papers, Speeches 1930-1934). Essentially, his concern for conservation emanated from a Turnerian belief in the closing of the frontier; that land must be used in the best possible way in light of the sociological conditions which pushed Americans to exploit and misuse land when confronted with its vastness and economic potential.

Hibbard's discussion of land tied in closely to his second strain of interpretation, the socioeconomic role of the American farmer. The fact that a cow on Hibbard's Wisconsin farm won the state milk production championship in 1921 was not insignificant, for farming consumed much of his private as well as his public life. Furthermore, his dissertation and his study of the public lands demonstrates that the main focus of his historical writing, and his economic research, was as much on the common people who settled the land as on the development of the economic and legislative machinery for the transmission of the public domain.

As Hibbard said later in his life, he first started to write the history of farmer movements because he wanted to discover why "the farmer sold his produce at a very low figure whereas the same products went on the market a little later much augmented in price"; why "city people refused to take farmers seriously, despite the fact that our democracy came from forebearers who were farmers"; and why "very few of our historians have appeared able to handle altogether well" the economic side of American agricultural history (Hibbard Papers, February 4-5, 1941). Farm power over economic and political affairs, he thought, was a key aspect in American history. This focus incorporated the historical idea that farmers had increasingly acquired an agricultural consciousness that had set them apart from the rest of American society. In *Marketing Agricultural Products* (1921) and in his textbook *Agricultural Economics* (1948) he outlined the predominating characteristic of the farmer movements: they "represented a revolt against the existing state of things and a plan for improvements, but at the same time the plan is one of many parts" (*Marketing Agricultural Products*, p. 188).

By the 1920s early agricultural historians like Solon Buck and Fred Haynes had already described the political background of some of the farmer movements. Hibbard, starting in *Marketing Agricultural Products*, defined the economic milieu of the Grange, Farmer's Alliance, American Society of Equity, the Farmer's Union, the Non-Partisan League, and the American Farm Bureau Federation, and added to these incipient analyses. From a Turnerian perspective he discussed the differences of farmers and laborers, efficiency versus overproduction, tenancy and settlement, population growth, and new technology. Inevitably, Hibbard placed his work within the often fiery debates over farm policy in the 1920s and 1930s. The farm revolt of the depression era showed that once again farmers had to reject orthodox economic views and learn that controlling the "land" meant that they could control the historical process. Although his suspicion of the farmers' penchant for stirring up "class trouble" in an effort to achieve "economic heaven" led Hibbard to reject most of the radical aspects of their programs, he defined their economic parameters in a concise and unique way.

The study of the economic influence of the farmer in American history also caused Hibbard to believe in the importance of the social impact of the agrarian lifestyle. Urban and rural life could be reconciled, he argued, only when the traditions of the country met the innovations of the city on equal ground. At the turn of the century, farm society was confronted with problems resulting from the disappearance of the frontier and the rise in modern "economic" farming as opposed to self-sufficient farming.

The movement of many farm people to the cities as a result of these processes made Hibbard wary of "modernization," for the "farm is not merely a factory or a business, it is a home. Farming is a mode of life, carrying with it a whole train of questions and problems involving education, religion, morality, and traits of character of the most fundamental kind" (Hibbard Papers, "General Files," ca. 1923). By studying the social particulars of farm movements, historians could discover the nonmaterial reasons why farmers moved to the frontier and other places; whether or not the lure to the city drained the country of its "better elements" and left the "dregs"; and what classes of people viewed from standpoints other than the ability to make money were the products of the farm. Ultimately, he believed that, once the historical frontier thirst for land was overcome and the arrogant technological urban spirit moderated, the city and the country would coexist in social balance.

Whether Hibbard's rather romantic interpretation of the social influence of the American farmer carried much weight in the historical profession is a moot point. Moreover, although drafting many outlines, he never published an inclusive monograph on farmer movements. Yet, as a recognized authority on the topic he influenced many historians, including his Wisconsin colleagues Frederic Paxson, John Hicks, and Theodore Saloutos. For instance, Hibbard reviewed manuscripts for Hicks while Hicks was chair of the Wisconsin history department. Even though Hibbard was somewhat jealous of Hicks's position as the Turnerian scholar at Wisconsin, he gave *The Populist Revolt* (1931) a semi-adulatory review, and edited to good effect the Hicks-Saloutos book, *Twentieth Century Populism* (1951). Hicks himself thought Hibbard's books had made excellent contributions to the literature on farmer movements.

In the same way, Theodore Saloutos, as a research assistant, advisee, and peer, drew many ideas from Hibbard while involved in a long career in agricultural history. In response to Saloutos' request for help in research on farmer organizations, Hibbard recommended dropping academic habits and then immersion in actual agricultural life to acquire a more "real" perspective on farmer history: "More than anything else you need a knowledge of farming and farmers," he said. "It would not take you a very great length of time to get a pretty fair insight into the general business features of farming. On the other hand, it takes longer to gain an intimate knowledge of the sociology of farmers, that is to say, their mental make-up and their views which they are likely to develop" (Hibbard Papers, November 6, 1940). So, similar to his work on land policy, Hibbard consolidated both practical and scholarly experience to produce innovative and influential work in the history of farmer movements.

By the late 1930s and early 1940s the majority of Hibbard's professional research and writing has been completed. But the initial assault on the frontier thesis after Turner's death in 1932, centering on the semantical definitions of the frontier, the safety-valve theory, and the relationship of democracy to western land settlement, prodded the elderly Hibbard to an explicit defense of the theory. In letters and articles Hibbard argued against all three lines of attack. The challenge to Turner, indeed, was a challenge to Hibbard's entire conception of history; history as he had written it in *Public Land Policies* and on farmer movements.

Hibbard's defense culminated in a long and impassioned letter sent to anti-Turnerian George Pierson of Yale in 1941 for inclusion in a series of articles published in the *Wisconsin Magazine of History* reviewing the state of the controversy (26: 36-60). For him, the frontier thesis remained an efficacious methodology, perhaps even more so than Turner himself might have advocated. Admitting his "provincial patriotism," Hibbard found in the "West" or "Middle West" a combination of elements that allowed Americans to escape from the confines of the East. The frontier was hard to define. But he had no doubt of its democratic influence, which resulted in expanded franchise, the growth of beneficial public institutions, free land and the amelioration of class strife, a new legal interpretation of human rights, and a new and fresh "Western man." He knew, however, that Turner's concept had failings; that it did not explain everything. But like many of the fervent Turnerians of the period who were incensed by the imbroglio, he believed that the attacks were ad hominem, that the critics harped on minor inconsistencies, that in essence the thesis had never been disproved by evidence, and that, in any case, the sheer number of Turner acolytes in the historical profession meant that frontier theory would have an indisputable intellectual impact for decades to come. Hibbard never doubted that his own historical work had underscored the importance of Turner.

When Hibbard died in 1955 he left many historical works uncompleted: on the Republican party, on tariffs and taxation, on demography, and on tenancy. Throughout his career he maintained that he "never got away from American History." But the kind of Turnerian analysis he practiced had become anachronistic. Caught between tradition and the new age, he was never able to overcome historical contradictions that, for instance, led him to extol western farm women as equal workers and voters on the one hand, but never reject the idea that blacks were best suited for tenancy on the other. His insistent exposition of the safety-valve theory proved inaccurate, as did his understanding of the Homestead Law and other important land policies. Furthermore, except for *Public Land Policies*, he seldom reinforced his historical statements with other than scanty evidence derived mostly from secondary sources. His historical admiration of farmer cooperation changed to worried conservatism when faced with agrarian radicalism, especially in the 1930s. And even many in his own profession, agricultural economics, had rejected the imaginative use of historical method, swinging-off instead into synchronic statistical analysis by the 1950s.

Yet Hibbard's contributions to American frontier history remain important. From Turner he acquired and then applied the idea that understanding the human relationship with the environment could produce historical scholarship of significant interpretive power. Like Turner, his ecumenical use of broad-ranging methodologies ignored the special interest barriers set up by many academic professions. In public land studies he drew upon new techniques and sources. With his work in conservation he showed the necessity of managing the American environment in national, not sectional, terms. And, his early study of farmer organizations helped define a new historical field. In retrospect, Benjamin Hibbard had the opportunity of living as a pioneer in two rather dissimilar areas: the agricultural frontier of nineteenth-century Iowa and the intellectual frontier of historical scholarship. His was both a long and productive life.

Bibliography

Books

Agricultural Economics. New York: McGraw-Hill, 1948.

Effects of the Great War upon Agriculture in the United States and Great Britain. Carnegie Endowment for International Peace, Preliminary Economic Studies of the War, Number 11. New York: Oxford University Press, 1919.

The History of Agriculture in Dane County. Vol. 101, Bulletin of the University of Wisconsin. Madison: University of Wisconsin, 1904.

A History of Public Land Policies. Madison: University of Wisconsin Press, 1924; reprinted 1965.

Marketing Agricultural Products. New York: D. Appleton and Co., 1921.

Articles

"Credit Needs of Settlers in Upper Wisconsin." *Agricultural Experiment Station Bulletin* (University of Wisconsin) 318 (1920).

"Indian Agriculture in Southern Wisconsin." In State Historical Society of Wisconsin, *Proceedings for 1904.* Madison: State Historical Society of Wisconsin, 1905. Pp. 144-155.

"Legislative Pressure Groups among Farmers." *Annals of the American Academy* 179(May, 1935):17-24.

"Tax Delinquency in Northern Wisconsin." *Agricultural Experiment Station Bulletin* (University of Wisconsin) 399 (1928).

Selected Reviews

Eastern Workingmen and the National Land Policy by Helena Zahler. *Journal of Political Economy* 49(August, 1941): 612-615.

The Farmer's Last Frontier by Fred Shannon. *Journal of Farm Economics* 28(November, 1946):1088-1091.

History of Agriculture in the Northern United States by P. Bidwell and J. Falconer. *Mississippi Valley Historical Review* 13(September, 1926):275-276.

Introduction to Agricultural Economics by L. C. Grey. *Journal of Land and Public Utility Economics* 1(January, 1925):119-121.

Revolution in Land by Charles Adams. *Journal of Political Economy* 49(December, 1941):909-912.

Studies of Benjamin Hibbard

Aydelotte, William, Allan Bogue, and Robert Fogel. *The Dimensions of Quantitative Research in History*. Princeton, NJ: Princeton University Press, 1972.

"Benjamin Horace Hibbard." *National Cyclopedia of American Biography* 43(1961):142-143.

Carstensen, Vernon, ed. *The Public Lands: Studies in the History of the Public Domain.* Madison: University of Wisconsin Press, 1963.

Erdman, Henry. "Benjamin Horace Hibbard." In *Pioneers in Marketing* edited by J. Wright and C. Dimsdale. Atlanta: Georgia State University Press, 1974. Pp. 69-70.

Gates, Paul W. "Pressure Groups and Recent American Land Policies." *Agricultural History* 55(April, 1981):103-127.

Hibbard, Benjamin, Papers. Steenbock Agricultural Library Archives, University of Wisconsin, Madison, WI.

Parsons, Kenneth. "Benjamin Horace Hibbard." *Journal of Farm Economics* 37(November, 1955):772.

Pierson, George. "American Historians and the Frontier Thesis in 1941." *Wisconsin Magazine of History and Biography* 26(September, 1942):36-60.

Schafer, Joseph. Review of *A History of Public Land Policies* by Benjamin Hibbard. *Journal of Land and Public Utility Economics* 1(March, 1925):238-241.

Swierenga, Robert. "Land Speculation and Its Impact on American Growth and Welfare: A Historiographical Approach." *Western Historical Quarterly* 8(July, 1977):283-302.

_________. "Quantitative Methods in Rural Landholding." *Journal of Interdisciplinary History* 13(Spring, 1983):787-808.

Taylor, Henry C., and Anne D. Taylor. *The Story of Agricultural Economics in the United States, 1840-1932: Men-Service-Ideas*. Ames: Iowa State University Press, 1952.

Wellington, Raynor. Review of *A History of Public Land Policies* by Benjamin Hibbard. *American Historical Review* 30(July, 1925):837-838.

24

JOHN D. HICKS

by Gerald D. Nash

Biography

During his lifetime John D. Hicks was not only a prominent student of the American West, but one of America's best known historians. His perspectives were always broad. Although dispassionate, he clearly reflected many of the values and beliefs of America's heartland in the first half of the twentieth century, from whence he sprang.

John D. Hicks was born in the small town of Pickering, Missouri, on January 25, 1890, of what he himself, with his customary impishness, designated as WASPish background. On his father's side he claimed descent from Mayflower settlers; his mother was born in a frontier log cabin. His father, John K. Hicks, was a devout Methodist preacher, an active revivalist, and as his son phrased it in his autobiography, *My Life with History* (1968), "an earnest seeker after souls" (p.19). During John's youth the elder Hicks held five pastorates in Missouri and three in Wyoming. Thus, John D. Hicks grew up in small Missouri and Wyoming towns at the turn of the century and came to know rural America intimately. Moreover, some of the men in the Hicks family felt the urge to move westward and settled in Colorado and Wyoming where young Hicks visited them during his impressionable years.

Hicks began most of his formal education in Wyoming where his father moved in 1903 to assume a succession of pastorates. Like most American boys in rural areas during this period, Hicks held a variety of jobs, including shepherding, ranch hand, and dairyman. In view of his father's meager salaries, he took it for granted that he would teach school for a few years before going on to college. In 1909 he began a two-year teaching career in a one-room school at Kaycee, Wyoming, arriving in a stagecoach, and learning to ride the range for cattle. By 1910 he set his sights on Northwestern University, a leading Methodist institution, where he enrolled with his meager savings. His father had fervently hoped that his son would become a preacher, but during his college years John abandoned this idea and became fascinated with history. In fact, he stayed at Northwestern for an extra year to earn an M.A. degree in the field.

Encouraged by his professors, in 1914 Hicks decided to pursue a doctorate and secured an assistantship at the University of Wisconsin. There he worked with a number of well-known historians including Carl Russell Fish, Winfred Root, Dana C. Munro, and Frederic L. Paxson. Since Hicks shared Paxson's interests in the American West and recent United States history, he chose him as his major professor. Hicks wanted to write a dissertation on Populism or some phase of agricultural reform, but Paxson insisted that he study the constitutional history of six northwestern states admitted into the Union in 1889 and 1890. That Hicks did, with some reluctance, because financial pressures made it imperative for him to secure his degree as rapidly as possible.

Armed with his doctorate in 1917, Hicks embarked on what was to become a distinguished teaching career. He got his start at Hamline University, a Methodist college in St. Paul, Minnesota. Here he was the sole member of the history department. He taught a wide range of courses in European and American history. After five years at Hamline he moved to North Carolina State at Greensboro. There he stayed for one year only because the University of Nebraska offered him a position where he could concentrate on western American and recent history. He also served as dean of the college of arts and sciences from 1929 to 1932. When Paxson left Madison for Berkeley in 1932, Hicks was chosen as his successor at the University of Wisconsin, teaching western and recent American history. He remained for a decade before following his mentor to the University of California in 1942. At Berkeley he also served for a year as dean of the graduate school before retiring in 1957. He continued to be active in lecturing, writing, and research until his death in 1972.

Themes

Unlike some historians of his generation, Hicks was not readily identified with any one historical theory or approach. As a scholar sensitive to the changing influences shaping American society, he tended to be eclectic. A superb synthesizer and an acute critic, he kept his options open to consider diverse approaches. His mind was particularly adept at creative synthesis, and he had the ability to crystallize the essential elements of a historical problem. He focused these talents on many aspects of American history, but he specialized in the history of the American West and recent United States. In the later stages of his career he began to merge these two interests by developing the history of California and the West in the twentieth century.

Four themes, among many, stand out in Hicks's diverse writings. First, he found the theme of sectionalism, particularly the unique growth of the West, to be significant. Although exposed to Turner's frontier hypothesis at the University of Wisconsin in the World War I era (after Turner had left for the East), Hicks early became aware of its limitations. "As time went on," Hicks wrote in later years, "I found my interest turning away from the frontier and more and more toward the history of the whole section" (*My Life*, pp. 145-146). True, he said that when he wrote *The Populist Revolt* (1931), "I was still uncritical, as were most American historians, of Turner's theories, and found greater significance in the passing of the frontier than I would now [1968] think reasonable" (p. 162).

Instead, he gradually came to place greater emphasis on the impact of technology on American development, a second main theme of his writings. Referring to agricultural changes, he notes in 1968 that "I would now give greater emphasis on the effects of the agricultural revolution, and particularly to the increasingly international aspects of American farm marketing" (pp. 162-163). Clearly, such influences were related to economic factors which constituted a third theme in Hicks's writings about American life. By 1954 he was writing about the significance of economic influences and indicated frankly in 1968 that industry had reached an overwhelming superiority over agriculture. A fourth major theme was his emphasis on the twentieth century, in contrast to most of his contemporary colleagues who felt that it was not within the province of professional historians, particularly with reference to the West.

Analysis

Hicks's first published book, *The Constitutions of the Northwest States*, was his doctoral dissertation, an analysis of the constitutions adopted by six western states in 1889 and 1890 upon their admission to the Union. Appearing in 1924, when Hicks was teaching at the University of Nebraska, the work received favorable reviews. Yet Hicks was never happy with it. "I was never very proud of my thesis," he later commented, and "came to regret that it was published" (*My Life*, p. 88). He did not touch the subject again during his lifetime. In good Turnerian fashion, Hicks, in the study, focuses on the political innovations made by the farmers of western state constitutions as they built on their eastern inheritance.

But once he had earned his degree, Hicks turned to his original interest in Populism. Despite job changes and a growing family he patiently combed newspapers, personal manuscripts, and archives for more than a decade. He wrote articles and reviews, but it was not until 1931 that he published his major work, *The Populist Revolt*. Appearing in the depth of the depression, the timeliness of this work, in addition to its sound research and judicious judgments, made it an immediate success. The book had a profound impact on the profession, then and in later years. In his analysis Hicks chronicles the destructive impact of industrialism on the nation's farmers, particularly those in the West. But Hicks is not so much bemoaning the changes that made the Populists dispossessed Americans as he is providing an understanding of their predicament, and of the political movement with which they hoped to salvage their agrarian heritage. The study is meticulously documented and dispassionately written even if Hicks's sympathies lay with those farmers who questioned uncritical acceptance of the new industrial order. Although innumerable specialized studies of Populism appeared in the five decades after the first appearance of *The Populist Revolt*, they did not really supercede it, either in content or in many of its judgments.

Ironically, in view of the intense interest in Populism after World War II, Hicks felt in the 1930s that the subject was a bit passé. Instead, he shifted his own interests and those of his graduate students to later reform movements, particularly progressivism and the New Deal. He himself embarked on the arduous task of writing a textbook on American history. *The Federal Union* appeared in 1937, and *The American Nation* four years later. Both volumes quickly established themselves as the most concise historical syntheses of the American experience in print and for several decades were widely used in hundreds of colleges and universities.

But *The Populist Revolt* had also kindled Hicks's interest in regionalism, and his next major project was a history of the Middle West. That book was never written, although he published several articles related to the project. "I conceived the idea of writing a history of . . . the Middle West . . . from the earliest times to the present that would point up its continuing significance in the life of the nation," he writes. "No longer could I regard the frontier--if ever I had--as an adequate key to American development; in particular, economic influences, both national and international, were essential to the understanding of nation and section alike" (*My Life*, pp. 162-163). But various circumstances conspired to prevent him from bringing the study to completion during the 1930s. Not only was he preoccupied with the writing of his textbook, he also collaborated with one of his doctoral students to write a history of agrarian reform movements after Populism, and that joint venture with Theodore Saloutos, *Agricultural Discontent in the Middle West, 1900-1939*, was ultimately published in 1951. It demonstrates how many of the proposals of the Populists and succeeding agrarian reformers were gradually institutionalized in federal farm programs in the first four decades of the twentieth century.

Moreover, Hicks moved to the University of California in 1942, where he broadened his interests. Paxson continued to teach his course on the westward movement there until 1947 so that Hicks tactfully concentrated more intensely on the twentieth century. "I had expected that my second lecture course would be the history of the West," Hicks recalled. "Paxson said as much during our negotiations. But I quickly sensed that he had no real desire to give up that course, so I filled in such neglected gaps as I noted in the history curriculum" (pp. 220-221). Although Hicks was now not teaching western history, he combined his lifelong interest in the West with twentieth-century history, not through his own publications but by directing more than a score of graduate students in the next fifteen years. Among the books that encompassed the twentieth-century history of California were those of George Mowry, Clarke Chambers, Vincent Carosso, Robert E. Burke, and Gerald D. Nash. With the exception of Mowry, who had finished his doctorate at the University of Wisconsin, all of these works originated as dissertations at Berkeley. They reflect Hicks's belief that historians should concentrate greater attention on the history of the West after 1900.

With retirement Hicks devoted increased time to research and produced three books, in addition to articles and reviews. He completed *Republican Ascendancy*, a volume that synthesized the decade of the 1920s in *The American Nation* series. The book reflects a neo-Populist or traditional liberal interpretation of the decade, critical of the politics of that era which Hicks considered to have contributed to the Great Depression. In a related book, *Rehearsal for Disaster*, Hicks perceptively analyzes the postwar crisis of 1919 which he perceives as a prelude to the Great Crash of 1929 and the depression of the 1930s. He continued to use the comparative approach by comparing the 1920s and the 1950s in numerous talks and published essays. In response to numerous requests he began to write his autobiography in the 1960s. It was published in 1968 as *My Life with History*. More than just a personal account, it is a fascinating analysis of far-reaching changes in the historical profession during his lifetime.

Hicks was a warmhearted individual who attracted undergraduates and graduates alike. His contributions to American history were diverse. In his day he was one of the ablest synthesizers in the field, as his textbooks indicate. His focus on the significance of the West as a region found expression in *The Populist Revolt*. His contributions to the development of recent American history took form in *Republican Ascendancy* and *Rehearsal for Disaster*. And in fusing the two major interests of his career--the West and twentieth-century America--he provided inspiration for the next generation of historians to explore the history of the twentieth-century West.

Bibliography

Books

Agricultural Discontent in the Middle West, 1900-1939. Co-authored with Theodore Saloutos. Madison: University of Wisconsin Press, 1951.

The American Nation: A History of the United States from 1865 to the Present. Boston: Houghton Mifflin Co., 1941.

The American Tradition. Boston: Houghton Mifflin Co., 1955.

The Constitutions of the Northwest States. Vol. XXIII, nos. 1-2, University Studies Series. Lincoln: University of Nebraska, 1924.

The Federal Union: A History of the United States to 1865. Boston: Houghton Mifflin Co., 1937.

My Life with History. Lincoln: University of Nebraska Press, 1968.

The Populist Revolt: A History of the Farmers' Alliance and the People's Party. Minneapolis: University of Minnesota Press, 1931.

Rehearsal for Disaster. Gainesville: University of Florida Press, 1961.

Republican Ascendancy, 1921-1933. New York: Harper and Bros., 1960.

A Short History of American Democracy. Boston: Houghton Mifflin Co., 1943.

Articles

"Adventures in Popular Scholarship." *Saturday Review of Literature* 35(June 14, 1952):14.

"American Foreign Policy in Perspective." *Social Education* 12(October, 1948):247-252.

"American History in Colleges." In *American History in Schools and Colleges* edited by Edgar B. Wesley. New York: Macmillan, 1944. Pp. 85-93.

"The American Professor in Europe." *The Pacific Spectator* 6(Autumn, 1952):428-441.

"The American Tradition of Democracy." *Hawaii Educational Review* 34(January, 1948):168.

________. *Utah Historical Quarterly* 21(January, 1953):25-41.

"The Birth of the Populist Party." *Minnesota History* 9(September, 1928):219-247.

"The Birth of Our Farm Protest." *Co-op Grain Quarterly* 13(August, 1955):39-44.

"The California Background--Spanish or American?" *The Westerner's Brand Book* 5(June, 1948):21-23, 26-28.

"California in History." *California Historical Society Quarterly* 24(March, 1945):7-16.

"Changing Concepts of History." *Western Historical Quarterly* 2(January, 1971):21-36.

"The Development of Civilization in the Middle West, 1860-1900." In *Sources of Culture in the Middle West* edited by Dixon Ryan Fox. New York: Appleton Century Co., 1934. Pp. 72-101.

"The 'Ecology' of Middle Western Historians." *Wisconsin Magazine of History* 24(June, 1941):377-384.

"Faith of Our Fathers: Recent Trends in American Democracy." *California Monthly* 61(September, 1950):12-13, 39-41.

"The Farmer's Alliance in North Carolina." *North Carolina Historical Review* 2(April, 1925):162-187.

"The Legacy of Populism in the Western Middle West." *Agricultural History* 23(October, 1949):225-236.

"Lincoln, Defender of Democracy." *Prairie Schooner* 4(Winter, 1930):16-25.

"Memorial to Joseph Schafer." *Wisconsin Magazine of History* 24(March, 1941):249-252.

"The Organization of the Volunteer Army in 1861, with Special Reference to Minnesota." *Minnesota History Bulletin* 2(February, 1918):324-368.

"The Origin and Early History of the Farmers' Alliance in Minnesota." *Mississippi Valley Historical Review* 9(December, 1922):203-226.

"Our Own Middle West, 1900-1940." In *Democracy in the Middle West, 1840-1940* edited by Jeannette P. Nichols and James G. Randall. New York: Appleton Century, 1941. Pp. 97-117.

"Our Pioneer Heritage." *Prairie Schooner* 2(Winter, 1928):16-28.

"The People's Party in Minnesota." *Minnesota History Bulletin* 5(November, 1924):531-560.

"The Persistence of Populism." *Minnesota History* 12(March, 1931):3-20.

"The Place of the State University in a Democratic Society." *Journal of Dental Education* 12(December, 1947):68-78.

"The Political Career of Ignatius Donnelly." *Mississippi Valley Historical Review* 8(June-September, 1921):80-132.

"The Postwar Generation in Arts and Letters--American History." *Saturday Review of Literature* 36(March 14, 1953):14-15, 63-64.

"The Responsibilities of Citizenship." *Social Education* 4(October, 1940):383-386.

"Revisionist Trends in American History." In *Western College Association, Addresses on War-Time Problems of Higher Education.* Berkeley: University of California, 1943. Pp. 19-21.

"The Revolution in American Foreign Policy." *California Monthly* 56(April, 1946):23, 36-37.

"The Roots of American Radicalism." *California Monthly* 59(September, 1948):12-13; 59(October, 1948):14-15, 43.

"Six Constitutions of the Far Northwest." *Proceedings of the Mississippi Valley Historical Association* 9(December, 1922):360-379.

"Some Parallels with Populism in the Twentieth Century." *Social Education* 8(November, 1944):297-301.

"The Sub-Treasury: A Forgotten Plan for the Relief of Agriculture." *Mississippi Valley Historical Review* 15(December, 1928):355-373.

"Teaching United States History and Civics in California." *California Journal of Secondary Education* 19(November, 1944):352-371.

"The Text Book in America: A Symposium--A College Professor." *Saturday Review of Literature* 35(April 19, 1952):22-23.

"Then (1891) and Now (1966): Some Comparisons and Contrasts." *Nebraska History* 47(June, 1966):139-155.

"The Third Party Tradition in American Politics." *Mississippi Valley Historical Review* 20(June, 1933):3-28.

"Two Postwar Decades." *Nebraska History* 40(December, 1959):243-264.

"The Urban Revolution." *Pacific Northwest Quarterly* 57(October, 1966):181-188.

"The Western Middle West, 1900-1914." *Agricultural History* 20(April, 1946):65-77

"Why We Fought: A Reconsideration." *Social Education* 6(May, 1942):200-204.

Selected Reviews

America is West: An Anthology of Middlewestern Life and Literature edited by John T. Flanagan. *American Historical Review* 51(July, 1946):734-735.

American Radicalism, 1865-1901: Essays and Documents by Chester McArthur Destler. *Pacific Historical Review* 16(May, 1947):193-194.

The Attainment of Statehood edited by Milo M. Quaife. *Mississippi Valley Historical Review* 17(December, 1930):471-473.

Benjamin Franklin, Printer by John Clyde Oswald. *Mississippi Valley Historical Review* 4(September, 1917):248-249.

Colorado: The Story of a Western Commonwealth by Le Roy R. Hafen. *American Historical Review* 39(July, 1934):790-791.

The Cowboy: His Characteristics, His Equipment, and His Past In The Development of the West by Philip Ashton Rollins. *Mississippi Valley Historical Review* 11(June, 1924):140.

Coxey's Army: A Study of the Industrial Army Movement of 1894 by Donald L. McMurry. *American Historical Review* 35(April, 1930):641-642.

The Culture of the Middle West by the Lawrence College Faculty. *American Historical Review* 50(April, 1945):624-625.

Current Problems of Public Policy: A Collection of Materials by Charles A. Beard and George H. E. Smith. *Mississippi Valley Historical Review* 23(March, 1937):595.

Discontent of the Polls: A Study of Farmer and Labor Parties, 1827-1948 by Murray S. Stedman, Jr., and Susan W. Stedman. *American Historical Review* 56(October, 1950):216-217.

The Farmers' Last Frontier: Agriculture, 1860-1897 by Fred A. Shannon. *Pacific Historical Review* 15(March, 1946):113-114.

Fighting Liberal: The Autobiography of George W. Norris by George W. Norris. *American Historical Review* 51(January, 1946):343-344.

George N. Peek and the Fight for Farm Parity by Gilbert C. Fite. *Mississippi Valley Historical Review* 41(September, 1954):359-360.

The Historian's Workshop: Original Essays by Sixteen Historians edited by L. P. Curtis, Jr. *Pacific Historical Review* 41(February, 1972):92-93.

The Historical World of Frederick Jackson Turner with Selections from His Correspondence by Wilbur R. Jacobs. *Journal of American History* 56(September, 1969):413-414.

The Hunting of the Buffalo by E. Douglas Branch. *Mississippi Valley Historical Review* 16(September, 1929):266-267.

Ignatius Donnelly: The Portrait of a Politician by Martin Ridge. *American Historical Review* 68(April, 1963):768-769.

J. Sterling Morton by James C. Olson. *Pacific Historical Review* 12(June, 1943):215-216.

Jay's Treaty: A Study in Commerce and Diplomacy by Samuel Flagg Bemis. *Mississippi Valley Historical Review* 11(June, 1924):130-132.

Joseph Schafer, Student of Agriculture by Edward Porter Alexander. *Pacific Historical Review* 12(December, 1943):431.

The Life of James J. Hill by Joseph Gilpin Pyle. *Mississippi Valley Historical Review* 5(September, 1918):223-225.

The Making of an American Community: A Case Study of Democracy in a Frontier County by Merle Curti *et al.* *Pacific Historical Review* 28(November, 1959):395-396.

Minnesota in the Spanish-American War and the Philippine Insurrection by Franklin F. Holbrook. *Mississippi Valley Historical Review* 10(September, 1923):195-197.

The Older Middle West, 1840-1880: Its Social, Economic, and Political Life and Sectional Tendencies before, during, and after the Civil War by Henry Clyde Hubbart. *American Historical Review* 42(January, 1937):358-360.

The Other Side of Main Street: A History Teacher from Sauk Centre by Henry Jackson. *Pacific Historical Review* 12(September, 1943):318-319.

The Pioneer West: Narratives of the Westward March of Empire by Joseph Lewis French. *Mississippi Valley Historical Review* 11(June, 1924):140.

The Pragmatic Revolt in American History: Carl Becker and Charles Beard by Cushing Strout. *Mississippi Valley Historical Review* 46(June, 1959):111-112.

Probing Our Past by Merle Curti. *Pacific Historical Review* 24(August, 1955):299-300.

The Public Papers of Francis G. Newlands edited by Arthur H. Darling. 2 volumes. *Mississippi Valley Historical Review* 19(December, 1932):450-451.

The Range Cattle Industry by Edward Everett Dale. *Mississippi Valley Historical Review* 17(March, 1931):645-647.

Sons of the Wild Jackass by Ray Tucker and Frederick R. Barkley. *Mississippi Valley Historical Review* 19(March, 1933):602-603.

Theodore Roosevelt and the Rise of American World Power by Howard K. Beale. *Pacific Historical Review* 26(August, 1957):302-303.

Theodore Roosevelt Cyclopedia edited by Albert B. Hart and Herbert R. Ferleger. *Mississippi Valley Historical Review* 28(September, 1941):279-280.

Tom Watson, Agrarian Rebel by C. Vann Woodward. *Journal of Southern History* 4(November, 1938):538-539.

The Union Colony at Greeley, Colorado, 1868-1871 edited by James F. Willard. *Mississippi Valley Historical Review* 6(December, 1919):426-427.

The United States, 1830-1850: The Nation and Its Sections by Frederick Jackson Turner. *American Historical Review* 41(January, 1936):354-357.

The Whig Myth of James Fenimore Cooper by Dorothy Waples. *American Historical Review* 45(October, 1939):173-174.

Studies of John D. Hicks

Blegen, Theodore C. Review of *Populist Revolt: A History of the Farmers' Alliance and the People's Party* by John D. Hicks. *American Historical Review* 38(January, 1933):347-349.

Billington, Ray Allen. Review of *My Life with History: An Autobiography* by John D. Hicks. *Journal of American History* 56(June, 1969):165-166.

Buley, R. Carlyle. Review of *Agricultural Discontent in the Middle West, 1900-1939* by Theodore Saloutos and John D. Hicks. *Mississippi Valley Historical Review* 38(December, 1951):530-532.

Clark, Dan E. Review of *The American Nation: A History of the United State from 1865 to the Present* by John D. Hicks. *Mississippi Valley Historical Review* 28(September, 1941):293-294.

Dale, Edward Everett. Review of *The American Tradition* by John D. Hicks. *Mississippi Valley Historical Review* 43(September, 1956):342-343.

Dyer, Brainerd. Review of *My Life with History: An Autobiography* by John D. Hicks. *Pacific Historical Review* 38(August, 1969):342-344.

"Hicks, John D." In *Who Was Who in America, 1969-1973*. Chicago: Marquis-Who's Who, Inc., 1973. P. 332.

Johnson, Walter. Review of *Republican Ascendancy, 1921-1933* by John D. Hicks. *Mississippi Valley Historical Review* 47(December, 1960):530-531.

Libby, O. G. Review of *The Constitutions of the Northwest States* by John D. Hicks. *Mississippi Valley Historical Review* 11(March, 1925):594-595.

Nichols, J. Harley. Review of *The Populist Revolt :A History of the Farmers' Alliance and the People's Party* by John D. Hicks. *Indiana Magazine of History* 27(December, 1931):345-347.

Nichols, Roy F. Review of *The Federal Union: A History of the United States to 1865* by John D. Hicks. *Mississippi Valley Historical Review* 24(March, 1938):559-560.

Noblin, Stuart. Review of *Agricultural Discontent in the Middle West, 1900-1939* by Theodore Saloutos and John D. Hicks. *Journal of Southern History* 18(May, 1952):253-254.

25

STEWART H. HOLBROOK

by Robert E. Ficken

Biography

Reading a Boston newspaper's survey of the state of American history as of 1950, Stewart Holbrook found himself ranked with George Bancroft, Francis Parkman, Henry Adams, and Samuel Eliot Morison as "eminent" chroniclers of the nation's past (Holbrook Papers, Diary, October 13, 1950). A posthumous Sinclair Lewis novel published the following year included a passage mentioning Carl Van Doren, Bernard DeVoto, and Holbrook as outstanding historians of the United States (Diary, March 25, 1951). Until budget conditions forced a reduction in positions, Holbrook served with DeVoto, J. Frank Dobie, and Arthur Schlesinger, Jr. on the original editorial board of the History Book Club (Diary, May 15, 1946). These were heady associations for an Oregon author who lacked academic credentials and pridefully regarded himself as a "low-brow historian" (Diary, November 8, 1935).

Stewart Hall Holbrook was born in Newport, Vermont, on August 12, 1893. Moving from place to place with his father, who at various times operated a drugstore and a hotel and dabbled in land investment, Stewart received the ragged schooling of rural New England. The Holbrooks eventually traveled to Manitoba for yet another fling in real estate speculation. His father's sudden death left Stewart, still in his teens, adrift in the Canadian prairies (Littleton, NH *Courier*, September 10, 1964).

At first, Holbrook worked as a reporter for a Winnipeg newspaper. Then, in 1913, he signed on for a season with "the worst dramatic stock company an accursed God ever permitted to roam." Passing back and forth across the international boundary, Holbrook became friendly with Boris Karloff, a fellow trouper, and met Charlie Chaplin. Stranded in Minneapolis when the company went bankrupt, Holbrook sang in theaters and developed a vaudeville routine based upon ethnic caricatures (Holbrook Papers, Crown, August 5, 1947).

Eventually, just prior to America's involvement in World War I, he returned to New England, where he continued to perform while supporting himself in the more mundane occupation of general store clerk. After wartime service as an artillery sergeant, Holbrook worked log drives on the Connecticut River and then set out for the unknown wilds of the West. "Yankees were born," he wrote many years later, "with an uncommon urge to see, with their own eyes, if the grass on the other side of the mountain really was greener" (*The Yankee Exodus*, p. 10).

Holbrook's curiosity took him in 1920 across the continent to the rugged and forested coast of British Columbia. Here was to be found, the newcomer believed, the last genuine frontier, the place "where men have their faces to the sea, and can go no further." In this land of towering firs was also to be rediscovered the true pioneering spirit, "the opening-up-of-the-country idea" (*Far Corner*, pp. 4, 6, 10, 30). There was, Holbrook later wrote, no respite from the exhilaration of expanded horizons and possibilities: "The whole place was filled with so much vitality, and there was so much going on and so many places and things to see, that I could not get up early enough nor stay up late enough to take it all in" (Holbrook Papers, Crown, August 5, 1947).

For three years, Holbrook worked as a clerk in the isolated logging camps of British Columbia. The insights and much of the material that would animate his subsequent writings were gathered in this period. He carried the broken bodies of injured loggers from the woods and fought a terrifying forest fire. He experienced wage cuts and the loneliness of life cut off from the civilized pursuits of urban culture (*Burning an Empire*, pp. 3-10). Throughout the remainer of his life, Holbrook's sensitivities would never be far from the timber and from the men whose task it was to transform the "round stuff" into logs and lumber.

Holbrook also sought an outlet for his artistic streak by sitting up nights writing stories. Sketches of life in the American Expeditionary Force were often accepted for publication by veterans' magazines. Submissions to such general interest periodicals as *Whiz Bang* and the original *Life* garnered rejection slips, those frustrating accompaniments to the fledgling writing career. Lumber industry trade publications, though, proved eager to print short pieces about the logging camps, often illustrated with the author's own rude cartoons.

Through this early mixture of success-and-failure, Holbrook determined to make a career as a professional writer. Nonfiction with a historical bent was his chosen route into the literary world. As an abortive effort or two demonstrated, he later recalled, he was incapable of writing "the crap that makes most 'popular' novels." But history offered enough drama to be a different matter. "There is so much good and unknown Americana to be written," observed an enthused Holbrook, "that I wish I could be subsidized to do it" (Holbrook Papers, Holbrook to M. T. Dunten, March 2, 1935; April 18, 1939).

The decision to become a writer required a return to the United States. In the spring of 1923, Holbrook relocated to Portland, Oregon, where he would maintain his home for most of the remainder of his life. As Holbrook knew, the writer of nonfiction, especially one at the beginning stages of an uncertain career, required an outside means of support. Upon arrival in Portland, therefore, he secured a position as associate editor of the *Four L Lumber News*, the editorial voice of a rather unique effort in regional labor organization. The Loyal Legion of Loggers and Lumbermen--usually referred to as the Four Ls--had been created during World War I by the army to join management and labor in a patriotic campaign to maximize lumber production. Following the war, employers continued the organization as something of an industry-wide company union. Its main purpose was to provide institutional opposition to the remnants of the Industrial Workers of the World (IWW or Wobblies). Until 1927, when he became editor of the *Lumber News*, Holbrook divided his time between writing copy and field organization work. At one time, he claimed to have visited every camp and mill in Oregon, Washington, and Idaho (Holbrook to Allan Nevins, March 9, 1959; *Far Corner*, p. 233).

Editorial labors did not provide a sufficient outlet for Holbrook-the-writer. The *Lumber News* was to literary quality, he once remarked, what Billy Sunday was to theology (Holbrook to Dunten, June 12, 1930). Happily, Holbrook began in mid-decade to achieve recognition as a magazine writer. In September, 1924, *Sunset* paid $50 for a piece on the IWW, "my first large check for an article." A year later, the *American Mercury* accepted an essay on Wobbly terminology, commencing a long relationship with that publication and its editor, H. L. Mencken. Other articles appeared in what Holbrook described as "such cultural journals as The Sat. Eve. Post and True Confessions" (Holbrook to Dunten, March 1, 1926; Diary, September 19, 1924 and October 31, 1925).

These writings focused on the lives of the men who worked in the timber. Popular forest literature of the time centered on such subjects as the Paul Bunyan legends assembled by Holbrook's friend, James Stevens. Holbrook, though, debunked the alleged folklore status of the Bunyan stories, contending that virtually all of them were the invention of Stevens and other literary confidence artists (Holbrook to Nancy Larrick, January 25, 1958). As for scholarly works of labor history, they dealt in his view almost exclusively with deadening administrative details. The "chief attention" in such studies was "paid to the exact moment that Local 89 of the Vulcanized Amalgamation of Tyrd Shovellers, Thinners & Heavers passed a resolution of faith in T. Powderly" (Holbrook to Dunten, June 16, 1931).

Holbrook's interest, in contrast, was in the actual--if sometimes embellished--experiences of everyday workers. His articles ignored economics and "conservation ideas . . . for the common logger, the guy I was writing about, never heard of either" (Holbrook to Emanuel Fritz, April 23, 1938). The material gathered during his years in the camps provided both dramatic color and genuine insight into the world of the forest industry. Writing in a breezy style about working people, Holbrook earned his original Oregon reputation as a "low-brow historian."

There developed within Holbrook a tension between the need to produce articles that would sell and the need to be taken seriously as a man of literature. "My philosophy of writing," he explained in early 1926, "is that [it] is far more important to know *what* to write and *where* to send it, than in the writing per se. Literary quality is quite secondary" (Holbrook to Dunten, March 1, 1926). Yet, as he noted on another occasion, "there is absolutely no satisfaction in writing for slicks other than the check" (July 1, 1939). The normal aggravations of the freelancer's life accompanied this internal struggle over quality versus quantity.

However frustrating, the mid-1920s was a period rich with promise in comparison to the aftermath of the crash on Wall Street. The Great Depression crushed alike the prospects of the lumber industry and regional authors. The Four Ls, caught between its financial dependence on management and the rise of new independent timber unions, declined amidst wage and salary cuts and internal bickering. Although privately vowing to terminate his association with the organization, a dispirited Holbrook continued to edit the *Lumber News* until 1934. A meal ticket was certainly a necessity because of the collapse of Holbrook's writing career. "The mss market," he lamented in mid-1931, "is as bad off as the so-called stock market" (June 16, 1931).

Caught in the vise of the depression, Holbrook suffered humiliation upon humiliation. For a time, he collaborated with H. L. Davis and James Stevens on a radio series based upon the latter's Paul Bunyan stories. Poor ratings, though, brought an early cancellation. Then, just as the nation's economic fortunes began to revive during the initial phase of the New Deal, so, too, did Holbrook's stalled career.

In 1934, he began writing a column for the Portland *Oregonian*, as well as frequent editorials and Sunday features. It was, wrote Holbrook, "like being turned into a new pasture." He could, among other joys, make regular use of words that "would have been uncomprehensible to 99 percent of Lumber News readers" (September 13, 1934). Magazines, ranging from detective pulps to *Esquire*, again purchased his articles. Holbrook also was appointed in 1935 to edit the WPA guide for the state. This assignment, which he described as "the turning out of boondoggerel," required six months of trying labor (December 29, 1935, February 1, 1936; Diary, December 2, 5, 7, 1935). Numerous and often bizarre government regulations had to be mastered. The prose submitted by a staff of fifty-four writers, of whom only four were regarded as competent, had to be assembled into readable copy. The final product was a state guide regarded by the literary bureaucrats of the WPA as a model for the series (Diary, March 25, 1936).

Fortified by the income from these assorted tasks, Holbrook also began in 1935 to write "the book," as he referred to his first full-length venture. Given the official working title, "Bughouse Camp," the manuscript distilled Holbrook's magazine pieces and personal experiences into a colorful protrayal of life and labor in the woods. Unfortunately, the would-be book was rejected by at least three New York publishers (October 20, 21, November 18, 1935; February 10, April 27, 1936; March 26, 1937). On a happier note, a fruitful meeting with the Macmillan Company's Harold Latham, famed as the "discoverer" of Margaret Mitchell, led in April, 1937, to a contract for the revised manuscript that became *Holy Old Mackinaw: A Natural History of the American Lumberjack* (April 17, 22, 23, 1937).

Published in 1938, *Mackinaw* surveyed the history of America's lumber industry from the pineries of New England to the firs of the Northwest coast. Holbrook focused on the idea of the logger as an elemental force of the nation's successive frontiers: "Before houses could be built and farms plowed there had to be a clearing and there had to be logs and boards." This was the vital task of the man of the woods, with his ax and saw and greased-down skidroad (pp. vii-viii). Part history and part folklore, *Mackinaw* made Holbrook an instant literary celebrity. An approving review, complete with a brooding author's photograph, appeared in *Time* magazine (31:70-71). The book spent over five months on national bestseller lists.

He was not so carried away, though, as to fail to recognize that here at last was a chance to establish the basis for a successful career. There was scant hope, Holbrook believed, that an Oregon author could earn a sustained and decent living from regional books. Rather, the money and the future lay in dealing with broad topics from a base close to national publishers. Thus, in July, 1938, Holbrook abandoned Portland and took up residence in Boston. Here Holbrook turned out book after book: a history of the steel industry, a biography of Ethan Allen, and a collection of murder mysteries derived from earlier articles in detective magazines. A disturbing trend, however, followed upon the outbreak of World War II in September, 1939. American readers, their attention diverted by the grim news from abroad, seemed to have lost interest in conventional books. Although Holbrook turned out a volume on the nation's initial battlefield heroes in 1942, he looked to alternative means of financial support for the duration.

James Stevens, who had become an official of a lumber trade association, invited Holbrook to return to the Pacific Northwest as director of the Keep Washington Green campaign. A cooperative venture between the state and private timber owners, the program meant to reduce losses from forest fires. Over the next four years, Holbrook spent the summers in Seattle, writing press releases and "canned" editorials and articles for publication in local newspapers. From the $500 monthly stipend for his work came the wherewithal to spend the remainder of each year writing for magazines.

Out of this wartime emphasis on timber protection came the decision to write a history of American forest fires. Holbrook determined in part to write a narrative account of such great conflagrations as the 1871 Peshtigo fire, the Hinckley fire of 1894, the Cloquet fire of 1918, and the Tillamook Burn of 1933. He would also go beyond the mere recounting of death and destruction to explain the historical causes and consequences of fire. It was a book, as Bernard DeVoto noted in a letter, that was "right up the alley of a man to whom summer will always have a whiff of smoke in it and a faint dullness in the sun" (Holbrook Papers, DeVoto to Holbrook, August 11, 1943).

Published in 1945, *Burning an Empire: The Story of American Forest Fires* established fire as a vital aspect of the frontier experience. "Smoke," argues Holbrook, "was for many years taken to be a sign of progress, of development. What fire burned, a man did not have to clear; and clearing the forest . . . was held to be the greatest duty of man" (p. 109). Through fire, the settler transformed an apparent wilderness into civilization. And, through fire, the abandoned detritus of logging became the barren back-country counties of New England and the Great Lakes. Here indeed was a demonstration of the profligacy of the national culture. "Probably no other people on earth," sums up Holbrook, "are so thoughtless, so careless with fire, as Americans" (p. 25).

Burning an Empire marked a transition in the emphasis of Holbook's work. The chronicler of the life of the working man became the defender--some would say the apologist--of the so-called Timber Baron. This latter personage had once been regarded as a heroic figure. But rising popular interest in conservation had transformed him into "one son of a bitch proper" as the despoiler of America's environment. To Holbrook, there could be nothing more ridiculous than the thought that lumbermen, those calculating creatures of profit, would wantonly destroy millions of dollars worth of timber. Rather, the true blame, if blame there was, lay in irresponsible land-clearing activities. The virtuous settler, however, was the prototypical American and could not be so easily given "whipping boy" status by the developers of the conservationist ethos (pp. 46-48).

Holbrook's long exposure to the woods and the unsentimental work of professional foresters enabled him to make a credible argument on this point. Logging, he contended, did not destroy the forest forever, as "the seeds for its rebirth are [left] on the ground" (p. 47). But if fire was allowed to pass over the cutover land, the basis for regeneration would be obliterated. Those who would preserve the nation's timber supply, therefore, would best concentrate on combatting the fire menace through patrols, permits, and careful removal of slash. If this sensible course had been taken in the past, Holbrook points out, "the northern states from Maine through Minnesota would still be founded on forest products" (Holbrook Papers, Holbrook to Henry Beston, May 14, 1943). *Burning an Empire*, then, was both history and polemic attempting to educate the public as to forest reality.

As suggested by this book's assault on conventional wisdom, Holbrook regarded himself as an iconoclast. To his way of thinking, "the goddamned stuffed-shirt historians" had long since concocted a standardized view of the nation's past and a conventional list of colorless characters. "Their heirs," noted Holbrook of the profession, "have simply been rewriting the story, adding little or nothing." Few educated Americans, for example, had ever heard of John Wesley Powell, yet the explorer of the arid West was more important "than a thousand Martin Van Burens and such." Holbrook now took upon himself the task of rescuing the truly significant figures of American history from the "dust" of "unread documentaries, historical quarterlies, monographs, unpublished diaries . . . and newspapers" (Holbrook to Joseph K. Howard, January 11, 1944; to George Savage, October 24, 1940).

This was the explicit purpose of Holbrook's first postwar effort, *Lost Men of American History* (1946). "The basic theory of the book," he noted in a letter to a friend, "is that thousands of unknown or forgotten Americans contributed more to our country than many of the stuffed-shirts they told you and me about in school" (Holbrook to John Guthrie, November 26, 1943). To ensure proper breadth of treatment, suggestions were solicited from H. L. Mencken, Bernard DeVoto, Henry Steele Commager, Pearl Buck, and other friends. Much of Holbrook's spare time during the war was devoted to preparatory reading. The summer of 1944 was given over to research in New York, where Allan Nevins proffered the use of his Columbia University office. The result was a volume that told the "true" story of the Boston Massacre and the War of 1812 and educated readers as to the significance of such neglected men and women as Herbert Spencer, Margaret Sanger, and Thorstein Veblen.

During the writing of *Lost Men*, Holbrook returned to Portland on a permanent basis. Working from this Oregonian base, he made the writing of further serious and large-scale historical works the focus of his career. In 1947, he began work on *The Yankee Exodus: An Account of Migration from New England*. Stirred by his own experiences, Holbrook had long been interested in the role played by emigrants from his native region. Yet the only extant treatment of the subject was a 1909 doctoral thesis, "a sound and unreadable book, done with the timidity and woodenness usual to professors" (Holbrook to H. S. Latham, May 31, 1949; Diary, September 5, 16, 1947). Appearing in 1950, *Exodus* detailed in a virtual state-by-state fashion the multifarious activities of voluntary exiles from the old Puritan heartland. "The Yankee exodus to all parts of the American West, and occasionally into the South," argues Holbrook, "is the most influential movement our country has known" (p. 10).

Within months of publication, Holbrook was engaged in writing *The Age of the Moguls* for Doubleday's "Mainstream of America" series. This most colorful of his postwar works dealt with the formative figures of American big business, from Astor and Commodore Vanderbilt to the industrialists of the late nineteenth century. Holbrook differed from the prevailing--to borrow the title of a popular rival treatment of similar subject matter--Robber Baron thesis. His moguls "plundered and wasted," but they "were also builders." In the latter counterpoint was to be found the true mogul significance: "no matter how these men accumulated their fortunes, their total activities were of the greatest influence in bringing the United States to its present incomparable position in the world of business and industry" (pp. x, 360-361).

A subsequent "Mainstream" volume by Holbrook, *Dreamers of the American Dream* (1957), tells the reverse side of the story. Here he writes of the reformers, visionaries, and radicals--from Dorothea Dix to Eugene Debs, from Alexander Graham Bell to Helen Keller--of the industrial epoch. This project, though, lacked the invigorating element of villainy and proved all but depressing to the author. *Dreamers*, confessed Holbrook upon the book's completion, "took more out of me than Moguls did." Always attuned to what was likely to sell, he anticipated a modest public reception. "My fellow Americans," reflected Holbrook, "had much rather read about pirates (Moguls) than assorted nuts (Dreamers)" (Holbrook Papers, Diary, April 11, 1957; Holbrook to Lewis Gannett, February 14, 1955). At least the latter continued the process of educating readers about the little-known aspects of their nation's history.

Interspersed among these large-scale books were a series of profitable, if often unsubstantial, works. In 1945, Holbrook edited an anthology of Pacific Northwest literature, a project which left him privately "amazed" that such contemporaries as Archie Binns, Vardis Fisher, and Nard Jones "should be considered even 2nd rate writers" (*Promised Land*; Holbrook Papers, Diary, June 26, 1953). Two years later, he was out with a history of railroading in the United States (*Story of American Railroads*). For a $10,000 fee from the Case farm implement company, he wrote an account of the development of agricultural machinery focusing on the firm's activities (*Machines of Plenty*). During the mid-1950's, Holbrook literally dashed off children's biographies of Wild Bill Hickok, Davey Crockett, and Wyatt Earp for the Random House "Landmark" series. Finally, a short biography of railroad magnate James J. Hill appeared in 1955.

Time was also found by Holbrook for his only book-length forays into Pacific Northwest history. In 1952, Macmillan published *Far Corner: A Personal View of the Pacific Northwest*. This volume combined an autobiographical account of the author's early years in the region with a reworked collection of previously-published articles on Oregon and Washington. The following year, Holbrook agreed to cover the Columbia River for Rinehart's "Rivers of America" series. Known among local authors as a "real jinx" because at least one writer had already failed to honor a contract for the book, *The Columbia* (1956) amounted to a general regional history.

Holbrook was obviously both a prolific and a successful author. During 1955, for example, he undertook five separate book projects. *Moguls* and *Dreamers* were selections of the Book-of-the-Month Club. The former spent five months on the bestseller list. Combined sales for the "Landmark" juvenile biographies, each requiring only a few weeks of labor, exceeded 200,000 copies. Holbrook's relative affluence--he earned $51,000 from his writings in 1954--was reflected in an elegant home and a Mercedes for his second wife. After casting four previous presidential ballots for Norman Thomas, he voted for Eisenhower in 1952 (Holbrook Papers, Diary, November 4, 1952).

Despite his popular success, Holbrook still regarded himself as falling short of the stature of a major serious historian. "I grow cautious these days," he reflected at the age of sixty-five, "for it is late, very late, and I want my next book to have a long life, with modest sales, rather than a B. of the M[onth] sale, then obsolescence" (Holbrook to Ken Williams, October 3, 1959). By 1960, he was engaged in the volume on the American Revolution for a series edited by Eric Goldman and was himself developing a series of historical works on western forts. These endeavors came to an end in 1963 when Holbrook suffered a major stroke. A partial recovery left him incapable of working more than an hour or two a day. His diary, kept in meticulous form over the decades, deteriorated into an occasional entry rendered in an illegible scrawl. Shortly after returning from a last visit to New England, Stewart Holbrook died in Portland on September 3, 1964.

Themes

The nonscholar writing narrative history for a general audience rarely develops consistent themes. Several constants, however, can be found in the works of Stewart Holbrook. Whether his subject was the logger, the financier, or the ameliorator of social evil, he always dealt with the pioneer. The lumberjack confronted the forested wilderness, the railroad baron drove tracks across arid plain and mountain crag, and the reformer attempted against all odds to rectify the ills of the industrial age. All typified the spirit--what Holbrook characterized as the desire to discover if the grass really was greener on the far side--of the actual pioneers crossing the continent.

These pioneers were readily grouped together as the outsiders of society. They turned their backs on conventional standards and institutions in order to seek new opportunities. The original overland migrants--and it made no difference whether the trail led from Boston to backcountry New York and Pennsylvania or from the Missouri to Oregon--did so in an especially dramatic fashion. But so did the logger who left comfort behind to toil in the forest. So, too, did an Astor or a Rockefeller, devising new means of organizing industry and gathering wealth. And so did the early reformers, who, if much admired by subsequent chroniclers, were often ridiculed by contemporaries as hapless visionaries.

Holbrook's historical world of pioneers, while occasionally peopled with such females as Dorothea Dix and Margaret Sanger, was overwhelmingly masculine. He reflected in this the traditional view of the frontier and of the Pacific Northwest. The most chauvinist of modern historians would likely admit that women also traveled the Oregon Trail, braved the ballyhooed Indian "menace," and even worked in camps and mills. But for Holbrook and most writers of his generation, the history of the West was the story of big men confronting equally big obstacles of nature and barbarism. According to his point-of-view, the significant past was to be found in the tall timber, not in the tearoom.

All of Holbrook's characters shared a passion for action. The great moguls, for example, had often been described "as rogues, robbers, and rascals. But never as feeble. The least of them had a splendid audacity and a vital energy that erupted in astonishing ways" (*Age of the Moguls*, p. viii). The industrial barons, and the other pioneers as well, shaped their own destiny and that of the nation. "I am an addict," confessed Holbrook, "to what is often dismissed by professors as the Hero Concept of History." The currents, movements, and other organizing concepts devised by scholars were of significance. Still, continued Holbrook, "I believe that men, even one man or one woman, often have had immense effect in slowing or hastening the forces that are said to make history; that they have had the ability, sometimes of genius, to catch or direct as through a funnel the great currents that are flowing and ebbing around them" (Holbrook Papers, notes to *The Oregon Story*, April 10, 1959).

Just such a process, Holbrook believed, had taken place in the far corner of the Pacific Northwest. This was especially true of Oregon, where the old Yankee individualist ethos had been most completely commingled with the heartiness of the frontier. Yet, at mid-century, the pioneer commonwealth was under seige from the alien ideas of effete easterners and rabid Californians. Holbrook in his later years thus became a progenitor of the unboosterish movement to save Oregon for genuine Oregonians. In articles, lectures, and books, he explained to a friend in 1951, "I always play [up] our vast rains, and gloomy skies; and of late have added a good line, viz, the danger to male glands of the Handford [sic], Wash., atomic plant" (Holbrook to Lucius Beebe, April 8, 1951). Like the near-extinct oldtime lumberjack, the pioneer spirit was both vital and endangered. Life would be more orderly with its demise, but it would also be much less interesting.

Readers of Holbrook would search in frustration for a clear and detailed exposition of these views about the meaning of the frontier. Nor could these themes, once deduced, be regarded as original to his work. In the year of Holbrook's birth, Frederick Jackson Turner had explained the historical importance of the American frontier. Turner had pointed as well to the possible malignant consequences of the erasure of the boundary between settled and unsettled territory. The great historian developed his ideas through research and mental effort. Holbrook, who probably never read Turner, came to his through experience and close observation of the final throes of the pioneer era. Down these contrasting avenues to understanding--the one intellectual and the other experiential--can be found a major difference between "high brow" and "low brow" history.

Analysis

Essays in historiography rarely take note of the so-called popular historians. Due, among other sins, to improper devotion to footnotes and colorless writing, these individuals are usually deemed unworthy of rank among scholars. In Stewart Holbrook's case, a chasm looms between the number of books he produced and the contribution he made to historical understanding. The irony of his career was that he would be least remembered for those works undertaken in the effort to earn recognition as a serious historian.

From *Lost Men* in 1946 through *Dreams* in 1957, Holbrook believed he was breaking new ground in American history. At last, the true story of forgotten events and the real contribution of neglected individuals were brought to light. Yet this confident assertion belied a limited exposure to extant literature. *The Age of the Moguls*, for example, was in the view of Thomas C. Cochran, "a retelling of old stories." If colorful details were desired, one might better consult Matthew Josephson. And the antidote to the Robber Baron poison existed in the Allan Nevins biographies of Rockefeller and Ford (*Saturday Review* 36:11-12). The same point held true for Holbrook's other large works. For the most part, the "lost men" had already been rescued and awareness of the "dreamers" had already been awakened.

Holbrook's significance depends more upon two earlier books. *Holy Old Mackinaw* is an early journalistic attempt to tell history from the "underside." As Holbrook noted prior to its writing, the literature of labor history tended toward turgid chronologies of internal union politics. *Mackinaw*, in contrast, successfully conveys a sense of the gritty drama of life in the woods. The book, though, is a harbinger of changes taking place in historiographical perception, rather than an influential agent in those changes. *Mackinaw* is more the product of personal experience than exhaustive research and modern historians pay it scant attention.

Of more importance, *Burning an Empire* is an original attempt to deal with the impact of fire on the course of American history. Holbrook sought not just to relate the horrible details of past forest conflagrations, but to explain the actual consequences of fire in remaking the national landscape. Until the appearance of Steven Pyne's massive *Fire in America* in 1982, Holbrook's book remained the most significant work on its topic. Because of the relatively sophisticated approach he brought to a complex phenomenon--forest fires, after all, were more than the simplistic product of the greed and stupidity of lumbermen--Holbrook deserves ranking as a pioneer of environmental history.

Throughout his career, in good and indifferent books alike, Holbrook displayed the virtues and the vices of the popular historian. He was, more than anything else, blessed with the knack for turning out lively and straightforward prose. Books, he observed, "ought to zip in every chapter" (Holbrook Papers, Holbrook to Latham, November 23, 1941). In a series of pithy sentences, he could convey the terror of being trapped by the advance of a forest inferno. This, given the bland standard of the historical profession, was an important point in his favor.

But Holbrook also regarded himself as a superb researcher. "We ought to have no little of what the professors term 'source material'," he wrote at the outset of one project, "by which I mean . . . first-hand stuff not yet in books" (Holbrook to Edmund Fuller, August 18, 1945). At least with respect to his larger works, this laudable aim was pursued in libraries and historical societies across the country. Indeed, Holbrook concluded that some of his books were actually overstuffed with "damned information" (Diary, August 3, 1949). Unfortunately, the effort was often haphazard, leaving important primary and secondary sources unconsulted. "Mr. Holbrook," observes John Garraty of this tendency, "does not try to overpower either himself or his readers with deep investigations of every aspect of his subjects" (*Saturday Review* 40:31). Selective research, of course, could lead to commission of error. Informed readers of *The Columbia*, for instance, blanch at the lengthy account of Kamiakin's plot to exterminate Washington and Oregon settlers in the mid-1850s (pp. 106-108).

Scholars reviewed Holbrook's books only upon rare occasion and then in a tone that was both critical and patronizing. Cochran, for example, found *The Age of the Moguls* to be both "entertaining" and a failure in terms of research and thought. "If the 'popularizer'," he contends, "does not take the time to read the up-to-date standard scholarly works to acquire the results of new primary research, he is not performing his educational function" (*Saturday Review* 36:10-11). Garraty considers *Dreamers*, if well-written, to be derivative: "When he offers interpretations they are usually the interpretations of others." At least, continues this critic, Holbrook was scrupulous in admitting his borrowings and crediting his sources (p. 32).

Holbrook bristled at these assaults, especially the casting of aspersions on his research efforts. The Cochran review of *Moguls*, he privately responded, "belong[s] in the son-of-a-bitch class" (Holbrook Papers, Holbrook to Gannett, December 16, 1953). With firm pride in his own attention to detail, Holbrook delighted in discovering factual errors in the work of scholars (Holbrook to H. L. Mencken, October 19, 1944). Of academic historians, he regarded only Henry Steele Commager and Allan Nevins--and he wasn't totally convinced about Nevins--as worthy of respect (Holbrook to Lee Barker, October 9, 1953; to Lloyd Lewis, October 1, 1945).

Over the long perspective, Stewart Holbrook's ultimate importance may well come to rest upon his status as a successful freelance historian. Through diligent effort and fortunate connections, he built a career that was at the least financially remunerative. Moreover, he personifies the debate over what is more valuable: second-rate history told in first-rate style to a wide audience, or first-rate history told in second-rate style to a limited audience.

Bibliography

Books

The Age of the Moguls. Garden City, NY: Doubleday & Company, Inc., 1953.

America's Ethan Allen. Boston: Houghton Mifflin Co., 1949.

Burning an Empire: The Study of American Forest Fires. New York: The Macmillan Company, 1945.

The Columbia. New York: Rinehart & Co., 1956.

Dreamers of the American Dream. Garden City, NY: Doubleday & Company, Inc., 1957.

Ethan Allen. New York: The Macmillan Company, 1940.
Far Corner: A Personal View of the Pacific Northwest. New York: The Macmillan Company, 1952.
The Golden Age of Quackery. New York: The Macmillan Company, 1959.
Green Commonwealth: A Narrative of the Past and a Look at the Future of One Forest Products Community. Seattle: Dogwood Press, 1945.
Holy Old Mackinaw: A Natural History of the American Lumberjack. New York: The Macmillan Company, 1938.
Iron Brew: A Century of American Ore and Steel. New York: The Macmillan Company, 1939.
James J. Hill: A Great Life in Brief. New York: Alfred A. Knopf, 1955.
Let Them Live. New York: The Macmillan Company, 1938.
Little Annie Oakley & Other Rugged People. New York: The Macmillan Company, 1948.
Lost Men of American History. New York: The Macmillan Company, 1946.
Machines of Plenty: Pioneering in American Agriculture. New York: The Macmillan Company, 1955.
Murder Out Yonder: An Informal Study of Certain Classic Crimes in Back-Country America. New York: The Macmillan Company, 1941.
A Narrative of Schafer Bros. Logging Company's Half Century in the Timber. Seattle: Dogwood Press, 1945.
None More Courageous: American War Heroes of Today. New York: The Macmillan Company, 1942.
Northwest Corner: Oregon and Washington, the Last Frontier. Garden City, NY: Doubleday & Company, Inc., 1948.
The Old Post Road: The Story of the Boston Post Road. New York: McGraw-Hill, 1962.
Promised Land: A Collection of Northwest Writing. Editor. New York: Whittlesey House, 1945.
The Rocky Mountain Revolution. New York: Holt, 1956.
The Story of American Railroads. New York: Crown Publishers, 1947.
The Yankee Exodus: An Account of Migration from New England. New York: The Macmillan Company, 1950.

Selected Articles
"Anarchists at Home." *American Scholar* 15(October, 1946):425-438.
"Annual Address to the Oregon Historical Society." *Oregon Historical Quarterly* 41(December, 1940):427.
"Beard of Joseph Palmer." *American Scholar* 13(October, 1944):451-458.
"Coast to Coast on the Steam Cars." *American Scholar* 16(April, 1947):183-191.
"First Bomb." *New Yorker* 20(October 7, 1944):42-46.
"Melancholy on a Hill." *American Scholar* 17(October, 1948):407-416.
"Murder at Harvard." *American Scholar* 14(October, 1945):425-434.

"My Grandfather Was Accessory after the Fact." *American Scholar* 20(January, 1951):57-70.
"Mythmakers." *New Yorker* 24(July 31, 1948):38-39.
"The Peshtigo Fire." *American Scholar* 13(April, 1944):201-209.
"There She Stands. . . ." *New England Quarterly* 23(March, 1950):3-18.
"There They Stand, the Yankees." *American Scholar* 10(April, 1941):220-227.
"You are a cheap cad, he said." *Saturday Review of Literature* 28(October 13, 1945):30-31.

Selected Reviews

The Klondike Fever: The Life and Death of the Last Great Gold Rush by Pierre Berton. *Saturday Review of Literature* 41(November 8, 1958):21.
Wiring a Continent: The History of the Telegraph Industry in the United States, 1832-1866 by Robert Luther Thompson. *Pacific Historical Review* 17(May, 1948):214-215.

Studies of Stewart H. Holbrook

Catton, Bruce. Review of *The Columbia* by Stewart H. Holbrook. *American Heritage* 7(April, 1956):109-110.
Cochran, Thomas C. Review of *The Age of the Moguls* by Stewart H. Holbrook. *Saturday Review of Literature* 36(October 10, 1953):10-11.
French, Allen. Review of *Ethan Allen* by Stewart H. Holbrook. *American Historical Review* 46(April, 1941):668-669.
Garraty, John. Review of *Dreamers of the American Dream* by Stewart H. Holbrook. *Saturday Review of Literature* 40(October 26, 1957):31-32.
Garver, Frank H. Review of *Lost Men of American History* by Stewart H. Holbrook. *Mississippi Valley Historical Review* 33(December, 1946):497-498.
Gates, Paul W. Review of *The Age of the Moguls* by Stewart H. Holbrook. *Pacific Historical Review* 23(August, 1954):288-289.
Goodykoontz, Colin B. Review of *The Yankee Exodus: An Account of Migration from New England* by Stewart H. Holbrook. *American Historical Review* 56(January, 1951):361-362.
Handlin, Oscar. Review of *The Yankee Exodus: An Account of Migration from New England* by Stewart H. Holbrook. *William & Mary Quarterly* 8(January, 1951):140-141.
Hicks, John D. Review of *Machines of Plenty: Pioneering in American Agriculture* by Stewart H. Holbrook. *Saturday Review of Literature* 38(August 6, 1955):21, 40.
Holbrook, Stewart H., Papers. University of Washington Library, University of Washington, Seattle, WA.
Lind, Katherine Miles, Review of *Holy Old Mackinaw: A Natural History of the American Lumberjack* by Stewart H. Holbrook. *American Journal of Sociology* 44(March, 1939):762-763.

Marx, Leo. Review of *The Story of the American Railroads* by Stewart H. Holbrook. *New England Quarterly* 21(September, 1948):416.

McMurry, Donald L. Review of *Iron Brew: A Century of American Ore and Steel* by Stewart H. Holbrook. *Mississippi Valley Historical Review* 27(June, 1940):151-152.

"Obituary." Littleton, NH *Courier*, September 10, 1964.

Paine, Clarence S. Review of *Little Annie Oakley & Other Rugged People* by Stewart H. Holbrook. *Pacific Historical Review* 18(May, 1949):259-260.

Powers, Alfred. *History of Oregon Literature*. Portland, OR: Metropolitan Press, 1935.

Pyne, Stephen J. *Fire in America: A Cultural History of Wildland and Rural Fire*. Princeton, NJ: Princeton University Press, 1982.

Shepard, H. B. Review of *Burning an Empire: The Study of American Forest Fires* by Stewart H. Holbrook. *New England Quarterly* 17(March, 1944):123-125.

Time 31(April 4, 1938):70-71.

Tryon, W. S. Review of *The Old Post Road: The Story of the Boston Post Road* by Stewart H. Holbrook. *American Historical Review* 68(April, 1963):822.

__________. Review of *The Yankee Exodus: An Account of Migration from New England* by Stewart H. Holbrook. *Mississippi Valley Historical Review* 37(December, 1950):525-527.

Tyler, Robert L. Review of *The Rocky Mountain Revolution* by Stewart H. Holbrook. *Pacific Historical Review* 26(May, 1957):189.

Walster, H. L. Review of *Machines of Plenty: Pioneering in American Agriculture* by Stewart H. Holbrook. *Agricultural History* 30(January, 1956):45-46.

Waterman, W. R. Review of *Lost Men of American History* by Stewart H. Holbrook. *American Historical Review* 52(July, 1947):746-747.

Winther, Oscar O. Review of *Far Corner: A Personal View of the Pacific Northwest* by Stewart H. Holbrook. *Mississippi Valley Historical Review* 39(December, 1952):574-575.

26

GEORGE TALBOT HUNT

by James P. Ronda

Biography

By any simple understanding of culture and geographical setting, George Talbot Hunt should not have become a leading student of the Iroquois and their eastern frontier neighbors. Born on Wyoming's Wind River Shoshone Indian Reservation in 1899, Hunt was the product of a western world far removed from the eastern woodlands. But those Atlantic reaches of a distant frontier held special attraction for a young man anxious to make his way in the world. After brief service in World War I, Hunt pursued a career in journalism writing for newspapers in both Philadelphia and Boston.

Early in the 1920s a restless George Hunt drifted to the isolated eastern Nebraska hamlet of Stella. Then as now Stella was a tiny cross-roads village serving the farmers of northern Richardson County. Armed only with a high school diploma and considerable writing experience, Hunt was hired as principal of the local high school. He stayed in Stella for a year (1922-1923) and then moved north to Weeping Water, Nebraska. For the next five years Hunt served as principal of the Weeping Water High School. It was during those early years at Weeping Water that Hunt decided to seek a college degree. The distance to Lincoln made attending the University of Nebraska impossible. Not to be thwarted, Hunt began taking classes at the state normal school in nearby Peru. He completed the undergraduate degree in 1927. The next year Weeping Water's school board promoted Hunt to superintendent of schools. George Hunt plainly loved rural Nebraska. When asked years later to review the Federal Writers' Project *Nebraska: A Guide to the Cornhusker State,* he spoke with knowing fondness about the place that had been his home for ten years.

But a new degree, earlier experiences in eastern cities, and a growing interest in American history drew Hunt beyond the world of Stella and Weeping Water. Early in 1930 he began graduate study in American history under John D. Hicks at the University of Nebraska. Hicks was then engaged in some of the most important research of his long career and his seminars were challenging and exciting. In 1932 Hunt received a master of arts degree in American history.

Hunt's years in Lincoln and his association with Hicks convinced him of his calling to advanced study and a university position. When John Hicks left Nebraska for the University of Wisconsin, Hunt followed him to pursue doctoral studies. It was in Madison that Hunt began to explore the Iroquois and the Beaver Wars. While Hicks was not especially interested in either Indian-white relations or eastern frontiers, he did encourage Hunt's research. Perhaps more important for Hunt's growing scholarship was the influence and support of Louise Phelps Kellogg, research associate at the Wisconsin State Historical Society. Kellogg's experience working with Reuben G. Thwaites on a massive edition of *The Jesuit Relations* and her own book *The French Regime in Wisconsin and the Northwest* (1925) had made her aware of the rich documentary sources for the study of Iroquois history and culture. Hunt's dissertation, a study of war and trade in the Iroquois world, made use of just those sources. At a time when most colonial historians believed Francis Parkman to be the last word on Iroquois-European relations, Hunt's topic was a daring choice.

Hunt spent most of the early 1930s in Madison. After receiving his Ph.D. in 1935, he moved to Cleveland to become acting head of the Department of History at Cleveland College-Western Reserve University. The following year he was confirmed as chairman of the department. Already burdened with administrative duties and the preparation of his dissertation for publication by the University of Wisconsin Press, Hunt eagerly entered into the public life of Cleveland.

Although Hunt was to make important contributions to the academic study of history, his long years in the public school system led him to see himself as more educator than professional historian. In 1939 he prepared a series of radio lectures on the theme of "Democracy." Hunt's broad knowledge of American history and his public speaking skills insured success, and more lectures were broadcast during the war years. Busy with these pursuits and departmental duties, Hunt wrote no more than an occasional book review. After the publication of *The Wars of the Iroquois* in 1940 there is no evidence that he intended to continue either Iroquois or colonial frontier research. By 1945-1946 his health began to fail. A hurried trip to Arizona in the winter of 1947 to regain his strength proved fruitless. In April, Hunt returned to Cleveland, entered University Hospital, and died on April 18.

Themes

Few groups of Native Americans have so fully captured the imagination of both the public and professional historians as the Iroquois of New York. Iroquois warriors and diplomats have come to symbolize both backwoods violence and highflown rhetoric. In American culture the Iroquois is the essential eastern woodlands Indian. By the time George Hunt came to write about what he called "the Iroquois Problem"--the hows and whys of the Beaver Wars of the seventeenth century--there had been at least two solutions offered to explain Iroquois violence and expansion. In his epic series on Anglo-French conflict in North America, *The Jesuits in North America in the Seventeenth Century* (1867), Francis Parkman insisted that Iroquois behavior was sparked by some innate passion for war and violence. Caught in the racial theories of his age, Parkman considered "insensate fury" and "homicidal frenzy" as keys to Iroquois motivation. Others, no less influenced by racial notions, simply accepted Iroquois success at face value and asked how that success was possible. One of these was Lewis Henry Morgan. Lawyer by profession but student of Iroquois culture by avocation, Morgan claimed in his *League of the Ho-De-No-Sau-Nee or Iroquois* (1851) that the Five Nations' strength was based on superior political organization. Morgan believed that the Iroquois confederacy had a political and military unity that no rival--neither native nor European--could match.

When George Hunt began his research on the Iroquois and the fur trade, he quickly rejected both Parkman and Morgan. Perhaps through Louise Kellogg he was introduced to an essay largely ignored by others studying the colonial frontier. In 1915 historian and political scientist Charles H. McIlwaine wrote a persuasive introduction to a collection of New York Indian documents, *An Abridgment of the Indian Affairs . . . transacted in the Colony of New York from the Year 1678 to the Year 1751* edited by Peter Wraxall. Where Parkman and Morgan had seen either bloodthirsty savages or astute diplomats, McIlwaine saw men dominated by powerful market forces. He argued that Iroquois imperialism was directed by a ceaseless search for fresh supplies of beaver and other pelts. Increasingly dependent on European manufactured goods, the Iroquois needed peltry to purchase guns and iron pots. McIlwaine maintained that Iroquois relations with Europeans and other Indians focused on a desire to serve as "middlemen between the 'Far Indians' and the English, a role that enabled them . . . to retain a position of superiority over the Indians of the eastern half of the United States" (p. xlii). Troubles between the Iroquois, the French, and their Huron neighbors were the result of a wholly economic drive for fur. McIlwaine's interpretation was very nearly a brand of economic determinism. Along with historians like Charles A. Beard and James Harvey Robinson, McIlwaine found such an economic view both logical and scientific. As Allen W. Trelease wrote years later in 1962, "the economic interpretation of history came like a fresh breeze to at least the younger generation of historians, dispelling the stale air of heroic and moralistic treatments which enveloped so much of the historical landscape during the nineteenth century" (*Mississippi Valley Historical Review* 44:35).

George Hunt was one of those younger historians captivated by the economic interpretation. He writes approvingly of McIlwaine's essay, calling it "the best historical writing yet done on the Iroquois" (*The Wars of the Iroquois*, p. 187). Uncritically accepting McIlwaine, Hunt refines and expands the economic view. In *The Wars of the Iroquois* Hunt limits his inquiry to the period from Champlain to the 1690s. These were indeed years of intense conflict--a time when confederacy warriors devastated

Huron villages and raided in the distant Illinois country. Applying McIlwaine's dictum that trade was an ultimate foreign policy goal, Hunt proceeds to cast all Iroquois behavior in an economic mold. Hunt believes that the commercial demands of the fur trade radically transformed Iroquois life. Denying any continuity with the precontact past, he writes that "old institutions and economies had profoundly altered or disappeared completely at the electrifying touch of the white man's trade" (p. 5).

Hunt sought to apply his economic master theme by looking at two central episodes in Iroquois history. By the 1640s the Hurons had become valued partners with the French in an extensive northern fur trade system. In that exchange network the French were the newcomers, junior partners, relying on Huron skill and knowledge to make trade profitable. In the late 1640s Iroquois warriors launched massive raids against the Huron towns. By 1650 those towns were smoking ruins and the Hurons a scattered people. For Hunt the destruction of Huronia provided a classic example of Iroquois behavior rooted in the iron laws of economic necessity. He argues that as beaver supplies in Mohawk and Seneca homelands dwindled, warriors dependent on Dutch (and later, English) trade goods were forced to find new and reliable sources for peltry. Shrewd Iroquois planners, so Hunt believes, saw Huron power and wealth built on brokering furs between northern hunters and French buyers. Putting words in Mohawk mouths, Hunt has native diplomats say, "furs they must have, and here [Huronia] were furs enough to satisfy their wildest desires" (p. 65). Hunt's Iroquois, bound in capitalist straitjackets, were intent on becoming the new fur trade middlemen, passing furs and guns around a circle of hands while reaping great rewards for themselves.

Having explained the costly Iroquois-Huron conflict in economic terms, Hunt turns to the Five Nations' expansion in the Great Lakes. Here too he finds that Iroquois raids in the Illinois country and the resultant French tensions all sprang from the unbending laws of fur trade supply and demand. As the Iroquois had done to the Hurons, so now Hunt insists they were doing to Indians in the middle Mississippi Valley. In one telling passage Hunt summarizes his entire argument, revealing both its economic assumptions and the tendency to exclude all noneconomic motives: "The fall of the Hurons, the rise to affluence and power of the Ottawa, the depopulation of western Ontario and Michigan, and the repopulation of Wisconsin, the conquest of Pennsylvania and Ohio--all these were the results of the efforts of the Five Nations to get furs and assume the position held by the Hurons before 1649" (p.54). Hunt is convinced that the Iroquois had become pawns in a fur trade capitalism that erased earlier ways and made the people of the longhouse prisoners in an alien economic system. As he argues near the end of his book, "European trade was the major circumstance of all intertribal relations in the Great Lakes area, and the Iroquois and all their works were phenomena of that context" (p. 161).

Analysis

Although *The Wars of the Iroquois* proposed a dangerously monistic and determinist interpretation of native behavior, the book gained quick approval from many historians. Randolph Downes, author of *Council Fires on the Upper Ohio* (1940), reviewed it for the *Mississippi Valley Historical Review.* Downes praises Hunt's careful use of the sources but evidently checked few if any citations. Downes also accepts without qualm the book's economic thesis (27:287-288). University of Toronto anthropologist T. F. McIlwraith, writing in the *American Historical Review,* raises no doubts about either Hunt's approach or his conclusions (46:615-616). Leo Srole's review in the *American Journal of Sociology* is equally positive, describing *The Wars of the Iroquois* as a "pioneer and important contribution to the field" (46:616).

When Hunt's book appeared in 1940, there were very few scholars qualified to review it. Historians of the eastern frontiers were busy studying elusive traces of democracy in Puritan towns while anthropologists generally neglected the documentary record. One of the very few who knew both the Iroquois past and present was William Fenton, an ethnologist working for the Federal Bureau of American Ethnology on New York Iroquois reservations. Fenton's comments in the *American Anthropologist* amounted to the only searching critique Hunt's book had either in 1940 or for many years after. While praising Hunt for rejecting Parkman and Morgan, Fenton expresses grave doubts about Hunt's methods and conclusions. Fenton's considerable field experience told him that Hunt's belief that the fur trade had wholly transformed Iroquois life was simply untrue. Fenton points to a number of important instances of cultural continuity, including examples that cast real doubt on Hunt's use of the sources. Most telling, Fenton challenges Hunt's interpretation of Iroquois warfare. Hunt maintains that Five Nations warriors were instruments of economic hegemony. Fenton observes that native warfare had many motives, including revenge, the taking of captives for adoption, and the acquisition of personal status. Fenton's review came at a time when few historians read journals outside Clio's domain. Thus, the red flags he raised went largely unnoticed for more than twenty years (42:662-664).

Despite Fenton's warnings, *The Wars of the Iroquois* soon became the standard source used in texts and cited with approval in bibliographies. Historians bent on finding Puritan capitalists and tidewater entrepreneurs could easily accept the notion of native people as participants in a larger capitalist system. It was not until the early 1960s that colonial historians began to chip away at what McIlwaine and Hunt had proposed. In 1962 Allen W. Trelease published "The Iroquois and the Western Fur Trade: A Problem in Interpretation" in the *Mississippi Valley Historical Review.* Trelease's essay was a direct, and largely successful, attack on the middleman thesis and Hunt's use of sources. Trelease undertook a careful evaluation of all Hunt's citations bearing on the middleman argument. What he found was that Hunt had misread much evidence and ignored even more. "Taking the evidence as a whole," Trelease writes, "there is no question that the Iroquois occasionally served or aspired to serve as middlemen in the western fur trade; but such activity was sporadic and of slight importance" (44:48). In this essay, and in his earlier book, *Indian Affairs in Colonial New York: The Seventeenth Century* (1960), Trelease makes it plain that the evidence simply did not support Hunt's economic approach.

While Trelease effectively evaluated Hunt's middleman thesis, he did not go to the heart of *The Wars of the Iroquois.* The economic interpretation declared that native cultures were radically transformed by white contact. This transformation involved not only material culture but values and behavior. Hunt assumes that European economic values could be generalized to all cultures. Those assumptions were challenged in Bruce Trigger's two volume *The Children of Aataentsic: A History of the Huron People to 1660* (1976). Using both historical and anthropological evidence, Trigger demonstrates the continuities in Huron life. He also continues the critique of Hunt by noting that beaver supplies were not declining in the 1640s. Trigger concludes that Hunt's arguments were simply without substance (2:843).

With so much of George Hunt's work either discredited or undermined, it appears that *The Wars of the Iroquois* is destined to be read merely as an exercise in colonial Indian historiography. The fate of Hunt's book is in many ways the tale of a traditional Indian-white relations approach giving way to more sophisticated ethnohistorical perspectives. Hunt did ignore important evidence while tailoring other documents to suit his thesis. Hunt assumed that economic values and motives were universal. His Iroquois were European merchants in forest garb. But in all of this it seems important to keep Hunt's contributions in mind. He wrote at a time when few historians of early North America considered Indians an important subject. Hunt's book rightly placed native people at center stage on the frontier. In many ways Hunt was the victim of the barriers between academic disciplines. During his years as an active scholar there was little contact between historians and anthropologists. Hunt's bibliography reveals few anthropological sources. The flowering of ethnohistory took place after Hunt's premature death. George Hunt needs to be remembered for his challenge to the historical wisdom of the time. That was the wisdom of Parkman and Morgan. Hunt sought, however unsuccessfully, to put a human face on the Iroquois. That effort was no mean achievement.

Bibliography

Book

The Wars of the Iroquois: A Study in Intertribal Trade Relations. Madison: University of Wisconsin Press, 1940.

Reviews

The Bloody Mohawk by T. Wood Clarke. *Mississippi Valley Historical Review* 27(September, 1940):451-453.

Nebraska: A Guide to the Cornhusker State by the Federal Writers' Project--WPA. *Mississippi Valley Historical Review* 26(March, 1940):621-622.

Schoolcraft-Longfellow-Hiawatha by Chase S. Osborn and Stellanova Osborn. *Mississippi Valley Historical Review* 30(September, 1943):272-273.

The Small Town in American Literature by Ima H. Herron. *Mississippi Valley Historical Review* 26(January, 1940):432-434.

Studies of George T. Hunt

Downes, Randolph. Review of *The Wars of the Iroquois* by George T. Hunt. *Mississippi Valley Historical Review* 27(September, 1940):287-288.

Fenton, William. Review of *The Wars of the Iroquois* by George T. Hunt. *American Anthropologist* 42(October, 1940):662-664.

Hicks, John D. *My Life wiih History: An Autobiography*. Lincoln: University of Nebraska Press, 1968.

Hunt, George T., Papers. Case Western Reserve University Archives, Case Western Reserve University, Cleveland, OH.

__________. University of Nebraska Alumni Association Records Department, University of Nebraska, Lincoln, NE.

McIlwraith, T. F. Review of *The Wars of the Iroquois* by George T. Hunt. *American Historical Review* 46(January, 1941):415-416.

"Obituary." *New York Times*, April 20, 1947.

__________. *School and Society*, April 26, 1947.

Srole, Leo. Review of *The Wars of the Iroquois* by George T. Hunt. *American Journal of Sociology* 46(January, 1941):616.

Trelease, Allen W. "The Iroquois and the Western Fur Trade: A Problem in Interpretation." *Mississippi Valley Historical Review* 44(June, 1962):32-51.

Trigger, Bruce. *The Children of Aataentsic: A History of the Huron People to 1660*. 2 volumes. Montreal: McGill-Queen's University Press, 1976.

27

MARQUIS JAMES

by Bruce J. Dinges

Biography

As a child growing up on the Cherokee Strip in and around Enid, Oklahoma, Marquis (pronounced "Markey") James was captivated by the myth and romance of the fading frontier. The Strip had only been opened to white settlement six months before Marquis and his mother arrived to join his father, an attorney who had participated in the 1893 rush to stake out claims in the virgin territory. A lonely child, isolated from playmates his own age, he found intellectual stimulus in his mother's large collection of history books and entertainment in old-timers' tales of Indians, trappers, and the cattle range. Through his father's criminal law practice, he met the outlaw Dick Yaeger and the flamboyant Temple Houston, both of whom he idolized. James spent his adult life in worlds far more cosmopolitan and places far removed from his boyhood home, but the West of his childhood remained with him always. At the time of his death in 1955, the *New York Times* remarked that the boy from Enid had come to town "by train or car, not on horseback. He never put on any Western airs or affected the manners of the wide open spaces." But, the newspaper concluded, "The West was in his bones and veins, nonetheless, and it gave ease and informality to himself and his work." In his lifetime, James coupled a passion for historical research with a relaxed and unaffected literary style that critics pronounced peculiarly "American," and which captured two Pulitzer prizes for biography. As works of scholarship, his major books have not always fared well at the hands of professional historians. And yet he managed, as have few other American writers, to breathe life and substance into his subjects.

The descendant of tidewater Virginia gentry, Marquis James was born at Springfield, Missouri, on August 29, 1891. His father, Houstin James, was forty-seven at the time of his son's birth, and his mother, Rachel Marquis, was forty-three. Two sisters had already married and moved away from home. Marquis experienced "considerable difficulty" with classes in the Enid, Oklahoma, public school. Even as an established man of letters, he confessed that "Grammar and arithmetic I could not understand, and cannot now." From an early age, however, he enjoyed history and read it voraciously, a habit he would retain throughout his life. He also was drawn to literature, because he "liked the sound of words," and he read literary biography, because he considered it "a branch of history." Fascinated by the printer's art, young James began hanging around the newspaper office and, at the age of fourteen, became a reporter for the Enid *Events*. His father died suddenly when Marquis was sixteen, and he was compelled to work to support himself and his widowed mother. He finished high school and briefly attended Oklahoma Christian University (now Phillips University), until he decided that he could learn more and enjoy his work better in a newspaper office (*Twentieth-Century Authors*, p. 714).

At the age of twenty, James took to the road as a journeyman reporter. In the course of his travels, he worked for almost two dozen papers in the South and Midwest, including the Kansas City *Journal*, the St. Louis *Globe-Democrat*, the Chicago *Inter-Ocean*, and the New Orleans *Item*. In 1914 he took a job as copy editor on the Chicago *Journal*. There, on June 25, he married Bessie Rowland, a reporter, whom he had met while working on the New Orleans *Item*. The couple had one daughter, Cynthia. James advanced to city editor of the *Journal* in 1915, and supplemented his income by writing fiction under a variety of pseudonyms for pulp magazines. A year later, he moved to New York, where he obtained a job as a rewrite man on the New York *Tribune*. Upon America's entry into World War I, James declined an assignment as war correspondent and enlisted in the army. He served with the infantry in France and near the close of the war was assigned as a captain to the Intelligence Section of the General Staff.

Back in the United States, James struggled to reestablish his journalistic career by working as a ghostwriter and press agent. His break came in 1920, when he took the job in Indianapolis as publicity director for the American Legion and helped found the *American Legion Weekly* (later the *American Legion Monthly*). He achieved national attention through a series of muckraking articles that led to a congressional investigation into the incompetent management of vocational training for disabled veterans, and exposed waste and fraud in war contracts and surplus property disposal. Appropriately, James's first book was *A History of the American Legion* (1923). He also contributed a series of well-researched historical sketches to the Legion magazine, which he later gathered together in book form as *They Had Their Hour* (1934). Ernest Hemingway included three of the stories ("Deguelo," "The Stolen Train," and "The Wrong Road") in his anthology, *Men at War: The Best War Stories of All Time* (1942).

James's work for the Legion organ attracted offers from elsewhere, and in 1925 he accepted an invitation from its former editor, Harold Ross, to moonlight on the editorial staff of the fledgling *New Yorker*. His tenure with the magazine was brief, as he soon left to begin work on a biography of Sam Houston, the hero of Texas independence. He devoted five years to researching and writing the life of Houston. Entitled *The Raven: A Biography of Sam Houston* (1929), the book won the Pulitzer Prize in 1930, and sold over 100,000 copies during the depression decade. James rightly prided himself on the original research that went into the biography, and in 1940 he sued Republic Productions for plagiarism of his work in the film *Man of Conquest*.

Encouraged by the success of his first foray into biography, James next turned to Houston's political mentor, Andrew Jackson. James and his wife traveled extensively, visiting the sites of Jackson's life and conducting research into repositories throughout the South. He examined over 40,000 manuscripts, and the project took seven years to complete. *Andrew Jackson, The Border Captain* was published in 1933 and covered Jackson's life up to 1824; the second volume, *Andrew Jackson, Portrait of a President*, appeared four years later and completed James's most ambitious undertaking. The Jackson volumes shared the 1938 Pulitzer Prize for biography with Odell Shepard's *Pedlar's Progress*, a life of Bronson Alcott. James was only the third American biographer to win the prestigious award on two occasions. Unfortunately, James's subsequent attempts at biography were less successful. *Mr. Gardner of Texas* (1939) and *Alfred I. Du Pont, The Family Rebel* (1941) failed to garner either the popular or critical acclaim of his earlier efforts.

During the war years, James successfully marketed his literary talents in corporate boardrooms. In 1940 the Insurance Company of America approached him to write a history of the firm. James agreed, with the proviso that he should have a free hand to interpret the corporate records as he saw fit. Assisted by his wife, who performed much of the research, over the next decade he turned out a series of solidly documented and well-written business histories of the Insurance Company of North America, Metropolitan Life, Texaco, and Bank of America. He also returned to his Oklahoma boyhood in *The Cherokee Strip, A Tale of an Oklahoma Boyhood* (1945), a nostalgic and engaging reminiscence of frontier life at the turn of the century. Meanwhile, he supplemented his income by writing radio scripts and contributing articles to national magazines such as the *New Yorker*, *Outlook*, and the *Saturday Evening Post*.

A lanky man with an air of informality about him, James stood six feet tall. His expressive face, with its slightly protruding upper lip, opened easily into an engaging smile. A full mat of rumpled hair crowned a high forehead, and his voice retained its soft Oklahoma drawl. James was an omnivorous reader, with a retentive memory, whose hobbies included riding, tennis, travel, and draw poker. Elected to the National Institute of Arts and Letters in 1953, he prided himself on having never attended a literary tea or cocktail party. He also was a member of the Society of American Historians, the National Press Club, and the American Yacht Club. In politics, he described himself as a "non-partisan New Dealer" (*Twentieth-Century Authors*, pp. 714-715).

James divorced in 1952, and on January 9, 1954, he married Jacqueline Mary Parsons. In the meantime, he had developed an interest in race relations and was working on a biography of Booker T. Washington when he was stricken by a cerebral hemorrhage on November 19, 1955, and died at the age of sixty-four at his home at Rye, New York. With Bernard De Voto and Robert E. Sherwood, America lost her third Pulitzer laureate within the space of a week. Although he was not a Quaker, James had attended services at the Friends meeting house near Rye Lake, and requested that his funeral be held there. Patrick Murphy Malin, executive director of the American Civil Liberties Union, presided, and historian Henry Steele Commager delivered the eulogy, after which James was laid to rest in Greenwood Union Cemetery at Rye. In a moving obituary, the *New York Times* (November 21, 1955) lamented the passing of "an excellent journalist, a citizen of the world and an engaging companion," whose biographies of Houston and Jackson would stand as enduring monuments.

Themes

After receiving his second Pulitzer Prize, James reflected that both his subjects had been men of action and ventured an opinion that such men were "simpler to handle" than intellectual figures. "When I feel capable of doing a man of thought," he speculated, "I want to tackle Jefferson and possibly Franklin. Maybe that will be the work of my very ripe years when I have actually settled down for good" (*Twentieth-Century Authors*, p. 715). Although at the time of his death James had commenced research for a biography of black educator Booker T. Washington, it seems improbable that he would have imparted to the project quite the same grasp of character, eye for dramatic detail, and sense of historic dimension that he displayed in his lives of Houston and Jackson. He may not have worn his western heritage on his coat sleeves, but beneath the cosmopolitan exterior beat the heart of a westerner. The secret to much of his appeal as a writer lay in his selection of subjects who conformed in the popular mind to widely held notions of the frontier, and his ability to translate their actions into simple and forceful prose.

James was not a professional historian; he considered himself a biographer and drew careful distinctions between biography and history. Nor did he publish primarily on western topics. Nonetheless, it is significant that his most popular and important books--the Houston and Jackson biographies and the memoirs of his boyhood--were essentially frontier studies. Viewing these works as a whole, at least three overarching themes emerge. Most important, James was intrigued by (and a master at portraying) the dramatic interplay between environment and character, one reviewer comparing him in this regard with Carl Sandburg in *The Prairie Years* (John H. Jenkins, *Basic Texas Books*, p. 269). A second theme was implied in his selection of subjects who embodied the frontier myth popularized by James Fenimore Cooper and a host of other nineteenth- and early-twentieth-century writers. Both Houston and Jackson were men of aristocratic antecedents who moved to the far fringes of the frontier (and in Houston's case beyond the frontier line to the Cherokee Nation and Texas), were regenerated, and achieved apotheosis as leaders and spokespersons for the inarticulate western masses. And finally, there is a dark and unsettling vision of frontier democracy. Like Frederick Jackson Turner, James discerned a heightened form of democratic action and expression in the western wilderness. But it was an often dangerous and potentially violent type of democracy. Among the supreme accomplishments attributed to Houston and Jackson was their ability to defuse, or at least temper, the more radical impulses of their frontier constituents and channel them toward socially and politically acceptable ends.

Analysis

James was fond of quoting Thomas Carlyle's observation that "a well written life is almost as rare as a well spent one." The problem, he felt, was that "so many good writers . . . are careless, lazy and shallow about their research, whereas most of the honest and competent researchists can't write for sour apples" (*Andrew Jackson, President*, p. 582). James was not alone in lamenting the "lowly state" of historical writing, as the 1920s and 1930s witnessed a flowering of American romantic biography. Carl Sandburg, Douglas Southall Freeman, Esther Forbes, and Marquis James all produced first-rate character studies that were at once meticulously researched and superbly literate.

James took pains to define the art of biography and to distinguish it from history. "Biography," he explains, "is not history in the general sense. It is a more personal and individual thing, and more difficult to do well" (*Andrew Jackson, Captain*, p. 429). The successful biographer must combine the novelist's craft of creating "dependable representations of life and character" with the historian's passion for exhaustive research (*Andrew Jackson, President*, p. 582). Because the primary responsibility of the biographer is to breathe life into his subject, James and his fellow "moderns" insisted that the spotlight remain ever firmly fixed on the central character. "Background," according to James, "must remain background and by selection and emphasis be kept from swamping the man we are trying to tell about" (*Andrew Jackson, Captain*, p. 429).

Of early American biographers, James most admired James Parton (1822-1891), who had penned the lives of Aaron Burr, Benjamin Franklin, Thomas Jefferson, Andrew Jackson, and others. Parton's shortcomings, he acknowledges, were "neither few nor small." "An indifferent and superficial historian," he failed to grasp the economic and political forces at work in Jeffersonian and Jacksonian America, and committed numerous errors of fact. Nonetheless, James insisted that Parton's failings as a historian in no way diminished his stature as a biographer. In biography, he observes, "as in other undertakings, there is a difference between fact and truth." In James's eyes, Parton possessed "the greatest of all literary gifts"--he was a "born storyteller." For all its flaws and errors, James writes of Parton's life of Jackson, "the fact remains that *a man* walks through the numerous pages of Mr. Parton, and that man, in the main, is Andrew Jackson, whom the reader comes to know as he knows a friend or neighbor" (pp. 428-429; "Opening New Horizons for the Biographer," pp. 7-8). James hoped that serious scholarship would elevate modern biography above the level of its nineteenth-century practitioners, but by-and-large his final goal was the same--to recreate accurately a living, breathing human being.

James selected as his subjects two men who epitomized the romantic frontier hero--Sam Houston and Andrew Jackson. In the foreword to a reprint edition of the *The Raven*, Henry Steele Commager describes the life of Sam Houston as "the stuff of which legend is made," and compares his role in Texas history to those of "Charlemagne and Alfred and Barbarossa and Vlademar Sejr . . . [in] the histories of the nations they helped to make." As much as his less fortunate contemporary, Davy Crockett, Houston took an active hand in shaping his own legend. In several campaign biographies, Houston portrayed himself as a Cooperian hero and as "the George Washington of Texas." A soldier-aristocrat and woodsman, he fled what James termed "disorderly civilization" to find tranquility among the Cherokee and repose amidst the beauties of nature. Like a backwoods Thoreau, he read *The Illiad* to pass the time. Rejuvenated, Houston eventually returned to civilization, where he donned the garb of soldier and politician, defeated the Indians, captured the governorship of Tennessee, and won the hand of the young and beautiful Eliza Allen.

Suddenly, for reasons that remain a mystery--and about which Houston always refused to speak--he left his bride, gave up his high office, and fled back to the Cherokee. After a bout with alcoholism and marriage to Tiana Rogers, an Indian "princess," he once again emerged from the wilderness regenerated, and embarked on his great odyssey as the father of Texas independence. Through his deeds and his own accounts of his career, as Richard Slotkin has perceptively noted, Houston "impressed the public by living or acting out the full scenario of the fantasy embodied in the Leatherstocking cycle and the larger Myth of the Frontier" (*The Fatal Environment*, p. 164).

These themes also impressed Marquis James as he effectively molded them into the cornerstone of *The Raven*. He had read and reread Charles Edward Lester's *Sam Houston and His Republic* (1846)--which apparently had been written under Houston's supervision--and as a child he had clung mesmerized to the knee of Temple Houston, as the son of the Texas hero recited the story of the Alamo. James later claimed that by reading and listening he had probably, by the age of twelve, formed "a better conception, ignoring details of course, of Houston, the man, and of his place in the southwestern scheme of things, than when I started my book about him."

James's great accomplishment as a biographer lay in the vibrancy with which he recreated the historic and mythic Houston, and the diligence with which he filled in the details of his life and career. After burning six or seven chapters that he had completed, based solely on secondary sources, he plunged into manuscript materials in search of Houston's personality, "the inner springs of his character, the ultimate and terrible personal things that shaped his character and changed a nation's destiny."

James proved a dogged and painstaking sleuth, visiting the scenes of Houston's boyhood and manhood, delving into public repositories in the United States and England, and gaining access to privately held family collections of Houston letters previously closed to researchers (*Texas Monthly* 6:1-8). To this rich trove of personal documents, James applied his considerable journalistic talents and created a portrait of Houston that, in the estimate of Texas bookdealer and bibliographer John Jenkins, "adds immeasurably to our understanding of Houston as Houston saw himself, without swallowing it but without letting it detract from his appreciation of Houston's genius" (*Basic Texas Books*, p. 269).

At the time of its publication, a critic commented that *The Raven* exhibited "all the merits and defects of the modern romantic biography" (*Mississippi Valley Historical Review* 17:465). Although James succeeded brilliantly in recreating the myth and romance that surrounded Houston, he fell short of his avowed intention "to portray him against the background of national affairs" (*The Raven*, p. 467). Questionable judgments, shallow analysis, and factual errors remind readers that James was not a trained historian. Contemporary scholars criticized his superficial understanding of the relationship between Houston and Jackson, his limited grasp of national politics, and his misconception of Houston's attitude toward annexation. Recent scholarship suggests that James overestimates the importance of Houston's role in the Texas Revolution and seriously underrates Anson Jones's significant part in annexation. His knowledge of Texas diplomacy is rudimentary, and he inflates Andrew Jackson's involvement in Texas affairs. More than once, James is carried away by the epic dimensions of his subject, as in his assessment of the battle of San Jacinto:

> The mastery of a continent was in contention between the champions of two civilizations--racial rivals and hereditary enemies, so divergent in idea and method that suggestion of compromise was an affront. On an obscure meadow of bright grass nursed by a water course named on hardly any map, wet steel would decide which civilization should prevail on these shores and which submit in the clash of men and symbols impending--the conquistador and the frontiersman, the Inquisition and the Magna Carta, the rosary and the rifle (p. 250).

And yet, for all its flaws as good history, *The Raven* remains a classic American biography. Jack Gregory and Rennard Strickland have treated Houston's Cherokee years at greater length and more dispassionately in *Sam Houston with the Cherokees* (1967), and Llerena Friend's *Sam Houston, The Great Designer* (1954) is a superb political study. Nonetheless, anyone who wishes to gain a true feeling for Sam Houston--the man and the legend--must turn first to James's biography.

Having captured a Pulitzer Prize and popular acclaim for his life of Houston, it was logical that James should next turn to Andrew Jackson. Like his young protege, Jackson seemed to play out popular notions of the frontier experience. In*Andrew Jackson, The Border Captain*, James portrays the "Young Hickory" as a landed aristocrat who squandered his South Carolina inheritance and migrated west to recoup his fortune. As an attorney on the Tennessee frontier, he championed the cause of creditors against debtors, and associated with property holders and land speculators. A natural leader, he briefly donned the robes of lawmaker and jurist, but found his greatest fame as a military chief--the conqueror of the Creeks and the hero of New Orleans. A man of forceful action and impeccable integrity, Jackson fought hard, dared much, and refused to shirk responsibility. Duels, horse races, his controversial marriage to Rachel Donelson Robards, and warfare dominate James's bold and vivid portrait of Jackson as "Celtic chieftain, a man of fire and tenderness, of strong and sincere, if sometimes rash, emotions--a product of the vibrant forces that had swept him . . . across the gusty Blue Ridge into the Western wilderness" (pp. 358-359).

At the close of *Andrew Jackson, The Border Captain*, James conjures up a Turnerian vision of democracy rising out of the frontier experience to challenge the seaboard for control of the nation's destiny:

> By virility, experience and, since the war [of 1812], the prestige of victory, pioneers compensated for the disparity of their numbers. They lived close to the machinery of government. They had seen it made: "offices" for the registration of land titles housed in immigrant wagons; courts in log cabins; Indian wars, Indian treaties; every man a soldier and a servant of the law. Thus county governments had taken shape, and over them territorial and state regimes from which it was an easy step for the frontiersman with all the aplomb in the world to shoulder into the councils of the nation (p. 359).

In the acknowledgments to *Andrew Jackson, Portrait of a President*, James accurately predicts that professional historians will likely be unimpressed "by the reverential mention of my obligation to history." "History," he reminds his critics, "has concerned me only as it touched Jackson or as Jackson touched it" (p. 583). It is no surprise then that Jackson's powerful personality dominates the portrayal of his presidency, while politics and economics are brushed over lightly or neglected entirely. The Peggy Eaton affair and Jackson's domestic difficulties share at least equal treatment with the nullification crisis and the Bank War. James's portrait once again is that of a man of deep passions and forthright action who "brought to the presidency fewer personal ambitions than any man excepting Washington." Although labeled "a man of the people," Jackson held few claims to the title. Rather than listen for the voices of his constituents, he "strode forth to inspire, to lead, to govern." No other president, in James's view, had confronted so powerful and well organized a group of political adversaries; and "he beat them to their knees." Nevertheless, Jackson was utterly lacking in pretension or the thirst for power for its own sake. "After eight years," James concludes, "he laid down his burden, unsuspecting that on his times was an impress so characteristic and so deep that posterity would accord to Andrew Jackson an honor not as yet vouchsafed another American--that of marking out an Epoch in our national history and calling it by the name of one man" (pp. 430-432).

To account for Jackson's popular support, James offers a somewhat cynical view of popular democracy. "All the catchwords of proletarianism notwithstanding," he suspects that in their secret hearts the people preferred to be governed, rather than govern themselves. Jackson, in James's opinion, intuitively sensed this "peculiarity" of human nature, and utilized it as had no president before him and few since. "He saw for the people what they could not see for themselves," and then lashed up public support for his policies. "When a majority was at hand," James argues, "Jackson used it. When a majority was not at hand he endeavored to create it. When this could not be done in time, he went ahead anyhow" (pp. 429-430). A towering figure of elemental forcefulness and character, Jackson as president completes the frontier cycle launched in volume one of James's study. A soldier-aristocrat who found regeneration in the West, he emerged reluctantly but inevitably to assume his natural role as the spokesman and guiding force behind an inarticulate, and potentially disruptive, frontier democracy.

As an outstanding example of the "new" biography, James's life of Jackson shares--along with his earlier study of Sam Houston--all of the strengths and weaknesses of that literary genre. Robert Remini, Jackson's most recent and distinguished biographer, has aptly characterized James's work as "a pulsating, full-blooded, vivid, and durable account of a heroic life written with imagination, enormous narrative power, and a distinctive and absorbing style" (*Dictionary of American Biography* Supplement 5:364). Historians have uniformly applauded the "color and brilliancy" of James's portrait of "Old Hickory," while faulting him for a background that lacks depth and is "too sketchily and somewhat incorrectly drawn" (*Journal of Southern History* 1:86; 4:525). Some topics, like Jackson's public land policy, are ignored completely, while cabinet affairs, the tariff, internal improvements, and diplomacy are imperfectly rendered. Where political campaigns and the Bank War are treated in depth, the emphasis is more on personalities than on conflicting policies and philosophies.

For all his research and forceful prose style, James offered a one-dimensional view of an individual of monumental complexity. Remini observes that "James could not see beyond Jackson as a man of action and honor. . . . As a writer, James matched his subject in terms of color and excitement; as an historian he failed to do him justice" (*Dictionary of American Biography* Supplement 5:364). The problem, however, was not peculiar to James; it was a flaw common to romantic biography. A perceptive contemporary critic carefully weighed James's impressive success in breathing life and feeling into his subject, against his failure to portray accurately the economic and political environment of the Jacksonian Age.

The shortcomings of *Andrew Jackson, Portrait of a President*, he concludes, "may suggest to the philosophical reader . . . some misgivings as to too great an emphasis upon the element of portraiture in biography" (*American Historical Review* 43:654-655).

James was conscious of having himself played a small role in the story of the settlement of the West, and as a pastime for over ten years he put together the recollections of his childhood on one of the nation's last frontiers. Published in 1945, *The Cherokee Strip*, according to its author, was prompted by his daughter's query: "Pop, why don't you write some of the things you tell about instead of what you do write?" ("Note of Explanation," n.p.). A nostalgic and gently humorous account of an Oklahoma boyhood, the work establishes James as an accomplished storyteller. Along the way, he gives colorful insights into life in a turn-of-the-century frontier boomtown and the antecedents of an American author.

Writing in typically unobtrusive and straightforward fashion, James recreates the wonderment of a bygone world as seen through boyish eyes. The effect was calculated, as he admits to checking carefully his recollections against newspapers and the remembrances of Enid oldtimers. As befits a biographer, James's youthful world is peopled by an eccentric collection of carefully drawn characters, each of whom in some manner, large or small, shaped his character and directed his interests. His father and mother had participated in the frontier migration, and their stories helped "to bring closer the epic of the Westward Movement" (p. 181). Mr. Howell--an old-time soldier, buffalo hunter, scout, stagecoach driver, and inveterate spinner of tall tales--enlivened the youngster's lonely hours with yarns of the Old West. Dick Yaeger--a "third-rate outlaw" in one critic's eyes--and Temple Houston were tangible and heroic links to a West that had all but disappeared (*Mississippi Valley Historical Review* 21:106).

Paul Wellman, a popular writer of some note and a fellow native of Enid, compares *The Cherokee Strip* with the adventures of Tom Sawyer and Huck Finn, and pronounces it a "superlative" expression of a "young, vital, exuberant period in American history, told with all the authority and flavor of a participant in it" (*Saturday Review of Literature*, October 20, 1945, p. 13). Once again, James attempts to recreate the romance of the frontier; thanks to his facile pen and a marvelous eye for character and setting he largely succeeds. The accomplishment is all the more impressive in view of the fact that James's childhood does not appear to have been all that idyllic. Reading between the lines, the reader discovers a lonely young man striving hard for acceptance among Enid "society." Fatherless and in debt, he abandoned schooling in order to support himself and his widowed mother. Whether in storytelling, reading, or cherished contacts with tramp printers, James sought avenues of escape from what must have been a stifling existence in a remote border community. Only later, one suspects--in the warm glow of a successful career--could he look back with affection and nostalgia on a way of life that seemed to have passed forever.

In his autobiography, as elsewhere, James appears torn between the lure of the mythic West and a newspaperman's eye for human interest, and the historian's demand for fact and objectivity. As in the tale of Walter Cook, Enid's first pioneer, who at the time of Marquis's acquaintance doubled as a bootlegger and the town drunk, James perceives the need to keep the two separate. "Walter Cook was still with us," he explains, "and I liked the way Enid treated him--distinguishing between the man and the historical figure. It was the right way. To have mixed up the two would have done Walter no good and it might have marred the figure" (p. 277). Given the choice between cold reality and colorful romance, James usually opted for the romance.

A reviewer characterized Marquis James as "a journalistic historian," then added, but "one of rare conscientiousness" (*Mississippi Valley Historical Review* 21:106). James no doubt would have substituted "biographer" for "historian"; otherwise, the assessment is accurate. Together with Sandburg, Freeman, and other practitioners of the "new" biography, he effectively coupled exhaustive research with an epic vision of American frontier history and a powerful narrative style. For all their shortcomings as serious history, James's biographies of Houston and Jackson remain vibrant human portraits that brilliantly encapsulate romantic notions of the frontier and frontier heroes. Similarly, his reminiscence of boyhood in the Cherokee Strip evokes nostalgic memories of a more recent frontier experience. James's failings were common, in one degree or another, to most of the so-called "modern" biographies. Unfortunately, he lacked the scholar's training and grasp of historical processes that would have enabled him to place his subjects in the proper context. By the same token, however, few academicians could match his grasp of the mythic westward movement or equal his considerable literary skills. More so than professional historians, James and the romantic biographers of the 1920s and 1930s conveyed to hundreds of thousands of Americans widely accepted notions of the nation's past.

Bibliography

Books

Alfred I. Du Pont, The Family Rebel. Indianapolis and New York: Bobbs-Merrill Co., 1941.

Andrew Jackson, The Border Captain. Indianapolis: Bobbs-Merrill Co., 1933.

Andrew Jackson, Portrait of a President. Indianapolis and New York: Bobbs-Merrill Co., 1937.

Biography of a Bank: The Story of Bank of America N.T. & S.A. Co-authored with Bessie Rowland James. New York: Harper, 1954.

Biography of a Business, 1792-1942: Insurance Company of North America. Indianapolis and New York: Bobbs-Merrill Co., 1942.

The Cherokee Strip, A Tale of an Oklahoma Boyhood. New York: Viking Press, 1945.

A History of the American Legion. New York: W. Green, 1923.

The Metropolitan Life, A Study in Business Growth. New York: Viking Press, 1947.
Morris L. Ernst . . . a Liberal Lawyer. New York: N.p., 1938.
Mr. Gardner of Texas. Indianapolis and New York: Bobbs-Merrill Co., 1939.
The Raven: A Biography of Sam Houston. Indianapolis: Bobbs-Merrill Co., 1929.
The Texaco Story: The First Fifty Years, 1902-1952, Written for the Texas Company. New York: N.p., 1953.
They Had Their Hour. Indianapolis: Bobbs-Merrill Co., 1934.

Articles
"A Different Andrew Jackson Emerges." *New York Times*, July 24, 1932, pp. 10-11.
"On the Trail of Sam Houston." *Texas Monthly* 6(July, 1930):1-8.
"Opening New Horizons for the Biographer," *New York Times Book Review*, October 6, 1946, pp. 7-8.

Studies of Marquis James
Branch, E. Douglas. Review of *They Had Their Hour* by Marquis James. *Mississippi Valley Historical Review* 21(June, 1934):106.
Caldwell, Robert G. Review of *The Raven: A Biography of Sam Houston* by Marquis James. *Mississippi Valley Historical Review* 17(December, 1930):465.
Hamer, Philip M. Review of *Andrew Jackson, The Border Captain* by Marquis James. *Journal of Southern History* 1(February, 1935):86.
__________. Review of *Andrew Jackson, Portrait of a President* by Marquis James. *Journal of Southern History* 4(November, 1938):525.
Jenkins, John H. Review of *The Raven: A Biography of Sam Houston* by Marquis James. In *Basic Texas Books.* Austin, TX: Jenkins Publishing Co., 1983. P. 269.
Kunitz, Stanley J., ed. *Twentieth-Century Authors, First Supplement: A Biographical Dictionary of Modern Literature.* New York: H. W. Wilson Co., 1955. Pp. 484-485.
__________, and Howard Haycroft, ed. *Twentieth-Century Authors: A Biographical Dictionary of Modern Literature.* Fifth edition. New York: H. W. Wilson Co., 1961. Pp. 714-715.
"Marquis James." In *The National Cyclopaedia of American Biography.* New York: James T. White & Co., 1893-1984. 44:167.
New York Times. May 3, 1938; February 24, 1940; November 20, 21, 23, 1955.
Remini, Robert V. "Marquis James." In *Dictionary of American Biography.* New York: Charles Scribner's Sons, 1946-1981. Supplement 5:364.
Sioussat, St. George L. Review of *Andrew Jackson, Portrait of a President* by Marquis James. *American Historical Review* 43(April, 1938):654-655.

Slotkin, Richard. *The Fatal Environment: The Myth of the Frontier in the Age of Industrialization, 1800-1890*. New York: Antheneum, 1985.

__________. *Regeneration through Violence: The Mythology of the American Frontier, 1600-1860*. Middletown, CT: Wesleyan University Press, 1973.

Wellman, Paul I. Review of *The Cherokee Strip* by Marquis James. *Saturday Review of Literature*, October 20, 1945, p. 13.

28

LOUISE PHELPS KELLOGG

by Dwight L. Smith

Biography

The Phelps and Kellogg families, both of Connecticut Yankee stock, were part of the first wave of New England and New York settlers to come to Wisconsin in its early territorial years. The marriage of Mary Isabella (Belle) Phelps and Amherst Kellogg established a family that became prominent in church and church-related activities such as temperance, charity, orphanages, and relief efforts. As an executive of Milwaukee and Chicago insurance companies, Amherst was able to provide his family with reasonably comfortable circumstances.

Their daughter, Louise Phelps Kellogg, was born May 12, 1862, in Milwaukee. As a child, she became a good horsewoman under the instruction of her father, but she did not do well with her mother-encouraged piano lessons, perhaps because she was handicapped with a hearing deficiency. She had learned to read and write, printing by copying from magazines and books, before entering the public schools in Chicago. Kellogg qualified to enter at the third grade level; but she was put in the first grade so she could learn to write in longhand.

This humiliation and a sleeplessness and nervousness induced in part by the fear of being tardy affected her attitude toward school; so she was sent to a private teacher under whom she adjusted and fared better. The school-entry handwriting problem was never forgotten, especially in later life when painful neuritis frequently forced her to adopt an awkward print style or even to delay major research projects.

After two years of instruction at Milwaukee College, Kellogg accepted a teaching position at a Milwaukee girls school. She read extensively in history and decided she wanted to pursue it for a career. In early 1895, she appeared with a letter of introduction at the doorstep of Frederick Jackson Turner, her elder by six months. He was recommended as the best person in the country with whom to talk about her desire to become a historian.

The Turner seminar at the University of Wisconsin that fall was almost too much for Kellogg; but under the spell of his charm, inspiration, and encouragement, she persisted. Her senior thesis removed any doubt about her ability and her promise as a historian. Graduating with honors and receiving one of the university's few graduate scholarships, she plunged into advanced study serving as Turner's assistant. Kellogg won a Boston Education Association fellowship for her second year of graduate study and used it to do research at the Public Record Office in London and to enroll at the Sorbonne. While in Paris, the first item in her subsequent impressive list of publications appeared, "Sur la translation des Restes de Voltaire au Pantheon, le 11 Juillet 1791," in *La Révolution Française* (37:271-277). She returned to the University of Wisconsin in the fall of 1899 to teach history courses for a member of the faculty on leave and to work on her dissertation. Her dissertation, "The American Colonial Charter: A Study of English Administration in Relation Thereto, Chiefly after 1688," was published by the American Historical Association and awarded its Justin Winsor Prize (*Annual Report AHA 1903*, 1:187-341).

The State Historical Society of Wisconsin, the University of Wisconsin, and the history of the state and the region became Louise Phelps Kellogg's magnificent profession and obsessions. She attained wide recognition and respect as an authority, particularly on the French and British eras in the Middle West. She was a frequent speaker and an active participant in the programs of professional historical societies, reaching the pinnacle of the profession by election to the presidency of the Mississippi Valley Historical Association, the present Organization of American Historians. She was a mainstay in the development of the state's historical society and its journal and a frequent speaker at and consultant to historical activities throughout Wisconsin. Other states' societies sought her advice and solicited journal contributions from her pen. That she was never granted an academic appointment at the University of Wisconsin was probably her greatest disappointment.

In her later years, physical impairments began to take their toll on her activities, her scholarly production, and her social and professional acceptance. Never retiring, she had to adjust to increasing deafness, failing eyesight, and diminished energy. She regretted her decreasing production as she came to realize that she had gained the most satisfaction in life from her research and writing, the driving force that had been her principal motivation. She died July 11, 1942, two months after her eightieth year.

Themes

Kellogg's lasting heritage is measured by her remarkable outpouring of books, essays, and reviews. The thrust of these is best understood if it is remembered that she was a Turner student and assistant; that for years she was closely associated with Reuben Gold Thwaites, Joseph Schafer, Milo M. Quaife, and Carl Russell Fish (Kellogg and Mrs. Fish were cousins and intimate friends), in the work that they were doing; and that the collections of Lyman Copeland Draper furnished the basis for several of her research projects. It must also be pointed out that considerable time was consumed responding to historical queries, serving as miscellany columnist for the state historical society and its journal, and speaking to and working with numerous local societies in their activities.

Aside from physical infirmities affecting her sight, hearing, and hands, which were overcome to some extent by sheer determination, Kellogg found composition and writing a very demanding and time consuming task. She was driven by the conviction that before anything appeared in print it must be virtually perfect, both from the standpoint of accuracy and thoroughness as well as clarity of statement. Although much of it was done in response to numerous requests from others--she declined a considerable number of such invitations--she wrote because of her dedication to history and her desire to share it with others.

Rather than themes or points of view or schools of thought or biases, in studying Kellogg's published efforts one is impressed that she was primarily in pursuit of something much more vital to her. She was on a lifelong pursuit of the documentary evidence upon which to base the historical account. It is not surprising, therefore, that she edited voluminous amounts of correspondence, official records, and other manuscript source materials that were used immediately in her own writings and have remained valuable sources for successive generations of scholars as well.

Transcription was not routine copying which could be trusted to an assistant, especially for the materials that had been generated in the years of her interests and often under difficult circumstances. For that matter, major portions of the documentary records with which she worked were such that only she possessed the essential knowledge to make faithful transcriptions, and, in many cases, meaningful translations. Deciphering barely legible and unschooled handwriting was only a part of the problem. In the earlier periods, especially in the seventeenth-century French-Canadian fur trading context, French and Indian words and abbreviations were used in bewildering combinations, as were symbols and codes. Kellogg became a recognized authority in such matters and other scholars and professional groups sought her help.

Accurate transcription, including translation if necessary, made the document available for research. Only then could it be put to its intended research use. For Kellogg, this meant studying the document in its context and content to make an accurate determination of what it said and had to contribute. Frequently this revealed that a document had been previously misread or misinterpreted and misused as a part of the historical record, perhaps by generations of scholars, perhaps even by those who were called upon to react to the contents of the document as it was first issued. Besides setting the record straight, Kellogg also uncovered other documentary materials hitherto unused or unknown to researchers and scholars.

Well schooled in research techniques and methods by graduate training under Frederick Jackson Turner at the University of Wisconsin and Charles V. Langlois and Charles Seignobos at the Sorbonne, it augured well that her own writing would bear the mark of sound scholarship. She established herself as a scholar while still studying at the Sorbonne with her first published effort, which appeared in French, and then with the prize-winning publication of her doctoral dissertation. Her writing was better than most of her contemporaries, but even though she was sometimes compared favorably with Francis Parkman as a literary stylist, it is fairer to say that she was a highly competent historian whose prose style was marked by clarity and simplicity, virtues in themselves that deserve the widest emulation.

Analysis

Any analysis of Kellogg's contribution to the literature of frontier history must center on an examination of her several volumes of documentary collections and two monographs. The bulk of her other numerous writings are generally related in subject matter to these efforts. They include the dozens of articles that appeared in popular as well as professional journals, as well as some forty-five short subject entries in the *Dictionary of American History* and seventy-three highly regarded biographical sketches of key figures in the *Dictionary of American Biography*.

Soon after receiving her doctorate, Kellogg became associated with Reuben Gold Thwaites in his monumental editorial projects at the State Historical Society of Wisconsin. It is not always possible to determine precisely what aspects or what amount of the intellectual and routine work she did. Some partial clues are offered by the acknowledgments Thwaites made in his prefaces. In the fifteen-volume *Original Journals of the Lewis and Clark Expedition* (1904-1905), he gave her credit for "the difficult work of comparing transcriptions with the original manuscripts" (1:lx). In the thirty-volume *Early Western Travels, 1748-1846* (1904-1907), he was more elaborate: "Throughout the entire task of preparing for the press this series . . . the Editor has had the assistance of Louise Phelps Kellogg, . . . Others have also rendered editorial aid, duly acknowledged . . . but from the beginning to the end, particularly in the matter of annotation, Dr. Kellogg has been the principal research colleague, and he takes great pleasure in asking for her a generous share of whatever credit may accrue from the undertaking" (30:19). For the five volumes he edited of the society's *Collections* (1902-1911), her "valuable assistance throughout" was acknowledged in the matters of annotation, indexing, and translation (17:xix). She then prepared the *Index to Volumes I-XX of the Wisconsin Historical Collections* (1915), which was published as a separate volume in the series.

With her research and editorial skills honed by this extensive experience in association with Thwaites, they now became partners to edit a series on the American Revolution in the Ohio Valley, derived from the Lyman Copeland Draper manuscripts at the historical society. Their initial effort in this new arrangement, *Documentary History of Dunmore's War, 1774* (1905), included about half of the Draper materials on that subject. The editors regarded the war as "a focal point" in frontier history that infused new vigor into westward expansion and the development of nationalism, the two paramount forces that were to characterize the eighteenth century. The soldier participants had already breached the Appalachian barrier with their American institutional baggage. The war trained and seasoned them for the coming American struggle for independence.

The publication of the documents was in itself a substantial contribution to the scholarship on the subject. High quality editorial introductions and annotations were Thwaites and Kellogg hallmarks here and in their other editorial efforts, presenting a more detailed and complete coverage of their subjects than heretofore. With the advantage of increased knowledge and new perspectives, subsequent scholarship offers interpretations that sometimes modify or are at variance with those of Thwaites and Kellogg, but that does not detract from their contributions in *Dunmore's War* and other efforts.

As the Draper manuscripts were to constitute the principal basis for the series, the editors designated the successive volumes as the Draper Series. The second, *The Revolution on the Upper Ohio, 1775-1777* (1908), continues the chronicle of events following the Battle of Point Pleasant and the peace talks at Camp Charlotte of the first volume. The provisional arrangement of Camp Charlotte kept the Ohio Indians neutral as the Revolution was beginning to flare up in the East. The Indian-Virginia peace conference at Pittsburgh in the autumn months of 1775 sought to make this a permanent arrangement. The proceedings of the Pittsburgh conference cover a major portion of this volume. *Dunmore's War* and *Revolution* document the transition from the Indian defense of their lands against aggressive frontiersmen to the western phase of the Revolution.

Frontier Defense on the Upper Ohio, 1777-1778 (1912) resumes the story of the Revolution on the western Pennsylvania and Virginia frontier. The fragile peace was jeopardized by the increased activity of the British from their western base at Detroit, by Pennsylvania-Virginia bickering over jurisdiction of the upper Ohio country, by irresponsible actions of border settlers, some of whom were Loyalists, and by increased Indian restlessness occasioned by these factors and such blatant provocation as the murder of Cornstalk. The regular troops and border counties militia under General Edward Hand were unequal to their responsibility, and key Loyalist defections to the British were a blow. George Rogers Clark's preparations for a campaign into the Illinois country held out some cause for optimism.

The first three volumes of the Draper Series were published with the support of the Sons of the American Revolution. Thwaites died in 1913, and Kellogg continued the project with the state historical society assuming the responsibility for publication. In her first solo volume in the series, *Frontier Advance on the Upper Ohio, 1778-1779* (1916), she broadened the base from which she selected items for inclusion. About one-fourth came from the Washington Papers in the Library of Congress. Others were excerpts from a transcript of the Morgan Letter Books that had been given to Kellogg. She added "recollections" of participants in the Draper collection and summaries and extracts from documents previously printed elsewhere.

Frontier Advance concerned the projected expeditions, negotiations with Indians, the frontier settlement defense measures against potential enemy attacks, the failed major offensive enterprises, and the general lack of harmony that prevailed under the command of General Lachlan McIntosh from mid-1778 to mid-1779. McIntosh and his small force did manage to keep the frontier intact while George Rogers Clark reduced some of the British-induced menace.

The final volume of the Draper series, *Frontier Retreat on the Upper Ohio, 1779-1781* (1917), concerns the years when Colonel Daniel Brodhead served as commandant at Fort Pitt. He ended Iroquois domination over the western tribes, but his pettiness made a cooperative expedition against British strongholds in the West impracticable. As a consequence, numerous frontier posts were abandoned.

As in the previous volume, *Frontier Advance*, Kellogg went beyond the Draper collection for her selection and also included summaries of some documents. This enhanced and diminished the contribution of Kellogg's volumes, and, to some extent, pointed up fundamental shortcomings of the series. To the extent that significant and unpublished non-Draper documents were known and available, the editor now had an obligation to present through their reproduction, supplemented by annotation, a reasonably complete account of the subject as indicated by the title of each of the volumes. In *Frontier Retreat*, for example, nearly one-half of the items are summaries of documents that had been published elsewhere. These might well have been reduced to footnotes, making crucial textual space available for other documents. Since either in entirety or by summary the five volumes neither include all of the documents of the Draper collection nor from other manuscript or published sources that are pertinent, the title of each volume might have accurately been prefaced by such as "An Introduction to the Documentation of . . ."

While she was still working on the Draper series, Kellogg found time and energy to contribute a volume to an American Historical Association sponsored nineteen-volume project, the *Original Narratives of Early American History*. Hers, *Early Narratives of the Northwest, 1634-1699* (1917), was the last of the series to appear. Its concern was the French conquest of the Great Lakes and upper Mississippi country. Kellogg carefully explained which text of each of the thirteen selections she made of travel accounts and episodes from already published English translations. Such discrimination was crucial because variant translations or transcriptions were sometimes unfaithful or inaccurate renderings of the originals thereby performing a disservice rather than making a contribution.

In keeping with the intended purpose of the series, Kellogg's volume brought together and annotated a collection of widely dispersed accounts into a convenient package, especially for use by students and laymen. Her selection of the accounts by such well known persons as Radisson, Father Allouez, Jolliet, Marquette, and Tonty, whose narratives are frequently reprinted, took up so much of the space in the volume, however, that there was little room left for lesser known documents. She did, however, include a Father St. Cosme 1699 letter, heretofore unpublished and of which she herself helped render into a revised translation. Kellogg's editorial craftsmanship of the contextual introductions and annotations was not as careful or thorough as in the Draper series, but this may well have been due to the general format of the series of which *Early Narratives* was a part.

Whatever contributions Louise Phelps Kellogg made through the editing and annotation skills which had established her as a respected scholar, her reputation rests on her monographic examination of the French and British years in the Old Northwest. In a very real sense, these volumes are a distillation of the storehouse of information and insights she had acquired in the many years of work in the archival sources, some of which she had already used for her numerous articles and other publications.

The French Regime in Wisconsin and the Northwest (1925) presented a new perspective from which to study the history of New France. It had previously been viewed from the vantage point of the St. Lawrence Valley. While historians of New France had considered expansion into the interior of the continent, the bulk of their efforts and emphases was centralized in the East. Kellogg acknowledged that New France's history started in the East, but her "Northwest" became the focal point of the *French Regime*, its exploration, occupation, economic development, relations with other parts of New France, and role in the demise of French power in North America.

To accomplish this, she did not synthesize the work of previous scholars, selecting and emphasizing whatever might support a "western outposts" centered approach. She went, instead, to the documentary sources to examine afresh what they had to offer. The yield was substantial both for new information and the resulting revision of previous conclusions, thereby establishing Kellogg's assertion that the western perspective was a valid one.

Specifically, for example, she gave the first satisfactory account of the changes that took place in intertribal Indian relations in the Lake Michigan environs in the early years following the initial French penetration; she seriously questioned the generally accepted itinerary of Pierre Esprit Radisson which previous scholars had deduced from the vague references in his journal; she broke new ground about the Fox Wars; she modified the traditional emphasis on the impact of the missionaries in the western country; and she accounted for the changes made in French fur trade methods in the interior. On this last point, however, she was on shaky ground, apparently unconsciously influenced by her extensive knowledge of post-New France fur trade developments. Kellogg was not a literary historian in the genre of Francis Parkman, but her *French Regime* took a well earned place alongside Parkman's studies of New France.

It was a logical sequence for Kellogg to focus attention on the British years for her next important monographic study. *The British Regime in Wisconsin and the Northwest* (1935) continued the history from the previous volume down through the end of the War of 1812. The post-French and Indian War transition from the French to the British, the British efforts to consolidate their control over their new domain, the attempted administrative redirection under the Quebec Act, the western theater of the American Revolution, the reluctant postrevolutionary British exodus, and the futility of British-Indian resistance efforts of the War of 1812 years furnish the narration guidelines for this volume.

Kellogg's principal theme in *British Regime* is the fur trade. Her analysis of the organized trade with the Indians, with all of its complicated rules and regulations persuasively shows that it had a greater impact on the frontier than did the military, politics, or the scattered settlers for these years. Remembering the full title to both this and *French Regime*, whether Kellogg was an Old Northwest historian with a Wisconsin perspective or a Wisconsin historian who viewed her subject in a larger context, matters little. She did alternate between Wisconsin and the larger context with skill and without disruption. Assuming a combination of both, her state of the art contributions to frontier history and to the history of Wisconsin merit all the credit they were given by her contemporaries and successive generations. Even though some of her observations and conclusions have been outdated by subsequent scholarship and considerable additional sources of information have since been uncovered, later scholars are heavily indebted to Kellogg for the solid foundations she established. At the same time, it must also be recognized that while she presented much new material, she built upon the works of her predecessors and included much in her monographs already told elsewhere, including some from her own extensive annotated documentary publications. Kellogg had the knack of placing things in their proper context and of assigning them their relative importance. It can only be conjectured that *The Pioneer Regime*, the projected next volume on which she had begun to work, would have been cast in the same mold.

Bibliography

Louise Phelps Kellogg's publications present a veritable bibliographer's nightmare. The sheer number of her published efforts makes it doubtful whether a definitive reckoning can ever be made, especially in light of three additional considerations. Apparently she made no effort to keep a record of what appeared. Her pieces were not always signed and attribution can sometimes only be deduced indirectly, if at all. She also contributed occasional articles to lesser well known publications whose locations are now discovered only by chance.

Her professional career was a part of the warp and woof of the State Historical Society of Wisconsin and its various publications. As already surmised, she had probably become co-editor with Rueben Gold Thwaites long before that was acknowledged on the title pages of many of his efforts. She also composed some of the regular features in the early volumes of the *Wisconsin Magazine of History*: "Historical Fragments," "The Question Box," and "The Society and the State." These are sometimes signed, sometimes not. The latter, the most substantial of the three features, was probably her responsibility from the beginning with volume I (1917). It first appeared under her signature with volume IX (1925) and continued into volume XXV (1942), the year of her death. Some of these efforts cannot be considered as "publications" for bibliographic listing, but many represented scholarly contributions and should be so recognized. For practical reasons, this general statement must suffice instead of specific identification, even if identification could be made.

Another genre poses a bibliographic problem. Kellogg became a master indexer. She was frequently enlisted to construct indexes for the works of other scholars. Her penchant for accuracy and thoroughness produced high quality tools that considerably enhanced the utility and the understanding of the volumes. As with her other endeavors, some were credited to her, some were not; but no account was kept of all of these efforts.

In this bibliography, only the initial publication of a book is noted, although in some instances there were subsequent reprints, widely scattered in time and place of publication. A number of articles have also been issued as reprints, a few were translated into French, and some were issued in pamphlet form as separates. Inasmuch as the initial imprints are generally available, no disservice is rendered in not going beyond them in this listing.

Books

The British Regime in Wisconsin and the Northwest. State Historical Society of Wisconsin *Publications.* Madison: State Historical Society of Wisconsin, 1935.

Documentary History of Dunmore's War, 1774. Compiled from the Draper Manuscripts in the Library of the Wisconsin Historical Society and Published at the Charge of the Wisconsin Society of the Sons of the American Revolution. Edited with Reuben Gold Thwaites. Madison: Wisconsin Historical Society, 1905.

Early Narratives of the Northwest, 1634-1699. Editor. New York: Charles Scribner's Sons, 1917.

The French Regime in Wisconsin and the Northwest. State Historical Society of Wisconsin *Publications.* Madison: State Historical Society of Wisconsin, 1925.

Frontier Advance on the Upper Ohio, 1778-1779. Editor. State Historical Society of Wisconsin, *Collections.* Vol. XXIII. Madison: Published by the Society, 1916.

Frontier Defense on the Upper Ohio, 1777-1778. Compiled from the Draper Manuscripts in the Library of the Wisconsin Historical Society and Published at the Charge of the Wisconsin Society of the Sons of the American Revolution. Edited with Reuben Gold Thwaites. Madison: Wisconsin Historical Society, 1912.

Frontier Retreat on the Upper Ohio, 1779-1781. Editor. State Historical Society of Wisconsin, *Collections.* Vol. XXIV. Madison: Published by the Society, 1917.

Index to Volumes I-XX of the Wisconsin Historical Collections. State Historical Society of Wisconsin, *Collections.* Vol. XXI. Madison: Published by the Society, 1915.

The Revolution on the Upper Ohio, 1775-1777. Compiled from the Draper Manuscripts in the Library of the Wisconsin Historical Society and Published at the Charge of the Wisconsin Society of the Sons of the American Revolution. Edited with Reuben Gold Thwaites. Madison: Wisconsin Historical Society, 1908.

Stage Coach and Tavern Tales of the Old Northwest by Harry Ellsworth Cole. Editor. Cleveland: Arthur H. Clark Co., 1930.

Articles and Pamphlets

"The Admission of Wisconsin to Statehood." In *The Movement for Statehood, 1845-1846* edited by Milo M. Quaife. State Historical Society of Wisconsin, *Collections.* Vol. XXVI. Madison: Published by the Society, 1918. Pp. 18-29.

"The Agency House at Fort Winnebago." *Wisconsin Magazine of History* 14(June, 1931):437-448.

"The Alien Suffrage Provision in the Constitution of Wisconsin." *Wisconsin Magazine of History* 1(June, 1918):422-425.

"The American Colonial Charter: A Study of English Administration in Relation Thereto, Chiefly after 1688." In *Annual Report of the American Historical Association for the Year 1903.* Washington, DC: Government Printing Office, 1904. 1:185-341.

"Angel Decorah Dietz." *Wisconsin Archeologist* 18(August, 1919):103-104.

"The Baker Papers." *Wisconsin Magazine of History* 4(September, 1920):116-122.

"Banker's Aid in 1861-62." *Wisconsin Magazine of History* 1(September, 1917):25-34.

"The Beginnings of Milwaukee." *Wisconsin Magazine of History* 1(June, 1918):417-418.

"The Bennett Law in Wisconsin." *Wisconsin Magazine of History* 2(September, 1918):3-25.

"Biographical Sketches of the Members of the Convention of 1846." In *The Convention of 1846* edited by Milo M. Quaife. State Historical Society of Wisconsin, *Collections.* Vol. XXVII. Madison: Published by the Society, 1919. Pp. 756-800.

"Biographical Sketches of Members of the Convention of 1847-1848." In *The Attainment of Statehood* edited by Milo M. Quaife. State Historical Society of Wisconsin, *Collections.* Vol. XXIX. Madison: Published by the Society, 1928. Pp. 900-931.

"The Capture of Mackinac in 1812." In State Historical Society of Wisconsin, *Proceedings for 1912.* Madison: Published by the Society, 1913. Pp. 124-145.

"Carl Russell Fish." *Wisconsin Magazine of History* 16(September, 1932):96-101.

"The Chicago-Milwaukee-Green Bay Trail." *Wisconsin Archeologist* n.s. 9(January, 1930):103-106.

"The Contemporary Scene in Wisconsin." *Wisconsin Archeologist* n.s. 17(April, 1937):34-37.

"Copper Mining in the Early Northwest." *Wisconsin Magazine of History* 8(December, 1924):146-159.

"David Starr Jordan in Wisconsin." *Wisconsin Magazine of History* 17(March, 1934):266-276.

"Diary of George W. Stoner--1862." Editor. *Wisconsin Magazine of History* 21(December, 1937):194-212; 21(March, 1938):322-336; 21(June, 1938):420-431; 22(September, 1938):74-89.

Dictionary of American Biography edited by Allen Johnson and Dumas Malone. 20 vols. New York: Charles Scribner's Sons, 1928-1937. Biographical sketches on Alemany, Jose Sadoc; Altham, John; Andre, Louis; Badin, Stephen Theodore; Bapst, John; Baraga, Frederic; Bienville, Jean Baptiste Le Moyne, Sieur de; Bourgmont, Etienne Venyard, Sieur de; Brodhead, Daniel; Brule, Etienne; Cadillac, Antoine de la Mothe, Sieur; Carver, Jonathan; Celeron de Blainville, Pierre Joseph de; Champlain, Samuel de; Charlevoix, Pierre Francois Xavier de; Chaumonot, Pierre Joseph Marie; Clark, William; Cornstalk; Dablon, Claude; De Langlade, Charles Michel; Druillettes, Gabriel; Duluth, Daniel Greysolon, Sieur; Dunmore, John Murray; Faribault, Jean Baptiste; Forsyth, Thomas; Garakonthie, Daniel; Gass, Patrick; Gravier, Jacques; Guignas, Michel; Hennepin, Louis; Iberville, Pierre Le Moyne, Sieur d'; Jogues, Isaac; Jolliet, Louis; Joutel, Henri; Juneau, Solomon Laurent; Kinzie, John; Lahontan, Louis-Armand de Lom d'Arce, Baron de; Lapham, Increase Allen; La Ronde, Louis Denis, Sieur de; La Salle, Robert Cavalier, Sieur de; Laudonniere, Rene Goulaine de; La Verendrye, Pierre Gaultier De Varennes, Sieur de; Legler, Henry Eduard; Lery, Joseph Gaspard Chaussegros de; Le Sueur, Pierre; Lewis, Meriwether; L'Halle, Constantin de; Marest, Pierre Gabriel; Marquette, Jacques; Membre, Zenobius; Menard, Rene; Monette, John Wesley; Nicolet, Jean; Nicollet, Joseph Nicolas; Ordway, John; Perrot, Nicolas; Pond, Peter; Rale, Sebastien; Ribaut, Jean; Rolette, Jean Joseph; Saenderl, Simon; St. Denis (Denys), Louis Juchereau de; St. Lusson, Simon Francois Daumont, Sieur de; Thwaites, Reuben Gold; Tonty, Henry de; Vaudreuil-Cavagnal, Pierre de Rigaud, Marquis de; Verwyst, Chrysostom Adrian; Vincennes, Francois Marie Bissot, Sieur de; Vincennes, Jean Baptiste Bissot, Sieur de; and Williams, Eleazar.

Dictionary of American Biography, Supplement One edited by Harris E. Starr. New York: Charles Scribner's Sons, 1944. Biographical sketches on Fish, Carl Russell; Henry, Alexander; and Hooper, Jessie Annette Jack.

Dictionary of American History edited by James Truslow Adams. 5 vols. New York: Charles Scribner's Sons, 1940. Articles on Big Knives; Boone, Jemima, and Calloway Girls Episode; Bourgeois; Butte des Morts Council; Champlain Fires a Shot; Charlevoix's Journey; Charlotte, The Treaty of Camp; Chequamegon Bay; Chiswell's

Mines; Connolly's Plot; Cornstalk, Murder of; Duluth's Explorations; Dunmore's War; "Forted"; Fox, The; Fox-French Wars, The; Fox-Wisconsin Waterway, The; Franquelin's Maps; Fur Trade, Goods for; Green Bay; Gwynn's Island; Hennepin Narratives; Howard, Fort; Indian and the Gun; Indian Barrier State; Jesuit Relations; Jolliet and Marquette Discovery; LaBalme's Expedition; Mascouten, The; McDonald's Expedition; Pluggy's Band; Point Pleasant, The Battle of; Powell's Valley; Prairie du Chien; Prairie du Chien, Indian Treaty at; St. Antoine, Fort; Sauk Indians; Sauk Prairie (1778); Squaw Campaign; Warrior's Path, Great; Winnebago, Fort; Winnebago; Wisconsin; Wisconsin Heights, Battle of; and Wisconsin Idea.

"The Disputed Michigan-Wisconsin Boundary." *Wisconsin Magazine of History* 1(March, 1918):304-307.

"The Early Biographers of George Rogers Clark." *American Historical Review* 35(January, 1930):295-302.

"The Electric Light System at Appleton." *Wisconsin Magazine of History* 6(December, 1922):189-194.

"The Fairchild Papers." *Wisconsin Magazine of History* 10(March, 1927):259-281.

"The Fame of Daniel Boone." *Register of the Kentucky State Historical Society* 32(July, 1934):187-198.

"The First Missionary in Wisconsin." *Wisconsin Magazine of History* 4(June, 1921):417-425.

"The First Traders in Wisconsin." *Wisconsin Magazine of History* 5(June, 1922):348-359.

"A Footnote to the Quebec Act." *Canadian Historical Review* 13(June, 1932):147-156.

"Fort Beauharnois." *Minnesota History* 8(September, 1927):232-246.

"The Fox Indians during the French Regime." In State Historical Society of Wisconsin, *Proceedings for 1907*. Madison: Published by the Society, 1908. Pp. 142-188.

"The Fox-Wisconsin Portage." *Wisconsin Magazine of History* 2(December, 1918):238-240.

"France and the Mississippi Valley: A Resume." *Mississippi Valley Historical Review* 18(June, 1931):3-22.

"The French Regime in the Great Lakes Country." *Minnesota History* 12(December, 1931):347-358.

"The Fur Trade in Wisconsin." *Wisconsin Archeologist* 17(September, 1918):55-60.

"General George Rogers Clark on American Antiquities." *Wisconsin Archeologist* n.s. 7(December, 1927):44-50.

"The Historic Brule." *Wisconsin Archeologist* n.s. 8(October, 1928):10-13.

"An Historic Collection of War Portraits." *Wisconsin Magazine of History* 6(June, 1923):414-418.

"Historic Trees in Wisconsin." *Wisconsin Magazine of History* 2(September, 1918):92-98.

"Historical Associations of Sinsinawa." *Wisconsin Magazine of History* 3(January, 1920):364-367.

"The Hudson['s] Bay Company Tokens." *Wisconsin Magazine of History* 2(December, 1918):214-216.

"Indian Diplomacy during the Revolution in the West." *Illinois State Historical Society Transactions for the Year 1929* (1929):47-57.

"Joseph Schafer, the Historian." In *Joseph Schafer: Student of Agriculture*. Madison: State Historical Society of Wisconsin, 1942. Pp. 1-20.

"Journal of a British Officer during the American Revolution." Editor. *Mississippi Valley Historical Review* 7(June, 1920):51-58.

"A Kentucky Pioneer Tells Her Story of Early Boonesborough and Harrodsburg." *History Quarterly of the Filson Club* 3(October, 1929):223-236.

"The Knapp Papers." *Wisconsin Magazine of History* 4(December, 1920):231-232.

"La Chapelle's Remarkable Retreat through the Mississippi Valley, 1760-61." Translator and editor. *Mississippi Valley Historical Review* 22(June, 1935):63-81.

"Letter of Thomas Paine, 1793." Editor. *American Historical Review* 29(April, 1924):501-505.

"Marquette's Authentic Map Possibly Identified." In State Historical Society of Wisconsin, *Proceedings for 1906*. Madison: Published by the Society, 1907. Pp. 183-193.

"Memorandum on the Spelling of 'Jolliet'." *Wisconsin Magazine of History* 1(September, 1917):67-69.

"The Menominee Treaty at the Cedars, 1836." *Transactions of the Wisconsin Academy of Sciences, Arts and Letters* 26(1931):127-135.

"The Mission of Jonathan Carver." *Wisconsin Magazine of History* 12(December, 1928):127-145.

"The Mission of St. Marc." *Wisconsin Archeologist* n.s. 14(September, 1934):1-8.

"Old Fort Howard." *Wisconsin Magazine of History* 18(December, 1934):125-140.

"The Old Indian Agency House Association." *Wisconsin Magazine of History* 22(March, 1939):280-285.

"'On Wisconsin'--The Football Song." *Wisconsin Magazine of History* 21(September, 1937):35-38.

"Organization, Boundaries, and Names of Wisconsin Counties." In State Historical Society of Wisconsin, *Proceedings for 1909*. Madison: Published by the Society, 1910. Pp. 184-231.

"The Origins of Milwaukee College." *Wisconsin Magazine of History* 9(June, 1926):386-408.

"Passerat de la Chapelle in the American Revolution." Translator and editor. *Mississippi Valley Historical Review* 25(March, 1939):535-538.

"The Passing of a Great Teacher--Frederick Jackson Turner." *Historical Outlook* 23(October, 1932):270-272.

"The Paul Revere Print of the Boston Massacre." *Wisconsin Magazine of History* 1(June, 1918):377-387.

"The Perrault Papers." *Wisconsin Magazine of History* 4(December, 1920):233-235.

"Petition for a Western State, 1780." Editor. *Mississippi Valley Historical Review* 1(September, 1914):265-269.

"Pocahontas and Jamestown." *Wisconsin Magazine of History* 25(September, 1941):38-42.

"A Portrait of Wisconsin." *Wisconsin Magazine of History* 25(March, 1942):264-282.

"The Recognition of George Rogers Clark." *Indiana Magazine of History* 25(March, 1929):40-46.

"Remains of a French Post Near Trempealeau: Historical Sketch." In State Historical Society of Wisconsin, *Proceedings for 1915.* Madison: Published by the Society, 1916. Pp. 117-123.

"The Removal of the Winnebago." *Transactions of the Wisconsin Academy of Sciences, Arts and Letters* 21(1924):23-29.

"The Rise and Fall of Old Superior." *Wisconsin Magazine of History* 24(September, 1940):3-19.

"Salling's Journey in the Mississippi Valley." Editor. *Mississippi Valley Historical Review* 1(September, 1914):262-265.

"Search for Wisconsin Manuscripts in Canada." In State Historical Society of Wisconsin, *Proceedings for 1911.* Madison: Published by the Society, 1912. Pp. 36-42.

"The Senatorial Election of 1869." *Wisconsin Magazine of History* 1(June, 1918):418-420.

"The Services and Collections of Lyman Copeland Draper." *Wisconsin Magazine of History* 5(March, 1922):244-263.

"Sioux War of 1862 at Superior." *Wisconsin Magazine of History* 3(June, 1920):473-477.

"The Smiley Papers." *Wisconsin Magazine of History* 5(June, 1922):421-422.

"The State Historical Society of Wisconsin." *Papers of the Bibliographical Society of America* 16(1922):47-52.

"The Stockaded Village." *Wisconsin Archeologist* n.s. 8(January, 1929):61-68.

"The Story of Wisconsin, 1634-1848." *Wisconsin Magazine of History* 2(March, 1919):257-265; 2(June, 1919):413-430; 3(September, 1919):30-40; 3(December, 1919):189-208; 3(March, 1920): 314-326; 3(June, 1920):397-412.

"Sur la translation des Restes de Voltaire au Pantheon, le ll Juillet 1791." *La Révolution Française* 37(Septembre, 1899):271-277.

The Tercentennial of the Discovery of Wisconsin. Madison: State Historical Society of Wisconsin, 1934. Pamphlet.

"The Underwood Journal." *Mississippi Valley Historical Review* 2(June, 1915):117-118.

"The United States and Japan." *Wisconsin Magazine of History* 4(March, 1921):347-349.

"West Virginia Material in the Draper Manuscripts." *West Virginia History* 2(October, 1940):5-11.
"Winnebago Villages on Rock River." *Wisconsin Magazine of History* 3(January, 1920):370-371.
"The Winnebago Visit to Washington in 1828." *Transactions of the Wisconsin Academy of Sciences, Arts and Letters* 29(1935):347-354.
"A Wisconsin Anabasis." *Wisconsin Magazine of History* 7(March, 1924):322-339.
"Wisconsin at the Centennial." *Wisconsin Magazine of History* 10(September, 1926):3-16.
"Wisconsin Indians during the American Revolution." *Transactions of the Wisconsin Academy of Sciences, Arts and Letters* 24(1929):47-51.
"Wisconsin's Eminence." *Wisconsin Magazine of History* 21(June, 1938):397-404.
"The Wood Papers." *Wisconsin Magazine of History* 4(December, 1920):232-233.

Reviews
An Abridgement of the Indian Affairs, Contained in Four Folio Volumes, Transacted in the Colony of New York, from the Year 1678 to the Year 1751 by Peter Wraxall, edited by Charles Howard McIlwain. *American Historical Review* 22(July, 1917):880-882.
Across the Plains in 1850 by John Steele, edited by Joseph Schafer. *Wisconsin Magazine of History* 14(December, 1930): 236-237.
America of Yesterday as Reflected in the Journal of John Davis Long by John Davis Long. *Mississippi Valley Historical Review* 11(June, 1924):145-147.
Anglo-French Boundary Disputes in the West, 1749-1763 edited by Theodore Calvin Pease. *Wisconsin Magazine of History* 20(June, 1937):462-463. Reprint. *Mississippi Valley Historical Review* 24(September, 1937):234-235.
An Annotated Bibliography of Robert M. La Follette by Ernest W. Stirn. *Wisconsin Magazine of History* 22(September, 1938):109.
Antique Dubuque, 1673-1833 by M. M. Hoffman. *Mississippi Valley Historical Review* 18(June, 1931):76-77.
Approaches to American History edited by William E. Lingelbach. *Wisconsin Magazine of History* 22 (December, 1938):232.
The Big Sandy Valley: A Regional History Prior to the Year 1850 by Willard Rouse Jillson. *Mississippi Valley Historical Review* 11(December, 1924):449-450.
A Brief History of Galesville University, 1854-1940 by Arthur F. Giere. *Wisconsin Magazine of History* 24(March, 1941):362.
The British Regime in Michigan and the Old Northwest, 1760-1796 by Nelson Vance Russell. *Mississippi Valley Historical Review* 27(June, 1940):95-96.
Caesars of the Wilderness: Medard Chouart, Sieur des Groseilliers, and Pierre Esprit Radisson, 1618-1710 by Grace Lee Nute. *Wisconsin Magazine of History* 27(September, 1943):94.

Canadian Currency, Exchange, and Finance during the French Period edited by Adam Shortt. 2 volumes. *Wisconsin Magazine of History* 4 (March 1927): 357.

The Catholic Church in Indiana, 1789-1834 by Thomas T. McAvoy. *Wisconsin Magazine of History* 24(June, 1941):468.

Chapters in Frontier History: Research Studies in the Making of the West by Gilbert J. Garraghan. *American Historical Review* 41(January, 1936):386-387.

Charles Henry Keyes: A Biography by Maud Keyes Decker. *Wisconsin Magazine of History* 21(December, 1937):240.

The Church Founders of the Northwest: Loras and Cretin and Other Captains of Christ by M. M. Hoffmann. *Mississippi Valley Historical Review* 24(December, 1937):400-401.

A Collection of Documents Relating to Jacques Cartier and the Sieur De Roberval edited by H. P. Biggar. *Mississippi Valley Historical Review* 18(September, 1931):249-250.

Colonial Women of Affairs: A Study of Women in Business and the Professions in America before 1776 by Elisabeth Anthony Dexter. *Mississippi Valley Historical Review* 11(December, 1924): 438-440.

Connecticut's Place in Colonial History: An Address Delivered before the Connecticut Society of Colonial Wars, 28 May 1923 by Charles McLean Andrews. *Mississippi Valley Historical Review* 11(December, 1924):440-441.

Contributions of the Canadian Jesuits to the Geographical Knowledge of New France, 1632-1675 by Nellis M. Crouse. *Minnesota History* 7(December, 1926):348-349.

Council Fires on the Upper Ohio: A Narrative of Indian Affairs in the Upper Ohio Valley until 1795 by Randolph C. Downes. *American Historical Review* 47(April, 1942):618-619.

Daniel Boone: Master of the Wilderness by John Bakeless. *Wisconsin Magazine of History* 23(December, 1939):238-239.

A Day with the Cow Column in 1843: Recollections of My Boyhood by Jesse Applegate, edited by Joseph Schafer. *Wisconsin Magazine of History* 18(December, 1934):233.

Dialogues Curieux entre l'Auteur et un Sauvage de Bon Sens qui a voyagé et Mémoires de l'Amérique Septentrionale by Baron de Lahontan. *American Historical Review* 38(October, 1932): 166-167.

The Era of the Civil War, 1848-1870 by Arthur Charles Cole. *Wisconsin Magazine of History* 3(March, 1920): 391-394.

The Fatal River: The Life and Death of LaSalle by Frances Gaither. *Mississippi Valley Historical Review* 18(March, 1932):553-555.

Father Louis Hennepin's Description of Louisiana, Newly Discovered to the Southwest of New France by Order of the King translated by Marion E. Cross with an introduction by Grace Lee Nute. *Minnesota History* 20(March, 1939):66-68.

Filson's Kentucke by Willard Rouse Jillson. *Filson Club History Quarterly* 4(January, 1930):29-31.

The First Explorations of the Trans-Allegheny Region by the Virginians, 1650-1674 by Clarence Wolworth Alvord and Lee Bidgood. *American Historical Review* 18(January, 1913): 372-374.

Five Fur Traders of the Northwest: Being the Narrative of Peter Pond and the Diaries of John Macdonell, Archibald N. McLeod, Hugh Faries, and Thomas Connor edited by Charles M. Gates with an introduction by Grace Lee Nute. *Minnesota History* 15 (March, 1934):90-92.

Flight into Oblivion by Alfred J. Hanna. *Wisconsin Magazine of History* 23(September, 1939):114-115.

Fort Ligonier and Its Times: A History of the First English Fort West of the Allegheny Mountains and an Account of Many Thrilling, Tragic, Romantic, Important but Little Known Colonial and Revolutionary Events in the Region Where the Winning of the West Began by C. Hale Sipe. *Mississippi Valley Historical Review* 21(June, 1934):89-90.

French Catholic Missionaries in the Present United States (1604-1791). A Dissertation by Mary Doris Mulvey. *Mississippi Valley Historical Review* 23(September, 1936):256.

The French Foundations, 1680-1693 edited by Theodore Calvin Pease and Raymond C. Werner. *Mississippi Valley Historical Review* 22(December, 1935):435-436.

The French in the Heart of America by John Finley. *Mississippi Valley Historical Review* 2(September, 1915): 286-289.

French Settlement in the Driftless Hill Land by Glenn T. Trewartha. *Wisconsin Magazine of History* 22(June, 1939): 467-468.

From Quebec to New Orleans: The Story of the French in America. Fort de Chartres by J. H. Schlarman. *Mississippi Valley Historical Review* 17(March, 1931):605-606.

Frontenac and the Jesuits by Jean Delanglez. *American Historical Review* 46(October, 1940):123-124.

George Croghan and the Westward Movement, 1741-1782 by Albert T. Volwiler. *Mississippi Valley Historical Review* 13(September, 1926):268-270.

George Rogers Clark and the Revolution in Illinois, 1763-1787: A Sesquicentennial Memorial by Theodore Calvin Pease and Marguerite Jenison Pease. *Mississippi Valley Historical Review* 17 (December, 1930):461-463.

The George Washington Atlas edited by Lawrence Martin. *Wisconsin Magazine of History* 16(September, 1932):118-119.

Guide to the Personal Papers in the Manuscript Collections of the Minnesota Historical Society compiled by Grace Lee Nute and Gertrude W. Ackermann. *Wisconsin Magazine of History* 19(September, 1935):109.

Henry de Tonty: Fur Trader of the Mississippi by Edmund Robert Murphy. *Wisconsin Magazine of History* 25(December, 1941):237-238.

Historic St. Joseph Island by Joseph Bayliss and Estelle Bayliss. *Minnesota History* 19(June, 1938):198-199.

History of the Battle of Point Pleasant, Fought between White Men and Indians at the Mouth of the Great Kanawha River (now Point Pleasant, West Virginia), Monday, October 10th, 1774: The Chief Event of Lord Dunmore's War by Virgil A. Lewis. *American Historical Review* 15(April, 1910):660-661.

Illinois on the Eve of the Seven Years' War, 1747-1755 edited by Theodore Calvin Pease and Ernestine Jenison. *Wisconsin Magazine of History* 24(September, 1940):111-112.

The Jesuits of the Middle United States by Gilbert J. Garraghan. 3 volumes. *Wisconsin Magazine of History* 23(September, 1939):113-114. Reprint. *American Historical Review* 45(October, 1939):169-170.

John Marsh, Pioneer: The Life Story of a Trail-blazer on Six Frontiers by George D. Lyman. *Minnesota History* 11(December, 1930):430-432.

The Jolliet-Marquette Expedition, 1673 by Francis Borgia Steck. *American Historical Review* 33(April, 1928):698-699.

The Journal of Jean Cavelier: The Account of a Survivor of La Salle's Texas Expedition, 1684-1688 translated and edited by Jean Delanglez. *American Historical Review* 44(July, 1939):978-979.

Journals and Letters of Pierre Gaultier de Varennes De La Verendrye and His Sons: With Correspondence between the Governors of Canada and the French Court, Touching the Search for the Western Sea edited by Lawrence J. Burpee. *Mississippi Valley Historical Review* 14(March, 1928):533-535.

The Kentuckie Country: An Historical Exposition of Land Interest in Kentucky prior to 1790, Coupled with Fascimile Reproductions of the London, 1786, Brochure of Alexander Fitzroy, and the "Whatman" Edition of John Filson's Map by Willard Rouse Jillson. *American Historical Review* 37(October, 1931):170.

King of the Fur Traders: The Deeds and Deviltry of Pierre Esprit Radisson by Stanley Vestal. *Minnesota History* 22(March, 1941):60-61.

The Kingdom of Saint James: A Narrative of the Mormons by Milo M. Quaife. *American Historical Review* 36(January, 1931):418-419.

L'Empire français d'Amérique, 1534-1803 by Gabriel Louis-Jarray. *American Historical Review* 44(January, 1939): 340-341.

La Salle by Ross P. Lockridge. *Mississippi Valley Historical Review* 18(September, 1931):250-251.

La Salle by L. V. Jacks. *Mississippi Valley Historical Review* 18(March, 1932):553-555.

Lewises, Meriwethers and Their Kin compiled by Sarah Travers Lewis. *Wisconsin Magazine of History* 22(December, 1938): 235-236.

Life and Work of Mother Benedicta Bauer by Mary Hortense Kohler. *Wisconsin Magazine of History* 21(September, 1937): 112-113.

The Life of George Rogers Clark by James Alton James. *American Historical Review* 34(January, 1929):353-354.

The Literature of the Middle Western Frontier by Ralph Leslie Rusk. 2 volumes. *Mississippi Valley Historical Review* 13(June, 1926):96-97.

Marches of the Dragoons in the Mississippi Valley: An Account of Marches and Activities of the First Regiment United States Dragoons in the

Mississippi Valley between the Years 1833 and 1850 by Louis Pelzer. *Mississippi Valley Historical Review* 5(September, 1918):230-231.

The Marcus W. Jernegan Essays in American Historiography edited by William T. Hutchinson. *Wisconsin Magazine of History* 22(March, 1939):360-361.

The Menomini Indians of Wisconsin: A Study of Three Centuries of Cultural Contact and Change by Felix M. Keesing. *Wisconsin Magazine of History* 23(March, 1940):366-367.

Meriwether Lewis of Lewis and Clark by Charles Morrow Wilson. *Mississippi Valley Historical Review* 21(September, 1934):269-270.

Minnesota: Its History and Its People. A Study Outline with Topics and References by Theodore C. Blegen and Lewis Beeson. *Wisconsin Magazine of History* 21(December, 1937):239-240.

My Seven Sons by Lilian Washburn. *Wisconsin Magazine of History* 24(March, 1941):361-362.

New England and New France: Contrasts and Parallels in Colonial History by James Douglas. *Mississippi Valley Historical Review* 1(June, 1914):132-133.

The Northwest Fur Trade, 1763-1800 by Wayne Edson Stevens. *Mississippi Valley Historical Review* 15(June, 1928): 120-122.

Norwegian Emigrant Songs and Ballads edited and translated by Theodore C. Blegen and Martin B. Ruud. *Wisconsin Magazine of History* 20(June, 1937):464-465.

Norwegian Sailors in American Waters by Knut Gjerset. *Wisconsin Magazine of History* 16(June, 1933):471.

Old Fort Crawford and the Frontier by Bruce E. Mahan. *Minnesota History* 7(December, 1926):351-353.

The Old Northwest as the Keystone of the Arch of American Federal Union: A Study in Commerce and Politics by Albert L. Kohlmeier. *Pennsylvania Magazine of History and Biography* 65(October, 1941):494-495.

Oliver Pollock: The Life and Times of an Unknown Patriot by James A. James. *Mississippi Valley Historical Review* 24(December, 1937):384-385.

One Hundred Years of Welsh Calvinistic Methodism in America by Daniel Jenkins Williams. *Wisconsin Magazine of History* 23(September, 1939):117.

One Hundred Years of Wisconsin Authorship by Mary Emogene Hazeltine. *Wisconsin Magazine of History* 21(March, 1938):356-357.

Our Catholic Heritage in Texas, 1519-1936 edited by Paul J. Foik. *Wisconsin Magazine of History* 20(March, 1937):357-358.

Our First Great West, In Revolutionary War, Diplomacy and Politics. (How It Was Won in War and Politics under Virginia's Lead and under John Jay's in Diplomacy) by Temple Bodley. *Mississippi Valley Historical Review* 25(December, 1938): 400-401.

The Paths of Inland Commerce: A Chronicle of Trail, Road, and Waterway by Archer B. Hulbert. *Mississippi Valley Historical Review* 7(September, 1920):153-154.

Peter Kalm's Travels in North America edited by Adolph B. Benson. 2 volumes. *Wisconsin Magazine of History* 22(September, 1938):111-112.

Records of the Original Proceedings of the Ohio Company edited by Archer Butler Hulbert. *Mississippi Valley Historical Review* 4(December, 1917):390-392.

Report of the Public Archives [of Canada] for the Year 1921 by Arthur G. Doughty. *Mississippi Valley Historical Review* 10(March, 1924):455-457.

Rise of Ecclesiastical Control in Quebec by Walter Alexander Riddell. *Mississippi Valley Historical Review* 5(September, 1918):240-242.

The Roots of American Civilization: A History of American Colonial Life by Curtis P. Nettels. *Wisconsin Magazine of History* 22(June, 1939):461-462.

A Second Epoch of Destructive Occupance in the Driftless Hill Land by Glenn T. Trewortha. *Wisconsin Magazine of History* 24(December, 1940):230-231.

Simon Kenton: His Life and Period, 1755-1836 by Edna Kenton. *Filson Club History Quarterly* 4(July, 1930): 142-145.

Some La Salle Journeys by Jean Delanglez. *American Historical Review* 44(January, 1939):340-341.

Tabeau's Narrative of Loisel's Expedition to the Upper Missouri edited by Annie Heloise Abel and translated by Rose Abel Wright. *American Historical Review* 45(July, 1940):908-909.

The Territorial Papers of the United States. Vol. IV., *Territory South of the River Ohio, 1790-1796* compiled and edited by Clarence Edwin Carter. *Wisconsin Magazine of History* 20(September, 1936):111.

This Is My Town by Marian Scanlan. *Wisconsin Magazine of History* 23(March, 1940):372.

Thomas Sumter by Anne King Gregorie. *Wisconsin Magazine of History* 15(March, 1932):383-384.

Trade and Politics, 1767-1769 edited by Clarence Wolworth Alvord and Clarence Edwin Carter. *Mississippi Valley Historical Review* 12(September, 1925):287-289.

Vanguard of the Caravans: A Life-Story of John Mason Peck by Coe Hayne. *Wisconsin Magazine of History* 21(June, 1938): 462.

The Voyageur by Grace Lee Nute. *Mississippi Valley Historical Review* 18(March, 1932):555-557.

The Voyageur's Highway by Grace Lee Nute. *Wisconsin Magazine of History* 25(September, 1941):112-114.

War Aims and Peace Ideals: Selections in Prose and Verse Illustrating the Aspirations of the Modern World edited by Tucker Brooke and Henry Seidel Canby. *Mississippi Valley Historical Review* 6(March, 1920):572-573.

Westward with Dragoons by Kate L. Gregg. *Wisconsin Magazine of History* 21(March, 1938):358-359.

Wisconsin Lives of National Interest by William L. Crow. *Wisconsin Magazine of History* 21(March, 1938):357-358.

Youngest Son by Chester Lloyd Jones. *Wisconsin Magazine of History* 22(September, 1938):110-111.

Studies of Louise Phelps Kellogg

Alvord, Clarence W. Review of *Early Narratives of the Northwest, 1634-1699* edited by Louise Phelps Kellogg. *Mississippi Valley Historical Review* 4(December, 1917):392-393.

__________. Review of *The French Regime in Wisconsin and the Northwest* by Louise Phelps Kellogg. *Minnesota History* 7(December, 1926):345-347.

Beers, Henry Putney. Review of *The British Regime in Wisconsin and the Northwest* by Louise Phelps Kellogg. *Pennsylvania Magazine of History and Biography* 61(April, 1937):224-225.

Burpee, Lawrence J. Review of *The French Regime in Wisconsin and the Northwest* by Louise Phelps Kellogg. *Mississippi Valley Historical Review* 12(March, 1926):589-591.

Byers, Inzer. "Louise Phelps Kellogg." In *American Women Writers: A Critical Reference Guide from Colonial Times to the Present* edited by Lina Mainiero and Langdon Lynne Faust. New York: Frederick Ungar Publishing Co., 1979-1982. 2:439-441.

Carter, Clarence E. Review of *The British Regime in Wisconsin and the Northwest* by Louise Phelps Kellogg. *Mississippi Valley Historical Review* 24(December, 1937):387-388.

__________. Review of *Frontier Advance on the Upper Ohio, 1778-1779* edited by Louise Phelps Kellogg. *American Historical Review* 22(July, 1917):908-909.

__________. Review of *Frontier Defense on the Upper Ohio, 1777-1778* edited by Louise Phelps Kellogg and Reuben Gold Thwaites. *American Historical Review* 18(January, 1913):403-404.

__________. Review of *Frontier Retreat on the Upper Ohio, 1779-1781* edited by Louise Phelps Kellogg. *American Historical Review* 23(July, 1918):906-907.

Creighton, D. G. Review of *The British Regime in Wisconsin and the Northwest* by Louise Phelps Kellogg. *Canadian Historical Review* 17(June, 1936):204-205.

Hafen, Le Roy R. Review of *Stage Coach and Tavern Tales of the Old Northwest* by Harry Ellsworth Cole and edited by Louise Phelps Kellogg. *American Historical Review* 36(January, 1931):452-453.

Hicks, John D. "Memorial." *Mississippi Valley Historical Review* 29(September, 1942):316.

Holmes, Oliver W. Review of *Stage Coach and Tavern Tales of the Old Northwest* by Harry Ellsworth Cole and edited by Louise Phelps Kellogg. *Mississippi Valley Historical Review* 17(December, 1930):470-471.

Innis, H. A. Review of *The French Regime in Wisconsin and the Northwest* by Louise Phelps Kellogg. *Canadian Historical Review* 7(March, 1926):64-65.

James, James Alton. Review of *Frontier Retreat on the Upper Ohio, 1779-1781* edited by Louise Phelps Kellogg. *Mississippi Valley Historical Review* 5(December, 1918):363-364.

Kellogg, Amherst Willoughby. "Recollections of Life in Early Wisconsin." *Wisconsin Magazine of History* 7(June, 1924):473-498; 8(September, 1924):88-110; 8(December, 1924):221-243.

Kinnett, David. "Miss Kellogg's Quiet Passion." *Wisconsin Magazine of History* 62(Summer, 1979):267-299.

Larson, Arthur J. Review of *Stage Coach and Tavern Tales of the Old Northwest* by Harry Ellsworth Cole and edited by Louise Phelps Kellogg. *Minnesota History* 11(September, 1930):309-310.

Lewis, Virgil A. Review of *The Revolution on the Upper Ohio, 1775-1777* edited by Louise Phelps Kellogg and Reuben Gold Thwaites. *American Historical Review* 14(October, 1908): 183-184.

"Memorial." *American Historical Review* 48(October, 1942):220-221.

__________. *Journal of the Illinois State Historical Society* 35(September, 1942):306-307.

Merrill, Ethel Owen. Review of *The British Regime in Wisconsin and the Northwest* by Louise Phelps Kellogg. *Mid-America* 18(July, 1936):214-215.

Nettels, Curtis. Review of *The British Regime in Wisconsin and the Northwest* by Louise Phelps Kellogg. *Wisconsin Magazine of History* 19(June, 1936):476-477.

__________, Gilbert H. Doane, and Edward P. Alexander. "Louise Phelps Kellogg, 1862-1942." *Wisconsin Magazine of History* 26(September, 1942):6-7.

Nute, Grace Lee. Review of *The British Regime in Wisconsin and the Northwest* by Louise Phelps Kellogg. *Minnesota History* 17(June, 1936):196-198.

Pease, Theodore Calvin. Review of *The British Regime in Wisconsin and the Northwest* by Louise Phelps Kellogg. *American Historical Review* 42(October, 1936):148-149.

Phillips, Paul C. Review of *Frontier Advance on the Upper Ohio, 1778-1779* edited by Louise Phelps Kellogg. *Mississippi Valley Historical Review* 4(September, 1917):257-258.

Potter, Franc M. Review of *Early Narratives of the Northwest, 1634-1699* edited by Louise Phelps Kellogg. *Minnesota History Bulletin* 2(August, 1917):189-190.

[Unsigned] Review of *Documentary History of Dunmore's War, 1774* edited by Louise Phelps Kellogg and Reuben Gold Thwaites. *American Historical Review* 11(October, 1905):200.

__________. *Virginia Magazine of History and Biography* 13(January, 1906):332-333.

[Unsigned] Review of *Early Narratives of the Northwest, 1634-1699* edited by Louise Phelps Kellogg. *American Historical Review* 23(October, 1917):179-180.

__________. *Dial*, May 31, 1917, pp. 485-486.

__________. *Illinois Catholic Historical Review* 1(July, 1918):124.

__________. *Nation* (June 28, 1917):762-763.

[Unsigned] Review of *Frontier Defense on the Upper Ohio, 1777-1778* edited by Louise Phelps Kellogg and Reuben Gold Thwaites. *Virginia Magazine of History and Biography* 21(January, 1913):110-111.

Schafer, Joseph. "Librarian Authors." *Library Journal*, June 1, 1932, p. 511.

Schapsmeier, Frederick H. Review of *The British Regime in Wisconsin and the Northwest* by Louise Phelps Kellogg. *Journal of the West* 10(October, 1971):734-735.

Sellers, J. L. "Louise Phelps Kellogg." *Wisconsin Magazine of History* 37(Summer, 1954):210.

Severance, Frank H. Review of *The French Regime in Wisconsin and the Northwest* by Louise Phelps Kellogg. *American Historical Review* 31(July, 1926):834-835.

Tramond, J. Review of *The French Regime in Wisconsin and the Northwest* by Louise Phelps Kellogg. *Revue de l'histoire des colonies Francaises* 1926(3e Trimestre):433-439.

W. B. W. Review of *Documentary History of Dunmore's War* edited by Louise Phelps Kellogg and Reuben Gold Thwaites. *English Historical Review* 21(July, 1906):622-623.

29

LAWRENCE KINNAIRD

by Jane E. Dysart

Biography

Lawrence Kinnaird was an unlikely prospect for the history graduate program at the University of California, Berkeley. When he first met Herbert E. Bolton, the distinguished borderlands historian, in 1925, he was a thirty-two-year-old oil field equipment salesman with an A.B. degree in chemistry and chemical engineering from the University of Michigan and only three lower division units of history to his credit. Bolton asked the obvious question, "Why do you want to study history?" "For fun," was the reply. That response was evidently acceptable, for Bolton admitted him into the program and supervised his graduate studies. Indeed, for the next sixty years Kinnaird did take great pleasure in the study, teaching, and writing of history.

The bare outline of Kinnaird's early life provides no hint of his later attraction to historical studies. Born in Williamstown, West Virginia, on July 9, 1893, he attended schools there and across the Ohio River in Marietta, Ohio. After graduating from the University of Michigan in 1915, he moved to Kansas City, Kansas, where he was principal of a small high school and part-time basketball coach. When the United States entered World War I in 1917, he enlisted in the army, completed officer's training, and then took flight instruction. Overseas he flew observation and combat missions with the Eighty-eighth Aero Squadron. In 1919, while he was still in France, he did graduate work at the University of Grenoble. On returning to the United States he became an oil field equipment and supplies salesman, traveling extensively from Wyoming to Texas. Eventually he grew tired of so much travel, and upon meeting Bolton, decided to turn what had been only a hobby into his life's work.

In 1925 Kinnaird joined Bolton's famous "round table" seminar and began to stake out his own section of the borderlands. His topic was "American Penetration into Spanish Louisiana," which he developed for his M.A. thesis in 1927 and expanded for his doctoral dissertation. After receiving the Ph.D. in 1928, he remained at Berkeley for four years as Bolton's assistant. To broaden the foundation of research by translating and editing the important historical documents found in the Bancroft Collection was a major responsibility assumed by Bolton and his students. Kinnaird set to work on the Louisiana Papers composed of Spanish governmental files from 1769 to 1809, the research materials he had plumbed for his own graduate studies. While he was at Berkeley he also met and married Lucia Burk, a political science graduate student who later received her own Ph.D. and collaborated with him in his borderlands studies.

Kinnaird spent most of his academic career in California. In 1932 he took his first teaching position at San Francisco State College. Four years later he moved to the University of California College of Agriculture at Davis, where he taught only one year. In 1937 he joined the faculty at Berkeley at the request of Bolton, who had decided to groom Kinnaird as his successor. Several of Bolton's students had more distinguished publication records, but Bolton was convinced that Kinnaird would best continue the "round table" tradition, carefully attending to the direction of graduate students and instilling in them the necessity of thorough archival research and critical analysis of documents. Kinnaird remained at Berkeley until he retired in 1960, taking leave from 1942 to 1945 to serve as cultural attaché to the U.S. Embassy in Santiago, Chile, and from 1954 to 1955 to be acting director of the Bancroft Library. After retiring from Berkeley, he went to the University of California at Santa Barbara, where he taught from 1960 to 1966, with one year's leave as visiting professor at Chatham College in Pittsburgh, Pennsylvania, in 1964.

During his thirty-year teaching career Kinnaird trained a sizable percentage of the third generation of borderlands scholars. Presiding over the "round table" seminars, he directed thirty-five doctoral candidates and 128 master's students on topics ranging from the early history of the Navajo Indians, to the army of New Spain, to Mormon missions. He was generous with his time and praise, believing that encouragement and patience were more effective than harsh criticism in developing scholars. At the same time, he held up to his students high standards of performance. He was a commendable model of kindness, integrity, and scholarly excellence for those students who crowded into his seminars and lecture halls.

Retiring from the classroom at age seventy-three, Kinnaird maintained contact with his former students and pursued his interest in historical studies. In his eighties he began to publish again, collaborating with his wife, Lucia, on six articles based on materials gleaned during his years of research in the Bancroft. When he died on September 27, 1985, at age ninety-three, he was laying plans for another book. A competent scholar and great teacher, Lawrence Kinnaird's influence extends not only to those who still benefit from his scholarship but to his academic progeny and their students, who now number in the thousands (Kinnaird Papers; *Arizona and the West* 2:185-187).

Themes

The Spanish borderlands, that "southern fringe" of the United States which Herbert Bolton called "once an area lightly sprinkled with Spanish outposts" (*Bolton and the Spanish Borderlands*, p. 32), was Lawrence Kinnaird's intellectual bailiwick. His dream, like that of Bolton, was to document and interpret the Spanish frontier as an integral chapter in American history. He chose the Mississippi Valley for his major research area of borderlands studies.

The list of Kinnaird's publications is not long compared to the scholarly records of many other Bolton students. His most important work was the three-volume *Spain in the Mississippi Valley, 1765-1794* (1949), edited translations of the Louisiana Papers in the Bancroft Library. Clustered around these volumes was a scattering of articles published in the 1930s and a series of articles written in collaboration with Lucia Burk Kinnaird during the last decade of his life. He also made short forays into other regions of the borderlands. In 1958 he added to the Quivira Society's shelf of notable publications a translation of Nicolás de Lafora's report of a tour on the northern frontier of New Spain from 1766 to 1768. His long time interest in California history resulted in another three-volume work, *History of the Greater San Francisco Bay Region* published in 1966.

In all aspects of his scholarship, Kinnaird demonstrated himself to be a Bolton disciple, following and expanding upon interpretive guidelines laid down by his mentor. The overarching theme implicit in all his studies is the defensive character of the Spanish presence in the Borderlands. Especially in the works dealing with the Southwest borderlands and California, he emphasizes the significance of missions and presidios as agencies of empire.

Kinnaird's major contribution to scholarship was to make available to scholars important Spanish historical sources. A central theme emphasized in his monographs is the value of Spanish documents to the study of American history. His dissertation had dealt with American penetration into Louisiana, a topic which held the promise of conveying a fresh synthesis to the history of American expansion. Although Kinnaird never gave full treatment to that subject, he did introduce various aspects of it in several of his articles. The focus of the majority of his articles, however, was Indian relations, a theme that his research in the Louisiana Papers had revealed was of major concern to the Spanish regime in Louisiana. Thematic development and interpretation emerged from the critical analysis of documents in Kinnaird's scholarly works.

Analysis

"Documents are the life-blood of history," writes Lawrence Kinnaird in the foreword to his three-volume edition of the Louisiana Papers. Transfusing more of that blood into historical accounts he designated as his principal scholarly task. Indeed, his edited documents formed a substantial part of the foundation for historical studies of the Mississippi Valley during the late eighteenth century.

Kinnaird employs several techniques to make documents more accessible for historical research. To some of his articles he appends one or more sources that shed light on an important event or a controversial issue. In two articles published in 1931 concerning international rivalry in the Creek nation, Kinnaird attaches four translated documents, three taken from the Louisiana Papers and one obtained directly from the archives of Cuba, which provided firsthand accounts of the flamboyant William Bowles's escapades in West Florida (*Florida Historical Quarterly* 9:156-192; 10:79-85). Illustrating a different use of source materials was an article published in 1932 on the 1781 Spanish expedition against Fort St. Joseph. Controversy among historians centered on Spanish motivation for the expedition. After surveying previous historical accounts and analyzing the evidence used by the historians, Kinnaird presents a letter found in the Louisiana Collection which clarified the issue. He then proceeds to reconcile the conflicting interpretations (*Mississippi Valley Historical Review* 19:173-191). Collecting a set of related documents and introducing them with a brief account of the historical context and provenance is another method Kinnaird employed to present original sources. In 1935 the *American Historical Review* published the Clark-Leyba Papers, a set of twenty-five letters originally from the Archivo General de Indias, Papeles de Cuba. These letters dealt with the American conquest of the Illinois country during the American Revolution and illustrated Kinnaird's point that a vast number of documents important for the study of American history were preserved in Spanish archives (*American Historical Review* 41:92-112).

The three volumes of translated sources from the Louisiana Papers of the Bancroft Library proved a rich treasure of materials for students of American history. This set, published as part of the American Historical Association's annual report for 1945, made available in print a large portion of the entire collection of more than 900 manuscripts and rare pamphlets obtained by Hubert Howe Bancroft from Alphonse Pinart during the 1800s. He omitted from the work all previously published materials, including those documents found in his earlier articles as well as those translated by Bolton in *Athanase de Mézières and the Louisiana-Texas Frontier*. Although Kinnaird translated and edited two more volumes of sources from the collection, they have never been published.

Each of the three *Spain in the Mississippi Valley* volumes contains an introduction, providing a straightforward account of the events documented in that book. Taken together the three introductions are an excellent survey of the history of Spanish colonial Louisiana. The sources themselves are arranged in strict chronological order without topical headings. The editor indicates the origin and the original language of each manuscript but does not include other types of explanatory notes. By adhering closely to the styles of the writers, Kinnaird preserves the flavor of the frontier atmosphere. Letters and reports written by all sorts of individuals--governors, commandants of remote posts, Indian agents, traders, even the Indians through their interpreters--discuss a wide range of subjects from war and defense to agriculture and religion (I:xiii-xiv).

Although Latin Americanists have been more inclined to use the original documents in the Spanish archives and microfilm copies of the entire Louisiana Collection are now available, students of United States history, particularly specialists in Indian studies and historians of the Old Southwest, have relied heavily on Kinnaird's translated sources. In *The Spanish in the Mississippi Valley, 1762-1804*, a collection of sixteen papers originally presented at a conference held in 1970 by leading historians in the field, Kinnaird's publications appear frequently in the notes. In a bibliographical article Charles Edward O'Neill cites Kinnaird's *Spain in the Mississippi Valley* as one of the leading collections of documents for the study of Spanish colonial Louisiana (*The Spanish in the Mississippi Valley*, p. 18). That Kinnaird's work is still an essential source for historians interested in the Spanish era in the Mississippi Valley is amply demonstrated in their bibliographies and notes. Among the more recent works relying on Kinnaird are Robert V. Haynes, *The Natchez District and the American Revolution* (1976), Gilbert C. Din and A. P. Nasatir, *The Imperial Osages: Spanish-Indian Diplomacy in the Mississippi Valley* (1983), and William S. Coker and Thomas D. Watson, *Indian Traders of the Southeastern Spanish Borderlands: Panton, Leslie & Company and John Forbes & Company, 1783-1847* (1986).

Kinnaird's other major documentary project was the 1958 Quivira Society publication of the Lafora diary. Nicolás de Lafora, an engineer who made a tour of inspection of the defenses of northern New Spain from 1766 to 1768, had kept a detailed account of his observations. Scholars have acclaimed it as the best single source of information about New Spain's northern frontier. In a forty-two-page introduction Kinnaird summarizes the diary's contents and places the expedition in the context of borderlands history (*The Frontiers of New Spain*, pp. 1-42). Again, as in the Louisiana Papers, the editor omits explanatory footnotes. The index is explicit and comprehensive, and an excellent foldout map drawn from Lafora's original is a noteworthy feature. A Spanish edition of Lafora's work had been published in 1939, but Kinnaird's translation for the Quivira Society fulfills its editors' objectives of making available in attractive format significant documents of borderlands history.

Kinnaird by nature was not given to polemic or overblown rhetoric, but he had the zeal of a missionary in commending to historians the value of Spanish records for the study of American history. "The accumulation of American historical materials by Spaniards," he writes, "may have as great a significance in the writing of the history of the West as the penetration of American settlers into Spanish territory had in its making" (*New Spain and the Anglo-American West* I:227). He reiterates this claim in the foreword to *Spain in the Mississippi Valley*, pointing out that the Louisiana Papers contained letters signed by "such noteworthy Americans as Thomas Jefferson, Patrick Henry, [and] John Hancock." Spain had unwittingly performed a significant service by preserving materials which give vitality to the study of American westward movement (I:xiv). In his introductory comments to the Clark-Leyba Papers he chides United States historians for their neglect of Spanish records concerning the American Revolution

(*American Historical Review* 41:93). Undoubtedly he realized that the lack of facility in reading Spanish, as much as the remoteness of the archives, prevented many historians from using the Spanish manuscripts. His translations and edited collections, along with hints of additional Spanish treasures, constituted his missionary activity on behalf of Spanish sources.

From Kinnaird's research in the Louisiana Papers for his doctoral dissertation emerges another theme--American penetration into Spanish Louisiana. He never published his dissertation, possibly because Arthur P. Whitaker's *The Spanish-American Frontier, 1783-1795*, covering similar subject matter and also based on material from the Spanish archives, came out in 1927. Ideas first suggested in the dissertation, however, appear in his articles. In his contribution to the first Bolton *festschrift, New Spain and the Anglo-American West* (1932), he maintains that the Spanish frontier in the Old Southwest was not really a barrier to American expansion. Instead, "under a very mild Spanish control French and English villages and settlements of Louisiana and West Florida attracted immigrants and served as centers for American colonization" (p. 212). Writing in 1976 on the American Revolution in the West, he points out that the Spanish presence along the Mississippi was "more beneficial than detrimental to American westward expansion" (*Western Historical Quarterly* 7:253-270). He cites as supporting evidence Spain's liberal land grant policy, a peaceful Indian frontier, freedom from taxes, and "in general, benevolent treatment by local authorities." To reinforce his position he demonstrates the considerable assistance which the Spanish had given Americans in securing supplies and munitions during the Revolutionary War. Kinnaird was no perpetrator of a "white legend" of Spanish good will and generosity, but he advocated fairness in acknowledging the positive aspects of Spain's role in North America.

Finally, the theme most thoroughly developed by Kinnaird was Indian relations. Trade and diplomacy provide thematic unity to Kinnaird's Indian studies. He is especially interested in the changes that the Spanish made in their Indian policy when they acquired Louisiana by diplomacy rather than conquest. There the Indians "had been in long contact with French traders, were well armed," and the "paucity of Spanish troops assigned to Louisiana precluded the use of force" as a means of controlling the tribes. Instead of employing the presidio to defend against Indian attack and missions to convert and civilize them, the Spanish turned to trade and diplomacy "for maintenance of safety on the Louisiana frontier" (*Western Historical Quarterly* 10:39). As a result of this more benign policy the "Spaniards, in marked contrast to the Americans farther east, avoided all serious Indian wars" in the Mississippi Valley (*Western Historical Quarterly* 7:270). When Spain did revert to the presidio system in the 1770s it was owing to "American pressure and not Indian troubles" (*West Tennessee Historical Society Papers* 35:26). Controlling the Indians by means of treaties and subsidies, Spain relied on the tribes in the Old Southwest as a buffer against the expansion of the United States (*Journal of Mississippi History* 42:1).

Although Kinnaird wrote from a non-native position using European-produced sources, he did not cloud his view of the Indians with a strong, ethnocentric bias. The Indians, as he saw them, were not mere pawns in the intrigues of international politics, but intelligent, independent agents acting on their own behalf. "The Choctaws made their first appearance in Spanish Louisiana history," he states, "by successfully blackmailing the government. They knew how to bargain from strength and rarely altered their strategy" (*Southwestern Historical Quarterly* 83:351). Discussing the leadership of Alexander McGillivray, Kinnaird emphasizes the Creek chief's independence and skill. He was a "master of intrigue," the "key to the whole southern Indian trade situation" (*Florida Historical Quarterly* 10:66,70). In a review of Robert S. Cotterill's *The Southern Indians*, Kinnaird writes, "Treating his subject sympathetically, the author presents the Indian view insofar as his sources permit" (*American Historical Review* 61:145). That declaration aptly summarizes Kinnaird's own approach to the Indians as subjects of his historical scholarship.

In his treatment of American frontier history Lawrence Kinnaird championed the borderlands perspective. He carried the Bolton approach eastward, viewing the Mississippi Valley and West Florida as an Anglo-Spanish frontier. His contributions to the study of American history, however, are found both in his publications and his influence as a teacher. The students in his seminars could find his precepts demonstrated in his scholarship. A careful search for Spanish as well as Anglo-American documents and the critical analysis of sources were values that he both taught and practiced. Trustworthy interpretation, he believed, depended on solid research as well as a fair-minded and discriminating use of materials. Thus he continued the Bolton tradition, but more importantly, Lawrence Kinnaird left his own legacy of scholarly integrity in his writings and in the work of his academic progeny.

Bibliography

Books

The Frontiers of New Spain: Nicolás de Lafora's Description, 1766-1768. Editor. Berkeley, CA: The Quivira Society, 1958.

History of the Greater San Francisco Bay Region. 3 volumes. New York: Lewis Historical Publishing Co., 1966.

Spain in the Mississippi Valley, 1765-1794. Editor. 3 volumes. *Annual Report of the American Historical Association, 1945.* Part 2: *The Revolutionary Period, 1765-1781*; Part 3: *Problems of Frontier Defense, 1792-1794*; Part 4: *Post War Decade, 1782-1791.* Washington, DC: Government Printing Office, 1949.

Articles

"American Penetration into Spanish Louisiana." In *New Spain and the Anglo-American West: Historical Contributions Presented to Herbert Eugene Bolton.* Lancaster, PA: Lancaster Press, Inc., 1932. I:221-237.

"Bolton of California." *California Historical Society Quarterly* 32(June, 1953):97-103.

"Choctaws West of the Mississippi 1766-1800." Co-authored with Lucia B. Kinnaird. *Southwestern Historical Quarterly* 83(April, 1980):349-370.

"Clark-Leyba Papers." Translator and editor. *American Historical Review* 41(October, 1935):92-112.

"Herbert Eugene Bolton, 1870-1953." Co-authored with George P. Hammond, James F. King, and Engel Sluiter. *Hispanic American Historical Review* 33(February, 1953):184-186.

"Herbert Eugene Bolton: Historian of the Americas." *Andean Quarterly* (Christmas, 1942):3-5.

"International Rivalry in the Creek Country: The Ascendancy of Alexander McGillivray, 1783-1789." *Florida Historical Quarterly* 10(October, 1931):59-85.

"Nogales: Strategic Post on the Spanish Frontier." Co-authored with Lucia B. Kinnaird. *Journal of Mississippi History* 42(February, 1980):1-16.

"The Red River Valley in 1796." Co-authored with Lucia B. Kinnaird. *Louisiana History* 24(Spring, 1983):184-194.

"Research Topics in Spanish Colonial History." Co-authored with Madaline Wallis Nichols. *Notes on Latin American Studies* 2(October, 1943):32-38.

"San Francisco de Las Barrancas: Spain's Last Outpost of Empire." Co-authored with Lucia B. Kinnaird. *West Tennessee Historical Society Papers* 35(October, 1981):25-39.

"Secularization of Four New Mexican Missions." Co-authored with Lucia B. Kinnaird. *New Mexico Historical Review* 54(January, 1979):35-41.

"The Significance of William August Bowles' Seizure of Panton's Apalachee Store in 1792." *Florida Historical Quarterly* 9(January, 1931):156-192.

"The Spanish Expedition against Fort St. Joseph in 1781, A New Interpretation." *Mississippi Valley Historical Review* 19(September, 1932):173-191.

"The Spanish Tobacco Monopoly in New Mexico, 1766-1767." *New Mexico Historical Review* 21(October, 1946):328-339.

"Spanish Treaties with Indian Tribes." *Western Historical Quarterly* 10(January, 1979):39-48.

"War Comes to San Marcos." Co-authored with Lucia B. Kinnaird. *Florida Historical Quarterly* 62(July, 1983):25-43.

"The Western Fringe of Revolution." *Western Historical Quarterly* 7(July, 1976):253-270.

Reviews

Before Lewis and Clark: Documents Illustrating the History of Missouri, 1785-1804 edited by A. P. Nasatir. *Pacific Historical Review* 23(November, 1954):388-389.

Borderland in Retreat: From Spanish Louisiana to the Far Southwest by Abraham P. Nasatir. *Western Historical Quarterly* 8(January, 1977):70-71.

Coronado's Quest: The Discovery of the Southwestern States by A. Grove Day. *American Historical Review* 47(January, 1942):397-398.

The Economic Aspects of the California Missions by Robert Archibald. *Western Historical Quarterly* 11(January, 1980):83-84.

Lost Harbor: The Controversy over Drake's California Anchorage by Warren L. Hanna. *Western Historical Quarterly* 11(July, 1980):337-338.

Narratives of the Coronado Expedition, 1540-1542 edited by George P. Hammond. *American Historical Review* 47(January, 1942):397-398.

The Natchez District and the American Revolution by Robert V. Haynes. *Journal of American History* 64(June, 1977):133-134.

Pichardo's Treatise on the Limits of Louisiana and Texas translated by Charles Wilson Hackett, Chairmion Clair Shelby, and Mary Ruth Splawn, edited and annotated by Charles Wilson Hackett. Vol. I. *Mississippi Valley Historical Review* 18(March, 1932):574-575. Vol. II. *Mississippi Valley Historical Review* 22(June, 1935):95-96.

The Plate of Brass Reexamined: A Report Issued by the Bancroft Library by James D. Hart. *Western Historical Quarterly* 9(April, 1978):227-228.

The Southern Indians: The Story of the Civilized Tribes before Removal by R. S. Cotterill. *American Historical Review* 61(October, 1955):145-146.

Who Discovered the Golden Gate? The Explorer's Own Accounts--How They Discovered a Hidden Harbor and at Last Found its Entrance by Frank M. Stanger and Alan K. Brown. *Western Historical Quarterly* 1(April, 1970):183-185.

Studies of Lawrence Kinnaird

Bobb, Bernard E. Review of *The Frontiers of New Spain: Nicolás de Lafora's Description, 1766-1768* edited by Lawrence Kinnaird. *Pacific Historical Review* 28(May, 1959):179-180.

Dahl, Victor C. Review of *The Frontiers of New Spain: Nicolás de Lafora's Description, 1766-1768* edited by Lawrence Kinnaird. *Montana: Magazine of Western History* 10(January, 1960):73.

Ellsworth, S. George. "News and Notes." Tribute in honor of Lawrence Kinnaird. *Western Historical Quarterly* 17(April, 1986):253.

Hamilton, John C. Review of *Spain in the Mississippi Valley, 1765-1781* edited by Lawrence Kinnaird. *Arkansas Historical Quarterly* 8(Autumn, 1949):259-260.

Kinnaird, Lawrence, Papers. Personal possession of S. George Ellsworth. Logan, UT.

"Lawrence Kinnaird Retires." *Arizona and the West* 2(Summer, 1960):185-187.

McGloin, John B. Review of *History of the Greater San Francisco Bay Region* by Lawrence Kinnaird. *California Historical Society Quarterly* 48(March, 1969):81-83.

Nasatir, Abraham P. Review of *The Frontiers of New Spain: Nicolás de Lafora's Description* edited by Lawrence Kinnaird. *Hispanic American Historical Review* 39(August, 1959):492.

O'Neill, Charles Edwards. "The State of Studies on Spanish Colonial Louisiana." In *The Spanish in the Mississippi Valley, 1762-1804* edited by John Francis McDermott. Urbana: University of Illinois Press, 1974. Pp. 16-25.

Worcester, Donald E. Review of *Spain in the Mississippi Valley, 1765-1781* edited by Lawrence Kinnaird. *Hispanic American Historical Review* 30(August, 1950): 369-371.

30

JAMES C. MALIN

by Robert P. Swierenga

Biography

James Claude Malin was rooted in Kansas. His education, career, research, and writings all revolved around the history and ecology of the Jayhawk State, which lies in the heart of the North American grassland. As a lifelong plainsman and professor of history, he tramped and photographed its landscape, imbibed its folk culture, studied the history of its farms and cities, and taught its young. Having worked as a youth on the farm and as a teenager in his father's farm implement business, Malin learned at first hand the slow process of adaptation by which local farmers experimented with new machines, methods, and crops for dryland agriculture. "There was no plan beforehand for these things," he realized later, "but they just fit together, that is, after they've happened you can see how they fit together. As a historian, I became interested in writing the history of that area of Kansas" (Colman-Malin interview, p. 4). Thus, the unique grassland environment that had long challenged its inhabitants--and defeated many--also attracted Malin, who devoted his long and productive career to the study of human adaptation to the grassland. All of Kansas became his laboratory. He achieved an unrivaled mastery of its historical literature and research materials by reading virtually every extant newspaper file in the rich Kansas State Historical Society collection, as well as regional periodicals and government documents.

James Malin was born on a 160-acre homestead in Edgely, North Dakota, on February 28, 1893, and died of a heart attack at Lawrence, Kansas, on January 26, 1979, at the age of eighty-five. He was the second of three children. His father, Jared Malin, with his two older brothers, had migrated in the mid-1880s from Illinois to Lewis in Edwards County, Kansas. Then, like the proverbial rolling stone on the frontier, Jared returned to Illinois for a bride, briefly homesteaded in North Dakota, became a small-town merchant-dealer first at Edgely and later at Kulm in North Dakota, and finally in 1893 he returned to Lewis, Kansas, and opened a farm implement business. Young James thus grew up with manure on his boots, dirt under his fingernails, and a firsthand knowledge of mules and machines and men, all of which he later believed was an excellent background for his life of scholarship (Bell, "Malin," p. 3).

In 1903 at age nineteen, Malin received his bachelor's degree from Baker University in Baldwin, Kansas, where he studied under a biologist, Charles Sylvester Parmenter, in addition to taking courses in history, philosophy, and psychology. This interdisciplinary focus in his undergraduate studies, Malin later explained, was "the foundation of my scientific thinking as related to the historian" (p. 4). After a brief stint of secondary school teaching, Malin in 1915 enrolled in the history graduate program of the University of Kansas under an academic fellowship. Here he studied under a professor of American history at the university, Frank Haywood Hodder, a scholar of the westward movement. The free-spirited Malin adopted Hodder's eclectic and unconventional methods and penchant for local history.

After completing his master's degree in 1916, Malin returned to high school teaching, but with the American entry into World War I, he was drafted into the army and served two years at a desk job in counseling and personnel work. With the war over in 1919 he continued secondary teaching and began doctoral studies with Hodder during the summer breaks. In 1921 he completed the then minimal course requirements and earned the Ph.D. degree in history from the University of Kansas, with a dissertation on the federal government's Indian policy in the trans-Mississippi West and its effects on the westward movement. At Hodder's insistence, the university broke precedent and appointed Malin to the faculty. At first Malin barely held a candle to his brilliant and ebullient colleagues, Hodder and Carl Becker. While teaching the standard fifteen hours per semester, however, Malin in his quiet and reserved manner soon established his reputation as a master tutor and mentor of graduate students. By 1935, he had supervised fifty-three master's theses and three dissertations. Ultimately during his long career of forty-two years at the University of Kansas, he directed seven dissertations and ninety-seven theses.

Malin's own scholarship was equally prolific. He published eighteen books and numerous articles during his career, beginning with two monographs in his first years.

Themes

Unlike many of his contemporaries, the innovative Malin demanded that the grassland be treated on its own terms as a unique region, distinct from the humid, forest lands of the East. He also stressed the importance of an interdisciplinary approach to grassland history. While other frontier and western historians readily acknowledged the need for such historical studies, Malin alone immersed himself in the literature of the natural and physical sciences as they related to the history of the grassland. In his own words, Malin explains that his ecological approach to history included "all the elements that enter into a situation as historical activity, especially facts and thoughts formulated by the sciences in areas not traditionally recognized by historians" (*On the Nature of History*, p. 27). He thus synthesized into regional human history such esoteric histories as land topography, rocks and substrata, climate, flora and fauna, fire, insects, and even soil microorganisms. In the words of an anonymous reviewer of one of his grassland books, Malin "summarized a whole new galaxy of auxiliary sciences represented by the plant sciences, climatology, animal and insect ecology, zoology, several physics, genetics, and agronomy" (*American Historical Review* 53:410). Malin's purpose in integrating the natural sciences with history is to gain greater insights into human life itself, which he believed could not be distinguished sharply from nonhuman history. "Both history and ecology," says Malin, "deal with groups or assembleges of living organisms in all their relations, living together, the differences between plant, animal and human ecology or history being primarily a matter of emphasis" (*Grassland of North America*, p. 408).

Malin's amazing reach into the scientific literature of ecology enabled him to view the grassland holistically and over long durations of time. Bisons, jackrabbits, grasshoppers, cactus, wild and tame grasses, cattle, and rainfall all contribute to the "unstable equilibrium" of the region and are significant variables in the endless harmonization process between human cultures and physical environment. In brief, Malin rejects fragmentation and also notions of regional deficiency, and he illustrates how to study the complete history of a region, including its prehistory, by drawing upon knowledge from all relevant academic disciplines. He was therefore a powerful publicist of the Great Plains and its people as well as an innovator in historical methodology.

James Malin's first book, *Indian Policy and Westward Expansion*, his dissertation, was published by the University of Kansas in late 1921. The work opened a new chapter in frontier historiography by treating the development of Indian removal policy in the Old Northwest as a response to the westward movement. Three years later, Malin published with the university an interpretative survey of American history in the period, 1865-1917, which a New York house soon reissued in a slightly revised version under the title, *An Interpretation of Recent American History* (1926). The book was one of the first to argue the case for the connection between the rise of American capitalism and imperialism. In the early 1930s, Malin completed a book on government agricultural policy and Populism in which he argues that the farmers' protest was not an indigenous movement but part of the larger progressive crusade. Malin reveals his conservative political philosophy by condemning national planning in agriculture by New Deal liberals as counterproductive and even dangerous to individual freedom.

In the mid-1930s, the most significant phase of Malin's career began with his studies of human adaptation to the grassland. Walter Prescott Webb's classic, *The Great Plains* (1931), stimulated his interest in the question of how early Kansas pioneers had learned to live in a low rainfall environment. Malin developed new social scientific and interdisciplinary methods that gave his work a lasting significance. Interestingly, Malin used a high school commencement address to present his initial findings on the folk process of adjustment among frontier farmers in the local Wayne township (*Agricultural History* 10:118-141). Soon he expanded the project into a massive ten-year study of population change and agricultural adjustment by white settlers in the broader prairie-plains region. In addition to the historical sources, notably the manuscript population and farm censuses, which Malin was one of the first scholars to use, he synthesizes the findings of the natural and social sciences relating to the grassland. The research culminated in three major books published in succession in the mid-1940s: *Winter Wheat in the Golden Belt of Kansas: A Study in Adaptation to Subhumid Geographical Environment* (1944); *The Grassland of North America: Prolegomena to Its History* (1947); and *Grassland Historical Studies: Natural Resources Utilization in a Background of Science and Technology* (1950). These works, with their exciting new ecological interpretations and quantitative research techniques, established Malin's reputation among the first rank of frontier historians, along with Webb and Frederick Jackson Turner.

As a Kansan scholar and student of Hodder, Malin was always deeply interested in the political struggles of the 1850s. He published two notable monographs on this subject: *John Brown and the Legend of Fifty-Six* (1942) and *The Nebraska Question, 1852-1854* (1954). The *Brown* study, which was based on newly discovered Kansas territorial court records and also the voluminous collections of the Kansas State Historical Society, reinterprets Brown's career in Kansas as primarily that of a land speculator rather than an antislavery fighter. This book, in Allan Bogue's words, is a "tour de force in the analysis of evidence and the demolition of historical myth" (*American Historical Review* 84:915). The *Nebraska* book similarly reevaluates the role and motives of the central actor, Senator Stephen A. Douglas. These fine books buttressed Malin's growing reputation as an iconoclast, tearing down the myths of John Brown, "bleeding Kansas," the "Nebraska question," the sod-house frontier (Malin preferred "sawed-house" frontier), and "the plow that broke the plains."

The emergence in the 1930s of the philosophy of historical relativism under the tremendous influence of Carl Becker and Charles Beard increasingly concerned the objectivist Malin. When the Committee on Historiography, sponsored by the Social Science Research Council, published its notable *Bulletin 54* in 1946, Malin felt compelled to respond to its overwhelming relativist slant with the publication of his *Essays on Historiography* (1946). When the committee issued its *Bulletin 64* in 1954, which in Malin's view continued to advocate the utility value of history for public policy formation, he followed with two new books that had a more strident tone: *On the Nature of History* (1954) and *The Contriving Brain and the Skillful Hand* (1955). Malin insisted that the purpose of history is neither social science nor biography; rather, it is the preservation of knowledge of the past in all its uniqueness. To make his point, Malin overstates the case and asserts that history is useless and historians should take pride in its uselessness (*On the Nature of History*, p. 39). But his main purpose was to insist on the possibility of objectivity and certainty of knowledge in scholarship, particularly when historians employed the detailed, case-study method that was his hallmark. The denial of certainty, Malin insists, involved a surrender to the nihilism of the "lost generation" of the interwar era, and opened the door to the "collectivist democracy" of the New Deal liberal agenda. While knowledge of the past is incomplete, Malin argues, it can be expanded by diligent scientific research and the boundaries of certainty can be enlarged. He also objects to the functionalist framework of the progressive school of historiography that distorted and perverted history by limiting it to the "ideological fashion of the hour." Historical research had no presentist function other than to expand knowledge; any usefulness was an incidental byproduct (Bell, "Malin").

Malin privately printed all three of these defenses of objectivity after the editor of the University of Kansas Press demanded unacceptable revisions of interpretations and conclusions. Malin welcomed stylistic changes but not intellectual censorship. "It is not a matter of particular terms," he wrote, "but a challenge to my whole position in major propositions which center particularly in the essays on science and social history and historiography" (p. 118). Malin contacted other publishers but none would consider the *Essays* volume. This unfortunate circumstance not only hurt and embittered Malin, but it had the long-term effect of severely limiting the dissemination of his research and writings. As Robert G. Bell notes, having "severed the umbilical cord" between himself and the University of Kansas Press, Malin lost the editor's pen, its bookmaking expertise, and especially its marketing capabilities (p. 119).

In the years immediately prior to his retirement from teaching in 1963, Malin pursued his long-term interest in the Populist movement and offered a new perspective on Kansas Populists in an important monograph, *A Concern about Humanity: Notes on Reform, 1872-1912 at the National and Kansas Levels of Thought* (1964). In contrast to the reigning orthodoxy at the time, which followed John Hicks, Walter T. K. Nugent, and Norman Pollack, all of whom placed the populists firmly in the liberal reform tradition as precursors of the progressives, Malin found the populists to be a coalition of older shopworn reformers with an anachronistic world view and a misguided "concern about humanity." They sought political office more for the spoils than reform. They were "not realistic," bankrupt of new ideas, weakened by internal struggles, and as a result, young progressive Republicans easily swept them aside.

In his publications during the postretirement years in the 1960s, Malin turned increasingly to cultural and philosophical themes in Kansas history. The Fort Scott poet-philosopher Eugene Fitch Ware particularly attracted him, as did the study of local theater troupes in early Kansas, and the religious philosopher Emmanuel Swedenbourg. In graduate school, Malin had described himself as a "free-thinker" and he joined the American Unitarian Society because it offered him the opportunity for "working on his own religious beliefs," which can be called naturalistic humanism. In his final book, published posthumously in 1981, *Power and Change in Society with Special Reference to Kansas, 1880-1890*, Malin refers to the "universal life process . . . of man evolving by random natural selection" (pp. 7-8, 19-25). Humans, Malin hopes, would use their contriving brains and skillful hands continuously to restructure society, including nonhumans. Humans must not be anthropocentric, he warns, and assume that they are the end product and purpose of creation. Rather, they must keep an open mind, avoid dogmatism, and hold to an open system. With such an inchoate philosophy of life and its meaning, Malin laid down his pen forever. In religion as in scholarship, Robert Johanssen's statement is apropos: "Malin as historian defies categorization; he is sui generis" (*Kansas Historical Quarterly* 38:457).

Analysis

The basic theoretical constructs of the new rural history--the systematic study of human behavior over time in the rural environment--rest on the work of the pioneering historian of the Midwest, James C. Malin. Malin integrated the study of history and natural ecology as no other modern scholar has done, and he developed innovative quantitative methods to chart grassland demographic and agricultural patterns that are the foundation of present social statistical research.

Malin's ecological interpretation of history is as imaginative and theoretically robust as the work of his better-known predecessors Frederick Jackson Turner, who tied the disciplines of history and cultural geography, and Walter Prescott Webb, who wedded technology and history. Turner stressed spatial relationships in human history, and Webb underscored human mechanical ingenuity. But Malin alone included the history of the natural habitat, as well as geography and cultural artifacts. If "land makes people," then Malin was correct to study the natural history of that land, and to insist on integrating human history with earth history. This was because Malin viewed the history of humankind as one infinitesimal segment of the time continuum stretching from prehuman geological time to pre-historical human time and, in the last few thousand years, to historical time.

Of the seminal scholars of the American West, Malin's work for a variety of reasons is least understood and appreciated. Yet he surpasses his predecessors in perceiving the interrelatedness of physical environment and human occupancy, in the interdisciplinary breadth of his scholarship, in his innovative research methods, and in his voluminous publications.

James Malin's interpretation of the grassland provided a foundation for the new rural history that developed in North America in the 1950s (*Great Plains Quarterly* 1:211-213). He broke free from the traditional methodologies and concepts that had often limited history to the study of past politics and elites, as derived from written records. Malin studied past human behavior systematically and comprehensively by going "to the field" along with the botanist and soil scientist. He sought to understand past human experience "as it was actually lived," the style of life and activities of farmers and villagers, their demographic behavior, farming practices, social structures, and community institutions. He considered the effects of economic, political, social, and environmental forces on human behavior as part of the larger picture. His was a unified conception of regional history in which human behavior is the key factor.

Malin's unique historical concepts closely resemble those of his contemporary, Marc Bloch, a founding father of the famous French Annales tradition, who did pioneering studies in French rural history in the 1920s and 1930s (*Agricultural History* 21:187-189). Rather than limiting himself to the traditional institutional and legal aspects, Bloch sought to understand the totality of French rural history. No Paris armchair scholar, he roamed over rural France to penetrate the peasant mentality and learn the daily routine of farming. His ideal was to unite historical perspective with local knowledge and experience. He immersed himself in the literature of all of the disciplines relating to land and agrarian communities--agronomy, cartography, economics, geography, philosophy, psychology, sociology, and folklore--and he asked "why" questions. Why did hamlets develop in one place and nucleated villages in another? Why were some farmers innovators? Why did crop patterns differ from one area to another? Bloch's innovative approach revolutionized the study of agrarian history in Europe and captivated countless young scholars who continued to work after World War II cut short Bloch's brilliant career.

Malin was cut from the same cloth as Bloch, although he had no acquaintance with Bloch's work or that of others of the Annales school of scholarship (Malin to Swierenga, September 15, 1973). Like Bloch, Malin urged colleagues to study history "as a whole" and to examine each topic "in relation to the cultural totality to which it belongs" (*Kansas Historical Quarterly* 38:460). Malin likewise raises the broad issues. Was the grassland a "natural environment?" Was it a finished product? Or was it ever-changing and never completed? Was the grassland "adequate" in resources for sustaining human life? What was the process of human adaptation? To what extent did human occupancy change this environment, and reciprocally, to what extent did the environment change the settlers? In answering these questions, Malin turned to the natural sciences, as Bloch had done a decade earlier. Malin's model integrates the human actors into the total cultural setting and especially stresses the adjustments forced upon farmers by the grassland environment. The natural landscape, cultural artifacts, and individual behavior all come within his range of vision, although the environmental forces receive more attention than the social forces.

Malin's amazing reach into the technical scientific literature of ecology is not his only accomplishment. Like the French scholars, he also pioneered in the quantitative, local-community approach to studying population changes over time. There are at least two roots of this methodological innovation. Most important is the influence of his teacher, Frank Hodder, who stressed the significance of local history for understanding change in its broader context. Malin and Hodder were doubtless swayed in their research methods by the grand designs of their contemporaries--Joseph Shafer's Domesday studies of Wisconsin frontier development and Frank Owsley's work on southern yeoman farmers. But

Malin never acknowledged a direct influence or cited the publications of either scholar.

A lesser factor was Malin's negative reaction to the historical relativism that was rampant in the profession in the 1930s. Like other founders of social scientific history, Malin became deeply dissatisfied with the unsupported and impressionistic generalizations that he found in writings on Kansas history. The careful counting of relevant populations on the basis of individual-level data, he became convinced, would show the actual facts and serve to correct mistaken notions and assumptions. Mass figures such as the United States census reports were inadequate. They were based on arbitrary boundaries and masked local differences either by "cancelling out" the behavior of smaller groups in the population or over-emphasizing the role of a dominant group. The writing of survey history from "the top down," Malin insists, "partakes too much of the fitting of generalizations to particular cases rather than arriving at the generalization from the study of the underlying detail." American history in general and population studies in particular, Malin contended in 1940, must "be written from the bottom up. . . . The mass statistics tell only part of the story, and it is necessary to balance one type of procedure against the other, recognizing that both are essential to a complete and balanced treatment of population problems" (*Cultural Approach to History*, p. 300).

Another asset of local-community history, in Malin's view, is that it recognizes the fact that people do not live compartmentalized lives. The units of analysis are small enough that all aspects of human behavior can be "envisioned as a whole" (p. 300). The problem of statistical validity can then be solved by comparative studies of a number of selected sample communities. Malin's remarkable insights regarding the potential of local-community studies and his call for history written from the bottom up became the guiding principles of the new behavioral historians, such as Allan G. Bogue, Lee Benson, Peter Knights, and Stephan Thernstrom.

To provide material grist for his scholarly mill, Malin exploited local serial records that few scholars of his generation deemed worthy of attention. These included land records, probates of wills, church and school records, and "most important of all," in Malin's words, the original census schedules of population and agriculture at both the state and federal levels. Based on these sources, Malin in the early 1930s launched a series of social scientific studies of farm behavior. He devised research strategies of areal sampling, individual-level analysis, and multifile nominal record linkage. Malin traced individual farm operators from one census to the next (including both federal and Kansas state censuses) and linked farm operators in the population and agricultural censuses of the same year. These innovative methods enabled him to chart rural persistence and turnover patterns, to determine the initial migration fields of pioneer Kansans, to measure changes in land tenure and farm size, and to describe the demographic characteristics of farm operations. Malin also began studies of urbanization in 1935; his work on the Kinsley boom is an example. But he expressed frustration later in life for not being able to identify new statistical methodologies for studying urban samples as he had done for rural populations.

Despite his modest disclaimer, Malin's powerful techniques of census analysis became the mainstay of the new social history and his findings challenged the prevailing wisdom on a number of points. Instead of a pattern of increasing farm turnover, which was the conventional view, Malin discovered a reverse trend: Kansas farmers were highly mobile only during the frontier period; subsequently they became less fluid, and after World War I they achieved a high level of stability. Moreover, the turnover rates in the eastern semihumid zones and in the western semiarid zones were similar for any given community age. Thus, Malin's fresh approach of studying communities in historical perspective by using local records and standardizing for time and place provides striking insights in population studies and lays the methodological base for all future geographical mobility research.

The Kansas historian's innovative techniques also yielded fresh conclusions about interstate migration. To measure the volume and direction of interstate population movement, Malin exploited the rich Kansas state census enumerations of 1875 to 1925, which listed each resident's state of birth and state of last residence. This enabled him to determine rates of direct and indirect, or multiple, migration and also in the case of large families to chart the migration routes based on the state of birth of successive children. Again, the Kansas historian is the first to employ the technique of birth-state data in the censuses to construct residential mobility indices. His findings show that the proportion of Kansans who migrated directly to the Sunflower State increased to sixty percent by 1875 and then declined sharply. Moreover, movement to Kansas until 1915 was mainly long-distance, i.e., from noncontiguous states. Furthermore, foreign-born residents increasingly displaced the native-born on Kansas farms. Both conclusions, in Malin's view, ran counter to Turner's picture of "rolling stones" on successive frontiers and the Americanization of the soil (pp. 304-305). Thus, Malin happily contributed to the revisionist critique of the Turner frontier thesis.

A second decisive influence on Malin's work is his strong reaction against the legacy of rank subjectivism that he found among the "new historians"--James Harvey Robinson, Carl Becker, and Charles Beard. If "everyman [is] his own historian," as Becker claimed in his presidential address to the American Historical Association in 1931 (*American Historical Review* 37:233-255), and if written history is an "act of faith," as Beard asserted in a similar setting in 1933, then each historian's reconstruction of the past is an imaginative figment of equal validity (*American Historical Review* 39:219-227). Malin openly rejected such subjectivist thinking and firmly held to the possibility of objective history, within the limits of human knowledge. Systematic sampling, counting, aggregation of individual-level data, and replicable research designs, Malin believed, would restore the necessary degree of objectivity to historical study. This is what drove him to quantify the migration, settlement, and cropping practices of the early residents of Kansas. He also immersed himself, as no scholar before or since, in the vast local newspaper collection and proceedings of agricultural societies in the archives of the Kansas State Historical Society. From these sources, he documented the folk wisdom by which the pioneer settlers by trial and error learned to farm in harmony with the ecological givens of the plains region.

Despite his methodological boldness, however, Malin refused to accept the logical outcome of quantitative analysis, that of generalizing and theorizing on the basis of aggregate data in order to establish laws of human behavior. The Kansas historian insisted on the uniqueness of each historical situation in space and time and on the distinct individuality of each person as a free moral agent within that particular historical reality. A person "does not follow laws in his behavior," Malin argues, "because, within limits, he possesses the power of choice. This freedom to choose leads to unique behavior" (*Kansas Historical Quarterly* 21:375).

Malin, it is clear, adopted the inductive method of science, but on philosophical grounds he rejected the scientist's goal of classification according to likeness and difference in order to derive laws of behavior of matter or living things. Man's "contriving brain and skillful hand," says Malin, is an elemental creative force not bound by environmental or cultural determinants. So opposed is Malin to any general theory that might encourage a closed system of thought that he rejected all theories and labels. He even objected when a sympathetic historian described his work, appropriately enough, as an "ecological" interpretation of history (*Grassland of North America*, p. 324). One suspects that the Kansas scholar overly enjoyed his lonely crusade against the reigning historical orthodoxy of relativism in the twenties and thirties. As he admits in a characteristic understatement: "Being an individualist and a bit stubborn about freedom of scholarship as against abject compliance with groupthink," he insists that no label could adequately encapsulate his scholarship (*The Contriving Brain*, p. 338).

Malin's grassland trilogy, more than his other work, exemplifies his unique scholarship and view of history. In studying any earth area such as the western grassland, Malin insists (in the preface to *Grassland Historical Studies*), "it is essential to avoid . . . any form of geographical determinism, . . . or gestalt dicta about the whole being greater than the sum of its parts." The historian should freely pursue a topic in all its aspects. He or she "has no thesis to prove, or problem to solve, and no necessity of formal organization" (p. v).

In spite of his many disclaimers, Malin's grassland studies did prove a thesis and establish major new interpretations of the midwestern frontier experience. The central thesis of his work is that agricultural adaptation by European forest-culture people to the treeless grassland environment was a painfully slow and disorganized folk process that succeeded only because of the ingenuity and resourcefulness of individual settlers. Not geographical space, but the human mind and skills are the cardinal factors in human progress, Malin writes. The physical environment is absolutely determinative only within fairly wide limits of tolerance. Geographical givens set the outer boundaries within which people have freedom to adapt in optimum ways. "The individual is the ultimate creative force in civilization," is Malin's dictum. He laments the fact that historians and geographers place "too much emphasis . . . upon space and not enough upon people in time and in the capacity of man to unfold the potentialities of the mind in discovery of new properties of the earth" (*Essays on Historiography*, p. 130).

Malin's treatment thus enlarges the concept of space to include multitudinous space-time units of limited duration--"partitioned space"--which are the result of ever-changing technological "discoveries." There is no end to the "world frontier," no closed space, because "man's capacity to discover new relations has no known limit." In the essay "Ecology and History," Malin gives the classic formulation of his main thesis:

> The earth possessed all known, and yet to be known, resources, but they were available as natural resources only to a culture that was technically capable of utilizing them. There can be no such thing as the exhaustion of the natural resources of any area of the earth unless positive proof can be adduced that no possible technological "discovery" can ever bring to the horizon of utilization any remaining property of the area. Historical experience points to an indeterminate release to man of such "new resources" as he becomes technologically capable of their utilization (*Grassland in North America*, pp. 410-411).

In short, land *use*, not its *availability*, is the crucial factor. The frontier was, and remains, an open-ended, perpetual process of intelligent use of resources.

A theme related to the openness of history and geography is that the time-space segments are interrelated. All ecological activity comprises a seamless web of past, present, and future. Malin perceives each chronological segment of space-time as part of a whole. Therefore, every vegetation map must be dated, Malin insists, because plant growth varies, depending on prevailing conditions that are always in flux. Never was there a time, even before human occupancy, when natural processes had produced a final "climax succession," such as the grassland-buffalo matrix in the presettlement prairie-plains, which many scientists believed was a finished product of nature best suited to the climate of the region. Such a concept of a pristine, stable "state of nature" is a myth, Malin believed, and he urged grassland soil scientists to posit a pattern of instability rather than "equilibrium" in the ecology of the Great Plains. Malin coined the phrase "unstable equilibrium" to express this concept of indeterminacy (pp. 441, 466-467).

With this revisionist view, Malin takes issue with the founding school of American plant ecology, that of the University of Nebraska professor Frederic E. Clements and his foremost disciple, John E. Weaver. The Clements school taught that the grassland had reached its climax after countless natural successions or adaptations by living species to soil and climate. Human occupation disrupted this steady state and threatened irreparable harm to the grassland equilibrium. Malin rejects this notion of a "permanent climax" and the assumption derived from it that the prairies must be saved from the plow. Rather, he espouses the alternative theory of Henry Chandler Cowles of the University of Chicago, leader of the so-called "Chicago School," who held that the grassland was an open ecological system in which vegetation continually changed, depending on climate, microorganisms in the soil, and the activity of plants and animals. No vegetation could ever be stable and any appearance of stability was deceptive (pp. 7-8).

When the United States Department of Agriculture in the dust bowl era of the 1930s adopted the Clements-Weaver interpretation and propagated it in the highly effective film, "The Plow That Broke the Plains," Malin wrote a scathing denunciation. He demonstrated from the writing of early explorers that floods, muddy rivers, and dust storms on the plains predated man's arrival and tillage. "There was no such thing as an undisturbed grassland in the conventional sense," Malin argued. "Man's turning over of the sod with the plow is only a more complete process of cultivation of the soil than took place continuously in nature" from the burrowings of prairie dogs, the cutting hooves of buffalo herds, and even the heaving of the ground during freezing and thawing (p. 152). Likewise, the Missouri River carried heavy silt long before the first plow broke the plains. The erstwhile "clean river" image was a myth. In short, disturbance is not only the normal condition in nature, according to Malin, but it is "a positive contribution to the well-being of vegetation and soil" (Colman-Malin interview, pp. 108-109, 119). For the emotionally charged terminology of "virgin land" and "rape of the land," Malin substitutes the sterile historical terms "native grassland" to designate the prehuman era, "domesticated native grassland" for the era of food-gathering habitation, and "plowed native grassland" after 1850 when European agriculture began (p. 152).

Another key point of Malin's historical perspective on the grassland is that throughout geological and historical time all regions of the earth--whether grassland or forestland, deserts, tropics, polar circles, or oceans--are adequate for all native vegetation and higher life forms within their limits. Human occupants must fit their culture into the natural givens of their environments. Each area is "biologically complete," deficient in nothing; and successful human habitation depends on utilizing available natural resources to the best advantage (pp. 154-155). As Malin aptly states: "The plains country is normal for hard spring and hard winter wheats, the bread wheats, and they do grow successfully where the rainfall is greater than about thirty inches. Western Kansas has a normal climate for the grain sorghums, but it is subhumid for corn. Likewise, white-faced cattle (Herefords) will thrive on the plains where buffaloes were most numerous but cannot compete with Shorthorns in the Bluegrass region of Kentucky." Thus, "an area is never super or sub anything for its native fauna or flora, and it is not deficient in anything that constitutes its natural condition." Malin, therefore, rejects the pejorative words super-humid, humid, subhumid, semi-humid, and arid, in favor of the descriptive words wet, high rainfall, mid-rainfall, low rainfall, and dry (*Geographical Review* 37:242).

It is notable that Malin shifts his thinking over the years on the issue of environment. In his early work in the 1930s, when Webb's influence was strong, Malin stresses the need for human adaptation to fixed, stable environments (*Kansas Historical Quarterly* 4:339-372). But later, after reading the geographer Carl Sauer's *Agricultural Origins and Dispersals* (1952), he came to believe that the stress on adaptation smacked of geographical determinism. Malin consciously tried to reorient his assumptions; he allowed that creative human beings enjoyed a considerable measure of freedom in learning to live with their environment, and perhaps to modify it (*Agricultural History* 46:418). Even the "natural resources" of a given region are culturally defined by the inhabitants rather than determined by climate, fire, or any "climax formations." Consequently, says Malin, "new skills acquired by man create new 'natural resources' and new opportunities. The process is indeterminate" (*On the Nature of History*, pp. 124-125). Thus, in geography as in history, the human mind is the crucial variable. Each landscape in every place and time is unique and subject to continuous, irreversible change, due to the interaction of numerous independent variables--climate, minerals, living species, even human cultural artifacts such as revolutions in transportation and communication. In a summation of his position in 1956, Malin stated his major proposition succinctly: "Each and every place and time is unique and change is continuous, irreversible, and indeterminate" (*Grassland of North America*, p. 404).

Malin enlarged the scope of the discipline of history by including the findings of the natural sciences in the story of human occupation of the plains. To this day, his is one of the few efforts to integrate biology and geology as part of historical analysis. Malin transformed prehistory into history by incorporating events prior to humans on the historical timeline of the Midwest. In addition to this vertical extension, he expanded history horizontally by bringing into each chronological segment that simultaneous interplay of all forces, natural as well as social. This is truly an interdisciplinary approach.

Quite properly, Malin is respected as an ecological historian. He first brought the findings of the natural and physical sciences into the purview of the historian, and conversely, he introduced to natural scientists the historical aspects of their disciplines and the role of ideas in shaping interpretations of their data. It is this synthesis: science, technology, and history--applied in a significant regional setting--that Malin deemed to be his primary contribution. He wrote: "Few scientists are trained in history and social science, and likewise, few historians and social scientists have training in science" (p. 326). This statement is unfortunately as true today as when Malin first wrote it in the mid-1940s.

Malin's iconoclastic mind and research methods influenced a generation of historians, geographers, and social scientists. His legacy has been profound and his heirs numerous. In the thirty years since his major writings on the grassland, rural historians have filled in many more details of plains agricultural development. Modern scholars have also explored a number of processes that Malin largely ignored, such as the ethnic and religious influences on farming practices, the life cycle changes of plains farm families, and the impact of the forces of commercialization on agriculture. No scholar can singlehandedly provide a complete regional history or a comprehensive general model of historical change. Research is a cumulative endeavor. For rural historians, Malin's innovative studies of the grassland are a lodestar that still shines brightly.

Bibliography

Portions of this essay have been adapted from Robert P. Swierenga, ed., *Ecology and History: Studies of the Grassland by James C. Malin* (Lincoln: University of Nebraska Press, 1984). The bibliography relies heavily upon Burton J. Williams, ed., *Essays in American History in Honor of James C. Malin* (Lawrence, KS: Coronado Press, 1973).

Books

A Concern about Humanity: Notes on Reform, 1872-1912 at the National and Kansas Levels of Thought. Lawrence, KS: The Author, 1964.

Confounded Rot about Napoleon: Reflections upon Science and Technology, Nationalism, World Depression of the Eighteen Nineties and Afterwards. Lawrence, KS: The Author, 1961.

The Contriving Brain and the Skillful Hand in the United States. Lawrence, KS: The Author, 1955.

Doctors, Devils and the Woman, Fort Scott, Kansas: 1870-1890. Lawrence, KS: Coronado Press, 1975.

Essays on Historiography. Lawrence, KS: The Author, 1946.

Grassland Historical Studies: Natural Resources Utilization in a Background of Science and Technology. Vol. I. *Geology and Geography*. Lawrence, KS: The Author, 1950.

The Grassland of North America: Prolegomena to Its History. Lawrence, KS: The Author, 1947. Revised, with Addenda. Lawrence, KS: The Author, 1956. Reprint. New York: Peter Smith, 1967.

H. H. Sargent and Eugene F. Ware on Napoleon: Professional and Amateur Military Historians. Lawrence, KS: Coronado Press, 1980.

Indian Policy and Westward Expansion. Vol. 1. Lawrence, KS: University of Kansas, Humanistic Studies, 1921.

Ironquill--Paint Creek Essays. Lawrence, KS: Coronado Press, 1972.

John Brown and the Legend of Fifty-Six. Philadelphia: The American Philosophical Society, 1942.

The Nebraska Question, 1852-1854. Lawrence, KS: The Author, 1954.

On the Nature of History: Essays about History and Dissidence. Lawrence, KS: The Author, 1954.

Power and Change in Society with Special Reference to Kansas, 1880-1890. Lawrence, KS: Coronado Press, 1981.

The United States, 1865-1917: An Interpretation. Vol. XIII. Lawrence, KS: University of Kansas, Humanistic Studies, 1924. Reprinted,

An Interpretation of Recent American History. New York: The Century Company, 1926.
The United States after the World War. New York: Ginn & Co., 1930.
Winter Wheat in the Golden Belt of Kansas: A Study in Adaptation to Subhumid Geographical Environment. Lawrence, KS: University Press of Kansas, 1944. Reprinted, New York: Octogon Books, 1973.

Articles
"The Adaptation of the Agricultural System to Sub-Humid Environment." *Agricultural History* 10(July, 1936):118-141.
"Adventure into the Unknown by Relativist 'Man-Afraid-of-His-Mind'." In *Relativism and the Study of Man* edited by Helmut Shoeck and James W. Wiggins. Princeton, NJ: D. Van Nostrand Company, Inc., 1961. Pp. 175-196.
"Agricultural Adaptation to the Plains." *Dictionary of American History* 1(1940):22-24.
"The Agricultural Regionalism of the Trans-Mississippi West as Delineated by Cyrus Thomas." *Agricultural History* 21(October, 1947):208-217.
"Aspects of the Nebraska Question, 1852-1854." *Kansas Historical Quarterly* 20(May, 1953):385-391.
"At What Age Did Men Become Reformers?" *Kansas Historical Quarterly* 29(Autumn, 1963):250-266.
"The Background of the First Bills to Establish a Bureau of Markets, 1911-1912." *Agricultural History* 6(July, 1932):107-129.
"Beginnings of Winter Wheat Production in the Upper Kansas and Lower Smoky Hill River Valleys: A Study in Adaptation to Geographical Environment." *Kansas Historical Quarterly* 10(August, 1941):227-259.
"Bluestem Pastures." *Dictionary of American History* 1(1940):205-206.
"The Burlington, Iowa, Apprenticeship of the Kansas Poet Eugene Fitch Ware, 'Ironquill'." *Iowa Journal of History and Politics* 57(July, 1959):193-230.
"C. A. Logan." *Dictionary of American Biography* 11(1933):357-358.
"Carlyle's Philosophy of Clothes and Swedenbourg's." *Scandanavian Studies* 33(August, 1961):155-168.
"Colonel Harvey and his Forty Thieves." *Mississippi Valley Historical Review* 19(June, 1932):57-76.
"The Contriving Brain as the Pivot of History." In *Issues and Conflicts in Twentieth Century American Diplomacy* edited by George L. Anderson. Lawrence, KS: University Press of Kansas, 1959. Pp. 339-363.
"The Democratic Party and Atchison: A Case Study, 1880." *Kansas Historical Quarterly* 28(Summer, 1962):154-166.
"Developments in History and Social Sciences in Kansas High Schools, 1926-1928." *Kansas Teacher* 29(May, 1929):7-10.

"Dodge City Varieties--A Summer Interlude of Entertainment, 1878." *Kansas Historical Quarterly* 22(Winter, 1956):347-353.
"Domestic Policies of the United States since the World War." *Historical Outlook* 18(October, 1927):249-259; (November, 1927):309-321.
"Dry-Farming." *Dictionary of American History* 2(1940):171.
"Dust Storms: Part One, 1850-1860." *Kansas Historical Quarterly* 14(May, 1946):129-144.
"_________: Part Two, 1861-1880." *Kansas Historical Quarterly* 14(August, 1946):265-296.
"_________: Part Three, 1881-1900--Concluded." *Kansas Historical Quarterly* 14(November, 1946):391-413.
"E. N. Morrill." *Dictionary of American Biography* 13(1934):197-198.
"Ecology and History." *Scientific Monthly* 70(May, 1950):295-298.
"Emanuel Swedenbourg and His Philosophy of Clothes." *Scandanavian Studies* 33(May, 1961):45-67.
"Emergency Housing at Lawrence, 1854." *Kansas Historical Quarterly* 21(Spring, 1954):34-49.
"Eugene F. Ware, Journeyman Poet--Acceptance by Fort Scott." *Kansas Historical Quarterly* 31(Winter, 1965):396-441.
"Eugene F. Ware, Master Poet--Acceptance by Fort Scott and the State of Kansas--History as Business (Commerce), and as War." *Kansas Historical Quarterly* 32(Winter, 1966):401-425.
"Eugene F. Ware's Literary Chronology." *Kansas Historical Quarterly* 37(Autumn, 1971):314-332.
"Eugene Ware and Dr. Sanger: The Code of Political Ethics, 1872-1892." *Kansas Historical Quarterly* 26(Autumn, 1960):255-266.
"Eugene Ware's Concern about a Woman, a Child, and God." *Kansas Historical Quarterly* 25(Winter, 1959):402-406.
"The Evolution of a Rural Community (Wayne Township, Edwards County, Kansas)." *The Lewis* [KS] *Press*, June 1, 8, 15, 22, 29, and July 6, 1933.
"F. H. Hodder's 'Stephen A. Douglas'." Editor. *Kansas Historical Quarterly* 8(August, 1939):227-237.
"The Farmers' Alliance, Subtreasury Plan, and European Precedents." *Mississippi Valley Historical Review* 31(September, 1944):255-260.
"Frank A. Root." *Dictionary of American Biography* 16(1935):146.
"Frank Heywood Hodder, 1860-1935." *Kansas Historical Quarterly* 5(May, 1936):115-121.
"Grassland, 'Treeless' and 'Subhumid': A Discussion of Some Problems of the Terminology of Geography." *Geographical Review* 37(April, 1947):241-250.
"The Grassland of North America: Its Occupance and the Challenge of Continuous Reappraisals." In *Man's Role in Changing the Face of the Earth* edited by William L. Thomas, Jr. Chicago: University of Chicago Press, 1956. Pp. 350-366.
"Haskell Institute." *Dictionary of American History* 3(1940):15.

"The Historian and the Individual." In *Essays on Individuality* edited by Felix Morley. Philadelphia: University of Pennsylvania Press, 1958. Pp. 146-167.

"The Hoogland Examination: *The United States v. John Brown, Jr. et al.*" *Kansas Historical Quarterly* 7(May, 1938):133-153.

"Housing Experiments in the Lawrence Community, 1855." *Kansas Historical Quarterly* 21(Summer, 1954):95-121.

"Identification of the Stranger at the Potawatomie Massacre." *Kansas Historical Quarterly* 9(February, 1940):3-12.

"In Commemoration of the Centennial Anniversary of the Admission of Kansas into the Union, 1861." [pamphlet] Lawrence, KS: University of Kansas Library, 1961.

"An Introduction to the History of the Bluestem-Pasture Region of Kansas: A Study in Adaptation to Geographical Environment." *Kansas Historical Quarterly* 11(February, 1942):3-28.

"Ironquill's 'The Washerwoman's Song'." *Kansas Historical Quarterly* 25(Autumn, 1959):257-282.

"J. A. Walker's 'Early History of Edwards County'." Editor. *Kansas Historical Quarterly* 9(August, 1940):259-284.

"James A. and Louie Lord: Theatrical Team -- Their Personal Story, 1869-1889." *Kansas Historical Quarterly* 22(Autumn, 1956):242-275.

"John A. Martin." *Dictionary of American Biography* 12(1933):341-342.

"John Brown and the Manes Incident." *Kansas Historical Quarterly* 7(November, 1938):376-378.

"The John Brown Legend in Pictures: Kissing the Negro Baby." *Kansas Historical Quarterly* 8(November, 1939):339-341 and 9(November, 1940):339-342.

"Judge Lecompte and the 'Sack of Lawrence,' May 21, 1856: Part One: The Contemporary Phase." *Kansas Historical Quarterly* 20(August, 1953):465-494.

"__________: Part Two: The Historical Phase." *Kansas Historical Quarterly* 20(November, 1953):553-597.

"Kansas." In *Britannica Book for the Year 1937*, pp. 365-366; *1938*, pp. 365-366; *1939*, p. 368; *1940*, p. 387; *1941*, p. 386; *1942*, p. 377; *1943*, pp. 379-381; *1944*, pp. 379-380; *1945*, pp. 381-384; *1946*, pp. 419-420.

"__________." *Dictionary of American History* 3(1940):194-195.

"__________." *Encyclopedia Americana* 16(1950):294-299.

"Kansas: Some Reflections on Culture, Inheritance, and Originality." *Journal of the Central Mississippi Valley American Studies Association* 2(Fall, 1961):3-19.

"Kansas or Kaw Indians." *Dictionary of American History* 3(1940):198.

"The Kansas-Missouri Border, 1854-1859." In *Atlas of American History* edited by James T. Adams. New York: Charles Scribner's Sons, 1943. Map 121.

"The Kinsley Boom of the Late Eighties." *Kansas Historical Quarterly* 4(February, 1935):23-49 and 4(May, 1935):164-187.

"Local Historical Studies and Population Problems." In *The Cultural Approach to History* edited by Caroline Ware. New York: Columbia University Press, 1940. Pp. 300-307.

"The Lower Missouri Valley." In *The North American Midwest: A Regional Geography* edited by John H. Garland. New York: John Wiley and Sons, Inc., 1955. Pp. 218-228.

"Man, the State of Nature, and Climax: As Illustrated by Some Problems of the North American Grassland." *Scientific Monthly* 74(January, 1952):29-37.

"Mary Elizabeth Lease." *Dictionary of American Biography: Supplement One* (1944):488-489.

"Mobility and History: Reflections on the Agricultural Policies of the United States in Relation to a Mechanized World." *Agricultural History* 17(October, 1943):177-191.

"The Motives of Stephen A. Douglas in the Organization of Nebraska Territory: A Letter Dated December 17, 1853." *Kansas Historical Quarterly* 19(November, 1951):321-353.

"*Mugler v. Kansas* and the Presidential Campaign of 1884." *Mississippi Valley Historical Review* 34(September, 1947):274-277.

"The Nebraska Question: A Ten-Year Record, 1844-1854." *Nebraska History* 35(March, 1954):1-15.

"Notes on Historical Literature of the Range Cattle Industry." *Kansas Historical Quarterly* 1(November, 1931):74-76.

"Notes on the Literature of Populism." *Kansas Historical Quarterly* 1(February, 1932):160-164.

"Notes on the Poetic Debts of Eugene F. Ware--Ironquill." *Kansas Historical Quarterly* 35(Summer, 1969):165-181.

"Notes on the Several Editions of Eugene F. Ware's *Rhymes of Ironquill.*" *Kansas Historical Quarterly* 33(Winter, 1967):481-511.

"Notes on the Writing of General Histories of Kansas: Part One: The Setting of the Stage." *Kansas Historical Quarterly* 21(Autumn, 1954):184-223.

"__________: Part Two: J. N. Holloway, *History of Kansas* (1868)." 21(Winter, 1954):264-287.

"__________: Part Three: The Historical and Philosophical Societies: Repositories of the Material of History and of Science." *Kansas Historical Quarterly* 21(Spring, 1955):321-378.

"__________: Part Four: The Kansas State Historical Society: Repository of the Material of History." *Kansas Historical Quarterly* 21(Summer, 1955):407-444.

"__________: Part Five: The 'Vanity' Histories." *Kansas Historical Quarterly* 22(Winter, 1955):598-643.

"On the Nature of Local History." *Wisconsin Magazine of History* 40(Summer, 1957):227-230.

"Plotting after Harper's Ferry: The 'William Handy' Letters." Editor. *Journal of Southern History* 8(February, 1942):81-87.

"Potawatomie Massacre." *Dictionary of American History* 4(1940):323.

"The Proslavery background of the Kansas Struggle." *Mississippi Valley Historical Review* 10(December, 1923):285-305.

"Professor W. Foster: An Identification." *Transactions of the Kansas Academy of Science* 58(1955):22-23.

"The Regional Concept and Regional Method." In *American Geography: Inventory and Prospect* edited by Preston James. Syracuse, NY: Syracuse University Press, 1954. Pp. 19-68.

"Research Projects in Kansas History." Co-authored with Nyle Miller. *Kansas Historical Quarterly* 8(May, 1939):175-183.

"Roosevelt and the Elections of 1884 and 1888." *Mississippi Valley Historical Review* 14(June, 1927):25-38.

"The Soft Winter Wheat Boom and the Agricultural Development of the Upper Kansas River Valley: Part I." *Kansas Historical Quarterly* 11(November, 1942):370-398.

"__________: Part II." *Kansas Historical Quarterly* 12(February, 1943):58-91.

"__________: Part III." *Kansas Historical Quarterly* 12(May, 1943):156-189.

"Soil, Animal, and Plant Relations of the Grassland, Historically Reconsidered." *Scientific Monthly* 76(April, 1953):207-220.

"Some Reconsiderations of the Defeat of Senator Pomeroy of Kansas, 1873." *Mid-America* 48(January, 1966):47-57.

"Space and History: Reflections on the Closed-Space Doctrines of Turner and Mackinder and the Challenge of Those Ideas by the Air Age." *Agricultural History* 18(April, 1944):65-74 and (July, 1944):107-126.

"Speaker Banks Courts the Free-Soilers, the Fremont-Robinson Letter of 1856." *New England Quarterly* 12(March, 1939):103-112.

"The Status of the Historical and Social Sciences in Kansas High Schools." *Historical Outlook* 18(January, 1927):22-28. Reprinted, *Kansas Teacher* 25(March, 1927):11-17.

"Status of History and Other Social Studies in Kansas High Schools." Co-authored with Annabel Pringle. *Kansas Teacher and Western School Journal* 9(March, 1941):20-21, 26.

"Theater in Kansas, 1858-1868: Background for the Coming of the Lord Dramatic Company to Kansas, 1869: Part I." *Kansas Historical Quarterly* 23(Spring, 1957):10-53.

"__________: Part II." *Kansas Historical Quarterly* 23(Summer, 1957):191-203.

"Thomas Jefferson Sutherland, Nebraska Boomer, 1851-1852." *Nebraska History* 34(September, 1953):181-214.

"The Topeka Statehood Movement Reconsidered: Origins." In *Territorial Kansas Studies Commemorating the Centennial.* Lawrence, KS: University of Kansas, Social Science Studies Publications, 1954. Pp. 33-69.

"The Turnover of Farm Population in Kansas." *Kansas Historical Quarterly* 4(November, 1935):339-372.

"United States Foreign Policy since the World War: Paper I." *Historical Outlook* 19(January, 1928):13-22.

"__________: Paper II." *Historical Outlook* 19(February, 1928):61-70.
"W. A. Philips." *Dictionary of American Biography* 14(1934):548-549.
"Walter Roscoe Stubbs." *Dictionary of American Biography: Supplement One* (1944):677-678.
"Was Governor John A. Martin a Prohibitionist?" *Kansas Historical Quarterly* 1(November, 1931):63-73.
"Wheat, Geology, and 'Professor' Foster." *Transactions of the Kansas Academy of Science* 59(1956):240-248.

Selected Reviews
Advancing the Frontier, 1830-1860 by Grant Foreman. *Mississippi Valley Historical Review* 20(March, 1934):580.
Adventures in American Diplomacy by Alfred L. P. Dennis. *Mississippi Valley Historical Review* 15(December, 1928):413-415.
America Moves West by Robert E. Riegel. *Annals of the American Academy of Political and Social Science* 1(March, 1931):191-192.
America's Foreign Policies, Past and Present by Thomas A. Bailey. *Pacific Historical Review* 12(December, 1943):417-418.
American History since 1865 by George M. Stephenson. *Mississippi Valley Historical Review* 26(June, 1939):102-103.
The Battle Against Isolation by Walter Johnson. *Pacific Historical Review* 14(June, 1945):235-236.
Bleeding Kansas by Alice Nichols. *Journal of Southern History* 20(November, 1954):548-550. Reprinted, *The Historian* 17(Autumn, 1954):112-114.
The Catholic Church on the Kansas Frontier, 1850-1877 by Peter Beckman. *American Historical Review* 50(January, 1945):414-415.
Civil War on the Western Border, 1854-1865 by Jay Monaghan. *American Historical Review* 61(January, 1956):421-422.
The Civil War Veteran in Minnesota Life and Politics by Frank H. Heck. *Mississippi Valley Historical Review* 29(June, 1942):108-109.
Crop Production and Environment by R. O. Whyte. *Geographical Review* 37(April, 1947):345-347.
Drought, Its Causes and Effects by Ivan R. Tannehill. *Journal of Economic History* 8(May, 1948):98-99.
Elias Boudinot, Cherokee, and his America by Ralph H. Gabriel. *Mississippi Valley Historical Review* 28(December, 1941):435-436.
Fifty Years of Public Life by Daniel C. Roper. *Mississippi Valley Historical Review* 29(September, 1942):272.
Franklin Pierce: Young Hickory of the Granite Hills by Roy F. Nichols. *Kansas Historical Quarterly* 1(May, 1932):295-297.
The Great Crusade and After, 1914-1928 by Preston W. Slosson. *Mississippi Valley Historical Review* 17(March, 1931):658-659.
Historical Geography of the United States by Ralph H. Brown. *Journal of Economic History* 8(November, 1948):189-190.
A History of Farmer Movements in the Southwest, 1873-1925 by Robert L. Hunt. *Mississippi Valley Historical Review* 23(March, 1937):610-611.

Indian Fighting Army by Fairfax Downey. *Mississippi Valley Historical Review* 29(June, 1942):128.

The Indian Journals: 1859-1862, Lewis Henry Morgan edited by Leslie A. White. *Professional Geographer* 12(September, 1960):38-39.

The Industrial History of a Midwestern Town: Lawrence, Kansas by K. A. Middleton. In *The United States, 1865-1900: A Survey of Current Literature*. Fremont, OH: The Hayes Foundation, 1943. P. 62.

Interpretations, 1931-1932 by Walter Lippmann. *Mississippi Valley Historical Review* 19(March, 1933):626-627.

Interpretations, 1933-1935 by Walter Lippmann. *Mississippi Valley Historical Review* 23(June, 1936):320-321.

Jesse Buel: Agricultural Reformer, Selections from His Writings edited by H. J. Carman. *Mississippi Valley Historical Review* 35(September, 1948):306-307.

The Kaw: The Heart of the Nation by Floyd B. Streeter. *Mississippi Valley Historical Review* 28(December, 1941):476.

The Liberal Republican Movement in Missouri, 1865-1871 by Thomas S. Barclay. *Mississippi Valley Historical Review* 14(September, 1927):264-265.

Maize in the Great Herbals by John J. Finan. *American Historical Review* 57(October, 1951):210.

A Man from Kansas: The Story of William Allen White by David Hinshaw. *American Historical Review* 51(April, 1946):553-554.

Men, Money, and Motors: The Drama of the Automobile by Theodore J. MacManus and Norman Beasley. *Mississippi Valley Historical Review* 16(December, 1929):432-433.

Midwest at Noon by Graham Hutton. *Mississippi Valley Historical Review* 33(September, 1946):322-324.

Missouri: Its Resources, People, and Institutions edited by N. P. Gist *et al. Mississippi Valley Historical Review* 38(September, 1951):302.

More They Told Barron: Conversations and Revelations of an American Pepys on Wall Street, the Notes of the Late Clarence W. Barron edited by Arthur Pound and Samuel T. Moore. *Mississippi Valley Historical Review* 19(June, 1932):137.

The New United States by E. E. Robinson. *Mississippi Valley Historical Review* 34(June, 1947):114-115.

No Man's Land by Carl Coke Rister. *Mississippi Valley Historical Review* 35(December, 1948):526-527.

Our Business Civilization by James T. Adams. *Mississippi Valley Historical Review* 17(September, 1930):342-343.

Our Human Rights by Rebecca C. Barton. *Wisconsin Magazine of History* 40(Autumn, 1956):66-68.

Overland Routes to the Gold Fields, 1859, from Contemporary Diaries edited by LeRoy R. Hafen. *Pacific Historical Review* 11(December, 1942):457-459.

Prisoners of War: A Study in the Development of International Law by William E. S. Flory. *Mississippi Valley Historical Review* 29(December, 1942):431-432.

Range Management by Arthur W. Sampson. *Scientific Monthly* 74(May, 1952):308-309.

Rendezvous with Destiny: A History of Modern American Reform by Eric F. Goldman. *Journal of Southern History* 19(August, 1953):405-407.

The Rise of American Economic Life by Arthur C. Bining. *Mississippi Valley Historical Review* 30(December, 1943):432.

Road to Survival by William Vogt. *Pacific Historical Review* 18(May, 1949):243-245.

Roosevelt and the Caribbean by Howard C. Hill. *Mississippi Valley Historical Review* 14(December, 1927):430-431.

Samuel Gridley Howe by Laura E. Richards. *Mississippi Valley Historical Review* 23(June, 1936):146.

A Second Look by Edward H. Faulkner. *Mississippi Valley Historical Review* 34(December, 1947):514-515.

Short Grass Country by Stanley Vestal. *Journal of Southern History* 8(August, 1942):442-443.

Toward Civilization by Charles A. Beard. *Mississippi Valley Historical Review* 17(September, 1930):343-344.

The Tragic Era: The Revolution after Lincoln by Claude G. Bowers. *Mississippi Valley Historical Review* 16(March, 1930):561-564.

Tulsa: From Creek Town to Oil Capital by Angie Debo. *American Historical Review* 49(January, 1944):369-370.

U.S. Foreign Policy: Shield of the Republic by Walter Lippmann. *Pacific Historical Review* 12(December, 1943):417-418.

Wartime Price Control by George P. Adams, Jr. *Mississippi Valley Historical Review* 29(December, 1942):431-432.

Water and the Power: Development of the Five Great Rivers of the West by Albert N. Williams. *Scientific Monthly* 75(September, 1952):197.

The West in American History by Dan E. Clark. *Mississippi Valley Historical Review* 24(September, 1937):257-258.

Western Land and Water Use by Mont H. Saunderson. *Pacific Historical Review* 19(December, 1950):429-430.

Words That Won the War: The Story of the Committee on Public Information, 1917-1919 by James R. Mock and Cedric Larson. *Political Science Quarterly* 55(June, 1940):298-299.

Studies of James C. Malin

Beard, Charles A. "That Noble Dream." *American Historical Review* 41(October, 1935):74-87.

__________. "Written History as an Act of Faith." *American Historical Review* 39(January, 1934):219-227.

Becker, Carl. "Everyman His Own Historian." *American Historical Review* 37(January, 1932):221-236.

__________. *Everyman His Own Historian.* Chicago: University of Chicago Press, 1935.

Bell, Robert Galen. "James C. Malin: A Study in American Historiography." Ph.D. dissertation, University of California, Los Angeles, 1965.

___________. "James C. Malin and the Grasslands of North America." *Agricultural History* 46(July, 1972):414-424.

Berkhofer, Robert F., Jr. Review of *A Concern About Humanity: Notes on Reform, 1872-1912 at the National and Kansas Levels of Thought* by James C. Malin. *American Historical Review* 70(October, 1964):198-199.

Bloch, Marc. *French Rural History: An Essay on Its Basic Characteristics*. Berkeley: University of California Press, 1966.

Bogue, Allan G. "The Heirs of James C. Malin: A Grassland Historiography." *Great Plains Quarterly* 1(Spring, 1981):105-131.

___________. "Obituary of James C. Malin." *American Historical Review* 84(July, 1979):915.

Cairns, James C. Review of *On the Nature of History: Essays about History and Dissidence* by James C. Malin. *American Historical Review* 61(January, 1956):354-356.

Clary, David A. Review of *Doctors, Devils, and the Woman: Fort Scott, Kansas, 1870-1890* by James C. Malin. *Western Historical Quarterly* 7(July, 1976):330.

Colman, Gould P. Interview with James C. Malin, March 29-31, 1972. Transcript, Cornell Program in Oral History, Cornell University Libraries, Cornell University, Ithaca, NY.

Craven, Avery. Review of *The Nebraska Question, 1852-1854* by James C. Malin. *Journal of Southern History* 20(May, 1954):270-271.

Debien, G. "Marc Bloch and Rural History." Translated by Helen E. Hart. *Agricultural History* 21(July, 1947):187-189.

Edwards, Everett E. Review of *Grassland Historical Studies: Natural Resources Utilization in a Background of Science and Technology*, Vol. 1, *Geology and Geography* by James C. Malin. *Mississippi Valley Historical Review* 37(September, 1950):333-334.

Entrikin, J. Nicholas. "Robert Park's Human Ecology and Human Geography." *Association of American Geographers Annals* 70(1980):43-58.

Farmer, Paul. Review of *Essays on Historiography* by James C. Malin. *Mississippi Valley Historical Review* 34(December, 1947):515-516.

Hamer, Philip M. Review of *John Brown and the Legend of Fifty-Six* by James C. Malin. *Mississippi Valley Historical Review* 30(March, 1944):581-582.

Johannsen, Robert. "James C. Malin: An Appreciation." *Kansas Historical Quarterly* 38(Winter, 1972):457-466.

Kraenzel, Carl F. Review of *Winter Wheat in the Golden Belt of Kansas: A Study in Adaptation to Subhumid Geographical Environment* by James C. Malin. *Rural Sociology* 9(December, 1944):403-404.

Le Duc, Thomas H. "An Ecological Interpretation of Grasslands History: The Work of James C. Malin as Historian and as Critic of Historians." *Nebraska History* 31(September, 1950):226-233.

Nichols, Roy F. Review of *John Brown and the Legend of Fifty-Six* by James C. Malin. *Political Science Quarterly* 58(December, 1943):614-615.

____________. Review of *The Nebraska Question, 1852-1854* by James C. Malin. *American Historical Review* 59(July, 1954):946-948.

Pressly, Thomas J. Review of *The Contriving Brain and the Skillful Hand in the United States* by James C. Malin. *Pacific Historical Review* 25(August, 1956):294-296.

Socolofsky, Homer E. Review of *The Grassland of North America: Prolegomena to Its History, with Addenda* by James C. Malin (reprint). *Agricultural History* 43(July, 1969):416.

Swierenga, Robert P. "The New Rural History: Defining the Parameters." *Great Plains Quarterly* 1(Fall, 1981):211-223.

____________. Letter from James C. Malin, September 15, 1973.

____________, ed. *Ecology and History: Studies of the Grassland (by James C. Malin)*. Lincoln: University of Nebraska Press, 1984.

Tobey, Ronald C. *Saving the Prairies: The Life Cycle of the Founding School of American Plant Ecology, 1895-1955*. Berkeley: University of California Press, 1981.

[Unsigned] Review of *The Grassland of North America: Prolegomena to Its History* by James C. Malin. *American Historical Review* 53(January, 1948):410.

Williams, Burton J. "A Dedication to the Memory of James C. Malin, 1893-1979." *Arizona and the West* 22(Autumn, 1980):207-210.

____________. "James C. Malin: Creative Iconoclast." *Heritage of the Great Plains* 16(Spring, 1983):18-28.

____________. "James C. Malin--In Memoriam." *Kansas History: A Journal of the Great Plains* (Spring, 1979):65-67.

____________., ed. *Essays in American History in Honor of James C. Malin* Lawrence, KS: Coronado Press, 1973.

Woodburn, James A. Review of *An Interpretation of Recent American History* by James C. Malin. *American Historical Review* 32(January, 1927):341-342.

Worster, Donald. *Dust Bowl: The Southern Plains in the 1930s.* New York: Oxford University Press, 1979.

31

D'ARCY McNICKLE

by Willard H. Rollings

Biography

D'Arcy McNickle was an extraordinary man. Born on an Indian reservation, McNickle left the insular world of the reservation to pursue an education. Although McNickle left the reservation, he never abandoned his Indian people. In the course of his long and busy life he gave of his energy and ability to improve the lives of the American Indian. He produced seven books and countless articles about Indian people. He pursued an active career with the Bureau of Indian Affairs and provided important leadership for nascent Indian activist groups. Until his death in 1977, McNickle distinguished himself as a novelist, historian, anthropologist, policy expert, and Indian rights advocate. He was an Indian man.

McNickle was born in the winter of 1904 on the Flathead Reservation in northwest Montana. His Irish father, William McNickle, was a rancher and sometime farmer on the Flathead Reservation, and his mother, Philomene, although a member of the Flathead nation, was a French-Chippewa-Cree. Her family, the Parenteau, were Canadian Metis who had participated in the Louis Riel Rebellion of 1885 and had later moved south to Montana (McNickle Papers, McNickle to Skinner, July 18, 1935).

As a boy, McNickle attended the Jesuit school on the reservation, but after his mother and father were divorced in 1913, he was removed from the mission school by the Flathead agent and sent to the Indian boarding school at Chemawa, Oregon. McNickle's mother objected to his removal, and when it came time for his departure, nine-year-old D'Arcy ran away. His escape was brief, and he was sent 400 miles away to the boarding school in Oregon (McNickle Papers, Philomene McNickle to BIA, October 27, 1914). McNickle later incorporated these experiences in his first novel, *The Surrounded.*

After high school, McNickle returned to Montana, and in 1921 he enrolled at the University of Montana just south of the Flathead Reservation at Missoula. At the university McNickle studied literature and began writing poetry. In 1925 he won a Montana state poetry contest, and no doubt inspired by this success, he decided to leave Montana after his junior year. Encouraged by an English professor and another friend who had won a Rhodes scholarship, McNickle decided to go to England to improve his writing and to complete his degree at Oxford. Without financial support, yet intent on going to England, McNickle made a crucial decision. He sold the only thing he owned, his eighty-acre allotment on the Flathead Reservation (McNickle Papers, McNickle to Sol Tax, December 24, 1962). Only those who share McNickle's intense love of the land can truly understand and appreciate the desperate nature of the sacrifice he made that summer of 1925.

The full extent of that sacrifice became more evident when McNickle arrived in England and found that his Montana professors had not prepared him for the academic rigors of Oxford. The university refused to recognize most of his Montana work, and McNickle soon realized it would require at least two more years to finish his degree there. With only enough money for one year, McNickle, without his Oxford degree and his Flathead land, returned to the United States in the summer of 1926 (McNickle Papers, McNickle to Sol Tax, December 24, 1962).

McNickle, however, did not return to Montana. Instead, he moved to New York City where he lived for the next nine years. Despite his lack of a degree he was a skillful writer, and he made his living, as he later described it "as a hackwriter" working for various publishing houses and encyclopedias (McNickle Papers, McNickle to R. B. Roberts, February 20, 1939). Not content to give up on his dream of a university degree, he saved enough money to travel to France and he completed a summer session at the University of Grenoble. Upon his return in the fall of 1931 he enrolled at Columbia University intending to complete his undergraduate work. He never completed his degree, for he soon married, and as the depression worsened, it was impossible for him both to support his family and to attend the university. It was in these bleak times that he finished his first novel, *The Surrounded*, which was published in 1936.

Drawing upon his own experiences, McNickle produced a powerful yet pessimistic description of Indian life. His depiction of mixed-blood Archilde Leon's attempt to return to the Flathead Reservation, and his description of American Indians surrounded by a hostile world is an outstanding piece of literature. His characterization, plot, and themes are pathbreaking, and all contribute to what is certainly the first modern novel about and by an American Indian. The book was well received by literary critics, and there were plans of turning it into a color motion picture. Unfortunately, the movie was never made and despite the positive reviews, royalties were pitifully small--six months royalties in 1937 were only $2.90 (McNickle Papers, Ruth Rae to McNickle, April 27, 1937).

McNickle was unable to follow *The Surrounded* with another manuscript, for in 1935 he left New York to take a job with the Federal Writers Project in Washington. He remained there for less than a year, and in March, 1936, he moved to the BIA where he would labor for the next sixteen years.

Coming to work for the BIA in 1936, McNickle became deeply involved in the changes that Commissioner John Collier was attempting to bring about in American Indian policies. McNickle, first as an administrative assistant, then as a field representative, and finally as the director of tribal relations, worked to shape and implement Collier's Indian New Deal. McNickle spent hours explaining Collier's policies and their benefits to Indian leaders across the United States. From icy tents on the North Plains to sweltering afternoons on Arizona mesa tops, McNickle brought Collier's policies to the Indians of the United States.

Work and travel, while providing him with firsthand knowledge of the living conditions of contemporary Indians, left him with little time or energy to write. In 1938 McNickle applied for a Guggenheim fellowship, intending to go to New Mexico to prepare a book about the Pueblo Indian leader, Popé, who had led the 1680 rebellion against the Spanish (McNickle Papers, McNickle to E. H. Dodd, November 26, 1937). He did not receive the fellowship, and he never wrote the Popé book. Unable to conduct research in the Southwest, McNickle wrote his next book about the land and people he knew so well, the Indians of the Northwest. "Flight of Featherboy" is a compelling, yet pessimistic description of Indian life in America. Dodd, Mead, the publishers of his first novel, were unwilling to publish "Featherboy" because "Indians aren't a particularly popular subject, and the book has got to be so framed that it will be made to appeal to the intelligent public" (McNickle Papers, R. T. Bond to McNickle, May 12, 1944). McNickle later revised the manuscript, and it was finally published by Harper and Row as *Wind from an Enemy Sky* in 1978, one year after McNickle's death.

During the war years McNickle continued to work tirelessly for the Indian Bureau, but it became obvious to him by the mid-1940s that the nation was reluctant to support Collier's policies any longer. Indeed, it was clear that most Americans were not interested in the welfare of American Indians. In response to the growing indifference, McNickle became an outspoken advocate for the protection of American Indian treaty rights, Indian land and resources, and American Indian cultural integrity. In the face of growing indifference to American Indians, McNickle helped to organize the National Congress of American Indians (NCAI) in 1944. The NCAI would become the principal national Indian organization responsible for advancing Indian interests. It would provide the most powerful Indian response to federal Indian policy until the advent of the Red Power movement in the 1960s. McNickle played a crucial role in NCAI for the rest of his life (*American Indian Journal* 4:15).

While organizing the NCAI, McNickle, as the director of tribal relations, became involved in another of Collier's Indian projects. Collier, intent on improving the lot of Native Americans, had created an anthropological unit within the Bureau and insisted that the social sciences be used to provide help for American Indians. McNickle worked closely with the anthropology unit from 1941 to 1945, and he participated in a University of Chicago-directed project to study Native American personality development. As the project examined personality development among the Navajo, Sioux, Hopi, and Papago, McNickle began reading the works of sociologists and anthropologists and became deeply interested in the scientific study of the impact of federal policies and programs on Indian peoples. He became an advocate of such studies, and his interest in social science continued after he left the BIA.

With the resignation of Collier in 1945, support for such projects began to disappear. Postwar America was not interested in American Indians, and Collier's policies of cultural autonomy and economic revitalization were rejected in favor of a new federal program of forced assimilation, an end to Indian treaty rights, and a final liquidation of Indian land and property.

As support for such policies grew, McNickle became increasingly dissatisfied with the BIA. The government began dismantling Collier's programs and destroying what McNickle had spent so much of his life creating. It was during this unhappy time that McNickle wrote his first nonfiction book about American Indians. Published in 1949, *They Came Here First* is a historical study of American Indians, which traces both the antiquity of their presence in this country and the evolution of United States Indian policy.

Unable to work within the BIA as it pursued its termination policy, McNickle resigned in 1952 and moved to Colorado to head a new organization, American Indian Development, Inc. (AID), a firm intended to help American Indian peoples. Headquartered in Boulder, AID applied social science principles to Indian problems. Initially, AID organized short-term community action workshops for Indian people. Community problems were analyzed and practical solutions were suggested to use human and material resources more effectively. In 1953 AID concentrated their community development programs on a single Indian community, Crownpoint, New Mexico. McNickle and AID were convinced that people suffered impairment when decision-making was denied them, and that they grew and improved when decision-making was restored to them. From 1953 to 1960, AID worked with the Indian people of Crownpoint to take control of their community for their own benefit (McNickle Papers, McNickle's Accomplishments).

To further enable Indian people to take control of their communities and their affairs, AID began another action program in the summer of 1956. While continuing the Crownpoint Project, AID began a series of summer workshops to train young Native Americans to lead their people. McNickle directed these summer leadership workshops until 1970 and helped train scores of young Indians who today lead many Indian nations

(Interview, Alfonso Ortiz to author, March, 1986; *American Anthropologist* 81:634).

While heading AID, coordinating the Crownpoint Project, and leading the summer leadership workshops, McNickle found the time to write. Throughout the 1950s and early 1960s McNickle produced a long series of historical articles reminding the American people of past injustices of American Indian policy and denouncing the continuing injustice of the termination policy. He also wrote fiction. In 1954 *Runner in the Sun* was published. This novel, unlike his pessimistic first novel, was a pleasant, positive story about the Pueblo people of the Southwest, pleasant perhaps because its setting was the Southwest before the Europeans arrived.

In 1961 McNickle became involved in the University of Chicago American Indian Conference. Sol Tax, an anthropologist long active in American Indian affairs, asked McNickle and the NCAI to help bring together American Indians to review past policies and to propose new ones. Over 500 Indians from sixty-seven nations came to Chicago in the summer of 1961. They met and discussed their problems and proposed solutions. They also produced a Declaration of Indian Purpose which articulated Indian goals and expectations. It called for Indian answers to Indian problems. McNickle, working with other NCAI members, played an important role in writing this Indian Declaration. The Chicago Conference was an important event in Native American history, for it provided the spark for the Indian activism of the 1960s and 1970s, and McNickle helped strike that spark (*Current Anthropology* 2:478-500).

It was during this time of Indian rights advocacy that McNickle wrote two additional books. He co-authored with the editor of the *Christian Century*, Harold Fey, *Indian and Other Americans*, a harsh examination of the history of Indian-white relations and the problems confronting Indians. Three years later he wrote *The Indian Tribes of the United States*, a survey of American Indian history that combined elements of anthropology and history to tell the story of the Native American in North America.

As an advocate for Indian rights McNickle became increasingly interested in the life of another Indian rights activist, Oliver La Farge. McNickle had worked with La Farge in the BIA in the thirties and wanted to write a biography of the artist-activist. In 1963 McNickle won a Guggenheim fellowship and used the money and time provided by the fellowship to go to New Mexico, La Farge's home, to conduct research for such a biography. Before he finished the La Farge book he was approached by the University of Saskatchewan at Regina to head their anthropology department. McNickle was eager to work in Canada, for he wanted to organize community self-help projects among Canadian Indian people as he had in the United States and believed he could use the university as a base for such work. He was, however, reluctant to accept the offer, for he had never received his Ph.D.; indeed, McNickle had never received his undergraduate degree. His uneasiness was dispelled when Saskatchewan assured him they were not concerned with his lack of degree, and McNickle accepted the position (Tax Papers, McNickle to Tax,

March 8, 1966). Prior to the move he was awarded an honorary doctorate from the University of Colorado, and then Dr. McNickle went to Canada where he taught until 1971. Although living in Canada, McNickle spent most of his summers in New Mexico working on the La Farge book. In 1971 Indiana University Press published his biography of Oliver La Farge entitled *Indian Man.* In that same year McNickle retired and moved to New Mexico.

His retirement was short, for in 1972, only a year after he left Canada, the Newberry Library in Chicago asked him to create an Indian research center at the library. The Newberry Library possessed a vast collection of American Indian research materials and wanted to create a center that would encourage the study of the history of the American Indian and help prepare scholars who wanted to specialize in Native American history. McNickle served as director of the Indian Center in its early years and remained the chairman of the Advisory Board until his death in 1977.

McNickle spent the last years of his life enjoying recognition and praise for his earlier work. He continued speaking and writing about American Indians. He remained an active member of the Advisory Council of the National Indian Youth Council and on the boards of the Institute for the Development of Indian Law and the Association on American Indian Affairs. In 1975 he became the historian for the American Indian Policy Review Commission, and the Smithsonian Institution selected him to edit the contemporary Indians volume of their *Handbook of the American Indians* (*American Anthropologist* 81:634).

McNickle welcomed the new interest in Native Americans in the late 1960s and 1970s, as a new generation of Americans turned to McNickle's books to provide them with information about Indian people and their history. He revised some of his earlier books. In 1970 his revised *Indians and Other Americans* was republished, in 1973 *The Indian Tribes of the United States* was revised and reissued as *Native American Tribalism: Indian Survivals and Renewals*, and in 1975 *They Came Here First* was republished. His first novel, *The Surrounded*, was also republished and "The Flight of Featherboy," rejected in 1944, was finally published as *Wind from an Enemy Sky* (1978). McNickle was unfortunately unable to enjoy fully the recognition and praise he so richly deserved, for in October, 1977, he died of a massive coronary at his home in Albuquerque (*American Indian Journal* 4:12).

Themes

As a novelist, historian, anthropologist, federal Indian policy expert, Indian advocate, and Indian man, D'Arcy McNickle produced three novels, three historical books, one biography, at least twenty-six articles, and numerous lengthy review essays.

In McNickle's novels there are several themes. *The Surrounded* and *Wind from an Enemy Sky* share similar ones. The overriding theme in these two books is the tragic clash between Indian and white cultures. Connected with the theme of culture clash is the theme of misunderstanding, distrust, and fear between cultures and individuals. Another topic is the ongoing attack on the Indian way of life, sometimes directed by malevolent individuals and other times by well-meaning, blundering outsiders. Although these rather pessimistic ideas are not present in *Runner in the Sun*, it does share a common thread. In all three, the Indian way of life is praised. McNickle consistently depicts the Indian culture with warmth and regard, and out of these sympathetic portrayals McNickle reveals some Indian attitudes about family, community, nature, and humankind's place in the universe.

The theme of regard for the Indian way of life is found in McNickle's nonfiction as well. McNickle describes and discusses Indian world views at some length, and while warning the reader of the danger of generalizing about Indians, he presents Indian people and their culture in an extremely positive light. The portrait of the essential goodness of Indian life in all its diversity is found throughout his nonfiction. Another related theme is the contention that this valuable, worthwhile way of life, while everchanging, will survive. McNickle dismisses the concept of the Indian as the vanishing American and insists that Indian cultures will survive. Another important topic found in his nonfiction is Indian self-determination. McNickle repeatedly calls for Indian answers and Indian-directed action for Indian problems.

When McNickle originally wrote most of his nonfiction in the late 1940s, 1950s and early 1960s, he was a consistent foe of the termination policy. As congressional leaders dismantled the Indian policies of John Collier, McNickle repeatedly defended Collier and denounced termination. His defense of Collier's Indian New Deal is a familiar topic in all of McNickle's work. Another familiar theme is the call for scientific studies of Indian problems. McNickle urged the government to use scientific means to examine problems and to assess Indian needs and resources. McNickle also favored a new methodology for Native American history: methodology that would examine the cultural context in which Native American history took place. McNickle weaves all of these themes together with skill and grace. He is able to show how reasonable and decent our Indian policy could be, and how truly unreasonable and indecent it had been.

Analysis

D'Arcy McNickle wrote three novels: *The Surrounded* (1936), *Runner in the Sun* (1954), and *Wind from an Enemy Sky* (1978). The central theme in *The Surrounded* and *Wind from an Enemy Sky* is essentially the same: Indians and whites have two very different sets of cultural values and world views, and because of these differences in world views there is misunderstanding, distrust, and fear between the cultures. Out of this comes tragedy. Although published over forty years apart the theme is essentially identical in both novels. The forty-two year gap, however, is perhaps misleading, for McNickle wrote a novel in the early forties entitled "The Return of Featherboy." This novel was rejected by several publishers in 1944, and although McNickle revised the manuscript, it seems certain that

"The Return of Featherboy" was essentially *Wind from an Enemy Sky* published in 1978 (McNickle Papers, R. T. Bond to McNickle, May 12 and 25, 1944). Thus, it appears that *The Surrounded* and *Wind from an Enemy Sky* were written only about seven years apart. Settings, characters, and theme are similar, and both present bleak, pessimistic visions of Indian-white relations.

> He was always forgetting that his way of seeing things was his own. His people could not understand it, but thought he was chasing after damn fool notions. All ideas were damn fool until they were understood and believed; and it was useless to wish them on to anybody else until the other person had come to them in the same way--by understanding and believing (p. 247).

These thoughts of the main character in *The Surrounded*, Archilde Leon, express the lack of understanding between individuals and cultures. The clash between the Indian and white worlds is represented graphically by Archilde's world. Mixed-blood Archilde is a product of the union of Indian and white. Son of a Salish mother and Spanish father, Archilde lacks a place in either culture. As Archilde returns home to the reservation after several years in the white world, the incompatibility of Indian and white worlds is shown within his own family. His father, Max, and mother, Catherine, live apart and have little to do with one another. Catherine refuses to live in her husband's ranch house preferring to live in a cabin set away from the house. There is little understanding between Max and Catherine. Catherine refuses to speak English, and Max is forced to speak Salish to communicate with her. The Leon family is a tragic picture. "That was how matters always stood in Max Leon's family. There was always this distrust, this warfare" (p. 11). This misunderstanding and distance is repeated throughout the book. Catherine and her Salish people gather at her cabin to visit and eat together. As they sit around the fire listening to the old Salish stories, Max does not join the group but goes to bed confused and upset. "Why was it that after forty years he did not know these people and was not trusted by them . . . ? What were they saying? Why didn't they talk to him?" (p. 75).

The gulf that separated Max and Catherine is as great as the gulf between the rest of the white world and the Salish people. The Salish have been surrounded by an alien world. Escape is impossible. "They called that place Sniel-emen (mountains of the surrounded) because there they had been set upon and destroyed" (p. 11). Escape is impossible, yet so is survival, for not only have the Indians been surrounded, they are attacked by the outside world. Louis, Archilde's brother, truly does not fit in the white world, but he is also not allowed to live as an Indian. McNickle, while pointing out the ill will of white Sheriff Quigley, also describes the shortcomings of well-intentioned outsiders. Then McNickle introduces Father Grepilloux, a Roman Catholic priest. Grepilloux has compassion for the Salish. He realizes that they have been mistreated, abused, and robbed, and yet he fails to see his role in the tragedy. Grepilloux, while sympathetic, is just as guilty as Quigley of misunderstanding the Salish.

McNickle shows that the church transformed the Salish. It altered the lives of Archilde and his brother Louis and was changing Archilde's nephews, Narcisse and Mike. The church takes away the Salish world, but it does not provide them with an adequate replacement (*Western American Literature* 19:277). Father Grepilloux is sympathetic: "these people have lost a way of life, and with it their pride, their dignity, their strength. Men like Jeff Irving have murdered their fathers and sons with impunity. Gross natured officials have despoiled them, they are insulted when they present their grievances" (p. 59). McNickle shows that Grepilloux ultimately fails to understand their plight, for he adds "since Grepilloux was a priest, and a faithful one, he added what in his heart seemed to balance all that he had set against it--'they have God'" (p. 59). Clearly, to McNickle the church takes away everything and gives nothing in return.

McNickle, who as a boy attended the Jesuit school at St. Ignatius, wrote from experience and clearly it was a bitter one. He apparently based some of the characters in *The Surrounded* upon actual people living on the Flathead Reservation, for a friend wrote him shortly after *The Surrounded's* publication delighting in the portrayals of known individuals. The friend further related to McNickle that the priest at St. Ignatius, Father Taelman, "read your book and he states that he thinks you have gone completely mad (McNickle Papers, J. V. Dusenberg to McNickle, June 3, 1936). McNickle was angry, *not* insane.

To McNickle the misunderstanding between the two worlds and lack of trust between the cultures is tragic. McNickle, however, hints that a reconciliation is possible. Archilde begins in time to accept his Indianness, and at the same time he works to break down the walls between Max and Catherine. It is, however, doomed to failure, for just as it seems that Archilde can find a place in both worlds, events ruin his life. Archilde takes his mother on a deer hunt, and while on the hunt Louis joins them and kills a doe. While killing a doe is acceptable to the Salish, it is a violation of the white man's game laws. When the game warden discovers them with the "illegal" game, there is trouble. Archilde tries to explain to the warden that Indians are exempt from game laws because of their treaty status, but the game warden ignores the argument, and as he arrests them, he kills Louis. Catherine then kills the game warden with an axe. Archilde quickly buries the bodies and takes his mother home. Sheriff Quigley notices the warden's disappearance, and although Archilde is innocent of the killings, Quigley suspects him of murder. Archilde attempts to leave the reservation with his girlfriend, Elise, but is stopped by the sheriff. Elise, intent on escape, kills Quigley, but before they can flee both are arrested, and the book ends as they are taken away in handcuffs (*Western American Literature* 19:278).

Many of these same themes are presented in *Wind from an Enemy Sky*. Again the Indian people, the Little Elk people, are surrounded by a hostile world. There is mistrust between whites and Indians, and again McNickle shows these divisions within an Indian family. Bull, the leader of the Little Elk, rejects the white world and takes his people into the mountains to live apart. His brother, Henry Jim, however, accepts the white world and lives in the valley on a prosperous farm. The two brothers never speak to one another. Henry Jim has alienated himself not only by adopting the ways of the white world, but also by committing sacrilege. As a young man Henry Jim had given away one of the important and sacred tribal bundles, Featherboy, to the whites.

An important character is Antoine, Bull's grandson. Antoine had been away at a boarding school in Oregon. McNickle, who was forcibly placed in an Indian boarding school in Chemawa, Oregon, writes from experience as he describes the dreadful conditions of the school, where the teachers impose a harsh discipline and steal the childrens' culture.

The whites are slowly strangling the Little Elk people, for not only did they take the tribal bundle and continue to take the children away to school, they constructed a dam in Little Elk country. The dam is located on a holy site and desecrates this spiritual place. It also stops the flow of water to the Little Elk people. Bull hates the dam, but there is little that he can do.

Once again McNickle shows the clash of the two cultures, a lack of communication between Indian and white worlds. Even when both speak English they do not speak the same language, for there is no real comprehension. Bull regrets that he never learned to talk to the whites, and the agent Rafferty also regrets that he never listened to the Little Elk people. This lack of understanding again causes death. Pock Face, a young Little Elk, unintentionally kills a young man working on the dam. The victim's uncle, the designer of the dam, Adam Pell, comes to the reservation looking for answers to his nephew's death. Pell is a sympathetic white. He does not want to hurt the Indian people, but because of his ignorance he can do little but hurt them. McNickle once again holds out the promise of reconciliation. The investigation of the death of the young Pell brings Bull, Rafferty, and Pell together. They begin to try to talk to one another. Pell, upon discovering that the Little Elk people want the bundle returned, promises to find it and return it to them.

Unfortunately this apparent accord is also shattered by a lack of understanding. Pell is unable to return Featherboy, because the bundle, so important to the Little Elk, had little importance to the whites. It was neglected by the museum and had been destroyed by vermin. Pell, unable to return Featherboy, thinks that he understands its significance and plans to replace it with a golden idol given to him by South American Indians. Pell, tragically ignorant of the meaning of Featherboy, offers the idol to Bull, and Bull, heartsick and outraged at the destruction of Featherboy and the arrogant ignorance of Pell, grabs his gun and kills Pell and Rafferty. Bull is then killed by the Indian policeman, The Boy.

In both *The Surrounded* and *Wind from an Enemy Sky*, McNickle shows the impossibility of communication between Indians and whites and the dire consequences of that misunderstanding. In both, however, despite the pessimistic themes, McNickle presents a positive image of Indian people and their lives. In both novels McNickle writes from his own experience on the Flathead Reservation. McNickle was the son of a white rancher and Indian mother, and he confronted the challenges that beset Archilde. There are many autobiographical elements in the novels. Agnes, Archilde's older sister, "was afraid of her younger brother, the first in the family to educate himself (through high school), who was not afraid of the world beyond the mountains" (*The Surrounded*, p. 15). McNickle's two older sisters probably had such thoughts about him, for he did educate himself, and he was not afraid of the world beyond the mountains.

McNickle, born an Indian, living among Indians, was urged to be white. His education at the mission school and the boarding school worked to make him a white man. His mother, sadly aware of what life offered for the Indian, also tried to erase his Indianness. In a leter to the Flathead agent she wrote, "I want to raise him as a whiteman and fit him for a better life, than the common indian [sic]" (McNickle Papers, Philomene McNickle to BIA, October 27, 1914). McNickle chose otherwise and determined his own cultural destiny, but he certainly knew of the conflict, and it was this personal knowledge of the clash between the worlds that enabled him to write about it so intimately. It is ironic that a man who clearly was successful in both worlds should paint such a grim picture. His success, however, was long in coming and the result of talent, intelligence, persistence, and luck. McNickle who spent so much of his life among Indian people knew only too well of the uniqueness of his life, hence the grim vision of his novels.

McNickle's third novel, *Runner in the Sun*, does not present such a bleak picture. It is a novel set in the pre-Columbian Southwest among the Pueblo peoples. After a schism within the pueblos, a young Pueblo boy, Salt, leaves his house in the Southwest and travels south to Aztecan Mexico. After an adventurous trip Salt returns to his people with a new, strong variety of maize and leads his people from their desert homes to the river valley. *Runner in the Sun* is considered juvenile literature. This is unfortunate, for too many adults will miss a gem of a story. It is a simple story, but a well told one that reveals a great deal about Pueblo life. It is significant that *Runner in the Sun* is perhaps the only piece of Native American fiction by a Native American author that deals solely with Indians and does not deal with any Indian-white themes at all (*American Indian Fiction*, p. 195).

An important aspect of McNickle's fiction is the time in which it was written. McNickle's novels contain themes of cultural conflict, complex characters, and involved plots. His use of Indian oral tradition, flashback, and complex plot schemes are all modern. They are solidly placed within the context of the modern American Indian novel, yet one or two of them were written well before other American Indian authors opted for such sophisticated approaches. McNickle's *The Surrounded* is the first modern American Indian novel. It belongs within the context of the Native American Renaissance, yet it preceded the works of such writers as N. Scott Momaday, James Welch, and Leslie Silko by twenty-five years (*American Indian Fiction*,p. 74; *American Indian Literature*, p. 165). McNickle was a pioneer in Indian fiction, and unfortunately he has never received the attention and critical acclaim that he deserves.

The themes of his fiction are also seen in his nonfiction. McNickle deals with the history of American Indians and relates the tragic consequences of the ignorance and ill will of the white invaders. McNickle produced four nonfiction books. In *They Came Here First* (1949/1975), *Indians and Other Americans: Two Ways of Life Meet* (1959/1970) written with Harold Fey in 1949, *Native American Tribalism* (originally *Indian Tribes of America*) (1962/1973) and *Indian Man* (1971), McNickle deals with several themes.

One important theme found in McNickle's nonfiction is the regard for quality and distinctiveness of Indian culture. McNickle describes the Indian way of life: their web of kinship, sense of place, regard for one another, sharing, reverence for nature; and he continually praises it. A related and equally important element of McNickle's work is the belief that despite years of attack and abuse, Indians still survive. McNickle challenges the notion of the vanishing American:

> In spite of oppression, contumely, appropriation of their wealth, even threats of extermination through wars and pestilence, they had remained viable, keeping their languages, their religions, their kinship systems and their self-views and world views. They have been adaptive and assimilative, yet faithful to the past (*Nation* 206:718).

This theme is repeated in *Indians and Other Americans*. McNickle wrote the book to explain how Indians had survived, and how they incorporated change in their lives in order to remain Indian. He and Fey begin the book with a powerful metaphor:

> In this matter of change, people are like the grass. They toss and sway and even seem to flow before the forces that make for change, as grass bows to the wind. But the rude force moves on, people are found still rooted in the soil of the past. Again, like grass, people produce seed; and the seed will fly with the wind and, finding a friendly soil and climate, start a new generation. To change, yet to remain steadfast--that would seem to be the need of all living things (p. 3).

This theme of Indian cultural survival is examined in his third historical book, *Native American Tribalism.* Indeed, the theme is incorporated into the revised subtitle *Indian Renewals and Survivals.* He once again claims, "Indians, for all that has been lost or rendered useless out of their ancient experience remain a continuing ethnic and cultural enclave with a stake in the future" (p. 15). McNickle deals with this theme with eloquence and power. This is important today, but it was essential when McNickle was writing his books. In the late 1940s, 1950s, and 1960s there was a movement in this country to force the assimilation of Indian people, to compel them into the mainstream culture by terminating all federal obligations to the Indian people. The federal government began to break up reservations, abolish tribal governments, and end federal health care and educational assistance. This attack on Native Americans, called termination, was a dangerous threat to Indian people, and McNickle attacks it relentlessly.

Termination reversed John Collier's policies. Most of McNickle's nonfiction is a defense of Collier and an attack on the injustices of termination. McNickle shaped his attack on federal Indian policy by providing a history of Indian people, a history that combined the features of both history and anthropology. He forcefully chronicled their abuse at the hands of the invading Europeans. McNickle's historical work is important for its methodology and its angry, forceful tone.

Despite his anger, McNickle shows clearly the atrocities committed against the Indian people and the justice due them. McNickle calls on the United States to restore self-determination for all its people. McNickle believed that Indian people should decide things for themselves, and that by permitting them to confront their problems and provide their own solutions they would be better off, not only because of the solution, but by the very act of deciding. "The time has come to show faith in the democratic process which the nation avowedly practiced" (*They Came Here First*, p. 284). He repeats this message in another passage:

> If the nation is ever to demonstrate the moral strength of the democractic process, it must find it possible to allow the Hopi villager to make his own adjustments with a changing world society. Men born out of Europe came to power by insisting on just such a course for themselves (p. 285).

These are powerful words of an angry man, angered by the injustices done to his people. It is a righteous anger, and its tone adds an important quality to his books. This tone, described as combining the precision of a surgeon with the rage of a street fighter, makes his books so important (*Meeting Ground* 1:2).

McNickle knew full well the condition of American Indians. He knew why their land had disappeared, their natural resources had been stolen, their health care was wretched, and their education was second rate. He is, however, more than simply a critic, for McNickle, pessimistic in his fiction, was more optimistic in his nonfiction. He saw the limited success of Collier's plans, but knew that therein lay the answer. He called on this country to expand the land and resource base for Native Americans, to provide decent health care and education, and to allow the Indian people the right to determine the course of their own lives. It is not a complex message, but a profound one. McNickle, relying on his credentials of experience, asked for respect for the rights of Indian people and called on the American people to support a policy of self-determination and cultural pluralism.

Another important theme of McNickle's concerns the methodology for Indian history. McNickle maintained that in order to study the history of American Indians one had to know something of the Indians and their culture:

> The historian for pre-literate people assumes a special burden, objectivity being the expected burden. His source material is drawn from the writing of intruders, some innocent and benign, others aggressively evil, who rarely understand the people they encounter and write about. He must dig beneath layers of misinformation, prejudice and self interest to find the semblance of reality (*Nation* 202:493).

McNickle urged historians to incorporate Indian culture into their history, for he insisted that without the Indians' cultural context their history is incomplete and inaccurate. In the mid-1960s, McNickle called for a new history, known today as ethnohistory, a combination of the methodology of history within the cultural context of anthropology. It is fitting that the Indian research center of The Newberry Library that bears McNickle's name is the leading center for ethnohistory and yearly provides support and encouragement for such work.

McNickle also wrote a biography. In 1971 *Indian Man*, the biography of Oliver La Farge, was published. La Farge was an important novelist, anthropologist, federal Indian Bureau worker, and Indian rights advocate. La Farge came from an upper class eastern American family. Trained as an anthropologist, La Farge went to the Southwest where he discovered Indians. La Farge, fascinated by their lives, began a life-long career devoted to restoring to the Indian people their land, resources, and independence. He wrote sympathetic novels depicting the tragedy of their oppression, and later he was an important member of Collier's BIA. McNickle's biography of La Farge is both a story of La Farge and of the history of Indian advocacy and the development of federal Indian policy. There is also an autobiographical tone to McNickle's biography, for McNickle, although from a far different background, was also an Indian novelist who became an anthropologist, federal Indian policy expert under Collier, and Indian rights advocate. When McNickle wrote of La Farge's troubles getting *Laughing Boy* published, it is clear that he incorporated his own experiences. La Farge's work in the BIA is also framed by McNickle's work there. McNickle points out that "What is probably most remarkable about *The Copper Pot* is what it reveals about Oliver La Farge." What is equally remarkable is how much D'Arcy McNickle is revealed in *Indian Man* (p. 133).

D'Arcy McNickle was an extraordinary man. McNickle left his mountain home and went into the larger world. He combined the best qualities of the white and Indian worlds, and distinguished himself as a novelist, historian, anthropologist, Indian policy expert, and Indian rights advocate. He wrote powerful novels filled with insight and sadness, and he wrote equally important and forceful historical studies of the Indian people. He worked throughout his life to help his people and, indeed, he left a profound legacy of achievement.

Bibliography

Books

Indian Man: A Life of Oliver La Farge. Bloomington: Indiana University Press, 1971.

The Indian Tribes of the United States: Ethnic and Cultural Survival. New York: Oxford University Press, 1962. Revised edition. *Native American Tribalism: Indian Renewals and Survivals.* New York: Oxford University Press, 1973.

Indians and Other Americans: Two Ways of Life Meet. Co-authored with Harold Fey. New York: Harper and Row, 1957. Revised edition. New York: Harper and Row, 1970.

Runner in the Sun: A Story of Indian Maize. New York: Winston, 1954.

The Surrounded. New York: Dodd, Mead, 1936. Reprint. Albuquerque: University of New Mexico Press, 1978.

They Came Here First: The Epic of the American Indian. New York: Lippincott, 1949. Revised edition. New York: Harper and Row, 1975.

Wind from an Enemy Sky. New York: Harper and Row, 1978.

Articles

"Afternoon on a Rock." *Common Ground* 5(Spring, 1945):71-76.

"American Indians Who Never Were." *New University Thought* 7(Spring, 1971):24-29.

"Americans Called Indians." In *North American Indians in Historical Perspective* edited by Eleanor Leacock and Nancy Lurie. New York: Random House, 1971. Pp. 29-63.

"The Clash of Cultures." In *The World of the American Indian* edited by Jules B. Billard. Washington, DC: National Geographic Society, 1974. Pp. 311-353.

"Commentary." In *Indian White Relations: A Persistent Paradox* edited by James Smith and Robert Kvasnicka. Washington, DC: Howard University Press, 1976. Pp. 251-257.

"The Dead Horse Walks Again." *Nation* 205(December 25, 1967):677-678.

"The Goals of the Group." *Nation* 201(September 27, 1965):167-168.

"The Golden Myth." *Common Ground* 9(Summer, 1949):65-74.

"The Healing Vision." *Tomorrow* 4(Spring, 1956):25-31.

"In Search of White Man's Guidance." *Nation* 202(April, 25, 1966):493-494.

"Indian and European: Indian-White Relations From Discovery to 1887." *Annals of the American Academy of Political and Social Science* 311(May, 1957):1-11.

"Indian Expectations." *Indian Truth* 38(July, 1961):1-7.

"The Indian in American Society." In *Social Welfare Forum: Official Proceedings of the 82nd Annual Forum, National Conference of Social Work*. New York: Columbia University Press, 1955. Pp. 68-77.

"The Indian Tests the Mainstream." *Nation* 203(September 26, 1966):275-279.

"The Indians of the United States." *America Indigena* 18(April, 1958):99-118.

"It Takes Two to Communicate." Co-authored with Viola G. Pfrommer. *International Journal of Health Education* 2(July, 1959):136-141.

"It's Almost Never Too Late." *Christian Century* 74(February 20, 1957):227-229.

"John Collier's Vision." *Nation* 206(June 3, 1968):718-719.

"North American Indians." *Encyclopedia Britannica* 12(1951):200-211.

"Peyote and the Indian." Co-authored with Emma Reh. *Scientific Monthly* 57(September, 1943):220-229.

"Private Intervention, the Role of Private Welfare Groups in Indian Affairs Administration in the United States and Canada." *Human Organization* 20(Winter, 1962):208-215.

"Process or Compulsion: The Search for a Policy of Administration in Indian Affairs." *America Indigena* 17(July, 1957):261-270.

"Snowfall." *Common Ground* 4(September, 1944):75-82.

"The Sociocultural Setting of Indian Life." *American Journal of Psychiatry* 125(August 2, 1968):219-223.

"A U.S. Indian Speaks." *Americas* 6(July, 1954):8-11, 27.

"United States Indian Affairs--1953." *America Indigena* 13(October, 1953):263-273.

"We Go On From Here." *Common Ground* 4(Autumn, 1943):26-31.

Selected Reviews

Education to the American Indian: The Road to Self-Determination, 1928-1973 by Margaret Szasz. *The Historian* 38(May, 1976):534-535.

The Hopi Child by Wayne Dennis. *Nation* 202(March 28, 1966):365-366.

The Last Americans: The Indian in American Culture by William Brandon. *Nation* 219(December 7, 1974):599-600.

The Nez Perce Indians and the Opening of the Northwest by Alvin M. Josephy, Jr. *Nation* 202(April 25, 1966):493-494.

Red Power: The American Indians' Fight for Freedom by Alvin M. Josephy, Jr. *Pacific Historical Review* 41(May, 1972):244-245.

Southern Indians in the American Revolution by James H. O'Donnell III. *North Carolina Historical Review* 51(October, 1974):428-429.

The Tewa World: Space, Time, Being, and Becoming in a Pueblo Society by Alfonso Ortiz. *Nation* 210(April 27, 1970):504-505.

Wilderness Kingdom: Indian Life in the Rocky Mountains, 1840-1847: The Journals and Paintings of Nicholas Point, S.J. translated and edited by Joseph P. Donnelly. *Nation* 205(December 25, 1967):692-693.

Studies of D'Arcy McNickle

Black, Mary B., and Edward S. Rogers. Review of *Indian Man: A Life of Oliver La Farge* by D'Arcy McNickle. *American Anthropologist* 78(September, 1976):665-666.

Cotterill, Robert S. Review of *They Came Here First: The Epic of the American Indian* by D'Arcy McNickle. *Mississippi Valley Historical Quarterly* 36(March, 1950):681-682.

Debo, Angie. Review of *Indian Man: A Life of Oliver La Farge* by D'Arcy McNickle. *Pacific Historical Review* 41(August, 1972):394.

Fey, Harold E. Review of *Indian Man: A Life of Oliver La Farge* by D'Arcy McNickle. *Christian Century* 89(May 17, 1972):585.

Green, Joseph C. Review of *They Came Here First: The Epic of the American Indian* by D'Arcy McNickle. *American Historical Review* 55(July, 1950):947-948.

Hoxie, Frederick. "Director's Notes: D'Arcy's Legacy and the Center's Future." *Meeting Ground* 1(Spring, 1984):2-3.

Jorgensen, Joseph G. Review of *Native American Tribalism: Indian Renewals and Survivals* by D'Arcy McNickle. *Western Historical Quarterly* 5(October, 1974):464-466.

Kluckhohn, Clyde. Review of *They Came Here First: The Epic of the American Indian* by D'Arcy McNickle. *New York Herald Tribune Book Review*, November 13, 1949, p. 30.

Larson, Charles R. *American Indian Fiction.* Albuquerque: University of New Mexico Press, 1978.

Le Duc, Thomas. Review of *Indian Man: A Life of Oliver La Farge* by D'Arcy McNickle. *American Historical Review* 78(June, 1973):742-743.

__________. Review of *Indians and Other Americans: Two Ways of Life Meet* by D'Arcy McNickle and Harold Fey. *Pacific Historical Review* 29(Winter, 1960):81-82.

Lurie, Nancy Oestreich. Review of *Native American Tribalism: Indian Renewals and Survivals* by D'Arcy McNickle. *Pacific Historical Review* 44(August, 1975):399-400.

__________. "The Voice of the American Indian: Report on the American Indian Chicago Conference." *Current Anthropology* 2(December, 1961):478-500.

McNickle, D'Arcy, Papers. Newberry Library, Chicago, IL.

McWilliams, Carey. Review of *Indian Man: A Life of Oliver La Farge* by D'Arcy McNickle. *Nation* 213(October 11, 1971):346.

Ortiz, Alfonso. "D'Arcy McNickle." *American Anthropologist* 81(September, 1979):632-636.

__________. "D'Arcy McNickle (1904-1977): Across the River and Up the Hill." *American Indian Journal* 4(April, 1978):12-16.

__________. Interview with Willard Rollings. March, 1986.

Owens, Louis. "The 'Map of the Mind': D'Arcy McNickle and the American Indian Novel." *Western American Literature* 19(Winter, 1984):275-283.

Prucha, Francis Paul. Review of *Native American Tribalism: Renewals and Survivals* by D'Arcy McNickle. *America* 134(May 22, 1976):456.

__________. *Journal of American History* 63(December, 1976):659.

Raymer, Robert G. Review of *They Came Here First: The Epic of the American Indian* by D'Arcy McNickle. *Pacific Historical Review* 19(February, 1950):59-60.

Roessel, Robert A., Jr. Review of *Native American Tribalism: Indian Renewals and Survivals* by D'Arcy McNickle. *Western Political Quarterly* 27(June, 1974):353.

Ruoff, A. La Vonne Brown. "Old Traditions and New Forms." In *Studies in American Indian Literature: Critical Essays and Course Designs* edited by Paula Gunn Allen. New York: Modern Language Association of America, 1983. Pp. 147-168.

Tax, Sol, Papers. University of Chicago Library; copies at the Newberry Library, Chicago, IL.

Trafzer, Clifford E. Review of *Indian Man: A Life of Oliver La Farge* by D'Arcy NcNickle. *Journal of the West* 11(January, 1972):182.

Underhill, Ruth. Review of *Indians and Other Americans: Two Ways of Life Meet* by D'Arcy McNickle and Harold Fey. *American Anthropologist* 61(December, 1959):1163.

__________. *New York Times*, August 9, 1959, p. 3

Vestal, Stanley. Review of *They Came Here First: The Epic of the American Indian* by D'Arcy McNickle. *Saturday Review of Literature* 32(October 15, 1949):21.

32

FREDERICK MERK

by Thomas C. McClintock

Biography

Of the most distinguished historians of the American frontier who were members of the generation immediately following that dominated by Frederick Jackson Turner, the one most closely associated with him was Frederick Merk. He not only was one of Turner's graduate students at Harvard, but subsequently Merk would assist him with and then succeed him as the instructor of his famous History 17 course, History of the West (Merk would change the title to History of the Westward Movement). Furthermore, there were earlier ties as well for Merk was a fellow native of Wisconsin and a student at the University of Wisconsin during Turner's last three years as a professor there before moving on to Harvard (*Journal of American History* 65:572-576; *New York Times*, September 27, 1977, p. 42).

Merk was born on August 15, 1887, in Milwaukee, Wisconsin; his family was of German origin. After graduating from high school in that city, he entered the University of Wisconsin. Although he had to work to finance his schooling (as a member of a hod carrier's union), he excelled as a student, and was elected to Phi Beta Kappa. For five years after receiving his bachelor's degree in 1911, he was a member of the editorial staff of the State Historical Society of Wisconsin. These were unusually productive years for Merk as a young scholar in that he published two books, *The Labor Movement in Wisconsin During the Civil War* (1912/1915), an edited volume of documents, and an *Economic History of Wisconsin During the Civil War Decade* (1916).

The latter was a remarkable piece of scholarship, especially considering the fact that Merk was "raw from his undergraduate degree," as he recalled in the preface to the 1971 reprint edition (p. 8). It was characterized by painstaking research, including a great reliance on primary documents and newspapers, a sophisticated analysis of economic and other statistical data, and a clarity of presentation that later would characterize both his lectures and his subsequent publications. As Paul W. Gates, one of Merk's most distinguished students, has reported, "At least a dozen scholars have taken his chapter subjects for long and excellent monographs but none has found error, nor have they altogether replaced his book" (*Journal of American History* 65:573). Evidence of the validity of this assessment was the reappearance of the book in a reprint edition in 1971. Probably even more important to Merk at the time were the facts that this book both facilitated his entry into Harvard as a graduate student and accelerated the completion of his Ph.D. degree. Since, as he later wrote Turner, "you had escaped me in Madison," Merk, as a graduate student, followed him to Harvard in 1916 (*Western Historical Quarterly* 9:141). And the *Economic History of Wisconsin* not only won him the Edward Austin Fellowship for graduate study at Harvard in that year, but it also subsequently would be accepted by the history department as his doctoral dissertation.

Even before he received his Ph.D. in 1920 (and Harvard's Toppan Prize), Merk had begun assisting Turner with the History 17 course; in 1918 he was appointed a tutor in history, government, and economics. In 1921, he became an instructor in American history, at which time he officially began sharing the History 17 course with Turner. In 1922, he was co-editor of a revised edition of Turner's *List of References on the History of the West*, assembled primarily for History 17 students and including what was, at the time, the definitive bibliography on the subject, as well as a detailed list of "Thesis Topics." And in 1924, upon Turner's retirement, Merk assumed full responsibility for History 17. That same year he was promoted to assistant professor.

During the thirty-three years prior to his retirement in 1957, Merk became one of the best-loved teachers at Harvard. His introduction to American history (History 5) course and, in particular, the History 17 course, which his students affectionately called "Wagon Wheels," not only became among the most popular courses for several generations of Harvard students but History 17 also became well-known nationally through the editorials and other writings of enthusiastic Nieman Fellows who were attracted to the course (it was even the inspiration for a novel by a former Nieman Fellow--A. B. Guthrie's *The Way West*).

Although Merk was a great teacher and would move steadily up through the professorial ranks at Harvard, being promoted to associate professor in 1930, to professor in 1936, and to the distinguished chair of Gurney Professor of History and Political Science in 1946, he became increasingly frustrated by the modesty of his published scholarship. In this deficiency, he seemed destined again to follow in his mentor's footsteps and for the same basic reason. As Rodman W. Paul, another of his most distinguished students, has reported, "He shared with Turner a perfectionism that made him a slow, careful, and reflective writer, never quite satisfied that he had all the evidence, never ready to call the job done" (*Western Historical Quarterly* 9:144). In 1929, having published, in addition to the *List of References on the History of the West*, only one article since he had come to Harvard, he took the drastic step of submitting his resignation "on the ground," as he reported to Turner, "that my tastes and abilities, such as they were, were in the direction of research, that at Harvard I was forced into the mold of teacher and administrator which did not fit me and which was increasingly distasteful to me" (p. 144).

Fortunately, members of the Harvard history department, determined to prevent the departure of such a valued colleague, quickly recommended his promotion to associate professor and, more encouragingly, assumed much of his nonteaching responsibilities. However, probably even more persuasive, as well as being a turning point in both his professional career and his personal life, was his marriage. In 1931, in a letter to Turner, he reported that

> This year I have had a very happy 20 course [Individual Studies] with a graduate student of Radcliffe, Lois Bannister. She and I have met on common ground in our admiration for your writings, and this past term we have found many other interests in common. Our conferences recently have not always been confined strictly to history, and I have just persuaded her to let me give her a diamond ring (p. 146).

It was an extremely happy and productive marriage, including the birth of a son and daughter. Lois Bannister Merk would become her husband's collaborator during his most productive years as a publishing scholar.

Nevertheless, although, during the remaining two and a half decades prior to his retirement, Merk became considerably more successful as a publishing scholar, the list of his publications was still comparatively modest. Between 1931 and his retirement in 1957, he was the editor of the 1824-1825 journal of George Simpson (1931), the author of a small volume on *Albert Gallatin and the Oregon Problem* (1950), co-author of the *Harvard Guide to American History* (1954), and author or editor of nine articles.

Finally, with his retirement from Harvard, Merk found the time for which he had so desperately longed. Although he agreed to continue teaching on a part-time basis for several years, he now, with the assistance of his wife, entered his most productive years as a scholar. Using the mass of notes that he had accumulated over the years, he produced five books and was awaiting the galley proofs of a sixth at the time of his death. This last book was also his most ambitious in scope; it was a *History of the Westward Movement* (1978). For Merk to have been so productive at such a late stage in his life was a truly remarkable achievement (at the time five of these books were published he was 76, 79, 80, 84, and 85 years of age and when he completed the sixth and last one he was 90). As the citation read when Clark University awarded him an honorary degree in 1977, "The Indian summer of his professional life has been more fruitful than most men's springtime" (*Harvard University Gazette* 74, No. 33).

On September 24, 1977, Merk died of a heart attack at Mt. Auburn Hospital in Cambridge. He was 90 years old.

Themes

Merk's publications fall into four major groups. The first and smallest one includes the two books he published while he was a member of the editorial staff of the Wisconsin Historical Society; an article on the "Eastern Antecedents of the Grangers," (*Agricultural History* 23:1-8) which was his address as president of the Agricultural History Society in 1948; and the *Harvard Guide to American History* (1954), of which he was one of the six co-authors. This group is a miscellaneous one since these publications not only are unrelated to each other (except for the two Wisconsin books) but also have no connection to his other publications.

The other three groups, on which his reputation as a distinguished American historian is based, are closely related in that they are concerned with the diplomacy and politics of American expansionism, particularly the role of Manifest Destiny in the 1840s and later in the century. What sets them apart is the region on which each concentrated. The first traces the long sequence of diplomatic and other events in the Oregon Country, the United States, and Great Britain that would culminate in the settlement of the Oregon boundary dispute in 1846. The publications covering this topic include nine articles published over a period of thirty-six years, the final one being his address as president of the Mississippi Valley Historical Association in 1960, plus three books and a long section of a fourth. The subject of the first of these books, *Fur Trade and Empire* (1931), is the early years of the Hudson's Bay Company in the Oregon Country and include George Simpson's journal describing his journey from York Factory to Fort George at the mouth of the Columbia and return in 1824-1825, edited by Merk, plus over 250 pages of related documents. The second one, *Albert Gallatin and the Oregon Problem: A Study in Anglo-American Diplomacy* (1950), a small volume of only ninety-seven pages, describes Gallatin's unsuccessful efforts as a special envoy to settle the Oregon question in the mid-1820s. In a third volume, *The Monroe Doctrine and American Expansionism* (1966), Merk included a long chapter in which he describes, critically, Polk's role in the Oregon boundary settlement, ground, incidentally, that he already had thoroughly covered in several of the earlier articles. Finally, in 1967, he brought together in one volume all of his scholarship on the Oregon boundary dispute. In this volume, *The Oregon Question: Essays in Anglo-American Diplomacy and Politics*, are reprinted the nine Oregon articles and the small volume on *Albert Gallatin and the Oregon Problem.* However, he also included three essays published for the first time plus a long "Résumé."

The region that is the focus of the second of these three groups of related publications was Texas and Mexico. In these publications Merk describes the diplomatic and political developments involved in the annexation of Texas and the war with Mexico. The publications covering these events include only one article, "A Safety Valve Thesis and Texas Annexation," but all or parts of five books, four of which, incidentally, were written "with the collaboration of Lois Bannister Merk." The first of these books was *Manifest Destiny and Mission in American History: A Reinterpretation* (1963). Although, in the final chapters of this book, Merk describes the transformation of Manifest Destiny into "insular imperialism," his major focus is on its original continental form as invoked by Polk and other expansionists in the conflict with Mexico. In the second book in this group, *The Monroe Doctrine and American Expansionism, 1843-1849* (1966), Merk traces the diplomatic and political controversies involved in the annexation of Texas and the war with Mexico, including a detailed and critical description of the efforts by Tyler and Polk to manipulate public opinion by the use of propaganda. The content of the third volume, *Dissent in the American Wars* (1970), are lectures presented by Samuel Eliot Morison, Frank Freidel, and Merk at meetings of the Massachusetts Historical Society in 1968-1969. In his lecture, "Dissent in the Mexican War," Merk pays tribute to Whig and other opponents of that war, suggesting that the Treaty of Guadalupe Hidalgo would have been harsher had it not been for the dissent. In the fourth book, *Fruits of Propaganda in the Tyler Administration* (1971), a relatively brief volume of two major sections plus 120 pages (almost half of the book) of related documents, he returned to the use by that administration of propaganda to achieve its diplomatic objectives. The first section concerns the settlement of the Maine boundary dispute (Webster-Ashburton Treaty) and the second is merely a revised version of his previously-published article, "A Safety Valve Thesis and Texas Annexation." The final book in this group, *Slavery and the Annexation of Texas* (1972), also is an expanded version of an earlier publication, in this case several chapters from *The Monroe Doctrine and American Expansionism.* And again included are over one hundred pages of supporting documents.

The third and final region that is a focus of Merk's publications on American expansionism included the Yucatan and other parts of Mexico and, in particular, islands in the Caribbean and the Pacific. His examination of this imperialistic form of Manifest Destiny appears in two of his books. In the last four chapters in *Manifest Destiny and Mission in American History*, he presents his most extended discussion of the movement, tracing it to the end of the nineteenth century. In addition, in *The Monroe Doctrine and American Expansionism*, he describes its initial appearance at the end of Polk's administration.

Standing alone among Merk's publications is his final one, *History of the Westward Movement* (1978). Although it obviously was related to his earlier publications on American westward expansion, it is a much more ambitious work. The moving force behind this book was the desire of his publisher, Alfred A. Knopf, to publish his History 17 lecture notes. However, when he finally agreed to do so, he typically insisted on incorporating additional research and widening its scope. Not only does it include an extremely detailed history of the westward movement from its beginnings on the Atlantic seaboard in the early seventeenth century to its conclusion in the trans-Mississippi West at the end of the nineteenth century but also one-fourth of it is devoted to developments in the West in the twentieth century. In this last section, the developments on which he concentrates include agriculture, reclamation, and land use planning. Although, again with the close collaboration of his wife, to whom it would be dedicated, he had completed the manuscript at the time of his death in 1977, it was not published until the following year.

Analysis

Certainly one of Merk's greatest achievements as a historian was the meticulous scholarship on which all of his publications were based beginning with his book on Wisconsin during the Civil War decade. It is difficult to believe that any available sources escaped his attention. Because the focus of so many of his publications was on the manipulation of public opinion in foreign affairs in the United States--and in Great Britain--"these raw materials," as he, on one occasion, referred to them, include not only the records of Congress, diplomatic correspondence, and other governmental documents but also newspaper editorials, congressional speeches, and "orations on the hustings" (*Manifest Destiny and Mission*, p. iii). And his research in such British sources as *Hansard's Parliamentary Debates*, documents in the Public Record Office, published memoirs and correspondence, private papers in the British Library, and newspapers covering the first half of the nineteenth century is equally impressive.

In his research, Merk particularly enjoyed the role of historical detective, discovering events or individuals previously unknown or filling in the details on events, individuals, and other subjects barely touched upon by other scholars. Probably the best example of the former is his identification of Christopher Hughes as the probable author of the communication, revealing that Gallatin was dissatisfied with his instructions, that fell into the hands of Canning during his negotiations with Gallatin on the Oregon boundary in the 1820s (*Albert Gallatin*, pp. 61-64). Examples of his success in at least filling in the details on subjects previously barely touched upon would include his description of the origins of the Caledonia River myth and its importance in the Oregon boundary negotiations in 1818 (*American Historical Review* 55:530-551); of the role of Francis O. J. Smith in winning the acceptance by the residents of Maine of the boundary settlement in the Webster-Ashburton Treaty (*Fruits of Propaganda*, pp. 9-10, 59-71, 87-89, 131-220) and of the role of Duff Green in the Texas annexation controversy (*Fruits of of Propaganda*, pp. 17-23; *The Monroe Doctrine*, 11-17; *Slavery*, pp. 12-17, 30-32); of the work of Dr. Edward Jarvis to expose the errors in the 1840 census statistics on the extent of insanity among northern Negroes, which were being used by Calhoun and other southerners to defend slavery and by Robert J. Walker in campaigning for the annexation of Texas (*Slavery*, pp. 61-68, 85-92, 113, 117-120); and of the unsuccessful efforts of Moses Y. Beach, editor of the New York *Sun*, to bring about a quick settlement of the Mexican War during a clandestine visit to Mexico City after the war was underway (*Manifest Destiny and Mission*, pp. 131-134).

Considering the complexity of the diplomatic and political developments covered by his publications and, in particular, the obvious mass of research notes on which they were based, also among his most impressive achievements as a scholar were both his mastery of his material and the clarity with which he presented it. He managed to trace diplomatic maneuvers and manipulations of public opinion by Tyler and Polk, as convoluted as they became at times, for example, without leaving his readers in a state of confusion. Especially noteworthy was his ability to present historical background and to sum up his publications. Representative examples of the former would include the introductions to *Fur Trade and Empire*, in which he traced the history of the Hudson's Bay Company, and to *Manifest Destiny and Mission*, and of the latter, the concluding "Résumé" in *The Oregon Question*.

In contrast to his mentor, Merk avoids sweeping generalizations, although he did propose a number of important theses. This is particularly true in his examination of the 1840s, the period on which his most important publications concentrate and during which, as he reported, occurred "the greatest expansionist drive in American history" (*The Monroe Doctrine*, p. vii). For example, he suggests that, in the final stages of the long Anglo-American negotiations over the Oregon boundary, "politics shaped diplomacy" both in the United States and in Great Britain (*The Oregon Question*, p. xiii; *Slavery*, p. xii). As he went on to report, in those final stages, it was the efforts of the Whigs and southern Democrats in the United States, combined with Lord Aberdeen's political and diplomatic maneuvers, that were successful in bringing "the reckless and noisy expansionists, seeking political profit from the exploitation of a dangerous international issue, under control" (*The Oregon Question*, pp. 416-417).

He sees a similar shaping of diplomacy by politics in the annexation of Texas and the war with Mexico, and also with somewhat similar results. Although both Tyler and Polk used propaganda in their efforts to achieve their expansionist goals, their political opponents and public opinion at least forced Tyler to change his annexation strategy and Polk to accept a Mexican treaty that, in its territorial provisions, was more limited than he and his fellow expansionists desired.

Another important thesis that Merk presents, in his discussion of Polk's use of propaganda in furthering his territorial ambitions, is calling attention to the fact that Polk invoked the Monroe Doctrine but, in doing so, fundamentally altered it. Whereas Monroe's declaration had been applied to both American continents and was "defensive" in that its purpose was to protect the two continents from European political intervention and future colonization, Polk, according to Merk, not only limited it just to North America and the Caribbean but also converted it to an expansionist doctrine, using it "to cover ambitions of the United States for the whole Oregon Country, parts of Mexico--California and Yucatan--and Cuba" (*The Monroe Doctrine*, pp. 281-289).

However, probably Merk's best-known thesis appears in his analysis of Manifest Destiny. It is the subject on which he concentrated in most of his published scholarship after his retirement, including one book, *Manifest Destiny and Mission in American History*, and parts of several others. However, for several reasons it also is the least persuasive of his theses. On one of the rare occasions when he went on record in disagreement with fellow historians, he rejected the view of Albert K. Weinberg and others who, he reported, credited a "single force," nationalism, as having generated Manifest Destiny. According to Merk, this view, which had "been suggested rather than carefully developed or defended," simply is "out of accord with the temper of the era" (*Manifest Destiny and Mission*, pp. 57, 218-219). He pointed out, for example, that the presidential election of 1844 "was filled with the extravagance of party campaigning, of the venom among Democrats, of factional infighting, and of bitterness produced in the sections by a clash over slavery." As a result,

> That a national spirit so strong and unified as to generate Manifest Destiny could have emerged from such a composite of disharmonies is inconceivable. The forces that produced Manifest Destiny were domestic for the most part. They were ample in number to account for Manifest Destiny, and among them one was undoubtedly powerful--the strong taste of expansionists for the doctrine of states' rights (p. 60).

Later, in returning again to this issue, he insists that

> continentalist and imperialist doctrines were never true expressions of national spirit. They were the very opposite. . . . They misrepresented the nation. . . . A thesis that continentalist and imperialist goals were sought by the nation regardless of party or section won't do. It is not substantiated by good evidence. A better-supported thesis is that Manifest Destiny and imperialism were traps into which the nation was led in 1846 and in 1899 . . . (p. 261).

One problem with these counter arguments of Merk is that they are based on what seems to be a misreading of Weinberg. The nationalism in the 1840s that Weinberg is referring to was not a national consensus but rather a form of nationalistic idealism, the belief that "America's providential mission or destiny" was an "extension of the area of freedom" or democracy (*Manifest Destiny*, pp. 100-101).

Ironically, Merk, at least at times, in his definition of Manifest Destiny is much closer to Weinberg than he was willing to acknowledge. For example, early in his analysis, he, too, suggests that Manifest Destiny, in contrast to earlier expansionism, was idealistic and the idealistic features he listed were virtually the same ones mentioned by Weinberg (*Manifest Destiny and Mission*, pp. 24-33). However, curiously, later on in his analysis he changed his mind. "Manifest Destiny," he now argues,

> seemed, despite its exaltation of language, somehow touched by a taint of selfishness, both national and individual. The sacrifices it asked were to be from others. Territory was to be taken, and all that was to be given in exchange was the prospect of American citizenship (p. 265).

But, he reports, there was a force operating at the same time as Manifest Destiny that was "a truer expression of the national spirit"--that is, "Mission." This force, he suggests,

> was present from the beginning of American history, and is present, clearly, today. It was idealistic, self-denying, hopeful of divine favor for national aspirations, though not sure of it. Its language was that of dedication--dedication to the enduring values of American civilization (p. 261).

More to the point, he continues, it was a force that had successfully curbed "expansionism of the aggressive variety" both in the 1840s and at the end of the century (pp. 262-263).

A more general problem, again particularly apparent in that series of books on expansionism in the 1840s that he published after his retirement, is that of repetitiousness. Predictably, it is most noticeable in *The Oregon Question* since in it were reprinted all of the articles, plus the small monograph, on the Oregon boundary dispute that he had published over a period of thirty-five years. Inevitably, as a result, the major events in that long dispute were covered several times in the volume. In the introduction, he acknowledges that reprinting these publications "entails some repetition" but, he adds, "this has been kept to a minimum." However, the only way he could have minimized such repetition was to revise each of these earlier publications and this he did not do. Moreover, he compounds the problem by including a summary of this scholarship both in the introduction and, even in greater detail, in the long "Résumé." Since, in several other books that he published in his postretirement years, he concentrates on the same topics--the diplomatic and political developments involved in the annexation of Texas and the Mexican War--repetition again is an ever-present problem. Nevertheless, it should be acknowledged that, at least in the case of *The Oregon Question*, for those interested in the Oregon boundary dispute the convenience of having the results of all Merk's painstaking research available in one volume far outweighs such repetition.

Another problem in Merk's later publications is an occasional lack of balance. This problem stems from a temptation with which any research scholar is very familiar--that is, having meticulously researched a topic, Merk at times could not resist reporting it all even though its importance did not justify such detail. One of the more obvious examples of this problem is the long and detailed description of the history, economy, and social structure of the Yucatan that he included in the chapter on "Yucatan and the Mare Clausum" in *The Monroe Doctrine and American Expansionism* (pp. 197-206).

However, it is in Merk's final book, *History of the Westward Movement*, in which the lack of balance is a particularly serious problem. It is apparent in the amount of space he devotes to each period of that movement as well as to specific developments that were part of it. Generally the geographic areas and topics that he discusses in the greatest detail were those on which his own research also had concentrated. An obvious example of this lack of balance is his one chapter on Oregon. As the title, "The Oregon Question," indicates, the subject of this chapter is the Anglo-American dispute, there being only a few references to the Hudson's Bay Company and only one brief paragraph on the American settlers (pp. 309-329). The explanation for the virtual absence of any account of the settlement of the region by American pioneers is Merk's conclusion, as he had reported elsewhere, that they "were merely marginal in their effects on the outcome of the Oregon [boundary] dispute" (*The Oregon Question*, p. xiii). However, although a chapter on this dispute was appropriate, his failure also to include a chapter on the British fur companies and the American settlers in the Oregon Country in such a detailed history of the westward movement is quite extraordinary. This last book of Merk's, then, "unfortunately," as Rodman W. Paul and Michael P. Malone have observed, "did not do him justice" (*Western Historical Quarterly* 16:33).

Nevertheless, though there were a number of problems in Merk's writings, compared to his contributions as a scholar they seem of minor importance. Without question he was one of the greatest historians of his generation in terms of both his influence as a teacher and the scholarly quality of his publications. That he was a master teacher is documented not only by the testimony of his students but also by the popularity of his History 5 and 17 courses. Moreover, as a teacher, Merk must have taken particular satisfaction in the outstanding careers of his former graduate students, of whom Paul Wallace Gates, William S. Greever, Mary W. M. Hargreaves, J. Orin Oliphant, Rodman W. Paul, and Francis Paul Prucha are notable examples.

As to the importance of his writings, there also is no dispute. As Thomas Le Duc reports in his review of Merk's *Manifest Destiny and Mission*, "The patient investigations and penetrating insights of Frederick Merk have for many years helped scholars understand the complex interplay of forces in the 1840s that attended the extension of American sovereignty to the Pacific Coast" (*Mississippi Valley Historical Review* 50:296). His detailed account of the Oregon boundary dispute, judged by Thomas A. Bailey as the "ablest scholarship on the subject" (*Diplomatic History*, 10th ed., 1980, p. 235) is definitive and his scholarship on the expansionist maneuvers of the Tyler and Polk administrations certainly approaches such distinction. In his inspiration as a teacher and in his meticulous research and mastery of his material, Frederick Merk set standards that will continue to be models for members of his profession.

Bibliography

Books

Albert Gallatin and the Oregon Problem: A Study in Anglo-American Diplomacy. Cambridge, MA: Harvard University Press, 1950.

Dissent in the American Wars. Co-authored with Samuel Eliot Morison and Frank Freidel. Cambridge, MA: Harvard University Press, 1970.

Economic History of Wisconsin During the Civil War Decade. Madison: State Historical Society of Wisconsin, 1916. Reprint. 1971.

Fruits of Propaganda in the Tyler Administration. With the collaboration of Lois Bannister Merk. Cambridge, MA: Harvard University Press, 1971.

Fur Trade and Empire: George Simpson's Journal . . . in the Course of a Voyage from York Factory to Fort George . . . 1824-1825; Together with Accompanying Documents. Editor. Cambridge, MA: Harvard University Press, 1931.

Harvard Guide to American History. Co-authored with Oscar Handlin et al. Cambridge, MA: Harvard University Press, 1954.

History of the Westward Movement. New York: Alfred A. Knopf, 1978.

The Labor Movement in Wisconsin During the Civil War. Editor. Madison: State Historical Society of Wisconsin, 1915.

List of References on the History of the West. Co-authored with Frederick Jackson Turner. Cambridge, MA: Harvard University Press, Revised editions. 1922.

Manifest Destiny and Mission in American History: A Reinterpretation. With the collaboration of Lois Bannister Merk. New York: Alfred A. Knopf, 1963. Reprint. New York: Vintage, 1966.

The Monroe Doctrine and American Expansionism, 1843-1849. With the collaboration of Lois Bannister Merk. New York: Alfred A. Knopf, 1966. Reprint. New York: Vintage, 1972.

The Oregon Question: Essays in Anglo-American Diplomacy and Politics. Cambridge, MA: Harvard University Press, 1967.

Slavery and the Annexation of Texas. With the Collaboration of Lois Bannister Merk. New York: Alfred A. Knopf, 1972.

Articles

"The British Corn Crisis of 1845-1846 and the Oregon Treaty." *Agricultural History* 8(July, 1934):95-123.

"British Government Propaganda and the Oregon Treaty." *American Historical Review* 40(October, 1934):38-62.

"British Party Politics and the Oregon Treaty." *American Historical Review* 37(July, 1932):653-677.

"Eastern Antecedents of the Grangers." *Agricultural History* 23(January, 1949):1-8.

"The Genesis of the Oregon Question." *Mississippi Valley Historical Review* 36(March, 1950):583-612.

"The Ghost River Caledonia in the Oregon Negotiation of 1818." *American Historical Review* 55(April, 1950):530-551.

"The Oregon Pioneers and the Boundary." *American Historical Review* 29(July, 1924):681-699. Reprint. *Oregon Historical Quarterly* 28(December, 1927):366-388.

"The Oregon Question in the Webster-Ashburton Negotiations." *Mississippi Valley Historical Review* 43(December, 1956):379-404.

"Presidential Fevers." *Mississippi Valley Historical Review* 47(June, 1960):3-33.

"A Safety Valve Thesis and Texas Annexation." *Mississippi Valley Historical Review* 49(December, 1962):413-436.

"Snake Country Expedition, 1824-1825: An Episode of Fur Trade and Empire." *Mississippi Valley Historical Review* 21(June, 1934):49-62. Reprint. *Oregon Historical Quarterly* 35(June, 1934):93-122.

"The Snake Country Expedition Correspondence, 1824-1825." Editor. *Mississippi Valley Historical Review* 21(June, 1934):63-77.

Reviews

A History of Agriculture in Wisconsin by Joseph Schafer. *American Historical Review* 29(October, 1923):153-154.

John McLean's Notes of a Twenty-Five Years' Service in the Hudson's Bay Territory edited by W. S. Wallace. *American Historical Review* 39(October, 1933):180-181.

Studies of Frederick Merk

Athearn, Robert G. Review of *History of the Westward Movement* by Frederick Merk. *American Historical Review* 84(June, 1979):835-836.

Bailey, Thomas A. *A Diplomatic History of the American People*. Tenth edition. Englewood Cliffs, NJ: Prentice-Hall, 1980. P. 235.

Bailyn, Bernard, et al. "Frederick Merk." *Harvard University Gazette* 74, No. 33(May 18, 1979).

Berge, Dennis E. "Manifest Destiny and the Historians." In *Historians and the American West* edited by Michael P. Malone. Lincoln: University of Nebraska Press, 1983. Pp. 83-86.

Bloom, John Porter. Review of *Manifest Destiny and Mission in American History: A Reinterpretation* by Frederick Merk. *American West* 1(Spring, 1964):65-66.

Brack, Gene. Review of *Fruits of Propaganda in the Tyler Administration* by Frederick Merk. *Southwestern Historical Quarterly* 76(July, 1972):98-99.

Brauer, Kinley J. Review of *The Monroe Doctrine and American Expansionism, 1843-1849* by Frederick Merk. *Journal of American History* 54(June, 1967):134-135.

Gates, Paul W. "Memorial Resolution to Frederick Merk." *Journal of American History* 65(September, 1978):572-576.

Haynes, Robert V. Review of *Slavery and the Annexation of Texas* by Frederick Merk. *American Historical Review* 79(April, 1974):578-579.

Hyman, Harold. Review of *Slavery and the Annexation of Texas* by Frederick Merk. *Political Science Quarterly* 88(December, 1973):753-754.

Le Duc, Thomas. Review of *Manifest Destiny and Mission in American History: A Reinterpretation* by Frederick Merk. *Mississippi Valley Historical Review* 50(September, 1963):296-297.

Lefeber, Walter. Review of *The Oregon Question: Essays in Anglo-American Diplomacy and Politics* by Frederick Merk. *American Historical Review* 73(December, 1967):598.

Nash, Gerald D. Review of *History of the Westward Movement* by Frederick Merk. *Western Historical Quarterly* 10(July, 1979):371-372.

Nute, Grace Lee. Review of *Fur Trade and Empire: George Simpson's Journal . . .* edited by Frederick Merk. *Mississippi Valley Historical Review* 19(September, 1932):281-282.

"Obituary on Frederick Merk." *Harvard University News*, September 27, 1977.

Paul, Rodman W. "Frederick Merk, Teacher and Scholar: A Tribute." *Western Historical Quarterly* 9(April, 1978):141-148.

__________., and Michael P. Malone. "Tradition and Challenge in Western Historiography." *Western Historical Quarterly* 16(January, 1985):27-53.

Perkins, Dexter. Review of *Albert Gallatin and the Oregon Problem* by Frederick Merk. *William & Mary Quarterly* 8(July, 1951):453-455.

Pratt, Julius W. Review of *The Monroe Doctrine and American Expansionism, 1843-1849* by Frederick Merk. *Political Science Quarterly* 82(December, 1967):636-638.

__________. Review of *The Oregon Question: Essays in Anglo-American Diplomacy and Politics* by Frederick Merk. *Political Science Quarterly* 83(September, 1968):453-454.

Price, Glenn W. Review of *Fruits of Propaganda in the Tyler Administration* by Frederick Merk. *Pacific Historical Review* 41(February, 1972):105-106.

Pomeroy, Earl. Review of *The Monroe Doctrine and American Expansionism, 1843-1849* by Frederick Merk. *Journal of Southern History* 33(May, 1967):257-258.

Seager, Robert, II. Review of *Fruits of Propaganda in the Tyler Adminstration* by Frederick Merk. *American Historical Review* 77(October, 1972):1177-1178.

Sellers, Charles. Review of *Manifest Destiny and Mission in American History: A Reinterpretation* by Frederick Merk. *American Historical Review* 69(January, 1964):479.

Swierenga, Robert P. Review of *Economic History of Wisconsin During the Civil War Decade* by Frederick Merk. *Civil War History* 20(September, 1974):278-279.

Thomas, Robert M., Jr. "Obituary on Frederick Merk." *New York Times*, September 27, 1977, p. 42.

Van Alstyne, Richard W. Review of *Albert Gallatin and the Oregon Problem* by Frederick Merk. *Mississippi Valley Historical Review* 37(March, 1951):717-719.

Weinberg, Albert K. *Manifest Destiny: A Study of Nationalist Expansionism in American History*. Baltimore: Johns Hopkins University Press, 1935.

Winther, Oscar O. Review of *The Oregon Question: Essays in Anglo-American Diplomacy and Politics* by Frederick Merk. *Journal of American History* 54(December, 1967):657-658.

33

FRANK LAWRENCE OWSLEY

by Frank L. Owsley, Jr.

Biography

Frank Lawrence Owsley, fourth of seven children, was born on January 20, 1890, in Montgomery County, Alabama, on a farm that his mother, Annie Scott McGehee, had inherited from her grandfather, Abner McGehee. This grandfather, believed to be a descendant of the outlawed Highland Scottish Clan of MacGregor, had been one of the pioneer settlers of Montgomery County and ultimately one of the largest slaveholders and planters. Owsley's father, Lawrence Monroe Owsley, had come from the more modest background of a middle class yeoman farmer. The nature of Owsley's family background had a strong influence on his work in his later life. Here in his own family were good examples of the social mobility of yeoman farmers and the influence of the frontier on the antebellum South.

Owsley's parents had grown up during the reconstruction period when nearly everyone lived in a state of poverty and an education was extremely difficult to obtain. Both Annie and Lawrence Owsley were, by the standards of the day, well educated; his father was a college graduate. At that time anyone in the South who obtained an education above the elementary level did so as a result of very hard work and family sacrifice. Lawrence Owsley and his wife Annie were both school teachers and met while they were teaching in a school owned and run by Annie's brother, Oliver Clark McGehee, a Methodist minister. Soon after their marriage the young couple turned to full-time farming. Lawrence Owsley tried for several years to farm the prairie land in Montgomery County, but finding it very difficult to cultivate, he persuaded his wife to sell the McGehee land and move to Elmore County.

Lawrence eventually bought a farm at Claude, Alabama, near Wetumpka. This was the place where Frank Owsley spent most of his childhood. The life of farming did not dull the family's interest in obtaining an education and all five children who reached maturity completed college. One was an engineer, another majored in agriculture, two became medical doctors, and Frank Owsley obtained a Ph.D. degree ("Memoir," Frank Owsley Papers).

Frank Owsley's mother died when he was fifteen years old and his father married his late wife's best friend, Ealon Welch, who had also taught at McGehee's school. Owsley's earliest schooling was in a one-room school on his great-grandfather's plantation, taught by a kinswoman. His views and those of his family on education are well expressed in this memoir: "My father and my mother and my step-mother were well educated, and all three had taught school. My father always taught us at home." Owsley continued to explain that although he and his brothers all loved the country and the farm, they were all "fully determined not to farm for a livelihood" ("Memoir," Frank Owsley Papers).

Owsley's determination not to be a farmer did not diminish his interest in agriculture. He attended high school in Wetumpka at the Fifth District Agricultural School which combined high school and junior college. When he graduated in 1909, he entered the junior class at Alabama Polytechnic Institute, later Auburn University. Owsley graduated from Auburn in 1911 with a double major in English and history. He had long wanted to be a fiction writer, but until he could establish himself, he did not think that he could make a living as a writer. He returned to Auburn where he had planned to study agriculture and perhaps become a county agent. However, his former mentor in history, Dr. George Petrie, offered him an assistantship in history which would pay his expenses. The result of Petrie's offer of financial aid was that Owsley took an M.S. in History in 1912. Owsley then accepted a position at his alma mater, the Fifth District Agricultural School, teaching history and Latin from 1912 to 1914. The following year he returned to Auburn as an instructor. However, he soon suffered with what was probably a case of stomach ulcers, and so he spent the year 1915-1916 farming, reading law, and trying to improve his health. Although not completely recovered from this ailment, he entered the University of Chicago in the fall of 1916 and began his studies for the Ph.D. degree in history.

During most of the year at Chicago, he suffered from stomach trouble, an illness which prevented him from doing his best work. Perhaps because of this, several of his professors including the chairman of the history department, did not encourage him to continue. He was, however, awarded the Master of Arts degree in June, 1917, and continued his studies for the Ph.D. degree at Chicago. In fact, by the fall of 1917, he had completed the greater part of the residency requirements for the Ph.D.

World War I was already in progress and Owsley applied for and was admitted to the Reserve Officers Training Camp at Fort Oglethorpe, Georgia. He remained at that post from September until November, 1917, when once again a gastrointestinal ailment forced his resignation. In May, 1918, he re-entered the military when he was drafted and sent to Camp Sevier, near Greenville, South Carolina. After a few weeks, however, again he was discharged, this time for flat feet, a congenital condition which had never troubled him. Following this discharge, he returned to the University of Chicago and enrolled for the summer session.

During the academic year of 1919-1920, Owsley taught at Birmingham Southern, where he married Harriet Chappell, one of his students. He accepted a position at Vanderbilt University in Nashville in the fall of 1920 and taught there until 1949. He continued his work for the Ph.D. in the summers and received the degree *magna cum laude* in 1924 ("Memoir," Frank Owsley Papers).

In a letter written February 24, 1921, to his former professor at Auburn, Dr. George Petrie, Owsley stated his career objectives. This letter proved prophetic, since he was able to accomplish during his professional life almost exactly what he had proposed. He wrote, "If I live long enough I want to write three books on American History--a thesis, as soon as I can, which I don't expect to be any more than the price of my Ph.D. which no one will read." This was *States Rights in the Confederacy* (1925) which was well received and read. He then wanted to write, "a book of about five hundred pages some ten years later, maybe on which I have spent years of work and thought." This was *King Cotton Diplomacy* (1931) and although it was published in less than ten years, this book was certainly the type of work he had in mind. The letter continued, "Then before 'I kick in' on my job, I want to write another book somewhat larger in which I have put the work and thought of my life." Not a long book, *Plain Folk of the Old South* (1949) was the most important work of his life, based on years of careful and innovative research. Like most people in the historical profession, Owsley is best remembered for his writings. He felt, however, that teaching was his greatest commitment and he expressed strong feelings on this subject. In the letter to Petrie he continued, "The greater part of my energy, I want to be spent on *Teaching*. Consequently, I am going to devote less time to publishing books--hoping of course to get in a few" (Owsley to Petrie, Owsley Papers).

Frank Owsley never abandoned his commitment to good teaching, and one needs only to talk with his former students to find that he had the reputation of being one of the best and most inspiring teachers. Owsley's influence on his students and their impact on the profession has probably been of as much significance as his writing. Both at Vanderbilt and at the University of Alabama where he moved in 1949, he directed a large number of students who have, on the whole, been a credit to scholarship and who have the reputation of being good teachers.

Frank Owsley died in Winchester, England, October 21, 1956, and an excerpt from the notice of his death in the *American Historical Review* calls attention to his influence on his students:

> Professor Owsley was not satisfied to pursue the beaten paths of historical interpretation; he worked with the passion of the explorer and instilled in his students the same spirit. He had a deep and abiding interest in his students, who held him in esteem and affection, and he developed a large number of highly capable and inspired young historians. His work as a

> productive scholar made a significant contribution toward a better understanding of the Old South and of the Civil War, but perhaps his most lasting influence will be seen through the continuation of that contribution of the work of more than fifty younger scholars who earned their doctorate under his inspiring guidance (62:525-526).

In all of his work, Owsley was greatly assisted by his wife, Harriet Chappell Owsley. In the foreword to *Plain Folk of the Old South*, he makes this statement, "As in former publications, my wife is essentially the joint author of this book. She has constantly aided in the research for this volume and for other projected works on this subject. . . . In this particular volume she made the statistical analysis, prepared the land maps and made the index." Prior to the publication of *Plain Folk*, Harriet Owsley co-authored several articles on land tenure and related subjects with her husband which were published in the *Journal of Southern History*. After her husband's death in 1956, she edited and revised *King Cotton Diplomacy* in 1959 and edited *The South's Old and New Frontiers: Selected Essays of Frank Lawrence Owsley*.

Owsley was both the historian of the South and the southerner as historian. He was a native of Alabama and he loved his state. In 1949, when his good friend, A. B. Moore, established an endowed chair of American History at the University of Alabama and offered him the position, he accepted and returned to his beloved Alabama. In the seven years he was the Victor Hugo Friedman Professor of American History, he directed ten or twelve doctoral students. In 1956, he was awarded a Fulbright Grant which gave him the opportunity for research in England, but also included a lectureship at St. John's College, Cambridge University. He planned to work on an enlarged study of American foreign policy during the Civil War which would include an examination of the diplomatic records of Lincoln's government. The study would include a new and revised edition of *King Cotton Diplomacy*, which had gone out of print. He had hardly begun the work when he died suddenly October 21, 1956. His wife, Harriet Owsley, was given a Fulbright Grant and completed the work for the revision of *King Cotton Diplomacy* but the larger study was not finished.

Perhaps a good summary of Owsley's career can be found in the statement of Bennett H. Wall who said Owsley was:

> warm and friendly. . . . He laughed easily. On his feet he could say the right things. . . . He never harbored grudges. . . . He had time for graduate students. His manner was gracious and hospitable. . . . An outstanding critic, he nevertheless was kind to everyone. He took off on the history snobs and the pretentious big shots. Always open-minded he never said he had the answers (*Plain Folk*, 1984, p. xvi).

Themes

Frank Owsley considered himself to be primarily a southern historian, with a specialty in the Old South. He believed that the South both old and new had a special relationship with the rural frontier. The antebellum South was his main concern and the focus of his most important scholarly works, and he believed this region to be a part of the great American frontier.

All of Owsley's scholarship concentrated on the South and with the exception of *Plain Folk of the Old South*, they were about the Civil War and its causes. His original contributions fell into two groups: essays of opinion, which include the Agrarian essays and the scholarly, more objective, and well-researched works which include his three books, *States Rights in the Confederacy*, *King Cotton Diplomacy: Foreign Relations of the Confederate States of America*, and *Plain Folk of the Old South*.

Analysis

Owsley joined a group of writers known as the Agrarians in 1929, and soon thereafter his essays of opinion were written. The Agrarian manifesto, *I'll Take My Stand*, was published in the fall of 1930. His essays published in this and related works were written for the general reader. Although he was careful to make his facts correct, the essays were not objective. They were deliberately provocative, as Owsley admitted in a statement made at the Fugitive Reunion in 1956 (Purdy, *Fugitive Reunion*, p. 205). The Agrarian essays include "The Foundations of Democracy," in *Who Owns America*; "The Pillars of Agrarianism," "The Soldier Who Walked with God," and "The Making of Andrew Jackson," all in the *American Review*.

Owsley's critics have been primarily concerned with these Agrarian essays, a number of which have been reprinted. Edwin Rozwenc reprinted a portion of the "Irrepressible Conflict" from *I'll Take My Stand*, in a collection on the causes of the Civil War and commented that "only Owsley still finds it necessary to write his interpretation in a highly partisan and emotional manner" (p. vii). Thomas Pressly called Owsley a "Modern fire eater" (*Americans Interpret Their Civil War*). Michael O'Brien's criticisms miss the mark. As an Englishman, O'Brien fails to grasp the fine points of the struggle between the North and the South, and he especially lacks any understanding of the frontier or its influence (*The Idea of the American South*, 1920-1940, pp. 162-184). Other critics of this work, like John Stewart and Edward Shapiro, are much more favorable (*The Burden of Time*; *Tennessee Historical Quarterly* 36:75-94).

The last and possibly the most carefully researched of all of Owsley's essays on the Civil War was his presidential address delivered to the Southern Historical Association in 1940. Not one of the original Agrarian essays, it was entitled "The Fundamental Cause of the Civil War: Egocentric Sectionalism." He did not believe that the Civil War was fought over slavery. Instead, he saw the real cause of the conflict as the failure of the two sections to observe the comity of nations. The people in each section failed to respect the wishes of the people of the other section. Abraham Lincoln stated that the Civil War was fought to "save the Union," but Owsley believed that the slavery issue was simply a convenient justification for the North (*Journal of Southern History* 7:3-18). He writes that the South was fighting for a variety of causes, including slavery, but there is little doubt that the North was fighting for the Union. This essay has been reprinted more than any other writing that Owsley had ever done.

Owsley's lack of objectivity noted by some of his critics was justified when the objects of criticism were his essays of opinion. These essays, as previously noted, were not intended to be objective. Owsley's scholarly books and articles were, on the other hand, as objective as he could make them. H. L. Mencken, the South's harshest critic, called *States Rights in the Confederacy*, an excellent book (*American Mercury* 22:379-381). Owsley did not believe that there was any such thing as complete objectivity. The fact that the ideas passed through the mind of an individual meant that they were colored by the background and knowledge of that person. Given that premise, he tried to be objective in all his scholarly writings.

Owsley's first two books, written before any of his essays of opinion, concerned the Civil War and the reason for the South's defeat. His dissertation at the University of Chicago, *States Rights in the Confederacy*, was an indictment of states rights, showing how the state governments, especially those of Georgia and North Carolina, withheld both troops and supplies from the Confederate government. In the author's words, "If a monument is ever erected as a symbolical gravestone over the lost cause, it should have engraved upon it, these words: 'Died of States Rights'" (p. 1).

King Cotton Diplomacy: Foreign Relations of the Confederate States of America was written after years of research in Washington and Europe, including research sponsored by a Guggenheim fellowship. This study also delved into the reasons for the South's defeat. Southern leaders believed that England and France would recognize the Confederacy and intervene to get cotton. This mistaken idea led them to institute an embargo on the shipment of cotton in order to force an early intervention. At the time when the blockade was ineffective and they could have built up credit abroad with stockpiles of cotton, they were burning it in southern ports to enforce the embargo. The final chapter on the reasons why Europe did not intervene undercuts the theory usually given that it was the great hostility to slavery which kept them from recognizing the Confederacy. According to Owsley, it was their enormous war profits and the belief that the South would win the war without outside intervention that caused Europe to remain neutral in the Civil War (pp. 1-52, 562-578).

In the 1930s when Owsley was writing his Agrarian essays, he had already begun the research for *Plain Folk of the Old South* and he had also signed a contract to write a two-volume American history textbook with Oliver Perry Chitwood. They were joined later by H. C. Nixon for part of Volume II. The first volume of the textbook was published in 1945 and the second volume in 1948. It was the first and only American history textbook, at that time, authored by southerners.

Plain Folk of the Old South, published first in 1949, established Owsley as a historian of frontier America. It was based on years of research by Owsley, his wife, and several of his graduate students. The project from the beginning was a search for the plain folk or as Owsley said, "the forgotten man." A number of books had been written about the planters who usually kept written records of their business transactions and many of these records had been preserved. Unfortunately for Owsley's research, the yeoman farmer seldom kept account books, and it was necessary to find him in the public records, church records, diaries, memoirs, journals, and newspapers. Circuit riders often kept journals containing information about the places where they preached. There were journals describing camp meetings, pioneer weddings, corn huskings, log rollings, quilting parties, and all sorts of games and celebrations. This was the type of material necessary to make the people come to life but more was needed to determine percentages of the population and sizes of their land holdings.

Owsley first discovered the unpublished Federal Census in the Alabama State Archives in Montgomery, and later he found that Duke University had the census records for other southern states. This material had never before been used by historians. Schedule IV, the Agricultural Schedule, contained much of the information needed but it had to be checked, name by name, with two other schedules in order to determine which people were slaveholders and which were landless tenants. Space does not permit a detailed description of the methods used to collect and assimilate this information. It was, however, a task requiring many years and was accomplished before the development of the computer, a device which would have greatly speeded up the research.

In the 1850s and 1860s there were very few towns of any size in the southern states. Large municipalities were mostly a product of the period following the Civil War. Many of the southerners who did live in urban areas during the antebellum period either owned land or made their living by serving the rural population as merchants or professional people. In any case *Plain Folk of the Old South* was not intended to be a study of the urban South.

The plain people were found and the census records contained figures for the amount of land they owned, improved and unimproved; the value of farm equipment; the number and value of livestock; the amounts of various crops produced during the census year; and from the two other schedules, it was determined how many slaves were owned and the people who were tenant farmers. This was the data needed to obtain the number of yeoman farmers and the size and value of their property holdings.

Owsley made his greatest contribution as a historian in *Plain Folk of the Old South*. The most important discovery of this research was that there was a large middle class in the South composed of yeomen farmers, many of whom owned their land and were politically active. Also the size and value of their holdings proved that the planters had not crowded the small farmers off the good soils.

In the years since it was published, *Plain Folk of the Old South* has created a storm of hostile criticism. When one considers that this study was logical and seemed to fill an otherwise unexplained void in history, the criticism is surprising. In addition to filling an obvious gap, Owsley's work contains innovative research and its documentation is far more complete that most historical studies. It is difficult to understand why this work was not universally accepted, or why it was ever considered to be controversial. Nevertheless, there were critics who tried to invalidate Owsley's conclusions.

Probably John Ray Skates, Jr., in his article "In Defense of Owsley's Yeomen," has the best explanation of the attack. Skates suggests that *Plain Folk* refutes the old *Gone with the Wind* tradition and that this angers many southern traditionalists who would prefer to pretend that the yeoman farmer did not exist. These people simply could not bring themselves to bury the traditional myth of the Old South with its spoiled belles and young men who would still fight duels over points of honor. The group most upset by the Owsley study was the Marxists. In their unending search for a class struggle, they did not want to find a large group of prosperous yeoman or middle class farmers in the South. A large and powerful middle class simply did not fit the Marxist model (*Southern Miscellany*, pp. 1-15).

The first and perhaps most widely quoted critic of the *Plain Folk* thesis was Fabian Linden who published an article in the *Journal of Negro History* in which he challenged Owsley's methodology and the choice of counties that he used. Linden went on to question the existence of a large and valuable cattle industry in the southern states. Interestingly enough, Linden's article is widely used by Owsley's critics and is usually considered to be a critical review of *Plain Folk*, even though the article was published three years before Owsley's book (*Journal of Negro History* 31:140-189).

Owsley's evidence shows rather conclusively that there was an extensive cattle industry in the South. As mentioned above, Linden denies the existence of this industry and the Linden conclusion is strongly endorsed by historian Eugene Genovese. He concludes that the southern cattle industry could not have been of much value since nearly all of the cattle and hides which were shipped out of the United States through the port of New Orleans had points of origin outside the South and also there was considerable evidence that southern planters were buying meat from the northern states (*Political Economy of Slavery*). What Genovese and Linden both ignore is that the southern climate made it difficult to preserve slaughtered cattle. It was, therefore, a very common practice in the South to drive or ship cattle to the northern states for slaughter and perhaps to buy back the processed meat. The subsequent studies of Grady McWhiney and Forrest McDonald have produced considerable research on cattle production in the antebellum South (*Journal of Southern History* 41:147-166). Another critic of *Plain Folk* was Idus Newby, who in his book, *The South: A History* (1978), attacks the idea of a strong southern middle class by suggesting that their power was tolerated by the planters because it promoted racial solidarity (p. 157).

One other point that critics especially dislike about Owsley's work is the fact that he gave strong support to the idea that there was no real class struggle among the white population of the old South. Marxists argue that the planters controlled too much of the wealth and therefore the power. The flaw in their argument is that there was almost an unlimited supply of land, and there was a great amount of social mobility in antebellum southern white society. This mobility was to a considerable extent the product of the frontier and its supply of cheap land, factors which urban-raised Marxist historians simply cannot place within their model.

Although Owsley never stressed it in his writings, in his classes and by implication in his writing, he argued that there was no significant class struggle in the antebellum South simply because there were no serious points of conflict between planters and yeomen. They all wanted cheap land; protection from the Indians and their removal to the West; good prices for their crops; law and order; protection for their slaves and their right to own them; and little else other than to be left alone by their government. These factors go farthest to answer the notion of a lack of a class struggle in the South.

Most of Owsley's critics have continued to use the article by Fabian Linden which is based on certain assumptions. Genovese asserts that "an attempt was made by Frank Owsley and his students to prove that the Southern yeomanry was strong and prosperous . . . this view was convincingly refuted by Fabian Linden (*Political Economy of Slavery*, p. 37). Michael O'Brien called Linden's article a devastating review of *Plain Folk in the Old South.* The comments were typical of the critics and almost every mention of Owsley's work is followed by one of Linden's statements. Interestingly enough, neither Linden nor any of the other critics have made any serious effort to check the validity of Owsley's statistics. Most of the charts, documents, and other statistical records and notes are on file in the library at Vanderbilt University, but not until very recently has anyone attempted to make a thorough examination of them.

Fortunately this situation is changing. Donald L. Winters has computerized the figures for eight Tennessee counties, compiled by the Owsley school. Although Winters is critical of some of the statistical methods used, he has found that Owsley's most important conclusions were correct according to the computer study. In Winter's article, "'Plain Folk' of the Old South Reexamined: Economic Democracy in Tennessee," Winters concludes that the "Plain Folk" are the "small and medium-sized landholders [who] represented the largest group in [Tennessee] society" (*Journal of Southern History* 53:584). He also contends that the most significant contribution of the Owsley school was the identification of this rural middle class which represented 60 percent or more of frontier southern population. To ignore the yeomanry, Winters believes, is to seriously distort history. He finds that Tennessee came closer to representing Owsley's model than the entire Cotton South, but "in neither region, however, does the evidence support the claim that small owners were routinely pushed off their land or relegated to inferior soils" (p. 585).

Owsley seems to have been ahead of his time in developing quantification as a methodology for historical research.

Nevertheless, Fabian Linden may have come closer than anyone to actually describing the plain folk when he suggested that they were "closer to the frontier" (*Journal of Negro History* 31:183). Linden is probably correct on this point. Herein is the major thrust of all of Owsley's research. Owsley believes that southern history was to a great extent the history of the frontier. The South was a rural farming area with the same life and economic style as that of the frontier. In this sense the planter and townspeople were simply attached to a deeply entrenched folk culture which had its roots on the frontier.

Bibliography

Books

King Cotton Diplomacy: Foreign Relations of the Confederate States of America Chicago: University of Chicago Press, 1931. Revised edition edited by Harriet Chappell Owsley, 1959.

Know Alabama: An Elementary History. Co-authored with John Craig Stuart and Gordon Thomas Chappell. Northport, AL: Colonial Press, 1957.

Plain Folk of the Old South. Baton Rouge: Louisiana State University Press, 1949.Reprint. 1984.

A Short History of the American People, vol. I. Co-authored with Oliver Perry Chitwood. New York:Van Nostrand, 1945. Revised edition, 1955.

A Short History of the American People, vol. II. Co-authored with Oliver Perry Chitwood and Herman Clarence Nixon. New York: Van Nostrand, 1948.

The South: Old and New Frontiers: Selected Essays of Frank Lawrence Owsley. Edited by Harriet Chappell Owsley. Athens: University of Georgia Press, 1969.

States Rights in the Confederacy. Chicago: University of Chicago Press, 1925.

The United States From Colony to World Power. Co-authored with Oliver Perry Chitwood and Herman Clarence Nixon. New York: Van Nostrand, 1949.

Articles

"Aaron Venable Brown." *Dictionary of American Biography* 3(1929):267-268.

"The Agrarians Today." *Shenandoah* 3(Summer, 1952):22-28.

"Ambrose Dudley Mann." *Dictionary of American Biography* 12(1933):239-240.

"America and the Freedom of the Seas." In *Essays in Honor of William E. Dodd* edited by Avery Craven. Chicago: University of Chicago Press, 1935. Pp. 194-256.

"The Clays in Early Alabama History." *Alabama Review* 2(October, 1949):243-268.

"The Confederacy and King Cotton: A Study in Economic Coercion." *North Carolina Historical Review* 4(October, 1929):371-397.

"Defeatism in the Confederacy." *North Carolina Historical Review* 3(July, 1926):446-456.

"Democracy Unlimited." *Georgia Review* 15(Summer, 1961):129-143.

"The Economic Basis of Society in the Late Ante-Bellum South." Co-authored with Harriet C. Owsley. *Journal of Southern History* 4(February, 1940):24-25. Reprint. Bobbs-Merrill Reprint Series in History, 1964.

"The Economic Structure of Rural Tennessee, 1850-1860." Co-authored with Harriet C. Owsley. *Journal of Southern History* 8(May, 1942):161-182.

"The Education of a Southern Frontier Girl." *Alabama Review* 6(October, 1953):268-288 and 7(January, 1954):66-73.

"Foreword." In *Joseph E. Brown and the Confederacy* by Louise Biles Hill. Chapel Hill: University of North Carolina Press, 1939. Pp. vii-viii.

__________. In *Mississippi Farmers, 1850-1860* by Herbert Weaver. Nashville, TN: Vanderbilt University Press, 1945. Pp. 11-12.

__________. In *Secession and Restoration of Louisiana* by Willie Melvin Caskey. Baton Rouge: Louisiana State University Press, 1938. Pp. xi-xii.

__________. In *Slavery in Tennessee* by Chase C. Mooney. Bloomington: Indiana University Press, 1957. Pp. vii-viii.

__________. In *The Tennessee Yeomen, 1840-1860* by Blanche Henry Clark. Nashville, TN: Vanderbilt University Press, 1942. Pp. xiii-xv.

"Foundations of Democracy." *Southern Review* 1(Spring, 1936):708-720. Reprint. In *Who Owns America? A Declaration of Independence* edited by Herbert Agar. Boston: Houghton Mifflin Co., 1936. Pp. 52-67.

"The Fundamental Cause of the Civil War: Egocentric Sectionalism." *Journal of Southern History* 7(February, 1941):3-18. Reprint. In *Vanderbilt Miscellany*. Nashville, TN: Vanderbilt University Press, 1944. Pp. 232-247; *The Literature of the South* edited by R. C. Beatty et al. Chicago: Scott, Foresman and Co., 1952. Pp. 659-668. Revised edition, 1968. Pp. 645-654; *The Pursuit of Southern History* edited by George B. Tindall. Baton Rouge: Louisiana University Press, 1964.

"The Irrepressible Conflict." In *I'll Take My Stand: The South and the Agrarian Tradition* with an introduction by Louis D. Rubin, Jr. New York: Harper & Brothers, 1930. Pp. 61-91. Reprint. New York: Peter Smith, 1951; in paperback, New York: Harper Torchbacks, 1962; in *The Causes of the American Civil War* edited by Edwin C. Rozwenc. Boston: D. C. Heath, 1961.

"Isham Green Harris." *Dictionary of American Biography* 8(1932):310-311.

"James Murray Mason." *Dictionary of American Biography* 12(1933):364-365.

"James Williams." *Dictionary of American Biography* 20(1936):267.

"John Larue Helm." *Dictionary of American Biography* 8(1932):513-514.

"John Williams Walker." *Alabama Review* 9(April, 1956):100-119.

"Joseph Anderson." *Dictionary of American Biography* 1(1928):267-268.

"Leonidas Campbell Houk." *Dictionary of American Biography* 9(1932):256-257.

"Local Defense and the Downfall of the Confederacy." *Mississippi Valley Historical Review* 11(March, 1925):492-525.

"The Patterns of Migration and Settlement on the Southern Frontier." *Journal of Southern History* 11(May, 1945):147-176. Reprint. Bobbs-Merrill Reprint Series in History, 1964.

"The Pillars of Agrarianism." *American Review* 4(March, 1935):529-547.

"Scottsboro, the Third Crusade: The Sequel to Abolition and Reconstruction." *American Review* 1(Summer, 1933):257-285.

"A Southerner's View of Abraham Lincoln." *Georgia Review* 12(Spring, 1958):5-17.

"The Third Annual Meeting of the Southern Historical Association." *Journal of Southern History* 4(February, 1938):55-67.

"William Selby Harney." *Dictionary of American Biography* 8(1932):280-281.

"The Writing of Local History." *Alabama Review* 7(April, 1954):113-126.

Review Essays

"Abolition and Secession." *Virginia Quarterly Review* 11(Summer, 1935):461-466. Reviews of *The Antislavery Impulse, 1830-1844* by Gilbert Hobbs Barnes and *The Secession Movement in Virginia* by Henry T. Shanks.

"The American Triangle." *Virginia Quarterly Review* 11(January, 1935):113-119. Reviews of *America's Tragedy* by James Truslow Adams and *The Eve of Conflict: Stephen A. Douglas and the Needless War* by George Fort Milton.

"The Anatomy of Military Command." *Virginia Quarterly Review* 19(Winter, 1943):436-439. Review of *Lee's Lieutenants: Cedar Mountain to Chancellorsville* by Douglas Southall Freeman.

"Civil War on Two Fronts." *Virginia Quarterly Review* 19(Winter, 1943):124-129. Reviews of *Lee's Lieutenants: A Study in Command, Manassas to Malvern Hill* by Douglas Southall Freeman and *The Hidden Civil War: The Story of the Copperheads* by Wood Grey.

"Confederate Justice." *Virginia Quarterly Review* 17(Autumn, 1941):630-632. Review of *Justice in Grey: A History of the Judicial System of the Confederate States of America* by William M. Robinson, Jr.

"The Everlasting South." *Sewanee Review* 54(Autumn, 1948):716-720. Reviews of *The Dixie Frontier* by Everett Dick and *The South Old and New* by Francis Butler Simkins.

"Fear May Come Too Late." *Sewanee Review* 55(Summer, 1947):514-517. Review of *The Shore Dimly Seen* by Ellis Gibbs Arnall.

"The Historical Philosophy of Frederick Jackson Turner." *American Review* 5(Summer, 1935):368-375. Review of *The United States, 1830-1850* by Frederick Jackson Turner.

"History of the Old South." *Yale Review* 29(Summer, 1940):849-853. Reviews of *The South to Posterity* by Douglas Southall Freeman and *Freedom of Thought in the Old South* by Clement Eaton.

"A House Divided." *Sewanee Review* 53(Summer, 1945):500-503. Review of *Divided We Stand: The Crisis of Frontierless Democracy* by Walter Prescott Webb.

"Jefferson Davis." *Southern Review* 3(Spring, 1938):762-768. Review of *Jefferson Davis*, 2 volumes, by Robert McElroy.

"A Key to Southern Liberalism." *Southern Review* 3(Summer, 1937):28-38. Review of *It's a Far Cry* by Robert W. Winston.

"The Life and Death of the Confederacy." *Virginia Quarterly Review* 24(Spring, 1950):280-284. Review of *A Diary From Dixie* by Mary Boykin Chesnut and edited by Ben Ames Williams.

"Lucius Quintus Cincinnatus Lamar." *American Review* 5(September, 1935):502-512. Review of *Lucius Q. C. Lamar* by Wirt Armistead Cate.

"The Making of Andrew Jackson." *American Review* 1(May, 1933):220-225. Review of *Andrew Jackson, the Border Captain* by Marquis James.

"Mr. Daniels Discovers the South." *Southern Review* 4(Spring, 1939):665-675. Review of *A Southerner Discovers the South* by Jonathan Daniels.

"The Old South and the New." *American Review* 4(February, 1936):475-485. Review of *The South Looks at Its Past* by Ben B. Kendrick and A. M. Arnett.

"Origins of the American Civil War." *Southern Review* 5(Spring, 1940):609-626. Review of *The Antislavery Origins of the Civil War in the United States* by Dwight Lowell Dumond.

"Paths of Glory." *Virginia Quarterly Review* 14(Winter, 1938):136-144. Reviews of *Andrew Jackson: Portrait of a President* by Marquis James, *Henry Clay: Spokesman of the New West* by Bernard Mayo, *The Life of Henry Clay* by Glyndon Van Deusen, *Winfield Scott: The Soldier and the Man* by Charles Winslow, *Old Fuss and Feathers: The Life and Exploits of Winfield Scott* by Arthur D. Bowden Smith, *Jefferson Davis* by Robert McElroy, and *The American Civil War* by Carl Russell Fish and edited by William Ernest Smith.

"Prelude to Conflict." *Virginia Quarterly Review* 24(Spring, 1948):297-300. Review of *The Ordeal of the Union*, 2 volumes, by Allan Nevins.

"President Lincoln." *Virginia Quarterly Review* 22(Spring, 1946):300-304. Review of *Lincoln, The President*, 2 volumes, by James G. Randall.

"A Rebel War Clerk and His Diary." *Southern Review* 1(Winter, 1936):680-685. Review of *A Rebel War Clerk's Diary at the Confederate States' Capital* by J. B. Jones, edited by Howard Swiggett.

"Reconciliation and Reunion." *Yale Review* 27(Autumn, 1937):171-173. Review of *The Road to Reunion, 1865-1900* by Paul H. Buck.

"Slavery and the Struggle of the Sections." *Yale Review* 24(Spring, 1934):643-644. Review of *American Tragedy* by James Truslow Adams.

"The Soldier Who Walked With God." *American Review* 4(February, 1935):435-459 and 5(April, 1935):62-74. Reviews of *R. E. Lee*, 4 volumes, by Douglas Southall Freeman.

"Two Agrarian Philosophers: Jefferson and DuPont de Nemours." *Hound and Horn* 6(October-December, 1932):166-172. Reviews of *The Correspondence of Jefferson and DuPont de Nemours* by Gilbert Chinard, *Correspondence Between Thomas Jefferson and Pierre Samuel DuPont de Nemours* edited by Dumas Malone, and *The Educational Work of Thomas Jefferson* by Roy J. Honeywell.

"The War of the Sections." *Virginia Quarterly Review* 10(October, 1934):630-635. Reviews of *The Secession of the Southern States* by Gerald Johnson and *The Irrepressible Conflict* by Arthur C. Cole.

Reviews

The Aaron Burr Conspiracy by Walter Flavious McCaleb. *Nashville, TN, Banner*, November 29, 1936.

Andrew Jackson: Portrait of a President by Marquis James. *Nashville, TN, Banner*, October 3, 1937.

Andrew Stevenson, Democrat and Diplomat, 1785-1857 by Frances Fry Wayland. *American Historical Review* 56(October, 1950):133-134.

The Arkansas Plantation, 1820-1849 by Donald Crichton Alexander. *Mississippi Valley Historical Review* 30(December, 1943):466.

The Army of Tennessee: A Military History by Stanley F. Horn. *Tennessee Historical Quarterly* 1(June, 1942):181-183.

Atlantic Impact, 1861 by Evan John. *Journal of Southern History* 19(November, 1953):540-541.

Auburn: Loveliest Village of the Plain by Mollie Hollifield. *Alabama Review* 10(April, 1957):155-156.

Beginnings of Tennessee in the Land of the Chickasaws, 1541-1641 by Samuel Cole Williams. *Mississippi Valley Historical Review* 17(September, 1930):320-322.

The Blue and the Gray: The Story of the Civil War as Told by Participants by Henry Steele Commager. *Journal of Southern History* 18(November 1951):559-561.

Confederate Georgia by Conn Bryan. *Mississippi Valley Historical Review* 40(March, 1954):741-742.

The Confederate Ironclad "Virginia" ("Merrimac") by Harrison A. Trexler. *Journal of Southern History* 4(August, 1938):401-402.

Confederate Leaders in the New South by William Hesseltine. *Alabama Review* 4(April, 1951):150-151.

David Wilmot: Free Soiler by Charles Buxton Going. *Nashville, TN, Tennessean*, November 30, 1924.

A Decade of Sectional Controversy, 1851-1861 by Henry M. Simms. *Journal of Southern History* 9(February, 1943):119-120.

The Development of Southern Sectionalism, 1819-1848 by Charles S. Sydnor. *Journal of Southern History* 15(February, 1949):108-110.

A Diary from Dixie by Mary Boykin Chesnut, edited by Ben Ames Williams. *Alabama Review* 3(July, 1950):234-236.

The Dixie Frontier: A Social History of the Southern Frontier from the First Transmontane Beginnings to the Civil War by Everett Dick. *Journal of Southern History* 14(August, 1948):413-415.

Everyday Things in American Life by William C. Langdon. *Mississippi Valley Historical Review* 29(September, 1942):276-278.

Freedom of Thought in the Old South by Clement Eaton. *Journal of Southern History* 6(November, 1940):558-559.

French Opinion on the United States and Mexico, 1860-1867: Extracts from the Reports of the Procureaurs Generaux edited by Lynn M. Case. *American Historical Review* 42(April, 1937):566-568.

The Gallant Hood by John Percy Dyer. *Alabama Review* 4(April, 1951):152-154.

Gideon Welles, Lincoln's Navy Department by Richard S. West, Jr. *Nashville, TN, Tennessean*, October 31, 1943.

George Rogers Clark: Life and Public Services by Temple Bodley. *Nashville, TN, Tennessean*, March 27, 1927.

Government in Business by Stuart Chase. *Nashville, TN, Banner*, September 30, 1935.

The Growth of Southern Nationalism, 1848-1861 by Avery O. Craven. *Annals of American Political Science* 91(January, 1951):165-166.

An Introduction to the Papers of the New York Prize Court, 1861-1865 by Madeline Russell Robinson. *American Historical Review* 52(April, 1947):524-525.

Jefferson Davis: His Rise and Fall by Allen Tate. *Mississippi Valley Historical Review* 16(March, 1930):570-572.

Jefferson in Power by Claude G. Bowers. *Nashville, TN, Banner*, September 6, 1936.

The Journal of Benjamin Moran, 1857-1865 edited by Sarah Agnes Wallace and Frances Emma Gillespie. *Journal of Southern History* 14(May, 1950):236-238.

Judah P. Benjamin, Confederate Statesman by Robert Douthat Meade. *American Historical Review* 49(April, 1944):506-507.

Lee: West Point and Lexington by Walter Creigh Preston. *Journal of Southern History* 1(May, 1935):237-239.

__________. *Nashville, TN, Tennessean*, October 20, 1929.

Letters of James Gillespie Birney, 1831-1857 edited by Dwight L. Dumond. *Journal of Southern History* 5(May, 1939):263-264.

The Life of Thomas Jefferson by Francis W. Hirst. *Nashville, TN, Tennessean*, March 21, 1926.

The Living Jefferson by James Truslow Adams. *Nashville, TN, Banner*, April 26, 1936.

Mainland by Gilbert Seldes. *Nashville, TN, Banner*, December 13, 1936.

The Memoirs of Lieutenant Henry Timberlake, 1756-1765 edited by Samuel Cole Williams. *Nashville, TN, Tennessean*, May 8, 1927.

Mobile: History of a Seaport Town by Charles G. Summersell. *Alabama Review* 3(January, 1950):77-78.

Origins of Class Struggle in Louisiana: A Social History of White Farmers and Laborers During Slavery and After, 1840-1875 by Roger W. Shugg. *Journal of Southern History* 6(February, 1940):116-117.

Ploughshares into Swords by Frank E. Vandiver. *Alabama Review* 5(October, 1952):291-292.

A Rebel War Clerk's Diary at the Confederate States' Capital by J. B. Jones, edited by Howard Swiggett. *Journal of Southern History* 1(August, 1935):402-404.

Reconstruction in Arkansas, 1862-1874 by Thomas S. Staples. *Misssissippi Valley Historical Review* 9(March, 1925):591-593.

Sectionalism and Internal Improvements in Tennessee, 1796-1845 by Stanley John Folmsbee. *American Historical Review* 46(January, 1941):425-426.

A Short History of the American People by Robert Granville Caldwell. *Nashville, TN, Tennessean*, January 3, 1926.

Simon Girty: The White Savage by Thomas Boyd. *Nashville, TN, Tennessean*, October 21, 1928.

Six Years with the Texas Rangers, 1875-1881 by James B. Gillett, edited by Milo M. Quaife. *Mississippi Valley Historical Review* 12(March, 1926):608-610.

The Soul of a Nation: The Founding of Virginia and the Projection of New England by Matthew P. Andrews. *Journal of Southern History* 10(February, 1944):95-96.

The Southern Poor-White Farmer from Lubberland to Tobacco Road by Roger S. Shugg. *Mississippi Valley Historical Review* 24(March, 1940):116-117.

The Texas Revolution by William C. Binkley. *Tennessee Historical Quarterly* 12(June, 1953):185-186.

Tom Watson, Agrarian Rebel by C. Vann Woodward. *Mississippi Valley Historical Review* 25(December, 1938):431-432.

A Two Party South? by Alexander Heard. *Mississippi Valley Historical Review* 39(December, 1952):587-588.

Two Soldiers: The Campaign Diaries of Thomas J. Key, C.S.A., December 7, 1863-May 17, 1865, and Robert J. Campbell, U.S.A., January 1, 1864-July 21, 1865 edited by Wirt Armstead Cate. *Journal of Southern History* 4(August, 1938):394-396.

__________. *Nashville, TN, Banner*, March 19, 1938.

War Memoirs of Robert Lansing by Robert Lansing. *Nashville, TN, Banner*, October 6, 1935.

The War of Independence by Claude H. Van Tyne. *Nashville, TN, Tennessean*, January 26, 1930.

War Years With Jeb Stuart by William W. Blackford. *Journal of Southern History* 12(May, 1946):285-286.

William G. Brownlow, Fighting Parson of the Southern Highlands by E. Merton Coulter. *Mississippi Valley Historical Review* 24(December, 1937):403-405.

Wilsonian Diplomacy: Versailles Peace and French Public Opinion by Bernard Noble. *Nashville, TN, Banner*, June 2, 1935.

Studies of Frank Lawrence Owsley

Atherton, Lewis. Review of *Plain Folk of the Old South* by Frank L. Owsley. *Mississippi Valley Historical Review* 37(June, 1950):127-128.

Bogue, Allan G. Review of *King Cotton Diplomacy: Foreign Relations of the Confederate States of America* by Frank L. Owsley. *Civil War History* 5(December, 1959):436-437.

Clark, Blanche Henry. *The Tennessee Yeoman, 1840-1860.* Nashville, TN: Vanderbilt University Press, 1942.

Clark, Thomas D. Review of *Plain Folk of the Old South* by Frank L. Owsley. *Alabama Review* 3(April, 1950):146-148.

Coles, Harry, Jr. "Some Notes on Slave Ownership in Louisiana." *Journal of Southern History* 9(August, 1943):381-393.

Eaton, Clement. Review of *Plain Folk of the Old South* by Frank L. Owsley. *American Historical Review* 55(April, 1950):617-618.

Genovese, Eugene D. *The Political Economy of Slavery: Studies in the Economy and Society of the Slave South.* New York: Random House, 1965.

Jordan, H. Donaldson. Review of *King Cotton Diplomacy: Foreign Relations of the Confederate States of America* by Frank L. Owsley. *American Historical Review* 38(October, 1932):135-137.

Linden, Fabian. "Economic Democracy in the Slave South: An Appraisal of Some Recent Views." *Journal of Negro History* 31(April, 1946):140-189.

McDonald, Forrest, and Grady McWhiney. "The Antebellum Southern Herdsman: A Reinterpretation." *Journal of Southern History* 41(May, 1975):147-166.

Mencken, H. L. *American Mercury* 22(March, 1931):379-381.

Mooney, Chase C. Review of *The South's Old and New Frontiers: Selected Essays of Frank Lawrence Owsley* edited by Harriet Chappell Owsley. *Journal of American History* 57(September, 1970):448-449.

___________. "Some Institutional and Statistical Aspects of Slavery in Tennessee." *Tennessee Historical Quarterly* 1(Summer, 1942):195-228.

Newby, Idus. *The South: A History.* New York: Holt, Rinehart & Winston, 1978.

O'Brien, Michael. *The Idea of the American South, 1920-1940.* Baltimore, MD: Johns Hopkins University Press, 1979.

["Obituary Notice."] *American Historical Review* 62(January, 1957):525-526.

Owsley, Frank, Papers. Family papers in possession of Harriet Owsley, Nashville, TN; Owsley Papers at Vanderbilt University Library, Vanderbilt University, Nashville, TN.

Owsley, Harriet, ed. *The South: Old and New Frontiers: Selected Essays of Frank Lawrence Owsley.* Athens: University of Georgia Press, 1969.

Pressly, Thomas. *Americans Interpret Their Civil War.* Princeton, NJ: Princeton University Press, 1954.

Purdy, Rob Roy, ed. *Fugitive Reunion.* Nashville, TN: Vanderbilt University Press, 1957.

Rozwenc, Edwin C., ed. *The Causes of the American Civil War.* Boston: D.C. Heath, 1961.

Schmidt, Louis Bernard. Review of *King Cotton Diplomacy: Foreign Relations of the Confederate States of America* by Frank L. Owsley. *Mississippi Valley Historical Review* 19(December, 1932):107-110.

Shapiro, Edward. "Frank L. Owsley and the Defense of the Southern Identity." *Tennessee Historical Quarterly* 36(Spring, 1977):75-94.

Skates, John Ray, Jr. "In Defense of Owsley's Yeomen." In *Southern Miscellany: Essays in Honor of Glover Moore* edited by Frank Allen Dennis. Jackson, MS: University Press of Mississippi, 1981. Pp. 1-15.

Stewart, John. *The Burden of Time: The Fugitives and Agrarians.* Princeton, NJ: Princeton University Press, 1965.

Sydnor, Charles S. Review of *Plain Folk in the Old South* by Frank L. Owsley. *South Atlantic Quarterly* 49(October, 1950):542-543.

Vance, Rupert B. Review of *Plain Folk in the Old South* by Frank L. Owsley. *Journal of Southern History* 16(November, 1950):545-547.

Weaver, Herbert. *Mississippi Farmers, 1850-1860.* Nashville, TN: Vanderbilt University Press, 1945.

Winters, Donald L. "'Plain Folk' of the Old South Reexamined: Economic Democracy in Tennessee." *Journal of Southern History* 53(November, 1987):565-586.

34

FREDERIC LOGAN PAXSON

by Tully Hunter

Biography

Philadelphia, Pennsylvania, is a city whose historical roots are deeply imbedded into the American past. Many important people have walked the streets of Philadelphia and numerous significant events have taken place there. In addition to the historical importance of the city, Philadelphia has contributed to the pursuit of history by producing one of the ablest American frontier historians of all, Frederic Logan Paxson.

Frederic Logan Paxson was born on February 23, 1877, in Philadelphia. In 1898 he graduated from the University of Pennsylvania. He received the Master of Arts degree from Harvard in 1902 and then returned to the University of Pennsylvania where, in 1903, he earned his Ph.D. in United States history (*American Historical Review* 54:479).

Paxson's career was long and productive. He served first as an assistant professor at the University of Colorado and then at the University of Michigan. In 1906 he married Helen Hale. The Paxsons raised three daughters, Jane, Emma, and Patricia. In 1910 he joined the history department at the University of Wisconsin. For the year 1917 he served as president of the Mississippi Valley Historical Association. When World War I began, Paxson entered the United States army in the war plans division, general staff. As a major he was in charge of the historical branch of the economic mobilization section. After the war he returned to his position at Wisconsin. In 1924, Frederic Paxson was awarded the Pulitzer Prize for the best book of the year in American history for his work, *History of the American Frontier, 1763-1893.* In 1932, he accepted the Margaret Byrne professorship in United States history at the University of California, Berkeley. From 1940, until his retirement in 1947, he served as the history department chairman at Berkeley (*American Historical Review* 54:479; *New York Times*, October 25, 1948, p. 23).

Throughout his career, Frederic Paxson was most concerned with the history of the United States, both as a teacher and as a writer. In teaching he attempted to reach a wide audience. For younger students he helped put together textbooks such as *Builders of Our Nation* (1939) and *Finding America* (1937). The general, more popular, audience was reached in various ways, most notably through his series of four radio programs during the early 1940s. His students at Berkeley, however, witnessed the strict historian in Paxson. The "Professor" had a reputation of being a very thorough, formal, and "no nonsense" type of instructor. Yet, as one former student of Paxson's recalls, he was very positive in his presentation of material to his students (Interview, Marie Thornton, October 1, 1985). Paxson oversaw approximately sixty-six dissertations in numerous areas of United States history, and he was considered to be an able administrator both by the history department and the university. Paxson was truly a valuable asset to Berkeley.

As a writer, Paxson was extremely active. He produced over forty books and essays. Not only did he write textbooks, but he wrote numerous narrative histories, edited archival work, and compiled bibliographical materials. The majority and best known of his works dealt with the West and the role of the American frontier.

On October 24, 1948, Frederic Logan Paxson, author, teacher, father, and lifelong member of the Society of Friends, died from an embolism after undergoing surgery at Alta Bates Hospital in Berkeley, California. He was seventy-one years old at the time of his death. Paxson had witnessed the end of the frontier and had left behind a wealth of material explaining the importance of its passing. Indeed, his professional life was dedicated to the ideals of the frontier (*New York Times*, October 25, 1948, p. 23).

Themes

Paxson wrote on a wide variety of topics in American history, but the bulk of his work dealt with the development of the frontier. Paxson looked west and saw the frontier of Frederick Jackson Turner. Paxson, like Turner, viewed the history and character of the United States in frontier terms, and like Turner he believed that this unique element and era of American history had passed by the end of the 1890s. Thus, Paxson interpreted the past and present of the United States in terms of the frontier:

> The West has gone, and it behooves us to look into our household and to examine the estate, to peregrinate our boundaries and to gaze across them to the world outside. We have hitherto regarded life from a setting in which the implicit condition was the West that was. Ever it was there, exercising its influence upon our course. When it was new, it formed our character as a nation, giving to the world in the process a new race whose advent was not foreseen and whose very existence

> was not realized until its character was formed beyond all repression or recall (*When the West is Gone*, p. 6).

Paxson was a Turnerian. He understood American history by looking at the influence of the frontier and the frontier alone.

In Paxson's works that specifically covered the frontier, four major themes appear. First, the frontier as a process was the means by which the frontier shaped America and Americans, and, second, Paxson understood history as a sequence of events, a very methodical listing of events that demonstrated the effect of the frontier. The cause and effect relationship of the events that took place on the frontier is a third theme that is complemented by a fourth, the end of the western frontier bringing the United States to new frontiers in international affairs.

Like most Turnerians, Paxson's concern for the process of the frontier received most of his attention. Yet, Paxson ably describes the sequence of events and presents the cause and effect relationship of the events in such a manner as to produce a very readable form of narrative history. The theme of the continued frontiers of the United States allowed Paxson to address the issues of "national character" and "national destiny," while others used history to play the role of the "prophet" (pp. 3-4). With this type of approach, Paxson is able to address a wide range of topics in American history, and yet remain ideologically close to the frontier.

Analysis

Frederick Jackson Turner believed the role of the frontier in the history of the United States was primarily in the reaction between the West and the East whereby American society took on its peculiar features (*American Historical Review* 1:70). That interaction and reaction among the parts of the nation that were settled and the parts of the nation being settled created a unique American country and people. Turner elaborated his thesis through the explanation of the location and ideals of the frontier. Likewise, Paxson recognized and wrote about the region and the process of the frontier experience.

The West as a region is of limited importance to the overall context of Paxson's writings. The frontier as a region did exist. For this historian, the demarcation of the frontier as a line was ambiguous, yet the frontier steadily moved from East to West. Along this line non-Native Americans reclaimed the land from nature as they pushed further into the interior of the continent. As the settlers migrated inland, the process basic to the frontier experience was created.

The frontier, for Paxson and Turner, was a process that reshaped and altered the settler. Lead westward by the pioneers, the colonies, and later the United States, were institutionally and culturally molded into a non-European nation. Old World institutions could not meet the needs of the settlers. Individuals were forced to do away with European societal means of status and well-being, and instead they developed their own unique blend of strength, courage, and institutions to adapt the West into a suitable environment for settlement.

From the very beginning, Paxson's frontier was more than a region. The western frontier was a process of reshaping and restructuring old customs into useful tools of the New World. With this perspective on American history, Paxson writes that, "The influence of the frontier has been the strongest single factor in American history, exerting its power from the first days of the earliest settlements down to the last years of the nineteenth century, when the frontier left the map" (*The Last American Frontier*, pp. 28-29). The theme of the process of the frontier was the basis of all of Paxson's works concerning the West. Paxson's Turnerian view of history saturates every page. As a result, the author sees the process of the frontier as of singular importance in the history of the United States.

One reviewer of Paxson's Pulitizer Prize-winning *History of the American Frontier, 1763-1893*, notes how the author traced with "scientific precision" virtually all aspects of frontier history. The reviewer, amazed with Paxson's handling of the topics of discovery, diplomacy, war, exploitation, penetration, and legislation, writes that the work is "the ablest one-volume history of the West" (*American Historical Review* 30:603-604). Indeed, such attention to the numerous phases of American history is typical of Paxson's work.

The organization of *The Last American Frontier* is representative of Paxson's propensity to use a natural sequence of events in order to cover the greatest amount of material possible. He moves from the Native American frontier to the Santa Fe and Oregon Trails, from the California to the Colorado migrations, from the railroad to the Native American wars on the Great Plains, and so forth. The author is not prone to reflection upon events to prove a point. Instead, correlations and analogies to be made are drawn from the same approximate time period. Not only did this technique allow Paxson to preserve the natural progression of events, but such an approach gave him the freedom to concentrate on the cause and effect relationships in history.

For Paxson, not only was the cause and effect relationship mandatory, but recent effects had recent causes. Also, one event usually had only one cause. Paxson's work concerning railroads is a prime example of this approach. Paxson demonstrated the prominence of the railroad after the settling of the eastern coast and the far western United States. The railroad was a movement to connect the two coasts. The obvious result was the crossing and eventual settlement of the "Great American Desert," thus bringing about the beginning of the end for the frontier (*American Historical Association Report*, pp. 107-109). In *The Last American Frontier* Paxson explains the role of the railroad in closing the frontier more fully, but he retains his cause and effect approach:

> The overland traffic had begun on the heels of the first migrations. Its growth during the fifties and its triumphant period in the sixties were great arguments in favor of the construction of railways to take its place. It came to an end when the first continental railroad was completed in 1869 (p. 191).

Such an approach to history might be considered simplistic to some, but Paxson's style enabled him to write very readable and informative histories which could easily be summarized. Paxson saw the frontiernot only as a force moving through the West, but also as the only constant tying the nation together. Since events are carefully limited to sequence and cause and effect, the frontier process becomes the only common denominator throughout American history.

Even though Paxson, like Turner, marks the end of the frontier in the 1890s, he does not envision an America which has completely come of age or lost its uniqueness. The loss of the western frontier did not spell instant doom for the United States in Paxson's writings. He saw the United States as pushing on to new frontiers, which facilitates both internal and external change. Internally, Paxson predicts a society which will continue to develop upon its own unique path. Due to the resources of America and the effects of the western frontier, the United States could not become a closed frontier like Europe, according to Paxson. Instead, movements like the populists of the 1890s demonstrated the ability of Americans to continue to develop within internal frontiers. Even though much had been lost with the passing of the frontier, the United States did not become stagnant nor, as Paxson wrote, "European" (*When the West is Gone*, pp. 102-126).

Externally, the United States began to flex its muscles on the international frontier. In his three-volume history of the First World War, *American Democracy and the World War*, the frontier is not mentioned. However, Paxson describes a countrythat continues to change in the same terms that he described as having taken place on the frontier. The experience of World War I furthers the development of a unique America and American people. In one work, *The United States in Recent Times*, Paxson openly admits that he believed the influence of World War I to be very similar to that of the frontier: "Through it all the American structure changes and grows, until in the World War it reveals unsuspected strength, and the power to deliver it" (p. 20). The frontier began the development of America and World War I was the hallmark of the formation of that unique America. Paxson saw a nation arriving on the international scene after having emerged from the North American continent by way of frontier processes. America continued to find new frontiers when the West was gone.

Overall, Paxson's writings prove readable and informative. His affinity to the general reader and dedication to teaching is attested to by his work with textbooks and in his preparation of books to familiarize the general reader with a broad perspective of United States history. His attention to detail and historical explanation make his works valuable to both the scholar and nonscholar alike.

Close examination of this Turnerian brings only three major criticisms. First, his desire to trace the history of the frontier gives the impression that, at times, the rest of the nation is historically void or stagnant. Second, Paxson seldom uses either footnotes or bibliographies in his works. When he does invoke notes, they contribute greatly to his scholarship. If a bibliography is present, it usually consists of a small collection of works at the end of each chapter. Finally, Paxson, like most historians of the time, gives little attention to Blacks, Native Americans, or other minority groups on the frontier. He limits his discussion of ethnic groups to their affect on Anglo-Americans. As a separate people, these groups retain little identity of their own in Paxson's writings.

In spite of his generalist work in United States history, Frederic Logan Paxson was first and foremost a historian of the American frontier. The ideas that are encapsulated by the frontier appear in all of his works to some degree. Due to his ability to reach the general reader and maintain his academic integrity, Paxson may have done more to anchor the Turner thesis as a basic component to American historiography than any other immediate post-Turnerian.

Bibliography

Books

The American Civil War. London: Williams and Norgate, 1911.

American Democracy and the World War: 1913-1917, Pre-War Years. Boston: Houghton Mifflin, 1936.

American Democracy and the World War: 1917-1918, America at War. Boston: Houghton Mifflin, 1939.

American Democracy and the World War: 1918-1923, Post-War Years. Berkeley: University of California Press, 1948.

American Political History: A Series of Twelve Lessons, by Frederic Logan Paxson . . . with Introductions, References, and Significant Questions, to be used in Connection with the American Statesman, Standard Library Edition. Boston: Houghton Mifflin, 1928.

Builders of Our Nation. Co-authored with Olive E. Smallidge. Boston: Houghton Mifflin, 1939.

Finding America, an Elementary History. Co-authored with Olive E. Smallidge. Boston: Houghton Mifflin, 1937.

The Great Demobilization and Other Essays. Co-edited with Graduate Students. Madison: University of Wisconsin Press, 1941.

Guide to the Materials in London Archives for the History of the United States Since 1783. Co-authored with Charles Paullin. Washington, DC: Carnegie Institution, 1914.

History of the American Frontier, 1763-1893. Boston: Houghton Mifflin, 1924.

A History of the United States. Co-authored with Reuben Gold Thwaites. Boston: Houghton Mifflin, 1936.

The Independence of the South American Republics: A Study in Recognition and Foreign Policy. Philadephia: Ferris and Leach, 1903.

The Last American Frontier. New York: Macmillan, 1910.

The New Nation. The Riverside History of the United States. Vol. IV. Edited by William E. Dodd. Boston: Houghton Mifflin, 1915.

Recent History of the United States. Boston: Houghton Mifflin, 1921.

T. Turnbull's Travels from the United States Across the Plains to California. Editor. Madison: State Historical Society of Wisconsin, 1914.

The United States in Recent Times: Reading with a Purpose. Chicago: American Library Association, 1926.

The United States in the Making. Co-authored with Leon Hardy Canfield. Boston: Houghton Mifflin, 1946.

War Cyclopedia: A Handbook for Ready Reference on the Great War. Co-authored with Edwin S. Corwin. Washington, DC: Government Printing Office, 1918.

When the West is Gone. New York: Henry Holt and Co., 1931.

Selected Articles

"The Admission of the 'Omnibus' States, 1889-1890." In State Historical Society of Wisconsin, *Proceedings for 1911*. Madison: State Historical Society of Wisconsin, 1912. Pp. 77-96.

"The American War Government, 1917-1918." *American Historical Review* 26(October, 1920):45-76.

"The Boundaries of Colorado." *University of Colorado Studies* 2(July, 1904):87-94.

"A Constitution of Democracy--Wisconsin, 1847." *Mississippi Valley Historical Review* 2(June, 1915):3-24.

"The Constitution of Texas, 1845." *Southwestern Historical Quarterly* 18(April, 1915):386-398.

"The Cow Country." *American Historical Review* 22(October, 1916):65-82.

"England and Mexico, 1824-1825." *University of Colorado Studies* 3(June, 1906):115-120.

"Finance and the Frontier." In *The Trans-Mississippi West* edited by James F. Willard and Colin B. Goodykoontz. Boulder: University of Colorado, 1930. Pp. 257-266.

"The Great Demobilization." *American Historical Review* 44(January, 1939):237-251.

"The Highway Movement, 1916-1935." *American Historical Review* 51(January, 1946):236-253.

"The Historical Opportunity in Colorado." *University of Colorado Studies* 3(November, 1905):19-24.

"The New Frontier and the Old American Habit." *Pacific Historical Review* 4(December, 1935):309-327.

"Organization or Anarchy?" In *World Resources and Peace* edited by T. H. Goodspeed. Berkeley: University of California Press, 1941. Pp. 131-151.

"The Pacific Railroads and the Disappearance of the Frontier in America." In *American Historical Association Annual Report for the Year 1907*. Washington, DC: American Historical Association, 1908. 1:105-118.

"A Preliminary Bibliography of Colorado History." *University of Colorado Studies* 3(June, 1906):101-114.

"Public Archives of the State of Colorado." In *American Historical Association Annual Report for the Year 1903.* Washington, DC: American Historical Association, 1904. 1:415-437.

"The Railroads of the 'Old Northwest' Before the Civil War." *Transactions of the Wisconsin Academy of Sciences, Arts and Letters* 17(1914):243-274.

"The Territory of Colorado." *American Historical Review* 12(October, 1906):53-65.

"The Territory of Jefferson: A Spontaneous Commonwealth." *University of Colorado Studies* 3(November, 1905):15-18.

"A Tripartite Intervention in Haiti, 1851." *University of Colorado Studies* 1(February, 1904):323.

"The Twain Have Met." *General Magazine and Historical Chronicle* 46(January, 1941):181-191.

"The West and the Growth of the National Ideal." *Transactions of the Illinois State Historical Society* 15(1910):24-33.

Selected Reviews

A. Barton Hepburn: His Life and Service for His Time by Joseph B. Bishop. *Mississippi Valley Historical Review* 11(June, 1924):132-133.

The Administration of President Rutherford B. Hayes by John W. Burgess. *Mississippi Valley Historical Review* 3(December, 1916):406.

Adventures of the First Settlers of the Oregon or Columbia River by Alexander Ross. *Mississippi Valley Historical Review* 11(June, 1924):150.

Afternoon Neighbors: Further Excerpts from a Literary Log by Hamlin Garland. *Mississippi Valley Historical Review* 22(June, 1935):126-127.

Alaska: A History of Its Administration, Exploitation, and Industrial Development During Its First Half Century under the Rule of the United States by Jeanette Paddock Nichols. *American Historical Review* 29(April, 1925):579-580.

Alexander Graham Bell by Catherine Mackenzie. *Mississippi Valley Historical Review* 15(March, 1929):572-573.

The American Livestock and Meat Industry edited by Rudolf Alexander Clemen. *American Historical Review* 29(January, 1924):359-361.

Anglo-American Relations During the Spanish-American War by Bertha Ann Reuter. *Mississippi Valley Historical Review* 11(December, 1924):434-435.

Anybody's Gold: The Story of California's Mining Towns by Joseph H. Jackson. *Mississippi Valley Historical Review* 28(December, 1941):441-442.

Applied History edited by Benjamin F. Shambaugh. *American Historical Review* 18(July, 1913):821-823.

Autobiography of George Dewey by George Dewey. *Mississippi Valley Historical Review* 4(June, 1917):118-120.

The Bozeman Trail by Grace Raymond Hebard and E. A. Brinistool. *Mississippi Valley Historical Review* 9(March, 1923):338-339.

The British Empire and the United States: A Review of Their Relations During the Century of Peace Following the Treaty of Ghent by William Archibald Dunning. *American Historical Review* 20(April, 1915):648-649.

The Canadian North-West edited by E. H. Oliver. *Mississippi Valley Historical Review* 2(December, 1915):455-457.

Civilization and Climate by Ellsworth Huntington. *Mississippi Valley Historical Review* 3(June, 1916):88-89.

The Course of Empire by Bernard DeVoto. *American Historical Review* 58(July, 1953):120-121.

The Diary of Nelson Kingsley, a California Argonaut of 1849 edited by Frederick J. Teggart. *Mississippi Valley Historical Review* 2(December, 1915):452-453.

E. A. Harriman: A Biography by George Kennan. *American Historical Review* 28(October, 1922):166-167.

E. I. Dupont de Nemours and Company by B. G. Dupont. *Mississippi Valley Historical Review* 8(June, 1921):189.

Early Life and Letters of General Thomas J. ("Stonewall") Jackson by Thomas Jackson Arnold. *Mississippi Valley Historical Review* 5(March, 1918):511.

Edward Fitzgerald Beale: A Pioneer in the Path of Empire, 1822-1903 by Stephen Bonsal. *American Historical Review* 18(October, 1912):173-174.

The Expansionist Movement in Texas, 1836-1850 by William C. Binkley. *American Historical Review* 31(January, 1926):366.

The Foreign Policy of James G. Blaine by Alice Felt Tyler. *Mississippi Valley Historical Review* 15(June, 1928):140-142.

49er's: The Chronicle of the California Trail by Archer Butler Hulbert. *American Historical Review* 37(April, 1932):567-568.

Forty Years of It by Brand Whitlock. *Mississippi Valley Historical Review* 1(September, 1914):314-315.

Galusha A. Grow, Father of the Homestead Law by James T. Dubois and Gertrude S. Mathews. *American Historical Review* 24(October, 1917):221-222.

George Hamilton Perkins, Commodore, USN by Carroll Storrs Alden. *Mississippi Valley Historical Review* 2(December, 1915):435.

George Harvey: "A Passionate Patriot" by Willis Fletcher Johnson. *Mississippi Valley Historical Review* 16(March, 1930):581-584.

The Granger Movement: A Study of Agricultural Organization and Its Political, Economic, and Social Manifestations by Solon J. Buck. *Mississippi Valley Historical Review* 1(June, 1914):136-139.

The Great Plains by Walter Prescott Webb. *American Historical Review* 37(January, 1932):359-360.

Hanna by Thomas Beer. *Mississippi Valley Historical Review* 16(March, 1930):580-581.

A History of American Life, Vol. VIII: The Emergence of Modern America, 1865-1878 by Allan Nevins. *Mississippi Valley Historical Review* 14(March, 1928):571-572.

A History of Muhlenberg County by Otto A. Rothert. *Mississippi Valley Historical Review* 1(September, 1914):317-318.

History of Road Legislation in Iowa by John E. Brindley. *American Historical Review* 18(July, 1913):821-823.

A History of the United States by Cecil Chesterton. *Mississippi Valley Historical Review* 6(December, 1919):407.

A History of the United States Since the Civil War by Ellis Paxson Oberholtzer. *Mississippi Valley Historical Review* 9(December, 1922):253-255.

A Hoosier Autobiography by William Dudley Foulke. *Mississippi Valley Historical Review* 10(December, 1923):327-328.

James Baird Weaver by Fred Emory Haynes. *American Historical Review* 25(October, 1919):144.

John Hay, Author and Statesman by Lorenzo Sears. *Mississippi Valley Historical Review* 2(June, 1915):140-141.

Joseph Ward of Dakota by George Harrison Durand. *Mississippi Valley Historical Review* 1(March, 1915):589.

The Life and Letters of John Hay by William Roscoe Thayer. *Mississippi Valley Historical Review* 2(March, 1916):578-581.

The Life and Times of Stephen B. Girard: Mariner and Merchant by John B. McMaster. *Mississippi Valley Historical Review* 6(June, 1919):120.

The Life of James J. Hill by Joseph Gilpin Pyle. *American Historical Review* 23(October, 1917):196-197.

The Life of Preston B. Plumb, 1837-1891, U.S. Senator from Kansas for the 14 Years from 1877-1891 by William Elsey Connelly. *Mississippi Valley Historical Review* 1(September, 1914):323-324.

The Life of Rutherford Birchard Hayes, Nineteenth President of the United States by Charles Richard Williams. *Mississippi Valley Historical Review* 1(March, 1915):582-584.

The Life of Thomas Brackett Reed by Samuel W. McCall. *Mississippi Valley Historical Review* 2(September, 1915):282-283.

The Life of William McKinley by Charles S. Olcott. *Mississippi Valley Historical Review* 3(March, 1917):543-545.

My Friendly Contemporaries, A Literary Log by Hamlin Garland. *Mississippi Valley Historical Review* 19(March, 1933):601-602.

New Spain and the Anglo-American West: Historical Contributions Presented to Herbert Eugene Bolton. Pacific Historical Review 2(May, 1933):231-233.

Notes of a Busy Life by Joseph Benson Foraker. *Mississippi Valley Historical Review* 3(September, 1916):248-250.

Official Report of the Debates and Proceedings in the Nebraska Constitutional Convention edited by Albert Watkins. *Mississippi Valley Historical Review* 1(December, 1914):468-469.

The Oxford History of the United States, 1783-1917 by Samuel Eliot Morison. *American Historical Review* 33(July, 1928):889-891.

The Pageant of America: A Pictorial History of the United States. The Lure of the Frontier, a Story of Race Conflict, Vol. II, by Ralph Henry Gabriel. *Mississippi Valley Historical Review* 17(June, 1930):172-174.

The Prairie and the Making of Middle America: Four Centuries of Description by Dorothy Anne Dondore. *American Historical Review* 32(July, 1927):892-894.

The Presbyterians, 1783-1840: A Collection of Source Materials edited by William Warren Sweet. *American Historical Review* 42(July, 1937):792-793.

The Quakers of Iowa by Louis Thomas Jones. *Mississippi Valley Historical Review* 1(September, 1914):315-316.

The Railroad Builders by John Moody. *Mississippi Valley Historical Review* 7(June, 1920):158.

Recollections of a Long Life, 1829-1915 by Isaac Stephenson. *Mississippi Valley Historical Review* 3(September, 1916):258-259.

The Rise of American Civilization by Charles A. Beard and Mary R. Beard. *Mississippi Valley Historical Review* 14(September, 1927):233-235.

Roadside Meetings by Hamlin Garland. *Mississippi Valley Historical Review* 17(March, 1931):652-653.

Samuel F. B. Morse: His Letters and Journals edited by Edward Lind Morse. *Mississippi Valley Historical Review* 2(June, 1915):142-143.

Samuel Jordan Kirkwood by Dan Elbert Clark. *Mississippi Valley Historical Review* 5(March, 1918):513-515.

Sixty Years of American Life by Everett P. Wheeler. *Mississippi Valley Historical Review* 4(September, 1917):254-255.

The Tall Sycamore of the Wabash: Daniel Woolsey Voorhees by Leonard S. Kenworthy. *Mississippi Valley Historical Review* 23(December, 1936):420-421.

Theodore Roosevelt and his Time: Shown in His Own Letters by Joseph B. Bishop. *American Historical Review* 26(April, 1921):552-554.

Ulysses S. Grant by Louis A. Coolidge. *Mississippi Valley Historical Review* 4(September, 1917):249-251.

Under Four Administrations from Cleveland to Taft by Oscar S. Straus. *Mississippi Valley Historical Review* 10(June, 1923):98-99.

William Rockhill Nelson by Members of the staff of the *Kansas City Star*. *Mississippi Valley Historical Review* 3(September, 1916):259.

The Year of Decision by Bernard DeVoto. *American Historical Review* 49(October, 1943):120-121.

Studies of Frederic Logan Paxson

Clark, Ira G. "A Dedication to the Memory of Frederic Logan Paxson, 1877-1948." *Arizona and the West* 3(Summer, 1961):107-112.

Coulter, E. Merton. Review of *History of the American Frontier, 1763-1893* by Frederic Logan Paxson. *Georgia Historical Quarterly* 10(December, 1926):343-344.

Cox, Isaac J. Review of *The New Nation* by Frederic Logan Paxson. *Mississippi Valley Historical Review* 2(September, 1915):274-278.

Dale, H. C. Review of *History of the American Frontier, 1763-1893* by Frederic Logan Paxson. *American Historical Review* 30(April, 1925):603-604.

"Dr. F. L. Paxson, 71, Won Pulitzer Prize." *New York Times*, October 25, 1948, p. 23.

Farrand, Max. Review of *The Last American Frontier* by Frederic Logan Paxson. *American Historical Review* 15(July, 1910):892-893.

Hollon, W. Eugene. "Paxson, Frederick Logan." In *The Reader's Encyclopedia of the American West* edited by Howard R. Lamar. New York: Thomas Y. Crowell Co., 1977. P. 897.

Meyer, B. H. "Discussion of Doctor Paxson's Paper." In *American Historical Association Annual Report for the Year 1907*. Washington, DC: American Historical Association, 1908. 1:119-122.

Pelzer, Louis. Review of *Recent History of the United States* by Frederic Logan Paxson. *Mississippi Valley Historical Review* 9(June, 1922):84-88.

Phillips, Ulrich B. Review of *History of the American Frontier, 1763-1893* by Frederic Logan Paxson. *Mississippi Valley Historical Review* 12(March, 1925):583-584.

Pomeroy, Earl. "Frederic L. Paxson and His Approach to History." *Mississippi Valley Historical Review* 39(March, 1953):673-692.

"Recent Deaths." *American Historical Review* 54(January, 1949):479.

Schafer, Joseph. Review of *American Democracy and the World War: 1913-1917, Pre-War Years* by Frederic Logan Paxson. *Wisconsin Magazine of History* 20(December, 1936):234-236.

Thornton, Marie. Interview with Tully Hunter. October 17, 1985. Berkeley, CA.

Turner, Frederick Jackson. "Western State-Making in the Revolutionary Era." *American Historical Review* 1(October, 1895):70-87; 1(January, 1896):251-269.

Webb, Walter Prescott. Review of *History of the American Frontier, 1763-1893* by Frederic Logan Paxson. *Southwestern Historical Quarterly* 28(January, 1925):247-252.

35

THEODORE CALVIN PEASE

by R. Douglas Hurt

Biography

When Theodore Calvin Pease was born on November 25, 1887, in Cassopolis, Michigan, the historical profession was on the verge of great change. At that time a new generation of scholars was beginning to revolt from the patrician dominated craft which heretofore had largely controlled the past. These young historians received their training in the seminars of the German universities and upon completion of their graduate work, returned home to provide training for a second generation of professional historians. In turn, these American educated historians continued to remove themselves from the literary past which the patricians, such as Hubert Howe Bancroft and Francis Parkman, had penned in broad, romantic, uncritical strokes. Instead, these new historians turned to scientific methodology to learn the facts and to base history, if not on immutable law, upon precise research and understanding.

The profession, however, soon changed again under the influence of the progressive movement and later still again with the unheaval of the Second World War. Yet, no single philosophical view governed the interpretation of the American past. Since the late nineteenth century, several schools of historical interpretation have, at any one time, produced substantive scholarship. The career of Theodore Calvin Pease spanned the first half of the twentieth century when new methodologies and schools of thought influenced the interpretation of the past, particularly that of the American frontier (*Writing American History*, p. 92; *The Development of Historical Studies*, p. 114).

When Pease graduated from Chicago's Lewis Institute in 1904, he entered the University of Chicago where he earned the degree of Bachelor of Philosophy three years later. Pease continued his studies at the university and, in 1914, upon completion of his dissertation entitled "John Lilburne and the Levellers," received a Ph.D. in history. After graduation, he took the position of associate in history at the University of Illinois, which he held until 1917, when World War I interrupted his career. Pease served as a first lieutenant in the 32nd Division of the American Expeditionary Force, and he was part of the army of occupation. On May 24, 1919, he was discharged. When Pease returned to civilian life, he resumed his duties at the University of Illinois, where he became assistant professor in 1920. The university elevated him to the associate rank in 1923, and he became a full professor three years later (*Journal of the Illinois State Historical Society* 41:354, 356).

Between 1920 and 1939, Pease edited the *Collections of the Illinois State Historical Library*. He also served as chairman of the Historical Manuscripts Commission of the American Historical Association from 1925 to 1931. In 1936, Pease became a founding member of the Society of American Archivists, and he edited *The American Archivist* from 1938 to 1946. In 1939, Pease served as director of the Illinois Historic Survey and, in 1942, he became chairman of the Department of History at the University of Illinois. His scholarly interest in Illinois history contributed to his appointment as president of the Illinois State Historical Society from 1946-1947. Pease died at the age of sixty on August 11, 1948 (p. 358; *American Historical Review* 54:256).

Themes

The theme of evolutionary progress permeates the work of Theodore Calvin Pease. Trained in the Scientific School, Pease believed history indicated the evolutionary, progressive change of civilization in general and American society in particular. This assumption, however, was based upon a conservative interpretation of the past. History provided stability and nationalistic focus, and it ensured the retention of the best achievements of the past. Moreover, history was cumulative. The events of the past shaped the present, which became larger than the past. History brought the present to a pinnacle of progress, which the next age would, in turn, supersede. He could not specifically measure this progress, of course, but he had an abiding faith that history slowly changed life for the better.

This philosophical premise, however, was mixed with acceptance of the Imperial and Turner Schools of historical interpretation in relation to the frontier. The Imperial School, which Charles M. Andrews best represented, saw American colonial history shaped by the process of salutary neglect, which a new British imperialism superseded after the conclusion of the French and Indian War in 1763. He also believed, however, as Frederick Jackson Turner suggested, that the frontier shaped the growth of democracy. Pease fit both historical interpretations into the philosophical constructs of his own Scientific School. As a result, he contended that both European design and the American environment combined to create a new civilization more progressively advanced than that which went before. These changes took time, of course, and the historical progress, which his work suggests, was evolutionary, not revolutionary. Indeed, this is the primary theme in the work of Pease, the evolutionary, conservative progress of history (*Journal of the Illinois State Historical Society* 41:354-362; *Mississippi Valley Historical Review* 25:168).

Analysis

In 1916, Pease began his scholarly career with the publication of *The Leveller Movement: A Study in the History and Political Theory of the English Great Civil War.* This work began in Andrew Cunningham McLaughlin's seminar at the University of Chicago. It was a sympathetic study of a minority group's attempt to keep England governed by law instead of men. In 1914, the university accepted this manuscript for his doctoral dissertation, and the next year it won the Herbert Baxter Adams Prize in European history. This was the only work which Pease conducted strictly in European history. Perhaps his midwestern origin and professional location turned his attention from European to American frontier studies and to the history of Illinois. In any event, in 1918, he published *The Frontier State, 1818-1848.* This book was a contribution to the multivolume *Centennial History of Illinois* under the editorship of Clarence W. Alvord. Because the war and military duty interrupted his work, however, Agnes Wright, his assistant, wrote the chapters on Indian affairs and socioeconomic changes on the eve of the Mexican War in order to meet the publication deadline (p. vii).

Pease's first venture into frontier history was topical in format and political in substance. Here, he traces the development of Illinois through the legislative process. As such, it is descriptive or narrative history with a faint tint of Frederick Jackson Turner's influence. Turner's frontier thesis, while not strong, is apparent when Pease writes that "half savage" hunters preceded the "advance of civilization." He hints at the democratization of the frontier by noting that: "Town government in so far as it was distinct from other local government was rudimentary. Towns were incorporated by individual acts which gave the trustees power to legislate for the order of the town and to levy taxes on town lots." He did not suggest, however, that the frontier affected the development of social and political institutions which improved or expanded democracy among the newly arrived immigrants. Pease recognizes that the "advance of population northward [was] one of the most significant facts in the history of the decade from 1830-1840," and that immigration influenced the ethnic mix in Illinois and placed new demands on political parties and state government. The frontier, however, did not foster the pure democracy that Turner suggested. Instead, political developments in Illinois sprang from "quarrels and rivalries" in an already developed democratic system. Personality and faction determined political development--not the frontier environment. Indeed, Pease never fully adopts or gives much attention to what became known as the Turner thesis (pp. 6, 173, 188, 193, 265).

Instead, Pease, schooled in scientific historical methodology, sees the development of American history as a cumulative, evolutionary, progressive process. The events of the past led to an improvement of life at any given moment. Stripped of romanticism, history was the process of cause and effect. In this respect, history provided guidance and stability. One could learn from the past, rest certain that the future would be even better than that which went before, and feel secure in the stability of the nation state. "The War of 1812," he writes, "offered a new stimulus to national pride." Moreover, it caused revolutionary stirrings in Europe and South America which made the United States "seem destined to an even nobler and more significant future as the standard bearer of republican principles" (p. 20).

By the Mexican War, Pease believed that great changes, mostly for the better, had occurred in Illinois. Where life had been "conventionalized and stiff," men now thought "broadly in terms of general political principles." "The Illinois of 1818," he writes, "like the nation it existed in was dreaming dreams and interpreting the future in terms of the past; in Illinois of 1848, there were many men of vigorous mind who had visions of the future" (p. 442). This closing sentence reveals the influence of a new Progressive School of historical interpretation. Thereafter, Pease would be torn between the new history of the progressive movement and the scientific history from which it developed. At the same time, he began to emulate the literary felicity of the patrician historians in his historical writing, but he was never able to break the bonds of his past training in the Scientific School. For Pease, history meant evolutionary progress which maintained the best of the past for the future.

Upon his return to the University of Illinois following service in the World War I, Pease focused his attention on editing documents relating to the Old Northwest and the state of Illinois. The first results of that work appeared in 1923 with publication of *Illinois Election Returns, 1818-1848*, which was his first contribution to the *Collections of the Illinois State Historical Library*. This study grew out of his research for *The Frontier State*. Here, Pease once again acknowledges the casual influence of Turner when he writes that, "In a rural frontier commonwealth the ideal of democracy had triumphed over the aristocracy of geniality," but he also acknowledges the growing influence of the Progressive School by adding "it now had to maintain itself in a state being rapidly transformed by railroads, cities, and business enterprises." New forces in historical development were now suitable for study, particularly the "economic motive" which must be considered when "determining the actions and beliefs of men." Pease, however, did not believe that economic determinism is the prime mover of history. Rather, history depended upon the mixture of economics among other things, such as personality, prejudice, vanity, arrogance, and hero worship. Tradition, not "pure economic motives," shapes the actions of humans. "Loyalty to a principle, an organization, an individual, determine them" (pp. lv, lviii-lix).

In 1925, Pease made his second contribution to the *Collections of the Illinois State Historical Library* with publication of *The Laws of the Northwest Territory, 1788-1800*. He now backed away from Turner's interpretation of frontier history. Pease concludes his introduction to that volume by seriously questioning, if not refuting, the significance of the frontier upon the political development of the early settlers in the Old Northwest. "The legislation of the Northwest Territory," he writes, "can be picked full of defects, but [it] is a question whether the scattered communities for which it was made would not generally have governed themselves in about the way they actually did whatever the legislation provided for them" (p. xxxvi). Pease did not elaborate on those thoughts, but he clearly suggests traditional practice rather than the frontier experience predominantly influenced governmental institutions. The political structures in the Northwest Territory, he implies, developed from the institutional baggage which the immigrants brought with them. Frontier democracy was a scion from the sturdy oak of eastern institutions; it was not born anew in the Old Northwest.

Pease published *The Story of Illinois* (1925) the same year in which *The Laws of the Northwest Territory* (1925) appeared. This state history, like its predecessor, *The Frontier State*, was a solid political and economic history of Illinois. Pease revised this book for reprint in 1949, and it was printed for a third time in 1965. Here, again, Pease reflects some of Turner's influence when he writes of the Illinois frontier that, "The first comer was the typical outlier of civilization, imbued with the love for the wilderness, a lone wolf, often scarcely more than a savage, with a savage's cruelty, ignorance, and superstition." The squatters and farmers, in turn, followed and lived in a "primitive" fashion, but they soon acquired the comforts of civilization. Yet, for all of the Turnerian implications of these thoughts, Pease still does not go beyond them. Life on the frontier might be "primitive," but economic improvement soon brought the benefits of civilization. Contrary to Turner's view, the frontier did not imbue the frontiersman with a new democratic rectitude. For Pease, "The Wilderness to the American pioneer was no mother but a terrible foe" (p. 84). The environment in itself did not enable the development of a new, superior civilization, only hard work with ax, plow, and muscle could do that. Pease concludes, "man knew that if he would, he might be greater than his environment and remake it to his use; and the thought ennobled him" (p. 100).

To the extent that the frontier shaped the development of democratic principles, it did so only in the sense that frontiersmen favored government which controlled them the least. Again, with a tinge of Turner's influence, but without elaboration, Pease writes that the Illinois Democratic party during the 1840s reflected the democractic elements of the frontier. Perhaps he expected his readers to understand those traits clearly and explicitly. Yet, if this sentiment was no more than a belief in the "dignity of labor and the rights of man," then the results of the frontier experience were hardly unique. Pease is ambivalent, or at least unclear, in his writing on this point. More important than the vague references to Turner's influence, *The Story of Illinois* reflects Pease's philosophical link to the Scientific School of historical interpretation. As a "conservative evolutionist," he often interprets the past in patriotic terms. "The death of Lincoln," for example, "marked the end of the heroic age of Illinois history" (pp. 115-116). While the Civil War destroyed the institution of slavery, racial bondage remained; abolitionist zeal faded once the war ended and little changed. Pease reflects, "The enthusiasm for the ideal was to pass because human nature cannot as yet long sustain the ideal; and to it were to succeed the ages of bronze and iron" (pp. 173-174).

In 1927, Pease published *The United States*, a survey of American history. It is a typical history which stresses political, diplomatic, and economic developments, with a smattering of social history. After a brief overview of America's European heritage, Pease plunges into colonial developments. He briefly comments that the frontier had a leveling influence upon aristocratic easterners. The frontier environment, he believes, changed the westward moving pioneers, and the clash of environment and eastern culture produced democracy. Certainly, this view is eminently Turnerian, but again Pease did not elaborate upon it, perhaps because he lacked space or because he accepted it at face value. Yet, if the democratic influence of the frontier was important to Pease, and he gave little indication that this was so, it is because the frontier enabled progress in every aspect of life. This involves not only the improvement of democracy but also the whole gamut of social, economic, and political changes which made life better for those who followed. Frontier and economic determinism occasionally niggles Pease, but it did not concern him for long. History was more important than the sum of its parts; its value lay instead in providing continuity from one generation to the next and in the steady advance of civilization.

In 1929, Pease's philosophical bent can be seen more clearly with publication of *George Rogers Clark and the Revolution in Illinois, 1763-1787*. Here, he seems to have left Turner's influences behind and moved more into the interpretive camp of the progressive historians. Pease reflects the economic determination of the progressives when he notes, "In the long run, economic necessity was sure to make the Indians dependent on the British." Yet, this brief passage is the strongest allegation Pease makes concerning the economic causes of the revolution in the Illinois country. Instead of joining the Progressive School, the conservative evolutionist reasserts himself by attributing the American Revolution to the new British imperialism. As Britain struggled to bring the American colonies back into the fold after a hundred and fifty years of neglect, the colonists revolted to protect their long-enjoyed liberties. As a result, Pease argues, "The Revolution had been necessary to override the faulty principles on which the British tried to organize [Illinois], and to set it in its true place in a system based on principles of liberty." The War of Independence resulted from cumulative grievances against Great Britain, and the colonists fought it to preserve their rights and their constitutional government. As such, the American Revolution was a conservative movement (pp. 32, 52, 87). Pease's philosophical and interpretive inclinations are even more clearly enunciated when he writes that the Ordinance of 1787 "represented a retreat from the democratic ideas of Jefferson on conservative lines; but perhaps no more of a retreat than was advisable. There was always liberty on the American frontier; the need was to prevent license and to ensure the supremacy of federal control. Both of these the ordinance with its appointive government in the first stage and its high suffrage qualifications, accomplished" (*Mississippi Valley Historical Review* 25:180).

Here, too, the past became not only larger than life, but faintly romantic, when, for example, he writes of Clark's "heroic little band" which fought with the "dogged resolution of the American soldier" (*George Rogers Clark*, p. 91). As a conservative evolutionist, Pease is a nationalistic and patriotic historian.

In 1930, Pease continued to reflect the philosophical inclinations of a conservative historian who revered the past. Perhaps the collapse of Italian and the failure of German democracy made him stress the need to study history to help preserve American liberty. He writes, "A quickened sense that this country of the Illinois, in which we live, is the product of a fine historic past, is the best insurance for a reverent attitude toward its institutions." Pease urges his readers to, "Learn the story of how men wrought and sacrificed and fought in this land in bygone days that more equal liberty might prevail in America, and ungirdled selfishness will appear the sacrilege it really is." The study of history, then, would preserve the virtues of American life. Historical study was not only a patriotic duty, it was a moral obligation (*Journal of the Illinois Historical Society* 23:664).

In spite of this strong nationalistic interpretation of the past by a historian from the Conservative School, the work of his colleagues in the progressive camp did not go unnoticed. As the progressive historians gave increasing attention to matters such as economics and business, Pease recognized the importance of these factors for historical interpretation. Moreover, while he respected Francis Parkman's romantic portrayal of the past and Clarence Alvord's sweeping pen, he recognizes that the "less dramatic and more practical" aspects of history were significant. In 1934, this belief led to the publication of *The French Foundations, 1680-1693*. In the introduction to this volume of documents in the *Collections* series of the Illinois State Historical Library, Pease writes that his intent is to "introduce the state's first businessmen and employers of labor on the distinctly financial and commercial side of their enterprise" (p. xiv). The documents, however, must stand by themselves, because Pease did not take the next step of analysis or synthesis to show the influence of the late seventeenth century entrepreneurs on the development of the Illinois Country. Pease merely provides the documents; he left the task of interpretation to other historians.

If Pease gave token recognition to the Progressive School for historical interpretation, he did not do so for long. By early 1935, he had returned to the conservative camp where he felt most comfortable. This meant the writing of broad narratives where the facts were allowed to speak for themselves--a characteristic of the Scientific School. At best, this meant the writing of consensus and rather unimaginative history; at worst, it bordered an antiquarianism. For Pease, it also meant writing history as literature, a technique which harkened to the past and which many of his contemporaries were increasingly leaving behind. This approach enables him to remark that William Pitt rode the "storm like Lucifer," and that he "intoxicated the English nation with the heady wine of victory" (*Indiana History Bulletin* 12:132). This made good reading occasionally, but he often sacrifices the analysis and detail that would have made his generalizations meaningful.

In 1936, his literary intent emerges again in "The French Regime in Illinois: A Challenge to Historical Scholarship." Pease notes that his generation of scholars contemptuously dismissed Bancroft for his "spread eagle" approach to historical writing. Pease, however, believes this criticism reflected the "insular and provincial" nature of contemporary scholarship. He maintains that Bancroft's narrative was not only broad but lyrical, and he contends that historians were beginning to resurrect that form of historical writing. Clarence Alvord also was among those who were writing broadly and treating history as literature, and Pease greatly admired him. In this spirit, Pease sought a "unified study" of the French in the Old Northwest. He believed that a synthesis had to depend upon manuscript sources, the study of which the documents in the *Collections* series of the Illinois State Historical Library would materially aid. Pease also suggests other collections and materials for the broad research which he envisioned.

Most importantly, Pease recognizes that the study of Illinois history required scholarly research far beyond the state's boundaries. As such, he is advocating painstaking scholarship for the writings of state and regional history--an approach far removed from the antiquarianism which plagued state, local, and regional history at the time. The result would not only provide good history but, more significantly, social "stability." Pease argues that society's "consciousness" of the past would provide a "sense of security" so that those who knew history could better understand their place in the universe. Life was a progressive continuum, he believes, because "the person of the present is merely carrying on the work of other human beings stretching farther and farther back into the distant past." Thus, state history "broadly conceived and truly recorded" would not only provide community and stability, but also a secure link with the past. Pease's relationship to the conservative evolutionists was never more clearly stated (pp. 71, 74-79).

Pease continued his archival work and next published the *Anglo-French Boundary Disputes in the West, 1749-1763*. This contribution to the *Collections* series, published in 1936, stresses the Franco-English diplomacy of the Seven Years' War. In his introduction, however, Pease begins to stray from the domain of the historian to that of the prophet, and his speculations about what might have been are bothersome to historians today. In essence, Pease argues that the Peace of 1763 upset the political equilibrium in the Old Northwest and that the Mississippi River Valley would not be peacefully and stably united until the Louisiana Purchase in 1803. That achievement, however, is significant because it created a strong nation thereby preordaining the doom of the Confederacy (pp. iii, clxix-clxxi).

In 1940, Pease continued his infatuation with the French in the Illinois Country with the publication of *Illinois on the Eve of the Seven Years' War, 1747-1755*. This was his last contribution to the *Collections* series of the Illinois State Historical Library. Here, Pease presents the cause of the French in the West. He maintains that the Illinois Country was the "keystone of the arch of French imperialism," but it was vulnerable to the mistakes of French Indian policy. Economic competition for the allegiance of the Indians provoked enmity and war--all of which made Britain's acquisition of the Illinois Country in 1763 "an integral part in the epic of the American Revolution" (pp. iii, xv, xxi, xxiv, lii). For Pease, the story of the Illinois Country always was history writ large, and with this work, he essentially ends his scholarly publications. Upon becoming department chairman in 1942, administrative duties took much of his time. When he died on August 11, 1948, he had just completed the revision of *The Story of Illinois* for publication as part of the golden anniversary celebration of the Illinois State Historical Society.

Today, much of his writing seems a classic example of old-fashioned political and diplomatic history which was characteristic of the Scientific School. Pease also wrote with a formal and often cumbersome style. Consequently, the broad narratives which he strove to craft frequently were far less informative than he intended. Certainly, he was part of the new movement in the historical profession which turned the study of the past from romanticism to realism. Yet, he never fully embraced the influences of the Progressive School, which emphasized the study of popular movements, social change, and economic determinism rather than institutions. Pease, while essentially democratic and egalitarian, did not follow the drums of either Frederick Jackson Turner or Charles A. Beard. Instead, he preferred the interpretive approach of the Scientific School while accepting some of the tenets of other theoretical frameworks. Consequently, Pease was no different from most historians who follow a multicausational approach to history while leaning toward one particular point of view. No matter the slight influences of the Turner and Progressive Schools, Pease essentially saw history as a stabilizing, progressive force that was both conservative and evolutionary (*American Historical Review* 55:705).

Bibliography

Books

Anglo-French Boundary Disputes in the West, 1749-1763. Edited with an introduction. Vol. XXVII, *Collections of the Illinois State Historical Library*. Springfield: Illinois State Historical Library, 1936.

The County Archives of the State of Illinois. Editor. Vol. XII, *Collections of the Illinois State Historical Library*. Springfield: Illinois State Historical Library, 1915.

The Diary of Orville Hickman Browning, 1850-1864. Co-edited with James G. Randall with an introduction. Vol. XX, *Collections of the Illinois State Historical Library*. Springfield: Illinois State Historical Library, 1925.

The French Foundations, 1680-1693. Co-edited with Raymond C. Werner and an introduction. Vol. XXIII, *Collections of the Illinois State Historical Library*. Springfield: Illinois State Historical Library, 1934.

The Frontier State, 1818-1848. Vol. II, *The Centennial History of Illinois.* Springfield: The Illinois Centennial Commission, 1918.

George Rogers Clark and the Revolution in Illinois, 1763-1787. Co-authored with Marguerite Jenison Pease. Springfield: Illinois State Historical Library, 1929.

Illinois Election Returns, 1818-1848. Edited with an introduction. Vol. XVIII, *Collections of the Illinois State Historical Library.* Springfield: Illinois State Historical Library, 1923.

Illinois on the Eve of the Seven Years' War, 1747-1755. Co-edited with Ernestine Jenison and with an introduction. Vol. XXIX, *Collections of the Illinois State Historical Library.* Springfield: Illinois State Historical Library, 1940.

The Laws of the Northwest Territory, 1788-1800. Edited with an introduction. Vol. XVII, *Collections of the Illinois State Historical Library.* Springfield: Illinois State Historical Library, 1925.

The Leveller Movement: A Study in the History and Political Theory of the English Great Civil War. Washington, DC: American Historical Association, 1916.

Selected Readings in American History. Co-edited with A. Sellew Roberts. New York: Harcourt, Brace & Co., 1928.

The Story of Illinois. Chicago: A. C. McClury & Co., 1925.

The United States. New York: Harcourt, Brace & Co., 1927.

Articles

"The Archives of the State of Illinois." Co-authored with Clarence W. Alvord. *Annual Report of the American Historical Association, 1909*, pp. 383-463.

"A Caution Regarding Military Documents." *American Historical Review* 26(January, 1921):282-284.

"Charles Benjamin Farwell." *Dictionary of American Biography* 6:294-295.

"The County Records of Illinois." *Journal of the Illinois State Historical Society* 7(January, 1915):374-378.

"The Diary of Orville H. Browning: A Lecture Delivered before the Chicago Historical Society, March 29, 1923." Chicago: University of Chicago Press, 1924.

"Evarts Boutell Greene, 1870-1947." *Journal of the Illinois State Historical Society* 41(March, 1948):7-15.

"The French Regime in Illinois: A Challenge to Historical Scholarship." *Transactions of the Illinois State Historical Society* 43(1936):69-79.

"Green Berry Raum." *Dictionary of American Biography* 15:391-392.

"Illinois." *1938 Britannica Book of the Year*, pp. 329-330. Reprinted with minor additions in 1939, 1940, and 1941 editions.

"The Illinois Historical Collections." *Transactions of the Illinois State Historical Society* 29(1922):66-67.

"Indiana in Contention between France and England." *Indiana History Bulletin* 12(February, 1935):113-132.

"Isaac Newton Arnold." *Dictionary of American Biography* 1:368-369.

"John Franklin Farnsworth." *Dictionary of American Biography* 6:284-285.
"John J. Hardin." *Dictionary of American Biography* 8:246.
"John Mason Peck." *Dictionary of American Biography* 1:381-382.
"Laurence Marcellus Larson, 1868-1938." *Journal of the Illinois State Historical Society* 31(September, 1938):245-261.
"The Mississippi Boundary of 1763: A Reappraisal of Responsibility." *American Historical Review* 40(January, 1935):278-286.
"Ninian Wirt Edwards." *Dictionary of American Biography* 6:42-43.
"The Ordinance of 1787." *Mississippi Valley Historical Review* 25(September, 1938):167-180.
"Orville Hickman Browning." *Dictionary of American Biography* 3:175-176.
"Otto Leopold Schmidt, 1863-1935." Co-authored with Laurence M. Larson. *Journal of the Illinois State Historical Society* 38(January, 1936):225-236.
"The Problem of Archive Centralization with Reference to Local Conditions in a Middle Western State." *Annual Report of the American Historical Association, 1916*, 1:151-154.
"Robert Roberts Hitt." *Dictionary of American Biography* 9:80-81.
"1780--The Revolution in Crisis in the West." *Journal of the Illinois State Historical Society* 23(January, 1931):664-681.
"Stephen Alfred Forbes, 1844-1930." *Journal of the Illinois State Historical Society* 23(October, 1930):543-548.
"Stephen Augustus Hurlbut." *Dictionary of American Biography* 9:425-426.
"Thomas Ford." *Dictionary of American Biography* 6:520-521.
"William Henry Herndon." *Dictionary of American Biography* 8:579.
"William Joshua Allen." *Dictionary of American Biography* 1:213-214.

Reviews
The British Regime in Wisconsin and the Northwest by Louise Phelps Kellogg. *American Historical Review* 42(October, 1936):148-149.
Checagou: From Indian Wigwam to Modern City, 1673-1835 by Milo M. Quaife. *American Historical Review* 39(April, 1934):588-589.
Competition for Empire, 1740-1763 by Walter L. Dorn. *Mississippi Valley Historical Review* 27(September, 1940):283-284.
England in the Age of the American Revolution by L. B. Namier. *American Historical Review* 36(April, 1931):583-585.
Englishe Geschichte im Achtzenhnten Jarhundert by Michael Von Wolfgang. *American Historical Review* 40(July, 1935):732-733.
A History of Chicago by Bessie Louise Pierce. *American Historical Review* 43(July, 1938):903-904.
The Illinois by James Gray. *Mississippi Valley Historical Review* 28(December, 1941):476-477.
The Illinois Central Railroad and its Colonization Work by Paul Wallace Gates. *American Historical Review* 40(January, 1935):352-354.

John Stuart and the Southern Colonial Frontier: A Study of Indian Relations, War, Trade, and Land Problems in the Southern Wilderness, 1754-1775 by John Richard Alden. *Mississippi Valley Historical Review* 31(December, 1944):452-453.

Leveller Manifestoes of the Puritan Revolution edited by Don M. Wolfe. *American Historical Review* 50(January, 1945):315-316.

The Leveller Tracts, 1647-1653 edited by William Haller. *American Historical Review* 50(January, 1945):315-316.

The Ohio Company of Virginia and the Westward Movement, 1748-1792: A Chapter in the History of the Colonial Frontier by Kenneth P. Bailey. *American Historical Review* 45(January, 1940):410-411.

The Planning of Civilization in Western Pennsylvania by Solon J. Buck. *Mississippi Valley Historical Review* 26(September, 1939):566-567.

Plans for World Peace through Six Centuries by Sylvester John Hemben. *Mississippi Valley Historical Review* 30(September, 1943):259-260.

Political Thought in England from Locke to Bentham by Harold J. Laski. *American Historical Review* 26(April, 1921):572-573.

Postwar Years: Normalcy, 1918-1923 by Frederic L. Paxson. *American Historical Review* 54(October, 1948):169-170.

Recent American History by Lester Burrell Shippee. *American Historical Review* 30(April, 1925):619-621.

S. O. Levinson and the Pact of Paris: A Study in the Technique of Influence by John Stoner. *Mississippi Valley Historical Review* 30(September, 1943):259-260.

The Structure of Politics at the Accession of George III by L. B. Namier. *American Historical Review* 34(July, 1929):824-826.

The Territorial Papers of the United States, vol. VI edited and compiled by Clarence E. Carter. *Mississippi Valley Historical Review* 25(March, 1939):565-566.

__________, vol. VIII edited and compiled by Clarence E. Carter. *Mississippi Valley Historical Review* 27(September, 1940):285-287.

Western Lands and the American Revolution by Thomas P. Abernathy. *Mississippi Valley Historical Review* 25(December, 1938):399.

The Works of Gerrard Winstainley, with an Appendix of Documents Relating to the Digger Movement edited by George H. Sabine. *American Historical Review* 47(January, 1942):326-327.

Studies of Theodore Calvin Pease

Billington, Ray Allen. Review of *The Story of Illinois* by Theodore Calvin Pease. *American Historical Review* 55(April, 1950):705.

Buffington, A. H. Review of *The Diary of Hickman Browning, 1850-1864* edited by Theodore Calvin Pease and James G. Randall. *American Historical Review* 33(January, 1928):449-450.

Carter, Clarence E. Review of *Illinois on the Eve of the Seven Years' War, 1747-1755* edited by Theodore Calvin Pease and Ernestine Jenison Pease. *American Historical Review* 46(July, 1941):927-928.

Deitz, Fred. Untitled Obituary. *Mississippi Valley Historical Review* 35(March, 1949):719-720.

Edwards, Martha L. Review of *The Frontier State, 1818-1848* by Theodore Calvin Pease. *American Historical Review* 24(July, 1919):708-709.

Higham, John. *The Development of Historical Studies in the United States*. Englewood Cliffs, NJ: Prentice-Hall, 1965.

__________. *Writing American History: Essays of Modern Scholarship*. Bloomington: Indiana University Press, 1970.

Quaife, Milo M. Review of *The French Foundations, 1680-1693* edited by Theodore Calvin Pease and Raymond C. Werner. *American Historical Review* 41(April, 1936):583-584.

Randall, James G. "Theodore Calvin Pease." *Journal of the Illinois State Historical Society* 41(December, 1948):353-366.

"Recent Deaths." *American Historical Review* 54(October, 1948):256-257.

Volwiler, A. T. Review of *Anglo-French Boundary Disputes in the West, 1749-1763* edited by Theodore Calvin Pease. *American Historical Review* 43(January, 1938):406-408.

__________. Review of *The Story of Illinois* by Theodore Calvin Pease. *Mississippi Valley Historical Review* 37(September, 1950):322-323.

W. O. L. Review of *Illinois on the Eve of the Seven Years' War, 1747-1755* edited by Theodore Calvin Pease and Ernestine Jenison Pease. *Indiana Magazine of History* 36(September, 1940):296.

36

LOUIS PELZER

by Malcolm J. Rohrbough

Biography

Louis Pelzer, who established a national reputation for his study of the American frontier and for his editorship of the *Mississippi Valley Historical Review*, was a man whose careers as teacher, scholar, and editor were closely identified with the University of Iowa and the Middle West.

Born in Griswold, Iowa, in 1879 into a large family that included two brothers and six sisters, Pelzer spent his early life on a farm. The values that he absorbed there--hard work, loyalty, and integrity--he carried with him into his profession and later transmitted to his graduate students. Pelzer graduated from Iowa State Teachers College in 1901, and after teaching in an Iowa high school for two years, he enrolled as a graduate student at the University of Iowa. There, he began an apprenticeship as a research assistant under Benjamin F. Shambaugh in the State Historical Society of Iowa. After six years of graduate study during which time he continued to research and write for the State Historical Society, he received the Ph.D. degree in 1909. Pelzer then accepted a teaching position at Montana State Normal School. In 1911, he returned to the University of Iowa as an assistant professor in the department of history. He advanced to the rank of associate professor in 1917 and to full professor in 1925 in a career that would span thirty-five years at the university in Iowa City.

Louis Pelzer's graduate training coincided with the founding and growth of a new organization of professional historians, the Mississippi Valley Historical Association [later the Organization of American Historians]. From the beginning of his professional career and through a generation as a professional historian, Pelzer was closely identified with the association. He presented a paper at its first meeting in 1908 at the age of twenty-nine. His name appeared on a committee in 1912, and over the next thirty-five years he served on every important committee. He urged his graduate students to join as soon as they could afford to do so. He also attended almost every annual meeting. William C. Binkley said on the occasion of Pelzer's death in 1946 that he had attended more annual meetings of the Mississippi Valley Historical Association than any other member. In addition to his committee work, Pelzer participated actively in the programs. He was also a regular reviewer. In 1918, the membership of the Association elected him to a three-year term on the executive committee. He was vice-president of the association in 1934-1935, president in 1935-1936, and thereafter until his death, a member ex-officio of the executive committee. He served on the board of editors from 1936-1939, and in 1941, he became managing editor of the *Review*, a position that he held at the time of his death in 1946.

Pelzer's long career was characterized by both great productivity and high standards of scholarship. His first article appeared in the October, 1904, issue of the *Iowa Journal of History and Politics*, and he was soon at work on two major biographies. He published his first book-length biography, a life of Augustus Caesar Dodge, one of Iowa's first senators, under the imprimatur of the State Historical Society in 1909. It was his doctoral dissertation. Two years later, he published a companion biography of Henry Dodge. He eventually published fourteen articles in the *Iowa Journal of History and Politics*, five in *The Palimpsest*, four in the *Mississippi Valley Historical Review*, and three in the *Proceedings* of the Mississippi Valley Historical Association. He also contributed articles to the *Transactions* of the Illinois State Historical Society, the *Harvard Journal of Economic and Business History*, and the *Bulletin* of the American Association of University Professors. His third book, *Marches of the Dragoons*, appeared in 1917. The Arthur H. Clark Company brought out his *The Cattleman's Frontier* in 1936. It was a volume that he had worked on for twenty years and was a fitting climax to a scholarly career that carried him from the prairie to the plains, with the American frontier always as the focal point of his work.

Among his many intellectual interests, none was more important to Pelzer than his work with the American Association of University Professors (AAUP). When he joined the AAUP in 1930, Pelzer found a fledgling organization promoting academic freedom, due process in higher education, and the security of tenure at a time when none of these principles found ready acceptance in society at large or even on university campuses across the nation. As president of the University of Iowa chapter of the AAUP, Pelzer was a moving force in bringing Blue Cross medical coverage to the faculty on the campus in Iowa City. He also labored energetically and successfully for the university's adoption of the retirement plan under the Teachers' Insurance and Annuity Association.

Pelzer served the University of Iowa in other ways, among them as a member of the Committee on Intercollegiate Athletics. Through this service to the university, he became secretary of the Western Athletic Conference (the ancestor of the Big Ten Conference) during an especially difficult and controversial period. The University of Iowa had been suspended from the conference for violations of conference rules. Pelzer was an eloquent spokesman on behalf of his institution. He never disguised or minimized the university's transgressions, but his honesty and integrity notably assisted the University of Iowa in its application for readmission to the conference.

After he joined the department of history in 1911, Pelzer became the advisor to a growing number of graduate students. At a long table surrounded by a dozen chairs in his office in Schaeffer Hall, he presided over a seminar that introduced a generation of graduate students to the excitement and challenge of studying the American frontier. The climax of the seminar was the student's report on a research topic. Pelzer's criticisms were insightful and thorough but never unfair or personal. He was a demanding teacher, for he sought in his students the same commitment to his craft that he displayed over a generation as a professional. Those who could not make such a commitment moved on to other professors or other careers.

Pelzer trained students to become professionals, and nothing gave him more satisfaction than the demonstration of professional accomplishment on the part of his successful graduates, especially in the form of a published article or monograph. He would often share such examples with the members of a seminar, simultaneously reminding its members of the level and expression of scholarship to which they should aspire, and at the same time giving them experience in criticism and analysis. Pelzer prized the book review as an important form of scholarly activity. With examples from scholarly journals, he conducted a continuous clinic on book reviewing, encouraging the beginner to perfect this professional skill under his direction.

Louis Pelzer demanded much of his students, and he was prepared to give much of himself in the collaborative venture of professional training as a historian. Accordingly, he gave unstintingly of his time to meet with students and to criticize their work. Pelzer knew that successful historical writing resulted from a combination of careful research and numerous drafts. He spent much time marking up drafts of student papers. He knew that the only way to write history effectively was to rewrite history on a regular basis, and he gave freely of his time to assist in the rewriting process.

One of Louis Pelzer's most distinctive features as a man and as a graduate advisor was his puckish sense of humor. It was restrained and gentle but pungent and pointed. Upon one occasion, a stranger came late into Pelzer's seminar. The seats were all occupied, but by rearranging some overcoats, the latecomer managed to find a precarious seat on the window ledge. Pelzer ignored his entrance and his seating arrangement. About ten minutes before the end of the hour, Pelzer switched the subject of discussion from a student report on a research topic to a general discussion on historians of the American frontier. He asked about some of the recent major publications in the field, gradually coming to rest on a new book by the young E. Douglas Branch. Pelzer pressed the students a bit and finally found one who expressed doubts about the Branch book. At this point, he suddenly noticed the visitor with a dramatic announcement that the Branch volume that had been started in the seminar at the table around which the seminarians were seated, and that the author for lack of a chair was now seated on the window ledge! The dramatic effect his words had in the seminar was probably just what he hoped to achieve. Pelzer was proud of Branch (as he was of all his publishing students) but he was not above teasing him a bit. The opportunity to combine a little joke on Branch with a large joke on the seminar was exactly the sort of afternoon exercise that he found irresistible.

In his personal life, Pelzer was a tall, distinguished figure of great public formality and great personal kindness. The loss of one arm in an accident as a young man gave him a distinctive appearance and added to his personal dignity and bearing. His wife, the former Mildred Leonore Weenick, was an established artist. During the New Deal arts program, she received a commission to paint murals of early Iowa City scenes on the walls of the Jefferson Hotel, a prominent building in the center of town. Louis and Mildred Pelzer frequently entertained graduate students and faculty in their home at 127 Ferson Avenue. Later, the Pelzers purchased a forty-acre tract north of Iowa City, and this place soon became a center of good conversation and a place of warm hospitality among students, faculty, and townspeople alike.

In the course of their quiet and pleasant lives in a small university town, Louis and Mildred Pelzer suffered two devastating losses. The outbreak of the World War II called into service the two Pelzer sons. Parker and Henry were both killed in the war, one in the Battle of the Bulge in the winter of 1944-1945, and the second as pilot of a plane that disappeared over the mountains in California on a training mission. The loss of their two sons (and only children) was a crushing blow that affected the Pelzers the rest of their lives. Few of Louis Pelzer's professional acquaintances--and they were legion--knew of the deep and abiding anguish that he and Mrs. Pelzer had suffered.

In 1941, Louis Pelzer became managing editor of the *Mississippi Valley Historical Review.* It was a position to which he ascended naturally by his established national reputation among his peers, by his years of service to the association, and by his long apprenticeship in editing his own work and that of his graduate students. It was recognition of the high regard in which he was held by his professional colleagues. The *Review* was the most important professional journal for American historians, and as editor Pelzer shaped its content to his own high standards of scholarship and reviewing. In addition to his post as editor, Pelzer worked on a number of special projects. The most important of these was a committee "to propose and to formulate in detail a series of projects in American History and culture." Under his direction and supported by a grant from the Rockefeller Foundation, Pelzer's committee prepared a report on "Projects in American History and Culture," published in a 1945 issue of the *Review.* It served as a guideline for the profession for the next decade.

Louis Pelzer died suddenly of a heart attack on June 28, 1946. The September, 1946, issue of the *Review* contained sixteen pages of expressions of sorrow and respect by his professional colleagues. His legacy lives on today in the form of the Pelzer Award of the Organization of American Historians, given annually to the best paper submitted to the journal by a graduate student. It was and is a fitting memorial to a man who had high standards of historical scholarship and spent much of his time imparting them to graduate students.

Themes

Louis Pelzer's research and writing over the first twenty-five years of his career as a professional historian dealt with the frontier of the upper Mississippi Valley from the opening of the nineteenth century to the close of the Civil War. To the broad area of the Old Northwest, Pelzer added Iowa, Missouri, and eventually the Great Plains to the Rockies as the setting for his description and analysis of American settlement and the creation of an American civilization. Within this vast geographic arena, he brought together a broad cross-section of frontier types: public land officers, army personnel (both militia and regular army), missionaries, Indians, traders, lead miners, pioneer homesteaders, and government officials (federal, state, and territorial).

The central theme of his story is the spread of American civilization and, most especially, American economic and political institutions. In his work, he delighted in showing how the powerful force of "American democracy" pulsed from the ordinary frontier farmers through vigorously contested local elections into the halls of the legislatures--in the territories, in the states, and eventually into the Congress of the United States.

Analysis

Pelzer's subjects for his panorama of American history over half a century were the Dodges, the families of Henry Dodge and his son, Augustus Caesar Dodge. Together these two families, and their heads, carried American civilization from the tiny French fur trading post of Vincennes to the foothills of the Rockies, from the log cabins of pioneers to the halls of the United States Congress, from a deserted wilderness in 1785 to a settled world of prosperous agriculturalists and five million Americans in 1860. It was a drama worthy of Francis Parkman or John Lothrop Motley, and Pelzer proceeded to fashion his own epic, with special attention to the influence of the American frontier.

Pelzer begins his story with the study of Augustus Caesar Dodge, the son. It was his doctoral dissertation, and the background work that he did on the Dodge family undoubtedly fired his vision of a larger and more complete canvas. But the earlier generation would come later. First came the son. Born in 1812, Dodge came into a world that was in the process of dramatic change. Pelzer emphasizes the significance in that year of the continuing conflict with Great Britian, the on-going struggle against the several Indian tribes of the Ohio Valley, and the continuing expansion of American pioneer farmers westward, and in the case of the Dodges, with lead miners as the spearheads of the frontier movement. Writes Pelzer of his subject, "born in the West and tempered in the atmosphere of its virgin forests and prairies, Augustus Caesar Dodge represented and reflected the life of a western frontier community, which without historic tradition or settled political formula has a free and natural growth" (*Augustus Caesar*

Dodge, p. v). It was a setting and character that Pelzer would develop in his first two books: the uneducated (in a formal sense) frontier leader, the military man drawn to civil government by the need to serve his neighbors, his service in a wide range of local, territorial, state, and federal offices, crowning his career as the first United States Senator of his new state, and the parallel maturing of his region and its democratic institutions and flowering agricultural economy of opportunity for all.

In his description and analysis of this broad panorama, Pelzer is little concerned with the complex struggles of internal politics. It was enough for him that the democratic processes worked to produce an expression of popular opinion. And for Pelzer it was sufficient that Dodge supported slavery and that he saw the Compromise of 1850 as a means of preserving the Union. That other northern senators voted against provisions of the compromise for more complex reasons did not disturb him. Nor does he analyze the political revolution of 1853 and 1854 under which the new Iowa Republican party of James Grimes overthrew the Democratic party and its principles on the campaign platform opposed to the principles of the compromise that Dodge had so vigorously supported. Presumably, the senior senator from Iowa had lost touch with this constituency. Yet Pelzer does not concern himself with this dramatic turn in Iowa politics. And, while he discusses in detail Dodge's subsequent career as minister to the court at Madrid from 1853 to 1859--an orthodox political appointment by a Democratic president--Pelzer has little to say about Dodge's final twenty years, which included the Civil War, Reconstruction, and the establishment of a Republican dominance in the state of Iowa that would last until well into the twentieth century. It is enough for him that Dodge had acted out the role of the frontiersman who served his territory in its transition to statehood. With the closing of the frontier, Pelzer seems to lose interest in his subject.

Pelzer has little sympathy for obstacles in the way of American expansion, including American Indians. For him, the Black Hawk War was the result of the persistent violation of legal treaties (signed and recognized by all parties), and the "massacre" of American pioneers by "marauding" Indians led by the Sac chief. Instead of analyzing the cultural conflict inherent in that unhappy incident, Pelzer sees the affair as a chapter in American military history, more especially the mobilization of the militia under Dodge's leadership; the military maneuvers of the two sides, which resulted in an overwhelming American victory; and finally, the unequal treaty-making exercise that permitted legal American expansion into what is today the state of Iowa. Pelzer concludes of the experience, "The far-reaching results of this war in opening up a vast area for settlement and agriculture and for the planting of permanent cities and home belong to the romantic rise of the West" (p. 17).

His main themes established, Pelzer now turned to the earlier generation in his second book, *Henry Dodge* (1911). Henry Dodge, the founding father of a new American dynasty, was born at Post Vincennes in 1782. Pelzer finds it significant that this small trading post had been a focal point of conflict among the French, Spanish, Indians, and most recently, the British and their former colonials, the Americans, now in revolt. The Dodge family emigrated to Missouri in search of economic opportunity in lead mining and some years later to the lead region in southwestern Wisconsin. Dodge began his public career as a militia officer, and his long and prominent service--he was a general in the Black Hawk War and later an important officer in the First Regiment of United States Dragoons--carried him to the front ranks of the territory's public men. President Andrew Jackson appointed him the first governor of the Wisconsin Territory in 1836, and Dodge served until 1841, when the election of the Whig William Henry Harrison led to his removal from office. Dodge promptly declared himself a candidate for territorial delegate, and, successful in the general election, he represented the Territory of Wisconsin in the Congress of the United States from 1841 to 1844, when the election of the Democrat James K. Polk restored him to the governorship.

Throughout his tenure as governor, Dodge focussed on the problems that confronted frontier people: lead-mining rights, Indian treaties, the preemption law, the militia, protection from the Indians, and the organization of local civil government. Pelzer considers Dodge's governorship as representing "the zenith of his career as a public man" (*Henry Dodge*, p. 200). It was a time when the frontier trained public servant could serve the citizens of the territory by resolving the kinds of frontier problems that he knew well. When Wisconsin entered the Union in 1848, the predominantly Democratic legislature chose him one of the state's first two senators. Thus, Henry Dodge and his son, Augustus Caesar Dodge, served in the Senate of the United States at the same time. As a senator, Dodge continued his interest in western issues. Pelzer concludes that the senior Dodge's noteworthy qualities were his "devotion to the needs and ideals of the West and to Jacksonian principles of Democracy." (p. 196).

Pelzer sees Henry Dodge's frontier background as the dominant influence on his career as a public official. "His training and talents fitted him for military life and administration rather than for the more abstract work of statesmanship and legislation," writes his biographer. In a world dominated by the Compromise of 1850 and the Kansas-Nebraska Act of 1854, Dodge remained largely concerned with local issues of interest to his constituents. On the great questions of the day, he followed the instructions of the state legislature. Pelzer was under no illusions about Dodge's stature in a legislative body that included, among others, Henry Clay, Daniel Webster, and John C. Calhoun. He concludes of his subject, "he cannot be given rank as a great Senator; he belongs to that class of Senators who are industrious and capable" (p. 192).

In 1917, Louis Pelzer published his third book, *Marches of the Dragoons*. In this volume that covered the history of the First United States Dragoons from their organization in 1833 to their decommissioning in 1861, he carefully documents the duties and contributions of the peace-time army to the advance of the frontier. These included "frontier defense, garrison duty, treaty negotiations, marches, expeditions, patrol duty, exploration, and the enforcement of federal laws" (p. vii). One of his most prominent subjects was Henry Dodge, and Pelzer drew heavily on his biography for the description of Colonel Dodge's service. The panorama that stretched from the Mississippi to the Rockies also let Pelzer give free voice to the romance of western expansion. "Every morning the reveille roused the troops to another day's march. They invaded a colony of chattering prairie dogs, with staring screech owls and rattlesnakes for neighbors; greyhounds chased the antelope through the tall grass; buffalo were pursued over the plains; and squalid wolves slunk over the hills and sandy ravines," he writes of General Stephen Watts Kearny's march over the Oregon Trail in 1845. "Emigrant caravans, driving before them great herds of cattle, were passed again and again" (p. 123). This was one of Pelzer's favorite frontiers: mounted dragoons in the service of American expansion, Indians in their native habitat, and nineteenth-century pilgrims on the way to Oregon and California. It was a story that he never tired of relating.

After twenty years of research and publication on the settlement and growth of the Upper Mississippi Valley, Louis Pelzer turned to a new area of interest: the frontier of the cattleman on the Great Plains from 1850 to 1890. He published his first articles on this subject in 1926, but he worked another ten years before he was completely satisfied with the results. The Arthur H. Clark Company published *The Cattlemen's Frontier* in 1936, the same year that Pelzer served as president of the Mississippi Valley Historical Association. The volume's subtitle, *A Record of the Trans-Mississippi Cattle Industry from Oxen Trains to Pooling Companies, 1850-1890*, was an accurate description of its contents, but it did not do justice to Pelzer's broad research and detailed account.

In this history of the cattle industry on the open range, Louis Pelzer found another sweeping canvas for his account of the American frontier--in the 1860s and 1870s, the plains of Texas north across Indian Territory to the railheads in the Kansas cattle towns, and, in the 1880s, the limitless expanses of waving grass in Montana and Wyoming to the Dakotas. Pelzer sees in the cattle trails of this vast region "the course of empire"--a unique experience through which the land was settled and tamed, in which the open range cattle industry served as a short but brilliant transitional interlude before the arrival of the individual farm. It was a dramatic setting with great human appeal, and he tells it well. To the natural panorama that would later become a staple of the motion picture industry, Pelzer adds intriguing local characters like John G. McCoy, promoter of the Kansas cow towns; international investors, especially the English and Scots, personified by Alexander H. Swan of the Swan Land and Cattle Company; and the great physical disasters of droughts and blizzard in the middle 1880s, followed immediately thereafter by parallel economic disasters for much of the range cattle industry. Simultaneous with the depletion of the great herds of the northern ranges and the bankruptcy of numerous large companies, Congress passed a law in 1885 against illegal fencing. By 1890, the age of the open range, with free land, free water, great trail drives, and the myth of the American cowboy, had passed, to be enshrined in American folklore. It was from this mythology that Pelzer proposed to retrive it, by blending with its natural attractions his own high standards of scholarship based on a careful examination of the sources.

The introduction of cattle to the plains began with the oxen used in freighting on the plains in the 1850s. After delivering supplies to Indian reservations and army posts, the drovers turned the exhausted stock out to graze on the grasslands. They soon noted that the cattle emerged sleek and fat in the spring after a winter on the dried grasses of the valleys. It was only a short step to an enterprise that proposed to fatten stock for market on the grasslands of the plains. There followed the great cattle drives from Texas to the Kansas cow towns and the eventual development of the livestock industry on the northern plains.

Pelzer finds the Kansas cattle towns especially rich in the lore of the frontier. "During the Texas cattle trade at Abilene a carnival of crime and lawlessness prevailed," he writes. "Desperadoes, thieves, gamblers, and courtesans flocked like vultures to the cattle market" (*The Cattleman's Frontier*, p. 55). Like the rest of the cattle trade frontier, the towns appeared and disappeared with striking abruptness; like other aspects of the trade, they added much to the romance of the frontier story.

Among the aspects of the cattle frontier that especially caught Pelzer's eye was the institutional organization that became part of the livestock industry on the northern plains. He sees this as another step in the evolving institutional framework that was so much a part of the frontier experience. "From successive frontiers of our American history have developed needed customs, laws, and organizations," he writes. "The era of fur-trading produced its hunters, its barter, and the great fur companies; on the mining frontier came the staked claims and the vigilance committees; the camp meeting and the circuit rider were heard on the religious outposts; on the margins of settlement the claim clubs protected the rights of the squatter farmers; on the ranchmen's frontier the millions of cattle, the vast ranges, the ranches, and the cattle companies produced pools and local, district, territorial, and national cattle associations" (p. 87). The most important of these was the Wyoming Stock Growers' Assocation, an institution that Pelzer analyzes from its records in great detail.

In spite of his admiration for the energy, savvy, and independence of these early cattle kings, Pelzer came to have reservations and eventually objections to their high handed intimidation of homesteaders and their wholesale evasion of federal law through illegal fencing of open range. In his chapter, "Illegal Fencing on the Western Range," Pelzer argues that the Congress was right to outlaw such illegal occupation of the public domain and that the General Land Office was correct in its vigorous enforcement of the law of 1885. The issue was the settlement and development of the northern plains. "In the settlement of the trans-Missouri West the individual settler meant more than the corporation; his plow was of greater promise than the cattleman's fence; land office records contain more constructive pioneering than the books of corporations that fenced," Pelzer judges. "The thousands of plain settler folk constituted a greater asset than the non-resident shareholders of cattle companies; the great fences could never remain deeply fixed in the soil; only to citizens did the government give quarter sections but for years foreign corporations with alien shareholders inclosed and appropriated kingdoms" (p. 191). Even more than the disastrous winters of 1886, 1887, and 1888 and the mismanagement of range cattle industries financed by absentee English and Scottish investors, the closing of the open range spelled the end to the cattle frontier. As Pelzer writes by way of benediction, "the era of free grass was gone" (p. 150).

Even with the preponderant balance on the side of the individual settler family, Pelzer could not resist the romance of the cattle frontier. The Cheyenne Club in Laramie was a good example of this lost world. "Here men dined generously, sang songs, debated politics, planned horse races and tennis matches, described travel in foreign lands, discussed the cattle business,and recounted twice-told tales of losses, profits, and hardship on the ranges," he writes (pp. 110-111). Pelzer's sympathetic interest also extends to cowboys and their limited world. His more scholarly accounts are in the tradition of the fiction of Owen Wister and the first person account of Philip Ashton Rollins.

With all his interest in the romance of the frontier across the vast colorful canvas, Pelzer wanted to bring his story the highest standards of scholarship. To this end, he traveled widely and read extensively in the manuscript accounts of the cattle trade from the plains of Texas across to the cattle towns of Kansas to the absentee corporations of the northern plains. His book includes an appendix of the "Cattle Brands owned by Members of the Wyoming Stock Growers' Association," and his bibliography is filled with newspapers, personal correspondence, and records of cattle companies. For the latter, he read endless quarterly reports, inventories, accounts, certificates, vouchers, and records of bankruptcies that illuminated his account.

In his conclusion, he writes a benediction that might have summed up his own career as a historian of the American frontier: "Transitory as it was, the cattlemen's frontier was the most picturesque and perhaps most American of America's frontiers, and the horsemen who invaded this vacant empire dismounted not without regret" (p. 248). It was an admirable valedictory to his own thirty years of work in what he regarded as the greatest and most American of all our national experiences. Subsequent generations of historians would fault his emphasis and his conclusions, but for Louis Pelzer and others of his world of professional historians, the frontier lay at the heart of the American nation.

Bibliography

Books

Augustus Caesar Dodge: A Study in American Politics. Iowa City: State Historical Society of Iowa, 1908.

The Cattleman's Frontier: A Record of the Trans-Mississippi Cattle Industry from Oxen Trains to Pooling Companies, 1850-1890. Glendale, CA: Arthur H. Clark Co., 1936.

Henry Dodge. Iowa City: State Historical Society of Iowa, 1911.

Marches of the Dragoons: An Account of Marches and Activities of the First Regiment of United States Dragoons in the Mississippi Valley between the Years 1833 and 1850. Iowa City: State Historical Society of Iowa, 1917.

The Prairie Logbooks: Dragoon Campaigns to the Pawnee Villages in 1844 and the Rocky Mountains in 1845 by James Henry Carlton. Editor. Chicago: Caxton Club, 1943.

A Topical Guide to the Mississippi Valley Historical Review, Vol. I-XIX, 1911-33, and the Mississippi Valley Historical Review Proceedings, Vol. I-XXI, 1907-24. Editor. Compiled with Charles H. Norby and Walker D. Wyman. Lincoln, NE: Mississippi Valley Historical Association, 1934.

Articles

"Captain Ford's Journal of an Expedition to the Rocky Mountains." *Mississippi Valley Historical Review* 12(March, 1926):550-579.

"A Cattleman's Commonwealth on the Western Ranges." *Mississippi Valley Historical Review* 13(June, 1926):30-49.

"The Diplomatic Correspondence of Augustus Caesar Dodge." *Mississippi Valley Historical Association Proceedings* 1(1907-1908):111-120.

"The Disintegration and Organization of Political Parties in Iowa, 1852-1860." *Mississippi Valley Historical Association Proceedings* 5(1911-1912):158-166.

"Early Burlington." *Palimpsest* 15(July, 1934):225-254.

"Economic Factors in the Acquisition of Louisiana." *Mississippi Valley Historical Association Proceedings* 6(1912-1913):109-128.

"The Election of Francis Gehon in 1839." *Iowa Journal of History and Politics* 5(October, 1907):534-543.

"Financial Manaagement of the Cattle Ranges." *Journal of Economic and Business History* 2(August, 1930):723-741.

"A Frontier Officer's Military Order Book." *Mississippi Valley Historical Review* 6(September, 1919):260-267.

"German Submarine Warfare against the United States, 1915-1917." *University Extension Division Bulletin* no. 29 (1917).

"The History and Principles of the Democratic Party of Iowa, 1846-1857." *Iowa Journal of History and Politics* 6(April, 1908):163-246.

"The History and Principles of the Democratic Party of the Territory of Iowa." *Iowa Journal of History and Politics* 6(January, 1908):3-54.

"The History and Principles of the Whig Party of the Territory of Iowa." *Iowa Journal of History and Politics* 5(January, 1907):46-90.

"History Made by Plain Men." *Iowa Journal of History and Politics* 11(July, 1913):307-322.

"The History of Political Parties in Iowa from 1857 to 1860." *Iowa Journal of History and Politics* 7(April, 1909):179-229.

"Iowa City: A Miniature Frontier of the Forties." *Iowa Journal of History and Politics* 29(January, 1931):3-26.

"A Journal of Marches by the First United States Dragoons, 1834-1835." *Iowa Journal of History and Politics* 7(July, 1909):331-378.

"The Negro and Slavery in Early Iowa." *Iowa Journal of History and Politics* 2(October, 1904):471-484.

"The Origin and Organization of the Republican Party in Iowa." *Iowa Journal of History and Politics* 4(October, 1906):487-521.

"Pioneer Stage Coach Travel." *Mississippi Valley Historical Review* 23(June, 1936):3-26.

"The Private Land Claims of the Old Northwest Territory." *Iowa Journal of History and Politics* 12(July, 1914):373-393.

"The Public Domain as a Field for Historical Study." *Iowa Journal of History and Politics* 12(October, 1914):568-578.

"The Scope of Iowa History." *Iowa Journal of History and Politics* 8(October, 1910):467-477.

"Seward and Douglas in Iowa." *Palimpsest* 7(October, 1926):297-308.

"The Shifting Cow Towns of Kansas." *Transactions of the Illinois State Historical Society* 33(1926):41-51.

"The Spanish Land Grants of Upper Louisiana." *Iowa Journal of History and Politics* 11(January, 1913):3-37.

"Squatter Settlements." *Palimpsest* 14(February, 1933):77-84.

"Trails of the Trans-Mississippi Cattle Frontier." In *The Trans-Mississippi West* edited by James F. Willard and Colin B. Goodykoontz. Boulder: University of Colorado, 1930. Pp. 139-161.

Reviews

America Moves West by Robert E. Riegel. *Mississippi Valley Historical Review* 18(March, 1932):575.

American Historical Review, General Index to Vol. XXXI-XL, October 1925 to July 1935 compiled by Eleanor D. Smith. *Mississippi Valley Historical Review* 26(September, 1939):293-294.

Atlas of American History edited by James Truslow Adams. *Mississippi Valley Historical Review* 30(September, 1943):261-262.

The Changing West and Other Essays by Laurence M. Larson. *Mississippi Valley Historical Review* 25(December, 1938):420-421.

Express and Stage Coach Days in California, from the Gold Rush to the Civil War by Oscar O. Winther. *Mississippi Valley Historical Review* 23(December, 1936):425.

Famous First Facts: A Record of First Happenings, Discoveries and Inventions in the United States by Joseph Nathan Kane. *Mississippi Valley Historical Review* 21(March, 1935):604-605.

The Flag of the United States by Milo M. Quaife. *Mississippi Valley Historical Review* 29(March, 1943):607-608.

Forty-Niners: The Chronicle of the California Trail by Archer B. Hulbert. *Mississippi Valley Historical Review* 18(March, 1932):578-579.

Grand Demobilization and Other Essays by Frederic L. Paxson. *Mississippi Valley Historical Review* 28(March, 1942):622-623.

Indian Slavery in Colonial Times within the Present Limits of the United States by Almon Wheeler Lauber. *Mississippi Valley Historical Review* 1(1914):123-124.

Intimate Letters of Carl Schurz, 1841-1869 edited and translated by Joseph Schafer. *Mississippi Valley Historical Review* 17(March, 1931):628.

The Long Road Home: An Autobiography by John Moody. *Mississippi Valley Historical Review* 21(March, 1935):599.

Michigan Historical Collections 35(1907). *Iowa Journal of History and Politics* 6(January, 1908):111-113.

A Recent History of the United States by Frederic L. Paxson. *Mississippi Valley Historical Review* 9(June, 1922):84-85.

Sixty-Years and other Discourses with Reminiscences by William Salter. *Iowa Journal of History and Politics* 6(April, 1908):290-292.

Stephen A. Douglas: A Study in American Politics by Allen Johnson. *Iowa Journal of History and Politics* 7(January, 1909):142-146.

Transactions of the Kansas State Historical Society, 1907-1908 10(1908) edited by George W. Martin. *Iowa Journal of History and Politics* 7(April, 1909):294-295.

Treasure Express: Epic Days of the Wells Fargo by Neill C. Wilson. *Mississippi Valley Historical Review* 23(June, 1936):141-142.

Webster's Biographical Dictionary: A Dictionary of Names of Newsworthy Persons with Pronunciation and Concise Biographies. *Mississippi Valley Historical Review* 30(December, 1943):424-425.

Westward with Dragoons: The Journal of William Clark on His Expedition to Establish Fort Osage, August 25 to September 22, 1808 edited by Kate L. Griggs. *Mississippi Valley Historical Review* 25(December, 1938):407.

Wisconsin: The Americanization of a French Settlement by Reuben Gold Thwaites. *Iowa Journal of History and Politics* 7(April, 1909):284-286.

Studies of Louis Pelzer

Binkley, William C., Ralph E. Himstead, Herbert A. Kellar, William J. Petersen, Elmer Ellis, and Philip D. Jordan. "Louis Pelzer: Scholar, Teacher, Editor." *Mississippi Valley Historical Review* 33(September, 1946):201-216.

Dale, Edward E. Review of *The Cattlemen's Frontier: A Record of the Trans-Mississippi Cattle Industry from Oxen Trail to Pooling Companies, 1850-1890* by Louis Pelzer. *Mississippi Valley Historical Review* 5(September, 1948):230-231.

Johnson, Allen. Review of *Augustus Caesar Dodge: A Study in American Politics* by Louis Pelzer. *American Historical Review* 14(July, 1909):857.

Kellogg, Louise Phelps. Review of *Marches of the Dragoons in the Mississippi Valley: An Account of Marches and Activities of the First Regiment of United States Dragoons in the Mississippi Valley between the Years 1833 and 1850* by Louis Pelzer. *Mississippi Valley Historical Review* 5(September, 1918):230-231.

Pelzer, Louis, Papers. State Historical Society of Iowa Library, Iowa City, IA.

Smith, J. H. Review of *Marches of the Dragoons: An Account of Marches and Activities of the First Regiment of United States Dragoons in the Mississippi Valley between the Years 1833 and 1850* by Louis Pelzer. *American Historical Review* 24(October, 1918):138.

Taylor, Edward Raymond. Review of *Henry Dodge* by Louis Pelzer. *American Historical Review* 17(April, 1912):669-670.

Watson, Walcott. Review of *The Cattlemen's Frontier: A Record of the Trans-Mississippi Cattle Industry from Oxen Trail to Pooling Companies, 1850-1890* by Louis Pelzer. *American Historical Review* 42(July, 1937):799-800.

37

MILO MILTON QUAIFE

by David A. Walker

Biography

In early fall, 1959, Milo Milton Quaife and his wife Letitia (Goslin) were driving through northern Michigan from their home in Highland Park, a Detroit suburb. A few miles south of Sault Ste. Marie their car was struck head on; Milo Quaife died on September 1, 1959, his wife, less seriously injured, recovered. Quaife was editorially eulogized as "the unofficial voice of Midwestern history," "a manuscript ferreter perhaps equal to Lyman Draper" (*Milwaukee Journal*, September 2, 1959), and "the foremost authority on the history of Michigan and the Old Northwest" (*Michigan History* 44:36).

Born near Nashua, Iowa, on October 6, 1880, the son of Albert E. and Barbara S. (Hinz), Milo Quaife received his undergraduate degree from Iowa College (now Grinnell) in 1903. Following graduation he taught high school Latin and German in Sheffield, Illinois, but left after one year to study history at the University of Missouri, earning an M.A. in 1905. Three years later he received the Ph.D., with honors, from the University of Chicago. His dissertation, entitled "The Doctrine of Non-Intervention with Slavery in the Territories," was published in 1910.

Quaife joined the history faculty of Chicago's Lewis Institute of Technology in 1908 and advanced to the rank of professor. In January, 1914, he moved to Madison as the newly appointed superintendent and editor of the State Historical Society of Wisconsin. Quaife faced a difficult situation. He replaced Reuben Gold Thwaites who had run the society with considerable political skill and a very firm administrative hand. He had trained a devoted staff that quickly resented changes of method, approach, and personality. Quaife was not Thwaites, but "he was a better scholar, a better editor, an equally hard worker. His great weakness lay in dealing with people. Shy, he gave the impression of being cold and aloof. Inexperienced, he never knew when to give a little to gain more" (*Clio's Servant*, p. 202). Yet Quaife established a proud record, expanding the activities and focus of the society. He initiated publication of the monthly *Wisconsin Historical Bulletin* that was distributed to state newspapers; prepared a monthly historical article that the United Press circulated nationwide to Sunday editions of newspapers; organized a special exhibit at the state fair; inaugurated an annual conference of local historical societies; increased the volumes in the society library; and in 1917 launched the *Wisconsin Magazine of History*, editing the first five volumes.

Unfortunately, these positive advances were counterbalanced by the devastating effect of World War I. The staff experienced great turnover, the book and newspaper collections were threatened, the research and publication programs ground to a halt, and museum attendance dropped. Quaife continued to face a cutback in appropriations and growing discontent from personnel inherited from the Thwaites years. This spilled over to the board of curators who expressed loss of confidence in Quaife as superintendent. "His scholarship and editorial capacity were beyond question, but they felt another man could do a better job with the public" (p. 253). A compromise settlement was reached when Joseph C. Schafer replaced Quaife in 1920, but the former superintendent remained in charge of society publications for two more years.

In March, 1924, Quaife assumed the positions of secretary and editor of the Burton Historical Collection in the Detroit Public Library. In that capacity he encouraged an interest in local and regional history with the founding of the Algonquin Club in 1934 and as editor and principal author of the monthly *Burton Historical Collection Leaflet* from March, 1924, to November, 1931. In addition, Quaife edited the *Mississippi Valley Historical Review* from June, 1924, to March, 1930, often using its columns to publish lively editorials on such diverse topics as germ warfare, accuracy in historical writing, unreliable travel narratives, and censorship of school history textbooks. He was also advisory editor for the initial volumes of the *Dictionary of American Biography* and the *Atlas of American History*; president of the Mississippi Valley Historical Association, 1919-1920; and lecturer in history at Wayne University, 1931-1942, and at the University of Detroit, 1932-1935. Quaife was awarded honorary degrees from Wayne University in 1951 and Eastern Michigan University in 1959. Following his retirement from the Burton Collection in 1947, he spent the last dozen years of his life writing, editing, and lecturing.

Themes

In half a century Milo M. Quaife edited and authored an imposing variety of scholarly materials in the fields of American history and the American West. His writing focused primarily on the region surrounding lakes Huron and Michigan. In addition to monographs and edited volumes, Quaife published more than two hundred articles, book reviews, and personal and professional commentaries in academic journals and the public press. In 1955 the Algonquin Club, an organization founded by Quaife and Detroit industrial salesman William F. Lawler to foster interest in the history of the Detroit-Windsor, Ontario, area, published a fifty-two page pamphlet that catalogued his bibliographic achievements.

Like many historians of his generation Quaife was influenced by the frontier thesis of Frederick Jackson Turner. Personal contact between the two scholars was limited to professional meetings although they were friendly rivals for an important administrative position. When Reuben G. Thwaites died, many individuals tried to persuade Turner to leave Harvard and return to Madison as superintendent of the State Historical Society of Wisconsin. Turner politely refused the offer and Milo Quaife succeeded Thwaites. There was little attempt made in any of Quaife's volumes to address directly the frontier thesis, but an analysis of his writings demonstrates clear support of the fundamental principles. Quaife's choices of subject matter and his historical focuses portray the frontier as creating distinguished and superior American institutions and a national character.

A second theme or purpose behind the Quaife scholarship was a strong desire to offer readable history to both a scholarly and particularly a nonacademic audience. Despite active participation in nationwide professional organizations, especially the Mississippi Valley Historical Association, he stressed the significance of local, narrative history with a strong human interest component. Quaife remained active in Detroit's Algonquin Club, the Anthony Wayne Memorial Association, the Michigan-Ontario History Conference, and the Maumee Valley Historical Convention. He wrote short historical articles for the employee publications of IBM, Pure Oil Company, Chesapeake and Ohio Railroad Company, and the Society of Surgery, Gynecology, and Obstetrics.

One major purpose dominated the historical record of Milo Quaife. He devoted a lifetime to proving the value of studying the Upper Midwest, the region surrounding the Great Lakes. He contributed substantially to making available exhaustively researched and carefully edited primary documents and personal narratives, often of historically unknown individuals. He was also particularly upset with what he perceived as an eastern bias to all American historical scholarship in the early decades of the twentieth century.

Analysis

Beginning with the publication in 1910 of his dissertation, *The Doctrine of Non-Intervention with Slavery in the Territories*, Milo Quaife remained an active author and editor for fifty years. Nearly all of the dozen books he wrote dealt with the Great Lakes region, yet the American reading public was most familiar with his history of the United States flag published in 1942.

Quaife co-authored a college textbook history of Michigan, writing the section that covered geologic times to statehood in 1836, and was the principal author and editor of a multivolume history of Wisconsin that included a general narrative review, topical chapters, and short biographical sketches of prominent living citizens. Two books focus on Detroit, one built around twenty-six biographical portraits, the other based on hundreds of paintings and photographs. A Michigan theme dominates two other publications. Quaife co-authored a history of the Saint Mary's

River at Sault Ste. Marie that details the background of the entire upper Great Lakes area. In a thoroughly documented study Quaife depicts the somewhat bizarre tale of James J. Strang, self-proclaimed "King of the Earth by direct appointment of God." Strang led nearly 2,600 Mormons from Nauvoo, Illinois, into Wisconsin and eventually onto Beaver Island in Lake Michigan (*Kingdom of St. James*). Using exhaustive research in diaries and reminiscences, Quaife tells the story of a helpless, suffering frontier people, bearing immense hardships, blindly trusting a vain prophet into the wilderness. During the 1940s Quaife organized and edited the American Lakes Series for Bobbs-Merrill Publishing Company. He wrote *Lake Michigan* (1944) establishing a pattern for the remaining nine volumes. The regional histories are based on sound research but designed for a popular audience.

Quaife's scholarly style is exemplified in three volumes about Chicago. *Chicago and the Old Northwest, 1673-1835* (1913) vividly describes the Indian campaigns of Anthony Wayne, the War of 1812 in the region, the importance of Fort Dearborn, and the significance of the Chicago portage. Nearly one-third of the book is devoted to an appendix that included official reports, personal journals, and military muster rolls. The anecdotal style of *Chicago's Highways* (1923) is written as a popular tour guide to historic events and sites. Its dominant Turnerian theme is the inevitable success of civilization conquering the frontier, human progress guided by various modes of transportation. Written for a youthful audience, *Checagau: From Wigwam to Modern City* (1933) includes one of the first laudatory accounts of Jean Baptiste Pierre Sable, considered the city's first settler. Quaife described him somewhat romantically as "a true pioneer of civilization, leader of the unending procession of Chicago's swarming millions. Even in his mixed blood he truly represented the future city" (p. 46).

Milo Quaife used a variety of scholarly journals, particularly the *Mississippi Valley Historical Review* and the *Wisconsin Magazine of History*, to detail minor events related to the Great Lakes frontier and to reprint little known letters and diaries. These include such diverse topics as the date of the Michilimackinac Massacre, pioneer recollections of southern Wisconsin, the murder of a Wisconsin territorial legislator, and the accuracy of reports that the French built a fort at present day Chicago. Quaife utilized the monthly *Burton Historical Collection Leaflets* to introduce readers to the minutia of local history. Each issue contains a brief historical narrative written by the editor followed by reprints of selected documents from the Burton Collection. These include a series of biographical sketches of French, British, and American pioneers, the value of naval vessels around Detroit, and historic buildings in the city.

Three articles are of particular interest to a broader, more professional audience. Quaife presented a general overview of the Northwest Ordinance of 1787. The author, writing with obvious regional pride, concludes that this was one of the most significant documents in United States history. Its provisions exemplified concepts well ahead of the times and was the key to future American expansion. Quaife also attempted to resurrect the historical reputation of General William Hull and soften criticism raised about his conduct of military campaigns around Detroit during the War of 1812. Quaife concludes that Hull was a scapegoat for American shortcomings. Although Quaife sees Hull as "no military genius," he excuses Hull "because of conditions over which he had no control" (*Ohio State Archaeological and Historical Quarterly* 47:168). Finally, Quaife expressed strong feelings concerning the accuracy of the Kensington Rune Stone that allegedly established the presence of Viking explorers in the western Great Lakes during the fourteenth century. He relegates the rune stone to the realm of myth and firmly rejects all collateral evidence as a "hoax of modern origin" (*Michigan History* 31:161).

Perhaps Milo Quaife's most significant historical contributions are edited volumes of primary sources. This activity formed natural parameters for a prolific career. From 1910, the year he received his Ph.D., to the year of his death, 1959, Quaife edited many volumes, including a variety of frontier residents' original works. During this near half century reviewers consistently praised the thoroughly researched and carefully edited works that often uncovered little known but historically valuable material.

Most of Quaife's edited efforts, like his written scholarship, focus on the Great Lakes region. These include a series of narratives on early Chicago, letters of an English settler in pioneer Wisconsin, and the papers of Detroit fur trader and merchant John Askin. Quaife also contributed to the historical record of the Lewis and Clark expedition by editing the journal of Sergeant John Ordway, one of the few participants who kept a daily account throughout the entire trip. The volume also contains the first publication of Meriwether Lewis's journey during the fall, 1803, from Pittsburgh to Camp Dubois opposite the mouth of the Missouri River. In another publication Quaife edited the original narrative of the principal combatants during the American Revolution battle at Vincennes. George Rogers Clark is praised as a "veritable military genius" while Henry Hamilton is described as a "brave and highminded soldier" (*Capture of Old Vincennes*, p. xix). In an effort to upgrade the British commander's historical reputation, Quaife concludes that Hamilton was carrying out his superiors' orders, "it is wholly unfair . . . to single him out for peculiar responsibility or infamy" (p. xx). One of Milo Quaife's most valuable editorial projects is the compilation of records surrounding Wisconsin's admission to the Union. He brought together, in four volumes, official proceedings, debates, participant journals, and newspaper accounts of the movement for statehood, constitutional conventions, and the ratification struggle. This provides the most complete record available of the often difficult transition from territorial status to statehood (*Wisconsin: Its History and Its People*).

Forty-three volumes of the Lakeside Classics form the backbone of Milo Quaife's prodigious editorial achievements. In 1903 Thomas E. Donnelley, a prominent Chicago business executive, initiated publication of a series of historical volumes. The books were not available for purchase but were distributed complimentarily during the Christmas season to the Donnelley Company's "friends and patrons and to others who may prize them" (*Autobiography of Benjamin Franklin*, p. ii). The publisher selected Quaife as general editor in 1916 because he believed "no one is more deeply versed in the history of the Old Northwest Territory or has a finer appreciation of its romance" (*Life of Black Hawk*, p. v). The initial volumes reprinted presidential inaugural addresses and memorable political speeches. A later format emphasized the personal relations of early frontier settlers. Each book portrays the reality of first hand experience to capture the general human interest. With one exception, Quaife prepared every annual volume from 1916 to 1959 when the series ended with the editor's death. The previous year, R. R. Donnelley Company had received an award of merit from the American Association of State and Local History commending the high quality of the Lakeside Classics.

The publisher never intended to reprint a precise copy of the original document. The editor added chapter titles, paragraphing, modern spelling and punctuation, and a brief historical introduction. Quaife began with the autobiography of Black Hawk whom he describes as "one of the pathetic tragedies of the development of our Middle border" (p. ix). Considering Quaife's intimate knowledge of the Midwest and willingness to ferret out relatively scarce narratives, it comes as no surprise that the Classics series contained many works of regional interest. These included settlers accounts written by pioneer men and women and the personal recollections of such prominent individuals as George Rogers Clark, Lamothe Cadillac, and Alexander Henry. Quaife also selected material that portrays events in the Far West. Recipients of these small volumes read about fur trappers and Indian traders, the Texas Rangers, gold rush California, and army life on the Great Plains. Readers also absorb the adventurous accounts of Zebulon Pike, Kit Carson, and Geronimo. Finally, the series includes several "classics" of western history, particularly *Commerce of the Prairies* by Josiah Gregg, *Vanishing Arizona* by Martha Summerhayes, and *My Life on the Plains* by George A. Custer.

Milo M. Quaife contributed substantially to American frontier history through original writings and more importantly through the prodigious quantity of his edited works. Although not introducing new historiographical insights, he established Great Lakes regional history as a respected field of scholarly research and presented to the general public readable, human interest historical works.

Bibliography

Books

Absaraka: Home of the Crows by Margaret I. Carrington. Editor. Chicago: Lakeside Press, 1950.

Across the Plains in Forty-Nine by Reuben Cole Shaw. Editor. Chicago: Lakeside Press, 1948.

Adventures of the First Settlers on the Oregon or Columbia River by Alexander Ross. Editor. Chicago: Lakeside Press, 1923.

Alexander Henry's Travels and Adventures in the Years 1760-1776 by Alexander Henry. Editor. Chicago: Lakeside Press, 1921.

Alexander Mackenzie's Voyage to the Pacific Ocean in 1793 by Alexander Mackenzie. Editor. Chicago: Lakeside Press, 1931.

Among the Indians: Eight Years in the Far West, 1858-1866 by Henry A. Boller. Editor. Chicago: Lakeside Press, 1959.

Army Life in Dakota: Selections from the Journal of Philippe Regis Denis de Keredern de Trobriand. Editor. Chicago: Lakeside Press, 1941.

The Attainment of Statehood. Editor. Vol. XXIX, *Wisconsin Historical Collections*. Madison: State Historical Society of Wisconsin, 1928.

The Bark Covered House: Or, Back in the Woods Again by William Nowlin. Editor. Chicago: Lakeside Press, 1937.

The Border and the Buffalo: An Untold Story of the Southwest Plains. Editor. Chicago: Lakeside Press, 1938.

Builders of Detroit. Detroit: J. L. Hudson Company, 1951.

The Capture of Old Vincennes: The Original Narratives of George Rogers Clark and of His Opponent Governor Henry Hamilton. Editor. Indianapolis: Bobbs-Merrill, 1927.

Checagau: From Indian Wigwam to Modern City, 1673-1835. Chicago: University of Chicago Press, 1933.

Chicago and the Old Northwest, 1673-1835: A Study of the Evolution of the Northwestern Frontier, Together with a History of Fort Dearborn. Chicago: University of Chicago Press, 1913.

Chicago's Highways, Old and New, From Indian Trail to Motor Road. Chicago: D. F. Keller, 1923.

The Commerce of the Prairies by Josiah Gregg. Editor. Chicago: Lakeside Press, 1926.

The Conquest of the Illinois by George Rogers Clark. Editor. Chicago: Lakeside Press, 1920.

The Convention of 1846. Editor. Vol. XXVII, *Wisconsin Historical Collections*. Madison: State Historical Society of Wisconsin, 1919.

Death Valley in '49 by William L. Manly. Editor. Chicago: Lakeside Press, 1927.

The Development of Chicago, 1674-1914: Shown in a Series of Contemporary Original Narratives. Editor. Chicago: Caxton Club, 1916.

The Doctrine of Non-Intervention with Slavery in the Territories. Chicago: M. C. Chamberlin, 1910.

The Early Days of Rock Island and Davenport: The Narratives of J. W. Spencer and J. M. D. Burrows. Editor. Chicago: Lakeside Press, 1942.

Echoes of the Past about California by General John Bidwell. Editor. Chicago: Lakeside Press, 1928.

An English Settler in Pioneer Wisconsin: The Letters of Edwin Bottomley, 1842-1850. Editor. Vol. XXV, *Wisconsin Historical Collections*. Madison: State Historical Society of Wisconsin, 1918.

Forty Years a Fur Trader on the Upper Missouri, the Personal Narrative of Charles Larpenteur, 1833-1872 by Charles Larpenteur. Editor. Chicago: Lakeside Press, 1933.

The Fur Hunters of the Far West by Alexander Ross. Editor. Chicago: Lakeside Press, 1924.

Growing Up with Southern Illinois, 1820 to 1861: From the Memoirs of Daniel Harmon Brush. Editor. Chicago: Lakeside Press, 1944.

A History of Illinois, From Its Commencement as a State in 1818 to 1847 by Governor Thomas Ford. Vol. I. Editor. Chicago: Lakeside Press, 1945.

__________. Vol. II. Editor. Chicago: Lakeside Press, 1946.

In Camp and Cabin by Reverend John Steele. Editor. Chicago: Lakeside Press, 1928.

The Indian Captivity of O. M. Spencer. Editor. Chicago: Lakeside Press, 1917.

The John Askin Papers, 1747-1795. Editor. Vol. I. Detroit: Detroit Library Commission, 1928.

The John Askin Papers, 1796-1820. Editor. Vol. II. Detroit: Detroit Library Commission, 1931.

John Long's Voyages and Travels in the Years 1768-1788. Editor. Chicago: Lakeside Press, 1922.

The Journals of Captain Meriwether Lewis and Sergeant John Ordway, Kept on the Expedition of Western Exploration, 1803-1806. Editor. Vol. XXII, *Wisconsin Historical Collections.* Madison: State Historical Society of Wisconsin, 1916.

The Kingdom of Saint James: A Narrative of the Mormons. New Haven: Yale University Press, 1930.

Kit Carson's Autobiography. Editor. Chicago: Lakeside Press, 1935.

Lake Michigan. Indianapolis: Bobbs-Merrill, 1944.

The Life of Blackhawk (Ma-Ka-Tai-Me-She-Kia-Kiak). Editor. Chicago: Lakeside Press, 1916.

The Life of John Wendell Anderson. Privately printed, 1950.

Michigan: From Primitive Wilderness to Industrial Commonwealth. Co-authored with Sidney Glazer. New York: Prentice-Hall, 1948, 1954.

Michigan and the Old Northwest: From the Ice Age to the End of French Rule. Editor. Detroit: Greyhound Corporation, 1945.

The Movement for Statehood, 1845-1846. Editor. Vol. XXVI, *Wisconsin Historical Collections.* Madison: State Historical Society of Wisconsin, 1918.

My Life on the Plains by George A. Custer. Editor. Chicago: Lakeside Press, 1952.

Narrative of the Adventures of Zenas Leonard, Written by Himself. Editor. Chicago: Lakeside Press, 1934.

Narrative of the Texan Santa Fe Expedition by George Wilkins Kendall. Editor. Chicago: Lakeside Press, 1929.

The Personal Narrative of James O. Pattie of Kentucky edited by Timothy Flint. Editor. Chicago: Lakeside Press, 1930.

Pictures of Gold Rush California. Editor. Chicago: Lakeside Press, 1949.

Pictures of Illinois One Hundred Years Ago. Editor. Chicago: Lakeside Press, 1918.

River of Destiny: The Saint Marys. Co-authored with Joseph E. Bayliss and Estelle L. Bayliss. Detroit: Wayne University Press, 1955.

The Siege of Detroit in 1763: The Journal of Pontiac's Conspiracy; John Rutherford's Narrative of a Captivity. Editor. Chicago: Lakeside Press, 1958.

Six Years With the Texas Rangers, 1875 to 1881, by James B. Gillett. Editor. Chicago: Lakeside Press, 1943.

The Southwestern Expedition of Zebulon M. Pike. Editor. Chicago: Lakeside Press, 1925.

The Struggle over Ratification, 1846-1847. Editor. Vol. XXVIII, *Wisconsin Historical Collections.* Madison: State Historical Society of Wisconsin, 1920.

This is Detroit, 1701-1951: Two Hundred and Fifty Years in Pictures. Detroit: Wayne University Press, 1951.

Three Years among the Indians and Mexicans by General Thomas James. Editor. Chicago: Lakeside Press, 1953.

A True Picture of Emigration by Rebecca Burlend. Editor. Chicago: Lakeside Press, 1936.

The Truth About Geronimo by Britton Davis. Editor. Chicago: Lakeside Press, 1951.

Uncle Dick Wootton, the Pioneer Frontiersman of the Rocky Mountain Region by Howard L. Conard. Editor. Chicago: Lakeside Press, 1957.

Vanished Arizona: Recollections of My Army Life by Martha Summerhayes. Editor. Chicago: Lakeside Press, 1939.

A Voyage to the Northwest Coast of America by Gabriel Franchere. Editor. Chicago: Lakeside Press, 1954.

War on the Detroit: The Chronicles of Thomas Vercheres de Boucherville; The Capitulation, by an Ohio Volunteer. Editor. Chicago: Lakeside Press, 1940.

War-Path and Bivouac: The Big Horn and Yellowstone Expedition by John F. Finerty. Editor. Chicago: Lakeside Press, 1955.

Wau-Bun, the "Early Day" in the North-West by Julliette A. Kinzie. Editor. Chicago: Lakeside Press, 1932.

The Western Country in the 17th Century: The Memoirs of Lamothe Cadillac and Pierre Liette. Editor. Chicago: Lakeside Press, 1947.

When Detroit Was Young: Historical Studies. Editor. Detroit: Burton Abstract & Title Company, 1951.

Wisconsin: Its History and Its People. 4 Volumes. Chicago: S. J. Clarke, 1924.

A Woman's Story of Pioneer Illinois by Christiana Holmes Tillson. Editor. Chicago: Lakeside Press, 1919.

"Yellowstone Kelly": The Memoirs of Luther S. Kelly. Editor. New Haven: Yale University Press, 1926.

Articles

"An Artilleryman of Old Fort Mackinac." *Burton Historical Collection Leaflet* 6(January, 1928):33-48.

"The British Take Detroit." *Burton Historical Collection Leaflet* 17(May, 1939):7-9.

"The Chicago Treaty of 1833." *Wisconsin Magazine of History* 1(March, 1918):287-303.
"Concerning Historical Inaccuracies, Correct Date of the Michilimackinac Massacre, and the First English Woman at Mackinac." *Michigan History* 23(Winter, 1939):109-112.
"Critical Evaluation of the Sources of Western History." *Mississippi Valley Historical Review* 1(September, 1914):167-184.
"Detroit and Early Chicago." *Burton Historical Collection Leaflet* 5(January, 1927):33-48.
"Detroit and George Rogers Clark." *Indiana History Bulletin* 5(April, 1928):38-54.
"Detroit Battles: The Blue Licks." *Burton Historical Collection Leaflet* 6(November, 1927):17-32.
"Detroit Biographies: Robert Rogers." *Burton Historical Collection Leaflet* 7(September, 1928):1-16.
"Detroit Biographies: The Sieur de Bourgmont." *Burton Historical Collection Leaflet* 6(March, 1928):49-63.
"Detroit in 1750." *Burton Historical Collection Leaflet* 17(May, 1939):12-13.
"A Diary of the War of 1812." Editor. *Mississippi Valley Historical Review* 1(September, 1914):272-278.
"Eleanor Little, Pioneer." *Burton Historical Collection Leaflet* 8(January, 1930):33-48.
"The Fort Dearborn Massacre." *Mississippi Valley Historical Review* 1(March, 1915):561-573.
"From Detroit to Montreal in 1810." *Canadian Historical Review* 14(September, 1933):293-296.
"From Detroit to the Mississippi in 1820." *Burton Historical Collection Leaflet* 8(March, 1930):49-64.
"General James Wilkinson's Narrative of the Fallen Timbers Campaign." Editor. *Mississippi Valley Historical Review* 16(June, 1929):81-90.
"General William Hull and His Critics." *Ohio State Archaeological and Historical Quarterly* 47(April, 1938):168-182.
"George Washington Enters Detroit." *Bulletin of the Detroit Historical Society* 9(February, 1953):5-9.
"An Indian Captive's Picture of Early Detroit." *Burton Historical Collection Leaflet* 3(May, 1925):65-80.
"Jonathan Carver and the Carver Grant." *Mississippi Valley Historical Review* 7(June, 1920):3-25.
"Journals and Reports of the Black Hawk War." *Mississippi Valley Historical Review* 12(December, 1925):392-409.
"The Kensington Myth Once More." *Michigan History* 31(June, 1947): 129-161.
"Marking the Site of Old Fort St. Joseph." *Journal of the Illinois State Historical Society* 6(January, 1914):490-495.
"More Light on Jonathan Carver." *Wisconsin Magazine of History* 4(March, 1921):345-347.

"The Myth of the Kensington Rune Stone: The Norse Discovery of Minnesota, 1362." *New England Quarterly* 7(December, 1934): 613-645.

"A Narrative of the Northwestern Campaign of 1813." *Mississippi Valley Historical Review* 15(March, 1929):519-525.

"The Ohio Campaigns of 1782." *Mississippi Valley Historical Review* 17(March, 1931):515-529.

"On the Attainment of Accuracy in Historical Writing." *Mississippi Valley Historical Review* 12(March, 1926):624-627.

"On the Censorship of School History Text Books." *Mississippi Valley Historical Review* 16(December, 1929):435-437.

"On the Destruction of Historical Manuscripts." *Mississippi Valley Historical Review* 16(December, 1929):437-439.

"On the Difficulties Attending the Writing of History." *Mississippi Valley Historical Review* 16(March, 1930):600-602.

"On the Supposed American Design to Annex Canada." *Mississippi Valley Historical Review* 16(June, 1929):140-141.

"On the Unreliability of Travelers' Narratives." *Mississippi Valley Historical Review* 13(December, 1926):454-456.

"The Panic of 1862 in Wisconsin." *Wisconsin Magazine of History* 4(December, 1920):166-195.

"Pioneer Recollections of Beloit and Southern Wisconsin." Editor. *Wisconsin Magazine of History* 1(March, 1918):266-286.

"Property of Jean Baptiste Point Sable." Editor. *Mississippi Valley Historical Review* 15(June, 1928):89-92.

"Resolutions concerning the Kensington Rune Stone." *Mississippi Valley Historical Review* 35(September, 1948):361.

"The Royal Navy of the Upper Lakes." *Burton Historical Collection Leaflet* 2(May, 1924):49-64.

"The Significance of the Ordinance of 1787." *Journal of the Illinois State Historical Society* 30(January, 1938):415-428.

"The Smallpox Epidemic on the Upper Missouri." *Mississippi Valley Historical Review* 17(September, 1930):278-299.

"Some Glimpses of Life in Ancient Detroit." *Burton Historical Collection Leaflet* 3(September, 1924):1-16.

"Some New-Found Records of the Lewis and Clark Expedition." Editor. *Mississippi Valley Historical Review* 2(June, 1915):106-117.

"Was There A French Fort At Chicago?" In *Illinois Historical Society Transactions* for 1914. Springfield: Illinois

"Wisconsin's Saddest Tragedy." *Wisconsin Magazine of History* 5(March, 1922):264-283.

Reviews

Around the Horn to the Sandwich Islands and California, 1845-1850 by Chester S. Lyman. *Mississippi Valley Historical Review* 11(March, 1925):608-609.

As Others See Chicago: Impressions of Visitors, 1873-1933 compiled and edited by Bessie L. Pierce. *Mississippi Valley Historical Review* 20(December, 1933):425-426.

The Bloody Mohawk by Thomas Wood Clarke. *Canadian Historical Review* 22(March, 1941):75-76.

Brigham Young by M. R. Werner. *Mississippi Valley Historical Review* 12(September, 1925):274-276.

Call It North Country: The Story of Upper Michigan by John B. Martin. *Pacific Historical Review* 13(December, 1944):444.

Champlain, The Life of Fortitude by Morris G. Bishop. *Wisconsin Magazine of History* 32(June, 1949):492-494.

Chicago: The History of Its Reputation by Lloyd Lewis and Henry Justin Smith. *Mississippi Valley Historical Review* 16(December, 1929): 431-432.

Clark of the Ohio: A Life of George Rogers Clark by Frederick Palmer. *Canadian Historical Review* 11(September, 1930):258-260.

Coronado's Children: Tales of Lost Mines and Buried Treasures of the Southwest by J. Frank Dobie. *Yale Review* 21(September, 1931): 180-182.

Council Fires on the Upper Ohio: A Narrative of Indian Affairs in the Upper Ohio Valley Until 1795 by Randolph C. Downes. *Canadian Historical Review* 22(March, 1941):75-76.

The Day of the Cattleman by Ernest Osgood. *Yale Review* 20(December, 1930):397-401.

Death Valley by Bourke Lee. *Yale Review* 20(December, 1930):397-401

The Diplomacy of the War of 1812 by Frank A. Updyke. *Mississippi Valley Historical Review* 2(March, 1916):574-575.

Every House a Frontier: Detroit's Economic Progress, 1815-1825 by Floyd R. Dain. *Wisconsin Magazine of History* 40(Winter, 1956-1957): 136-137.

Father Louis Hennepin's Description of Louisiana Newly Discovered in the Southwest of New France by Order of the King translated from the original edition by Marion E. Cross. *Mississippi Valley Historical Review* 26(June, 1939):77-78.

The First Michigan Frontier by Calvin Goodrich. *Canadian Historical Review* 22(March, 1941):75-76.

Fort Laramie and the Pageant of the West, 1834-1890 by LeRoy R. Hafen and Francis Marion Young. *American Historical Review* 44(January, 1939):466-467.

The Forty-Niners: A Chronicle of the California Trail and El Dorado by Stuart Edward White. *Mississippi Valley Historical Review* 6(June, 1919):138-141.

The French Foundations, 1680-1693 edited by Theodore C. Pease and Raymond C. Werner. *American Historical Review* 41(April, 1936):583-584.

The Fruits of Mormonism by Franklin S. Harris and Newbern I. Butts. *Mississippi Valley Historical Review* 13(June, 1926):126-127.

A History of Minnesota, Vol. I by William W. Folwell. *Mississippi Valley Historical Review* 8(March, 1922):385-389.

A History of Minnesota, Vol. II by William W. Folwell. *Mississippi Valley Historical Review* 11(September, 1924):284-287.

The Illinois Country, 1673-1818 by Clarence W. Alvord. *American Historical Review* 26(January, 1921):341-344.

Illinois in 1818 by Solon Justus Buck. *Mississippi Valley Historical Review* 4(December, 1917):396-398.

Indians and Pioneers: The Story of The American Southwest before 1830 by Grant Foreman. *Yale Review* 20(December, 1930):397-401.

The Keelboat Age on Western Waters by Leland D. Baldwin. *Mississippi Valley Historical Review* 28(March, 1942):602-603.

Land of Promise: The Story of the Northwest Territory by Walter Havighurst. *American Historical Review* 52(April, 1947):512-513.

The Land of the Miamis: An Account of the Struggle to Secure Possession of the Northwest from the End of the Revolution until 1812 by Elmore Barce. *American Historical Review* 28(April, 1923):588-589.

The Last Frontier by Zachery T. Sutley. *Yale Review* 20(December, 1930):397-401.

The Location of the Chicago Portage Route of the Seventeenth Century by Robert Knight and Lucius M. Zeuch. *Mississippi Valley Historical Review* 15(March, 1929):535-536.

Meriwether Lewis of Lewis and Clark by Charles Morrow Wilson. *American Historical Review* 40(October, 1934):149-150.

The National Road by Philip D. Jordan. *Wisconsin Magazine of History* 33(December, 1949):233-235.

An Old Frontier of France: The Niagara Region and Adjacent Lakes under French Control by Frank H. Severance. *Mississippi Valley Historical Review* 4(March, 1918):519-520.

On the Old West Coast: Being Further Reminiscences of a Ranger by Major Horace Bell. *Yale Review* 21(September, 1931):180-182.

The Passing of the Frontier: A Chronicle of the Old West by Emerson Hough. *Mississippi Valley Historical Review* 6(June, 1919):138-141.

Peter Melendy: The Mind and the Soul by Luella M. Wright. *Mississippi Valley Historical Review* 30(December, 1943):448.

Quaker Forty-Niner: The Adventures of Charles E. Pancoast on the American Frontier edited by Alberta P. Hannum. *Yale Review* 20(December, 1930):397-401.

Sacajawea, A Guide and Interpreter of the Lewis and Clark Expedition: With an Account of the Travels of Toussaint Charbonneau and Jean Baptiste, The Expedition Papoose by Grace R. Hebard. *Mississippi Valley Historical Review* 20(September, 1933):280-281.

The Santa Fe Trail by Robert L. Duffus. *Yale Review* 20(December, 1930):397-401.

Six Horses by William Banning and George Hugh Banning. *Yale Review* 20(December, 1930):397-401.

Southwest on the Turquoise Trail. The First Diaries on the Road to Santa Fe edited by Archer B. Hulbert. *American Historical Review* 39(October, 1933):177-178.

The Story of Old Fort Dearborn by J. Seymour Currey. *The Dial* 53(September 1, 1912):129-131.

Trail Makers of the Northwest by Paul L. Haworth. *Mississippi Valley Historical Review* 8(March, 1922):395-396.

Transactions of the Supreme Court of the Territory of Michigan, 1805-1836 edited by William Wirt Blume. *American Historical Review* 47(October, 1941):144-147.

The Truth about Mormonism by James H. Snowden. *Mississippi Valley Historical Review* 13(March, 1927):594-595.

Uncle Sam's Camels: The Journal of Mary Humphreys Stacy, Supplemented by the Report of Edward Fitzgerald Beale edited by Lewis Burt Leslie. *Yale Review* 20(December, 1930):397-401.

United States Soldiers Invade Utah by E. Cecil McGavin. *American Historical Review* 43(April, 1938):720-721.

The Voyageur by Grace L. Nute. *Indiana Magazine of History* 52(June, 1956):216-217.

Wah-To-Yah and the Taos Trail by Lewis H. Garrard. *American Historical Review* 44(April, 1939):741.

Westward: The Romance of the American Frontier by E. Douglas Branch. *Yale Review* 21(September, 1931):180-182.

Westward from Vinland: An Account of Norse Discoveries and Explorations in America, 982-1362 by Hjalmar R. Holand. *Minnesota History* 21(September, 1940):302-304.

Zebulon Pike's Arkansaw Journal in Search of the Southern Louisiana Purchase Line, Interpreted by His Newly Recovered Maps edited by Stephen H. Hart and Archer B. Hulbert. *American Historical Review* 38(July, 1933):774-775.

Studies of Milo Milton Quaife

Adams, Randolph G. "Remarks at the Luncheon in Honor of Dr. Milo M. Quaife." *Michigan History* 27(Winter, 1943):9-15.

Bald, F. Clever. "Dr. Milo Milton Quaife, 1880-1959." *Michigan History* 44(March, 1960):36-38.

Blegen, Theodore C. Review of *Wisconsin: Its History and Its People* by Milo M. Quaife. *Mississippi Valley Historical Review* 12(June, 1925):105.

Buley, R. Carlyle. Review of *Lake Michigan* by Milo M. Quaife. *Indiana Magazine of History* 40(December, 1944):396-398.

Cox, Isaac J. Review of *Chicago and the Old Northwest, 1673-1835: A Study of the Evolution of the Northwestern Frontier, Together with a History of Fort Dearborn* by Milo M. Quaife. *Mississippi Valley Historical Review* 1(September, 1914):305-307.

Henderson, Archibald. Review of *The Capture of Old Vincennes: The Original Narratives of George Rogers Clark and of His Opponent*

Governor Henry Hamilton edited by Milo M. Quaife. *North Carolina Historical Review* 7(July, 1930):419-423.

Hollon, W. Eugene. "Quaife, Milo Milton." In *The Reader's Encyclopedia of the American West* edited by Howard R. Lamar. New York: Thomas Y. Crowell Co., 1977. Pp. 988-989.

Holmes, Oliver W. Review of *The Attainment of Statehood* edited by Milo M. Quaife. *Mississippi Valley Historical Review* 17(December, 1930):471.

Kellogg, Louise Phelps. Review of *The Kingdom of Saint James :A Narrative of the Mormons* by Milo M. Quaife. *American Historical Review* 36(January, 1931):418-419.

Lord, Clifford L., and Carl Ubbelohde. *Clio's Servant: The State Historical Society of Wisconsin.* Madison: State Historical Society of Wisconsin, 1967.

"Milo Milton Quaife." *Mississippi Valley Historical Review* 46(December, 1959):576-577.

Norris, Joe L. *Forty-Six Years: The Published Writings of Milo M. Quaife, 1910-1955.* Detroit: Algonquin Club, 1956.

Pease, Theodore. Review of *Checagou: From Indian Wigwam to Modern City, 1673-1835* by Milo M. Quaife. *American Historical Review* 39(April, 1934):588-589.

Quaife, M. M. "Some Memories of Forty Years." *Wisconsin Magazine of History* 38(Summer, 1955):217-224, 250-252.

Quaife, Milo Milton, Papers. Detroit Public Library, Detroit, MI.

Utter, William T. Review of *Michigan: From Primitive Wilderness to Industrial Commonwealth* by Milo M. Quaife and Sidney Glazer. *Mississippi Valley Historical Review* 35(September, 1948):293.

Who Was Who in America. Chicago: A. N. Marquis, 1960. 3:705-706.

38

ROBERT EDGAR RIEGEL

by Richard Saunders, Jr.

Biography

Robert Riegel was born in Reading, Pennsylvania, in 1897. He was educated at Carroll College in Wisconsin, and three years after earning his B.A., he completed work on a doctorate at the University of Wisconsin in 1922. He worked under Frederic Paxson who interested him in writing a dissertation on railroads west of the Mississippi. Out of that dissertation, he extracted a number of articles that began to appear even before he received his degree. A highly modified version of the dissertation came out as a book, *The Story of the Western Railroads*, in 1926, and the young man was recognized as a rising star in the profession.

He took a job at Dartmouth College immediately out of graduate school, and there he would spend his career. Being a published scholar in a department where that was still the exception, he was something of a celebrity from the beginning. Though his dissertation and publications up to that point were on railroad history, a topic that seemed to put him in the category of an economic historian, he was never an economic historian. Indeed, his grasp of economic concepts was limited. He regarded himself as a social and intellectual historian, and the courses he taught were in social and intellectual history. His research interests never returned to railroads after *The Story of the Western Railroads*. In his early years at Dartmouth, he teamed up with a young colleague, Lawrence Eager, a political scientist with an interest in medical history, to write an article on birth control in frontier New England. It was to be part of a larger work on medicine and social attitudes on the frontier that was never completed. Later in life, his research interests turned to women's history, although it did not seem to be out of any commitment to the feminist cause.

By the post-World War II period, Riegel was an institution at Dartmouth. He lectured, really read, from meticulously typed notes, and so would dawdle over lengthy cups of coffee each morning with colleagues, then go to class, open his notebook, and begin reading a lecture that had been given each year for decades. His courses were described by a colleague as not terribly popular for their intrinsic interest, but not too demanding, not the worst of the "guts" but tending in that direction. Hence, they were usually packed with fraternity boys. Riegel was said to attend virtually every one of the cocktail parties the fraternities threw for faculty members who had been particularly helpful. Riegel's personal conservatism in political matters seemed to fit well with the ambience of fraternity row in the 1950s. In the late 1940s, he co-authored a high school text in American history that was a great financial success and was believed to be the reason he could afford a new Cadillac automobile each year. But there were disappointments in those years. He co-authored a college text in American history which he used in his own courses but which his colleagues refused to adopt, a matter which caused considerable rift at the time.

Carroll College, his alma mater, honored him with a Doctor of Laws degree in 1946. He received a Guggenheim Fellowship in 1960-1961. He liked to teach summer school away from Dartmouth, at Columbia, University of Wisconsin, University of Missouri, University of Colorado, and University of California. He retired from Dartmouth in 1964 and became Benedict Professor of History at Texas Western College (University of Texas-El Paso after 1967) where he stayed until 1969. He returned to his home near Dartmouth. His retirement years were unhappy, however, particularly after an automobile accident, following a party in Vermont, in which his second wife was killed. He was hospitalized for a long time, although he eventually recovered and remarried. He died December 11, 1984.

Themes

Robert Riegel emphasized synthesis. All of his books characteristically brought together vast amounts of diverse material and attempted to integrate it into a comprehensive whole. In his most famous book, *The Story of the Western Railroads*, he attempted to follow the strand of a single story, the building of railroads through a complex diversity of time periods, geographic subdivisions, economic conditions, and political attitudes. In his other books, he emphasized the diversity of the human experience, de-emphasizing famous people and leaders in favor of ordinary people and how they lived their ordinary lives.

Famous people, from presidents to outlaws, appear in Riegel's books, but the effect of his emphasis on ordinary people is to paint a picture of a West that was built step-by-step by everyday people pursuing their everyday goals. Their motives were mixed. Their methods were honorable sometimes and dishonorable at other times. This takes myth out of the history of the West, even as Riegel repeats a tall tale here and there that sometimes seems like myth at its worst. Riegel emphasizes that westerners were not always the self-reliant individualists they like to portray themselves as, but people like all people who needed each other, who needed community support, who needed money from the outside, and who needed government to help them and keep order.

Otherwise, Riegel is notoriously weak on theory, unifying ideas, and themes. His technique was to compile a vast amount of information, reduce it to its essence, deposit it in the readers' laps, and let them make of it what they wished.

Analysis

Robert Riegel's most important contribution to historical writing on the West was *The Story of the Western Railroads.* It was an expanded version of a dissertation he wrote under Frederic Paxson at the University of Wisconsin in 1922. The book version was published by Macmillan in 1922 and was reissued by the University of Nebraska Press in 1964 and again in 1977.

The Story of the Western Railroads combines, in a little over three hundred pages, the whole panorama of railroad building west of the Mississippi River from the first dreams and agitations of the 1830s to the titanic struggles of the swashbuckling capitalists--Hill, Gould, and Harriman--to dominate the West in the 1880s. It ends with the completion of the last western mainlines, the Milwaukee Road's Pacific Extension in 1909 and Gould's Western Pacific in 1911. The book's strength is that it integrates so much material, puts it into context, and gives the reader a quick and comprehensive grasp of a complex topic. It was bold in its conceptualization and its execution. At the time of its publication, James Hedges, who reviewed it for the *Mississippi Valley Historical Review*, called it a "pioneer venture and subsequent workers in the field must follow the trail which he has blazed" (13:592). Twenty years after its publication, Harold Briggs, also writing in the *Mississippi Valley Historical Review*, called it "the best account" and "the only attempt at a synthesis" (34:85). Forty years after its appearance, on the occasion of its first reissue by the University of Nebraska Press, it was still accorded the significance of a groundbreaking work (*Choice* 1:337).

The Story did not receive universal acclaim when it was published. Stuart Daggett, whose *Chapters on the History of the Southern Pacific* (1922) had just appeared, reviewed the original publication for the *American Historical Review* and for his final summation, found nothing more laudatory to say than "the narrative is on the whole accurate" (32:373). This dubious endorsement was what the University of Nebraska Press inexplicably chose for the cover blurb on its reissue of the book in 1964.

The Story's most serious weakness was not a few factual errors, but that it never found grand themes to match its grand scope. There is no conclusion, no thesis, no judgment, no analysis, just an arbitrary (and debatable) statement at the end that after about 1910, there was nothing to distinguish western railroads and their problems from American railroads in general. This was no thesis at all, just a convenient way to end the book. An inability to reach conclusions was a problem for Riegel in all of his works, including *The Story*, *Young America, 1830-1840* (1949), the grand work of his mature years, and *American Feminists* (1963) from his later years. They, too, had no themes to give them unity.

Another weakness of *The Story* is that it did not, and really could not in its three hundred-page format, give the reader much information about any one topic. When Riegel did take the time to tell a story, as with Gould's controversial rate-busting railroad, the Wabash (that went from Buffalo to Kansas City and thus invaded the territory of eastern as well as western railroads), he is a delightful storyteller. But there are many topics he flies over with little more than a sentence. The building of Hill's Great Northern Railway is a very significant story if one is to understand the nature of swashbuckling capitalism, or the shadowy role of the Canadian Pacific (and through it, the British Empire) in United States railroad affairs are good examples of important issues Riegel ignores.

Sixty years after its publication, a reader's typical response to *The Story* is that surely we know a lot more about all these things now. On many of the topics, the answer is yes. There have been histories (of uneven qualities) of the individual railroads Riegel talks about, and the heart of *The Story*, its discussion of the highstakes battles of Hill, Gould, and Harriman, has been largely supplanted by Julius Grodinsky's *Trans Continental Railway Strategy, 1869-1893* (1963), although the lasting place of *The Story* is saved somewhat by Grodinsky's turgid writing style. But there is much in *The Story* that has not been treated elsewhere. There are still a hundred dissertations to be wrung from the material Riegel introduced.

Already in 1926, Riegel's primary interest was social history. Hence his treatment of railroad labor and labor organizations is very good. But his treatment of the politics of railroads is sketchy, and his command of economics is poor. Railroads were being built all over the West, but he offers little explanation as to why, or what they hauled, or whether they made any money hauling it, or what this did to the western economy. And though he tried to keep the names of railroads to a minimum, his efforts got away from him. Readers had better have a pretty good knowledge of the routes of various railroad companies after they emerged as regional systems in the late 1800s and before the consolidations of the 1970s or they will be lost because *The Story* has no maps.

America Moves West, a textbook on the westward movement, first came out in 1930, with a second edition in 1947, a third in 1956, and a fourth and fifth (with Robert G. Athearn) in 1964 and 1971. It was an ideal vehicle for Riegel's talents. He could talk about many subjects. His delightful storytelling was appropriate. He did not have to probe anything in depth. He could include all the social and cultural history that he loved. And he did not have to draw conclusions of his own. After the first edition, the book ended with a discussion of the Turner thesis and its critics, which gave the illusion that Riegel himself had brilliantly tied all the loose ends together, a perfect frosting on the cake.

The first edition suffered from too much emphasis on railroads, material that came straight out of *The Story*. His prose still had a graduate school stiffness. But by the second edition, he was in his prime. Much of the railroad material was dropped, making room for the social history that fascinated him. He talks at length about daily life, violence, sports, schools and colleges, religion, medicine, technology, art, literature, Indians, and Mormons. He is weak on politics, and as in *The Story*, economics is negligible. Reviews were critical of this, that, for example, he spent more time talking about the James Brothers' robberies than about the financing of railroads, that he describes Billy the Kid at length as one of the most remarkable characters of the West but says not a word about the organizing and financing of the great cattle companies (*Mississippi Valley Historical Review* 18:575).

Riegel could turn a good phrase -- "some men found outlawry more interesting than cutting trees," (p. 94, 2d ed.) for example, or, describing Creole women, "voluptuous charms on a moonlit river helped one forget the clouds of mosquitoes" (p. 264). He often thought in the stereotypes of his era and background. Steamboat daredevils were "the sporting southern element" (p. 227). He talks about the "happy and carefree Negroes on the river" (p. 230) and followed this with the words of a "Negro" song that took up a page and a half and began "A dancin' up de river, a dancin' down again." An example he offered of the colorfulness of western speech was unfortunate--"dumb as a dead nigger in a mudhole" (p. 230). But his flip phrases often reflected an inner sensitivity, that westerners did things that were wrong--"killing Indians was like killing snakes," for example (p. 57), or that the Chickasaw met smallpox and the Choctaw and "subsequent Chickasaw history is no subject for the sensitive investigator" (p. 311). He describes at length the significance of the Mormons in settling the desert West, but in a few pungent sentences, conveys unmistakably that the origin of the denomination was bizarre in the extreme. Similarly, just a few sentences on the Chivington Massacre leaves the reader thoroughly jolted, even one who has read it elsewhere.

The second edition probably deserves to be kept in print as a pleasant supplement to whatever more scholarly history one wishes to read about the West. The third edition retains much of the second's flavor, but he tempers some of his more pungent phrases. The fourth edition, written with Robert Athearn, eliminated most of what made the earlier editions fun. The anecdotes were mostly gone, like the one about "Col. Plug" who ran a tavern at Cairo, Illinois, whose wife "Pluggy" would entertain the river boys in her boudoir while the colonel robbed their boat and drilled a hole in the bottom so the victims and the evidence would vanish shortly after they left dock (p. 94, 2d ed.). These stories were probably apocryphal--Riegel suggests as much--and were responsible for giving "cowboys and Indians" courses a bad name in days gone by. But without them, the fourth edition has no color. The incisive phrases about the Mormons are gone. Now they are protrayed as just another denomination on the smorgasbord of denominations. There is nothing in the way of ideas or theories to replace the color. The fifth edition has extensive illustrations and maps interspersed through the text to give color to what is otherwise a dull book.

Riegel's college textbook in American history, *The American Story*, written with David F. Long, and published in 1955, had the clear and delightful style that Riegel had perfected, but there was little to distinguish it. It spends only thirty-six pages on the colonial period before 1763 (and that includes paragraphs that attempt to integrate all of European history since the Renaissance). It is disasterously weak on politics and economics. It did make a stab at integrating events in Europe with those in the United States, and it did attempt to incorporate some Latin American history (although no attempt is made to compare the United States and Latin America). It includes the social history that he loved. It is good on Indians. But overall, it is not a memorable textbook.

Young America, 1830-1840 was published in 1949 by the University of Oklahoma Press. It was a project dear to Riegel's heart and the flower of his mature writing. His idea was to examine every facet of life in the republic at a moment when a culture shaped by self-reliance and the frontier was becoming organized, industrialized, corporatized, and civilized. He describes life in the seaboard cities, in the West, on the frontier, in factories, on farms, on plantations, the life of slaves, the life of Indians, the life of women, the life of children, their homes, their churches, their schools, their doctors, their teachers, their sports, their art, their literature, their science--everything. It is based on newspapers, periodicals, travel accounts, some diaries, and letters.

Riegel's readable writing style is at its peak, although he never lets himself go, nor takes the time to tell stories in the way that made Mark Sullivan's treatment of the period 1900 to 1920 so delightful in the *Our Times* series. Riegel avoids a pitfall that damaged other examinations of a specific period of time, namely a subtitle like "fabulous forties" or "feminine fifties" which tended to emphasize eccentricities. In some ways, his attention to women and feminism is ahead of his time, and on this matter, including sex, he did not speak in euphemisms. His frankness caught at least one reviewer, Wood Grey, by surprise, who thought the frank references were intrusive while admitting that he, the reviewer, was probably a "fuddy duddy" (*American Historical Review* 55:925). The work did manage to develop a theme of sorts, although it never quite emerges as a hypothesis, that the age was characterized by the hypocrisy between its mawkish righteousness and its no-holds-barred pursuit of money.

But *Young America* was not received well at the time nor is it a great book now. Like *The Story of the Western Railroads*, it tries to do too much without doing anything very well. Grey, in the review cited above, said its opening chapter was like an operatic overture that was followed by a flying trip of a tourist who sees everything but only for a momentary glimpse. There is no analysis, no interpretation, just an enormous pile of stuff left for the reader to sort out. It is peppered with generalizations that have no supporting evidence. These generalizations sometimes contradict each other, sometimes within the space of a single page--the statement saying that immigrants were "fleeced of their small funds" (p. 29), for example, was followed by one saying they "with rare exceptions, were given excellent treatment in the United States" (p. 30). In his review for the

Journal of Southern History, Bennett Wall says he simply questions the value or meaning of such statements (16:540). "The social historian has learned his craft but not his art," says Alice Felt in her review in *Saturday Review*. "He's a good craftsman--precision of detail of the intricacy of a jigsaw puzzle, but when the picture is complete, it has no life or meaning. The stage is set with all the props, but without the action whose motives might give it significance" (33:11).

Riegel's last two books were about women in the United States. The first, *American Feminists*, describes and compares the lives of women whose primary reform interest was feminists--Elizabeth Cady Stanton, Susan B. Anthony, Lucy Stone, and others. It is a slender volume, written in his usually delightful style, that brings together a lot of material on a few key women. It was criticized for being too narrow in its focus, however, by excluding men who contributed to the feminist cause and women who were active in other causes besides feminism. His portraits are tempered. He describes women who were moral, rational, and complex, dedicated but not obsessed, who worked for limited goals within the structure of society. There is no sensationalism. Even his speculation on their sex lives is unsensational, perhaps because he concludes they did not have sex lives. He is sympathetic to their cause, but in the past tense, that changes were appropriate once upon a time but everything is arranged satisfactorily in the present. There are gaps, "frustrating blanks where some climaxes are expected" said Gerald Christoph in his review in the *American Quarterly* (16:502). His conclusions are weak, limited to summarizing the obvious. He ends with a gratuitous statement that people are happiest when sex roles are well defined. The book appeared in 1963 on the eve of the women's movement of the late twentieth century, but Riegel seems to have little sense he was in the vanguard of something new. Instead, the tone is that of preserving, as in a museum, something that was over and done.

His last book, *American Women*, is a failed book. It is another of his kaleidoscopic treatments, this one tracing women's role in society from Revolutionary War times to what he calls "to date," although his treatment of the entire twentieth century is too sketchy to have any value. The book was published in 1970, but incorporated none of the research or ideas that were exploding in that field from the mid-1960s on. It was not widely reviewed, and its few notices suggested it was not an important contribution.

Riegel wrote a number of articles in his lifetime. Most of them were by-products of his book research, the railroad articles limited to his early career, most of his articles on women coming in the 1960s. His talents as a writer showed brilliantly when he dealt with a limited topic that had a precise focus. His article, "The American Father of Birth Control," that appeared in the *New England Quarterly* in 1933, was probably his best single piece of writing. It is a wonderful story about a Dr. Charles Knowlton, a not-very-likeable eccentric who paid his way through what passed for a medical education on the New England frontier by robbing graves, who described the concept of behaviorism fifty years before it as called behaviorism, and whose book on contraception sold hundreds of thousands of copies in the United States and England. It is a story that weaves together attitudes toward women and sex, medical education in the early nineteenth century, and the practice of medicine on the frontier. Riegel's articles on phrenology are similarly valuable and memorable contributions.

Riegel sought to take the myth out of subjects he wrote about. He tells a few tall tales in *America Moves West* to show how the concept of the West came to loom so large in the world's imagination. But mostly, he de-romanticizes--the cowboy, the Indian wars, railroad building. He does not see American domination of the West as some God-sanctioned Manifest Destiny. He sees westerners as rather self-centered people, though not bad people, who went out and took what they wanted and who did not have too many scruples about what they did. "Whether at the Boston Tea Party or in the snowy wastes of Alaska, Americans have seldom been docile conformists," he writes in *America Moves West.* "When conditions served them badly, they acted directly and vigorously--if on the right side or the law, then well and good, but the mere existence of law has never been an effective deterrent"(p. 534, 2d ed.).

He was sharply critical of others who did try to perpetuate myths. Of *Stagecoach North*, Storrs Lee's history of frontier Vermont, he notes the author's insistence on the independence and self-reliance of the early settlers was belied by virtually all the evidence he brought to bear (*American Historical Review* 47:428). He wrote a scathing review of Walter McCaleb's book, *The Conquest of the West.* McCaleb protrayed the defenders of the Alamo as God-like heroes, Santa Ana and his men as curs, Andrew Jackson as the greatest patriot whoever lived, John Quincy Adams as a traitor and tool of European monarchies. Riegel says these conclusions did not square with the facts. McCaleb fired off a sneering communication to the *Mississippi Valley Historical Review* about the "learned professor" who was "saturated with New England bias." Riegel was cool, and responded again that facts did not support McCaleb's interpretation no matter how much "yahoo" westerners might want to believe it (35:536-538).

Despite his personal political conservatism, Riegel was a quintessential academic liberal of the 1940s and 1950s era. He questioned certain prevailing attitudes but felt no great need to try to change them. In *The Story of the Western Railroads*, he emphasizes that government, not private enterprise, made possible the initial railroad construction in the West, but he never really hits the reader with what the implications of this were. In *America Moves West*, he leaves no doubt that he thought what was done to the Indians was morally repugnant, and yet he seems to accept that what was done was done, and in the long run was probably for the best, or at least inevitable. In 1945, when Robert S. Henry published his now famous article, "The Railroad Land Grant Legend in American History Texts" (which demonstrated that railroads probably received less land and paid more for land than was generally perceived), Riegel was one of several historians who responded with denunciations (*Mississippi Valley Historical Review* 32:171-194). Riegel was not among those who impugned Henry simply because he (Henry) worked for the Association of American Railroads. (Henry's historical method was good and stood the test of time no matter who his employer was at the time.) But in a knee-jerk kind of way, Riegel reasserted that it was known fact that railroads were bloodsuckers (32:565-566). Henry responded to Riegel, easily refuting the few facts Riegel had offered to make his point, even catching Riegel in contradictions of the facts he had offered (33:116).

In all of Riegel's work, it seemed he wanted to tell a story first, and then sought out the materials he needed to tell it--newspapers, periodicals, a few archival sources here and there, old secondary accounts. It never appeared to be an exhaustive or definitive research. This is not to say he reached foregone conclusions. He never reached many conclusions at all. But though he wanted to tell a good story, he was too conscientious to exaggerate and was critical of those (like McCaleb) who did. That is why his books are flat without being good history. He was criticized for being too short on statistics and interpretation and too long on adjectives and generalities. But in a review of *Then Came the Railroads*, Riegel complains that author Ira G. Clark had too many names, too much detail, called for a "more generous use of adjectives," and wanted "factual details pruned ruthlessly." He said the advice came to him from Frederic Paxson who warned not to bog the readers down in details they would never remember (*American Historical Review* 64:198).

Riegel could spot his own inability to draw conclusions in others. He complained that John Stover's book, *American Railroads*, needed a lot more stress on analysis and interpretation (*Mississippi Valley Historical Review* 48:318-319). Yet he never seemed to see the fault in himself. And by the 1960s, new historical techniques were clearly passing him by. In his review of Robert Fogel's *The Union Pacific Railroad: A Case Study in Premature Enterprise*, he misses the significance of the new statistical method entirely. Judging the book by the standards of traditional history, he could only find it puzzling (*American Historical Review* 68:820). By the time he reviewed Fogel's next book, *Railroads and American Economic Growth*, he is aware, or had been made aware, that the new econometric approach was significant and controversial, but he could not seem to explain why, and ends with something of a sigh, that historians would probably have to get used to mathematical tools (*Journal of American History* 52:635-636).

It is the tragedy of Robert Riegel that his significant contribution to historical writing was *The Story of the Western Railroads*, a product of his professional youth, limited by its origin as a doctoral dissertation. The rest of his work was too constrained by gentility, by the limits of his imagination, and by an unwillingness to do tough work in the archives to have lasting value. Even *The Story*, though it remains an important volume, is neither brilliant nor exciting nor definitive and will almost certainly be replaced someday by a volume that is one or all of those things. And yet his work helped shape thinking about the West, by scholars who read *The Story*, and by countless students in countless American frontier courses who read *America Moves West* and chuckled over the likes of Col. Plug and his lovely wife Pluggy, sitting in their tavern, waiting for the next raft to come down the Ohio.

Bibliography

Books

America Moves West. New York: Henry Holt & Company., 1930; 2d ed., 1947; 3d ed., 1956. Co-authored with Robert G. Athearn, 4th ed., New York: Holt, Rinehart & Winston, 1964; 5th ed., 1971.

American Feminists. Lawrence: University Press of Kansas, 1963.

The American Story. Co-authored with David F. Long. 2 volumes. New York: McGraw-Hill, 1955.

American Women. Rutherford, NJ: Fairleigh Dickenson University Press, 1970.

Introduction to the Social Sciences. Edited with W. L. Eager, Francis E. Merrill, and others. New York: D. Appleton-Century, 1941.

The Story of the Western Railroads. New York: Macmillan, 1926. Reprint. Lincoln: University of Nebraska Press, 1964 and 1977.

United States of America. Co-authored with Helen Haugh. New York: Scribners, 1947, 1948, 1949, 1951, and 1953.

Young America, 1830-1840. Norman: University of Oklahoma Press, 1949. Reprint. Westport, CT: Greenwood Press, 1973.

Articles

"American Father of Birth Control." *New England Quarterly* 6(September, 1933):470-490.

"The Birth Control Controversy." Co-authored with Lawrence Eager. *Current History* 36(August, 1932):563-568.

"Changing Attitudes Towards Prostitution, 1800-1920." *Journal of the History of Ideas* 29(July, 1968):437-452.

"Early Phrenology in the United States." *Medical Life* 37(July, 1930):361-376.

"Federal Operation of Southern Railroads During the Civil War." *Mississippi Valley Historical Review* 9(September, 1922):126-138.

"Introduction of Phrenology to the United States." *American Historical Review* 39(October, 1933):73-78.

"The Missouri Pacific Railroad to 1879." *Missouri Historical Review* 18(April, 1923):3-26.

"The Missouri Pacific Railroad, 1879-1900." *Missouri Historical Review* 18(July, 1924):173-196.

"The Omaha Pool." *Iowa Journal of History and Politics* 22(October, 1924):569-582.

"The Southwestern Pool." *Missouri Historical Review* 19(April, 1924):12-24.

"The Split in the Feminist Movement in 1869." *Mississippi Valley Historical Review* 49(December, 1962):485-496.

"Standard Time in the United States." *American Historical Review* 33(October, 1927):84-89.

"Trans Mississippi Railroads During the Fifties." *Mississippi Valley Historical Review* 10(September, 1923):153-172.

"Western Railroad Pools." *Mississippi Valley Historical Review* 18(December, 1931):364-377.

"Women's Clothes and Women's Rights." *American Quarterly* 25(Fall, 1963):390-401.

Reviews

The American Diaries of Richard Cobden by Elizabeth Coon Hawley. *American Historical Review* 58(April, 1953):507.

The American Lyceum: Town Meeting of the Mind by Carl Bode. *Mississippi Valley Historical Review* 43(June, 1956):120-121.

American Railroads by John Stover. *Mississippi Valley Historical Review* 48(September, 1961):318-319.

American Railroads: Four Phases of Their History by Winthrop M. Daniels. *Mississippi Valley Historical Review* 19(November, 1933):631-632.

Andrew D. White and the Modern University by Walter P. Rogers. *Mississippi Valley Historical Review* 29(December, 1942):418-419.

Ben Holliday, the Stagecoach King: A Chapter in the Development of Transcontinental Transportation by J. V. Frederick. *American Historical Review* 46(April, 1941):683.

Brigham Young, the Colonizer by Milton R. Hunter. *Mississippi Valley Historical Review* 29(March, 1943):598-599.

British Essays in American History edited by H. C. Allen and C. P. Hill. *American Historical Review* 63(October, 1957):130.

Centennial History of the South Carolina Railroad by Samuel M. Derrick. *Mississippi Valley Historical Review* 18(December, 1931):445.

The Conquest of the West by Walter F. McCaleb. *Mississippi Valley Historical Review* 35(June, 1948):120-121.

Dear Preceptor: The Life and Times of Thomas Wentworth Higginson by Anna Mary Wells. *Mississippi Valley Historical Review* 50(December, 1963):508-509.

End of Track by James H. Kyner. *Mississippi Valley Historical Review* 24(June, 1937):126.

The First Transcontinental Railroad: Central Pacific, Union Pacific by John Debo Galloway. *Mississippi Valley Historical Review* 37(March, 1951):732-733.

The Great American Desert Then and Now by W. Eugene Hollon. *American Historical Review* 72(October, 1966):304.

Gulf to the Rockies: The Heritage of the Fort Worth & Denver and Colorado & Southern Railways by Richard C. Overton. *Mississippi Valley Historical Review* 41(June, 1954):146-147.

A History of Texas Railroads by S. G. Reed. *Mississippi Valley Historical Review* 29(June, 1942):110-111.

A History of Transportation in the Ohio Valley with Special Reference to its Waterways, Trade, Commerce from the Earliest Period to the

Present Time by Charles H. Ambler. *Mississippi Valley Historical Review* 19(June, 1932):118.

The Jacksonian Persuasion: Politics and Belief by Marvin Meyers. *Mississippi Valley Historical Review* 44(March, 1958):730-731.

The Katy Railroad and the Last Frontier by V. V. Masterson. *American Historical Review* 58(January, 1953):469.

Mapping the Trans-Mississippi West, 1540-1861: Volume II, from Lewis and Clark to Fremont, 1804-1845 by Carl I. Wheat. *American Historical Review* 65(October, 1959):139.

Mapping the Trans-Mississippi West, 1540-1861: Volume III from the Mexican War to the Boundary Surveys, 1846-1854 by Carl I. Wheat. *American Historical Review* 66(October, 1960):233.

March of the Iron Men: A Social History of the Union through Invention by Roger Burlingame. *Mississippi Valley Historical Review* 24(March, 1939):583-584.

Men, Cities and Transportation: A Study in New England History, 1820-1900 by Edward C. Kirkland. *Mississippi Valley Historical Review* 35(December, 1948):508-509.

Men of Erie: A Story of Human Effort by Edward Hungerford. *Mississippi Valley Historical Review* 33(March, 1947):662.

The Northern Railroads in the Civil War, 1861-1865 by Thomas Weber. *Mississippi Valley Historical Review* 39(March, 1953):770.

A Pathfinder in the Southwest: The Itinerary of Lieutenant A. W. Whipple During his Exploration for a Railway Route from Fort Smith to Los Angeles in the Years 1853 and 1854 edited by Grant Foreman. *Mississippi Valley Historical Review* 28(September, 1941):302-303.

The Persistence of the Westward Movement and Other Essays by John Carl Parish. *Mississippi Valley Historical Review* 30(September, 1943):260-261.

A Pioneer in Northwest America, 1841-1858: The Memoirs of Gustaf Unonius, Volume I edited and translated by Nils William Olsson. *Mississippi Valley Historical Review* 38(June, 1951):114-115.

The Railroad in Literature: A Brief Survey of Railroad Fiction, Poetry, Songs, Biography, Essays, Travel and Drama in the English Language Particularly Emphasizing the Place in American Literature by Frank P. Donovan. *Mississippi Valley Historical Review* 28(June, 1941):121-122.

Railroad Leaders, 1845-1890: The Business Mind in Action by Thomas C. Cochran. *American Historical Review* 59(April, 1954):648.

Railroads and American Economic Growth: Essays in Econometric History by Robert Fogel. *Journal of American History* 52(December, 1965):635-636.

Railroads and Rivers: The Story of Inland Transportation by William H. Clark. *Mississippi Valley Historical Review* 26(December, 1939):415.

Readings in the Economic and Social History of the United States edited by Felix Flugel and Harold U. Faulkner. *Mississippi Valley Historical Review* 17(March, 1931):662-663.

Singin' Yankees by Philip D. Jordan. *American Historical Review* 52(January, 1947):340.

Son of Thunder: Patrick Henry by Julia H. Carson. *American Historical Review* 51(January, 1946):382.

Stagecoach North: Being an Account of the First Generation of the State of Vermont by Storrs Lee. *American Historical Review* 47(January, 1942):428.

State of Vermont by Storrs Lee. *American Historical Review* 47(January, 1942):428.

Their Majesties the Mob by John W. Caughey. *Mississippi Valley Historical Review* 47(September, 1960):333-335.

Then Came the Railroads: The Century from Steam to Diesel in the Southwest by Ira G. Clark. *American Historical Review* 64(October, 1958):198.

They Built the West: An Epic of Rails and Cities by Glenn Chesney Quiett. *Mississippi Valley Historical Review* 21(March, 1935):572.

Trails, Rails and War: The Life of General G. M. Dodge by J. R. Perkins. *Mississippi Valley Historical Review* 16(December, 1929):416-418.

The Union Pacific Railroad: A Case Study in Premature Enterprise by Robert Fogel. *American Historical Review* 66(April, 1961):820.

Studies of Robert Edgar Riegel

Benson, Mary S. Review of *American Feminists* by Robert Riegel. *Mississippi Valley Historical Review* 50(March, 1964):690-691.

Briggs, Harold. "An Appraisal of Historical Writings of the Great Plains Region Since 1920." *Mississippi Valley Historical Review* 34(June, 1947):83-100.

Carstensen, Vernon. Review of *America Moves West* by Robert Riegel. *Mississippi Valley Historical Review* 34(September, 1947):279-280.

Christoph, Gerald. Review of *American Feminists* by Robert Riegel. *American Quarterly* 16(Fall, 1964):502.

"Communications." *Mississippi Valley Historical Review* 32(January, 1946):565-566; 33(June, 1946):116; 35(December, 1948):536-538.

Craven, Avery. Review of *Young America, 1830-1840* by Robert Riegel. *Mississippi Valley Historical Review* 37(September, 1950):327-328.

Daggett, Stuart. Review of *The Story of the Western Railroads* by Robert Riegel. *American Historical Review* 32(January, 1927):372-373.

Felt, Alice. Review of *Young America, 1830-1840* by Robert Riegel. *Saturday Review of Literature* 33(January 21, 1950):11.

Grey, Wood. Review of *Young America, 1830-1840* by Robert Riegel. *American Historical Review* 55(July, 1952):925.

Hedges, James B. Review of *The Story of the Western Railroads* by Robert Riegel. *Mississippi Valley Historical Review* 13(March, 1927):592-593.

Jensen, Billie Barnes. Review of *America Moves West* by Robert Riegel. *Journal of the West* 11(January, 1972):188.

Lindeman, Edward C. Review of *Introduction to the Social Sciences* edited by Robert Riegel. *American Journal of Sociology* 47(March, 1942):772.

Pelzer, Louis. Review of *America Moves West* by Robert Riegel. *Mississippi Valley Historical Review* 18(March, 1932):575.

Taylor, A. Elizabeth. Review of *American Feminists* by Robert Riegel. *American Historical Review* 69(Junary, 1964):546-547.

[Unsigned] Review of *The Story of the Western Railroads* by Robert Riegel. *Choice* 1(October, 1964):337.

Wall, Bennett. Review of *Young America, 1830-1840* by Robert Riegel. *Journal of Southern History* 16(November, 1950):540.

White, Howard. Review of *Introduction to the Social Sciences* edited by Robert Riegel. *American Political Science Review* 35(1941):1022.

Wyllys, Rufus K. Review of *America Moves West* by Robert Riegel. *American Historical Review* 37(January, 1932):811.

39

CARL COKE RISTER

by Rebecca Herring

Biography

Named for the county of his birth, Carl Coke Rister was born to Craton and Sarah Parker Rister on June 30, 1889, near the small post office community of Hayrick, Texas. The Risters settled in the new village of McCaulley in Fisher County, Texas, while he was still a boy. His father, a Baptist preacher, ministered to small congregations on Sundays, and worked at temporal tasks throughout the week to support his growing family.

Strongly influenced by his father's religious faith, as well as by the stark power of the West Texas landscape and the hardiness of those who inhabited it, Rister grew to young manhood with three passions; Baptist fundamentalism, southwestern history, and baseball. Each would follow him throughout his life.

After attending McCaulley High School, Rister considered briefly a career in professional baseball. As a left-handed pitcher for the local scrub team, he attracted not only the admiration of local boys such as future historian William Curry Holden, but also the attention of an Abilene, Texas, banker who offered him a job if he would play out the season with the Abilene Baseball Club. A late train, Rister reported years later, was all that prevented his pursuing this opportunity. While waiting with bags packed for the local that would carry him to a new life as a professional athlete, he had time to reconsider his decision. Fearing the instability and short life of a baseball career, he changed his mind and left the station (*Arizona and the West* 14:317).

He did go to Abilene within the year, however, this time to attend Simmons College. There his interest in the Southwest and its heritage was nurtured. Working his way through school as a tailor, he was graduated in 1915 with a B.A. in social science. He married Mattie May of Hamlin, Texas, in 1916. They would remain childless, both dedicated to Rister's work as an evangelist of the Southwest's unique heritage.

The young couple lived first in McCaulley, where Rister served as superintendent of the community schools for one year before moving to Washington, DC. There he worked for the U.S. Treasury Department and attended night classes at George Washington University, earning a M.A. in 1920. Drawn back to the Southwest, he spent the next several years teaching classes at Simmons, and attending summer classes at the University of California at Berkeley under borderlands historian Herbert Eugene Bolton. A return to George Washington University as both instructor and student allowed him to complete his graduate work, receiving a Ph.D. in 1925. His dissertation, one of the first frontier histories focusing on the Southwest, was published as *The Southwestern Frontier, 1865-1881* by the Arthur H. Clark Company in 1928.

Once again returning to Abilene, he resumed teaching at his alma mater and continued his research work in southwestern topics. Instrumental in the formative years of the West Texas Historical Association, he served as editor of the organization's yearbook from 1925 to 1929. Hoping to fill a void in the formal historical study of the region, he combed both government documents and public records heretofore ignored by historians. From these sources he pulled the stories of buffalo hunters, land speculators, Indian raiders, and pioneers that he would tell, and retell, in his writings.

In 1929 Rister was offered a position as associate professor at the University of Oklahoma in Norman. During his twenty-two years there he would earn a national reputation for his work, producing ten books as well as dozens of articles and book reviews for scholarly journals. In addition to teaching classes, he served for a short time as chair of the history department, and later as professor, and research historian. He often spent summers as a visiting professor, teaching classes at various universities and colleges throughout the country in order to make use of research facilities at each institution. George Washington University, the University of Texas at Austin, Denver University, the University of Colorado, the University of Missouri, and Highlands University of New Mexico, all were recipients of these working research trips.

A serious man who looked askance at frivolity and idleness, Rister devoted all his time to his profession. His "strong sense of moral rectitude," "firm belief in rugged individualism" and the "virtues of hard work," as well as his "unwavering faith in the ultimate triumph of good over evil," affected his entire life (*Great Plains Journal* 18:120-121). Although he remained a sports fan, and loved to fish and play golf, he rarely was comfortable away from his work. While humorless and uninspiring in the classroom, he was dedicated and detailed, rarely referring to notes while lecturing for hours on his beloved Southwest. His students respected his knowledge of the subject and his willingness to make time for serious inquiries or discussions. He formed strong relationships with young scholars, giving advice on research topics, primary resources, and research and writing techniques. His life-long devotion to the Baptist church and adherence to temperate behavior, however, did not make him totally intolerant to intemperance in others. Although he neither smoked, drank, nor cussed, he was known on at least one occasion to pour a glass of wine for a bewildered graduate student. He did frown, however, on practical jokes and any lack of devotion to scholarship in his students.

This no-nonsense approach to hard work was not without its rewards. He served as president of the Mississippi Valley Historical Association from 1949-1950, and as a member of its executive board from 1946-1955. He, in addition, was a fellow of the Society of American Historians, the Social Science Research Council of New York, the American Philosophical Society, the American Geographical Society, and the Texas State Historical Association. He was a member of nine professional organizations, serving as an officer in almost all of them. In 1942, Hardin-Simmons University awarded him with an honorary LL.D. degree.

In 1951, lured by a high salary, the expectation of more time for research, and the possibility of greater prestige, Rister accepted the position of Distinguished Professor at Texas Technological College. Established by Graduate Dean William Curry Holden who hoped to strengthen Tech's graduate and research programs, the distinguished professorship had been designed to attract nationally renowned scholars to the college. Unfortunately, neither the program, nor Rister's stay at Texas Tech, proceeded as envisioned.

Rister arrived in Lubbock planning to continue work on his new-found research interest, the western oil industry. He also was charged to begin formal organizational plans for the "Southwest Collection," a regional repository designed to document West Texas, South Plains, and southwestern history. Instead he was faced with the ill will of fellow faculty members, and with a non-cooperative administration that did not fulfill promises for office facilities and clerical help to pursue research projects. Although local newspaper articles issued a call for family papers, business records, and photographs, little was accomplished formally on the proposed manuscript repository (Holden interview; Rister file).

Denied both the academic respect and the facilities he felt he deserved, Rister instead concentrated his efforts on editing and preparing for publication two manuscripts concerning Indian/Anglo conflicts in nineteenth-century Texas. He, in addition, worked tirelessly, traveling throughout West Texas in order to speak to interested groups in small communities. It was while in the midst of one such trip that his work ended. Rister died unexpectedly of a heart attack in Rotan, Texas, on April 16, 1955, at the age of sixty-five. Memorial services were conducted at the First Baptist Church in Lubbock, Texas.

There were those who felt that these traumatic final years at Texas Tech hastened Rister's death. A worrier by nature, his dissatisfaction with his situation at the college possibly had caused ulcers and other health problems. He accomplished in death, however, what he had been unable to in life. Mattie May Rister, his widow, sold to the college his southwestern library and personal papers containing the research material that documented his historical career. This material, when added to the ranch records and southwestern books already held by the college, would become the core of Texas Tech's modern-day Southwest Collection, a regional manuscript repository dedicated to perpetuating the heritage of the American Southwest.

Themes

When Carl Coke Rister was born in newly created Coke County, Texas, in mid-1889, the region was as yet a part of that southwestern frontier he would devote his professional life to describing. Then thinly populated by struggling farm and ranch families, West Texas would grow within Rister's lifetime to one of the richest agricultural areas in the nation. Attributing that growth to the optimism, resourcefulness, hard work, and adaptability of the Southwest's Anglo settlers, Rister dedicated his historical writing to glorifying their accomplishments and defending their offenses.

Rister's thirteen books and dozens of articles focus on the American Southwest's evolution from wilderness to a "land of prosperous communities and happy homes." (*Southwestern Frontier*, p. 19). Before this change could take place, however, many obstacles had to be overcome. A hostile environment was the most obvious hindrance. Bitter winter cold contrasted with dry, wind-blown summer heat, and timber for both shelter and fuel was scarce. Threatening animal life, from lobo wolves and coyotes to rattlesnakes and scorpions, provided an ever present danger. To these annoyances were added the constant fear of Indian attack, both real and imagined. The forced isolation resulting from the absence of transportation and communication lines intensified these problems. Rister's pioneers, however, "brought law and order to a land without law, dug a meager subsistence from a wind-blown soil, and survived the extreme hardships of pioneering" (*No Man's Land*, p. vi).

Underlying Rister's work is the assumption that continued U.S. territorial expansion throughout the Southwest was not only inevitable, but desirable. The Indians who stood in the way of that expansion were not always to blame for their actions, but nevertheless were "vindictive savages" and "backward people" (*Border Captives*, p. ix; *Greater Southwest*, p. 28). The Indian condition would be improved by exposure to both the hard-working, God-fearing example of Anglo pioneer stock, and the educational opportunities and moral training provided by agents of the government. The United States therefore was justified in using military force to defeat and control the native population. While a few innocent Indians possibly were harmed in the process, the end results of "enlightenment and progress" more than justified the means (*Southwestern Frontier*, pp. 20-21; *Greater Southwest*, p. 486). Anglo settlement, Rister maintains, added "to the wealth of the nation and the happiness of all the people" (*Border Command*, p. 196). "Order followed chaos; millions of homeless people found prosperous homes in what . . . had been a desolate lonely Indian country; and hundreds of thriving towns and cities supplanted squalid Indian encampments. Thus, the white man's culture transformed the 'desert'" (p. 215).

Rister's southwestern frontier is characterized by both good and evil. The latter was personified by unscrupulous traders, dishonest agents, outlaws, claim jumpers, vigilantes, prostitutes, and gamblers, as well as by Indians. The failure of those Indians to "adopt civilization," he reports, was due at least in part to exposure to this "low plane of morality." The early absence of government and formal legal restraints made the region a haven of sin and corruption where "the revolver settled more differences among men than the judge" (*Fort Griffin*, p. 132).

This "wild west" image was tempered, however, by the enterprising citizens and "border heroines" who brought eventual stability and order to the region. In an era when traditional historians focused their attention on the dastardly deeds or heroic accomplishments of men, Rister purposely points out the many contributions of--and unusual hardships faced by--the region's women settlers. Although he concentrates his praise on women's traditional role of making "easier and more endurable the lives of those they loved (p. 46)." his interest in the cultural aspects of southwestern history allowed him to explore nontraditional subjects. Typical forms of entertainment, housing, household goods, clothing, hospitality, home remedies, and religion all receive his attention.

The Southwest, Rister stresses, was unique, and therefore required unique people to settle it. Only strong, optimistic, adaptable frontierspeople could survive the combined hardships of aridity, inhospitable terrain, lawlessness, and Indian raids offered by the region. The same characteristics that allowed them to survive, in addition, ensured that the social, economic, and political institutions developed in the Southwest would differ from those of the East. The cultural baggage they carried west, he maintains, was soon adapted to southwestern realities.

While much of his writing seems to glorify the stories of Indian atrocities, buffalo hunts, military campaigns, and vigilante justice of a wild and romantic Southwest, Rister did not mourn the frontier's passing. Always concentrating on the "foundations of civilization in the Southwest," he boasts that "the region which was once the hunting grounds of the nomadic red man now supports one of the most prosperous centers of Anglo-Saxon civilization to be found in the United States" (*Southwestern Frontier*, p. 307).

Analysis

Rister, dedicated to narrative history, rarely ventures into analysis or interpretation. To Rister, the facts, when presented in a meticulous and orderly fashion, provided all the information a reader required to gain an understanding of the region's past. Rendering the utmost attention to detail, Rister often begins his books with an in-depth survey of the Southwest's land forms, wildlife, vegetation, earliest inhabitants, and first European explorers. This emphasis on factual details is most obvious in his handling of military subjects. Play-by-play accounts of battles, military campaigns, construction of forts, and descriptions of daily life often make up the bulk of these monographs.

Almost Victorian in nature, Rister's earliest works are tied more closely to the nineteenth century than to the twentieth. Boasting five and six line subtitles, tables of contents providing in-depth descriptions of each chapter, and romantic introductions comparing America's search for free land with Moses leading the children of Israel across the Red Sea, or prairie schooners with sixteenth-century sailing ships, these books relate stories of heroic white settlers pitted against border ruffians and "bloodthirsty savages."

Rister's ethnocentric views of southwestern cultural differences sometimes are subtle, more often blatantly stated. To him, Indians, among other traits similarly uncomplimentary, are "cruel," "vindictive," "backward," "primitive," "savage," and "given to sexual improprieties" (*Border Captives*, pp. ix, 24; *Greater Southwest*, p. 28). Because Mexican inhabitants were generally very poor and often of Indian blood (and therefore of a lower form of life), they readily adopted Indian ways when taken captive by warring tribes. Their captors soon discovered, on the other hand, "that 'Indianizing' Texas [Anglo] women was far more difficult. . . . The vast gulf between red and white cultural plains was too wide to be easily bridged" (*Border Captives*, pp. 58-59, 62). Even Anglo men who frequented border outposts were "cruelly changed" by "border rawness." "Some were Mexicanized, and others were Indianized," rendering them unrecognizable (*Border Command*, p. 36). Those who successfully settled the region, he maintains, "were of Anglo-Saxon ancestry. A bold, progressive race of people attacked these problems with all the aggressiveness characteristic of this race and soon brought about a better era" (*Southwestern Frontier*, p. 263).

Rister's work shows a preoccupation with proving that America's native population had "too often been cast in a noble role" (*Border Captives*, p. 196) while at the same time defending the actions of the United States military. In his description of the Battle of Washita, he states adamantly that Custer ordered his men to not fire on women and children. A few were killed in the confusion of the battle, however, when they "subjected themselves to the danger of stray bullets" (*Border Command*, p. 107). "In all truth," he maintains, "the savagery of the Southern plains tribes was remarkable even to their Indian contemporaries" (*Border Captives*, p. 196). Concentrating on the "stark realism, of primitive Indian life, and of terrible cruelty and grim tragedy," he claims to "reveal to . . . readers the price which our pioneers paid for laying well the basis of our present southwestern life" (*Comanche Bondage*, p. 17).

Between 1925 and 1955 Rister authored, or co-authored, thirteen books and an estimated fifty articles and book reviews. Published in 1928, *The Southwestern Frontier* was his first major work. Asserting that the Southwest had been ignored by former historians, he traces the Indian/Anglo conflict, the problems faced by settlers, the development of the cattle industry, and the growth and economic impact of southwestern railroads. Although the book is criticized for presenting a "rather dreary story of Indian wars," and dwelling too much on early details, Rister is complemented for the "extensive use of sources which hitherto . . . received little attention," and for providing the "most satisfactory unified account" of the region for that time period (*American Historical Review* 34:625-627).

Rister moved to the University of Oklahoma the following year, and would produce ten additional books during his twenty-two year stay there. Two more, polished during his four years at Texas Tech, would be published after his death. *The Greater Southwest* with Rupert Richardson in 1934, and *Western America* with LeRoy R. Hafen in 1941, are text books designed to provide students with an overview of western exploration and the economic, social, and military history of the American West and Southwest. *Southern Plainsmen* (1938), on the other hand, is a cultural account of the region--focusing on the Anglo settlers who "civilized" the area and the unique institutions they developed to combat the problems posed by the region's harsh environment. In these four works Rister introduces the themes and stories that he simply would expand in most of his other works. With the exception of one book, he never deals with a new topic again.

Each of these four works is commended for breaking new ground in western and southwestern studies, for utilizing documents that had been ignored up to that time, and for humanizing history by presenting character sketches of individuals. Each is criticized, however, for sloppy, uneven work, for errors in fact, and for concentrating too heavily on details not always pertinent to the subject (*American Historical Review* 40:794-795, 47:368-369; *Mississippi Valley Historical Review* 21:567-569, 25:573-574; *Southwestern Historical Quarterly* 42:418-419, 45:117-119). All of these characteristics, both good and bad, would continue in the balance of Rister's work.

Border Captives, released in 1940, and *Comanche Bondage*, published posthumously in 1955, concern the trade in captive Mexican and Anglo women and children practiced by the southern plains Indians between 1835 and 1875. *Comanche Bondage* contains an edited reprint of the *Narrative of the Captivity of Mrs. Horn and Her Two Children, With Mrs. Harris, by the Comanche Indians*, first published in 1839. In an additional seventy-page introduction setting the stage for the story, and explanatory footnotes which help to elucidate events, Rister presents a fascinating account of the failed colonization attempt by Englishman John Charles Beale, and subsequent capture of Mrs. Horn and Mrs. Harris.

Border Captives, on the other hand, presents an overview of the South Plains environment, a description of South Plains Indian culture and social structure, a synopsis of the development of United States/Indian relations, and an account of the economic impact of the trade in Anglo captives. This background is followed by a grim recounting of captivity stories, including those of Cynthia Ann Parker, the Putnam girls, Mrs. Horn, and Mrs. Harris. It is in these two books that Rister is most damning of Indians and their negative impact on southwestern settlement. He claims, however, to neither "condemn or to condone," but to be "only interested in picturing the red man as he was, and as he created a cultural problem" (*Border Captives*, p. ix).

Border Command (1944), *Robert E. Lee* (1946), and *Fort Griffin* (1956) focus on the other side of the Indian/United States conflict. Each deals with the U.S. Army and its commanders who led the battle against warring southern plains Indians during the last half of the nineteenth century. *Border Command* traces the career of General Phil Sheridan from the end of the Civil War to his death in 1888. The bulk of the book concerns his years as commander of the borderlands area where he actively opposed the "Peace Policy" initiated by President Ulysses S. Grant at the encouragement of Quaker reformers. According to Rister, Sheridan single-handedly ended the Indian wars and opened the Southwest for secure settlement by pursuing a course which punished Indians for transgressions against settlers. Rister applauds this action. It is with this book that reviewers begin to mention two consistent characteristics of Rister's work: first, his anti-Indian, pro-civilizing settler approach to the Indian/Anglo conflict; and second, his tendency to retell the same stories over and over in each of his books (*American Historical Review* 51:730; *Mississippi Valley Historical Review* 33:349-350; *Southwestern Historical Quarterly* 48:126-127).

Robert E. Lee, concentrating on Lee's almost two years spent on the Texas frontier prior to the Civil War, is criticized as adding detail and local color, but no new information to the study of Lee's life. It is noted also that "he tells many of the same stories [as biographer Douglas Southall Freeman] even to the extent of occasional identical quotations." He, in addition, is rebuked for using extensive quotes, with no note as to their origin (*Mississippi Valley Historical Review* 33:330-331).

In *Fort Griffin*, his final book published after his death, Rister primarily reworks material touched on in his earlier books dealing with southwestern frontier settlement and Indian conflicts. This work can be divided into two major sections, the first dealing with Rister's oft-told tales of Indian depravations, subsequent need for a military fort to provide protection for settlers, and final confinement of Indians to reservations in Indian Territory. The second part concerns the boisterous community referred to as the "Flat" that developed outside the gates of Fort Griffin. "The Flat," Rister claims, "was classed as one of the West's four wildest towns, giving harbor to unwanted outlaws, whores, gamblers, and killers" (p. ix). In this work he particularly stresses the "wild west" aspects of his Southwest.

In two books, *Land Hunger* (1942), and *No Man's Land* (1948), Rister takes advantage of his Oklahoma location to present information on the settlement of two of the state's regions; the unassigned lands first known as "Oklahoma" near the center of the present state, and the Oklahoma Panhandle. The latter work, *No Man's Land*, once again concentrates on the stories of lawlessness and hardship endemic to a harsh region not controlled by an adminstrative arm of the government. Many of these stories he gathered from interviews with original settlers in the area. Soundly criticized for lack of documentation and feeble attempts to popularize his writing (*Mississippi Valley Historical Review* 35:526-527), the book is also lauded as a "model study in regional history" (*Southwestern Historical Quarterly* 53:92-93).

In *Land Hunger* Rister relates the tale of charismatic David L. Payne and the Oklahoma Boomers he initially led in a decade-long fight for the right to settle an area the federal government protected as Indian land. Payne's followers, who believed the region to be a part of the eminent domain and therefore available for homesteading, eventually opened the region to settlement. This work, once again, is unfootnoted. Reviewers, however, are so taken by his tales of adventure that one describes it as having "no footnotes to mar the narration," and compliments him on his "thorough research" and "very full bibliography of local materials" (*Southwestern Historical Quarterly* 46:283-284; *Mississippi Valley Historical Review* 30:94-95). Perhaps they should have been more careful in their praise. A manuscript, "On to Oklahoma!," written by journalist W. W. Bloss in 1885 and now housed in the Oklahoma Historical Society Archives, Thomas Athey Collection, when compared to Rister's noteless *Land Hunger*, is far too similar to be explained away as simply "sloppy" research or notetaking. Entire paragraphs, especially biographical sections on Payne, follow Bloss's work word for word. Other sections are constructed in a similar order, with interspersed sentences worded exactly the same in each manuscript. Whether Rister was pressed for time, under self-imposed or administrative pressure to publish, or assumed that the manuscript--buried deep in the Archives (and deep in his bibliography)--would never be found, by today's standards of scholarship *Land Hunger* would be considered plagiarism.

Rister's two remaining books cannot be grouped topically with others, though *Baptist Missions* (1944) follows the same patterns established in his earlier writing. It too expands a theme--the role of religion as a civilizing agent on the frontier--that had been introduced in his earliest works. It stresses the desirability of using Anglo institutions to "civilize," and thus control, America's native populations. Published by the Home Mission Board of the Southern Baptist Convention, it demonstrates Rister's life-long commitment to his Baptist roots.

In his remaining book, *Oil! Titan of the Southwest* (1949), Rister strays from his usual focus on nineteenth-century settlers and Indians, concentrating instead on the development of southwestern oil production. Although financed by a grant from the Standard Oil Company of New Jersey, Rister claims to present his research impartially. The oil industry, he emphasizes, had a major impact on the social and economic state of the nation, and therefore required formal historical study. His approach to the subject, however, lacks the analysis necessary to fulfill adequately this need. Once again telling stories and listing the particulars of the discovery of oil field after oil field, he presents a detailed, though sometimes tedious, account of the industry. It is ironic that in his conclusion he criticizes historians for depending so heavily on the work of those who had gone before, when *Oil!* was the first piece of original research he had produced in at least six books (pp. 393-405). Although criticized for its repetition, errors in fact, and uncritical presentation of the oil industry (*Mississippi*

Valley Historical Review 36:491-492), Rister was pleased when *Oil!* won the Texas Institute of Letters prize in 1950.

This incongruity, a work criticized roundly by some, yet lauded by others, was typical of the history produced by Rister. While his books often are censured as repetitious, sloppy, and trite by reviewers in professional journals with a national readership, he consistently is praised for his strong dedication to scholarship in reviews written by his colleagues in journals published in the Southwest. The only exception to this tendency occurred following his death, when all those who reviewed his final two books described his present and past works in glowing terms. In light of this observation, one might question the objectivity of the Southwest history "good-old-boy" network which may have existed during the first half of the twentieth century.

Since much of Rister's work was undocumented, one could ask if it was written to appeal to a popular audience, or the product of lazy scholarship and an overanxiousness to publish. His dependence on sensationalistic tales and lack of analysis imply a popular audience, yet his extensive use of quotes (often uncited) and annotated bibliographies indicate an effort to appear scholarly. In the words of a later Sheridan biographer describing *Border Command*, Rister's work often is "limited in scope . . . offer[s] no documentation, [has] a shallow analysis of frontier warfare, and [is] repeatedly marred by an antiquated viewpoint toward Native Americans" (*Phil Sheridan and His Army*, p. xiii).

Whatever his intentions, Rister did provide one of the first bodies of historical works that focused totally on the American Southwest. His attempts to present an overview of the region's cultural traits and institutions, as well as his concerns that women be included in formal historical study, only can be applauded. He, in addition, laid the groundwork for future historical work by providing the facts on which others could build. Carl Coke Rister, one of the Southwest's first historians, was also one of its best storytellers.

Bibliography

Books

Baptist Missions Among the American Indians. Atlanta: Southern Baptist Home Mission Board, 1944.

Border Captives: The Traffic in Prisoners by Southern Plains Indians, 1835-1875. Norman: University of Oklahoma Press, 1940.

Border Command, General Phil Sheridan in the West. Norman: University of Oklahoma Press, 1944.

Comanche Bondage: Dr. John Charles Beale's Settlement of La Villa Dolores on Las Moras Creek in Southern Texas of the 1830s. Glendale, CA: Arthur H. Clark Co., 1955.

Fort Griffin on the Texas Frontier. Norman: University of Oklahoma Press, [ca.] 1956.

The Greater Southwest: The Economic, Social, and Cultural Development of Kansas, Oklahoma, Texas, Utah, Colorado, Nevada, New Mexico, Arizona, and California From the Spanish Conquest to the Twentieth

Century. Co-authored with Rupert Richardson. Glendale, CA: Arthur H. Clark Co., 1934.

Land Hunger: David L. Payne and the Oklahoma Boomers. Norman: University of Oklahoma Press, 1942.

No Man's Land. Norman: University of Oklahoma Press, 1948.

Oil! Titan of the Southwest. Norman: University of Oklahoma Press, 1949.

Robert E. Lee in Texas. Norman: University of Oklahoma Press, 1946.

Southern Plainsmen. Norman: University of Oklahoma Press, 1938.

The Southwestern Frontier, 1865-1881: A History of the Coming of the Settlers, Indian Depredations and Massacres, Ranching Activities, Operations of White Desperadoes and Thieves, Government Protection, Building of Railways, and the Disappearance of the Frontier. Cleveland: Arthur H. Clark Co., 1928.

Western America: The Exploration, Settlement, and Development of the Region Beyond the Mississippi. Co-authored with LeRoy Hafen. New York: Prentice-Hall, 1941.

Articles

"The Border Post of Phantom Hill." *West Texas Historical Association Year Book* 14(1938):3-13.

"Carlotta, A Confederate Colony in Mexico." *Journal of Southern History* 11(February, 1945):33-50.

"Colonel A. W. Evans' Christmas Day Indian Fight (1868)." *Chronicles of Oklahoma* 16(September, 1938):275-301.

"A Diary Account of a Creek Boundary Survey." *Chronicles of Oklahoma* 27(Autumn, 1949):268-302.

"Documents Relating to General W. T. Sherman's Southern Plains Indian Policy, 1871-1875," Part 1. *Panhandle-Plains Historical Review* 9(1936):7-27.

"Documents Relating to General W. T. Sherman's Southern Plains Indian Policy, 1871-1875," Part 2. *Panhandle-Plains Historical Review* 10(1937):48-63.

"Early Accounts of Indian Depredations." *West Texas Historical Association Year Book* 2(1926):18-63.

"A Federal Experiment in Southern Plains Indian Relations, 1835-1845." *Chronicles of Oklahoma* 14(December, 1936):434-455.

"Fort Griffin." *West Texas Historical Association Year Book* 1(1925):16-26.

"Free Land Hunters of the Southern Plains." *Chronicles of Oklahoma* 22(Winter, 1944-45):392-401.

"Harmful Practices of Indian Traders of the Southwest, 1865-1876." *New Mexico Historical Review* 6(July, 1931):231-248.

"The Oilman's Frontier." *Mississippi Valley Historical Review* 37(June, 1950):3-16.

"'Oklahoma' The Land of Promise." *Chronicles of Oklahoma* 23(Spring, 1945):2-15.

"Outlaws and Vigilantes of the Southern Plains, 1865-1885." *Mississippi Valley Historical Review* 19(March, 1933): entire issue.

"Possibilities in the Field of West Texas History." *West Texas Historical Association Year Book* 5(1930):188-195.
"The Rio Grande Colony." *Southwest Review* 25(July, 1940):429-441.
"Satanta: Orator of the Plains." *Southwest Review* 17(October, 1931):77-99.
"The Significance of the Destruction of the Buffalo in the Southwest." *Southwestern Historical Quarterly* 33(July, 1929):34-49.
"The Significance of the Jacksboro Indian Affair of 1871." *Southwestern Historical Quarterly* 29(January, 1926):181-200.
"Social Activities of the Southwestern Cowboy." *West Texas Historical Association Year Book* 7(1930):40-55.
"When Camels Came to Texas." *Southwest Review* 31(Fall, 1945):88-91.
"Yates, an 'Oil Klondike'." *West Texas Historical Association Year Book* 25(1949):3-10.

Reviews
Anson Jones: The Last President of Texas by Herbert Gambrell. *Journal of Southern History* 14(August, 1948):416-418.
Apache Agent: The Story of John P. Clum by Woodworth Clum. *Mississippi Valley Historical Review* 23(September, 1936):285-286.
The Arkansas by Clyde B. Davis. *Mississippi Valley Historical Review* 27(December, 1940):471-472.
The Blazing Frontier by Herman Edwin Mootz. *Mississippi Valley Historical Review* 23(March, 1937):609.
Charles Goodnight: Cowman and Plainsman by J. Evetts Haley. *Mississippi Valley Historical Review* 23(September, 1936):310-311.
The Cherokee Strip: A Tale of an Oklahoma Boyhood by Marquis James. *Mississippi Valley Historical Review* 32(March, 1946):628-629.
The Comanches, Lords of the South Plains by Ernest Wallace and E. Adamson Hoebel. *West Texas Historical Association Year Book* 28(1952):127-129.
Democracy's College: The Land-Grant Movement in the Formative Stage by Earle D. Ross. *Mississippi Valley Historical Review* 29(June, 1942):108.
Famous Texas Feuds by C. L. Douglas. *Mississippi Valley Historical Review* 23(March, 1937):610.
The Founding of Stillwater: A Case Study in Oklahoma History by Berlin Basil Chapman. *Mississippi Valley Historical Review* 36(September, 1949):333-334.
General George Crook: His Autobiography edited by Martin F. Schmitt. *Journal of Southern History* 12(August, 1946):442-443.
Life and Death of an Oilman: The Career of E. W. Marland by John Joseph Mathews. *Mississippi Valley Historical Review* 38(March, 1952):728-729.
The March of Empire: Frontier Defense in the Southwest, 1848-1860 by Averam B. Bender. *Southwestern Historical Quarterly* 56(January, 1953):480-481.

Maverick Town: The Story of Old Tascosa with Chapter Decorations by Harold D. Bugbee. *Panhandle-Plains Historical Review* 19(1946):98-99.

Narratives of the Coronado Expedition, 1540-1542 edited by George P. Hammond and Agapito Rey; *Coronado Quarto Centennial Publication, 1540-1940*, vol. II, edited by George P. Hammond. *Mississippi Valley Historical Review* 27(March, 1941):618-619.

Pageant in the Wilderness: The Story of the Escalante Expedition to the Interior Basin, 1776 by Herbert E. Bolton. *Southwestern Historical Quarterly* 56(July, 1952):170-171.

A Southwestern Utopia by Thomas A. Robertson. *Mississippi Valley Historical Review* 35(September, 1948):329-330.

Texas: The Lone Star State by Rupert Norval Richardson. *Mississippi Valley Historical Review* 30(June, 1943):105.

This Reckless Breed of Men: The Trappers and Fur Traders of the Southwest by Robert Glass Cleland. *Journal of Southern History* 16(August, 1950):356-357.

The Western Journals of Washington Irving edited and annotated by John Francis McDermott. *Mississippi Valley Historical Review* 32(June, 1945):111-112.

Westward the Briton by Robert G. Athearn. *Southwestern Historical Quarterly* 57(April, 1954):531-532.

Wild Bill and His Era by William E. Connelley. *West Texas Historical Association Year Book* 9(1933):132-133.

The XIT Ranch of Texas and the Early Days of the Llano Estacado by J. Evetts Haley. *Mississippi Valley Historical Review* 41(June, 1954):147-148.

The Year of Decision: 1846 by Bernard DeVoto. *Journal of Southern History* 9(August, 1943):415-416.

Studies of Carl Coke Rister

Bennett, Patrick. "Golden Age of Texas Historians: An Interview with Rupert N. Richardson." *Southwest Review* 67(Winter, 1982):33-43.

Binkley, William C. Review of *Robert E. Lee in Texas* by Carl Coke Rister. *Mississippi Valley Historical Review* 33(September, 1946):330-331.

Bloom, Lansing B. Review of *The Greater Southwest* by Carl Coke Rister and Rupert Richardson. *Mississippi Valley Historical Review* 21(March, 1935):567-569.

Bloss, W. W. "On to Oklahoma!" Thomas Athey Collection, Archives and Manuscripts Division, Oklahoma Historical Society, Oklahoma City, OK.

Claussen, Martin P. Review of *Border Command, General Phil Sheridan in the West* by Carl Coke Rister. *Mississippi Valley Historical Review* 33(September, 1946):349-350.

Douglas, Jesse S. Review of *Border Command, General Phil Sheridan in the West*. *American Historical Review* 51(July, 1946):730.

Ewing, Floyd F., Jr. Review of *Fort Griffin on the Texas Frontier* by Carl Coke Rister. *West Texas Historical Association Year Book* 32(1956):166-167.

Friend, Llerena. Review of *Border Command, General Phil Sheridan in the West* by Carl Coke Rister. *Southwestern Historical Quarterly* 48(July, 1944):126-127.

Giddens, Paul H. Review of *Oil! Titan of the Southwest* by Carl Coke Rister. *Mississippi Valley Historical Review* 36(December, 1949):491-492.

Goodykoontz, Colin B. Review of *Western America* by Carl Coke Rister and LeRoy Hafen. *American Historical Review* 47(January, 1942):368-369.

Hedges, James B. Review of *The Southwestern Frontier--1865-1881* by Carl Coke Rister. *American Historical Review* 34(April, 1929):625-627.

Holden, W. C. Review of *No Man's Land* by Carl Coke Rister. *Journal of Southern History* 15(February, 1949):116-117.

__________. Taped interview, March 1970. Southwest Collection, Texas Tech University, Lubbock, TX.

Hollon, Gene. Review of *Robert E. Lee in Texas* by Carl Coke Rister. *Southwestern Historical Quarterly* 50(July, 1946):176-178.

Jackson, W. Turrentine. "Materials for Western History in the Department of the Interior Archives." *Mississippi Valley Historical Review* 35(June, 1948):61-76.

Landers, Emmett M. Review of *Border Captives* by Carl Coke Rister. *West Texas Historical Association Year Book* 16(1940):147.

__________. Review of *Southern Plainsmen* by Carl Coke Rister. *West Texas Historical Association Year Book* 14(1938):141-142.

Leckie, William H. "Carl Coke Rister." *Great Plains Journal* 18(1979):120-123.

Malin, James C. Review of *No Man's Land* by Carl Coke Rister. *Mississippi Valley Historical Review* 35(December, 1948):526-527.

Mecham, Kirke. Review of *Southern Plainsmen* by Carl Coke Rister. *Mississippi Valley Historical Review* 25(March, 1939):573-574.

Morton, Ohland. Review of *Border Captives* by Carl Coke Rister. *Southwestern Historical Quarterly* 44(July, 1940):151-152.

"Obituary." *Mississippi Valley Historical Review* 42(June, 1955):156-157.

__________. *Southwestern Historical Quarterly* 59(July, 1955):101-102.

Peckham, Howard H. Review of *Comanche Bondage* by Carl Coke Rister. *Mississippi Valley Historical Review* 42(March, 1956):748-749.

Richardson, Rupert. Review of *Border Captives* by Carl Coke Rister. *American Historical Review* 46(January, 1941):487.

__________. "A Dedication to the Memory of Carl Coke Rister, 1889-1955." *Arizona and the West* 14(Winter, 1972):317-320.

__________. Review of *Fort Griffin on the Texas Frontier* by Carl Coke Rister. *Southwestern Historical Quarterly* 61(July, 1957):190-191.

__________. Review of *Land Hunger* by Carl Coke Rister. *American Historical Review* 48(July, 1943):825-826.

__________. Review of *Southern Plainsmen* by Carl Coke Rister. *Southwestern Historical Quarterly* 42(April, 1939):418-419.

Richardson, T. C. Review of *Land Hunger* by Carl Coke Rister. *Southwestern Historical Quarterly* 46(January, 1943)):283-284.

Rister, Carl Coke, Papers, 1934-1963, and Reference File. Southwest Collection, Texas Tech University, Lubbock, TX.

Robbins, Roy Marvin. Review of *Land Hunger* by Carl Coke Rister. *Mississippi Valley Historical Review* 30(June, 1943):94-95.

Rundell, Walter, Jr. "Texas Petroleum History: A Selective Annotated Bibliography." *Southwestern Historical Quarterly* 67(October, 1963):267-278.

Strickland, Rex W. Review of *No Man's Land* by Carl Coke Rister. *Southwestern Historical Quarterly* 53(July, 1949):92-93.

Wallace, Ernest. Review of *Comanche Bondage* by Carl Coke Rister. *West Texas Historical Association Year Book* 31(1935):161-163.

Waller, J. L. Review of *Western American* by Carl Coke Rister and LeRoy Hafen. *Southwestern Historical Quarterly* 45(July, 1941):117-119.

Watson, Walcott. Review of *Southern Plainsmen* by Carl Coke Rister. *American Historical Review* 44(July, 1939):1012-1013.

Westermeier, Clifford P. Review of *Fort Griffin on the Texas Frontier* by Carl Coke Rister. *Mississippi Valley Historical Review* 43(March, 1957):687-688.

Wyllys, Rufus Kay. Review of *The Greater Southwest* by Carl Coke Rister and Rupert Richardson. *American Historical Review* 40(July, 1935):794-795.

40

DOANE ROBINSON

by H. Roger Grant

Biography

Before graduate training of frontier historians became commonplace, there existed scores of self-educated amateurs, usually without a college or university affiliation, who contributed mightily to the literature. One of these often unheralded individuals was the remarkable Doane Robinson, a man who did yeoman service recording and promoting South Dakota's past. He showed a real zeal for objectivity and exactitude that placed him in an elite class.

Born near the western Wisconsin community of Sparta on October 19, 1856, son of George McCook and Rhozina Grow Robinson, Doane was christened Jonah Leroy, names he later rejected for the more lyrical Doane. Typical of lads of the mid-nineteenth century, he attended public schools, but unlike most of his peers, he had some post-high school training. For one academic year, 1882-1883, Robinson enrolled in the law school of the University of Wisconsin. (He would receive an honorary doctorate from tiny Yankton College seven years later.) But between the time Robinson left his family's farm in 1877 and his matriculation at the state university, he homesteaded near Marshall, in southwestern Minnesota, where the area's rich prairie lands were then being settled. When not farming, he read law with a local attorney.

In 1883, the twenty-seven year old lawyer decided to return to the "Last Best West," but now he made his home across the Minnesota border in Dakota Territory. At that time the "Great Dakota Boom" was in full swing, and thousands of settlers streamed into the region. Robinson soon married Jennie Austin of Leon, Wisconsin, and hung out his legal shingle in bustling Watertown, the recently established seat of Codington County. Within a year, however, he abandoned the law for journalism. Rather than joining the staff of an established newspaper, he launched his own organ, the *Watertown Courier-News*, a daily publication. After a decade in Watertown he became proprietor of the nearby *Gary Interstate*, and then two years later, 1896, he acquired the *Yankton Daily Gazette.* In 1898 Robinson made another foray into publishing; he founded the *Monthly South Dakotan*, a magazine that for the next seven years promoted his adopted state through essays, short-stories, and poetry of South Dakotans. Included in the pages of this remarkably successful journal were numerous historical pieces, for "[Robinson] viewed history as a source of state pride, and preservation of the heritage of South Dakotans soon became the magazine's primary goal" (*South Dakota History* 11:53). Indeed, the *Monthly South Dakotan* (the title varied over its life) emerged as the principal outlet for works on local history, many of which Robinson himself contributed.

Doane Robinson, though, had other ways of sharing his literary efforts. As early as 1893 a Huron editor pridefully remarked that "Mr. Robinson is known to all magazine readers, having been for nearly three years a contributor to the Century, Arena and other high class publications" *(Daily Huronite* [Huron, S.D.] September 23, 1893). In 1899 Robinson even produced a book of poetry, *Midst the Coteaus of South Dakota*, which his Yankton printing firm published.

Coinciding with Robinson's developing literary career were various public-spirited activities. He served between 1889 and 1891 as secretary of the last territorial and the first state railroad commission. His friendship with fellow Republican and first South Dakota governor, Arthur C. Mellette, made this appointment possible. Robinson's enthusiasm for education led to a long stint as a trustee of Yankton College beginning in 1908. A devout Congregationalist, he had a special attachment to his denomination's Dakota school. In the early 1920s he served as president of the South Dakota Academy of Science and the South Dakota State History Teachers' Association. And most important of all, when the state legislature created the Department of History (State Historical Society) in January 1901, he became its executive secretary. He would remain active in that post until 1926, when his son, Will Grow Robinson, assumed his position. (For a time Doane Robinson also performed in the dual capacity as state librarian.) During Robinson's twenty-five-year tenure as State Historical Society head he made a major contribution to the historical profession by collecting and editing a wide variety of records and writing numerous studies, including several lengthy ones. Most of these involved Dakota Indians and the process of white settlement.

Doane Robinson gained much state-wide attention for his work with the State Historical Society, and he truly became "Mr. South Dakota History." It was a suggestion, however, that he made in 1923 for granite carvings in the Black Hills that gave him a measure of immortality. Yet Robinson did not envision the grand design that Gutzon Borglum later followed with his internationally recognized images of George Washington, Thomas Jefferson, Abraham Lincoln, and Theodore Roosevelt. Rather, as Robinson wrote, "I am thinking of some notable Sioux as Red Cloud, who lived and died in the shadow of these peaks." Although he later wrote to sculptor Lorado Taft that "In my imagination I can see all the old heroes of the West peering out from the rocks" (*South Dakota History* 4:465).

In his retirement years Robinson largely ended his labors as an historian. Instead he ranched near Pierre. A widower since his wife Jennie's death in 1902, he had two sons, Harry Austin, born in 1888, and Will, who arrived five years later, who remained in South Dakota and close to their father. Harry practiced law in Yankton, and Will served as the historical society's head in Pierre.

Themes

Doane Robinson was almost exclusively a regional historian. His works represent the first historical collections and the first synthesis of South Dakota history. Within his numerous publications dealing with South Dakota's past, Robinson stressed two substantial areas: political history and Native American history.

Analysis

A cursory glance at the historical works of Doane Robinson suggests that he merely compiled and chronicled South Dakota's past and that his efforts are antiquarian in tone. This assessment is partially correct. Such activities were unquestionably in vogue during Robinson's time of greatest historical productivity. After all, Western history benefited enormously from the collecting and editing efforts of Hubert Howe Bancroft and Benjamin F. Shambaugh. Indeed, the volumes produced by these men and their contemporaries frequently became essential building blocks for future and better trained historians. Robinson realized that before any comprehensive study of South Dakota's past could be written, sources must be found, organized, and preserved. He gathered, for example, the yellowing documents of the Dakota constitutional debates of 1885 and 1889. When printed in 1907, this publication immediately emerged as the standard reference on territorial politics, although it would be joined shortly by George W. Kingsbury's heavily documented *History of Dakota Territory* (1915). Howard R. Lamar, for one, would later consult both works for his widely acclaimed study, *Dakota Territory, 1861-1889: A Study of Frontier Politics* (1956).

Robinson's most imaginative and in all likelihood his most popular reference work appeared in 1925, *Doan Robinson's Encyclopedia of South Dakota.* After a maudlin dedication, which in part read, "South Dakota, my South Dakota, for half a century my homeland! I have loved you as a father loves his own; your abounding plains, your mighty rivers, your glorious mountains, and your purling brooks are all mine; the flowers bloom on the prairies and perfume the summer breezes for me; the spicy breath of your forest is for my benediction. From your infancy I have adored you" (p. iii), users found a rich smorgasbord of entries. Yet, they discovered more than the expected political happenings, personal and business biographies, and major events in the state's past, for the publication contained some wonderfully original material. Outstanding is a nearly sixteen thousand word essay on "Sports in South Dakota." Instead of simply a listing of various records compiled by local schools and colleges, much of the text reviews the wide variety of games played by the Sioux, often with a careful explanation of playing rules and related details. Included in this coverage are the popular "Hoop Game," "Woskate Takapsice" (game of men's shinney), "Woskate Tawinkapsice" (game of women's shinney), Woskate Canwiyusna" (guessing the old stick), and eighteen others. Moreover, the entry reviews a vast array of white residents' sports, from "Lawn Tennis" and "Polo" to "Base Ball" and "Golf." The scope is truly catholic (pp. 679-700).

Compiler-editor Robinson offered the public more than documents and encyclopedia sketches. His most acclaimed work, *A Brief History of South Dakota*, published by the Cincinnati-based American Book Company in 1905, immediately became the leading historical study of the Sunshine state. In fact, it would not be fully superseded until 1968, when the University of Nebraska Press released Herbert S. Schell's masterful volume, *History of South Dakota*. Robinson's book, which went through five revisions between 1912 and 1931, unmistakably reveals his worldview. Most of all, he saw history as something useful. South Dakota was a young state that lacked the historical complexity of Massachusetts or New York or for that matter of Iowa or Minnesota. But in Robinson's mind, the events that constituted "our heritage" warranted close scrutiny. As he aptly argued in the preface, "The student who learns the story of his community, the sacrifices and successes of the pioneers, the worthy accomplishments of his relatives of an earlier generation, the history of the soil upon which he lives, will hardly fail to develop pride in his locality, and that pride is an almost certain guaranty of good citizenship" (p. 5). Today Robinson might be classified as an advocate of "nearby" or "common person" history, but actually he is better labeled as the quintessential booster, a figure whom George Babbitt would understand and appreciate.

Unlike Herbert Schell's finely tuned monograph, which is the effort of a talented professional, Robinson's *Brief History* is somewhat disjointed and really more a series of newspaper-type pieces. Still, its organization is logical and reflects in a chronological fashion the author's historical interests, particularly Indians and public officials. While Robinson, like virtually all Americans of his day, saw the arrival of whites as a positive force, he, nevertheless, admired Native Americans. He undoubtedly was in a minority of South Dakotans when he blasts the federal government for commonly cheating and abusing them. And there is clearly an Indian hero for Robinson, Red Cloud. This chieftain of the Oglalas fascinates him; he admires greatly his tenacity, skill, and honesty. In his adoration of Red Cloud he shows his acceptance of the "Great Man" interpretation of history. Similarly, when Robinson discusses the state's leading politicians, namely its governors and United States senators, he once again demonstrates his commitment to this same interpretation of the importance of significant individuals to history. Interestingly, he would later spotlight minor elective officeholders in his *Encyclopedia*, perhaps to increase sales or more likely to indicate that South Dakotans frequently displayed a keen sense of public service. Yet, Robinson carefully avoided political controversy; he virtually ignored the significant, albeit disruptive, activities of the Farmer's Alliance and its successor body, the People's

Party. This would not be an omission in Schell's history. Maybe Robinson's potentially sensitive position with the State Historical Society prompted an apolitical approach. And, too, he was a person who sought out the "facts," information that likely was devoid of much interpretative meaning. Of course, Robinson lacks total consistency; he discusses Indians in that obviously sympathetic framework.

While few people probably still read *A Brief History of South Dakota* or for that matter pull *Doane Robinson's Encyclopedia of South Dakota* off the shelf, Robinson's various collected works, most of which he did for the State Historical Society, continue to be consulted; they have lasting value. Perhaps not many of these users realize that Robinson had a long career, distinguished most of all by a sense of mission. His loyalty to his chosen state knew no bounds. Thanks to Doane Robinson's considerable labors, large segments of South Dakota history have been preserved and remembered.

Bibliography

Books

A Brief History of South Dakota. Cincinnati: American Book Co., 1905.

A Brief Outline of the History of South Dakota. Aberdeen: News Printing Co., 1904.

Constitutional Debates: South Dakota, 1885, 1889. Huron: Huronite Printing Co., 1907.

Dam Sites on the Missouri River. Pierre: South Dakota Department of Immigration, 1917.

Doane Robinson's Encyclopedia of South Dakota. Pierre: Privately printed, 1925.

History of South Dakota. Logansport, IN: B. G. Bowen & Co., 1904.

A History of South Dakota: From Earliest Times. Mitchell: The Educator School Supply Company, 1900.

A History of the Dakota or Sioux Indians from Their Earliest Traditions and First Contact with White Men to the Final Settlement of the Last of Them Upon Reservations and the Consequent Abandonment of the Old Tribal Life. Aberdeen: News Printing Company, 1904.

The Lesueur Tradition, in *State Historical Society of South Dakota Historical Collections.* Pierre: State Historical Society, 1918.

Lewis and Clark in South Dakota., in *State Historical Society of South Dakota Historical Collections.* Pierre: State Historical Society, 1918.

Memoirs of General William Henry Harrison Beadle, in *State Historical Society of South Dakota Historical Collections.* Pierre: State Historical Society, 1906.

More Boulder Mosaics, in *State Historical Society of South Dakota Historical Collections.* Pierre: State Historical Society, 1914.

Progress of South Dakota, in *State Historical Society of South Dakota Historical Collections.* Pierre: State Historical Society, 1916.

Revised Compendium of Information Relating to South Dakota. Aberdeen: News Printing Company, 1908.

Sioux Indian Courts. Sioux Falls: H. C. Sessions & Sons, 1909.

The Sioux of the Dakotas. Worcester, MA: Home Geographic Society, 1932.

Some Sidelights on the Character of Sitting Bull, in *Mississippi Valley Historical Association Proceedings.* Cedar Rapids: Mississippi Valley Historical Association, 1911.

South Dakota: Sui Generis, Stressing the Unique and Dramatic in South Dakota History. Chicago: American Historical Society, 1930.

Verendrye, in *State Historical Society of South Dakota Historical Collections.* Pierre: State Historical Society, 1914.

Verendrye Calendar, in *State Historical Society of South Dakota Historical Collections.* Pierre: State Historical Society, 1914.

La Verendrye's Farthest West, in *State Historical Society of Wisconsin Proceedings.* Madison: State Historical Society of Wisconsin, 1914.

Articles

Gary Interstate (Gary, SD), 1893-1895.

Monthly South Dakotan, 1898-1905.

Watertown Courier-News (Watertown, SD), 1883-1893.

Yankton Daily Gazette, 1896-1898.

Studies of Doane Robinson

The Daily Argus-Leader (Sioux Falls, SD), November 27, 1946.

Daily Huronite (Huron, SD), September 23, 1893.

"Doane Robinson." In *Who Was Who in America.* Chicago: A. N. Marquis & Co., 1960. P. 735.

__________. In *Who's Who in America.* Chicago: A. N. Marquis & Co., 1924. P. 2730.

Fite, Gilbert C. "South Dakota: Some Observations by a Native Son." *South Dakota History* 4(Fall, 1974):465.

Fox, Lawrence K., ed. "Doane Robinson." In *Fox's Who's Who Among South Dakotans.* Pierre: Statewide Services Co., 1924. P. 171.

McLaird, James D. "The Monthly South Dakotan." *South Dakota History* 11(Winter, 1980):53-76.

Schafer, Joseph. Review of *South Dakota: Sui Generis, Stressing the Unique and Dramatic in South Dakota History* by Doane Robinson. *Mississippi Valley Historical Review* 38(September, 1931):274.

41

THEODORE ROOSEVELT

by Michael Collins

Biography

It is a forbidding country of timeless prairies and eternal winds. For millions of years nature's weathering forces have warped and scarred the earth, carving towering formations of hard limestone and huge boulders. Throughout the geologic ages meandering streams have cut slowly but deeply into vast beds of white alkaline sands and red rock, sculpting a twisted maze of jagged escarpments and gloomy canyons. For centuries the Sioux called this windswept emptiness the Mako Shika, or "bad earth." United States Army General Alfred Sulley once described it as "hell with fires out." Not much survives there, only sparse and tangled sagebrush, a few gnarled and stunted cedars, an occasional dwarfed pine, and the seemingly endless sea of short buffalo grasses. The climate is one of extremes, scorching, almost desert-like in summer, frigid and bitter cold during the arctic squalls of winter. Yet there is something mystical, almost spiritual about this most desolate country, a haunting beauty that can best be observed each sunset when the day's last light bursts across the landscape into a breathtaking rainbow of brilliant colors. As darkness descends over these bleak and barren Badlands of Dakota, all that remains is a ghostly stillness, a silence broken only by the murmurings and mournings of the evening winds. It seems then that a human can almost hear forever--and hear nothing.

Little wonder that Theodore Roosevelt was enchanted by what he called the "devil's wilderness" of Dakota. In 1884, following the deaths of his wife Alice and mother Martha, young Roosevelt was drawn to the alluring land of the Little Missouri River which seemed to symbolize his inner feelings of desolation and loneliness. (Roosevelt Papers, Personal Diaries, February 14-June 21, 1884). With his adoring Alice and beloved "Mittie" gone, his world had suddenly turned dark and silent and empty. So maybe it was fitting that he disappeared for a time into the hidden recesses of the Badlands where he could confront his sorrows, alone, and forsake his fear of living without Alice. Perhaps no man in America, therefore, could have profited more from publisher Horace Greeley's advice to all aspiring young men than a twenty-six year-old Theodore Roosevelt. "When you have no family or friends to aid you, and no prospects open to you," Greeley had urged, "turn your face to the Great West, and there build up a home and fortune" (*A Representative Life of Horace Greeley*, p. 553).

So much has already been said and written about the life of Theodore Roosevelt, twenty-sixth president of the United States. The events of his boyhood in New York City, his days at Harvard, and his cowboy years in Dakota have been told and retold. So have accounts of his rising political career from the Albany State House to the White House. Every American school child has learned about the stories and legends of the Rough Rider who charged up San Juan Hill and into history.

But few realize that, before Roosevelt assumed his proper place among the pantheon of American heroes, he aspired not to make history, but to write it. And too few recognize that the man behind the familiar president is actually a forgotten pioneer among frontier historians. As an impressionable and impatient youth in a hurry to leave his mark upon the world, Roosevelt followed his fertile and far-reaching interests from the confines of New York politics to the open ranges of stockraising, then on to the intellectual frontiers of history. Between 1884 and 1889, while ranching and hunting on the remote borders of the Badlands, he observed the closing of the last cattleman's frontier and the passing of a way of life. At the same time he accomplished some of his most creative writing. His experiences during the Dakota years profoundly altered his conception of America's past as well as his vision of the nation's future. So it was not at all surprising that the promising historian looked to the American West for a subject for his pen.

Themes

Although an easterner by birth, background, and education, Roosevelt grew to embrace many attitudes, values, and ideals that were identifiably western. His acceptance of physical strength as the greatest of virtues, the origins of his concept of the "Big Stick," his strident belief in Manifest Destiny and expansionism, his racial views, even his support for the conservation of the vanishing North American wilderness--all evolved directly from his experiences on the frontier as well as his interpretation of the past westward movement (*Roosevelt in the Bad Lands*).

Four dominant themes appear throughout Roosevelt's narratives on the West. Perhaps most obvious, he reflected his generation's almost feverish *nationalism* and acceptance of muscular patriotism, ambitious militarism, and territorial expansionism--all of which seemed confirmed in the American frontier experience. Like so many contemporaries, he was captivated by Darwinism--both scientific and social--and his historical works heralded the coming of a new generation of scholars whose quest for a distinctively native interpretation of the American experience led to *environmental determinism.* Roosevelt also viewed the mighty contest for the North American continent, above all else, in terms of the bloody *"racial warfare"* between Anglo and Indian cultures. Lastly, he recognized the leveling influence of the frontier experience, and he emphasized the process of *democratization* that resulted from man's interaction with the hostile forces of the wilderness (*Journal of the West* 17:105-111).

Analysis

During the winter of 1885-1886, Roosevelt accepted a commission from Houghton-Mifflin to write a biography of former Missouri senator and ardent expansionist Thomas Hart Benton for the *American Statesman* series. Although the *Life and Times of Thomas Hart Benton* did not sell particularly well when published in 1887, and despite receiving reviews that were something less than laudatory, the study would stand unchallenged for almost a quarter of a century as the standard biography of "Old Bullion" Benton.

During the spring and summer of 1886 Roosevelt wrote most of the Benton biography at his Elkhorn Ranch in the Badlands. Every page of the manuscript bore the unmistakable imprint of his recent experiences in the West. For instance, while conceding that the Mexican War was "bloody and unrighteous," Roosevelt contends that the American conquest was inevitable as well as "desirable for the good of humanity." On the Oregon question, he likewise defends American claims to the Pacific Northwest because only the United States could have put these territories to best use and thus "ought to have taken it all." Predictably too, he vindicates the "frontier view" of Indians which he believes to be "more right than the. . .so-called humanitarian or Eastern view" (pp. 7-9, 12-27, 37-39, 44-45, 50, 75).

More than just a colorful and insightful portrait of Benton, the book offers a revealing profile of Theodore Roosevelt. Specifically, the biography presented a manifesto of ideas and ideals that the author had recently come to accept while in Dakota. Clearly now Roosevelt was beginning to view the great issues of American history in terms of the westward movement and the frontier experience. More than just transplanted Europeans and different from their kin in the East, he maintains, American frontier inhabitants had been forged "by the hard and stern surroundings of their life" into a peculiar and characteristically "American type." He therefore points out that those men and women who had ventured beyond the borders of civilization had been altered, somehow "Americanized" by their contact with the frontier. Equally significant, he stresses the importance of a vast and vacant continent which drew a surplus population westward like a natural magnet. Understandably then, the entire monograph sounded a clarion call for Manifest Destiny (pp. 4, 8-9, 12, 27, 66-67).

The views and values expressed by Roosevelt in the Benton biography were typically western. Nowhere is this more evident than in his treatment of the War of 1812. Whereas five years earlier, in his monumental history of *The Naval War of 1812*, he interprets that conflict as simply a "contest for the rights of seamen," he now emphasizes western land hunger as a primary cause of the war. No longer does he see the fighting in 1812 as merely a dispute over maritime issues, but instead he views the war as one of territorial conquest. While in his earlier naval history he had simply dismissed the backwoods campaigns on the frontier as being merely in the backwash of history, he now recognizes the long-range significance of these events in pushing the advancing frontier line westward. "On the [Atlantic] seaboard . . . [the war] was regarded as . . . a revolt against Great Britain's domineering insolence," he summarizes, whereas "west of the [Appalachian] mountains . . . it was a renewal on a large scale of the Indian struggles" (*Thomas Hart Benton*, pp. 7-8, 22).

Not content merely to live out his boyhood fantasies while admittedly "playing cowboy" in the Badlands, Roosevelt decided sometime during the winter of 1885-1886 to explore the vast historic landscape of the American frontier. At his Long Island home of Sagamore Hill he began preliminary research on what he hoped would be a monumental multi-volume history of the American West. He envisioned the work to be not just a dusty chronicle of persons, places, and events, but a sprawling narrative tracing the westward movement of men, institutions, and ideas. He conceived the work to be in the literary style and tradition of the eminent American historian, Francis Parkman, whose works he much admired. Roosevelt wanted to begin where Parkman had left off and to follow the century-long path of Anglo-American conquests, beginning with the French and Indian War. On a grand historical and geographic stage, he could dramatize the importance of the continuing westward expansion of the English-speaking peoples as well as analyze the significance of the American frontier experience.

By January, 1888, Roosevelt was thinking more seriously about this ambitious literary undertaking that could possibly consume several years of his already crowded life. Recently he wrote that he would like to produce a study that would "really take rank in the very first class." Months earlier he had confided to Henry Cabot Lodge: "If I write another historical work of any kind . . . my dream is to make . . . [it my own] *magnum opus*" (*The Letters of Theodore Roosevelt I*: 119-122). He pondered that this work would trace the westward movement from the Alleghenies to the Mississippi River and beyond to the Great Plains. He planned, in perhaps six, possibly eight volumes, nothing less than a sweeping history of pioneers, an epic and heroic saga of hardship, conquest, courage, and warfare. With the turning of each page he would make his readers hear the whizzing of Ottawa arrows, the steady creaking of Conestogas, and the distant thunder of Shawnee war drums. He would almost cause them to smell the smoke of Ohio campfires and the gunpowder flashing from Kentucky long rifles. He would even make them dodge the awful skull-crushing blows of a Creek tomahawk. Appropriately, he would dedicate this effort to Francis Parkman, who he once termed the "greatest historian . . . the United States has yet produced (*The Works of Theodore Roosevelt XII*: 246)." And he would entitle it, *The Winning of the West* (1905).

In March, 1888, Roosevelt contracted with publisher George Haven Putnam to produce within the next fifteen months the first two volumes of his history of westward expansion. Without delay he then set about the tedious and tiresome task of researching, collecting materials, gathering sources, and compiling stacks of notes. For weeks he lived an almost monastic existence, cloistering himself in a small and quiet world of books and papers, then withdrawing to his study at Sagamore Hill where he would begin writing.

Roosevelt believed that, if he were to take a place someday alongside the famous, it would be as a writer of history rather than as a statesman. As he wrote an ailing Francis Parkman in 1888, "literature must be my mistress . . . for though I really enjoy politics, I appreciate the exceedingly short nature of . . . [its] tenure" (*The Letters of Theodore Roosevelt* I:210-211). Early in the summer of 1889 the first two volumes of his "big work" were finished and turned off the presses. Despite obvious shortcomings, the study showed great promise of becoming a worthy achievement and an important contribution to the annals of the American frontier. His research appeared too hasty, almost superficial by modern standards of scholarship, his narrative too often repetitious, his conclusions too much an exercise in unnecessary moralizing.

But the opening volumes of *The Winning of the West* also broke new ground and seemed bold, imaginative, even controversial. For instance, Roosevelt challenges traditional interpretations of the origins of the American Revolution. According to Roosevelt, that monumental collision between the colonies and the British empire is "rendered inevitable" not by oppressive taxation and the tyranny of the Navigation Acts, but by the Proclamation of 1763, which imposed a foolish and impractical artificial barrier to Anglo expansion west of the Appalachians (I:57).

As evidenced in each chapter of the narrative, Roosevelt the historian is unable to transcend the racial prejudices of Roosevelt the cowboy. His attitudes toward the Native American thus prevent him from offering a balanced and unbiased view of the struggles between Anglo and Indian cultures. Page after page drips with the bloody and hideous atrocities committed by the "savage" Indians--who were always the "first aggressors." Roosevelt describes in all too vivid detail how the "heathen redman," usually unprovoked, mercilessly fell upon helpless settlers, burning and scalping and torturing innocent whites, braining babies againt trees, raping their mothers, and then mutilating their bodies in unspeakable ways. But he fails to account for the equally barbarous acts of the Anglo settlers. This monumental clash between the "civilized" and the "savage" is the dominant theme in the westward movement, according to Roosevelt, and the outcome of the struggle furnished unmistakable proof of the English-speaking peoples' superiority over Native Americans who were "devils, not men," something less than human (I: 78-79, 96, 115, 117-120, 274, 276-279; II: 52-53; IV: 7, 199-202; V: 222-229; VI:63-64).

Roosevelt saw no reason why North America should have remained an unpeopled and uncivilized waste, a "vast hunting ground for squalid savages," when God had intended the country as a sprawling pastoral paradise for hardy yeomen-farmers (I: 117-118). The "racial warfare" in the American wilderness was unavoidable, inevitable, even righteous and divinely ordained. After all, the Indians had neither owned the land by permanent occupation nor cultivated the soil, Roosevelt insists, but had merely hunted the forests and prairies and fished the teeming streams. And since the long warring Indian nations had settled their claims only by "mercilessly butchering weaker rivals," there was "no right [on the frontier] save that of the strongest." For these reasons Roosevelt attacks the "eastern sentimentalists" and "maudlin fanatics" who believed whites and Indians could coexist peacefully. He simply dismisses as "worse than valueless," even "beneath criticism" Helen Hunt Jackson's assaults upon past Indian removal and resettlement policies expressed in *A Century of Dishonor* (I:117-118).

Roosevelt's racial attitudes were typical of the times and consistent with the cowboy ethic he had recently adopted in the West. Despite this stain of racism, however, Roosevelt was emerging quickly at the vanguard of a new movement of narrative school writers who perceived their discipline not as a science but as a literary art. More importantly, by examining the significance of the frontier in the American experience, he also established himself as a forerunner of the landmark frontier thesis advanced in 1893 by Frederick Jackson Turner, who had already acknowledged that it was Roosevelt who first "rescued an entire movement in American development from the hands of unskilled analysts (*Journal of the West* 17:105-106)." Clearly, Roosevelt presages the monumental Turner thesis in several respects. Most noticeably, he foreshadows Turner by suggesting that Americans were not simply transplanted English, but a unique and identifiable people, "natives to the soil" who were markedly different from their Old World ancestors. He insists, too, that a people isolated for generations beyond the borders of civilization had been "Americanized," forged into a peculiar and new national type as they interacted with the "hard surroundings" of the wilderness. Like Turner, who came after him, he writes of frontiersmen, forced to adapt to the harsh conditions of their environment, who lost their Europeanness. Environmental pressures, he believes, shaped the pioneers of the trans-Allegheny borderlands and molded them into natural by-products.

Roosevelt anticipates Turner by stressing how Americans had become "one in speech, thought, and character" because of their struggles in the wilderness (*The Genesis of the Frontier Thesis*, p. 40). He also contends that the universal experience of the frontier stood as a "compact and continuous whole" (*Journal of the West* 17:110). No less significant, he emphasizes the democratization that had occurred in the West, maintaining that "there was everywhere great equality of conditions" since "land was plenty and all else was scarce" (*The Winning of the West* 1:147). He even antedates the frontier thesis by pointing out that western settlement had developed in succeeding waves: first, the fur trappers and explorers, next the long hunters, then the surveyors, and finally the permanent settlers who established government and order. In short, like Turner, Roosevelt writes of a free people, settling on free lands, founding free institutions.

Roosevelt's opening volumes on the westward movement received considerable acclaim, most contemporaries hailing the study for its sound scholarship and lively literary style. One Roosevelt admirer was the promising young Turner who applauds the work as a "revelation" and credits the author with having done a "real service to history." Only after reviewing the first two volumes of the Roosevelt narrative did Turner begin viewing American development in terms of the continuous and steady progress of Anglo civilization across the North American continent. Turner's careful study of *The Winning of the West* was, without a doubt, a watershed in the evolution of his thinking, as evidenced by the many handwritten notes and marked passages that appear throughout his personal copies of the work (*American Historical Review* 2:171).

That Roosevelt influenced Turner's emerging synthesis of ideas seems certain. On January 24, 1893, Roosevelt delivered the featured biennial address before the members of the State Historical Society of Wisconsin assembled in Madison. In his keynote speech entitled "The Northwest in the Nation," he referred to the American West as the "heart of the country" and of "true American sentiment." Confidently he spoke of the westward movement as perhaps the most important theme in the national experience. He encouraged those scholars present to devote more of their efforts to studying the historic development of the frontier. He lectured about the continual rebirth and growth of democracy in the wilderness and commented on the unique and "typically American" characteristics produced by the primitive conditions of pioneer life. He also noted the unifying nationalistic influence of the frontier and pointed out the obvious--that "there is no longer any frontier." No doubt, one of his most attentive listeners was the thirty-four year-old Turner who just several months later would capture the attention of the American Historical Association in Chicago with his essay entitled "The Significance of the Frontier in American History" (Theodore Roosevelt Collection).

Turner rightfully maintains that Roosevelt depicted the westward movement "as probably no other man of his time could have" (*The Life and Times of Theodore Roosevelt*, p. 66). Unlike most previous historians and writers who had treated the movement of the frontier [with the exception of Parkman], Roosevelt was neither a westerner of limited education nor a provincial easterner with a narrow national perspective. Firmly rooted in eastern traditions, a scion of the New York aristocracy, he held a unique perspective of the West since he had actually lived and experienced the hardships of the frontier. According to friend and author Owen Wister, Roosevelt seemed to be the only writer of his generation who "felt . . . [the] poetry" of the West (*Roosevelt*, p. 29).

Although Roosevelt generally concurred with Turner in interpreting the frontier experience, he differed sharply with him on several critical issues. While admitting that Turner had "put into definite shape a good deal of thought which . . . [had] been floating around rather loosely," Roosevelt devotes less attention to "land politics" and claims to be "more interested in the men themselves than in institutions" (*Letters of Theodore Roosevelt* 1:363, 440). He also emphasizes the "fundamental unity" of the West as opposed to regional differences in development. Neither does he put aside his racial predilections long enough to view the frontier as rationally as Turner. Nor does he offer an arrangement of ideas as systematic and orderly (*Pacific Historical Review* 29:379-386).

In expressing his generations's belief in Manifest Destiny, Roosevelt remains absolutely convinced that the greatness of the United States was the result of an expanding frontier. Moreover, he is equally certain that the extension of democratic institutions to the Pacific--and then beyond--was the ordained fate of the American people. Historically, he insists, American leaders had imposed their control over the borderlands of the West where Native Americans were incapable of governing themselves. Jefferson had established the precedent of extending the American "Empire of Liberty" with the Louisiana Purchase; Andrew Jackson had applied the same principle to the Seminoles of Florida; Ulysses S. Grant had extended it to the Sioux and Cheyenne of the northern Great Plains. Logically, in 1898, Roosevelt therefore argues the rationale that William McKinley should bestow the same "blessing of liberty" upon the Hawaiians and Filipinos (*Winning of the West* 3:45-46, 175-176).

By 1898 there was no longer any need to "push the Indians back," but there still remained for Roosevelt the challenge of world frontiers. To Roosevelt, the conquest of North America had been the "crowning and greatest achievement" in the continuing spread of English-speaking peoples around the globe. To the remote regions and native peoples of the world, civilization had come only in recent centuries by the "armed settlement" of a superior culture over the "heathen savage." Regardless of whether the experience was between Boer and Zulu, Englishman and Sepoy, New Zealander and Maori, or Anglo-American and Indian, the resulting advance of progress and civilization was the same. Specifically, in reference to the United States' seizure of the Philippines during the Spanish-American War, Roosevelt warns that "to grant self-government to Luzon and Aguinaldo would be like granting . . . [freedom] to an Apache reservation under some local chief [like Geronimo]" (*The Works of Theodore Roosevelt* 16:236-237).

Roosevelt was not only a trailblazer among frontier historians, but he emerged, too, as a pioneer of the American conservation movement. Roosevelt believed that, throughout the American experience, people moving onto the frontier had always been forced to make the most of what nature provided. On the other hand, however, he viewed as tragic--if not dangerous--the traditional attitudes of westerners toward their own wilderness environment, the careless and wanton waste of renewable natural resources having been deeply ingrained in the fabric of the American frontier. Typically, those pioneers who have hewn and plowed their way westward across the continent looked upon mountain ranges, rivers, and forests as natural obstacles, enemies to be conquered and exploited, not precious natural treasures to be preserved. When the early settlers had felled the trees and had exhausted the soil, they needed only to move westward, on to new frontiers, to more fertile and verdant valleys. If they had hunted and trapped out their wooded environs and fished their streams empty, they could always trek farther west to find still more virgin wilderness. But now all of that had changed forever, Roosevelt realized. The frontier was closed.

Throughout most of his literary career, Theodore Roosevelt dedicated himself to his favorite subject--the American West. Among the products of his labors was a trilogy narrating his own ranching and hunting experiences. In 1886 he produced a colorful and captivating narrative of his early adventures in the Badlands entitled "Hunting Trips of a Ranchman." Besides recording his general impressions about life on the Dakota frontier, the essay offers a detailed description of the flora, fauna, and physiography of the region. Then in 1889 he finished another manuscript detailing his personal observations in the West. The chapters were serialized into six monthly installments for *Century* magazine, then published in book form under the title *Ranch Life and the Hunting Trail.* Then in 1893, while serving on the United States Civil Service Commission, he somehow found time to complete a third project, *The Wilderness Hunter*, describing his travels on the Northern Great Plains and in the Great Rockies. In future years he produced several narratives on big game hunting in the West. But his most important contribution to historical literature remained unfinished. In 1896, after completing the last of his four volumes of *The Winning of the West*, which ended with the Lewis and Clark expedition, he reluctantly abandoned his dream of finishing the study.

Still Roosevelt remained, for the rest of his days, a serious student of the American frontier. In the end his contributions were justifiably overshadowed by Turner and others, and thus as a historian of the frontier he has been too easily overlooked, even ignored. Perhaps had he never become president, had he not gone on to become a shaper of history, his illuminating narratives of the westward movement would not have been all but forgotten. To Roosevelt, the American West continued to represent not just a geographic region or a romantic idyll, but a state of mind. As Owen Wister describes Roosevelt the warrior, the hunter, the stateman, the historian: "deep in his spirit dwelt the pioneer eternal" (*The Works of Theodore Roosevelt* 1:263).

Bibliography

Books

The Life and Times of Thomas Hart Benton. New York: Houghton Mifflin, 1887.

The Naval War of 1812: The History of the United States Navy During the Last War With Great Britain. New York: G. P.Putnam's Sons, 1882.

Ranch Life and the Hunting Trail. New York: Century Co., 1899.

Theodore Roosevelt: An Autobiography. New York: Charles Scribner's Sons, 1927.

The Winning of the West. 4 volumes. New York: Current Literature Publishing Co., 1905.

The Works of Theodore Roosevelt. 20 volumes. New York: Charles Scribner's Sons, 1926.

Articles

"Big Game Disappearing in the West." *Forum*, August, 1893, pp. 767-776.

"Forests Vital to Our Welfare." *National Geographic*, November, 1905, pp. 515-516.

"The Northwest in the Nation: Biennial Address Before the State Historical Society of Wisconsin." In *Proceedings of the Fortieth Annual Meeting of the Wisconsin State Historical Society, 1893.* Theodore Roosevelt Collection, Harvard University Library, Cambridge, MA.

Studies of Theodore Roosevelt

Billington, Ray Allen. *Frederick Jackson Turner: Historian, Scholar, Teacher.* New York: Oxford University Press, 1973.

__________. *The Genesis of the Frontier Thesis: A Study in Historical Creativity.* San Marino, CA:Huntington Library, 1971.

Burton, Davis H. "The Influence of the American West on the Imperialist Philosophy of Theodore Roosevelt." *Arizona and the West* 4(January, 1962):5-26.

Cowles, Anna Roosevelt, ed. *Letters From Theodore Roosevelt to Anna Roosevelt Cowles.* New York: Charles Scribner's Sons, 1924.

Drinnon, Richard. *The Metaphysics of Indian Hating and Empire Building.* New York: New American Library, 1980.

Ferris, Joseph A. "When Roosevelt Came to Dakota." *Wide World*, March, 1921, pp. 435-439.

Hagedorn, Hermann. *Roosevelt in the Bad Lands.* Boston: Houghton Mifflin Company, 1921.

Harbaugh, William H. *The Life and Times of Theodore Roosevelt.* Revised edition. London: Oxford University Press, 1978.

Knee, Stuart. "Awakening in the West." *Journal of the West* 17(April, 1978):105-111.

Lang, Lincoln A. *Ranching with Roosevelt.* Philadelphia: J. B. Lippincott Co., 1926.

Lewis, Merrill E. "The American Frontier as Literature: The Historiography of George Bancroft, Frederick Jackson Turner, and Theodore Roosevelt." Ph.D. diss., University of Utah, 1968.

Morison, Elting E., ed. *The Letters of Theodore Roosevelt.* 8 volumes. Cambridge: Harvard University Press, 1951.

Morris, Edmund. *The Rise of Theodore Roosevelt.* New York: Coward, McCann, Geoghegan, Inc., 1979.

New York Times, May 15, 1897.

Putnam, Carleton. *Theodore Roosevelt: The Formative Years, 1858-1886.* New York: Charles Scribner's Sons, 1958.

Roosevelt, Theodore, Collection. Harvard University Library, Cambridge, MA.

Roosevelt, Theodore, Papers. Library of Congress, Washington, DC.

"Roosevelt's Benton." *Nation*, March 29, 1888, p. 264.

Sewall, William Wingate. *Bill Sewall's Story of T. R.* New York: Harper and Brothers, 1919.

Turner, Frederick Jackson. Review of *The Winning of the West* by Theodore Roosevelt. *American Historical Review* 2(October, 1896):171.

__________. Review of *The Winning of the West* by Theodore Roosevelt. *The Dial* 10(August, 1889):71-73.

White, G. Edward. *The Eastern Establishment and the Western Experience: The West of Frederick Remington, Theodore Roosevelt, and Owen Wister.* New Haven: Yale University Press, 1968.

Williams, William Appleman. "The Frontier and American Foreign Policy." *Pacific Historical Review* 29(November, 1955):379-395.

Wister, Owen. *Roosevelt: The Story of a Friendship.* New York: Macmillan, 1930.

42

WALTER RUNDELL, JR.

by Anne M. Butler

Biography

Walter Rundell, Jr., assumed the presidency of the Western History Association at the twenty-second annual conference at Phoenix, Arizona. On Saturday, October 23, 1982, he boarded his flight for home and, once in the air, set to work on a presidential memo that concerned the just announced plans of John and La Ree Caughey to establish an annual prize for distinguished writing in the field of western American history. The Caugheys requested that the Western History Association administer the award, so it fell to the newly-installed president to draft the plans for its implementation. Upon arrival in Dallas, Texas, Rundell, a son of the Lone Star State, put aside his papers and announced he would take a "stretch-of-the-legs," his usual practice during a layover, since a few hours in flight always cramped his long frame.

During this interval, Rundell stood in the busy airport corridor and took leave of WHA member, David Baird, who would shortly catch a connecting flight to his home in Oklahoma. The two chatted about the Phoenix meeting, and Baird, then chairman of the history department at Oklahoma State University, commented on some of his hopes for future development at that campus. He pointed to the outdoor ranching museum at Texas Tech University in Lubbock, Texas, as a model for the promotion of frontier history through utilization of the regional environment. Rundell, ever the champion of vigorous endeavor, concurred in Baird's assessment and spoke favorably of an agricultural history project for Oklahoma. Rundell, with regards to the Baird family, completed his farewell and reboarded the plane, expressing, as he strode down the ramp, his great admiration and affection for Baird, whom he had known since the younger man's student days.

On the second leg of the journey from Dallas to Washington, DC, Rundell, satisfied with his first presidential labors, relaxed and chatted with his traveling companions. In his long career, Rundell supervised to completion the doctoral programs of only two students, each of whom had written on some aspect of western history. Recent events--a manuscript accepted for one, a dissertation to be defended in ten days for the other--had prompted Rundell to encourage his graduate students to journey with him to Phoenix. He reveled in the role of mentor and brought to it the full force of his knowledge and influence. In Phoenix, he seized every opportunity to introduce his students to his friends, to involve them in his professional activities and social functions. On the flight home with them, he contentedly reviewed the events that the three had shared.

Rundell's topics ranged back and forth over the conference: he spoke with pleasure of the Caughey prize, the excellence of the final Saturday session when he heard Terry Jordan speak on his book, *Trails to Texas*, his good fortune at securing Jordan's inscription in a copy of the work, his own response to Jordan's assessment of Walter Prescott Webb, his warm regard for Norris Hundley, William Hagan, and a dozen other friends. He reserved his greatest glee, however, for the subject of his new and cherished Green River knife, symbol of the WHA presidency. An annual presentation made by Colorado businessman, Sam Arnold, the knife tickled Rundell's fancy, and he asked his students for suggestions about where to display the treasure. His own first choice would have been his University of Maryland office, but a recent burglary there had resulted in the theft of a mounted collection of currency, a valuable gift that commemorated Rundell's publication of *Military Money* in 1980. Reluctant to risk a similar fate for the Green River knife, Rundell seemed inclined to keep his new prize safely in his personal study.

About mid-trip, he turned his attention to the latest volume of the *Pacific Historical Review* and passed the time reading an article written by a former student. The constant pace of the week overtook him after a bit; he stopped reading, placed his boarding pass into the journal as a marker, said he would nap until landing, and drifted off to sleep--his hands folded lightly in his lap, his silver hair glittery in the dim cabin light hinted of future snow-white beauty, his features calm in repose with the inner dignity that always characterized his bearing.

At Dulles Airport, his spirits revived, Rundell scooped up his luggage and bounded down the stairs, declaring it "a matter of principle" to avoid the easy escalator descent. During the drive along the Capital Beltway, Rundell's festive humor soared and he burst into a rousing song, a sure sign of his overall satisfaction and pleasure. Rundell arrived at his Hyattsville, Maryland, home shortly before ten o'clock in the evening. He greeted his wife, Deanna, poured himself a glass of cider from a jug on the side porch, and settled into a wicker rocker in the living room as he prepared to report on the Arizona trip.

A bit subdued from the wearying travel, but with no lessening of his enthusiasm, Rundell shared with his wife a full account of the outstanding conference and listed the names of their many old friends who had demanded that he explain her absence. To each, Rundell said he had promised, "Wait until next year. We will see you in Salt Lake City." Over and over, the new president pronounced it, "a fine meeting, a fine meeting." He began to talk of plans for the coming year and reviewed possible topics for his 1983 presidential address to the WHA. He mentioned several possibilities, but felt most drawn to the subject of the West as an artistic setting, long one of his favorite research interests that he hoped to develop into a major publication when he finished his work on Walter Prescott Webb.

Rundell rested on Sunday, for he had to teach during the first half of the week and then return to Texas on Thursday. There he would attend the Levelland Junior College oil symposium to present a slide lecture entitled, "Using Photographs as Historical Evidence." Sunday evening, he and Deanna attended a small birthday party for Paul Scheips, a friend from Rundell's graduate school days and a fellow member of the Potomac Corral of Westerners. Among the guests was Dan Mortensen, son of Rundell's friend, A. Russell Mortensen, a one-time chief historian for the National Park Service and a past director of the Utah State Historical Society. It was a warm gathering of friends, but with the busy week ahead, the Rundells departed early.

On Monday, October 25, 1982, Walter Rundell did not awaken; sometime past the hour of midnight he died in his sleep. He was fifty-three years old; in eight more days, he would have reached his next birthday.

The final week of Walter Rundell's life mirrored the twenty-five years that had preceded it. In five days, from Maryland to Arizona and back again, Rundell occupied himself with the primary concerns of his career: devotion to teaching, encouragement of scholarship, pursuit of research, solidness in friendship, commitment to students, and an untiring dedication to the systematic advancement of the historical profession, with a special emphasis on all matters related to the study of the American West. Rundell's actions during that late October soon touched all who knew him with a bittersweet sense of "unfinished business." Yet, those days celebrate the contributions of an extraordinary American scholar, who died as he had lived--happily surrounded by friends and colleagues and joyfully immersed in the professional and personal ambience of his discipline.

The saga of this remarkable man began in Austin, Texas, on November 2, 1928. The only child of Walter and Olive Rundell, young Walter grew up in Baytown, Texas, where his father served as the dean of the local junior college. His parents, in a home notable for its grace and charm, instilled in their son the most attractive of personal traits. The senior Rundells valued their close ties with church and school and drew on these institutions to form their guides in raising their child. Early on, Walter learned the merit of hard work, the significance of good schooling, the nature of integrity, and the essence of justice. In all things, his parents taught that courtesy and human decency bonded these basic values. Healthy doses of Texas courtliness, good humor, and warm laughter rounded out the Rundell's home environment.

It was an equation that could not miss. By the time he was twelve, Walter, serious and honorable, demonstrated that he had absorbed the lessons of his family. That year he determined that he should seek employment, as the Christmas season approached. Despite a disheartening job market where the few plums had gone to older boys, he persisted until he found an after-school position with a local jeweler. The shopkeeper hired him at lower than the going rate, but promised to improve the salary and keep the boy on after the holiday season. Once the new year started the jeweler suddenly refused to allow the boy to use the back alley door to haul the trash, insisting it should be carried out the front and around an entire block. Chagrined, Walter realized the man had never intended to keep him or to give him a raise, and now added insult to injury by asking that he haul the trash bins an unreasonable distance. Embarrassed at his own naiveté and angered by the injustice, Walter quit. The senior Rundells felt only pride at their son's response to unfair treatment on that occasion and for the remainder of his life, as his unswerving opposition to injustice in any form became one of his most striking points (Olive Rundell to Butler, July 20, 1984).

Among his many talents, Rundell possessed a rich singing voice. Throughout his lifetime, he graced the choirs of several Methodist churches and sang with the Cathedral Choral Society and the University of Maryland Chorus. Personal performance certainly did not define the scope of his musical zest. Upon completion of his studies at Lee Junior College in Baytown, Rundell entered the University of Texas at Austin, determined to become a professional music critic. He shaped an academic program that could lead to such a future and graduated in 1951 with combined skills in music and journalism.

Before he could establish himself in the music field, Rundell faced a military obligation. He entered the United States Army in 1951, but his mind remained fixed on his goal in music. Of all the recruits who marched to the sergeant's cadence during basic training, surely only Rundell spotted a small group of children peering through the post fence at the inductees and allowed his thoughts to drift to the opening scene of the opera, "Carmen."

Fate intervened during Rundell's military stint and set the would-be music critic upon a different path in life, that of professional historian. Fellow Texan, Edith H. Parker, held a position as chief historian in the Office of Finance of the United States Army. Parker had known Rundell since 1948 and, once she learned he was in uniform, saw him as the perfect candidate to attend the Army Finance School and join her staff as one of the historical officers. Rundell grasped the advantages of such a move and sensed that the atmosphere in the historical office would be much more to his liking than many other stations. Once attached to Parker's staff, Rundell became responsible for writing a history of the Army's overseas fiscal activities during World War II. These sudden events and the enjoyment he extracted from being thrust amongst a near avalanche of military documents propelled Rundell in the direction of advanced training in history (Rundell Papers, April 7, 1954).

Posted to Washington, DC, Rundell surveyed the possible graduate programs available in the immediate area and settled on the one at The American University. With the approval of the department and his major professor, Louis C. Hunter, Rundell shaped the previously unculled records he needed for his Army assignment into a dissertation about military currency management (Rundell Papers, June 24, 1954). With the dispatch he brought to every task, Rundell completed his masters' degree in 1955 and his doctorate in 1957. His proud parents presented him with his academic robes as a graduation gift.

Although these events seem far afield of Rundell's later connections with western history, such was not the case. As a student at American, Rundell enrolled in a course entitled, "The Frontier in U.S. History," taught by Richard A. Bartlett. This proved to be Rundell's only formal course work on the subject, but the experience quickened his already warm appreciation for the West. Bartlett, who became an important and lasting friend to Rundell, emphasized at the outset that the class would be expected to develop a keen understanding of the works of Walter Prescott Webb (Rundell Papers).

This spark Rundell carried to the requirements of a historiography course and used an assignment there as the reason to read and analyze the writings of Webb. During his undergraduate days at Austin, Rundell had known about, but never studied with Walter Prescott Webb. As a graduate student, far beyond the borders of Texas, Rundell, prompted by the urgings of his professors at an eastern university, launched his lifelong intellectual commitment to Walter Prescott Webb.

Upon completion of his graduate work, Rundell returned to his home state and taught at Del Mar College in Corpus Christi, Texas, from 1957-1958 and Texas Woman's University at Denton from 1958-1961. During the spring semester of 1959, Rundell, through a college political group, met the young woman who was to become his wife. In perhaps the only impetuous move of his life, but one guided by impeccably good judgment, Rundell courted and married Deanna Boyd of Denton, Texas, in little more than three months. The correctness of their decision became apparent in the gracious and solid blending of their lives that produced an unfaltering relationship, a cordial home, and a family of three children.

Rundell, calling on his own reserves of energy and determination, methodically built a career that led him to greater and greater recognition as a reputable scholar, an efficient administrator, and a champion of western history. He served as assistant executive secretary for the American Historical Association (1961-1965) and director of a survey of graduate school training conducted by the National Historical Publications Commission (1965-1967). During these years, visiting lecturer opportunities convinced Rundell that he wanted to return to academia, and he did with a position at the University of Oklahoma. In 1969, his career entered a new administrative phase when he accepted the chairmanship of the Iowa

State University history department at Ames. In 1971, the history department at the University of Maryland beckoned, and Rundell returned to the East, where he would finish his career. In each of his professional positions, Rundell made contributions that earned for him a growing reputation as a national figure in the fields of American history and higher education (Rundell Papers, Rundell vita).

However, it had been in 1961 that Rundell made the move that permanently linked his name with those scholars of major significance in the field of western American history. At the instigation of historians John Alexander Carroll and K. Ross Toole, Rundell joined a committee of six who hoped to convene a western history conference in Santa Fe during October. The committee's broader goal, inspired by a conviction there existed a strong grassroots interest and a serious professional vacuum, was to establish a formal organization that ultimately came to be known as the Western History Association. Rundell enthusiastically responded to the call of his good friend, Carroll; he spent the spring and summer of 1961 helping to implement the program. The project appealed to Rundell, for it touched on both his love for the West and his passion for system in scholarship. Accordingly, Rundell involved himself in all stages of the coming conference, always with an eye to making the venture an annual event under the auspices of a regularized society. He worked on plans for financial structure and conference logistics, he organized a Santa Fe session and offered to present a paper, prophetically entitled, "The West as an Operatic Setting" (Rundell Papers, WHA file).

The organizers tried to anticipate every possible snag but despite their intensive efforts felt uncertain about what sort of response to expect from the simple green brochure they distributed that invited those "seriously interested in the historical phenomena of the American West," to register for the Santa Fe experiment (Rundell Papers, WHA file). By early July, the number of preregistrants so impressed committee member Robert Utley that he wrote to Rundell, "Business is booming--this may blow-up in our faces!" His fears proved groundless (Rundell Papers, WHA file).

In October, when 293 participants flocked to Santa Fe, the committee was ready. It had arranged for a conference hotel that provided rooms at the unbeatable bargain rates of $6 and $12. More importantly, it boasted of a meeting with eleven sessions, twenty-seven papers, and John F. Kennedy's Assistant Secretary of the Interior, John A. Carver, as the keynote speaker. Carver, a last minute substitute for Secretary of the Interior Stewart Udall, in a burst of oblique logic told the assembled historians, "The West being closer to the . . . Old Frontier, is in a position to make the major contribution to the philosophy of the New Frontier. You are the professional custodians of that responsibility" (Rundell Papers, WHA file).

His blatantly political charge fell upon a group, slightly disgruntled by the Interior Secretary's default, keenly aware of its professional responsibility, and anxious to formalize its future through a written constitution. That became the next order of business, and it was in these constitutional discussions that Rundell placed his stamp upon the burgeoning Western History Association. Committed to clarity and legality, Rundell vigorously assisted in drafting the document that would give shape to the western history interests of professionals, amateurs, and students. With the adoption of that constitution at the Denver meeting in 1962, the Western History Association formally assumed its place among the historical organizations of the nation.

This did not conclude Rundell's constitutional work, and in 1963, at the annual meeting in Salt Lake City, he used the hotel stationery to rough out new by-laws that defined the various types of memberships that the association offered to both individuals and institutions. Always concerned about the well-being of students, whom he recognized to be notoriously poverty-stricken, Rundell wrote in an attractive discounted rate for that group (Rundell Papers, WHA file). The importance of his work in this area left a lasting mark on the structure of the Western History Association and prompted John A. Carroll, upon the occasion of Rundell's nomination to the vice-presidential slot, to write, "Your efforts on the Constitution . . . I personally vividly recall, and your special part in the birthing of the WHA ought to be known by the present membership" (Rundell Papers, Carroll file). Only one year later, in 1982, a grieving John A. Carroll remembered Walter Rundell as the "James Madison" of the writing of the Western History Association constitution (John A. Carroll to Butler, October 14, 1983).

Rundell's enthusiasm for the WHA never slackened. It was a rare conference that he was not seen in the halls, at the sessions, on the tours, with friends. The scope of his participation touched on every aspect of the organization's life. He served on the executive council, assumed special investigative tasks, chaired awards committees, and supported the society's efforts to encourage a western history program for secondary school teachers, attract student members, publish a western bibliography, and stabilize the chronic management problems with the *American West* journal (Rundell Papers, WHA file).

Four times Rundell served on the program committee, and twice he accepted the enormous job of chairman, once in 1965 and again in 1980. He prided himself on being able to organize a well-balanced conference designed to appeal to the interests of all who attended, regardless of their connection to western history. He was particularly skilled at casting his net through the history profession and drawing to a regional conference scholars who, although not regarded as "frontier historians," had research expertise that could be interestingly applied to the West. Additionally, he liked to sprinkle the program with the known "big names in the field," to provide professional ballast, while at the same time he was generous with arrangements for those just entering the field and anxious for a chance to make a mark at a respected conference.

Both of the programs that he organized, the first in Helena, Montana, and the second in Kansas City, Missouri, elicited praise from those who attended. As for Rundell, he was quick to turn the compliments back upon those who had performed special tasks for him. Shortly after the completion of these annual meetings, his letters of thanks went out around the country. Always the epitome of courtesy, Rundell did not simply dash off a form letter but pointed to some notable contribution that had pleased him--thanks to members of the program committee, appreciation to a person who pinch-hit in a last minute conference snarl, compliments to a panelist with a stimulating paper, gratitude to the organizer of local transportation arrangements (Rundell Papers, WHA file).

Quick to acknowledge the hard work and accomplishments of others, Rundell spoke up with comparable briskness if he thought that a situation deserved criticism. Although satisfied with the "intellectual fare" of the Helena conference, Rundell concluded that the WHA had outgrown its original format, as each year a healthy increase in attendees stretched the time frame and the room space during sessions. With his usual directness, Rundell wrote immediately to the next program chairman about his concerns (Rundell Papers, WHA file).

He pointed to the WHA's traditional plan of two separate morning sessions and pronounced it "too crowded," for it eliminated time for questions and discussion at the end of a presentation. Rundell thought it regretable that pertinent issues could not be raised from the floor, as he viewed this procedure as one of the most stimulating aspects of professional presentations. He conceded that part of the problem stemmed from the "tragic condition" that "we can just expect historians to be long-winded" (Rundell Papers, WHA file). Nonetheless, he declared that the WHA needed some "intellectual elbow room," and called for a schedule with concurrent sessions. This move, when adopted, greatly expanded the varieties of subjects offered at the annual meeting, broadened the intellectual scope of the organization, and improved the dynamics of the daily conference sessions. Yet, few who crisscrossed the halls of a WHA meeting ever knew that these practical adjustments began with Rundell, who with constant attention to efficiency, first defined the problem only four years after the Santa Fe meeting.

Beyond the confines of the organization, Rundell excelled as a champion for the Western History Association. In 1972, when chairman at the University of Maryland history department, Rundell secured a pledge from the school to become a sponsor of the WHA. He understood that support from a major academic institution enhanced the national reputation of the essentially regional organization, as well as added to the financial well-being of the association (Rundell Papers, WHA file).

Rundell did not permit these many administrative duties to inhibit his participation as a scholar in the WHA. Happy to chair a session, present a paper, or offer the commentary, Rundell accumulated a long list of appearances at the annual meetings. Rundell clearly ranked as a major patron of the Western History Association. His labors to insure the organization and continuation of the WHA were monumental. When the association recognized his stature by selecting him as the 1981 vice-presidential candidate, a nomination that would automatically elevate him to the presidency in 1982, Rundell was unabashedly thrilled. He and Deanna hosted a party for friends in the College Park, Maryland, area to celebrate the occasion; it proved a festive gathering, in part because the well-wishers knew it marked but the latest accolade in a career filled with past accomplishments and future honors.

Themes

Rundell's scholarly activities at the Western History Association meetings captured his primary research interests. They represent those subjects to which he dedicated much of his intellectual energy: the West and art, archives and record keeping, and Walter Prescott Webb. These themes often provided him with the subjects for his WHA presentations and his frontier history publications.

Rundell also had professional interests beyond his ties to the WHA that thematically explain his research activities. An active member in the Organization of American Historians, the American Historical Association, the Southern Historical Association, the Society of American Archivists, the Maryland Historical Society, and the Texas State Historical Society, Rundell directed attention to each of these groups. A popular speaker, he gave more than fifty addresses in addition to his scholarly papers, served on at least that many professional committees, received numerous awards, and was the first nonarchivist elected president of the Society of American Archivists (Rundell Papers, Rundell vita). Along with an impressive array of essays, articles, and pamphlets, he found time to publish three major works outside the field of the American West: *Black Market Money* (1964), *In Pursuit of American History* (1970), which received the Waldo G. Leland Prize for 1971, and *Military Money* (1980).

None of these enterprises, projects, or publications slowed Rundell's productivity in the area of the American West. The scope of his western interests, always highlighted by his love for the trans-Mississippi West in general and Texas in particular, reflected concerns that had intrigued him since his first days as a historian.

Analysis

Any analysis of Walter Rundell's works must start with documents. A priority interest for Rundell concerned the management of archival sources, as well as the availability with which scholars could secure research materials. Rundell found this topic especially relevant to the American West, where scattered sources, often carelessly held in far-flung areas, plagued researchers of almost every frontier topic. He reminded historians not to overlook valuable government documents and cautioned that if scholars would not limit their own ingenuity, "practically all aspects of American life . . . can be researched in federal records" (Rundell Papers, WHA file).

He wanted professionals to be concerned with the records of the West and records in the West, insisting that the number of federal repositories beyond the Mississippi River and the quantity of documents generated by public domain issues justified a heightened demand for improved record keeping by frontier scholars. He applauded efforts at the state and local levels to develop retention and disposition schedules, and he called for increased funds for the National Historical Publications and Records

Commission. In all, he was guided by his own enormous love for the records themselves, and was well known for repeatedly urging his seminar students to "treat the documents with care--they are all that we have" (Butler's seminar notes, 1974). True to his own philosophy, he promptly deposited appropriate WHA papers with the Western History Collection at the University of Colorado.

In his insistence upon system at every archival level, Rundell demonstrated his personal conviction that history could only be defined as both art and science. He knew that in the arena of frontier history these components had suffered from a sometimes fuzzy past. He decried lack of scholarship in western writings but recognized the frustrations of scholars who found it almost impossible to develop continuity in research materials. Walter Rundell's answer to this dilemma was to promote both the art and science of western history through the orderly preservation of the public record.

Many of Rundell's concerns about records, document preservation, and research spilled over into his evaluation of scholarly publications. Perhaps nowhere can Rundell's personal intellectual construct be more quickly seen than in his style as a book reviewer. He enjoyed the form and used the assignments as a means of keeping abreast of recent publications. He unswervingly believed that one should review a book and not the author. This professional attitude, coupled with his punctual attention to publishing deadlines, made him a popular reviewer with the editors of several important journals. In his career, he published more than one hundred book reviews, most of which focused on publications with a western theme.

As a reviewer, Rundell expected certain qualities in a western manuscript. He grasped quickly the weakness in those scholars who thought the American West could be used as simply a colorful background to make a bland topic more glamorous. He dismissed such writers as having no real sense of the meaning of frontier, either as place or process, and found the works too formless for his liking. He was equally displeased by the manuscript that represented little more than previously published articles strung together under the guise of "chapters," for he felt that type of work lacked originality, or worse yet, smacked of intellectual laziness.

He enjoyed scholarship that had been drawn from extensive research in a wide variety of archives and sources, for he thought this reflected the "growth and . . . vitality of frontier studies" (*Western Historical Quarterly* 13:430). Nothing pleased him more than the scholar who could retell an old story with new insights, for this type of thinker offered the rich synthesis of frontier concepts that Rundell believed the highest intellectual endeavor of western scholars (*American Historical Review* 84:1150-1151).

The cardinal virtues of writing for Rundell included grace, clarity, and vigor; among these he ranked clarity as most important. He disliked involved syntax and excelled at expressing an idea with linguistic economy. He conceded that grace seemed the most elusive element of style and that as a concept, he found it difficult to teach. Ultimately, he recommended that historians turn to the wisdom of Walter Prescott Webb, who had once asserted that to be judged a real scholar, one must choose truth in writing (Butler's seminar notes, 1974).

Rundell lived by these standards of publication with his own research and writing. His major publications in the area of the American West focused on the subject of the Texas petroleum industry. His two volumes, *Early Texas Oil* (1977) and *Oil in West Texas and New Mexico* (1982) earned for Rundell national and international attention, a satisfying monetary return, special acclaim in his home state, and an expansion of his basic archival interests into the realm of photography collections.

Both books recreate the Texas petroleum business through the use of photographs. Rundell, who had grown up in the oil district of East Texas, knew only too well that the story of this particular industry often hung on contradictions. The former lad from Baytown had seen first hand that oil brought jobs to Texans and profits to Texas, but he could not overlook that along with industrial development had come questionable labor practices and environmental exploitation (*Arizona and the West* 2:190-192).

Rundell brought these warring elements together into two exquisite volumes that captured the history of the Texas oil boom days. His careful presentation, concern for accuracy, and insightful analysis converted essentially mundane photographs into a fascinating odyssey of western development. Most notable, Rundell's strong emphasis upon the human experience in the oil bonanza never diluted his lucid explanations of technological information, nor did the business aspects override the impact of the events on the men and women of Texas. In short, Rundell balanced regional industrial phenomena with regional social dynamics.

In so doing, and true to his basic sense of honesty and justice, Rundell refused to gloss over traditional racial discrimination in the oil fields. He presented the ugly cast of racial relations that had erupted by 1921 and added that the retention of jobs by Mexicans and blacks hardly ended their problems, as they always received less pay than white workers (*Early Texas Oil*, p. 123). The directness of his remarks in no way detracted from the "Texasness" of these volumes. Quite the opposite, for Rundell's unflagging devotion to truth intensified the validity of the historical portrait he drew. Indeed, the two oil books represented Rundell's love song to the Lone Star State, and they will stand as monuments to Rundell's commitment to scholarly integrity, people, and Texas.

In Rundell's intellectual development, these works opened an added archival vista for him. His experiences of traveling through Texas and gathering the pictorial documentation from several different museums and libraries impelled Rundell to consider more deeply the research benefits of photographs. This was not a new concept for him; he had long chided historians for their apparent willingness to depend on over-used and familiar photographs. His work in the Texas oil book reinforced his interest in the use of refreshingly new materials. He thought that what appeared to be an ordinary and dull picture could be fleshed out through research and take on meaningful historic terms (Butler's seminar notes, 1974).

Always quick to harness his activities into a coherent form, Rundell began to think systematically about the subject of photographs as a source of historical evidence. Rundell argued that photographs must be collected in accord with a research plan, that each should add something clear to the project, and that the captions should provide for the movement of ideas from image to image, much like the logical development in a well-constructed paragraph (Rundell Papers, Lecture Notes file). To illustrate his points, Rundell organized a slide presentation entitled, "Oil History through the Camera Lens: Research Adventures and Misadventures." Here he bonded his passionate interest in orderly research to a growing fascination with the uses of photography as documentation and his great affection for Texas history. Accordingly, his efforts represented the best in western scholarship, for he drew upon universal professional standards to investigate a regional event, but he transformed a localized topic into a format applicable to any scholarly audience. His welding of standard to subject and his meshing of subject into standard made his slide presentation on photographs as documentary evidence an oft-demanded lecture in and out of Texas.

Despite these impressive credentials in several areas of western scholarship, Rundell's name will be best remembered as the foremost biographer of Walter Prescott Webb. In 1954, Rundell had written to Webb, "The thing I find most significant about your works is that you have pioneered by introducing new concepts to the social studies. Shedding new and different light on fundamental problems is to me the highest achievement of scholarship" (Rundell Papers, Webb file). That early respect of a young graduate student evolved into the major scholarly project of the professional historian.

In part, Webb, himself, kindled the interest. Webb received a copy of Rundell's first essay efforts from Edith Parker, who had done her doctoral studies with the renowned scholar. The essay delighted Webb and he quickly wrote to Rundell and asked for permission to copy the paper. Rundell felt honored by the request, especially since in those pre-xerox days the copy would be time-consumingly made by typewriter (Rundell Papers, Webb file). The exchange led to a cordial relationship between the two Texans, although theirs had never been the teacher/student relationship that many had erroneously assumed.

Rundell's original correspondence to Webb captured the essence of his respect for the older Texan. Rundell's sentiments of 1954 became his intellectual beacons as he pursued a nearly three decade-long devotion to the "human and literary sensitivity" of Walter Prescott Webb. He transformed his personal regard and interest into twelve scholarly articles and, in 1982, moved toward the completion of a major Webb biography.

Rundell's premise centers on Walter Webb as a product of the Great Plains of Texas, and he argues Webb's writings reflected the impact of his environment on his intellectual development. Accordingly, Rundell showed himself comfortable with traditional frontier perspectives, but always when used as catalysts for bold thought and imaginative synthesis. Thus, Rundell was less concerned with absolute validity in Webb's theories and more elated by his suggestive concepts and the stimulating debates and research they provoked.

Rundell saw the biography as a way to use life events to trace the configurations of ideas and to understand the emergence of concepts in the mind of an influential scholar whose impact reached far beyond the Texas borders. For Rundell, the underpinnings of Webb's intellectual structure could be found on the Texas Plains as the frontier era wound to a close. There, in Rundell's view, an environment and an intellect melded and the result produced one of the major scholars of the twentieth century.

Rundell, with his own roots deep in Texas, valued Webb's status as a state-wide educator, a regional historian, a national and international scholar. He understood that for one to consider Walter Prescott Webb, one had to also consider the elements that made Texas: the essence of frontier living, the struggle with aridity, the costs of isolation. Major issues, provocative questions, scholarly reassessments, spirited discussions--these became Webb's legacy to frontier history, not only through his own work, but from the quantities of subsequent scholarship his concepts generated. Rundell perceived that Webb forced Texans and non-Texans to confront the West as an intellectual problem, worthy of scholarly analysis from myriad angles. The academic scenario, where Webb fired the thought and work of others, contained the captivating ingredients that held intellectual fascination for Rundell.

Rundell fashioned his interests into a lucid and intelligent analysis of how an environment shaped a man, who in turn touched the contours of American thought. Rundell moved his work far beyond mere biographical storytelling to embrace regional and national issues fundamental to the American experience. This work alone would win Rundell a high place among western scholars. Yet, Rundell's contributions were so many and diversified that not even his outstanding Webb studies give him his just due as a frontier historian.

Rundell's personal love for region and state guided his work in American western history, but he empowered his efforts with an overall dedication to professional standards. With his expansive interests and massive productivity, Rundell fits no easy category as a historian, in the West, or generally. His willingness to embrace the concepts of Frederick Jackson Turner and Walter Prescott Webb might label his frontier philosophy, "slightly old school." He fits that mold only partially, for his exhaustive, all-encompassing scholarship and his vast administrative endeavors, coupled with his receptive regard for the ideas of others, mark him--to use one of his favorite phrases--a "shaker and mover" in his own right.

Rundell once wrote about Walter Webb, "Probably more than any other contemporary historian, he left an unmistakable record of what he thought about historical methods, the aim of history, and how historians practice their craft" (*Arizona and the West* 5:19). It is a statement aptly applied to Rundell, whose twenty-five year career reflected his passionate love for history as art and science. As a practitioner, an administrator, a teacher, a champion, Rundell brought his historical zeal to frontier history.

He left it a better discipline -- more scholarly, more orderly, more accomplished, and guided by a strong professional association, in which his charter membership had been critical. Walter Rundell made this impact through the winning power of his fine, personal character and through his ever apparent intellectual conviction that the American West had, by virtue of place and process, altered the cultural and political structures of the nation.

In 1978, when Ray Allen Billington suffered a serious illness, Rundell, in an encouraging note to his friend, said, "It would be mighty unhandy for us to have to do without you" (Rundell Papers, Billington file). Since October 25, 1982, frontier historians across the United States say the same of Walter Rundell, Jr.

Bibliography

Books

Black Market Money: The Collapse of United States Military Currency Control in World War II. Baton Rouge: Louisiana State University Press, 1964.

Early Texas Oil: A Photographic History, 1866-1936. College Station: Texas A&M University Press, 1977.

In Pursuit of American History: Research and Training in the United States. Norman: University of Oklahoma Press, 1970.

Military Money: A Fiscal History of the United States Army Overseas in World War II. College Station: Texas A&M University Press, 1980.

Oil in West Texas and New Mexico: A Pictorial History of the Permian Basin. College Station: Texas A&M University Press, 1982.

Articles

"Agriculture with Hoof and Horn: An Analysis of the Historical Literature of the Cattle Industry." Co-authored with Anne M. Butler. In *Agricultural Literature--Proud Heritage--Future Promise* edited by Alan Fusonie and Leila Moran. Washington, DC: United States Department of Agriculture, 1977. Pp. 87-106.

"Buchel August." In *Handbook of Texas.* Austin: Texas State Historical Association, 1976. 3:118-119.

"Concepts of the Frontier and the West." *Arizona and the West* 1(Spring, 1959):13-41.

"A Historian's Impact on Federal Policy: W. P. Webb as a Case Study." *Prologue* 15(Winter, 1983):214-228.

"Interpretations of the American West: A Descriptive Bibliography." *Arizona and the West* 3(Spring, 1961):69-88 and (Summer, 1961):381-399.

"Music about the West." In *The Reader's Encyclopedia of the American West* edited by Howard R. Lamar. New York: Crowell, 1977. Pp. 791-792.

"Opera." In *The Reader's Encyclopedia of the American West* edited by Howard R. Lamar. New York: Crowell, 1977. Pp. 377-378.

"Photographs as Historical Evidence: Early Texas Oil." *American Archivist* 41(October, 1978):373-398.

"Steinbeck's Image of the West." *American West* 1(Spring, 1964):4-17, 19.

"Taverns and Hotels." In *The Reader's Encyclopedia of the American West* edited by Howard R. Lamar. New York: Crowell, 1977. Pp. 1157-1161.

"Texas Petroleum History: A Selective Annotated Bibliography." *Southwestern Historical Quarterly* 67(October, 1963):267-278.

"Theater." In *The Reader's Encyclopedia of the American West* edited by Howard R. Lamar. New York: Crowell, 1977. Pp. 1175-1177.

"The Training of Western Historians." In *Reflections of Western Historians* edited by John Alexander Carroll. Tucson: University of Arizona Press, 1969. Pp. 265-266.

"W. P. Webb." *Dictionary of American Biography* 7:770-772.

"W. P. Webb's 'Divided We Stand'." *Western Historical Quarterly* 13(October, 1982):391-407.

Walter Prescott Webb [pamphlet]. Austin, TX: Steck-Vaughn, 1971.

"Walter Prescott Webb: Product of Environment." *Arizona and the West* 5(Spring, 1963):4-28.

"Walter Prescott Webb and the Texas State Historical Association." *Arizona and the West* 25(Summer, 1983):109-136.

"Webb: The Schoolteacher." In *The Walter Prescott Webb Memorial Lectures: Essays on Walter Prescott Webb* edited by Kenneth R. Philp and Elliott West. Austin: University of Texas Press, 1976. Pp. 95-123.

"Webb as Businessman." *Great Plains Journal* 18(1979):130-139.

"Webb at Wisconsin." *Panhandle-Plains Historical Review* 50(1977):81-89.

"Webb to Bolton." *Western Historical Quarterly* 2(April, 1971):229-231.

"The West as an Operatic Setting." *El Palacio* 49(Spring, 1962):5-19. Reprint. *Probing the American West* edited by K. Ross Toole, John Alexander Carroll, Robert M. Utley, and A. R. Mortensen. Santa Fe: Museum of New Mexico Press, 1962. Pp. 49-61.

Selected Reviews

The Ambidextrous Historian: Historical Writers and Writing in the American West by C. L. Sonnichsen. *Journal of the West* 21(July, 1982):73-74.

Bartlett's West: Drawing the Mexican Boundary by Robert V. Hine. *Southwestern Historical Quarterly* 72(October, 1968):276-278.

Black Hills, White Sky: Photographs from the Collection of the Arvada Center Foundation, Inc. compiled by Alvin M. Josephy, Jr. *South Dakota History* 10(Fall, 1980):342-343.

Community on the American Frontier: Separate but Not Alone by Robert V. Hine. *History Review of New Books* (May, 1981):320-321.

Comparative Frontiers: A Proposal for Studying the American West by Jerome O. Steffen. *South Dakota History* 11(Spring, 1981):145-146.

Country Music, U.S.A. by William Malone. *American Historical Review* 74(December, 1969):609-610.

"Dear Lady": The Letters of Frederick Jackson Turner and Alice Forbes Perkins Hooper edited by Ray Allen Billington. *Arizona and the West* 13(Winter, 1971):379-380.

Frederick Jackson Turner: Historian, Scholar, Teacher by Ray Allen Billington. *Journal of American History* 60(December, 1973):832-833.

The Frontier Challenge: Responses to the Trans-Mississippi West edited by John G. Clark. *American Historical Review* 77(February, 1972):207-208.

The Genesis of the Frontier Thesis: A Study in Historical Creativity by Ray Allen Billington. *Journal of American History* 59(September, 1972):435-436.

Herbert Eugene Bolton: The Historian and the Man, 1870-1953 by John Francis Bannon. *Journal of the West* 19(January, 1980):94.

The Historical World of Frederick Jackson Turner by Wilbur Jacobs. *American Historical Review* 74(October, 1969):224-225.

History of the Humble Oil and Refining Company by Henrietta Larson and Kenneth Wiggins Porter. *Arizona and the West* 2(Summer, 1960):190-192.

The Making of a History: Walter Prescott Webb and the Great Plains by Gregory Tobin. *Arizona and the West* 19(Autumn, 1977):267-268.

More Burs Under the Saddle by Ramon F. Adams. *New Mexico Historical Review* 55(April, 1980):165-166.

The New Country: A Social History of the American Frontier by Richard Bartlett. *Journal of Southern History* 41(May, 1975):255-256.

People of the Plains and Mountains: Essays in the History of the West Dedicated to Everett Dick edited by Ray Allen Billington. *History Review of New Books* (August, 1973):202.

Photographing the Frontier by Dorothy Hoobler. *South Dakota History* 10(Fall, 1980):342-343.

Regeneration Through Violence: The Mythology of the American Frontier by Richard Slotkin. *American Archivist* 38(January, 1975):57.

The Saloon on the Rocky Mountain Mining Frontier by Elliott West. *History Review of New Books* (January, 1980):53-54.

Taos: A Painter's Dream by Patricia Janis Broder. *Western Historical Quarterly* 12(October, 1981):439.

The Trans-Appalachian Frontier by Malcolm Rohrbough. *American Historical Review* 84(October, 1979):1150-1151.

Walter Prescott Webb by Necah Furman. *Southwestern Historical Quarterly* 80(October, 1976):238-239.

Westward Expansion: A History of the American Frontier by Ray Allen Billington and Martin Ridge. *Western Historical Quarterly* 13(October, 1982):429-430.

Westward Vision: The Story of the Oregon Trail by David Lavender. *California Historical Quarterly* 44(March, 1965):50-51.

Studies of Walter Rundell, Jr.

Charlton, Thomas L. Review of *Early Texas Oil: A Photographic History, 1866-1936* by Walter Rundell, Jr. *Western Historical Quarterly* 9(July, 1978):374-375.

Hagan, William T. "Walter Rundell, Jr." *Western Historical Quarterly* 14(April, 1983):141-144.

Huntsman, Jeffrey. Review of *Oil in West Texas and New Mexico: A Pictorial History of the Permian Basin* by Walter Rundell, Jr. *Western Historical Quarterly* 14(October, 1983):479-480.

Loos, John L. Review of *Oil in West Texas and New Mexico: A Pictorial History of the Permian Basin* by Walter Rundell, Jr. *Journal of American History* 70(June, 1983):191-192.

Rundell, Walter, Jr., Papers. In the private possession of Deanna Rundell, Hyattsville, MD.

43

MARI SANDOZ

by William E. Unrau

Biography

The agrarian frontier on which Mari Sandoz was born at the close of the last century was the windswept short-grass country of Sheridan County, in northwestern Nebraska. It was a remote country, one of the last to be settled under the government's cheap land policies of the nineteenth century.

The high plains of that region, broken only occasionally by treacherous ravines, received less than twenty inches of rain per year, thus requiring a major modification of traditional farming methods in order to be productive. To the southeast were the ever-shifting sandhills, with their grass-covered valleys so vital to the ranchers who in the 1880s were threatening the economy of the homesteaders.

The twisting Niobrara River, which joins the mighty Missouri some 200 miles to the east, bisected the region. Forty miles north was the Pine Ridge Indian Reservation, where only recently the Wounded Knee tragedy had erupted, and to the west, by way of the Agate Fossil Beds that told of life centuries earlier, lay the remote Wyoming border country. As a region struggling to overcome the privations of the frontier circumstance, it was a virgin setting for historical appraisal, particularly if the appraiser were an individual of acute historical awareness.

Jules Sandoz, with a medical education from the University of Zurich and the volatile temperament of an outrageously spoiled emigrant who viewed life in a new country as an escape from family problems and the restrictive socioeconomic structure of central Europe, came to America in 1881. He first tried homesteading in Knox County, Nebraska, just south of Yankton, South Dakota. Three years later he abandoned his first wife and the homestead, and headed up the Niobrara to Mirage Flats in Sheridan County, some eighteen miles southeast of the nearest town of Hay Springs. Following two more failures at marriage, Jules married Mary Fehr (also a Swiss emigrant) in 1895. Mari (her given name was Mary), first of the six Sandoz children, was born at Mirage Flats on May 11, 1896 (*Sandoz, Story Catcher*).

Mari spoke only her mother's Swiss-German until she entered country grammar school at the age of nine. But she quickly mastered English, and her need for self-expression was soon evident in the short stories she wrote prior to her graduation from grammar school at the age of seventeen. As the eldest of the Sandoz children Mari was obliged to spend long hours tending to her younger siblings, performing household duties, and dealing with the often abusive treatment at the hands of her father. Her mother, almost wholly dominated by her tempestuous husband, attempted to keep the routine farm operations going, while Jules busied himself with fighting ranchers and promoting the surrounding countryside for future agrarian development.

It was a burdensome and occasionally terrifying experience, albeit instructive in the rigors of pioneer life. Following a short career as a rural school teacher and a brief marriage to Wray McCumber that ended in divorce in 1919, Mari broke with her family and Mirage Flats to attend business school in Lincoln, Nebraska. Later, because she had no high school diploma, she attended the University of Nebraska as a special adult student and established a pattern of supporting herself with temporary jobs, taking classes (including one under Professor John D. Hicks), and devoting her spare time to writing.

The publication of "The Vine" in the Nebraska English department's *Prairie Schooner* in 1927 established Mari Sandoz as a writer of promise, but by then she was moving away from the short story to the novel, with the Niobrara frontier as her main focus. It was a regional setting that would dominate her writing for the rest of her life. The death of her father in 1928, however, was a major turning point in her literary career. Shortly thereafter she began serious research on his biography, which under the title of *Old Jules* was published by Little, Brown in 1935, after having been rejected by more than a dozen other publishers.

This blunt, earthy study of her father and his world on the Nebraska plains was awarded the Atlantic Press Nonfiction Prize for 1935 and later that year was designated the November Book-of-the-Month selection. National recognition came quickly and most reviewers responded favorably. The distinguished Bernard DeVoto called the book a magnificent achievement and Sandoz's handling of her father "without passing a single wart . . . something between a dirge and a Gloria" (*Saturday Review of Literature* 19:5-6). Practically, the Atlantic prize money provided the foundation for financial security in the future and the time to do what she enjoyed most--research and writing.

The publication in 1939 of *Capital City*, a biting allegory of a mythical midwestern city and its proto-fascist inhabitants, prompted many citizens of Lincoln to believe that Sandoz had exceeded the bounds of propriety by insulting them and their city. This, of course, was not her intent--in fact, Lincoln was one of her most beloved places--but life in that city was difficult thereafter (Sandoz Papers, Sandoz to *Lincoln Journal and Star*, May 25, 1960). In 1940 she moved to more hospitable Denver, which had the advantage of important resources for research in western history and a literary-artistic community that welcomed her with open arms.

A recurring complaint of Sandoz was the insularity and aloofness of the eastern publishing establishment, while from a more practical standpoint it was difficult to deal with obstinate editors whose offices were halfway across the continent. Following the publication of *Crazy Horse* in late 1942, she moved to New York's Greenwich Village, which, though contemplated as a temporary move, became her residence for the rest of her life.

Nevertheless, Mari Sandoz did not consider New York as her real home. She traveled for months at a time in the West and Midwest, promoting her publications, lecturing, researching, and teaching creative writing courses during nine summer sessions at the University of Wisconsin in Madison. Her wish to be buried on the Nebraska plains was honored following her death of cancer in New York, on March 10, 1966, and a burial site was selected on a low hill on the Sandoz Fruit Ranch some twenty miles east of her birthplace at Mirage Flats.

Themes

Mari Sandoz was a prolific and versatile writer of novellas, novels, short stories, essays, recollections, and pedagogical studies regarding the western writers' craft. Several of these publications have professional merit, the best, perhaps, being *The Horsecatcher* (1957), a novella dealing with a nonconformist, peace-loving Cheyenne youth embroiled in traditional village values and a culture consecrated to the importance of warfare.

But it is in her nonfiction that Sandoz clearly excelled. Certainly there is widespread consensus that her social history of the Great Plains and her penetrating analyses of Lakota and Cheyenne culture at the close of the nineteenth century are her most sophisticated and scholarly works. Some of her conclusions have been challenged, some of her data has been questioned, and much of her narrative dialogue flies in the face of conventional historical writing. Yet her canny perception of frontier society, cultural conflict, and the individual confronting nature at a harsh, rudimentary level seldom have been equaled in frontier historiography.

Fundamental to an understanding of the various themes Sandoz developed in the Great Plains series (sometimes called the Trans-Missouri series) are the childhood and early adolescent experiences at Mirage Flats. Indeed, few professional historians have profited more from the environment in which they came to their maturity.

The farmstead of Jules Sandoz was near a long-established crossing of the Niobrara River. Closer still was a road heading to the sandhill country to the east. As a remote but important crossroads the Sandoz's were visited by traders, trappers, and prospectors of yesteryear, as well as foreign emigrants and various domestic shifters seeking Jules's advice on how best to reduce the wilderness to a garden. Storytelling and reminiscing about the past, not infrequently with ingenious embellishment or blatant exaggeration, were commonplace in these encounters, as was the earthy, colloquial style of those recalling their real or fantastic roles in taming the frontier. And from the Sioux and Cheyenne reservations only a short distance to the north came Indians to camp near Mari Sandoz's home and provide her with important insights into traditional Native American culture and its response to the white invaders.

For Mari Sandoz it was an exciting and enriching experience. With an unusually curious and fertile mind, coupled with a strong determination to become a professional writer and an unwavering commitment to chronicle the grand sweep of history in the region she knew best, she plunged ahead with the grand project. In addition to *Old Jules* (1935), the Great Plains series eventually included *Crazy Horse* (1942), *Cheyenne Autumn* (1953), *The Buffalo Hunters* (1954), *The Cattlemen* (1958), and *The Beaver Men* (1964). In these, and to a lesser degree in her three additional works of nonfiction; *These Were the Sioux* (1961), *Love Song to the Plains* (1961), and *The Battle of the Little Bighorn* (1966), several themes may be identified as basic to the Sandoz approach to western frontier history.

Standing majestically above the rest is the relationship among earthy humans and the Great Plains environment they attempted to occupy and exploit. Implicit in this is a colossal confrontation between beings and nature through time, with the latter hopefully providing the direction for improvement of the former.

The courageous and often mystical powers of the Indian constitute secondary themes that attracted Sandoz. She firmly believed that the Indians of the Great Plains had been conspicuously dispossessed by avaricious whites oblivious to the cultural viability and integrity of the Native American. Human greed in general, whether displayed by eastern capitalists against beleagured western Populists or by western ranchers and farmers against Indians or the native flora and fauna, is another theme permeating the nonfiction of Sandoz. Finally, in the last three volumes of the Great Plains series, she uses animals as focal points to demonstrate how human antagonism toward the lower animal kingdom disrupted the balance and well-being of all life on the Great Plains.

Analysis

Notwithstanding her considerable talents in the area of fiction, Mari Sandoz viewed herself primarily as a historian. She perceived *Old Jules* as mainly biography. One critic insisted on calling it "fictionalized biography" (*Sandoz, Story Catcher*, p. 85), but in fact it is a penetrating social history of a particular community on the Nebraska frontier. Determined to describe in great detail how her father tried to function in a raw, inhospitable setting, Sandoz utilizes an enormous amount of documentary material she had carefully collected over a period of more than half a decade.

In addition to newspaper accounts, the extensive Eli Ricker Collection in the Nebraska Historical Society, journals, government records, diaries, and numerous personal interviews, Sandoz fashioned three large notebooks of holograph notes based on her father's extensive personal correspondence and records. These constitute the empirical foundation of *Old Jules* and, at the same time, reveal much of Sandoz's strategy for the construction of frontier history.

More than anything else she sought to obtain material, preferably of a personal nature, that was what she called "close" to the events she was attempting to chronicle. In a particularly revealing letter she penned less than a year following the publication of *Old Jules*, Sandoz writes:

> The greatest difficulty encountered when working with frontier material is the dearth of source material written close to the date of observation--close enough to be fairly free from the tricks memory plays and written by an observer occupied and conquered by non-writers--sometimes illiterates, sometimes refuges [sic] from justice who have no desire to leave records, and always by men of action. The occasional visitor leaves letters, manuscripts and books behind but his observation is often faulty or completely misleading and valueless because he just isn't "posted" as one man said of Parkman's discussion of Indians in his *Oregon Trail.* The deeper you get into your problem the more cautious you become. The temptation is to research all your life and never be sure enough of anything to write down (Sandoz Papers, Sandoz to J. Glenn McFarland, February 1, 1936).

Years later, following the publication of *Son of the Gamblin' Man*, a less than successful novel in which she tries to develop the narrative based only on ascertainable facts, Sandoz described her intention to integrate the individual, the community, the place, and the time into a comprehendable unity:

> I started on the book, to which I had really been committed from my childhood, for this was the story of three formative periods in one: a region, a community, and a youth. . . . Such periods reminded me of the growth of a garnet from its gray matrix, and I wanted to study the components of that matrix, the pressures and heats put upon it, the crystalizations often partial and flawed, but now and then perfect, a well-faceted jewel (Sandoz Correspondence, "Some Thoughts," August 14, 1960).

On still another occasion she emphasizes the authenticity of her nonfiction. "Every individual and every incident," she wrote, "is, of course, factual, as true a portrayal of the actuality as it is within my power to present" (Sandoz Papers, Sandoz to W. Blenkinsop, August 28, 1961). In this instance she is referring to George A. Custer's allegedly having violated the smoke he performed in the presence of the Southern Cheyennes' Sacred Arrows on the Sweetwater in Texas, in 1869. For authorities she listed the Lakeside edition of Custer's *My Life on the Plains* and George B. Grinnell's *The Fighting Cheyennes*. But, insists Sandoz, this "well authenticated incident" was all the more factual because "I heard it from the Indians in my childhood, long before they, or I, knew it was in print anywhere" ("Some Thoughts"). Here, then, is an indication of a critical aspect of the Sandoz methodology--the importance she attached to long-standing oral tradition and personal interviews with individuals who had experienced or who had close associations with the participants in the events themselves.

No less important is the setting itself. Again and again she would visit the locale of her subject matter, possibly as much for personal empathy as for possible confirmation of written documents. In preparation for *Crazy Horse*, for example, Sandoz traveled more than 3,000 miles to visit battle sites and the Pine Ridge and Rosebud reservations, and in the research for *Cheyenne Autumn* she spent five weeks on the Northern Cheyenne Reservation in Montana, followed by a visit to the Indian Territory reservation and a trip along the route of the Indian flight through western Kansas and Nebraska (*Boise State Writers*, pp. 20-23).

Complimented by the use of the Indian dialect in dialogue form and often abstruse native symbolism, such on-the-scene conditioning seems to have strengthened her preference for the Indian point of view. Certainly a careful reading of *Cheyenne Autumn* within the context of analyses more recently published by Donald J. Berthrong and Ramon S. Powers on the same subject raises serious questions regarding the objectivity of Sandoz's account. More than anything else the death and destruction wrought by the Northern Cheyennes in 1878 remains, in the Sandoz version, obliquely apart from the main thread of her story.

Others have called attention to Sandozian subjectivity. In his 1966 review of *Old Jules Country* (1965), John Brennan concedes that Mari "wrote with vigor, grace, and research," but he stresses her largely negative role in the continuing "verbal warfare between the admittedly subjective and hopefully objective historians" (*Colorado Magazine* 43:249). His point was not unlike that of Edgar I. Stewart, who, while recognizing *Cheyenne Autumn* as "equal to anything Sandoz has written," nevertheless complains that the reader "sometimes loses the historical narrative in the brilliant sweep of the literary style" (*Montana: Magazine of Western History* 4:54-55).

Less generous was the *Mississippi Valley Historical Review* when it characterized *The Cattleman* as "an imaginative account that is not a study or an interpretation . . . but rather an attempt to re-create the cattlemen's way of life through the portrayal of its major personages" (45:360). Similarly, a reviewer describes *The Beaver Men* as "not so much an historical study as a careful and intelligently drawn portrait of a world." Her concern was less historical than ecological, concludes reviewer Don Berry, the emphasis being "relations of living creatures with each other and with their physical world" (*Colorado Magazine* 42:75-76).

For the professional historian the chronic absence of footnotes for major statements of "fact," coupled with conjectural dialogue and bibliographies that are selective at best, presents the dilemma of ferreting fact from fiction in much of Sandoz's nonfiction, and at worst, dealing with fabrications that distort the best evidence on a given event. In his review of *The Buffalo Hunters*, Carl Coke Rister cautions that "Miss Sandoz is not, of course, trying to supply the needs of professional historians, but her book has certain weaknesses, that one like myself cannot help regretting, notably of lack of cohesiveness and the over-use of imaginative fill-in dialogues (*Saturday Review of Literature* 37:11-12)."

Rister illustrates his lament by establishing that Sandoz had wrongly charged John R. Crook with instructing his troops to kill women and children in a retaliatory expedition against the Comanche in the Texas Panhandle, when in fact Crook's cautionary orders were, "And boys *don't* [emphasis added] kill any of the women and children if you can help it." Included in the fill-in, says Rister, is Sandoz's fabrication, obviously paraphrased from the mouth of the Reverend John M. Chivington just prior to the Sand Creek Massacre of 1864, "Get the nits with the lice" (p. 12).

Even the enormously popular *The Battle of the Little Bighorn*, Sandoz's last book, is not without conjecture. The book was commissioned in 1960 by Lippincott, as part of their "Great Battle and Leaders Series," with the formula that it be short, well written, and interpretative as to precisely what went right or wrong in the battle. Sandoz, always fiercely independent, was opposed to directive writing, as had happened in 1935 when a Brandt and Brandt agent in New York offered her a formula for her short stories. "That finished me," she recalled. "I cancelled every engagement I had and caught the Wednesday plane for Lincoln" (Sandoz Correspondence, Sandoz to Paul Hoffman, July 16, 1935). On another occasion she confided to her friend, Paul Hoffman, "Why is it that publishers never have any idea what the books they buy really *are*?" (July 17, 1935).

Yet from the start she was attracted to the project. A large amount of material she had collected for *Crazy Horse* two decades earlier could be used, and the opportunity to put Custer (whom she intensely disliked) in his proper place encouraged her to write the book. Predictably, nefarious military contractors, ambitious and petty army officers worried about their jobs, bureaucratic snarl and corruption among Indian Office employees, and seething tribal discontent all receive their due. In the final analysis, however, the focus is on Custer himself. Suffering from an aggravated case of egoism and professional insubordination, the catalyst for his stupendous error at the Little Bighorn is his sense of "desperate destiny" and the conviction that a smashing victory over the Sioux would gain him the presidency. "Custer," insists Sandoz, "was very well aware that no one voted against a national hero" (pp. 181-182).

Eschewing, as usual, uncryptic documentation by way of footnotes, Sandoz calls attention to certain newspaper accounts, Custer's childhood letters and statements "from West Point on," and presumed corroboration provided by Arikara scout Red Star in an interview at the home of Bear Belly, on the Fort Berthold Reservation in August, 1912, and published by University of North Dakota Professor O. G. Libby in 1920 (pp. 181-182).

Red Star did, in fact, report Custer's presidential aspirations (although he qualified them by stating that even a minor victory against "only five tents of Dakotas" would do the trick), and there is every reason to believe that Sandoz had read the Libby account sometime prior to her completion of the Little Bighorn book in 1966. But her personal correspondence suggests that the "presidential theory" dates back to the very beginning of her career as a historian, and more important, that the theory has a very personal touch (p. 58).

On October 27, 1937, some twenty-five years before she began working on *The Battle of the Little Bighorn*, Sandoz wrote to *Atlantic* editor Paul Hoffman about a camping experience she had had in July, 1930, while engaged in field observations in preparation for the *Crazy Horse* study. The letter sheds important light on how Sandoz arrived at her conclusions regarding Custer:

> I'm glad you saw the Custer battlefield. It was up that draw to your right, when you face the Little Big Horn, that Crazy Horse led his Sioux and cut off the retreat of Custer for all time. I pitched a tent just at the breaks of this draw at nine o'clock one night in July, 1930, and the next day when the sun came up, there was my first view of the battlefield. I was once more overwhelmed by the astonishing helplessness of civilized man (if not backed up completely by the mechanical jaugernaut he has built) when brought face to face with natural man in his own environment. Still it probably would have seemed worth the risk to Custer even if he had been able to appreciate the gravity of the situation. Had he succeeded that warm, dusty day *he would have been President* (Sandoz Correspondence, Sandoz to Hoffman, October 27, 1927 [emphasis added]).

Here is vintage Sandoz at her very best. It was all there: the raw, physical setting; the personal experience; the empathy with natural man confronted by the dynamo of industrial civilization; and most important, the irrationality of ego urged on by mindless ambition. Red Star's statement at Fort Berthold was less a directive for determining human motive than it was a confirmation of what Sandoz so poignantly *wanted* to conclude regarding Custer's monumental miscalculation on the Little Bighorn. And it is a deductive style that pervades much of the exciting historical writing of Mari Sandoz.

Of this there is no better example than a letter she wrote to Bernard DeVoto in 1936. DeVoto, then with the *Saturday Review of Literature*, had suggested that Sandoz do a piece on the Mormons, in response to the recent dedication of a monument at the site of the Mormon Winter Quarters near Omaha. In reply Sandoz provided DeVoto with ample evidence that she was informed regarding the major documents for such an endeavor. But she declined, simply because matters were not falling in place:

> I've given your suggestions considerable thought while pursuing the wily pheasant through the weeds [of northwestern Nebraska] and always I am reduced to a return to the gray matrix of my own reactions. . . . Worse, nothing crystalized from the matrix, no matter how much heat and pressure I exert upon it. . . . I feel very apologetic about it and see that there is no promising crystalization that you might select for enlargement or shaping or polishing. But I had fun thinking about this once more (Sandoz Papers, Sandoz to DeVoto, December 22, 1936).

Bibliography (Historical)

Books

The Battle of the Little Bighorn. Philadelphia: J. B. Lippincott Co., 1966.

The Beaver Men: Spearheads of Empire. New York: Hastings House, 1964.

The Buffalo Hunters: The Story of the Hide Men. New York: Hastings House, 1954.

The Cattlemen: From the Rio Grande across the Far Marias. New York: Hastings House, 1958.

Cheyenne Autumn. New York: McGraw-Hill, 1953.

Crazy Horse: The Strange Man of the Oglalas. New York: Alfred A. Knopf, 1942.

Love Song to the Plains. New York: Harper and Row, 1961.

Old Jules. Boston: Little, Brown, 1935.

These Were the Sioux. New York: Hastings House, 1961.

Selected Articles

"Anybody Can Write." *The Writer* 57(April, 1944):99-101.

"The Homestead in Perspective." In *Land Use Policy and Problems in the United States* edited by Howard W. Ottoson. Lincoln: University of Nebraska Press, 1963. Pp. 47-62.

"How I Came to Write." *Baltimore Bulletin of Education* 35(May-June, 1958):19-24.

"I Wrote a Book." *Nebraska Alumnus* (November, 1935):6-7.

"The Kinkaider Comes and Goes." *North American Review* 6(April, 1930):422-431; 6(May, 1930):576-583.

"Look of the Last Frontier." *American Heritage* 12(June, 1961):42-53.

"The Look of the West." *Nebraska History* 35(December, 1954):243-254.

"Martha of the Yellow Braids." *Prairie Schooner* 21(Summer, 1947):139-144.

"Musky, the Narrative of a Muskrat." *Nature* 132(November, 1933):199-202.

"Nebraska." *Holiday* 19(May, 1956):103-114.

"The Neighbor." *Prairie Schooner* 30(Winter, 1956):340-349.

"Outpost in New York." *Prairie Schooner* 37(Summer, 1963):95-106.

"Sandhill Sundays." In *Folksay: A Regional Miscellany* edited by B. A. Botkin. Norman: University of Oklahoma Press, 1931. Pp. 291-301.

"Search for the Bones of Crazy Horse." *Westerners (New York) Brand Book* (Autumn, 1954):4-5.

"Some Notes on Wild Bill Hickok." *Westerners (New York) Brand Book* (Winter, 1954):8.

"There Were Two Sitting Bulls." *Bluebook* 90(November, 1949):58-64.

"What the Sioux Taught Me." *Reader's Digest* 60(May, 1952):121-124.

Selected Reviews

Beyond the Hundredth Meridian: John Wesley Powell and the Second Opening of the West by Wallace Stegner. *Westerners Brand Book, New York Posse* (Autumn, 1954):17.

The City of Trembling Leaves by Walter Van Tilburg Clark. *Atlantic Monthly* 176(July, 1945):130.

Corn Country by Homer Croy. *New York Times Book Review*, June 1, 1947, p. 16.

Gulch of Gold: A History of Central City, Colorado by Caroline Bancroft. *Westerners Brand Book, New York Posse* (Autumn, 1958):72.

Indians of the Northwest Coast by Philip Drucker. *Westerners Brand Book, New York Posse* (Autumn, 1956):18.

In Time of Harvest by John L. Sinclair. *New York Times Book Review*, August 29, 1943, p. 6.

Kansas Irish by Charles B. Driscoll. *New York Times Book Review*, May 23, 1943, p. 7.

Overland Routes to the Gold Fields, 1859, from Contemporary Diaries. edited by LeRoy R. Hafen. *American Historical Review* 48(July, 1943):820-821.

Prairie City: The Story of an American Community by Angie Debo. *New York Times Book Review*, May 21, 1944, p. 3.

Sheehan's Mill by John Henry Reese. *New York Times Book Review*, October 17, 1943, p. 16.

The Sod-House Frontier, 1854-1890 by Everett Dick. *Saturday Review of Literature* 20(December 18, 1937):27.

Warpath and Council Fire by Stanley Vestal. *American Indian* 5(1949):48-49.

Westward the Women by Nancy Wilson Ross. *New York Times Book Review*, October 15, 1944, p. 4.

Studies of Mari Sandoz

Berry, Don. Review of *The Beaver Men: Spearheads of Empire* by Mari Sandoz. *Colorado Magazine* 42(January, 1965):75-76.

[Book Notes]. Summary of *The Cattleman: From the Rio Grande across the Far Marias* by Mari Sandoz. *Mississippi Valley Historical Review* 45(September, 1952):360.

Brennan, John. Review of *Old Jules Country* by Mari Sandoz. *Colorado Magazine* 43(October, 1966):249.

DeVoto, Bernard. Review of *Old Jules* by Mari Sandoz. *Saturday Review of Literature* 19(November 2, 1936):5-6.

Josephy, Alvin M., Jr. Review of *The Battle of the Little Bighorn* by Mari Sandoz. *New York Times Book Review*, July 3, 1966, p. 6.

Neihardt, John G. Review of *Crazy Horse: The Strange Man of the Oglalas* by Mari Sandoz. *New York Times Book Review*, December 20, 1942, p. 4.

Rister, Carl Coke. Review of *The Buffalo Hunters: The Story of the Hide Men* by Mari Sandoz. *Saturday Review of Literature* 37(August 21, 1954):11-12.

Robbins, Roy Marvin. Review of *Old Jules* by Mari Sandoz. *Mississippi Valley Historical Review* 23(June, 1936):284.

Sandoz, Mari, Correspondence and Manuscripts. George Arents Research Library, Syracuse University, Syracuse, NY.

__________, Papers. University of Nebraska Library, Lincoln, NE.

Stauffer, Helen Winter. "Mari Sandoz." In *Boise State Western Writers Series* 63(1948):20-23.

__________. *Mari Sandoz, Story Catcher of the Plains*. Lincoln: University of Nebraska Press, 1982.

Stewart, Edgar I. Review of *Cheyenne Autumn* by Mari Sandoz. *Montana, Magazine of Western History* 4(Fall, 1954):54-55.

Williams, Stanley T. Review of *Old Jules* by Mari Sandoz. *Yale Review* 25(December, 1935):391-392.

44

JOSEPH SCHAFER

by Richard Maxwell Brown

Biography

Joseph Schafer was born on December 29, 1867, near Muscoda in Grant County, Wisconsin. He was the son of German immigrants Mathias and Anna Joseph (Bremmer) Schafer. Mathias Schafer had been a schoolmate of Karl Marx in a Trier *gymnasium*, but in later years he rejected Marx's radical ideology of class conflict. Joseph Schafer's lifelong devotion to education and agricultural history was influenced by his father's double occupation of farmer and schoolmaster. Young Joseph's attendance at Madison (South Dakota) Normal, 1888-1890, and two years of high school teaching, 1890-1892, was followed by his enrollment as a junior in the University of Wisconsin, where he fell under the spell of Frederick Jackson Turner and his frontier thesis of American history. Schafer's 1894 graduation with honors in history was the prelude to teaching at Valley City (North Dakota) Normal, 1894-1898, and marriage in 1895 to Lily Abbott of Columbia, South Dakota. A return to the University of Wisconsin brought Schafer graduate degrees in history (M.L., 1899; Ph.D., 1906) under Turner's direction.

Meanwhile, Schafer had taken a job at the University of Oregon in 1900 where he initiated an up-to-date program in history, becoming department head in 1904. Schafer remained in Eugene until 1920, where he was a popular teacher, a successful administrator of the summer session and extension service as well as his own department, and one of a band of dynamic young faculty who made Oregon one of the leading universities in the West. Schafer had established himself as a scholar with three books published from 1901 to 1905 and with a steady stream of articles on the history of Oregon and the Pacific Northwest.

Schafer was, then, a successful historian, teacher, and administrator when the State Historical Society of Wisconsin called him to its superintendency in 1920. As operating head of this citadel of research and writing on American frontier history, Schafer had, however, little taste or talent for the duties of publicity, fundraising, and legislative lobbying. While others bore the burden of run-of-the-mill routine, Schafer buried himself in the more congenial tasks of editing the *Wisconsin Magazine of History* (which he made into a first-class historical journal) and carrying out his own prodigious program of publication. Schafer remained a conscientious, faithful head of the society until his death in 1941, but the organization languished in the absence of the strong leadership which Schafer lacked the personal qualities to provide. For his prolific and distinguished scholarship, Schafer was honored with an LL.D. degree (1933) from the beloved University of Oregon; the presidencies of the Mississippi Valley Historical Association (now the Organization of American Historians), 1926-1927, and the Agricultural History Society, 1931-1932; and a Commonwealth Fund lecturership at the University of London in 1936.

An early supporter of the League of Nations, Schafer was haunted by the clouds of World War II which he saw gathering over America at the same time his body was invaded by cancer. Courageous to the end, Schafer continued to work at his desk until within a week of his death in Madison on January 27, 1941, at the age of seventy-four. Surviving him were his wife, Lily, and their six children: Max, Paul A., Elizabeth, Sidney P., Joseph, and Frederick. Of average size with an appearance that combined the look of both a scholar and a farmer, Joseph Schafer was positive, extremely personable, and in politics an outspoken and consistent liberal.

Themes

There are three strong continuities in the research and writing of Joseph Schafer: the frontier factor in the tradition of his mentor, Frederick Jackson Turner; the relationship between land and people; and agricultural history. Schafer was deeply devoted to Turner, whose inspiration is implicit (or, much less often, explicit) in virtually all of his work, but these three themes are also inherent in Schafer's local and family background: his parents were frontier settlers of Wisconsin who were tightly tied to the land by the family occupation of farming. Far from being embittered by his youth on the soil, as many of his generation were, Schafer had a nostalgic love for the lovely landscape of his home country in rural southwestern Wisconsin. In almost all of his books and articles, the three themes of frontier, land-and-people, and agriculture are interwoven. Related to them are certain other significant themes.

Schafer's years in Oregon coincided with his notion that the last frontier of the Pacific Coast had an inspiring potential to combine the modern material growth of the twentieth century with the spiritual values of the pioneer age. To probe the historical background of this ideal, Schafer provided a series of articles, 1905-1912, dealing with the diplomacy of the Oregon question and the pioneers of the old Oregon country. These studies were prefaced by two general works, *The Pacific Slope and Alaska* (1904) and *History of the Pacific Northwest* (1905; revised 1918)--the first textbook on the subject by a scholar. Nor did Schafer drop the subject of the Far West when he went back to Wisconsin, for in 1930-1931 he edited the works of two Wisconsinites who went to California in the gold rush era.

It was not in the nature of the mild, positive Schafer either to debunk or to romanticize the pioneers of Wisconsin and the Far West. Rather, he struck what was for him a happy medium between myth and reality--a stance exemplified by his classic 1912 sketch of Oregon pioneer Jesse Applegate. For Schafer, the prototypical pioneer was the farmer whose history he persistently tracked in the *Wisconsin Domesday Book* series, 1922-1937. As a long-time resident of the small but cosmopolitan cities of Eugene and Madison, Schafer was much too sophisticated and judicious to ignore the urban factor in American life, and, indeed, the rural-to-urban transition is a motif in his massive *Domesday Book* case study. Yet, his *summa apologia* was *The Social History of American Agriculture* (1936), a graceful synthesis which reflects his Turnerian faith in the rural way of life as the nucleus of American democracy.

Close to Schafer's heart and heritage was a theme which united all the others: the German experience in Wisconsin as an example of immigrant acculturation to American life. This appears time and again in the *Domesday Book* volumes, in his 1930 biography of the Schafer family hero, Carl Schurz, and in one of his most appealing works, a five-part monograph on "The Yankee and the Teuton in Wisconsin" (1922-1923). Schafer was fascinated by the constructive interaction in Wisconsin of Yankees from New England and New York and Teutons from Germany. He sees the Yankees advancing the frontier and the Germans consolidating it with superior farming. Deep research in the primary sources of the *Domesday Book* series convinced Schafer that the pressure of economic survival, along with attendance in English-language schools, had been the most effective Americanizer of the Germans. Schafer noted that the same factors were, in the early twentieth century, acculturating to American society eastern Wisconsin's "new immigrant" factory workers from southern and eastern Europe. An ironic twist to Schafer's work on German immigrants was his last publication (1941) which used minute analysis of voting to shatter the long-held belief that Germans had swung the presidential election to Lincoln in 1860 (*American Historical Review* 47:51-63). It was a mark of Schafer's integrity that he, the biographer of Carl Schurz, felt obliged to deprive his own ethnic stock of what had been viewed as one of their greatest contributions to American history.

Analysis

The paradox of Joseph Schafer's scholarly career is that his magnum opus, the *Wisconsin Domesday Book* series, was his greatest failure as well as his greatest success. Largely neglected in Schafer's own lifetime, the *Domesday Book* volumes can now be seen as remarkably innovative forerunners of the "new social history" and the "new rural history" of the 1960s-1980s. There were some defects in the *Domesday Book* series that limited its appeal to scholars and the public, but the main difficulty was that Schafer was far ahead of his time. Not until the 1960s would historians favor the local-history emphasis and the advanced research and method represented by the *Domesday Book*, and by that time Schafer's monumental but flawed work was all but forgotten.

Borrowing the title *Domesday Book* from the great land survey of William the Conqueror, Schafer envisioned a project of the State Historical Society of Wisconsin that would investigate neglected historical sources to reveal the contributions of ordinary people to the civilization of Wisconsin. Schafer called for a huge cooperative effort of scholars and local citizens to produce an enormous, all-inclusive "domesday book" of Wisconsin history and life from the 1820s to 1920, county-by-county, town-by-town, and farm-by-farm. The high point of Schafer's scholarly life came at the December, 1920, annual meeting of the American Historical Association where he was a sensation with his plan for the *Domesday Book*. All agreed that Schafer's strikingly original project would have to be replicated throughout the Mississippi Valley, but the excitement faded after the appearance of the first two volumes in 1922 and 1924, and the reception to the last (and best) volume in 1937 was apathetic.

Schafer's *Domesday Book* begins as an avant-garde work of historical scholarship and ends in obscurity. What went wrong? First was an unexpected lack of funding by the historical society; this drastically reduced the scope of the project. With the funding shortfall, Schafer had to abandon plans for a large staff of researchers in Madison, and it turned out that he himself lacked the personal qualities and the follow-up ability to energize the rank-and-file of school children and local historians whom he had counted on to provide crucial research in the field. Yet, he refused to give up and settled down to a virtually one-man project.

The keynote volume, *A History of Agriculture in Wisconsin* (1922), was solid but unexciting, while the next, *Wisconsin Domesday Book: Town Studies* (1924), was an atlas of frontier settlement. As a piece of historical research the atlas was awesome in its coverage of the pioneer farms and farmers of twenty-three towns (really townships), but reviewers found it difficult to plumb the significance of the research, which lacked an effective design for comparison among the towns studied or with those not treated. Learning from this criticism, Schafer's next three installments of the *Domesday Book* were county-bloc case studies: *Four Wisconsin Counties. Prairie and Forest* (1927); *The Wisconsin Lead Region* (1932), of three counties; and *The Winnebago-Horicon Basin* (1937), of four counties. A brief summary does not do justice to the wealth of data and perception in these three volumes, but in each Schafer investigates "community creation" in terms of land selection (and land speculation) and the contrasting experiences of native-born citizens and immigrants in terms of economic success, geographic mobility, schooling, and voting behavior. Also emphasized is the agricultural progression from primitive farming to advanced new dairying and the rise of factory-dominated cities of the early twentieth century.

Schafer's heroic research achievement in the *Domesday Book* was not emulated in his own era. The growing eclipse of Turner's reputation in the 1930s dimmed interest in Schafer's *Domesday Book* application of the master's frontier thesis. Meanwhile, historians had turned to other topics that seemed more timely and exciting--for example, the industrial and urban factors which Charles A. and Mary R. Beard explored in their *Rise of American Civilization* (1927). There were flaws in Schafer's execution of the project: he never found an engaging style of presentation, and his volumes were popular neither with the people nor with scholars. Schafer was a good writer, but the mass of evidence in the *Domesday* books swamped his literary gift (*Mississippi Valley Historical Review* 12:99-105).

Conceptual fuzziness eroded Schafer's appeal to his peers in the historical guild. He had an agenda of worthy topics but lacked a comprehensive research design that would enable him to test key propositions of historical interpretation with sufficient precision. Lacking, also, is a Turnerian ability to assimilate historical complexity in one grand conception. Thus, no "Schafer thesis" emerges to excite historians and attract both critics and defenders. Finally, Schafer's sunny and positive disposition as well as his liberal centrism predisposed him to find consensus rather than conflict in history. Without the tang of conflict, Schafer's cuisine of history was too bland for all but a few.

One must not belabor the failure of the *Domesday* project. From the vantage point of the 1930s it was an intellectual backwater, but from the perspective of the 1980s it is in the mainstream. Schafer's sources and method placed him a generation or two ahead of his time. As the first historian to make major, sustained use of federal manuscript census returns and similar local records, Schafer anticipates a favorite strategy of the new social history. In common, also, with the new social historians of our own time was Schafer's quantification of landholding and other data and his focus on wealth and property distribution, geographic mobility, and "history from the bottom up"--all through the medium of the now fashionable community history. Conceptually more sophisticated and using more advanced quantitative techniques, the frontier historians of today are where Joseph Schafer was a half-century ago.

Bibliography

Books

The Acquisition of Oregon Territory: Discovery and Exploration. Eugene: University of Oregon, 1908.

Across the Plains in 1850 by John Steele. Editor. Chicago: Caxton Club, 1930.

California Letters of Lucius Fairchild. Editor. State Historical Society of Wisconsin, *Publications.* Vol. XXXI. Madison: State Historical Society of Wisconsin, 1931.

Carl Schurz: Militant Liberal. State Historical Society of Wisconsin, Publications. Biography Series, vol. I. Madison: State Historical Society of Wisconsin, 1930.

A Day with the Cow Column in 1843 by Jesse Applegate and Recollections of My Boyhood by Jesse A. Applegate. Editor. Chicago: Caxton Club, 1934.

Democracy in Reconstruction. Co-edited with Frederick A. Cleveland. Boston: Houghton Mifflin, 1919.

Four Wisconsin Counties: Prairie and Forest. Wisconsin Domesday Book, General Studies, vol. II. Madison: State Historical Society of Wisconsin, 1927.

The Government of the American People. Co-authored with Frank Strong. Boston: Houghton Mifflin, 1901.

A History of Agriculture in Wisconsin. Wisconsin Domesday Book, General Studies, vol. I. Madison: State Historical Society of Wisconsin, 1922.

A History of the Pacific Northwest. New York: Macmillan, 1905. Revised edition, 1918.

Intimate Letters of Carl Schurz, 1841-1869. Editor and translator. State Historical Society of Wisconsin, *Publications*. Vol. XXX. Madison: State Historical Society of Wisconsin, 1928.

Memoirs of Jeremiah Curtin. Editor. State Historical Society of Wisconsin, *Publications*. Biography Series, vol. II. Madison: State Historical Society of Wisconsin, 1940.

The Origin of the System of Land Grants for Education. Madison: University of Wisconsin, 1902.

The Pacific Slope and Alaska. The History of North America series edited by Guy Carleton Lee, vol. X. Philadelphia: George Barrie & Sons, 1904.

Prince Lucien Campbell. Eugene: University of Oregon Press, 1926.

The Social History of American Agriculture. New York: Macmillan, 1936.

University Extension and Commonwealth Service. Eugene: University of Oregon, 1912.

The Winnebago-Horicon Basin: A Type Study in Western History. Wisconsin Domesday Book, General Studies, vol. IV. Madison: State Historical Society of Wisconsin, 1937.

Wisconsin Domesday Book: Town Studies. Vol. I. Madison: State Historical Society of Wisconsin, 1924.

The Wisconsin Lead Region. Wisconsin Domesday Book, General Studies, vol. III. Madison: State Historical Society of Wisconsin, 1932.

Articles

"Abernethy, George." *Dictionary of American Biography* 1:29-30.

"Adams, William Lysander." *Dictionary of American Biography* 1:102.

"Albert John Ochsner: A Wisconsin Gift to Chicago." *Wisconsin Magazine of History* 24(September, 1940):83-109.

"American Social History." *Wisconsin Magazine of History* 13(March, 1930):305-312.

"Applegate, Jesse." *Dictionary of American Biography* 1:325-326.

"Assembling Historical Manuscripts." *Wisconsin Magazine of History* 17(December, 1933):232-242.

"Atkinson, George Henry." *Dictionary of American Biography* 1:408-409.

"The Author of the 'Frontier Hypothesis'." *Wisconsin Magazine of History* 15(September, 1931):86-103.

"Beginnings of Civilization in the Old Northwest: The Ordinance of 1787." *Wisconsin Magazine of History* 21(December, 1937):213-236.

"Boise, Reuben Patrick." *Dictionary of American Biography* 2:414.
"The British Attitude toward the Oregon Question, 1815-1846." *American Historical Review* 16(January, 1911):273-299.
"California Diary of Charles M. Tuttle, 1859." Editor. *Wisconsin Magazine of History* 15(September, 1931):69-85 and 15(December, 1931):219-233.
"Campbell, Prince Lucien." *Dictionary of American Biography* 3:462.
"Carl Schurz, Immigrant Statesman." *Wisconsin Magazine of History* 11(June, 1928):373-394.
"Chancellor John Hiram Lathrop." *Wisconsin Magazine of History* 23(December, 1939):207-236.
"Christian Traugott Ficker's Advice to Emigrants." Translator. *Wisconsin Magazine of History* 25(December,1941):217-236; 25(March, 1942):331-355; and 25(June, 1942):456-475.
"Church Records in Migration Studies." *Wisconsin Magazine of History* 10(March, 1927):328-337.
"Civil War Historiography: Carl Russell Fish." *Wisconsin Magazine of History* 21(December, 1937):151-159.
"Concerning the Frontier as Safety Valve." *Political Science Quarterly* 52(September, 1937):407-420.
"Corbett, Henry Winslow." *Dictionary of American Biography* 4:435-436.
"The Courts and History." *Wisconsin Magazine of History* 9(March, 1926):347-357.
"The Courts and History--Again." *Wisconsin Magazine of History* 16(March, 1933):321-335.
"Death of Professor Turner." *Wisconsin Magazine of History* 15(June, 1932):495-499.
"DeSmet, Pierre-Jean." *Dictionary of American Biography* 5:255-256.
"Documenting Local History." *Wisconsin Magazine of History* 5(December, 1921):142-159.
"Documents Relative to Warre and Vavasour's Military Reconnoisance in Oregon, 1845-6." Editor. *Oregon Historical Quarterly* 10(March, 1909):1-99.
"Doolittle, James Rood." *Dictionary of American Biography* 5:374-375.
"Doty, James Duane." *Dictionary of American Biography* 5:390-391.
"The Draper Collection of Manuscripts." State Historical Society of Wisconsin, *Proceedings*, 1922. Madison: State Historical Society of Wisconsin, 1923. Pp. 51-76.
"Draper, Lyman Copeland." *Dictionary of American Biography* 5:441-442.
"The Epic of a Plain Yankee Family." *Wisconsin Magazine of History* 9(December, 1925):140-156 and 9(March, 1926):285-309.
"Excerpts from a Whaler's Diary by George Burchard." Editor. *Wisconsin Magazine of History* 18(June, 1935):422-441; 19(September, 1935):103-107; 19(December, 1935):227-241; and 19(March, 1936):342-355.
"Farnham, Thomas Jefferson." *Dictionary of American Biography* 6:283-284.

"Ferries and Ferryboats." *Wisconsin Magazine of History* 21(June, 1938):432-456.

"Five Years in America (*Cinq Ans en Amérique*): Journal of a Missionary among the Redskins--Journal, 1859, by Father Anthony Maria Gachet." Translator. *Wisconsin Magazine of History* 18(September, 1934):68-76; 18(December, 1934):191-204; and 18(March, 1935):345-359.

"Francis Parkman, 1823-1923." *Mississippi Valley Historical Review* 10(March, 1924):351-364.

"Frederic G. Young: A Wisconsin Gift to Oregon." *Wisconsin Magazine of History* 23(March, 1940):342-365.

"Gaines, John Pollard." *Dictionary of American Biography* 7:94-95.

"Genesis of Wisconsin's Free High School System." *Wisconsin Magazine of History* 10(December, 1926):123-149.

"Great Fires of Seventy-One." *Wisconsin Magazine of History* 11(September, 1927):96-106.

"Greenhow, Robert." *Dictionary of American Biography* 7:580.

"Grover, La Fayette." *Dictionary of American Biography* 8:29.

"Harvey W. Scott, Historian." *Oregon Historical Quarterly* 34(September, 1933):191-201.

"Henry Baird Favill: A Wisconsin Gift to Chicago." *Wisconsin Magazine of History* 24(December, 1940):199-227.

"Hiram Moore, Michigan-Wisconsin Inventor." *Wisconsin Magazine of History* 15(December, 1931):234-243.

"The Horicon Dam Question." *Wisconsin Magazine of History* 18(December, 1934):212-231.

"Immigrant Letters." *Wisconsin Magazine of History* 13(June, 1930):409-416.

"__________." 16(December, 1932):211-215.

"Introduction." In *History of the Conspiracy of Pontiac, and the War of the North American Tribes against the English Colonies after the Conquest of Canada* by Francis Parkman. New York: Macmillan, 1929.

"Jackson, Mortimer Melville." *Dictionary of American Biography* 9:551-552.

"Jesse Applegate: Pioneer and State Builder." *University of Oregon Bulletin* n.s. 9(February, 1912):n.p.

"Kelley, Hall Jackson." *Dictionary of American Biography* 10:297-298.

"Keyes, Elisha Williams." *Dictionary of American Biography* 10:365.

"Know-Nothingism in Wisconsin." *Wisconsin Magazine of History* 8(September, 1924):3-21.

"Knowledge Is Not Enough." *Wisconsin Magazine of History* 23(September, 1939):89-109.

"La Pointe Letters by Florantha Thompson Sproat." Editor. *Wisconsin Magazine of History* 16(September, 1932):85-95 and 16(December, 1932):199-210.

"Lands across the Sea." *Wisconsin Magazine of History* 13(June, 1930):417-429.

"Lane, Joseph." *Dictionary of American Biography* 10:579-580.

"Letters of Charles Richard Van Hise." Editor. *Wisconsin Magazine of History* 23(June, 1940):439-447; 24(September, 1940):66-82; 24(December, 1940):189-198; 24(March, 1941):315-335; 24(June, 1941):453-467; and 25(September, 1941):73-109.

"Letters of Richard Emerson Ela." Editor. *Wisconsin Magazine of History* 19(June, 1936):430-453 and 20(September, 1936):72-88.

"Letters of Sir George Simpson, 1841-1843." Editor. *American Historical Review* 14(October, 1908):70-94.

"The Life of a Lumberman: John E. Nelligan as told to Charles M. Sheridan." Editor with an introduction. *Wisconsin Magazine of History* 13(September, 1929):3-65; 13(December, 1929):131-185; and 13(March, 1930):241-304.

"McLoughlin, John." *Dictionary of American Biography* 12:134-135.

"Memorials of John H. Tweedy." *Wisconsin Magazine of History* 8(March, 1925):349-360.

"The Microscopic Method Applied to History." *Minnesota History Bulletin* 4(February-May, 1921):3-20.

"Muscoda, 1763-1856." *Wisconsin Magazine of History* 4(September, 1920):27-43.

"Nesmith, James Willis." *Dictionary of American Biography* 13:430-431.

"New Glarus in 1850: Report of Rev. Wilhelm Streissguth." Editor and translator. *Wisconsin Magazine of History* 18(March, 1935):328-345.

"Notes on the Colonization of Oregon." *Oregon Historical Quarterly* 6(December, 1905):379-390.

"On Teaching Social Studies." *Wisconsin Magazine of History* 22(September, 1938):90-107.

"Oregon Pioneers and American Diplomacy." In *Essays in American History Dedicated to Frederick Jackson Turner* edited by Guy Stanton Ford. New York: Henry Holt & Co., 1910. Pp. 35-56.

"Origin of Wisconsin's Free School System." *Wisconsin Magazine of History* 9(September, 1925):27-46.

"Peopling the Middle West." *Wisconsin Magazine of History* 21(September, 1937):85-106.

"The Place and Date of Jeremiah Curtin's Birth." *Wisconsin Magazine of History* 22(March, 1939):344-359.

"Popular Censorship of History Texts." *Wisconsin Magazine of History* 6(June, 1923):450-461.

"Praying for Rain--Droughts in Wisconsin." *Wisconsin Magazine of History* 20(March, 1937):337-353.

"Prohibition in Early Wisconsin." *Wisconsin Magazine of History* 8(March, 1925):281-299.

"Public Schools One Hundred Years Ago as Seen through Foreign Eyes." *Wisconsin Magazine of History* 22(June, 1939):435-459.

"Randall, Alexander Williams." *Dictionary of American Biography* 15:344-345.

"Rodney Howard True: A Wisconsin Gift to Washington and Philadelphia." *Wisconsin Magazine of History* 24(March, 1941):336-356.

"The Rump Council." Editor. In State Historical Society of Wisconsin *Proceedings*, 1920. Madison: State Historical Society of Wisconsin, 1921. Pp. 62-155.

"A Rural Life Survey of a Western State." In *The Trans-Mississippi West* edited by James F. Willard and Colin B. Goodykoontz. Boulder: University of Colorado, 1930. Pp. 291-308.

"Rusk, Jeremiah McClain." *Dictionary of American Biography* 16:235-236.

"Scandinavian Moravians in Wisconsin." *Wisconsin Magazine of History* 24(September, 1940):25-38.

"Sectional and Personal Politics in Early Wisconsin [1835-1843]." *Wisconsin Magazine of History* 18(June, 1935):442-465.

"Smith, Jedediah Strong." *Dictionary of American Biography* 17:290-291.

"Social Prognosis." *Wisconsin Magazine of History* 17(September, 1933):77-92.

"Some Enduring Factors in Rural Polity." *Agricultural History* 6(October, 1932):161-180.

"Some Facts Bearing on the Safety-Valve Theory." *Wisconsin Magazine of History* 20(December, 1936):216-232.

"State Boundaries in the Old Northwest." *Wisconsin Magazine of History* 21(March, 1938):337-355.

"Stevens, Isaac Ingalls." *Dictonary of American Biography* 17:612-614.

"Stormy Days in Court--the Booth Case." *Wisconsin Magazine of History* 20(September, 1936):89-110.

"The Surrender of Rastatt by Carl Schurz." Translator. *Wisconsin Magazine of History* 12(March, 1929):239-270.

"Thomas James Walsh: A Wisconsin Gift to Montana." *Wisconsin Magazine of History* 23(June, 1940):448-473.

"Trailing a Trail Artist of 1849." *Wisconsin Magazine of History* 12(September, 1928):97-108.

"Turner's America." *Wisconsin Magazine of History* 17(June, 1934):447-465.

"Turner's Early Writings." *Wisconsin Magazine of History* 22(December, 1938):213-231.

"Turner's Frontier Philosophy." *Wisconsin Magazine of History* 16(June, 1933):451-469.

"Was the West a Safety Valve for Labor?" *Mississippi Valley Historical Review* 24(December, 1937):299-314.

"Washington and His Biographers." *Wisconsin Magazine of History* 11(December, 1927):218-228.

"Whitman, Marcus." *Dictionary of American Biography* 20:141-143.

"Who Elected Lincoln?" *American Historical Review* 47(October, 1941):51-63.

"The Wisconsin Domesday Book." *Wisconsin Magazine of History* 4(September, 1920):61-74.

"The Wisconsin Phalanx." *Wisconsin Magazine of History* 19(June, 1936):454-474.

"Wisconsin's Farm Loan Law, 1849-1863." In State Historical Society of Wisconsin *Proceedings*, 1920. Madison: State Historical Society of Wisconsin, 1921. Pp. 156-191.

"Wyeth, Nathaniel Jarvis." *Dictionary of American Biography* 20:576-577.

"The Yankee and the Teuton in Wisconsin." *Wisconsin Magazine of History* 6(December, 1922):125-145; 6(March, 1923):261-279; 6(June, 1923):386-402; 7(September, 1923):3-19; and 7(December, 1923):148-171.

"A Yankee Land Speculator in Wisconsin." *Wisconsin Magazine of History* 9(June, 1925):377-392.

Selected Reviews

Adventurers of Oregon: A Chronicle of the Fur Trade by Constance L. Skinner. *American Historical Review* 26(October, 1920):117-118.

Autobiography of John Ball compiled by Kate Ball Towers, Flora Ball Hopkins, and Lucy Ball. *American Historical Review* 32(October, 1926):177.

A Brief History of Rocky Mountain Exploration, with Especial Reference to the Expedition of Lewis and Clark by Reuben Gold Thwaites. *American Historical Review* 9(July, 1904):831-832.

The Call of the Columbia: Iron Men and Saints Take the Oregon Trail edited by Archer Butler Hulbert. *American Historical Review* 40(April, 1935):527-528.

The Discovery of the Oregon Trail: Robert Stuart's Narratives edited by Philip Ashton Rollins. *American Historical Review* 41(January, 1936):357-360.

Early Records of Gilpin County, Colorado, 1859-1861 by Thomas Maitland Marshall. *Mississippi Valley Historical Review* 9(June, 1922):86-87.

Francis Drake and Other Early Explorers along the Pacific Coast by John W. Robertson. *American Historical Review* 33(January, 1928):410-411.

From Millwheel to Plowshare: The Story of the Contribution of the Christian Orndorff Family to the Social and Industrial History of the United States by Julia A. Drake and James R. Orndorff. *Mississippi Valley Historical Review* 26(June, 1939):114-115.

From Quebec to New Orleans: The Story of the French in America, Fort de Chartres by J. H. Schlarman. *American Historical Review* 36(July, 1931):865-866.

A History of California: The American Period by Robert Glass Cleland. *American Historical Review* 28(January, 1923):334-336.

A History of California: The Spanish Period by Charles E. Chapman. *American Historical Review* 27(July, 1922):804-806.

History of the State of Washington by Edmond S. Meany. *American Historical Review* 15(October, 1909):167-169.

Israel, Elihu, and Cadwallader Washburn: A Chapter in American Biography by Gaillard Hunt. *Mississippi Valley Historical Review* 13(September, 1926):291-293.

Jason Lee, Prophet of the New Oregon by Cornelius J. Brosnan. *American Historical Review* 38(April, 1933):605.

Marcus Whitman, Crusader edited by Archer Butler Hulbert and Dorothy P. Hulbert. *American Historical Review* 42(April, 1937):560-562 and 44(April 1939):740-741.

Marcus Whitman, M.D., Pioneer and Martyr by Clifford Merrill Drury. *American Historical Review* 44(October, 1938):154-156.

Old Fort Crawford and the Frontier by Bruce E. Mahan. *American Historical Review* 32(April, 1927):669-670.

Opening a Highway to the Pacific, 1838-1846 by James Christy Bell. *American Historical Review* 27(January, 1922):331-333.

The Oregon Crusade: Across Land and Sea to Oregon edited by Archer Butler Hulbert and Dorothy P. Hulbert. *American Historical Review* 41(January, 1936):357-360.

The Transition of a Typical Frontier by Wilson Porter Shortridge. *Mississippi Valley Historical Review* 9(March, 1923):348-349.

Vikings of the Pacific by A. C. Laut. *American Historical Review* 11(April, 1906):680-681.

Where Rolls the Oregon: Prophet and Pessimist Look Northwest edited by Archer Butler Hulbert. *American Historical Review* 39(July, 1934):788-789.

The Whitman Mission, the Third Station on the Old Oregon Trail by Marvin M. Richardson. *American Historical Review* 46(January, 1941):429-430.

Woodrow Wilson, the Man, His Times, and His Task by William Allen White. *Mississippi Valley Historical Review* 12(September, 1925):270-273.

Studies of Joseph Schafer

Buck, Solon J. Review of *Wisconsin Domesday Book: Town Studies* by Joseph Schafer. *Mississippi Valley Historical Review* 12(June, 1925):101-105.

Carman, Harry J. Review of *The Social History of American Agriculture* by Joseph Schafer. *American Historical Review* 42(July, 1937):777-778.

Craven, Avery O. Review of *Four Wisconsin Counties: Prairie and Forest* by Joseph Schafer. *Mississippi Valley Historical Review* 14(March, 1928):561-564.

Duncan, Otis Durant. Review of *The Social History of American Agriculture* by Joseph Schafer. *American Sociological Review* 1(December, 1936):1040-1041.

Duniway, C. A. Review of *Prince Lucien Campbell* by Joseph Schafer. *American Historical Review* 32(July, 1927):935-936.

Edwards, Everett E. Review of *The Winnebago-Horicon Basin* by Joseph Schafer. *Mississippi Valley Historical Review* 25(March, 1939):569-570.

Goebel, Julius. Review of *Intimate Letters of Carl Schurz, 1841-1869* edited and translated by Joseph Schafer. *American Historical Review* 35(October, 1924):178-179.

Hicks, John D. "Memorial to Joseph Schafer: Presented to the Faculty [of the University of Wisconsin], February 3, 1941." *Wisconsin Magazine of History* 24(March, 1941):249-252.

__________. Review of *The Social History of American Agriculture* by Joseph Schafer. *Wisconsin Magazine of History* 20(December, 1936):238-239.

Joseph Schafer: Student of Agriculture. Madison: State Historical Society of Wisconsin, 1942. Includes a complete bibliography of Schafer's publications with book reviews and minor publications not listed above.

Kellar, Herbert A. Review of *The Social History of American Agriculture* by Joseph Schafer. *Mississippi Valley Historical Review* 24(June, 1937):113-114.

Lord, Clifford L., and Carl Ubbelohde. *Clio's Servant: The State Historical Society of Wisconsin, 1846-1954*. Madison: State Historical Society of Wisconsin, 1967.

Meany, Edmond S. Review of *A History of the Pacific Northwest* by Joseph Schafer. *Mississippi Valley Historical Review* 5(September, 1918):235-236.

Merk, Frederick. Review of *A History of Agriculture in Wisconsin* by Joseph Schafer. *American Historical Review* 29(October, 1923):153-154.

Osgood, Ernest S. Review of *The Wisconsin Lead Region* by Joseph Schafer. *Mississippi Valley Historical Review* 21(June, 1934):91-92.

Powers, Alfred. "Debt of Pacific Northwest to Dr. Joseph Schafer." *Oregon Historical Quarterly* 42(March, 1941):88-97.

Schmidt, Bernard. Review of *A History of Agriculture in Wisconsin* by Joseph Schafer. *Mississippi Valley Historical Review* 12(June, 1925):99-101.

Wellington, Raynor G. Review of *Wisconsin Domesday Book: Town Studies* by Joseph Schafer. *American Historical Review* 30(April, 1925):622-623.

Who's Who in America, 1940-1941, p. 2277.

45

FLORA WARREN SEYMOUR

by Deborah Welch

Biography

Flora Warren Seymour is best remembered today for her long and unwavering opposition to Commissioner of Indian Affairs John Collier and his reform policies implemented during the Franklin Roosevelt administration. A sincere proponent of acculturation and assimilation as the basis for Indian progress, Seymour viewed Collier's cultural pluralism values as a foolishly romantic deterrent to necessary Indian advancement. Her stature as the first woman member of the United States Board of Indian Commissioners provided a public platform for her arguments defending assimilationist policies. Beginning in 1924 and continuing throughout the next two decades, Seymour published a series of articles warning the American public of the dangerous and ill-informed sentimentality of many would-be reformers, chief among them, Collier, a man she would later seek to brand a communist.

Ironically, it is Seymour, perhaps more than any other popular historian of the early twentieth century, whose works sought to imbue a whole generation with romantic images of the frontier. Between 1928 and 1946, she published over ten books written for young boys and girls. Primarily biographies, these heavily moralistic narratives relate the ideals and actions of well-known heroes such as Daniel Boone, Sam Houston, Meriwether Lewis, and Kit Carson. Only two of these individual biographies deal with Indians, *Bird Girl: Sacagawea* (1945) and *Pocahontas: Brave Girl* (1946). Notably these are the only heroines who appear in the young people's series and, again, the moral of their stories is clear as Seymour recommends to young readers the examples of these women's right-thinking allegiance to Anglo heroes.

Seymour also wrote historical studies dealing with Indian peoples and the frontier, though again these are written for a popular, not scholarly, audience. In these books, like the children's stories, her profoundly assimilationist views of the American Indian as essentially "primitive people" whose only hope lay in rapid acculturation into Anglo-American society are clearly argued. No less than Collier, Seymour sincerely believed herself to be a champion of Indian peoples. Accordingly, she fought for the Indian's right to share in the progress and opportunities available to all Americans rather than remain chained to what she considered archaic tribalism, a state such persons as John Collier sought to impose.

Born in Cleveland, Ohio, to Charles and Eleanor De Forest Smith, Seymour received her B.A. in 1906 from George Washington University. Following graduation, she chose to remain in Washington, DC, and went to work as a clerk in the United States Indian Service (*Official Register of the United States*, vol. 1). She also began to study law earning her LL.B. from the Washington College of Law in 1915. In that year also, she married George Steele Seymour, a railroad accountant some ten years her senior.

The Seymours took up residence in Chicago following their marriage where both resumed legal studies at the Kent College of Law. Flora Seymour graduated Phi Beta Kappa earning her LL.M. in the following year while her husband received his LL.B. Both were admitted to the Illinois Bar in 1916 (*Who's Who in America* 22:1970-1971).

In addition to law, an active interest in literature and writing drew the Seymours together. In 1919, they organized a national society, the Order of Bookfellows, and began publishing a monthly magazine, the *Step Ladder*, edited by George Seymour. Clearly, Flora shared her husband's enjoyment of writing and their literary circle of friends (she served as secretary of the *Step Ladder* for over a decade), but she could not match his zeal for purely literary pursuits.

In 1920, Flora Seymour completed her first book, a review of the work of writer William De Morgan. Only seventy-two pages in length, *William De Morgan: A Post-Victorian Realist* is a stilted biography which devotes more attention to Morgan's character than his books (pp. 22-23). Published by the Bookfellows, the biography was scarcely a success and, hereafter, Seymour left the writing of book-length literary analysis to her husband. Flora Seymour possessed a far broader interest in history than did her husband and a keen interest in Indian peoples. Nonetheless this first short book is important in developing Seymour's skills in writing biographies and her commitment to providing an uplifting moral lesson, which pervades all of her work.

Seymour's advanced education in law, interest in Indian peoples, and six years spent in the Indian Service brought her to the attention of the Board of Indian Commissioners. In 1922, President Calvin Coolidge selected her as the first woman member of that Board, a capacity in which she would serve until 1933. This appointment gave Seymour the forum she sought to educate the American public on the absolute necessity of steady assimilation for Indian young people into Anglo-American society. Increasingly alarmed by a growing call for Indian policy reform in the early 1920s, notably by John Collier's American Indian Defense Association, Seymour was determined that the country not be swayed by "the delusion of the sentimentalists" (*The Forum* 71:273).

Seymour spent the next twenty-two years fighting those sentimentalists who, first challenged and after 1933, took control of Indian policy with the appointment of Collier as Commissioner of Indian Affairs. Her efforts seemed futile as Collier dismantled the assimilationist policy of the past and implemented the "Indian New Deal" creating tribal governments and protecting Indian lands and cultures. Yet, she never wavered; indeed, her attacks grew more vitriolic as the years passed (*Missionary Review* 58:397-400; *New Outlook* 163:22-25).

Seymour lived to see Collier's decline, though she possessed no sense of victory. In her view, too much damage had been done and her warnings too long ignored. Isolated from the formulation of Indian policy after 1933, Seymour nonetheless refused to be silenced and she took pride in her individual stance, "I seem to have the misfortune of being considered by my conservative friends as a wild-eyed radical, while my radical friends look upon me as a hidebound conservative. . . . I realize now that the successful game is 'Follow-the-leader,' but I have thought things out for myself too long" (*Current Biography*, p. 755).

Themes

Despite the wide variety of her work, ranging from heroic biographies for children to reasoned analyses of United States Indian policy, one overriding theme pervades all of Seymour's work and that is a total commitment to all things American. Seymour defends and celebrates the American character as it evolved through an allegiance to the principles of honor, the work ethic, and the Christian faith. She embraced the uniqueness of the American experience, and like Frederick Jackson Turner, she looked to the frontier for the foundation of the American way of life.

Accordingly, all of Seymour's stories for young people emphasize the bravery, ingenuity, and personal honor of the pioneers, in particular, the pathfinders--Fremont, Carson, Boone, among others. "America had sons," she writes, who opened the West, and succeeding generations could do no better than to emulate their virtues and protect their legacy (*Fremont*, p. 16). America had daughters as well, and in telling their stories, Seymour wrote about Indian women in three books, *Bird Girl: Sacagawea* (1945); *Pocahontas: Brave Girl* (1946); and *Women of Trail and Wigwam* (1930). The latter is a compilation of stories about women such as Holy Rainbow, who accompanied the Overland Astorians; Owl Woman, the wife of William Bent; and the Seneca sisters who adopted captive Mary Jemison. Throughout, Seymour emphasizes the bravery of these women who rejected the "primitive" customs of their Indian society and allied themselves with Euro-American pioneers.

The "primitive," often barbaric, society that Seymour insists Indian people endured before the coming of American civilization is another oft-repeated theme used not only in the children's books, but in Seymour's historical studies. In every case, Seymour begins by stressing the heathen conditions of Indian peoples prior to Euro-American contact.

The benefits brought to Indian peoples by that extension of Christianity and civilization (used synonymously) constitute another principal theme in all of Seymour's writings. Once living only a barbaric, brutal life, Indian peoples had evolved into societies of peaceful, productive men and women by the early twentieth century. Moreover, Seymour repeatedly explains to her readers, this transformation was part of the natural development of Indian societies, which, like all cultures, must evolve or stagnate.

The injustice of the Collier administration's attempts to halt that natural progress and revert Indians to a tribal existence "which they had given up years ago" forms a final theme that can be found throughout Seymour's books and articles (*We Called Them Indians*, p. 258). Over and over, Seymour warns of the injustice imposed by Collier's efforts to block all Indian progress and keep native peoples only "as a curio or a speciman for the museum" (*We Called Them Indians*, Foreword). What could happen to Indian peoples once the attention of the American public, now heightened by a misplaced sense of guilt over perceived past wrongs, was distracted by another cause, another issue? "To-day, we ride on the crest of a great wave of feeling;" she wrote, "to-morrow we collapse feebly into the trough of indifference" (*Outlook* 141:442). To Seymour the problems facing American Indian peoples demanded a considered, informed policy, not runaway emotion: "the real and serious need is for less sentimentality and more information" (*The Forum* 71:273).

Analysis

In order to gather the most current information on Indian peoples for her books and articles, Seymour traveled throughout the country. Beginning during her tenure as an Indian commissioner and continuing every year until the onset of gas rationing during World War II, the Seymours spent their summers driving through reservations in the West. During these months, George Seymour took leave from his work as an accountant to accompany his wife. An amateur photographer, his pictures illustrate many of her works.

Automobile travel over long distances was still a novel undertaking in the 1920s and 1930s. These journeys enabled Seymour to speak with the authority of a first-hand observer to Indian life. The clash of her observations with the Hollywood image of the Indian and the romantic illusions of Collier became the principal impetus of her writing.

Two years after being appointed to the Board of Indian Commissioners, Seymour published four monographs and an article attacking "The Delusion of the Sentimentalists." The latter appeared in the March, 1924, issue of *The Forum* magazine. Here she takes to task the Indian reformers whose policy proposals would "plunge them [Indian peoples] back into a Stone Age civilization." She also criticizes the gullible American public who "experiences a vague feeling of mingled guilt and sympathy" at the image of "the once care-free savage, robbed of his ancestral heritage" (p. 274). The truth is far different from the Hollywood dichotomy of villain and saint, Seymour charged. The American Indian, she thought, was living a primitive existence at the time of European contact, making no use of America's rich natural resources. While Seymour does not deny that injustice was done, she forcefully argues that the benefits of Christianity, civilization, education, health care, and land ownership given to the Indian far outweigh any harm. Moreover, Indian peoples have embraced this progress; the average Indian, no more than Seymour herself, would not want to return to the barbarism of the past, "If we have wronged the Indian by what we have taken from him, we cannot right the wrong by taking from him what our civilization has given him" (p. 274).

This transition of a "primitive" people into acculturated citizens is discussed at further length in two monographs of case studies, *The Story of the Sioux Indians* (1924) and *The Indians of the Pueblos* (1924). Once a "remote warlike people," the Sioux, Seymour concludes, were peaceful farmers as a result of the allotment policy legislated in 1887. The return to communal land holdings proposed by Collier and other reformers would be a gross injustice to these hard-working farmers and would benefit only the lazy, indolent members of the race who had lost or sold their land and now looked to their neighbors and the government for rescue. "[I]n the end there will be a realization that they are no more exempt than others from the rule that man must earn his bread by the sweat of his brow" (*Story of Sioux*, p. 58).

Seymour had every confidence that if allowed a free choice, the younger generation of Indian children educated in the ways of Anglo-American society would not permit the sentimentalists to rob them of their constitutional rights to land ownership as well as all other benefits and obligations of American citizenship. Seymour notes, "as the young people become educated Pueblo life will become better particularly as the older generation becomes less powerful." But, "whether he clings to his conservative ways or adopts the new, the choice must be his own" (*Indians of Pueblos*, pp. 63-64).

Seymour's belief that the energies of reformers like Mary Austin and John Collier would soon dissipate "proved wildly premature" (*The Vanishing American*, p. 297). Instead the American Indian Defense Association (AIDA) grew in strength, listing among its members and directors such prominent Americans as Harold Ickes, Hamlin Garland, George Foster Peabody, and General Nelson A. Miles, among others. These were the men whom Seymour had called uninformed, charged Mary Austin in a 1924 response to *The Forum* article, "Delusion of the Sentimentalists." Moreover, Austin countered, the AIDA had been joined in its call for reform by the General Federation of Women's Clubs and the American Association for the Advancement of Science. Who was Seymour to challenge the motives and wisdom of such people whose "sanity and the extent and accuracy of their information on public questions had never before been questioned" (*The Forum* 71:286). It is Seymour, Austin charged, who was ignorant of history by calling Indian societies primitive when "the whole economic system of the American Colonies was founded on a corn and potato culture which we took over from the Indians and have improved very little since" (p. 282).

Despite these criticisms and the impressive membership of those in opposition to Seymour's views, she continued to call for an end to "unavailing sentimentality" regarding the American Indian. In 1925, she rose to the defense of the Indian Bureau against Carlos Montezuma's attack in an article using the Yavapai physician and reformer's most famous phrase, "Let My People Go," subtitled "a painful article on the American Indian for the sentimentalists to read--a good article for any one to whom a fact does not give a headache" (*Outlook* 141:441). Again, Seymour acknowledges that "we all share more or less the dim feeling that our very presence on this continent wrongs the Indian," but the "stone age is over" (p. 441). Again, she argues, all cultures must evolve and it is the Indian's right to share fully in the American way of life, "a race cannot be kept in its infancy" (p. 442).

Seymour was not alone in her views during this decade. Many prominent Indian leaders of the national pan-Indian organization, the Society of American Indians, notably Arthur C. Parker and Marie Baldwin, shared Seymour's dismay at Montezuma's abrupt call for the abolition of the Bureau (*Quarterly Journal of the Society of American Indians* 3:261). Nor was she the only American interested in Indian policy who was alarmed by the growing reform movement fostered by Collier, Stella Atwood, and others active in the American Indian Defense Association (*Papers of IRA*, "Accomplishments and Aims").

In 1926, Seymour published her first book-length history, *The Indians Today*. Heavily anecdotal, lacking notes on sources, and written in a simplified prose for young students as well as the adult public, *The Indian Today* offers a state-by-state survey of Indian peoples. Seymour includes histories of the Iroquois, Sioux, Osage, Pueblo, Navajo, Hopi, and Nez Perce peoples before turning to a discussion of their present-day lives. Of all of Seymour's works, these chapters offer the most blatant example of the author's ethnocentrism. In examining the Osage, Seymour concludes that only those with white blood had been able to handle their wealth. She is dismayed that the new healthy ways taught to the Zuni Pueblo young people were squashed by powerful tribal elders. Among the Hopi, she observes that the Snake Dance and other rituals were no longer done to ensure rain and good crops but to gain tourist dollars. A final chapter devoted to Indian education reaffirms Seymour's commitment to acculturationist policies promoted by nonreservation boarding schools such as Carlisle.

The Indian Today was well-received as an "interesting humanized presentation" of Indian history (*New York Times*, June 20, 1926, p. 26). Encouraged by the favorable review, Seymour published two additional books for young people in rapid succession, *The Boys' Life of Fremont* in 1928 and *The Boys' Life of Kit Carson* in 1929. Both are written as simple narratives which include imagined conversations and events. Anxious as always to provide a moral example of American decency for young people, Seymour exalts the qualities of both men as dutiful, hardworking, possessed of high purpose, and willing to sacrifice for the nation.

Also, in 1929 Seymour published her second history of the American Indian, *The Story of the Red Man.* Though primarily a sketch of the Indian wars, this lengthy volume represents a more serious attempt at scholarship, and Seymour is careful here to include bibliographical notes. Again, however, her writing is obsessed with a defense of American assimilationist policy. Indian peoples were "primitive" and consisted of only a sparse native population at the time of European contact, Seymour writes. The development of American society required land, which was not being used in any case, and, in return, rescued the Indian from barbarism. Finally, Seymour cannot resist slipping into the narration used in previous works as she creates a conversation between Sacagawea and her small son.

The Story of the Red Man was well-received by those reviewers who treated it as a useful school textbook. Others, such as John Collier, recognizing Seymour's more serious intent, charged that the book was severely marred by "an unconscious race prejudice" (*New York Herald Tribune*, September 29, 1929, p. 38). Perhaps stung by these criticisms, Seymour retreated during the next three years to the writing of only children's stories, producing three books, *Lords of the Valley, Sir William Johnson and his Mohawk Brothers* (1930); *Sam Houston, Patriot* (1930); and *Women of Trail and Wigwam* (1930). The latter two were dedicated to her nephews and nieces, respectively.

By 1933, the threat of the "sentimentalists" as Seymour persistently called Collier and his reformer colleagues had become a reality with the election of Franklin Roosevelt to the presidency and the appointment of John Collier as Commissioner of Indian Affairs. The Board of Indian Commissioners, upon which Seymour still served, was abolished by executive order. In 1934 Congress passed the Indian Reorganization Act (IRA) ending allotment in severalty and opening a new era in American Indian policy.

Seymour immediately resumed publication of articles attacking the reform policies being implemented under Collier's broad interpretation of the Reorganization Act. A longstanding supporter of the nonreservation boarding schools, she turned first to education in an article, "The Pedagogues Hunt Indians." Here she challenges the so-called experts being brought into the Indian Bureau, "a great influx of new employees whose strings of college degrees are matched only by their exquisite ignorance of the Indian and his ways" (*American Mercury* 29:437). Taxpayers' money was being wasted, she charges, by the employment of teachers who knew nothing of English, history, or arithmetic, but who, instead, were paid high salaries to teach traditional culture, "Native Navajo rug weavers are employed to teach the girls their art, just as they would do on the desert in any case. Without their salary from the school funds, however, they might not be 'conditioning skill outcomes,' they might be merely producing rugs" (p. 445).

Final passage of the Indian Reorganization Act in 1934 drove Seymour to new extremes in her attacks on Collier. In "Trying It on the Indian," she calls the IRA, "the most extreme gesture yet made by the administration in this country toward a Communistic experiment" (*New Outlook* 163:22). Indian opposition, she charges, was fast growing to this blatant move to segregate and "de-individualize" the Indian.

The measures contained in the Reorganization Act were bad enough in Seymour's view. Collier's broadly interpretive administration of the Act to protect and encourage native religious practices goaded Seymour to still greater fury at the "deliberate fostering of native religions and primitive ritualism" (*Missionary Review* 58:397). Indeed, Collier was promoting "fetishism," in her view, and Bureau employees who opposed these immoral policies did so at peril to their jobs (p. 399). This final assault on the Christian civilization brought to the Indian by American society disgusted Seymour as "typical of the whole illogical, unintelligent attitude which has prevailed in the Indian office in the past two years" (p. 400).

Seymour never ceased in her efforts to discredit Collier and emphasize the "confusion and misery" his policies brought to Indian peoples "from those who have always loudly publicized themselves as 'friends of the Indian'" (*Saturday Evening Post* 211:23). The bitter anger of the Navajo at Collier's stock reduction policy and their rejection of reservation schools were two examples of Collier's failure which Seymour quickly brought to the attention of the American public (*Missionary Review* 62:448-450).

In addition to her constant attacks on Collier through her articles, Seymour continued to write her books during these years. In 1937, she published yet another biography for young people, a study of Meriwether Lewis, followed two years later with a biography of the French explorer, La Salle. In 1940, she produced an additional history of American Indians, *We Called Them Indians*, dedicated to her friend, Elaine Goodale Eastman. The book is essentially a narrative history which emphasizes the basic and continuing misunderstanding of Indians by Anglo-American policy makers. Much of the information contained here was taken from Seymour's earlier works as once again she reviews the Indian wars and highlights the leadership of well-known figures--Sacagawea, Pontiac, Joseph Brant, Tecumseh, and others. While offering little new information, the book did afford her another opportunity to attack the Indian Reorganization Act as "a backward step in Indian progress" (p. 238).

Indian Agents of the Old Frontier, published in 1941, represents a final attempt by Seymour to produce a scholarly, well-researched refutal to the sentimental perception of Indians as a saintly people whose land had been stolen by greedy whites. Perhaps no frontiersmen were so deeply villified by Hollywood and in popular novels as the Indian agents, often portrayed as dirty, shiftless, scheming perpetrators of Indian misfortune. Correction of this image is the stated purpose of the book as Seymour offers a multitude of facts, citing numerous sources, as well as a number of intriguing stories of a large number of good and dedicated men whose efforts were poorly repaid by Indians and the Indian Bureau. Seymour's account of the relationship between Cochise and Thomas Jeffords is particularly poignant and is an example of her story-telling abilities at their best.

Seymour's last published assault on Collier appears in the essays she contributed to G. E. E. Lindquist's *The Indian in American Life* published in 1944. Once again she pleads with Americans to set aside their romantic notions of the Indian and return to a fair and just policy. Allotment, she insists, was a realistic policy whereas the Indian Reorganization Act is "a complete violation of Constitutional principles" (p. 60).

In the four remaining years of her life, Seymour published only two more books, both of them children's biographies of Indian women: *Bird Girl: Sacagawea* (1945) and *Pocahontas: Brave Girl* (1946). These are the simplest of Seymour's books written for elementary school children, and they provide a fitting close to her career. Throughout her life she had always looked to the next generation as inheritors of the American ideals. Thus, she had devoted so much of her time to writing biographies for children to read and pattern their lives on the example of America's bravest and best forefathers--the men who had opened the West. Similarly, she looked to the next generation of Indian children who, once carefully educated in the ideals and values of American society, would bring progress to their people enabling them to take their place as productive citizens of the world's greatest country. John Collier threatened to destroy this natural evolution, and Seymour opposed him bitterly lest he obliterate the American legacy she believed should be available to Indian, no less than Anglo, children.

Their differing backgrounds, unrelenting personalities, and, most importantly, their opposing views of American society combined to make the clash between Seymour and Collier inevitable. Whereas Seymour celebrated all that was good in the Anglo-American character and society, Collier had spent much of his early life laboring for better conditions among the immigrant populations of eastern cities. This experience had left him deeply disillusioned with American society as it had evolved in the throes of late nineteenth-century industrial development. A visit to Taos in 1920-1921 gave Collier the inspiration he sought to deal with the troubled American society and the problems of cultural survival. Indian peoples, he wrote, "possessed the fundamental secret of human life--the secret of building great personality through the instrumentality of social institutions" (*Assault on Assimilation*, p. 120).

Seymour was among the first who recognized the danger Collier posed to past acculturation policies. Her writing offers a case study of assimilationist thinking about United States Indian policy as it existed in the late nineteenth and early twentieth centuries. Her histories of the American frontier were heavily anecdotal and imbued with moral overtones unencumbered by subtlety. Her narrative writing style bears close resemblance to other women authors of her generation also involved in Indian affairs. Unlike many others who shared her interests, however, Seymour never evolved in her perception or consideration of her stance. Collier's rise to power and his implementation of far-sweeping reform policies had the effect of entrenching Seymour's views. Her arguments in 1944 differed little from the case against reform she first presented twenty years earlier. The attacks grew more strident but their basic premise anchored in assimilationist thinking remained unaltered. Seymour's books and articles offer a rich source for anyone seeking knowledge of the arguments which lay behind the sincerely motivated, if totally ethnocentric, assimilationist view of United States Indian policy.

Bibliography

Books

Bird Girl: Sacagawea. New York: Bobbs-Merrill Co., 1945.
The Boys' Life of Fremont. New York: The Century Co., 1928.
The Boys' Life of Kit Carson. New York: The Century Co., 1929.
Daniel Boone, Pioneer. New York: The Century Co., 1931.
The Five Civilized American Indian Tribes. Girard, KS: Haldeman-Julius Co., 1924.
History of the New York Indians. Girard, KS: Haldeman-Julius Co., 1924.
Indian Agents of the Old Frontier. New York: D. Appleton-Century Co., 1941.
The Indians of the Pueblos. Girard, KS: Haldeman-Julius Co., 1924.
The Indians Today. Chicago: H. B. Sanborn and Co., 1926.
La Salle: Explorer of Our Midland Empire. New York: D. Appleton-Century Co., 1939.
Lords of the Valley, Sir William Johnson and His Mohawk Brothers. New York: Longmans, Green, and Co., 1930.
Meriwether Lewis, Trail-Blazer. New York: D. Appleton-Century Co., 1937.
Pocahontas: Brave Girl. New York: Bobbs-Merrill Co., 1946.
Sam Houston, Patriot. New York: The Century Co., 1930.
The Story of the Red Man. New York: Longmans, Green, and Co., 1929.
The Story of the Sioux Indians. Girard, KS: Haldeman-Julius Co., 1924.
We Called Them Indians. New York: D. Appleton-Century Co., 1940.
William De Morgan, A Post-Victorian Realist. Chicago: The Bookfellows, 1920.
Women of Trail and Wigwam. New York: The Woman's Press, 1930.

Selected Articles

"Delusion of the Sentimentalists." *The Forum* 71(March, 1924):273-280.
"A Desert Domain--Among the Indians." *Missionary Review of the World* 62(October, 1939):448-450.
"Fear of TB." *Survey* 36(August 26, 1916):545.
"Federal Favor for Fetishism." *Missionary Review of the World* 58(September, 1935):397-400.
"Indian-White Relations." In *The Indian in American Life* edited by G. E. E. Lindquist. New York: Friendship Press, 1944. Pp. 46-66.
"Indians and Reading." *Library Journal* 60(November 15, 1935):893.
"Let My People Go." *Outlook* 141(November 18, 1925):441-444.

"The Pedagogues Hunt Indians." *American Mercury* 29(August, 1933):437-445.
"Thunder Over the Southwest." *Saturday Evening Post* 211(April 1, 1939):23, 71-76.
"Trying It on the Indian." *New Outlook* 163(May, 1934):22-25.

Studies of Flora W. Seymour

Austin, Mary. "The Folly of the Officials." *The Forum* 71(March, 1924):281-288.
Babcock, Willoughby M. Review of *The Story of the Red Men* by Flora W. Seymour. *Mississippi Valley Historical Review* 16(March, 1930):589-590.
Buell, E. L. Review of *We Call Them Indians* by Flora W. Seymour. *New York Times*, March 31, 1940, p. 10.
Carter, Clarence E. Review of *Lords of the Valley, Sir William Johnson and his Mohawk Brothers* by Flora W. Seymour. *American Historical Review* 36(January, 1931):408-410.
Collier, John. Review of *The Story of the Indian* by Flora W. Seymour. *New York Herald Tribune*, September 29, 1929, p. 38.
Cotterill, Robert S. Review of *Indian Agents of the Old Frontier* by Flora W. Seymour. *Journal of Southern History* 8(May, 1942):265-266.
Dippie, Brian W. *The Vanishing American: White Attitudes and U.S. Indian Policy*. Middletown, CT: Wesleyan University Press, 1982.
Eastman, Elaine Goodale. "Does Uncle Sam Foster Paganism?" *Christian Century* 51(August 8, 1934):1016-1018.
"Flora Warren Seymour." In *Current Biography* edited by Maxine Block. New York: H. W. Wilson Co., 1942. P. 755.
Green, Joseph C. Review of *The Story of the Red Men* by Flora W. Seymour. *American Historical Review* 35(July, 1930):881-882.
Henderson, Archibald. Review of *Lords of the Valley, Sir William Johnson and his Mohawk Brothers* by Flora W. Seymour. *North Carolina Historical Review* 9(April, 1932):214-218.
__________. Review of *The Story of the Red Men* by Flora W. Seymour. *North Carolina Historical Review* 9(April, 1932):214-218.
Kelly, Lawrence C. *The Assault on Assimilation: John Collier and the Origins of Indian Policy Reform.* Albuquerque: University of New Mexico Press, 1983.
Litton, Gaston. Review of *Indian Agents of the Old Frontier* by Flora W. Seymour. *Mississippi Valley Historical Review* 28(March, 1942):601-602.
Mead, Margaret. Review of *The Story of the Red Men* by Flora W. Seymour. *Annals of the American Academy of Political and Social Science* 152(November, 1930):413-414.
Moffitt, James W. Review of *Indian Agents of the Old Frontier* by Flora W. Seymour. *American Historical Review* 47(July, 1942):954-955.
Official Register of the United States Containing a List of the Offices and Employees in the Civil, Military, and Naval Services, vol. I. Washington, DC: Government Printing Office, 1907, 1909, 1911.

Olson, James S., and Raymond Wilson. *Native Americans in the Twentieth Century*. Provo, UT: Brigham Young University Press, 1984.

Parker, Arthur C. "Certainly Abolish the Indian Bureau." *Quarterly Journal of the Society of American Indians* 3(October-December, 1915):261-263.

Prucha, Francis Paul. *The Great Father: The United States Government and the American Indian.* Vol. II. Lincoln: University of Nebraska Press, 1984.

Review of *The Indians Today* by Flora W. Seymour. *New York Times*, June 20, 1926, p. 26.

"Seymour, Flora." In *Who's Who in America.* Chicago: A. N. Marquis Co., 1942. 22:1970.

"Seymour, George." In *Who's Who in America.* Chicago: A. N. Marquis Co., 1942. 22:1970-1971.

"A Statement Covering the Accomplishments and Aims of the American Indian Defense Association." In *Papers of the Indian Rights Association.* Philadelphia: Historical Society of Pennsylvania, April, 1924.

Thompson, L. W. Review of *The Story of the Red Men* by Flora W. Seymour. *New York Times*, September 22, 1929, p. 3.

Vestal, Stanley. Review of *Indian Agents of the Old Frontier* by Flora W. Seymour. *New York Herald Tribune*, August 31, 1941, p. 13.

46

BENJAMIN F. SHAMBAUGH

by Alan M. Schroder

Biography

Benjamin Shambaugh's writings on frontier history focus on the place where he lived nearly all of his adult life--eastern Iowa, and more specifically Iowa City. He was born on the Shambaugh family farm near Elvira in Clinton County in 1871 and grew up as a second-generation pioneer in an environment that must have seemed a living demonstration of the efficacy of frontier virtues. His parents, John and Eva Ann Shambaugh, built their original 120-acre purchase into a substantial 720-acre farming operation (Aurner, *Benjamin Shambaugh*, p. 10). One of the benefits of the Shambaugh's prosperity was that it enabled their son Benjamin to follow his brother in 1886 to the Iowa Academy in Iowa City, a prep school that channeled its students into the nearby State University of Iowa. Benjamin Shambaugh followed the usual course, entering the University of Iowa in 1888 and receiving his bachelor's degree there in 1892.

He exhausted the university's modest graduate program with a master's degree in 1893, then moved on to the University of Pennsylvania's Wharton School of Finance and Economy. Shambaugh completed his doctoral work in 1895 and, in the customary acknowledgment of the sources of professional historical training, conducted an intellectual grand tour of the German universities of Halle, Leipzig, and Berlin. He was back in Iowa City by January, 1896, however, to settle in to his lifelong career as a professor in what would shortly become the political science department at the University of Iowa. At this time he also married Bertha Horack, a member of a prominent Iowa City family and a fellow student with Shambaugh at the university.

Shambaugh's master's and doctoral research on early Iowa history had awakened in him an interest in the State Historical Society of Iowa, which was also located in Iowa City, and he quickly became one of the leaders among the local scholars who set out to make it a true research institution, rather than the museum of curios and storage facility for old newspapers and manuscripts that it was then. Shambaugh was elected to the Society's board of curators in 1897 and became the editor of its journal, the *Iowa Historical Record*, in 1900. By 1903 he had converted what had been a repository of reminiscences and local antiquarianism into a modern scholarly journal, the *Iowa Journal of History and Politics*. First as a member of the Society's executive committee and then, beginning in 1907, as its superintendent and editor, Shambaugh converted the Society itself into a major research and publishing organization in local, state, and regional history. This was not a state historical society in the model that came to be followed later in the century. Instead, it was what Shambaugh called a "laboratory of scientific historical research," in which the public benefited, not by visiting a museum (which the Society did not have) or by doing its own (usually genealogical) research, but by reading the articles and books produced by the Society's own professional historians.

Under Shambaugh, the supply of these historians came mainly from the master's and doctoral students and junior faculty of the University of Iowa's political science department. Shambaugh became the head of the department when it was created in 1900 and, as he had at the Society, immediately set out to make it an important institution in the new field of political science as it was developing during the Progressive Era. Shambaugh's early career coincided, in fact, with a strong national movement toward professionalization in the social sciences, and as an energetic participant in this movement, he served as one of the charter members of the American Political Science Association and one of the founders of the Mississippi Valley Historical Association, now the Organization of American Historians.

During and after World War I, Shambaugh began to turn the emphasis of both the State Historical Society and the political science department toward an active involvement with the general public. At the Society this took the form of such public programs as essay contests for students, radio programs, and even a filmed recreation of Marquette and Joliet's 1673 canoe trip down the Mississippi. In the Society's publications, Shambaugh began to emphasize a lighter, more impressionistic, regionalist approach to history, most notably in its new magazine of popular history, *The Palimpsest*. At the university, the new emphasis could be seen in the annual sessions of the Iowa Commonwealth Conference, which were held from 1923 to 1930. The conference brought together nationally recognized authorities on contemporary problems and representatives of the press and the general public for roundtable discussions that were attended by very large audiences and that received very wide state and national attention.

The onset of the depression curtailed many of these activities. The Society's public programs and its publications were sharply cut back, and the university's Commonwealth Conferences came to an end. Even in the 1930s, however, Shambaugh's imagination and energy were unchecked. At the university he began an innovative interdisciplinary course that was formally called "Approaches in Liberal and Cultural Education" and that was commonly known as the "Campus Course." In this, Shambaugh made full use of his talents as an engaging lecturer to introduce his students to the full range of the cultural heritage of the society in which they lived. At the State Historical Society, Shambaugh inaugurated a planned multi-volume centennial history of Iowa. Though he was sixty-nine at the time of his death in 1940, Shambaugh's plans and the energy he still showed in seeking to fulfill them make his death seem premature.

Themes

Just as Benjamin Shambaugh pursued a dual career in political science and history, the themes of his writings diverge fairly clearly between a concern for the contemporary issues of government policy during the Progressive Era and the historical issues of Iowa's frontier government. Between the two areas, it is his writing on the Iowa frontier that is the focus of this essay and the accompanying bibliography.

The central theme of Shambaugh's frontier history is that the origins of government can be found in the values and practices of the people governed rather than the tenets of political philosophy or the dictates of an external governmental power, and that the location of these origins was the frontier. In his most prominent essay, "Frontier Land Clubs or Claim Associations," he traces the origins of effective government to the claim club, which he sees as a popular institution for the establishment of a government that would protect the legitimate interests of law-abiding citizens from the unlawful assaults of claim jumpers and land sharks.

Shambaugh continued this theme in his *History of the Constitutions of Iowa*, published in 1902. In this he describes the formation of Iowa's state government in the Constitutions of 1844 and 1846 as an effort of the people's elected delegates to protect them from the dictates of a powerful governor and the whims of a succession of General Assemblies. Throughout this discussion of frontier government making, Shambaugh stresses that the principles of the founders were those of Jeffersonian democracy and of the Declaration of Independence. These principles, he believes, were modified in the frontier environment to produce a distinctive western democracy, of which the Iowa frontier was the highest expression.

In fact, although his scholarly interest in the frontier predated the Turner thesis (and was probably, like Turner's, rooted in his personal background among the pioneers themselves), Shambaugh quickly adopted a Turnerian outlook in his writing. He traces the frontier back to Plymouth Rock, thus making American history essentially frontier history and American values essentially the frontier values of equality, democracy, and practicality. Unlike many of his contemporaries, Shambaugh held to this classic Turnerian view throughout his career, expressing essentially the same views in the 1932 edition of his history of Iowa constitutions as he had in the original 1902 edition and repeating them again in his popular history, *The Old Stone Capitol Remembers*, published in 1939.

Shambaugh was similarly consistent throughout his career in stressing the values of the scholarly study of state and local history. This is an inductive, Platonic view that in general can best be understood by studying the particular rather than by first establishing a body of theoretical principles. While the Turnerian ideas that Shambaugh made such an important part of his writing have seen successive periods of enthusiastic acceptance, staunch rejection, and qualified acceptance, Shambaugh's emphasis on the validity of studying local history--when such study is held to high standards of scholarship--as a basis for working outward toward national history and beyond is still accepted and is vigorously being pursued in modern writing on the frontier.

Analysis

Shambaugh is best known for his work on the claim club as a frontier institution. He recognized that settlers had established such clubs in the earliest settlements in Kentucky and Tennessee and that there was also evidence for them in Illinois and Wisconsin and most recently in Oklahoma shortly before he was writing. He also believed that there had been dozens of claim clubs in Iowa (*Annual Report AHA* 1:69, 71-72). But, though he discusses the clubs at Fort Dodge and at the North Fork of the Maquoketa River to some extent, he focuses his attention on the Claim Association of Johnson County. This is no doubt partly due to the fact that Iowa City and the Johnson County area were the focus of his local history research as a whole, but it is also true that this was the only Iowa claim club for which he had located detailed records. The Iowa historian Jesse Macy had already published the club's constitution, but Shambaugh also had access to the records of the members' claims and the various transactions involving these claims in the four years of the club's existence (*Constitution and Records*, pp. 17-192). It may have been the very completeness of these records that led him to declare in 1900 that "it was upon the Iowa frontier that land clubs or claim associations reached their most perfect organization and attained their greatest influence," and that among the Iowa clubs "the Claim Association of Johnson County was in its organization and administration, one of the most perfect, not only in Iowa, but in all the West" (*Annual Report AHA* 1:69, 72).

Shambaugh found the origins of this club in the 1839 decision to locate the seat of government for the Territory of Iowa in Johnson County at the site of what would become Iowa City and to donate the one-mile-square federal survey section that contained the site to the Territory and reserve it and the surrounding sections from sale. The settlers who had already moved to this area, Shambaugh asserts, quite accurately concluded that the decision would create an "influx of 'new-comers' and land speculators" to the site while at the same time negating their own claims, which they had supposedly already begun to develop as homes and farms. The claim club, Shambaugh concludes, was intended to protect the original settlers' claims and to secure them the right eventually to purchase the land encompassed by the claims at the federal land auction at the $1.25 per acre minimum price (*Constitution and Records*, pp. xviii-xix).

Interpreting the issue more broadly, Shambaugh asserts that the early Iowa settlers were justified in forming these inherently extralegal organizations because they were effectively beyond the rule of law. He points out that while the land that would become the state of Iowa was technically under a succession of territorial governments, these governments were neither powerful enough nor well enough organized to extend this jurisdiction to the Iowa frontier in practice. Beyond this, the claim club members were technically trespassers on the public lands and could be forcibly removed under the provisions of an 1807 law. Shambaugh realizes that this law had never been consistently enforced, but he contends that the squatters were honest farmers, not criminals, and that they had a right to be protected in their possessions, and since formal government could not provide this, they were justified in forming their own governments (*Constitution and Records*, pp. xi-xii; *Annual Report AHA* 1:71).

Shambaugh thus generalizes from the idea of claim clubs as protectors of land claims to claim clubs as protogovernments, and he sees their constitutions as the first written constitutions by which government operated on the frontier. In a distinctly Turnerian approach, Shambaugh argues that the Squatter Constitutions, as he calls them, grew out of a perceived need of the "lawful men of the neighborhood" for some form of governmental protection, that the provisions of the constitutions followed the usages and customs of the community, and that the resulting documents constituted the "fundamental laws of the pioneers" (*History of the Constitutions of Iowa*, pp. 31-32). Beyond this he suggests that they formed the basis for the state homestead exemption laws and the federal preemption and homestead acts (*History of the Constitutions of Iowa*, pp. 63-64; *Annual Report AHA* 1:83). Shambaugh sums up his view of the Squatter Constitutions in his statement that "above all they expressed and, in places and under conditions where temptations to recklessness and lawlessness were greatest, they effectively upheld the foremost civilizing principle of Anglo-Saxon polity--the Rule of Law" (*History of the Constitutions of Iowa*, p. 65).

To counter the possible criticism that this was saying a lot for a document that was essentially intended to protect the land interests of a clique of early arrivals who had sufficient solidarity to enforce it by mob violence, Shambaugh notes that the clubs followed standards for the establishment of land claims that stretched back to the earliest days of the public land system, that the system protected "all bona fide settlers," that there were limits on the size of the claims, that disputes were to be settled in "regularly constituted courts," and that the affairs of the clubs were conducted in open meetings of all the people (*Annual Report AHA* 1:82-83). Shambaugh, then, sees the claim clubs and their constitutions as the charter oaks of government that honest, hardworking settlers planted in the virgin soil of the frontier.

Historians generally accepted this view until the publication in 1958 of Allan Bogue's essay, "The Iowa Claim Clubs: Symbol and Substance" (*Mississippi Valley Historical Review* 45:231-253). Bogue could find definite evidence of only twenty-six claim clubs in Iowa, not the hundred or more that Macy and Shambaugh had speculated about, so the great majority of settlers would not have received whatever protection they provided. Further, when he examines the narrative evidence in such sources as newspaper reports and reminiscences in county histories and the quantitative evidence in claim records that have survived from three of the clubs, Bogue finds that the classic case of a settler locating a choice farm-sized plot of land for his claim, recording it with the local claim club, and then purchasing that land at the appropriate federal land auction is the distinct exception. In the Johnson County club, for example, Bogue finds that only 26 percent of the people who simply entered a claim in the club's records, without any further transactions, went on to purchase land from the federal government in the townships covered by the club. Much more common was the individual who entered much larger than farm-sized claims and used the income he gained from selling part of the claim to latecomers to pay for a land purchase from the government. The land so purchased was not even necessarily part of the original claim. Other individuals actively speculated in claims, buying and selling undeveloped and unoccupied claims right up to the time of the auction. Still others obtained title to land in the area through the time-entry system, in which a speculator entered the land but agreed to deed it over to another purchaser within a specified period after receiving a stated price plus a usually substantial interest payment (pp. 244-246).

Bogue did find variations in the character of claim club activity in different parts of the state. The business of speculating in claims was most active in Johnson County, where the anticipated prosperity from locating the seat of government there would make claims especially desirable. In the Poweshiek County claim club there was more evidence of the time-entry system, and in the Fort Dodge club there was less evidence either of speculation or of a time-entry system, though here the club revised its constitution in 1851 in an apparent attempt to rid itself of just such activity. Bogue concludes that, on the whole, the Iowa claim clubs did protect the settlers who were simply interested in filing a claim on enough land to serve as a farm, but it also protected the much larger number of individuals who had "far more complex motives" (pp. 247-253).

This conclusion is supported by Robert P. Swierenga in his further study of the Fort Dodge claim club. Swierenga discovers that nonresidents filed a substantial number of claims in the club's records, either by using local land agents to locate claims or by purchasing claims from residents. He also finds that the residents themselves often engaged in claim speculation, filing a quit claim on one piece of land and immediately filing a new claim on another. Swierenga's conclusions are published as the introduction to a letter written in 1896 by Charles B. Richards, a resident of Fort Dodge when the claim club was in operation there. Richards described the club as being made up of people who were seeking to prevent the lands from being taken up by actual settlers and who in at least two cases used intimidation to prevent such settlers from entering unoccupied land upon which no preemption claim had been filed. Swierenga notes that Charles Aldrich, who was the editor of the *Annals of Iowa* and who had invited

Richards to prepare the letter, never in fact published it, perhaps, Swierenga suggests, because it ran counter to the prevailing image of the claim club Shambaugh and others had created (*Annals of Iowa* 39:513-518).

Shambaugh may never have seen the Richards letter, but he did publish more than one hundred pages of land claims and claim transactions of the Johnson County club in 1894. Quantitative analysis of the kind done by Bogue and Swierenga would have been much more laborious then, and such analysis was certainly not then the vogue in historical research. But it would have been reasonable for Shambaugh at least to wonder about the implications of the numerous multiple entries by individuals in the club records and to compare the claim records against the county deed records.

It may be that Shambaugh was more concerned about the principles of law and government that the claim clubs established on the frontier than about the imperfect functioning of these principles in day-to-day affairs. But even in this, Shambaugh's conclusion that the clubs represented protogovernments is contradicted by the course of events he describes elsewhere. The Johnson County club dissolved after the federal land auction at Marion, Iowa, in 1843, and the founding fathers of Iowa government proved to be distinctly averse to establishing any other local government in the Iowa City area. In his study of early Iowa City, Shambaugh points out that prior to the incorporation of Iowa City by the Iowa General Assembly in 1853, there had been only one attempt to form a local government. The officers elected to this government had been audacious enough to issue an order that the citizens clean up their streets and alleys, which order they ignored, and to pay a municipal tax, which they refused to do, so the town government, Shambaugh observes, "dropped their official duties and returned to their ordinary pursuits" (*Iowa City*, p. 107). Thus, for the first fourteen years of its existence Iowa City had essentially no local government, not by necessity but by choice.

Beyond this, Iowa's earliest citizens proved to be decidedly reluctant to move from territorial status to statehood. It required three popular votes between 1840 and 1844 (votes that Shambaugh repeatedly chronicles in his writings) to convince them that the benefits of state government outweighed the costs of supporting it (*History of the Constitutions of Iowa*, pp. 152-174). Though part of the opposition was due to a Whig reluctance to form a state government while the state was still dominated by Democrats, the repeated rejections do not reflect the striving toward established government Shambaugh sees in the formation of the claim clubs.

In his writing on Iowa's territorial government Shambaugh makes it clear that he considered it to be the highest product of an evolution that stretched back past the Ordinance of 1787 to the colonial period, but he also sees it as a form of colonial government, a government handed down by a distant power to people who had never really given their consent to be ruled by it (pp. 106-108). Governments based on popularly derived constitutions are superior, he believes, because they rise up from below. He writes:

> Members of constituent assemblies and constitutional conventions neither manufacture nor grow Constitutions--they simply formulate current political morality. It is in the social mind back of the convention, back of the government, and back of the Law that the ideals of human rights and justice are conceived, born, and evolved. A Constitution is a social product. It is the embodiment of popular ideals (pp. 13-14).

He sees the conflict between the territorial governor, Robert Lucas, and the Legislative Assembly--a prominent element in early Iowa history--not as a political battle or a contest of wills, but as the representatives' declaration of independence from the territorial administration (pp. 142-143). He records the same attitude reflected in the early constitutional conventions' efforts to limit severely the governor's influence on the state government, though he notes that the delegates also showed a preference for writing even minor legislative matters into the constitution itself rather than trusting to later General Assemblies to decide the questions (p. 202; *Iowa City*, pp. 114-115).

In chronicling the debates on the various issues before the constitutional conventions of 1844 and 1846, Shambaugh uncovers numerous examples of the influence of a spirit of western democracy and a determination to keep control of the state government very much in the people's hands. In the delegates' decision to prohibit any form of religious test in the performance of public or private duties, Shambaugh sees a liberal spirit of religious toleration, and in their decision to limit the governor's veto powers to those allowed to the president in the federal constitution and in sharply limiting his powers of appointment to the judiciary, he posits further evidence of the pioneers' distrust of a strong executive (*History of the Constitutions of Iowa*, pp. 186-196, 202-212).

One area that Shambaugh considers a test of whether the delegates were prepared to extend the principles of Jeffersonian democracy and of the Declaration of Independence to everyone is on the question of the admission of blacks into the state on an equal basis with whites, and here the delegates failed the test. As Shambaugh reviews the debates, he sees the delegates as torn between their own expressed dedication to the formal principles of equality and of inalienable rights as expressed in the Declaration of Independence and, Shambaugh believes, as revitalized on the frontier, and the fear that a liberal policy in Iowa in the context of restrictive policies in other states would, in the words of the select committee appointed to study the question, "drive the whole black population of the Union upon us" (pp. 28-29, 216). The committee ultimately recommended that blacks should not be totally excluded from the state but that their admission should be severely restricted, a proposal that the convention as a whole simply tabled. To Shambaugh, the committee's recommendation represents the triumph of expediency over principle. In this instance Shambaugh is clearly disappointed with such a triumph, concluding that "Our pioneer forefathers believed that the negroes were men entitled to freedom and civil liberty. But more than a score of years had yet to elapse before there was in their minds no longer 'a doubt that all men [including the negroes] are created free and equal'"(p. 218).

Earlier in the same volume, however, Shambaugh had praised this frontier reliance on expediency, concluding that, because of their experiences on the frontier, the pioneers had been freed from traditions, and that "henceforth they turned with impatience from historical arguments and legal theories to a philosophy of expediency. Government, they concluded, was after all a relative affair" (pp. 27-28). In more concrete terms, Shambaugh clearly supports the kind of expedient justice dealt out to people the local claim club considered to be claim jumpers. In one Johnson County case, he notes, "a prisoner was taken from the officers and whipped and choked till he confessed his crime," and in another case an "obnoxious citizen" was simply taken to the Iowa River and drowned. Shambaugh concludes that "in the frontier settlements of the West the people were justified in taking the law into their own hands; for in the absence of courts and local government the vigilance committee was often absolutely necessary to the proper administration of justice" (*Iowa City*, p. 55). If he had considered the contradictions inherent in these applications of frontier expediency, he might have concluded that it could be a two-edged sword, slashing at both good and evil in an effort to clear a path through to a convenient solution.

Beyond his discussion of the frontier as it was experienced in Iowa, Shambaugh's ideas were classic Turnerian. He defines the West as stretching back to the earliest colonial settlements, so that the history of the West is the history of America, and beyond this it is "the story of evolving, developing, progressive mankind--the story of the pioneer, to which America has contributed the latest chapter" (*Proceedings*, 1910, p. 134). The frontier required that the succession of people from the explorer to the fur trader to the pioneer be able to adapt to new conditions. It was a wellspring of liberal and democratic ideals, including equality of social conditions and equality before the law, a liberal ideal that clearly was sometimes sacrificed to that other frontier characteristic--expediency (*History of the Constitutions of Iowa*, pp. 26-29). The pioneers were, in turn, "young, strong, energetic men--hardy, courageous, and adventurous," plus law-abiding and "religious but not ecclesiastical" (pp. 23-24). None of this was particularly original with Shambaugh; for decades after 1893 such ideas permeated the intellectual atmosphere of the study of American history.

But Shambaugh links these ideas to a belief in the validity of the study of local history. This history of communities and states is not, of course, necessarily the history of their frontier period, but such studies often do focus on this, and Shambaugh's certainly do. Shambaugh said his own interest in local history derived from his undergraduate years, when a University of Iowa professor, William R. Perkins, asked his students, "Why doesn't someone write the story of Iowa towns? They are just as important as those of New England or of Greece" (Aurner, *Shambaugh*, pp. 11-12). Shambaugh took up this idea, writing a history of early Iowa City for his master's thesis and a history of early Iowa government (which was essentially Iowa City history) for his doctoral dissertation. His work on the Johnson County claim club is also, of course, local history. The idea fit in very well with his belief that governments arise out of the needs, and reflect the values, of the communities they govern.

Generalizing from this in his 1910 essay, "The History of the West and the Pioneers," Shambaugh asserts that the traditional approach was to look at American history from the viewpoint of Washington. But "the real life of the American nation," he contends, "is lived in the very commonplaces of the shop, the factory, the store, the office, in the mine, and on the farm. Through the commonwealths the life and spirit of the nation are best expressed. And every local community, however humble, participates in the formation and expression of that life and spirit." The idea is to look at history from the bottom up, and from the particular to the general. "The family, the clan, the tribe, the nation," he writes, "this is the order of social evolution. Why not follow it in historical research?" (*Proceedings*, 1910, p. 143).

Beyond his own writing, Shambaugh promoted the study of local history in editing the journals and monographs of the State Historical Society and in directing the research by his graduate students in the university's political science department. Even in studies of the contemporary issues of state government during the Progressive Era, he insisted that researchers trace the origins of the problems back to their earliest history in the area under study. This is the basis for his applied history approach. Today many historians are turning again to a search for the historical sources of contemporary problems in policy studies--appropriately enough, under the rubric of applied history--and for the universal in the particular in a wide range of strongly conceptualized, often interdisciplinary, community studies, many of which again focus on the frontier period. Shambaugh would have been pleased.

Bibliography

Books

The Constitution and Records of the Claim Association of Johnson County, Iowa. Editor. Iowa City: State Historical Society of Iowa, 1894.

The Constitutions of Iowa. Iowa City: State Historical Society of Iowa, 1934.

Documentary Material Relating to the History of Iowa. Editor. 3 volumes. Iowa City: State Historical Society of Iowa, 1895-1901.

Executive Journal of Iowa, 1838-1841: Governor Robert Lucas. Editor. Iowa City: State Historical Society of Iowa, 1906.

The First Census of the Original Counties of Dubuque and Demoine (Iowa) Taken in July, 1836. Editor. Des Moines: Historical Department of Iowa, 1897.

Fragments of the Debates of the Iowa Constitutional Conventions of 1844 and 1846, Along with Press Comments and Other Materials on the

Constitutions of 1844 and 1846. Editor. Iowa City: State Historical Society of Iowa, 1900.

History of the Constitutions of Iowa. Des Moines: Historical Department of Iowa, 1902.

Iowa City: A Contribution to the Early History of Iowa. Iowa City: State Historical Society of Iowa, 1893.

The Messages and Proclamations of the Governors of Iowa. Editor. 7 volumes. Iowa City: State Historical Society of Iowa, 1903-1905.

The Old Stone Capitol Remembers. Iowa City: State Historical Society of Iowa, 1939.

Proceedings of the Fiftieth Anniversary of the Constitution of Iowa. Editor. Iowa City: State Historical Society of Iowa, 1907.

A Second Report on the Public Archives. Des Moines: Historical Department of Iowa, 1907.

Articles

"Applied History." *Proceedings of the Mississippi Valley Historical Association* 2(1908-1909):137-139.

"The Beginnings of a Western Commonwealth." In *Biographies and Portraits of the Progressive Men of Iowa*. Des Moines: Conaway & Shaw, 1899. 2:1-72.

"A Brief History of the State Historical Society of Iowa." *Iowa Journal of History and Politics* 1(April, 1903):139-152.

"The Case of Mr. Lorin(g) Wheeler: His Appointment and Resignation as Chief Justice of the County Court of Dubuque." *Annals of Iowa* 3rd series 3(April-July, 1898):454-457.

"The Creation of a Commonwealth." *Palimpsest* 15(March, 1934):81-126.

"Documentary Study of Western History." *The Dial* 31(June 16, 1897):353.

"Documents Relating to Governor Lucas." Editor. *Iowa Historical Record* 16(April, 1900):56-73.

"The Founding of Iowa City." *Palimpsest* 20(May, 1939):137-176.

"From the Standpoint of a Pioneer." Editor. *Iowa Historical Record* 14(July, 1898):310-317.

"Frontier Land Clubs or Claim Associations." In *Annual Report of the American Historical Association* 1900. Washington, DC: Government Printing Office, 1901. 1:67-84.

"An Historical Journal." Editor. *Iowa Historical Record* 18(April, 1902):460-462.

"The History of the West and the Pioneers." In *State Historical Society of Wisconsin Proceedings*, 1910. Madison: State Historical Society of Wisconsin, 1911. Pp. 133-145.

"An Important Manuscript." Editor. *Iowa Historical Record* 9(January, 1893):414-420.

"Iowa History from 1699 to 1821: A History of Governments." *Iowa Historical Record* 16(January, 1900):29-46.

"The Iowa Pioneers." *Palimpsest* 8(January, 1927):1-4.

"Maps Illustrative of the Boundary History of Iowa." Editor. *Iowa Journal of History and Politics* 2(July, 1904):369-380.

"The Naming of Iowa." *Palimpsest* 5(October, 1924):370-372.

"Notes on the Early Church History of Iowa City." *Iowa Historical Record* 15(October, 1899):564-573.

"The Origin of the Name Iowa." *Annals of Iowa* 3rd series 3(January, 1899):641-644.

"Report on the Public Archives of Iowa." In *Annual Report of the American Historical Association,* 1900. Washington, DC: Government Printing Office, 1901. 2:39-46.

"Statutory Adoption of the Common Law in the West, and Herein of Its Introduction into Iowa." *Annals of Iowa* 3rd series 2(April, 1896):372-375.

Reviews

The American Nation: A History edited by Albert Bushnell Hart. Vols. I-V. *Iowa Journal of History and Politics* 3(April, 1905):304-307.

Biographical Story of the Constitution: A Study of the Growth of the American Union by Edward Elliott. *American Historical Review* 16(October, 1910):174-175.

Constitution and Admission of Iowa into the Union by James Alton James. *Iowa Historical Record* 16(October, 1900):198-199.

The Early History of Banking in Iowa by Fred D. Merritt. *Iowa Historical Record* 16(October, 1900):199-200.

Iowa: The First Free State in the Louisiana Purchase by William Salter. *Iowa Journal of History and Politics* 3(July, 1905):465-467.

The Making of Iowa by Henry Sabin. *Iowa Historical Record* 16(October, 1900):197-198.

Rhode Island: A Study in Separatism by Irving B. Richman. *Iowa Journal of History and Politics* 4(January, 1906):136-137.

Studies of Benjamin F. Shambaugh

Ames, Herman V. Review of *History of the Constitutions of Iowa* by Benjamin F. Shambaugh. *Annals of the American Academy of Political and Social Science* 21(March, 1903):152-153.

Aurner, Nellie Slayton. *Benjamin Franklin Shambaugh.* Iowa City: University of Iowa Press, 1947.

Benjamin Franklin Shambaugh, As Iowa Remembers Him, 1871-1940. Iowa City: State Historical Society of Iowa, 1941.

Bogue, Allan G. "The Iowa Claim Clubs: Symbol and Substance." *Mississippi Valley Historical Review* 45(September, 1958):231-253.

Briggs, John Ely. "Benj. F. Shambaugh." *Palimpsest* 21(May, 1940):133-139.

Brigham, Johnson. Review of *History of the Constitutions of Iowa* by Benjamin F. Shambaugh. *Annals of Iowa* 3rd series 5(October, 1902):547-550.

Gallaher, Ruth A. "Benjamin F. Shambaugh." *Iowa Journal of History and Politics* 38(July, 1940):227-233.

Herriott, F. I. Review of *Executive Journal of Iowa, 1838-1841* edited by Benjamin F. Shambaugh. *Annals of Iowa* 3rd series 7(January, 1907):630-634.

Jordan, Philip D. Review of *The Old Stone Capitol Remembers* by Benjamin F. Shambaugh. *Mississippi Valley Historical Review* 26(December, 1939):437-438.

Merriam, C. E. Review of *History of the Constitutions of Iowa* by Benjamin F. Shambaugh. *Political Science Quarterly* 18(June, 1903):331-332.

Pickard, Josiah L. Review of *Documentary Material Relating to the History of Iowa*, vol. II, edited by Benjamin F. Shambaugh. *Iowa Historical Record* 14(January, 1898):216-217.

__________. Review of *Documentary Material Relating to the History of Iowa*, vol. III, edited by Benjamin F. Shambaugh. *Iowa Historical Record* 17(July, 1901):351-352.

Schroder, Alan M. "A Dedication to the Memory of Benjamin Franklin Shambaugh, 1871-1940." *Arizona and the West* 24(Winter, 1982):301-304.

Springer, John. Review of *Fragments of the Debates of the Iowa Constitutional Conventions of 1844 and 1846* edited by Benjamin F. Shambaugh. *Iowa Historical Record* 16(April, 1900):88-91.

Steiner, Bernard C. Review of *Executive Journal of Iowa, 1838-1841* edited by Benjamin F. Shambaugh. *American Political Science Review* 2(November, 1907):148-149.

Still, Bayrd. Review of *The Constitutions of Iowa* by Benjamin F. Shambaugh. *Mississippi Valley Historical Review* 22(June, 1935):122-123.

Swierenga, Robert P. "The Fort Dodge Claim Club, 1855-1856: Recollections of Charles B. Richards." *Annals of Iowa* 3rd series 39(Winter, 1969):511-518.

47

FRED ALBERT SHANNON

by Peter H. Argersinger

Biography

Looking back on his youth, Fred Shannon once observed that "if, as some say, God made the country and man made the city, then the devil made the small town, and the devil took pains to fashion the job perfectly" (*Agricultural History* 37:117). A difficult childhood in a struggling family in a series of small midwestern towns not only convinced Fred Albert Shannon of his ability to recognize the devil's handiwork but early disabused him of any illusions about American society and helped shape both his personality and subsequent scholarship.

He was born in Sedalia, Missouri, on February 12, 1893, the son of Sarah Margaret Sparks Shannon and Louis Tecumseh Shannon, a tenant farmer who had been raised in a family of frontier farmers and who had previously worked as a section hand on the railroads and in mines and sawmills. In the depression of the 1890s, the Shannons futilely sought opportunities by moving to Clay City, Indiana, and thereafter moved on to Terre Haute, Clinton, and Brazil, Indiana. As a boy, Shannon worked in a series of difficult and often dangerous jobs: in a sawmill at age ten, on neighboring farms, in a small-town bakery, in a canning factory at age fourteen, then in a glass factory, and at seventeen as a farm hand in western Kansas. These experiences helped give him a habit of working hard, a sympathetic understanding of common Americans and their difficulties, and a corresponding disdain for the people of power and privilege. All would be expressed in his scholarly writings.

Shannon simultaneously worked hard to achieve a formal education. He earned a B.A. at Indiana State Teachers College in 1914 and thereafter financed his further education by teaching in grade school and serving as principal of an Indiana high school. He received an M.A. at Indiana University in 1918 and began his college teaching career at Iowa Wesleyan College. In 1924 he received his Ph.D. at the University of Iowa, where he worked with Arthur M. Schlesinger, Sr., and was appointed assistant professor of history at Iowa State Teachers College. From 1926 to 1939 Shannon was a member of the faculty at Kansas State College, and from 1939 he was a professor at the University of Illinois, except for one year as a visiting professor of economic history at Williams College and for summer teaching stints at Cornell, Ohio State, West Virginia, Missouri, Harvard, Wisconsin, Stanford, and Columbia universities. After his retirement from Illinois in 1961, he was a visiting professor at the University of South Carolina in 1962 and was to be a visiting professor at the University of Texas in 1963, but he died on February 4, 1963, at his son's home in Wickenburg, Arizona.

Shannon was both active and prominent in professional organizations, particularly in the Mississippi Valley Historical Association (MVHA), the forerunner of the Organization of American Historians. In 1934, for example, he was chairman of the Association's membership committee, chaired a session at the annual meeting, wrote the official account of the meeting, and served on the MVHA's executive committee, a position he held, either by election or ex officio, for seventeen years. In 1953 he was elected president of the MVHA. Shannon was also an active member of the American Historical Association, the Agricultural History Society, the American Association of University Professors, and the American Civil Liberties Union.

Shannon's historical scholarship early won critical acclaim. His dissertation was published in 1928 in two volumes as *The Organization and Administration of the Union Army, 1861-1865*, which was awarded both the Justin Winsor Prize of the American Historical Association and a Pulitzer Prize. His textbook, *The Economic History of the People of the United States*, first published in 1934 and revised in 1940 as *America's Economic Growth*, became a standard for generations of college students. His most important contributions, however, were in the fields of agricultural and western history. These included *The Farmer's Last Frontier: Agriculture, 1860-1897*, published in 1945 as one volume of the nine-volume *Economic History of the United States*, a distinguished series he co-edited as well; *American Farmers' Movements* (1957); a book-length critique of Walter Prescott Webb's *The Great Plains*; and many important articles in major journals.

Themes

Fred Shannon made major contributions to many aspects of the writing of American history but there were certain underlying themes in his work that unified his investigation, interpretation, and explanation of such varied subjects as western settlement practices, land policy, farming customs, rural economic conditions, and military finance. Believing that history was too often written from the point of view of elite groups or important individuals and too rarely from that of "people in the mass," Shannon always focused his history from the perspective of the experience of common Americans (*Mississippi Valley Historical Review* 37:491). His sympathies, moreover, were always and obviously with the hopeless farm worker, the hapless sharecropper, the mortgaged farmer, the exploited laborer, the betrayed soldier. Simultaneously, as Paul Wallace Gates notes, "he had little respect for the rich and well born in American life and delighted in scorning them and their works" (*Dictionary of American Biography* 7:684). This focus on "people in the mass" also influenced Shannon's historical methodology and writing, for it often required the painstaking analysis and presentation of census statistics, which he regarded as the major source of "mass data readily available" (*Mississippi Valley Historical Review* 37:491). Although conceding that such studies might sometimes be tiresome or even boring, he believed they were necessary, and he must have enjoyed the fact that their prosaic quality was appropriate to the often dreary conditions he found characteristic in American history.

Indeed, from this perspective another distinctive theme in Shannon's work emerged naturally: his determination to puncture the easy illusions that shroud too much of America's past, to dismantle the myths which often simply reflected the cultural dominance of the groups he disdained. From this objective, in turn, developed a final characteristic of Shannon's professional work: caustic criticism of other historians, whether expressed in book reviews, essays, or comments at professional meetings. A rigorous scholar, unwilling to tolerate what he termed "slipshod scholarship" (*American Historical Review* 49:198), Shannon prided himself on his abilities as a critic and was often merciless in attacking the work of those whose attitudes and interpretations were more conservative than his own. One historian describes both Shannon's sympathies and his style by observing that Shannon would have been a "natural born prosecuting attorney for the Populist government of Kansas" (*Agricultural History* 37:119). Robert Wiebe also accurately describes Shannon's "singular style: the stabbing criticism, the earthy metaphors, the use of statistics as frontal assault in argument" (*American Historical Review* 73:612). But this approach to scholarship, because it reflected Shannon's own consistent commitment to thorough research, factual accuracy, and precise presentation, was a persistent theme as well as the style of his work. Effectively employing his own research, using statistical evidence to give his arguments the weight of authenticity, Shannon not only attacked his opponent's major contentions but relentlessly exposed his misspellings, typographical errors, and incorrect citations as well, thereby implying (as one beleaguered target complained) "that they indicate the unsoundness of the entire work" (*American Historical Review* 49:197).

Such victims sometimes arraigned Shannon as a "sadistic reviewer," but John W. Caughey, in evaluating book reviews in the *Mississippi Valley Historical Review*, described Shannon's critical work as "brilliant reviewing" (*Mississippi Valley Historical Review* 44:526). And Walter Prescott Webb, the object of Shannon's most famous critical attack, once observed (albeit after a cooling-off period of a decade and a half) that if a Pulitzer Prize were ever established for criticism, Shannon would have "a good claim to several *ex post facto* awards" (*Agricultural History* 37:119).

Analysis

Fred Shannon's concern for the experience of the common American, his interest in quashing romantic images of American history, and his critical and methodical approach were apparent in nearly all his scholarly work. In his first major publication, *The Organization and Administration of the Union Army* (1928), his prize-winning study of the Union Army in the Civil War, for example, he focuses not on the famous generals and great battles but on the recruiting, feeding, clothing, arming, training, and daily life of the common soldiers in the ranks. He debunks the glorious imagery still surrounding the conflict in the 1920s, exposes the sordid and corrupt "ways in which moneyed and money-making patriots helped to save the country" by profiteering at the expense of the suffering soldiers, and emphasizes the pervasiveness of the desire to *avoid* military service, the wealthy by exploiting the inequitable draft law to hire substitutes and others by fleeing to the West or even resorting to self-mutilation. Shannon's stress is so much on the "shoddy uniforms," "sleazy and rotten blankets," and "rusty and putrid pork" provided the poor souls who did serve that one reviewer complains that Shannon "lays on the darker colors of the picture with so heavy a hand that the result is unduly somber" and that he "over-emphasizes the disagreeable" in order that "our complacency should be punctured" (*American Historical Review* 34:621-623).

Beginning in the 1930s, Shannon turned his attention to exploding some of the comforting generalizations about western settlement which were either explicit or implicit in the frontier thesis of Frederick Jackson Turner, then at the peak of its academic acceptance. In particular, he attacked the concept of the safety valve, or what Shannon called the "myth" of the safety valve. This "attractive" hypothesis that the West was a land of opportunity which acted as a safety-valve to minimize labor discontent in the East by drawing workers westward in periods of depression, said Shannon, "was based only on unsupported rationalization" (*Agricultural History* 19:37). In an important 1936 article in the *American Historical Review*, "The Homestead Act and the Labor Surplus," he deflates the pleasant mythology surrounding the Homestead Act and denies that it promoted significant social fluidity as previously claimed. Its limitations, he argues, rendered the law of benefit only to "monopolists or persons of fairly ample means" (*American Historical Review* 41:644). By detailed examination of land entries under the legislation, the growth of population, and the course of economic development, Shannon concludes that "the much vaunted cheap or free public lands . . . have not been of measurable consequence as the alleviator of labor conditions" (p. 651).

In a second tightly-reasoned essay, published several years later, Shannon uses careful analysis of the statistics of land ownership and population to deny that, after the Civil War at least, the frontier had even operated as an indirect safety valve by attracting eastern farmers who might otherwise have become urban factory workers. Indeed, he stands the traditional safety-valve thesis on its head by arguing that the city served as a safety valve for rural discontent. Only a small fraction of the increased population between 1860 and 1900 settled on farms anywhere in the

United States and still fewer people went to the West to become farmers. In fact, Shannon calculates that "at least twenty farmers moved to town for each industrial laborer who moved to the land, and ten sons of farmers went to the city for each one who became the owner of a new farm anywhere in the Nation." The industrial violence in the eastern cities during the 1870s and 1880s further convinced him that "there never was a free-land or even a western safety-valve for industrial labor" (*Agricultural History* 19:34, 37).

Although Shannon believed that the safety-valve theory could "be sealed in its coffin and laid to rest" (p. 37), it, of course, continued to be a subject of controversy, and characteristically Shannon was often involved in the debates. No episode was more famous perhaps than that which occurred at the 1958 annual meeting of the Mississippi Valley Historical Association when Shannon and Norman J. Simler engaged in a vigorous argument over the validity of the concept. Simler charged that Shannon "portrays both the industrial and the agricultural situations in an unnecessarily gloomy way," and Shannon rejected Simler's attempts to "breathe new life into the cadaver of the safety-valve theory" as mere "legerdemain"(*Agricultural History* 32:254-255; 32:257; 36:123-142).

Fred Shannon became involved in another famous controversy when he turned his attention to a second major thesis describing the course of western settlement. In 1939, the Social Science Research Council held a conference at Skytop, Pennsylvania, to appraise Walter Prescott Webb's *The Great Plains*, published in 1931 and already regarded as a book of great historiographical significance. Shannon was appointed the appraiser, and he delivered a devastating critique of the work, proceeding methodically (as he himself observed) "to break down the author's major contentions" (*Critiques of Research*, p. 112). Shannon's appraisal, as Gregory Tobin notes in his biography of Webb, became "a classic . . . and its echoes were to run through the ranks of the profession for many years afterward" (*The Making of a History*, p. 116). Indeed, the confrontation between Shannon and Webb, George Wolfskill writes, became "part of the folklore of the profession for years afterward" and had "the general effect of badly dividing the profession" (*Reviews in American History* 12:300-301).

In his critique, Shannon charged that Webb's use of geography was so vague that the Great Plains themselves were insufficiently identified, that his central argument as to the unique influence of the Plains on American settlers and their institutions was altogether inaccurate, and that in trying to demonstrate its validity Webb had deliberately ignored contrary evidence while unfairly generalizing from doubtful data. Shannon particularly objected to Webb's unsupported claims and inadequate research, both so contrary to his own approach, which Webb in turn contemptuously and inaccurately dismissed, in Tobin's words, as "mindless factgrubbing" (*The Making of a History*, pp. 119-120). But in truth Shannon was concerned with Webb's failure to apply the basic principles of historical methodology and simply argued that valid conclusions could not be derived from factual errors and the exclusion of relevant data. Indeed, Webb sought to defend his work by denying that it was intended to be history; it was, he maintained, "a work of art." Convinced that Shannon had failed to understand the book, Webb rejected his criticism as an attack but not an appraisal (*Critiques of Research*, pp. 114, 122, 186-188).

Other scholars came to Webb's defense. John W. Caughey condemned Shannon's narrow critique for not recognizing the techniques by which anthropologists defined cultural areas (*Mississippi Valley Historical Review* 27:442-444). Avery Craven denounced Shannon's criticism as a mean-spirited failure. With invective rarely used in academic disputes, Shannon and Craven then exchanged insults through the pages of the *American Historical Review*, with Shannon ridiculing errors made by Craven in his own work, impugning his personal and professional motives, and suggesting that he deliberately falsified and fabricated data (*American Historical Review* 47:627-630; 48:587-589). Craven retorted that Shannon engaged in "flagrant distortions of fact for the purpose of injury" and was unqualified "either by research or production" to judge the work of others (*American Historical Review* 49:195-197). Shannon had the last laugh by subjecting Craven's reply to the same damaging close analysis of words and assumptions which he had originally applied to Webb's work (pp. 197-198). Shannon's appraisal of *The Great Plains* remains a crushing critique of the factual accuracy and methodological weaknesses of Webb's book, but its very thoroughness and its needlessly (though characteristically) harsh tone have caused many western historians to reject it and support Webb's central thesis, although their arguments have often been on subjective grounds and thus, ironically, confirm Shannon's original analysis.

Fred Shannon's rejection of pleasant generalizations, reliance on exhaustive research and particularly statistical data, and concern for the experience of common Americans also characterized his subsequent work, most of which investigated the American farmer. In his major book, *The Farmer's Last Frontier: Agriculture, 1860-1897* (1945), for example, he sought to focus on "the scene as the farmer saw it and to picture the farmer himself as he affected and was influenced by the world in which he worked and lived" (p. viii). And his technique, as Harry J. Carman notes in reviewing the book, was to be "a stickler for ascertaining the exact facts" and to use "them mercilessly to expose many traditional notions that were accepted as gospel" (*Mississippi Valley Historical Review* 32:426).

Some of this work covered topics he had earlier analyzed. Again rejecting what he called the "easy" assumption that pioneers "generally took up free homesteads," for instance, Shannon warns that the truth was more "prosaic--even painfully so" and he demonstrates how few pioneer farmers actually succeeded in claiming land under the famous Homestead Act (*Farmer's Last Frontier*, p. 51). He again attacks Webb's concept of abrupt cultural change on the Great Plains and denies that there was "any sudden departure from old customs and methods" as the agricultural frontier moved westward (p. 21). But Shannon also considered new topics as well. His examination of the livestock frontier seeks "to offset the glamour of cowboy literature and Western 'movies'" and to have "a salubrious effect on the overwrought imagination" by describing the cowboy's work and life as "prosaic, monotonous, and deadeningly tiresome" (pp. 202, 207). In discussing the frontier farmer, Shannon similarly emphasizes the typical tasks and problems encountered which, although far from exciting, were of paramount importance to the average farmer. Thus he examines the role of soils, climate and insects, marketing problems, credit arrangements, and farm mechanization. This approach produced a comprehensive account of the development of agriculture in the late nineteenth century from the standpoint of the actual settler, an account which still retains great value.

In *American Farmers' Movements* (1957), still the best brief survey of its subject, Shannon again refutes many prevailing beliefs about agricultural history while explaining the factors behind the recurring rural rebellions of small farmers from the colonial period to the Great Depression of the 1930s. He dismisses, for instance, the contention that average farmers profited greatly from land appreciation as "largely nonsense," maintaining instead that farmers generally expanded their operations during periods of prosperity when land prices were high and lost the land and any profits in the subsequent economic decline. He argues that despite "a spate of twaddle about the agricultural ladder," it led only downward after the mid-nineteenth century (pp. 8-9). In other writings Shannon also reverses the traditional imagery of the agricultural ladder, "down which," he declares, the "sons of the soil" "had climbed from ownership to tenancy, from tenancy to hired labor, and from which they had fled to the city" (*Mississippi Valley Historical Review* 37:504). Tenancy to Shannon was a sign of rural distress; tenants were "the victims of the land monopolists," unable to acquire their own land from speculators or to afford the increasingly expensive and necessary machinery to farm successfully (*Farmer's Last Frontier*, p. 146). By the end of the frontier period, in 1900, he gloomily calculated from census data, nearly three-fourths of those working the land even in the productive Midwest were "making less than subsistence," and he feared that figure was "too optimistic" (*Mississippi Valley Historical Review* 37:504).

Shannon's own blunt assertations, of course, never won universal assent. Edward Everett Dale was not alone in believing that Fred Shannon's "keen sympathy for the poor and oppressed has at times prevented an entirely objective treatment of some phases of his subject" (*American Historical Review* 51:334). And subsequent generations of scholars have often sharply modified many of his contentions. His indictment of the government's land policies, his dismissal of the efficacy of the agricultural ladder, his negative evaluation of the role of tenancy in the rural economy: all these and more have been disputed by modern historians who have applied computer technology and more sophisticated statistical analysis to the mass data that Shannon always insisted had to be investigated (*Journal of Interdisciplinary History* 13:787-808; *Indiana Magazine of History* 78:128-153; *Great Plains Quarterly* 1:105-131). An uncompromising scholar, Fred Shannon would have welcomed the light their work sheds on the previously dark corners and hidden processes of

American development. But as an agrarian, he would have been troubled by their focus on questions of efficiency rather than equity. And as an individual he would have rejected their arguments for "dispassionate" analysis and the avoidance of value judgments and vigorously denied their claims to have eliminated any "ideological bias" from their work (*Indiana Magazine of History* 78:149).

His own view of history, both as the past and as a discipline, he best revealed in 1956 in a sentence in one of the reviews for which he was justly famous. It indicates his own distinctive style, his confidence in his own opinions and scholarship, his identification with the underprivileged and distaste for the activities of the powerful, and his belief that moral judgment was a necessary part of the historian's craft. "In these days," wrote Fred Albert Shannon, "when the Hayek influence seems to be tightening its grip on a vociferous group of American sycophants--those who go so far as to tell us that there never was a Robber Baron and that stealing a cow was justifiable if the thief later gave back a calf and a pound of butter--it is refreshing to read a book on a controversial subject where the author is perfectly uninhibited in his feeling of unabashed sympathy with the underdog, and who lights anew the fire of liberalism and tolerance" (*Journal of Economic History* 16:63).

Bibliography

Books

American Farmers' Movements. Princeton, NJ: Van Nostrand Co., 1957.

America's Economic Growth. New York: Macmillan, 1940.

The Centennial Years: A Political and Economic History of America from the Late 1870s to the Early 1890s. Garden City, NY: Doubleday and Co., 1967.

The Civil War Letters of Sergeant Onley Andrus. Editor. Urbana: University of Illinois Press, 1947.

Critiques of Research in the Social Sciences: III. An Appraisal of Walter Prescott Webb's The Great Plains: A Study in Institutions and Environment. New York: Social Science Research Council, 1940.

The Economic History of the People of the United States. New York: Macmillan, 1934.

The Farmer's Last Frontier: Agriculture, 1860-1897. New York: Farrar and Rinehart, 1945.

The Organization and Administration of the Union Army, 1861-1865. Cleveland: Arthur A. Clark Co., 1928.

Articles

"C. W. Macune and the Farmers' Alliance." *Current History* 28(June, 1955):330-335.

"Culture and Agriculture in America." *Mississippi Valley Historical Review* 41(June, 1954):3-20.

"The Homestead Act and the Labor Surplus." *American Historical Review* 41(July, 1936):637-651.

"Is Oral History Really Worth While?" In *Ideas in Conflict: A Colloquium on Certain Problems in Historical Society Work in the United States and Canada* edited by Clifford L. Lord. Harrisburg, PA: American Association for State and Local History, 1958. Pp. 17-57.

"The Life of the Common Soldier in the Union Army, 1861-1865." *Mississippi Valley Historical Review* 13(March, 1927):465-482.

"The Mercenary Factor in the Creation of the Union Army." *Mississippi Valley Historical Review* 12(March, 1926):523-549.

"A Post Mortem on the Labor-Safety-Valve Theory." *Agricultural History* 19(January, 1945):31-37.

"State Rights and the Union Army." *Mississippi Valley Historical Review* 12(June, 1925):51-71.

"The Status of the Midwestern Farmer in 1900." *Mississippi Valley Historical Review* 37(December, 1950):491-510.

"The Twenty-Seventh Annual Meeting of the Mississippi Valley Historical Association." *Mississippi Valley Historical Review* 21(September, 1934):207-224.

Selected Reviews

American Agriculture: Its Structure and Place in the Economy by Ronald L. Mighell. *Agricultural History* 30(January, 1956):45.

The American Civil War by David Knowles. *American Historical Review* 32(April, 1927):665-666.

The American Civil War: A Brief Sketch by David Knowles. *Mississippi Valley Historical Review* 14(June, 1927):113-116.

The American Iliad: The Epic Story of the Civil War as Narrated by Eyewitnesses and Contemporaries by Otto Eisenschiml and Ralph Newman. *Minnesota History* 29(March, 1948):63-64.

American Problems of Today: A History of the United States since the World War by Louis M. Hacker. *American Historical Review* 45(April, 1940):720-721.

American Regionalism: A Cultural-Historical Approach to National Integration by Howard W. Odum and Harry E. Moore. *American Historical Review* 44(July, 1939):1002.

America's Sheep Trails: History, Personalities by Edward Norris Wentworth. *Journal of Economic History* 8(November, 1948):196-197.

Certain Aspects of Land Problems and Government Land Policies by the Land Planning Committee of the National Resources Board. *American Historical Review* 43(October, 1937):175-176.

The Coming of the Civil War by Avery Craven. *American Historical Review* 48(April, 1943):587-589.

Corn and Its Early Fathers by Henry A. Wallace. *Agricultural History* 31(July, 1957):69.

Democracy and Military Power by Silas Bent McKinley. *Mississippi Valley Historical Review* 21(March, 1935):600-601.

Dry Farming in the Northern Great Plains, 1900-1925 by Mary Wilma M. Hargreaves. *American Historical Review* 63(October, 1957):231-232.

DuPont: One Hundred and Forty Years by William S. Dutton. *American Historical Review* 48(January, 1943):370.

Ersatz in the Confederacy by Mary Elizabeth Massey. *Journal of Economic History* 13(Summer, 1953):330-331.

The Farmer's Tools, 1500-1900: The History of British Farm Implements, Tools, and Machinery before the Tractor Came by G. E. Fussell. *Journal of Economic History* 14(Winter, 1954):75.

John G. Carlisle, Financial Statesman by James A. Barnes. *Mississippi Valley Historical Review* 19(June, 1932):128-130.

Harvard Guide to American History by Oscar Handlin et al. *American Historical Review* 60(October, 1954):115-116.

Hood's Tennessee Campaign by Thomas Robson. *Mississippi Valley Historical Review* 16(September, 1929):278-280.

J. Laurence Laughlin: Chapters in the Career of an Economist by Alfred Bornemann. *Mississippi Valley Historical Review* 28(September, 1941):277-278.

John C. Fremont and the Republican Party by Ruhl Jacob Bartlett. *Mississippi Valley Historical Review* 18(September, 1931):259.

Lee's Lieutenants: A Study in Command by Douglas Southall Freeman. *Mississippi Valley Historical Review* 29(March, 1943):611-613.

The Life of Billy Yank: The Common Soldier of the Union by Bell Irvin Wiley. *American Historical Review* 58(October, 1952):141-143.

Mississippi Farmers, 1850-1860 by Herbert Weaver. *Journal of Economic History* 6(November, 1946):226-227.

A Narrative History of the People of Iowa by Edgar R. Harlan. *Mississippi Valley Historical Review* 20(June, 1933):120-121.

Ordeal by Fire: An Informal History of the Civil War by Fletcher Pratt. *Mississippi Valley Historical Review* 36(September, 1949):325-326.

People of Plenty: Economic Abundance and the American Character by David M. Potter. *Mississippi Valley Historical Review* 41(March, 1955):733-734.

Plain Folk of the Old South by Frank L. Owsley. *Journal of Economic History* 10(May, 1950):92.

Political Prairie Fire: The Nonpartisan League, 1915-1922 by Robert L. Morlan. *Journal of Economic History* 16(Winter, 1956):63.

Reveille in Washington, 1860-1865 by Margaret Leech. *Mississippi Valley Historical Review* 28(December, 1941):447-448.

Rural Hunterdon: An Agricultural History by Hubert G. Schmidt. *Mississippi Valley Historical Review* 32(March, 1946):592-593.

Social Science Research Methods by Wilson Gee. *Mississippi Valley Historical Review* 37(December, 1950):567-568.

Two Blades of Grass: A History of Scientific Development in the U.S. Department of Agriculture by T. Swann Harding. *Journal of Economic History* 7(November, 1947):254-255.

Wheat and the AAA by Joseph S. Davis. *Mississippi Valley Historical Review* 22(December, 1935):463-464.

Communications
Letter to the Editor. *Agricultural History* 32(October, 1958):257.
__________. *American Historical Review* 49(October, 1943):197-198.
__________. *Mississippi Valley Historical Review* 32(March, 1946):572-574.

Studies of Fred A. Shannon
Anonymous. Review of *The Organization and Administration of the Union Army* by Fred A. Shannon. *American Historical Review* 34(April, 1929):621-623.
Bogue, Allan G. "The Heirs of James C. Malin: A Grassland Historiography." *Great Plains Quarterly* 1(Spring, 1981):105-131.
Buck, Solon J. Review of *American Farmers' Movements* by Fred A. Shannon. *Agricultural History* 32(July, 1958):206.
Carman, Harry J. Review of *The Farmer's Last Frontier* by Fred A. Shannon. *Mississippi Valley Historical Review* 32(December, 1945):425-427.
Caughey, John W. "A Criticism of the Critique of Webb's The Great Plains." *Mississippi Valley Historical Review* 27(December, 1940):442-444.
__________. "Under Our Strange Device: A Review of the 'Review'." *Mississippi Valley Historical Review* 44(December, 1957):526.
Craven, Avery. Letter to the Editor. *American Historical Review* 49(October, 1943):195-197.
__________. Review of *Critiques of Research in the Social Sciences: III. An Appraisal of Walter Prescott Webb's The Great Plains* by Fred A. Shannon. *American Historical Review* 47(April, 1942):627-630.
Dale, Edward Everett. Review of *The Farmer's Last Frontier* by Fred A. Shannon. *American Historical Review* 51(January, 1946):333-335.
Gates, Paul W. "Fred Albert Shannon." *Dictionary of American Biography*. Supplement Seven, 1961-1965. New York: Charles Scribner's Sons, 1981. Pp. 684-685.
Jarchow, Merrill E. Review of *The Farmer's Last Frontier* by Fred A. Shannon. *Minnesota History* 26(December, 1945):360-362
Kohlmeyer, Fred W. "Fred Albert Shannon." *Agricultural History* 37(April, 1963):117-119.
Loehr, Rodney C. Review of *The Farmer's Last Frontier* by Fred A. Shannon. *Journal of Economic History* 6(May, 1946):97.
McGuire, C. E. Review of *Economic History of the People of the United States* by Fred A. Shannon. *American Historical Review* 41(July, 1936):818-819.
Paxson, Frederic L. Review of *Critiques of Research in the Social Sciences: III. An Appraisal of Walter Prescott Webb's The Great Plains* by Fred A. Shannon. *Pacific Historical Review* 10(March, 1941):91-92.
Simler, Norman J. "The Safety-Valve Doctrine Re-Evaluated." *Agricultural History* 32(October, 1958):250-257.

Swierenga, Robert P. "Quantitative Methods in Rural Landholding." *Journal of Interdisciplinary History* 13(Spring, 1983):787-808.

Tobin, Gregory M. *The Making of a History: Walter Prescott Webb and "The Great Plains."* Austin: University of Texas Press, 1976.

Von Nardroff, Ellen. "The American Frontier as a Safety-Valve -- The Life, Death, Reincarnation, and Justification of a Theory." *Agricultural History* 36(July, 1962):123-142.

Wiebe, Robert. Review of *The Centennial Years: A Political and Economic History of America from the Late 1870s to the Early 1890s* by Fred A. Shannon. *American Historical Review* 73(December, 1967):612-613.

Winters, Donald L. "Agricultural Tenancy in the Nineteenth-Century Middle West: The Historiographical Debate." *Indiana Magazine of History* 78(June, 1982):128-153.

Wolfskill, George. "Walter Prescott Webb and *The Great Plains*: Then and Now." *Reviews in American History* 12(June, 1984):300-301.

Woodburn, James A. Review of *The Organization and Administration of the Union Army* by Fred A. Shannon. *Mississippi Valley Historical Review* 15(March, 1929):530-533.

48

EDWARD H. SPICER

by Evelyn Hu-DeHart

Biography

Edward H. Spicer was by training and reputation a cultural anthropologist of the American Southwest. He merits inclusion in this volume because of his contribution to the ethnohistorical knowledge and understanding of the native peoples and cultures of this vast southwestern region.

Born in November 29, 1906, to a Quaker family in Cheltenham, Pennsylvania, raised as a child in the single-tax colony founded by Henry George disciples located in Arden, Delaware, educated by liberal parents who imbued him with intellectual curiosity, humanistic concerns, and creative interests, later by schools in Wilmington, Delaware, and Louisville, Kentucky, Spicer was nevertheless most identified--professionally as well as personally--with the Southwest and the state of Arizona in particular.

His first introduction to the Southwest came in 1918, when he went to Arizona to nurse his pulmonary tuberculosis. Except for brief stints to study and work in other states, he rarely left Arizona. At the University of Arizona, he received a B.A. in Economics in 1931 and went on to study archaeology with Byron Cummings, receiving his M.A. in 1933. He then attended the University of Chicago, to study with Radcliffe-Brown and Robert Redfield, receiving his Ph.D. in anthropology in 1939. His dissertation was based on field work conducted in 1936-1937 at the Yaqui Indian village of Pascua in Tucson. He was accompanied and ably aided by his new wife and lifelong collaborator, Rosamond Pendleton Brown, fellow anthropology student at Chicago.

In 1939, he began a lifelong professional association with the University of Arizona, his alma mater, advancing from instructor in Anthropology to full professor in 1950, and finally professor emeritus upon his retirement in 1978. Actually, he began his teaching career at Dillard University, a black college in New Orleans, in 1938. He also accepted visiting appointments at a number of major universities, including Cornell and the University of California at Santa Barbara. During the war years, from 1942 to 1946, he served as an analyst in the United States War Relocation Authority. He and other social scientists undertook an important study of this controversial move to intern Japanese-Americans on the West coast.

At the University of Arizona, after a brief archaeological stint, he began producing a large body of ethnographic material on the peoples and cultures of the Southwest, making him the indisputable foremost authority on this broad subject. Furthermore, he developed a legendary reputation as a teacher, whose ability to inspire his students was demonstrated by many teaching awards during his long career as well as over one hundred M.A. theses and Ph.D. dissertations completed under his direction.

Measures of the professional respect that he earned from colleagues in anthropology can be easily demonstrated by the numerous high awards and honors he received. Spicer enjoyed two Guggenheims (1941-1942 and 1955-1956), and fellowships from the National Science Foundation (1963-1964), the National Endowment for the Humanities (1970-1971), and the National Academy of Sciences (1975). He received the Malinowsky Award of the Society for Applied Anthropology (1976), the Distinguished Service Award of the American Anthropological Association (1979), the Outstanding Scholarship Award of the Southwestern Anthropological Association (1980), and honorary life membership in the Society of Borderland Scholars (1980). Furthermore, from 1956 to 1963, he became associate editor, then editor of *American Anthropologist*, journal of the American Anthropological Association. In 1974, he achieved perhaps the singular highest honor in his discipline when he was elected president of the American Anthropological Association.

Until the day he died, at his historic Fort Lowell home in Tucson, Spicer continued his writing. Unfortunately, he left unfinished a manuscript on "Enduring Peoples" (Communications, Rosamond Spicer to Hu-DeHart, 1985-1986).

Themes

Spicer's primary field of inquiry focused on a wide area which, "for want of a better name," can be termed the "Southwest." The name is problematic because the area actually includes parts of Mexico--her "Northwest." But Spicer's precise definition of the region, in both geographical and cultural terms, eliminates any confusion:

> This region extends from the southern Sierra Madre Mountains in Mexico to the San Juan River in Utah, and from the Pecos River in New Mexico to the Gulf of California. It is a region in which at the time of the arrival of the Spaniards the Indians were predominantly agricultural, but their level of political organization was much below that of the Aztecs and Tarascans who adjoined them to the south (*Cycles of Conquest*, p. viii).

What attracted him to the Southwest in the first place was the large number of surviving Indian peoples and cultures. What continuously fascinated him, and engaged him in a lifetime of research and analysis, was why and how these Indians have survived, especially in light of the fact that most came under the cultural and political domination of other groups, notably Spaniards and North Americans.

He was keenly aware of the changes these cultures must have undergone in the process of surviving. Thus, Spicer integrated into his analysis of these "persistent cultures," or "cultural enclaves," the process of what he called "culture change" that was in turn the result of "cultural contact." The emphasis is on the dynamic process of acculturation. He gathered data primarily from field work, supplemented by historical material. Incorporating historical information into the description based on contemporary field work was Spicer's methodology, which he called "ethnohistory," or "history in its cultural context."

> This consists in the interpretation of documented events of the past by means of the knowledge of situations which anthropologists have gained through direct study of living societies. Just as geologists assume that processes which currently affect the earth's crust may be regarded as having done so in the same manner in the past, anthropologists may assume uniformities running through the whole experience of humans--past, present, and future (*The Yaquis*, p. xiii).

Analysis

Through a series of publications, Spicer developed his expertise on the Southwest, at the same time refining his ethnohistorical approach. His first major contribution in cultural anthropology was his dissertation, published as *Pascua, A Yaqui Village in Arizona*, in 1940. In 1954, after considerable fieldwork among Yaquis in their native Sonora, he published the companion monograph, *Potam, A Yaqui Village in Sonora*. These two pioneering monographs, together with a number of journal and popular magazine articles on the Yaqui, firmly established Spicer as the preeminent Yaqui scholar, in all academic disciplines and on both sides of the border.

Without abandoning interest in the Yaqui, his next two publications, which appeared in succession in the early sixties, displayed a broader scope of interest in the Southwest and on the question of culture change, and more fully developed the ethnohistorical approach. He also demonstrated a mastery of the art of synthesis, producing highly readable essays for specialists and the public alike.

In *Perspectives in American Indian Culture Change* (1961), Spicer edited the essays of an interuniversity summer research seminar on comparative study of acculturation. He contributed a study on the Yaqui, one of seven Indian cultures in North America included (the others being the Rio Grande Pueblo, Kwakiutl, Navajo, Mandan, Wasco, and Wishram). While acknowledging variations and unique cultural traits, Spicer and his colleagues concluded that "the repetition of certain combinations of Indian and Anglo-American ways becomes unmistakable." In other words, Indians in America experienced similar patterns of acculturation when subjugated by, or confronted with, dominant societies, resulting in the "existence of similar social and cultural processes at work under the surfaces of reservation life." From reservation to reservation, these studies find that "attitudes and views of life seem essentially the same; and, perhaps most definitely, the way of dealing with non-Indians has the same quality," this conclusion being all the more astounding given the geographic separation and widely different historical experiences of the Indian peoples studied (pp. 1-2).

Spicer's essay on the Yaqui, entitled "Yaqui Contact History," at some ninety pages almost a monograph in itself, offers the first full sketch of Yaqui history, in English or in Spanish, that spans the entire length from first contact with Spaniards in 1533, to 1957. The sketch follows his periodization of Yaqui history, roughly along the lines of either directed culture change (e.g. Jesuit mississionaries from 1617 to 1767), or nondirected change (e.g. a long period he identifies as "autonomous communities," from 1740 to 1887). His references include a handful of historical sources, from Jesuit accounts, to eyewitness reports, to official military histories, from relatively well-known books to others that he probably rescued from oblivion. In addition, of course, he utilizes freely and fully his own extensive field notes gathered over more than ten years and several visits. In short, Spicer offered the first well-developed example of the kind of ethnohistory he advocated.

In 1962 Spicer published *Cycles of Conquest: The Impact of Spain, Mexico, and the United States on the Indians of the Southwest, 1533-1960*. This time the focus was on the surviving cultures of the Southwest only, and Spicer himself wrote all the essays. This volume, still in print from the University of Arizona Press, justly established Spicer's national reputation as a leading ethnohistorian, cultural anthropologist, and authority on the Southwest.

As the title indicates, his intention in *Cycles* was to continue the work set out in *Perspectives*, both thematically and methodologically, that is, to examine the processes of acculturation, or culture change. "A feature of the basic conception of the study is that there has been a similarity in the results of culture contact over a wide area which is called . . . the Southwest" (p. viii). In addition to an essay on the Yaqui and Mayo (a neighboring group whose history paralleled that of the Yaqui until the end of the nineteenth century), the others, on the Tarahumara, Lower Pima and Opata, Seri, Upper Pima, Eastern Pueblo, Western Pueblo, Navajo, Western Apache, and Yuman, all provide a historical sketch from initial contact with Anglos to about 1960. As with his essays on the Yaqui in both volumes, he synthesizes available published sources with field work, his own or that of other anthropologists.

According to Spicer, the European conquest of America resulted in a common culture, with the invaders imposing their ways on the Indians far more than in the other direction, that is, borrowing from the Indian cultures. At the same time, this "Europeanization of the Indians" did not mean that the Indians did not find ways to resist "submergence in the conquering societies." Indeed, having studied the major surviving cultures of the Southwest, Spicer concludes that in this region of America, the most striking feature is not so much the growth of the common culture as that so many Indian groups continued to exist as "identifiable and self-conscious entities" (p. 567). Spicer notes:

> This persistence of ethnic identification in the region seemed remarkable because of the smallness of the groups at the beginning of contact, their military weakness, and the ultimate invasion of their territory in overwhelming numbers by the European and European-derived peoples. The explanation of the persistence, despite such apparently unfavorable conditions, requires us to consider as much the effects of contact on the dominant peoples as on the Indian societies. The intensity with which a sense of distinct identity was maintained by any given Indian group was quite unrelated to the extent to which its customs and beliefs had been replaced by those of the conquerors; the sense of identity was not at all proportional to the number of aboriginal traditions persisting. The processes of cultural assimilation were in fact distinct from the processes of group identification (p. 576).

What, then, were the factors affecting the Indian sense of identity if not related to retention of traditional customs and beliefs? Spicer believes the factors to be many, and no one to be decisive in all instances. He suggests two to consider. The conditions affecting the relationship of Indians to the land is of primary importance: "The retention of land bases was an important basic condition permitting a continuity of tribal sense among Indians and, in later phases of contact, constituting fixed boundaries in an increasingly mobile enveloping society." Another important factor consisted of conditions which "promoted working solidarity among tribal members," such as the ability to wage successful warfare against the invaders, as the Yaqui had demonstrated throughout their history, or the nativistic religious movements identified with the Tarahumara, Mayo, Western Apache, and others (p. 577).

The pathbreaking syntheses of southwestern Indian histories embodied in *Cycles of Conquest* and the resultant conclusions drawn from his comparative analysis are perhaps the highlights of Spicer's scholarly contributions. For good reason, this book is still in print, widely used in college classrooms, and invaluable as the first point of reference for anyone doing research on the Southwest, historians, archaeologists, and anthropologists alike.

During the next two decades after its publication and up to his death, Spicer essentially devoted his scholarly energies to two related projects that grew out of his works to date: a comprehensive cultural history of the Yaqui and a very ambitious, worldwide analysis of persistent cultures that would include not just the Yaqui as the leading example from the Southwest, but other American Indian groups, the Maya, Seneca, Cherokee, and Navajo, as well as Basques, Welsh, Irish, Catalans, and Jews--peoples who "retained their cultural identities in nation-states that sought to assimilate them" (*American Anthropologist* 86:381). The cultural history of the Yaqui was published in 1980. Regrettably, he left upon his death an unfinished manuscript entitled "Enduring Peoples."

The idea of his unfinished manuscript, "Enduring Peoples," first appeared in a seminal article in *Science*, entitled "Persistent Cultural Systems" (pp. 795-800). Quite clearly, however, the concept of persistent cultures first occurred to Spicer when he worked on *Cycles of Conquest*, if not earlier. In this new but unfinished study, his plan was to broaden the scope to include enduring peoples from across the globe. In the *Science* article, he was able to go beyond *Cycles* to identify the key factor in explaining cultural persistence: "Its formation and maintenance are intimately bound up with the conditions of opposition. Tentatively, on the basis of our limited data, it appears that the oppositional process is the essential factor in the formation and development of the persistent identity system" (p. 797).

Spicer also suggested that in the struggle between the dominant and the subjugated, persistent group, "the possession of state power dissipates the kind of identity system under discussion. . . . Apparently, the condition of holding state power may result in either the breakdown of an identity system or the reinforcement of it, but the latter results would seem to be a product of certain rather special conditions" (p. 797). Aside from the external, or oppositional, relationships, Spicer also emphasizes internal characteristics and maintenance processes of such systems, that is, the identity symbols, behavioral and emotional associations with these symbols, and institutionalized social relations that maintain the system of meanings (p. 798).

In *The Yaquis: A Cultural History* (1980), Spicer fleshes out the historical outline he had already sketched for the Yaqui people in earlier works. He also fills out the details for the important cultural aspects of Yaqui life: religion and religious arts, town (pueblo), and identity. By making use of his own accumulated field experience, secondary sources, some primary documents, contemporary observations of Yaqui ways during three centuries, as well as other anthropolgical studies based on direct observation, Spicer affirms his confidence in the ethnohistorical approach, that knowledge gained through direct observation of the present can help interpret the past. Published ten years after the *Science* article, *The Yaquis: A Cultural History* is quite clearly the first in-depth case study of a persistent culture, an example of the "enduring people of the world" (p. 362).

No review of Spicer's life and work would be complete without mention of his commitment to applied anthropology. His concern for the application of anthropology was clearly expressed in his teaching, his professional activities, and in some of his writings, notably *Human Problems in Technological Change: A Casebook* (1952). He edited the volume, contributed three case studies, and wrote the concluding chapter on

"Conceptual Tools for Solving Human Problems," an essay that affected a generation of Peace Corp volunteers, technical assistance and community development workers, and community policy makers. Equally important are his work and publications in connection with experiences with social scientists, administrators, and those Japanese-Americans interned during World War II under the War Relocation Authority (WRA), 1942-1946 (*Impounded People*). A colleague who knew him well notes:

> This was a troublesome period for Ned, serving first as social science analyst, then later as Head of the Community Analysis Section of WRA. The involvement of social scientists in the WRA constituted a pioneering effort in applied social science, under the most difficult of conditions, and he played an important role in a controversial exercise (*American Anthropologist* 86:382).

Finally, Spicer's applied anthropology applied most of all to the Yaqui, whom he not only spent a lifetime studying, but a lifetime helping and championing. He was identified with Yaqui people in Arizona and in Mexico both personally and professionally. A conclusion he reached regarding the interned Japanese-Americans could well be said of the Yaqui: "Public policy involving the future of human communities *must be made by those communities*, or the destruction of some of the most important human qualities is certain to take place, resulting in frustration, apathy, and dependency" (*Impounded People*, p. 20).

In a sense it would not be fair to offer a critique of Spicer from the historian's perspective, since he was a cultural anthropologist and never pretended to be an "orthodox" historian. Nevertheless, by emphasizing the importance of history in his cultural studies--his ethnohistorical approach--he has, wittingly or not, drawn close to the historian in a number of ways. First and most simply, the cultural and historical syntheses he provides for the Yaqui and other native peoples of the Southwest (as in *Cycles of Conquest*) constitute perhaps the best departing point for historians to begin a research project on the American Southwest (or Mexico's Northwest).

Second, it appears that Spicer was trying to bridge the gap between anthropologists and historians, certainly a call that noted historians of American Indians have sounded. Robert Berkhofer, for example, argues for a "new Indian history" with a new focus, that of "ethnic survival and cultural continuity and change," the very theme that preoccupied Spicer. Spicer realized that cultural change (or persistence) can only be studied within a historical context (*Pacific Historical Review* 40:357). He also appreciated the usefulness of historical documents to identify important events of the past. Then, by assuming uniformities running through time, not only in terms of the peculiarities of Yaqui history but also as general rules of culture change, he proceeds from the known ethnologic present--what is observed during field work--backwards to the less known or unknown past, to pinpoint the origins of these cultural patterns, and to determine whether and how much change has occurred.

This ethnohistorical approach has been graphically termed by one of its proponents, William N. Fenton, as "upstreaming" (*American Anthropologist* 54:329-339). And this is where Spicer first makes traditional historians uneasy. They are not convinced of the validity of "upstreaming" and its underlying assumption about uniformity. They are wary of using the observable present as historical evidence. Even Fenton (though not apparently Spicer) acknowledges the problem: "this method must be used with caution because it contains a built-in fallacy which historians will recognize as the doctrine of uniformitarianism, which infers past from present" (*American Indian and White Relations*, p. 22).

Historians have also found fault with the way Spicer depicts the past, as well as the way he uses historical sources (*The Americas* 38:143-145). In part because of the limited sources he avails himself of--certain published regional and local histories and accounts, and a random selection of documents--his history ends up being a chronological string of key events. This history-as-espisodes can leave large unfilled gaps, result in misplaced emphases, and overlook significant developments or individuals. Moreover, his heavy and largely uncritical use of the secondary sources, some only barely documented, lead him to some conclusions that were either not corroborated or directly contradicted by the abundant and readily available primary sources not consulted. Some of his interpretations are too broadly conceived, based on insufficient evidence, with missing or inadequate citation to sources. Certain myths, exaggerations, or plain mistakes are also perpetuated. In other words, by not being an archival researcher, Spicer has chosen not to examine a rich body of materials, although he is well aware of their existence. Indeed, he urged others to dig deeper into the historical records than he had and to search for the rich details. In doing so, of course, the historian is likely not only to come up with new information, but on that basis, reach new interpretations as well (*Missionaries, Miners and Indians*; *Yaqui Resistance and Survival*).

Bibliography

Books

A Brief Introduction to Yaqui: A Native Language of Sonora. Co-authored with William Kurath. University of Arizona Social Science Bulletin, Vol. 18, No. 1. Tucson: University of Arizona, 1947.

Cycles of Conquest: The Impact of Spain, Mexico, and the United States on the Indians of the Southwest, 1533-1960. Tucson: University of Arizona Press, 1962.

Ethnic Medicine in the Southwest. Editor. Tucson: University of Arizona Press, 1977.

Human Problems in Technological Change: A Casebook. New York: Russell Sage Foundation, 1952. Translation, *Problemas humanos en el cambio technológico: Una exposición de casos*. Editorial Letras, S.A., Mexico City, D.F.

Impounded People: Japanese-Americans in the Relocation Centers. Co-authored with Katharine Luomala, A. T. Hansen, and Marvin K. Opler. Washington, DC: United States Department of Interior, 1946. Reprint. Tucson: University of Arizona Press, 1969.

Pascua, A Yaqui Village in Arizona. Chicago: University of Chicago Press, 1940. Reprint. 1971, 1981; Tucson: University of Arizona Press, 1984.

People of Pascua. Co-edited by Kathleen M. Sands and Rosamond B. Spicer. Tucson: University of Arizona Press, 1988.

Perspectives in American Indian Culture Change. Editor. Chicago: University of Chicago Press, 1961.

Plural Society in the Southwest. Co-edited with R. H. Thompson. Interbook, NY: Weatherford Foundation, 1972. Reprint. Albuquerque: University of New Mexico Press, 1975.

Pótam, A Yaqui Village in Sonora. American Anthropological Association Memoir, No. 77. Springfield, IL: American Anthropological Association, 1954. Reprint. Millwood, NJ: Kraus Reprint, 1975.

A Short History of the Indians of the United States. New York: Van Nostrand Reinhold Co., 1969.

Tuzigoot: The Excavation and Repair of a Ruin on the Verde River Near Clarkdale, Arizona. Co-authored with Louis R. Caywood. Berkeley, CA: United States National Park Service, 1935.

Two Pueblo Ruins in West Central Arizona. Co-authored with Louis R. Caywood. University of Arizona Social Science Bulletin, Vol. 7, No. 10. Tucson: University of Arizona, 1936.

The Yaquis: A Cultural History. Tucson: University of Arizona Press, 1980.

Articles

"American Indians" and "American Indians, Federal Policy Toward." In *Harvard Encyclopedia of American Ethnic Groups* edited by Stephen Thernstrom. Cambridge, MA: Belknap Press of Harvard University Press, 1980. Pp. 114-122.

"Anthropologists and the War Relocation Authority." In *The Uses of Anthropology* edited by Walter F. Goldschmidt. Washington, DC: American Anthropological Association, 1979.

"Anthropology and the Policy Process." In *Do Applied Anthropologists Apply Anthropology*? edited by M. V. Androsino. Southern Anthropological Society Proceedings, No. 10. Athens: University of Georgia Press, 1976. Pp. 118-133.

"Applied Anthropology in a Dislocated Community." Co-authored with Alexander H. Leighton. In *The Governing of Men* edited by Alexander H. Leighton. Princeton, NJ: Princeton University Press, 1945. Pp. 371-397.

"Apuntes sobre el tipo de religión de los Yuto-Aztecas Centrales." In *XXXV Congreso Internacional de Americanistas, Actas y Memorias.* Segunda parte del Tomo 1, Mexico City, D.F., 1962.

"Assessing Public Opinion in a Dislocated Community." Co-authored with Alexander H. Leighton, et al. *Public Opinion Quarterly* 7(Winter, 1943):652-668.

"Beyond Analysis and Explanation? Notes on the Life and Times of the Society for Applied Anthropology." *Human Organization* 35(Winter, 1976):335-343.

"Capturing the Feeling." In *The Seris* edited by David L. Burckhalter. Tucson: University of Arizona Press, 1976. Pp. 5-12.

"Comments on Current Problems of Japanese-American Adjustment." *Journal of Social Issues* 1(May, 1945):28-29.

"Contrasting Forms of Nativism Among the Mayos and Yaquis of Sonora, Mexico." In *The Social Anthropology of Latin America* edited by Walter Goldschmidt and Harry Hoijer. Los Angeles: Latin American Center of UCLA, 1970. Pp. 104-125.

"Culture Contact and Change in Northwestern Mexico." In *Homenaje a Gonzalo Aquirre Beltrán.* Jalapa, Mexico City, Mexico: Universidad Veracruzana e Instituto Indigenista Interamericano, 1974. Tomo II:177-194.

"La danza yaqui del venado en la cultura mexicana." *America Indígena* 4(No. 4, 1965):371-373. Mexico City, D.F.

"Developmental Change and Cultural Integration." In *Perspectives of Developmental Change* edited by Art Gallaher, Jr. Lexington: University of Kentucky Press, 1968. Pp. 172-200.

"Early Applications of Anthropology in North America." In *Perspectives on Anthropology 1976* edited by Anthony F. C. Wallace, J. Lawrence Angel, Richard Fox, Sally McLendon, Rachel Sady, and Robert Sharer. Washington, DC: American Anthropological Association, 1977. Pp. 116-141.

"European Expansion and Enclavement of Southwestern Indians." *Arizona and the West* 1(Summer, 1959):132-145. Reprint. *The American Indian: Past and Present* edited by Roger L. Nichols. New York: John Wiley, 1971. Pp. 74-82.

"The History of Federal Indian Policy in Relation to the Government of Indian Communities." In *Report and Recommendations, Community Development Seminar, Chinle Agency.* Washington, DC: United States Bureau of Indian Affairs, Navajo Area, 1969.

"Indigenismo in the United States, 1870-1960." *America Indígena* 24(No. 4, 1964):349-363. Mexico City, D.F.

"The Issues in Indian Affairs." *Arizona Quarterly* 21(Winter, 1965):293-307.

"The Japanese Family in America." *Annals of the American Academy of Political and Social Sciences* 229(September, 1943):150-156.

"Linguistic Aspects of Yaqui Acculturation." *American Anthropologist* 45(July, 1943):410-426.

"El mestizaje cultural en el suroeste de Estados Unidos y noroeste de México." *Revista de Indias* 24(No. 95-96, 1964):1-26. Madrid, Spain.

"The Military Orientation in Yaqui Culture." In *For the Dean: Essays in Anthropology in Honor of Byron Cummings on His 89th Birthday, September 20, 1950* edited by Erik K. Reed and Dale S. King. Tucson and Santa Fe: Southwestern Monuments Association and Hohokam Museums Association, 1950. Pp. 171-187.

"Northwest Mexico." In *Handbook of Middle American Indians* edited by Evon Z. Vogt. Austin: University of Texas Press, 1969. 8:830-845.

"Parentescas Uto-Aztecas de la Lengua Seri." *Yan* 1(No. 1, 1953). Mexico City, D.F.

"Patrons of the Poor." *Human Organization* 28(Spring, 1970):12-20. Reprint. *City Ways: A Selective Reader in Urban Anthropology* edited by John Friedle and Noel Chrisman. New York: Thomas Y. Crowell Co., 1975. Pp. 416-428.

"Persistent Cultural Systems." *Science* 174(November, 1971):795-800.

"Política gubernamental e integración indigenista en México." *Anuario Indigenista* 29(1969):49-64. Instituto Indigenista Interamericano, Mexico City.

"Political Incorporation and Cultural Change in New Spain: A Study in Spanish-Indian Relations." In *Attitudes of Colonial Powers Toward the American Indian* edited by Howard Peckham and Charles Gibson. Salt Lake City: University of Utah Press, 1969. Pp. 107-135.

"El Problema Yaqui." *America Indígena* 5(No. 4, 1945):273-286. Mexico City, D.F.

"The Process of Cultural Enclavement in Middle America." In *XXXVI Proceedings, International Congress of Americanists.* Vol. III. Sevilla, Spain: 1966.

"Social Structure and Cultural Process in Yaqui Religious Acculturation." *American Anthropologist* 60(June, 1958):433-441.

"Southwestern Chronicle, Ethnology." *Arizona Quarterly* 9(Summer, 1953):163-172.

"Southwestern Chronicle, Ethnology of the Navaho, Apache, and Others." *Arizona Quarterly* 4(Spring, 1948):162-171.

"Southwestern Chronicle, Pueblo Ethnology." *Arizona Quarterly* 4(Spring, 1948):78-89.

"Spanish-Indian Acculturation in the Southwest." *American Anthropologist* 56(August, 1954):663-678.

"Training for Non-Academic Employment: Major Issues." Co-authored with Theodore E. Downing. In *Training Programs for New Opportunities in Applied Anthropology* edited by Eleanor Leacock, Nancie L. Gonzalez, and Gilbert Kushner. Washington, DC: American Anthropological Association, 1974. Pp. 1-12.

"The Use of Social Scientists by the War Relocation Authority." *Applied Anthropology* 5(Spring, 1946):16-36.

"Ways of Life." In *Six Faces of Mexico: History, People, Geography, Government, Economy, Literature, and Art* edited by Russell Ewing. Tucson: University of Arizona Press, 1966. Pp. 66-102.

"Worlds Apart, Cultural Differences in the Modern Southwest." *Arizona Quarterly* 13(Autumn, 1957):197-230.

"Yaqui Militarism." *Arizona Quarterly* 1(Autumn, 1947):40-48.

Selected Reviews

Man Takes Control by Charles J. Erasmus. *American Anthropologist* 63(December, 1961):1351.

Realidades y projectos by Alfonso Caso, et al. *American Anthropologist* 67(December, 1965):1318.

A Record of Travels in Arizona and California, 1775-1776 by Francisco Garces. *American Anthropologist* 68(August, 1966):824.

The Teachings of Don Juan: A Yaqui Way of Knowledge by Carlos Castaneda. *American Anthropologist* 71(April, 1969):320.

Studies of Edward H. Spicer

Gallaher, Art, Jr. "Edward Holland Spicer (1906-1983)." *American Anthropologist* 86(April, 1984):381-382.

Spicer, Rosamond. Communications with Evelyn Hu-DeHart, 1985-1986.

Voss, Stuart. Review of *The Yaquis: A Cultural History* by Edward H. Spicer. *The Americas* 38(July, 1981):143-145.

Other References

Berkhofer, Robert F., Jr. "The Political Context of a New Indian History." *Pacific Historical Review* 40(August, 1971):357.

Fenton, William N. "Indian and White Relations in Eastern North America: A Common Ground for History and Ethnology." In *American Indian and White Relations to 1830: Needs and Opportunities for Study*. Institute of Early American History and Culture Conference Proceedings. Chapel Hill: University of North Carolina Press, 1957. Pp. 3-27.

__________. "The Training of American Historical Ethnologists in America." *American Anthropologist* 54(April, 1952):329-339.

Hu-DeHart, Evelyn. *Missississionaries, Miners and Indians: Spanish Contact with the Yaqui Nation of Northwestern New Spain, 1533-1820.* Tucson: University of Arizona Press, 1981.

__________. *Yaqui Resistance and Survival: The Struggle for Land and Autonomy, 1821-1910.* Madison: University of Wisconsin Press, 1984.

49

K. ROSS TOOLE

by Steven F. Mehls

Biography

Montana, known today for its hundreds of scenic attractions and vacation memories, not only produced a number of western historical episodes but also noted western historians. Among them, none devoted more of his career or life to his native state than Kenneth Ross Toole. Toole had roots as deep as anyone in Montana's Anglo-American history. On both sides of his family, his ancestors arrived in the northern Rockies during the gold rush of the 1850s and 1860s. They and their immediate descendents experienced much of the history that the later Toole would write about. Two of them, John R. Toole and Kenneth Ross, worked as minor officials for the Anaconda Copper Company and its subsidiaries, the object of many of K. Ross' studies (*Montana and the West*, p. 5).

Born as the nation and the West reeled under the psychological letdown at the end of World War I and the time of the first great radical hunt of the twentieth century precipitated by Attorney General A. Mitchell Palmer's raids, the young Toole grew up, unscathed by these events, in the then rather sleepy town of Missoula. By 1920, the year young Kenneth Ross Toole came into this life, the community already was home to the University of Montana, an institution that would dominate much of his life. He grew up in what can be assumed to have been a comfortable environment. Toole later stated that his family life was not "an ordinary one, which implies, of course, that it has been an extraordinary one" (p. 5).

Toole had little trouble completing the required work to earn his high school degree on the eve of World War II. However, if his early collegiate career serves as any indication Toole had little, if any, future plans when he graduated and then entered the University of Montana, one of his four undergraduate institutions. During his attempts to find a suitable career Toole explored many different possibilities, from foreign service to the law. His undergraduate odyssey spanned eight years, with some time off for military service during World War II. By the late 1940s, still apparently seeking to delay the inevitable day of reckoning in the job market, Toole enrolled in graduate school, eventually finishing his Ph.D. in 1955. Ironically, not until his graduate years did Toole discover history. He embraced the discipline without hesitation and it became his life's work in a variety of forms.

Toole's first job came not at a university, but rather with the Montana Historical Society, where he worked for seven years before the nearly legendary Toole temper flared and he left the society (pp. 5-11). From then until his death, Toole would continue to have problems with employers, most rooted in the fact that he could seldom control his temper. While describing Montana's history, Toole also unknowingly gave a characterization of his own professional life:

> There is little or nothing moderate about the story of Montana. It has ricocheted violently down the corridor of possibilities. What is good in reasonable measure is often bad in full measure, and Montana has been a place of full measure (*Montana: An Uncommon Land*, p. 5).

Indeed, as Montana has been a land of full measure, so Ross Toole's life as a scholar and writer was one of full measure. Not content to manage museums, he also, during one of his self-imposed exiles, tried his hand at ranching, and then for what proved to be the last years of his career took a position at the University of Montana. There he taught the local history course, Montana and the West, which, in the eyes of his admirers, he made famous. From the scholarly pulpit Toole preached his thesis to hundreds of eager young minds.

But not satisfied to simply be a part of the faculty and rest on his past accomplishments, Toole's life took a turn during the 1970s as, in his eyes, Montana history began to repeat itself. Energy companies moved into the state, threatening, behind the smokescreen of environmental legislation, to start a new era of raping the land and its resources. Toole found the analogies irresistable. This spurred the historian to new heights of activity, not historically directed, but rather indirectly, as he took Clio's lessons and applied them to the modern situation, seeking out the villains and bringing them before the court of public opinion.

During these struggles, Toole's health began to deteriorate and after a short (1980-1981) battle with cancer, K. Ross Toole passed away, still active in his causes and teaching at the university. As Wallace Stegner described Toole, "There was no neutral in him, there was no way he could disengage his clutch and simply idle" (*Montana and the West* p. ix).

Themes

Kenneth Ross Toole, known to most as K. Ross, some as simply, Toole, and many others who sought to despoil Montana as "that [expletive deleted] Toole," left behind volumes of his ideas on western history. Only frequently does a historian appear who can elicit such reactions, especially in more recent times as many in the profession seem to have forgotten that history is, or should be, for everyone, not just the few in their particular area of specialization. Toole, during his thirty years as an active historian, remembered that lesson. Also, he frequently got backs up and tempers blazing. This came from his ability to use the written word with as much impact as Henry Plummer had wielded pistols earlier in Montana's history. Much like the local vigilantes that ended Plummer's career with a long drop and short rope, Toole used history as a noose to slow down the corporate abuses of Montana's natural resources.

Toole recognized early in his career that one underlying truth existed that explained Great Plains-Rocky Mountain history. He believed themes of economic exploitation explained settlement. Frederick Jackson Turner or those who followed his lead were not as direct. A few have labelled this the "Toole Thesis." Briefly, he argues that western history could best be explained by looking for the corporate giants that exploited western resources, including the people and their political organizations. Once the natural recourse, whether it came in the form of furs, copper, timber, gold, or coal, had been exhausted, the companies left the area and its people empty-handed. More damning than the "plundering" and abandonment in Toole's eyes, the corporations frequently channeled their profits away to people with little interest in the land other than how large their dividends would be (pp. 11-12; *Pacific Northwest Quarterly* 44:23-29). While based on the experience of his native Montana, his ideas proved somewhat viable throughout the region. This thesis of economic exploitation of the West by the East, while appearing parochial, nevertheless has been used by many in both serious history and polemical works, such as Richard D. Lamm and G. Michael McCarthy's *The Angry West* (1982). Toole himself made frequent use of the idea throughout his writings.

Indeed, even in his master's thesis, "Marcus Daly: A Study of Business in Politics," the reader can, from the title, start to recognize the seed of the "Toole Thesis" beginning to germinate in the young scholar's mind. Continuing his educational career in what could best be described as a gentleman's way to kill time, the young historian enrolled in the UCLA doctorate program (*Montana and the West*, pp. 5-6). More importantly, he remained enthralled with the abuse of power by one of Montana's largest corporations, Anaconda Copper. It became the subject of his dissertation. From here Toole's writings blossomed into other areas of Montana's history, but always the underlying struggle between the people and the companies remained present. In his purely historical writings, the "Toole thesis" remains as the cornerstone of his arguments.

However, he refused to limit his attentions only to the past. Rather, he wrote on topics of his everyday life as well. Spending many years as director of the Montana Historical Society and later the Museum of the City of New York and the Museum of New Mexico in Santa Fe, it is not surprising to find that Toole published articles on museum management and programs with organizations such as the American Association for State and Local History. In these writings Toole tries to convince his audience that the purpose of history, be it in writing or through exhibits, is to inform the public about the lessons to be learned from the past. Undoubtedly, Toole believed if present generations learned from the past they would avoid the same mistakes. It remains for people fifty to 100 years from now to evaluate if Toole's preachings in Montana proved effective.

Toole, believing there were lessons to be found in history, especially when viewed through his "thesis," wrote on problems of contemporary society. He chastized the campus radicals of the late 1960s and the developers of Montana's coal resources through the construction of the Coalstrip Power Plants during the 1970s. At times his arguments, while forceful against the corporations, approached angry diatribes, that for all his passion lost some of their perspective. In these writings Toole exhibits both conservative and liberal biases, proenvironmental but antistudent movement. Despite the inability to attach a political label to him, Toole succeeded in making people think, whether they agreed with his point of view or not. Possibly no better honor can go to a writer than to have readers take a sense of provocation and appreciation after finishing a book or article. K. Ross Toole's themes varied from area to area, but in whatever topic--history, museum studies, or contemporary affairs--Toole advocated his position most forcefully.

Analysis

K. Ross Toole proved to be a prolific writer throughout his career, yet unique in that he never completed a book-length study of his own. Nevertheless his contributions to over fifty books and articles leave a widely varied field of material for analysis. The best of his articles and books he wrote or edited form the bulk of Toole's original contributions in the realm of history.

Beginning with his earliest scholarly publication, "The Anaconda Copper Mining Company: A Price War and a Copper Corner," published in the October, 1950, *Pacific Northwest Quarterly*, Toole's fascination with Montana business and "the company's [Anaconda Copper]" abuse of the area began. His compassion for the victims of Anaconda, this time the miners of Butte during the 1880s, becomes readily apparent. As Toole phrases it:

> However, in spite of a concerted effort on the part of the local press to reassure jittery miners and businessmen, in August the Anaconda closed completely. J. B. A. Haggin left Butte for London after extended conversations with Daly, and dismal quiet settled over Butte.
>
> The camp shivered through the winter of 1886-87 while blizzard after blizzard piled snow over railroad rights-of-way and banked it high in the empty streets. The unemployed miners stared out at the black and smokeless chimneys of a thousand cold calcinating furnaces, and the Hotel de Mineral was jammed with cattlemen who had fled the worst winter they could recall, leaving the frozen corpses of thousands of cattle beneath the drifts. It was not a winter in which to be unemployed, and for the first time, but not the last, the com-

> pany's executives heard bitter and resentful comment from the miners (41:312).

This suffering came about, as Toole carefully and meticulously explains, due to the uncaring actions of people far removed from Montana, in this case financiers from San Francisco, the East, and Europe. One senses from Toole's writings that those entrepreneurs almost went out of their way to increase the suffering in Montana. But like many tales of good and evil, there is a settling of accounts as Toole indicates when he describes the downfall of Hyacinthe Secretan, the French financier behind the attempted market corner:

> While the copper producers were at sea, the banks of France were in such critical condition that catastrophe was avoided only when the bank of France came to the aid of the Comptoir with a loan of 120,000,000 francs. A proposition in the Chamber of Deputies to indict the men responsible for the panic on criminal charges was only defeated by a vote of 339 to 312. Hyacinthe Secretan left Paris and was not heard from again (p. 328).

True to what became the Toole style, goodness enjoyed only a very brief triumph before the forces of monopoly reexerted themselves in the exploitation of Montana's copper. Toole seems almost pleased by the turn of events, "for it was destined to be Standard Oil itself, through the Anaconda Company, which next attempted a copper corner--an attempt that would put Secretan to shame" (p. 329). Actually, for Ross Toole such an outcome was mandatory for the march of history. Without his villains life had little meaning.

In another early article, "When Big Money Came to Butte: The Migration of Eastern Capital to Montana," published in the *Pacific Northwest Quarterly* in January of 1953, as the "Toole thesis" germinated, he continues his attacks on "the company," Anaconda Copper. However, in this work Toole starts to develop the idea that the Montana experience, specifically the copper mining operations, held historical lessons that could be extrapolated to the entire Rocky Mountain West. Toole writes, "Butte, Montana, between 1876 and 1903, is a case study in the westward movement of Eastern capital and the consequences of that movement" (44:23). A few pages later Toole further explains the migration of money to the mining camps and what it meant:

> This westward movement of capital, however, was not an unmixed blessing. Gradually, as capital moved from east to west, control moved from west to east and outside interests began to exploit local political schisms. After 1888 there was a notable admixture of mining and politics in Montana which developed into the notorious "War of the Copper Kings." The

original participants in the war were Montanans, and the issues involved were local, but they did not long remain so (p. 25).

At the end of that passage Toole hints at a significant factor that he never really fully explores--local involvement, the active booster work to attract outside capital to the region. In Toole's thinking this was the ultimate folly as the local residents eventually came to suffer at the hands of "foreign capital."

What Toole does not account for inside and outside Montana are those other westerners who reversed the trend, convincing outside investors to put their money into western enterprises, such as cattle ranches or mines, the outsiders only to find themselves left empty-handed while the westerners' pockets filled. Toole's failure to address adequately that type of concern seriously limits the region-wide application of Toole's thesis. Admittedly, such a criticism may be somewhat unfair because subsequent findings post-date Toole's efforts. But, nonetheless, his failure to recognize the possibility that the flow of money and power might be a two-way street with a flow to the West as well as to the East seriously limits the Toole Thesis. This shortcoming marks Toole as rather parochial in his historical perspective.

Even if Toole was a bit limited in his view, or maybe because of it, Toole shaped frontier Montana historiography. The abuses of capital locally and how turn-of-the-century residents of the state viewed their peculiar situation helped explain Montana's uniqueness. "It is unfortunately true with regard to Montana that the advent of the trust's movement into the state generated hatred, suspicion and--ultimately--a peculiar apathy" (p. 29).

Toole prepared to interpret the history of Montana by the end of the 1950s. In *Montana: An Uncommon Land*, Toole took information from a number of other writers and assembled it into a book-length study. Amazingly, he accomplishes that work without a single footnote, even following passages that were printed as direct quotations. Despite such lack of scholarly trappings, the volume does allow glimpses of the Toole Thesis applied to historical questions beyond the Anaconda Copper Company. Toole ventures into the twentieth century examining such topics as progressive tax reform efforts and the dryland farming boom. In looking at the dryland or "honyocker" movement, Toole places it firmly in his view of the Montana tradition when he writes:

Had they come in slowly, in single families, over a period of years, and passed their experiences on to those who followed, had they even been wary, it would seem that enormous human misery could have been avoided. But that is not the way it happened; and, in fact, the way it did happen was more in the Montana tradition of too much too soon with too little (p. 229).

If the reader took the impression that somehow the movement lacked corporate capitalist abuse, Toole rectifies that a few pages later:

> Land dealers, merchants, and the grain industry all joined the railroads in this campaign. So did local residents, merchants, and bankers, who had lived on the land for a long time. Indeed, the campaign became public policy in Montana. Here was the old cry for outside capital in a new guise, but it was the old cry just the same (p. 235).

Montana: An Uncommon Land, emphasizes another Toole characteristic--that history had to have conflict between the people and corporations. After the failure of the honyockers during the 1920s, history apparently ended for Montana, at least until the book's publication in 1959. As such Toole tends to reinforce, at least for himself, the Toole thesis.

Toole almost refused to admit that anything happened in Montana after the 1920s when he assembled another volume, *Twentieth Century Montana: A State of Extremes*, published in 1972. Again he wrote a book based largely on the work of others without source notations except a bibliography. The footnotes for this book are limited to comments or explanations. Further weakening this work is the fact that it ends with the failure of progressivism in the 1920s, though from the title one is led to believe that topics such as the Great Depression or World War II might be given more than a cursory glance. Even so, Toole does not forget to continue to argue his thesis throughout the book.

Co-authoring works gave Toole more opportunities to reach audiences and, whenever possible, he hammered the reader with his views on capitalist abuses of Montana's resources. In 1968 he and Edward Butcher collaborated on an article, "Timber Depredations on the Montana Public Domain, 1885-1918," for the *Journal of the West*. Toole and Butcher point out in their opening arguments that the federal suits to end the uncontrolled use of public timber lands created a situation where, "the majority of Montanans were at first incredulous and then angry. Because Montana's economy was based on industries requiring great quantities of timber, the litigation was considered senseless, arbitrary and vengeful" (7:362). Nor did Toole and Butcher fail to examine the corporate control behind the scenes that not only prompted the federal court actions but also led the opposition. In particular, the Northern Pacific Railroad, beneficiary of the mid-nineteenth century federal land grant policies for railroads, became not only one of the primary actors in the authors' drama, but also the target of many of their criticisms. Not wanting to ignore Montana's arch villains, the copper companies were also indicted by Toole and Butcher. Finally, as with many of his other works, Toole extrapolates the Montana experience beyond the state's borders:

> The story of timber depredations in Montana is more typical than extraordinary. There were larger poachers in Oregon and California, there were smaller operators all over the West. And

> in all regions the depredations pose the same ethical and moral problems for the student of forest policy. Neither statistics nor close analysis of the legislation pertaining to forest lands wholly resolve these problems. The laws designed to produce revenue from private utilization of a public resource were fine in theory but malfunctioned in fact. In both cases Congress showed a lamentable ignorance of Western circumstances and Western needs (p. 360).

Despite such attempts to break out of his parochialism, K. Ross Toole remained a historian of Montana. The attention he paid to his native state and the material the Montana experience gave him to work with proved to be too fascinating for him to ignore. By the early 1970s Toole passed from being a historian, at least in his writing, toward becoming a polemicist more akin to the sky pilots of early Montana than the new social historians of the 1970s. Toole preached on sins other than those of the capitalist abuse of "his" youth. These efforts earned him a national reputation, particularly his writings against the youth movement of the late 1960s and early 1970s, fueling the fires of the so-called generation gap. As the writer of *An Angry Man Talks Up to Youth* and *The Time Has Come*, Toole ceased being a scholar or historian and became the writer he may have always wanted to be--a commentator on current events. But at that point his contributions to frontier history also all but ceased, with his later historical publications, such as *Montana: Images of the Past* (1978), being recyclings of earlier efforts and again frequently done in collaboration with others.

Bibliography

What follows is a fairly complete bibliography of K. Ross Toole's works. However, he also used some pen names and offered some writings anonymously, particularly while with the Montana Historical Society. According to the assemblers of a *festschrift* in his honor, "Not even Toole himself could remember all the items he had written" (*Montana and the West*, p. 189).

Books

An Angry Man Talks Up to Youth. New York: Award Books, 1970.

Historical Essays on Montana and the Northwest. Co-authored with John W. Smurr. Helena, MT: Western Publishing Co., 1957.

A History of Montana. Co-authored with Merrill G. Burlingame. 3 volumes. New York: Lewis Historical Publishing Co., 1957.

Montana: An Uncommon Land. Compiler. Norman: University of Oklahoma Press, 1959.

Montana: Images of the Past. Co-authored with William E. Farr. Boulder, CO: Pruett Publishing Co., 1978.

Probing the American West. Co-edited with John Alexander Carroll, Robert M. Utley, and A. R. Mortensen. Santa Fe, NM: Museum of New Mexico, 1962.

The Rape of the Great Plains: Northwest America, Cattle and Coal. Boston: Little, Brown and Co., 1976.

The Time Has Come. New York: William Morrow, 1971.

Twentieth Century Montana: A State of Extremes. Compiler. Norman: University of Oklahoma Press, 1972.

Articles

"Address: Eulogy to Charles M. Russell." *Congressional Record* 105(March, 23, 1959):A-2575.

"Amateurs Can Abet Academic Historians." *Pacific Northwesterner: Spokane Corral of Westerners* 22(Summer, 1978):46-48.

"The Anaconda Copper Mining Company: A Price War and a Copper Corner." *Pacific Northwest Quarterly* 41(October, 1950):312-329.

"Anne McDonnell: A Tribute." *Montana: Magazine of Western History* 3(Fall, 1953):63.

"Art in the Intermountain West." *The Lotus Leaf*, March, 1958, pp. 3-5.

"Beloved Westerner: Charles M. Russell." *Montana: Magazine of Western History* 8(Fall, 1958):3-5.

"Business History Records in Montana." In *American Philosophical Society Yearbook 1967.* Philadelphia: American Philosophical Society, 1968. Pp. 423-425.

"The Changing Winds of Montana." *Montana Business Quarterly* 7(Winter/Spring, 1969):7-10.

"E. S. Paxson: Neglected Artist of the West." *Montana: Magazine of Western History* 4(Spring, 1954):26-29.

"Early Montana Banking." *Out West Magazine* 3(February, 1953):26.

"Education and History." *Museum News* 37(March, 1959):12-13.

"Environmental Degradation in Montana." *Montana Business Quarterly* 8(Winter, 1970):5-9.

"Fort Benton: Hub of Empire." *Out West Magazine* 2(November, 1952):12-13.

"The Forty-Seventh Legislature in Review." *Montana Magazine* 11(July/August, 1981):10-16.

"The Future of Higher Education in Montana." *Rocky Mountain Magazine*, February, 1980.

"The Future of the Northern Rockies." *Rocky Mountain Magazine*, November, 1979.

"The Genesis of the Clark-Daly Feud." *Montana: Magazine of Western History* 1(April, 1951):21-34.

"The Harney Scandal." *Montana Lawyer* 5(November, 1979):4, 14-15.

"The Historical Society and Its Function Today." *Nebraska History* 38(September, 1957):221-227.

"The Honyockers." In *Small Business Administration Directory, 1979.* Washington, DC: Small Business Administration, 1979.

"How Montanans View America: Independent Cusses vs. Glittery Suits." *Montana Business Quarterly* 13(Spring, 1975):33-38.

"I Am Tired of the Tyranny of the Spoiled Brats." *U.S. News and World Report* 68(April, 13, 1970):76-78. Reprinted, *Reader's Digest* 96(June, 1970):129-132.

"The Impact of the Museum in the Hinterlands." *Clearing House for Western Museums* 201(November, 1956):991-996.

"An Industrialist Asks a Question: Are We Really Spreading the American Heritage?" In *Ideas in Conflict: A Colloquium on Certain Problems in Historical Society Work in the United States and Canada* edited by Clifford L. Lord. Harrisburg, PA: American Association for State and Local History, 1958. Pp. 117-150.

"Is Local History Really Passe?" *Montana Historian* 6(June, 1976):54.

"Is Local History Really Important? In *Ideas in Conflict: A Colloquium on Certain Problems in Historical Society Work in the United States and Canada* edited by Clifford L. Lord. Harrisburg, PA: American Association for State and Local History, 1958. Pp. 151-181.

"Montana." *Daughters of the American Revolution Magazine* 87(March, 1953):440, 460.

"Montana: The New Place and the Old." *Champion Magazine* 6(1980):3-10.

"Montana: The Peculiar Enclave." In *Small Business Administration Directory, 1979*. Washington, DC: Small Business Administration, 1979.

"Montana's Potential." *Out West Magazine* 2(January, 1953):26.

"The Northern Great Plains." In *The Rape of the Great Plains*. Boston: Little, Brown & Co., 1976. Pp. 13-32. Reprinted, *The Great Plains Experience: Readings in the History of a Region* edited by James E. Wright and Sarah Z. Rosenberg. Lincoln, NE: University of Mid-America, 1979. Pp. 431-441.

"Notes: Why I Live Here." *Northwest America* 1(May, 1979):22.

"Old Man Thomas and the Stuff of History." *Montana Historian* 3(Winter, 1973):21.

"The Opening Door." *University of Montana, President's Newsletter*, Fall, 1968.

"The Other Side of the Montana Fact." *Montana Opinion* 1(June, 1956):25-27.

"The Role of the Museum in the Great Plains." In *Cultural Leadership in the Great Plains: A Report of the Great Plains Conference on Higher Education* edited by Paul G. Ruggiers. Norman: University of Oklahoma, 1957. Pp. 92-99.

"The Sandwich Man: A Hard Role." *Museum News* 52(June, 1974):41-42.

"Surprises for the Museum-Going Vacationist." *New York Times*, May 24, 1959.

"Things Will Never Be the Same." *University (of Montana) Outreach* 1(1976):1-2.

"Timber Depredations on the Montana Public Domain, 1885-1918." Co-authored with Edward Butcher. *Journal of the West* 7(July, 1968):351-362.

"The Tourist and the Museum." *New York Times*, May 14, 1959.

"A Tribute to Dr. Paul C. Phillips." *Montana: Magazine of Western History* 5(Winter, 1955):68.

"Urban and Non-Urban Museums: A Subjective Comparison." *Curator* 3(Winter, 1960):20-25.

"The War of the Copper Kings." In *The Westerners: New York Posse Brand Book* 6(1959):1, 3, 10, 12.

"When Big Money Came to Butte: The Migration of Eastern Capital to Montana." *Pacific Northwest Quarterly* 44(January, 1953):23-29.

"When Copper Was King." *Out West Magazine* 2(November, 1952):26.

"Where Are the Ranch Records?" *Montana Stockgrower* 38(October, 1966):32-33.

Selected Reviews

A History of Phelps Dodge, 1834-1950 by Robert Glass Cleland. *Pacific Historical Review* 21(August, 1952):282-283.

Montana Adventure: The Recollections of Frank B. Linderman by Harold G. Merriam. *Pacific Historical Review* 38(May, 1969):230-231.

The Peaks of Lyell by Geoffrey Blainey. *Pacific Historical Review* 24(November, 1955):412-413.

Miscellaneous

Author, syndicated newspaper series entitled "Montana History" (10 weeks).

Editor, 1951-1957, *Montana: Magazine of Western History*.

Founder (1959), supervising editor (1959-1960), and contributor (1959-1960), *Our Town*.

Script writer for films and television: "Montana As Science Sees It" (1977); "The Economics and the Myth: A History of the Western Cattle Industry" (1978); "The Blue Sky Blues" (1979).

Studies of K. Ross Toole

Caughey, John W. Review of *Probing the American West* edited by K. Ross Toole *et al. American Historical Review* 68(July, 1963):1081-1082.

Elliot, Russell R. Review of *A History of Montana* by K. Ross Toole and Merrill G. Burlingame. *Mississippi Valley Historical Review* 46(December, 1959):540-541.

Fritz, Harry W. "An Uncommon Man: K. Ross Toole." In *Montana and the West: Essays in Honor of K. Ross Toole* edited by Rex C. Myers and Harry W. Fritz. Boulder, CO: Pruett Publishing Co., 1984. Pp. 1-15.

Lamm, Richard D., and G. Michael McCarthy. *The Angry West*. Boston: Houghton Mifflin Co., 1982.

Larson, T. A. Review of *A History of Montana* by K. Ross Toole and Merrill G. Burlingame. *Pacific Historical Review* 28(November, 1959):403-404.

__________. Review of *Twentieth Century Montana: A State of Extremes* compiled by K. Ross Toole. *American West* 10(March, 1973):52.

McAvoy, Thomas T. Review of *Probing the American West* edited by K. Ross Toole *et al.* *Indiana Magazine of History* 59(March, 1963):73.

Myers, Rex C., and Harry W. Fritz, eds. *Montana and the West: Essays in Honor of K. Ross Toole.* Boulder, CO: Pruett Publishing Co., 1984.

Parker, Watson. Review of *Twentieth Century Montana: A State of Extremes* compiled by K. Ross Toole. *Journal of the West* 11(October, 1972):683.

Pomeroy, Earl. Review of *Probing the American West* edited by K. Ross Toole *et al.* *Pacific Historical Review* 32(May, 1963):191-193.

Rollins, George W. Review of *Twentieth Century Montana: A State of Extremes* compiled by K. Ross Toole. *Western Historical Quarterly* 5(April, 1974):210-212.

Ruetten, Richard T. Review of *Twentieth Century Montana: A State of Extremes* compiled by K. Ross Toole. *Pacific Historical Review* 42(August, 1973):431-432.

Smith, Robert T. Review of *Montana and the West: Essays in Honor of K. Ross Toole* edited by Rex C. Myers and Harry W. Fritz. *Western Historical Quarterly* 17(April, 1986):224-225.

Winther, Oscar O. Review of *Probing the American West* edited by K. Ross Toole *et al.* *American West* 1(September, 1964):65.

50

FREDERICK JACKSON TURNER

by Richard White

Biography

What makes the career of Frederick Jackson Turner historically significant is precisely what would make his life seem commonplace today. Turner was an academic historian of middle-class origins and progressive sympathies whose professional career centered on university teaching. Turner taught at the history departments of the University of Wisconsin (1885-1910) and Harvard University (1910-1924) with a final research appointment at the Huntington Library (1927-1932). He never seems to have aspired to be anything more than a professional historian and a university professor. If he had any ambitions for political office, they were satisfied by a term as president of the American Historical Association (see *Frederick Jackson Turner: Historian, Scholar, Teacher*). What made such a career seem new in the late nineteenth and early twentieth centuries was precisely its narrow professional focus, its dependence on universities and professional organizations, and its devotion to a history aimed more at specialists than the general public (although, in this respect, Turner probably had no idea how far academic historians would go).

Born on November 14, 1861, Turner lived during a period in which academics had just begun to dominate the writing of history, and the teaching of history had only recently become a distinct profession. In the mid-nineteenth century the study of history remained a genteel accomplishment rather than a profession (*Progressive Historians*, pp. 1-43, 69, 85). Historians tended to stress, some with very good reason, their breeding more than their research. Even Henry Adams, by far the most eminent and accomplished historian of his generation, was the grandson and great-grandson of presidents, and the writing of history was hardly his career in any conventional sense. This older idea of history as either an adjunct to or a preparation for other careers persevered in Turner's own generation. Two contemporaries who might loosely be called historians--Woodrow Wilson and Theodore Roosevelt--served as presidents not of the

American Historical Association but of the United States. In distinction Turner, as his biographer, Ray Allen Billington, has emphasized, was above all a professor. It is within the prosaic boundaries of the university that his life and work is best understood (*Frederick Jackson Turner*, p. vi).

In pursuing his career Turner helped to create the day-to-day world that conditioned the lives and work of later academic historians. As department chairman at the University of Wisconsin (1891-1910), he shaped one of the first modern history departments in an American state university. As a leading member and president of the American Historical Association (1909-1910), he helped to build a major professional organization. Finally, as a graduate instructor without equal in his time (at least by the testimony of his students), he did much to shape graduate instruction in history and thus the teaching of American history for more than a generation. Taken as a whole, these activities probably influenced the kind of history written in this country almost as thoroughly as did Turner's own writing (pp. 88-97, 242-250, 287-290, 329-343; *American Masters*, pp. 273-295; *Pacific Historical Review* 23:184-208).

As a writer, it was Turner's frontier thesis that made him famous, but despite his biographer's efforts to bathe his boyhood in the afterglow of the Wisconsin frontier, this was a product of his intellectual life, not a residue of his youth in Portage, Wisconsin, during the 1860s and 1870s (*Frederick Jackson Turner*, p. 11). The argument that had Turner been city-born he would never have evolved his frontier thesis both exaggerates the frontier elements of Portage and ignores the wider context of Turner's outlook. Such personal qualities as Turner's love of the outdoors or his "Emersonian" fascination with the wilderness seem more in harmony with the romantic East than with the West, while his passionate devotion to hunting and fishing was, in this period, as congenial to the outlook of the eastern Boone & Crockett Club as to a small town upbringing in Portage. If the frontier elements of his Wisconsin upbringing can be easily exaggerated, the sectional influences emphasized by Richard Hofstadter deserve greater attention. Turner was a son of the Middle West in its most vital and self-confident period, and this is everywhere reflected in his work. The West for Turner, in so far as it was a specific place at all, was the Midwest; the Far West usually concerned him only as an afterthought (*Progressive Historians*, pp. 77-78).

The blending of Turner's midwestern interests with academic history took place both at the University of Wisconsin, where Turner received both his B.A. and M.A., and at the Johns Hopkins University, where he participated for a single year (1888-1889) in the famous seminars of Herbert Baxter Adams and received his Ph.D. After his acquisition of the Ph.D., the key credential of the new academic historians, Turner's personal and professional fortunes rose steadily through the 1890s. He married Mae Sherwood in 1889, and together they had three children. Turner was promoted to professor at Wisconsin in 1891 and made department chair the same year. As a scholar, Turner's progress was not so rapid. Probably no major historian has based his reputation on so little published work, but Turner did write steadily during this period. Retrospectively, of course, the highlight of these years was the delivery of his paper on "The Significance of the Frontier in American History" at the Columbian Exhibition at Chicago in July of 1893. The paper made a small splash that produced big ripples, and Turner's reputation and influence increased as the paper gained recognition over the next decade (*Frederick Jackson Turner*, pp. 24-81, 124-131, 184-208).

The 1890s were probably the happiest and certainly the most intellectually fruitful decade of Turner's life, but they ended in tragedy. In 1899 Turner's youngest daughter, Mae Sherwood Turner, died of diphtheria, and in October, his only son, Jackson Allen Turner, died of a ruptured appendix. It took Turner years to recover from the blows, and writing, always a burden, became for a period nearly impossible (pp. 153-159).

Turner was hardly a broken man, but scholarly writing, including the only monograph he published during his lifetime, *The Rise of the New West* (1906), came painfully. His editor, Albert B. Hart, later wrote that: "It ought to be carved on my tombstone that I was the only man in the world that secured what might be classed an adequate volume from Turner (p. 222)." Much of his energy during the first decade of the century continued to go into concerns other than scholarship. He became a major figure in the fight to reform college football in the early twentieth century. He took an active role in defending the University of Wisconsin against those who wished to purge it of radicals and fought against those public officials who denied that there was any place for humanistic research in a state-funded university. And, finally, he was a leading figure in the American Historical Association.

Few of these efforts ended well. There were only token reforms in college football; the American Historical Association eventually exploded into conflict as younger scholars attacked the influential clique of which Turner was a part; and Turner felt that the political opponents of the university who denounced the release time granted him for research made his position there untenable. He resigned his position at Wisconsin to begin teaching at Harvard in 1910 (pp. 263-279; 292-307; 337-343). Turner finished his teaching career at Harvard, but it was as much a case of voluntary exile as a significant advance in his career. He was, he said, in 1913 "still a western man in all but my place of residence" (*Progressive Historians*, p. 80).

The Harvard years often found Turner ill and vaguely discontented. His work during the period often speaks better of his patriotism than his scholarship (*Frederick Jackson Turner*, pp. 308-336, 364-390). Turner had long matched his professional concerns with American ideals and institutions with an ardent enthusiasm for America and American institutions that fired the best of his history. With the outbreak of World War I, however, Turner the patriot and Turner the historian fell into conflict. In 1917 Turner, like the nation, dramatically changed from a wary isolationist to a belligerent interventionist, but, given his age and health, Turner had only scholarship to put at the service of his country. In helping to organize the National Board for Historical Services he chose a particularly troublesome means of doing do. Ostensibly an organization dedicated to keeping alive traditional values and ideals, the board looked to many of his colleagues suspiciously like a government propoganda tool (pp. 347-349). His health, never good, declined rather steadily during these years, leaving him even less time for writing the major work on sectionalism which he had been planning and researching since the turn of the century. He retired from Harvard with few regrets in 1924, intending to spend his last years in Wisconsin. The winters there proved too hard on the now chronically ill Turner, however, and in 1927 he accepted a position as senior research associate at the Huntington Library, where he worked until his death in 1932 (pp. 391-419).

Themes

As an American historian, Frederick Jackson Turner is remembered primarily for his frontier thesis and secondarily for his work on sectionalism. Centainly any consideration of Turner's work must concentrate on his ideas about the frontier and sections, but Turner's significance both as a historian and as an American intellectual should not rise or fall with these particular interpretations of American history. Turner thought deeply about history, and if most historians no longer accept his analysis of the American past, the way in which he approached the past continues to illuminate the history of the nation, his own time, and the study of history itself. Turner's theories on the frontier and on sections form avenues into enduring problems of American development. These roads may today seem poorly constructed and seldom traveled, but the destinations Turner sought are as alluring and important as ever.

Following Turner's death, some scholars have tended to divide Turner's thought into his work on the frontier and his work on sections. Major differences undeniably exist. More forcefully stated than rigorously developed, the frontier thesis was a product of Turner's essays; he lavished two books as well as numerous essays on sectionalism, but there is no "sectional thesis" that can be stated with anything like the cogency and force of the frontier thesis. Turner's later concern with sectionalism cannot, however, be taken as a sharp break in his historical concerns. It is best understood as a logical extension of themes first set forth in his frontier thesis and can only be fully grasped through these themes (p. 183; *New England Quarterly* 16:224-255; *Progressive Historians*, p. 103).

The frontier thesis, as first and most clearly stated by Turner, was that "The existence of an area of free land, its continuous recession, and the advance of American settlement westward, explains American development" (*The Frontier in American History*, p. 1). Certainly this formulation was an overstatement, but it was, nonetheless, a brilliant overstatement. Precisely because it was so sweeping, monocausal, and without nuance, it compelled attention. Turner summoned the frontier from the dim historical backcountry and made it the key to reinterpreting American history as a whole.

Like any historical explanation that commands wide attention, Turner's frontier thesis spoke as much to contemporary issues, both scholarly and public, as it did to the past. By insisting on the special American qualities derived from the frontier, Turner was breaking with a reigning academic orthodoxy--the germ theory--but it was an orthodoxy already under attack. The germ theory postulated an American history based on the development of European "seeds" which, once carried to this side of the Atlantic, replicated ancient Teutonic institutions. The theory was most effectively promoted in the Johns Hopkins seminars of Herbert Baxter Adams, and Turner himself referred favorably to it in an early essay even as he sought to modify its emphasis. Well before Turner's arrival, however, two other products of the seminar, J. Franklin Jameson and Charles McLean Andrews, had already effectively begun to attack the idea that American institutions grew out of Teutonic germs. Turner's own break was thus neither particularly early nor unique (*American Historical Review* 89:1225-1239; *Selected Essays*, p. 30).

Turner's substitution of the frontier and free land for Teutonic germs as the determinative factors in American history is also understandable within the intellectual context of the 1890s. As Lee Benson has demonstrated, the idea that arable lands available for homesteading would soon be exhausted was widely, if loosely, discussed at the time (*Turner and Beard*, pp. 5-10; *The Frontier*, pp. 4-8). Turner took this popular concern and linked it to the ideas of the Italian economist Achille Loria. Loria asserted that the existence of free land was the single critical force in shaping economic life and, therefore, political and social life. According to Loria, only a simple economy could exist as long as workers could easily take possession of the soil and add their labor to it. No land in the United States, of course, was literally free. Even homesteaders had to pay fees, but Turner apparently interpreted Loria's free land within the conventional economic discourse of the time. "Free land" was land so economically marginal, either from lack of fertility or distance from markets, that purchasers could obtain it for a pittance because the land returned only actual capital or labor expended on it. It yielded no profit or "rent." As long as such land existed, a simple economy with an egalitarian political and social structure would also exist (*Frederick Jackson Turner*, pp. 78-79).

This idea became the foundation for Turner's own theory, but he did more than copy it. His formulation was both more complex and more contradictory than Loria's. In analyzing the results of free land in American history, Turner introduced a series of subsidiary themes which would appear repeatedly in his work. The first of these was that the American experience replicated the stages of a universal history of society: it began when population was sparse and land abundant and culminated in a populous industrial society. For Turner, like John Locke before him, the whole world had once been America. Turner, later so closely associated with American exceptionalism, quoted Loria approvingly that in the United States, "the land which has no history reveals luminously the course of universal history" (*The Frontier in American History*, p. 11).

When coupled with the crude borrowings from evolutionary thought popular in the social sciences of the time, universal history provided Turner with his repeated images of society retreating to a primitive state only to recapitulate subsequent social development (*Rise of New West*, pp. 88-89, 134).

In this retreat to the primitive Turner found a second theme which somewhat contradicts and modifies the first. The United States, although a replication of universal history, also became exceptional and fundamentally different from Europe because of the confrontation of settlers with the American environment. The source of American uniqueness was the place itself. According to Turner, society on the frontier initially was overwhelmed by an environment that Turner always characterized as wilderness (p. 111): "Environment is too strong for the man. He must accept the conditions it furnishes or perish" (*The Frontier in American History*, p. 4).

Turner's environmentalism allowed him to present American distinctiveness as a counterweight to universal history, but when Turner initially listed the ways that the wilderness had changed the pioneers, he very clearly confused environment and culture. In Turner's examples, frontiersmen did not accept what the environment offered; instead they accepted what Indian cultures offered. Canoes, hunting shirts, moccasins, and war cries were not natural products of the forest. Birch trees and deer were natural to the forest. Canoes and moccasins were not. Culture, not wilderness, created them (p. 4).

This initial confusion of nature and culture brought Turner stumbling as it were into his third theme: the relationship of culture to material conditions. Turner rarely uses the word culture in his later work, instead he writes of ideals--nationalism, individualism, democracy, equality. By ideals he meant the concepts by which Americans organized and understood their public life; such concepts are an important part of what scholars now label American culture.

Taken as a whole, Turner's frontier essay provided a powerful but confusing formulation. Turner was the American exceptionalist who saw the national experience as a replication of universal history. He was an economic determinist and materialist whose real concern was ideals. Finally, he was an environmental determinist who confused culture and environment.

Analysis

In his contraditions Turner found a lifetime of fruitful work as a historian. The basic themes he outlined with such vigor and lack of consistency in his most famous essay continued to drive his later work. His frontier thesis had only scouted the historical terrain. Turner had asserted an ill-defined but supposedly critical relationship between three things: free lands as an economic phenomenon, a "wilderness" environment, and the cultural values that guided American public life. He spent the rest of his life trying to understand the problems he had raised under the guise of a solution.

In a sense, Turner, having in his original frontier essay reached the conclusion that the material life of the frontier had produced distinctive American cultural traits, could not accept the implications of his own unmodified theory. The frontier thesis originally argued that American democracy resulted from the operation of universal laws. By creating economic equality, free lands promoted political equality, democracy, and individualism. But since free lands were only a transitory stage in an ongoing historical process, these ideals, too, would vanish. European conditions would inevitably replicate themselves in the United States. Turner's theory thus explained the origins of American culture while simultaneously predicting its inexorable and relatively rapid demise. Turner, the patriot, never reconciled himself to American ideals being as transitory as the free lands he believed had produced them (*Significance of Sections*, pp. 86-90).

Turner's original formulation created his dilemma, but the theory's contradictions also offered him an avenue of escape. Because Turner had presented the United States both as a window into a universal past and also as a new and unique product of a wilderness encounter, he could, without abandoning his frontier thesis, choose to present the United States as a "new chapter in man's struggle for a higher type of society" rather than as a transitory stage in universal history (*The Frontier in American History*, p. 261). The frontier presented an opportunity that could "never again come to the sons of men," but one which, once seized, might have lasting consequences (p. 261).

Pursuing this emphasis obviously involved Turner in a rather drastic revision of his ideas on universal history, but it also necessarily forced changes in his approach to historical causation. His later theoretical formulations would not be the result of abstract thought; rather they were products of his struggle with the concrete problem of maintaining democratic ideals once free land was exhausted. Since the frontier thesis argued that material conditions produced cultural beliefs, new conditions would obviously produce a new culture. Rather than accept this, Turner modified his ideas on historical causation. Turner was not, it must be emphasized, altering his ideas on what were the significant historical forces. On this he was consistent. He never abandoned his conviction that "social and economic tendencies" were the "vital forces that work beneath the surface and dominate the external form" (p. 323).

Throughout his career Turner puzzled over the relationship of these forces. The younger Turner clearly thought that economics and the environment determined all else. He wrote of American history being "determined by natural conditions" and of free lands having "determined the larger lines of American development (*Significance of Sections*, pp. 86, 90). This emphasis on free lands tilted Turner toward economic determinism. Free lands created economic equality, and this, in turn, promoted political equality, democracy, and individualism (*Frontier and Section*, p. 30).

Turner of the early essays clearly seems a determinist, and numerous historians have read him this way, but the Turner his graduate students remembered was a historian who rejected simple determinisms. Their memories deserve some credit since a man who resorted to both economic and environmental determinism could not have held either very deeply. Certainly the Turner of the later essays has turned away from ultimate laws. He argues for multiple causation and "the study of forces that operate and interplay in the making of society" (*The Frontier in American History*, p. 334). Turner came to contend that economic forces were not as preeminent as he had earlier indicated and thus could not infallibly predict historical change. Free land and the environment remained critical, but they were now influences not determinants. In his essay on "Geographical Influences," for example, Turner warned "there is not absolute geographical control" and trying to understand the geographical distribution of capitalism demanded "the use of the multiple hypothesis." When compared to the more extreme environmental determinists of the period, Turner was quite moderate. He concluded his final attempt to formulate an explanation of sectional voting patterns by stating flatly that exceptions "prevent the historian from formulating a law of political distribution on physical or economic grounds" (*Significance of Sections*, pp. 191-192).

Turner's partial retreat from materialism was necessary if the ideals produced by his frontier were to survive the passing of the free lands. Turner's interest in American political ideals--democracy, political equality, and individualism--never waned, but in his mature work the emphasis is on how they could be preserved rather than on how they originated. It is this preoccupation with preserving culture or ideals that makes Turner's turn toward sectionalism in his twentieth-century scholarship a logical extension of his early work on the frontier. The frontier for Turner had not been a particular place, but "a form of society" that occurred wherever old institutions came into contact with free land. It was a stage in society and so must pass (*The Frontier in American History*, p. 205). The section, however, was a place with relatively permanent topography, soil types, vegetation and climate, and also, according to Turner, with a distinctive ethnic make up or, in his terms, with differing racial stocks. The section had a solidity and permanence that the frontier lacked (p. 155; *Signficance of Sections*, p. 183).

The frontier produced American ideals, while the sections--particularly the Midwest--preserved them. In making this argument, Turner relies on the double significance he had given land in his original essay. Land as a "free" commodity was not unique to the United States, and Turner continued to assert that "free" lands in this universal sense produced economic equality on the frontier which in turn yielded American political ideals. Land as a particular place in an American landscape was, however, unique, and Turner went on to argue that these specific American environments had altered the original equality in complex ways (*Rise of New West*, pp. 67-95; *United States, 1830-1850*, pp. 1-31).

Here one should note in passing a seemingly remarkable omission in Turner's work. Turner at no time provides any evidence that free lands had actually produced economic equality. He asserted it repeatedly. Vacant lands, he claimed, "broke down social distinctions in the West, and by causing economic equality, they promoted political equality and democracy" (*Significance of Sections*, p. 90). He wrote that the "early society of the Middle West was not a complex, highly differential and organized society. Almost every family was a self-sufficing unit, and liberty and equality flourished" (*The Frontier in American History*, p. 153). Or, as he puts it elsewhere, "Where everybody could have a farm, almost for taking it, economic equality easily resulted and this involved political equality" (p. 212). Studies have since demonstrated that the distribution of wealth on the frontier was very similar to the distribution elsewhere in the country. Turner may have realized how weak his ground was on this issue, because he eventually backed away from economic equality per se. He retreated to an assertion that he had previously often coupled with his claim of economic equality; he argued that pioneers perceived of the West as a place of equal opportunity rather than of actual equality. It was, he wrote in his last book, a society "based upon the idea of the fair chance for all men, not on the conception of leveling by arbitrary methods and especially by law." (*United States, 1830-1850*, p. 20).

Economic equality is measurable; equal opportunity, particularly a perception of economic opportunity, is not. In shifting his claim from western equality to western opportunity, Turner was doing more than escaping the problem of evidence for his assertions. Far more significantly, he was making perceptions and ideals rather than material facts the critical elements in his thinking.

Turner's partial shift away from materialism toward idealism is marked in his later work. Ideals took on a life of their own. They sprang from the frontier, but no longer depended on it. They survived in his sections--particularly in the Midwest--even after the frontier had passed. As Turner wrote in "The Middle West":

> The ideals of equality, freedom of opportunity, faith in the common man are deep rooted in all of the Middle West. . . . The peculiar democracy of the frontier has passed away with the conditions that produced it; but the democratic aspirations remain. They are held with passionate determination (*The Frontier in American History*, p. 155).

This passionate determination changed everything. Turner had condescended to the Populists in his first frontier essay as hopeless throwbacks to a simpler world. By 1901 he has reincarnated the Populist as a pioneer standing on the prairies of Kansas "striving to adjust present conditions to his old ideals." Here is an odd twist in environmental or economic determinism. "Passionate determination" alone now challenged changing economic conditions. Turner still attributes particular Populist positions to the environment ("the physiographic province itself decreed that the destiny of this new frontier should be social rather than individual"), but ideals produced by the frontier had nevertheless taken on an independent life (pp. 155, 258).

The struggle for the preservation of frontier ideals in particular sections became an underlying theme in the collection of essays Turner eventually gathered as *The Frontier in American History*. In "The Significance of the Mississippi Valley in American History" (1909-1910), Turner forthrightly asks if "the Mississippi Valley [has] a permanent contribution to make to American society, or is it to be adjusted into a type characteristically Eastern and European?" For Turner it was "ideals" that were "the most significant fact in the Mississippi Valley." The real question became "Can these ideals of individualism and democracy be reconciled and applied to the twentieth century type of civilization?" Here, in bastions created not only by geography but by the cultural legacy of earlier revolts, Turner thought democracy could withstand the modern forces attacking it. Implicit in his answer was the conviction that ideals had become to a large degree independent of the conditions that produced them. In formulating both his question and his answer in this manner, Turner's history had taken a turn away from the dictation of material forces toward a more complex view of the reciprocal influences of culture and material life (pp. 202, 204).

Looked at in this way, sectionalism was integral to Turner's later thought. He had made the section a vehicle for carrying forward his ideas on the relationship between culture and environment. Where Turner's frontier environment in his 1893 paper had transformed the pioneer, Turner's sections now balanced these "transforming influences" with "conservative" tendencies that preserved older "types." The meeting of environment and "racial stocks" produced distinctive regional cultures. The section thus provided more permanence than the transitory frontier; here was a place where particular American ideals could take root and thrive after the frontier and free land had vanished (p. 239).

Turner's attempts to give a precise statement to how these complex relations had produced sections and how sections had shaped American history was the work not only of his later essays but also of his only two scholarly monographs: *The Rise of the New West* (1906) and *The United States, 1830-1850: The Nation and Its Sections* (1935). Both were ambitious books; both, in terms of their larger aims, were failures.

In *The Rise of the New West* Turner attempts to explain the interaction of economics and geography--"the vast physiographic provinces"--which formed the sections and shaped the political attitudes of their populations and leaders. Turner reiterated the classic premises of his frontier thesis. American democracy arose in the West; it "came strong and full of life from the American forest" to become the dominant force in American life. In its frontier stage, the West, for all the differences between its northern and southern components, "possessed a fundamental unity in its democratic ideals." Turner traveled easily over this familiar ground, but he did less well in meeting the real challenge of the book: explaining how sections at once altered and preserved this frontier heritage, and how this heritage--on the level of political ideals--spread, albeit unequally, throughout the nation (pp. 6, 68-69, 72).

Turner employed two techniques in answering these questions. The first, an approach he would repeat in his second book, was to use a series of symbolic sketches of representative political leaders: Jackson was the "west itself," Calhoun was the South, Adams and Webster were New England. Turner justified this approach, so different from his usual social and economic emphasis, by insisting that these men were important because they are expressions of their sections, but what this meant was never clear. New England was hardly a collection of little Adamses nor was the West Andrew Jackson writ large. All Turner really did was select aspects of the personalities and positions of these men and then ascribe them to their sections. Turner's second technique was more rigorous, but his ambitions exceeded the tools at his disposal. Turner sought to determine sectional divisions and values by charting the distribution of votes in presidential elections and congressional votes on particular issues. The results were not impressive. Not only are the measurements statistically primitive, but Turner's own data did not always support his sectional generalizations. His analysis of votes sometimes revealed united sections; more often, his sections divided. And as he admitted, in many elections, issues were not clearly enough drawn to make sectional analysis possible (pp. 172-198).

Turner's second book, a product of his old age, lacked the grace and aphoristic flair of most of his writing. As published, it was a ponderous journey through the sectional conflicts of the two decades between 1830 and 1850, but with all its faults it is an underrated book. In it Turner offered a far more elaborate discussion of how cultural, economic, and environmental factors interacted to create and subdivide sections than he had ever done before. Turner begins with environmental influences--the "design made by physical geography was reflected in human geography"--but he cautioned that numerous exceptions prevented historians from formulating laws of political behavior based on physical or economic grounds. Cultural and social factors now complicated Turner's schema. Calvinism not only helped shape New England, but settlers from that region carried it west to influence the emerging Northwest. Similarly, in the South, Turner argued that it was a social institution--slavery--that united a region which climate and geography otherwise separated into two different sections. And in the country as a whole, party politics acted to provide a "flexible bond of union" (pp. 2-13, 41-43, 146).

How these various factors combined to shape a section, however, remained elusive. Turner's major gauge of sectionalism was politics, but sections themselves lacked political unanimity and so Turner was forced to delineate regions within sections and here he fell into a morass. Since party votes even in a region were often close, he contended that "the nuclear portions of these areas--those portions that carried the characteristics of the region to the highest point--were politically homogeneous "according to the quality of the region." What determined quality? "Several factors: not only soil and illiteracy, but also communication, inheritance, personal leadership, etc., must be considered" (p. 232).

The farther Turner traveled from simple determinisms, the less clear the determinants of a section's boundaries became. When Turner attempted to demonstrate the power of political sectionalism, the argument grew even denser. Since an analysis of congressional votes on specific issues failed to reflect consistent political sectionalism, Turner contended that it lurked deeper still, hidden among the votes of congressional committees. Track it as he would, sectionalism never emerged clearly from the political thicket where Turner claimed to have cornered it. At times Turner seemed to give up the chase entirely, and his book lapsed into traditional political narrative (p. 381).

Turner never was able to elucidate sectionalism with enough strength and clarity so that sections could carry the intellectual freight he intended for them. Sectionalism, as Turner developed it, did not provide a convincing explanation of the relationship between material and cultural factors in American history, nor did it explain how cultural ideals survived in different forms in different sections. And perhaps the task was beyond Turner or any scholar of his period. Turner was, in a sense, a prisoner of his times. He might modify his materialism, but he never escaped the confining bounds of biological analogies which made understanding social change on its own terms almost impossible. For all his efforts to work out a model of a multicausal history, for all his emphasis on ideals, he could not stop conceiving of society as an organism and redefining social change as a mere adaptation. New southern lands, for example, produced a seemingly biocultural result. The lands produced "greater energy and initiative," and this in turn transformed a social institution, slavery, from a patriarchal to a commercial form. This, coming full circle, became evidence for the modification of people--the "original stock"--in a new environment. That people and societies "adapt" is, of course, always true in the sense that any person or society radically unsuited to its environment will not survive. The natural environment is, however, usually generous enough to allow a wide variety of options for human societies and, even more critically, human beings can alter their environment. Turner could have with more precision said that slavery transformed the southern environment. Turner recognized that human beings changed the environment, but, conceiving of society as an organism, he continued to regard all change as adaptation. He attached little analytical significance to changes humans made in the environment itself (*Significance of Section*, p. 289; *The Frontier in American History*, p. 139).

This intellectual roadblock stymied Turner. Replacing determinants with influences and asserting that many factors shape human history is an eminently safe and reasonable position, but unless the relationship of these factors is stated with some precision, little is gained. Turner's biological analogies were neither precise, new, nor convincing.

Turner's remarkable intellectual edifice for American history did not long survive him. Once the attack began, much of the frontier thesis crumbled quickly. His evidentiary foundations were weak, his claims were too sweeping, and the comparative basis of the thesis was virtually nonexistent. Eventual testing of Turner's generalizations has reduced most of them to rubble (*Frederick Jackson Turner*, pp. 449-472; *Progressive Historians*, pp. 118-164). And yet, nearly a century after the publication of the frontier thesis, Turner still commands respect. Most historians admit that the frontier certainly had *something* to do with the way in which American society and the American economy developed. And in figuring out what that something might be, Turner's thought remains the departure point. He does not provide the answers, but the questions remain his.

As effective as they were against the specifics of his frontier thesis, many of Turner's critics have been less impressive when they have attacked his larger plan for interpreting American history. They did him wrong in refusing to view the whole edifice of his thought. Concentrating almost solely on the frontier thesis, they dismissed sectionalism as a failed and oddly quixotic enterprise. Yet to ignore Turner's sectionalism is to ignore the sweep of his ambition. With sectionalism restored, some of the early criticisms of Turner seem almost willfully misplaced. Critics as diverse as Lee Benson and George Pierson have arraigned Turner, on the basis of his early materialism and economic determinism, for ignoring cultural influences, but such charges can be quickly dismissed with evidence from the later Turner. Turner, perhaps more than any other major American historian of his generation, tried to understand both material and cultural life in this country. Turner's persistent attempts in his studies of sectionalism to understand how ideals might survive in altered material circumstances indeed anticipated some other arguments later made against the frontier thesis. Critics wondered why, if free lands alone produced Turner's American ideals, other countries with frontiers and free lands did not develop them too? Also why did countries with neither free lands nor frontiers become democratic? Turner escaped the full impact of these objections in his later work on sections where he gave democratic and egalitarian ideals more complex origins, and made their spread and survival to other areas a major concern (*Turner and the Sociology of Frontier*, pp. 15-42; *The Frontier in American History*, pp. 6, 9).

Other larger criticisms of Turner, however, do take his work as a whole and are not so easily escaped. Richard Hofstadter delivered one of the most eloquent and telling critiques when he asked why so much is missing from Turner's history. Turner's West largely ignores Indians, Mexican-Americans, environmental destruction, and greed. The point, Hofstadter stresses, was not to arouse shame or to pick moral quarrels with ancestors, but rather "that the anguish of history, as well as its romance and charm, is there for the historian who responds to it" (*Progressive Historians*, p. 105). Turner's patriotic intent, his search for American identity, in the end robbed his history of the tragedy necessary to put its triumphs in context.

Having said all that, having granted the evidentiary and analytical failures, Turner remains the major frontier historian in large part because he never considered himself merely a historian of the West. He was first and foremost an American historian. He set out not just to explain problems in western development but instead larger questions of American development. He sought to explain his country to himself and his contemporaries. He asked big questions and he thought deeply about their answers. If he now seems on close examination too celebratory and too simple, the wider sweep of his work still looks impressive. Turner opened doors not just to major questions in America's past but also to the nature of history itself. He was a new historian when the "new history" was actually new. Although his work did not always follow his own strictures, he from the beginning stressed underlying structural changes and not just political narrative. He wanted a history of peoples and not simply of great men. But beyond that he wanted to know the sources of change; the relationships between human cultures and the physical world in which they existed, the relationship between how people earned their livings and how they spent the rest of their lives. The real vigor of his western history originated in these basic questions that powered his analysis. The specific interpretations Turner offers may have failed, but his true legacy is his approach to history itself. Carl Becker, perhaps the best of Turner's remarkable graduate students, memorialized Turner while he still lived in a way that admirably summarizes his signifiance as a historian:

> For my part, I do not ask of any historian more than this, that he should have exerted in his generation a notable influence upon many scholars in humanistic study. That is enough, and this, I think, must be accorded Turner (*American Masters*, p. 317).

Bibliography

Books

The Character and Influence of the Indian Trade in Wisconsin: A Study of the Trading Post as an Institution. Baltimore, MD: Johns Hopkins University Press, 1890.

The Frontier in American History. New York: Henry Holt & Co., 1920.

Guide to the Study and Reading of American History. Co-authored with Edward Channing and Albert Bushnell Hart. Boston: Ginn & Co., 1912.

List of References on the History of the West: List of References in History 17: History of the West. Editor. Cambridge, MA: Harvard University Press, 1911; second edition, 1913; third edition, 1915; fourth edition co-edited with Frederick Merk, 1922; fifth edition co-edited with Frederick Merk, 1928.

Rise of the New West, 1819-1829. New York: Harper & Bros., 1906.

The Significance of Sections in American History. Introduction by Max Farrand. New York: Henry Holt & Co., 1932.

The United States, 1830-1850: The Nation and Its Sections. New York: Henry Holt & Co., 1935.

Articles and Pamphlets

"American Development, 1789-1829: Syllabus of a Course of Six Lectures" [pamphlet]. Madison: Tracy, Gibbs & Co., 1895. Pp. 1-14.

"American Historical Review: An Historical Statement Concerning the American HIstorical Review" [pamphlet]. Washington, DC: American Historical Association, 1915. Pp. 1-8.

"Architecture through Oppression." *University Press* (Madison, WS), June 21, 1884, p. 12.

"Carondelet on the Defense of Louisiana, 1794." Editor. *American Historical Review* 2(April, 1897):474-505.

"The Character and Influence of the Fur Trade in Wisconsin." In State Historical Society of Wisconsin, *Proceedings*, 1888. Madison: State Historical Society of Wisconsin, 1889. 36:52-98.

"The Children of the Pioneers." *Yale Review* 15(July, 1926):645-670. Reprint. *The Significance of Sections in American History*. New York: Henry Holt & Co., 1932. Chapter 10.

"[Clark-Genet Correspondence]: Selections from the Draper Collection in the Possession of the State Historical Society of Wisconsin, to Elucidate the Proposed French Expedition under George Rogers Clark against Louisiana in the Years 1793-1794." Editor. In *Annual Report, American Historical Association, 1896*. Washington, DC: Government Printing Office, 1897. 1:930-1107.

"The Colonization of the West, 1820-1830." *American Historical Review* 11(January, 1906):303-327.

"Contributions of the West to American Democracy." *Atlantic Monthly* 91(January, 1903):83-96. Reprint. *American Ideals* edited by Norman Forester and W. W. Pierson, Jr. Boston: Houghton Mifflin, 1917. Pp. 72-97; *The Frontier in American History*. New York: Henry Holt & Co., 1920. Chapter 9.

"Correspondence of the French Ministers to the United States, 1791-1797." Editor. In *Annual Report, American Historical Association, 1903*. Washington, DC: Government Printing Office, 1904. 2:1-1110.

"The Democratic Education of the Middle West." *World's Work* 6(August, 1903):3754-3759.

"The Development of American Society." *Alumni Quarterly* (University of Illinois) 2(July, 1908):120-136.

"The Diplomatic Contest for the Mississippi Valley." *Atlantic Monthly* 93(May, 1904):676-691 and (June, 1904):807-817.

"Documents on the Blount Conspiracy, 1795-1797." Editor. *American Historical Review* 10(April, 1905):574-606.

"Documents on the Relations of France to Louisiana, 1792-1795." Editor. *American Historical Review* 3(April, 1898):490-516.

"Dominant Forces in Western Life." *Atlantic Monthly* 79(April, 1897):433-443. Reprint. *The Frontier in American History*. New York: Henry Holt & Co., 1920. Chapter 8.

"Editor's Note." In *The Geographical Distribution of the Vote of the Thirteen States on the Federal Constitution, 1787-1788* by Orin Grant Libby. Madison: University of Wisconsin, 1894. Pp. iii-vii.

"English Policy toward America in 1790-1791." *American Historical Review* 7(July, 1902):706-735 and 8(October, 1902):78-86.

"The Extension Work of the University of Wisconsin." *University Extension: A Monthly Journal Devoted to the Interests of Popular Education* 1(April, 1892):311-324.

"The First Official Frontier of the Massachusetts Bay." In *Publications, Colonial Society of Massachusetts 1913-1924.* Boston: Colonial Society of Massachusetts, 1915. Pp. 250-271. Reprint. *The Frontier in American History.* New York: Henry Holt & Co., 1920. Chapter 2.

""Frontier." In *Johnson's Universal Cyclopaedia.* New York: A. J. Johnson Co., 1894. 3:606-607.

"Frontier in American Development." In *Cyclopedia of American Government* edited by Andrew C. McLaughlin and Albert Bushnell Hart. New York: D. Appleton & Co., 1914. 2:61-64.

"Geographic Sectionalism in American History." *Annals* (Association of American Geographers) 16(June, 1926):85-93. Reprint. *The Significance of Sections in American History.* New York: Henry Holt & Co., 1932. Chapter 7.

"Geographical Influences in American Political History." *Bulletin* (American Geographical Society) 46(August, 1914):591-595. Reprint. *The Significance of Sections in American History.* New York: Henry Holt & Co., 1932. Chapter 6.

"Geographical Interpretations of American History." *Journal of Geography* 4(January, 1905):34-37.

"George Rogers Clark and the Kaskaskia Campaign, 1777-1778." *American Historical Review* 8(April, 1903):491-506.

"Greater New England in the Middle of the Nineteenth Century." In *Proceedings, American Antiquarian Society 1919.* Worcester, MA: American Antiquarian Society, 1919. 29:222-241.

"A Half Century of American Politics, 1789-1840: Syllabus of a Course of Six Lectures" [pamphlet]. Madison, WS: Tracy, Gibbs & Co., 1894. Pp. 1-12.

"The Harvard Commission on Western History." *Harvard Graduates' Magazine* 10(June, 1912:606-611. Reprint. *History Teacher's Magazine* 3(September, 1912):146-147.

"The Historical Library in the University." In *The Dedication of the Library Building May the Seventeenth. . . .* Providence, RI: Brown University, 1905. Pp. 41-58.

"History of the 'Grignon Tract' on the Portage of the Fox and Wisconsin Rivers." *State Register* (Portage, WS), June 23, 1883.

"The Intellectual Influence of the West upon the Nation." *Minnesota Daily* (Minneapolis), June 7, 1900, p. 1.

"Introductory Words." *University Record* (University of Chicago) 6(January, 1902):293-294.

"Is Sectionalism in America Dying Away?" *American Journal of Sociology* 13(March, 1908):661-675. Reprint. *The Significance of Sections in American History.* New York: Henry Holt & Co., 1932. Chapter 11.

"Jefferson to George Rogers Clark, 1783." Editor. *American Historical Review* 3(July, 1898):672-673.

"The Mangourit Correspondence in Respect to Genet's Projected Attack upon the Floridas, 1793-1794." Editor. In *Annual Report, American Historical Association 1897*. Washington, DC: Government Printing Office, 1898. Pp. 569-679.

"The Middle West." *International Monthly* 4(December, 1901):794-820. Reprint. *The Frontier in American History*. New York: Henry Holt & Co., 1920. Chapter 4.

"Middle Western Pioneer Democracy." *Minnesota History Bulletin* 3(August, 1920):393-414. Reprint. *The Frontier in American History*. New York: Henry Holt & Co., 1920. Chapter 13.

"New England, 1830-1850." *Huntington Library Bulletin* 1(May, 1931):153-198. Reprint. *The United States, 1830-1850*. New York: Henry Holt & Co., 1935. Chapter 3.

"The Old West." In State Historical Society of Wisconsin, *Proceedings*, 1909. 56:184-233. Reprint. *The Frontier in American History*. New York: Henry Holt & Co., 1920. Chapter 3; "The Colonial Frontier." In *Readings in the Economic History of American Agriculture* edited by L. B. Schmidt and E. D. Ross. New York: Macmillan, 1925. Pp. 107-125.

"The Origin of Genet's Projected Attack on Louisiana and the Floridas." *American Historical Review* 3(July, 1898):650-671. Reprint. *The Significance of Sections in American History*. New York: Henry Holt & Co., 1932. Chapter 3.

"Outline Studies in the History of the Northwest" [pamphlet]. Chicago: C. H. Kerr & Co., 1888. Pp. 1-12.

"Pioneer Ideals and the State University." *Bulletin* (Indiana University) 8(June, 1910):6-29. Reprint. *The Frontier in American History*. New York: Henry Holt & Co., 1920. Chapter 10.

"The Place of the Ohio Valley in American History." *Ohio Archaeological and Historical Quarterly* 20(January, 1911):32-47. Reprint. *History Teacher's Magazine* 2(March, 1911):147-152; "The Ohio Valley in American History." *The Frontier in American History*. New York: Henry Holt & Co., 1920. Chapter 5.

"The Poet of the Future." *University Press* (Madison, WS), May 26, 1883, p. 4.

"The Policy of France toward the Mississippi Valley in the Period of Washington and Adams." *American Historical Review* 10(January, 1905):249-279. Reprint. *The Significance of Sections in American History*. New York: Henry Holt & Co., 1932. Chapter 5.

"The Problem of the West." *Atlantic Monthly* 78(September, 1896):289-297. Reprint. *The Frontier in American History*. New York: Henry Holt & Co., 1920. Chapter 7.

"Problems in American History." *Aegis* 7(November 4, 1892):48-52.

"__________." In *International Congress of Arts and Science, Universal Exposition, St. Louis, 1904* edited by Hoard J. Rogers. Boston: Houghton Mifflin Co., 1906. Pp. 183-194. Reprint. *The Signif-*

icance of Sections in American History. New York: Henry Holt & Co., 1932. Chapter 1.

"Report of the Conference on the Relation of Geography and History." In *Annual Report, American Historical Association 1907*. Washington, DC: Government Printing Office, 1908. 1:45-48.

"Reuben Gold Thwaites: A Memorial Address." In *Reuben Gold Thwaites*. Madison: State Historical Society of Wisconsin, 1914. Pp. 13-59.

"The Rise and Fall of New France." *Chautauquan* 24(October, 1896):31-34 and (December, 1896):295-300. Reprint. "An Unfamiliar Essay by Frederick J. Turner" edited by Fulmer Mood. *Minnesota History* 18(December, 1937):381-398.

"Sectionalism in the United States." In *Cyclopedia of American Government* edited by Andrew C. McLaughlin and Albert Bushnell Hart. New York: D. Appleton & Co., 1914. 3:280-285.

"Sections and Nation." *Yale Review* 12(October, 1922):1-21. Reprint. *The Significance of Sections in American History*. New York: Henry Holt & Co., 1932. Chapter 12.

"The Significance of History." *Wisconsin Journal of Education* 21(October-November, 1891):230-234, 253-256.

"The Significance of the Frontier in American History." In *Annual Report, American Historical Association 1893*. Washington, DC: Government Printing Office, 1894. Pp. 199-227. Reprint. State Historical Society of Wisconsin, *Proceedings*, 1893. Madison: State Historical Society of Wisconsin, 1894. 41:79-112; and in numerous other publications.

"The Significance of the Louisiana Purchase." *Atlantic Monthly Review of Reviews* 27(May, 1903):578-584.

"The Significance of the Mississippi Valley in American History." In *Proceedings, Mississippi Valley Historical Association 1909-1910*. Cedar Rapids, IA: Torch Press, 1911. 3:159-184. Reprint. *The Frontier in American History*. New York: Henry Holt & Co., 1920. Chapter 6.

"The Significance of the Section in American History." *Wisconsin Magazine of History* 8(March, 1925):255-280. Reprint. *The Significance of Sections in American History*. New York: Henry Holt & Co., 1932. Chapter 2.

"Since the Foundation." In *Publications, Clark University Library*. Worcester, MA: Clark University, 1924. 7:9-29. Reprint. "Since the Foundation of Clark University, 1889-1924." *Historical Outlook* 15(November, 1924):335-342; *The Significance of Sections in American History*. New York: Henry Holt & Co., 1932. Chapter 8.

"Social Forces in American History." *American Historical Review* 16(January, 1911):217-233. Reprint. *Magazine of History* 13(March, 1911):111-118; *The Frontier in American History*. New York: Henry Holt & Co., 1920. Chapter 12.

"The South, 1820-1830." *American Historical Review* 11(April, 1906):559-573.

"Studies of American Immigration." *Chicago Record-Herald*, August 28; September 4, 11, 18, 25; October 16, 1901.

"Suggestive Outlines for the Study of the History of the Middle West, Kentucky, and Tennessee" [pamphlet]. Madison, WS: Democrat Printing Co., 1901. Pp. 1-29.

"Syllabus of a University Extension Course of Six Lectures on the Colonization of North America" [pamphlet]. Madison, WS: Tracy, Gibbs & Co., 1891. Pp. 1-20. Revised reprint. 1893. Pp. 1-28; 1894. Pp. 1-16.

"The Territorial Development of the United States." In *The Harvard Classics University Extension Course I*. Cambridge, MA: Harvard University, 1913. Pp. 35-40.

"Turner's Autobiographic Letter." *Wisconsin Magazine of History* 19(September, 1935):91-103.

"United States--History, 1865-1910." In *Encyclopaedia Britannica.* New York: Cambridge University Press, 1911. 23:711-735. Revised reprint. "From 1865-1910." 1929. 22:810-830.

"The West--1876 and 1926: Its Progress in a Half-Century." *World's Work* 52(July, 1926):319-327. Reprint. *The Significance of Sections in American History*. New York: Henry Holt & Co., 1932. Chapter 9.

"The West and American Ideals." *Washington Historical Quarterly* 5(October, 1914):243-257. Reprint. *The Frontier in American History*. New York: Henry Holt & Co., 1920. Chapter 11.

"The West as a Factor in American Politics." In *Cyclopedia of American Government* edited by Andrew C. McLaughlin and Albert Bushnell Hart. New York: D. Appleton & Co., 1914. 3:668-675.

"The West as a Field for Historical Study." In *Annual Report, American Historical Association 1896*. Washington, DC: Government Printing Office, 1897. 1:281-287. Reprint. State Historical Society of Wisconsin, *Proceedings*, 1897. Madison: State Historical Society of Wisconsin, 1897. 44:107-113.

"Western State-Making in the Revolutionary Era." *American Historical Review* 1(October, 1895):70-87 and 1(January, 1896):251-269. Reprint. *The Significance of Sections in American History*. New York: Henry Holt & Co., 1932. Chapter 4.

"What Others Say: Prof. Turner on Runestones." *Wisconsin State Journal* (Madison), February 10, 1910.

"Wisconsin." In *Encyclopaedia Britannica.* 9th edition. New York: Charles Scribner's Sons, 1888. 24:616-619.

Reviews

The American Revolution, Part I, 1766-1776 by G. O. Trevelyan. *American Historical Review* 5(October, 1899):141-144.

Conquest of the Country Northwest of the River Ohio, 1778-1783; and *Life of Gen. George Rogers Clark* by W. H. English. *American Historical Review* 2(January, 1897):363-366.

Early Western Travels, 1748-1846 edited by Reuben Gold Thwaites. Vols. I-VIII. *The Dial* 37(November, 1904):298-302.

__________. Vols. 5-20. *The Dial* 41(July, 1906):6-10.

The Economic and Social History of New England, 1620-1789 by W. B. Weeden. *Atlantic Monthly* 77(June, 1896):837-844.

Economic History of Virginia in the Seventeenth Century by P. A. Bruce. *Atlantic Monthly* 77(June, 1896):837-844.

English Politics in Early Virginia History by Alexander Brown. *American Historical Review* 7(October, 1901):159-163.

Francis Parkman's Works by Francis Parkman. Vols. I-XII. *The Dial* 25(December, 1889):451-453.

Franklin in France by E. E. Hale and E. E. Hale, Jr. Vol. I. *The Dial* 8(May, 1887):7-10.

__________. Vol. II. *The Dial* 9(December, 1888):204-206.

The Growth of the American Nation by H. P. Judson. *American Historical Review* 1(April, 1896):167-170.

History of Early Steamboat Navigation on the Missouri River: Life and Adventures of Joseph La Barge . . . by Hiram M. Chittenden. *American Historical Review* 11(January, 1906):443-444.

A History of Political Parties in the United States by J. P. Gordy. Vol. I. *Political Science Quarterly* 12(March, 1897):163-164.

A History of the American People by Woodrow Wilson. *American Historical Review* 8(July, 1903):762-765.

History of the Expedition under the Command of Lewis and Clark, to the Sources of the Missouri River, Thence across the Rocky Mountains and down the Columbia River to the Pacific Ocean, Performed during the Years 1804-5-6, by Order of the Government of the United States edited by Elliott Coues. *The Dial* 16(February, 1894):80-82.

History of the New World Called America by E. J. Payne. Vol. I. *The Dial* 13(December, 1892):389-391.

A History of the People of the United States by J. B. McMaster. Vol. IV. *Atlantic Monthly* 77(June, 1896):837-844.

History of the United States from the Compromise of 1850 by J. F. Rhodes. Vol. III. *Atlantic Monthly* 77(June, 1896):837-844. Revised, *Political Science Quarterly* 11(March, 1896):167-170.

History of the United States under the Constitution by James Schouler. *Atlantic Monthly* 77(June, 1896):837-844.

Journal of William Maclay, United States Senator from Pennsylvania, 1789-1791 edited by E. S. Maclay. *The Dial* 12(July, 1891):78-81.

The Middle Period, 1817-1858 by J. W. Burgess. *Educational Review* 14(November, 1897):390-395.

New Light on the Early History of the Greater Northwest: The Manuscript Journals of Alexander Henry . . . and of David Thompson . . . 1799-1814. Exploration and Adventure among the Indians on the Red, Saskatchewan, Missouri, and Columbia Rivers. Edited with Copious Critical Commentary edited by Elliott Coues. *American Historical Review* 3(October, 1897):157-159.

Reconstruction during the Civil War in the United States of America by E. G. Scott. *Atlantic Monthly* 77(June, 1896):837-844.

A Short History of the Mississippi Valley by J. K. Hosmer. *American Historical Review* 7(July, 1901):801-803.

The Story of a Great Court: Being a Sketch History of the Supreme Court of Wisconsin by J. B. Winslow. *American Historical Review* 17(July, 1912):859-860.

A Students' History of the United States by Edward Channing. *Educational Review* 18(October, 1899):301-304.

The Westward Movement by Justin Winsor. *American Historical Review* 3(April, 1898):556-561.

The Winning of the West by Theodore Roosevelt. Vols. I-II. *The Dial* 10(August, 1899):71-73.

__________. Vols. I-III. *Nation* 60(March 28, 1895):240-242.

__________. Vol. IV. *American Historical Review* 2(October, 1896):171-176. Reprint. *Nation* 63(October 8, 1896):277.

Studies of Frederick Jackson Turner

Becker, Carl. "Frederick Jackson Turner." In *American Masters of Social Science* edited by Howard W. Odum. New York: Henry Holt & Co., 1927. Pp. 273-295.

Benson, Lee. "The Historian as Mythmaker: Turner and the Closed Frontier." In *The Frontier in American Development: Essays in Honor of Paul Wallace Gates* edited by David M. Ellis. Ithaca, NY: Cornell University Press, 1969. Pp. 1-9.

__________. *Turner and Beard: American Historical Writing Reconsidered.* New York: Free Press, 1960.

Billington, Ray Allen. *Frederick Jackson Turner: Historian, Scholar, Teacher.* New York: Oxford University Press, 1973.

__________. *The Frontier Thesis, Valid Interpretation of American History?* New York: Holt, Rinehart and Winston, 1966.

__________, ed. *Frontier and Section: Selected Essays of Frederick Jackson Turner.* Englewood Cliffs, NJ: Prentice-Hall, Inc., 1961.

Curti, Merle, *et al. The Making of an American Community.* Stanford, CA: Stanford University Press, 1959.

Hicks, John D. Review of *The United States, 1830-1850: The Nation and Its Sections* by Frederick Jackson Turner. *American Historical Review* 41(January, 1936):354-357.

Hofstadter, Richard. *The Progressive Historians: Turner, Beard, Parrington.* New York: Alfred A. Knopf, 1968.

__________, and Seymour Martin Lipset. *Turner and the Sociology of the Frontier.* New York: Basic Books, 1968.

Jacobs, Wilbur R. "Frederick Jackson Turner--Master Teacher." *Pacific Historical Review* 23(February, 1954):49-58.

__________, ed. *Frederick Jackson Turner's Legacy: Unpublished Writings in American History.* San Marino, CA: Huntington Library, 1965. Reprinted, *America's Great Frontiers and Sections:*

Frederick Jackson Turner's Unpublished Essays. Lincoln: University of Nebraska Press, 1969.

Johnson, Allen. Review of *The Frontier in American History* by Frederick Jackson Turner. *American Historical Review* 26(April, 1921):542-543.

McBride, George M. Review of *The Significance of Sections in American History* by Frederick Jackson Turner. *Pacific Historical Review* 3(November, 1934):451-452.

Mood, Fulmer, ed. *The Early Writings of Frederick Jackson Turner with a List of all His Works compiled by Everett E. Edwards.* Freeport, NY: Books for Libraries Press, 1938.

Moore, Frederick W. Review of *Rise of the New West, 1819-1829* by Frederick Jackson Turner. *American Historical Review* 12(October, 1906):162-164.

Paxson, Frederic L. "A Generation of the Frontier Hypothesis: 1893-1932." *Pacific Historical Review* 2(February, 1933):34-51.

__________. "The New Frontier and the Old American Habit." *Pacific Historical Review* 4(November, 1935):309-327.

__________. Review of *The Significance of Sections in American History* by Frederick Jackson Turner. *American Historical Review* 38(July, 1933):773-774.

Pierson, George. "The Frontier and American Institutions: A Criticism of the Turner Theory." *New England Quarterly* 16(June, 1942):224-255.

Robbins, Roy M. Review of *The United States, 1830-1850: The Nation and Its Sections* by Frederick Jackson Turner. *Mississippi Valley Historical Review* 22(September, 1935):295-297.

Schafer, Joseph. "Death of Professor Turner." *Wisconsin Magazine of History* 15(June, 1932):495-499.

__________. "Turner's Early Writings." *Wisconsin Magazine of History* 22(December, 1938):213-231.

__________. "Turner's Frontier Philosophy." *Wisconsin Magazine of History* 16(June, 1933):451-469.

Sioussat, St. George L. Review of *Rise of the New West, 1819-1829* by Frederick Jackson Turner. *The Dial* 43(July, 1907):15.

Soltow, Lee. "Inequality Amidst Abundance: Land Ownership in Early Nineteenth-Century Ohio." *Ohio History* 88(Spring, 1979):133-151.

Steiner, Michael C. "The Significance of Turner's Sectional Thesis." *Western Historical Quarterly* 10(October, 1979):437-466.

Wunder, John R., and Rebecca J. Herring. "Frontier Conspiracy: Law, Turner, and the Cordova Rebellion." *Red River Valley Historical Review* 7(Summer, 1982):51-67.

51

JOHN D. UNRUH, JR.

by Doyce B. Nunis, Jr.

Biography

In canvassing the historians who are included in this volume, a singular truism stands out: John David Unruh, Jr., is by far the youngest scholar in this biographical litany of historians of the American frontier. But more. He earned his place among these eminent and senior colleagues on the basis of a single, magnificent book, *The Plains Across: The Overland Emigrants and the Trans-Mississippi West, 1840-1860*, published by the University of Illinois Press in 1979.

The irony of that triumphant scholarly achievement, a book which has been acclaimed as definitive, indeed a seminal work, was wrought by untimely tragedy. He died on January 18, 1978, two days after undergoing surgery for the removal of a brain tumor which proved malignant. The pleasure of seeing his superb book in print and reading the laudatory critical acclaim that greeted it was thus denied him--though the knowledge that it was accepted for publication by a distinguished university press was surely a source of deep personal satisfaction.

Born on a South Dakota farm at Marion, Turner County, on October 4, 1937, John was the descendant of Mennonite pioneers who had settled on nearby Turkey Creek in the spring of 1874. His formative education was completed in Freeman, with the exception of the sixth grade, which was taken by correspondence when his parents were in the service of the Mennonite Central Committee in the Netherlands. In 1957, after completing two years at Freeman Junior College, he transferred to Bethel College in North Newton, Kansas, majoring in history. He took his bachelor's degree "with highest distinction" and spent the ensuing two years with the Peace Section of the Mennonite Central Committee, serving for a time in Akron, Pennsylvania (Communications with John D. Unruh, Sr., and Elda M. Unruh).

After that church-related duty, John decided to pursue graduate work, no doubt influenced by his father, who earned a doctorate in history and who has published several books dealing with the Mennonites. John also had early taken an interest in the history of his faith and family and later joined his father in a collaborative research effort on both subjects as time and circumstances permitted.

Determined on being a historian, John earned his M.A. at the University of Kansas, where he was elected to Phi Beta Kappa. Following the example of his parents, he then decided on a teaching career, accepting an instructorship at Bluffton College in Bluffton, Ohio. Two years later he returned to Kansas to work full time on his doctorate with Professor George L. Anderson, supported by several university fellowships. Three arduous years of study culminated in advancement to candidacy. That hurdle behind, on June 11, 1967, John married Elda M. Waltner, whom he had known from high school days in Freeman, and the Unruhs returned to Bluffton, where John resumed teaching.

Through the intervening years as he labored on his dissertation, he established a solid reputation as a demanding and excellent classroom teacher. His good humor and deep humanitarian qualities won him much admiration as well. His love of nature and his enthusiasm for sports provided him with pleasant diversions, but his dissertation research was all-pervasive: he was a scholar first.

His scholarship was of a high quality. This fact was made clear when he published "The Burlington and Missouri River Railroad Brings the Mennonites to Nebraska, 1873-1878" in the March and June, 1964, issues of *Nebraska History*. Later, during his dissertation research and writing years, he co-authored two additional articles, one with his Bluffton College colleague, Von Hardesty. As he approached the culmination of his long graduate labors on his doctoral dissertation, he also published two studies based on his research topic, one in the *Kansas Historical Quarterly* (1973) and another essay in the Los Angeles Corral of Westerners *Brand Book* No. 14 (1974).

The following year, in October, 1975, Unruh successfully defended his doctoral dissertation. Unfortunately, his mentor, George L. Anderson, had died in the meantime. Thus, John Unruh's Ph.D. work was completed under the guidance of Clifford S. Griffin. A distinguished career as a historian loomed bright. Death, however, intervened. Unruh's doctoral *alma mater* posthumously awarded him the George L. Anderson prize for 1976 for the most outstanding dissertation completed that year in the History Department, an honor well deserved.

Themes

When Richard Wentworth, director of the University of Illinois Press, asked me to serve as a referee for Unruh's submitted manuscript, *The Plains Across*, in 1977, I readily accepted. I had only met the young historian once, but knew the quality of his scholarship having served as editor of the Los Angeles Corral's *Brand Book* No. 14, which included a masterful bibliographical essay solicited from Unruh for publication in that volume. When the book manuscript arrived, I was bowled over by its size. It was *huge*! This was one of the primary concerns of the University of Illinois Press--the bulk of the text. The expense in printing and manufacturing was obvious. I set diligently to work with note pad ready and pen in hand.

I readily became overwhelmed by the breath and depth of the scholarship and stimulated by the insightful observations which splashed across each chapter like high tides slamming into craggy rocks. It was a once-in-a-life time experience to read the work of a young scholar and immediately recognize the brilliance of his achievement. I wrote the strongest possible recommendation to the University of Illinois Press, urging publication. But the press was duly concerned about the financial investment and hesitated. I am no prophet, but I declared to the University of Illinois Press that the manuscript was a prize winner and would be a best seller. Those two prognostications proved true. The University of Illinois Press accepted it.

With John's premature death, the manuscript had to be steered through publication. In that endeavor three people played unsung roles. Professor Von Hardesty, a colleague then at Bluffton College, came to the assistance of Unruh's widow, and together the two labored on galleys and related publication details. Elizabeth G. Dulany, managing editor at the University of Illinois Press, prepared the manuscript copy for the printer; her editorial work was a model in all respects--skillful, thorough, restrained.

As publication neared, the University of Illinois Press invited me to author a foreword. I was honored, indeed, privileged to do so. At the outset I declared that the book was a "magisterial study." The young historian had invested eight years of tireless research and writing in completing the manuscript as a dissertation: that it was destined for publication was all too obvious.

There is no doubt: *The Plains Across* is a superb achievement. The research, both in printed and manuscript sources, is near-exhaustive, as the extensive bibliography reveals. Emigrant diaries, journals and letters, contemporary newspapers, book and articles, theses and dissertations--little escaped Unruh's attention. What he fashioned from that prodigious research was the first synthesis on overland travel via the central route in the antebellum period. I prophetically opined in my foreword that it "will surely be a classic." And it is! Why?

Although a large body of books and articles have touched on some of the subjects included in the narrative--the role played by the federal government, the Indians, and the Mormons in the overland endeavor, ferrying and other entrepreneurial activities, sickness and disease, equipment and costs--this is the first study to present an overall synthesis on overland emigration via the central route for the 1840-1860 period. Unruh's "Introduction," which ably surveys and critiques the existing body of pertinent literature, makes this point abundantly clear.

Not only did the author structure a comprehensive synthesis, he also fashioned a hypothesis. He applies "the concept of change through time" in order to increase our understanding and to offer us new perspectives about overland emigration. The fulcrum on which this innovative study balances is found in the focus on "the interaction between the overlanders and other groups in the West--the army, the Indians, the Mormons, the traders and other entrepreneurs--as well as the interaction of the overlanders with the flora and fauna of the West." Utilizing a broad scope and incorporating new data from the neglected decade of the 1850s, the author traces "the ways in which trails, the West, and the overlanders themselves were changing." By examining such interactions and interfaces the historian can then discern "the real explanation of how the feat [of overland emigration] was successfully accomplished" (pp. xi-xiii). In this endeavor Unruh succeeds admirably. *The Plains Across* is a major contribution to the history of the American West and has earned the author his place in this volume of historians of the American frontier.

Analysis

Historians in their reviews of *The Plains Across* were overwhelmingly effusive in their praise. Merrill J. Mattes heralds it as "monumental," "the most penetrating and comprehensive study of the epic Oregon-California migrations to date." He notes the "encyclopedic scope" of the work which was "enlivened by the author's refreshing insights and overviews and by his sustained, vigorous prose style, buoyed up by subtle humor and ironic overtones" (*Pacific Historical Review* 49:372-373). John Logan Allen could only apply superlatives to "a superb book. Many cliches are relevant--seminal work, definitive study, formidable scholarship . . . at the same time, skillfully and sensitively written" (*American Historical Review* 84:1474).

Francis Paul Prucha observes that Unruh "corrects the stereotypes of the overland migration that have crept into textbooks and the movies" (*America*, April 7, 1979, p. 287), by moving away from concentration on the '49ers to give closer attention to the larger migrations of the 1850s, a view echoed by Joseph Barbato (*Smithsonian* 10:132). Ray Allen Billington was effusive in his review for the *Washington Post*, declaring that *The Plains Across* was "the best book yet written on the overland journey," one which "has also laid laid to rest a multitude of popular myths." "Remarkably," Billington declares, "he has accomplished this miracle in a highly unlikely medium--a doctoral dissertation--that is so rich in anecdote, so sparklingly written, and so free of academic gobbledy-gook that it might have come from the pen of a best-selling popularizer" (April 1, 1979).

Robert H. Becker, who revised the Wagner-Camp *Plains and Rockies* bibliography, was equally generous in his comments, concluding: "It was a long time in preparation, and in the opinion of this reviewer, it will endure for yet a longer time" (*American West* 16:49). W. Turrentine Jackson offers praise in another context. He writes: "The author has proved in this volume that historians with imagination can find a new approach to the evidence, and with deep research and thoughtful analysis, offer a new synthesis that contributes to the understanding of our nation's history" (*Montana: Magazine of Western History* 29:71). Allan G. Bogue hailed the book as "a great achievement," worthy of Pulitzer Prize consideration--which it was (*Reviews in American History* 8:221-227). *The Plains Across* was one of the three finalists in that competition.

Martin Ridge of the Huntington Library concludes: "There is no doubt that *The Plains Across* will stand as a milestone in western historical scholarship" (*Western Historical Quarterly* 11:69-71), while his then library colleague and former mentor, Ray Allen Billington writes that Unruh in his book "could not have erected a finer or more enduring monument to himself" (*Washington Post*, April 1, 1979).

With all the praise heaped on *The Plains Across*, it is no wonder that the book won seven awards, among them the prestigious American Historical Association's John H. Dunning Prize, the Organization of American Historian's first Ray A. Billington Book Award, the National Historical Society Book Prize, as well as four other regional and state awards.

However, even award-winning books are not without blemish. Thomas G. Alexander, though holding a high opinion for "a significant volume" and noting that Unruh's book "must rank as one of the major achievements of the decade in the literature of the American West," faulted "the author's apparent lack of familiarity with economic analysis" (*Journal of Historical Geography* 6:355-356). Robert Becker quibbled that more time should have been spent on the southern overland routes (*American West* 16:49), as did several other reviewers, among them Richard W. Etulain. The latter was also critical of some omissions or slights on the part of the author, among them failure to comment on human aspects of the trip--the roles of women and families--as well as "the attitudes, values, and outlooks" of the overlanders along with the squabbles and legal issues which westbound immigrants encountered. Unlike Ray Billington, Etulain finds Unruh's narrative "less lively and colorful" than those by Wallace Stegner and George Stewart in way of comparison (*Idaho Yesterdays* 24:30-31). Earl Pomeroy, though opining that the book "would have enhanced the reputation of any historian of the United States," cavils about "some all-too-familiar slips in choice of words" (*Journal of American History* 67:403-404). So much for picking the specks out of the pepper.

But the fact remains, *The Plains Across* will long remain the most definitive treatment of the Oregon-California overland emigration between 1840 and 1860. That fact is underscored by the appearance of a paperback edition from the publisher in 1982 and the inclusion of Unruh in this volume. He is in good company, rightly so, including his first mentor and several of his laudatory critics.

Bibliography

Book

The Plains Across: The Overland Emigrants and the Trans-Mississippi West, 1840-1860. Urbana: University of Illinois Press, 1979. Paperback edition with Notes and Bibliography omitted. Urbana: University of Illinois Press, 1982.

Articles

"Against the Grain: West to East on the Overland Trail." *Kansas Historical Quarterly* 5(Spring, 1973):72-84.

"The Burlington and Missouri River Railroad Brings the Mennonites to Nebraska, 1873-1878." *Nebraska History* 45(March, 1964):3-30.

"The Burlington and Missouri River Railroad Brings the Mennonites to Nebraska, 1873-1878--Part II." *Nebraska History* 45(June, 1964):177-206.

"Daniel Unruh and the Mennonite Settlement in Dakota Territory." Co-authored with John D. Unruh, Sr. *Mennonite Quarterly Review* 49(July, 1975):203-216.

"Daniel Unruh, 1820-1893.". Co-authored with John D. Unruh, Sr. In *General Conference Mennonite Pioneers* edited by Edmund G. Kaufman. North Newton, KS: Privately printed, 1973. Pp. 30-40.

"The Enigma of Degaev-Pell." Co-authored with Von Hardesty. *South Dakota History* 3(Winter, 1972):1-29.

"The Golden History of the Overland Emigrations." In the Los Angeles Corral of Westerners *Brand Book*, No. 14. Los Angeles: Los Angeles Corral of Westerners, 1974. Pp. 79-101, 229-235.

"Isaiah Harris' 'Minutes of a Trip to Kansas Territory' in 1855." Co-edited with Michael J. Brodhead. *Kansas Historical Quarterly* 35(Winter, 1969):373-385.

"This was George Anderson: A Student's View." In *Essays on Kansas History: In Memoriam, George L. Anderson, Jayhawker-Historian* edited by Burton J. Williams. Lawrence, KS: Coronado Press, 1977. Pp. 11-18.

Studies of John D. Unruh, Jr.

Alexander, Thomas G. Review of *The Plains Across: The Overland Emigrants and the Trans-Mississippi West, 1840-1860* by John D. Unruh, Jr. *Journal of Historical Geography* 6(October, 1980):355-356.

Allen, John Logan. Review of *The Plains Across: The Overland Emigrants and the Trans-Mississippi West, 1840-1860* by John D. Unruh, Jr. *American Historical Review* 84(December, 1979):1474.

Athearn, Robert G. Review of *The Plains Across: The Overland Emigrants and the Trans-Mississippi West, 1840-1860* by John D. Unruh, Jr. *Great Plains Quarterly* 1(Winter, 1981):68-69.

Barbato, Joseph. Review of *The Plains Across: The Overland Emigrants and the Trans-Mississippi West, 1840-1860* by John D. Unruh, Jr. *Smithsonian* 10(June, 1979):132.

Becker, Robert H. Review of *The Plains Across: The Overland Emigrants and the Trans-Mississippi West, 1840-1860* by John D. Unruh, Jr. *American West* 16(September/October, 1979):49.

Billington, Ray Allen. Review of *The Plains Across: The Overland Emigrants and the Trans-Mississippi West, 1840-1860* by John D. Unruh, Jr. *Washington Post*, April 1, 1979, Book World section, front page.

Bogue, Allan G. Review of *The Plains Across: The Overland Emigrants and the Trans-Mississippi West, 1840-1860* by John D. Unruh, Jr. *Reviews in American History* 8(June, 1980):221-227.

Etulain, Richard W. Review of *The Plains Across: The Overland Emigrants and the Trans-Mississippi West, 1840-1860* by John D. Unruh, Jr. *Idaho Yesterdays* 24(Summer, 1980):30-31.

Jackson. W. Turrentine. Review of *The Plains Across: The Overland Emigrants and the Trans-Mississippi West, 1840-1860* by John D. Unruh, Jr. *Montana: Magazine of Western History* 29(Autumn, 1979):71.

Mattes, Merrill J. Review of *The Plains Across: The Overland Emigrants and the Trans-Mississippi West, 1840-1860* by John D. Unruh, Jr. *Pacific Historical Review* 49(May, 1980):372-373.

__________. *Nebraska History* 60(Summer, 1979):296-297.

__________. *New Mexico Historical Review* 55(July, 1980):157-163.

Pomeroy, Earl. Review of *The Plains Across: The Overland Emigrants and the Trans-Mississippi West, 1840-1860* by John D. Unruh, Jr. *Journal of American History* 67(September, 1980):403-404.

Prucha, Francis Paul. Review of *The Plains Across: The Overland Emigrants and the Trans-Mississippi West, 1840-1860* by John D. Unruh, Jr. *America*, April 7, 1979, p. 287.

Ridge, Martin. Review of *The Plains Across: The Overland Emigrants and the Trans-Mississippi West, 1840-1860* by John D. Unruh, Jr. *Western Historical Quarterly* 11(January, 1980):69-71.

Spence, Mary Lee. Review of *The Plains Across: The Overland Emigrants and the Trans-Mississippi West, 1840-1860* by John D. Unruh, Jr. *Arizona and the West* 21(Autumn, 1979):280-281.

Unruh, John D., Jr., Papers. In the private possession of Elda M. Unruh, Bluffton, OH.

Williams, Burton J. "In Memoriam." In *Essays on Kansas History: In Memoriam, George L. Anderson, Jayhawker-Historian.* Lawrence, KS: Coronado Press, 1977. P. 10.

52

WILLIAM T. UTTER

by Clarke L. Wilhelm

Biography

William Thomas Utter wrote of early Ohio. While not extensive, his published works provide valuable insights into the years when Ohio changed from a rather raw wilderness into a stable agricultural society with the first stirrings of industry.

Born in California in 1895, Utter earned a B.S. from Northwest Missouri State Teachers College and an M.A. and Ph.D. from the University of Chicago. At Chicago he wrote a doctoral dissertation on "Ohio Politics and Politicians, 1802-1815." After teaching at the Ohio State University, the University of Chattanooga, and Eureka College, Utter moved to Denison University in Granville, Ohio, in 1929.

He would remain at Denison until his death shortly before retirement in 1962, and it would be both Denison and Granville that would shape Utter's professional growth and accomplishments. An effective teacher of frontier history for more than thirty years, Utter also headed his department until 1954 and was generally considered by his colleagues as one of the major figures on the faculty. Former associates recall his gentle and ironic wit, which is also reflected in his writings, his relaxed manner, and his stubborn integrity when he felt principle was at stake. As a teacher, he spoke without notes, trying to communicate directly with his students. He particularly attempted to create empathy in them for the experiences of the early settlers, often by bringing in small pioneer artifacts and then developing his discussion from examination of a tool or utensil (Interviews, G. Wallace Chessman, Granville, OH, August 13, 1985; Horace F. King, Granville, OH, October 30, 1985).

During his years at Denison, Utter also became somewhat of an institution in Granville, a village of about three thousand, situated on the side of a valley at the western edge of the Appalachian plateau. A town leader, he served on the village council and as mayor. He loved Granville and his extensive civic activities surely stemmed in large part from his desire to preserve Granville's picturesque, small town atmosphere. Utter, however, also devoted so much time to Granville because he found it fascinating professionally. Granville began as an authentic frontier community, hewed out of the huge deciduous Ohio forest by an organized group of settlers from New England. Some of the town's pioneer lineaments were still faintly visible and for Utter, to study Granville was a way of examining frontier Ohio. He would help establish a historical society in Granville and write a history of the village.

Beyond college and town, Utter was active in the Ohio Academy of History, serving as its president in 1940-1941. He worked with the Ohio Historical Society and as a further example of his desire to recapture past experiences through the tangible, served as a consultant to the Society in restorations of the Zoar utopian community, early Ohio statesman Thomas Worthington's house in Chillicothe, and the home of John and William Tecumseh Sherman in Lancaster.

Themes

Utter, in his writings on frontier Ohio, pursues three major themes. His first interest, stemming from his dissertation, is the emergence of political and legal structures in Ohio. In mid-career, he broadened his focus. With *The Frontier State: 1803-1825* (1942), he continued his investigation of governmental questions, but then shifted much of his attention to the ordinary settlers, those who did not have much time to consider political issues. Through a mixture of economic and social history, Utter attempts to depict the mosaic of life that was reality for most early Ohioans (p. xii). This emphasis upon the people themselves also dominates his last major work: *Granville: The Story of an Ohio Village* (1956); yet in both books a third theme is also present. Utter was intrigued by the forces that brought the frontier era to an end. The early appearance of industry and transportation improvements which connected farmers with markets and Ohio with the East spells for Utter a new phase in the state's development. He gives considerable space in both books to the process of change and clearly believes that Ohioans gained as they became a more integral part of the larger American society. Yet one senses in William Utter, especially in his Granville book, a nostalgic ambivalence, a feeling that perhaps some important personal relationships and values as well as a simpler way of life were unfortunately lost with the passing of the frontier.

Analysis

To arrive at an analysis of William Utter's importance as a historian and particularly as a frontier historian, one must examine his two books. *The Frontier State: 1803-1825* and *Granville: The Story of an Ohio Village* contain his themes and insights.

Utter published *The Frontier State*, the second of a six-volume history of the state sponsored by the Ohio State Archaeological and Historical Society, in 1942. He begins his study with party politics and the evolution of state government. He moves easily through such complex matters as creating a constitution, land squabbles, taxes, schools, internal improvements, and judicial review. He interweaves these issues with more dramatic questions like the Burr affair, the War of 1812, and the constant conflicts between the liberal and conservative Jeffersonians who dominated the state. While granting that Ohio had some particular problems such as Indian defense and lack of capital, Utter continually points out how closely linked Ohio was with the rest of the nation in both concerns and approaches. He sees much of the state's political wrangling as mirroring that of the national scene and stresses how often Ohioans relied upon Washington, DC, and the older states for ideological and material assistance.

William Utter had first attracted scholarly attention with articles on Ohio politics and law, and it was these writings that brought him the commission from the historical society for *The Frontier State*, but he now sought to locate the essence of the pioneer past elsewhere (p. xi). After a few chapters on political history, he moves on to his larger purpose: "to write a history *of the people of Ohio* . . . emphasizing what they considered of most importance and disregarding what to them seemed unessential" (p. xiii). And as he transfers his concern to the pioneers and their struggles to subdue the wilderness and find first subsistence and then profit, the book's pace quickens.

It was a hard time. Utter's settlers faced many different environments in Ohio and found various ways to eke out a living from the land: corn, wheat, apples, and the raising of livestock. They had their disasters: natural, financial, and moral. They lived with death and loneliness, and at times they had little but frontier religion for comfort, a religion that sought not only to save them, but to restrain them, especially from excessive sinning. Yet, while these Ohioans may have been pioneers, they were soon in the process of leaving that stage behind, fashioning a more civilized and substantial existence. They started schools and imported eastern clothes and culture. They began small industries, improved river transport, built roads, and dug canals. By 1825, with the beginnings of the Ohio canal system and extension of the National Road into Ohio, the state in Utter's judgment was passing beyond the frontier phase (p. 319).

Utter provides a complex picture of the life and cares of the Ohio settlers. He ranges from election campaigns to damnation, from disease to canal building. His cast includes not only farmers, but speculators, statesman, flatboatmen, and frontier merchants. Despite the breadth, he is not superficial. He gives twenty-four pages to sickness and health care and another twenty-five to considering what he calls "the struggle with human depravity" (p. 362): the churches' efforts to curb frontier vice. With almost every subject, whether it is planting crops, poling barges, or distilling whiskey, he goes into considerable detail.

Utter, however, is reluctant to venture too far beyond description to search for wider meanings of the Ohio experience. There is examination of change, particularly in terms of transportation, but it is closer to narrative than analysis. He does address one of the more contentious historiographical issues at the time he was writing: the causes of the War of 1812. Breaking with the traditional interpretation of the war as a nationalistic response to hostile British actions on the seas and along the Indian border, Louis Hacker and Julius Pratt had recently argued for the war being largely caused by expansionist desires, especially among southerners and westerners. William Utter would be among the first historians to challenge land hunger as a major factor. He does not find his westerners seeking war for more territory. While admitting that expansion may have been a contributing element, he returns to the older understanding, arguing that at least for Ohioans "defense of national honor was uppermost in their minds as war approached" (p. 87).

Basically, Utter avoids the larger generalizations. While specific observations about how typical or how singular were the problems faced by Ohio settlers are scattered throughout the book, they can be overlooked in the accumulation of detail. They could be gathered together and developed into a fuller assessment as to the extent Ohio can serve as a representative pioneer example. Utter also hesitates to speculate on what later frontiers may have learned from Ohio's experiences. He is no advocate of Frederick Jackson Turner. The book is replete with evidence that refutes the frontier thesis. Utter clearly believes that while the wilderness environment effected some changes, the settlers carried their heritage with them, looked eastward for help, and tried to recover their former culture as quickly as possible. But Utter will not overtly develop these insights. Except for a short statement at the end of the book, he side steps direct involvement in the Great Debate. In his conclusion he suggests the frontier had only a limited impact on the pioneers, and states, perhaps with anti-Turnerian irony:

> With the nice problem of the extent to which the pattern of western culture was "evolved" or "borrowed," or whether society on the frontier was atomized, as if in some giant cyclotron, this study cannot concern itself, for these are naked abstractions which had better be left to writers more capable of giving them a wordy clothing. It has been a sufficient task to describe, with honesty, how things actually were among Ohioans of the first quarter of the last century, without attempting to explain how they came to be that way, save where the explanation seemed fairly obvious (pp. 420-421).

Utter does furnish a solid description that has served ever since as a course for other histories that treat the Ohio frontier, including: Eugene Roseboom and Francis P. Weisenburger, *A History of Ohio* (1958); R. Carlyle Buley, *The Old Northwest* (1951); and Reginald Horsman, *The Frontier in the Formative Years: 1783-1815* (1970). Nonetheless, the professional historian might wish that William Utter had been more willing to explore those "naked abstractions" that might further illuminate Ohio's significance as a frontier state.

In *Granville: The Story of An Ohio Village*, Utter turned to the town that had come to mean so much to him. Granville was founded by people from Granville, Massachusetts, and from Granby, a neighboring town just over the border in Connecticut. Moving as a preplanned community much as did their Puritan forebears, these settlers established a functioning village even as the last ox-drawn wagons reached the town site. As he had in his state history, Utter seeks primarily to capture the personal nature of the frontier and with the smaller setting he is able to evoke an even greater sense of every day life. Almost one fourth of the book deals with the village's birth. He evaluates the leaders, showing how they chose the location, their negotiations with speculators, their careful preparation for moving over a hundred people to Ohio, and their administration of plot determination, land clearing, and problems of local government. Drawing on reminiscences, Utter recreates the trek west and the accompanying alternating moods of exhilaration and depression. He tells of the years of home building, the exhausting work of preparing the land, and the satisfaction found in cooperating to establish the new community.

Utter then portrays the village as it grew and changed. Granvillians began to supplement their agricultural base with small industry, such as distilling, tanning, and iron work. Better roads and canal feeders appeared and Granville as well as the rest of Ohio started to leave the frontier behind. Socially and morally, Granville was a bit loose in the beginning, with the local tavern as a social center, dancing a favorite pastime with the young, and hard drinking not uncommon among the men. Eventually, however, religious conservatism, spurred on by the Great Revival and the local Protestant churches, insisted upon temperance and a more sober approach to life. Utter actually places religion at the core of much of Granville's early history, discussing not only how it affected social behavior, but increasingly how religious concerns and controversy permeated most aspects of village life, especially education. The local churches' emphasis upon education that would be doctrinally acceptable helped make Granville an educational center, creating several frontier academies and colleges and eventually Utter's own Denison University in 1831.

The town would know misfortune. Floods, drought, and financial panic would come and as Granville became caught up in national issues, its sons would fight in the War of 1812 and the town itself would divide over the issues of slavery and abolition. But Granville as William Utter depicts it was essentially a happy place up through the Civil War, prosperous and sharing a fundamental sense of community. In spirit, William Utter ends his account in 1865. The following years clearly do not appeal to him. While he does limn the town's later developments, it is a quick sketch. The first sixty years of Granville's existence receive 247 pages, the remaining years only seventy-nine. He seems in a hurry and the sense of Granville's organic unity lessens. Granville's frontier and the early decades that follow are what command William Utter's scholarly interest and affection.

A capsule review of the Granville book in the *Mississippi Valley Historical Review* basically dismisses it as a "modest" subject (43:722). The book does appear at first as local history, locally conceived, but it actually can be an important source for the frontier historian. Granville's founding was distinctive. Planned community migrations were not totally unique, but they were hardly the norm and because of their exceptional nature they can be utilized by the scholar to throw light on possible options for other settlers had they been able to organize. While being different in its origins, Granville was in other ways typical of pioneer settlement. Especially after its first few years, Granville can be seen as a microcosm of the passing of the frontier. Utter does provide some help in understanding the wider lessons and connections that can be made by considering Granville as both exception and as model. He argues that the homogeneous background would be crucial for the village's success, provides examples of the judicious planning that ameliorated problems of settlement, and indicates areas where Granville's evolution was part of the common frontier, especially in terms of religion and the impact of better transportation.

These types of generalizations, however, are infrequent and often indirect. Granvillians as Utter presents them definitely do not fit into the frontier thesis, but there is not even a whisper about Turner in this book. As in *The Frontier State*, Utter's strength is descriptive. He prefers to observe the settlers rather than probe their activities for insights. While later social historians might fault *Granville* for lacking statistical data and a quantitative structure, the book does present a complex, coherent, and ultimately empathetic picture of a changing pioneer town. If one approaches *Granville* with a background in frontier and Ohio history, including knowledge of *The Frontier State*, and with questions already in mind, then one can glean from Utter's narrative account useful evidence for dealing with more profound questions about the frontier.

Utter also wrote six articles and several book reviews, but almost none of them are likely to attract sustained historical interest. His first three articles dealing with Jeffersonian politics and the issues of judicial review and the common law were absorbed into *The Frontier State* (*Mississippi Valley Historical Review* 14:3-24; 15:321-340; 16:321-333). He also contributed a brief treatment of early Ohio statesman Samuel Huntington for the *Dictionary of American Biography* and wrote an essay in *American Heritage* dealing with the efforts of Chillicothe to win statehood for Ohio which is more a slightly filled-in outline than a study of substance. In a posthumously published article, Utter returned at the end of his career to an issue he had treated in *The Frontier State*, the causes of the War of 1812. Although his analysis is somewhat blurred, perhaps because he died before he could make revisions, he evidently still sees national honor as the prime cause of the war (*After Tippecanoe*, pp. 9-16). Only once did Utter venture into a different field, providing in 1937 an essay on literary historian Vernon Lewis Parrington in a *festschrift* to Marcus Jernegan, a former professor at the University of Chicago. Utter's approach is historiographical, examining Parrington's methods as a historian rather than the content of his ideas, but nonetheless this essay can still be a useful starting place for critical analysis of Parrington (*The Marcus W. Jernegan Essays*, pp. 394-408).

Except for the Parrington study, William Utter devoted himself to explicating the experiences of those who settled early Ohio. *Granville: The Story of an Ohio Village* and *The Frontier State*, his main contributions to this purpose, have limitations, yet each is also a useful source for the frontier historian. It does not appear that many scholars have noticed *Granville*, but after more than forty years *The Frontier State* continues to stand as the major work for this period of Ohio's past and its importance seems unlikely to diminish in the foreseeable future.

Bibliography

Books

The Frontier State: 1803-1825. Vol. II, *The History of the State of Ohio* series edited by Carl Wittke. Columbus: Ohio State Archaeological and Historical Society, 1942.

Granville: The Story of an Ohio Village Granville, OH: Granville Historical Society and Denison University, 1956.

Articles

"Chillicothe Juncto." *American Heritage* 4(Spring, 1953):38-39, 70-71.

"The Coming of the War." In *After Tippecanoe: Some Aspects of the War of 1812* edited by Philip P. Mason. Westport, CT: Greenwood Press, 1973. Pp. 9-16.

"Introduction." In *Ohio Town Names* by William D. Overman. Akron: Atlantic Press, 1959. Pp. iii-iv.

"Judicial Review in Early Ohio." *Mississippi Valley Historical Review* 14(June, 1927):3-24.

"Ohio and the English Common Law." *Mississippi Valley Historical Review* 16(June, 1929; March, 1930):321-333.

"Saint Tammany in Ohio: A Study in Frontier Politics." *Mississippi Valley Historical Review* 15(December, 1928):321-340.

"Samuel Huntington." *Dictionary of American Biography* 9:419-420.

"Vernon Louis Parrington." In *The Marcus W. Jernegan Essays in American History* edited by William T. Hutchinson. Chicago: University of Chicago Press, 1937. Pp. 394-408.

Reviews

Michigan: From Primitive Wilderness to Industrial Commonwealth by Milo M. Quaife and Sidney Glazer. *Mississippi Valley Historical Review* 35(September, 1948):293.

Old Illinois Houses by John Drury. *Mississippi Valley Historical Review* 37(December, 1950):528-529.

Pennsylvania Agriculture and Country Life, 1640-1840 by Stevenson Whitcomb Fletcher. *Ohio State Archaeological and Historical Quarterly* 62(January, 1953):87-89.

Two Captains West: An Historical Tour of the Louis [sic] and Clark Trail by Albert and Jane Salisbury. *Ohio State Archaelogical and Historical Quarterly* 60(January, 1951):108-110.

Studies of William T. Utter

Barnhart, John D. Review of *The Frontier State: 1803-1825* by William T. Utter. *Indiana Magazine of History* 38(June, 1942):214-215.

"Bibliographical Notices." Review of *Granville: The Story of an Ohio Village* by William T. Utter. *Mississippi Valley Historical Review* 43(March, 1957):722.

Cole, Arthur C. Review of *The Frontier State: 1803-1825* by William T. Utter. *Ohio State Archaeological and Historical Quarterly* 52(October-December, 1943):373-381.

Havinghurst, Walter. Review of *Granville: The Story of an Ohio Village* by William T. Utter. *Ohio Historical Quarterly* 66(January, 1957):113-115.

Monaghan, Jay. Review of *The Frontier State: 1803-1825* by William T. Utter. *American Historical Review* 48(October, 1942):129-131.

Utter, William T., Publications File. Denison University Library, Granville, OH.

Volwiler, A. T. Review of *The Frontier State: 1803-1825* by William T. Utter. *Mississippi Valley Historical Review* 29(September, 1942):260-262.

53

STANLEY VESTAL

by Sherry L. Smith

Biography

Stanley Vestal had two names. "Walter S. Campbell" was the Oxford graduate, the scholarly university professor, the teacher of writers. "Stanley Vestal" was the western writer, the rugged outdoorsman, the lover of Indian life. He was born on his parents' homestead near Severy, Kansas, in 1887 and named Walter S. Vestal. But his father died soon after Walter's birth and when his mother remarried in 1896, James Robert Campbell adopted the boy and gave him his surname. As a writer, however, Vestal chose a pen name to honor the father he never knew (*American West*, p. 1225).

Vestal seemed destined to write about Indians. He had many boyhood opportunities to glimpse the nineteenth century Plains Indians, the people who became a lifetime interest. He dated his fascination with Native Americans to an encounter with an Indian Service employee who showed him an array of war bonnets and beadwork. At age seven Vestal was enthralled with the beauty and romance of these objects.

That was just the beginning. Vestal's stepfather was a man with an interest in history and a decided sympathy toward the Cheyenne. Earlier in his career Campbell had worked on Hubert H. Bancroft's research staff studying, among other things, the Sand Creek Massacre. The stepfather's enthusiasms no doubt influenced his stepson, but Campbell's career took Vestal even closer to Indians when he moved the family to Guthrie, Oklahoma, in 1898. Walter spent the summer in the Cheyenne-Arapaho country of western Oklahoma, frequenting an Indian camp near his uncle's ranch. The next winter he set up a tipi back in town, a practice he continued into adulthood when he argued it offered more cold weather comfort than a regular home.

Adolescence did not dim Vestal's ardor for Indians. He read Ernest Thompson Seton's column about Indians in *The Ladies Home Journal.* Vestal even organized one of the hundreds of "Seton Indians" tribes that cropped up across the country for boys who wanted to camp out in tipis, or master bows, arrows, and Indian woodcraft. By age fifteen Vestal admitted to his grandmother that he was "a mighty big kid to be playing Indian but it is in my system and will stay in, I suppose, until at some date in the dim future the interest in girls will supplant it" (*Stanley Vestal*, p. 36). It is open to debate whether that time ever came.

In 1903 Vestal's stepfather took a new position as president of Southwestern State Normal School in Weatherford, Oklahoma, smack in the middle of Cheyenne-Arapaho country. Vestal often visited the agency at Colony where he befriended agent John Homer Seger and some of the older Indian men. They taught him a good deal about Plains Indian life, but the old men would not discuss their personal war exploits, a subject of great interest to Vestal, with someone who had no wartime experience.

Vestal's idylls in Indian country came to a close when he chose to pursue a college education. Distinguishing himself at Southwestern State, in 1908 Vestal was off for three years at Merton College, Oxford, as a Rhodes Scholar. He left England with an A.B. and an M.A. with honors in English Literature. This English sojourn proved central to his eventual drift not only toward writing, but also toward his western and Indian subjects. From Oxford he wrote his parents that Indians deserved more accurate characterizations than previously given in romantic writings (p. 74).

Heady days at Oxford were followed not by literary success, but by dreary days of making a living as a high school teacher in Kentucky. Frustrated with recalcitrant students and his inability to sell his prose, Vestal accepted his parents' offer, in 1914, to return to Oklahoma, live at home, and research Indians in anticipation of making a go at a professional writing career. He published several articles in *American Anthropologist*, but that did not make a living. And so, the following year, he joined the faculty at the University of Oklahoma as a member of the English department.

Vestal found more satisfactions in college than high school teaching, but money troubles plagued him. He longed for the "literary jackpot" and claimed "money is the inevitable answer to every question I ask of life--the one end of every quest" (p. 88). Believing Indian warfare topics would prove lucrative, he again appealed to old warriors to talk of their experiences. Still, they refused. World War I provided his chance to break through. He served as a captain of field artillery with the American Expeditionary Force and, although he never saw combat, his army affiliation proved sufficient to lower the barrier between himself and Indian informants.

Vestal's publication career began in earnest in 1925 with articles, stories, and ballads appearing in periodicals such as *American Mercury, Poetry*, and *Southwest Review*. In 1926 his *Kit Carson, Fandango*, and *Happy Hunting Grounds* manuscripts were circulating among publishers.

During the next thirty years Vestal published over twenty books, about 150 magazine pieces, five radio scripts, and countless book reviews and newspaper articles. He also established the School of Professional Writing at the University of Oklahoma, earned a reputation as a brilliant teacher, and won a number of honors including a Guggenheim Fellowship, a Rockefeller Foundation award, and a membership in the Oklahoma Hall of Fame. His wife, Isabel Jones, was also a writer, although she did not experience her husband's commercial success. The couple had two daughters, but the marriage eventually ended in divorce.

In December, 1957, Vestal became ill while attending a University of Oklahoma football game. He died soon after and was buried in the National Cemetery at Custer Battlefield National Monument--in the company of Sioux warriors.

Themes

Stanley Vestal thought the book *Sitting Bull* his best work. It is rather interesting that this plainsman penned a biography of the Sioux leader while living with his family on the French Riviera. But in some respects, such a juxtaposition of place and subject was appropriate. For what Vestal hoped to do in all his writing was make his readers understand that his native place, the American West, contained all the material necessary for the creation of a universal literature. More precisely Vestal wanted his countrymen to see the epic dimensions of their American, rather than European, heritage.

If there is one dominant theme in Vestal's work, then, it is his effort to present Anglo-American mountain men and occasionally Plains Indians as figures of epic proportion. He believed such men could rightfully take their place next to Homer's heroes or the knights errant of the Middle Ages. And he believed their stories symbolized an important element in American culture. Vestal was convinced this tradition was "most clearly expressed in the heroic age of the Old West. Therefore," he explained, "that heroic age became my chosen field" (p. 229).

Within this framework, Vestal attributes to his American heroes a number of characteristics which serve as subthemes in his works. First, a Vestal hero is self-reliant for the author believed wholeheartedly in rugged individualism. Second, these heroes usually prove their mettle in warfare, in most cases, Indian warfare. Third, his protagonists are always male. More to the point, they are emphatically virile, masculine figures. Vestal's West was a place of conquest, violence, courage, aggression, and adventure. There was no room for qualities which Vestal would label as more feminine--doubt, diplomacy, vulnerability, or appeasement. His heroes' souls remain untouched by life's complexities. They resent authority and champion notions of self-reliance which did not cohere in a social context.

Indians' presence in the West certainly loom large as a theme in Vestal's work, too. Sometimes Native Americans play the role of epic hero. More often, they operate as mere foils to the white men whose struggles with Indians transformed them into American heroes. As a consequence, Vestal's image of Indians is clearly ambivalent. When Plains

Indians encountered farmers, army personnel, or government bureaucrats, however, this writer's sympathies are unmistakable. "Probably no American now wishes to give the Plains back to the Indian," he writes, "though many have an uneasy feeling that the Indian has received a raw deal." In several works Vestal deliberately sets out to present Indian points of view, motivated not "by love for the underdog--but shame for my own people" (*Warpath and Council Fire*, p. xii).

One other major theme of Vestal's work concerns his method rather than his subject. He certainly perceived himself as a writer of western nonfiction, but he is not an academic historian. He did not want to be. Instead, Vestal wrote for a popular audience. His books often rest on minimal primary research (several Indian books serving as exceptions). He preferred color to footnotes. C. L. Sonnichsen calls this approach "informal history" and adds that writers like Vestal took "history off the library shelves and put it into the hands of the people" (*El Paso Herald Post*, September 2, 1939). Not all reviewers are as positive in their assessments.

In several works on writing nonfiction, Vestal provides explanation and justification for his style and approach to historical nonfiction. Vestal believed that the formula for successful nonfiction, which he defines as both art and commerce, is a blend of fact with passion. Such an approach to his subject matter, then, is not only an important theme in his work, but an important theme in others' appraisals of the value of his work.

Analysis

Recalling boyhood jaunts over the prairie north of his schoolhouse, Vestal noted that he had always "superimposed the Homeric scenes and actions of the *Iliad* upon that place." Not that Kansas and Oklahoma resembled the Mediterranean in any physical sense, but "the underneath bedrock of Homeric topography" rested there. "Helen of Troy looks into the schoolhouse windows from the walls of the sacred city," he wrote. "Queerly, almost every story I know has this definite location underlying the dream--Why I cannot say. . . . Perhaps my historical interest led me to seek a local habitation for every dream" (*Chronicles of Oklahoma* 51:477).

Whatever the reason, there is no doubt that Vestal most often chose the High Plains as the setting for his tales. He was convinced that region posed special challenges for American frontiersmen and provided the greatest opportunity for heroic endeavor. The Virginian and the New Englander extended westward, he wrote in *The Missouri*, overwhelming all barriers until they reached the plains. There a country, a climate, a tradition, and a material culture stopped them for "it could not and would not be assimilated" (pp. 162-163). Reflecting the influence of Walter Prescott Webb on his image of the plains, Vestal argues that "civilization on the Short Grass was a *natural* growth. Institutions were sketchy or non-existent. The only controls of conduct were the sense of shame and fear or blame in the hearts of individual Plainsmen" (*Short Grass Country*, p. 38). In such a vast land every man met the same hazardous conditions and the "great man was great simply because he did what others did, and did it better--like Achilles, like Ulysses. Those Greek heroes would have felt perfectly at home with Sitting Bull or Buffalo Bill or 'Dad' Lemmon" (*The Missouri*, p. 163). Tides of humans eventually swept in to overwhelm the Indians' way of life and that of the "old-time white population." But the memory and tradition of those people remained, Vestal believed, to serve as foundation for truly American epics.

Vestal adds, however, that the plainsman had one "advantage" over both Homeric heroes and Arthurian knights. He was a common man who required only a gun, a horse, and a blanket. Thus, any man could be a hero on the plains "if he had the stuff, and nearly every man was forced to be a hero at some time or other." This "advantage" made Vestal's plainsmen quintessentially American. While men of the woodlands and hill country to the east of the Great Plains might turn their back on their own country as they cast nostalgic glances toward Europe, the same was not true of people of the plains. "There the American came into his own," Vestal claims in a statement somewhat reminiscent of Frederick Jackson Turner. "There he became an independent man, looking in four directions, instead of only one. . . . For in that big, open country--so different from the tidy pettiness of Europe--no sane man can long go on pretending to be a European living, like some ungrateful, carping refugee, in an inferior' country. The bluff is too thin" (*Short Grass Country*, pp. 40, 5-6).

And what forces helped forge this new man, this plainsman? The land and climate certainly played a role. The plains was a place of extremes and excesses including the shortest and tallest grasses, the widest and driest rivers, the heaviest downpours and the least rain. Moreover, once on the plains, a woodlands man finds himself adrift in a sea, of sorts, where none of the old rules applied. He could not determine the points of the compass, for instance, by looking for moss on the north side of trees. There were no trees. "All around there was nothing. Only the grass and sky. And--of course--the lost greenhorn" (*The Old Santa Fe Trail*, p. 101).

Beyond the forces of environment, Vestal believes the Indians of the High Plains shaped the frontier, the plainsman, and much that was distinctly American. Sitting Bull, for example, is "the strongest, boldest, most stubborn opponent of European influence, was the very heart and soul of that Frontier. . . . Sitting Bull was one of the Makers of America." In fact, Vestal maintains, Americans owed a great debt to Sitting Bull and others like him for foes, not friends, forge character. Conflicts with Indians molded the history of the United States into something more than "a dull chronicle of plodding clodhoppers, placidly moving each year a little farther into the vacant lands, carrying along their petty, outworn European ideas and institutions, their bastard European culture, unchanged and changing--so many rubber stamps" (*Sitting Bull*, p. 315).

So, Indians shape the plainsman's unique character. But they are also heroes in their own right, American originals untainted by European influences. Moreover, they endure. If by mid-twentieth century it appeared that dudes had replaced genuine western heroes, the Indian was one figure who had not changed. If the trappers, explorers, fur barons, scouts, soldiers, showmen, bandits and cowmen, who merely imitated the Indian in the course of adapting to the plains had disappeared, "the Red Man . . remains" (*Short Grass Country* p. 183).

This, then, is the stuff of American legend. In his drive to write western epics Vestal, the artist, was determined to define a unique American culture and literature. To be sure, few artists or writers play a role in Vestal's books. But one does appear in *Sitting Bull*, interestingly in the form of a menopausal woman. In some respects Catherine Weldon, Indian reformer and artist, represents Vestal himself. Weldon, as artist, "had no use for shams. And yet, in that pallid imitation of Europe which then passed for American culture, she herself . . . could only be a sham" for she had "no authentic relation" to the European world. Then she met Sitting Bull and saw in him "the integrity, the wholeness that her battled heart looked for in vain in that travesty of culture which had frittered her talents away. To her he seemed a rock in a weltering sea" (*Sitting Bull*, p. 265). And so he appeared to Vestal, too.

Yet it was not Sitting Bull but Kit Carson who first serves as Vestal's vehicle for an American epic. Vestal chose Carson, he explains, to rescue him from biographers and showmen who either left Carson "blameless and colorless" or made of him a "cheap burlesque" by commercializing the Western Hero. What Vestal intends in his biography is to convey a sense of the real man, to present "an authentic portrait." At the same time, he went on to say, Kit Carson was as much a symbol of the American frontier "as Odysseus was of the Greek seafarings." So, he should take his place among classical heroes. Actually, Vestal argues, Carson deserves a rank *above* the most legendary heroes:

> Kit Carson's endless journeys through the wilderness make the fabled Mediterranean wanderings of Odysseus seem weekend excursions of a stay-at-home; his humanity rivals Robin Hood's; in readiness to fight and in chivalry to women he rates a *seige* at the Round Table; his courage and coolness against hopeless odds may be matched but not surpassed by the old Norse heroes; while his prowess in innumerable battles--all quite without the aid of invulnerable armor or the encouragement of indulgent goddesses--makes Achilles look like a wash-out (*Kit Carson*, p. 3-4).

Vestal, of course, did not intend Carson's example as unique. Rather, he sees the mountain man as the archetype of the American pioneer. The Old West was an heroic age precisely because it offered every man equal chance to show "the stuff that was in him." Kit was a "hero who personified American enterprise in the Far West--the banner which was to wave the pioneers forward into the Great American Desert" (p. 188).

Vestal would repeat this refrain in other books about mountain men, Santa Fe Trail merchants, and even the Missouri River. But mountain men especially appealed to him for they represented the three major subthemes of his work--individualism, violence, and virility. Not the least of the attractive aspects of the mountain man's life, according to Vestal, is his presumed self-reliance and independent character. "The free trapper had to be a man of infinite resource," he states, "able to do everything for himself. . . . He stood on his own feet. . . . He was independent as a hog on ice" (*Mountain Men*, p. 90). The same held true for Santa Fe Trail merchants--"rugged individuals" who "frequently left the regular ruts and cut trails of their own"; people who quickly tired of the gaiety of Santa Fe for they found "something a little indecent about a crowd, something less than human, something offensive and dangerous to their personal identity" (*The Old Santa Fe Trail*, p. 274). The plainsman, Vestal maintains, is simply more individualistic than other Americans.

In Vestal's West every man carries arms to insure his individualism went unchecked. Fighting, in fact, seems central to Vestal's vision of heroic action. His protagonists fought the elements, the Mexicans of the Southwest, and most notably of all, the Plains Indians. Survival, let alone success, requires courage, quick action, and a willingness to kill, for in "a land where every stranger was a potential enemy," a frontiersman "would not live long if he were beset by doubts, by scruples, by conflicting theories of conduct." Vestal never expresses doubt about the necessity and even value of violence. In the Carson biography, subtitled *The Happy Warrior*, Vestal makes it clear Kit never picked a fight. He fought only in open warfare against Indians, bandits, or soldiers opposing the United States' interests. Admittedly, Carson did engage in the cold-blooded killing of non-combatants at the start of the Mexican War in California. But, Vestal insists, there was provocation. Besides, Kit could have offered plenty of examples where Mexicans had similarly gunned down Americans. In the end, Vestal concludes, Carson was probably motivated by "the mountain man's ingrained distrust of and contempt for the Mexicans. As the saying ran, 'If Spaniards warn't made for shootin, what are rifles for?'" (Pp. 216, 228).

Ultimately, however, the western hero's courage was tested in the crucible of Indian warfare. At age nineteen Kit Carson passed this crucial test when he killed and scalped an Apache. But the greatest challenge to Vestal's hero comes from Plains Indians. "No mission slaves these, to run away and let him burn their town. No miserable Diggers, no skulking Apaches crawling into camp at night to steal a trap. Blackfoot!" Plains Indians are Vestal's proudest fighters. They pose the ultimate test of a frontier hero's valor. Carson passes this one, too. He is "the greatest Indian fighter in the army. He had crushed the Apaches, the most dreaded and crafty of mountain Indians. He had tamed the Navajo, most manly and treacherous and numerous of all the tribes of the desert" (pp. 64, 280).

He would have a hand in the conquest of the southern Plains Indians as well.

Warfare, Vestal believes, plays an enormous role in all human affairs. Moreover, it created the United States. Every generation, in fact, should be prepared to defend itself through resort to arms. Writing in 1941 about life on the nineteenth-century plains, Vestal cautions the reader that "the Road to Appeasement leads to Death in any country." On the High Plains that road was short and led straight to Boot Hill. Fighting was not only right, it was natural. If a male did not look forward to war, "people would think there was something wrong with his glands" (*Short Grass Country*, pp. 22, 28, 43).

Besides, Vestal argues elsewhere, few of his generation needed to be reminded that tyranny was worse than war. "Abolish war, and you abolish revolution; abolish the possibility of revolution, and you abolish liberty. Our Constitution provides that Congress shall pass no law forbidding American citizens to own and bear arms; for, to be free, men must have bullets as well as ballots" (*Warpath*, p. 94). Individual freedom and a willingness to fight to protect that freedom, then, make the West and America.

So did *men.* The Great Plains, Vestal maintains, was a man's country. "Women and weaklings shrank from the vastness." But the men, "hard drinking, hard fighting warriors and wanderers, gamblers and explorers," love the Plains with its "moods of violence." "Not since the days of the Vikings had the virile white man found a country so congenial to his heart's desire." The mountain men, in particular, "left America an ideal of manhood to cherish, a memory to be proud of." Even the Missouri River, whose story was "an heroic poem, an epic," was a "thoroughly masculine river." So insignificant were women to Vestal's West that he transforms the noun "woman" into a verb, meaning to mate or to marry as in "Kit decided it was about time he womaned," thus making it a word that could be applied only in the context of male action and initiative (*Kit Carson*, p. 181; *Mountain Men*, p. 90).

In a most remarkable and significant passage, Vestal amplifies the virility theme:

> In the good old days on the Buffalo Plains, when an Indian orator had reached the passionate climax of his speech, and wished to overwhelm his hearers with the force and validity of his remarks, he would suddenly step forward, let fall his blankets, jerk off his breech-cloth, and display the tokens of his manhood to the admiration of the world.... Since those days, that virile, magnificent gesture has been the inspiration of countless Westerners, who have imitated it (in essentials, if not in detail) to their own great profit, and the glory of their kind. . . . One may say, metaphorically, that the history of the American Frontier is strewn with discarded breech-cloths (*Short Grass Country*, p. 172).

He goes on to say that one cannot understand the West "without constant reference to vanishing gee-strings. It all boils down to What a Man!" Vestal's point here surpasses the issue of virility. He believes that the Plains Indians, with his manliness, independence, and warlike spirit, made the nineteenth-century plains frontier a heroic age and place. Without Indians there would have been no adventure, no war, "only a mob of lusterless clodhoppers moving into the empty wilds a little farther each season" (pp. 173-174).

Vestal's Anglo-American heroes, as noted above, owe their renown not only to fighting Indians, but to imitating them. This poses a dilemma for Vestal, however. On the one hand, he presents Sioux warriors as "gentlemen of the Epic mold." On the other hand, when Anglo-Americans took center stage, Vestal recasts Indians into villains, whose role was limited to testing the mettle of mountain men and others. In *Jim Bridger*, Vestal presents Indians as "angry savages driven from their towns, thirsting for the white man's blood, scornful of their peace" (p. 40). "Hostile Injuns gave the trappers more trouble than all other things combined," Vestal writes elsewhere, "and of all the hostiles on the Missouri, the Blackfeet were the worst." "Anyways you fix it," he explains, "a Blackfoot was a Blackfoot, the orneriest skunk in the mountains" (*Mountain Men*, p. 9; *Joe Meek*, p. 104). He reserves his darkest image for the Comanches--a kindly folk, he claims, before their contacts with the Spaniards. "After centuries of contact with the Spanish outposts, however, the Comanches acquired peculiarly repulsive traits," including lack of art, myth, courage, and compassion for captives (*The Old Santa Fe Trail*, p. 121). In his own defense, Vestal might argue that he simply presented the mountain man's attitude toward Indians and Mexicans in these books. But Vestal did not research mountain man attitudes. He simply accepts, and perpetuates, stereotype. His work, then, presents an irreconcilable ambivalence about Indians.

Yet on this fundamental point he remains consistent. Plainsmen, whether Indian or white, afford ample scope to any lover of heroics. Indians such as Sitting Bull and Chief White Bull earn their distinction through warfare with other Indians. But they also achieve a measure of heroic stature through conflicts with Anglo-Americans--not mountain men, of course, but bureaucrats, army officers, and farmers. Representatives of these groups never reach Vestal's realm of epic heroes and so they serve nicely as foils to Indian protagonists. Emigrant farmers receive little but contempt. They are "alternately arrogant and panic-stricken, and tried to make up for the boredom of plodding along the endless trail by writing home highly-colored accounts of imaginary Indian raids" (*New Sources of Indian History*, p. 189).

As for officer and bureaucrat, "From the point of view of the Indians, it was generally a toss-up as to whether the Army was to kill them or the Indian Bureau was to rob or starve them." Vestal's problem with both institutions is the curb they placed on individual liberty. The Indian Bureau is particularly un-American, in his view, because it allowed for no liberty of person, property, or conscience; no free speech, no self-determination; no separation of church and state on the reservation. In a line he must have liked since he used it several times, Vestal concludes, "the Rights of Man had been lost somewhere between Thomas Jefferson's study and the cabin of Sitting Bull" (*Warpath*, pp. 30, 291; *New Sources of Indian History*, p. 279). Stanley Vestal did not attempt careful, judicious assessment of Indian policy in the nineteenth century West. He offers comments about these matters in the context of his heroic themes where all is black and white. If Sitting Bull was the hero, then someone must be the villain, and the Indian Bureau fit the bill.

Vestal did take pride, however, in writing what he claimed to be the first biography of a great American Indian statesman. Anxious to present Indian points of view, Vestal made an important contribution in original research, spending several months interviewing old timers among the Sioux in South Dakota before penning *Sitting Bull.* This kind of intensive primary research did not typify Vestal's work, though, and his shallow research became an important theme for his academic critics.

Vestal did not hesitate to defend himself on this score. In the preface of his textbook, *Writing Non-Fiction*, he indicates that writing was both art and business. A successful book, according to Vestal, finds a wide audience and produces royalties. His formula for popular appeal was fact combined with passion. While some writers would maintain facts and ideas could stand on their own without embellishment, Vestal believed the author must add emotion and enthusiasm to attract readers. Without the "passion" a writer should expect to be satisfied with a university press and a small readership. Vestal explains that he did read widely in primary and secondary sources before composing his books, but he never wrote from notecards. Academic critics note that the consequence was often inaccurate information and inappropriate generalizations. But Vestal believed that university library shelves were already packed with Ph.D. dissertations produced by "embryo scholars [who] have to print their theses at their own expense and donate them to their university--for even the very university which granted the degree for the thesis would never dream of paying money for such writing. The principal reason why these theses are so unreadable is that they were, as a rule, written directly from notes" (*Writing Non-Fiction*, p. 65).

The University of Oklahoma professor of writing argued for a popularization of American western history for ideological reasons as well as commercial ones. The skilled writer should be "a propagandist for the democratic way of life" because "every writer must practice independence, self-reliance, self-sacrifice, and good will to man. Though all the world go soft and rest in the arms of the government from cradle to the grave, there is no such security for the author. He knows from daily experience that *security is an illusion*; that the only solid thing on which a man can count is his own personal character. The writer cannot function except as a rugged individualist" (pp. 54-55).

Further, he maintains that every scholar's duty was to make himself understood. In an industrial society, men must be informed "if science and democracy are to continue to advance. We cannot maintain our culture if only a few experts understand it." Vestal argues, then, that writers had a civic duty to write in language that all could comprehend. "It is noteworthy that so far, no genius has ever written anything worth understanding which nobody else could understand. The greatest authors in the past have been the most popular" (p. 189).

Understandably, some academic historians took issue with Vestal's concept of scholarship and popular style, if not his politics. Fur trade historian Leroy Hafen understood the dilemma of attempting scholarship and commercial success simultaneously. He grants that by manufacturing detail, dialogue, and thoughts for Jim Bridger, Vestal enables the popular readers to envision the character. But Hafen also believes that a writer could not maintain scholarly definitiveness and popular readability at the same time (*Pacific Historical Review* 16:325). Vestal, for his part, chose a wider audience and for this choice could not be criticized. Dale Morgan, another fur trade historian, is more severe. He criticizes popularizers as writers who lack the novelist's imagination and so use reality as a "crutch," distorting it in the process. Of this breed, Morgan admits, Vestal was one of the most talented writers. The problem was Vestal would not work at research. "Except as entertainments, and a source of income," Morgan concludes, "the majority of Vestal's fur-trade books should never have been written; they added nothing to knowledge, and by merely existing, by preempting the field, may have inhibited scholars and publishers alike from going ahead with books that needed doing" (*American West* 3:31).

In an attempt to categorize Vestal's work, A. R. Mortensen rhetorically asks if *Joe Meek* was biography, history, literature, folklore, or a combination of several genres. He knew it was certainly not history for the historian. Vestal is careless with facts and dates and the writing style would raise professional eyebrows. "However," Mortensen admits, "for the average reader this will be a virtue rather than a shortcoming. Apparently Vestal little cares what the professor says or thinks. With much justification he can say, 'My books are read. Are yours?'" (*Pacific Historical Review* 2:66). Almost thirty years after his death, seven of Vestal's books remain in print.

Bibliography

Books

Adventures of Kit Carson: Frontier Hero. Girard, KS: Haldeman-Julius, 1927.

Bigfoot Wallace: A Biography. Boston: Houghton Mifflin, 1942.

The Book Lover's Southwest: A Guide to Good Reading. Norman: University of Oklahoma Press, 1955.

'Dobe Walls, A Story of Kit Carson's Southwest. Boston: Houghton-Mifflin, 1929.

Early Days among the Cheyenne and Arapaho Indians by John Homer Seger. Editor. Norman: University of Oklahoma Press, 1924.

Fandango: Ballads of the Old West. Boston: Houghton Mifflin, 1927.

Happy Hunting Grounds. Chicago: Lyons and Carnahan, 1928.

The Indian Tipi . . . with a History of the Tipi by Stanley Vestal edited by Reginald Laubin. Norman: University of Oklahoma Press, 1957.

Jim Bridger, Mountain Man: A Biography. New York: W. Morrow & Co., 1946.
Joe Meek: The Merry Mountain Man, A Biography. Caldwell, ID: Caxton Printers, 1952.
King of the Fur Traders: The Deeds and Deviltry of Pierre Esprit Radisson. Boston: Houghton Mifflin, 1940.
Kit Carson: The Happy Warrior of the Old West, A Biography. Boston: Houghton Mifflin, 1928.
The Missouri. New York: Farrar and Rinehart, 1945.
Mountain Men. Boston: Houghton Mifflin, 1937.
New Sources of Indian History, 1850-1891; The Ghost Dance--the Prairie Sioux; a Miscellany. Norman: University of Oklahoma Press, 1934.
The Old Santa Fe Trail. Boston: Houghton Mifflin, 1939.
The Oregon Trail: Sketches of Prairie and Rocky Mountain Life by Francis Parkman. Editor. Oklahoma City: Harlow Publishing Co., 1927.
Professional Writing. New York: Macmillan, 1938.
Queen of the Cowtowns: Dodge City, "the Wickedest Little City in America," 1872-1886. New York: Harper, 1952. Reprint. *Dodge City: Queen of the Cowtowns.* London: P. Nevill, 1955.
Revolt on the Border. Boston: Houghton Mifflin, 1938.
Sallow Moon by Walter D. Merton (pseudonym). Privately printed, ca. 1937.
Short Grass Country. New York: Duell, Sloan, and Pearce, 1941.
Sitting Bull: Champion of the Sioux, A Biography. Boston: Houghton Mifflin, 1932.
Wagons Southwest: Story of Old Trail to Santa Fe. New York: American Pioneer Trails Association, 1946.
Wah-to-Yah and the Taos Trail by Lewis H. Garrard. Editor. Oklahoma City: Harlow Publishing Co., 1927.
Warpath: The True Story of the Fighting Sioux Told in a Biography of Chief White Bull. Boston: Houghton Mifflin, 1934.
Warpath and Council Fire: The Plains Indians' Struggle For Survival in War and Diplomacy, 1851-1890. New York: Random House, 1948.
The Wine Room Murder. Boston: Little, Brown and Co., 1935.
Writing: Advice and Devices. Garden City, NY: Doubleday, 1950.
Writing Magazine Fiction. New York: Doubleday, Doran, & Co., 1940.
Writing Non-Fiction. Boston: The Writer, Inc., 1944.

Selected Articles

"Amerindian Traits." *Southwest Review* 28(Autumn, 1942):53-62.
"Ballads of Kit Carson" [poems]. *American Mercury* 5(July, 1925):270-272.
"Ballads of the Old West: Belle Starr, Boggy Depot, Cynthia Ann." *American Mercury* 7(April, 1926):402-403.
"The Battle of the Little Big Horn." *Bluebook* 57(September, 1933):52-58.
"Best Seller Making." *Saturday Review of Literature* 37(October 16, 1954):22.
"Brave Alone." *Boys' Life* (June, 1937):14-15, 46-50.

"Characterization." *The Writer* 52(December, 1939):369-373.
"The Cheyenne Dog Soldiers." *Chronicles of Oklahoma* 1(January, 1921):90-97.
"The Cheyenne Tipi." *American Anthropologist* 17(October-November, 1915):685-694.
"The Culture is Here." *Southwest Review* 14(July, 1929):478-480.
"Cynthia Ann" [poem]. *Literary Digest* 89(April, 17, 1926):34.
"Dakotah Courtship." *Southwest Review* 24(January, 1939):148-163.
"Death of Satank." *Southwest Review* 12(October, 1926):29-30.
"Dream to Pattern." *The Writer* 55(June, 1942):174-176.
"Duel with Yellow Hand." *Southwest Review* 26(Autumn, 1940):65-77.
"Early Days among the Northern Cheyenne." *Westerners (Chicago) Brand Book* 6(August, 1949):41-42.
"El Rancho Magnifico." *Saturday Review of Literature* 40(September 14, 1957):51-52.
"First Families of Oklahoma." *American Mercury* 5(August, 1925):489-494.
"Fuss and Feathers: Indian Warfare on the Plains." *Westerners (Chicago) Brand Book* 13(May, 1956):17-19, 21-24.
"Hats: Beaver vs. Silk." *Rotarian* 57(November, 1940):17-20.
"The Histrionic West." *Space* 1(June, 1934):13-16.
"The Hollywooden Indian." *Southwest Review* 21(July, 1936):418-423.
"How Not to Write a Story." *The Writer* 53(November, 1940):330-332.
"Imitating the Indian." *Southwest Review* 15(July, 1930):444-451.
"Indians of Oklahoma." *Southwest Review* 14(January, 1929):138-152.
"Irish Flathead." *Catholic Digest* 9(April, 1945):38-40.
"Jim Bridger." *Boys' Life* (March, 1947):22, 40.
"John Colter's Race for Life." In *Adventures for Americans* edited by Wilbur Schramm *et al.* New York: Harcourt, Brace & Co., 1956. Pp. 113-120.
"Kit Carson." *Boys' Life* (November, 1945):16-17, 45.
"Last of the Pioneers." *New Mexico* (November, 1935):22-23, 44.
"Little Soldiers." *Boys' Life*, October, 1936.
"Lynn Riggs: Poet and Dramatist." *Southwest Review* 15(October, 1929):64-71.
"The Man Who Killed Custer." *American Heritage* 8(February, 1957):6-9.
"Making Yourselves Wolves." In *Best Short Stories for Boys and Girls* compiled by Carol Ryrie Brink. 6th edition. Evanston, IL: Row, Peterson and Co., 1940. Pp. 325-351.
"Modern Article Technique." *The Writer* 57(January, 1944):9-12.
"Mountain Gardens." *New Mexico* (February, 1937):14-15, 33.
"No Encore." *Southwest Review* 20(October, 1934):56-60.
"Oxford Revisited." *Southwest Review* 40(Spring, 1955):151-155.
"Plains Indians and the War." *Saturday Review of Literature* 25(May 16, 1942):9-10.
"The Plains Indian in Literature--and in Life." In *The Trans-Mississippi West* edited by James F. Willard and Colin B. Goodykoontz. Boulder: University of Colorado, 1930. Pp. 175-194.

"Prairie Pictographs: Prairie Dog, Burrowing Owl, Rattlesnake, Spider, Buffalo." *Poetry, Magazine of Verse* 32(August, 1928):252-253.

"Ree Horse Race: An Incident in the Life of Sitting Bull." *Southwest Review* 17(Autumn, 1931):72-76.

"Re-Tooling for the War Market." *The Writer* 56(August, 1943):231-233.

"The Saga of the Corncob Pipe." *Southwest Review* 30(Summer, 1945):354-356.

"Sailing Over the Prairies." *Southwest Review* 23(July, 1938):428-435.

"Sans Arc." *Space* 1(May, 1934):9.

"Settlers in the Territory." *Saturday Review of Literature* 18(September 14, 1935):12.

"Significant Form." *The Writer* 54(January, 1941):9-12.

"Sioux in Ambush." *Bluebook* 57(August, 1933):44-50.

"Sitting Bull." *Adventure* 81(January 15, 1932):138-152 and (February 15, 1932):50-63.

"Sitting Bull's Maiden Speech." *Frontier and Midland* 12(March, 1932):269-271.

"The Soldiers." In *This is the West* edited by Robert West Howard. Chicago: Rand McNally & Co., 1957. Pp. 66-71.

"Sooner Songs and Ballads: Saddle Songs, Kit Carson's Mule, Kit Carson of U.S.N., The Lost Trail." *Poetry, Magazine of Verse* 26(July, 1925):177-184.

"They Dance in Oklahoma." *Southwest Review* 20(July, 1935):336-346.

"Three Ballads of Kit Carson" [poems]. *Southwest Review* 10(April, 1925):77-82.

"The Tipis of the Crow Indians." *American Anthropologist* 29(January, 1927):87-114.

"The Troubled Life of Billy Bonney." *Saturday Review of Literature* 39(July 21, 1956):27.

"The West Rewrites its History." *Saturday Review of Literature* 38(July 16, 1955):16.

"Western Stuff." *Southwest Review* 15(January, 1930):171-176.

"What Price Tradition?" *Southwest Review* 21(October, 1935):83-88.

"White Bull and One Bull." *Westerners (Chicago) Brand Book* 4(October, 1947):45, 47-48.

"Who Will Win the War?" *Woman's Home Companion* 69(November, 1942):17.

"Wooden Indian." *American Mercury* 13(January, 1928):81-86.

"The Works of Sitting Bull: Real or Imaginary." *Southwest Review* 19(April, 1934):265-278.

"Writing Historical Fiction." *The Writer* 54(June, 1941):165-168.

"Writing Non-Fiction." *The Writer* 56(October, 1943):298-301.

"Your Intimate Subject." *The Writer* 53(September, 1940):268-269.

Selected Reviews

Across the Wide Missouri by Bernard de Voto. *American Historical Review* 53(April, 1948):560-561; and *Pacific Historical Review* 17(May, 1948):201-208.

The Apache Indians by Frank C. Lockwood. *Mississippi Valley Historical Review* 25(June, 1938):125-126.

The Cheyenne Way: Conflict and Case Law in Primitive Jurisprudence by K. N. Llewellyn and E. Adamson Hoebel. *Pacific Historical Review* 11(March, 1942):88.

The Comanche Barrier to South Plains Settlement: A Century and a Half of Savage Resistance to the Advancing White Frontier by Rubert Norval Richardson. *Mississippi Valley Historical Review* 21(September, 1934):272-273.

Land of the Spotted Eagle by Chief Standing Bear. *Mississippi Valley Historical Review* 22(December, 1933):442-443.

The Missouri Valley: Land of Drought, Flood, and Promise by Rufus Terrel. *Pacific Historical Review* 17(February, 1948):78.

Plains Indian Painting: A Description of an Aboriginal American Art by John C. Ewers. *Mississippi Valley Historical Review* 27(December, 1940):472-473.

This Reckless Breed of Men: The Trappers and Fur Traders of the Southwest by Robert Glass Cleland. *American Historical Review* 55(July, 1950):919-920.

The Wild Horse of the West by Walker D. Wyman. *Mississippi Valley Historical Review* 32(September, 1945):287-288.

Studies of Stanley Vestal

Austin, Mary. Review of *Sitting Bull* by Stanley Vestal. *Saturday Review of Literature* 9(October 22, 1932):188.

Berthrong, Donald. "Walter Stanley Campbell: Plainsman." *Arizona and the West* 7(Summer, 1965):91-104.

Branch, E. Douglas. Review of *Mountain Men* by Stanley Vestal. *Mississippi Valley Historical Review* 24(September, 1937):255-256.

Commager, Henry Steele. Review of *Warpath: The True Story of Fighting the Sioux Told in a Biography of Chief White Bull* by Stanley Vestal. *Yale Review* 28(Summer, 1934):847.

DeVoto, Bernard. Review of *Jim Bridger* by Stanley Vestal. *Weekly Book Review*, October 6, 1942, p. 6.

Dobie, J. F. Review of *Kit Carson* by Stanley Vestal. *Nation* 126(June 6, 1928):650.

Foreman, Grant. Review of *New Sources of Indian History* by Stanley Vestal. *Mississippi Valley Historical Review* 21(December, 1934):420-421.

Gabriel, R. H. Review of *Kit Carson* by Stanley Vestal. *Yale Review* 18(September, 1928):185.

Hafen, Le Roy R. Review of *Jim Bridger* by Stanley Vestal. *Pacific Historical Review* 16(August, 1947):325-326.

Hollon, W. Eugene. "Stanley Vestal." In *The American West: The Reader's Encyclopedia* edited by Howard R. Lamar. New York: Thomas Y. Crowell Co., 1977. P. 1225.

Morgan, Dale L. Review of *Jim Bridger* by Stanley Vestal. *Saturday Review of Literature* 29(October 26, 1946):37.

Mortensen, A. R. Review of *Joe Meek* by Stanley Vestal. *Pacific Historical Review* 22(February, 1953):65-66.

Nevins, Allan. Review of *The Old Santa Fe Trail* by Stanley Vestal. *Saturday Review of Literature* 20(September 9, 1939):17.

Short, Julee. "Walter S. Campbell." *Chronicles of Oklahoma* 51(Winter, 1974):473-486.

Sonnichsen, C. L. Review of *The Old Santa Fe Trail* by Stanley Vestal. *El Paso Herald Post*, September 2, 1939.

Swain, Dwight V. "A Dedication To the Memory of Walter Stanley Campbell, 1877-1957." *Arizona and the West* 7(Summer, 1965):87-90.

Tassin, Ray. *Stanley Vestal.* Glendale, CA: The Arthur H. Clark Co., 1973.

Van de Water, F. F. Review of *Bigfoot Wallace* by Stanley Vestal. *New York Times*, August 23, 1942, p. 21.

Webb, Walter Prescott. Review of *Queen of the Cowtowns* by Stanley Vestal. *Saturday Review of Literature* 35(February 23, 1952):13.

54

WALTER PRESCOTT WEBB

by Gregory M. Tobin

Biography

Like many of those who entered the expanding higher education system in the early years of the century and went on to notable academic careers, Walter Prescott Webb had to work his way out of an isolated rural setting and contrive the kind of education that a later generation would come to regard as a routine progression. Born in Panola County, East Texas, in 1888, the son of an itinerant school teacher, Webb was taken at a very early age to a raw farming community in Stephens County, west of Fort Worth and on the edge of the Great Plains. His father taught school wherever he could find work in a three-county area and in 1902 began farming a small tract of land near Ranger in Stephens County. He worked the farm on weekends, teaching during the rest of the week to generate an income until the land could be brought into production. While he was away, his fourteen-year-old son was left in charge; in later years, Walter Webb would point to those years of drudgery as evidence of his personal knowledge of life on the plains and as the basis for his understanding of the ways of its people, although at the time he hated the boredom of farm routine and the poverty that went with it.

The irregular schooling Walter Prescott Webb received alerted him to a far more attractive world beyond the farm, and he gradually constructed a way to escape. A voracious reader and keen to work with words, Webb inched his way toward college by teaching in a number of rural communities, and gained admission to the University of Texas in 1909. He had hoped that the study of literature would train him to become a writer for quality magazines; but he reacted against the approach to literature then in vogue, and instead turned to courses offered in what was then known as the department of institutional history. This rather unusual unit was devised by the university to accommodate Lindley Miller Keasbey, a formidable scholar with interests in sociology, anthropology, economics, and broad social science theory, who was cast adrift as the result of a departmental reorganization within the college of arts. Several years after graduation, Webb was hired by the more orthodox department of history, and but for short periods as a visiting professor at Harvard and Oxford, he was to remain at Texas for the rest of his working life. He died in 1963 at the age of seventy-four, the victim of a car accident, and was buried in the state cemetery at Austin--itself a striking indication of his status as a public figure in his home state (*The Making of a History*).

Partly by choice and partly due to circumstances outside his control, Webb's scholarly development generally ran behind the conventional schedule. He was twenty-one when he began his undergraduate studies in 1909, did not graduate until 1915, was thirty-four when he entered graduate school in 1922 and his first major publication--*The Great Plains*--established his academic reputation at the age of forty-three. That success provided him with the security of tenure; he had been given a minor position in the history department at the University of Texas in 1918, when the influx of returning veterans put a heavy strain on the department's resources, and the need to upgrade his qualifications had taken him to graduate school at the University of Chicago. His failure there deeply humiliated Webb, and left him almost permanently estranged from his profession. *The Great Plains* was in part his reply to that earlier verdict of failure, and was accepted by his own university as the graduate qualification required before tenure could be granted. Though a well-respected and influential figure in his own department, he studiously maintained a rather jaundiced view of the profession at large. He rarely published in major journals, and preferred to see his occasional pieces appear in newspapers or magazines where they would be judged by the wider community rather than by his academic peers. A profoundly loyal Texan, he promoted local history at a time when it was unfashionable and enjoyed the kind of close contact with the life of his own community that many academics tend to avoid.

Because his introduction to his craft was delayed and irregular, Webb's outlook and personality were already shaped by the time professional conventions began to make demands on him; but he was also unlucky in that at two critical points in his life those conventions bore down on him with considerable force. The first was his failure as a graduate student, an event which owed as much to his own lack of effort and interest than any inherent defect in the system of graduate training. The second was the famous appraisal of *The Great Plains* by the Social Sciences Research Council in 1939, an exercise planned with the best of scholarly intentions and fatally compromised by profound disagreement between Webb and the appraiser, Fred Shannon (*An Appraisal of Webb*). On each occasion Webb was severely affronted and retreated to his Texas enclave in high dudgeon. When toward the end of his career his peers honored him with the presidency of the American Historical Association and the University of Chicago awarded him an honorary degree, Webb accepted with customary grace. But there can be little doubt that he saw such gestures of recognition as victories to be enjoyed and belated acknowledgment that his maverick ways had been justified. It had been the profession that had come to terms with Webb, and not vice versa.

Long before he retired the broad outlines of Webb's biography were well established, both in his own community and in the profession at large. It was an attractive story, and one that struck familiar chords: a farm boy, whose appeal for advice in the columns of a southern magazine had caught the attention of a generous benefactor in New York, and had won his way to college with his patron's unselfish assistance. An independent and unconventional thinker, he had been frustrated in his first efforts by more conservative academics, but then went on to prove them wrong by becoming a famous scholar in his own right. It was a portrait that Webb carefully shaped and gradually revealed to his audience in a series of gestures that seem to reflect more than the normal tendency in middle life to locate oneself retrospectively and to define identity by reference to past experience.

For several decades before his retirement, Webb discreetly laid out a line of autobiographical detail, leaving skillfully arranged clues to the stages of his growth as a personality and as an intellect, and making sure that the image that he found in his own contemplation of self was taken up and reproduced by others. This is not to suggest deception or the existence of a persona radically different from that accepted by his contemporaries. It is rather to emphasize the extent to which he reflected in private on his experience of life as an academic and the care with which he released details of his private identity to the public. A rather reticent, modest, and self-contained personality as his friends and colleagues saw him, Webb had rather more than the normal concern for acceptance and recognition by his peers and by the general public. To Webb, the significance of what he had written derived from the fact that it was in some sense anchored in his own experience of life, and it was important that others understood that a view of history that had that element of personal authentication was not amenable to change simply at the behest of scholarly critics.

This element of personal reflection on his own past and the relationship between experience and interpretation was also triggered by his long-standing interest in the technique of writing, and especially short story writing. One of his undoubted strengths as a historian was his ability to recognize a good story line and work simple material into a compelling format. In his youth he had hoped to establish himself as a writer of fiction set in the Southwest, but he found that he was much more comfortable with material drawn from life. Throughout his career he made good use of what might be termed historical parables. The subject that best lent itself to the short story technique, however, was the story of his own life, and there is probably no better testimonial to his ability to work with words than the success of the account of his discovery by his benefactor, William E. Hinds, that Webb wrote for *Harper's Magazine* (223:62-69) and which later appeared in *Reader's Digest* (79:35-40). For a historian who placed special value on the approval of the general public, it was an especially satisfying achievement to have a segment of his life story read by millions. The cumulative effect of this kind of autobiographical revelation, appearing in magazines, newspapers, and occasional addresses, was quite impressive. It has always been Webb's own account of his journey from the Cross Timbers of West Texas to a position of eminence in his profession that has shaped the public and professional perception of his life and its significance, and that in itself is a tribute to his shrewd understanding of human nature and the way in which public reputations are made.

Themes

Webb remains one of a small number of western historians to have made an impact on his profession at the national and international levels. That someone so deeply locked into a local and provincial setting should have gradually worked his way out to a global frame of reference may seem ironic at first sight, but it was precisely the urge to assert the importance of regional concerns within larger structures that determined his choice of themes and the manner in which they were presented. In the 1920s Webb's resentments were not directed solely at the obstructions that he felt had been put in the way of his career, but also at what he regarded as the indifference of conventional historical scholarship to the experience of communities in the more remote and recently settled parts of the country, and in particular the communities he had known in his early years. When he began the research that would culminate in *The Great Plains*, Webb was privately sympathetic with rural America's distrust of the pretensions of city life and the apparent dilution of Anglo-American civilization by decades of exposure to European influences. Although Webb was never as strident in his criticisms of the East as the old-guard westerners whom he so much admired in the 1920s--Eugene Manlove Rhodes and Emerson Hough--he shared their resentment of the eastern establishment's refusal to recognize that part of the national experience that lay west of the Mississippi.

The success of *The Great Plains* in 1931 established Webb's credentials as a historian, and at the same time provided his region with an acceptable historical self-portrait; but his distrust of the East and its ways spilled over into his polemical *Divided We Stand: The Crisis of a Frontierless Democracy*, published in 1935 as an angry attack on the economic exploitation of the South by grasping and arrogant corporations of the East. Although the book was to a large extent a tract for the times, its subtitle signaled Webb's growing interest in the wider theme to which Turner had drawn attention three decades earlier, the impact on American life of the loss of the frontier dynamic. For another fifteen years he brooded over the approaches that had worked so well in *The Great Plains*, and began to widen his terms of reference. Pausing only to tidy up an old project on the Texas Rangers that had been superseded by his study of the Plains, Webb began to delve into fields far beyond his basic regional framework.

When *The Great Frontier* appeared in 1952, it became clear how far he had travelled as a historian over the two decades since his first success. Now confident of his abilities as a wide-angle theorist, Webb startled Americanists and Europeanists alike by extending the notion of the West far beyond its regional origins and stretching it across the entire Atlantic rim and over four centuries. The West that Theodore Roosevelt had cherished was now the West as his cousin Franklin saw it during World War II and as the Cold War generation understood it in relation to the Eastern European bloc. The frontier was no longer Turner's purely American dynamic, but the engine of European expansion since the fifteenth century. *The Great Frontier* marked the furthest extension of Webb's lifelong effort to give shape to a perspective that had its roots in the life of a small farming community in West Texas at the turn of the century. By joining the small group of scholars willing to operate at a global level of generalization, Webb ignored the convention that historians of the American West converse only with each other and on matters of parochial concern.

Analysis

Two works, *The Great Plains* and *The Great Frontier*, some fifty years apart, are basic to any assessment of Webb's significance as a historian. Though it has stood unrevised for more than half a century, *The Great Plains* continues to be the essential starting point for any discussion of the region. In a sense, it gave definition to an area that at the time was less obviously a regional entity than other parts of the nation, and at the same time encased it in a historical narrative that ensured its special place within the broader American epic. For an unknown scholar at odds with his profession, this was no mean achievement; but the elements that went into that achievement were in themselves an intriguing mixture of personality traits and a variety of intellectual influences. That he worked at a conscious remove from the Turnerian tradition can be generally accepted, and although no one working with western materials in the 1920s could claim to be immune from Turner's influence, Webb's local sensitivities inevitably put him at odds with any outlook centered on the experience of the eastern half of the country, however rural its emphasis.

By taking up the relationship between the natural environment and social development that had figured so large in the lectures he had heard from Lindley Miller Keasbey in his undergraduate years at the University of Texas, Webb found that he could identify within the Plains environment so distinctive a combination of environmental extremes--level terrain, semiaridity, and lack of timber--that he could explain the character of the various human incursions into the region, incursions that resulted in defeat for those groups unable to adapt and success for those which could supply the elements needed to counteract the critical deficiencies in the environment. What he produced was an account which could stand quite apart from the Turner canon and could generate admiration for the special achievements of the Plains communities.

Yet it was also an account that owed little to the conventional forms of historical writing. There was no account of the political history of the region, no state history, no customary narrative line--in fact, none of the categories that would have been exposed as patently thin if they had been applied to the history of the Great Plains. The structure of Webb's work was determined by the patterns he saw in the relationship between the natural environment and social institutions, and to challenge the book was to deny the environmental assumptions on which it was based. It was Webb's strong sense of the interdependence of its component parts, combined with his anger at its treatment at the hands of Fred Shannon in 1939, that made him refuse to revise *The Great Plains*. Since he was convinced that his conclusions had been validated by the approval given to his work by those familiar with the region, any suggestion that it could be improved by revision smacked of a malicious and destructive assault on historical truth as he understood it, and he refused to join such a debate.

To argue that from the vantage point of half a century Webb's portrait of the Plains is seriously flawed is not to denigrate the original achievement or to suggest that its status as a historical artifact in its own right is undeserved. It remains a bold and innovative study, but it reflects the weaknesses as well as the strengths of Webb's historical perspective at the time, and it must be seen in the light of both the insights and the findings generated by the research that has accumulated since it first appeared.

Like a number of historians of his generation, Webb absorbed too much of the emphasis given to environmental influences by the first generation of American geographers, and did not detect the shift toward a more cautious view of the relationship between environment and culture that began to take hold in the mid-1920s. Nor does he appear to have monitored the development of a body of detailed geographical and scientific information that began to accumulate as the Plains environment came under closer scrutiny in the years that followed his successful publication, information that would have suggested useful elements of revision. Though he had already demonstrated a commendable willingness to search for information and ideas in sources that would have seemed unusual to the more conventional historians of his day, he stopped well short of the kind of comprehensive investigation that was to characterize James C. Malin's work.

It was this impatience with close detail when larger formulations were there to be flushed out that left Webb vulnerable to Fred Shannon's relentless testing during the Social Science Research Council's appraisal exercise in 1939, and to which Webb reacted with such bitterness. Webb was a hunter after clues and insights rather than a methodical accumulator and assessor, and given the range of his topic and the lack of a body of systematic research from which he might launch his own investigation, his preference for the broad sweep may have been justifiable in the late 1920s. What is unfortunate was his apparent determination to see his account of the Plains as fixed and incapable of modification in the light of new knowledge.

Although Webb argued that the strength of his interpretation of the Plains experience lay in his direct experience of life in that environment, his knowledge of the Plains region was orientated to its southeastern corner, and he remains open to the criticism that he saw the region from a Texan perspective. He had not travelled extensively in much of the region prior to 1931, and he did not have a detailed knowledge of its central or northern tiers; the kind of detailed critique that Fred Shannon developed in relation to Webb's definition of the eastern perimeter of the plains can now be developed by geographers and historians specializing in the study of the northern Great Plains.

Nor is Webb's account of the specifically Texan component of the Plains experience immune from revision; for example, Terry G. Jordan's studies of the earlier manifestations of the cattle industry in the South appear to have undermined Webb's account of the origins of the industry in South Texas (*Trails to Texas*). At a more general level, Webb's discussion of the Indian and Spanish experience of the Plains reflects both the limitations of contemporary scholarship and the prevailing cultural assumptions of the Anglo community in the 1920s, and as such needs revision in the light of later research.

The more fundamental problem, however, remains Webb's inability to detect the shift in attitudes towards the relationship between culture and environment that had already set in at the time the book went to press and that subsequently undercut many of its basic assumptions. By the late 1920s Carl Sauer had already discussed culture as an active rather than passive element in relation to the natural environment, and a later generation of scholars would tease out the considerable variations within the cultural factor itself as interacted with specific geographic settings. As Frederick C. Luebke has pointed out, the communities that settled on the Plains came from a variety of ethnic backgrounds and brought with them specific cultural traditions that reacted with the local environment in a number of ways (*Western Historical Quarterly* 15:33).

The process of settlement was a good deal more complex than Webb's general account suggested, and it must be studied in smaller units and specific time frames before a satisfactory general account can emerge. Webb was not interested in the kind of detailed studies of farm ownership and settler mobility that Malin developed in the 1940s, or the probing of the immigrant experience carried out more recently by Luebke. The Shannon appraisal in 1939 had revealed with some precision the contrast between Webb's research methods and those of his colleagues, a contrast that Webb confirmed both at the Skytop Conference and in his later comments on the development of his career: he worked intuitively, elaborating a general theory first and then searching for the evidence to confirm it, acting rather like an advocate for a brief rather than an impartial investigator. There can be no doubt that Webb's perceptions were often shrewd and amenable to confirmation, and that they provided an excellent starting point for research and testing. But by virtue of his temperament, his training, and his alienation from the working practices of his profession,

Webb balked at the kind of testing that broad generalizations require if they are to be of value.

A Webb formulation, once advanced, remained locked into place, and despite his description of his work as available for further development and elaboration by others, he found it difficult to distinguish between constructive criticism and personal attack. The notion of scholarly debate as an instrument in the advancement of knowledge did not sit comfortably with him, and he preferred to nail his flag to the mast and let others try to reach it. For Webb, the writing of history was an aspect of the presentation of self as well as a contribution toward a collective exploration of a segment of the past, and it was as the founder of a school of historical research, rather than as a member of one, that he hoped to be remembered.

That hope was central to the great enterprise which dominated the second half of his career--the formulation and elaboration of what he termed the Great Frontier concept. Webb's interest in the social implications of the disappearance of the frontier--with all that meant in terms of access to land and resources--had its source in the harsh realities of the depression. Although able to keep his family in modest comfort during those years, he was close enough to his roots in rural and small-town Texas to grieve for those who saw their lives shattered by deprivation and to detest the corporations that used their power to exploit the weak and the impoverished. *Divided We Stand*, Webb's polemic against the economic predators of the East, made it clear that he had begun to think about the wider economic context that lay beyond the specific case of regional exploitation before him. For another decade and a half he was to devote most of his efforts toward trying to understand the wider framework within which the great crises of his day--the massive economic dislocation of the thirties and World War II--were set.

The Great Frontier appeared in 1952, and set out Webb's global variant of the original Turner thesis: the frontier was a great deal more than the dynamic element underlying the entire American experience through to the late nineteenth century and should be seen as the central element in the expansion of European civilization across the world during the last four centuries. Just as Turner expressed concern about the impact on American life of the closing of the frontier, Webb pointed to the implications for the western world of the disappearance of that vast stockpile of natural resources. He shared with Turner an interest in the ideas of the nineteenth-century Italian economist Achille Loria, whose major work had been translated into English by Lindley Miller Keasbey, Webb's mentor at the University of Texas, and whose ideas on the place of land in the economic expansion of Western Europe provided both with a useful conceptual framework. But Webb was especially concerned with the problems of his own day, believing that it was possible to understand great economic and political issues confronting the western world in the mid-twentieth century by tracing their source in deep-rooted changes in the relationship between population and land, and in the social institutions that developed around that relationship over the previous four centuries.

What he found convinced him that the western world would have to come to terms with a general contraction of its supply of natural resources, a process that he describes as the collapse of a 400-year boom in the Atlantic economy. Just as Turner had expressed anxiety about the capacity of American institutions to adjust to the loss of the frontier dynamic, Webb became increasingly pessimistic about the impact of the end of the boom on the values and institutions of western civilization, which he saw as shaped and solidified by their long exposure to an affluence based on New World resources. It was a pessimism that would be reflected in many of his statements on public issues in his later years, and at times it put him at odds with those who equated short-term economic advantage with long-term public benefit. When he returned in the late 1950s to the regional rather than global framework, his designation of a large part of the American West as a desert region attracted the kind of criticism that he had by then come to accept as almost routine (*American Historical Review* 58:963; *William & Mary Quarterly* 11:121-126; *Past and Present* 5:79-93). To suggest that current prosperity could not be maintained permanently if it was based on the regular depletion of water resources was to challenge assumptions that were embedded in every section of the local community, and Webb understood the hostility his ideas evoked. His response was not to retreat, but to try to make his point more effectively.

There is some irony in the fact that Webb's portrait of a western world poised at the end of an unusually prolonged resources boom appeared at the beginning of a decade in which his profession was to define affluence and consensus as key elements in the national experience and to confirm the public view of the promise of American life. Had he lived through the 1960s, he would have found himself less isolated in a community that was beginning to question the wisdom of conventional attitudes to the exploitation of resources and to doubt the capacity of the natural environment to cope with the pressures placed on it by the growth of population and the extension of industrialization. The energy crises of the 1970s would have confirmed his pessimistic view of the long-term prospects for the industrialized world, and he would have been intrigued by discussion of the problems confronting postindustrial societies. Yet the arrival of some of the elements of crisis that Webb had forecast in the early 1950s has not led to any significant amplification of his Great Frontier thesis.

The man himself remains a source of considerable interest, and the general outline of his Great Frontier thesis has become almost as familiar as his portrait of the plains; but in neither case has a body of Webb-related studies emerged. The lecture series sponsored by the University of Texas at Arlington as a memorial to Webb has produced some excellent probes in comparative history; but then careful and detailed studies of the frontier experience across the globe tend to point up the diversity and complexity of that experience, and rather than providing support for a general theory, underline the importance of an understanding of the specific cultural and institutional context in each case (*Essays on Walter Prescott Webb*; *Essays on Frontiers in World History*).

In some respects, *The Great Frontier* is more seriously flawed than *The Great Plains*, in that it is based on a limited knowledge of the complex and dense history of European societies and appears to make far too sweeping a claim for the impact of the overseas frontier on European civilization. Even discounting for the traditional reluctance of Europeanists to concede significance to the experience of the outer continents, there is some basis for the view that Webb's general theory contained very little that was new and that his supporting arguments revealed a rather elementary grasp of European history (*The Old World and the New*). The problem for those who consider further development of the Webb thesis is to define what aspects lend themselves to further study. For many, it will be the study of Webb as a theorist rather than the study of *The Great Frontier* that will seem the more fruitful line of research.

It is as boundary markers for Webb's personal view of history, rather than as seminal studies, that *The Great Plains* and *The Great Frontier* continue to have an impact. Turner's ideas triggered a whole range of commentary and amplification, and it was not until many years after his death that Lee Benson and Ray Allen Billington began to map out the processes that formed Turner's historical outlook and to locate him in a specific intellectual environment. Webb, on the other hand, was very conscious of his own identity as a historian and tried to understand why his approach to historical inquiry was different than that of his peers. It comes as no surprise that he found part of the answer in environmental influences; but he also stressed the effectiveness of the research techniques he had slowly developed over the years, and especially his use of the graduate seminar as a test bed for his ideas. Others might find his methods idiosyncratic and, despite their pedagogical value, less rigorous than they ought to have been.

The element in his own training that Webb did not fully understand and that to a large extent explains why so few have attempted to follow his lead, was his unusually heavy exposure to elements of late nineteenth-century social and cultural theory that were already fading when he first came across them. His period with Keasbey introduced him to the expansive theorizing characteristic of nineteenth-century social science, and it is to this influence that he owed his lifelong orientation as a thinker and researcher. He knew something of Loria and Ratzel, and as Donald K. Pickens has noted, he probably owed a good deal to William Graham Sumner (*Red River Valley Historical Review* 6:25-34). What he did not receive from Keasbey was exposure to the kind of grounding in archival research and in the evaluation of carefully accumulated bodies of information which by that time had come to be characteristic of the training in the new graduate schools of history. It is that contrast in intellectual styles and in approaches to research that lay at the root of his lifelong suspicion of conventional historians, explains his venture into global history, and provides the context for his celebrated clash with Shannon over the 1939 appraisal.

At the time Webb was puzzled by the Social Science Research Council's selection of *The Great Plains* as the best example of interdisciplinary research in American history since World War I. He had little sense of what the Council meant by interdisciplinary research, simply because he had not been thoroughly trained within a single discipline, and drew ideas and information from any source that seemed appropriate because that was the way in which he had been trained to work. He had found it rewarding. Ironically, it was precisely because he had been so heavily influenced by a body of literature and a way of thinking which predated the division of the social sciences into discrete disciplines that his colleagues, and the Council, saw his work as genuinely interdisciplinary--which it certainly was.

Since he did not understand what the appraisal exercise was about, the confrontation with Shannon was inevitable; yet if he had observed what was happening with a less jaundiced eye, Webb would have found much that was of interest. What the Social Science Research Council was engaged in was a remarkably ambitious attempt to define social science methodology and reestablish something akin to the sense of purpose and cohesion that the nineteenth-century social scientists felt they had achieved. Angry and confused by his own part in the proceedings, Webb asserted the importance of personal experience and insight as against barren empiricism as his defense against Shannon's critique; in doing so, he stumbled into what became the central dilemma of the entire appraisal exercise, the question of whether it would ever be possible--or desirable--to factor out the subjective element in social science research.

The sociologists Thomas and Znaniecki confronted that problem in *The Polish Peasant*, the subject of one of the other appraisals conducted by the Council, and a fruitful discussion resulted (*An Appraisal of Thomas and Znaniecki*). Webb, on the other hand, saw the evaluation of his work solely in terms of personal affront, and missed the opportunity to engage in a much more significant debate about the nature of the social sciences, the place of historical inquiry within that context, and the role of insight and personal experience in shaping knowledge of the past. Yet the latter theme, in particular, lay at the basis of many of his private and public reflections on his own life history and its relationship to his writing and research.

An outsider by temperament and a provincial by choice, Webb carried also the handicap of a skewed intellectual formation, elements of which were at the same time the source of his distinctive historical outlook and the barrier that separated him from the give-and-take of professional discourse. That he was not anti-intellectual is shown by the intriguing exchange of ideas he shared in his later years with his Texan friends Roy Bedichek and J. Frank Dobie, an exchange so formal and literary in its structure that it seems to suggest a conscious effort to reproduce an eighteenth-century salon in miniature, and perhaps assert that civilized discourse need not be incompatible with the wearing of a Stetson and a preference for life in a provincial setting (*Three Friends*).

The membership of the group was itself revealing; like Webb, Dobie and Bedichek were both highly individualistic and eclectic in their interests. Webb appears not to have shown much interest in developing the same level of discourse with his fellow historians, and might have benefited considerably if he had been able to operate with more comfort and composure in the forums of his own profession. Since he saw no reason to value the opinions of his peers, his only option when he needed confirmation and reassurance was to turn to his close friends or to the public mind and seek approval there for his view of the past and its relationship to contemporary life. In the case of *The Great Plains*, he received the answer he hoped for; *The Great Frontier*, however, did not lend itself to public adjudication.

In the long run, Webb came to acknowledge how fickle the public mind could be when his ideas scraped across the popular grain, as they did in his articles on the West as, in part, a desert region. These were risks he was more than willing to accept, especially in his later years, because age if anything sharpened his sense of the public interest and his determination to use his standing and his flair for advocacy to draw attention to the crass and mindless exploitation of natural resources. A decade later, he might have been singled out for praise as a social scientist with a strongly developed sense of commitment to contemporary environmental issues. He may even have been described as relevant. Webb, one suspects, would have been as puzzled by that designation as he was by most attempts to put a collar on him and make him amenable; he was an original, and very much aware of that.

Bibliography

Books

The Building of Our Nation. Co-authored with Eugene C. Barker and Henry Steel Commager. Evanston, IL: Row, Peterson and Co., 1937.

Divided We Stand: The Crisis of a Frontierless Democracy. New York: Farrar and Rinehart, 1937.

Flat Top: A Story of Modern Ranching. El Paso, TX: Carl Hertzog, 1960.

The Great Frontier. Boston: Houghton Mifflin, 1952.

The Great Plains. Boston: Ginn and Co., 1931.

The Growth of a Nation: The United States of America. Co-authored with Eugene C. Barker and William E. Dodd. Evanston, IL: Row, Peterson and Co., 1928.

History as High Adventure by Walter Prescott Webb. Edited by E. C. Barksdale. Austin, TX: Pemberton Press, 1969.

An Honest Preface and Other Essays. Boston: Houghton Mifflin, 1959.

More Water for Texas: The Problem and the Plan. Austin: University of Texas Press, 1954.

Our Nation Begins. Evanston, IL: Row, Peterson and Co., 1932.

Our Nation Grows Up. Co-authored with Eugene C. Barker and William E. Dodd. Evanston, IL: Row, Peterson and Co., 1938.

The Story of Our Nation. Co-authored with Eugene C. Barker and William E. Dodd. Evanston, IL: Row, Peterson and Co., 1929.
The Texas Rangers: A Century of Frontier Defense. Boston: Houghton Mifflin, 1935.

Articles
"The American Revolvers and the West." *Scribner's Magazine* 81(February, 1927):171-178.
"The American West: Perpetual Mirage." *Harper's Magazine* 214(May, 1957):25-31.
"Caldwell Prize in Local History." *Texas History Teachers' Bulletin*, October 22, 1924, pp. 5-19.
"Folklore of Texas." *Journal of American Folklore* 28(July/September, 1915):290-301.
"Geographical-Historical Concepts in American History." *Annals of the Association of American Geographers* 50(June, 1960):85-93.
"The Great Plains and the Industrial Revolution." In *The Trans-Mississippi West* edited by James F. Willard and Colin B. Goodykoontz. Boulder: University of Colorado, 1930. Pp. 309-339.
"The Great Plains Block the Expansion of the South." *Panhandle-Plains Historical Review* 2(1929):3-21.
"History as High Adventure." *American Historical Review* 64(January, 1959):278-281.
"An Honest Preface." *Southwest Review* 34(Autumn, 1951):312-314.
"Increasing the Functional Value of History by the Use of the Problem Method of Presentation." *Texas History Teachers' Bulletin*, February 15, 1916, pp. 16-40.
"The Land and Life of the Great Plains." *West Texas Historical Association Yearbook* 4(June, 1928):58-85.
"The Last Treaty of the Republic of Texas." *Southwestern Historical Quarterly* 25(January, 1922):151-173.
"Miscellany of Texas Folklore." In *Coffee in the Gourd* edited by J. Frank Dobie. Austin, TX: Texas Folklore Society, 1923.
"Search for William E. Hinds." *Harper's Magazine* 223(July, 1961):62-69.
"__________." *Reader's Digest* 79(August, 1961):35-40.
"Some Vagaries of the Search for Water in the Great Plains." *Panhandle-Plains Historical Review* 3(1930):28-37.
"A Texas Buffalo Hunt." *Holland's Magazine* 46(October, 1927):10-11, 101-102.
"Texas Rangers: Riders and Fighters of the Lone Star State. Part III." *Owenwood Magazine* 1(April, 1922):39-46; "Part IV," 1(May, 1922):47-54.
"The West and the Desert." *Montana: Magazine of Western History* 9(January, 1958):2-12.
"Wild Horse Stories of Southwest Texas." In *Round the Levee* edited by Smith Thompson. Austin, TX: Texas Folklore Society, 1916. I:58-61.

Reviews

The Comanche Barrier to South Plains Settlement: A Century and a Half of Savage Resistance to the Advancing White Frontier by Rupert Norval Richardson. *American Historical Review* 40(January, 1935):356-357.

Conquering Our Great American Plains by Stuart Henry. *Mississippi Valley Historical Review* 17(March, 1931):644-645.

Cowboys and Cattle Kings: Life on the Ranch Today by C. L. Sonnichsen. *American Historical Review* 56(January, 1951):365-366.

History in a Changing World by Geoffrey Barraclough. *American Historical Review* 62(April, 1957):594-595.

History of the American Frontier by Frederic L. Paxson. *Southwestern Historical Quarterly* 28(January, 1925):247-252.

In Blood and Ink by Maury Maverick. *Mississippi Valley Historical Review* 26(March, 1940):632.

Legends of Texas by J. Frank Dobie. *Southwestern Historical Quarterly* 28(January, 1925):243-247.

Studies of Walter Prescott Webb

Barraclough, Geoffrey. "Metropolis and Macrocosm: Europe and the Wider World, 1492-1939." *Past and Present* 5(May, 1954):77-93.

Bellot, H. Hale. Review of *The Great Frontier* by Walter Prescott Webb. *William and Mary Quarterly* 11(January, 1954):121-126.

Blegen, Theodore C. "The Twenty-Fifth Annual Meeting of the Mississippi Valley Historical Association." *Mississippi Valley Historical Review* 19(September, 1932):243-254.

Blumer, Herbert. *An Appraisal of Thomas and Znaniecki's "The Polish Peasants in Europe and America."* Critiques of Research in the Social Sciences, Vol. I. New York: Social Sciences Research Council, 1939.

Caldwell, Robert G. Review of *The Great Plains* by Walter Prescott Webb. *Mississippi Valley Historical Review* 18(March, 1932):581-583.

Cole, Arthur C. Review of *Divided We Stand: The Crisis of a Frontierless Democracy* by Walter Prescott Webb. *Mississippi Valley Historical Review* 25(September, 1938):294-295.

Dale, E. E. Review of *The Texas Rangers: A Century of Frontier Defense* by Walter Prescott Webb. *Mississippi Valley Historical Review* 23(September, 1936):288-289.

Dugger, Ronnie, ed. *Three Men in Texas: Bedichek, Webb and Dobie: Essays by Their Friends in the Texas Observer.* Austin: University of Texas Press, 1967.

Elliott, J. H. *The Old World and the New, 1492-1650.* Cambridge: Cambridge University Press, 1970.

Friend, Llerena, ed. and comp. *Talks on Texas Books: A Collection of Book Reviews.* Austin: Texas State Historical Association, 1970.

__________. "Walter Prescott Webb and Book Reviewing." *Western Historical Quarterly* 4(October, 1973):381-404.

Furman, Necah Stewart. *Walter Prescott Webb: His Life and Impact.* Albuquerque: University of New Mexico Press, 1976.

Hexter, J. H. Review of *The Great Frontier* by Walter Prescott Webb. *American Historical Review* 58(July, 1953):963.

Jacobs, Wilbur R., John W. Caughey, and Joe B. Frantz. *Turner, Bolton and Webb: Three Historians of the American Frontier.* Seattle: University of Washington Press, 1965.

Jordan, Terry G. *Trails to Texas: Southern Roots of Western Cattle Ranching.* Lincoln: University of Nebraska Press, 1981.

Lemons, William E. "The Western Historical Perspectives of DeVoto, Webb, Dobie and Hyde." Ph.D. diss., University of Minnesota, 1973.

Lewis, Archibald R., and Thomas F. McGann, eds. *The New World Looks at Its History.* Austin: University of Texas Press, 1963.

Luebke, Frederick C. "Regionalism and the Great Plains: Problems of Concept and Method." *Western Historical Quarterly* 15(January, 1984):19-38.

Morris, Margaret. "Walter Prescott Webb, 1888-1963, A Bibliography." In *Essays on the American Civil War* edited by William F. Holmes and Harold H. Hollingsworth. Austin: University of Texas Press, 1968.

Owens, William A. *Three Friends: Roy Bedichek, J. Frank Dobie and Walter Prescott Webb.* Garden City, NY: Doubleday and Co., 1969.

Paxson, Frederic L. Review of *The Great Plains* by Walter Prescott Webb. *American Historical Review* 37(January, 1932):359-360.

Philp, Kenneth R., and Elliott West, eds. *Essays on Walter Prescott Webb.* Austin: University of Texas Press, 1976.

Pickens, Donald K. "Walter Prescott Webb's Tomorrows." *Red River Valley Historical Review* 6(Winter, 1981):25-34.

__________. "Westward Expansion and the End of American Exceptionalism: Sumner, Turner and Webb." *Western Historical Quarterly* 12(October, 1981):409-418.

Rundell, Walter, Jr. "W. P. Webb's *Divided We Stand*: A Publishing Crisis." *Western Historical Quarterly* 13(October, 1982):391-407.

__________. "Walter Prescott Webb: Product of Environment." *Arizona and the West* 5(Spring, 1963):4-28.

__________. "Walter Prescott Webb and the Texas State Historical Association." *Arizona and the West* 25(Summer, 1983):109-136.

__________. "Walter Prescott Webb as Businessman." *Great Plains Journal* 18(1979):130-139.

Shannon, Fred A. *An Appraisal of Walter Prescott Webb's "The Great Plains: A Study in Institutions and Environment."* Critiques of Research in the Social Sciences, Vol. III. New York: Social Sciences Research Council, 1940.

Tobin, Gregory M. *The Making of a History: Walter Prescott Webb and "The Great Plains."* Austin: University of Texas Press, 1976.

Wolfskill, George. "Walter Prescott Webb and the Great Plains:Then and Now." *Reviews in American History* 12(June, 1984):296-307.

____________, and Stanley Palmer, eds. *Essays on Frontiers in World History.* College Station: Texas A&M University Press, 1983.

55

EDWARD N. WENTWORTH

by Paul H. Carlson

Biography

Because he was born in New England, it may be surprising that Edward Norris Wentworth spent much of his life studying and writing about the western livestock industry; but he did. Wentworth produced several books and many articles that deal with topics associated with the West, a region he came to know and appreciate through his careful research, professional activities, personal acquaintances, and extensive travel. Scholars continue to judge some of his studies as standard works on the livestock industry of the American West.

Wentworth, who could trace his ancestry back through eight generations to 1636 when one William Wentworth from England settled in America, was born on January 11, 1887, in Dover, New Hampshire. When Edward was still a youth, his father, Elmer Wentworth, a railway freight agent, took the family to State Center in Marshall County, Iowa. Here, with his brothers and sister, Edward received an elementary education in Iowa rural schools. After graduation from high school Edward attended Iowa State College of Agricultural and Mechanical Arts at Ames, receiving a B.S. degree in agriculture in 1907 and a M.S. degree two years afterward. Later he completed additional graduate work at Cornell University and at Harvard University, and in 1951 he received an honorary Doctor of Agriculture degree from Iowa State University.

From 1907 to 1913 Wentworth was assistant and later associate professor of animal husbandry at Iowa State College. During the year 1913-1914 he was associate editor of the *Breeders' Gazette* and taught zootechnics at Chicago Veterinary College, and from 1914 to 1917 he was professor of animal breeding at Kansas State Agricultural College in Manhattan. His career in education was well-established when war intervened.

After the United States entered World War I, Wentworth enlisted in the United States Army Field Artillery. Sent to France and promoted first to captain and then major, he served as assistant director of the College of Agriculture, American Expeditionary Forces University in Beaune, France. For this work the French government in 1919 nominated him *officer du merite agricole.* Following the war Wentworth attained the rank of colonel in the United States Army Reserve Corps, a title he held the rest of his life.

Back in the United States, Wentworth in 1919 joined the public relations department of Armour & Company, a large Chicago meatpacking firm. He moved to the company's Bureau of Agricultural Research in 1920, and in 1923 he became director of the Armour Livestock Bureau, a position he held until his retirement in 1954. Meanwhile, from 1923 to 1931, he also lectured at the University of Chicago. During World War II, Wentworth was a member of the advisory committee to the United States Quartermaster General and served on the Wartime Swine Industry Council.

A member of more than a dozen agricultural and historical associations, Wentworth was active in professional organizations. He served as president of the Agricultural History Society for 1952-1954, and he was an honorary fellow of the American Society of Animal Production. He also belonged to many social clubs and fraternities, including the Military Order of the World Wars, of which he was national commander in 1938-1939, the American Legion, and the Reserve Officers' Association of the United States.

Medium in heighth, broad-shouldered, and stocky, Wentworth possessed a high forehead, distinctive, dark eyes, and a small moustache on his large, round face. An open, easy to approach, and enthusiastic personality, he enjoyed a friendly familiarity with most people who knew him and a wide acquaintance among America's specialists in both agricultural science and history (*National Wool Grower* 39:67-68).

Wentworth married Alma B. McCulla in 1911 at Saint Ansgar in Mitchell County, Iowa. The couple had two sons, Edward Norris and Raymond Howard (who died in infancy). In religion Wentworth was a Congregationalist. Politically he was a Republican. Horseback riding was his chief recreation, but he was also fond of reading, especially history; his personal library of 1400 volumes was donated to the University of Wyoming. He also maintained a lively interest in genetics and animal breeding. Edward Norris Wentworth died at his home near Chesterton, Indiana, on April 21, 1959. He is remembered most often as author of *America's Sheep Trails: History, Personalities,* for stimulating others to special efforts in livestock breeding and history, and for the bright smile on his face (*Encyclopedia of American Agricultural History*, p. 375; *Journal of American History* 46:361; *Agricultural History* 33:153).

Themes

In his long career, Edward N. Wentworth wrote or co-authored nine books, contributions to another, two scholarly book reviews, and many articles. Nearly all of them deal with the American livestock industry. Most are history and biography, but a few are scientific and technical manuals for livestock raisers. Wentworth was an agricultural scientist who specialized in animal breeding. He was trained in animal husbandry, taught the science at respected agricultural colleges, and spent much of his life encouraging others in the subject. In addition, he retained all his life a special interest in agricultural history and in men and women who made a living on America's farms and ranches.

It is not surprising, therefore, that in his writing there emerge four major themes related to his professional interests: biography, breeding adaptation, adaptation to natural conditions, and adjustment to a changing economy. The latter two themes are present in most of his historical writings, but they are most clearly developed in *Shepherd's Empire* (1945) and *Cattle and Men* (1955). Breeding adaptation is a central theme in *Pigs: From Cave to Corn Belt* (1950). In *America's Sheep Trails* (1948), Wentworth's most ambitious work, and in many of his articles, adaptation to natural conditions is the dominant theme, but biography is also important and, in a submerged form, so is the theme of breeding adaptation.

Analysis

In his foreword to *America's Sheep Trails*, Wentworth writes: "Some readers may find too many personalities. But history is neither lived nor written, except by the actors that move across its pages, and those who disapprove the recording of many names will remember that those very names provide many clues for further research" (p. ix). Beyond that statement Wentworth offers no apology for his emphasis on biography. In nearly all his historical works he uses the lives of people as important focal points in his studies of the livestock industry. "Flocks came into being," he writes, "only as an expression of the flockmaster behind them. Sheep trails cross the American horizon because someone herded the flocks, picked the bedgrounds, dispersed the predators, and turned ram, ewe, wether, lamb, and wool into living achievement" (p. ix).

In his own studies, therefore, biography plays a major role in the narrative. *America's Sheep Trails* and his articles on the Texas and southwestern sheep industry describe the men, and occasional women, who drove flocks, developed new techniques for treating diseases, designed unique marketing schemes for sheep and wool, or led the way in popularizing new breeds. Indeed, in an article in *Agricultural History* he maintains that "livestock history is personalized history" (25:53). In his foreword to *Cattle and Men*, which Wentworth co-authored with Charles W. Towne, Colin Campbell Sanborn writes: "Men and cattle developed together; each had a powerful influence on the life of the other . . . so this book is a history, not only of cattle, but a history of men" (p. xii).

In *Cattle and Men* and *Shepherd's Empire*, also written with Towne, the authors' themes throughout are of adaptation to natural conditions and adjustments to a changing economy. Consequently, both books contain significant material on the general economic history of the United States. In his review of *Cattle and Men*, Earle D. Ross notes that "while the survey is global, emphasis is placed upon the North American scene. The authors record the formation in Europe of the basic types and breeds, and trace their place in the successive regions of the expanding nation" (*Mississippi Valley Historical Review* 42:252-253). In the same work they show how cattle raisers were often forced to adapt their herding methods and breeding schemes to "changing preferences of consumers" (p. 752). Reviewer Ross indicates that the authors argue impressively for "the variant conditions and influences of physiography, soil, vegetation, and climate" on the matter of a "superior" breed (p. 752). In *America's Sheep Trails*, Wentworth notes that "Americans developed systems of management that made existing breeds efficient under differing and highly specialized conditions" (p. 257).

Breeding adaptation, Wentworth's academic speciality as a college professor, naturally enough is an important theme in many of his works, but it takes on special meaning in *Pigs: From Cave to Corn Belt*, coauthored with Towne, and, to a lesser extent, in *America's Sheep Trails*. In the latter work Wentworth writes: "Inherently the Merinos possessed the qualifications for the American range," and "the development of mutton quality in [American Merino] descendants made the permanent occupation of the trans-Missouri country a certainty" (p. 80).

In their major historical works Wentworth and his collaborator, Charles W. Towne, combine the expertise of a distinguished animal husbandry man and the narrative skills of a veteran journalist and freelance writer. They recount in *Shepherd's Empire*, writes Earle D. Ross, "the dramatic, often tragic story of the origins and establishment of the sheep husbandry and industry in the Far West" (*Mississippi Valley Historical Review* 32:271). The result, Ross suggests, "has been carried out with thoroughness and sympathetic understanding" (p. 271). In his review of *Cattle and Men*, Ross indicates that the two authors by reason of technical competence and intimate contact with cattle and cattlemen produced "numerous distinguished writings on the history of livestock." They possess, he concludes, "the essential skills of the historian's craft without the conventional inhibitions" (*Mississippi Valley Historical Review* 42:252).

Each of Wentworth's historical works is characterized by thoroughness, revealing quotations, apt anecdotes, carefully selected illustrations, and reliability. Sympathetic toward his topics and personalities, Wentworth in historical articles and books he produced alone is rarely critical. His writings stress information over analysis, and where he uses careful analysis, it is in the main positive, as opposed to negative, in emphasis. He typically uses a wide range of sources, printed and manuscript, and he draws upon pertinent special studies in the various disciplines associated with his topic. Of *Pigs: From Cave to Corn Belt*, Ben H. Wall writes: "The index and bibliography to *Pigs* is complete and accurate"

(*Mississippi Valley Historical Review* 37:341). About *America's Sheep Trails*, Jay Monaghan writes: "The author has prepared an extensive bibliography, rich in unpublished manuscripts and government documents. In addition, he has used hundreds of letters written to him by 'old-timers' on the range" (*Mississippi Valley Historical Review* 35:311). The personal letters furnish new and sometimes valuable source material.

Thus, Wentworth and Towne combine a vivid narrative with an informing, well-documented monograph. Monaghan notes that "Wentworth writes well, and his research has been prodigious" (p. 311). Ross says of *Cattle and Men* that the authors have produced an "informing, interesting, and attractively designed book" (*Mississippi Valley Historical Review* 42:252). Wall in reviewing *Pigs: From Cave to Corn Belt* notes that the "material covered . . . represents an imaginative culling of references to all kinds of pigs in all eras of the history of mankind" (*Mississippi Valley Historical Review* 37:342). Not only do Towne and Wentworth cover the sources but they also provide information of interest to a wide audience. "They have succeeded," writes Wall, "in making an entertaining and informative story" (p. 342).

If there is weakness in his historical writings, it relates to Wentworth's reliance on personal letters for information. The letters have serious shortcomings if used uncritically. Jay Monaghan, for example, present at two skirmishes in the sheepman-cattleman war that in part led in 1934 to the federal government's Taylor Grazing Act, argues in his review of *America's Sheep Trails* that Wentworth's descriptions of the fights, taken from two interviews with neighboring sheepmen who were not present, "bears no resemblance to the events seen by an eyewitness" (*Mississippi Valley Historical Review* 35:311). Since Wentworth's narratives often rely upon such personal notes and letters, scholars must be on guard against accepting hearsay evidence for established fact. To the contrary, however, R. H. Burns indicates that "the handling of the material in *Cattle and Men* shows not only scholarly and orderly display of materials, but also a love of livestock and land" (*Agricultural History* 30:92-93).

In short, Wentworth produced several thoughtful and attractive books and many scholarly articles, and by doing so he performed a valuable service to the livestock industry and the agricultural history of the American West. His work represents no mean achievement. *America's Sheep Trails: History, Personalities*, for instance, continues, forty years after its publication, to be recognized as the standard work on the history of the sheep industry in America. Clearly, his respect for extensive research, the importance of biography, scientific breeding, and economic and natural forces that influence livestock production characterize Wentworth's scholarly contributions as a historian of the American frontier.

Bibliography

Books

America's Sheep Trails: History, Personalities. Ames: Iowa State College Press, 1948.

A Biographical Catalogue of the Portrait Gallery of the Saddle and Sirloin Club. Chicago: Union Stock Yards, 1920.

Cattle and Men. Co-authored with Charles W. Towne. Norman: University of Oklahoma Press, 1955.

Marketing Livestock and Meats. Co-authored with Tage U. H. Ellinger. Chicago: Armour's Livestock Bureau, 1925.

Pigs: From Cave to Corn Belt. Co-authored with Charles W. Towne. Norman: University of Oklahoma Press, 1950.

Progressive Beef Cattle Raising. Co-authored with Tage U. H. Ellinger. Chicago: Armour's Livestock Bureau, 1920.

Progressive Hog Raising. Co-authored with Tage U. H. Ellinger. Chicago: Armour's Livestock Bureau, 1922.

Progressive Sheep Raising. Co-authored with Tage U. H. Ellinger. Chicago: Armour's Livestock Bureau, 1925.

Shepherd's Empire. Co-authored with Charles W. Towne. Norman: University of Oklahoma Press, 1945.

Articles

"The Age Factor in Register-of-Merit Jerseys." *American Breeders Magazine* 2(1911):97-103.

"Another Sex-limited Character." *Science* n.s. 35(June 28, 1912):986.

"Color Inheritance in the Horse." *Zeit F. ind. Abstammungs-und Vererbungslehre*. 11(1913):14.

"Dried Meat--Early Man's Travel Ration." *Agricultural History* 30(January, 1956):2-11. Reprint. *Annual Report*. Smithsonian Institution, Publication no. 4272 (1956):557-581.

"Eastward Sheep Drives from California and Oregon." *Mississippi Valley Historical Review* 28(March, 1942):507-538.

"The Evolution of Sheep Shearing in America." *Sheep and Goat Raiser* 25(June, 1945):20, 24-27, 30, 32.

"Foreword." *Agricultural History* 27(January, 1953):1.

"The Golden Fleece in Texas." *Sheep and Goat Raiser* 24(December, 1943):16-17, 20, 25-33.

"Inheritance in Swine." Co-authored with Jay L. Lush. *Journal of Agricultural Research* 23(February 17, 1923):557-581.

"Inheritance of Fertility in Southdown Sheep." *American Naturalist* 51(1917):662-682.

"Inheritance of Fertility in Swine." Co-authored with C. E. Aubel. *Journal of Agricultural Research* 5(March 20, 1916):1145-1160.

"Inheritance of Mammae in Duroc Jersey Swine." *American Naturalist* 47(1913):257-278.

"A Livestock Specialist Looks at Agricultural History." *Agricultural History* 25(April, 1951):49-53.

"On the Nature of Heredity." *American Breeders Magazine* 2(1911):310-311.

"Prepotency." *Journal of Heredity* 6(1915):17-20.

"A Search for Cattle Trails in Matto Grosso." *Agricultural History* 26(January, 1952):8-16.

"Sex in Livestock Breeding." *Journal of Heredity* 7(1916):29-32.
"A Sex-limited Color in Ayrshire Cattle." *Journal of Agricultural Research* 6(April 24, 1916):141-147.
"Sex-linked Factors in the Inheritance of Rudimentary Mammae in Swine." *Iowa Academy of Science Proceedings* 21(1914):265-268.
"Sheep Trails of Early Texas (Part I)." *Southwestern Sheep and Goat Raiser* 9(June, 1939):7, 35, 37, 39.
"Sheep Trails of Early Texas (Part II)." *Southwestern Sheep and Goat Raiser* 9(July, 1939):23, 34.
"The Story of Texas Sheep." *The Cattleman* 25(April, 1939):47, 49, 51.
"Trailing Sheep from California to Idaho in 1865: The Journal of Gorham Gates Kimball." *Agricultural History* 28(April, 1954):49-83.

Reviews
American History in Schools by Committee on American History in Schools and Colleges of the American Historical Association. *Mississippi Valley Historical Review* 31(June, 1944):108-109.
The Golden Hoof: The Story of the Sheep of the Southwest by Winifred Kupper. *Mississippi Valley Historical Review* 32(December, 1945):454.

Studies of Edward N. Wentworth
Burns, R. H. Review of *Cattle and Men* by Charles W. Towne and Edward N. Wentworth. *Agricultural History* 30(April, 1956):92-93.
"Edward N. Wentworth." *National Cyclopedia of American Biography* 47(1965):335-336.
"In Memoriam." *Agricultural History* 33(April, 1959):153.
__________. *Journal of American History* 46(September, 1959):361.
__________. *National Wool Grower* 49(May, 1959):18.
Monaghan, Jay. Review of *America's Sheep Trails: History, Personalities* by Edward N. Wentworth. *Mississippi Valley Historical Review* 35(September, 1948):311-312.
National Wool Grower 39(March, 1949):67-68.
Ross, Earle D. Review of *Cattle and Men* by Charles W. Towne and Edward N. Wentworth. *Mississippi Valley Historical Review* 42(March, 1956):252-253.
__________. Review of *Shepherd's Empire* by Charles W. Towne and Edward N. Wentworth. *Mississippi Valley Historical Review* 32(September, 1945):271-272.
Schapsmeier, Edward L. and Frederick A. Schapsmeier. "Edward N. Wentworth." In *Encyclopedia of American Agricultural History*. Westport, CT: Greenwood Press, 1975. P. 375.
Shannon, Fred A. Review of *America's Sheep Trails: History, Personalities* by Edward N. Wentworth. *Journal of Economic History* 8(November, 1948):196-197.
Wall, Ben H. Review of *Pigs: From Cave to Corn Belt* by Charles W. Towne and Edward N. Wentworth. *Mississippi Valley Historical Review* 37(September, 1950):341-342.

56

OSCAR O. WINTHER

by Bonny O. Van Orman and Richard A. Van Orman

Biography

Oscar Osburn Winther was born near Weeping Water, Nebraska, on a raw December night in 1903. A son of the Middle Border, he grew up in a land steeped in history. Ponca and Omaha had hunted there; explorers and fur traders had journeyed there. Nearby snakes the Platte River, which had been the principal highway to the Pacific Northwest, a region Winther would live in and write about.

He was the youngest of seven children born to Danish immigrants who had arrived in the United States in 1895. After four hard years in Massachusetts, the family moved to Nebraska. Following a decade of toil, the Winthers migrated to a dairy farm near Eugene, Oregon. One of Winther's lasting boyhood memories was of Conestoga wagons lumbering past the homestead.

Life on the farm was a dull routine of daily chores that would make school an adventure. Because of the encouragement he received from high school teachers, by the time he graduated he had become a convert to Clio. After he entered the University of Oregon, his love of history grew because of the help given him by Professor Walter C. Barnes and through the histories of Edward Channing, Charles A. Beard, and James Harvey Robinson. It was while at the university that he witnessed a historical pageant starring Oregon pioneer, Ezra Meeker.

Following his graduation in 1925, he taught high school and worked double shifts in a cannery to earn enough money to enroll in Harvard's master's program. Decades later he was convinced that it was "the biggest decision of my life" (*Western Historical Quarterly* 1:128). His year at Harvard was a great awakening. He was stimulated by the savants of the history department--Hart, Schlesinger, Channing, and Morison--while life in Cambridge and Boston was unlike anything he had ever experienced. At one point he ran out of money and learned the humiliation of hunger. And when a Jewish friend was kicked out of the rooming house that

Winther lived in, he was so outraged by the anti-Semitic act that he also left.

After receiving his master's degree in 1926, he moved back to the Pacific Northwest and taught school for two years in order to finance his Ph.D. degree in history. In 1929 he enrolled at Stanford University. There Edgar Eugene Robinson's western history seminar convinced him to specialize in the American West. And while working in the library that housed the Wells, Fargo Collection, he decided to do his dissertation on "The Express and Stagecoach Business in California, 1848-1860."

Granted his doctorate in 1934, Winther became assistant curator of the Wells, Fargo Collection, worked as a Danish translator at the Hoover War Library, and taught at Stanford and at the San Jose Adult Education Center. These were productive years. In 1934 his first article appeared. The next year the California Historical Society published his history of San Jose, one of the first scholarly studies of a western town. His dissertation was published in 1936. The following year he was hired by Indiana University as an instructor in history. In the same year, 1937, he married Mary Galey. Besides being his wife for thirty-four years and mother of their children, Ingrid and Eric, she acted as his "best critic, and my high chief typist" (*The Old Oregon Country*, p. x).

At Indiana he served on numerous faculty committees and for almost a decade was either the associate or acting dean of the Graduate School. In 1965 he was made University Professor. He was also a visiting professor at a number of universities, including New Mexico, Johns Hopkins, and Stanford. It was as a teacher that Winther felt he made his "most worthwhile contribution" (*Western Historical Quarterly* 1:135).

In 1963 he was elected the second president of the Western History Association and six years later was chosen president of the Oral History Association. With Allan Nevins, Winther was one of the first professional historians to become interested in oral history. In the mid-1960s he was managing editor of the *Mississippi Valley Historical Review* when it became the *Journal of American History*.

To his friends he was a witty raconteur, to fellow historians he was a gracious colleague, and to his students he was a concerned and congenial teacher. Indeed, he looked upon the relationship with his graduate students "as a lifetime partnership" (*Reflections of Western Historians*, p. 289).

Winther died of cancer at the age of 66 on May 22, 1970. Before his death the Western History Association in recognition of his importance to the field made him an honorary life member; it annually presents in his name an award for the best essay appearing in the *Western Historical Quarterly*.

Themes

Oscar Winther was a man of the West. There he was born and bred, and there he returned to travel the routes of trade and transportation in the Herbert E. Bolton tradition. His interests were as broad and varied as the western landscape, as can be seen in his dozen books, seventy articles, and 125 book reviews. Among the topics covered were climate as a means of promoting migration, the soldier vote in the election of 1864, agricultural problems in Denmark, and the fourteenth-century Danish king Valdemar Atterdag. He edited two volumes of letters. He translated the diary of a Danish politician. And he co-authored a junior high history text.

But his major area of research was in the field of nineteenth-century western transportation. Nearly one-third of his works deal with that subject. He was not just concerned with the facts and figures of transportation but also its tremendous impact on the economic, social, and political affairs of the West. His goal was "to round out, if possible, the pre-railroad (inland) aspect" of the trans-Mississippi West (*Western Historical Quarterly* 1:135).

His second major theme was the history of the Pacific Northwest. In *The Great Northwest* he demonstrated how the region's past had had a profound effect on its "ever-changing culture pattern that is rugged and vigorous" (p. vii). Though he lived over thirty years in the Midwest, his heart was in the Northwest.

Winther felt that as a professor he was obliged to perform "academic chores," and so he believed that as a professional historian he also had certain obligations. One of them was to turn out a series of comprehensive bibliographies of the periodical literature of the trans-Mississippi West, even though there was no remuneration and little recognition for such publications.

In part because of his family's immigrant experience, one of his scholarly interests was the English in the American West, the impact they had on the West, and its effect upon them. After writing a number of articles on this theme, he had hoped to write a book on the subject, but death intervened. At the time of his passing, he was also working on an interpretive history of the West for Hill and Wang publishers.

Analysis

For decades, writings on the history of western transportation had been fragmentary and anecdotal. Although tons of information had been collected and thousands of pages written, the field attracted eager amateurs committed to parochial interests. In their works, anecdotes were more important than analysis, and emphasis was placed on penny-dreadful heroes such as outlaws, Pony Express riders, and "knights of the reins."

Oscar Winther was one of the first historians to break with this romantic and random approach. His work was different in part because of the vast amount of research he did. "Research," he said, "can be as much fun as it is compulsive" (*Western Historical Quarterly* 1:133). Much of it was done at his favorite library, the Henry E. Huntington in San Marino, California. Another reason his work was different was his splendid talent to generalize. W. Turrentine Jackson believes that Winther's works are unique "because he displayed exceptional ability to place a large amount of historical material in its proper perspective" (*Historians and the American West*, p. 123).

Winther recognized that transportation was the alpha and omega in the opening and development of the frontier. It was not by chance that in his first book on transportation, *Express and Stagecoach Days in California*, he quoted a sentence from Emerson Hough's *The Passing of the Frontier*: "There is in history no agency so wondrous in events, no working instrumentality so great as transportation" (p. vi). In *Express and Stagecoach Days in California*, published in 1936, Winther discusses the vital role that the stage lines and express companies played in the social and economic life of California from 1849 to 1860. Though there were over 250 companies before consolidation, his emphasis is on the larger ones such as Wells, Fargo and Company, Adams and Company, and the California Stage Company. He writes about their rapid growth and the various functions that these firms performed, such as issuing bills of exchange, transporting gold dust, and carrying the mail. But to him these companies are more than just businesses; they acted as civilizing agencies for the citizens of California (p. vii). More than a succinct economic survey, this volume skillfully demonstrates how these companies fitted into the general fabric of California history.

Winther was convinced that historians had obligations to two audiences--historians and the general public. Thus while *Express and Stagecoach Days in California* was a scholarly work that dealt with the world of balance sheets and tonnages, *Via Western Express and Stagecoach*, published in 1945, was a more exciting and colorful version of the earlier work. Covering the years between 1849 and 1869 in California's history, the book's emphasis is "upon the more human, the more picturesque and exciting aspects of overland transportation" (p. vii).

Besides continuing the story of the express companies, Winther covered the activities of the Butterfield Overland Mail, the Pony Express, Ben Holladay, and Russell, Majors and Waddell. Noting the connections between the two works, a reviewer of *Via Western Express* wrote, "It is a pleasure to see an historian who can make one set of notes stretch so far" (*Mississippi Valley Historical Review* 32:620). Both books touch on the larger themes of how transportation held together the people of California and how it ended the state's isolation from the rest of the nation.

Winther's three decades of research on western transportation culminated in *The Transportation Frontier: Trans-Mississippi West, 1865-1890* (1964), the second volume published in the Histories of the American Frontier series. This was the first scholarly synthesis of western transportation. Ray Allen Billington noted that the work was the "first to recognize that water transportation played an important role in the occupation of the Far West." Also important to Billington was the fact that it was also the first scholarly work "to allot the now-forgotten bicycle its proper credit in stimulating the Good Roads movement across the nation" (p. vii).

On the subject of transportation, no one knew more or wrote so well in both a scholarly and popular vein. Billington labeled the works "classics." He believed they were "touched with greatness partly because Oscar Winther subjected each problem not only to exhaustive research but to systematic and detailed analysis, partly because his own excitement permeated his narratives" (*Indiana Magazine of History* 63:58).

In 1947 Winther published his favorite work, *The Great Northwest.* This popular survey went through five printings and was for many years the best one-volume study of the region. Fully one-third of the book dealt with the neglected topic of the twentieth century. After dealing with the planting of American civilization in the Pacific Northwest, he notes the awakening of that region to its real strength and potential. In sum, it is a restatement of the frontier process that had occurred throughout the nation.

Three years later Winther turned out his "largest and most far-ranging research project," *The Old Oregon Country* (*Western Historical Quarterly* 1:133). Some of the material on trade, travel, and transportation had already appeared in *The Great Northwest.* But in the newer work he offers an extended and more detailed treatment. As with the earlier works on California, his main theme is how trade and transportation overcame the physical obstacles that made that region distant and inaccessible. A quote from William Ellery Channing that he uses set the major thrust of the work: "Commerce is a noble calling. It mediates between distant nations, and makes men's wants . . . bonds for peace" (p. vii).

In all his works, Winther showed an avid interest in bibliography, and reviewers of his books noted his bibliographical skills. During his life he published three bibliographies of the periodical literature of the trans-Mississippi West. From his first in 1942 to his last in 1970, he was the outstanding bibliographer in his field. In the first volume, which covered the years 1811 to 1938, he listed 3,501 items. The second volume appeared in 1961; it covered the years 1811 to 1957 and combined all the items listed in the first volume with articles that appeared between 1938 and 1957, or 9,244 items, nearly a twofold increase in nineteen years. In 1970 a supplement appeared, taking in the years 1957 to 1967 in 4,559 items, equal to half the total of the previous 146 years. Because of this tremendous proliferation of articles, Winther was convinced that the West would survive as a field of study. As important as the increase in the number of articles was the appearance of new periodicals and important changes in the types of articles published. Articles on vigilantism, cattle kings, and Spanish and American exploration declined in numbers, while studies in such new areas as the urban West, blacks in the West, immigrants, the Klan in the West, and Alaska grew significantly.

Whatever field Winther wrote about, he was its foremost authority. Meticulous in scholarship, a writer of style and substance, Winther's works have stood the test of time. Ray Allen Billington wrote that his "books are fun to read because he had fun writing them" (*Indiana Magazine of History* 63:58). Among the second generation of western historians, Oscar Osburn Winther is among the giants.

Bibliography

Books

A Classified Bibliography of the Periodical Literature of the Trans-Mississippi West (1811-1957). Bloomington: Indiana University Press, 1961.

A Classified Bibliography of the Periodical Literature of the Trans-Mississippi West: A Supplement (1957-1967). Co-authored with Richard A. Van Orman. Bloomington: Indiana University Press, 1970.

Diary of a Dying Empire by Hans Peter Hanssen. Translator. Co-edited with Ralph H. Lutz and Mary Schofield. Bloomington: Indiana University Press, 1955.

Express and Stagecoach Days in California: From the Gold Rush to the Civil War. Stanford, CA: Stanford University Press, 1936.

A Friend of the Mormons: The Diaries and Letters of Thomas L. Kane. Editor with a biographical introduction. San Francisco: Grabhorn Press, 1937.

The Great Northwest: A History. New York: Alfred A. Knopf, 1947.

The Old Oregon Country: A History of Frontier Trade, Transportation, and Travel. Bloomington: Indiana University Press, 1950.

The Story of San Jose, 1777-1869. San Francisco: California Historical Society, 1935.

The Trans-Mississippi West: A Guide to Its Periodical Literature (1811-1938). Bloomington: Indiana University Press, 1942.

The Transportation Frontier: Trans-Mississippi West, 1865-1890. New York: Holt, Rinehart and Winston, 1964.

Via Western Express and Stagecoach. Stanford, CA: Stanford University Press, 1945.

With Sherman to the Sea: The Civil War Letters, Diaries, and Reminiscences of Theodore F. Upson. Editor with an introduction and critical notes. Baton Rouge: Louisiana State University Press, 1943.

Selected Articles

"The British in Oregon Country: A Triptych View." *Pacific Northwest Quarterly* 58(October, 1967):179-187.

"California as a Factor in the Pacific Northwest Trade, 1829-69." *Huntington Library Quarterly* 6(November, 1942):13-16.

"California Stage Company in Oregon." *Oregon Historical Quarterly* 35(June, 1934):131-138.

"Commercial Routes in the Pacific Northwest, 1792-1843." *Oregon Historical Quarterly* 42(September, 1941):230-247.

"The Development of Transportation in Oregon, 1843-49." *Oregon Historical Quarterly* 40(December, 1939):315-326.

"Early Commerical Importance of the Mullan Road." *Oregon Historical Quarterly* 46(March, 1945):22-35.

"The English and Kansas, 1865-1890." In *The Frontier Challenge: Responses to the Trans-Mississippi West* edited by John G. Clark. Lawrence: University Press of Kansas, 1971. Pp. 235-273.

"The English in Nebraska, 1857-1880." *Nebraska History* 48(Autumn, 1967):209-223.

"English Migration to the American West, 1865-1900." *Huntington Library Quarterly* 27(February, 1964):159-173.

"History of Transportation in Oregon, 1843-1849." *Oregon Historical Quarterly* 41(March, 1940):40-52.

"Pack Animals for Transportation in the Pacific Northwest." *Pacific Northwest Quarterly* 34(April, 1943):131-146.

"The Persistence of Horse-Drawn Transportation in the Trans-Mississippi West, 1865-1900." In *Probing the American West: Papers from the Santa Fe Conference* edited by K. Ross Toole, et al. Santa Fe: Museum of New Mexico Press, 1962. Pp. 42-48.

"The Place of Transportation in the Early History of the Pacific Northwest." *Pacific Historical Review* 11(December, 1942):383-396.

"Promoting the American West in England, 1865-1890." *Journal of Economic History* 16(December, 1956):506-513.

"The Rise of Metropolitan Los Angeles, 1870-1900." *Huntington Library Quarterly* 10(August, 1947):391-405.

"The Soldier Vote in the Election of 1864." *New York History* 25(October, 1944):440-458.

"The Southern Overland Mail and Stagecoach Line, 1857-1861." *New Mexico Historical Review* 32(April, 1957):81-106.

"Stage-Coach Service in Northern California, 1849-1852." *Pacific Historical Review* 3(December, 1934):386-399.

"The Story of San Jose, 1777-1869, California's First Pueblo." *California Historical Society Quarterly* Part I, 14(March, 1935):3-27; Part II, 14(June, 1935):147-174.

"Strictly Personal." *Western Historical Quarterly* 1(April, 1970):127-136.

"The Use of Climate as a Means of Promoting Migration to Southern California." *Mississippi Valley Historical Review* 33(December, 1946):411-424.

Selected Reviews

California Gold Rush Voyages, 1848-1849: Three Original Narratives edited by John E. Pomfret. *Mississippi Valley Historical Review* 42(June, 1955):124-125.

Conestoga Wagon, 1750-1850 by George Shumway. *American Historical Review* 70(January, 1965):567.

The Course of Empire by Bernard DeVoto. *Mississippi Valley Historical Review* 40(December, 1953):519-520.

Empire on the Pacific: A Study in American Continental Expansion by Norman A. Graebner. *Mississippi Valley Historical Review* 42(March, 1956):753-754.

The Far Western Frontier by Ray Allen Billington. *American Historical Review* 62(April, 1957):638-640.

Forty-Niners: The Chronicle of the California Trail by Archer B. Hulbert. *Mississippi Valley Historical Review* 36(June, 1949):139.

"He Built Seattle": A Biography of Judge Thomas Burke by Robert C. Nesbit. *Mississippi Valley Historical Review* 48(March, 1962):718-720.

Sea Routes to the Gold Fields: The Migration by Water to California in 1849-1852 by Oscar Lewis. *Mississippi Valley Historical Review* 36(March, 1950):713-714.

Three Years in California by Walter Colton. *Mississippi Valley Historical Review* 37(December, 1950):533-534.

West of the Great Divide: Norwegian Migration to the Pacific Coast, 1847-1893 by Kenneth O. Bjork. *Mississippi Valley Historical Review* 45(December, 1958):505-506.

Studies of Oscar O. Winther

Angus, H. F. Review of *The Great Northwest: A History* by Oscar O. Winther. *American Historical Review* 53(April, 1948):561-562.

Armstrong, Sinclair W. Review of *Diary of a Dying Empire* translated and co-edited by Oscar O. Winther. *American Historical Review* 61(April, 1956):708.

Billington, Ray Allen. "Memorial Tribute to Oscar Osburn Winther." *Indiana Magazine of History* 67(March, 1971):56-61.

Bynum, Lindley. Review of *The Story of San Jose, 1777-1869* by Oscar O. Winther. *Pacific Historical Review* 5(Fall, 1936):382-383.

Carroll, John Alexander, ed. *Reflections of Western Historians.* Tucson: University of Arizona Press, 1969. Pp. 288-290.

Clark, Dan E. Review of *The Old Oregon Country: A History of Frontier Trade, Transportation, and Travel* by Oscar O. Winther. *Mississippi Valley Historical Review* 37(December, 1950):529-530.

Cole, Arthur C. Review of *With Sherman to the Sea: The Civil War Letters, Diaries, and Reminiscences of Theodore F. Upson* edited by Oscar O. Winther. *Mississippi Valley Historical Review* 30(June, 1943):127-128.

Coy, Owen C. Review of *Express and Stagecoach Days in California: From the Gold Rush to the Civil War* by Oscar O. Winther. *Pacific Historical Review* 6(Summer, 1937):297-298.

Dale, Edward Everett. Review of *The Trans-Mississippi West: A Guide to Its Periodical Literature (1811-1938)* by Oscar O. Winther. *American Historical Review* 49(October, 1943):169.

Farnham, Wallace P. Review of *The Transportation Frontier: Trans-Mississippi West, 1865-1890* by Oscar O. Winther. *American Historical Review* 71(January, 1966):705-706.

Gates, Charles M. Review of *A Classified Bibliography of the Periodical Literature of the Trans-Mississippi West (1811-1957)* by Oscar O. Winther. *American Historical Review* 67(April, 1962):800.

__________. Review of *The Old Oregon Country: A History of Frontier Trade, Transportation, and Travel* by Oscar O. Winther. *American Historical Review* 56(October, 1950):130-131.

Hafen, Le Roy R. Review of *The Trans-Mississippi West: A Guide to Its Periodical Literature (1811-1938)* by Oscar O. Winther. *Mississippi Valley Historical Review* 30(September, 1943):292.

Harlow, Alvin F. Review of *Express and Stagecoach Days in California: From the Gold Rush to the Civil War* by Oscar O. Winther. *American Historical Review* 42(July, 1937):844-845.

Heck, Frank H. Review of *With Sherman to the Sea: The Civil War Letters, Diaries, and Reminiscences of Theodore F. Upson* edited by Oscar O. Winther. *American Historical Review* 49(October, 1943):158.

Holmes, Oliver W. Review of *Via Western Express and Stagecoach* by Oscar O. Winther. *Mississippi Valley Historical Review* 32(March, 1946):620-621.

Hunt, Rockwell D. Review of *Via Western Express and Stagecoach* by Oscar O. Winther. *American Historical Review* 51(July, 1946):779.

Karlin, Jules Alexander. Review of *The Great Northwest: A History* by Oscar O. Winther. *Mississippi Valley Historical Review* 35(September, 1948):309-310.

Kirkland, Edward C. Review of *The Transportation Frontier: Trans-Mississippi West, 1865-1890* by Oscar O. Winther. *Journal of American History* 51(September, 1964):309-310.

Malone, Michael P., ed. *Historians of the American West.* Lincoln: University of Nebraska Press, 1983.

Parker, Frances V. Review of *A Classified Bibliography of the Periodical Literature of the Trans-Mississippi West (1811-1957)* by Oscar O. Winther. *Southwestern Historical Quarterly* 65(January, 1962):457-458.

Pelzer, Louis. Review of *Express and Stagecoach Days in California: From the Gold Rush to the Civil War* by Oscar O. Winther. *Mississippi Valley Historical Review* 23(December, 1936):425.

Rundell, Walter, Jr. Review of *A Classified Bibliography of the Periodical Literature of the Trans-Mississippi West: A Supplement (1957-1967)* co-authored by Oscar O. Winther and Richard A. Van Orman. *Southwestern Historical Quarterly* 75(January, 1972):394-395.

Van Orman, Richard A. "Oscar Osburn Winther." *Great Plains Journal* 18(1979):60-63.

57

CHARLES L. WOOD

by John R. Wunder

Biography

Box Butte County, located in northwestern Nebraska, is a beautiful land of a hardy people. A rolling plains country, it is a place of escarpment; and it is the home of many flora and fauna, most notably grass and cattle. To the north of Box Butte County lies the twisting Niobrara. Mari Sandoz in *Old Jules* (p. 13) describes the Niobrara as a gash cutting river "sank deep between sandstone and magnesia-white bluffs." Running Water, the Niobrara to the Cheyenne and Sioux nations, is surrounded by Nebraska's Sand Hills and its waves of rich grasslands. The Niobrara guides Highway 2 over and around the gentle magnificent greens and browns as it finds its way to the county seat of Box Butte County, Alliance, and again north to Hemingford, population at or around a thousand. This windswept grassland is the country of Crazy Horse, of Mari Sandoz, and of Charles Louis Wood. It is a land of plenty and a people of plenty that command respect.

Here Charles L. Wood, agricultural historian, was born on March 15, 1937, grew up in a large family on a family farm, prayed at St. Bridget's in Hemingford, and became educated. A religious man with a strong desire for higher education, he graduated in 1959 from Benedictine College in Atchison, Kansas, with a bachelor of arts degree in philosophy. After three years in the United States Army stationed at Fort Leonard Wood, Missouri, Wood returned to the Great Plains and learning. He taught history at Hayden High School in Topeka, Kansas, from 1963 to 1970 and from 1974 to 1976. During this time, he commuted to Lawrence receiving a Masters of Arts degree in history in 1974 from the University of Kansas.

At this juncture in his life, Wood began to focus his historical interests on agricultural history, particularly farming and ranching in the Great Plains. In 1976 the Woods' journeyed to the southern plains where the now Dr. Wood accepted an assistant professorship in the department of history at Texas Tech University. Here he developed courses on agricultural history at the graduate and undergraduate levels, and he became an adjunct professor at The Museum of Texas Tech University. In addition, he pioneered in college education with the teaching of "The History of Cattle Ranching" and "The Great Plains Experience." After four years, Wood was tenured and promoted to associate professor of history.

On June 16, 1981, Wood died in Lubbock, Texas, at St. Mary's of the Plains Hospital. Chuck Wood, at the age of 44, had lost a brief but heroic battle with acute leukemia. Unlike many who perish, historians or not, Wood left a legacy of wisdom in his writings.

Themes

Charles L. Wood was a man of the Great Plains. These Plains roots were firmly anchored in his world view and in his conceptualization of the history of a land and its people. Chuck Wood shared the beliefs of another Nebraskan. "A history of society's life on the plains," penned John Janovy, Jr., in *Keith County Journal*, "is a history of pioneers, of survival in what at first appeared a harsh and unyielding environment, of determination, of dependence upon one's neighbors and upon use of the soil and its products and inhabitants" (pp. 1-2). It is this intersection of people and the land, first of Nebraska, then of Kansas, the Great Plains, North America, and the world that is so obviously present in the writings of Wood.

In Wood's brief academic career, he wrote one book, *The Kansas Beef Industry*, five scholarly articles, and five reviews, and he co-edited one article that was published posthumously. Within these writings are a myriad of ideas and a plethora of information, but for purposes of synthesis, four themes emerge: demythification, particularly of the ranching industry; the mutually dependent roles of environment and culture; the merger of agriculture with technology and industry; and the value of the case study in historical methodology.

Of these four themes, demythification is clearly the most developed by Wood. He concentrates around those aspects crucial to the ranching industry. This theme is clearly stated in all of his writings, but it is most succinctly addressed in *The Kansas Beef Industry*. The other two substantive themes, environment and cultural dependency and the evolution of agribusiness, are mutually related and often times submerged. The last theme is methodological rather than substantive, and in many ways it is as crucial as Wood's ideas on myth and agriculture.

Analysis

"These ranchers of the late nineteenth century and after, who transformed beef raising into the important national industry that it is today, are the real heroes of the cattle business," observed Wood in his *The Kansas Beef Industry*. "The greater credit is due to them rather than to their forefathers, who in fact helped themselves to the public's grass, paid few if any taxes, and wasted the lives of cows and men, all in the process of producing rather poor beef" (p. 2). These are bold words from an agricultural historian; they are also words of truth.

Demythification of the importance of the cowboy, the cattle trails, the early cattlemen, and even the sixshooter is present throughout Wood's writings. In his 1982 review of *The Kansas Beef Industry*, Gene M. Gressley succinctly summarized this trait: "Wood wanted to escape the romance of the nineteenth-century setting to excavate the concrete stage of the twentieth century, specifically the rancher as businessman" (*American Historical Review* 87:280).

Reviewing *Beef, Leather and Grass*, in 1981, a first-hand account of the Mexican-Montana livestock trade, Wood comments, "Most of the descriptions are interesting and avoid the romantic, although a few seem a bit fanciful" (*Journal of the West* 20:93). Ever vigilant for historical imagery, Wood cautions historians of agriculture to beware. Of cattlemen, saving their livestock from disease required association and cooperation with each other and government, belying "the hallowed myth of cattlemen as rugged individualists" (*Agricultural History* 54:92). Of cattle drives and cowtowns, it was the farmer and economics that caused the drive to be short-lived. Peaceful business and commerce prevailed rather than conflict. "The fame of Kansas cattle towns as dens of western rowdyism" Wood wryly warns, "continued to grow, however, and reached new heights as novels, movies and television continue to overdramatize the exchanges--commercial and otherwise--that supposedly occurred between the unreconstructed trail hands and the local citizens" (*Journal of the West* 16:16). And of the cowboys and his gun, Wood discovered a concern of the Kansas cattlemen, "contradictory to the modern myth surrounding the cowboy" (*Kansas Historical Quarterly* 43:135). The Kansas Livestock Association without dissent banned the possession of firearms during roundups. Guns were unnecessary and usually troublesome.

In the search for historical light, Wood frequently unearthed misstatements that encouraged myth making. His biographical article depicting the contributions of Clarence D. Perry, land speculator-township developer-farmer-rancher,did not allow Perry credit for the founding of Englewood, Kansas (*Kansas Historical Quarterly* 39:454). Perry was not listed on the Corporation Charters at the Kansas Historical Society as an original director of the town company. Olive M. Franklin had previously been assumed to be the discoverer of blackleg vaccine, but Wood's research uncovered the contributions of several other scientists, notably Francis S. Schoenleber and Thomas P. Haslam (*Agricultural History* 54:84-85). Like the misinformation surrounding Perry and Franklin, most secondary sources attributed the founding of the Kansas Livestock Association to a May, 1884, protest meeting in Emporia. Wood proved it did not happen until over three years later under completely different circumstances (*Kansas Historical Quarterly* 43:129-130).

Perhaps fencing more than any other facet of the agricultural West has encouraged exaggeration. An avid barbed wire collector himself, Wood was not above poking fun at his hobby. He noted the various modifications of fencing designs and the reasons behind such experimentation, and then appends that these developments were "much to the satisfaction of modern barbed wire collectors" (*The Trail Guide* 14:14). In the history of land enclosure, Wood wrote of how laws merely reflected practice rather than encouraged barbed wire adoption and of the gradual evolution of fencing with minimum comment, let alone wars and feuds. Wood intones, "let it be said that fencing can be an engaging subject. One must, however, guard against ascribing too much importance to it" (*The Trail Guide* 14:18).

Frederick Jackson Turner, James C. Malin, and Walter Prescott Webb have influenced countless western historians. Their theories entered the works of Charles Wood, but his subjects frequently did not exactly fit the Turner-Malin-Webb hypotheses. Returning to fencing, Webb believed the invention of barbed wire to be the greatest technological development to allow for the economic triumph of farming on the Great Plains. In *The Great Plains* (p. 295) Webb states, "It was barbed wire and not the railroads or the homestead law that made it possible for the farmers to resume, or at least accelerate, their march across the prairies and onto the Plains." Wood was skeptical. For five northern Kansas counties (Marshall, Washington, Clay, Cloud, and Republic), he found that Webb's statements contained only "a grain of truth." Any suggestion that "barbed wire made conquest of the grasslands possible was just not true for the five counties of this study," and then Wood adds, "one is led to suspect that there were other areas in the Great Plains where the statements did not apply" (*The Trail Guide* 14:17).

Wood also found that the individualism so lauded by Turner in his thesis did not always apply to the Great Plains, and certainly not to the cattle frontier. Essential to Kansas cattlemen was the Kansas Livestock Association, the KLA. Wood describes the KLA as "rather the antithesis of individualistic self-help, except in the broad sense that a group of people who had a community of interests cooperated to promote a single industry" (*Kansas Historical Quarterly* 43:138). Webb and Malin emphasized throughout their works the agriculturalist's need to adapt methods more conducive to an arid environment. But to Wood, the physical environment was not the determining factor for successful settlement beyond the 100th meridian. He even went so far as to challenge both interpretations, suggesting that the environment "probably [was] not even the most important consideration, in the adaptation process" (*Kansas Historical Quarterly* 39:451).

The search for demythifying the history of agriculture should not be seen as irreverential. Wood had a profound respect for the ideas of Turner, Webb, and Malin, and he often turned to them for sustenance and guidance. To not be knowledgeable of their contributions, particularly those of Webb and Malin, was to be flawed, to be somehow intellectually lesser than had one taken their ideas into account. Nevertheless, Wood was equipped to challenge Webb and Malin, and in his works that challenge became a force for agricultural historians to consider. William W. Savage wrote of Wood's *The Kansas Beef Industry*: "Indeed, the book provides a model that might be applied to other state experiences, and it will demand attention from any who contemplate preparation of the synthesis of western cattle industry--overdue by at least two decades" (*Western Historical Quarterly* 12:333).

A second theme present throughout the writings of Wood is the complementary duality of culture and ecology. Wood put it succinctly in *The Kansas Beef Industry* (p. 3) when he states, "Environmental traits, along with human adaptation to them, accounted in large part for the variations that were found in the Kansas beef industry" or in the settlement of the Great Plains or the Trans-Mississippi West. Reciprocity may be the word that best captures Wood's concept. The land and climate begot the rules of survival, and the human factor provided a resourcefulness based upon past experience and a fertile mind.

It is not surprising that Wood was struck by this duality. His upbringing in the Sand Hills of Nebraska and his studies of the Flint Hills of Kansas dictated this outcome. But balance was crucial, both to the agriculturalists he chronicled and to the interpretive importance of environment and culture as factors affecting human actions. By maintaining a balance, experimentation could occur. C. D. Perry diversified his economic activities and attempted projects in irrigation and upbreeding. He became involved in the Claremont Land and Irrigation Company that combined a curious blend of land speculation, breeding and sale of domestic animals, and construction of irrigation works. Culture demanded certain kinds of beef that could only be raised in certain kinds of climates.

Why did this significant melding occur on the Great Plains? Wood held that the Great Plains environment accelerated differences as perceived by agriculturalists. They became quickly conscious of the aridity factor, and consequently plains men and women allowed for environmental variation through experimentation. The by-product then was a dynamic culture capable of rapid adjustment but suspicious of change not influenced by environmental considerations. Basic to the region of Wood's studies, were grass, bison and cattle, and humanity. This interaction adequately explained the history of a unique region to Wood who hoped through his studies to preserve the beauty of the land and the quality of life for its people.

Closely related to ecology and myth in agricultural history is technology. The embrace of science by farmers and ranchers had a profound influence upon human relationships and their lands. For example, disease control required a commitment of finances, governmental leadership and intervention, and the subservience of individual desires to the interests of agricultural groups. This was accomplished in Kansas under the skillful management of Joseph H. Mercer.

But this marriage was not easily consummated. Impediments kept agriculturalists and technology apart. Foremost, according to Wood, was the railroad industry. Its monopolization of transportation and political power inhibited experimentation for an entire era, the 1870s to the 1900s. Government could not offer its services until constitutional changes were made. In some of Wood's most compelling conceptualization, he posited that during the technology lag, agriculturalists were forced to favor legal interventionist activities. Herd law variations are but one of numerous examples cited. This constituted a significant attitudinal change, and made twentieth-century agricultural technological advances readily acceptable to farmers and ranchers. As a result agriculture and industry functioned together in harmony.

The method chosen by Wood to convey his important observations including agricultural myth, ecology, and technology was the case study. Each of his contributions included a discussion of the land, climatically and geopolitically, and the people, particularly as they related to the land. Then a problem or problems were posed, and most importantly the answers suggested were placed in a perspective--a perspective of another time, place, or person. This methodology is not effective without a historical dimension outside a narrow time and place, and it was here--spatially and temporally--that Wood specialized. One must always remember, Wood wrote in a review that it was the duty of historians "to place the many facts into their larger regional, national, and international perspectives" (*Agricultural History* 53:821). Adherence by Wood himself to such a creed, not necessarily a trait of agricultural and western historians, would result in a significant impact on his chosen profession.

At the time of his death, Charles Wood was researching the career of Murdo Mackenzie, long-time manager of the Matador Ranch. This project had already taken Wood to Colorado and Scotland. Trips to New England and Brazil were in the offing. Materials regarding Murdo Mackenzie research by Wood are located in the Southwest Collection, Texas Tech University, Lubbock, Texas. These manuscripts may be viewed with the permission of Alma Wood, Lubbock, Texas. Other materials concerning Wood are deposited in the Charles L. Wood Papers, also located in the Southwest Collection.

In an opening paragraph to his last chapter in *The Kansas Beef Industry*, Wood sought to summarize his work:

> From a national perspective the Kansas industry, like that in states surrounding it, was transitional in beef-producing techniques. Here, in a state located strategically at the threshold of the Great Plains, were stockmen engaged in full-feeding cattle on grain, a practice that dominated the Midwest, and those involved in more expansive grazing operations that characterized the cattle industry to the west and south. This transitional character reflected to a large degree the state's environment and its agriculture as a whole. As one moved from east to west, rainfall declined, long grass gave way to short, and corn yielded to wheat as the basic crop. Kansas producers, who had chosen to specialize in calf production, maturing of stocker cattle, or grain fattening of feeder stock, had adapted well to their environment (p. 281).

This paragraph highlights what one review called "Wood's masterful account of the twentieth-century cattlemen." Continuing, the reviewer notes, Wood "has made a contribution to the historiography of the cattle industry, and a major one--a chronicle, as far as Kansas is concerned, which will not need to be written again" (*American Historical Review* 87:280). This paragraph also underlines the contribution Charles L. Wood made to history beyond Kansas cattlemen. His desire for historical truth through research and analysis, demythification, the balancing of environment and culture, and the important role of technology and industry in agriculture--all are a part of his works and will be enduring.

Bibliography

Book

The Kansas Beef Industry. Lawrence: Regents Press of Kansas, 1980.

Articles

"C. D. Perry: Clark County Farmer and Rancher, 1884-1903." *Kansas Historical Quarterly* 39(Winter, 1973):449-477.

"Cattlemen, Railroad, and the Origin of the Kansas Livestock Association--the 1890s." *Kansas Historical Quarterly* 43(Summer, 1977):121-129.

"Cowboy Life on a Western Ranch: Reminiscences of Alexander Mackay." Co-edited with James E. Brink in *At Home on the Range: Essays on the History of Western Social and Domestic Life* edited by John R. Wunder. Westport, CT: Greenwood Press, 1985. Pp. 177-195.

"Development of an Enclosure System for Five Kansas Counties, 1875-1895." *The Trail Guide* 14(March, 1969):1-20.

"Science and Politics in the War on Cattle Diseases: The Kansas Experience, 1900-1940." *Agricultural History* 54(January, 1980):82-92.

"Upbreeding Western Range Cattle: Notes on Kansas, 1880-1920." *Journal of the West* 16(January, 1977):16-28.

Reviews

Beef, Leather and Grass by Edmund Randolph. *Journal of the West* 20(October, 1981):93.

The Dakota Image: A Photographic Celebration by Bill Schneider. Co-authored with John R. Wunder. *Journal of the West* 21(July, 1982):77.

Environment and Man in Kansas: A Geographical Analysis by Huber Self. *Agricultural History* 53(October, 1979):821-822.

Shanley: Pennies Wise--Dollars Foolish by Grant B. Harris. *Journal of the West* 20(July, 1981):99.

Temple Houston: Lawyer with a Gun by Glenn Shirley. *Journal of the West* 19(July, 1980):124.

Studies of Charles L. Wood

Gressley, Gene M. Review of *The Kansas Beef Industry* by Charles L. Wood. *American Historical Review* 87(February, 1982):280.

Hargreaves, Mary W. M. Review of *The Kansas Beef Industry* by Charles L. Wood. *Journal of American History* 68(June, 1981):168-169.

Savage, William W. Review of *The Kansas Beef Industry* by Charles L. Wood. *Western Historical Quarterly* 12(July, 1981):333.

Wood, Charles L., Papers. Southwest Collection, Texas Tech University, Lubbock, TX.

Wunder, John R., ed. *At Home on the Range: Essays on the History of Western Social and Domestic Life.* Westport, CT: Greenwood Press, 1985.

__________. *Working the Range: Essays on the History of Western Land Management and the Environment.* Westport, CT: Greenwood Press, 1985.

INDEX

Page numbers in **boldface** indicate the location of the main entry.

CONTRIBUTORS

The contributors to this volume represent a diverse group of scholars. They include prominent members of the historical profession as well as new members. The contributors come from many subdisciplines of frontier history, and they are located throughout the United States, from Florida to Washington to Arizona to New Hampshire. One scholar presently resides in Australia. In addition, these historians include persons who hold positions in college history departments; practice public history in museums, historical societies, and archives; and compose history as free lance writers. An attempt was made to include as much diversity among the contributors as was provided within the subjects of this volume. It should be noted that two contributors, William H. Graves and Bonny O. Van Orman, died after the completion of their respective essays.

In alphabetical order, the contributors include:

Peter H. Argersinger
University of Maryland, Baltimore County
Catonsville, MD

Gordon Morris Bakken
California State University, Fullerton
Fullerton, CA

Francisco E. Balderrama
California State University, Los Angeles
Los Angeles, CA

Jo Tice Bloom
Stockton, CA

Richard Maxwell Brown
University of Oregon
Eugene, OR

Kimberly Moore Buchanan
Hobbs, NM

Anne M. Butler
Gallaudet College
Washington, DC

Paul H. Carlson
Texas Tech University
Lubbock, TX

Andrew R. L. Cayton
Ball State University
Muncie, IN

Michael Collins
Midwestern State University
Wichita Falls, TX

Bruce J. Dinges
Arizona Historical Society
Tucson, AZ

Gordon B. Dodds
Portland State University
Portland, OR

Jane E. Dysart
University of West Florida
Pensacola, FL

Robert E. Ficken
Issaquah, WA

H. Roger Grant
University of Akron
Akron, OH

William H. Graves
Prestonsburg Community College
Prestonsburg, KY

Michael D. Green
Dartmouth College
Hanover, NH

Mark W. T. Harvey
North Dakota State University
Fargo, ND

Rebecca Herring
Sausalito, CA

Michael Q. Hooks
Texas State General Land Office Archives
Austin, TX

Deborah J. Hoskins
Indiana University
Bloomington, IN

Evelyn Hu-DeHart
University of Colorado
Boulder, CO

Thomas Huffman
University of Wisconsin-Madison
Madison, WI

Tully Hunter
Georgia Southwestern College
Americus, GA

R. Douglas Hurt
Historical Society of Missouri
Columbia, MO

William L. Lang
Montana Historical Society
Helena, MT

David J. Langum
Samford University
Birmingham, AL

Thomas C. McClintock
Oregon State University
Corvallis, OR

Steven F. Mehls
Lafayette, CO

David J. Murrah
Texas Tech University
Lubbock, TX

Gerald D. Nash
University of New Mexico
Albuquerque, NM

Doyce B. Nunis, Jr.
University of Southern California
Los Angeles, CA

James H. O'Donnell III
Marietta College
Marietta, OH

Richard E. Oglesby
University of California, Santa Barbara
Santa Barbara, CA

Frank Owsley, Jr.
Auburn University
Auburn, AL

Malcolm J. Rohrbough
University of Iowa
Iowa City, IA

Willard H. Rollings
Southwest Missouri State University
Springfield, MO

James P. Ronda
Youngstown State University
Youngstown, OH

Richard Saunders, Jr.
Clemson University
Clemson, SC

Alan M. Schroder
University of Arizona Press
Tucson, AZ

Steven C. Schulte
College of the Ozarks
Clarksville, AR

Dwight L. Smith
Miami University
Miami, OH

Sherry L. Smith
University of Texas, El Paso
El Paso, TX

Robert P. Swierenga
Kent State University
Kent, OH

Gregory M. Tobin
Flinders University of South Australia
Bedford Park, SA, Australia

Carl Ubbelohde
Case Western Reserve University
Cleveland, OH

William E. Unrau
Wichita State University
Wichita, KS

Daniel H. Usner, Jr.
Cornell University
Ithaca, NY

Bonny O. Van Orman
Hammond, IN

Richard A. Van Orman
Purdue University, Calumet
Hammond, IN

David A. Walker
University of Northern Iowa
Cedar Falls, IA

Deborah Welch
Elon College
Elon, NC

Thomas R. Wessel
Montana State University
Bozeman, MT

Elliott West
University of Arkansas
Fayetteville, AR

Richard White
University of Utah
Salt Lake City, UT

Clarke L. Wilhelm
Denison University
Granville, OH

Burton J. Williams
Central Washington University
Ellensburg, WA

John R. Wunder
University of Nebraska
Lincoln, NE